Twelfth Canadian Edition

FOUNDATIONS OF
FINANCIAL
MANAGEMENT

STANLEY B. BLOCK
Texas Christian University

BARTLEY R. DANIELSEN
North Carolina State University

J. DOUGLAS SHORT
Northern Alberta Institute of Technology

GEOFFREY A. HIRT
DePaul University

Mc
Graw
Hill

Foundations of Financial Management
Twelfth Canadian Edition

The Internet addresses listed in the text were accurate at the time of publication. The inclusion of a Web site does not indicate an endorsement by the authors or McGraw-Hill Ryerson, and McGraw-Hill Ryerson does not guarantee the accuracy of the information presented at these sites.

ISBN-13: 978-1-26-032691-8
ISBN-10: 1-26-032691-8

2 3 4 5 6 7 8 9 M 23 22 21

Printed and bound in Canada.

Care has been taken to trace ownership of copyright material contained in this text; however, the publisher will welcome any information that enables them to rectify any reference or credit for subsequent editions.

Product Director: Rhondda McNabb
Portfolio Managers: Jade Fair & Alwynn Pinard
Senior Marketing Manager: Loula March
Content Developer: Krisha Escobar
Portfolio Associate: Tatiana Sevciuc
Senior Supervising Editor: Jessica Barnoski
Photo/Permissions Editor: Nadine Bachan
Copy Editor: Karen Rolfe
Plant Production Coordinator: Heitor Moura
Manufacturing Production Coordinator: Jason Stubner
Cover Design: Katherine Strain
Cover Image: © niserin © 123RF.com
Interior Design: Pixel Hive Studio
Page Layout: SPi Global
Printer: Marquis

Life is just a leap of faith. Do it with passion and conviction.

To my family, whom I love.

My ancestors who built our life and my descendants who will continue to live it.

My mum, Ruth, and dad, Jock, and my brothers, Rob and Kevin.

My wife, Devika (my life's love), and our children, Erin and Jason, and their families, Clayton, Stephanie, Connor, and Alice.

–Doug

BRIEF CONTENTS

CONTENTS

PREFACE

The daily events of the business world, the dynamics of the capital markets, and the deals that change enterprises encompass the world of finance. The dynamics of recent history, especially Covid-19, are particularly startling. Too often, the finance discipline is considered challenging by students because we make its concepts overly complicated. Although finance has unique language and terms, it relies on some fairly basic, commonsensical ideas. The 12th Canadian edition of *Foundations of Financial Management* **is committed to making finance accessible to you.**

As always, this edition incorporates content and presentation revisions to make the text an even better tool for providing you with the skills and confidence you'll need to be an effective financial manager. Concepts are explained in a clear and concise manner with numerous "Finance in Action" boxes highlighting real-world examples and employing Internet resources to reinforce and illustrate these concepts. The extensive and varied problem material helps to reinforce financial concepts in more detail. The text is committed to presenting finance in an enlightening, interesting, and exciting manner.

REINFORCING PREREQUISITE KNOWLEDGE

Employers of business graduates report that the most successful analysts, planners, and executives have both ability and confidence in their financial skills. We couldn't agree more. One of the best ways to increase your ability in financial planning is to integrate knowledge from prerequisite courses. Therefore, this text is designed to build on your knowledge from basic courses in accounting and economics, with some statistics thrown in for good measure. By applying tools learned in these courses, you can develop a conceptual and analytical understanding of financial management.

For some of you, a bit of time has passed since you've completed your accounting courses. Therefore, included in Chapter 2 is a basic review of financial statements based on Accounting Standards for Private Enterprises (ASPE) and International Financial Reporting Standards (IFRS) for public companies, finance terminology, and basic tax effects. With a working knowledge of that chapter, you will have a more complete understanding of financial statements, the impact of your decisions on financial results, and how financial statements can serve you in making effective financial decisions. Furthermore, as you are about to begin your career, you will be better prepared when called on to apply financial concepts.

FLEXIBILITY

The 12th Canadian edition of *Foundations of Financial Management* covers all core topics taught in a financial management course. However, it is almost impossible to cover every topic included in this text in a single course. This book has therefore been carefully crafted to ensure flexibility to accommodate different course syllabi and a variety of teaching approaches. We encourage instructors to use an approach to the text that works best for them and for the student.

Financial management's three basic concerns are the management of working capital, the effective allocation of capital by means of the capital budgeting decision, and the raising of long-term capital with an appropriate capital structure. These topics are covered in Parts 3, 4, and 5 of the text. An introduction to financial management in Part 1 and to financial analysis and planning in Part 2 precede these central parts. A broader perspective on finance is addressed in Part 6.

There is continued debate on the best method to present the time-value-of-money concepts. To allow for the range of opinion, formulae, tables, and calculator presentations and solutions are available. Although this is sometimes cumbersome, an attempt has been made to separate the different approaches with colour shading. Choose the method that works best for you.

NEW FOR THE 12TH CANADIAN EDITION

Throughout the 12th edition there have been timely updates to the "Finance in Action" (FIA) boxes, figures, and tables as finance continually changes, often in a dramatic fashion. With a mix of familiar and new examples from the markets, these illustrate financial concepts in action. Instructors who have used this text before will find it familiar and significantly improved since the last edition. Some of the topics and updates include:

- Lessons learned from the 2008 financial crisis and our period of low interest rates. Covid-19 impacts have been added where appropriate.
- Streamlined discussions in bullet-point form where appropriate to allow for greater focus and attention to key ideas.
- All FIA boxes have been re-examined for appropriateness and have been updated. Some new FIAs have been added in light of Covid-19 and its impacts. Web links have also been updated to help students explore further research on these topics. The impacts identified in the FIAs change constantly, but the related lessons are invaluable.
- Problem sets have been extensively reviewed from the previous edition. Numerous problems are different from the previous edition, as suggested and requested by reviewers.

In the introduction to Part 1, The Goals and Functions of Financial Management, the groundwork is set for the dynamic nature of finance, including a discussion of the pricing mechanism of the financial markets especially as it relates to tech company valuation with limited current earnings, and the trend to less widely held companies exhibited in Table 1-1. Of particular note the Finance in Action box "Change is Coming" reflects on the modification of the corporate goal.

In Part 2, Financial Analysis and Planning, we reflect on the changes in accounting and for tax rules, as well as financial presentation. We examine concerns over accounting preparation that tends to mislead investors, such was the case with Valeant Corporation; analyze firms such as Nvidia, considered the world's smartest company by MIT; and provide continuing examples of firms taking "the big bath."

In Part 3, Working Capital Management, we note the changes in working capital positions due to the cash hoarding by firms, which in turn reflect the financial conservatism that occurred as a result of the 2008 recession, the most severe financial recession since the 1930s. Weakened working capital positions came into prominence with the Covid-19 pandemic. This can be tied to the appropriateness of healthy dividends and share repurchases discussed in Chapter 18. This conservatism and risk aversion is seen in the significant drop of short-term financing with commercial paper and asset-backed securities. The implications of the low-interest-rate environment, amongst volatility of these rates, is also noted.

In Part 4, the Capital Budgeting Process, we add where appropriate screen shots of spreadsheets to illustrate calculations. Dramatic changes in security yields with changing risk affecting prices during the Covid-19 pandemic is noted. In the FIAs we highlight the low level of R&D spending in Canada. Capital budgeting strategies related to cyclical resource is highlighted, including the ongoing reversal of fortunes at Teck. Adjustments have been made for the impact of the lower-tax-rate environment and its impact on capital budgeting decisions. WestJet, now an established airline, has been successful in a very risky business and has been followed by airlines such as Porter.

In Part 5, Long-Term Financing, the capital markets chapter is extensively revised to show the significant increase in corporate borrowing, the continuing domination in financial intermediation by banks (although activity is tempered by pension and mutual funds), and ongoing globalization controlled to some extent by local regulatory concerns. Income trusts and asset-backed securities have retreated in influence, and the Finance in Action box "Don't Forget to Read the Fine Print," in Chapter 16, points out how we sometimes forget to examine the assets behind the financial security. Saudi Aramco, the oil and gas company, became the largest IPO in history, while Shopify and Canada Goose were significant recent IPOs. The shifting markets, from bond rates and tax changes (dividend tax credit) to Microsoft entering the stage of its life cycle where growth has slowed and dividends have replaced capital gains, are all examined and noted. The use of convertible securities by less creditworthy firms is also seen in the derivatives chapter.

In Part 6, Expanding the Perspective of Corporate Finance, the mergers and acquisitions chapter notes the presence of sovereign governments, such as China and Malaysia, as key players in the energy sector. The chapter identifies reorganizations taking place in the retail sector (e.g., Hudson's Bay/Saks, Loblaws, Amazon). Mergers were rejected for PotashCorp, now Nutrien, and then approved with a different player. The international financial management chapter continues to emphasize the significance of the global market plays for Canada, the volatility of the exchange markets, and the challenges to the European Monetary Union (EMU).

ETHICAL BEHAVIOUR AND CORPORATE GOVERNANCE

Our approach is to lay out in Chapter 1 an ethical framework from which financial management practices can be examined. The agency conflict related to good corporate governance can be examined in the context of establishing the goal of the firm. Numerous FIA boxes raise issues for discussion and research by students. The discussion in Chapter 1 begins with socially desirable actions with examples of responsible Canadian corporations.

A good ethical practice framework focuses first on fairness, tying into the rules and regulatory environment within which the firm operates and the changes that take place over time. It then identifies honesty as requiring timely, relevant, and reliable financial reporting. (This framework can be used to discuss several FIA topics.)

Good corporate governance practices and recent changes are tied into several chapters and to resources that include academic research and the Canadian Coalition for Good Governance (CCGG).

The discussion on market efficiency and securities regulation in Chapter 14 and what makes for good regulation should be tied into any examination of good corporate governance.

RISK

Risk is identified in Chapter 1 as one of the key concepts of finance (that is sometimes neglected) in determining value. Consideration of risk is interwoven throughout the text with discussion and FIA boxes. The general concept of volatility is illustrated, to be examined more extensively, particularly in Chapter 13 through statistical measures. Chapter 1 suggests the early warning signs of the 2008 market downturn were found in the Treasury bill–commercial paper yield spread.

In Chapter 2 rule-of-thumb risk measures of price-earnings and market to book ratios are examined from a financial statement perspective. Additionally, tax rule changes identify risk.

In Chapter 3 ratio analysis is seen in the context of gauging pressure points increasing risk within the firm, while Chapter 4 explores the risks and sensitivities of forecasting. Chapter 5 is the first full chapter exploring risk from the leverage perspective, identifying business, operating, and financial risk.

Hedging across the balance sheet is established in the context of risk reduction in Chapter 6, while volatility is viewed through interest rate changes. Chapter 8 assesses the credit crunch phenomenon that reappears time and time again.

In Chapter 10 there is the risk premium discussion on required rates of returns (yields), with Chapter 11 exploring risk within the overall concept of the cost of capital. Additionally the CAPM risk return model is introduced. It is within Chapter 13 that three significant questions related to risk are identified. The distinction between total risk (coefficient of variation) and systematic risk (beta) is highlighted. Risk reduction through the portfolio effect is constructed statistically with important conclusions and follow-up problems.

In Chapter 19 risk reduction from derivatives is illustrated, and is tied back to leverage in Chapter 5 and hedging in Chapter 6. Chapter 21 examines risk reduction through international diversification, and the volatility of the Canadian dollar in 2007–2017 (Figure 21–9) is illustrated.

FINANCE IN ACTION (FIA) BOX LISTING

Chapter 1

The Foundations

Nobel Prize Winners for Finance (Economics)

Change is Coming

Are Executive Salaries Fair?

Functions of Finance

The Pricing Mechanism of Financial Markets—What'sApp

The Markets Reflect Value, Yields (Rates of Return), and Risk

Chapter 2

Where Did Those Earnings Go?

Apparently Earnings Are Flexible

Meeting the Targets!

Earnings and Cash Flow: The Difference at Teck

Corporate Tax Rules

Chapter 3

Applying DuPont Analysis to the Rails

Combat in 3D

Taking a Big Bath

Chapter 4

Pro Forma Financial Statements: A Critical Tool For Entrepreneurs

Cannabis Sales Not Up To Snuff

Oil Prices! How About a Forecast?

Operational Cash Flows Exceeds Earnings and Allows Capital Expenditures

Chapter 5

On the Red to in the Black

Big Leverage! Big Losses! Big Gains! Insolvency! Rebirth!

Leverage of Seventeen Times Equity

Why Japanese Firms Tend to Be So Competitive

Chapter 6

Working Capital Is a Large Investment at Loblaw

Seasonal Sales

Loblaw's Cash Conversion Almost Generates Cash

Managing Working Capital

Chapter 7

Why Are Firms Holding Such High Cash Balances?

Cash Management Systems: The Octopus

U.S Overnight Money Market Rates Soar

Treasury Bills, or Commercial Paper, for Liquidity and Safety

Receivables, Credit Card Receivables, Securitizations

No Wine Before Its Time

JIT for Money and Inventory Control

Tsunami Shuts Down Global Supply Chains

Chapter 8

CN Rail Maintains a Negative Trade Credit Position

PEDAGOGY

WITHIN THE CHAPTER

To provide guidance and insights throughout the text, we incorporate a number of proven pedagogical aids. These include:

LO1 **Learning Objectives** At the beginning of each chapter, learning objectives will help focus your learning as you proceed through the material. The summary at the end of each chapter responds to each of these objectives. Learning objectives are tagged in-chapter and with end-of-chapter questions.

LEARNING OBJECTIVES

LO1 Illustrate how finance builds on the disciplines of accounting and economics, with connections to other disciplines.

LO2 Identify the analysis and decision-making nature of finance while considering return and risk.

LO3 Examine the primary goal of finance as the maximization of shareholder wealth as measured by share price.

LO4 Debate alternative goals of the firm on the basis of social or management interests.

Calculators When the use of a calculator is illustrated, a calculator icon appears in the text. Appendix E demonstrates the use of the three most commonly used business calculators, with the illustrations in the text tending to conform to the Sharp calculator. Chapter 9 demonstrates the use of a calculator with time lines, and the use of tables (as an option). The formulas for present value analysis, which are the basis for calculators, tables, or computers, have been included. Answers computed with the calculator will be more accurate than those provided by the tables, due to the rounding of the table factors.

Finance in Action (FIA) Boxes These popular boxes address topics related to the chapter subject matter and deal with the difficulties and opportunities in the financial markets. Questions appropriate to the topic often require Internet searches for background information and for help with analyses.

Rewarding discussions of current and historical financial events, issues, and practices can begin with this material. Most Finance in Action boxes include at least one website (URL) relevant to the discussion, which will allow for updating the events outlined in the box.

FINANCE IN ACTION

Change Is Coming

The Business Roundtable (businessroundtable.org) an association of CEOs of leading U.S. companies for almost 50 years, recently modified its statement on the purpose of a corporation. From the sole purpose of maximizing shareholder wealth it reintroduced a broader focus. The purpose now encompasses all stakeholders including employees, communities, customers, suppliers, and shareholders. The environment, diversity, and inclusion are also given consideration.

 Small Business Icons Small business references and examples are highlighted throughout the text with an icon.

Examples and Tables For problem solving and its methodologies, we have employed many examples and tables to illustrate the development of solutions. This is integrated with discussion of the concepts that are illustrated through the "number crunching." Problem solving is integrated throughout the text material, as in Chapter 2 where an income statement is developed over several pages. The use of tables brings your attention to a problem-solving methodology.

END-OF-CHAPTER MATERIAL

Practice makes perfect. Each chapter concludes with review and problem materials to help students review and apply what they've learned.

Summary Each chapter ends with a summary that ties the material back to the specific chapter objectives presented at the beginning of the chapter.

Review of Formulas At the end of every chapter that includes formulas, a list of all formulas used in that chapter is provided for easy reference.

Discussion Questions and Problems To reinforce and test your understanding of the chapter, the material in the text is supported by approximately 300 questions and over 500 problems in this 12th edition. The problems are a very important part of the text and have been written with care to be consistent with the chapter material. The problems for this edition have been revised, while maintaining the extensive variety and the range of difficulty from previous editions.

Comprehensive Problems Several chapters have comprehensive problems that integrate and require the application of several financial concepts into one problem.

Mini Cases These are more intense extensive problems that may involve several concepts and cover material from more than one chapter, often involving discussion.

MINI CASES
Glen Mount Furniture

Furniture magnate Carl Thompson couldn't believe the amount of pressure security analysts could put on a firm. The Glen Mount Furniture Company was a leading manufacturer of fine home furnishings and distributed its products directly to department stores, independent home furnishing retailers, and a few regional furniture chains. The firm specialized in bedroom, dining room, and living room furniture and had three plants in Quebec and two in Ontario. Its home office was in Granby, Quebec.

In a recent presentation to the Montreal chapter of the Financial Analysts Federation, Carl Thompson barely had taken a bite out of his salad when two analysts from a stock brokerage firm began asking questions. They were particularly concerned about Glen Mount's growth rate in EPS.

AWARD-WINNING TECHNOLOGY

 McGraw Hill Connect® is an award-winning digital teaching and learning solution that empowers students to achieve better outcomes and enables instructors to improve efficiency with course management. Within Connect, students have access to SmartBook®, McGraw Hill's adaptive learning and reading resource. SmartBook prompts students with questions based on the material they are studying. By assessing individual answers, SmartBook learns what each student knows and identifies which topics they need to practise, giving each student a personalized learning experience and path to success.

Connect's key features also include analytics and reporting, simple assignment management, smart grading, the opportunity to post your own resources, and the Connect Instructor Library, a repository for additional resources to improve student engagement in and out of the classroom.

Instructor resources for *Foundations of Financial Management,* 12th Canadian Edition:

- Instructor's Solutions Manual
- Test Bank
- Microsoft® PowerPoint® Presentations

End-of-Chapter Problems Connect for *Foundations of Financial Management* provides assignable, gradable end-of chapter content to help students learn how to solve problems and apply concepts. Advanced algorithms allow students to practise problems multiple times to ensure full comprehension of each problem.

Writing Assignments The Writing Assignment tool delivers a learning experience to help students improve their written communication skills and conceptual understanding. As an instructor you can assign, monitor, grade, and provide feedback on writing more efficiently and effectively.

Test Builder Available within Connect, Test Builder is a cloud-based tool that enables instructors to format tests that can be printed or administered within a Learning Management System. Test Builder offers a modern, streamlined interface for easy content configuration that matches course needs, without requiring a download.

Test Builder allows you to:

- access all test bank content from a particular title
- easily pinpoint the most relevant content through robust filtering options
- manipulate the order of questions or scramble questions and/or answers
- pin questions to a specific location within a test
- choose the layout and spacing
- add instructions and configure default settings

Test Builder provides a secure interface for better protection of content and allows for just-in-time updates to flow directly into assessments.

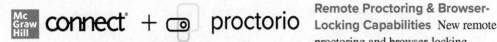 **Remote Proctoring & Browser-Locking Capabilities** New remote proctoring and browser-locking capabilities, hosted by Proctorio within Connect, provide control of the assessment environment by enabling security options and verifying the identity of the student.

Seamlessly integrated within Connect, these services allow instructors to control students' assessment experience by restricting browser activity, recording students' activity, and verifying students are doing their own work.

Instant and detailed reporting gives instructors an at-a-glance view of potential academic integrity concerns, thereby avoiding personal bias and supporting evidence-based claims.

ACKNOWLEDGMENTS

We are indebted to the many reviewers who have offered their thoughts and insights to improve this text. We are impressed by the ongoing support for the text and the willingness of so many to offer suggestions and advice. **Please continue to forward your ideas, thoughts, or suggestions to us.** Thanks go out to all for the source of stimulation. We hope we've been able to address most of the concerns raised, as we believe that we continue to make the text more effective for our students. As always, we've tried to balance competing thoughts and accommodate individual classroom styles.

To those colleagues across the country whom we have visited over the years, thank you for your continued support. We look forward to meeting with other instructors in the future. Special thanks go to the individuals who over several editions have always been there to help find an answer. Robert Short acts as a guide through the capital markets. In working through this latest edition my thanks go to Dr. Anna Beukes for her input and insights. For this 12th edition there was wonderful help from Devika Short in the preparation and review of several support documents.

Many individuals contributed in innumerable ways to earlier editions, and their efforts live on in this edition. Thank you to Allan Conway, Michael Perretta, Peter Nissen, Pan Zhang, Susan Rae Hurley, and Luigi Figliuzzi. I would like to express my gratitude to Stanley B. Block, Geoffrey A. Hirt, and Bartley R. Danielson for the work and care that they continue to put into the U.S. editions. The latitude that they have allowed in adapting the book for the Canadian environment and student is appreciated.

To my Portfolio Managers, Jade Fair and Alwynn Pinard, my thanks for their commitment to a text focused on the student. Their efforts to keep me on course were appreciated and the oversight was much appreciated. As always, Alwynn and Jade were sensitive to concerns and desires in producing a first-rate text, while carefully considering the trends of the marketplace. Their ideas sparked rewarding research and consideration of these ideas.

To my Content Developer, Krisha Escobar, a sincere thanks. Krisha carefully perused my e-files with great skill, with an eye to my oversights and errors. Her thoughts and comments were well considered and most helpful. Furthermore, Krisha persisted in keeping me on task.

I would like to thank Jessica Barnoski, our Supervising Editor, who pulled everything together on this project. An amazing feat!

Nadine Bachan, our Permissions Editor, was of great assistance in examining all reference material for appropriate permissions.

In working with the new technology that combines the text and online version, I have been impressed by the care taken by the many who put it all together. A special mention to Karen Rolfe who conscientiously examined every aspect of the text.

Thank you also to Basil Chen, Centennial College, for his diligent review of the end-of-chapter questions and solutions.

To the marketing representatives, a special thanks for doing such a great job of keeping in touch with the current and future users of this text. **Call anytime!**

Finally, thanks to my students and all student users of the text. Finance is fascinating because it changes every day and it reflects the future. It is like you.

—*J. Douglas Short*

Effective. Efficient. Easy to Use.

McGraw Hill Connect is an award-winning digital teaching and learning solution that empowers students to achieve better outcomes and enables instructors to improve course-management efficiency.

Personalized & Adaptive Learning

Connect's integrated SmartBook helps students study more efficiently, highlighting where in the text to focus and asking review questions to give each student a personalized learning experience and path to success.

High-Quality Course Material

Our trusted solutions are designed to help students actively engage in course content and develop critical higher-level thinking skills, while offering you the flexibility to tailor your course to meet your needs.

Analytics & Reporting

Monitor progress and improve focus with Connect's visual and actionable dash-boards. Reporting features empower instructors and students with real-time performance analytics.

Seamless Integration

Link your Learning Management System with Connect for single sign-on and gradebook synchroniza-tion, with all-in-one ease for you and your students.

Impact of Connect on Pass Rates

72.5%
Without Connect

85.2%
With Connect

SMARTBOOK®

NEW SmartBook 2.0 builds on our market-leading adaptive technology with enhanced capabilities and a streamlined interface that deliver a more usable, accessible, and mobile learning experience for both students and instructors.

Available on mobile smart devices – with both online and offline access – the ReadAnywhere app lets students study anywhere, anytime.

SUPPORT AT EVERY STEP

McGraw Hill ensures you are supported every step of the way. From course design and set up, to instructor training, LMS integration and ongoing support, your Digital Success Consultant is there to make your course as effective as possible.

CHAPTER

1

The Goals and Functions of Financial Management

LEARNING OBJECTIVES

LO1 Illustrate how finance builds on the disciplines of accounting and economics, with connections to other disciplines.

LO2 Identify the analysis and decision-making nature of finance while considering return and risk.

LO3 Examine the primary goal of finance as the maximization of shareholder wealth as measured by share price.

LO4 Debate alternative goals of the firm on the basis of social or management interests.

LO5 Identify financial manager functions connected to the efficient raising and investing of funds, as well as daily cash management.

LO6 Outline the role of financial markets in allocating capital, determining value, and establishing yields.

Finance is a dynamic, rigorous discipline built on the foundations of accounting and economics. The focus of finance is on increasing value, as measured by market share price, and this theme is played out daily in the world's financial markets. The financial manager performs many functions to enhance value for the shareholder.

FINANCE MANAGEMENT

Demands of Finance

A financial manager must perform effectively in today's competitive business environment for the firm to be successful. The task requires analysis and evaluation of the changing influences on the firm:

- Variable interest and exchange rates
- Volatile commodity prices
- Acquiring and investing capital (stock, bond, derivative markets)
- Analyzing and controlling risk
- Technological innovations
- Shifting consumer demand (particularly after the Covid-19 pandemic)

These and other changes immediately affect the flow of cash in and out of the firm, impacting its value. In the dynamic business environment, managers are challenged to maintain the firm's financial viability.

Financial management is concerned with the following:

- Managing the capital (assets and liabilities) of the firm efficiently
- Understanding global financial markets
- Assessing, enhancing, and creating value

The various tools of financial management guide the financial manager through a sophisticated financial marketplace in which assets are valued on the basis of their current and best use. Increasingly, these financial markets and the firm's operations are international in scope.

THE FIELD OF FINANCE

The finance discipline has developed rigorous decision-oriented analysis models that focus on creating value within the firm by

- Raising capital efficiently (debt from creditors and equity from shareholders)
- Investing in value-creating assets (current [short-term] and capital [long-term])

Creating value is done in a world of uncertainty. Thus, the financial manager is continually monitoring, adjusting to, and trying to control risk.

LO1 Financial management builds upon the disciplines of economics and accounting, with interplay with other disciplines.

Economics provides the financial manager with

- A broad picture of the economy and the key measures that influence the corporation's decisions and performance (gross domestic product, industrial production, disposable income, unemployment, inflation, interest rates, taxes).
- An understanding of the institutional structure of our mixed capitalist system (government regulation, Bank of Canada, chartered banks, investment dealers, trusts, insurance companies, financial markets). Capital is accumulated and valued in competitive financial markets, affecting its cost and availability to the firm.
- A structure for decision making (risk analysis, pricing theory through supply and demand relationships, and comparative return analysis).

Bank of Canada
bankofcanada.ca

Accounting provides the financial manager with

- Much of the language of finance (assets, liabilities, cash flow).
- Financial data (income statements, balance sheets or statement of financial position, statement of cash flows, changes in equity). The financial manager must know how to interpret and use this data in allocating the firm's financial resources to generate the best value on the basis of return and risk.

Finance links economic theory with the numbers of accounting, and all corporate managers—whether in the area of production, sales, research, marketing, management, or long-run strategic planning—must know what it means to assess the financial performance of the firm.

The field of finance offers career opportunities as varied as banker, corporate treasurer, stockbroker, financial analyst, portfolio manager, investment banker, financial consultant, and personal financial planner. You will become familiar with many of these roles in the financing and decision-making processes. A financial manager in the firm might be responsible for decisions ranging from where to locate a new plant to raising funds via a public share issue. Sometimes, the task is simply to figure out how to get the highest return on a million dollars of temporarily idle cash between 5 p.m. one afternoon and 8 a.m. the next morning.

For the small business operator, these many roles are often undertaken by one person. Nevertheless, it is important for that individual to have knowledge of accounting and economics to assist them in financial decision making. Finance focuses on creating value, and these disciplines will help to focus the small business owner on that goal.

EVOLUTION OF FINANCE AS A DISCIPLINE

To appreciate finance as a field of study, a historical perspective is instructive. Finance is

A Descriptive Discipline

- Toronto and Montreal stock exchanges were formed in the 1870s, outlining functions and procedures in raising capital.
- Financial instruments (shares and bonds) were defined.
- Financial institutions were delineated (investment dealers, brokers, and securities regulators).
- Capital preservation, liquidity, reorganization, and bankruptcy were described through the 1930s Depression.
- Securities regulations resulted from company failures and the questionable treatment of outside investors' interests by insiders.

Toronto Stock
Exchange
tmx.com

- Published data of corporate performance developed, laying the groundwork for later analytical techniques. Accounting scandals (Nortel, Enron, Valeant) and the financial crisis of 2007–08 again led to increased requirements for regulation, disclosure, and better corporate governance.

LO2 An Analytical, Decision-oriented Discipline

- By the 1950s, focus was on the allocation of financial capital (money) for the purchase of real capital (plant and equipment) and the creation of value from the interplay of possible returns and risks.
- Capital budgeting analysis and other sophisticated techniques objectively evaluated long-term decisions (strategies, technologies, real capital) to allocate the firm's scarce resources.
- Proposals were valued on the basis of their expected earnings, cash flows, risk, and an acceptable rate of return, usually suggested by the financial markets.
- The financial market's ability to reflect true or intrinsic value and its processing of information became the study of market efficiency.
- Asymmetric information questioned the appropriate functioning of financial markets when an imbalance of pertinent information among investors and the managers of firms existed.
- Sophisticated analysis was applied to other decision-making issues such as cash, inventory management, and other important day-to-day decisions affecting the short- and long-term well-being of the firm.
- Capital structure theory, the study of the relative importance of debt and equity in influencing the firm's value, received analytical investigation.
- Theories were developed for risk-return relationships in valuing assets and risk reduction, such as diversification.
- Models valuing options assisted in the development of the derivatives markets.
- Behavioural finance examined departures from rational market decision making.

 FINANCE IN ACTION

The Foundations

Accounting provides information the financial analyst can use to illuminate asset values of the firm. If financial statements are not prepared with integrity and diligence, the analyst's ability to use these statements to establish reliable valuations is weakened.

Sometimes there is considerable divergence between the accounting or book value and the market value of a shareholders' investment in a firm, known as *equity*.

Teck (TECK.B) versus Rogers Communication (RCI.B) shareholders' equity in late 2019 (billions)		
	Book Value	Market Value
TECK.B	$22	$13
RCI.B	8	34

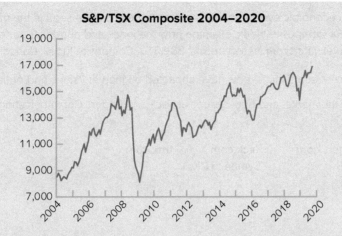

S&P/TSX Composite 2004–2020

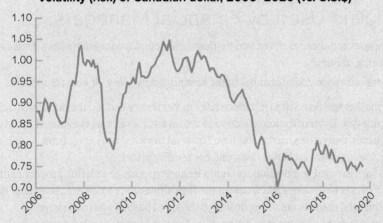

Volatility (risk) of Canadian dollar, 2006–2020 (vs. U.S.$)

Market value reflects investor expectations of a firm's ability to generate cash flows from its operations and assets. In late 2019, investors valued the ownership position in Rogers Communication, the communications and media company, as significantly higher than ownership in Teck, Canada's biggest mining company. However, the accounting numbers based on past performance showed a different story. Interestingly, Teck's book value was about three times greater than that of Rogers.

Economics, another building block of finance, provides us with useful theories in order to understand value formation. The financial markets rise or fall in value, reflecting investor expectations modified by economic events that affect potential risks and returns. The stock market volatility of 2004–20, with a collapse in 2009, was triggered by difficulties in the short-term credit market and subsequent interest rate uncertainty. But by 2011 and again by 2020 it had recovered beyond 2008 levels. During the same period, the Canadian dollar rose and fell dramatically against the U.S. dollar.

Accounting and economics provide indispensable tools for understanding how value is determined in financial markets.

Examine the financial statements of Rogers and Teck for significant differences between GAAP income and pro forma income. Compare the book value of equity to the market value of equity (available at the TSX site).

A Discipline Used by Financial Managers

* The techniques and theories developed by finance are employed when making decisions and implementing strategies.
* Adjustments are made due to changes in the economy, new ideas, or new competition.

Many firms that had diversified to reduce risks as per theory had, by the late 1990s, refocused on their core businesses. Diversification, effective at the investor level, was questioned at the corporate level. The dynamic derivatives market, built on financial theories, is used by firms to reduce the risks of changes in interest rates, exchange rates, and commodity prices.

Vigorous international competition and rapid technology change redefine product markets, and production processes have sharpened focus on the firm's financial objectives. Analytical decision making and financial theories are as applicable to the small business as to the large corporation, although the analysis may not be as in-depth. The small business owner will be better prepared to adapt to the rigours of the changing marketplace if they know the theories and techniques of decision analysis.

Today e-commerce presents more efficient ways to interact with customers—the business-to-consumer-model (B2C)—and with suppliers—the business-to-business model (B2B). In the B2C model, the Internet plays an increasing role, producing instantaneous cash flow to organizations such as Chapters Indigo and eBay. In the B2B model, orders can be placed, inventory managed, and bids to supply product accepted online. The B2B model can help companies lower their cost of managing inventory, accounts receivable, and cash. As the pace of business increases, analytical decision making needs to occur effectively and quickly using well-founded techniques.

GOALS OF FINANCIAL MANAGEMENT

Financial management is concerned with the efficient management of the firm by employing its resources in the most productive manner. Several goals or objectives might be suggested:

* Customer satisfaction
* Product quality
* Happy employees
* Payment of taxes for society's welfare
* Contributing to the local community
* Enriching management
* Creating value for shareholders

However, is there one goal that best encompasses the productive use of the firm's resources? Might one goal capture the other suggested objectives of the firm?

LO3 Maximizing Shareholder Wealth

The diverse interests at play in formulating company strategy are probably best served by creating as much value in the firm as possible. Although we might question for whom the value is created, the broad goal·of the firm can be brought into focus if we say the financial manager's goal is shareholder wealth maximization. The firm is owned by the shareholders and they retain its residual value. Analysis of the motivations and actions of the firm are best explained with maximization of shareholder wealth considered the firm's goal.

There are suggestions that other goals may explain the actions of the firm. Agency theory, a branch of financial research, examines the potential for conflict between the owners of the firm and the firm's managers who make the day-to-day decisions. Diversified ownership interests may allow managers to follow their own interests that differ from those of the shareholders and other interested parties. This can affect the financial decisions of the firm.

Agency theory is important in assessing management's effect on the goals and value of the firm. Good corporate governance oversight and practices strive for transparency in decisions, ethical dealings, avoidance of conflicts of interest, and diversity of opinion. Many of the difficulties experienced in the financial markets relate to deficient corporate governance.

To some extent, management power is checked by institutional investors such as pension funds and mutual funds that own a large percentage of major Canadian companies. They have more to say about the way publicly owned corporations are managed through their ability to vote large blocks of shares and replace poorly performing boards of directors. Since these institutions represent individual workers and investors, they have a responsibility to see that the firm is managed in an efficient and ethical way.

FINANCE IN ACTION

Nobel Prize Winners for Finance (Economics)

Several individuals have been awarded the Nobel Prize in economic sciences for their body of work in the discipline of finance. Financial managers, analysts, and investors employ techniques derived from the theories and models developed by these Nobel laureates on capital structure, dividend policy, portfolio management, risk-return relationships, the reduction of risk through the use of derivatives, and how financial markets incorporate information into share values.

The Nobel laureates are

- Franco Modigliani   1985
- Harry Markowitz, Merton Miller, William Sharpe   1990
- Robert Merton, Myron Scholes   1997
- Joseph Stiglitz, Michael Spence, George Akerlof   2001
- Eugene Fama, Lars Peter Hansen, Robert Shiller   2013
- Richard Thaler   2017

Brief descriptions of the men, their theories, and their influence on the discipline of finance, in theory and in practice, can be viewed at the Nobel website. Search for each laureate by name.

Q1 Why were each of these individuals awarded the Nobel Prize?

nobelprize.org

Measuring the Goal

We may agree that maximizing shareholder wealth is an appropriate goal for the firm. However, how can we measure whether we have been successful in achieving this goal? Is it

- Market share?
- Earnings or profits?
- Size of the firm?
- Share price?
- Return on investment?

"Earning the highest possible profit for the firm" is often suggested as the firm's goal, and this is reinforced by income statements in which the bottom line is earnings. Under this criterion, every decision would be evaluated on the basis of its overall contribution to the firm's earnings. However, selecting profit maximization as the primary goal of the firm may not increase its value, because a profit-only focus has several drawbacks:

- Risk may increase as profit changes. More debts or investment in projects with cyclical earnings to increase profits also increase risk. Shareholders may consider the potential for increased earnings insufficient for the greater risk.

- Profit fails to take into account the timing of benefits. We might be indifferent between the following alternatives if our emphasis were solely on maximizing earnings, as the total is the same. However, alternative B is clearly superior, because larger benefits occur earlier; we could reinvest the difference in earnings for alternative B for an extra period.

	Earnings per Share		
	Period 1	Period 2	Total
Alternative A	$1.50	$2.00	$3.50
Alternative B	2.00	1.50	3.50

- Accurately measuring profit is almost impossible. Economics and accounting define profit (earnings) differently. Furthermore, earnings may not correspond to current values due to the methods used to capture accounting accruals and the amortization of capital expenditures. As well, financial statements can be subject to manipulation by managers, in which case reported earnings will be misleading.

Market Share Price

Although profits are connected to the goal of maximizing shareholder wealth, they don't necessarily measure it well. Wealth is best measured in our mixed capitalist system by what people are currently willing to pay for something, and what investors are willing to pay for a firm is its market-determined share price. Share price is a value that investors collectively are prepared to pay, whereas earnings are a paper entry prepared by management and their accountants. Market share price directly ties the firm's success back to the goal of shareholder wealth maximization.

In an analysis of the firm's market share value, the investor will consider

- The risk inherent in the firm (nature of its operations and how the firm is financed)
- The time pattern of the firm's earnings and cash flows
- The quality and reliability of reported earnings (as a guidepost to future earning power)
- Economic and political factors

As share price is a more complete measure of the achievement of shareholder wealth, the financial manager must be sensitive to the effect of each decision on the firm's overall valuation. If a decision maintains or increases the firm's overall value, it is acceptable from a financial viewpoint;

otherwise, it should be rejected. This is the one basic principle upon which everything in this text is predicated.

However, achieving the highest possible share price for the firm is not a simple task. The financial manager cannot directly control the firm's share price as it is affected by investors' future expectations as well as by the general economic environment. This is exhibited in "The Foundations" Finance in Action box. Even firms with good earnings and favourable trends do not always perform well in the financial markets. Effective financial management to help achieve this measurement yardstick is therefore quite important.

Investor expectations change over time from periods of high exuberance with risk taking, as in the late 1990s, to periods of caution, focusing on cash with lower growth. Caution in recent times followed the largest global financial crisis since the Depression and with the Covid-19 pandemic great uncertainty prevailed.

The key model of finance is the present value model that determines the value of assets on the basis of their future expected cash flows. "Expected" implies that there is uncertainty as to the amount and the timing of these cash flows, and therefore valuation must consider how risk will influence asset values and the return to investors. The present value model, with risk-return considerations, requires an appropriate discount rate to value cash flows. We look to the financial markets to supply us with this discount rate.

LO4 Management and Shareholder Wealth

In line with the earlier discussion of agency theory, one might ask, "Does modern corporate management actually follow the goal of maximizing shareholder wealth and does it try to increase market share price?" Management likely has its own interests to look after in operating the firm. Financial managers are interested in

- Maintaining their jobs (may discourage value-enhancing takeovers)
- Protecting "private spheres of influence"
- Maximizing their own compensation package
- Arbitrating among the firm's different stakeholders (shareholders, creditors, employees, unions, environmentalists, consumer groups, Canada Revenue Agency, government regulatory bodies, customers)

Pursuit of these interests may emphasize short-term results over long-term wealth building. Management may also perceive the risk of investment decisions differently from shareholders, leading to different points of view as to the best decision regarding the investment of the firm's resources.

Recognizing that there may be different motivations between managers and shareholders introduces the need to monitor the performance of management through independent boards of directors, compensation packages, audited financial statements, and regulatory bodies. The conflicts or frictions that exist, and the devices established to control them, impose "agency" costs on the firm that may reduce share values. Other agency costs are imposed by banks and bondholders that place restrictions on the actions of management to protect their positions in exchange for providing debt. Therefore, tradeoffs exist among the agency costs of monitoring management actions, allowing sufficient discretion for management decision making and designing compensation packages to motivate management to perform in the interests of the shareholders.

Managers often have their compensation determined from a combination of measurement yardsticks focused on several objectives. Stock options and bonuses are paid according to accounting measures that are subject to manipulation by managers and do not necessarily correlate well with the goal of maximizing shareholder wealth. These measures that have enriched many executives do not necessarily produce the same results experienced by long-term owners of shares. This has led to a divergence of interests between managers and investors, often resulting in questionable business decisions.

Despite their own interests, there are still reasons for management to act to maximize shareholders' wealth:

- Poor stock price performance often leads to takeovers and proxy fights to remove management.
- Share ownership by managers motivates them to achieve market value maximization for their own benefit.
- Institutional investors are increasingly making management more responsive to shareholders.

Share ownership that is widely held among many investors may allow management to pursue its own interest, although patterns of share ownership in Canada may mitigate this tendency. Share ownership in Canada is often tightly held, with Table 1–1 revealing widely diffused stock ownership for only 29 of our 100 largest companies. Slightly more than half of our top 500 firms are publicly traded. Many are subsidiaries of U.S. or other foreign multinational companies, and several are controlled directly by one family, such as the Desmarais family through Power Corporation. However, through pension funds, insurance companies, and mutual funds, the average Canadian is participating indirectly in share ownership to the tune of hundreds of billions of dollars. Pension fund managers are taking a more active role in the corporations in which they have an investment and are holding managers accountable. These ownership patterns suggest that management interests at least coincide with at least one shareholder.

Power Corporation
powercorporation.com

Table 1–1 Ownership of Canada's 100 largest companies*

Widely held	29
Foreign controlled (U.S. dominant)	29
Family or individually controlled	22
Government controlled	9
Other controlled (Coops, members, partners)	11
	100

*As determined by revenues, 2018.

The patterns of share ownership and concentration of wealth provide hints as to the reasons for the difficulties experienced by the smaller entrepreneur in accessing capital in Canada.

Social Responsibility

 FINANCE IN ACTION

Change Is Coming

The Business Roundtable (businessroundtable.org) an association of CEOs of leading U.S. companies for almost 50 years, recently modified its statement on the purpose of a corporation. From the sole purpose of maximizing shareholder wealth it reintroduced a broader focus. The purpose now encompasses all stakeholders including employees, communities, customers, suppliers, and shareholders. The environment, diversity, and inclusion are also given consideration.

Corporations play a dominant role in our society and are brought into existence with society's consent. As such, they have a responsibility to the communities in which they operate. Is, however, the goal of shareholder wealth maximization consistent with a concern for social responsibility? We believe that in most instances the answer is yes. By adopting policies that maximize values in the market, the firm can attract capital, provide employment, and offer benefits to its host community. This is the basic strength of the private enterprise system. Successful business firms can support the fundraising for endeavours by fine arts organizations, social assistance groups, and post-secondary institutions.

Corporations, which receive their operational charters from society, should consider socially desirable actions that include

- Community works (charitable giving, employment opportunities for marginalized groups)
- Customer respect (safe products, fair pricing, appropriate advertising and communication)
- Strong employee relations (fair benefits and compensation, equitable hiring, education, health and safety)
- Environmental health (pollution controls, appropriate use and renewal of resources)
- Human rights promotion (respecting the dignity of individuals globally)

There are good examples of responsible Canadian corporations. Canfor (canfor.com) aspires to certification for all its forestry operations by the Forestry Stewardship Council, an international coalition stressing forestry conservation and respect for the people and wildlife of our forests. Suncor Energy (suncor.com) has a commitment to stewardship of its valuable resources, to sustainability, and to a mutually beneficial relationship with Aboriginal peoples.

Nevertheless, certain socially desirable actions may at times be inconsistent with earning the highest possible profit or achieving maximum valuation in the market. For example, pollution control projects frequently offer a negative return on investment. Does this mean firms should not exercise social responsibility in regard to pollution control? The answer is no—but certain cost-increasing activities may have to be mandatory rather than voluntary, at least initially, to ensure that the burden falls equally over all business firms.

Ethical Behaviour

The ethical behaviour of firms is questioned when we hear of illegal financial practices, on Bay and Wall Streets, by corporate financial "deal makers." Ethics in business has perhaps two key aspects:

- Fairness (obeying the established rules of regulatory bodies and the company bylaws, appropriate compensation to managers and employees, and equitable share voting)
- Honesty (timely and full disclosure of pertinent company developments, rigorous financial reporting and scrutiny)

Fairness is often questioned when employee salaries are compared to those of top executives. Executive compensation is generally composed of base salary, bonuses, stock options, and lucrative pension entitlements. Currently missing from these corporations is an appropriate disclosure of the connection between the compensation schemes for top executives and the performance of the corporation in wealth creation for other shareholders.

Honesty, within the capitalist system, comes into question when the top executives seem to benefit from "confidential information" at the expense of regular shareholders. Insider trading has been a widely publicized issue in recent years. Insider trading occurs when someone has information that is not available to the public and then uses this information to profit from trading in a company's common stock. This practice is illegal and is protected against by the various securities commissions across Canada. Sometimes the insider is a company manager or friend; other times it is the company's lawyer, investment dealer, or even the printer of the company's financial statement. Anyone who has knowledge before public dissemination of that information stands to benefit from either good news or bad news. Insider trading is hard to prosecute successfully.

Are Executive Salaries Fair?

In 2017, Canada's top 100 CEOs (chief executive officers) earned an average of $10 million each, in contrast to an average worker's salary of $50,759, as reported by the Canadian Centre for Policy Alternatives (policyalternatives.ca). CEO compensation was 197 times the average worker's salary. Ironically, this occurred with greater disclosure of executive compensation in financial statements, which was required following the accounting scandals in the early 1990s. CEO salaries in the U.S. peaked at 376 times average worker salaries in 2000, up from 20 times average in the late 1960s. They were at 278 times in 2018.

The increase in executive compensation seems to be a North American phenomenon that has not extended to Europe. This has been identified in a paper by Emmanuel Saez and Michael Veall (eml.berkeley.edu/~saez/saez-veallAER05canada.pdf).

When investors doubt the integrity of a firm's leadership, there is a loss of value in the markets. The Ontario Securities Commission in 2004 introduced new governance standards to replace the Toronto Stock Exchange (TSX) guidelines of 1994. The TSX had been largely self-governing at the time in these matters.

Q1 Do you think CEO salaries properly reflect their value to a firm?

Q2 Are these high salaries in society's best interests?

The rules of fairness are laid out by the securities commissions, stock exchanges, accounting bodies, government laws, and employees of firms. The Canada Business Corporations Act (laws-lois .justice.gc.ca/eng/acts/C-44) states in Section 122 that directors and officers of the firm should "act honestly and in good faith with a view to the best interests of the corporation." Nevertheless, we have also heard of financial officers manipulating financial results, sometimes with the collaboration of accounting firms, to enrich themselves at the expense of the ordinary investor. Strong ethical standards for a corporation should be established by the board of directors. Good corporate governance results from

- Board composition (strong leadership, competent education, balanced competencies)
- Director and officers' ownership positions in the firm (other than by stock options)
- A published code of ethics
- Independent audits and a financially literate audit committee

There is some academic research (Gompers, Ishii, Motrick) that suggests that good governance leads to superior wealth creation in firms. Institutional investors realizing the importance of ethical leadership formed the Canadian Coalition for Good Governance (ccgg.ca) to promote best practices.

There have been increased demands for additional corporate governance practices by firms, despite the increased costs of compliance and the possibility of delays in timely reporting of financial results. These measures include

- Separating the roles of CEO and chair of the board
- Independent directors on the board
- Improved accounting standards (stock options, internal audit controls, "off-balance sheet items") (Chapter 2)
- More stringent reporting and disclosure requirements (Chapter 14)
- Closer monitoring by regulatory bodies (securities commissions) (Chapter 14)
- Questioning the use of "dual class" shares (Chapter 17)

Activities such as insider trading or the manipulation of financial statements to distort the true financial results of the firm serve no beneficial economic or financial purpose, and it could be argued that they have a negative impact on shareholders' interests. Illegal security trading and poor corporate governance destroy confidence in securities markets, making it more difficult to achieve shareholder wealth maximization.

FUNCTIONS OF FINANCIAL MANAGEMENT

The study of finance leads to a variety of functions within the capital and real markets of our system. These include

- Corporate finance
- Banking
- Securities trading and underwriting
- Money management
- Financial planning
- Risk management (insurance)

Financial managers allocate the firm's funds to current and capital assets, obtain the best mix of financing from the capital markets, and develop an appropriate dividend policy consistent with the firm's objectives. The daily activities of financial management, outlined in Figure 1–1, require careful monitoring of the cash position of the firm and consume most of a financial manager's time. Less-routine functions of a longer-term nature often require extensive analysis, as these decisions are often of strategic importance and may require large capital investment.

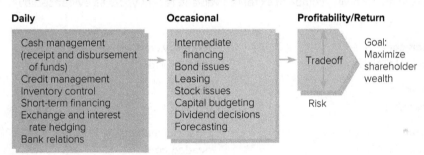

Figure 1–1 Functions of the financial manager

As these functions are carried out, an appropriate risk-return (profitability) tradeoff needs to be determined to maximize the market value of the firm for its shareholders.

LO5 The tasks of the financial manager are being reshaped by increased domestic and international competition, by advances in information technology and management techniques, and by innovations in the types of financial markets and products. A chief financial officer usually takes responsibility for long-term financing and investment; the controller looks after informational flows related to planning, control, and external reporting; and the treasurer looks after external relations, particularly as they apply to daily cash management. A large firm often has many individuals who report to these positions and specialize in the duties required of the functions identified in the figure.

FINANCE IN ACTION

Functions of Finance

Amazon is a leader in online selling and delivery, coupled with extensive data collection and sophisticated analysis of its customers. This allows it targeted deals for customers and effective management of its inventories. In mid-2017 it purchased Whole Foods. Has its GPS technology (Amazon Go) meant no cashiers, online grocer shopping, and delivery? This is a working capital decision on managing a minimal investment in current assets and liabilities.

Cenovus purchased oil sands assets of ConocoPhillips for almost $18 billion in the down oil markets of early 2017. Within a few months the price of its shares had fallen by almost 50 percent. Has this been a good long-term acquisition. Back in 2008, Teck purchased Fording Canadian Coal Trust for $12 billion in mostly borrowed cash and Teck shares. Teck almost failed in the subsequent credit market difficulties but in 2016 had a fantastic share price return. Mergers, takeovers, and company expansion are capital budgeting decisions made to create value; they require an appropriate assessment of risk to determine a rate of return, known as the *cost of capital.*

In 1999, TransCanada Corporation (now TC Energy) decreased its dividend unexpectedly, attempting to increase internal cash flow to reduce its debt and improve earnings. Share prices declined initially but by 2001, as investors saw the improved results, the share price increased. Following the liquidity crisis of 2008, corporations decreased their reliance on debt, sold equity, and hoarded cash. In 2014, Tim Hortons announced the repurchase of 1.5 million common shares. By the end of 2014 Tim Hortons was part of Restaurant Brands International, a Brazilian investment firm. Decisions to alter the relationship between debt and equity in the firm are referred to as capital structure decisions.

These are some of the decisions made by corporations as they attempt to create value for the shareholders. By going to the TSX website, you can see how the share prices of these companies have performed since these decisions were made.

Q1 Have the following companies created value in recent years as evidenced by increased share prices?

amazon.com
Symbol: AMZN (Nasdaq)

cenovus.com
Symbol: CVE

teck.com
Symbol: TECK.B

tcenergy.com
Symbol: TRP

rbi.com
Symbol: QSR

Financial markets:
nasdaq.com
tmx.com

FORMS OF ORGANIZATION

The finance function may be carried out within a number of different forms of organization. Of primary interest are the sole proprietorship, the partnership, and the corporation.

Sole Proprietorship

A sole proprietorship is characterized by

- Single-person ownership
- Simplicity of decision making
- Low organizational and operating costs
- Unlimited liability to the owner (can lose personal assets in settlement of firm's debts)
- Profits or losses taxed in hands of individual owner

Many small businesses with only a few employees are sole proprietorships. The unlimited liability is a serious drawback and few lenders are willing to advance funds to a small business without a personal liability commitment from the owner.

Partnership

A partnership is characterized by

- Multiple ownership
- Ability to raise more capital and share ownership responsibilities
- Unlimited liability for the owners (one wealthy partner may have to bear a disproportionate share of losses in a general partnership)
- Taxation of profits or losses is allocated in percentages to partners

Most partnerships are formed through an agreement between the participants, known as the **partnership agreement,** which specifies the ownership interest, the methods for distributing profits, and the means for withdrawing from the partnership.

To circumvent the unlimited liability feature, a special form of partnership called a limited partnership can be utilized. Under this arrangement one or more partners are designated general partners and have unlimited liability for the debts of the firm; other partners are designated limited partners and are liable only for their initial contribution. The limited partners are normally prohibited from being active in the management of the firm. Limited partnerships are common in real estate and trust syndications.

Corporation

A corporation is characterized by

- Being a legal entity unto itself (may sue or be sued, engage in contracts, acquire property)
- Ownership by shareholders (each with limited liability, although bankers may require small business owners to give their personal guarantee)
- Divisibility of the ownership (many shareholders)
- Continuous life span (not dependent on life of one shareholder)
- Taxation on its own income (individual shareholders pay tax on dividends or capital gain tax when shares are sold)
- A partnership-corporation blend known, in the U.S., as a LLC (limited liability corporation), with income flowing through to partners enjoying limited liability (taxed as a corporation in Canada)

In terms of revenue and profits produced, the corporation is by far the most important form of economic unit. Thus, the effects of many decisions in this text are considered from the corporate viewpoint.

Of growing significance and perhaps concern are state-owned enterprises (SOEs) which are politically and economically protected within certain countries such as China where 80 percent of companies are SOEs or even Brazil with 38 percent of companies being SOEs.

The corporation is generally incorporated federally or in a single province, with registration in all other provinces in which it conducts business. Although the incorporating procedure varies across Canada, to proceed with **articles of incorporation,** a firm will require a **company charter** and **company bylaws.** The charter contains the organization's founding principles and is relatively unalterable. The bylaws contain details of company policies and procedures and can be changed by vote of the board of directors and shareholders.

The Pricing Mechanism of Financial Markets—WhatsApp

Google (Alphabet (GOOG)), formed in 1998, has become the world's largest Internet search engine. It first sold shares (an IPO, or initial placement offering) in 2004 valuing the firm at $23 billion, and by 2019 they traded to value the firm at over $853 billion, making Google one of the most valuable companies in the world. In 2006, Google purchased YouTube for $1.65 billion, a company that had started only in 2005 and had not yet made any money. WhatsApp, a mobile instant data messaging company with negligible revenues, was purchased by Facebook in 2014 for $19 billion. The 450 million active users and rapid growth in users were the potential value.

Capital was being reallocated to companies that suggested a new business model. This reallocation is the pricing mechanism of the financial markets. As prices rise, capital flows to these "new age" companies with little in the way of tangible or hard assets. Their value comes from their ability to manipulate and supply information, suggesting that in the future they would be able to generate large cash flows for shareholders.

Gold traditionally has been a hard asset. It has been used to conduct business transactions, as a store of wealth, and, due to its scarcity, had at one time been used to back the major currencies of the world. Gold that sold for US$850 per ounce in 1980 sold for US$278 per ounce in 2002. In an age in which capital can be transferred instantaneously around the globe and many governments have learned to effectively manage their economies with low rates of inflation, gold seemed to have lost its significance as a store of wealth and as a reserve currency. But has it? By fall 2011 it was trading above US$1,900 per ounce, but by 2019 it was down to $1,500 per ounce.

Q1 Where will the pricing mechanism of the financial markets allocate capital resources next?

There are several noteworthy financial markets:

TSX **tmx.com**	LSE **londonstockexchange.com**
Japan Exchange Group **www.jpx.co.jp/english**	NYSE Euronext **euronext.com**
NASDAQ **nasdaq.com**	CME **cmegroup.com**

A corporation may have thousands of registered shareholders, each with the right to vote. The shareholders' interests are ultimately managed by the corporation's board of directors. The board, which generally includes key management personnel as well as outside directors not permanently employed by it, serves in a stewardship capacity and may be liable for the mismanagement of the firm or for the misappropriation of funds.

The corporation is established with capital supplied by the shareholders and recorded on its books as contributed capital (common stock). Earnings generated by the corporation are owned equally by each shareholder, and the board of directors has two choices for these earnings. Earnings can be

- Paid out as dividends (shareholders pay tax on dividends; a dividend tax credit reduces the effect of double taxation)
- Reinvested in the firm (recorded as retained earnings)

THE ROLE OF THE FINANCIAL MARKETS

Managerial efforts and ethical (or unethical) behaviour affect company value through the daily change of share prices in the financial markets. But what are the financial markets? Financial markets are the meeting place for people, corporations, and institutions that either need money or have money to lend or invest. They exist as a vast global network of individuals and financial institutions. Governments also participate in the financial markets primarily as borrowers of funds for public activities; their markets are referred to as public financial markets. Corporations such as Bombardier, Shopify, and CN Rail, on the other hand, raise funds in the corporate financial markets. Governments have for many years sold assets through share issues, such as the Government of Ontario's sale of Hydro One.

Structure and Functions of the Financial Markets

Financial markets have a diverse array of specialized areas with a broad distinction between money and capital markets. Money markets refer to those markets dealing with short-term securities that have a life of one year or less. Securities in these markets can include Treasury bills offered by the federal or provincial government, commercial paper sold by corporations to finance their daily operations, or certificates of deposit with maturities of less than one year sold by banks. Examples of money market securities are presented more fully in Chapter 7.

The capital markets are generally defined as those markets in which securities have a life of more than one year. While capital markets are long-term markets as opposed to short-term money markets, it is often common to break down the capital markets into intermediate markets (1 to 10 years) and long-term markets (greater than 10 years). The capital markets include securities such as common stock, preferred stock, and corporate and government bonds. The capital markets are fully presented in Chapter 14.

LO6 Allocation of Capital

Corporations rely on the financial markets to provide funds for short-term operations and for new plant and equipment. Financial capital is raised either by borrowing money through a debt offering of corporate bonds or short-term notes or by selling ownership in the company through an issue of common stock. When a corporation uses the financial markets to raise new funds, the sale of securities is said to be made in the primary market by way of a new issue. After the securities are sold to the public (institutions and individuals), they are traded in the secondary market between investors. Trading may take place in an open transparent market where all buyers and sellers have access to security prices, in the traditional auction market, or by way of negotiation with institutions that hold securities in inventory, the dealer market, which is considerably less transparent.

In the secondary market, prices change continually, as investors buy and sell securities based on their expectations of the corporation's prospects. Financial managers receive feedback about their firm's performance as the markets determine value and allocate capital to its most profitable uses. The present value calculations of Chapters 9 and 10 value financial assets in much the same way as properly functioning markets.

How does the market allocate capital to the thousands of firms that are continually in need of money? Suppose as a finance graduate you are hired to manage $250 million. You might buy common stock in Bombardier, the Canadian transportation manufacturer; in Nestlé, the Swiss food company; or in Telefonos de Mexico, the Mexican telephone company. You might choose to lend money to the Canadian or Japanese government by purchasing their bonds, or you might lend money to Rogers Corporation. Of course, these are only some of the endless choices you would have.

Your investment strategy would try to maximize return and minimize risk. Underpriced securities with the potential for high returns will be bid up in price, and overpriced securities of equal risk will be avoided. All market participants play the risk-return game, with the financial markets becoming the playing field and prices recording the winning or losing score. Given companies of equal risk, those with expectations for high return will have higher common share prices relative to those companies with poor expectations. Market share prices reflect the combined judgment of all the players in the market, and, as a result, securities price movements provide feedback to corporate managers on performance.

As the market rewards companies with higher-priced securities, they have an easier time raising new funds than their competitors. They are also able to raise funds at a lower cost. Go back to that $250 million you might manage. If the Royal Bank wants to borrow money from you at 5 percent and Baytex Energy is willing to pay 5 percent but is also riskier, to which company will you lend money? If you choose the Royal Bank you are on your way to understanding finance. The competition between the two firms for your funds will eventually cause Baytex to either offer higher returns than the Royal Bank or go without funds. In this way, the financial markets allocate funds efficiently to the highest-quality companies at the lowest cost and to the lowest-quality companies at the highest cost. In other words, there is a penalty for firms that fail to perform up to competitive standards.

Risk

As the markets allocate capital through the pricing of securities, a major consideration is risk and its impact on value. Risk is the uncertainty inherent in the future cash flows from a company's assets. The company cash flows will provide (or not provide) the returns to the investors that buy securities. Increasing risk in the financial markets or in a firm's prospects will put downward pressure on the share price. There are many factors at play that determine our collective perceptions of risk. Some of these are as follows:

- *Debt* is an important component of a firm's capital structure. However, too much debt can erode a firm's ability to generate sufficient cash flow to comfortably cover its interest expenses. This increases the firm's risk. The financial crisis of 2008–09 forced Lehman Brothers, Chrysler, and General Motors into bankruptcy because of their debt loads.

   Governments, and in particular the federal government, are heavy borrowers in the capital markets, and compete with corporations. The federal fiscal deficit represents the difference between the revenues and expenses of the government of Canada. The federal deficit reached $55 billion in 2009–10. Deficits, which accumulate to become the total net debt of the federal government, totalled $770 billion by 2019. A government accumulating too much debt limits its ability to properly manage the economy, adding risk to the domestic and foreign exchange financial markets. In 2019 the Government of Canada had the lowest debt to GDP of the G7 countries.

   When generating surpluses and lowering its debt as a percentage of GDP, the federal government has the decreased supply of relatively risk-free government securities, forcing investors into riskier financial securities.

- *Liquidity* is always a concern within the financial system. The financial crisis of 2008 required unprecedented intervention by governments to provide liquidity to their banking systems. The exchange of money dried up as people lost confidence because of the housing bubble, poor credit risks, a lack of scrutiny of financial instruments and questionable surveillance by securities commissions and rating agencies. Without liquidity the economies of the world slowed significantly.

   As a result of the financial crisis, governments resorted to regulation to keep institutions in check. The Dodd-Frank Act of 2010 required greater accountability and transparency to address systemic risks, moral hazards, and limits to speculative investing. Some have said that the Act over-regulated, reducing the flexibility of the financial markets.

The Markets Reflect Value, Yields (Rates of Return), and Risk

The S&P/TSX Composite Index represents the equity market value of the top companies listed on Canada's premier stock exchange. In June 2008 it had a value of over 15,000, but by November it was below 8,000. Shareholder market value had dropped considerably in half a year. By 2011 it had climbed back above 15,000, the heights reached in 2008. In the fall of 2019 it was almost to 17,000. Search for the Composite's current value at tmx.com.

The bedrock interest rate, or *yield,* in the economy is the overnight rate, the rate at which financial institutions lend money among themselves for one day. Other yields in the economy take their cues from this rate. In 1981, Canada's overnight rate reached 21.57 percent. In late 2019, the overnight rate was at 1.75 percent while in England it was 0.75 percent (gilt repo rate), and in Japan it was a negative 0.10 percent.

The U.S rate, generally at 2.00 percent in 2019, jumped to 10.00 percent with a temporary liquidity concern. Increased government borrowing and tighter regulations were suggested reasons for the jump.

In 2007 the short-term money markets reacted quickly to increased risk. Asset-backed commercial paper (ABCP) used to finance poor-credit-quality housing loans (*subprime mortgages*) in the United States became a major and far-reaching concern. Commercial paper generally offers a slightly higher yield than government-backed Treasury bills, but in August 2007 the yields between these two financial assets began to diverge significantly, as seen in the figure below. This signaled a liquidity crisis.

Q1 What are current overnight rates in these countries?

Q2 What is the current value of the S&P/TSX Composite Index?

Q3 What is the current spread (difference in yield) between Treasury bills and commercial paper?

bankofcanada.ca   **bankofengland.co.uk**   **boj.or.jp/en**

Treasury bill, commercial paper yield divergence, 2007 (one-month maturity)

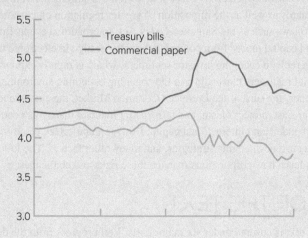

- **Interest rates,** or **yields,** are the rates of return required on investments that help establish the allocation of capital. Securities with the better yields attract the capital. Volatile interest rates generate risk in the marketplace. Short-term interest rates that were above 20 percent in the 1980s were down to 4 percent by 2001 and under 2 percent in 2014, where generally they have remained till 2020. The low stable interest rates of the 1990s acted to spur the stock and bond markets to record levels. Lower interest rates result in investors placing higher values on corporate securities. Furthermore, lower rates result in cheaper financing for new capital projects of the firm.

A major determinant of interest rates is the rate of inflation. Figure 1–2 portrays the annual rate of inflation, as measured by the changes in the consumer price index (CPI) along with the prime interest rate. Generally, the prime rate exceeds the average rate of inflation. Phantom profits and undervalued assets develop during periods of high inflation. The benefits, drawbacks, and implications of disinflation (a slowing of price increases) will be explored in Chapter 3 on financial analysis.

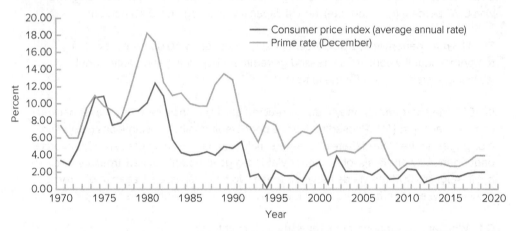

Figure 1–2 Prime rate versus percent change in the CPI

Greater risk increases the spread between inflation and yield.

- **Global competition.** Brand names such as Sony, Bombardier, Coca-Cola, Nokia, and Mercedes-Benz raise funds on most major international money and capital markets by searching for the cheapest sources of funds. This has led to mergers of the world's largest financial markets to reduce risks and inconveniences. Technology has given us electronic communication networks (ECNs) to trade securities. Increased costs come from the requirements of international accounting standards as well as the imposition of greater regulation on corporate governance and disclosure due to laws such as the Sarbanes-Oxley Act. International events impact economies of all countries, and capital moves from country to country easily via electronic networks. Markets are quickly vulnerable to changing investor sentiment, which is rapidly expressed over the Internet. Financial managers must adjust to the changing economic environment, the creation of the free trade zones, the euro of the European Common Market, the emergence of the industrial nations of the Far East, protectionism, and terrorism. Financial managers need to have the sophistication to understand international capital flows, computerized electronic funds transfer systems, foreign currency hedging strategies, and many other factors. The following chapters should help you learn how corporations manage these risks and challenges.

FORMAT OF THE TEXT

The material in this text is covered under six major parts. You progress from the development of basic analytical skills in accounting and finance to the utilization of decision-making techniques in working capital management, capital budgeting, long-term financing, and other related areas. The length, 21 chapters, makes the text appropriate for one or two semester coverage.

You are given a thorough grounding in financial theory in a highly palatable and comprehensive fashion—with careful attention to definitions, symbols, and formulas. The intent is, above all, that you develop a thorough understanding of the basic concepts in finance.

Parts

1. **Introduction** This part examines the goals and objectives of financial management. The emphasis on decision making and risk management is stressed, with an update of significant events influencing the study of finance.

2. **Financial Analysis and Planning** You are first given the opportunity to review the basic principles of accounting as they relate to finance (financial statements and funds flow). You may judge whether you need this review before progressing through the section.

   Additional material in this part includes a thorough study of ratio analysis, budget construction techniques, and development of comprehensive pro forma statements. The effect of heavy fixed commitments, in the form of either debt or plant and equipment, is examined in a discussion of leverage.

3. **Working Capital Management** The techniques for managing short-term assets of the firm and the associated liabilities are examined. The material is introduced in the context of risk-return analysis. The financial manager must constantly choose between liquid, low-return assets (perhaps marketable securities) and more profitable, less-liquid assets (such as inventory). Sources of short-term financing are also considered.

4. **The Capital Budgeting Process** The decision on capital outlays is among the most significant a firm will have to make. In terms of study procedure, we attempt to carefully develop "time value of money" calculations; we then proceed to the valuation of bonds and stocks, emphasizing present value techniques. The valuation chapter develops the traditional dividend valuation model and examines bond price sensitivity in response to discount rates and inflation. An appendix presents the supernormal dividend growth model, or what is sometimes called the two-stage dividend model. After careful grounding in valuation practice and theory, we examine the cost of capital and capital structure. The text then moves to the actual capital budgeting decision, using previously learned material and employing the concept of marginal analysis. The concluding chapter in this part covers risk-return analysis in capital budgeting, with a brief exposure to portfolio theory and a consideration of market value maximization.

5. **Long-Term Financing** You are introduced to Canadian financial markets as they relate to corporate financial management. You consider the sources and uses of funds in the capital markets, with coverage given to warrants and convertibles as well as the more conventional methods of financing. Derivative instruments are also explored. The guiding role of the investment dealer in the distribution of securities is also analyzed. Furthermore, you are encouraged to think of leasing as a form of debt.

6. **Expanding the Perspective of Corporate Finance** A chapter on corporate mergers considers external growth strategy and serves as an integrative tool to bring together topics such as profit management, capital budgeting, portfolio considerations, and valuation concepts. A second chapter on international financial management describes the growth of the international financial markets, the rise of multinational business, and the effects on corporate financial management. The issues discussed in these two chapters highlight corporate diversification and risk-reduction attempts over the years.

SUMMARY*

1. Finance builds on analytical techniques for decision making from economics and calls on financial data produced from accounting statements. Finance links these two disciplines. (LO1)

2. With the development of sophisticated analytical techniques for financial management, its focus has broadened to include not only adequate returns but also returns in the context of risk assumed by the firm. (LO2)

3. The primary goal of the firm is the maximization of shareholder wealth as measured by share price. This is a more satisfactory goal than profit maximization, because it incorporates the risk and timing of cash flows and because share value is objectively determined in the marketplace. Furthermore, this goal best helps to explain decisions made by corporations. (LO3)

4. The management of corporations may not always act in the best interests of shareholders. Management has other demands, including its own interests. Agency theory studies the conflicts between shareholders and management, and measures adopted to control the conflicts. The pursuit of socially or ethically acceptable goals may come at the expense of shareholders' wealth. (LO4)

5. Financial managers are involved in raising funds for the firm and in investing those funds in the most efficient way. The activities of the financial manager include working capital management, capital budgeting, and capital structure financing decisions. (LO5)

6. Financial markets allocate capital to its best use if they operate freely and properly. The markets determine value, a key variable in decision making. The markets also establish appropriate rates of return or yields for investments. (LO6)

*Each chapter summary is keyed to the learning objectives at the beginning of the chapter.

DISCUSSION QUESTIONS

1. What effect did the recession of 2007–09 have on regulation? (LO1–3)

2. If shares of both a high-tech startup company and the Royal Bank promised cash flow of $2 per share over the next year, for which shares would you be prepared to pay the higher price? Why? (LO2)

3. What is meant by the goal of maximization of shareholder wealth? Why is profit maximization, by itself, an inappropriate goal? (LO3)

4. What issue does agency theory examine? Why has it become more important in recent times? (LO4)

5. Why are institutional investors important in today's financial markets? (LO4)

6. When does insider trading occur? What government agency is responsible for protecting against the unethical practice of insider trading? (LO4)

7. The government has passed regulations over the years that require pollution controls, development restrictions, hiring equity, and pay equity. Can a firm still achieve the maximization of shareholder wealth? (LO4)

8. The senior management of corporations have often received generous compensation even after the firms have suffered significant losses. Are senior managers paid too much? (LO4)

9. Suggest two forms of daily functions and two forms of occasional functions that the financial manager performs. (LO5)

10. Contrast the liability provisions for a sole proprietorship, a partnership, a limited partnership, and a corporation. (LO5)

11. Why is the corporate form of organization best suited to a large organization? (LO5)

12. In terms of the life of securities offered, what is the difference between money and capital markets? (LO6)

13. What is the difference between a primary and a secondary market? (LO6)

14. What effect do government debt loads have on the financial markets? (LO6)

15. Who are the stakeholders in the corporation? (LO4)

INTERNET RESOURCES AND QUESTIONS

The Nobel website has a brief description of the work of the winners of the Nobel Prize in finance (economics): nobelprize.org.

The federal government's finances are available from the Department of Finance: fin.gc.ca.

The Bank of Canada has statistics on interest rates and the CPI: bankofcanada.ca.

1. Select one of the Nobel laureate professors in finance and briefly describe their contribution to the field of finance.

2. What is the current federal government's deficit and accumulated debt?

3. What is the current prime interest rate and CPI?

4. Contrast the stated goal(s) of Onex Corporation (onex.com) with those of the Royal Bank (rbc.com/aboutus/visionandvalues.html).

5. Who does BCE Inc. (bce.ca/en/responsibility/corporateresponsibility) identify as its stakeholders, and what objectives does it set to meet the desires of these stakeholders?

PROBLEMS

1. Incubus Corporation began with an investment by shareholders of $40,000.
   a. In its first year, its income showed a deficit of $7,000. What would the equity section of its balance sheet show?
   b. In the second year, it had an income of $15,000 and a dividend of $6,000 was paid. What would the equity section of its balance sheet show?
   c. In the third year, Incubus sold more shares for a value of $20,000, earned income of $12,000, and paid a dividend of $6,000. What would the equity section of its balance sheet show?

2. Puppet Corporation began with an investment by shareholders of $20,000.
   a. In its first year, the income earned was $2,000. What would the equity section of its balance sheet show?
   b. In the second year, it had an income of $9,000 and a dividend of $3,000 was paid. What would the equity section of its balance sheet show?
   c. In the third year, Puppet sold more shares for a value of $10,000, earned income of $5,000 and paid a dividend of $2,500. What would the equity section of its balance sheet show?

3. Two-to-Ten Dollar Corporation has expected earnings per share of $2.00 in its first year, $4.00 its second year, and $10.00 per year for many more years. Ten Dollar Corporation has expected earnings of $10.00 a share for three years only. Which company would you value higher and why?

4. A well-known financial institution expects that it will have no earnings for the next three years as the result of restructuring activities. Then it will begin to return to earnings of $3.00 a share. A somewhat new health services company expects $3.00 a share beginning immediately. Which company would you value higher and why?

5. The board of directors is faced with making a decision on one of the following projects:

   a. A new product with high profit margins and with preliminary research showing strong consumer acceptance.

   b. New software that will produce more-detailed disclosure of relevant and required financial information in a user-friendly, web-based environment.

   c. Pollution control mechanisms that will reduce effluent into the nearby river, which is popular with local residents, to zero.

   d. A report from compensation experts that will closely align executive compensation and its motivation with the goals of the shareholders.

   e. Discuss the merits of each project and identify which project you believe will create the most shareholder wealth and why.

CHAPTER

2

Review of Accounting

LEARNING OBJECTIVES

LO1 Prepare and analyze the four basic financial statements.

LO2 Examine the limitations of the income statement as a measure of a firm's profitability.

LO3 Identify the effects of IFRS (International Financial Reporting Standards) on financial analysis.

LO4 Examine the limitations of the balance sheet as a measure of a firm's financial position.

LO5 Explain the importance of cash flows as identified in the statement of cash flows.

LO6 Outline the effect of corporate tax considerations on aftertax cash flow.

LO7 Identify the different forms of investment income and the effects on investors' taxes payable.

LO8 Explain the concept of tax savings for companies.

Understanding and utilizing financial statements for the analysis of the firm's performance, for comprehending the dynamics revealed within the balance sheet, and for forecasting the future financial situation of the firm are key skills required of the financial manager. Much of the language of finance flows from accounting.

INCOME STATEMENT

The statement of income

- Measures the profitability of a firm over a time period (month, year).
- Assists financial decision making and analysis, utilizing past patterns for predicting the timing, uncertainty, and amount of future earnings and cash flows.

The income statement as presented in Table 2–1 for the Kramer Corporation is presented in a multi-step format to better allow the user to analyze and examine the profit or loss after each major type of expense item.

Table 2–1 Income statement

KRAMER CORPORATION
Income Statement
For the Year Ended December 31, 20XX

1. Sales	$2,000,000
2. Cost of goods sold.	1,500,000
3. Gross profit	500,000
4. Selling and administrative expenses	220,000
5. Amortization expense	50,000
6. Operating profit (EBIT)*	230,000
7. Interest expense.	$ 20,000
8. Earnings before taxes (EBT).	$ 210,000
9. Taxes	99,500
10. Earnings after taxes (EAT)	$ 110,500

Earnings per Share Calculations:

EAT − Preferred shares dividends (from Retained earnings).	10,500
= Earnings available to common shareholders.	100,000
divided by Common shares outstanding.	100,000
= Earnings per share.	$ 1.00

*Earnings before interest and taxes.

- Gross profit: Sales (revenues) less cost of goods sold (direct costs related to sales). May contain some fixed costs but exclude overheads.
- Contribution margin (not presented here): Sales less variable costs.

FINANCE IN ACTION

Where Did Those Earnings Go?

For 2018, the Swiss National Bank announced a loss of 14.9 billion Swiss Francs (1 Swiss Franc = $1.33 Canadian). This was after record profits of 54.4 billion Swiss francs in 2017.

	2018	2017	2016
Equity	118.2	137.2	84.5

Equity rose dramatically in 2017 to fall significantly 2018.

Q1 How did the Swiss National Bank lose 14.9 billion Swiss francs of equity in 2018?

snb.ch
Symbol: SNE

After subtracting selling and administrative expenses and amortization[1] (or fixed costs from contribution margin) we determine the operating income or profit.

- Operating profit (earnings before interest and taxes): A measure of how efficient management is in generating revenues and controlling expenses.

---

[1] Amortization was not treated as part of cost of goods sold in this instance, but rather as a separate expense. Depending on the circumstances, all or part of amortization may be treated as cost of goods sold. Amortization as recommended in the **CPA Canada Handbook** recognizes the declining value of a capital asset over its life. Depreciation or depletion are other acceptable terms for amortization.

Amortization can be a significant expense derived from the capital assets developed or purchased by the firm and identified on the balance sheet. A high gross profit margin (25 to 50 percent) can be eroded to a low operating income as a result of high expenses incurred in marketing products and managing the company.

- Earnings (net income or loss): Operating profit is adjusted for revenues and expenses not related to operational matters resulting in *net earnings*. Interest reflecting the financing policies of the firm or its financial leverage, as explored in Chapter 5, and taxes reflecting government policies are of particular note.

Earnings under IFRS may be further modified to report comprehensive income resulting from the reclassification of certain items (usually due to the revaluation of assets), subsequent to determining net earnings.

Earnings are not the same as the cash flow because of accrual accounting that matches revenues earned to expenses incurred, whether or not they are paid. Earnings represent a longer-run view of the firm, while the cash flow statement, which complements the income statement, focuses on the firm's cash position and survival in the short term. Financial managers must monitor performance (income statement) and liquidity (cash flow statement).

Return on Capital

We should note the return on capital to the three primary sources provided by investors:

Creditors (Bonds, etc.)	$20,000 in interest
Preferred shareholders	$10,500 in dividends
Common shareholders	$100,000 of earnings available

Earnings (or income) can be paid to shareholders (preferred and common) as dividends or retained in the firm for reinvestment on behalf of the common shareholders. The reinvested funds, identified on the balance sheet, theoretically belong to the common shareholders but do not represent cash. These funds will be invested in accounts receivable, inventories, capital, or other assets, and, it is hoped, provide future earnings and dividends to shareholders appropriate to the risk assumed.

The statement of changes in shareholders' equity (Table 2–2), the link between the income statement and balance sheet, shows the increase or decrease resulting from net income or loss from the income statement, distribution of earnings (dividends), and prior period adjustments.[2] A dividend of $50,000 for common shareholders has been declared in our example.

Table 2–2 Statement of changes in shareholders' equity

Statement of Changes in Shareholders' Equity For the Year Ended December 31, 20XX	
Balance, January 1, 20XX	$600,000
Add: Earnings available to common shareholders, 20XX	100,000
Deduct: Cash dividends declared in 20XX.........................	50,000
Balance, December 31, 20XX	$700,000

Note: "Prior period adjustments" for errors of past years may be added or subtracted in the statement of changes in shareholders' equity.

Valuation Basics from the Income Statement

The goal of the firm was identified in Chapter 1 as the maximization of shareholder value. This value is easy to measure immediately, based on today's market share price. However, shareholders, investors, and analysts will be interested in attempting to forecast future value. Over time, these future values will determine shareholders' return on their capital. Effective 2011, public companies

---

[2] The statement will also be affected by application of IFRS as well as any restriction on cash dividends.

must report their financial statements based on IFRS or Accounting Standards for Private Enterprises (ASPE), if no securities are issued to the public. Both have numerous effects on the presentation and interpretation of the income statement and other statements.

Shareholders' claim on earnings is a fundamental measure of value. Common shareholders are sensitive to the number of shares outstanding, with more shares resulting in lower earnings available to each shareholder. Therefore, to gauge shareholder returns we compute both basic and diluted earnings per share (EPS). For simplicity, only basic EPS is used in our illustrations.

$$\text{Earnings per share} = \frac{\text{Earnings available to common shareholders}}{\text{Number of shares outstanding}} \quad (2\text{--}1)$$

As indicated in item 14 of Table 2–1,

$$\text{EPS} = \frac{\$100,000}{100,000 \text{ shares}} = \$1$$

A caution to this is that before any new shares are issued, the financial manager must be sure that the capital raised by issuing the new shares will eventually generate sufficient earnings to increase earnings per share. Past trends and forecasts of earnings per share are key factors to investors. Market share prices react immediately to announced earnings particularly if they are different from the expectations of investors.

Shareholders will also be interested in what percentage of earnings is paid out immediately as dividends and this is referred to as the payout ratio.

$$\text{Payout ratio} = \frac{\text{Dividend per share}}{\text{Earnings per share}} \quad (2\text{--}2)$$

With $50,000 paid out by Kramer to 100,000 shareholders, or dividends per share of $0.50,

$$\text{Payout ratio} = \frac{\$0.50}{\$1} = 0.50 \text{ or } 50\%$$

Growth in earnings is important to all companies but especially for the survival of small businesses requiring increasing amounts of capital. Small businesses are often forced to rely on reinvested earnings to fund expansion as their access to the capital market and banking system is restricted. If these sources of external capital are prepared to lend or invest in the small firm they will carefully study the progress made by the firm in earnings growth. Furthermore, any valuation of the firm's shares, which are not publicly traded, will focus on current and future earnings.

Shareholders' reliance on earnings per share will influence the price they are prepared to pay for shares of the firm. A relationship between earnings per share and current market value is the price-earnings ratio (P/E ratio). This ratio may also be referred to as the earnings multiplier. Its magnitude is often a reflection of future expected earnings.

$$\text{P/E ratio} = \frac{\text{Market share price}}{\text{Earnings per share}} \quad (2\text{--}3)$$

If the market value per share for Kramer Corporation were $12, the price-earnings ratio would be

$$\text{P/E ratio} = \frac{\$12}{\$1} = 12$$

The price-earnings ratio of a firm will change as the shares' market price changes and is influenced by

- Earnings after taxes and sales growth
- Risk (business performance and debt-equity structure)
- Dividend payment policy
- Quality of management decisions
- Many other factors

This ratio allows comparison of the relative market value of many companies on the basis of $1 of earnings per share. Firms expected to provide greater than average future returns often have P/E ratios higher than the market average P/E ratio. As investors' expectations for future returns change, a company's P/E ratio, as indicated in Table 2–3, can shift substantially.

Table 2–3 Price-earnings ratios for selected companies

Corporation	Industry	P/E Ratio				
		1992	2001	2008	2017	2019
BCE (BCE)	Telecommunications	11.2	24.8	7.2	18.4	19.3
Bank of Montreal (BMO)	Banking	8.8	11.0	11.2	14.4	10.8
Loblaw (L)	Grocery chain	18.5	27.8	25.1	30.8	25.4
MolsonCoors (TPX.b)	Brewery	13.5	21.3	17.7	37.7	253.4
Open Text (OTEX)	Technology software	n.a.	43.5	50.0	7.3	36.4
Encana (ECA)(Ovintiv)	Petroleum	143.4	7.0	13.6	n.a.	3.2
TSX Composite*	Index	110.2	−81.9	17.7	25.1	18.6

*No P/E ratios are reported on negative earnings that would result in a negative stock price. A general average for P/E ratio is about 15 times. The TSX Composite Index is the exception in 2001 due to huge losses at Nortel and JDS.

Price-earnings ratios consolidate a great deal of information about a company and yet can be confusing. When a firm's earnings are dropping rapidly, perhaps even approaching zero, the decline in its share price may be more gradual. This process can give rise to the appearance of an increasing P/E ratio under adversity. This happens occasionally in cyclical industries such as Canada's resource-based companies.

In 1992, many shares were trading at high P/E ratios due to depressed earnings. Through the 1990s, P/E ratios were high by historical standards due to very low interest rates and good economic growth prospects. Encana (now Ovintiv) was at a ratio well above 100 in 1992, a reflection of the poor earnings in the petroleum industry. As earnings improved, P/E ratios became more reasonable, and by 2001 with record earnings in the oil patch, Encana's P/E ratio had dropped considerably on expectations of subdued growth due to expected declines in oil and gas prices. OpenText, a company in the high-tech business, trades at a large P/E ratio on the basis of future expected earnings, not its current low earnings. P/E ratios are closer to normal with stable stock markets and economic conditions.

Encana (now Ovintiv)
ovintiv.com

OpenText Corporation
opentext.com

Shareholders may place a higher value on income received from aftertax dividends as compared to future expected earnings that may result from reinvested earnings. Therefore, dividends often form the basis of the valuation of the firm's performance. The yield in immediate returns via dividends is the dividend yield.

$$\text{Dividend yield} = \frac{\text{Dividends per share}}{\text{Market share price}} \quad (2\text{–}4)$$

For Kramer Corporation this is,

$$\text{Dividend yield} = \frac{\$0.50}{12} = 0.0417 \text{ or } 4.17\%$$

LO2 Limitations of the Income Statement

A financial analyst examines the income statement with knowledge of how earnings or profits are defined. While the accountant records past events, the financial analyst builds models and suggests values based on the future. Like the economist, the analyst views past events as somewhat irrelevant for valuation purposes. It is the timing of cash flows in the future that is relevant for valuation and decision making. The accountant imposes a specific time period on the income statement, requiring accruals for both income and expenses that don't necessarily reflect the timing of cash flows or changes in a corporation's value. The accountant, tax auditor, economist, and financial analyst would likely have different numbers to reflect a company's profits.

The economist defines income as the change in real worth that occurs between the beginning and the end of a specified time period. To the economist, an increase in the value of a firm's land as a result of a new airport being built on an adjacent property is an increase in the real worth of the firm. It therefore represents income. Similarly, the elimination of a competitor might also increase the firm's real worth and, therefore, result in income in an economic sense. The accountant does not ordinarily employ such a broad definition of income.

Accounting values are established primarily by actual transactions, and income that is gained or lost during a given period is a function of verifiable transactions. While the potential sales price of a company's property may go from $10 million to $20 million as a result of new developments in the area, its shareholders may notice only a much smaller gain from operations, as reported in the accounting statements, until the gains are realized, unless IFRS is applied. IFRS requires gains to be recognized yearly whether or not assets are disposed of.

Also, as will be pointed out in Chapter 3, there is some flexibility in the reporting of transactions. This means similar events may result in different measurements of income at the end of the period. The choices accountants make in accounting policies and methods used for value determination should be clearly indicated in the notes to financial statements. The intent of this section is not to criticize the accounting profession—for it is certainly among the best-organized, best-trained, and most-respected professions—but to alert students to the fact that significant judgment is involved in financial reporting. Therefore, consumers of financial statements must also be prepared to exercise judgment, look at the notes to the financial statements, and draw their own conclusions and decisions. Because finance focuses on cash flows and their timing, one must be careful not to equate accounting income with cash flow.

 FINANCE IN ACTION

Apparently Earnings Are Flexible

Many expressed concern with the "quality" of earnings reported by publicly traded companies. This has led to new reporting and regulatory standards that require increased rigour for GAAP financial statements, as well as the introduction of international standards under IFRS. In efforts to meet earnings targets, accountants and managers had resorted to stretching accounting standards beyond their reasonable limits. Furthermore, firms have resorted to preparing non-GAAP, adjusted or pro-forma statements that they feel present a more accurate picture of the firm's financial performance or health. These variety of statements are potentially misleading to less than diligent investors.

Earnings can be affected by flexibility in accounting principles and management estimates. Estimates such as allowance for doubtful accounts or warranty expenses, and write-downs of assets (inventories and investments) are by their nature discretionary. Margins can also be managed by classification of "overhead" as a cost of goods rather than administrative expenses. Management has this discretion due to its experience and the need to make estimates of many of the revenues and expenses that will flow through the firm.

There is pressure on companies to meet earnings targets, and share prices often decline when targets are not met. Financial statement audits rely, to a significant extent, on company management. The securities commission in each province has the power to force public companies to clarify or reissue financial statements. Current accounting concerns are identified under proposed instruments, rules, and policies at the Ontario Securities Commission (OSC) website.

During this past decade, senior managers at several companies have been dismissed because of alleged manipulation of the company's financial statements. In the footnotes to financial statements, under "significant accounting policies," there is a statement that the firm "makes estimates and assumptions that affect the reported amounts of revenues and expenses during the reporting period." Sometimes this practice leads to misleading financial statements and regulatory investigations.

Several theories have suggested factors that may contribute to the management or "manipulation" of reported earnings:

- Bonuses (Compensation is tied to reported earnings.)
- Political considerations (High reported earnings attract societal attention.)
- Smoothing (Less-volatile earnings are viewed favourably by the market.)
- Debt covenants (Debt contracts are often based on book value calculations.)
- Big bath (New CEOs will look better in the future if assets are written down as they take over companies, avoiding future amortization charges.)

Q1 Identify and judge the validity of estimates/judgments made by TELUS in reporting income (noted in the notes to its financial statements).

Q2 What is the mandate of the Ontario Securities Commission?

telus.com/en/about   **osc.gov.on.ca**
Symbol: T

BALANCE SHEET

The balance sheet (statement of financial position) is a "snapshot picture" that indicates the firm's

- Holdings (what the firm owns)
- Obligations (financing as liabilities or equity [ownership interest])
- Measure of its value at a point in time (cost basis compared to various IFRS valuation methods)

A balance sheet for the Kramer Corporation as presented in Table 2–4 allows us to examine the firm's ability to accept opportunities and to deal with difficulties. It is the cumulative results of the company's transactions since its inception. In contrast, the income statement measures results only over a short, quantifiable period. Good income statement results usually produce healthy balance sheets. Generally, balance sheet items are stated on an original-cost basis rather than at market values. Public companies are now also preparing their financial statements based on IFRS (International Financial Reporting Standards), which allows reporting options, to make them comparable with companies in other countries.

LO3 Effects of IFRS on Financial Analysis

Most countries have accepted IFRS after the results of years of research by members of the IFAC (IFRS Advisory Council). CPA Canada made significant contributions to the research that was supervised by IASB (International Accounting Standards Board) and that resulted in IFRS. Accounting standards have moved from rules to principles-based preparation.

Public companies now report their annual financial statements with IFRS, a principles-based approach, along with comparative previous-year figures. The U.S still uses U.S. GAAP (Generally Accepted Accounting Principles) a more rules-based approach set out by FASB

(Financial Accounting Standards Board). Other companies in Canada may continue to report their financial statements on revised GAAP, which is referred to as ASPE (Accounting Standards for Private Enterprises). Therefore, financial comparisons must be made among companies that are reporting on the same basis of accounting; otherwise, the results will be significantly distorted, leading to inappropriate decisions by investors, lenders, and other users of financial statements.

Most financial topics will be affected by IFRS applications, especially

- Financial statement values
- Ratio analysis
- Determination of cost of capital
- Capital budgeting decisions

The financial analyst should always determine whether the financial statements are based on IFRS, GAAP, or ASPE before comparisons are made, to ensure the analysis results in relevant and reliable data.

Significant differences between IFRS and GAAP include the following: IFRS allows only the FIFO method for inventory, and IFRS allows inventories, capital assets, and intangibles that have been written down to be reversed if their value rises. Decreased values are reported in income; reevaluations are reported in equity unless they are reversals of previous write-downs. On the income statement IFRS requires that amortization more closely approximate a true cost allocation and extraordinary expenses must be included. IFRS allows more flexibility in recording between the three categories of the cash flow statement.

IFRS applications affect the accounting for many accounts on all four financial statements, but the most significant effect is the conversion of assets recorded at historical costs to market values based on appraisals at the balance sheet date. The format of the balance sheet is also significantly different since IFRS places emphasis on the materiality of the accounts, resulting in capital assets—usually the largest amounts—listed first and current assets listed after. Tables 2–4A and 2–4B compare the balance sheet without and with application of IFRS.

Table 2–4A Balance sheet

KRAMER CORPORATION		
Balance Sheet		
December 31, 20XX		
Assets		
Current assets:		
Cash		$ 40,000
Marketable securities		10,000
Accounts receivable	$ 220,000	
Less: Allowance for bad debts	20,000	200,000
Inventory		180,000
Prepaid expenses		20,000
Total current assets		450,000
Other assets:		
Investments		50,000
Capital assets:		
Plant and equipment, original cost	$1,100,000	
Less: Accumulated amortization	600,000	
Net plant and equipment		500,000
Total assets		$1,000,000

KRAMER CORPORATION
Balance Sheet
December 31, 20XX

Liabilities and Shareholders' Equity		
Current liabilities:		
Accounts payable.....................................		$ 80,000
Notes payable (bank indebtedness)......................		100,000
Accrued expenses......................................		30,000
Total current liabilities.............................		210,000
Long-term liabilities:		
Bonds payable, 2030....................................		90,000
Total liabilities.....................................		300,000
Shareholders' equity:		
Preferred stock, 500 shares...........................		50,000
Common stock, 100,000 shares..........................		350,000
Retained earnings.....................................		300,000
Total shareholders' equity............................		700,000
Total liabilities and shareholders' equity............		$1,000,000

Note: IFRS values and format would be significantly different as shown below.

Table 2–4B Statement of financial position (public company with IFRS)

KRAMER CORPORATION
Statement of Financial Position
December 31, 20XX

Assets		
Capital assets (non-current assets):		
Plant and equipment, appraised values..................	$2,100,000	
Less: Accumulated amortization.....................	600,000	$1,500,000
Current assets:		
Prepaid expenses......................................		20,000
Inventory...		180,000
Marketable securities.................................		10,000
Accounts receivable...................................	220,000	
Less: Allowance for bad debts......................	20,000	200,000
Cash..		40,000
Total current assets..................................		450,000
Other assets:...		50,000
Total assets:...		$2,000,000
Shareholders' equity:		
Preferred stock, 500 shares...........................	$ 50,000	
Common stock, 100,000 shares..........................	350,000	
Retained Earnings.....................................	300,000	
Unrealized Gains......................................	1,000,000	
Total shareholders' equity............................		1,700,000
Long-term liabilities:		
Bonds payable...		90,000
Total		
Current liabilities:		
Notes payable, short term.............................	100,000	
Accrued expenses......................................	30,000	
Accounts payable......................................	$ 80,000	
Total current liabilities.............................		210,000
Total liabilities and shareholders' equity............		$2,000,000

Note: The above IFRS balance sheet is only a basic example. Actual IFRS statements are more complex.

Readers should note that the explanation and comparisons of IFRS applications herein are only a basic introduction to the effects of IFRS, and more detailed preparation and formal presentations of financial statements should be studied in accounting courses.

Interpretation of Balance Sheet Items

For private companies, asset accounts are listed in order of liquidity. Public companies (IFRS) list noncurrent assets first, followed by current assets. Liquidity is a measure of how quickly an asset can be converted to cash. Current assets are items that may be converted to cash within one year (or the normal operating cycle of the firm). This is an important consideration, as significant increases can quickly tie up cash resources. The financial manager must monitor these resources carefully and plan to finance any increases. Capital demands are covered in Chapters 6 to 8.

- **Marketable securities** are temporary investments of excess cash (lower of cost or current market value).
- *Accounts receivable* less allowance for bad debts (based on estimates) is the net collection value.
- **Inventory valued at cost** may be in the form of raw material, goods in process, or finished goods.
- **Prepaid expenses** represent future expenses that have already been paid (insurance premiums, rent).

Investments, unlike marketable securities, are a longer-term commitment of funds, including stocks, bonds, or investments in other corporations (often for acquisition).

Plant and equipment is identified as original cost minus accumulated amortization. **Accumulated amortization** is not to be confused with the amortization expense item of the income statement in Table 2–1. It is the sum of all past and present amortization charges on currently owned assets, whereas amortization expense is the current year's charge. Public companies' (IFRS) values are generally adjusted yearly to reflect market values.

Obligations of the Kramer Corporation that finance assets are represented by $300,000 in debt and $700,000 of shareholders' equity. Current liabilities are short-term obligations due within one year.

- **Accounts payable** represent amounts owed on unpaid accounts to suppliers.
- **Notes payable** are generally short-term signed obligations to the banker or other creditors.
- **Accrued expense** is an obligation incurred but payment has not yet occurred. (It includes unpaid wages for services provided, expenses incurred but not paid, and amortizations of assets.)

Shareholders' equity represents the total contribution and ownership interest of preferred and common shareholders. The **preferred stock** investment position is $50,000, on the basis of 500 shares. In the case of **common stock,** 100,000 shares have been issued for $350,000.[3] We can assume that the 100,000 shares were originally sold at $3.50 each. Finally, $300,000 in retained earnings from the statement of retained earnings (Table 2–2) represents the firm's cumulative earnings since inception, minus dividends and any other adjustments.

Valuation Basics from the Balance Sheet

Shareholders' equity minus the preferred stock component represents the net worth, or book value, of the firm. If you take everything that the firm owns and subtract the debt and preferred stock

---

[3] In most current Canadian circumstances, new common stock and preferred stock is issued on a no-par-value basis. However, some corporate balance sheets still reflect the historical split between the par value of shares on issue and the premium, termed **contributed surplus,** paid by investors above that par value (predetermined nominal value).

outstanding, the remainder belongs to the common shareholder and represents net worth.[4] In the case of the Kramer Corporation, we show

Total assets......................................	$1,000,000
Total liabilities................................	300,000
Shareholders' equity.............................	700,000
Preferred stock outstanding	50,000
Net worth assigned to common	$ 650,000
Common shares outstanding	100,000
Net worth, or book value, per share..............	$ 6.50

The original investment in the firm by shareholders was $350,000, and $300,000 of earnings has since been reinvested in the firm. Together, these totals also represent the net worth of $650,000.

Because the concept of net worth (book value) is based on historical asset costs (Assets − Liabilities − Preferred stock), net worth may bear little relationship to value currently put on shareholders' equity by investors or the marketplace via share price. This will occur because the assets held by the firm have increased in value but this increased value is not yet recognized by the financial statements. Analysts often calculate the relationship between market value per share and historical book value per share.

$$\frac{\text{Market value}}{\text{Book value}} = \frac{\text{MV}}{\text{BV}} = \frac{\text{Market value per share}}{\text{Book value per share}} \quad (2\text{--}5)$$

For the Kramer Corporation with a market value of $12,

$$\frac{\text{MV}}{\text{BV}} = \frac{\$12}{\$6.50} = 1.85 \text{ times}$$

In examining this ratio we have to ask ourselves why market value has moved away from book value, and whether this is justified. IFRS restates yearly the cost values to year-end market values for public companies. A higher ratio suggests that the assets have achieved synergies beyond their original cost and are expected to generate increasing returns by way of cash flows in the future. A lower ratio may suggest the opposite. The Kramer ratio appears reasonable.

In Table 2–5 we look at disparities between market value and book value for a number of publicly traded companies, as identified by the ratio in the last column. Besides asset valuation, a number of other factors may explain the wide differences, including industry outlook, growth prospects, quality of management, and risk-return expectations. Shopify is a software company with a lot of human capital, which doesn't show up on the balance sheet, and it is a firm with solid growth potential. BCE and Bank of Montreal are solid, stable performers. Encana, in the gas business, and Teck, in mining, with large investments in tangible capital assets, have been subject to depressed commodity prices and increased competition.

Table 2–5 Comparison of market value to book value per share, December 2019

Corporation	Market Value per Share	Book Value per Share	Ratio of Market Value to Book Value
BCE (BCE)	63.94	22.67	2.82
Bank of Montreal (BMO)	102.22	71.51	1.43
Encana (ECA)(Ovintiv)	5.21	10.38	0.50
Loblaw (L)	71.60	32.60	2.20
OpenText (OTEX)	57.83	19.11	3.03
Shopify (SHOP)	445.45	25.14	17.72
Teck.B (TECK.B)	20.80	40.10	0.52

---

[4] An additional discussion of preferred stock is presented in Chapter 17. Preferred stock represents neither a debt claim nor an ownership interest in the firm. It is a *hybrid,* or intermediate, security.

LO4 Limitations of the Balance Sheet

The values on the balance sheet are often subject to interpretation or revaluation.

- Values are stated on a historical or original-cost basis for private companies, but public companies must report IFRS at market values (some assets may be worth considerably more than their original cost or may require many times the original cost for replacement).

FINANCE IN ACTION

Meeting the Targets!

Baush Health, formerly Valeant Corporation, formerly Biovail, is a Canadian pharmaceutical company. Between 2001 and 2004, according to the OSC and the Securities and Exchange Commission (SEC) of the United States, Valeant manipulated its financial statements. It was suggested that Valeant

- Used outdated and misleading exchange rates in its valuation
- Recorded phony sales at the end of financial quarters
- Moved research and development expenses off its balance sheet to the pharmaceutical technologies division
- Overstated the impact of a truck accident and product loss

The overall impact was misleading to investors. Valeant settled out of court, paying a fine to the OSC.

Nevertheless, Valeant continued to aggressively prepare financial statements that were "potentially misleading." Its "adjusted earnings" took out one-time costs for acquisitions that were quite reliant on increased debt and were seriously questioned for any value creation.

Valeant in 2015 was the highest valued firm on the TSX at $88 billion but by 2017 was valued at less than $7 billion. Investors had seen through the "adjusted earnings." In 2018 Valeant changed its name to Bausch Health, because of the negative publicity, and in late 2019 its market capitalization had grown to $13.2 billion.

Q1 How has Bausch Health's share price performed during the last 12 months?

Q2 What are Bausch Health's comments on these events and charges?

bauschhealth.com   **sec.gov/litigation/litreleases/2008/lr20506.htm**
Symbol: BHC

- Accounting policies, which are disclosed in notes to financial statements, will influence the recorded values.
- Contingent liabilities are omitted from the balance sheet, but for items such as intangibles that are included, it may be difficult to determine the economic value. Contingent liabilities, events that may result in future liabilities, are also disclosed in the notes to financial statements, alerting statement users to their possible impact.

The accounting profession has grappled with the valuation problem for decades, and there have been moves toward more market-based orientation for financial statements. In the 1980s, the profession recommended the use of the current cost (replacement cost) method, in which assets were revalued at their current costs; this method has been abandoned but IFRS requires public companies to report assets at market (current) values.

There has also been evidence that the financial statements adjusted to more fully reflect current values do not impact significantly on the valuation perspective of investors. Investors quickly reflect the value changes of a company's assets or liabilities by raising or lowering market share prices. Investors required only sufficient information from statements on which to base their valuations, but whether it is historically or current value-based does not seem to matter. Efficient markets, as discussed in Chapter 14, appear to be indifferent to how financial information is displayed.

LO5 STATEMENT OF CASH FLOWS

In evaluating investment opportunities, finance considers cash flows and their timing of utmost importance. Accrual accounting attempts to match expenses incurred to revenues earned over time through the income statement and the subsequent impact on the balance sheet at a point in time, even if the related cash flows occur at quite different times. Therefore, these two statements do not provide adequate information on the amount and timing of cash flowing into and out of the business.

A fourth financial statement is required to translate income statement and balance sheet data into cash flow information. The statement of cash flows identifies the sources and uses of the firm's cash from beginning to the end-of-year balance sheet. The International Accounting Standards Board (IASB), through International Financial Reporting Standards (IFRS), has initiated the global standardization of accounting information, and has brought CPA Canada and to some extent the Financial Accounting Standards Board (FASB) in the United States to a common format and valuation for the four financial statements (financial position, comprehensive income, changes in equity, and statement of cash flows) of public companies.

International Accounting Standards Board
ifrs.org

Financial Accounting Standards Board
fasb.org

The statement of cash flows reports changes in cash and cash equivalents (rather than working capital) resulting from the activities of the firm during a given period. For many internal and external users of a firm's financial information, cash flow information is critical. The cash flow statement allows an analyst to identify

- Cash flow generated from the firm's assets
- Financial obligations (interest on debt and dividends to owners' equity)
- Commitment to new assets, debt, and equity obligations

Cash equivalents are highly liquid investments (usually with maturities of less than three months) less any bank overdrafts. They should have little risk of change in value, because they are held to meet short-term commitments. In contrast, values of equity investments do change but gains are excluded from the income statement. The firm should disclose its policy distinguishing between cash equivalents and investments and if their use is restricted due to bank requirements or by foreign currency exchange controls. Movements between cash and cash equivalents are not reported, nor are financing and investing activities that do not use cash or equivalents, such as buying a business for shares or by assuming debts.

The statement of cash flows can highlight

- The relative buildup in short-term and long-term assets
- The means of financing used to support any growth in the firm's asset base
- The appropriateness and the future implications of the financing used

Historical cash flows are often useful in estimating future cash flows. Financial forecasting, discussed in Chapter 4, projects cash flow statements for future operating periods. A corporation that has $1 million in accrual-based accounting profits can determine whether it can actually afford to pay a cash dividend to shareholders, buy new equipment, or undertake new projects.

The cash flow statements for the small business are particularly important since cash flow is more relevant to the firm's short-term survival than its reported income. One is likely to be concerned about the quality, timing, and amount of earnings, and hence the firm's ability to acquire assets and meet its obligations. In the very competitive corporate environment of today, precise cash flow analysis is essential for a firm's survival.

Developing an Actual Statement

We use the information previously provided for the Kramer Corporation to illustrate how the statement of cash flows is developed.

But first, let's identify the three primary sections of the statement of cash flows. These sections are

1. Operating activities (data from income statement and current section of balance sheet)
2. Investing activities (data from noncurrent assets)
3. Financing activities (data from noncurrent section of balance sheet)

After each of these sections is completed, the results are added together to compute the net increase or decrease in cash and cash equivalents for the corporation. An example of the process is shown in Figure 2–1. Let's begin with cash flows from operating activities.

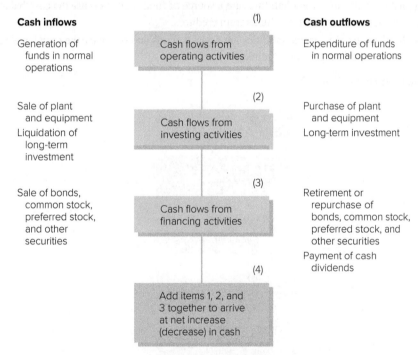

Figure 2–1 Illustration of concepts behind the statement of cash flows

Determining Cash Flows from Operating Activities

Basically, we are going to translate *income from operations* from an accrual to a cash basis. There are two ways to accomplish this objective. First, the firm may use a *direct method,* in which every item on the income statement is adjusted from accrual accounting to cash accounting. This is a tedious process that requires the adjustment of all sales to cash sales, all purchases adjusted to cash purchases, and so on. The *CPA Canada Handbook* encourages the use of the direct method. This may be a method that appeals to smaller firms that have their financial information on an easily accessible cash basis.

However, a more popular method that is favoured by larger firms is the *indirect method,* in which net income represents the starting point and then adjustments are made to convert net income to cash flows from operations.[5] This is the method we will use here. This method provides more information on the dynamics of cash flow. Regardless of whether the direct or indirect method is used, the same final answer is achieved.

Note: Accounting students might consider a debit and credit method to determine the effect of change for each line on the balance sheet to the increase or decrease in cash. For example, an increase in inventory during the year (debit to inventory) results in a decrease in cash (credit to cash). Similarly, an increase in accounts payable from beginning to end of year (credit to accounts payable) results in an increase in cash (debit cash). A worksheet could be used to determine the effect on cash for all changes from beginning to end of year on the balance sheet.

We follow these procedures to compute cash flows from operating activities using the indirect method:[6]

- Start with net income or net loss from the income statement.
- Recognize that noncash deductions in computing net income should be added back to net income to **increase** the cash balance. These include items such as amortization, deferred income taxes, restructuring charges, and foreign exchange losses. Any gains should be deducted. This produces cash flow from operations.
- Next, identify changes from beginning of year to end of year in noncash current assets and liabilities.
- Recognize that increases in current assets are a use of funds and **reduce** the cash balance (indirectly); as an example, the firm spends more funds on inventory.
- Recognize that decreases in current assets are a source of funds and **increase** the cash balance (indirectly); that is, the firm reduces funds tied up in inventory.
- Recognize that increases in current liabilities are a source of funds and **increase** the cash balance (indirectly); that is, the firm gets more funds from creditors.
- Recognize that decreases in current liabilities are a use of funds and **decrease** the cash balance (indirectly); that is, the firm pays off creditors.

These steps are illustrated in Figure 2–2.

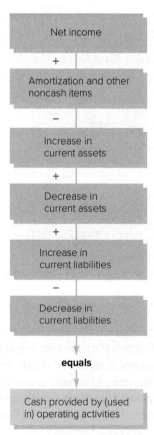

Figure 2–2 Steps in computing cash provided by operating activities using the indirect method

---

[5] The indirect method is similar to procedures used to construct the old sources and uses of funds statement.

[6] In addition to the items mentioned, we may need to recognize the gains or losses on the sale of operating and non-operating assets. We exclude these for ease of analysis.

We follow these procedures for the Kramer Corporation, drawing primarily on material from Table 2–1 (the previously presented income statement) and from Table 2–6 (which shows balance sheet data for the most recent two years). A quick look at the changes in assets on the balance sheets from one year to the next tells us of increased demands for cash resources.

Table 2–6 Comparative balance sheets (APSE, GAAP)

KRAMER CORPORATION

Balance Sheets

	December 31	
	20XX	20XW
Assets		
Current assets:		
Cash	$ 40,000	$ 30,000
Marketable securities	10,000	10,000
Accounts receivable (net).	200,000	170,000
Inventory	180,000	160,000
Prepaid expenses	20,000	30,000
Total current assets.	450,000	400,000
Investments (long-term)	50,000	20,000
Plant and equipment.	1,100,000	1,000,000
Less: Accumulated amortization	600,000	550,000
Net plant and equipment	500,000	450,000
Total assets.	$1,000,000	$ 870,000
Liabilities and Shareholders' Equity		
Current liabilities:		
Accounts payable	$ 80,000	$ 45,000
Notes payable	100,000	100,000
Accrued expenses.	30,000	35,000
Total current liabilities.	210,000	180,000
Long-term liabilities:		
Bonds payable, 2020	90,000	40,000
Total liabilities	300,000	220,000
Shareholders' equity:		
Preferred stock	50,000	50,000
Common stock	350,000	350,000
Retained earnings.	300,000	250,000
Total shareholders' equity	700,000	650,000
Total liabilities and shareholders' equity	$1,000,000	$ 870,000

The analysis is presented in Table 2–7. We begin with net income (earnings after taxes) of $110,500 and add back amortization of $50,000 (noncash expenses). We then show that increases in current assets (accounts receivable and inventory) reduce funds and that decreases in current assets (prepaid expenses) increase funds. Also, we show increases in current liabilities (accounts payable) as an addition to funds and decreases in current liabilities (accrued expenses) as a reduction of funds.

Table 2–7 Cash flows from operating activities

Operating Activities			
Net income (earnings after taxes) (Table 2–1).............	$110,500		
Add items not requiring an outlay of cash:			
Amortization (Table 2–1)...........................	50,000		
Cash flow from operations............................		160,500	
Changes in noncash working capital:			
Increase in accounts receivable (Table 2–6)	(30,000)		
Increase in inventory (Table 2–6)	(20,000)		
Decrease in prepaid expenses (Table 2–6)...............	10,000		
Increase in accounts payable (Table 2–6)	35,000		
Decrease in accrued expenses (Table 2–6)	(5,000)		
Net change in noncash working capital		(10,000)	
Cash provided by operating activities		$150,500	

We see in Table 2–7 that the firm generated $150,500 in cash flows from operating activities. This figure is $40,000 larger than the net income figure reported to shareholders ($150,500 – $110,500). You can also envision that a firm with little amortization and a massive buildup of inventory might show lower cash flow than reported net income. Once cash flows from operating activities are determined, management has a better idea of what can be allocated to investing or financing needs, such as paying cash dividends.

Determining Cash Flows from Investing Activities

The second section in the statement of cash flows relates to long-term investment activities in other issuers' securities or, more importantly, in plant and equipment. Increasing investments represent a *use* of funds, and decreasing investments represent a *source* of funds.

Examining Table 2–6 for the Kramer Corporation, we show the cash flow information in Table 2–8.

Table 2–8 Cash flows from investing activities

Investing Activities	
Increase in investments (long-term securities) (Table 2–6).....................	($ 30,000)
Increase in plant and equipment (Table 2–6)...............................	(100,000)
Cash used in investing activities	($130,000)

Determining Cash Flows from Financing Activities

In the third section of the statement of cash flows, we show the effects of financing activities on the corporation. Financing activities apply to the sale or retirement of bonds, common stock, preferred stock, and other corporate securities. Also, the payment of cash dividends is considered a financing activity. The sale of the firm's securities represents a *source* of funds, and the retirement or repurchase of such securities represents a *use* of funds.

Using the data from Tables 2–1, 2–2, and 2–6, the financing activities of the Kramer Corporation are shown in Table 2–9.

Table 2–9 Cash flows from financing activities

Financing Activities	
Increase in bonds payable (Table 2–6).	$50,000
Preferred stock dividends paid (Table 2–1)	(10,500)
Common stock dividends paid (Table 2–2)	(50,000)
Cash used in financing activities	($10,500)

Combining the Three Sections of the Statement

We now combine the three sections of the statement of cash flows. This statement of cash flows reveals information not readily available from the other two statements.

Because it reveals the patterns of cash flows in the firm, the information from this statement is valuable information to bankers, creditors, and investors who focus on dividends. These groups are particularly concerned with the liquidity of the firm and its ability to generate cash flow. Highly profitable firms have been known to go bankrupt because of the firm's inability to generate the cash needed to meet its obligations. The statement of cash flows also reveals information on the firm's management of, and requirements for, financing and investment.

We see in Table 2–10 that Kramer Corporation created excess funds from operating activities that were utilized heavily in investing activities and somewhat in financing activities. As a result, there is a $10,000 increase in the cash balance, and this can also be reconciled with the increase in the cash balance of $10,000, from $30,000 to $40,000, as indicated in Table 2–6.

Cash demands and funding are examined by way of

- Chapters 6 to 8: Working capital (current assets and liabilities) from operating activities
- Chapter 12: Capital budgeting from investing activities
- Chapter 16 to 18: Capital structure needs (bonds, preferred, common shares) from financing activities

One might also further analyze how the buildups in various accounts were financed. For example, if there is a substantial increase in inventory or accounts receivable, is there an associated buildup in accounts payable and short-term bank loans? If not, the firm may have to use long-term financing to carry part of the short-term needs. An even more important question might be, how are increases in long-term assets being financed? Most desirably, there should be adequate long-term financing and profits to carry these needs. If not, then short-term funds (trade credit and bank loans) may be utilized to carry long-term needs. This is a potentially high-risk situation, in that short-term sources of funds may dry up while long-term needs continue to demand funding. In the Problems at the end of this chapter, you will have an opportunity to further consider these points.

Simplification of Table 2–10 can occur by eliminating the "Changes in noncash working capital" and using the consolidated line "Net change in working capital." This simplification loses some of the dynamics of the changes within various accounts.

The direct method would be similar to Table 2–10 with an adjustment to operating activities recording receipts and payments for operational expenses, although the "Cash provided by operating activities" would be the same.

Table 2–10 Statement of cash flows

KRAMER CORPORATION
Statement of Cash Flows
For the Year Ended December 31, 20XX

Operating Activities		
Net income (earnings after taxes)		$110,500
Add items not requiring an outlay of cash:		
Amortization	50,000	50,000
Cash flow from operations.		160,500
Changes in noncash working capital:		
Increase in accounts receivable	(30,000)	
Increase in inventory	(20,000)	
Decrease in prepaid expenses	10,000	
Increase in accounts payable	35,000	
Decrease in accrued liabilities	(5,000)	
Net change in noncash working capital		(10,000)
Cash provided by (used in) operating activities		**$150,500**
Investing Activities		
Increase in investments (long-term securities).	(30,000)	
Increase in plant and equipment.	(100,000)	
Cash used in investing activities		**($130,000)**
Financing Activities		
Increase in bonds payable	50,000	
Preferred stock dividends paid.	(10,500)	
Common stock dividends paid.	(50,000)	
Cash used in financing activities		**($ 10,500)**
Net increase (decrease) in cash during the year*		**$ 10,000**
Cash, beginning of year*		30,000
Cash, end of year*		**$ 40,000**

*This would include cash equivalents if there were any.

AMORTIZATION AND CASH FLOW

One of the most confusing items for finance students is whether amortization is a source of funds to the corporation. In Table 2–7, we added amortization to net income in determining the cash flow from operations. The reason we added back amortization was not because amortization was a source of new funds, but rather because we had subtracted this noncash deduction in arriving at net income and have to add it back to determine the actual cash flow effect of operations.

Amortization represents an attempt to allocate the initial cost of an asset over its useful life. In essence, we attempt to match the annual expense of plant and equipment ownership against the revenues being produced. Nevertheless, the charging of amortization is purely an accounting entry and does not directly involve the movement of funds. To go from accounting flows to cash flows in Table 2–7, we restored the noncash deduction of $50,000 for amortization that was subtracted in Table 2–1, the income statement.

Earnings and Cash Flow: The Difference at Teck

Teck is one of the world's leading diversified natural resource companies, with interests from Northern Canada to Chile in South America. As an integrated natural resource company, its activities include mineral exploration, mining, smelting, and refining.

Teck's net earnings are sensitive to change in commodity prices and the U.S. dollar. A 10 percent change in the price of copper would increase/decrease net earnings by $21 million; a $0.10 percent change in the U.S. dollar would increase/decrease comprehensive income by $408 million. Research how Teck did in 2019 as commodity prices fluctuated.

To remain competitive in these world markets, Teck must continually reinvest in modern equipment. These capital investments are funded by borrowing in the capital markets and also from funds generated from Teck's operations. The table here shows that although earnings were volatile over a recent period, capital expenditures remained strong. An important observation is the significant difference between cash flow from operations and earnings. The most significant contributor to the difference is amortization (or depreciation) charges, which, of course, are related to previous and current capital expenditures. It was this cash flow that partially funded the capital investments. In finance our focus is primarily on cash flow.

	Earnings	Cash Flow from Operations	Capital Expenditures
2018	$3,145	$4,438	$1,906
2015	−2,484	1,748	1,581
2013	1,376	2,878	1,858
2010	1,975	2,743	810
2007	1,661	2,001	577
2006	2,395	2,606	391
2005	1,345	1,647	326
2002	30	201	187

Note: Figures in millions, available with the latest financial statements.

Q1 Is Teck continuing this substantial investment? Update the table.

Q2 Where is all that cash flow going?

teck.com
Symbol: TECK.B

Let us examine a very simple case involving amortization. Assume we purchase a machine for $500 with a five-year life and we pay for it in cash. Our amortization schedule calls for equal amortization of $100 per year for five years. Assume further that our firm has $1,000 in earnings before amortization and taxes and the tax obligation is $300. Note the difference between accounting flows and cash flows for the first two years in Table 2–11.

Table 2–11 Comparison of accounting and cash flows

	Year 1	
	(1) Accounting	(2) Cash Flows
Earnings before amortization and taxes (EBAT)........	$1,000	$1,000
Amortization	100	100
Earnings before taxes (EBT)	900	900
Taxes	300	300
Earnings after taxes (EAT)	$ 600	600
Purchase of equipment............................		−500
Amortization charged without cash outlay		+100
Cash flow..		$ 200
	Year 2	
Earnings before amortization and taxes (EBAT).......	$1,000	$1,000
Amortization	100	100
Earnings before taxes.............................	900	900
Taxes	300	300
Earnings after taxes (EAT)	$ 600	600
Amortization charged without cash outlay		+100
Cash flow..		$ 700

Since we took $500 out of cash flow originally (column 2), we do not wish to take it out again. Thus, we add back $100 in amortization each year to offset the subtraction in the income statement.

FREE CASH FLOW

A term that has received significant attention is free cash flow (FCF). This is actually a by-product of the previously discussed statement of cash flows.

However, there are several interpretations of what is meant by this term. In some calculations, explicit returns to suppliers of capital (interest, preferred and common dividends) are excluded from the determination of free cash flow, as the suggested focus is on operating performance and the maintenance of capital capacity.

Free cash flow for our purposes will include the anticipated return to the suppliers of capital and is equal to (using Table 2–11 and dividends of $100):

Cash flow from operating activities	$700
Minus: Capital expenditures (required to maintain the productive capacity of the firm)	500
Minus: Dividends (needed to maintain the necessary payout on common stock and to cover any preferred stock obligation)	100
Free cash flow	$100

The concept of free cash flow forces the stock analyst or banker not only to consider how much cash is generated from operating activities but also to subtract the necessary capital expenditures on plant and equipment to maintain normal activities. Similarly, dividend payments to shareholders must be subtracted, as these dividends must generally be paid to keep shareholders satisfied.

Please note that some will calculate free cash flow by adjusting working capital positions and by not adjusting for expected dividends.

The balance, free cash flow, is then available for *special financial activities.* In the 1990s, special financing activities were often synonymous with leveraged buyouts, in which a firm borrows money to buy its stock and take itself private with the hope of restructuring its balance sheet and perhaps going public again in a few years at a higher price than it paid. Leveraged buyouts are discussed more fully in Chapter 15. The analyst or banker normally looks at **free cash flow** to determine whether there are sufficient excess funds to pay back the loan associated with the leveraged buyout.

INCOME TAX CONSIDERATIONS

Taxpayers, including corporations, must pay taxes on taxable income, thereby reducing available cash flows. Therefore, virtually every financial decision is influenced by federal and provincial income tax considerations. We briefly examine tax rates and in a general way note how they will influence corporate financial decisions by reducing income and cash flows. The primary orientation is toward the principles governing corporate tax decisions, though many of the same principles apply to a sole proprietorship, partnership, and other forms of business entities.

We also examine personal tax considerations to identify how various investment returns are taxed differently under the Income Tax Act. This is of interest from a corporate point of view because investors prefer the investment returns that receive the most favourable tax treatment. Although the capital markets generally express yields or rates of return on a before-tax basis, the astute investor is usually focused on the aftertax yield or return.

Later chapters, especially Chapter 12, refer to the specific nature of income tax effects. Tax-allowable amortization (**capital cost allowance** in the Tax Act) is explored in detail and applied to the capital budgeting decision. The Income Tax Act sets rules by which capital expenditure (capital cost allowance) can be deducted from income over several years, and these usually differ from how the firm amortizes a capital expenditure for accounting purposes. For cash flow effects, we are concerned only with what is permissible under the Income Tax Act.

Given the complexity and ever-changing nature of the Canadian tax environment, an individual is well advised to get current advice from a tax expert in cases where tax implications may be important.

It is the incremental changes in the firm that come under analysis. When a firm undertakes an investment, it wants to know the rate of tax that will be applied to the income generated. An investor will also want to know how much the tax bite will be on any returns they receive from an investment. Therefore, as investment analysts we are concerned with the marginal tax rate, which is the rate of tax on the last dollar of cash flow or income earned.

LO6 Corporate Tax Rates

Corporate federal and provincial tax rates are continually changing, both in accordance with governments' need for revenue and their policies for achieving fiscal policies and economic objectives. In this section, we use rates for 2020, knowing these may be changed in subsequent budgets by the government of the day. Recently, the general trend in tax rates has been slightly downward.

The federal corporate tax rate attempts to be in line with competing international jurisdictions. This federal rate is reduced to allow the provinces to levy their own taxes on corporate income. Table 2–12 outlines the tax rates after combining the federal and provincial rates. Small business and manufacturing income are generally accorded reduced tax rates. Corporations should also be aware that some provinces have tax holidays (usually for Canadian-controlled private corporations [CCPCs] and designated industries), capital taxes on large corporations, and payroll taxes. These we will leave to a tax course.

Canada Revenue Agency
canada.ca/en/r evenue-agency

The general working definition of a small business in Canada is a firm that employs fewer than 100 persons, but small market share and ownership concentration also serve to define a small business. For tax purposes, the first $500,000 of active business income earned per year by a CCPC gets a 17.5 percent deduction of federal tax payable. These reductions

Table 2–12 Combined federal and provincial corporate income tax rates, 2020

	Manufacturing and Processing Income	Active Business Income	(CCPC) Small Canadian-Controlled Active Business Income < $500,000
British Columbia	27.0%	27.0%	11.0%
Alberta	26.0	26.0	10.0
Saskatchewan	25.0	27.0	11.0
Manitoba	27.0	27.0	9.0
Ontario	25.0	26.5	12.5
Quebec	26.5	26.5	14.0
New Brunswick	29.0	29.0	11.5
Nova Scotia	31.0	31.0	12.0
Prince Edward Island	31.0	31.0	12.0
Newfoundland & Labrador	30.0	30.0	12.0
Yukon	17.5	27.0	11.0
Northwest Territories	26.5	26.5	13.0
Nunavut	27.0	27.0	12.0

aim to encourage small businesses. Active income is interpreted to exclude personal services revenue and specified investment income. Manufacturing and processing industries in some provinces receive a reduced rate. A small manufacturing business is taxed federally at the same rate as other small businesses. These considerations are included in the marginal tax rates of Table 2–12.

Effective Tax Rate Examples

Let us look at three examples of estimating tax payable for a corporation. Active business income is determined by reducing income by allowable expenses, including capital cost allowance. (Note: Rates subject to change.)

1. Non-manufacturing company CCPC operating in Ontario:

    Active business income $100,000

    Combined federal and provincial tax rate   12.5%

    Total tax payable 12,500

2. Manufacturing company CCPC operating in Manitoba:

    Active business income $100,000

    Combined federal and provincial tax rate   9%

    Total tax payable 9,000

3. Manufacturing company foreign-controlled operating in British Columbia:

    Active business income $100,000

    Combined federal and provincial tax rate   27%

    Total tax payable 27,000

LO7 Personal Taxes

As of 2020, individuals are taxed by the federal government at rates of 15, 20.5, 26, 29, and 33 percent of taxable income. These rates are applied progressively as higher amounts of taxable income are reported by the individual. Provincial tax payable, as of 2020, is also calculated on taxable income (which is sometimes defined differently) with the percentage varying across provinces and territories. Furthermore, various surtaxes are payable in some provinces on higher income. For investment purposes, the taxpayer makes decisions on the basis of the marginal tax rate, the tax that will be paid on the last dollar of income received. It is aftertax income (the bottom line) that counts.

The Income Tax Act distinguishes between income received as interest (bonds), dividends (shares), or capital gains (sale of capital assets) and taxes each type of income differently. Investors' tax liability is of interest to corporations as it influences the types of securities issued to investors. Investors prefer one form of income (capital gains), over another (interest), all other things being equal. Table 2–13 shows the top marginal tax rates in each province on incomes in excess of $214,000 and the rate on midrange incomes ($90,000) for each type of investment income.

Table 2–13 Marginal tax rates (2020)

Province	Interest Income		Dividends (Eligible)		Capital Gains	
	Top	Medium	Top	Medium	Top	Medium
British Columbia	49.80%	31.00%	31.44%	5.49%	24.90%	15.50%
Alberta	48.00	30.50	31.71	7.56	24.00	15.25
Saskatchewan	47.50	33.00	29.64	9.63	23.75	16.50
Manitoba	50.40	37.90	37.78	20.53	25.20	18.95
Ontario	53.53	33.89	39.34	12.24	26.76	16.95
Quebec	53.31	41.12	40.10	23.28	26.65	20.56
New Brunswick	53.30	37.02	33.51	11.04	26.65	18.51
Nova Scotia	54.00	37.17	41.58	18.35	27.00	18.59
Prince Edward Island	51.37	37.20	34.22	16.12	25.69	18.60
Newfoundland & Labrador	51.30	36.30	42.61	21.91	25.65	18.15
Yukon	48.00	29.50	28.93	3.40	24.00	14.75
Northwest Territories	47.05	32.70	28.33	8.53	23.53	16.35
Nunavut	44.50	28.50	33.08	9.62	22.25	13.75

Medium rate at approximately $90,000 of taxable income
Top rate generally in effect at about $214,000, except Ontario, Alberta, and the Yukon have slightly higher brackets

Dividends for income tax purposes are increased, or grossed up, and have a tax credit available as an attempt to overcome double taxation. This occurs because the individual pays both personal tax and corporate tax as a shareholder. Capital gains are tax-free on personal residences. Only 50 percent of other capital gains, added to taxpayers' other income, are taxable. The special treatment of capital gains is an attempt to encourage capital investments. With this cursory look at personal taxation, the student should be aware that different forms of income received from the corporation are taxed differently and that there are numerous effects on the exact calculations of taxes on investment income.

The tax rates of Table 2–13 should be considered marginal tax rates as they apply to the last dollar of investment income received. As has been noted, the investor is concerned with the aftertax yield on an investment. This is determined by the formula

$$\text{Investment yield} = (1 - \text{tax rate})$$

LO8 Cost of a Tax-deductible Expense

The businessperson often states that a tax-deductible item, such as interest on business loans, travel expenditures, or salaries, costs substantially less than the amount expended, on an aftertax basis. To investigate how this process works, let us examine the tax statements of two corporations—the first pays $100,000 in interest, and the second has no interest expense. An average tax rate of 30 percent is used for each computation.

	Corporation A	Corporation B
Earnings before interest and taxes	$400,000	$400,000
Interest	100,000	0
Earnings before taxes (taxable income)	300,000	400,000
Taxes (30%)	90,000	120,000
Earnings after taxes	$210,000	$280,000
Difference in earnings after taxes—$70,000		

Although Corporation A paid $100,000 more in interest than Corporation B, its earnings after taxes are only $70,000 less than those of Corporation B. Thus, we say the $100,000 in interest costs the firm only $70,000 in aftertax earnings. The aftertax cost of a tax-deductible expense can be computed as the actual expense times 1 minus the tax rate. In this case, we show $100,000 (1 − tax rate), or $100,000 × 0.70 = $70,000. The reasoning in this instance is that the $100,000 is deducted from earnings before determining taxable income, thus saving us $30,000 in taxes and costing only $70,000 on a net basis. The tax savings, or tax shield, is computed by multiplying the expense times the tax rate: ($100,000 × 0.30 = $30,000).

Because a dividend on common stock is not tax deductible, we say it cost us 100 percent of the amount paid. From a purely corporate cash flow viewpoint, the firm would be indifferent between paying $100,000 in interest (expense) and $70,000 in dividends (distribution out of retained earnings).

Amortization (Capital Cost Allowance) as a Tax Shield

Amortization often leads to confusion. It is often the major noncash expense of the income statement, and yet our focus in finance is on actual cash flows. Confusion also arises because, in Canada, amortization that is allowable for tax purposes is referred to as *capital cost allowance.* We explore capital cost allowance in more depth in Chapter 12.

Corporations must file the T2S(1), Reconciliation of Accounting Income with Income for Tax Purposes, with the T2 corporate tax return. The major differences are income and expenses that are treated differently for accounting compared to the Income Tax Act requirements, such as the amortization charge. Let us examine a situation in which the accounting amortization charge and the capital cost allowance are the same. We will examine Corporations A and B again, this time with an eye toward amortization rather than interest. Corporation A deducts $100,000 in amortization (capital cost allowance = CCA), while Corporation B doesn't claim any CCA.

	Corporation A	Corporation B
Earnings before CCA and taxes	$400,000	$400,000
CCA	100,000	0
Earnings before taxes (taxable income)	300,000	400,000
Taxes (30%)	90,000	120,000
Earnings after taxes	$210,000	$280,000
+ Amortization deducted without cash outlay	100,000	0
Cash flow	$310,000	$280,000
Difference—Corporation A has $30,000 higher cash flow		

We compute earnings after taxes and then add back amortization to get cash flow. The difference between $310,000 and $280,000 indicates that Corporation A enjoys $30,000 more in cash flow. The reason is that amortization allowable for tax purposes shielded $100,000 from taxation in Corporation A and saved $30,000 in taxes, which eventually showed up in cash flow. Though amortization is not a new source of funds, CCA does provide tax shield benefits that can be measured as CCA times the tax rate, or in this case $100,000 × 0.30 = $30,000. A more comprehensive discussion of amortization's effect on cash flow is presented in Chapter 12 as part of the long-term capital budgeting decision.

Corporate Tax Rules

In the 2008 federal budget the government announced significant corporate tax rate changes to make Canada a very competitive tax regime. However, other countries have been following this pattern of decreasing rates. These changes have had an impact on the decision making of corporations.

The federal tax rate was reduced in 2008 to 15 percent (10.5 percent with small business deduction) from 19.5 percent. With provincial tax rates included, this brings the overall rate down to a range of 17.5 to 31 percent for 2020, depending on the province.

Internationally, corporate tax rates in early 2020 ranged from 0 percent to 34 percent. Since the 1980s when corporate tax rates were in the high 40 percent range they have been brought down to roughly the mid-20 percent range on average.

Bermuda, Isle of Mann	0%
Hungary	9
Ireland	12.5
United Kingdom	19
United States	21
France	31
Brazil	34

Periodically the government tries to promote specific types of economic activity by way of tax rules. Income trusts, for example, had been developed to encourage new business activity, while providing high yields with favourable tax treatment for investors. However, the result tended to be the recycling of old businesses to gain a tax advantage. As a result, the Tax Act was changed to eliminate the tax advantages of trusts. Today real estate investment trusts remain popular.

Q1 Identify and describe tax rules or rates that affect your decision making.

Q2 Examine a real estate income trust to identify its attractiveness.

fin.gc.ca   **choicereit.ca**
Symbol: ref.un.creit

SUMMARY

1. The financial manager must be thoroughly familiar with accounting and tax rules in order to administer the financial affairs of the firm and to prepare an income statement, retained earnings balance sheet, and statement of cash flows. (LO1)

2. The income statement provides a measure of the firm's profitability over a specified time period. Earnings per share represent residual income available to the common shareholders that may either be paid out in the form of dividends or reinvested in productive assets to generate future profits and dividends. A limitation of the income statement is that it reports income and expenses primarily on an accounting (accrual) basis and thus may not recognize certain important economic changes as they occur. The statement of retained earnings consists of the beginning retained earnings, plus aftertax net income, minus declarations of dividends, plus or minus any amounts for prior period adjustments (errors) resulting in the ending retained earnings, which also appears in the equity section of the balance sheet. (LO2)

3. Canadian public companies must report their financial statements using IFRS, which replaces historical costs with market values. Private companies have the choice of using IFRS or ASPE. Many still use GAAP as well. (LO3)

4. The balance sheet is a snapshot of the financial position of the firm at a point in time, with the shareholders' equity section representing the ownership interest. Because the balance sheet is (usually) presented on a historical cost basis, it may not represent the true value of the firm. (LO4)

5. The cash flow statement reflects the changes in cash from beginning to end of year. Through this statement we get a rough picture of cash flows from operations and the nature of the firm's investment and financing activities. (LO5)

6. The corporate tax structure and the tax implications of interest, jurisdiction, type of business, and amortization affect finance decisions. The aftertax cost and cash flow implications of these items are important throughout the text and are examined in more detail in other chapters. (LO6)

7. The aftertax cash flow to the individual varies depending on whether investment income is in the form of interest, dividends, or capital gain. Generally, interest results in higher taxes compared to dividends and gains. (LO7)

8. A tax shield, or savings, is the reduction of taxes otherwise payable as a result of an allowable deduction of an expense from income. (LO8)

REVIEW OF FORMULAS

$$\text{Earnings per share (EPS)} = \frac{\text{Earning available to common shareholders}}{\text{Number of shares outstanding}} \qquad \textbf{(2-1)}$$

$$\text{Payout ratio} = \frac{\text{Dividend per share}}{\text{Earnings per share}} \qquad \textbf{(2-2)}$$

$$\text{P/E ratio} = \frac{\text{Market share price}}{\text{Earnings per share}} \qquad \textbf{(2-3)}$$

$$\text{Dividend yield} = \frac{\text{Dividends per share}}{\text{Market share price}} \qquad \textbf{(2-4)}$$

$$\frac{\text{Market value}}{\text{Book value}} = \frac{MV}{BV} = \frac{\text{Market value per share}}{\text{Book value per share}} \qquad \textbf{(2-5)}$$

DISCUSSION QUESTIONS

1. Discuss some financial variables that affect the price-earnings ratio. (LO2)

2. What is the difference between book value per share of common stock and market value per share? Why does this disparity occur? (LO2, LO3)

3. Explain how amortization generates actual cash flows for the company. (LO4)

4. What is the difference between accumulated amortization and amortization expense? How are they related? (LO2, LO3)

5. Compare the balance based on IFRS with that based on ASPE, and describe limitations of the balance sheet information for financial analysis. (LO3, LO5)

6. Explain why the statement of cash flows provides useful information that goes beyond income statement and balance sheet data. (LO4)

7. What are the three primary sections of the statement of cash flows? In which section would the payment of a cash dividend be shown? (LO1, LO4)

8. How can we use a statement of cash flows to analyze how a firm's assets were financed? (LO4)

9. What is free cash flow? Why is it important to leveraged buyouts? (LO4)

10. Why is interest expense said to cost the firm substantially less than the actual expense, whereas dividends cost it 100 percent of the outlay? (LO6)

INTERNET RESOURCES AND QUESTIONS

For current individual and corporate tax rates: kpmg.ca, ey.com/ca/en/services/tax/tax-calculators (search tax facts)

The International Accounting Standards Board: ifrs.org

The Canadian Institute of Chartered Accountants: cpacanada.ca

Taxes—Canada: canada.ca/en/services/taxes

1. Describe the role of CPA Canada in accounting research.

2. CPA Canada identifies current trends in accounting and reporting. What are some of the emerging issues in accounting?

3. What is the IASB and what are its objectives?

4. IASB financial statements (IFRS) are accepted by many countries around the world. Are these statements required in Canada?

PROBLEMS

1. Bradley Bus Inc. had earnings last year of $600,000 with 300,000 shares outstanding. On January 1 of the current year, the firm issued 40,000 new shares. Earnings after tax increased by 25 percent over last year.
   a. Calculate earnings per share (EPS) for last year.
   b. Calculate EPS for the current year.

2. Dover River Company has current operating profit of $200,000 before taxes. Interest expense is $10,000, dividends paid on preferred shares were $18,750, and common dividends paid of $30,000. The company paid taxes of $38,250. The company has 20,000 outstanding common shares.
   a. Calculate the EPS and common dividends per share.
   b. Calculate the payout ratio.
   c. Determine the increase in retained earnings for the year.
   d. If the share price is $41.23, calculate the price-earnings (P/E) ratio.

3. Far East Fast Foods had earnings after taxes of $230,000 in the year 20XX with 200,000 shares outstanding. On January 1, 20XY, the firm issued 30,000 new shares. Because of the proceeds from these new shares and other operating improvements, earnings after taxes increased by 25 percent.
   a. Compute EPS of the year 20XX.
   b. Compute EPS of the year 20XY.

4. Sheridan Travel had earnings after taxes of $700,000 in 20XX with 400,000 common shares outstanding. On January 1, 20XY, the firm issued 50,000 new common shares. There is a 35 percent increase in aftertax earnings resulting from the issue of the new shares.

    a. Compute EPS for the year 20XX.

    b. Compute EPS for the year 20XY.

5. Botox Facial Care had earnings after taxes of $370,000 in 20XX with 200,000 shares of stock outstanding. The share price was $31.50. In 20XY, earnings after taxes increased to $436,000 with the same 200,000 shares outstanding. The share price rose to $42.50.

    a. Compute earnings per share and the P/E ratio for 20XX.

    b. Compute earnings per share and the P/E ratio for 20XY.

    c. Give a general explanation of why the P/E ratio changed.

6. Stillery Corporation had earnings after taxes of $436,000 in 20XX with 200,000 shares of stock outstanding. The share price was $42.00. In 20XY, earnings after taxes declined to $206,000 with the same 200,000 shares outstanding. The share price declined to $27.80.

    a. Compute earnings per share and the P/E ratio for 20XX.

    b. Compute earnings per share and the P/E ratio for 20XY.

    c. Give a general explanation of why the P/E ratio changed.

7. Brad Gravel Pitt Company has sales of $327,000 and cost of goods sold of $135,000.

    a. What is the gross profit margin?

    b. If the average firm in the gravel industry has a gross profit margin of 52 percent, how is this firm doing?

8. The Moore Enterprise has gross profit of $880,000 with amortization expense of $360,000. The Kipling Corporation has $880,000 in gross profits but only $60,000 in amortization expense. The selling and administration expenses are $120,000; the same for each company. If the tax rate is 40 percent, calculate the cash flow for each company. Explain the causes of differences in cash flow between the two firms.

9. The Aztec Book Company sold 1,400 finance textbooks to High Tuition College for $84 each in 20XX. These books cost $63 to produce. In addition, Aztec Books spent $2,000 (selling expense) to persuade the college to buy its books. Aztec Books borrowed $50,000 on January 1, 20XX, on which it paid 10 percent interest. Both interest and principal were paid on December 31, 20XX. Aztec Books' tax rate is 20 percent. Amortization expense for the year was $5,000. Did Aztec Books make a profit in 20XX? Verify your answer with an statement of income presented in good form.

10. Carr Auto Wholesalers had sales of $900,000 in 20XX, and cost of goods sold represented 65 percent of sales. Selling and administrative expenses were 9 percent of sales. Amortization expense was $10,000, and interest expense for the year was $8,000. The firm's tax rate is 30 percent.

    a. Compute earnings after taxes using percentage-of-sales method.

    b. Assume the firm hires Ms. Hood, an efficiency expert, as a consultant. She suggests that by increasing selling and administrative expenses to 12 percent of sales, sales can be increased to $1,000,000. The extra sales effort will also reduce cost of goods sold to 60 percent of sales (there will be a larger mark-up in prices as a result of more aggressive selling). Amortization expense will remain at $10,000. However, more automobiles will have to be carried in inventory to satisfy customers, and interest expense will go up to $15,000. The firm's tax rate will remain at 30 percent. Compute revised earnings after taxes based on Ms. Hood's suggestions for Carr Auto Wholesalers. How much will her ideas increase or decrease profitability?

11. Arrange the following income statement items so they are in the proper order of an statement of income:

Taxes	Earnings after taxes
Shares outstanding	Earnings available to common shareholders
Gross profit	Cost of goods sold
Interest expense	Earnings per share
Amortization expense	Earnings before taxes
Preferred stock dividends	Selling and administrative expense
Sales	Operating profit

12. Dog River Company has an operating profit of $250,000. Interest expense for the year was $21,000; preferred dividends paid were $23,450; and common dividends paid were $50,000. The tax was $45,550. The Dog River Company has 40,000 shares of common stock outstanding.

   a. Calculate the EPS and the common dividends per share for Dog River Company.

   b. What is the payout ratio?

   c. What was the increase in retained earnings for the year?

   d. If Dog's share price is $62.00 what is its price-earnings ratio (P/E)?

13. Thermo Dynamics had $450,000 of retained earnings on December 31, 20XX. The company paid dividends of $25,000 in 20XX and had retained earnings of $400,000 on December 31, 20XW.

   a. How much did Thermo earn during 20XX?

   b. What would EPS be if 20,000 shares of common stock are outstanding?

   c. What is the payout ratio?

   d. If Thermo's share price is $30.00 what is its price-earnings ratio (P/E)?

14. Brandon Fast Foods Inc. has operating profit of $210,000. The company has 16,000 common shares outstanding and paid corporate taxes of $59,300. Interest expense for the year was $30,000, preferred dividends paid were $24,700, and common dividends paid were $36,000.

   a. Compute EPS and common dividends per share.

   b. Calculate the increase in retained earnings for the year.

15. Given the following information, prepare an income statement for the Dental Drilling Company.

Selling and administrative expenses	$112,000
Amortization expense	73,000
Sales.	489,000
Interest expense	45,000
Cost of goods sold	156,000
Taxes	47,000

16. Classify the following balance sheet items as current or noncurrent:

Common stock	Investments
Accounts payable	Marketable securities
Preferred stock	Accounts receivable
Prepaid expenses	Plant and equipment
Bonds payable	Accrued wages payable
Inventory	Retained earnings

17. Arrange the following items in proper balance sheet presentation:

Accumulated amortization.	$300,000
Retained earnings.	96,000
Cash.	10,000
Bonds payable	136,000
Accounts receivable.	48,000
Plant and equipment—original cost.	680,000
Accounts payable.	35,000
Allowance for bad debts.	6,000
Common stock, 100,000 shares outstanding	188,000
Inventory	66,000
Preferred stock, 1,000 shares outstanding	50,000
Marketable securities.	20,000
Investments	20,000
Notes payable.	33,000

18. Bengal Wood Company has current assets of $100,000 and capital assets of $140,000. Current liabilities are $60,000 and long-term liabilities are $90,000. There is $20,000 in preferred stock outstanding and the firm has issued 17,500 shares of common stock. Compute book value (net worth) per share.

19. Monique's Boutique has assets of $600,000, current liabilities of $150,000, and long-term liabilities of $120,000. There is $75,000 in preferred stock outstanding; 30,000 shares of common stock have been issued.

    a. Compute book value (net worth) per share.

    b. If there is $33,600 in earnings available to common shareholders and Monique's stock has a P/E ratio of 12 times EPS, what is the current price of the stock?

    c. What is the ratio of market value per share to book value per share?

20. Phelps Labs has assets of $1,800,000, current liabilities of $595,000, and long-term liabilities of $630,000. There is $165,000 in preferred stock outstanding; 20,000 shares of common stock have been issued.

    a. Compute book value (net worth) per share.

    b. If there is $45,000 in earnings available to common shareholders and Phelp's stock has a P/E ratio of 13 times EPS, what is the current price of the stock?

    c. What is the ratio of market value per share to book value per share?

21. In the previous problem, what is the P/E ratio if the firm sells at two times book value per share?

22. Fill in the blank spaces with categories 1 through 7:

    1. Balance sheet (BS)

    2. Income statement (IS)

    3. Current assets (CA)

    4. Capital assets (Cap A)

    5. Current liabilities (CL)

    6. Long-term liabilities (LL)

    7. Shareholders' equity (SE)

Indicate whether

Item is on Balance Sheet (BS) or Income Statement (IS)	If on Balance Sheet, Designate Which Category	Item
_____	_____	Retained earnings
_____	_____	Income tax expense
_____	_____	Accounts receivable
_____	_____	Common stock
_____	_____	Bonds payable, maturity 2022
_____	_____	Notes payable (six months)
_____	_____	Net income
_____	_____	Selling and administrative expenses
_____	_____	Inventories
_____	_____	Accrued expenses
_____	_____	Cash
_____	_____	Plant and equipment
_____	_____	Sales
_____	_____	Operating expenses
_____	_____	Marketable securities
_____	_____	Accounts payable
_____	_____	Interest expense
_____	_____	Income tax payable

23. Identify whether each of the following items increases or decreases cash flow:

Increase in inventory	Increase in short-term notes payable
Decrease in prepaid expenses	Amortization expense
Decrease in accounts receivable	Decrease in accounts payable
Decrease in inventory	Increase in long-term investments
Dividend payment	

24. The Rogers Corporation has a gross profit of $880,000 and $360,000 in amortization expense. The Evans Corporation has $880,000 in gross profit, with $60,000 in amortization expense. Selling and administrative expense is $120,000 for each company. Given that the tax rate is 30 percent, compute the cash flow for both companies. Explain the difference in cash flow between the two firms.

25. The following information is provided for the Solitude Corporation.

Balance Sheets		
	December 31, 20XX	December 31, 20XW
Assets		
Cash	$ 77,490	$ 29,520
Accounts receivable...................	59,040	66,420
Inventory	154,980	132,840
Equipment 136,530		110,700
Less: accumulated amortization........ 33,210		22,140
Net equipment	103,320	88,560
Total assets........................	$394,830	$317,340
Liabilities and Equity		
Accounts payable....................	$ 62,730	$ 36,900
Taxes payable.......................	7,380	14,760
Common stock......................	243,540	221,400
Retained earnings....................	81,180	44,280
Total liabilities and equity	$394,830	$317,340

During 20XX, the following occurred:

1. Net income was $73,800.
2. Equipment was purchased for cash, and no equipment was sold.
3. Shares were sold for cash.
4. Dividends were declared and paid.

    a. Prepare a statement of cash flows for the Solitude Corporation.

    b. Identify the major accounts contributing to the change in cash position, from the three different components of the cash flow statement.

26. The following information is provided for the Waif Corporation.

Balance Sheets

	December 31, 20XX		December 31, 20XW	
Assets				
Cash...........................		$ 54,500		$ 17,400
Accounts receivable..................		64,800		52,200
Inventory		142,200		149,300
Land........................		60,000		87,000
Plant and equipment.................	206,000		158,000	
Less: Accum. amortization	55,000		33,000	
Net plant and equipment		151,000		125,000
Total assets.....................		$472,500		$430,900
Liabilities and Equity				
Accounts payable...................		$ 27,000		$ 37,000
Bonds payable		118,000		158,000
Common stock....................		170,000		130,000
Retained earnings..................		157,500		105,900
Total liabilities and shareholders' equity		$472,500		$430,900

During 20XX, the following occurred:

1. Net income was $91,000.
2. Bonds were retired by issuing new common stock.
3. No equipment was sold.
4. Cash dividends were paid.

    a. Prepare a statement of cash flows for the Waif Corporation.

    b. Identify the major accounts contributing to the change in cash position, from the three different components of the cash flow statement.

27. Prepare a statement of cash flows for the Maris Corporation.

MARIS CORPORATION

Income Statement

Year ended December 31, 20XX

Sales...	$3,300,000
Cost of goods sold	1,950,000
Gross profits.......................................	1,350,000
Selling and administrative expense	650,000
Amortization expense	230,000
Operating income....................................	470,000
Interest expense	80,000
Earnings before taxes.................................	390,000
Taxes	140,000
Earnings after taxes	250,000
Preferred stock dividends...............................	10,000
Earnings available to common shareholders	$ 240,000
Shares outstanding....................................	150,000
Earnings per share	$1.60

Statement of Retained Earnings
For the Year Ended December 31, 20XX

Retained earnings, balance, January 1, 20XX....................................	$800,000
Add: Earnings available to common shareholders, 20XX......................	240,000
Deduct: Cash dividends declared and paid in 20XX..........................	140,000
Retained earnings, balance, December 31, 20XX.............................	$900,000

Comparative Balance Sheets

	December 31, 20XX		December 31, 20XW
Assets			
Current assets:			
Cash..........................	$ 120,000		$ 100,000
Accounts receivable (net).........	510,000		500,000
Inventory	640,000		610,000
Prepaid expenses	30,000		60,000
Total current assets.............	1,300,000		1,270,000
Investments (long-term securities)...	80,000		90,000
Plant and equipment..............	2,600,000	2,000,000	
Less: Accumulated amortization ..	1,230,000	1,000,000	
Net plant and equipment	1,370,000		1,000,000
Total assets......................	$2,750,000		$2,360,000
Liabilities and Shareholders' Equity			
Current liabilities:			
Accounts payable................	$ 550,000		$300,000
Notes payable...................	500,000		500,000
Accrued expenses................	50,000		70,000
Total current liabilities..............	1,100,000		870,000
Long-term liabilities:			
Bonds payable, XX +10...........	160,000		100,000
Total liabilities................	1,260,000		970,000
Shareholders' equity:			
Preferred stock..................	90,000		90,000
Common stock..................	500,000		500,000
Retained earnings................	900,000		800,000
Total shareholders' equity	1,490,000		1,390,000
Total liabilities and shareholders' equity	$2,750,000		$2,360,000

The following questions apply to the Maris Corporation, as presented in the previous problem.

28. Describe the general relationship between net income and net cash flows from operating activities for the firm.

29. Has the buildup in plant and equipment been financed in a satisfactory manner? Briefly discuss.

30. Compute the book value per common share for 20XW and 20XX for the Maris Corporation.

31. If the market value of a share of common stock is 2.8 times book value for 20XX, what is the firm's P/E ratio for 20XX?

32. Prepare a statement of cash flows for the Winfield Corporation for 20XX.

WINFIELD CORPORATION
Balance Sheets

	December 31, 20XX		December 31, 20XW	
Assets				
Current Assets:				
Cash		$ 1,750		$ 1,400
Accounts receivable.		7,875		5,425
Inventory		33,250		28,000
Prepaid expenses		1,225		1,050
Total current assets.		44,100		35,875
Investments (long-term).		17,500		21,000
Capital assets:				
Land		15,750		7,000
Buildings	100,000		100,000	
Less: accumulated amortization. . .	61,500		58,000	
Net buildings		38,500		42,000
Equipment	36,750		28,000	
Less: accumulated amortization. . .	10,500		7,000	
Net equipment		26,250		21,000
Total assets.		$142,100		$126,875
Liabilities and Shareholders' Equity				
Current liabilities:				
Accounts payable		$ 15,750		$ 17,500
Notes payable.		8,750		6,125
Accrued expenses.		9,275		7,350
Interest payable		1,225		1,400
Total current liabilities.		35,000		32,375
Long-term liabilities:				
Bonds payable, XX + 8		43,750		38,500
Total liabilities		78,750		70,875
Shareholders' equity:				
Common stock		24,500		24,500
Retained earnings.		38,850		31,500
Total shareholders' equity		63,350		56,000
Total liabilities and shareholders' equity		$142,100		$126,875

WINFIELD CORPORATION
Income Statement
Year Ended December 31, 20XX

Sales.	$210,000
Cost of goods sold	87,500
Gross profits.	122,500
Selling and administrative expense	95,900
Amortization expense	10,500
Operating income.	16,100
Interest expense	3,500
Other income and losses:	
Gain on sale of investment.	5,250
Dividend income	1,575
Loss on sale of equipment	1,050
Net other income and losses.	5,775
Earnings before taxes.	18,375
Income taxes	4,375
Net income	$ 14,000

During 20XX, the following occurred:

1. From the long-term investments, a dividend of $1,575 was received. Shares originally costing $3,500 were sold for $8,750 from the investment account.

2. Land was purchased for $8,750. Purchase was completed with a note payable of $8,750, with interest and principal due in 12 months.

3. New equipment was purchased for $15,750 cash. Old equipment originally costing $7,000 with accumulated amortization of $3,500 was sold for $2,450.

4. Notes payable at $6,125 were paid.

5. Bonds were sold at par for $5,250.

6. A dividend of $6,650 was paid.

The 20XX amortization expense was $3,500 for buildings and $7,000 for equipment.

33. For December 31, 20XX, the balance sheet of the Gardner Corporation is as follows:

Balance Sheet

Current Assets			Liabilities	
Cash		$ 10,000	Accounts payable	$ 12,000
Accounts receivable		15,000	Notes payable	20,000
Inventor		25,000	Bonds payable	50,000
Prepaid expenses		12,000		
Capital Assets.			Shareholders' Equity	
Plant and equipment.	250,000		Common stock	75,000
Acc. amortization.	50,000		Retained earnings.	105,000
Net plant and equipment		200,000		
Total assets.		$262,000	Total liabilities and	
			shareholders' equity	$262,000

Sales for 20XY were $220,000, with cost of goods sold being 60 percent of sales. Amortization expense was 10 percent of plant and equipment (net) at the beginning of the year. Interest expense for the bonds payable was 8 percent, while interest on the notes payable was 10 percent. These are based on December 31, 20XX, balances. Selling and administrative expenses were $22,000, and the tax rate averaged 18 percent.

During 20XY, the cash balance and prepaid expense balance were unchanged. Accounts receivable and inventory each increased by 10 percent, and accounts payable increased by 25 percent. A new machine was purchased on December 31, 20XY, at a cost of $35,000. A cash dividend of $12,800 was paid to common shareholders at the end of 20XY. Also, notes payable increased by $6,000 and bonds payable decreased by $10,000. The common stock account did not change.

a. Prepare an income statement for 20XY.

b. Prepare a balance sheet as of December 31, 20XY.

c. Prepare a statement of cash flows for the year ending December 31, 20XY.

Identify the major accounts contributing to the change in cash position, from the three different components of the cash flow statement.

34. Ron's Aerobics Ltd., a CCPC located in downtown Winnipeg, Manitoba, has the following taxable income for 20XX.

20XX	$ 95,000

a. Compute the total tax obligation for Ron's Aerobics in 20XX and income after taxes (assume 9 percent tax rate).

b. If Ron pays a dividend of $95,000, what are the total taxes paid (corporate and individual as medium income)? What is the combined tax rate? Assume that Ron's Aerobics has accumulated retained earnings from previous periods.

c. If Ron pays a salary of $95,000 what are the total taxes paid (corporate and individual as medium income)? What is the combined tax rate?

d. Would Ron's taxes be less if he operated as a proprietorship instead of a corporation?

35. Coastal Pipeline Corp. anticipates cash flows from operating activities of $8 million in 20XX. It will need to spend $1.5 million on capital investments in order to remain competitive within the industry. Common share dividends are projected at $0.6 million and preferred dividends at $0.25 million.

a. What is the firm's projected free cash flow for the year 20XX?

36. Inland Fisheries Corp. anticipates cash flows from operating activities of $6 million in 20XX. It will need to spend $2 million on capital investments in order to remain competitive within the industry. Common share dividends are projected at $0.75 million and preferred dividends at $0.35 million.

a. What is the firm's projected free cash flow for the year 20XX?

b. What does the concept of free cash flow represent?

37. Given the following information, prepare, in good form, an income statement for the Nix Corporation. Use the corporate tax rates in Chapter 2 (11%) to calculate taxes. Nix is a CCPC manufacturer in Vancouver.

Selling and administrative expense	$ 70,000
Amortization expense	60,000
Sales	485,000
Interest expense	25,000
Cost of goods sold	205,000

38. For Nix Corporation, what is the tax savings due to amortization expense?

39. R. E. Forms Ltd., a CCPC, had taxable income of $75,000 from an active business in 20XX. Calculate both federal and provincial tax payable if it operates in Alberta (10.0%) as compared to operating in Ontario (12.5%).

40. J. B. Wands has $14,000 to invest. He lives in Saskatchewan and has other income of $90,000 for the year. A current bond issue is paying 6 percent, while a popular share issue offers a 4.7 percent dividend return.

a. Calculate the better return on an aftertax basis (assume 33.0% marginal rate on bonds and 9.63% on shares). What is the aftertax yield?

b. What other factors should be considered?

41. Billie Fruit lives in Alberta and her income fluctuates from year to year, ranging from over $320,000 to about $90,000. She has two investments of $20,000 each in shares, both achieving a return of 7 percent; one by dividend, the other by capital gain.

a. Calculate the higher return on an aftertax basis if this is a high income year (assume 31.71% tax on dividends and 24.00% on capital gains). What is the aftertax yield?

b. Calculate the higher return on an aftertax basis if this is a middle income year (assume 7.56% tax on dividends and 15.25% on capital gains). What is the aftertax yield?

42. Jasper Corporation has determined that its average bondholder has a marginal tax rate of 45 percent. Jasper's corporate tax rate is 27 percent. A current bond issue would require a 7 percent yield. Considering the tax savings to the firm and the taxes to be paid by the individual bondholder, what are the overall tax consequences of this issue from the government's perspective?

Financial Analysis

LEARNING OBJECTIVES

LO1 Calculate 13 financial ratios that measure profitability, asset utilization, liquidity, and debt utilization.

LO2 Assess a company's source of profitability using the DuPont system of analysis.

LO3 Examine the ratios in comparison to industry averages.

LO4 Examine the ratios and company performance by means of trend analysis.

LO5 Interpret ratios and identify corrective action for abnormal results.

LO6 Identify sources of distortion in reported income.

In Chapter 2, we examined the basic assumptions of accounting and the various components that make up the financial statements of the firm. We now use this fundamental material as a springboard into financial analysis to evaluate the financial performance of the firm. From gaining an understanding of the firm's financial performance we are better able to value the firm.

We examine the firm's performance in light of industry norms and past trends. In dissecting the financial statements, we learn how the various components influence each other and add or subtract from the firm's value. Later, we explore the distortions that may exist in cost-based financial statements.

IFRS-based financial statements for public companies are significantly different from generally accepted accounting principles (GAAP) in both valuation and financial analysis. Comparisons of ratios can be made only among companies using the same accounting basis; otherwise, results will be misleading and inappropriate decisions are likely to result.

When calculating ratios year over year it is important that the financial statements are based on the same accounting principles.

Future financial managers, and students, can begin to appreciate the effect of inflation, or sometimes deflation, on the various financial ratios.

Terms such as net income to sales, return on investment, and inventory turnover take on much greater meaning when they are evaluated through the eyes of a financial manager who analyzes the interrelationships of accounts.

RATIO ANALYSIS

Ratios such as litres of gas per 100 kilometres, or hockey player shooting percentages, are used in much of our daily lives. We should know what is being measured in order to construct a ratio and also to understand the significance of the resultant number.

Financial ratios are used to

- Weigh and evaluate the operating performance of the firm now and in the past
- Judge comparative performance between firms
- Determine relative as opposed to absolute performance

Are earnings of $50,000 actually good? If we earned $50,000 on $500,000 of sales (10 percent profit margin ratio), that might be quite satisfactory; whereas earnings of $50,000 on $5 million (a meagre 1 percent return) might be disappointing.

Ratio analysis measures and judges acceptability in relation to other values, but should be supplemented with an evaluation of company management, physical facilities, and numerous other factors. Ultimately, we hope to establish a link with valuation. We often use ratios of past financial performance to determine our expectations regarding the firm's future success. The ratios may help us to determine the current value of the firm's assets, liabilities, and equity on the basis of those future expectations.

Ratios for Comparative Purposes

Dun & Bradstreet
dnb.com/ca-en/

Comparative ratios are available from many sources, usually for a fee, but many university and public libraries subscribe to financial services that produce ratios. These include

D & B	Data on 330 million companies worldwide. Partnered with Mergent, available through libraries, this source provides key business ratios.
Infomart, PostMedia:	fpinfomart.ca, publicly traded companies, industry reports in 30 industry groups. A sample is available.
Government of Canada:	Ratios for major industry groups in "Canadian Industry Statistics"; available at Innovation, Science and Economic Development Canada
TD Waterhouse	The research section has limited ratios (P/E, P/B) for different sectors
University & Public Libraries	Bloomberg, Value Line Investment Survey, Mergent, S&P Industry Surveys, and for individual company ratios finance.yahoo.com

Classification System

The ratios classified in this chapter represent the most commonly used categories and ratios, but others can also be constructed. In Chapter 2 we identified five valuation ratios commonly used in the investment industry. These complement the ratios discussed in this chapter. We will separate 13 significant ratios into four primary categories.

A. Profitability ratios
   1a. Profit margin
   1b. Gross profit margin
   2. Return on assets (investment)
   3. Return on equity (common shareholders)

B. Asset utilization ratios
   4a. Receivable turnover
   4b. Average collection period (day's sales outstanding)
   5a. Inventory turnover
   5b. Inventory holding period
   6a. Accounts payable turnover
   6b. Accounts payable period
   7. Capital asset turnover
   8. Total asset turnover

C. Liquidity ratios
   9. Current ratio
   10. Quick ratio (acid test)

D. Debt utilization ratios
   11. Debt to total assets
   12. Times interest earned
   13. Fixed charge coverage

Profitability ratios—purposes
- Measure return (profit) on sales, total assets, and shareholders' capital
- Examine the effective employment of resources
- Are usually dependent on an adequate sales level
- Influence share price performance, and thus are important to equity investors and security analysts

Asset utilization ratios—purposes
- Measure the speed or efficiency of turning over assets resulting in the cash conversion cycle
- Identify the times per year inventory is sold, the accounts receivable collected, or the productivity of capital assets in generating sales
- Are primary responsibilities of management

Liquidity ratios—purposes
- Emphasize the ability to pay off short-term obligations as they come due
- Quickly impact day-to-day operations
- Focus bankers and creditors on the ability to generate timely cash flows

Debt utilization ratios—purposes
- Evaluate the overall debt position of the firm compared to the asset base and earning power
- Are examined by debt holders in relation to security behind debt obligations

The users of financial statements attach different degrees of importance to the four categories of ratios. Of course, the shrewd analyst and financial manager considers all the ratios, but with different degrees of attention.

The Analysis

Definitions alone carry little meaning in analyzing or dissecting the financial performance of a company. For this reason we apply our four categories of ratios to a hypothetical firm, the Saxton Company, as presented in Table 3–1, and then compare Saxton to representative industry data.

Table 3–1 Non-IFRS financial statements for ratio analysis of private companies

SAXTON COMPANY
Statement of Income
For the Year 20XX

Sales (all on credit)	$4,000,000
Cost of goods sold	3,000,000
Gross profit	1,000,000
Selling and administrative expense*	450,000
Operating profit	550,000
Interest expense	50,000
Extraordinary loss	100,000
Net income before taxes	400,000
Taxes (50%)	200,000
Net income	$ 200,000

*Includes $50,000 in lease payments.

SAXTON COMPANY
Balance Sheet
As of December 31, 20XX

Assets

Cash	$ 30,000
Marketable securities	50,000
Accounts receivable	350,000
Inventory	370,000
Total current assets	800,000
Net plant and equipment	800,000
Total assets	$1,600,000

Liabilities and Shareholders' Equity

Accounts payable	$ 50,000
Notes payable	250,000
Total current liabilities	300,000
Long-term liabilities	300,000
Total liabilities	600,000
Common stock	400,000
Retained earnings	600,000
Total liabilities and shareholders' equity	$1,600,000

Ratio analysis is like solving a mystery. It often suggests questions that need to be answered in coming to grips with the efficiency and the viability of the firm under analysis. No one value is correct, although we investigate ratios that appear unreasonable in comparison to certain standards, and hence raise questions: Is the ratio hinting at problems or very good performance? Is the ratio's calculation distorted by easily explained factors? How does one assess a combination of ratios that give conflicting signals?

LO1 **A. Profitability Ratios** In the table "A. Profitability ratios," the ratios shown relate income earned to an investment base, attempting to gauge the efficiency or performance of the firm. It is appropriate to compare these ratios (returns) to other investments of similar risk to determine if they are adequate. Rates of return can often be determined from the yields (returns) currently available in the financial markets.

The profit margin reflects a firm's pricing policies and its ability to control costs, varying among firms based on competitive strategy and product mix. (Saxton Company's lower return on sales is 5 percent; the industry average is 6.5 percent.)

The return on assets (ROA), or investment (ROI), measures the firm's overall efficiency in the use of capital. The creditors, bondholders, and shareholders all expect that an adequate return will be achieved on their investment. One should be careful in interpreting this ratio, because the income figure can be distorted by financial decisions (interest costs and dividends), and because the total assets figure is based on historical valuation, which may not reflect recent developments (12.5 percent exceeds the industry norm of 9.75 percent). Part of the advantage of IFRS statements is that current market values are used in the calculations of ratios, which makes ratio analysis better at making comparisons to previous years and to other firms in the same industry.

Return on equity (ROE) indicates a return to the owners of the firm and is closely followed by investment analysts. The owners of Saxton Company appear more amply rewarded than other shareholders in the industry (20 percent exceeds the industry norm of 15 percent).

This ratio has deficiencies because it

- Focuses on past results rather than on future, expected results
- Does not focus on share price, the goal of the firm
- Relies on book value and not the actual market value of the investment
- Doesn't capture the firm's assumed risk to generate earnings

Often a firm makes decisions that sacrifice earnings today for the future benefit of the firm. Although these prudent decisions will likely be reflected in the firm's market share price, its current earnings and return-on-equity ratio will probably suffer. Excessive debt or new business ventures may increase earnings in the short term but create a higher risk of business failure. Nevertheless, return on shareholders' equity is a closely watched ratio, and it indicates a firm's performance.

Profitability can also be examined by the gross profit margin, which is gross profit divided by sales. Generally, this ratio is an attempt to identify the relationship between variable costs and sales by factoring out fixed costs. A company with high fixed costs will suffer large declines in overall profitability if its sales decline. For the Saxton Company, the gross profit margin is 25 percent (1,000,000/4,000,000).

Finally, as a general statement in computing all the profitability ratios, the analyst must be sensitive to the age of the assets. Plant and equipment purchased 15 years ago may be carried on the books far below its replacement value in an inflationary economy. IFRS statements eliminate this problem since assets are converted to current values. ASPE statements (historical cost basis) showing a 20 percent ROA purchased many years ago may be inferior to a 15 percent return on newly purchased assets.

A. Profitability ratios

		Saxton Company	Industry Average
(3–1a)	Profit margin $= \dfrac{\text{Net income}}{\text{Sales}}$	$\dfrac{\$200,000}{\$4,000,000} = 5\%$	6.5%
(3–1b)	Gross profit margin $= \dfrac{\text{Gross profit}}{\text{Sales}}$	$\dfrac{\$1,000,000}{\$4,000,000} = 25\%$	22%
(3–2a)	Return on assets (ROA) investment (ROI) $= \dfrac{\text{Net income}}{\text{Total assets}}$	$\dfrac{\$200,000}{\$1,600,000} = 12.5\%$	9.75%
(3–2b)	Return on assets (ROA) investment (ROI) $= \dfrac{\text{Net income}}{\text{Sales}} \times \dfrac{\text{Sales}}{\text{Total assets}}$	$5\% \times 2.5 = 12.5\%$	$6.5\% \times 1.5$ $= 9.75\%$
(3–3a)	Return on equity (ROE) $= \dfrac{\text{Net income}}{\text{Shareholders' equity}}$	$\dfrac{\$200,000}{\$1,000,000} = 20\%$	15%
(3–3b)	Equity multiplier $= \dfrac{\text{Total assets}}{\text{Equity}}$	$\dfrac{\$1,600,000}{\$1,000,000} = 1.6$	$\dfrac{1}{0.6667} = 1.5$
(3–3c)	Return on equity (ROE) = ROA × Equity multiplier	$0.125 \times 1.60 = 20\%$	0.10×1.50 $= 15\%$

LO2 DuPont Analysis

The DuPont system, illustrated in Figure 3–1, causes the analyst to examine the sources of a company's profitability. The DuPont company was a forerunner in stressing that satisfactory ROA may be achieved through one or a combination of

- High profit margins
- A rapid turnover of assets
- The use of debt

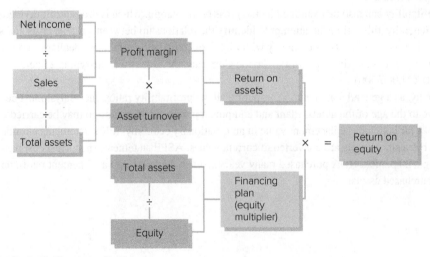

Figure 3–1 DuPont analysis

Since the profit margin is an income statement ratio, a high profit margin indicates good cost control, whereas a high asset turnover ratio demonstrates efficient use of the assets on the balance sheet. Different industries have different operating and financial structures. For example, in the heavy capital goods industry, the emphasis is on a high profit margin with a low asset turnover; in food retailing, the profit margin is low, and the key to satisfactory returns on total assets is a rapid turnover of assets, especially with inventory that will quickly become spoiled.

For the Saxton Company, it is noteworthy that the ROA is higher than the industry average (2.5 to 1.5), but its return on sales is lower. Thus, Saxton generates more sales on its asset base than the industry on average. This can be beneficial, as it shows a more efficient operation, but it may also suggest overuse of the assets. This might be the result of underinvestment in new assets.

Return on total assets as described through the two components of profit margin and asset turnover is part of the DuPont system of financial analysis.

$$\text{ROA (investment)} = \text{Profit margin} \times \text{Asset turnover}$$

A high ROE (return on equity) may be the result of one or two factors: a high return on total assets or a generous utilization of debt, or a combination thereof. This can be seen through formula 3–3*c*, which represents a modified or second version of the DuPont formula.

$$\text{ROE} = \text{ROA} \times \text{Equity multiplier}$$

Note that ROA is taken from formula 3–2*b*, which represents the initial version of the DuPont formula (ROA = Net income/Sales × Sales/Total assets). ROA is then increased or leveraged by the amount of debt to equity in the capital structure. Return to shareholders (ROE) is greater than the ROA when multiplied by the equity multiplier greater than 1. In other words, positive financial leverage (debt) caused by returns being higher than the cost of debt causes a higher equity multiplier, resulting in higher ROE.

$$\text{Equity multiplier} = \frac{\text{Total assets}}{\text{Equity}}$$

The use of debt, in relation to equity, has magnified the return to shareholders. Leverage is explored in more detail in Chapter 5.

 FINANCE IN ACTION

Applying DuPont Analysis to the Rails

In 2001, one of the great holding companies of Canada, Canadian Pacific (CP), was split into five separate companies (Canadian Pacific Railway, Fairmont Hotels, CP Ships, Fording Coal, Encana (now Ovintiv)). This split is sometimes referred to as "unlocking the asset value" of a vast conglomerate. CP had been synonymous with Canada—it had been formed to help build the nation in the early days of Confederation—and was often considered the means by which a global investor could buy a piece of Canada.

The DuPont method provides insight into the components of profitability, and may also highlight weaknesses or opportunities. It is worthwhile to examine the profit margins, asset turnovers, and debt structure (see *financial leverage* in Chapter 5) for a company such as CP in relation to that of a rival.

We will consider CN Rail, a transcontinental rival to CP with extensive interests in Canada and the United States. It is also insightful to examine firms in other lines of business (as illustrated) to examine their sources of profitability.

CN and CP are roughly equal on profit margin and ROA but CP has a higher ROE because of greater leverage. The low profit margins at the retail firm Empire is increased by high asset turnover by higher leverage (equity multipliers). Canadian Tire increases its ROE through leverage. The latest financial statements of these companies, analyzed by means of the DuPont method, will show if there has been a change in how they achieve ROE.

Q1 How has the ROE changed for each firm from results of late 2019 in table below to the current year, as revealed by DuPont analysis?

cpr.ca	cn.ca	empireco.ca	canadiantire.ca
Symbol: CP	Symbol: CNR	Symbol: EMP.A	Symbol: CTC

	Profit Margin	×	Asset Turnover	=	Return on Assets	×	Equity Multiplier	=	Return on Equity
CP Rail.........	30.03%		0.3543		10.64%		3.0414		32.36%
CN Rail	29.63		0.3591		10.64		2.3355		24.85
Empire	1.76		2.250		3.96		2.881		11.41
Canadian Tire.....	5.62		.774		4.35		3.871		16.84

In the case of the Saxton Company, the modified version of the DuPont formula shows

$$\text{Equity multiplier} = \frac{\text{Total assets}}{\text{Equity}} = \frac{\$1,600,000}{\$1,000,000} = 1.6$$

$$\text{ROE} = \text{ROA} \times \text{Equity multiplier} = 0.125 \times 1.60 = 20\%$$

Actually, the ROA of 12.5 percent is higher than the industry average of 9.75 percent, and the equity multiplier of 1.6 is higher than the industry norm of 1.5. Both ROA and leverage contribute to a higher ROE than the industry average (20 percent versus 15 percent). Note that if the firm had a 50 percent debt-to-assets ratio, ROE would be 25 percent.[1]

$$\text{Equity multiplier} = \frac{\text{Total assets}}{\text{Equity}} = \frac{\$1,600,000}{\$800,000} = 2.0$$

$$\text{ROE} = \text{ROA} \times \text{Equity multiplier} = 0.125 \times 2.0 = 25\%$$

This does not necessarily mean debt is a positive influence, only that it can be used to leverage ROE. The ultimate goal for the firm is to achieve maximum valuation for its securities in the marketplace, and this goal may or may not be advanced by using debt to increase ROE. Because debt represents increased risk, a lower valuation of higher earnings is possible.[2] Every situation must be evaluated individually.

B. Asset Utilization Ratios These ratios may explain why one firm can turn over its assets more rapidly than another. All of these ratios relate the balance sheet (assets) to the income statement (sales). The Saxton Company's rapid turnover of assets is explained in these formulas.

Generally, a firm will desire higher turnover ratios, which indicate that the assets are being used efficiently to generate sales. If the turnover ratios slow down, the firm might be concerned that inventories will become obsolete or that accounts receivable will turn to bad debts. On the other hand, too-rapid turnover of assets may indicate a lack of capital to fund assets, leading to undue wear on capital assets, inventory stockouts, and/or credit policies that inhibit sales because they are too strict.

When calculating ratios using the income statement, a flow concept, and the balance sheet representing the stock position of the firm at a point in time, distortions may occur because of fluctuations in the firm's level of activity. Sometimes, the ratios are calculated on the basis of an average of balance sheet positions between two points in an attempt to overcome these distortions. The ratios shown below have not made this adjustment.

The receivables turnover, or its reciprocal, the average collection period, suggests how long, on average, customers' accounts stay on the books. (Turnover of 11.4 times is faster than the industry average

---

[1] The return would be slightly less than 25 percent because of increased financing costs (interest) with higher debt.
[2] Further discussions of this point are presented in Chapters 5 and 10.

of 10 times per year; collection period of 32 days versus 36 days shows less time to collect receivables.) A quick collection period for accounts receivable is important; it demonstrates efficient management and has a positive influence on cash flow. However, one must be careful that the collection policies do not hamper credit sales. Of note is the fact that average daily credit sales are $10,959 ($4,000,000/365).

Inventory turnover, or its reciprocal, the inventory holding period, indicates sales per dollar of inventory and the efficiency of inventory ordering and cost-control methods.[3] (Turnover 8.1 times per year in contrast to industry average of seven times, and holding period of 45 days in contrast to industry average of 52 days, suggest greater efficiency at Saxton.) Although high inventory turns are generally good, they may be evidence of underinvestment in assets and may result in stockouts, which have a high opportunity cost due to customers buying from competitors.

The accounts payable turnover, or its reciprocal, the accounts payable period, identifies the effective use of trade credit as opposed to bank credit. By decreasing the turnover of payables, a firm can significantly reduce short-term borrowing and the resultant interest costs. This concept is explored more fully in Chapter 7. (Turnover of 60 times is well above the industry average of 12 times; accounts payable period of 6 days versus industry average of 30 days shows low trade credit use by Saxton.) This ratio can be distorted if we must use cost of goods sold (COGS) rather than purchases on credit. Small businesses, which have a tough time arranging borrowing from banks, must effectively balance their credit position between current assets and liabilities. This can be done by watching collection, holding, and payable periods. If Saxton is collecting from its customers in slightly over 30 days, it might expect to be paying its suppliers in a similar period of time.

Capital asset turnover and total asset turnover examine if an appropriate amount of capital is deployed in the firm to support sales and if reinvestment is occurring at proper intervals. (Turnover of capital assets [plant and equipment] at 5 is less than the industry's 5.4; the turnover of total assets is at 2.5 versus 1.5.)

B. Asset utilization ratios

			Saxton Company	Industry Average
(3–4a)	Receivables turnover =	$\dfrac{\text{Sales (credit)}}{\text{Receivables}}$	$\dfrac{\$4,000,000}{\$350,000} = 11.4$	10.0 times
(3–4b)	Average collection period =	$\dfrac{\text{Accounts receivable}}{\text{Average daily credit sales}}$	$\dfrac{\$350,000}{\$10,959} = 32$	36 days
(3–5a)	Inventory turnover =	$\dfrac{\text{Cost of goods sold}}{\text{Inventry}}$ or $\dfrac{\text{Sales}}{\text{Inventory}}$	$\dfrac{\$3,000,000}{\$370,000} = 8.1$	7.0 times
(3–5b)	Inventory holding period =	$\dfrac{\text{Inventory}}{\text{Average daily COGS}}$	$\dfrac{\$370,000}{\$8,219} = 45$	52 days
(3–6a)	Accounts payable turnover =	$\dfrac{\text{Cost of goods sold}}{\text{Account payable}}$	$\dfrac{\$3,000,000}{\$50,000} = 60.0$	12.0 days
(3–6b)	Accounts payables period =	$\dfrac{\text{Accounts payable}}{\text{Average daily purchases (COGS)}}$	$\dfrac{\$50,000}{\$8,219} = 6$	30 days
(3–7)	Capital asset turnover =	$\dfrac{\text{Sales}}{\text{Capital assets}}$	$\dfrac{\$4,000,000}{\$800,000} = 5$	5.4 times
(3–8)	Total asset turnover =	$\dfrac{\text{Sales}}{\text{Total assets}}$	$\dfrac{\$4,000,000}{\$1,600,000} = 2.5$	1.5 times

Note: Formula 3–4b can also be solved by Receivables/Sales × 365, formula 3–5b by Inventory/COGS × 365, and formula 3–6b by Payables/COGS × 365.

---

[3]Turnover is sometimes shown as sales divided by inventory, when cost of goods sold information cannot be obtained. However, if sales is used, ratio comparisons should be made using only sales for other years.

C. Liquidity Ratios The current ratio and quick (or acid test) ratio, which excludes inventories, examine current assets and liabilities (working capital) of the firm focusing on the need to meet cash requirements quickly. Today, with sophisticated means of managing current assets, one does not want to see ratios that are too high, as this would be evidence of inefficient management. A firm is expected to handle maturing short-term liabilities without overly large precautionary current asset balances.

Deteriorating liquidity ratios and cash flow problems often stem from weakening asset utilization ratios. Further liquidity analysis might call for cash budgets (as developed in Chapter 4) to determine whether Saxton can meet each maturing obligation as it falls due. For the small business, cash budgets will be crucial to stay in operation and will be carefully scrutinized by any lender. Liquidity allows the small business to remain flexible and able to meet short-term obligations, because bank loans and capital markets are difficult, if not impossible, to access. Many profitable firms have failed because they ran out of cash and were not able to pay bills when due. Creditors can then apply to put the firm into receivership or bankruptcy. A current ratio of 2.0+ and quick ratio of 1.0+ are generally acceptable levels.

C. Liquidity ratios

			Saxton Company	Industry Average
(3–9)	Current ratio =	$\dfrac{\text{Current assets}}{\text{Current liabilities}}$	$\dfrac{\$800,000}{\$300,000} = 2.67$	2.1
(3–10)	Quick ratio =	$\dfrac{\text{Current assets} - \text{inventory}}{\text{Current liablities}}$	$\dfrac{\$430,000}{\$300,000} = 1.43$	1.0

D. Debt Utilization Ratios These ratios allow the analyst to measure the prudence of the debt management policies of the firm. Debt utilization, referred to as *leverage,* is explored in Chapter 5 under risk-and-return considerations with the potential impact on the performance of the firm. (Debt to total assets of 37.5 percent is slightly above the industry average of 33 percent, but well within the prudent range of 50 percent or less.) Another common variation of debt to assets is the debt/equity ratio. This is basically the same thing, since

$$\frac{D}{TA - D} = \frac{D}{E} = \frac{0.375}{1 - 0.375} = 0.60, \text{ or } 60 \text{ percent}$$

Often this ratio is calculated only with long-term debt obligations (including their current portion). Whatever method is used, it is important to remain consistent when examining all ratio trends over time.

D. Debt utilization ratios

			Saxton Company	Industry Average
(3–11)	Debt to total assets =	$\dfrac{\text{Total debt}}{\text{Total assets}}$	$\dfrac{\$600,000}{\$1,600,000} = 37.5\%$	33%
(3–12)	Times interest earned =	$\dfrac{\text{Income before interest and taxes}}{\text{Interest}}$	$\dfrac{\$550,000}{\$50,000} = 11$	7 times
(3–13)	Fixed charge coverage =	$\dfrac{\text{Income before fixed charges and taxes}}{\text{Fixed charges}}$	$\dfrac{\$600,000}{\$100,000} = 6$	5.5 times

Coverage ratios demonstrate the debt management of the firm and the ability to meet financial obligations from income before interest and taxes (operating profit). Failure to meet financial obligations may endanger the firm. Times interest earned indicates the degree to which operating profit covers interest obligations (11 to 7 for the industry is very safe coverage). Fixed charge coverage measures the firm's ability to meet all fixed obligations including interest payments, leases etc. (6 times exceeds the industry norm of 5.5 times).

Income before interest and taxes	$550,000
Add: Lease payments (fixed charges)	50,000
Income before fixed charges and taxes	$600,000

LO3 The various ratios are summarized in Table 3–2. The conclusions reached in comparing the Saxton Company to industry averages are generally valid, though exceptions may exist. In summary, Saxton more than compensates for a lower return on the sales dollar by a rapid turnover of assets, principally inventory and receivables, and a wise use of debt. The student should be able to use these 13 measures to evaluate the financial performance of any firm.

Table 3–2 Ratio analysis

	Saxton Company	Industry Average	Conclusion
A. Profitability			
1a. Profit margin	5.0%	6.5%	Below average
1b. Gross margin	25.0%	28.0%	Below average
2. Return on assets	12.5%	10.0%	Above average due to high turnover
3. Return on equity.	20.0%	15.0%	Good due to ratios 2 and 11
B. Asset Utilization			
4a. Receivable turnover	11.4	10.0	Good
4b. Average collection period	32	36	Good
5a. Inventory turnover	8.1	7.0	Good
5b. Inventory holding period	45	52	Good
6a. Accounts payables turnover . . .	60.0	12.0	Poor
6b. Accounts payable period	6	30	Poor
7. Capital asset turnover.	5.0	5.4	Below average
8. Total asset turnover	2.5	1.5	Good
C. Liquidity			
9. Current ratio.	2.67	2.1	Good
10. Quick ratio	1.43	1.0	Good
D. Debt Utilization			
11. Debt to total assets	37.5%	33.0%	Slightly more debt, but reasonable
12. Times interest earned.	11	7	Good
13. Fixed charge coverage	6	5.5	Good

LO4 Interpretation of Ratios by Trend Analysis

In our examination of ratios, we have compared Saxton Company's results only to the industry average during a particular year in an attempt to identify possible problems. However, one might ask if a comparison to industry averages is appropriate. Would it be more appropriate to compare with the industry leader? How comparable is this company's business to the industry? Furthermore, is a look at a company at a point in time sufficient, or do trends that develop over time tell a more complete story?

Over the course of the business cycle, sales and profitability may expand and contract, and ratio analysis for any one year may not present an accurate picture of the firm. Therefore, we look at trend analysis of performance over a number of years. However, without industry comparisons, even trend analysis may not present a complete picture. For example, in Figure 3–2, we see

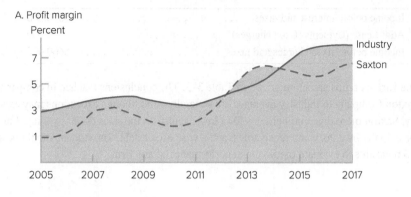

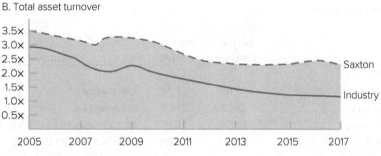

Figure 3–2 Trend analysis

that the profit margin for the Saxton Company has improved, but asset turnover has declined. This by itself may look good for the profit margin and bad for asset turnover. However, when compared to industry trends, we see the firm's profit margin is still below the industry average. On asset turnover, Saxton has improved in relation to the industry even though it is in a downward trend. Similar data could be generated for the other ratios, but we must convert all years to the same basis for IFRS statements of public companies.

By analyzing companies in the same industry, one company can compare its performance to its competitors. In comparing the Bank of Montreal and the Royal Bank of Canada, we assume that the goal of management is to become the best, not just to match the average performance for the industry. Using ROA and ROE as selected ratios, Table 3–3 compares these two companies. Notice the very low ROA, which is a characteristic of the highly leveraged banking industry. Leverage will be further explored in Chapter 5. Despite low returns on assets, the shareholders enjoyed healthy returns on equity.

Bank of Montreal
bmo.com
Royal Bank of Canada
rbc.com

Table 3–3 Trend analysis of competitors

| | Bank of Montreal | | Royal Bank | |
Year	Return on Assets	Return on Equity	Return on Assets	Return on Equity
2006	0.83%	17.7%	0.88	21.4
2008	0.50	13.0	0.63	18.1
2010	0.44	14.9	0.58	13.2
2012	0.69	15.9	0.86	18.25
2014	0.96	14.9	0.97	19.5
2016	0.64	10.4	0.79	13.1
2019	0.84	14.06	1.04	17.4

The Royal Bank has generally outperformed the Bank of Montreal. The better return on assets has translated into better returns on shareholders' equity. The market has been willing to pay a higher current share price for each dollar of profitability. In other words, the price/earnings multiple of the Royal Bank has been higher than that of the Bank of Montreal over the last several years.

Another technique for the examination of company trends is to prepare common-size financial statements. This method expresses the items on the balance sheet as a percentage of total assets and presents the items on the income statement as a percentage of total sales. This is demonstrated for the Saxton Company in Table 3–4. With the statements expressed in this manner, we can examine financial statement items that are changing relative to other items. As a certain item becomes more or less significant on the balance sheet or income statement, we want to determine if this is a healthy trend. When the lines of the income statement are expressed as a percentage of revenues, the firm can focus on its cost structure, identifying areas for improvement.

Table 3–4 Common-size income statement and balance sheet

Saxton Company
Statement of Income
For Year Ended Dec. 31, 20XX

Sales	100%
Cost of goods sold	75%
Gross profit	25%
Selling and administration	11%
Operating profit	14%
Interest expense	1%
Extraordinary loss	3%
Net income before taxes	10%
Taxes	5%
Net income	5%

Saxton Company
Balance Sheet
As of December 31, 20XX

Assets

Cash	2%
Marketable securities	3%
Accounts receivable	22%
Inventory	23%
Total current assets	50%
Net plant and equipment	50%
Total assets	100%

Liabilities and Shareholders' Equity

Accounts payable	3%
Notes payable	16%
Total current liabilities	19%
Long-term liabilities	19%
Total liabilities	38%
Common stock	25%
Retained earnings	37%
Total liabilities and shareholders' equity	100%

Key points for examination are operating ratios such as the gross profit and operating profit margins. The firm would like to examine how these margins compare to competitors and how they improve or deteriorate over time.

Before concluding this brief interpretation of ratios, it is important to recap some of the limitations of ratio analysis. Of major concern is whether or not financial statements correctly portray a company's financial situation, particularly in comparison to other companies that may use different methods to report financial performance. The question of market values, IFRS-based, versus book values, old GAAP, has been raised. The impact of inflation and other sources of distortion on the financial reporting of the firm are discussed more fully in the next sections.

LO5 Ratios do not, by themselves, suggest whether or not the firm is operating optimally. There are no accepted standards, although comparison with industry averages may be of some help. However, even in comparison with industry averages, we must raise questions: Are we comparing to the appropriate industry? What if the firm is a conglomerate? Furthermore, we may want to compare to the industry leader and not the average. Firms tend to follow the financing patterns of their competition, and one should wonder whether the industry norms are indeed appropriate. Is the industry operating optimally? Financial ratios are based on the past performance of a firm. Are they indicative of future performance? And finally, how are conflicting signals between ratios resolved?

 FINANCE IN ACTION

Combat in 3D

AMD and NVidia are serious competitors in 3D graphics, video, and multimedia technology, including 3D graphics accelerators. This is the dynamic digital entertainment field.

If we examine the two firms as of the end of 2011 and 2019 on the basis of common-size income statements, we find that NVidia had much healthier margins as well as better. Both spend about 25 percent of their revenues on R&D, a necessity in this competitive field.

The question is whether the firms can improve their margins, and whether the resources devoted to R&D will pay off over the long run. The longer-run share price performance of these companies will be the result of cost efficiencies and the impact of effective R&D.

Q1 Compare recent AMD and NVidia margins.

Q2 Which share price has performed better over the last year?

amd.com
Symbol: AMD (NYSE)

nvidia.com
Symbol: NVDA (NASDAQ)

	AMD		NVidia	
	2011	**2019**	**2011**	**2019**
Gross margin	44.8%	41.7%	39.8%	60.8%
R&D	22.0	25.0	23.9	26.8
Operating margin	5.6	6.1	19.7	23.8
Profit margin	5.6	3.7	7.2	23.7

LO6 DISTORTION IN FINANCIAL REPORTING

Coincident with the computation of financial ratios, we should also identify possible distortions that can occur in the reported results of companies. Historical-based accounting in an environment of changing prices due to inflation, disinflation, and possible deflation will distort financial results. Price changes will show immediately in revenues, but the impact of changing prices will be delayed in asset values, such as inventory and capital assets. Accrual-based accounting is subject to interpretation and the judgment of those who prepare the results. This can result in significant differences in the reporting of revenue, the treatment of cost of goods sold, and the write-off policies of the firm. These distortions cause a number of problems for the financial manager or analyst evaluating a company. The use of IFRS for public companies significantly reduces this distortion since assets are stated at current values. However, trend analysis is difficult since IFRS statements are available since only 2011. Reliable trend analysis will require years prior to 2011 to be converted to IFRS basis, which will be unlikely and costly since appraisals are required.

Inflationary Impact

The major problem during inflationary times is that revenue is almost always stated in current dollars, whereas plant and equipment or inventory may have been purchased at lower price levels. Thus, profit may be more a function of increasing prices than of satisfactory performance. Therefore, ratio analyses are only general, rather than absolute, indicators of the firm's performance. Qualitative factors should also be considered for appropriate decision making.

Bank of Canada
bankofcanada.ca

Consider the Stein Corporation's income statement for 20XX in Table 3–5. At year-end, the firm also has 100 units still in inventory at $1 per unit and $200 worth of plant and equipment with a 20-year life.

Table 3–5 Stein income statement, 20XX

Stein Corporation Net Income for 20XX		
Sales...	$200	(100 units at $2)
Cost of goods sold...	100	(100 units at $1)
Gross profit	100	
Selling and administrative expense	20	
Amortization	10	
Operating profit...	70	
Taxes (40%)..	28	
Aftertax income..	$ 42	

Assume that in 20XY the number of units sold remains constant at 100. However, inflation causes a 10 percent increase in price, from $2 to $2.20. Total sales go up to $220, but with no actual increase in physical volume. FIFO (first in, first out) causes higher profits during inflation. Assume that the firm uses FIFO inventory pricing, so inventory first purchased will be written off against current sales. In this case, 20XY inventory will be written off against 20XX sales revenue, causing greater profit due to inflation.

The 20XY income statement of the Stein Corporation is shown in Table 3–6. The company appears to have increased profit by $11 simply as a result of inflation. These are inventory profits. But not reflected is the increased cost of replacing inventory. Presumably, its replacement cost has increased in an inflationary environment.

Table 3–6 Stein income statement, 20XY

Stein Corporation Net Income for 20XY		
Sales...	$220	(100 units at 20XX price of $2.20)
Cost of goods sold...........................	100	(100 units at $1)
Gross profit..................................	120	
Selling and administrative expense...............	22	(10% of sales)
Amortization..................................	10	
Operating profit..............................	88	
Taxes (40%)..................................	35	
Aftertax income..............................	$ 53	

A replacement cost accounting method, such as the current price to buy the inventory, would reduce income but at the same time increase assets. This increase in assets would lower the debt-to-assets ratio since debt is a monetary asset that is not revalued because it is paid back in nominal (original value) dollars. A decreased debt-to-assets ratio would indicate the financial leverage of the firm has decreased. However, the interest coverage ratio, which measures the operating income available to cover interest expense, will have decreased.

Disinflation Effect

As long as prices continue to rise in an inflationary environment, profits appear to feed on themselves. However, when price increases moderately (disinflation), there will be a rude awakening for management and unsuspecting shareholders as expensive inventory is charged against softening retail prices. A 15 or 20 percent growth rate in earnings may be little more than an inflationary illusion. Industries most sensitive to inflation-induced profits are those with cyclical products, such as commodities, and also those in which inventory is a significant percentage of sales and profits. The value of assets must also be challenged if deflation comes into play. Additionally, the real value of debt will rise if deflation occurs.

Valuation Basics with Changing Prices

Inflation-induced corporate profits may go down during disinflation periods, but investors may be more willing to place their funds in financial assets such as stocks and bonds. The reason for the shift may be a belief that declining inflationary pressures will no longer seriously impair the purchasing power of the dollar. Lessening inflation means that the required return investors demand on financial assets will be lower and future expected earnings or interest should receive a higher current valuation.

None of the above happens with a high degree of certainty. Lower rates of inflation will not necessarily produce high stock and bond prices unless the price pattern appears sustainable over a reasonable period and disinflation or deflation is not coincident with a recessionary economy. Recessions will significantly lower the future returns from stocks and bonds.

Although financial assets such as stocks and bonds have the potential to do well during disinflation, such is not the case for tangible (real) assets. Precious metals, such as gold and silver, gems, and collectibles, which boomed in the high inflation of the late 1970s, fell off sharply in the 1980s as softening prices caused less perceived need to hold real assets as a hedge against inflation. Some commodities, such as copper and nickel, achieved strong price gains in the late 1980s due to supply shortages. Generally, in the 1990s, financial assets outperformed real assets during a period of low inflation. After 2000, with poor financial markets, real estate and commodities became better investments. Since 2010, low inflation and interest rates have caused an increase in stocks and other securities.

Accounting Discretion

Accrual-based accounting allows certain flexibility in matching the revenues and expenses of the firm, because some estimates are necessary when exact amounts are not available. This can result in a wide variance in reported results across different firms. Furthermore, many companies have taken to producing pro forma or adjusted earnings statements that are significantly different from traditional accounting standards. These adjusted statements often receive more public attention.

To illustrate some of these discretions in financial reporting, the income statements for two hypothetical companies in the same industry are presented in Table 3–7. Both firms had identical operating performances for 20XY, but Company A is very conservative in reporting its results, whereas Company B has attempted to maximize its reported income. If both companies had reported income of $200,000 in 20XX, Company B would be thought to be showing substantial growth in 20XY, with net income of $780,000, while Company A is reporting a "flat" or no-growth year of $240,000. Let us examine how the inconsistencies in Table 3–7 could occur. Emphasis is given to a number of key elements on the income statement.

Table 3–7 Income statement

Income Statement for the Year 20XY	Conservative (A)	High Reported Income (B)
Sales..	$4,000,000	$4,200,000
Cost of goods sold	3,000,000	2,400,000
Gross profit	1,000,000	1,800,000
Selling and administrative expense	450,000	450,000
Operating profit	550,000	1,350,000
Interest expense	50,000	50,000
Net income before taxes...................	500,000	1,300,000
Taxes (40%)	200,000	520,000
Net income................................	300,000	780,000
Extraordinary loss (net of tax)	60,000	—
Net income transferred to retained earnings	$ 240,000	$ 780,000

Sales Company B reported $200,000 more in sales dollars although actual volume in units was the same. This may be the result of different concepts of revenue recognition and estimates of allowances.

For example, certain assets may be sold on an instalment basis over a long period. A conservative firm may defer recognition of the revenue until each payment is received, but other firms may attempt to recognize a fully effected sale at the earliest possible date. A matter for debate is the question of when the risks and rewards of ownership are effectively transferred. Furthermore, sales are expressed net of an allowance for doubtful accounts. This account, which reduces the reported sales, is based on management estimates that may vary across firms.

Although the accounting profession attempts to establish appropriate methods of financial reporting through GAAP, reporting varies, using IFRS for public companies compared to ASPE for private companies.

Cost of Goods Sold Company B reported $600,000 less for cost of goods sold, which may be the result of different assumptions used to account for inventory costs and overhead charges against cost of goods sold. It is the discretion of management on the inventory method used when goods are moving in and out of inventory over a period of time. Management also decides what is appropriate to be considered an overhead expense included in cost of goods sold.

Conservative Company A may well be using LIFO accounting that charges the last-purchased, usually more expensive items against sales, whereas Company B may use FIFO accounting that charges the first purchased, usually less expensive inventory, against sales. The LIFO method, by generally charging the more-expensive items against sales, results in a lower value of inventory on the balance sheet. FIFO (mandated for income tax purposes) achieves the opposite. Note that although LIFO is not used in Canada, other countries may still be using LIFO.

Cost of goods sold may also be affected by varying treatments for research and development costs. These costs may be expensed against revenues over a lengthy time period or expensed more immediately. This can have a dramatic effect on reported earnings. Bombardier, for example, at one time expensed the R & D costs of new planes over the anticipated future sales. This caused problems for reported earnings when the sales did not materialize.

Asset Write-Downs Gains or losses may occur from the sale of corporate capital assets, lawsuits, the write-down in value of certain assets, or similar events. Unfortunately, there is not always agreement on when these gains or losses should be recognized in the income statement.

 FINANCE IN ACTION

Taking a Big Bath

The "big bath" is the tendency of corporations to write off large portions of corporate assets during times of financial stress in order to restart with a leaner balance sheet. The large write-offs usually result in substantial losses recorded on the income statement for one year. However, the large loss reported now will likely increase future reported earnings, because the amortization expense is lowered due to the decrease in capitalized assets. This may distort ratio calculations over time and across companies. An analyst should be able to adjust for these effects.

Often the big bath is taken during reorganization or a change in CEO. If a firm has to report a loss, why not report a big one? A large loss can be blamed on the past leadership. With lower amortization costs and, thus, higher earnings in the future, the new CEO will look better. Interestingly, executive compensation, which is often tied into profits, will also be better.

During the technology meltdown in the early 2000s, Nortel reported a loss of $19.4 billion, which included a write-down of $13.6 billion to goodwill. Nortel in the late 1990s had been Canada's most highly valued company. The market share value of Nortel dropped considerably and many people lost their jobs. The financial reports of the previous years had seemed to favour management while misleading investors. In 2009, Nortel sought bankruptcy protection.

After large asset write-downs (impairments) in 2015 ($6.5 billion) and in 2016 ($2.9 billion), Encana (now Ovintiv) suggested it was poised for growth in 2017 after the weak energy markets of the previous two years. Its assets were expected to earn significantly lower returns in the future. Earnings improved in 2017 and 2018.

In 2019 with continued poor returns, Encana announced it was moving its headquarters from Calgary to Denver, changing its name to Ovintiv with a 1 share for 5 share consolidation that would increase the individual share price but not the overall equity value.

Q1 Have energy firms had significant write-offs recently?

Q2 How has the share price of Encana (Ovintiv) performed recently?

ovintiv.com (Encana)
Symbol: ECA

Conservative Company A has taken a write-off of $100,000 ($60,000 after tax). This is shown as an extraordinary loss (defined in the *CPA Canada Handbook*). Company B, which holds similar assets, has chosen not to take a write-down in asset value and has, thus, avoided the extraordinary loss. Gains and losses occur among large companies fairly often, although they may be buried in the notes to financial statements. An item cannot be reported as an extraordinary gain/loss if the decision to expense it is within management's discretion. This means that if management decides to expense the item, it is likely to be included as part of other operational expenses elsewhere on the income statement.

Chartered Professional
Accountants Canada
cpacanada.ca

Net Income Company A has reported net income of $240,000, whereas Company B claims $780,000 before subtraction of extraordinary losses. The $540,000 difference is attributed to different methods of financial reporting, and it should be recognized as such by the analyst. No superior performance has actually occurred. The analyst must remain ever alert in examining each item in the financial statements rather than accepting bottom-line figures.

Distortions occur in reported financial statements despite the best efforts and intentions of accountants. Basic financial statements can hide much of what they purport to represent, but by careful examination, inquiry, analysis of notes to financial statements, and ratio analysis, we can gain a truer picture of the performance of a firm. This will allow us to better estimate the value of the assets held by the firm and also the value of the firm itself.

SUMMARY

1. Under ratio analysis, we develop four categories of ratios: profitability, asset utilization, liquidity, and debt utilization. We used the balance sheet and income statement to calculate the 13 ratios. (LO1)

2. The DuPont system of analysis breaks ROE, the shareholders' investment, into three components. The profit margin, asset turnover, and debt usage each contribute to ROE. (LO2)

3. Each ratio should be compared to industry averages to identify possibilities for inquiry. Ratio analysis is rather like solving a mystery in which each clue leads to a new area of inquiry. (LO3)

4. Each ratio should also be developed over a number of time periods to identify any positive or negative trends. (LO4)

5. The primary purpose of ratio analysis is to allow management to identify financial problems and plan corrective action to make the firm more profitable. (LO5)

6. Financial analysis calls for an awareness of the distortions that can occur in the financial reports of the firm. Historical-based accounting can report values significantly different from the current values of assets and can misrepresent income, especially in periods of inflation or deflation. Alternative methods of financial reporting may allow firms with equal performance to report different results. (LO6)

REVIEW OF FORMULAS

A. Profitability ratios

$$\text{Profit margin} = \frac{\text{Net income}}{\text{Sales}} \tag{3-1a}$$

$$\text{Gross profit margin} = \frac{\text{Gross profit}}{\text{Sales}} \tag{3-1b}$$

$$\text{Return on assets (ROA) investment (ROI)} = \frac{\text{Net income}}{\text{Total assets}} \tag{3-2a}$$

$$\text{Return on assets (ROA) investment (ROI)}$$
$$= \frac{\text{Net income}}{\text{Sales}} \times \frac{\text{Sales}}{\text{Total assets}} \tag{3-2b}$$

$$\text{Return on equity (ROE)} = \frac{\text{Net income}}{\text{Shareholders equity}} \tag{3-3a}$$

$$\text{Equity multiplier} = \frac{\text{Total assets}}{\text{Equity}} \tag{3-3b}$$

$$\text{Return on equity (ROE)} = \text{ROA} \times \text{Equity multiplier} \tag{3-3c}$$

B. Asset utilization ratios

$$\text{Receivables turnover} = \frac{\text{Sales (credit)}}{\text{Receivables}} \tag{3-4a}$$

$$\text{Average collection period} = \frac{\text{Accounts receivable}}{\text{Average daily credit sales}} \tag{3-4b}$$

$$\text{Inventory turnover} = \frac{\text{Cost of goods sold}}{\text{Inventory}} \text{ or } \frac{\text{Sales}}{\text{Inventory}} \tag{3-5a}$$

$$\text{Inventory holding period} = \frac{\text{Inventory}}{\text{Average daily COGS}} \tag{3-5b}$$

$$\text{Accounts payable turnover} = \frac{\text{Cost of goods sold}}{\text{Accounts payable}} \tag{3-6a}$$

$$\text{Accounts payables period} = \frac{\text{Accounts payable}}{\text{Average daily purchases (COGS)}} \qquad \text{(3–6b)}$$

$$\text{Capital asset turnover} = \frac{\text{Sales}}{\text{Capital assets}} \qquad \text{(3–7)}$$

$$\text{Total asset turnover} = \frac{\text{Sales}}{\text{Total assets}} \qquad \text{(3–8)}$$

C. Liquidity ratios

$$\text{Current ratio} = \frac{\text{Current assets}}{\text{Current liabilities}} \qquad \text{(3–9)}$$

$$\text{Quick ratio} = \frac{\text{Current assets} - \text{Inventory}}{\text{Current liabilities}} \qquad \text{(3–10)}$$

D. Debt utilization ratios

$$\text{Debt to total assets} = \frac{\text{Total debt}}{\text{Total assets}} \qquad \text{(3–11)}$$

$$\text{Times interest earned} = \frac{\text{Income before interest and taxes}}{\text{interest}} \qquad \text{(3–12)}$$

$$\text{Fixed charge coverage} = \frac{\text{Income before fixed charges and taxes}}{\text{Fixed charges}} \qquad \text{(3–13)}$$

DISCUSSION QUESTIONS

1. If we divide users of ratios into short-term lenders, long-term lenders, and shareholders, which ratios would each group be most interested in, and for what reasons? (LO5)

2. Inflation can have significant effects on income statements and balance sheets and, therefore, on the calculation of ratios. Discuss the possible impact of inflation on the following ratios and explain the direction of the impact according to your assumptions. (LO6)
   a. Return on investment
   b. Inventory turnover
   c. Capital asset turnover
   d. Debt-to-assets ratio

3. Explain how the DuPont system of analysis breaks down ROA. Also explain how it breaks down return on shareholders' equity. (LO2)

4. What advantage does the fixed charge coverage ratio offer over simply using times interest earned? (LO5)

5. How would our analysis of profitability ratios be distorted if we used income before taxes? Income before interest and taxes? (LO5)

6. Is there any validity in rule-of-thumb ratios for all corporations—for example, a current ratio of 2 to 1 or debt to assets of 50 percent? (LO3)

7. Why is trend analysis helpful in analyzing ratios? What are the problems of trend analysis when different bases of accounting are applied to different years? (LO4)

8. What effect will disinflation (after a high inflationary period) have on the reported income of the firm? (LO5)

9. Why might disinflation prove to be favourable to financial assets? (LO5)

10. Comparing the incomes of two companies can be very difficult even though they sell the same products in equal volume. Why? (LO3)

INTERNET RESOURCES AND QUESTIONS

Electronic documents including financial statements filed with the Canadian Securities Commissions are available through the System for Electronic Document Analysis and Retrieval (SEDAR): sedar.com

Financial ratios on some Canadian companies are available at ca.reuters.com

Some ratios are available on individual company sites such as globeinvestor.com

Innovation, Science and Economic Development Canada has available industry statistics at Research and Business Intelligence

Dun & Bradstreet outlines its services and describes its directories: dnb.com/ca-en

The Business Development Bank has a ratio calculator for many of the common financial ratios: bdc.ca

1. Using a site such as globeinvestor.com, select industry groupings for analysis.

    a. Compare two companies within an industry group over four years on the basis of ROE, profit margin, market to book value, and P/E ratio.

    b. Compare two companies within different industry groups over four years on the basis of ROE, profit margin, market to book value, and P/E ratio.

2. Using a site such as SEDAR, locate the financial statements of any corporation and calculate the 13 ratios used in this chapter over a three-year period.

3. Update the trends exhibited in Table 3–3. Has there been a change?

PROBLEMS

1. Griffey Junior Wear has $800,000 in assets and $200,000 of total debt. It reports net income of $100,000.

    a. What is its ROA (return on assets)?

    b. What is the return on shareholders' equity?

    c. If the firm has an asset turnover ratio of 2.75 times, what is the profit margin?

2. Bunny Hip and Hop Brewery has $750,000 in assets and $300,000 of debt. It reports net income of $55,000.

    a. What is its ROA?

    b. What is the return on shareholders' equity?

    c. If the firm has an asset turnover ratio of 2.2 times, what is the profit margin?

3. The Haines Corp. shows the following financial data for 20XX and 20XY:

	20XX	20XY
Sales.	$3,230,000	$3,370,000
Cost of goods sold	2,130,000	2,850,000
Gross profit	$1,100,000	$520,000
Selling & administrative expense.	298,000	227,000
Operating profit	$ 802,000	$ 293,000
Interest expense	47,200	51,600
Income before taxes	$ 754,800	$ 241,400
Taxes (35%)	264,180	84,490
Income after taxes	$ 490,620	$ 156,910

For each year, compute the following and indicate whether it is increasing or decreasing profitability in 20XY as indicated by the ratio:

a. Cost of goods sold to sales.

b. Selling and administrative expense to sales.

c. Interest expenses to sales.

4. Diet Health Foods Inc. has two divisions. Division A has a profit of $100,000 on sales of $2,000,000. Division B is able to make only $25,000 on sales of $300,000. On the basis of profit margin, which division is superior?

5. Dr. Gupta Diagnostics' income statement for 20XX is as follows:

Sales...	$2,000,000
Cost of goods sold	1,400,000
Gross profit	600,000
Selling and administrative expense	300,000
Operating profit....................................	300,000
Interest expense	50,000
Income before taxes................................	250,000
Taxes (30%).......................................	75,000
Income after taxes	$ 175,000

a. Compute the profit margin in 20XX.

b. Assume in 20XY sales increase by 10 percent and cost of goods sold increases by 20 percent. The firm is able to keep all other expenses the same. Once again, assume a tax rate of 30 percent. What are the income after taxes and profit margin in 20XY?

6. Watson Data Systems is considering expanding into a new product line. New assets to support expansion will cost $500,000. It is estimated that Watson can generate $1.2 million in annual sales, with a 6 percent profit margin. What would net income and return on assets (investment) be for the year?

7. Walker Glove and Bat Shop can open a new store that will have annual sales of $1,250,000. It will turn over its assets 3.4 times per year. The profit margin on sales will be 8 percent. What would net income and return on assets (investment) for the year be?

8. Hugh Snore Bedding has assets of $400,000 and turns over its assets 1.5 times per year. ROA is 12 percent. What is the firm's profit margin?

9. Billy's Crystal Stores Inc. has assets of $5,960,000 and turns over its assets 1.9 times per year. Return on assets is 8 percent. What is the firm's profit margin (return on sales)?

10. Sharpe Razor Company has total assets of $2,500,000 and current assets of $1,000,000. It turns over its capital assets five times a year and has $700,000 of total debt. Its return on sales is 3 percent. What is Sharpe's return on shareholder's equity?

11. Fondren Machine Tools has total assets of $3,310,000 and current assets of $879,000. It turns over its fixed assets 3.6 times per year. Its return on sales is 4.8 percent. It has $1,750,000 of debt. What is its return on shareholders' equity?

12. Global Healthcare Products has the following ratios compared to its industry for 20XX.

	Global Healthcare	Industry
Return on sales.....................................	2%	10%
Return on assets....................................	18%	12%

Explain, with supporting calculations, why the return-on-assets ratio is so much more favourable than the return-on-sales ratio, compared to the industry.

13. Acme Transportation Company has the following ratios compared to its industry for 20XX.

	Acme Transportation	Industry
Return on assets	9%	6%
Return on equity	12%	24%

Explain, with supporting calculations, why the return-on-equity ratio is so much less favourable than the return-on-assets ratio, compared to the industry.

14. The King Card Company has a ROA (investment) ratio of 12 percent.

   a. If the debt-to-total-assets ratio is 40 percent, what is the ROE?

   b. If the firm had no debt, what would the ROE be?

15. Using the DuPont method, evaluate the effects of the following relationships for the Lollar Corporation.

   a. Lollar Corporation has a profit margin of 5 percent and its ROA (investment) is 13.5 percent. What is its asset turnover?

   b. If Lollar Corporation has a debt-to-total-assets ratio of 60 percent, what would the firm's ROE be?

   c. What would happen to the ROE if the debt-to-total-assets ratio decreased to 40 percent?

16. Pony Express Company has $750,000 in assets and $300,000 of debt. The income for the year is $55,000.

   a. Calculate the ROA.

   b. Determine the return on shareholders' equity.

   c. If the asset turnover ratio is 2.2 times, what is the profit margin?

17. Baker Oats had an asset turnover of 1.6 times per year.

   a. If the return on total assets (investment) was 11.2 percent, what was Baker's profit margin?

   b. The following year, on the same level of assets, Baker's assets turnover declined to 1.4 times and its profit margin was 8 percent. How did the return on total assets change from that of the previous year?

18. K Y Shoe Stores has $2,000,000 in sales and turns over its assets 2.5 times per year. The firm earns 3.8 percent on each sales dollar. It has $60,000 in current liabilities and $140,000 in long-term liabilities.

   a. What is its return on shareholders' equity?

   b. If the asset base remains the same as computed in part *a,* but total asset turnover goes up to 3, what will be the new return on shareholders' equity? Assume the profit margin stays the same as does current and long-term liabilities.

19. Assume the following data for Interactive Technology and Silicon Software.

	Interactive Technology (IT)	Silicon Software (SS)
Net income	$ 15,000	$ 50,000
Sales	150,000	1,000,000
Total assets	160,000	400,000
Total debt	60,000	240,000
Shareholders' equity	100,000	160,000

a. Compute return on shareholders' equity for both firms. Which firm has the higher return?

b. Compute the following ratios for both firms:
   Net income/sales
   Net income/total assets
   Sales/total assets
   Debt/total assets

c. Discuss the factors that added or detracted from each firm's return on shareholders' equity.

20. A firm has sales of $1.2 million, and 10 percent of the sales are for cash. The year-end accounts receivable balance is $360,000. What is the average collection period?

21. The Chamberlain Corporation has accounts receivable turnover equal to 12 times. If accounts receivable are $90,000, what is the value for average daily credit sales?

22. A firm has net income before interest and taxes of $193,000 and interest expense of $28,100.
   a. What is the times-interest-earned ratio?
   b. If the firm's lease payments are $48,500, what is the fixed charge coverage?

23. 2GFU Corporation the following financial data for the years 20XX and 20XY:

	20XX	20XY
Sales.	$3,500,000	$4,200,000
Cost of goods sold	2,500,000	3,500,000
Inventory	250,000	300,000

a. Compute inventory turnover based on sales for each year.

b. Compute inventory turnover based on cost of goods sold for each year.

c. What observations can you reach based on the calculations in parts *a* and *b*?

24. Jim Kovacs Company makes supplies for schools. Sales in 20XX were $4,000,000. Assets were as follows:

Cash	$ 100,000
Accounts receivable.	800,000
Inventory	400,000
Net plant and equipment	500,000
Total assets.	$1,800,000

a. Compute the following:
   1. Accounts receivable turnover
   2. Inventory turnover
   3. Capital asset turnover
   4. Total asset turnover

b. In 20XY, sales increased to $5,000,000 and the assets for that year were as follows:

Cash........................	$ 100,000
Accounts receivable..............	900,000
Inventory	975,000
Net plant and equipment	550,000
Total assets....................	$2,525,000

Compute the same four ratios as in part **a.**

c. Indicate if there is an improvement or decline in total asset turnover, and based on the other ratios, explain the reasons this development has taken place.

25. The balance sheet for Bryan Corporation is given below. Sales for the year were $3,040,000, with 75 percent of sales sold on credit.

BRYAN CORPORATION
Balance Sheet Dec. 31, 20XX

Assets		**Liabilities and Equity**	
Cash....................	$ 60,000	Accounts payable..............	$ 220,000
Accounts receivable.......	240,000	Accrued taxes.................	30,000
Inventory	350,000	Bonds payable (long term).......	150,000
Plant and equipment.......	410,000	Common stock................	280,000
		Retained earnings.............	380,000
Total assets..............	$1,060,000	Total liabilities and equity	$1,060,000

Compute the following ratios:

a. Current ratio

b. Quick ratio

c. Debt-to-total-assets ratio

d. Asset turnover

e. Average collection period

26. The Simmons Corporation's income statement is given below.

a. What is the times interest earned ratio?

b. What would be the fixed charge coverage ratio?

SIMMONS CORPORATION

Sales.......................................	$200,000
Cost of goods sold	116,000
Gross profit	84,000
Fixed charges (other than interest).................	24,000
Income before interest and taxes	60,000
Interest	12,000
Income before taxes............................	48,000
Taxes	24,000
Income after taxes	$ 24,000

27. Using the income statement for the Sports Car Tire Company, compute the following ratios:

a. The interest coverage

b. The fixed charge coverage

The total assets for this company equal $40,000. Set up the formula for the DuPont system of ratio analysis, and compute *c, d,* and *e.*

c. Profit margin

d. Total asset turnover

e. Return on assets (investment)

THE SPORTS CAR TIRE COMPANY	
Sales..	$20,000
Less: Cost of goods sold	9,000
Gross profit	11,000
Less: Selling and administrative expense	4,000
Less: Lease expense............................	1,000
Operating profit*	6,000
Less: Interest expense	500
Earnings before taxes............................	5,500
Less: Taxes (40%)	2,200
Earnings after taxes	$ 3,300

*Equals income before interest and taxes

28. Century Plaza Enterprises has three subsidiaries:

	Grand Vista	Bronte	Caledon
Sales	$16,000,000	$4,000,000	$8,000,000
Net income after tax	1,000,000	160,000	600,000
Assets	5,000,000	2,000,000	5,000,000

a. Which subsidiary has the lowest return on sales?

b. Which subsidiary has the highest ROA?

c. Calculate the ROA for the whole company.

d. If Century Plaza sells the $5,000,000 investment in Caledon and reinvests same amount in Grand Vista at the same rate of ROA as currently in Grand Vista, calculate the new ROA for the whole company.

29. In January 2010 the Status Quo Company was formed. Total assets were $500,000, of which $300,000 consisted of capital assets. Status Quo uses straight-line amortization, and in 2010 it estimated its capital assets to have useful lives of 10 years. Aftertax income has been $26,000 per year each of the last 10 years. Other assets have not changed since 2010.

a. Compute ROA at year-end for 2010, 2012, 2015, 2017, and 2019.

b. To what do you attribute the phenomenon shown in part *a*?

c. Now assume income increased by 10 percent each year. What effect would this have on your above answers? Comment.

30. JAS Clocks Corp. shows the following data:

Year	Net Income	Total Assets	Shareholders' Equity	Total Debt
20XW	$110,000	$1,500,000	$ 750,000	$ 750,000
20XX	125,000	1,900,000	825,000	1,075,000
20XY	150,000	2,400,000	900,000	1,500,000
20XZ	175,000	3,000,000	1,000,000	2,000,000

a. Compute the ratio of net income to total assets for each year and comment on the trend.

b. Compute the ratio of net income to shareholders' equity and comment on the trend. Explain why there may be a difference in the trends between parts *a* and *b.*

31. Quantum Moving Company has the following data. Industry information is also shown.

	Company Data		Industry Data on
Year	Net Income	Total Assets	Net Income/Total Assets
20XX	$ 350,000	$2,800,000	11.5%
20XY	375,000	3,200,000	8.4
20XZ	375,000	3,750,000	5.5
Year	Debt	Total Assets	Debt/Total Assets
20XX	$1,624,000	$2,800,000	54.1%
20XY	1,730,000	3,200,000	42.0
20XZ	1,900,000	3,750,000	33.4

As an industry analyst comparing the firm to the industry, are you likely to praise or criticize the firm in terms of:

a. Net income/total assets?

b. Debt/total assets?

32. The United World Corporation has three subsidiaries.

	Computers	Magazines	Cable TV
Sales.....................................	$16,000,000	$4,000,000	$8,000,000
Net income (after taxes).................	1,000,000	160,000	600,000
Assets.................................	5,000,000	2,000,000	5,000,000

a. Which division has the lowest return on sales?

b. Which division has the highest ROA?

c. Compute the ROA for the entire corporation.

d. If the $5,000,000 investment in the cable TV division is sold and redeployed in the computer subsidiary at the same rate of ROA currently achieved in the computer division, what will be the new ROA for the entire corporation?

33. The Quinn Corporation shows the following income statement. The firm uses FIFO inventory accounting.

QUINN CORPORATION
Income Statement for 20XX

Sales...	$100,000	(10,000 units at $10)
Cost of goods sold	50,000	(10,000 units at $5)
Gross profit	50,000	
Selling and administrative expense	5,000	
Amortization	10,000	
Operating profit	35,000	
Taxes (34%)....................................	11,900	
Aftertax income................................	$ 23,100	

a. Assume that the same 10,000 unit volume is maintained in 2016, but the sales price increases by 10 percent. Because of FIFO inventory policy, old inventory will still be charged off at $5 per unit. Also assume that selling and administrative expense will be 5 percent of sales and amortization will be unchanged. The tax rate is 34 percent. Compute aftertax income for 20XY.

b. In part *a,* by what percent did aftertax income increase as a result of a 10 percent increase in the sales price? Explain why this impact occurred.

c. Now assume in 20XZ the volume remains constant at 10,000 units, but that the sales price decreases by 15 percent from its 20XY level. Also, because of FIFO inventory policy, cost of goods sold reflects the inflationary conditions of the prior year and is $5.50 per unit. Further assume that selling and administrative expense will be 5 percent of sales and amortization will be unchanged. The tax rate is 34 percent. Compute aftertax income.

34. Construct the current assets section of the balance sheet from the following data.

Yearly sales (credit)	$420,000
Inventory turnover (from sales)	7 times
Current liabilities	$80,000
Current ratio.	2
Quick ratio	1.25
Average collection period	36 days
Current assets:	
Cash	$_____
Accounts receivable	_____
Inventory	_____
Total current assets.	_____

35. The Shannon Corporation has sales of $750,000, all on credit and COGS of $500,000. Given the following ratios, fill in the balance sheet below.

Total assets turnover	2.5 times
Cash to total assets	2.0%
Accounts receivable turnover.	10.0 times
Inventory turnover	10.0 times
Current ratio.	2.0 times
Debt to total assets	45.0%

SHANNON CORPORATION
Balance Sheet Dec. 31, 20XX

Assets		Liabilities and Shareholders' Equity	
Cash	_____	Current debt	_____
Accounts receivable	_____	Long-term debt	_____
Inventory	_____	Total debt	_____
Total current assets.	_____	Equity.	_____
Capital assets	_____	Total debt and	
Total assets.	_____	shareholders' equity	_____

36. We are given the following information for Pettit Corporation.

Sales (credit)	$3,000,000
Cash	150,000
Inventory	850,000
Current liabilities	700,000
Asset turnover	1.25 times
Current ratio	2.50 times
Debt-to-assets ratio	40%
Receivables turnover	6 times

Current assets are composed of cash, marketable securities, accounts receivable, and inventory. Calculate the following balance sheet items:

a. Accounts receivable

b. Marketable securities

c. Capital assets

d. Long-term debt

37. The following data are from U Guessed It Company's financial statements.

U Guessed It manufactures board games for young adults, and it competes with Marker Brothers and Bilton Radley. Sales (all credit) were $20 million for 20XX. COGS were 80 percent of sales.

Sales to total assets	2.0 times
Total debt to total assets	40%
Current ratio	3.0 times
Inventory turnover	4.0 times
Average collection period	18.0 days
Capital asset turnover	5.0 times

Fill in the brief balance sheet:

Cash	_____	Current debt	_____
Accounts receivable	_____	Long-term debt	_____
Inventory	_____	Total debt	_____
Total current assets	_____	Equity	_____
Capital assets	_____	Total debt and shareholders'	
Total assets	_____	equity	_____

38. Using the financial statements for the Snider Corporation, calculate the 13 basic ratios found in the chapter.

SNIDER CORPORATION
Balance Sheet December 31, 20XX
Assets

Current assets:

Cash		$ 50,000
Marketable securities		20,000
Accounts receivable (net)		160,000
Inventory		200,000
Total current assets		430,000
Investments		60,000
Plant and equipment	600,000	
Accumulated amortization	190,000	
Net plant and equipment		410,000
Total assets		$900,000

Liabilities and Shareholders' Equity

Current liabilities:

Accounts payable	$ 90,000
Notes payable	70,000
Accrued taxes	10,000
Total current liabilities	170,000

Long-term liabilities:

Bonds payable	150,000
Total liabilities	320,000

Shareholders' equity

Preferred stock	100,000
Common stock	270,000
Retained earnings	210,000
Total shareholders' equity	580,000
Total liabilities and shareholders' equity	$900,000

SNIDER CORPORATION
Income Statement
Year ending December 31, 20XX

Sales (on credit)	$1,980,000
Cost of goods sold	1,280,000
Gross profit	700,000
Selling and administrative expenses*	475,000
Operating profit (EBIT)	225,000
Interest expense	25,000
Earnings before taxes (EBT)	200,000
Taxes	80,000
Earnings after taxes (EAT)	$ 120,000

*Includes $35,000 in lease payments.

39. Using the financial statements of Jet Boat Ltd., calculate the 13 basic ratios found in this chapter. Comment briefly on the ratios that might be worth further investigation. Explain why.

JET BOAT LTD.
Balance Sheet
December 31, 20XX
Assets

Current assets:

Cash	$ 40,000
Marketable securities	85,000
Accounts receivable (net)	100,000
Inventory	375,000
Total current assets	600,000
Net plant and equipment	600,000
Total assets	$1,200,000

Liabilities and Shareholders' Equity

Current liabilities:

Accounts payable	$ 100,000
Bank loans	125,000
Accrued expenses	25,000
Total current liabilities	250,000

Long-term liabilities:

Bonds payable*	500,000
Total liabilities	750,000

Shareholders' equity:

Common stock	350,000
Retained earnings	100,000
Total shareholders' equity	450,000
Total liabilities and shareholders' equity	$1,200,000

*Sinking fund provision of $50,000 a year.

JET BOAT LTD.
Income Statement
Year ending December 31, 20XX

Sales (on credit)	$2,900,000
Less: cost of goods sold	2,465,000
Gross profit	435,000
Selling and administrative expenses	250,000
Operating profit (EBIT)	185,000
Interest expense	94,000
Earnings before taxes (EBT)	91,000
Taxes (20%)	18,200
Earnings after taxes (EAT)	$ 72,800

---

40. The financial statements for Jones Corporation and Smith Corporation are shown below.

a. To which company would you, as credit manager for a supplier, approve the extension of (short-term) trade credit? Why? Compute all ratios before answering.

b. In which corporation would you buy shares? Why?

JONES CORPORATION

Current Assets		Liabilities	
Cash	$ 20,000	Accounts payable	$100,000
Accounts receivable	80,000	Bonds payable (long-term)	80,000
Inventory	50,000		
Total current assets	150,000	Total liabilities	180,000
Long-Term Assets		**Shareholders' Equity**	
Capital assets	500,000	Common stock	220,000
Acc. amortization	150,000	Retained earnings	100,000
Net capital assets	350,000		
	$500,000		$500,000

Sales (on credit)	$1,250,000
Cost of goods sold	750,000
Gross profit	500,000
Selling and administrative expense*	257,000
Amortization expense	50,000
Operating profit	193,000
Interest expense	8,000
Earnings before taxes	185,000
Tax expense (50%)	92,500
Net income	$ 92,500

*Includes $7,000 in lease payments.
Note: Jones Corporation has 75,000 shares outstanding.

SMITH CORPORATION

Current Assets		Liabilities	
Cash	$ 35,000	Accounts payable	$ 75,000
Marketable securities	7,500	Bonds payable @ 10%	
Accounts receivable	70,000	(long-term)	210,000
Inventory	75,000		
Total current assets	187,500	Total liabilities	285,000
Long-Term Assets		**Shareholders' Equity**	
Capital assets	500,000	Common stock	105,000
Acc. amortization	250,000	Retained earnings	47,500
Net capital assets	250,000		
	$437,500		$437,500

Sales (on credit)	$1,000,000
Cost of goods sold	600,000
Gross profit	400,000
Selling and administrative expense*	224,000
Amortization expense	50,000
Operating profit	126,000
Interest expense	21,000
Earnings before taxes	105,000
Tax expense (50%)	52,500
Net income	$ 52,500

*Includes $7,000 in lease payments.Note: Smith Corporation has 75,000 shares outstanding.

41. The following ratio calculations are based on three years of financial statements and are compared to the industry standards. The retail company has had some growth during this period but has found that its profitability is less than satisfactory. Examine the ratios to identify possible reasons for the profitability concerns.

	20XX	20XW	20XV	Industry
Profit margin	4.3%	4.0%	3.5%	4.2%
Return on assets	5.6%	4.8%	3.9%	6.4%
Return on equity.	11.2%	9.8%	7.7%	13.7%
Gross margin	43 %	43 %	43 %	40 %
Receivables turnover	7.8×	7.93×	8.1×	7.3×
Average collection period	47 days	46 days	45 days	50 days
Inventory turnover	8.1×	8.23×	8.3×	8.3×
Capital asset turnover.	3.3×	3.03×	2.7×	3.5×
Total asset turnover	1.3×	1.23×	1.1×	1.5×
Current ratio.	2.2	2.3	2.3	2.1
Quick ratio	1.9	2.0	2.0	1.7
Debt to total assets	50 %	50 %	50 %	54 %
Times interest earned.	8.1×	8.23×	8.1×	7.2×
Fixed charge coverage	5.5×	4.53×	4.0×	5.1×

COMPREHENSIVE PROBLEMS

42. You are the manager of a credit department. The sales team has presented a large order from a new purchaser, Wizard Industries. For approximately 12 years, Wizard has been installing security and water sprinkler systems in office buildings.

The salespeople have been well trained, as they have also presented you with the following financial statements and industry ratios (from your files). In their report they note that sales have increased in the last two years due to Wizard's more aggressive selling approach.

The sales team is eager for you to grant credit to Wizard Industries. Of course, you must do a complete analysis noting any ratios that are cause for concern or require a further explanation.

What is your recommendation? Do you grant credit?

WIZARD INDUSTRIES Income Statements Year Ended			
	20XX	20XW	20XV
Sales (all on credit)	$1,605,100	$1,841,300	$1,542,700
Cost of goods sold	1,258,900	1,397,400	1,174,800
Gross profit	346,200	443,900	367,900
Selling and administrative expense	265,650	256,850	294,200
Amortization	14,000	14,400	16,000
Operating profit	66,550	172,650	57,700
Interest expense	65,100	50,550	50,100
Earnings before taxes.	1,450	122,100	7,600
Taxes	350	27,100	2,200
Earnings available to common shareholders	$ 1,100	$ 95,000	$ 5,400
Dividends declared.	$ 70,000	$ 65,000	$ 60,000

WIZARD INDUSTRIES
Balance Sheet December 31,

	20XX	20XW	20XV
Assets			
Cash	$ 14,900	$ 24,700	$ 11,500
Marketable securities	7,000	7,000	7,000
Accounts receivable	410,800	361,800	297,300
Inventory	256,600	330,000	289,900
Prepaid expenses	5,200	800	5,500
Total current assets.	694,500	724,300	611,200
Net plant and equipment	162,000	172,900	184,300
Goodwill	25,400	28,200	30,600
Total assets.	$881,900	$925,400	$826,100
Liabilities and Shareholders' Equity			
Accounts payable	$145,900	$196,700	$209,700
Bank loan	254,000	202,000	169,000
Accrued expenses.	3,700	23,700	14,400
Total current liabilities.	403,600	422,400	393,100
Long-term debt	225,800	181,600	141,000
Total liabilities	629,400	604,000	534,100
Common stock	14,000	14,000	14,000
Retained earnings.	238,500	307,400	278,000
Total shareholders' equity	252,500	321,400	292,000
Total liabilities and shareholders' equity	$881,900	$925,400	$826,100

Selected Industry Ratios

Profit margin	5.8%
Return on assets (investment)	8.1%
Return on equity.	20.3%
Receivables turnover	6.3×
Average collection period	58.3 days
Inventory turnover	4.3×
Capital asset turnover.	8.0×
Current ratio.	1.6
Total asset turnover	1.7×
Quick ratio	1.1
Debt to total assets	60%
Times interest earned	4.3×

43. Al Thomas has recently been approached by his brother-in-law, Robert Watson, with a proposal to buy a 20 percent interest in Watson Leisure Time Sporting Goods. The firm manufactures golf clubs, baseball bats, basketball goals, and other similar items.

Mr. Watson is quick to point out the increase in sales that has occurred over the past three years as indicated in the following income statement. The annual growth rate is 20 percent. A balance sheet for a similar time period and selected industry ratios are also presented. Note the industry growth rate in sales is only 10 percent per year.

There was a steady real growth of 2 to 3 percent in gross domestic product during the period under study. The rate of inflation was in the 3 to 4 percent range.

The stock in the corporation has become available due to the ill health of a current shareholder, who needs cash. The issue here is not to determine the exact price for the stock but rather to determine whether Watson Leisure Time Sporting Goods represents an attractive investment situation. Although Mr. Thomas has a primary interest in the profitability ratios, he will take a close look at all the ratios. He has no fast and firm rules about required return on investment; rather, he wishes to analyze the overall condition of the firm. The firm does not currently pay a cash dividend, and return to the investor must come from selling the stock in the future. After doing a thorough analysis (including ratios for each year and comparisons to the industry), what comments and recommendations can you offer to Mr. Thomas?

WATSON LEISURE TIME SPORTING GOODS
Income Statements Year Ended

	20XX	20XW	20XV
Sales (all on credit)	$2,160,000	$1,800,000	$1,500,000
Cost of goods sold	1,300,000	1,120,000	950,000
Gross profit	860,000	680,000	550,000
Selling and administrative expense*	590,000	490,000	380,000
Operating profit (EBIT)	270,000	190,000	170,000
Interest expense	85,000	40,000	30,000
Net income before taxes	185,000	150,000	140,000
Taxes	64,850	48,720	46,120
Net income	$ 120,150	$ 101,280	$ 93,880
Shares	46,000	40,000	40,000
Earnings per share	$ 2.61	$ 2.53	$ 2.35

*Includes $15,000 in lease payments for each year.

WATSON LEISURE TIME SPORTING GOODS
Balance Sheet Dec. 31,

	20XX	20XW	20XV
Assets			
Cash	$ 20,000	$ 30,000	$ 20,000
Marketable securities	50,000	35,000	30,000
Accounts receivable	330,000	230,000	150,000
Inventory	325,000	285,000	250,000
Total current assets	725,000	580,000	450,000
Net plant and equipment	1,169,000	720,000	550,000
Total assets	$1,894,000	$1,300,000	$1,000,000
Liabilities and Shareholders' Equity			
Accounts payable	$ 200,000	$ 225,000	$ 100,000
Accrued expenses	300,000	100,000	100,000
Total current liabilities	500,000	325,000	200,000
Long-term liabilities	550,740	331,120	250,000
Total liabilities	1,050,740	656,120	450,000
Common stock	540,000	450,000	450,000
Retained earnings	303,260	193,880	100,000
Total shareholders' equity	843,260	643,880	550,000
Total liabilities and shareholders' equity	$1,894,000	$1,300,000	$1,000,000

Selected Industry Ratios

	20XX	20XW	20XV
Growth in sales	10.02%	9.98%	—
Profit margin	5.81%	5.80%	5.75%
Return on assets (investment)	8.48%	8.24%	8.22%
Return on equity	10.10%	13.62%	13.26%
Receivables turnover	9.31×	9.50×	10.00×
Average collection period	35.6 days	37.9 days	36.0 days
Inventory turnover	5.84×	5.62×	5.71×
Capital asset turnover	2.20×	2.66×	2.75×
Total asset turnover	1.46×	1.42×	1.43×
Current ratio	2.15×	2.08×	2.10×
Quick ratio	1.10×	1.02×	1.05×
Debt to total assets	40.10%	39.50%	38.00%
Times interest earned	5.26×	5.20×	5.00×
Fixed charge coverage	3.97×	3.95×	3.85×
Growth in earnings per share	9.80%	9.70%	—

Financial Forecasting

LEARNING OBJECTIVES

LO1 Explain why financial forecasting is essential for the sustainable growth of the firm.

LO2 Prepare the financial statements for forecasting—the pro forma income statement, the cash budget, and the pro forma balance sheet (financial position).

LO3 Perform the specific accounts method and the percent-of-sales method for forecasting on a less-precise basis.

LO4 Determine the need for new funding resulting from sales growth, while giving consideration to seasonal and other effects on cash flow.

LO5 Calculate the required new funds (RNF) and sustainable growth rate (SGR).

Forecasting the future has never been easy, but today our vision of that future changes constantly. The Internet provides us with instant access to these changes; however, we have to be prepared to use this constant stream of information effectively. The old notion of the corporate treasurer working all night to find new avenues of financing before dawn is no longer realistic. One talent that is essential to the financial manager is the ability to plan ahead and to make necessary adjustments before actual events occur. We likely could construct the same set of external events for two corporations (inflation, recession, severe new competition, and so on), and one would survive, while the other would not. The outcome might be a function not only of their risk-taking desires but also of their ability to hedge against risk with careful planning.

Although we may assume that no growth or a decline in volume is the primary cause for a shortage of funds, this is not necessarily the case. A rapidly growing firm may witness a significant increase in accounts receivable, inventory, and plant and equipment to facilitate that growth, and these increasing investments in assets cannot be financed solely through profits. Suppliers, financial institutions, and perhaps the shareholders will be required to contribute more capital to the firm. A comprehensive financing plan with pro forma statements must be developed to anticipate these capital needs. Too often, small business, and sometimes big business, is mystified by an increase in sales and profits but a decrease of cash in the bank. Recognizing the differences between income statements and actual cash is often crucial to ensure the continuing success of a business.

FINANCE IN ACTION

Pro Forma Financial Statements: A Critical Tool for Entrepreneurs

Creating forecasts and producing detailed pro forma financial statements rarely start out as anyone's idea of a good time. The level of detail required, the complexity of the decisions necessary, and the research required to make any of those decisions can be daunting, especially for a first-time entrepreneur. So why is it important for entrepreneurs to thoughtfully develop their financial forecasts? The answer is twofold. First and foremost, a startup entrepreneur must not run out of money. Thinking through how much cash you have, how much cash you need, and the different scenarios you may face is the ultimate responsibility for an entrepreneur, and your financial statements are your toolbox.

The second reason that pro formas are so important is that potential investors want to be able to evaluate the financial outlook for the firm. Many entrepreneurs will seek investment either from "angel" investors or venture capital funds, and what these investors are looking for are:

1. To clearly understand the short-term (12- to 18-month) cash forecasts.

2. To comprehend key operational factors such as the firm's

   a. Burn rate (how fast it is spending money).

   b. Runway (how long it will have enough cash to operate).

   c. Value-changing milestones (key points at which the company's value changes because of a significant accomplishment).

In the end, the difference between well-crafted and poorly done financial forecasts comes down not only to the accuracy and the depth of the analysis but also to the entrepreneur's ability to simply articulate and discuss the numbers. Venture capitalists like Bahram look for aspiring entrepreneurs who focus first on detailed monthly cash-based financials, especially for seed and early-stage ventures. Too often, entrepreneurs use templates that introduce complexity that is not needed in the start-up phase. Simple metrics are frequently the most important. Time is better spent on operating and improving the business.

LO1 THE FINANCIAL PLANNING PROCESS

Financial planning is a key component in the development of a focused corporate strategy that is necessary for a firm's success. The strategic plan is like a road map that examines the different opportunities available for the trip, considers the trends that will influence the route taken, and contemplates possible changes to how the trip has been taken in the past. The "road map" can be adapted as the trip progresses and as circumstances change with new information coming to light, but it serves as a communication device to suggest where one is going and the route(s) to take. With the rapid changes in today's environment, it provides a focus and a means to evaluate progress. Finance performs the critical analysis and modification of the alternatives and objectives suggested by the strategic planning process.

Strategic planning and the financial planning process usually involve the following steps:

- **Thinking.** Consideration of the firm's current businesses, as well as its challenges and opportunities. Careful collection of data and analysis are required.
- **Decisions.** Key directions, strategic resource commitments, and business models evolve. Finance should play an important role evaluating alternatives by modelling asset values and risk with long-term objectives.
- **Planning.** Priorities, objectives, and outcomes are established. Financial plans and budgets are developed with short-term objectives.
- **Performance.** Work plans for all departments, monitoring, evaluating, and corrective action.

The "thinking" and "decision" stages should incorporate good corporate governance practices and strong ethical standards as the mission and key business initiatives are established. Shareholder wealth maximization as examined in Chapter 1 is a major motivator for the firm, but there are other important considerations that contribute to the firm's success.

Long-run investment and financing decisions of the firm are moulded into the overall corporate strategy through the financial planning process that relies on financial forecasting. These decisions should be analyzed with the capital budgeting techniques examined in Chapter 12. Scenarios that cover the best-case, worst-case, and most-likely case outcomes are often produced to enable management to better appreciate the possible results of the different investment alternatives, as they affect the short-run operations of the firm.

In the process of building a financial plan, it is important that consensus is built among all stakeholders of the company, such as the marketing, production, human resources, treasury, and accounting personnel. If certain stakeholders are alienated from the process of building the plan, it will not have their support, and the financial plan will likely fail. If stakeholders don't feel part of the process they will be reluctant or unwilling to contribute reliable information that will be needed to construct an effective plan.

Financial forecasting tends to focus more on the short run, and is usually based on the overall strategies developed as part of the financial plan. Forecasting financial results, particularly over the next 12 months, are essential to ensure the firm has sufficient cash to remain in business. This helps the firm avoid surprises, and the forecasts can be used by the firm to measure performance. Difficulties arise in preparing the financial forecasts because there are seldom direct relationships between projected sales and cash requirements. Furthermore, sales projections, cost estimates, and the timing of cash flows often rely on the estimates of persons within the company, based on past experience, and these must be tempered with the changing business environment. This is why it is essential that all stakeholders see the value of the process and believe their participation gives tangible results.

Results are usually different than forecasted, sometimes to a great extent. The importance of a forecasted plan is that it allows the firm to identify what went wrong and correct it in the future. Furthermore, a flexible plan allows the firm to adjust to changing conditions so the firm knows where it should be going and can identify when things go wrong. A good plan will be adapted continually as new information becomes available, but it allows the firm to better assess its past and future financial capabilities.

LO2 CONSTRUCTING PRO FORMA STATEMENTS

The most comprehensive means of financial forecasting is to develop a series of pro forma, or projected, financial statements. Projections should be based on knowledge of the local and global economic environment, on social and political change, on anticipation of competitors' strategies, and on prediction of innovation in product markets.

A systems approach to developing pro forma statements allows construction, as depicted in Figure 4–1, of

- A pro forma income statement (based on sales projections and a production plan)
- A pro forma statement of retained earnings
- A cash budget resulting from inflows (receipts) and outflows (payments) of cash
- A pro forma balance sheet

Extensive financial planning and application templates are available through the Business Development Bank of Canada at bdc.ca. The projections allow us to anticipate asset and liability levels, profits, and borrowing requirements. Lenders will see how repayment will occur and financial officers can track actual events against the plan to make necessary adjustments.

Without realistic financial forecasts, the small business in particular will likely

- Have liquidity problems (lack of funds)
- Demonstrate poor management planning and control measures
- Have difficulty securing business loans
- Face possible business failure

The construction of pro forma statements is greatly enhanced by computerized spreadsheets, which will allow sensitivity (changes in variables such as sales and expenses) and scenario ("what-if" situation changes) analysis. These tools allow us to easily calculate multiple forecasts under different assumptions resulting in multiple levels of forecasted profits. We can also apply probability analysis to forecast the most likely levels of revenues and expenses, as covered in more

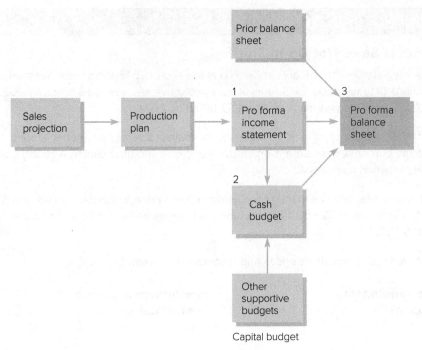

Figure 4–1 Development of pro forma statements

detail in Chapter 13. There are numerous economic and political changes that occur during the year that has been forecasted; computer software can facilitate changes to the forecast as new events affect the original forecast, allowing management to take corrective action immediately. A flexible budget is essential given the frequent changes that occur in our global environment.

LO2 PRO FORMA INCOME STATEMENT

Assume the Goldman Corporation has been requested by its bank to provide pro forma financial statements for midyear 20XX. The pro forma income statement provides a projection of how much profit the firm anticipates making over the ensuing time period. In developing the pro forma income statement, we will follow four important steps:

1. Establish a sales projection in dollars and units.
2. Determine a production schedule and the associated use of new material, direct labour, and overhead to calculate cost of goods produced and arrive at gross profit.
3. Compute other expenses, including indirect labour, supplies, and other costs.
4. Determine profit by completing the actual pro forma statement.

Ultimately, a firm's continued success is written with income statement results showing an acceptable return to investors. However, it is the appropriate management of the firm's short-term cash position that allows the long-term success to be realized.

Establish a Sales Projection

For purposes of analysis, we assume the Goldman Corporation has two primary products: wheels and casters. Our sales projection by the marketing department calls for the sale of 1,000 wheels and 2,000 casters at prices of $30 and $35, respectively. As indicated in Table 4–1, we anticipate total sales of $100,000.

Table 4–1 Projected wheel and caster sales (first six months, 20XY)

	Wheels	Casters	Total
Quantity	1,000	2,000	
Sales price	$ 30	$ 35	
Sales revenue	$30,000	$70,000	
Total			$100,000

Sales estimates are the cornerstone of the entire process of constructing pro forma statements. Sales revenue, we are reminded, is the product of demand for a company's products or services and their prices. A firm's financial results will likely prove to be sensitive to differences between projected demand and realized demand. Our concern for the precision of forecasted demand depends on the seriousness attached to a potential cash shortfall. This, in turn, determines if daily, weekly, or monthly estimates are required.

The projected price is based on the firm's cost structure, the marketing effort, and the anticipated response of competitors to the firm's price. A forecast of the quantity sold needs to consider price, knowledge of the continuing and growing needs of a firm's clientele, and estimates of new clients. The forecast uses past relationships and ratios, builds on the estimates suggested by the sales force, and is influenced by economic, social, and political events. In addition, the limitations and opportunities of the production facilities and human resources must be considered. The forecasts vary according to the needs of the firm and the industry dynamics.

Sales projections are best derived from both an external and an internal viewpoint. Using external factors, we analyze our prospective sales in light of economic conditions affecting our industry and our company. Statistical techniques such as regression and time series analysis may be employed in the process. Internal analysis calls for the sales department to survey our own salespeople within their territories. Ideally, we would proceed along each of those paths in isolation of the other and then assimilate the results into one meaningful projection.

Determine a Production Schedule and the Gross Profit

We determine the necessary production plan for the six-month period based on anticipated sales. The number of units produced depends on the beginning inventory of wheels and casters, our sales projection, and the desired level of ending inventory. Assume that on January 1, 20XX, the Goldman Corporation had in stock the items shown in Table 4–2.

Table 4–2 Stock of beginning inventory

	Wheels	Casters	Total
Quantity	85	180	
Cost	$ 16	$ 20	
Total value	$1,360	$3,600	
Total			$4,960

Oil Prices! How About a Forecast?

For oil producers and marketers, the future price of oil is very important for their projections of the firm's revenues and costs. It will also determine their spending plans and the returns to shareholders. In early 1999, oil was priced just above US$12 per barrel, while by mid-2008 it was over US$145 but only US$33 by the end of the year. More recently, oil was US$108 in July 2014 but below US$25 in February 2016. In late 2019 oil was priced at about US$60. What is expected for the future? Being a finite resource, oil is expected to remain expensive to produce, and Canada is one of the few countries with substantial reserves.

We should consider the past for guidance as to where oil prices might go in the future. (bp.com). In 1974, when the OPEC oil embargo was in its stage of infancy (or infamy), the price of oil had jumped to US$10.41, about the same as it was in early 1999. By 1980, the price of oil had reached US$36, which in real dollars (2017) would be over US$110. If we look at the price of a barrel of oil since 1946 we find that the average price, adjusted for inflation, has been about US$45. The average inflation-adjusted price of oil since 1973, when OPEC was formed, is about US$56. It would seem that the oil prices of the 1970s, the 1980s, and 2008 were abnormal by historical standards, but prices are likely to continue at fairly high levels. In 2020 we were about average, although during the Covid-19 pandemic oil prices briefly reached a <u>negative</u> $37.

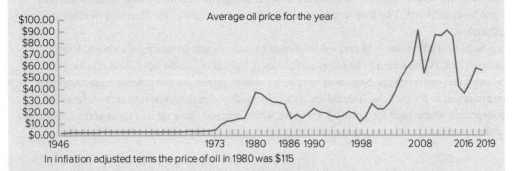

Average oil price for the year

In inflation adjusted terms the price of oil in 1980 was $115

Estimates from various sources for average oil prices for 2020 ranged from US$55 to US$60 (for WTI, about $5 higher for Brent). It is on these prices that oil firms would forecast their revenues and cash flows for the immediate future. Current oil prices can be found at bloomberg.com.

Q1 Compare the current prices of West Texas Intermediate (WTI) oil and Brent Crude.

Q2 What is your forecast for the price of oil in one and two years?

USIndependentEnergyAdministration

We add the projected quantity of unit sales for the next six months to our desired ending inventory and subtract our stock of beginning inventory (in units) to determine our production requirements.

Units
+ Projected sales
+ Desired ending inventory
− Beginning inventory
= Production requirements

In Table 4–3 we see a required production level of 1,015 wheels and 2,020 casters.

Table 4–3 Production requirements for six months

	Wheels	Casters
Projected unit sales (Table 4–1)............................	+1,000	+2,000
Desired ending inventory (assumed to represent 10% of unit sales for the time period)	+100	+200
Beginning inventory (Table 4–2)...........................	−85	−180
Units to be produced	1,015	2,020

We must now determine the cost to produce these units. In Table 4–2 we saw that the cost of units in stock was $16 for wheels and $20 for casters. However, we assume the price of materials, labour, and overhead going into the products is now $18 for wheels and $22 for casters, as indicated in Table 4–4.

Table 4–4 Unit costs

	Wheels	Casters
Materials	$10	$12
Labour	5	6
Overhead	3	4
Total............................	$18	$22

The *total* cost to produce the required items for the next six months is shown in Table 4–5.

Table 4–5 Total production costs

	Wheels	Casters	Total
Units to be produced (Table 4–3)................	1,015	2,020	
Cost per unit (Table 4–4)......................	$ 18	$ 22	
Total cost	$18,270	$44,440	$62,710

We must also determine whether the firm has the production facilities to meet the projected demand. Sales and production should be the same only over the long term, as seasonal and cyclical patterns will cause demand to fluctuate. Inventory positions and price adjustments can be used to handle the short-term differences between demand and production. However, without the required long-run production capabilities, the firm must reconsider its sales projections or make capital investments (buildings, machinery, vehicles, etc.). Either of these possibilities affects financial forecasts. Capital investments in particular require large fundraising efforts with concurrent costs.

Cost of Goods Sold The main consideration in constructing a pro forma income statement is the costs specifically associated with units sold during the time period. Note that in the case of wheels, we anticipate sales of 1,000 units, as indicated in Table 4–1, but are producing 1,015, as indicated in Table 4–3, to increase our inventory level by 15 units. For profit-measurement purposes, we do **not** charge these extra 15 units against current sales.[1] Furthermore, in determining the cost of the 1,000 units sold during the current time period, we do **not** assume all of the items sold represent

---

[1] Later on in the analysis we show the effect these extra units have on the cash budget and the balance sheet.

inventory manufactured in this period. We assume Goldman Corporation uses FIFO (first-in, first-out) accounting, and it first allocates the cost of current sales to beginning inventory and then to goods manufactured during the period.

In Table 4–6 we look at the revenue, associated cost of goods sold, and gross profit for both products. For example, 1,000 units of wheels are to be sold at total revenue of $30,000. Of the 1,000 units, 85 units are from beginning inventory at a $16 cost (see Table 4–2), and the balance of 915 units are from current production at an $18 cost. The total cost of goods sold for wheels is $17,830, yielding a gross profit of $12,170. The pattern is the same for casters, with sales of $70,000, cost of goods sold of $43,640, and gross profit of $26,360. The combined sales for the two products are $100,000, with cost of goods sold of $61,470 and gross profit of $38,530.

Table 4–6 Allocation of manufacturing cost and determination of gross profit

		Wheels		Casters	Combined
Quantity sold (Table 4–1)		1,000		2,000	3,000
Sales price		$ 30		$ 35	
Sales revenue		$30,000		$70,000	$100,000
Cost of goods sold:					
Old inventory (Table 4–2)					
Quantity (units)	85		180		
Cost per unit.	$ 16		$ 20		
Total		$ 1,360		$ 3,600	
New inventory (the remainder):					
Quantity (units)	915		1,820		
Cost per unit (Table 4–4)	$ 18		$ 22		
Total		16,470		40,040	
Total cost of goods sold		17,830		43,640	$ 61,470
Gross profit		$12,170		$26,360	$ 38,530

At this point, we also compute the value of ending inventory for later use in constructing financial statements. As indicated in Table 4–7, the value of ending inventory is $6,200.

Table 4–7 Value of ending inventory

+ Beginning inventory (Table 4–2)	$4,960
+ Total production costs (Table 4–5).	62,710
Total inventory available for sales	67,670
− Cost of goods sold (Table 4–6)	61,470
Ending inventory	$6,200

Other Expense Items

Having computed total revenue, cost of goods sold, and gross profit, we must now subtract other expense items to arrive at a net profit figure. We deduct selling, marketing, general and administrative, research and development, and interest expenses from gross profit to arrive at earnings before taxes. We then subtract taxes to determine aftertax income, and finally we deduct dividends (these are not expenses but they do require cash outflow) to ascertain the net contribution to retained earnings. Goldman Corporation's selling, general, and administrative expenses are $12,000, interest expense is $1,500, and dividends are $1,500.

Actual Pro Forma Income Statement

Combining the gross profit in Table 4–6 with our assumptions on other expense items, we arrive at the pro forma income statement presented in Table 4–8. We anticipate earnings after taxes of $20,024, dividends of $1,500, and an increase in retained earnings of $18,524.

Table 4–8 Pro forma income statement

Pro Forma Income Statement June 30, 20XX	
Sales revenue	$100,000
Cost of goods sold	61,470
Gross profit	38,530
Selling, general, and administrative expense	12,000
Operating profit (EBIT)	26,530
Interest expense	1,500
Earnings before taxes (EBT)	25,030
Taxes (20%)	5,006
Earnings after taxes (EAT)	$ 20,024
Change in Retained Earnings	
Common stock dividends declared	1,500
Increase in retained earnings	$ 18,524

Note: For simplicity amortization has not been included.

The following illustrations and formats are for private corporations. Public corporations will prepare actual and pro forma financial statements based on international standards (IFRS).

LO2 CASH BUDGET

The cash budget is perhaps the most important forecast, particularly for the small business. The ability to meet cash flow demands on a timely basis with efficient management of working capital, including having short-term financing such as a line of credit available as required, allows a firm to survive in the long term. Profitable sales may generate accounts receivable in the short run but no immediate cash to meet financial obligations including suppliers and debt payments.

Therefore, we must translate the pro forma income statement into cash flows, producing a cash budget. In this process, we divide the longer-term pro forma income statement into smaller and more precise time frames to appreciate the seasonal and monthly patterns of cash inflows and outflows. Some months may present particularly high cash requirements from low sales volume, or less in regular payments such as dividends, taxes, or capital expenditures.

The timing of cash flows is particularly crucial. One must consider the nature of the firm's business, terms of trade, and general economic conditions to appropriately reflect the timing of cash flows in the cash budget. The cash flow cycle, discussed further in Chapter 6, outlines the process from inventory to sale to accounts receivable to cash.

Cash Receipts

In the case of the Goldman Corporation, we break down the pro forma income statement for the first half of 20XX into a series of monthly cash budgets. In Table 4–1 we showed anticipated sales of $100,000 over this time period; we shall now assume these sales can be divided into monthly projections, as indicated in Table 4–9.

Table 4–9 Monthly sales pattern

January	February	March	April	May	June
$15,000	$10,000	$15,000	$25,000	$15,000	$20,000

A careful analysis of past sales and collection records indicates that 20 percent of sales are collected in the month of sales and 80 percent are collected in the following month. The cash receipt pattern related to monthly sales is shown in Table 4–10. It is assumed that sales for December 20XW were $12,000. The cash receipts could be adjusted to reflect any uncollectible accounts based on previous experience and future expectations.

Table 4–10 Monthly cash receipts

	December	January	February	March	April	May	June
Sales.	$12,000	$15,000	$10,000	$15,000	$25,000	$15,000	$20,000
Collections: (20% of current sales)		3,000	2,000	3,000	5,000	3,000	4,000
Collections: (80% of previous month's sales). . . .		9,600	12,000	8,000	12,000	20,000	12,000
Total cash receipts		$12,600	$14,000	$11,000	$17,000	$23,000	$16,000

The cash inflows vary between $11,000 and $23,000, with the high point in receipts coming in May. We now examine the monthly outflows.

FINANCE IN ACTION

Operational Cash Flow Exceeds Earnings and Allows Capital Expenditures

Ovintiv, formerly Encana, is one of North America's largest energy companies. Much of its activity is in Canada, although it has operations around the world. Ovintiv has a high drilling success, which suggests capital expenditures on exploration should bring good returns.

In 2002, PanCanadian and Alberta Energy merged to form Encana. In 2008 Encana split into two firms with Cenovus taking the bulk of the oil operations. In 2020 Encana changed its name to Ovintiv and moved its head office from Calgary to Denver.

As oil and gas prices pick up, cash flow improves, and capital expenditures can increase, sometimes significantly. The impact of oil and gas prices can be seen in Encana's (now Ovintiv) results for the period 2010–18. The weak energy prices result in a drop in profits. although cash flow can still support capital expenditures. When cash flow drops significantly so do capital expenditures. The current high price of oil is a significant variable in most firms' operations and cash forecasts.

Ovintiv prepares a sensitivity analysis as part of a regular "Guidance Report." It suggests how major variables will impact cash flow (unhedged).

	2018	2016	2014	2012	2010
			(US$ millions)		
Revenue	$5,939	$2,443	$8,019	$5,160	$8.870
Cash flow from operations.	2,330	625	2,667	3,107	2,329
Net income.	1,065	<1,124>	3,397	<2,700>	2,573
Capital expenditures.	1,975	1,132	2,526	3,476	4,779
ROE	14%	n.a.	35%	n.a.	27%
Average oil price (/bbl)	$64.77	$45.91	$66.40	$66.25	$79.43
Average gas price (/mbtu)	$3.09	$2.58	$4.16	$5.02	$4.03
US$/C$ (year-end).	$0.73	$0.75	$0.86	$1.01	$1.01

		Cash Flow (US$ millions)	
Crude oil	US$5/barrel (WTI)	<$81>	$71
Natural gas	US$0.25/MMBtu	<35>	32
Cdn/US$		<67>	82

These projections, when tied in with forecasts of crude oil and natural gas prices, show the potential for weakened results at Ovintiv if energy prices drop. Ovintiv is able to offset declining prices by increased production and from its hedging activities. Hedging activities preset the prices on the future production of oil and gas.

Q1 What are current oil and gas prices?

Q2 Identify Ovintiv's recent financial results.

ovintiv.com   **bloomberg.com**
Symbol: ECA

Cash Payments

The primary considerations for cash payments are monthly costs associated with inventory manufactured during the period (material, labour, and overhead) and disbursements for general and administrative expenses, interest payments, taxes, and dividends. We must also consider cash payments for any new plant and equipment, an item that does not show up on our pro forma income statement because it is a capital expenditure, not an expense.

Costs associated with units manufactured during the period may be taken from the data provided in Table 4–5. In Table 4–11 we simply recast these data in terms of material, labour, and overhead.

Table 4–11 Component costs of manufactured goods

	Wheels			Casters			
	Units Produced	Cost per Unit	Total Cost	Units Produced	Cost per Unit	Total Cost	Combined Cost
Materials	1,015	$10	$10,150	2,020	$12	$24,240	$34,390
Labour	1,015	5	5,075	2,020	6	12,120	17,195
Overhead	1,015	3	3,045	2,020	4	8,080	11,125
							$62,710

We see that the total costs for components in the two products are material, $34,390; labour, $17,195; and overhead, $11,125. We assume that all these costs are incurred on an equal monthly basis over the six-month period. Even though the sales volume varies from month to month, we assume we are employing level monthly production to ensure maximum efficiency in the use of various productive resources. Average monthly costs for materials, labour, and overhead are as shown in Table 4–12.

Table **4–12** Average monthly manufacturing costs

	Total Costs	Time Frame	Average Monthly Cost
Materials	$34,390	6 months	$5,732
Labour	17,195	6 months	2,866
Overhead	11,125	6 months	1,854

We pay for materials one month after the purchase has been made. Labour and overhead represent direct monthly cash outlays. Other major expenses occur at less frequent but fairly predictable intervals. These include interest (coupon payments), taxes, dividends, and new equipment purchases. We summarize all of our cash payments in Table 4–13. Past records indicate that $4,500 in materials was purchased in December.

Table **4–13** Summary of all monthly cash payments

	Dec.	Jan.	Feb.	March	April	May	June
From Table 4–12:							
Monthly material purchase	$4,500	$5,732	$5,732	$5,732	$5,732	$5,732	$5,732
Payment for material (prior month's purchase)		4,500	5,732	5,732	5,732	5,732	5,730*
Monthly labour cost .		2,866	2,866	2,866	2,866	2,866	2,866
Monthly overhead . .		1,854	1,854	1,854	1,854	1,854	1,854
From Table 4–8:							
Selling, general, and administrative expense ($12,000 over 6 months)		2,000	2,000	2,000	2,000	2,000	2,000
Interest expense							1,500
Taxes (two equal payments)				2,503			2,503
Cash dividend.							1,500
Also:							
New equipment purchases			8,000				10,000
Total payments.		$11,220	$20,452	$14,955	$12,452	$12,452	$27,953

Note: Amortization should not be included in overhead because there is no cash outflow.
*Monthly materials cost from Table 4-12 has been rounded up from $5,731.67. After six months this requires a $2.00 adjustment.

LO4 Actual Budget

We are now in a position to bring together our monthly cash receipts and payments into a cash flow statement, illustrated in Table 4–14. The difference between monthly receipts and payments is net cash flow for the month.

Table 4–14 Monthly cash flow

	Jan.	Feb.	March	April	May	June
Total receipts (Table 4–10)	$12,600	$14,000	$11,000	$17,000	$23,000	$16,000
Total payments (Table 4–13)	11,220	20,452	14,955	12,452	12,452	27,953
Net cash flow	$1,380	($ 6,452)	($ 3,955)	$ 4,548	$10,548	($11,953)

The primary purpose of the cash budget is to allow the firm to anticipate the need for outside funding at the end of each month. In the present case we assume the Goldman Corporation wishes to have a minimum cash balance of $5,000 at all times. If it goes below this amount, the firm borrows funds from the bank. If it goes above $5,000 and the firm has a loan outstanding, it uses the excess funds to reduce the line of credit. This pattern of financing is demonstrated in Table 4–15, which shows a fully developed cash budget with borrowing and repayment provisions.

Table 4–15 Cash budget with borrowing repayment provisions

	Jan.	Feb.	March	April	May	June
1. Net cash flow . .	$1,380	($6,452)	($3,955)	$4,548	$10,548	($11,953)
2. Beginning cash balance	5,000*	6,380	5,000	5,000	5,000	11,069
3. Cumulative cash balance	6,380	(72)	1,045	9,548	15,548	(884)
4. Monthly loan or (repayment)	—	5,072	3,955	(4,548)	(4,479)	5,884
5. Cumulative loan balance	—	5,072	9,027	4,479	—	5,884
6. Ending cash balance	6,380	5,000	5,000	5,000	11,069	5,000

*We assume the Goldman Corporation has a beginning cash balance of $5,000 on January 1, and it desires a minimum monthly ending cash balance of $5,000.

The first line in Table 4–15 shows net cash flow, which is added to the beginning cash balance to arrive at the cumulative cash balance. The fourth entry is the additional monthly loan or loan repayment, if any, required to maintain a minimum cash balance of $5,000. To keep track of our loan balance, the fifth entry represents cumulative loans outstanding for all months. Finally, we show the cash balance at the end of the month, which becomes the beginning cash balance for the next month.

At the end of January, the firm has $6,380 in cash, but by the end of February, the cumulative cash position of the firm is negative, necessitating a loan of $5,072 to maintain a $5,000 cash balance. The firm has a loan on the books until May, at which time there is an ending cash balance of $11,069. During the months of April and May, the cumulative cash balance is greater than the required minimum cash balance of $5,000, so loan repayments of $4,548 and $4,479 are made to retire the loans completely in May. In June, the firm is once again required to borrow **$5,884** to maintain a **$5,000** cash balance.

Adjustments could be made at this time. The cash budget indicates that operating loans will be required at certain times, which will necessitate the payment of monthly interest. Operating loans or self-liquidating loans are required as temporary current assets are built up in a firm due to seasonal fluctuations in demand. This buildup requires the use of short-term financing and is examined later in Chapters 6 and 8. We have included only interest on long-term debt on the summary of cash payments. Offsetting the payment of interest on short-term loans, to a certain extent, will be the receipt of interest from marketable securities received during periods with excess cash balances. These adjustments have not been included in our example.

Before proceeding to the pro forma balance sheet, we may want to return to the income statement and make some adjustments based on the results from the cash budget. For example, severe cash shortages may require additional borrowing, which in turn would increase the interest expense.

LO2 PRO FORMA BALANCE SHEET

Now that we have developed a pro forma income statement and a cash budget, it is relatively simple to integrate all of these items into a pro forma balance sheet, another important small business tool. Because the balance sheet represents cumulative changes in the corporation over time, we first examine the *prior* period's balance sheet and then translate these items through time to represent June 30, 20XY. The last balance sheet, dated December 31, 20XX, is shown in Table 4–16.

Table 4–16 Balance sheet (APSE)

Balance Sheet December 31, 20XX	
Assets	
Current assets:	
Cash	$ 5,000
Marketable securities	3,200
Accounts receivable	9,600
Inventory	4,960
Total current assets	22,760
Plant and equipment	27,740
Total assets	$50,500
Liabilities and Shareholders' Equity	
Accounts payable	$ 4,500
Long-term debt	15,000
Common stock	10,500
Retained earnings	20,500
Total liabilities and shareholders' equity	$50,500

In constructing our pro forma balance sheet for June 30, 20XX, some of the accounts from the old balance sheet remain unchanged, and others will take on new values, as indicated by the pro forma income statement and cash budget. The process is depicted in Figure 4–2.

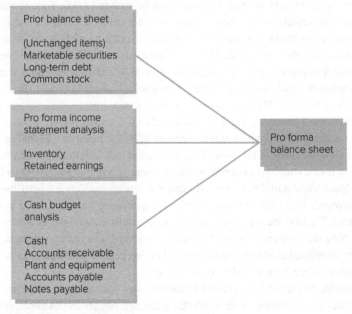

Figure 4–2 Development of pro forma balance sheet

We present the new pro forma balance sheet as of June 30, 2015, in Table 4–17.

Table 4–17 Pro forma balance sheet (ASPE format)

Pro Forma Balance Sheet
June 30, 20XX

Assets

Current assets:

1. Cash	$ 5,000
2. Marketable securities	3,200
3. Accounts receivable	16,000
4. Inventory	6,200
Total current assets	30,400
5. Plant and equipment	45,740
Total assets	$76,140

Liabilities and Shareholders' Equity

6. Accounts payable	$ 5,732
7. Notes payable	5,884
8. Long-term debt	15,000
9. Common stock	10,500
10. Retained earnings	39,024
Total liabilities and shareholders' equity	$76,140

Explanation of Pro Forma Balance Sheet

Each item in Table 4–17 can be explained on the basis of a prior calculation or assumption.

1. Cash ($5,000)—minimum cash balance as shown in Table 4–15.

2. Marketable securities ($3,200)—remains unchanged from prior period's value in Table 4–16. Note that firms will likely liquidate marketable securities positions before increasing short-term borrowings. In that case, Table 4–15 would require revision. To simplify matters, that has not been done in this example. Furthermore, due to cash flow timing considerations, firms often have positions in marketable securities and short-term loans on reporting dates.

3. Accounts receivable ($16,000)—based on June sales of $20,000 in Table 4–10. Twenty percent is collected that month and 80 percent becomes accounts receivable at the end of the month.

$20,000	sales
× 80%	receivables
$16,000	

4. Inventory ($6,200)—ending inventory as shown in Table 4–7.

5. Plant and equipment ($45,740).

Initial value (Table 4–16)	$27,740
Purchases* (Table 4–13)	18,000
Plant and equipment	$45,740

*For simplicity, amortization is not explicitly considered.

1. Accounts payable ($5,732)—based on June purchases in Table 4–13. They are not to be paid until July and, thus, are accounts payable.

2. Notes payable ($5,884)—the amount we must borrow to maintain our cash balance of $5,000, as shown in Table 4–15.

3. Long-term debt ($15,000)—remains unchanged from the prior period's value in Table 4–16. The firm may increase long-term debt to hedge the additional purchase of plant and equipment. The hedging concept is explored in Chapter 6.

4. Common stock ($10,500)—remains unchanged from prior period's value in Table 4–16.

5. Retained earnings ($39,024).

Initial value (Table 4–16).	$20,500
Transfer of pro forma income to retained earnings (Table 4–8)	18,524
Retained earnings.	$39,024

Analysis of Pro Forma Statement

In comparing the pro forma balance sheet (Table 4–17) to the prior balance sheet (see Table 4–16) we note that assets are up by $25,640.

Total assets (June 30, 20XY).	$76,140
Total assets (Dec. 31, 20XX).	50,500
Increase	$25,640

The growth must be financed by accounts payable, notes payable, and profit (as reflected by the increase in retained earnings). Though the company enjoys a high degree of profitability, it must still look to bank financing. At the end of June, this amounts to $5,884 to support the increase in assets. This represents the difference between the $25,640 buildup in assets and the $1,232 increase in accounts payable, as well as the $18,524 buildup in retained earnings.

However, the cash budget, Table 4–15, reveals that the borrowing need peaks at $9,027 in March. If Goldman has not anticipated this peak in borrowing need and had not made arrangements with the bank to advance funds to meet this peak requirement, there may be liquidity problems.

By failing to properly anticipate the fluctuations in borrowing requirements, the small business is often forced to return to the bank to renegotiate further loan advances. Bankers are obviously not too pleased by surprises resulting from poor forecasts and may view this as evidence of ineffective planning. This is not to say that forecasts turn out exactly as planned. However, by knowing the forecasts and the underlying assumptions, the firm is able to adapt its plan as conditions change.

LO3 PERCENT-OF-SALES METHOD

An alternative to tracing cash and accounting flows to determine financial needs as the firm grows is to assume that balance sheet accounts maintain a given percentage relationship to sales. As the sales level increases, we can ascertain our required financing needs if we rely on the assumption that certain assets and liabilities spontaneously increase with sales. This spontaneity without any conscious action by management is discussed in Chapter 7. This technique for determining financing needs is known as the percent-of-sales method. It makes some strong assumptions and is probably more applicable to longer-term forecasting. For immediate cash needs, a budget is more exact.

The Howard Corporation, introduced in Table 4–18, shows its balance sheet accounts in dollars and their percent of sales, based on a current sales volume of $200,000. For example, the cash balance of $5,000 represents 2.5 percent of the $200,000 in current sales. No percentages are computed for notes payable, common stock, and retained earnings, because they are not assumed to maintain a direct relationship with sales volume and often require a less spontaneous, more deliberate action to change.

Table 4–18 Percent-of-sales.table

Howard Corporation
Balance Sheet

Assets		Liabilities and Shareholders' Equity	
Cash	$ 5,000	Accounts payable	$ 40,000
Accounts receivable	40,000	Accrued expenses	10,000
Inventory	25,000	Notes payable	15,000
Total current assets	$ 70,000	Common stock	10,000
Equipment	50,000	Retained earnings	45,000
Total assets	$120,000	Total liabilities and equities	$120,000

$200,000 Sales
Percent of Sales

Cash . . . .($5/$200 =)	2.5%	Accounts payable . . . .($40/$200 =)	20.0%
Accounts receivable . . . .($40/$200 =)	20.0	Accrued expenses . . . .($10/$200 =)	5.0
Inventory . . . .($25/$200 =)	12.5	Total current liabilities percent	25.0%
Total current assets . . . .($70/$200 =)	35.0		
Equipment($50/$200 =)	25.0		
Total assets/sales percent	60.0%		

In this example we assume that equipment increases in proportion to sales. However, in most cases, capital asset investment is more tenuously connected to sales increases, expanding in a multi-step fashion. If there is excess capacity, equipment (and/or plant) will not increase, and more deliberate action from management is required for capital assets to be acquired.

In this example, if sales increase from $200,000 to $300,000, an increase of $100,000, additional financing will be required:

- A 60 percent spontaneous increase in assets
- Offset by a 25 percent spontaneous increase in current liabilities
- And offset by an increase in retained earnings (we assume the Howard Corporation has an aftertax return of 6 percent on sales and 50 percent of profits are paid out as dividends)[2]

Therefore, the $100,000 sales increase requires new financing of

• Spontaneous asset increase	$100,000 × 60%	$60,000
• Spontaneous liability increase	$100,000 × 25%	−25,000
• Increase in retained earnings	$300,000 × 6% × (1 − 50%)	−9,000
		$26,000

LO5 The financing alternatives for the $26,000 are identified in Figure 6–11. It is worth noting that the asset and liability increases are based on the sales increase from the previous period, and the retained earnings increase is based on total sales. Our formula to determine the need for new funds (required new funds, or RNF) is

RNF = Spontaneous increase in assets
− Spontaneous increase in liabilities
− Increase in retained earnings

---

[2]Some may wish to add back amortization under the percent-of-sales method. Most, however, choose the assumption that funds generated through amortization (in the sources and uses of funds sense) must be used to replace the capital assets to which amortization is applied.

$$RNF = \frac{A}{S_1}(\Delta S) - \frac{L}{S_1}(\Delta S) - PS_2(1 - D) \quad \textbf{(4–1)}$$

Where

$\dfrac{A}{S_1}$ = Percentage relationship of assets varying with sales to sales (60%)

ΔS = Change in sales ($100,000)

$\dfrac{L}{S_1}$ = Percentage relationship of liabilities varying with sales to sales (25%)

P = Profit margin (6%)

S_1 = Existing sales level

S_2 = New sales level ($300,000)

D = Dividend payout ratio

Plugging in the values, we show

RNF = 60% ($100,000) − 25% ($100,000) − 6% ($300,000)(1 − 0.5)

= $60,000 − $25,000 − $18,000(0.5)

= $35,000 − $9,000

= $26,000 required sources of new funds

Presumably, the $26,000 can be financed at the bank or through some other appropriate source.

We can see how this formula works by comparing pro forma balance sheets before and after the sales expansion, as in Table 4–19. The spontaneous increase in current assets and capital assets (equipment) from the increased sales is $60,000 and is the first term in the formula. This requirement for new funding is partially offset by the increase in current liabilities of $25,000 and by the increase in retained earnings of $9,000. The increase in retained earnings is based on the profit generated from total sales less the dividend payout. These increases are tied to the sales increase by a fixed percentage, but could be changed if we have superior knowledge.

We notice in Table 4–19 that in order to achieve balance, the amount of RNF, $26,000, is entered on the new balance sheet as notes payable. These RNF are needed to support the sales expansion and are the same value given by the formula. If the firm was not operating at capacity and did not require the $25,000 in additional equipment to support the new sales the RNF would be only $1,000. Therefore, our assumptions about what assets will increase proportionately with a sales increase are quite important.

If the RNF are financed through operating loans (notes payable), as is suggested in this example, there will be a significant change in certain relevant ratios. The debt to total assets increases from 0.54 to 0.64 and the current ratio decreases from 1.08 to 0.91. This would likely be interpreted as deterioration in these ratios. It is important to determine if the firm can obtain this funding from its financial institution(s).

If the firm cannot obtain additional short-term financing or perhaps long-term financing, sales and growth will have to be scaled back or, alternatively, additional equity contributions will have to be made by shareholders with a cash injection or by decreasing the dividend payout. Alternatively, the firm might improve its asset utilization ratios, which would generate additional cash flow. These utilization ratios were identified in Chapter 3.

It may be appropriate in this example to obtain long-term financing to match the increase in capital assets. This matching of the maturity of assets with liabilities is called a hedging approach and is discussed in Chapter 6. For the Howard Corporation, long-term funding has already been supplied by equity of $9,000. Further long-term financing of $16,000 would match the long-term investment in capital assets totalling $25,000. With this mix of long-term debt and a smaller portion of short-term debt, the current ratio would improve.

Observe that using the percent-of-sales method is much easier than tracing through the various cash flows to arrive at the pro forma statements. Nevertheless, the output is much less meaningful, and we do not get a month-to-month breakdown of the data. The percent-of-sales method is a broad-brush approach, whereas the detailed development of pro forma statements is more exact. Of course, whatever method we use, the results are only as meaningful or reliable as the assumptions about sales and production that went into the numbers.

Table 4–19 RNF with sales expansion (percent-of-sales method)

<table>
<tr><td colspan="5" align="center">**HOWARD CORPORATION**</td></tr>
<tr><td>Sales</td><td></td><td>$200,000</td><td></td><td></td></tr>
<tr><td>Sales increase</td><td>50.00%</td><td>$100,000</td><td></td><td></td></tr>
<tr><td align="center">**Assets**</td><td align="center">**Before**</td><td align="center">**Increase**</td><td align="center">**RNF**</td><td align="center">**After**</td></tr>
<tr><td>Cash . . . .</td><td>$ 5,000</td><td>$ 2,500</td><td></td><td>$ 7,500</td></tr>
<tr><td>Accounts receivable . . . .</td><td>40,000</td><td>20,000</td><td></td><td>60,000</td></tr>
<tr><td>Inventory . . . .</td><td>25,000</td><td>12,500</td><td></td><td>37,500</td></tr>
<tr><td>   Total current assets . . . .</td><td>$ 70,000</td><td>$35,000</td><td></td><td>$105,000</td></tr>
<tr><td>Equipment . . . .</td><td>50,000</td><td>25,000</td><td></td><td>75,000</td></tr>
<tr><td>   Total assets . . . .</td><td>$120,000</td><td>$60,000</td><td></td><td>$180,000</td></tr>
<tr><td colspan="5" align="center">**Liabilities and Shareholders' Equity**</td></tr>
<tr><td>Accounts payable . . . .</td><td>$ 40,000</td><td>$20,000</td><td></td><td>$ 60,000</td></tr>
<tr><td>Accrued expenses . . . .</td><td>10,000</td><td>5,000</td><td></td><td>15,000</td></tr>
<tr><td>Notes payable . . . .</td><td>15,000</td><td>0</td><td>26,000</td><td>**41,000**</td></tr>
<tr><td>   Total liabilities . . . .</td><td>$ 65,000</td><td>**25,000**</td><td></td><td>$116,000</td></tr>
<tr><td>Common stock . . . .</td><td>10,000</td><td></td><td></td><td>10,000</td></tr>
<tr><td>Retained earnings . . . .</td><td>45,000</td><td>9,000</td><td></td><td>54,000</td></tr>
<tr><td>   Total liabilities and shareholders' equity . . . .</td><td>$120,000</td><td>$34,000</td><td></td><td>$180,000</td></tr>
<tr><td>**Required new funds (RNF)**</td><td></td><td>$26,000</td><td>**26,000**</td><td></td></tr>
<tr><td colspan="5" align="center">**Selected Ratios**</td></tr>
<tr><td>Debt/Total assets</td><td colspan="2">65/120 = 0.54</td><td colspan="2">116/180 = 0.64</td></tr>
<tr><td>Debt/Equity</td><td colspan="2">65/(10 + 45) = 1.18</td><td colspan="2">116/(10 + 54) = 1.81</td></tr>
<tr><td>Current ratio</td><td colspan="2">70/65 = 1.08</td><td colspan="2">105/116 = 0.91</td></tr>
</table>

Sustainable Growth Rate

From the preceding discussion, the question arises: What level of growth can the corporation attain and still be able to raise the RNF through additional bank borrowings? The general answer is that highly profitable companies can sustain a high rate of growth, but marginally profitable companies can sustain only low growth.

We use the following formula to determine the maximum rate of growth obtainable without increasing the debt ratio. The formula, known as the sustainable growth rate (SGR), assumes that the performance ratios and balance sheet-to-sales ratios remain the same and that no new shares are issued.[3]

---

[3] A derivation follows:

$$\frac{A}{S_1}(\Delta S) = P(S_1 + \Delta S)(1 - D) + P(S_1 + \Delta S)(1 - D)\left(\frac{D_T}{E}\right)$$

$$\frac{A}{S_1}(\Delta S) = P(S_1 + \Delta S)(1 - D)\left(1 + \frac{D_T}{E}\right)$$

$$\frac{A}{S_1}(\Delta S) = S_1\left[P(1 - D)\left(1 + \frac{D_T}{E}\right)\right] + \Delta S\left[P(1 - D)\left(1 + \frac{D_T}{E}\right)\right]$$

$$\frac{A}{S_1}(\Delta S) - \Delta S\left[P(1 - D)\left(1 + \frac{D_T}{E}\right)\right] = S_1\left[P(1 - D)\left(1 + \frac{D_T}{E}\right)\right]$$

$$\Delta S_1\left[\frac{A}{S_1} - P(1 - D)\left(1 + \frac{D_T}{E}\right)\right] = S_1\left[P(1 - D)\left(1 + \frac{D_T}{E}\right)\right]$$

$$SGR = \frac{\Delta S}{S_1} = \frac{P(1 - D)\left(1 + \frac{D_T}{E}\right)}{\frac{A}{S_1} - P(1 - D)\left(1 + \frac{D_T}{E}\right)}$$

An approximate formula is SGR = ROE (1 − D). In other words, the lower the level of current debt, the greater the potential for the firm to borrow more funds for higher future growth.

$$SGR = \frac{\Delta S}{S_1} = \frac{P(1-D)\left(1+\dfrac{D_T}{E}\right)}{\dfrac{A}{S_1} - P(1-D)\left(1+\dfrac{D_T}{E}\right)} \quad (4\text{–}2)$$

where

$$\frac{D_T}{E} = \text{Debt to equity ratio}$$

For the Howard Corporation, the calculation is

$$SGR = \frac{0.06(1 - 0.5)(1 + 1.1818)}{0.60 - 0.06(1 - 0.5)(1 + 1.1818)}$$
$$= 0.1224 \text{ or } 12.24\%$$

This suggests that sales can increase by 12.24 percent, or $24,480, while maintaining the debt-to-equity ratio at 1.18. Using the RNF formula, assets will increase by $14,688, current liabilities by $6,120, and retained earnings by $6,734. This will require new funds of $1,834, as shown in Table 4–20. With the RNF financed by an operating loan (notes payable), the key ratios remain the same.

Table 4–20 RNF, based on SGR

HOWARD CORPORATION				
Sales		$200,000		
Sales increase	12.24%	$ 24,480		
Assets	**Before**	**Increase**	**RNF**	**After**
Cash	$ 5,000	$ 612		$ 5,612
Accounts receivable	40,000	4,896		44,896
Inventory	25,000	3,060		28,060
Total current assets	$ 70,000	$ 8,568		$ 78,568
Equipment	50,000	6,120		56,120
Total assets	$120,000	$14,688		$134,688
Liabilities and Shareholders' Equity				
Accounts payable	$ 40,000	$ 4,896		$ 44,896
Accrued expenses	10,000	1,224		11,224
Notes payable	15,000	0	1,834	16,834
Total current liabilities	$ 65,000	6,120		$ 72,954
Common stock	10,000			10,000
Retained earnings	45,000	6,734		51,734
Total liabilities and shareholders' equity	$120,000	$12,854		$134,688
Required new funds (RNF)		1,834	1,834	
Selected Ratios				
Debt/Total assets	65/120 = 0.54		73/135 = 0.54	
Debt/Equity	65/(10 + 45) = 1.18		73/(10 + 52) = 1.18	
Current ratio	70/65 = 1.08		79/73 = 1.08	

Although the forecasting approach is the same for all companies, whether it follows IFRS (public) or ASPE (private), the dollar amounts will vary due to different valuations of both income statement and balance sheet accounts. Therefore, the forecasted amounts will not be comparable between IFRS (public) versus ASPE (private) companies' forecasts.

SUMMARY

1. Financial forecasting allows the financial manager to anticipate events before they occur, particularly the need for raising funds externally. Growth itself may call for additional sources of financing because profit is often inadequate to cover the net buildup in receivables, inventory, and other asset accounts. (LO1)

2. We develop pro forma financial statements from an overall corporate systems viewpoint. We must identify whether it is a private (ASPE) or public corporation (IFRS) because the format and amounts will be significantly different. Today computerized spreadsheets greatly facilitate this process. The time perspective is usually six months to a year in the future. In developing a pro forma income statement, we begin by making sales projections; then, we construct a production plan. Finally, we consider all other expenses. From the pro forma income statement we proceed to a cash budget in which the monthly or quarterly cash inflows and outflows related to sales, expenditures, and capital outlays are portrayed. All of this information can be assimilated into a pro forma balance sheet in which asset, liability, and shareholders' equity accounts are shown. Any shortage of funds is assumed to be financed through notes payable (bank loans). (LO2)

3. We may take a shortcut to financial forecasting through the use of the percent-of-sales method. Under this approach, selected balance sheet accounts are assumed to maintain a constant percentage relationship to sales, and thus we can ascertain balance sheet values for any given sales amount. Once again, a shortage of funds is assumed to be financed through notes payable. (LO3)

4. Based on its forecasting, a firm must decide if new funds will be required, whether to grow sales or replace old machinery and equipment. Seasonal and other effects on cash flow must be considered. Management might decide what funding will be required for research and development to become more competitive. (LO4)

5. Required new funding can be estimated by using the RNF formula (4–1). We can also calculate the SGR, which will provide management with an estimate of its growth potential using its current resources. (LO5)

REVIEW OF FORMULAS

$$\text{RNF} = \frac{A}{S_1}(\Delta S) - \frac{L}{S_1}(\Delta S) - PS_2(1 - D) \tag{4–1}$$

$$\text{SGR} = \frac{\Delta S}{S_1} = \frac{P(1-D)\left(1 + \dfrac{D_I}{E}\right)}{\dfrac{A}{S_1} - P(1-D)\left(1 + \dfrac{D_I}{E}\right)} \tag{4–2}$$

DISCUSSION QUESTIONS

1. What are the basic benefits and purposes of developing pro forma statements and a cash budget? (LO1, LO2)

2. Explain how the collections and purchases schedules are related to the borrowing needs of the corporation. (LO1)

3. With inflation, what are the implications of using different inventory valuation methods? How do they affect the cost of goods sold? (LO3)

4. Explain the relationship between inventory turnover and purchasing needs. (LO3)

5. Rapid growth in sales and profits can cause financing and other problems. Elaborate on this statement. (LO4)

6. Discuss the advantage and disadvantage of level production schedules in firms whose sales are cyclical. (LO4)

7. What conditions would help make a percent-of-sales forecast as accurate as pro forma financial statements and cash budgets? Describe a more detailed approach to prepare pro forma statements. (LO3)

8. How will the calculations of required new funds (RNF) and SGR help management to make better decisions for the company? (LO5)

9. Research the current forecasts for GDP growth, inflation, and unemployment in Canada, Europe, and your particular region of the country. (LO1)

INTERNET RESOURCES

The major financial institutions have economic departments that regularly report on economic trends and their possible impact on the economy, regions of the country, and industries.
economics.bmo.com/en
rbc.com/economics/

Sample business plans can be found at several websites.
bplans.com

The New York–based U.S. Conference Board regularly reports on consumer confidence in the United States. Consumer spending is the major component of U.S. economic activity.
conference-board.org/us

Oracle's Crystal Ball demonstrates its time series forecasting tool for sales and other projections.
Oracle.com

Amazon also has a time series forecasting tool based on algorithms that it has used for many years.
aws.amazon.com/forecast

PROBLEMS

1. The Alonso Corporation has forecasted to sell the following units of copper cables, at prices indicated, under three different economic conditions. The probability of each outcome is shown below. What are the total sales projected in each situation?

Outcome	Probability	Units	Price
A	.30	200	$15
B	.50	320	30
C	.20	410	40

2. Philip Morris expects the sales for his clothing company to be $550,000 next year. Philip notes that net assets (Assets – Liabilities) will remain unchanged. His clothing firm will enjoy a 12 percent return on total sales. He will start the year with $150,000 in the bank. What will be Philip's ending cash balance?

3. Galehouse Gas Stations Inc. expects sales to increase from $1,550,000 to $1,750,000 next year. Galehouse believes that net assets (Assets – Liabilities) will represent 50 percent of sales. His firm has an 8 percent return on sales and pays 45 percent of profits out as dividends.
   a. What effect will this growth have on funds?
   b. If the dividend payout is only 25 percent, what effect will this growth have on funds?

4. Eli Lilly is very excited because sales for his nursery and plant company are expected to increase from $560,000 to $1,200,000 next year. Eli's net assets (Assets – Liabilities) will remain at 50 percent of sales. His firm will enjoy an 8 percent return on total sales. He will begin the year with $120,000 in the bank and is already bragging about the Jaguar and luxury townhouse he will buy. Does his optimistic outlook for his cash position appear to be justified? Compute the likely cash balance for the end of the year.

5. In the previous problem, if there is no increase in sales and all other facts remain the same, what would be Eli's ending cash balance? What observation can be reached from these two problems? Show calculations to support your observations.

6. Gibson Manufacturing Corporation expects to sell the following number of units of steel cables at the prices indicated, under three different scenarios in the economy. The probability of each outcome is indicated. What is the expected value of the total sales projection?

Outcome	Probability	Units	Price
A	0.20	100	$20
B	0.50	180	25
C	0.30	210	30

7. Brampton Truck Parts expects to sell the following number of units at the prices indicated under three different scenarios in the economy. The probability of each outcome is indicated below. What is the expected value of the total sales projection?

Probability	Units	Price
0.20	300	$16
0.50	500	25
0.30	1,000	30

8. Central Networks had sales of 3,000 units at $50 per unit last year. The marketing manager projects a 20 percent increase in unit-volume sales this year with a 10 percent increase in price. Returned merchandise will represent 6 percent of total sales. What is your net dollar sales projection for this year?

9. All Metal Bearings had sales of 10,000 units at $20 per unit last year. The marketing manager projects a 30 percent increase in unit-volume sales this year with a 5 percent price decrease (due to a price reduction by a competitor). Returned merchandise will represent 3 percent of total sales. What is your net dollar sales projection for this year?

10. Sales for Ross Pro's Sports Equipment are expected to be 4,800 units for October. The company likes to maintain 10 percent of unit sales for each month in ending inventory (that is, end of October). Beginning inventory for October is 300 units. How many units should the firm produce for the coming month?

11. Digitex Inc. had sales of 6,000 units in March. A 50 percent increase is expected in April. The company will maintain 5 percent of expected unit sales for April in ending inventory. Beginning inventory for April was equal to 200 units. How many units should the company produce in April?

12. Hoover Electronics has beginning inventory of 22,000 units, will sell 60,000 units for the month, and desires to reduce ending inventory to 30 percent of beginning inventory. How many units should Hoover produce?

13. Biomedical Products anticipates sales of 80,000 units for the first six months of the year. Beginning inventory is maintained at 16 percent of anticipated sales. Ending inventory will be equal to 20 percent of the projected sales of 92,000 units for the last six months of the year. How many units should the firm produce during the first six months of the year?

14. On December 31 of last year, Wolfson Corporation had 400 units in inventory of its product, which cost $21 per unit to produce. During January, the company produced 800 units at a cost of $24 per unit. Assuming Wolfson Corporation sold 700 units in January, what was the cost of goods sold (assume FIFO inventory method)?

15. At the end of January, Mineral Labs had an inventory of 775 units, which cost $12 per unit to produce. During February, the company produced 900 units at a cost of $16 per unit. If the firm sold 1,500 units in February, what was the cost of goods sold?

    a. Assume LIFO inventory accounting.

    b. Assume FIFO inventory accounting.

16. At the end of January, Higgins Data Systems had an inventory of 600 units, which cost $16 per unit to produce. During February the company produced 850 units at a cost of $19 per unit. If Higgins sold 1,100 units in February, what was its cost of goods sold?

    a. Assume average cost inventory accounting.

    b. Assume FIFO inventory accounting.

17. Cox Corporation produces a product with the following costs as of July 1, 20XX:

Material	$2 per unit
Labour	4 per unit
Overhead	2 per unit

    Assuming Cox sold 13,000 units during the last six months of the year at $16 each, beginning inventory at these costs on July 1 was 3,000 units. From July 1 to December 31, 20XY, Cox produced 12,000 units. These units had a material cost of $3 per unit. The costs for labour and overhead were the same. If Cox uses FIFO inventory accounting, what would gross profit be? What is the value of ending inventory?

18. Assume in the previous problem that Cox Corporation used average cost inventory accounting instead of FIFO. What would gross profit be? What is the value of ending inventory?

19. Jerrico Wallboard Co. had a beginning inventory of 7,000 shoes on January 1, 20XX. The costs associated with the inventory were as follows:

Material	$9.00 per shoe
Labour	5.00 per shoe
Overhead	4.10 per shoe

    During 20XX, the firm produced 28,500 units with the following costs:

Material	$11.50 per shoe
Labour	4.80 per shoe
Overhead	6.20 per shoe

    Sales for the year were 31,500 units at $29.60 each. Jerrico uses average cost accounting. What was the gross profit? What was the value of ending inventory?

20. Power Ridge Corporation has forecast credit sales for the fourth quarter of the year as follows:

September (actual)	$50,000
Fourth Quarter	
October	40,000
November	35,000
December	60,000

Experience has shown 20 percent of sales are collected in the month of sale, 70 percent are collected in the following month, and 10 percent are never collected. Prepare a cash receipts schedule for Power Ridge Corporation covering the fourth quarter (October through December).

21. Donna's Fashions Corporation has the following sales forecast in units:

    January 1,000; February 800; March 900; April 1,400; May 1,550; June 1,800; July 1,400

    Donna always keeps ending inventory equal to 120 percent of the next month's expected sales. The ending inventory for December (January's beginning inventory) is 1,200 units, consistent with company policy.

    Materials cost $14 per unit and are paid for in the month after production. Labour cost is $7 per unit and is paid in same month the cost is incurred. Overhead costs are $8,000 per month. Interest of $10,000 will be paid in March, and employee bonuses of $15,500 paid in June.

    Prepare a monthly production schedule and a monthly summary of cash payments for January through June. Donna produced 800 units in December.

22. Simpson Glove Company has made the following sales projections for the next six months. All sales are credit sales.

March	$41,000
April	50,000
May	32,000
June	47,000
July	58,000
August	62,000

    Sales in January and February were $41,000 and $39,000, respectively. Experience has shown that of total sales receipts 10 percent are uncollectible, 40 percent are collected in the month of sale, 30 percent are collected in the following month, and 20 percent are collected two months after sale.

    Prepare a monthly cash receipts schedule for the firm for March through August.

23. Ed's Waterbeds has made the following sales projections for the next six months. All sales are credit sales.

March	$12,000	June	$14,000
April	16,000	July	17,000
May	10,000	August	18,000

    Sales in January and February were $13,500 and $13,000 respectively.

    Experience has shown that 10 percent of total sales are uncollectible, 30 percent are collected in the month of sale, 40 percent are collected in the following month, and 20 percent are collected two months after sale.

    Prepare a monthly cash receipts schedule for the firm for March through August.

    Of the sales expected to be made during the six months from March to August, how much will still be uncollected at the end of August? How much of this is expected to be collected later?

24. Ultravision Limited anticipates sales of $240,000 from January through April. Materials will represent 50 percent of sales and because of level production, material purchases will be equal for each month during these four months.

    Materials are paid for one month after the month purchased. Materials purchased in December of last year were $20,000 (half of $40,000 in sales). Labour costs for each of the four months are slightly different due to a provision in the labour contract in which bonuses are paid in February and April. Fixed overhead is $6,000 monthly. The labour figures are:

January	$10,000	March	10,000
February	13,000	April	15,000

    Prepare a schedule of cash payments for January through April.

25. The Prince Albert Corporation has forecast the following sales for the first seven months of the year.

January	$10,000	March	$14,000	May	$10,000	July	$18,000
February	12,000	April	20,000	June	16,000		

Monthly material purchases are set equal to 30 percent of forecasted sales for the next month. Of the total material costs, 40 percent are paid in the month of purchase and 60 percent are paid in the following month. Labour costs will run $4,000 per month, and fixed overhead is $2,000 per month. Interest payments on the debt will be $3,000 for both March and June. Finally, the Prince Albert salespeople will receive a 1.5 percent commission on total sales for the first six months of the year, to be paid on June 30.

Prepare a monthly summary of cash payments for the six months from January through June. (Note: Compute prior December purchases to help get total material payments for January.)

26. The Boswell Corporation forecasts its sales in units for the next four months as follows.

March	6,000
April	8,000
May	5,500
June	4,000

Boswell maintains an ending inventory for each month in the amount of one and one-half times the expected sales in the following month. The ending inventory for February (March's beginning inventory) reflects this policy. Materials cost $5 per unit and are paid for in the month after production. Labour cost is $10 per unit and is paid for in the month incurred. Fixed overhead is $12,000 per month. Dividends of $20,000 are to be paid in May. Five thousand units were produced in February.

Complete a production schedule and a summary of cash payments for March, April, and May. Remember that production in any one month is equal to sales plus desired ending inventory minus beginning inventory.

27. The Ace Battery Company has forecast its sales in units as follows:

January	800	March	600	May	1,350	July	1,200
February	650	April	1,100	June	1,500		

Ace always keeps an ending inventory equal to 120 percent of the next month's expected sales. The ending inventory for December (January's beginning inventory) is 960 units, which is consistent with this policy.

Materials cost $12 per unit and are paid for in the month after production. Labour cost is $5 per unit and is paid in the month the cost is incurred. Overhead costs are $6,000 per month. Interest of $8,000 is scheduled to be paid in March, and employee bonuses of $13,200 will be paid in June.

Prepare a monthly production schedule and a monthly summary of cash payments for January through June. Ace produced 600 units in December.

28. Prince Charles Island Company has expected sales of $6,000 in September, $10,000 in October, $16,000 in November, and $12,000 in December. Cash sales are 20 percent and credit sales are 80 percent of total sales. Historically, 40 percent of receivables are collected in the month after the sale, and the remaining 60 percent collected two months after. Determine collections for November and December.

Assume that the company's cash payments for November are $13,000, and December $6,000. The beginning cash balance in November is $5,000, which is the desired minimum balance.

Prepare a cash budget and calculate borrowing or repayments for November and December.

29. Jim Daniels Health Products has eight stores. The firm wants to expand by two more stores and needs a bank loan to do this. Mr. Hewitt, the banker, will finance construction if the firm can present an acceptable three-month financial plan for January through March. Following are actual and forecasted sales figures:

Actual		Forecast		Additional Information	
November	$200,000	January	$280,000	April forecast	$330,000
December	220,000	February	320,000		
		March	340,000		

Of the firm's sales, 40 percent are for cash and the remaining 60 percent are on credit. Of credit sales, 30 percent are paid in the month after sale and 70 percent are paid in the second month after the sale. Materials cost 30 percent of sales and are purchased and received each month in an amount sufficient to cover the following month's expected sales. Materials are paid for in the month after they are received. Labour expense is 40 percent of sales and is paid in the month of sales. Selling and administrative expense is 5 percent of sales and is also paid in the month of sales. Overhead is $28,000 in cash per month; amortization expense is $10,000 per month. Taxes of $8,000 will be paid in January and dividends of $2,000 will be paid in March. Cash at the beginning of January is $80,000 and the minimum desired cash balance is $75,000.

For January, February, and March prepare a schedule of monthly cash receipts, monthly cash payments, and a complete monthly cash budget with borrowings and repayments.

30. Ellis Electronics Company's actual sales and purchases for April and May are shown here, along with forecasted sales and purchases for June through September.

	Sales	Purchases
April (actual)	$320,000	$130,000
May (actual)	300,000	120,000
June (forecast)	275,000	120,000
July (forecast)	275,000	180,000
August (forecast)	290,000	200,000
September (forecast)	330,000	170,000

The company makes 10 percent of its sales for cash and 90 percent on credit. Of the credit sales, 20 percent are collected in the month after the sale and 80 percent are collected two months after. Ellis pays for 40 percent of its purchases in the month after purchase and 60 percent two months after.

Labour expense equals 10 percent of the current month's sales. Overhead expense equals $12,000 per month. Interest payments of $30,000 are due in June and September. A cash dividend of $50,000 is scheduled to be paid in June. Tax payments of $25,000 are due in June and September. There is a scheduled capital outlay of $300,000 in September.

Ellis Electronics' ending cash balance in May is $20,000. The minimum desired cash balance is $15,000. Prepare a schedule of monthly cash receipts, monthly cash payments, and a complete monthly cash budget with borrowing and repayments for June through September. The maximum desired cash balance is $50,000. Excess cash (above $50,000) is used to buy marketable securities. Marketable securities are sold before borrowing funds in case of a cash shortfall (less than $15,000).

31. Carter Paint Company has plants in four provinces. Sales last year were $100 million, and the balance sheet at year-end is similar in percent of sales to that of previous years (and this will

continue in the future). All assets and current liabilities will vary directly with sales. Assume the firm is already using capital assets at full capacity.

Balance Sheet (in $ millions)

Assets		Liabilities and Shareholders' Equity	
Cash........................	$ 5	Accounts payable........................	$15
Accounts receivable............	15	Accrued wages..........................	6
Inventory	30	Accrued taxes..........................	4
Current assets..............	50	Current liabilities......................	25
Capital assets	40	Long-term debt	30
		Common stock.........................	15
		Retained earnings.......................	20
Total assets..................	$90	Total liabilities and shareholders'equity	$90

The firm has an aftertax profit margin of 5 percent and a dividend payout ratio of 30 percent.

a. If sales grow by 10 percent next year, determine how many dollars of new funds are needed to finance the expansion.

b. Prepare a pro forma balance sheet with any financing adjustment made to long-term debt.

c. Calculate the current ratio and total debt to assets ratio for each year.

32. The Longbranch Western Wear Company has the following financial statements, which are representative of the company's historical average.

Income Statement

Sales...	$200,000
Expenses	158,000
Earnings before interest and taxes	42,000
Interest	2,000
Earnings before taxes.............................	40,000
Taxes	20,000
Earnings after taxes	$ 20,000
Dividends......................................	$ 10,000

Balance Sheet

Assets		Liabilities and Shareholders' Equity	
Cash........................	$ 5,000	Accounts payable............	$ 5,000
Accounts receivable...........	10,000	Accrued wages..............	1,000
Inventory	15,000	Accrued taxes...............	2,000
Current assets..............	30,000	Current liabilities............	8,000
Capital assets	70,000	Notes payable...............	7,000
		Long-term debt	15,000
		Common stock..............	20,000
		Retained earnings............	50,000
Total assets..................	$100,000	Total liabilities and equity	$100,000

Longbranch is expecting a 20 percent increase in sales next year, and management is concerned about the company's need for external funds. The increase in sales is expected to be carried out without any expansion of capital assets; instead, it will be done through more efficient asset utilization in the existing stores. Of liabilities, only current liabilities vary directly with sales. (Refer to the example in the chapter and show all calculations).

a. Using a percent-of-sales method, determine whether Longbranch Western Wear has external financing needs.

b. Prepare a pro forma balance sheet with any financing adjustment made to notes payable.

c. Calculate the current ratio and total debt to assets ratio for each year.

33. Clyde's Well Servicing has the following financial statements. The balance sheet items, profit margin, and dividend payout have maintained the same relationships the past couple of years; these relationships are anticipated to hold in the future. Clyde's has excess capacity, so there is no expected increase in capital assets.

Income Statement	
Sales..	$2,000,000
Cost of goods sold	1,260,000
Gross profit	740,000
Selling and administrative expense	400,000
Amortization	55,000
Earnings before interest and taxes	285,000
Interest	50,000
Earnings before taxes.............................	235,000
Taxes	61,000
Earnings available to common shareholders	$ 174,000
Dividends paid...................................	$ 104,400

Balance Sheet			
Assets		**Liabilities and Shareholders' Equity**	
Cash	$ 30,000	Accounts payable.............	$ 105,000
Accounts receivable...........	260,000	Accruals....................	20,000
Inventory	210,000	Bank loan...................	150,000
Current assets..............	500,000	Current liabilities............	275,000
Capital assets	550,000	Long-term debt	200,000
		Common stock	175,000
		Retained earnings............	400,000
Total assets.................	$1,050,000	Total liabilities and equity	$1,050,000

a. Using a percent-of-sales method, determine whether Clyde's can handle a 30 percent sales increase without using external financing. If so, what is the need?

b. If the average collection period of receivables could be held to 43 days, what would the need be for external financing? All other relationships remain the same.

c. Suppose the following results with the increased sales of $600,000.

Cash increases by................................	$5,000
Average collection period	43 days
Inventory turnover (COGS)........................	6 ×
Capital assets increase by..........................	$125,000
Accounts payable increase.........................	in proportion to sales
Accruals.......................................	no change
Long-term debt decreases by.......................	$25,000
Gross profit margin	40%
Selling, general, and administrative expense increase by .	$50,000
Amortization increases by	$12,500
Interest decreases by	$10,000
Tax rate	35%
Dividends increase to.............................	$120,000

What new funds would be required? The first $75,000 of any new funds would be short-term debt and then long-term debt. Prepare the pro forma balance sheet.

34. Harvard Prep Shops, a national clothing chain, had sales of $300 million last year. The business has a steady net profit margin of 15 percent and a dividend payout ratio of 30 percent. The balance sheet for the end of last year is shown below:

Balance Sheet
December 31, 20XX ($ millions)

Assets		Liabilities and Shareholders' Equity	
Cash	$ 7	Accounts payable	$ 55
Accounts receivable	28	Accrued expenses	15
Inventory	60	Other payables	20
Plant and equipment	115	Common stock	30
		Retained earnings	90
Total assets	$210	Total liabilities and equity	$210

Harvard's anticipates a large increase in the demand for tweed sport coats and deck shoes. A sales increase of 25 percent is forecast.

All balance sheet items are expected to maintain the same percent-of-sales relationships as last year, except for common stock and retained earnings. No change in the number of common shares outstanding is scheduled, and retained earnings will change as dictated by the profits and dividend policy of the firm.

a. Will external financing be required for the Prep Shop during the coming year?

b. What would the need for external financing be if the net profit margin went up to 20 percent and the dividend payout ratio was increased to 65 percent? Explain.

COMPREHENSIVE PROBLEMS

35. The Mansfield Corporation had 20XX sales of $100 million. The balance sheet items that vary directly with sales and the profit margin are as follows:

	Percent
Cash	5%
Accounts receivable	15
Inventory	20
Net capital assets	40
Accounts payable	15
Other payables	10
Profit margin after taxes	10

The dividend payout rate is 50 percent of earnings, and the balance in retained earnings at the beginning of 20XY was $33 million. Common stock and the company's long-term bonds are constant at $10 million and $5 million, respectively. Notes payable are currently $7 million.

a. How much additional external capital will be required for next year if sales increase 35 percent? (Assume that the company is already operating at full capacity.)

b. What will happen to external fund requirements if Mansfield Corporation 1) reduces the payout ratio, 2) grows at a slower rate, or 3) suffers a decline in its profit margin? Discuss all three of these separately with an example for each variable.

c. Prepare a pro forma balance sheet for 20XY, assuming that any external funds being acquired will be in the form of notes payable. Disregard the information in part **b** in answering this question (that is, use the original information and part **a** in constructing your pro forma balance sheet).

d. Calculate debt to total assets, debt to equity, current ratio, return on assets, and return on equity before and after the sales increase.

e. Calculate Mansfield's SGR.

36. The Adams Corporation makes standard-size 2-inch fasteners, which it sells for $155 per thousand. Mr. Adams is the majority owner and manages the inventory and finances of the company. He estimates sales for the following months to be:

January	$263,500 (1,700,000 fasteners)
February	$186,000 (1,200,000 fasteners)
March	$217,000 (1,400,000 fasteners)
April	$310,000 (2,000,000 fasteners)
May	$387,500 (2,500,000 fasteners)

Last year, Adams Corporation's sales were $175,000 (1,129,030 fasteners) in November and $232,500 (1,500,000 fasteners) in December.

Mr. Adams is preparing for a meeting with his banker to arrange the financing for the first quarter. Based on his sales forecast and the following information provided by him, your job as his new financial analyst is to prepare a monthly cash budget, a monthly and quarterly pro forma income statement, a pro forma quarterly balance sheet, and all necessary supporting schedules for the first quarter.

Past history shows that Adams Corporation collects 50 percent of its accounts receivable in the normal 30-day credit period (the month after the sale) and the other 50 percent in 60 days (two months after the sale). It pays for its materials 30 days after receipt. In general, Mr. Adams likes to keep a two-month supply of inventory on hand in anticipation of sales. Inventory at the beginning of December was 2,600,000 units. (This was not equal to his desired two-month supply.)

The major cost of production is the purchase of raw materials in the form of steel rods that are cut, threaded, and finished. Last year raw material costs were $52 per 1,000 fasteners, but Mr. Adams has just been notified that material costs have increased, effective January 1, to $60 per 1,000 fasteners. The Adams Corporation uses FIFO inventory accounting. Labour costs are relatively constant at $20 per thousand fasteners, since workers are paid on a piecework (per unit) basis. Overhead is allocated at $10 per thousand units, and selling and administrative expense is 20 percent of sales. Labour expense and overhead are direct cash outflows paid in the month incurred, while interest and taxes are paid quarterly.

The corporation usually maintains a minimum cash balance of $25,000, and it invests its excess cash into marketable securities. The average tax rate is 40 percent, and Mr. Adams usually pays out 50 percent of net income in dividends to shareholders. Marketable securities are sold before funds are borrowed when a cash shortage occurs. Ignore the interest on any short-term borrowings. Interest on the long-term debt, taxes, and dividends are paid in March.

ADAMS CORPORATION
Balance Sheet
December 31, 20XX
Assets

Current assets:

Cash		$ 30,000
Accounts receivable		320,000
Inventory		237,800
Total current assets		587,800

Capital assets:

Plant and equipment	1,000,000	
Less: Accumulated amortization	200,000	800,000
Total assets		$ 1,387,800

Liabilities and Shareholders' Equity

Accounts payable	$ 93,600
Notes payable	0
Long-term debt, 8 percent	400,000
Common stock	504,200
Retained earnings	390,000
Total liabilities and shareholders' equity	$ 1,387,800

37. Toys for You, a manufacturing company, has been growing quickly but has found that its financial situation is continually under pressure. Production has fluctuated to meet demand in an attempt to provide first-class service, resulting in larger inventory positions. Also, the collection of accounts has worsened to approximately 60 days, which is well above the terms of 30 days. To address the financial concerns, Toys for You has proposed level production and an effort by the credit department to bring the average collection period down to 35 days.

Estimated sales for the upcoming months are:

July	$1,957,500	October	2,362,500
August	2,070,000	November	2,475,000
September	2,205,000	December	2,565,000

Sales for May were $1,732,500 and will be approximately $1,845,000 for the current month of June.

It is projected that the current collection period of 60 days will be reduced to 50 days for July and August, 42 days for September and October, and will meet the target of 35 days in November and December.

Purchases are forecast to be $585,000 a month beginning in July, until December. In May they were $630,000, and in June they are expected to be $592,500. The purchases are paid in 40 days. Labour expense will be paid as incurred and will be $195,000 a month. Other expenses of manufacturing will also be paid as incurred and are expected to be $375,000 a month. Cost of goods sold has regularly been 70 percent of sales.

Amortization is $38,000 per month. Selling and administrative expenses are expected to be 13 percent of sales. The tax rate is 42 percent.

There will be payments on notes of $675,000 in each of August and November. Interest of $270,000 and income taxes of $338,000 are both due in October. Dividends of $22,500 are payable in July and October.

TOYS FOR YOU
Balance Sheet (estimated)
June 30, 20XY ($ thousands)
Assets

Current assets:

Cash....................................		$ 666
Accounts receivable....................		3,578
Inventory		8,231
Total current assets.....................		12,475

Capital assets:

Plant and equipment......................	11,273	
Less: Accumulated amortization............	4,784	6,489
Total assets...............................		$18,964

Liabilities and Shareholders' Equity

Current liabilities

Accounts payable........................		$ 945
Notes payable...........................		3,700
Accrued liabilities		2,596
Total current liabilities..................		7,241
Long-term debt		4,725
Common stock...........................		4,500
Retained earnings........................		2,498
Total liabilities and shareholders' equity........		$18,964

Using the information above, prepare pro forma statements for Toys for You for the three months ending September and December 20XY. Also construct a cash budget for the six-month period and identify any need for short-term financing. There are no changes in accounts not mentioned above. Comment on the policy changes and examine the consequences if the collection period remains at 60 days. Assume capital assets are sufficient for increased sales.

Operating and Financial Leverage

LEARNING OBJECTIVES

LO1 Define leverage as a method to magnify earnings available to the firm's common shareholders.

LO2 Calculate break-even in units and in dollars to determine the magnitude of operations to avoid losses.

LO3 Define and calculate operating leverage and assess its opportunities and limitations.

LO3 Define and calculate financial leverage and assess its opportunities and limitations.

LO4 Calculate the indifference point between financing plans using EBIT/EPS analysis.

LO5 Define and calculate combined leverage.

In the physical sciences, as well as in politics, the term leverage has been popularized to mean the use of special force and effects to produce more than normal results from a given action. In business the same concept is applied. The use of fixed-cost items, in particular capital assets and debt, can magnify returns to shareholders at high levels of operation. Although leverage may produce highly favourable results when things go well, it is a two-edged sword. The opposite will occur under negative economic conditions. This potential for higher gains or greater losses is an exposure to a greater variability of returns, which we define as risk. We explore the concept of risk in Chapter 13. Greater risk will affect share value as will the higher expected gains/losses.

LO1 LEVERAGE IN A BUSINESS

There are two major risks that are faced by any firm:
- Business Risk Based on the nature of the business operations together with the mix of labour and capital assets
- Financial Risk Based on the nature of capital employed to fund the firm (debt and/or share equity)

 FINANCE IN ACTION

On the Red to in the Black

There are some intriguing examples of business risk. One of the more daring or perhaps desperate "gamble" was taken by Fred Smith, who founded FedEx in 1971.

FedEx had quickly run through its initial capital in its early years, primarily due to rising fuel costs. The company was down to its last $5,000, investors were unwilling to advance the company more funds, and a fuel bill of $24,000 was due Monday. Fred Smith knew that if payment was not made the company would fail.

Smith flew to Las Vegas with the $5,000 and won $27,000 at the blackjack tables. FedEx survived and by 1976 was turning a profit. This is not a recommended business strategy, but if you're going to lose the business anyway. . . .

By employing more capital assets and/or more debt, the firm increases its leverage and its risk. However, the firm also increases the potential for greater returns to shareholders (to magnify earnings).

Operating leverage reflects the extent to which capital assets and fixed costs are utilized in the business firm. As operations approach full production and sales capacity, costs per unit decrease, resulting in higher profits.

Financial leverage reflects the amount of debt used in the capital structure (debt/equity mix) of the firm.

It is helpful to think of operating leverage as primarily affecting the left side (fixed charges) of the balance sheet and financial leverage (interest charges) the right side. Whereas operating leverage influences the mix of plant and equipment (capital assets), financial leverage determines how the operation is to be financed (mix of debt/equity).

Balance Sheet			
Assets		**Liabilities and Equity**	
Operating leverage {	Current assets	Debt (Loads, bonds, leases)	} Financial leverage
	Capital assets	**(interest charges)**	
	(fixed charges)	Equity (Shares)	

From an income statement viewpoint, operating leverage determines return from operations, but financial leverage determines how earnings are allocated to debt holders and, more importantly, to shareholders in the form of earnings per share. Table 5–1 shows the combined influence of operating and financial leverage on the income statement.

Table 5–1 Income statement

Sales (total revenue) (80,000 units @ $2)	$160,000	
– Variable costs ($0.80 per unit)	64,000	
Contribution margin	96,000	Operating leverage
– Fixed costs	60,000	←
Operating income	36,000	
Earnings before interest and taxes	36,000	
– Interest	12,000	←
Earnings before taxes	24,000	Financial leverage
– Taxes	12,000	
Earnings after taxes	$ 12,000	
Shares	8,000	
Earnings per share	$1.50	

Observe that operating leverage influences the top half of the income statement—determining operating income. The last item under operating leverage, operating income, becomes the initial item for determining financial leverage. "Operating income" and "earnings before interest and taxes" are the same, representing the return to the corporation after production, marketing, and administration costs, but before interest and taxes are paid. In the second half of the income statement, we show the extent to which earnings before interest and taxes are translated into earnings per share. Note that earnings per share (EPS) shown in examples apply to public firms (IFRS).

The use of fixed-cost plant and equipment (capital assets) in the firm's operations or production process can decrease its need for labour. At high volumes, the firm can do quite well, as most of its costs are fixed. At low volume, however, the firm will have difficulty in making fixed payments for plant and equipment. Using expensive labour rather than machinery will lessen the opportunity for profit, but at the same time will lower the exposure to risk (part of the work force can be laid off).

The use of debt financing requires that the fixed costs (interest and repayment) must be covered by revenues. However, debt reduces the need to distribute profits with other shareholders (selling equity is the alternative to debt financing), if the firm is successful and substantial profits are generated. Of course, if the business starts off poorly, the contractual obligations related to debt could mean bankruptcy.

The degree of operating and financial leverage employed by the firm stems from its strategic decisions related to its operations. The analysis of the firm's opportunities, challenges, economic environment, and its access to capital (real and financial) influence the extent to which it is prepared to accept the risks of leverage. The amount of leverage a firm employs is often conditioned by its pattern of cash flows as they are required to service the fixed costs incurred with leverage.

The goal of the firm is the maximization of shareholders' wealth by increasing the share price. Expected earnings can be affected by leverage, but so can risk of not achieving desired results. Share price is a complicated mixture of many things, including a tradeoff between expected cash flows and risk.

LO3 OPERATING LEVERAGE

Operating leverage is the degree to which capital assets and associated fixed costs are utilized by the firm. Strategic capital budgeting decisions (Chapter 12) made by the firm as part of its investment strategy determine the extent of operating leverage. Larger capital projects demand substantial revenues to repay the investment and, if healthy revenues are generated by the project, then economies of scale can be exploited. Efficiency is obtained through better profit margins, although the firm's risk increases and will be evident if the capital projects do not generate the expected returns. As indicated in Table 5–2, a firm's operational costs may be classified as fixed, variable, or semivariable.

Table 5–2 Classification of costs

Fixed	Variable	Semivariable
Rental	Raw material	Utilities
Amortization	Factory labour	Repairs and maintenance
Executive salaries	Sales commissions	
Property taxes		

For purposes of analysis, variable and semivariable costs are combined. To evaluate the implications of heavy capital asset use, we employ the technique of break-even analysis. We are unable to change the fixed costs that come with capital assets in the short run.

LO2 Break-Even Analysis

Simulated break-even tool
https://.hbswk.hbs.edu/ Documents/ archive/docs/breakeven/xls

How much do changes in volume affect cost and profit? At what point does the firm break even? What is the most efficient level of capital assets to employ in the firm? A break-even chart is presented in Figure 5–1 (based on Table 5–1) to answer some of these questions. The number of units produced and sold is shown along the horizontal axis, and revenue and costs are shown along the vertical axis.

Fixed costs are $60,000 regardless of volume, and variable costs (at $0.80 per unit) are added to fixed costs to determine total costs at any point.[1] The total revenue line is determined by multiplying price ($2) and volume.

In Figure 5–1, the break-even point is 50,000 units and when multiplied by $2 (the price) results in BE of $100,000, when total costs and total revenue lines intersect. The numbers are as follows:

Break-even in Units = 50,000, in Dollars = $100,000				
Total Variable Costs (TVC)	Fixed Costs (FC)	Total Costs (TC)	Total Revenue (TR)	Operating Income (Loss)
(50,000 × $0.80)			(50,000 × $2)	
$40,000	$60,000	$100,000	$100,000	0

The break-even point in units may also be determined by use of a simple formula in which we divide fixed costs by the contribution margin on each unit sold. The contribution margin (CM) is defined as price (**P**) minus variable cost (VC) per unit.

$$CM = P - VC \quad (5–1)$$

$$BE = \frac{\text{Fixed costs}}{\text{Contribution margin}} = \frac{FC}{\text{Price} - VC} = \frac{FC}{CM} \quad (5–2)$$

$$\frac{\$60,000}{\$2 - \$0.80} = \frac{\$60,000}{\$1.20} = 50,000 \text{ units}$$

---

[1] Fixed costs, as used in the operating leverage analysis, include only fixed operating costs and do not include fixed financing charges.

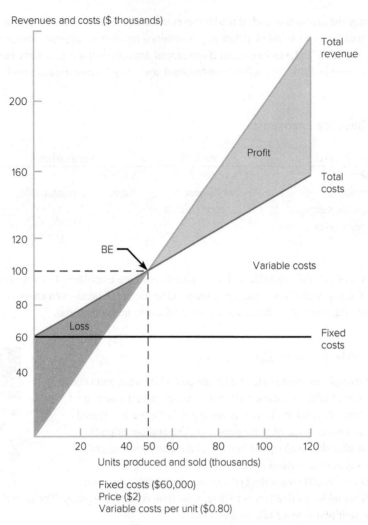

Figure 5–1 Break-even chart in dollars and units: leveraged firm

To calculate break-even in dollars, contribution margin must be calculated as a percentage as follows:

$$\frac{CM}{P} = \frac{\$2 - \$0.80}{\$2} = 0.60 = 60\%$$

To calculate break-even on a dollar–sales basis, fixed costs must be divided by the contribution margin of 60 percent as follows:

$$\frac{FC}{CM\%} = \frac{\$60,000}{0.60} = \$100,000$$

Since we are getting a $1.20 ($2 − .80) contribution toward covering fixed costs from each unit sold, minimum sales of 50,000 units will allow us to cover our fixed costs (50,000 units × $1.20 = $60,000 fixed costs). Once fixed costs are covered, we move into a highly profitable range in which each unit of sales brings an increase in operating profit of $1.20 per unit to the company. As sales increase from 50,000 to 60,000 units, operating profits increase by $12,000 as indicated in Table 5–3; as sales increase from 60,000 to 80,000 units, profits increase by another $24,000; and so on. As further indicated in Table 5–3 below, at low sales volumes such as 40,000 or 20,000 units, our losses are substantial ($12,000 and $36,000 in the red).

Assume that the firm depicted in Figure 5–1 is operating with a high degree of leverage. The situation is analogous to that of an airline, which must carry a certain number of people on board to break even; a very profitable range, however, is beyond that point.

Table 5–3 Volume-cost-profit analysis: leveraged firm

Units Sold	Total Variable Costs	Fixed Costs	Total Costs	Total Revenue	Operating Income (Loss)
0	0	$ 60,000	$ 60,000	0	$ (60,000)
20,000	$ 16,000	60,000	76,000	$ 40,000	(36,000)
40,000	32,000	60,000	92,000	80,000	(12,000)
50,000 (BE)	40,000	60,000	100,000	100,000	0
60,000	48,000	60,000	108,000	120,000	12,000
80,000	64,000	60,000	124,000	160,000	36,000
100,000	80,000	60,000	140,000	200,000	60,000

Limitations of break-even analysis include that it ignores the following:

- The timing of cash flows (time value of money (present value) analysis in Chapter 9)
- The opportunity cost of having monies invested in the capital assets and not available for other uses
- Cash flows; only accounting income is considered at this point

This is of major importance, as the fixed costs (cash outflows) are usually incurred at the beginning of a project when assets are bought, compared with discounted cash inflows, reduced to present values, received in later years.

A More Conservative Approach

Not all firms would choose to operate at the high degree of operating leverage exhibited in Figure 5–1. Fear of not selling the 50,000-unit break-even level may discourage some companies from heavy utilization of capital assets. More expensive variable costs may be substituted for automated plant and equipment. Assume that fixed costs for a more conservative firm can be reduced to $12,000, but that variable costs will go from $0.80 to $1.60. If the same price assumption of $2 per unit is employed, the break-even level is 30,000 units.

$$BE = \frac{FC}{CM} = \frac{\$12,000}{\$2 - \$1.60} = \frac{\$12,000}{\$0.40} = 30,000 \text{ units}$$

With fixed costs reduced from $60,000 to $12,000, the loss potential is small. Furthermore, the break-even level of operations is a comparatively low 30,000 units. Nevertheless, the use of a virtually unleveraged approach has cut into the potential profitability of the more conservative firm due to high variable costs, as indicated in Figure 5–2.

Even at high levels of sales, the potential profit is rather small. As indicated in Table 5–4, at a 100,000-unit volume, operating income is only $28,000, which is $32,000 less than that of the leveraged firm in Table 5–3.

Table 5–4 Volume-cost-profit analysis: Conservative firm

Units Sold	Total Variable Costs	Fixed Costs	Total Costs	Total Revenue	Operating Income (Loss)
0	0	$12,000	$12,000	0	$(12,000)
20,000	$32,000	12,000	44,000	$40,000	(4,000)
30,000 (BE)	48,000	12,000	60,000	60,000	0
40,000	64,000	12,000	76,000	80,000	4,000
60,000	96,000	12,000	108,000	120,000	12,000
80,000	128,000	12,000	140,000	160,000	20,000
100,000	160,000	12,000	172,000	200,000	28,000

Figure 5–2 Break-even chart: conservative firm (low risk)

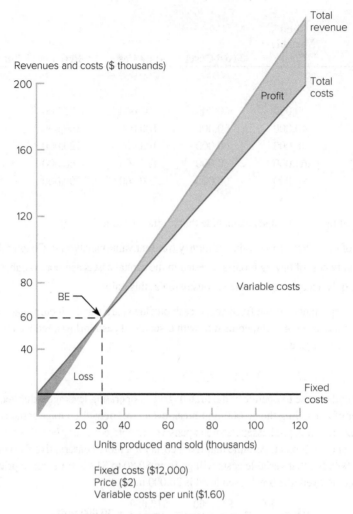

Fixed costs ($12,000)
Price ($2)
Variable costs per unit ($1.60)

The Risk Factor

Greater leverage (higher risk) can be taken on

- When the source of repayment appears to have greater certainty
- In more mature industries with larger capital requirements
- In times of strong and continuing economic growth
- To maintain or establish a competitive position
- To achieve the best possible return within an acceptable level of risk

For a small business competing in an emerging industry in which the market potential is not yet fully understood and the technology is not standardized, locking the firm into fixed costs that require high sales volume based on unproven technology is highly risky. On the other hand, a firm competing in the pulp and paper industry, where the markets are large but growing slowly and the production processes are highly developed, must invest in high-cost (but very efficient at high volumes) plant and equipment.

If management is apprehensive about economic conditions, a more conservative plan may be undertaken. To a certain extent, management should tailor the use of leverage to meet its own risk-taking policy. Those who are risk-averse (prefer less risk) will invest less in fixed assets but production capacity is limited. Firms willing to take higher risk may be willing to invest in more fixed assets resulting in greater capacity. The pace of technological change today may dictate the need to reinvest continually to remain competitive.

Cash Break-Even Analysis

Our discussion to this point has dealt with break-even analysis in accounting flows rather than cash flows. For example, amortization is included in fixed expenses, but it represents an accounting entry rather than an explicit expenditure of funds. To the extent that we were doing break-even analysis on a strictly cash basis, noncash expenses (amortization) would be excluded from fixed expenses. Accounting break-even analysis by including amortization gives a longer-term perspective to our analysis. In the example of the leveraged firm in formula 5–2, if we eliminate $20,000 of assumed amortization from fixed costs, the break-even level is reduced to 33,333 units.

$$\frac{FC - Amortization}{CM} = \frac{\$60,000 - \$20,000}{\$2 - \$0.80} = \frac{\$40,000}{\$1.20} = 33,333 \text{ units}$$

Other adjustments could also be made for noncash items. For example, sales may initially take the form of accounts receivable rather than cash, and the same can be said for the purchase of materials and accounts payable. An actual weekly or monthly cash budget would be necessary to isolate these items.

While cash break-even analysis is helpful in analyzing the short-term outlook of the firm, particularly when it may be in trouble, most break-even analysis is conducted on the basis of accounting flows rather than strictly cash flows. Most of the assumptions throughout the chapter are based on concepts broader than pure cash flows. This is a longer-term focus. In the short term, nothing is more important than cash flow.

Degree of Operating Leverage

Degree of operating leverage (DOL) may be defined as the percentage change in operating income that occurs as a result of a percentage change in units sold.

$$DOL = \frac{\text{Percent change in operating income}}{\text{Percent change in unit volume}} \quad (5\text{--}3)$$

Highly leveraged aggressive firms, such as those in the auto or construction industry, are likely to enjoy a rather substantial increase in profits as sales volume increases, whereas more conservative firms with less capacity will have lower sales and less profit. The degree of operating leverage should be computed only over a profitable range of operations. However, the closer DOL is computed to the company break-even point, the higher the number is, due to a large percentage increase in operating income.[2]

Let us apply the formula to the leveraged and conservative firms previously discussed. Their income or losses at various levels of operation are summarized in Table 5–5.

Table 5–5 Operating income or loss

Units	Leveraged Firm (Table 5–3) Income (Loss)	Conservative Firm (Table 5–4) Income (Loss)	
0	$(60,000)	$(12,000)	
20,000	(36,000)	(4,000)	
40,000	(12,000)	4,000	
60,000	12,000	12,000	Indifference point
80,000	36,000	20,000	
100,000	60,000	28,000	

---

[2] Although the value of DOL varies at each level of output, the beginning level of volume determines the DOL regardless of the location at the end point.

We now consider what happens to operating income as volume moves from 80,000 to 100,000 units, a 25 percent increase.

Leveraged Firm

$$DOL = \frac{\text{Percent change in operating income}}{\text{Percent change in unit volume}} = \frac{\frac{\$24,000}{\$36,000} \times 100}{\frac{\$20,000}{\$80,000} \times 100} = \frac{66.7\%}{25\%} = 2.67$$

Conservative Firm

$$DOL = \frac{\text{Percent change in operating income}}{\text{Percent change in unit volume}} = \frac{\frac{\$8,000}{\$20,000} \times 100}{\frac{\$20,000}{\$80,000} \times 100} = \frac{40\%}{25\%} = 1.60$$

We see that the degree of operating leverage is much greater for the leveraged firm, indicating at 80,000 units a 1 percent increase in volume will produce a 2.67 percent change in operating income versus a 1.60 percent increase for the conservative firm. The 25 percent sales increase has increased profits 67 percent (25% × 2.67) with the leveraged plan and 40 percent (25% × 1.60) with the conservative plan.

The degree of operating leverage measures the sensitivity of a firm's operating income to a change in sales. The higher the DOL, the more concerned the firm should be about any potential decrease in sales because of the potential negative impact on operating results. For instance, our leveraged firm is more susceptible to the loss of a major client.

The formula for DOL may be manipulated algebraically to produce

$$DOL = \frac{\text{Contribution margin}}{\text{Operating profit (EBIT)}} = \frac{CM}{EBIT} \quad (5\text{--}4)$$

For the leveraged firm (from Table 5–1),

$$DOL = \frac{\$96,000}{\$36,000} = 2.67$$

Sales less variable costs equals contribution margin. Sales, less variable costs, less fixed costs is operating profit, or EBIT. Therefore, the formula for degree of operating leverage may also be written as

$$DOL = \frac{Q(P - VC)}{Q(P - VC) - FC}$$

Where

Q = Quantity at which DOL is computed

P = Price per unit

VC = Variable costs per unit

FC = Fixed costs

Or, we can rewrite the second terms as

$QP = S$, or sales (Quantity × Price)

QVC = TVC, or total variable costs (Quantity × Variable costs per unit)

FC = Total fixed costs (remains the same term)

We then have

$$DOL = \frac{S - TVC}{S - TVC - FC}$$

Limitations of Analysis

Operating leverage analysis is limited by

* Assuming a constant, or linear, function exists for revenues and costs as volume changes
* Focusing on a limited time period

- Not accounting for the timing of cash flows
- Opportunity cost of an investment

In the real world, however, we may face price weakness as we attempt to capture an increasing market, or we may face cost overruns as we move beyond an optimum-size operation. Relationships are not as fixed as we have assumed. Nevertheless, the basic patterns we have studied are reasonably valid for most firms over an extended operating range (in our example, it might be between 20,000 and 100,000 units). It is only at the extreme levels that linear assumptions break down and nonlinear break-even analysis is required, as is indicated in Figure 5–3.

Figure 5–3 Nonlinear break-even analysis

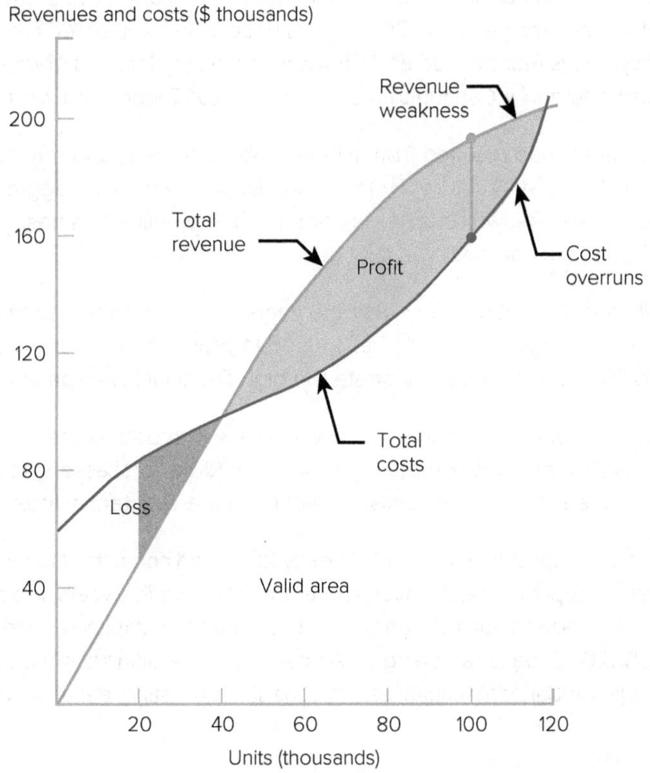

Analysis is usually over one year, although a new product or venture probably will not break even for a few years until the market for the product has developed. In such cases, one should analyze the break-even possibilities for the situation a few years later. Sales might increase at a lower rate while costs increase at higher rates due to production bottlenecks or dis-economies that result in higher repairs and labour costs. The result is the second break-even point leading to losses. The firm should aim for revenue and cost curves to be at the point which maximizes profits (100 thousand units in Figure 5–3).

LO4 FINANCIAL LEVERAGE

Financial leverage reflects the capital structure of the firm (mix of debt and equity [shares]). Debt carries a fixed obligation of interest payments and can greatly magnify the results at higher levels of operations. You may have heard of the real estate developer who borrows 100 percent of the costs of his project and enjoys an infinite return on his zero investment if all goes well. However, if revenues sag the interest payments still have to be made, whereas shareholders (equity) can wait for their returns if shares are issued to raise funds.

Leverage is a strategic choice by management based on its assessment of the risk, its potential cash flow, and the availability of financing. The overall financial choices available between short- and long-term financing options are identified in later chapters through Figures 6–11, 8–1 and 14–8. Corporate use of the capital markets in Canada is highlighted in Figure 14–4, with the tradeoffs for short-term financing alternatives examined in Chapter 8 and the longer-term choices covered in Chapters 16 (debt, leases) and 17 (shares).

Two firms can have equal operating capabilities and yet show widely different results because of differing uses of financial leverage.

 FINANCE IN ACTION

Big Leverage! Big Losses! Big Gains! Insolvency! Rebirth!

Air Canada is an international air carrier that, like many other carriers, has experienced financial difficulties over the years. By 2003 it was under court-appointed creditor protection due to insolvency. It was restructured as ACE Aviation Holding Inc. and gradually sold shares in the restructured Air Canada to the public until 2012 when ACE was liquidated.

Air Canada's problems had resulted from a slow global economy, decreased air travel after 9/11, and a high-cost structure. Furthermore, its problems were aggravated by its high degree of leverage, which is not uncommon in the airline business. Today, Air Canada is profitable and competitive.

Return on equity has fluctuated wildly over the years, and is often tied to the health of the economy. High leverage at Air Canada has helped to produce these dramatic swings in return on equity. The graphs below illustrate the high financial leverage at Air Canada.

Negative equity has been experienced in several years with debt sometimes representing over 100 percent of the capital structure (debt/total assets; formula 3–11). A high degree of financial leverage is also exhibited in the substantial interest payments.

On the operating leverage side, Air Canada in early 2020 had committed to more than $4.5 billion in capital expenditures for aircraft over the following five years, in addition to the $13 billion (book value) in aircraft currently in use.. The huge capital requirements for aircraft (over US$320 million for a Boeing 777) ensure that the airline business is one of high operating leverage. Air Canada's capital assets consist of operating leases and its own planes.

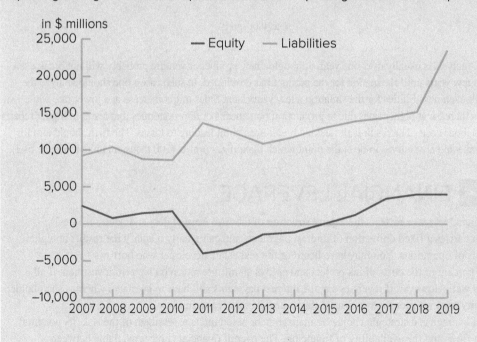

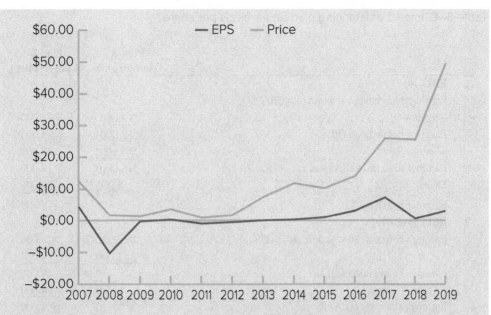

The combined effect of operating and financial leverage in the airline business requires the generation of large revenues and good control of operating costs to remain profitable. The combined leverage at Air Canada demonstrates the high risk combined with the potential for reward. Air Canada shares that were worth below $1 in 2011, were up to $50 by early 2020. However the Covid-19 pandemic reduced the shares to $12 within 2 months of the high. When earnings are positive, leverage magnifies returns on equity, but when the earnings are negative, losses are magnified and can be huge.

Q1 What is Air Canada's current capital structure?

Q2 Does it still have high operating and financial leverage?

aircanada.com/ca/en/aco/home/about/index.html   **boeing.com**
Symbol: AC   Symbol: BA (NYSE)

Impact on Earnings

In studying the impact of financial leverage, we examine two financial plans for a firm, each employing a significantly different amount of debt in the capital structure. Financing totalling $200,000 is required to carry the assets of the firm.[3]

	Total Assets—$200,000			
	Plan A (Leveraged)		**Plan B (Conservative)**	
Debt (8% interest)	$150,000	($12,000 interest)	$ 50,000	($4,000 interest)
Common stock	50,000	(8,000 shares at $6.25)	150,000	(24,000 shares at $6.25)
Total financing	$200,000		$200,000	

Under *leveraged* Plan A, we borrow $150,000 and sell 8,000 shares of stock at $6.25 to raise an additional $50,000; *conservative* Plan B calls for borrowing only $50,000 and acquiring an additional $150,000 in common stock with 24,000 shares.

---

[3]We have assumed that the share price does not change under the different plans for purposes of illustration. In reality, the different risk exposure of leverage and the potential for greater returns to shareholders would affect the share price.

Table 5–6 Impact of financing plan on earnings per share

		Plan A (Leveraged)	Plan B (Conservative)
1.	**EBIT (0)**		
	Earnings before interest and taxes (EBIT).............	0	0
	– Interest (*I*)......................................	$(12,000)	$ (4,000)
	Earnings before taxes (EBT)	(12,000)	(4,000)
	– Taxes (*T*)*......................................	(6,000)	(2,000)
	Earnings after taxes (EAT)	$(6,000)	$ (2,000)
	Shares..	8,000	24,000
	Earnings per share (EPS)...........................	$(0.75)	$(0.08)
2.	**EBIT ($12,000)**		
	Earnings before interest and taxes (EBIT).............	$12,000	$12,000
	– Interest (*I*)......................................	12,000	4,000
	Earnings before taxes (EBT)	0	8,000
	– Taxes (*T*)......................................	0	4,000
	Earnings after taxes (EAT)	$ 0	$ 4,000
	Shares..	8,000	24,000
	Earnings per share (EPS)...........................	0	$0.17
3.	**EBIT ($16,000) – Indifference Point (Same EPS)**		
	Earnings before interest and taxes (EBIT).............	$16,000	$16,000
	– Interest (*I*)......................................	12,000	4,000
	Earnings before taxes (EBT)	4,000	12,000
	– Taxes (*T*)	2,000	6,000
	Earnings after taxes (EAT)	$ 2,000	$ 6,000
	Shares..	8,000	24,000
	Earnings per share (EPS)...........................	$0.25	$0.25
4.	**EBIT ($36,000)**		
	Earnings before interest and taxes (EBIT).............	$36,000	$36,000
	– Interest (*I*)......................................	12,000	4,000
	Earnings before taxes (EBT)	24,000	32,000
	– Taxes (*T*)	12,000	16,000
	Earnings after taxes (EAT)	$12,000	$16,000
	Shares..	8,000	24,000
	Earnings per share (EPS)...........................	$1.50	$0.67
5.	**EBIT ($60,000)**		
	Earnings before interest and taxes (EBIT).............	$60,000	$60,000
	– Interest (*I*)......................................	12,000	4,000
	Earnings before taxes (EBT)	48,000	56,000
	– Taxes (*T*)	24,000	28,000
	Earnings after taxes (EAT)	$24,000	$28,000
	Shares..	8,000	24,000
	Earnings per share (EPS)...........................	$3.00	$1.17

*The assumption is that large losses can be written off against other income, perhaps in other years, thus providing the firm with a tax savings benefit. The tax rate is 50 percent.

In Table 5–6 we compute earnings per share (EPS) for the two plans at various levels of EBIT. These earnings represent the operating income of the firm—before deductions have been made for financial charges or taxes. We assume EBIT levels of 0, $12,000, $16,000, $36,000, and $60,000.

The impact of the two financing plans is dramatic. Although both plans assume the same operating income, or EBIT, for comparative purposes at each level (say $36,000 in calculation 4), the reported income per share is vastly different ($1.50 versus $0.67). It is also evident that the conservative plan produces better results at low income levels, but the leveraged plan generates much better EPS as operating income, or EBIT, goes up. The firm would be indifferent between the two plans at an EBIT level of $16,000, as indicated in Table 5–6.

In Figure 5–4, we graphically demonstrate the effect of the two financing plans on EPS. With an EBIT of $16,000 we are earning 8 percent on total assets of $200,000—precisely the percentage cost of borrowed funds to the firm. The use or nonuse of debt does not influence the answer. Beyond $16,000, Plan A, employing heavy financial leverage, really goes to work, allowing the firm to greatly expand EPS as a result of a change in EBIT.

Figure 5–4 Financing plans and earnings per share

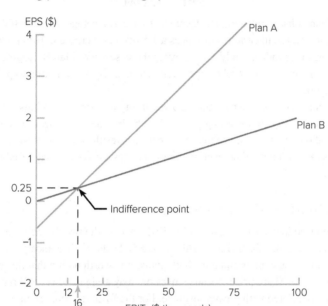

Degree of Financial Leverage

As was true of operating leverage, degree of financial leverage measures the effect of a change in one variable on another variable. Degree of financial leverage (DFL) may be defined as the percentage change in earnings (EPS) that occurs as a result of a percentage change in earnings before interest and taxes (EBIT).

$$DFL = \frac{\text{Percent change in EPS}}{\text{Percent change in EBIT}} \quad (5\text{–}5)$$

For purposes of computation, DFL may be stated as

$$DFL = \frac{\text{EBIT}}{\text{EBIT} - I}$$

$$I = \text{Interest}$$

The formula[4] for degree of financial leverage (DFL) related to the income statement is operating profit divided by earnings before taxes (EBT).

---

[4]If preferred shares are part of the capital structure, the denominator of the formula must be adjusted by subtracting the preferred dividend that has been increased to account for the non-tax-deductibility of dividend payments. This is achieved by dividing the preferred dividend by (1 − tax rate).

$$DFL = \frac{\text{Operating profit}}{\text{Earning before taxes (EBT)}} = \frac{\text{EBIT}}{\text{EBT}} \quad (5\text{--}6)$$

Let's compute the degree of financial leverage for Plan A and Plan B, presented in Table 5–6, at an EBIT level of $36,000. Plan A calls for $12,000 of interest at all levels of financing, and Plan B requires $4,000.

Plan A (Leveraged)

$$DFL = \frac{\text{EBIT}}{\text{EBT}} = \frac{\$36,000}{\$24,000} = 1.5$$

Plan B (Conservative)

$$DFL = \frac{\text{EBIT}}{\text{EBT}} = \frac{\$36,000}{\$32,000} = 1.1$$

As expected, Plan A has a much higher degree of financial leverage. At an EBIT level of $36,000, a 1 percent increase in earnings produces a 1.5 percent increase in EPS under Plan A. The same increase in earnings produces only a 1.1 percent increase under Plan B. Degree of financial leverage may be computed for any level of operation, and it changes from point to point, but Plan A always exceeds Plan B.

The degree of financial leverage measures the sensitivity of a firm's earnings available to shareholders, EPS, to a change in operating profits. The higher the DFL, the more concerned the firm should be about any potential decrease in operating results because of the potential impact on earnings. As with operating leverage, sales changes can have a magnified impact the greater the leverage.

LO5 The Indifference Point

A firm may be interested in determining the point, EBIT, where the two financing plans have an equal effect on earnings per share (EPS). This is the EBIT/EPS indifference point and will occur where net income per share is equal for both plans. It is worth noting that this point may not have an equal effect on share price, because investors may assign a lower P/E ratio to earnings with the higher risk associated with greater leverage. For the firm, it is important to assess the likelihood of exceeding or not exceeding the indifference point in operating results when deciding on a financing plan.

The indifference point between two financing plans is determined mathematically by

$$\frac{(\text{EBIT}^* - I_A)(1 - t)}{S_A} = \frac{(\text{EBIT}^* - I_B)(1 - t)}{S_B}$$

Where

$\text{EBIT}^* = $ Operating income at the indifference point
$I = $ Interest costs under Plans A and B
$S = $ Shares outstanding under Plans A and B
$t = $ Corporate tax rate

This formula can be simplified to

$$\text{EBIT}^* = \frac{S_B \times I_A - S_A \times I_B}{S_B - S_A} \quad (5\text{--}7)$$

For our example the indifference point is

$$\text{EBIT}^* = \frac{(24,000 \times \$12,000) - (8,000 \times \$4,000)}{24,000 - 8,000}$$

$$= \$16,000$$

This is the same result we obtained in Table 5–6.

Valuation Basics with Financial Leverage

The question arises that if debt is such a good thing, why sell any stock? (Perhaps one share for yourself!) With exclusive debt financing at an EBIT level of $36,000, we would have a DFL factor of 1.8.

$$\text{DFL} = \frac{\text{EBIT}}{\text{EBIT} - I} = \frac{\$36,000}{\$36,000 - \$16,000} = 1.8$$

(With no stock, we would borrow the full $200,000.)

$$(8\% \times \$200,000 = \$16,000 \text{ interest})$$

As is stressed throughout the text, debt financing and financial leverage offer unique advantages, but only up to a point. Beyond that point, debt financing may be detrimental to the firm. As the firm expands the use of debt in its capital structure, lenders may perceive a greater risk for the firm. They may then raise the interest rate to be paid, and may demand that certain restrictions be placed on the firm. Furthermore, concerned common shareholders may drive down the price of the stock because of their increased risk. This moves the firm away from the *objective of maximizing the firm's overall value* in the market. The overall impact of financial leverage must be carefully weighed.

This is not to say that financial leverage does not work to the benefit of the firm. It does, if properly used within an acceptable risk level. Further discussion of appropriate debt-equity mixes is covered in Chapter 11. For now, we accept the virtues of financial leverage, knowing that we face a tradeoff between the higher potential returns to shareholders and the greater risk of failing to meet our financial obligations.

The use of some debt is recommended for firms in industries that offer some stability, are in positive stages of growth, and are operating in favourable economic conditions. In the cases of large utilities, operating cash flows can be forecasted within narrow ranges, thus favouring the use of higher leverage to maximize share values. This is because of the relative certainty of the cash flows. On the other hand, for companies in industries open to cyclicality or other causes of revenue volatility, the use of high levels of leverage may become the cause of significant financial distress and depressed share prices. The small business may be limited in its ability to borrow from banks or capital markets, but it should consider the use of trade credit from suppliers as a means of leveraging its investment. Trade credit is a debt obligation that, if prudently used, can enhance the performance of the small firm.

FINANCE IN ACTION

Leverage of Seventeen Times Equity

The Royal Bank is the largest bank in Canada, with assets of over $1.4 trillion by 2019. With these assets, the Royal Bank received only a 0.80 percent return on its assets. This still represented a rather large net annual income of about $11.4 billion. Personally, we might expect to maybe receive this return on our savings accounts at the banks. However, the common shareholders at the Royal Bank did receive a 13.7 percent return on their equity investment (book value).

This large difference in the return to equity as compared to return on assets is the result of the tremendous financial leverage employed by the Royal Bank (and all banks). The majority of the bank's liabilities are loans from the general public by way of deposit accounts. Chequing and savings accounts are loans to the bank! The Royal Bank's debt accounts for 94 percent of total liabilities and equities. Total assets were 17.1 times its equity. This allowed it to magnify its low return on assets to achieve a quite satisfactory return to shareholders.

Before the Great Recession of 2008 some banks operated with leverage at 40 to 50 times equity capital. This was ripe for problems.

In effect, the ROA is multiplied by the degree of financial leverage to obtain the ROE:

$$0.80\% \times 17.1 = 13.7\%$$

The leverage employed by our banks helps to explain their conservative lending practices. They must ensure that revenues are maintained or the leverage will work against them.

Q1 What is the latest ROA and ROE at the Royal Bank?

rbc.com
Symbol: RY

Leveraged Buyout

During the late 1980s, leveraged buyouts were all the rage. These buyouts are act of purchasing a corporation's common shares (control) with borrowed money. Buyers hope to eventually repay that borrowed money by selling assets of the acquired corporation or by borrowing monies against the remaining assets of the corporation. These borrowings are often referred to as junk bonds, as the security is weak with leverage ratios, or debt-to-equity ratios, often in double digits. In effect, a corporation is bought with its own assets and borrowing power. It is, however, a much riskier (high debt) corporation after the changes. During the 1980s, the Canadian firm Campeau Corporation acquired Federated Department Stores (Macy's) and Allied Stores of the United States for a total of $11.6 billion, with about 97 percent borrowed money. Both U.S. companies went into bankruptcy protection (referred to as "Chapter 11" in U.S. bankruptcy law), as their cash flows were insufficient to meet the huge debt burden. The parent company, Campeau Corporation, had its common share price plunge below $1 from above $22 in less than half a year. It was a spectacular failure.

Macy*s (Federated Department Stores Inc.)
macysinc.com

With cheap money in the 2000s, leveraged buyouts returned. From 2004 to 2007, during a good economy and low interest rates, a leveraged buyout was a good strategy to acquire other firms. However, it is less common during the recessions and tight money policies.

In 2008, the Ontario Teachers' Pension Fund and a partner attempted to acquire BCE for $35 billion with $32 billion in debt provided by a syndicate of financial institutions. Sport teams that are failing in one city are often acquired by investors in another city using high levels of debt to be paid, it is hoped, with higher revenues from fans.

As firms in a given industry tend to face similar levels of business risk, investors and financial analysts often compare a firm's level of financial leverage to industry averages to estimate whether it is excessive. It is, therefore, incumbent on management to justify any decision to employ a higher amount of leverage than most other firms in its industry.

Information on financial leverage for selected Canadian industries is presented in Figure 5–5. We note that more volatile industries, such as oil and gas or mining, have a lower proportion of long-term debt to equity as compared to an industry such as utilities that tends to have more stable cash flows. It is the stability of cash flows that allows firms to commit more significant interest payments without inviting trouble if cash flows and income drop. Real estate seems to be an exception to this "rule of thumb" because of its requirement for long-term funding through mortgages. Also noteworthy is the heavy reliance on short-term debt in the agricultural and retail trade sectors, because of the large proportion of short-term assets in these industries.

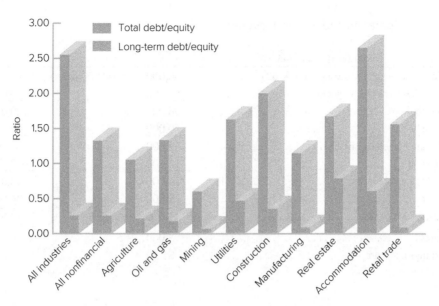

Figure 5–5 Financial leverage and earnings in selected industries

LO6 COMBINING OPERATING AND FINANCIAL LEVERAGE

If both operating and financial leverage allow us to magnify our returns, we get maximum leverage through combined leverage. We have said that operating leverage affects primarily the asset structure of the firm, whereas financial leverage affects the debt-equity mix. Combined leverage identifies the business and financial strategic decisions of the firm and the overall risk that it faces. This is represented in Figure 5–6.

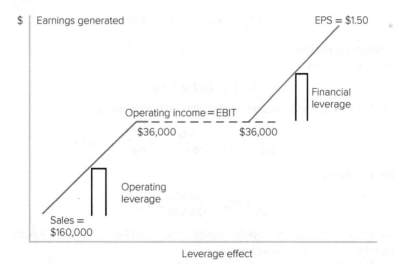

Figure 5–6 Combining operating and financial leverage

Degree of Combined Leverage

Degree of combined leverage (DCL) uses the entire income statement and shows the effect of a change in sales or volume on bottom-line earnings per share. Degree of operating leverage and degree of financing leverage are, in effect, being combined. Table 5–7 shows what happens to profitability as the firm's sales go from $160,000 (80,000 units) to $200,000 (100,000 units).

Table 5–7 Operating and financial leverage

(Taken from Table 5–6)			
Sales (total revenue) (80,000 units @ $2)	$160,000	(100,000 units)	$200,000
– Variable costs ($0.80 per unit)	64,000		80,000
Contribution margin	96,000		120,000
– Fixed costs	60,000		60,000
Operating income = EBIT	36,000		60,000
– Interest	12,000		12,000
Earnings before taxes	24,000		48,000
– Taxes	12,000		24,000
Earnings after taxes	$ 12,000		$ 24,000
Shares	8,000		8,000
Earnings per share	$1.50		$3.00

The formula for degree of combined leverage (DCL) is stated as

$$DCL = \frac{\text{Percent changes in EPS}}{\text{Percent change in sales (or volume)}} \quad (5\text{--}8)$$

Using our previous calculations we find

$$\underset{\substack{\text{Degree of operating}\\\text{leverage (DOL)}}}{} \times \underset{\substack{\text{Degree of financial}\\\text{leverage (DFL)}}}{} = \underset{\substack{\text{Degree of combined}\\\text{leverage (DCL)}}}{}$$

$$\frac{\% \text{ change in EBIT}}{\% \text{ change in unit volume}} \times \frac{\% \text{ change in EPS}}{\% \text{ change in EBIT}} = \frac{\% \text{ change in EPS}}{\% \text{ change in unit volume}}$$

Combining both leverage formulas:

$$DCL = DOL \times DFL \quad (5\text{--}9)$$

From previous calculations:
For Plan A (Leveraged)

$$DCL = 2.67 \times 1.5 = 4$$

The formula for DCL may be manipulated algebraically to produce

$$DCL = \frac{\text{Contribution margin}}{\text{Earnings before taxes}} = \frac{CM}{EBT} \quad (5\text{--}10)$$

For Plan A (Leveraged)

$$DCL = \frac{\$96,000}{\$24,000} = 4$$

This tells us that every percentage-point change in sales will be reflected in a 4 percent change in EPS at this level of operation (quite an impact).

The formula for degree of combined leverage (DCL) may also be written as

$$DCL = \frac{Q(P - VC)}{Q(P - VC) - FC - I}$$

$$\text{or } DCL = \frac{S - TVC}{S - TVC - FC - I}$$

The combined leverage is the result of the reduction in earnings from FC (fixed costs of operating leverage) and from I (interest expense of financial leverage).

A Word of Caution

In a sense, we are piling risk on risk as the two different forms of leverage are combined. Perhaps a firm carrying heavy operating leverage may wish to moderate its position financially, and vice versa. One thing is certain—the decision will have a major impact on the operations of the firm.

 FINANCE IN ACTION

Why Japanese Firms Tend to Be So Competitive

What do firms such as Sony, Honda, Fujitsu, Hitachi, and Mitsubushi have in common? They all are not only Japanese companies but also highly leveraged, from both operational and financing perspectives.

Japanese companies are world leaders in bringing high technology into their firms to replace slower, more expensive labour. They are known for automated factories, laser technology, robotics, memory chips, digital processing, and other scientific endeavours. Furthermore, the country has government groups such as the Ministry of International Trade and Industry (MITI) and the Science and Technology Agency encouraging further investment and growth through government grants and shared research.

To enjoy the benefits of this technology, Japanese firms have a high fixed-cost commitment. Obviously high initial-cost technology cannot be easily "laid off" if business slows down. Even the labour necessary to design and operate the technology has somewhat of a fixed-cost element associated with it.

Not only does the Japanese economy have high operating leverage as described above, but also Japanese companies have high financial leverage. The typical Japanese company has a debt-to-equity ratio two to three times higher than its counterparts in Canada. The reason is that credit tends to be more available in Japan because of the traditional relationship between an industrial firm and its bank. They may both be part of the same cartel or trading company with interlocking directors (directors that serve on both boards). Under such an arrangement, a bank is willing to make a larger loan commitment to an industrial firm, and there's a shared humiliation if the credit arrangement goes bad. Canadian banks move in immediately to cancel loans at the first sign of a borrower's weakness. None of these comments imply that Japanese firms do not default on their loans. There were, in fact, a number of bad loans sitting on the books of Japanese banks in the early 2000s.

The key point is that Japanese firms have high operating leverage as well as high financial leverage, and that makes them act very competitively. If a firm has a combined leverage of 6 or 8 times, as many Japanese firms do, the loss of unit sales can be disastrous. Leverage magnifies not only returns as volume increases but also losses as volume decreases. As an example, a Japanese firm that is in danger of losing an order is likely to drastically cut prices or take whatever action is necessary to maintain its sales volume. A general rule of business is that firms that are exposed to high leverage are likely to act aggressively to cover their large fixed costs, and this rule certainly applies to leading Japanese firms. This, of course, may well be a virtue, because it ensures that a firm will remain market-oriented and progressive.

Q1 Determine the leverage ratios for one of these identified firms.

sony.com

honda.com

fujitsu.com

hitachi.com

mitsubushi-motors.com

SUMMARY

1. Leverage may be defined as the use of fixed-cost items to magnify returns at high levels of operation. (LO1)

2. Break-even, in terms of unit sales volume, occurs when the total revenues equal the total costs for a period of time, usually for a one-year period. Linear break-even analysis assumes a linear relationship between revenues and costs, resulting in higher profits as revenues increase. Nonlinear break-even, a more realistic approach, considers a slow-down in revenue increases while dis-economies and bottlenecks contribute to a greater increase in costs resulting in a second break-even point. (LO2)

3. Operating leverage primarily affects fixed versus variable-cost utilization in the operation of the firm. An important concept, degree of operating leverage (DOL) measures the percentage change in operating income as a result of a percentage change in volume. With heavier utilization of fixed-cost assets, DOL is likely to be higher. Once the break-even point is reached, returns are magnified by the more efficient use of the fixed resource. Break-even is often calculated on accounting income for a longer-term perspective, whereas cash flow break-even focuses on more immediate needs. (LO3)

4. Financial leverage reflects the extent to which debt is used in the capital structure of the firm. Substantial use of debt places a great burden on the firm at low levels of profitability but helps to magnify earnings per share (EPS) as volume or operating income increases. The degree of financial leverage (DFL) measures the percentage change in earnings per share (EPS) for a percentage change in earnings before interest and taxes (EBIT). (LO4)

5. A level of operating income where the firm's results based on earnings per share are equal between two financing plans is calculated as the indifference point. The two financing plans usually involve the degree of financial leverage (DFL) being applied in each plan. (LO5)

6. We combine operating and financial leverage to assess the effect of all types of assets on the firm. There is a multiplier effect when we use the two different types of leverage. Because leverage is a two-edged sword, management must be sure the level of risk assumed is in accord with its desires for risk and its perceptions of the future. High operating leverage may be balanced against lower financial leverage if this is deemed desirable, and vice versa. (LO6)

REVIEW OF FORMULAS

$$CM = P - VC \tag{5-1}$$

P = Price
VC = Variable costs

$$BE = \frac{FC}{CM} \tag{5-2}$$

BE = Break-even point
FC = Fixed costs

$$DOL = \frac{CM}{EBIT} \tag{5-4}$$

DOL = Degree of operating leverage
EBIT = Earnings before interest and taxes

$$DFL = \frac{EBIT}{EBT} \tag{5-6}$$

DFL = Degree of financial leverage
EBT = Earnings before taxes

$$EBIT^* = \frac{S_B \times I_A - S_A \times I_B}{S_B - S_A}$$ (5–7)

EBIT*is operating income at the indifference point
I is interest costs under Plans *A* and *B*
S is shares outstanding under Plans *A* and *B*

$$DCL = \frac{\text{Percent changes in EPS}}{\text{Percent change in sales(or volume)}}$$ (5–8)

$$DCL = DOL \times DFL$$ (5–9)

DCL = Degree of combined leverage

$$DCL = \frac{CM}{EBT}$$ (5–10)

Alternatively the formulas can be written as

$$DOL = \frac{Q(P - VC)}{Q(P - VC) - FC} = \frac{S - TVC}{S - TVC - FC}$$

$$DFL = \frac{EBIT}{EBIT - I}$$

$$DOL = \frac{Q(P - VC)}{Q(P - VC) - FC - I} = \frac{S - TVC}{S - TVC - FC - I}$$

Where
  Q = Quantity
  P = Price per unit
  VC = Variable cost per unit
  FC = Fixed costs
  S = Sales
  TVC = Total variable costs
  I = Interest

DISCUSSION QUESTIONS

1. Discuss the various uses for both linear and nonlinear break-even analysis. (LO2)

2. Which factors would cause a difference between the use of financial leverage for a utility company and an automobile company? (LO1)

3. Explain how the break-even point and operating leverage are affected by the choice of manufacturing facilities (labour-intensive versus capital-intensive). (LO1, LO2)

4. What role does amortization play in break-even analysis based on accounting flows? Based on cash flows? Which perspective is longer term in nature? (LO2)

5. What does risk taking have to do with the use of operating and financial leverage? (LO3, LO4)

6. Discuss the limitations of financial leverage. (LO4, LO5)

7. How does the interest rate on new debt influence the use of financial leverage? (LO4, LO5)

8. Explain how combined leverage brings together operating income and EPS. (LO6)

9. Explain why operating leverage decreases as a company increases sales and shifts away from the break-even point. (LO2, LO3)

10. Why does the starting level of sales determine the degree of operating leverage (DOL) rather than the ending level of sales? (LO3)

11. One could say that financial leverage has its most important impact on EPS rather than net income after taxes. How would you support this statement? (LO4)

12. Does being at the EPS indifference point mean that you are always indifferent between two financing plans? Explain. (LO5)

13. Discuss the concept of operating leverage as it would apply to a major, independent television broadcaster. (LO3)

14. Explore the failure of leveraged buyouts (LBO) in the 80s and 90s by Campeau Corporation and other firms in comparison to LBOs between 2005 and 2008. What are the current factors that affect the use of LBO? (LO4)

INTERNET RESOURCES AND QUESTIONS

The latest financial statements of publicly traded Canadian companies are available at sedar.com.

1. Based on the latest available financial results (note the date), calculate and comment on the DOL, DFL, and DCL of the following companies:
   a. Air Canada
   b. Royal Bank
   c. Onex
   d. Encana (Ovintiv)

Explain the relationship between operating and financial leverage for each company and the resultant combined leverage. What accounts for the differences in leverage among these companies?

PROBLEMS

1. SUS Appliance toasters sell for $20 per unit, and the variable cost to produce them is $15. SUS estimates that the fixed costs are $80,000.
   a. Compute the break-even point in units.
   b. Fill in the table below (in dollars) to illustrate that the break-even point has been achieved.

Sales	_____
– Variable costs	_____
Contribution margin	_____
– Fixed costs	_____
Total operating profit (loss)	_____

2. The Harmon Corporation manufactures bats with Larry Walker's autograph stamped on them. Each bat sells for $25 and has a variable cost of $14. There is $40,000 in fixed costs involved in the production process.
   a. Compute the break-even point in units.
   b. Find the sales (in units) needed to earn a profit of $25,000.

3. Ensco Lighting Company has fixed costs of $100,000, sells its units for $28, and has variable costs of $15.50 per unit.
   a. Compute the break-even point.

b. Ms. Watts comes up with a new plan to cut fixed costs to $75,000. However, more labour will now be required, which will increase variable costs per unit to $17. The sales price will remain at $28. What is the new break-even point?

c. Under the new plan, what is likely to happen to profitability at very high volume levels (compared to the old plan)?

4. Air Filter Ltd. sells its products for $6 per unit. It has the following costs.

Rent	$100,000	Factory labour	$1.20 per unit
Executive salaries	89,000	Raw materials	0.60 per unit

Separate the expenses between fixed and variable costs per unit. Using this information and the sales price per unit of $6, compute the break-even point.

5. Shawn Penn and Pencils has fixed costs of $80,000. Its product currently sells for $5 per unit and has variable costs per unit of $2.50. Mr. Bic, the head of manufacturing, proposes to buy new equipment that will cost $400,000 and increase fixed costs to $120,000. Although the price will remain at $5 per unit, the increased automation will reduce variable costs per unit to $2.00.

a. Calculate the break-even point before and after acquiring the new equipment.

b. Find the required sales (in units) to generate a profit that represents a 30 percent return on the fixed costs before and after acquiring the new equipment.

6. Calloway Cab Company computes its break-even point strictly on the basis of cash expenditures related to fixed costs. Its total fixed costs are $400,000, but 20 percent of this value is represented by amortization. Its contribution margin (price minus variable cost) for each unit sold is $3.60. How many units does the firm need to sell to reach the cash break-even point?

7. Air Purifier Inc. computes its break-even point strictly on the basis of cash expenditures related to fixed costs. Its total fixed costs are $2,450,000, but 15 percent of this value is represented by amortization. Its contribution margin (price minus variable cost) for each unit is $40. How many units does the firm need to sell to reach the cash break-even point?

8. Base Timber Company computes its break-even point strictly on the basis of cash expenditures related to fixed costs. Its total fixed costs are $6,500,000, but 10 percent of this value is represented by amortization. Its contribution margin (price minus variable cost) for each unit is $9. How many units does the firm need to sell to reach the cash break-even point?

9. Draw two break-even graphs—one for a conservative firm using labour-intensive production and another for a capital-intensive aggressive firm. Assuming these companies compete within the same industry and have identical sales, explain the impact of changes in sales volume on both firms' profits.

10. The Sterling Tire Company's income statement for 20XX is as follows:

STERLING TIRE COMPANY
Income Statement
Year Ended December 31, 20XX

Sales (20,000 tires at $60 each)	$1,200,000
Less: Variable costs (20,000 tires at $30)	600,000
Contribution margin.	600,000
Less: Fixed costs	400,000
Earnings before interest and taxes (EBIT).	200,000
Interest expense	50,000
Earnings before taxes (EBT)	150,000
Income tax expense (34%).	51,000
Earnings after taxes (EAT)	$ 99,000

Given this income statement, compute the following:

a. Degree of operating leverage.

b. Degree of financial leverage.

c. Degree of combined leverage: Comment on the impact of a 20 percent increase in sales. Does financial or operating leverage have the greater impact?

d. Break-even point in units.

e. Break-even point considering the interest expense as a fixed cost.

11. Freudian Slips and Gowns, Inc.'s income statement for 20XX is as follows:

FREUDIAN SLIPS AND GOWNS
Income Statement
Year Ended December 31, 20XX

Sales (30,000 units at $25).............................	$750,000
Less: Variable costs (30,000 units at $7)................	210,000
Contribution margin.....................................	540,000
Less: Fixed costs	270,000
Operating profit or (EBIT)..............................	270,000
Interest expense	170,000
Earnings before taxes (EBT)	100,000
Income tax expense (25%)................................	25,000
Earnings after taxes (EAT)	$ 75,000

Given this income statement, compute the following:

a. Degree of operating leverage.

b. Degree of financial leverage.

c. Degree of combined leverage: Comment on the impact of a 30 percent increase in sales. Does financial or operating leverage have the greater impact?

d. Break-even point in units.

e. Break-even point considering the interest expense as a fixed cost.

12. Mo's Delicious Burgers Inc. sells food to university cafeterias for $15 a box. The fixed costs of this operation are $80,000, while the variable cost per box is $10.

a. What is the break-even point in boxes?

b. Calculate the profit or loss on 15,000 boxes and 30,000 boxes.

c. What is the DOL at 20,000 boxes and 30,000 boxes? Why does the DOL change as quantity sold increases?

d. If the firm has an annual interest payment of $10,000, calculate the DFL at both 20,000 and 30,000 boxes.

e. What is the DCL at both sales levels?

13. Cain Auto Supplies and Able Auto Parts are competitors in the aftermarket for auto supplies. The separate capital structures for Cain and Able are presented below.

Cain		Able	
Debt @ 10%..............	$ 50,000	Debt @ 10%..............	$100,000
Common stock............	100,000	Common stock............	50,000
Total..................	$150,000	Total..................	$150,000
Common shares...........	10,000	Common shares...........	5,000

a. Compute EPS if EBIT are $10,000, $15,000, and $50,000 (assume a 30 percent tax rate).

b. Explain the relationship between EPS and level of EBIT.

c. If the cost of debt went up to 12 percent and all other factors remained equal, what would be the indifference point for EBIT?

14. In the previous problem, compute the stock price for Cain Auto Supplies if it sells at 12 times EPS and EBIT is $40,000.

15. International Data Systems' information on revenue and costs is relevant only up to a sales volume of 105,000 units. After 105,000 units, the market becomes saturated and the price per unit falls from $14.00 to $8.80. Also, there are cost overruns at a production volume of over 105,000 units, and variable cost per unit goes up from $7.00 to $8.00. Fixed costs remain the same at $55,000.

a. Compute operating income at 105,000 units.

b. Compute operating income at 205,000 units.

16. Black Berry Farms and Pea Pod Farms are each able to generate EBIT of $120,000. The separate capital structures for Black Berry and Pea Pod are presented below.

Black Berry		Pea Pod	
Debt @ 7%...............	$ 600,000	Debt @ 7%...............	$ 200,000
Common stock............	500,000	Common stock............	900,000
Total.................	$1,100,000	Total.................	$1,100,000
Common shares	80,000	Common shares	144,000

a. Compute EPS for both firms (assume a 20 percent tax rate).

b. Assuming a P/E ratio of 18 for each firm, what would be each firm's share price?

c. Assume the P/E ratio would be 15 for the riskier company in terms of heavy debt utilization in the capital structure and 21 for the less risky firm. What would the share price now be for each firm?

d. Based on the evidence in part c, should management be concerned about the impact of financing plans on EPS or should share price also be considered?

17. Firms in Japan often employ both high operating and financial leverage because of the use of modern technology and close borrower-lender relationships. Assume the Mitaka Company has a sales volume of 125,000 units at a price of $25 per unit; variable costs are $5 per unit and fixed costs are $1,800,000. Interest expense is $400,000. What is the DCL for this Japanese firm?

18. The capital structure for Cain Supplies is presented below. Compute the share price for Cain if it sells at 19 times earnings per share and EBIT is $50,000. The tax rate is 20 percent.

Debt @ 9%...	$100,000
Common stock $10 par	200,000
Total...	$300,000
Common shares	20,000

19. Sterling Optical and Royal Optical both make glass frames and each is able to generate earnings before interest and taxes of $132,000. The separate capital structures for Sterling and Royal are shown here:

	Sterling	Royal
Debt @ 12%	$ 660,000	$ 220,000
Common stock, $5 par	440,000	880,000
Total	$1,100,000	$1,100,000
Common shares	88,000	176,000

a. Compute earnings per share for both firms. Assume a 25 percent tax rate.

b. In part a, you should have reached the same answer for both companies' earnings per share. Assuming a P/E ratio of 22 for each company, what would its share price be?

c. Now as part of your analysis, assume the P/E ratio would be 16 for the riskier company in terms of heavy debt utilization in the capital structure and 24 for the less risky company. What would the share prices for the two firms be under these assumptions? (Note: Although interest rates also would likely be different based on risk, we will hold them constant for ease of analysis.)

d. Based on the evidence in part c, should management be concerned only about the impact of financing plans on earnings per share, or should shareholders' wealth maximization (share price) be considered as well?

20. Sinclair Manufacturing and Boswell Brothers Inc. are both involved in the production of tile for the home-building industry. Their financial information is as follows:

Capital Structure		
	Sinclair	**Boswell**
Debt @ 12%..	$ 600,000	0
Common stock, $10 per share	400,000	1,000,000
	$1,000,000	$1,000,000
Common shares	40,000	100,000
Operating Plan		
Sales (50,000 units at $20 each).........................	$1,000,000	$1,000,000
Less: Variable costs	800,000	500,000
	($16 per unit)	($10 per unit)
Fixed costs	0	300,000
Earnings before interest and taxes (EBIT).................	$ 200,000	$ 200,000

a. If you combine Sinclair's capital structure with Boswell's operating plan, what is the DCL?

b. If you combine Boswell's capital structure with Sinclair's operating plan, what is the DCL?

c. Explain why you got the results you did in parts a and b.

d. In part b, if sales double, by what percentage will EPS increase?

21. DeSoto Tools, Inc. is planning to expand production. The expansion will cost $300,000, which can either be financed by bonds at an interest rate of 14 percent or by selling 10,000 shares of common stock at $30 per share. The current income statement before expansion is as follows:

DESOTO TOOLS, INC.
Income Statement
Year Ended Dec. 31, 20XX

Sales..	$1,500,000
Variable costs (30%)	450,000
Contribution margin.................................	1,050,000
Fixed costs	550,000
EBIT..	500,000
Interest expense	100,000
Earnings before taxes................................	400,000
Taxes @ 34%	136,000
Earnings after taxes	$ 264,000
Shares...	100,000
EPS...	$ 2.64

After the expansion, sales are expected to increase by $1,000,000. Variable costs will remain at 30 percent of sales, and fixed costs will increase to $800,000. The tax rate is 34 percent.

a. Calculate the DOL, the DFL, and the DCL before expansion. Explain the effects on earnings of a sales increase.

b. Construct the income statement for the two financial plans.

c. Calculate the DOL, the DFL, and the DCL, after expansion, for the two financing plans.

d. Calculate the EBIT/EPS indifference point with the formula in the chapter.

e. Explain which financing plan you favour and the risks involved.

22. Dickinson Company has $12 million in assets. Currently, half of these assets are financed with long-term debt at 10 percent, and half are financed with common stock. Ms. Smith, vice-president of finance, wishes to analyze two refinancing plans, one with more debt (D) and one with more equity (E). The company earns a return on assets before interest and taxes of 10 percent. The tax rate is 45 percent.

Under Plan D, a $3 million long-term bond would be sold at an interest rate of 12 percent and 375,000 shares of stock would be purchased in the market at $8 per share and retired.

Under Plan E, 375,000 shares of stock would be sold at $8 per share and the $3 million in proceeds would be used to reduce long-term debt. Show all calculations to support your answers.

a. How would each of these plans affect EPS? Consider the current plan and the two new plans.

b. Which plan would be most favourable if return on assets fell to 5 percent? Increased to 15 percent? Consider the current plan and the two new plans.

c. Calculate the EBIT/EPS indifference point with the formula in the chapter.

d. If the market price for common stock rose to $12 before the restructuring, which plan would then be most attractive? Continue to assume that $3 million in debt will be used to retire stock in Plan D and $3 million of new equity will be sold to retire debt in Plan E. Also assume that return on assets is 10 percent.

e. Calculate the EBIT/EPS indifference point at the new share price.

23. The Lopez-Portillo Company has $10 million in assets, 80 percent financed by debt and 20 percent financed by common stock. The interest rate on the debt is 15 percent, and the stock book value is $10 per share. President Lopez-Portillo is considering two financing plans for an expansion to $15 million in assets.

Under Plan A, the debt-to-total-assets ratio will be maintained, but new debt will cost 18 percent! New stock will be sold at $10 per share. Under Plan B, only new common stock at $10 per share will be issued. The tax rate is 40 percent.

a. If EBIT is 15 percent on total assets, compute earnings per share (EPS) before the expansion and under the two alternatives.

b. What is the DFL under each of the three plans?

c. Calculate the EBIT/EPS indifference point.

d. If shares could be sold at $20 each due to increased expectations for the firm's sales and earnings, what impact would this have on EPS for the two expansion alternatives? Compute EPS for each.

e. Calculate the EBIT/EPS indifference point at the new share price.

f. Explain why corporate financial officers are concerned about their share values.

24. Mr. Katz is in the widget business. He currently sells 2 million widgets a year at $4 each. His variable cost to produce the widgets is $3.00 per unit, and he has $1.5 million in fixed costs.

His sales-to-assets ratio is 4 times, and 40 percent of his assets are financed with 9 percent debt, with the balance financed by common stock at $10.00 per share. The tax rate is 30 percent.

His brother-in-law, Mr. Doberman, says he is doing it all wrong. By reducing his price to $3.75 a widget, he could increase his volume of units sold by 40 percent. Fixed costs would remain constant, and variable costs would remain $3.00 per unit. His sales-to-assets ratio would be 5 times. Furthermore, he could increase his debt-to-assets ratio to 50 percent, with the balance in common stock. It is assumed that the interest rate would go up by 1 percent and the price of shares would remain constant.

a. Compute earnings per share under the Katz plan.

b. Compute earnings per share under the Doberman plan.

c. Mr. Katz's wife does not think that fixed costs would remain constant under the Doberman plan; she believes they would go up by 20 percent. If this is the case, should Mr. Katz shift to the Doberman plan, based on earnings per share?

25. Phelps Canning Company is considering an expansion of its facilities. Its current income statement is as follows:

Sales	$5,000,000
Less: Variable expense (50% of sales)	2,500,000
Fixed expense	1,800,000
Earnings before interest and taxes (EBIT)	700,000
Interest (10% cost)	200,000
Earnings before taxes (EBT)	500,000
Tax (34%)	170,000
Earnings after taxes (EAT)	$ 330,000
Shares of common stock	200,000
EPS	$ 1.65

Phelps Canning Company is currently financed with 50 percent debt and 50 percent equity (common stock). To expand facilities, Mr. Phelps estimates a need for $2 million in additional financing. His investment dealer has laid out three plans for him to consider:

1. Sell $2 million of debt at 13 percent.

2. Sell $2 million of common stock at $20 per share.

3. Sell $1 million of debt at 12 percent and $1 million of common stock at $25 per share.

Variable costs are expected to stay at 50 percent of sales, while fixed expenses will increase to $2,300,000 per year. Mr. Phelps is not sure how much this expansion will add to sales, but he estimates that sales will rise by $1 million per year for the next five years. Mr. Phelps is interested in a thorough analysis of his expansion plans and methods of financing. He would like you to analyze the following:

a. The break-even point for operating expenses before and after expansion (in sales dollars).

b. The DOL before and after expansion. Assume sales of $5 million before expansion and $6 million after expansion.

c. The DFL before expansion at sales of $5 million and for all three methods of financing after expansion. Assume sales of $6 million for the second part of this question.

d. Compute EPS under all three methods of financing the expansion at $6 million in sales (first year) and $10 million in sales (last year).

e. What can we learn from the answer to part d about the advisability of the three methods of financing the expansion? Make your selection of the financing method that best suits Mr. Phelps' objective of maximizing shareholders' wealth.

COMPREHENSIVE PROBLEMS (CHAPTERS 2–5)

26. Ryan Boot Company

RYAN BOOT COMPANY
Balance Sheet
December 31, 20XX

Assets		Liabilities and Shareholders' Equity	
Cash.....................	$ 50,000	Accounts payable...........	$2,200,000
Marketable securities.......	80,000	Accrued expenses..........	150,000
Accounts receivable........	3,000,000	Notes payable (current)	400,000
Inventory	1,000,000	Bonds (10%)...............	2,500,000
		Common stock	
Gross plant and equipment ..	6,000,000	(1.7 million shares)	1,700,000
less: accumulated			
amortization.............	2,000,000	Retained earnings..........	1,180,000
Total assets...............	$8,130,000	Total liabilities and	
		shareholders' equity........	$8,130,000

Income Statement
Year Ended Dec. 31, 20XX

Sales (credit)	$7,000,000
Variable costs (0.60)	4,200,000
Contribution margin	2,800,000
Fixed costs*	2,100,000
Operating profit	700,000
Less: Interest	250,000
Earnings before taxes.................................	450,000
Less: Taxes @ 34%	153,000
Earnings after taxes	$ 297,000
Deduct: Dividends	118,800
Increased retained earnings............................	$ 178,200

*Fixed costs include (*a*) lease expense of $200,000 and (*b*) amortization of $500,000.Note: Ryan Boot also has $66,000 per year in sinking fund obligations associated with its bond issue. The sinking fund represents an annual repayment of the principal amount of the bond. It is not tax deductible.

Ratios

	Ryan Boot (to be filled in)	Industry
Profit margin	_____	5.75%
Return on assets	_____	6.90%
Return on equity.......................	_____	9.20%
Receivables turnover	_____	4.35 ×
Inventory turnover (sales based)	_____	6.50 ×
Accounts payable turnover...............	_____	3.8 ×
Capital asset turnover...................	_____	1.85 ×
Total asset turnover	_____	1.20 ×
Current ratio..........................	_____	1.45 ×
Quick ratio	_____	1.10 ×
Debt to total assets....................	_____	25.05%
Interest coverage	_____	5.35 ×
Fixed charge coverage	_____	4.62 ×

a. Analyze Ryan Boot Company using ratio analysis. Compute the ratios above for Ryan Boot and compare them to the industry data that is given. Discuss the weak points, strong points, and what you think should be done to improve the company's performance.

b. In your analysis, calculate the overall break-even point in sales dollars and the cash break-even point. Also compute the DOL, DFL, and DCL.

c. Use the information in parts *a* and *b* to discuss the risk associated with this company. Given the risk, decide whether a bank should loan funds to Ryan Boot. Ryan Boot Company is trying to plan the funds needed for 20XY. The management anticipates an increase in sales of 20 percent, which can be absorbed without increasing capital assets.

d. What would be Ryan Boot's need for external funds based on the current balance sheet? Compute RNF (required new funds). Notes payable (current) and bonds are not part of the liability calculation.

e. What would be the RNF if the company brings its ratios into line with the industry average during 20XY? Specifically examine receivables turnover, inventory turnover, and the profit margin. Use the new values to recompute the factors in RNF (assume liabilities stay the same).

f. Do not calculate, only comment on the following questions. How would RNF change if the company
   1. Were at full capacity?
   2. Raised the dividend payout ratio?
   3. Suffered a decreased growth in sales?
   4. Faced an accelerated inflation rate?

27. Rockway Framers Ltd. has requested a bank loan for a one-year period to refinance most of its notes payable. It would be supported by Rockway's current assets. The following statements and industry averages accompanied the loan request.

Prepare a statement of changes in financial position as at December 31, 20XX, for Rockway, and complete a ratio analysis. Also prepare pro forma statements for 20XY on the basis of the same financial relationships as in 20XX, no new capital asset purchases, and a sales increase of 25 percent. Recommend support or rejection of the loan request.

ROCKWAY FRAMERS LTD.
Balance Sheets
December 31

	20XX	20XW
Current assets:		
Cash	$ 1,300	$ 20,000
Accounts receivable	36,000	28,000
Inventories	101,000	64,500
Total current assets	138,300	112,500
Land	57,700	44,500
Buildings and equipment	222,000	155,000
Less: Accumulated amortization	85,000	62,000
Total assets	$333,000	$250,000
Current liabilities:		
Accounts payable	$ 48,770	$ 23,250
Notes payable	104,500	37,750
Total current liabilities	153,270	61,000
Long-term debt	51,000	64,000
Common stock	70,000	70,000
Retained earnings	58,730	55,000
Total liabilities and equity	$333,000	$250,000

ROCKWAY FRAMERS LTD.
Income Statements
Year Ended Dec. 31,

	20XX	20XW
Sales.	$355,200	$277,500
Cost of goods sold	213,120	166,500
Contribution margin.	142,080	111,000
Sales and administration expenses.	82,140	74,370
Amortization	23,000	10,000
Operating income.	36,940	26,630
Interest	14,200	6,800
Earnings before taxes.	22,740	19,830
Taxes	5,685	4,958
Net income.	$ 17,055	$ 14,872

Industry Averages

Profit margin	3.50%
Return on assets	4.00%
Return on equity.	8.20%
Gross margin	38.00%
Receivables turnover	9.73 times
Average collection period	37.51 days
Inventory turnover	2.50 times
Capital asset turnover.	2.08 times
Total asset turnover	1.14 times
Current ratio.	1.80
Quick ratio	0.70
Debt to total assets	58.00%
Times interest earned.	3.80 times

28. R. C. Dare is considering an investment in Deval Leasehold Improvements Ltd., a growing company that has been in business for five years. The good growth is the result of a reputation built on high-quality workmanship, the use of first-class materials, and fair prices.

However, Deval has experienced cash flow difficulties, and some of Deval's suppliers have expressed concern with the slow payment on their accounts. This can be attributed in part to the increasing number of government jobs awarded Deval. Although the government jobs are steady work, payment is slower than from private work.

Examine the financial statements of Deval Leasehold for the past three years and decide if you would recommend an equity investment of approximately $15,000 by R.C. Dare. Prepare the 13 ratios of Chapter 3 as well as the asset utilization variations to support your recommendation. Also comment on the firm's leverage.

DEVAL LEASEHOLD IMPROVEMENTS LTD.

Income Statement

	20XX	20XW	20XV
Sales..................................	$142,481	$195,200	$245,109
Cost of goods sold	83,351	130,198	168,145
Gross profit	59,130	65,002	76,964
Other expenses.........................	54,416	60,133	71,672
Operating profit	4,714	4,869	5,292
Interest expense	1,100	950	800
Earnings before taxes...................	3,614	3,919	4,492
Taxes	650	705	809
Earnings available to common shareholders ..	2,964	3,214	3,683
Dividends declared......................	612	612	612

Balance Sheet

Assets

	20XX	20XW	20XV
Cash	$ 1,775	$ 1,178	$ 215
Accounts receivable.....................	21,920	32,534	43,770
Inventory	5,699	7,808	10,204
Prepaid expenses	309	191	770
Capital assets	6,200	8,124	10,492
Total assets...........................	$35,903	$49,835	$65,451

Liabilities and Shareholders' Equity

	20XX	20XW	20XV
Accounts payable.......................	$10,658	$19,766	$31,351
Customer deposits	4,238	7,961	9,420
Term loan.............................	9,500	8,000	7,500
Common stock.........................	6,120	6,120	6,120
Retained earnings......................	5,387	7,988	11,060
Total liabilities and shareholders' equity	$35,903	$49,835	$65,451

MINI CASES

Glen Mount Furniture

Furniture magnate Carl Thompson couldn't believe the amount of pressure security analysts could put on a firm. The Glen Mount Furniture Company was a leading manufacturer of fine home furnishings and distributed its products directly to department stores, independent home furnishing retailers, and a few regional furniture chains. The firm specialized in bedroom, dining room, and living room furniture and had three plants in Quebec and two in Ontario. Its home office was in Granby, Quebec.

In a recent presentation to the Montreal chapter of the Financial Analysts Federation, Carl Thompson barely had taken a bite out of his salad when two analysts from a stock brokerage firm began asking questions. They were particularly concerned about Glen Mount's growth rate in EPS.

Carl was aware that security analysts considered earnings performance to be important, but he was somewhat distressed by the fact that this seemed to be their overriding concern. It bothered him that the firm had just spent over $10 million to develop exciting new product lines, modernize production facilities, and expand distribution capabilities, and yet all the questions seemed to deal with near-term earnings performance. He believed he would eventually have an opportunity to discuss the above-mentioned management initiatives and their impact on the company for the next decade, but current EPS seemed to gather the attention of the analysts.

Carl knew only too well from past experience that the earnings performance of the firm would affect the company's price-earnings ratio and its market value. Furthermore, before Carl became president of Glen Mount Furniture Company, he had attended a six-week executive development program at the Western Business School in which he heard a number of professors stress the importance of the goal of shareholder wealth maximization. He often wondered if other items were not equally important to the company, such as community service. (The firm donated $60,000 a year to a local university to help supplement faculty salaries for outstanding professors.) He also had a sense of pride that his firm provided employment to over 500 people in the area. He was not sure that the security analysts would consider these items important.

With all of these thoughts in mind, his upcoming meeting with Chief Financial Officer Barbara Bainesworth became particularly important.

When Barbara arrived, she had a number of financial documents to review before making key decisions. In Table 1 she showed the earnings performance of the company over the past five years. Table 2 provided a current balance sheet, and Table 3 represented an abbreviated income statement for 20XX.

Table 1 Earnings per share (EPS) for the past five years

Year	1st Quarter	2nd Quarter	3rd Quarter	4th Quarter	Yearly Total
20XS	$0.23	$0.25	$0.19	$0.34	$1.01
20XT	$0.26	$0.28	$0.27	$0.41	$1.22
20XU	$0.34	$0.36	$0.33	$0.48	$1.51
20XV	$0.35	$0.37	$0.34	$0.49	$1.55
20XW	$0.35	$0.36	$0.36	$0.49	$1.56

Table 2

Glen Mount Furniture Company
Comparative Balance Sheets December 31, 20XX
Assets

Current Assets:

Cash..		$ 350,000
Marketable securities..............................		90,000
Accounts receivable.............................		5,000,000
Inventory......................................		7,000,000
Total current assets		12,440,000
Other assets:		
Investments....................................		5,000,000
Capital assets:		
Plant and equipment.............................	27,060,000	
Less: accumulated amortization...................	4,000,000	
Net plant and equipment		23,060,000
Total assets....................................		$40,500,000

Liabilities and Shareholders Equity

Current liabilities:

Accounts payable................................	$ 4,400,000
Wages payable	150,000
Accrued expenses................................	950,000
Total current liabilities	5,500,000
Long-term liabilities:	
Bonds payable, 10.625%..........................	12,000,000
Shareholders equity:	
Common stock...................................	10,000,000
Retained earnings................................	13,000,000
Total shareholders equity	23,000,000
Total liabilities and shareholders equity.	$40,500,000

Table 3

Glen Mount Furniture Company
Abbreviated Income Statement
For the Year Ending Dec. 31, 20XX

Sales...................................	$45,000,000
Less: Variable costs	26,100,000
Fixed costs	12,900,000
Operating profit (EBIT).................	6,000,000
Interest	1,275,000
Earnings before taxes (EBT)	4,725,000
Taxes @ 34%.........................	1,606,500
Earnings after taxes	$3,118,500
Common Shares outstanding...............	2,000,000
EPS...................................	$1.56

The firm was considering buying back 625,000 shares of stock outstanding at $16 per share. This would represent $10 million in total. The funds to purchase the shares would be acquired from a new bond issue that would carry an interest rate of 11.25 percent. The bond would have a 15-year life. The firm was in a 34 percent tax bracket.

a.   Project EPS for 20XY assuming that sales increase by $500,000. Use Table 3 as the model for the calculation. Further assume that the capital structure is not changed.

b.   By what percent did EPS increase from 20XX to 20XY?

c.   Now assume $10 million of debt replaces 625,000 shares of common stock as described in the case. The interest on the new debt will be 11.250 percent. What will projected EPS be for 20XY based on the anticipated sales increase of $500,000?

d.   Based on your answer to part c, by what percent would EPS increase from 20XX to 20XY?

e.   Compute the degree of financial leverage (DFL) for the answers to part a and part c.

f.   Compute degree of combined leverage (DCL) for the answer to part a and the answer to part c.

g.   What is the total-debt-to-total-assets ratio as shown in the 20XX balance sheet (Table 2)? What will it be if $10 million worth of shareholders' equity is replaced with debt?

h.   What do you think might happen to the share price as a result of replacing $10 million worth of shareholders' equity with debt? Consider any relevant factors.

Chem-Med Company

April 1, 20XX: Dr. Nathan Swan, age 40, chairman of the board of directors, chief executive officer, and founder of the Chem-Med Company, was in his office staring at the ceiling, wondering if he would not have been better off still teaching biochemistry at the University of Toronto. This business was getting to be a headache. Only a short time ago he was able to spend most of his time in the company lab comfortably working with test tubes and formulas. Lately, though, it seemed that all his waking hours were spent with financial statements and spreadsheets, and in meetings. He wanted the firm to grow and make money, but he had no idea that the financial end of the business would be so demanding and complex.

Dr. Swan was a little mystified by financial matters. How could one describe a company in financial terms? How could financial statements indicate whether or not a firm was in good or bad shape? (The balance in the company chequing account didn't seem to be an indicator.) How could one convince a group of hard-nosed investors that the company was capable of making a lot of money in the next few years, if it just had more money now? (Dr. Swan was always puzzled by the fact that Chem-Med was growing and making money, but it never seemed to have enough cash.)

Chem-Med began operations 18 years ago after Dr. Francois Swan completed the development of commercial-scale isolation of sodium hyaluronate (hereafter referred to as HA), a naturally occurring biological fluid that is useful in eye surgery and other medical and veterinary uses. The isolation process, complex and proprietary to the company, involves extracting and purifying HA from rooster combs. Initial seed money for the enterprise came from research grants from the University of Toronto and the federal government, plus contributions from Dr. Swan's colleagues and associates, who were now classified as the company's shareholders (254 as of April 20XX, all closely held; not traded publicly).

In mid-20XU Chem-Med commenced the manufacture and distribution of its first product, VISCAM, which is used to hold tissues in place during and after surgery of the retina. In March 20XV Chem-Med received regulatory approval to market another HA product known as VISCHY, which is used for the treatment of degenerative joint diseases in horses. The two products, VISCAM and VISCHY, are the only ones Chem-Med currently produces; however, the company has an active R & D (Research & Development) program investigating other applications.

There are only two other manufacturers of FDA-approved HA products in the world: AB Fortia, a Swedish corporation, which manufactures a product called Healon in Sweden and distributes it in

North America through a subsidiary, Pharmacia Inc., and Cilco Inc. in West Virginia.

Chem-Med has about a 25 percent share of the market (for HA products in eye surgery) against Cilco's 16 percent and Pharmacia's 59 percent. Pharmacia, with the power of giant AB Fortia behind it, waged a continuing marketing war with Chem-Med, undercutting Chem-Med's prices and wooing its customers away at every opportunity. The matter came to a head in September 20XX, when Chem-Med filed a $13 million suit against Pharmacia, charging unfair trade practices. Dr. Swan was reasonably confident that Chem-Med would prevail in the suit, and in fact, Pharmacia had recently offered to settle out of court for $500,000.

Dr. Swan's primary problem was that although he was convinced the company was sound and would grow, he wasn't sure how to communicate that to potential investors in the financial community in a way that would convince them. Just handing out past income statements and balance sheets (shown in Tables 1 and 2) that he received from the accountants didn't seem to be enough. Further, he wasn't even sure the company needed outside financing, let alone how much. He just believed they would need it, since they had always had to ask for money in the past.

Table 1

CHEM-MED COMPANY
Income Statements

	20XU–20XW (in thousands)			Pro Forma Income Statements		
	20XU	**20XV**	**20XW**	**20XX**	**20XY**	**20XZ**
Net sales (all credit)	$ 777	$3,051	$3,814	$5,340	$7,475	$10,366
Cost of goods sold	257	995	1,040	1,716	2,154	2,954
Gross profit	520	2,056	2,774	3,624	5,321	7,412
Selling, etc., expenses . .	610	705	964	1,520	2,120	2,645
Other income (expenses)*	0	0	0	500	0	0
Operating profit	(90)	1,351	1,810	2,604	3,201	4,767
Interest expense	11	75	94	202	302	434
Income before tax.	(101)	1,276	1,716	2,402	2,899	4,333
Income taxes . . . . (40% in 20XV; 33% thereafter)	0	510	566	793	957	1,430
Net income	($101)	$ 766	$1,150	$1,609	$1,942	$2,903
Dividends paid	0	0	0	0	0	0
Increase in retained earnings	$(101)	$ 766	$1,150	$1,609	$1,942	$2,903
Average number of shares**	2,326	2,326	2,347	2,347	2,347	2,347
Earnings per share	($0.04)	$0.33	$0.49	$0.69	$0.83	$1.24

*Other income (expenses) refers to extraordinary gains and losses. In 20XX, $500,000 is expected from Pharmacia Inc., in settlement of the lawsuit. **Shares are not publicly traded.

Table 2

CHEM-MED COMPANY

Balance Sheets (in thousands)

	Pro Forma Balance Sheets as of Dec. 31, years ended:					
	20XU	20XV	20XW	20XX	20XY	20XZ
Assets						
Cash and equivalent..........	$ 124	$ 103	$ 167	$ 205	$ 422	$ 101
Accounts receivable..........	100	409	564	907	1,495	2,351
Inventories	151	302	960	1,102	1,443	798
Other current	28	59	29	41	57	11
Total current assets.........	403	873	1,720	2,255	3,417	3,261
Property, plant, & equipment...	1,901	2,298	2,917	4,301	5,531	8,923
Less: Accumulated amortization...............	81	82	346	413	522	588
Property, plant, & equipment net........................	1,820	2,216	2,571	3,888	5,009	8,335
Other capital assets	0	101	200	200	215	399
Total assets................	$2,223	$3,190	$4,491	$6,343	$8,641	$11,995
Liabilities						
Accounts payable............	$ 210	$ 405	$ 551	$ 771	$1,080	$ 1,512
Short-term debt	35	39	42	59	82	135
Total current liabilities......	245	444	593	830	1,162	1,647
Long-term debt	17	19	21	27	50	17
Total liabilities............	262	463	614	857	1,212	1,664
Equity						
Common stock..............	2,062	2,062	2,062	2,062	2,062	2,062
Retained earnings............	(101)	665	1,815	3,424	5,366	8,269
Total equity	1,961	2,727	3,877	5,486	7,428	10,331
Total liabilities and equity	$2,223	$3,190	$4,491	$6,343	$8,640	$11,995

Dr. Swan had lunch with his banker recently, and the banker mentioned several restrictive covenants the company would have to meet if it came to the bank for financing. The three covenants were

- The current ratio must be maintained above 2.25 to 1.

- The debt-to-assets ratio must be less than 0.3 to 1.

- Dividends cannot be paid unless earnings are positive.

Dr. Swan didn't think he would have any trouble with those, but he wasn't sure. He would have to analyze the numbers before the next board of directors meeting, but he now had to meet with a representative of a supermarket chain.

As an investor considering the addition of Chem-Med to your portfolio, you are interested in the company's record of profitability, prospects for the future, degree of risk, and how it compares with others in the industry (shown in Table 3). From that point of view, answer the following questions:

Table 3

	Biotechnology Industry Statistics—Median Company in Biological Products		
	20XU	20XV	20XW
Current ratio............................	2.5	2.3	2.4
Quick ratio	1.2	1.1	1.3
Inventory turnover	5.5	5.6	5.7
Total asset turnover	1.15	1.16	1.18
Return on sales.........................	4.00%	4.00%	5.00%
Return on assets........................	4.60%	4.64%	5.90%
Return on equity........................	7.64%	8.44%	12.29%
Total debt to assets.....................	0.40	0.45	0.52
	Selected Statistics, Pharmacia Company		
	20XU	20XV	20XW
Current ratio............................	2.8	2.7	2.8
Quick ratio	1.5	1.3	1.6
Inventory turnover	5.6	5.7	5.8
Total asset turnover	1.9	2	1.9
Return on sales.........................	6.00%	6.50%	7.00%
Return on assets........................	11.40%	13.00%	13.30%
Return on equity........................	19.04%	27.66%	29.56%
Total debt to assets.....................	0.40	0.53	0.55
Price-earnings ratio	13.7	14	15
Average share price	$21.78	$24.92	$31.50

a. What was Chem-Med's rate of sales growth in 20XW? What is it forecasted to be in 20XX, 20XY, and 20XZ?

b. What is the company's rate of net income growth in 20XX, 20XY, and 20XZ? Is projected net income growing faster or slower than projected sales? After computing these values, take a hard look at the 20XX income statement data to see if you want to make any adjustments.

c. How does Chem-Med's current ratio for 20XW compare to Pharmacia's? How does it compare to the industry average? Compute Chem-Med's current ratio for 20XZ. Is there any problem with it?

d. What is Chem-Med's total debt-to-assets ratio in 20XW, 20XX, 20XY, and 20XZ? Is any trend evident in the four-year period? Does Chem-Med in 20XW have more or less debt than the average company in the industry?

e. What is Chem-Med's average accounts receivable collection period for 20XW, 20XX, 20XY, and 20XZ? Is the period getting longer or shorter? What are the consequences?

f. How does Chem-Med's ROE compare to Pharmacia's and the industry for 20XW? Using the DuPont method, compare the positions of Chem-Med and Pharmacia by computing ROE from its components. Using the results, compare the sources of ROE for each company.

g. For 20XW, 20XX, 20XY, and 20XZ calculate the overall break-even point in sales dollars and the cash break-even point. Also compute the DOL, DFL, and the DCL. Discuss the risk of the company.

PART 3 WORKING CAPITAL MANAGEMENT

CHAPTER 6	CHAPTER 7	CHAPTER 8
Working Capital and the Financing Decision	Current Asset Management	Sources of Short-Term Financing

CHAPTER

6

Working Capital and the Financing Decision

LEARNING OBJECTIVES

LO1 Define working capital management.

LO2 Describe the effect asset growth has on working capital positions.

LO3 Identify working capital management considerations for permanent components, the effect of sales/production schedules, and liquidity versus risk.

LO4 Identify the cash flow cycle of the firm.

LO5 Explain financing of assets in terms of hedging.

LO6 Describe the term structure of interest rates, explain the theories that suggest its shape, and assess how it may be of use to a financial manager.

LO7 Examine risk and profitability in determining the financing plan for current assets.

The financial manager's major focus is the efficient management of the firm's short-term assets and liabilities. Inventories and accounts receivable are significant investments and there are several competing financing sources available to the financial manager. The proper use of the techniques for managing these resources allows the firm to plan and implement its long-run strategies.

FINANCE MANAGEMENT

LO1 The Short Term

Working capital management entails arranging short-term financing (current liabilities) to facilitate investment in the current assets of the firm. With increasing sales there will be growth in the firm's inventories and receivables, representing more and more cash (capital) tied up in current assets, as was demonstrated in Chapter 4. The current asset investment must be sufficiently liquid and achieve appropriate returns. Liquidity in the firm is influenced by asset growth, the sales and production schedule, and the cash flow cycle.

This increased capital invested in current assets can be financed to some extent from profits reinvested in the firm, but in most cases, internal funds do not provide enough financing. Short-term external sources of financing are found from trade credit (accounts payable), bank loans, and short-term securities. Some longer-term financing may also be utilized to support the working capital investment. The financial manager seeks to minimize the costs of these sources of financing.

Some theories and general considerations in the interaction between current assets and liabilities that contribute to the firm's success are examined in this chapter. The financial risk and return aspects of working capital management are identified in light of different financing patterns and interest rate changes, which leads to the development of optimum policy considerations. Chapter 7 will examine effective management of current assets and Chapter 8 will examine the effective management of current liabilities.

Financial managers probably devote more time to working capital management than to any other activity, in order to ensure adequate liquidity for the firm to meet its immediate obligations. For the small business, the maintenance of liquidity is critical to its survival, as the small firm is unlikely to have as much flexibility in short-term financing as the larger corporation. Although long-term decisions involving capital assets or market strategy may determine the eventual success of the firm, short-term decisions on working capital determine whether the firm gets to the long term.

FINANCE IN ACTION

Working Capital is a Large Investment at Loblaw

Loblaw Companies Ltd. is Canada's largest food and pharmacy firm, with sales in 2019 over $48 billion. It is represented in all provinces. President's Choice brand-name products, the Real Canadian Superstore, and Shoppers are all part of Loblaw, which has George Weston Limited as its majority shareholder.

The food business operates on very narrow margins. In 2019, Loblaw's operating profit was $2.3 billion, about 4.7 percent of sales. Net earnings were $1.1 billion, for a profit margin of about 2.4 percent (formula 3–1).

What is striking about Loblaw in comparison to companies in other industries is the large investment in current assets. In 2019, over $11.3 billion was invested in current assets, with almost half invested in inventory. Current assets were about the same magnitude as capital assets. Like many corporations, Loblaw had built up and was sitting on a cash hoard of $1.1 billion in cash. To finance this position in current assets, Loblaw relied heavily on its suppliers with accounts payable at $5.3 billion. In comparison to shareholders' equity of $11.3 billion, the suppliers of short-term capital also had a significant stake in the firm.

Net working capital (current assets less current liabilities) was $2.1 billion, whereas in 2000 it had been a negative $291 million. Loblaw tries to maintain a balance between its current assets and liabilities, although the shift to a positive net working capital position is possibly due to supply chain management problems at Loblaw, the new pharmaceutical inventory mix, and the cash hoarding of corporations in recent years.

As Loblaw is not in the manufacturing or "growing" business as a distributor; its primary investment is in its inventories. On a continuing basis, inventories, accounts receivable, and accounts payable are perhaps the most significant components of Loblaw's balance sheet. In a business with a low profit margin, it is important that Loblaw maintain a high degree of liquidity in these assets.

Q1 What is Loblaw's latest working capital position?

Q2 Have the margins at Loblaw improved or deteriorated?

Q3 How does Loblaw compare to Sobeys (part of Empire Co.)?

empireco.ca
Symbol: EMP. A

loblaw.com
Symbol: L

LO2 THE NATURE OF ASSET GROWTH

Any company that produces and sells a product, whether the product is consumer or industry oriented, has current assets and capital assets. As a firm grows, those assets are likely to increase. The key to current asset planning is the ability of management to forecast sales accurately and then to match the production schedules with the sales forecast. Whenever actual sales are different from forecasted sales, unexpected buildups or reductions in inventory occur that eventually affect receivables and cash flow.

In the simplest case, stage 1, all of the firm's current assets are self-liquidating assets (sold at the end of a specified time period). For example, assume that at the start of the summer you buy 100 tires to be disposed of by September. It is your intention that all tires be sold, receivables collected, and bills paid over this time period. In this case, your working capital (current asset) needs are truly short term.

In stage 2, you expand the business by adding radios, seat covers, and batteries to your operation. Some of your inventory is again completely liquidated, but other items form the basic stock for your operation. To stay in business, you must maintain floor displays and multiple items for selection. Furthermore, not all items will sell. As you eventually grow to more than one store, this permanent aggregate stock of current assets continues to increase. Problems of inadequate financing arrangements are often the result of the businessperson's failure to realize that the firm is not only carrying self-liquidating inventory but also is likely to require permanent current assets.

If we look at the balance sheet at any time during the year, we are likely to see minimum levels of cash, accounts receivable, and inventory necessary to maintain sales. Although the individual receivable or inventory item is not always with the business, one can say these minimum levels are a permanent component of current assets.

Figure 6–1 depicts the movement from stage 1 to stage 2 growth for a typical business. Panel A shows a buildup in temporary current assets, and in Panel B part of the growth in current assets is temporary and part is permanent. (Capital assets are included in the illustrations, but they are not directly related to the present discussion.)

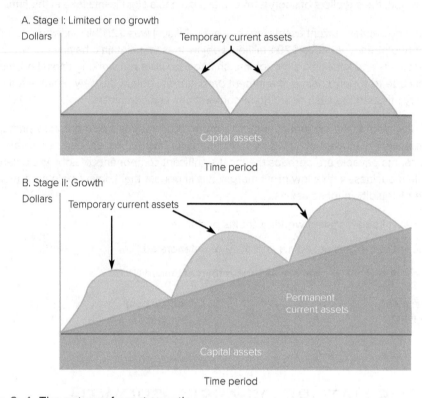

A. Stage I: Limited or no growth
Dollars
Temporary current assets
Capital assets
Time period

B. Stage II: Growth
Dollars
Temporary current assets
Permanent current assets
Capital assets
Time period

Figure 6–1 The nature of asset growth

LO3 CONTROLLING ASSETS—MATCHING SALES AND PRODUCTION

In most firms, capital assets grow slowly as productive capacity is increased and old equipment is replaced, but current assets fluctuate in the short run, depending on the level of production versus the level of sales. When the firm produces more than it sells, inventory rises. When sales rise faster than production, inventory declines and receivables rise.

As discussed in the treatment of the cash budgeting process in Chapter 4, some firms employ level production methods to smooth production schedules and to use labour and equipment efficiently at a lower cost. One consequence of level production is that current assets go up and down when sales and production are not equal. Other firms may try to match sales and production as closely as possible in the short run. This allows current assets to increase or decrease with the level of sales and eliminates the large seasonal bulges or sharp reductions in current assets that occur under level production.

Publishing companies are good examples of companies with seasonal sales, requiring careful working capital management and control. Quarterly sales and earnings of Canadian book publisher McGraw Hill Education are depicted in Figure 6–2. This major publishing company (publisher of **Foundations of Financial Management**) is a good example of a company with seasonal sales, with the largest sales component in the third quarter of each year. If company management has not planned its inventory correctly, then lost sales or excess inventory could be a serious problem. Even with good planning, McGraw Hill Education experiences negative earnings in some quarters because of significant fixed costs.

McGraw Hill Education
mheducation.ca

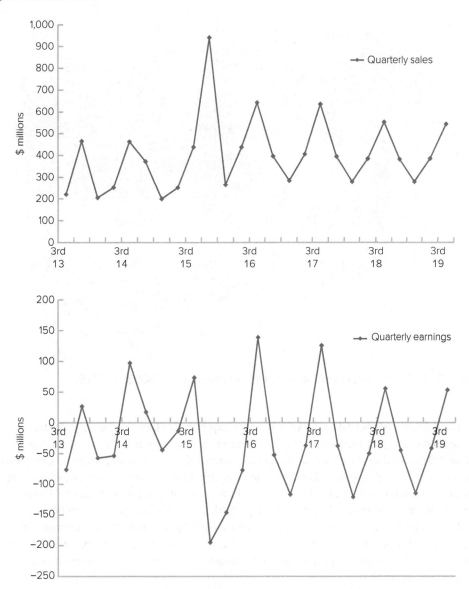

Figure 6–2 Sales and earnings for McGraw Hill Education from 2013 to 2019.

The fixed costs of printing and binding a book are most efficiently handled by contracting with a printing company for a fixed number of copies. The copies ordered are based on expected sales over at least a one-year period (sometimes several years). If the books sell better than expected, the publishing company orders a second or third printing. As textbooks cannot be reproduced on demand, orders are placed months ahead of actual sales. If the book declines in popularity, the publisher could get stuck with a large inventory of obsolete books.

The fluctuation in current assets at McGraw Hill Education is identified in Figure 6–3, with the sales patterns peaking in September and ebbing in March. Inventories are relatively constant, and accounts receivable peak in September, becoming cash one quarter later as they are collected. Cash is lowest in June when it is used to help finance the next season's production of books. In recent years, there has been an accumulation of a significant cash position. The fairly constant inventory position over the period is a reflection of this effort at control using measures (such as JIT), which helps to minimize the current asset investment.

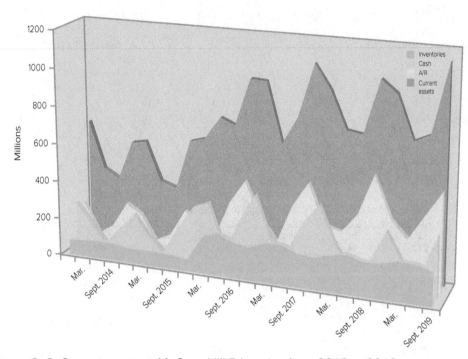

Figure 6–3 Current assets at McGraw Hill Education from 2013 to 2019.

Retail firms, such as Hudson's Bay or Indigo (Chapters), also have seasonal sales patterns, with the end-of-the-year fiscal quarter often accounting for over 40 percent of annual earnings. Although these retail stores are not involved in deciding level versus seasonal production, they would like to match sales and inventory. Therefore, their suppliers must bear inventory risk and make the decision to produce on either a level or a seasonal basis, affected by the weather and holiday periods. Inventory not sold during the Christmas season probably ends up being discounted in January.

Highly seasonal sales can cause asset management challenges. A financial manager must be aware of these to either avoid getting caught short of cash or being prepared to borrow if necessary. This pattern of fluctuating sales demonstrates the impact of operating leverage on earnings, as discussed in Chapter 5.

Many retail firms have been more successful in matching sales and orders using computerized inventory control systems linked to online point-of-sale terminals. Digital input and optical scanners record inventory levels item by item, allowing managers to adjust ordering and production schedules. The predictability of the market influences the speed with which the manager reacts to this information, and the length and complexity of the ordering and production processes dictating how fast inventory levels can be changed.

Temporary Assets Under Level Production— An Example

To get a better understanding of how current assets fluctuate, let us use the example of the hypothetical Yawakuzi Motorcycle Company, which manufactures in southern Ontario and sells throughout Canada. Not many Canadians buy motorcycles during October through March, but sales pick up in early spring and summer and trail off during the fall. Because of the capital assets and the skilled labour involved in the production process, Yawakuzi decides that level production is the least expensive and the most efficient production method.

Table 6–1 is a **sales forecast** (October through September) provided by the marketing department.

Table 6–1 Yawakuzi sales forecast (in units)

1st Quarter	2nd Quarter	3rd Quarter	4th Quarter
October....... 300	January.......... 0	April........ 1,000	July......... 2,000
November...... 150	February......... 0	May 2,000	August 1,000
December....... 50	March......... 600	June 2,000	September 500

Total sales of 9,600 units at $3,000 each = $28,800,000 in sales.

- Sales forecast   9,600 for the year
- Sales price $3,000 per unit

Table 6–2, the **production schedule**, shows how level production and seasonal sales combine to create fluctuating inventory rising to $9 million in March, the last consecutive month in which production is greater than sales, and then falling to $1 million in August, the last month in which sales are greater than production.

Table 6–2 Yawakuzi's production schedule and inventory

	Beginning Inventory	+	Production	–	Sales	=	Ending Inventory	Inventory (at cost of $2,000 per unit)
October	800		800		300		1,300	$2,600,000
November	1,300		800		150		1,950	3,900,000
December	1,950		800		50		2,700	5,400,000
January	2,700		800		0		3,500	7,000,000
February	3,500		800		0		4,300	8,600,000
March	4,300		800		600		4,500	9,000,000
April	4,500		800		1,000		4,300	8,600,000
May	4,300		800		2,000		3,100	6,200,000
June	3,100		800		2,000		1,900	3,800,000
July	1,900		800		2,000		700	1,400,000
August	700		800		1,000		500	1,000,000
September	500		800		500		800	1,600,000

- Level production   800 (9,600/12)
- Production cost $2,000 per unit
- Beginning inventory   800 units in October

Table 6–3 is a cash budget combining the sales forecast (Table 6–1), a **cash receipts** schedule, and a **cash payments** schedule to determine cash flow.

Table 6–3 Sales forecast, cash receipts and payments, and cash budget ($ millions)

	Oct.	Nov.	Dec.	Jan.	Feb.	March	April	May	June	July	Aug.	Sept.
Sales Forecast												
Sales (units)	300	150	50	0	0	600	1,000	2,000	2,000	2,000	1,000	500
Sales (unit price, $3,000)	$ 0.9	$ 0.45	$ 0.15	$ 0	$ 0	$ 1.8	$ 3.0	$ 6.0	$ 6.0	$ 6.0	$3.0	$1.5
Cash Receipts Schedule												
50% cash	$ 0.45	$ 0.225	$ 0.075	$ 0.000	$ 0	$ 0.9	$ 1.5	$ 3.0	$ 3.0	$ 3.0	$1.5	$0.75
50% from prior month's sales	0.75*	0.450	0.225	0.075	0	0.0	0.9	1.5	3.0	3.0	3.0	1.50
Total cash receipts	$ 1.20	$ 0.675	$ 0.300	$ 0.075	$ 0	$ 0.9	$ 2.4	$ 4.5	$ 6.0	$ 6.0	$4.5	$2.25
Cash Payments Schedule												
Constant production of 800 units/month (cost, $2,000 per unit)	$ 1.6	$ 1.6	$ 1.6	$ 1.6	$ 1.6	$ 1.6	$ 1.6	$ 1.6	$ 1.6	$ 1.6	$1.6	$1.6
Overhead	0.4	0.4	0.4	0.4	0.4	0.4	0.4	0.4	0.4	0.4	0.4	0.4
Dividends and interest	—	—	—	—	—	—	—	—	—	—	1.0	—
Taxes	0.3	—	—	0.3	—	—	0.3	—	—	0.3	—	—
Total cash payments	$ 2.3	$ 2.0	$ 2.0	$ 2.3	$ 2.0	$ 2.0	$ 2.3	$ 2.0	$ 2.0	$ 2.3	$3.0	$2.0
Cash Budget (required minimum balance is $0.25 million)												
Cash flow	$(1.10)	$(1.325)	$(1.70)	$(2.225)	$(2.00)	$(1.10)	$ 0.10	$ 2.50	$ 4.00	$ 3.70	$1.5	$0.25
Beginning cash	0.25†	0.250	0.25	0.250	0.25	0.25	0.25	0.25	0.25	0.25	1.1	2.60
Cumulative cash balance	$(0.85)	$(1.075)	$(1.45)	$(1.975)	$(1.75)	$(0.85)	$ 0.35	$ 2.75	$ 4.25	$ 3.95	$2.6	$2.85
Monthly loan or (repayment)	1.10	1.325	1.700	2.225	2.000	1.10	(0.10)	(2.50)	(4.00)	(2.85)	0	0
Cumulative loan	1.10	2.425	4.125	6.350	8.350	9.45	9.35	6.85	2.85	0.0	0	0
Ending cash balance	$ 0.25	$ 0.250	$ 0.250	$ 0.250	$ 0.250	$ 0.25	$ 0.25	$ 0.25	$ 0.25	$ 1.1	$2.6	$2.85

*Assumes September sales of $1.5 million.
†Assumes cash balance of $0.25 million at the beginning of October and that this is the desired minimum cash balance.

- Cash receipts   50 percent during the month of sale, 50 percent from the prior month's sales
- Cash payments   Production cost of $1.6 million and $0.4 million overhead monthly dividends, interest, and taxes as reported

From the cash flow of the table, borrowing needs and the accumulation of cash are determined. Negative cash flows (cumulative cash balance) necessitate expanding the bank loan, which reaches its highest level (cumulative loan) in March. These external funds finance current asset accumulation. Positive cash flows allow Yawakuzi to retire the loan and accumulate large cash balances by September.

- Minimum cash balance $0.25 million

The total current asset buildup as a result of level production and fluctuating sales is presented in Table 6–4, rising to $10.35 million in April. Inventory peaks in March, followed by accounts receivable in May through July and cash by September (the cash flow cycle).

Table 6–4 Total current assets, first year ($ millions)

	Cash	Accounts Receivable	Inventory	Total Current Assets
October............	$0.25	$0.45	$2.6	$3.30
November..........	0.25	0.225	3.9	4.375
December..........	0.25	0.075	5.4	5.725
January............	0.25	0.000	7.0	7.25
February...........	0.25	0.000	8.6	8.85
March.............	0.25	0.90	9.0	10.15
April..............	0.25	1.50	8.6	10.35
May	0.25	3.00	6.2	9.45
June	0.25	3.00	3.8	7.05
July...............	1.10	3.00	1.4	5.50
August	2.60	1.50	1.0	5.10
September	2.85	0.75	1.6	5.20

- Cash   From the last line of Table 6–3 (cash budget)
- Accounts receivable   50 percent of monthly sales
- Inventory   From the last column of Table 6–2 (production schedule and inventory)

In October the cycle starts again, but now the firm has accumulated cash that it can use to finance next year's asset accumulation, pay a larger dividend, replace old equipment or—if growth in sales is anticipated—invest in new equipment to increase productive capacity. Table 6–5 presents the cash budget and total current assets for the second year. Under a simplified, no-growth assumption, the monthly cash flow is the same as that of the first year, but beginning cash in October is much higher from the first year's ending cash balance. This lowers the borrowing requirement and increases the ending cash balance. Total current assets accumulate to high levels once again.

Table 6–5 Cash budget and assets for second year with no growth in sales ($ millions)

EndofFirstYear:	Sept.	Oct.	Nov.	Dec.	Jan.	Feb.	March	April	May	June	July	Aug.	Sept.
						SecondYear							
Cash flow.	$0.25	$(1.10)	$(1.325)	$(1.700)	$(2.225)	$(2.00)	$ (1.10)	$ 0.10	$2.50	$4.00	$3.70	$ 1.5	$0.25
Beginning cash.	2.60	2.85	1.750	0.425	0.250	0.25	0.25	0.25	0.25	0.25	0.25	3.7	5.20
Cumulative cash balance . .		1.75	0.425	(1.275)	(1.975)	(1.75)	(0.85)	0.35	2.75	4.25	3.95	5.2	5.45
Monthly loan or (repayment) . .		—	—	1.525	2.225	2.00	1.10	(0.10)	(2.50)	(4.00)	(0.25)	—	—
Cumulative loan.		—	—	1.525	3.750	5.75	6.85	6.75	4.25	0.25	0.00	—	—
Ending cash balance.	$2.85	$ 1.75	$ 0.425	$ 0.25	$ 0.25	$ 0.25	$ 0.25	$ 0.25	$0.25	$0.25	$3.70	$ 5.2	$5.45
Total Current Assets													
Ending cash balance.	$2.85	$ 1.75	$ 0.425	$ 0.250	$ 0.25	$ 0.25	$ 0.25	$ 0.25	$0.25	$0.25	$3.70	$ 5.2	$5.45
Accounts receivable.	0.75	0.45	0.225	0.075	0.00	0.00	0.90	1.50	3.00	3.00	3.00	1.5	0.75
Inventory	1.60	2.60	3.900	5.400	7.00	8.60	9.00	8.60	6.20	3.80	1.40	1.0	1.60
Total current assets.	$5.20	$ 4.80	$ 4.550	$ 5.725	$ 7.25	$ 8.85	$10.15	$10.35	$9.45	$7.05	$8.10	$ 7.7	$7.80

Figure 6–4 is a graphical presentation of the current asset cycle. It corresponds to Figure 6–1B, which demonstrates the nature of asset growth. Figure 6–4 includes the two years covered in Tables 6–4 and 6–5, assuming level production and no sales growth. We observe that there are minimum levels of current assets, considered permanent current assets. McGraw Hill Education demonstrates comparable patterns in Figure 6–3.

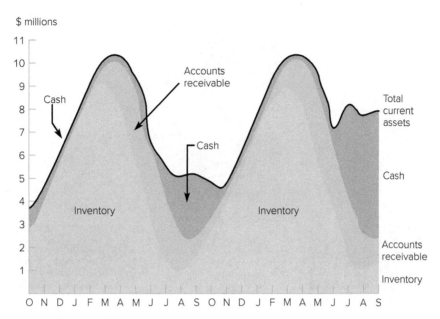

Figure 6–4 The nature of asset growth (Yawakuzi)

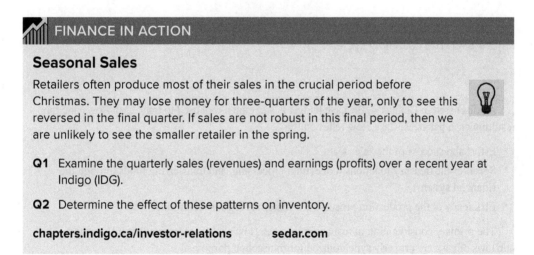

FINANCE IN ACTION

Seasonal Sales

Retailers often produce most of their sales in the crucial period before Christmas. They may lose money for three-quarters of the year, only to see this reversed in the final quarter. If sales are not robust in this final period, then we are unlikely to see the smaller retailer in the spring.

Q1 Examine the quarterly sales (revenues) and earnings (profits) over a recent year at Indigo (IDG).

Q2 Determine the effect of these patterns on inventory.

chapters.indigo.ca/investor-relations   **sedar.com**

Cash Flow Cycle

Managers continually monitor the state of these current assets to ensure liquidity, which is the ability to convert to cash quickly as the need arises. Many businesses hold current assets to better serve clients. In Chapter 3, we identified the ratios that can be used to monitor the firm's liquidity.

On the other side of the ledger, it is important that management have well-developed credit facilities with the support of suppliers and financial institutions to enhance the firm's liquidity. When a firm's liquidity is called into question it often is difficult to continue in business.

LO4 Liquidity is largely determined by cash flowing through the company on a daily, weekly, and monthly basis as determined by the cash flow cycle, illustrated in Figure 6–5. Sales produce accounts receivable that are collected as cash-in-the-future and, in turn, used for inventory or services. This cyclical process then repeats, but because the cash flow may be unpredictable and uneven, the firm will experience asset buildup and growth.

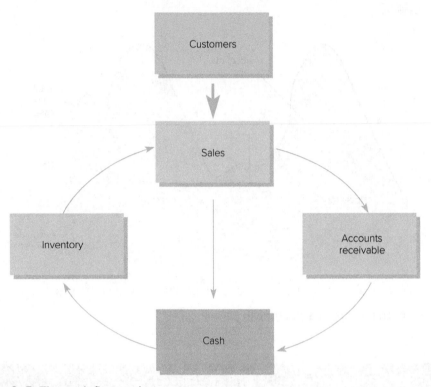

Figure 6–5 The cash flow cycle

As discussed in Chapter 4, the cash budget is a common tool used to track cash flows and the resulting cash balances. Cash flow relies on the

- Effort and success of the sales team
- Speed of the treasury functions (collecting, processing, and transferring funds through the financial system)
- Efficiency of the production process (raw materials to finished product)

The primary consideration in managing the cash flow cycle is to ensure that inflows and outflows of cash are properly synchronized for transaction purposes.

Although sales, receivables, and inventory form the basis for the cash flow cycle, Figure 6–7 expands the detail and activities that influence cash. Cash inflows are driven by sales and are influenced by the type of customers, their geographical location, the product being sold, and the industry. A sale can be made for cash or swipe card (e.g., Tim Hortons) or on credit (e.g., Dell). Some industries, such as textbook publishing (see Figure 6–3), will grant credit terms of 60 days to bookstores; others, such as department stores, will grant customers credit for 30 days. When receivables are collected, cash balances increase and the firm uses cash to pay interest to lenders, dividends to

Tim Hortons
timhortons.com
Dell
dell.ca

shareholders, taxes, suppliers, and wages, and to repurchase inventory. When the firm has excess cash, it invests in marketable securities, and when it needs cash for current assets, it usually either sells marketable securities or borrows funds from short-term lenders.

The time it takes from the initial outlay of funds for raw materials until the firm collects funds from its clients for the finished product, offset to some degree by the firm's purchases bought on credit, is referred to as the cash conversion cycle, shown in Figure 6–6. This cycle utilizes the asset utilization formulas developed in Chapter 3. Since cash flow is so important to the firm, we can understand why the utilization of assets is a major focus of management.

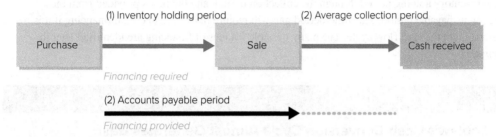

Figure 6–6 Cash conversion cycle (linear representation)

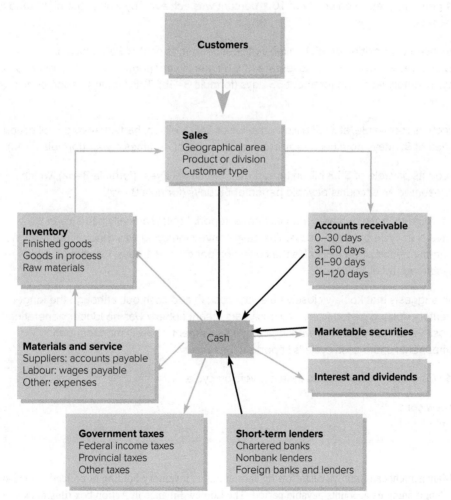

Figure 6–7 Expanded cash flow cycle

Basically, the cash conversion cycle will consist of

1. The time materials are in inventory (calculated as the inventory holding period, formula 3–5b)

2. Plus the time it takes to collect sales from clients (calculated as the average collection period, formula 3–4b)

3. Less the time the firm is allowed to delay payment to its suppliers (calculated as the accounts payable period, formula 3–6b)

Examining Figure 6–6 we observe that there is a cash gap between the funds required for the inventory holding period through the collection period, and the funds provided from the accounts payable period. This time-period gap will require that the firm obtain financing if it is to maintain the cash flow cycle. The many possible sources of financing are identified later in Figure 6–11.

 FINANCE IN ACTION

Loblaw's Cash Conversion Cycle Almost Generates Cash

The assets at Loblaw must be turned over quickly to obtain reasonable returns for shareholders because of its low profit margin. Despite 2019's low profit margin of 2.4 percent, a return on equity of 10.1 percent was achieved by way of the high turnover of assets.

The inventory position of $5.1 billion, with cost of goods sold at $33.3 billion, represented an inventory turnover rate of 6.5 times a year (formula 3–5a) or, put another way, inventory was held for about 56 days (formula 3–5b). This holding period continues to grow.

Accounts receivable, at $1.2 billion on sales of $48.1 billion, had an average collection period of 9.1 days (formula 3–4b), or a turnover rate of 40 times a year (formula 3–4a).

Accounts payable of $5.3 billion turned over 6.3 times a year (formula 3–6a), which represented an accounts payable period of 58 days (formula 3–6b).

According to these numbers from its annual report, Loblaw actually had a cash conversion cycle of about 7 days. The cash conversion cycle was determined from the inventory period of 56 days plus the collection period of 9.1 days, less the accounts payable period of 58 days.

This suggests that Loblaw closely balances cash in and cash out, although the longer inventory holding period from previous years meant Loblaw was no longer generating a positive cash flow from its working capital investment. Closely monitoring the components of the cash cycle is important for success.

Q1 Calculate Loblaw's latest cash conversion cycle.

loblaw.com
Symbol: L

Management can improve cash flow by shortening its inventory holding or collection periods or by lengthening its accounts payable period. The Loblaw Finance in Action box illustrates how the cash conversion period may produce positive cash flows for the firm. The cash conversion cycle, because it is repeated continuously by most firms, will create an ongoing or permanent need for financing to fill the cash gap, if it is negative as shown in Figure 6–6.

PATTERNS OF FINANCING

The financial manager's selection of external sources of funds to finance current assets may be one of the firm's most important decisions. The axiom that all current assets should be financed by current liabilities (accounts payable, bank loans, commercial paper, etc.) is subject to challenge when one sees the permanent buildup that can occur in current assets. In the Yawakuzi example, the buildup in inventory was substantial at $9 million. The example had a logical conclusion in that the motorcycles were sold, cash was generated, and current assets became very liquid. What if a much smaller sales level had occurred? Yawakuzi would be sitting on a large inventory that needed to be financed and would be generating no cash. Theoretically, the firm could be declared technically insolvent (bankrupt) if short-term sources of funds were used but were unable to be renewed when they came due. How would the interest and principal be paid without cash flow from inventory liquidation? The most appropriate financing pattern would be one in which asset buildup and length of financing terms are perfectly matched, as indicated in Figure 6–8.

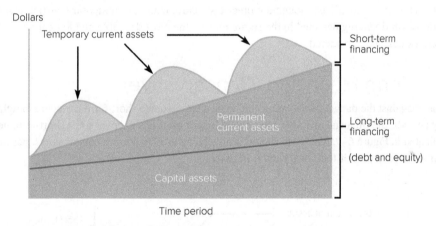

Figure 6–8 Matching long-term and short-term needs (hedged)

In the upper part of the figure we see that the temporary buildup in current assets is financed by short-term funds. More importantly, however, permanent current assets as well as capital assets are financed with long-term funds from the sale of stock, issuance of bonds, or retention of earnings. The financial liabilities are matched so that they are covered by assets converted to cash as they come due. Covering your risks with appropriate assets or insurance is known as a hedged approach.

LO5 Hedging is the matching of the maturities of assets and liabilities to reduce or cover risk. A financial manager is interested in techniques that help deal with risk. This is one instance of a hedged approach. Purchasing insurance and utilizing derivatives (Chapter 19) are other hedging techniques. Of course, a perfectly hedged approach is almost impossible to achieve in practice.

Hedged Corporation			
Balance Sheet			
As at December 31, 20XX (000s)			
Temporary current assets.........	6	Accounts payable..............	2
		Bank loans	4
Permanent current assets	10	Debt	15
Capital assets	20	Equity.......................	15
Total assets...................	36	Total liabilities and equity	36

The balance sheet for the perfectly hedged firm as illustrated in Figure 6–8 might look as shown above. The long-term assets (permanent and capital) are financed with both long-term debt and equity. Equity has an implicit cost. In some chapter problems we will input a cost for equity as part of the long-term financing cost.

Alternative Plans

Only a financial manager with unusual insight and timing could construct a financial plan for working capital that adhered perfectly to the design in Figure 6–8. The difficulty rests in precisely determining which part of current assets is temporary and which part is permanent. Even if dollar amounts could be ascertained, the exact timing of asset liquidation is a difficult matter. To compound the problem, we are never quite sure how much short-term or long-term financing is available at a given time. Even though the precise synchronization of temporary current assets and short-term financing depicted in the figure may be the most desirable and logical plan, other alternatives must be considered.

Long-Term Financing (Conservative)

To protect against the danger of not being able to provide adequate short-term financing in tight money periods, the financial manager may rely on long-term funds to cover some short-term needs. As indicated in Figure 6–9, long-term capital is now being used to finance capital assets, permanent current assets, and part of *temporary current assets*.

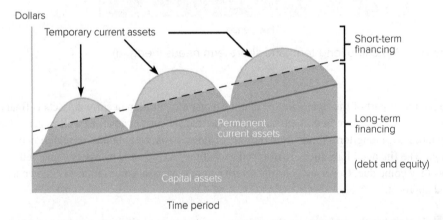

Figure 6–9 Using long-term financing for part of short-term needs (conservative)

By using long-term capital to cover short-term needs, the firm virtually assures itself of having adequate capital at all times. The firm may prefer to borrow a million dollars for 10 years—rather than attempt to borrow a million dollars at the beginning of each year for 10 years and pay it back at the end of each year.

This is a conservative approach. Although it provides adequate funds, it is less profitable. Generally, longer-term interest rates are more expensive. Additionally, as can be seen from Figure 6–9, the firm pays interest on funds during periods when the funds are not needed.

Short-Term Financing (Risky)

This is not to say that all financial managers utilize long-term financing on a large scale. To acquire long-term funds, the firm must generally go to the capital markets with a bond or stock offering or must privately place longer-term obligations with insurance companies, wealthy individuals, and so forth. Many small businesses do not have access to such long-term capital and are forced to rely heavily on short-term bank and trade credit. In the capital shortage era of the past decade, even some large businesses were forced to operate with short-term funds.

This is a risky approach. If sales lag and cash flows are not as projected, the firm may not be able to meet its short-term financing obligations as they come due. In addition, the suppliers of credit, the financial institutions and trade creditors, may be reluctant or unable to extend credit any longer. This approach is likely to show up in lower liquidity ratios, examined in Chapter 3.

The upside is that short-term financing offers some advantages over more extended financial arrangements. As a general rule, the interest rate on short-term funds is lower than that on long-term funds. In addition, short-term obligations are generally paid off sooner. We might surmise then that a firm could develop a working capital financing plan in which short-term funds are used to finance not only temporary current assets but also part of the permanent working capital needs of the firm. As depicted in Figure 6–10, bank and trade credit as well as other sources of short-term financing are now supporting part of the permanent current asset needs of the firm.

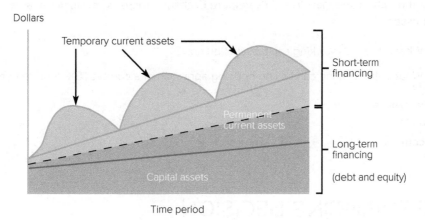

Figure 6–10 Using short-term financing for part of long-term needs (risky)

Managing Working Capital

Small businesses may have access to bank loans, but they tend to be expensive and, therefore, it is important to make good use of the trade credit available through suppliers. If a firm is offering its customers credit, it should seek to balance this accounts receivable position with trade credit (accounts payable) available to it. Trade credit is generally available without interest charges, whereas bank loans definitely have an explicit cost.

Freshii Inc. is a Canadian healthy food company started in 2005 that had grown to 300 franchises in 20 countries by 2020. Freshii was inspired by the "mom and pop" delis of New York. After listing on the TSX Venture Exchange it moved in 2017 to the senior TSX exchange with a public offering of $125 million in common shares. These funds would fund expansion and improve its capital structure. It had been relying heavily on accounts payable as a source of financing. This was an aggressive approach.

In 2014 Freshii had $2 million in accounts payable and only $460,000 in accounts receivable. An injection of equity capital was needed as Freshii moved beyond a heavy reliance on short-term accounts payable and short-term debt financing. In late 2016 accounts payable were $5 million with $15 million in debt due within one year. The equity issue in excess of $40 million reduces the reliance on short-term financing. By early 2020 it had $0.8 million in accounts payable and $1.7 million in accounts receivable.

Company websites generally have financial statements available under investor relations. The TSX site lists the securities that make up its TSX Venture Composite Index through its site map. The TSX Venture Exchange focuses on small Canadian businesses.

Q1 What is Freshii's working capital situation now?

Q2 What is the working capital and hedging approach of a current TSX Venture firm?

freshii.com/ca
Symbol: FRII

tmx.com

THE FINANCING DECISION

Some corporations are more flexible than others, because they are not locked into a few available sources of funds. Corporations would like many financing alternatives to minimize their cost of funds at any point in time. Unfortunately, not many firms are in this enviable position through the duration of a business cycle. During an economic boom period a shortage of low-cost alternatives exists, and firms often minimize their financing costs by raising funds in advance of forecasted asset needs.

The financial manager not only encounters a timing problem but also needs to select the right type of financing. Even for companies with many alternative sources of funds, there may be only one or two decisions that look good in retrospect. At the time the financing decision is made, the financial manager is never sure it is the right one. Should the financing be long term or short term, debt or equity, and so on? Figure 6–11 is a decision-tree diagram that shows many of the financing decisions that can be made. At each point a decision is made until a final financing method is reached. In most cases, corporations use a combination of these financing methods. At all times, the financial manager must balance short-term versus long-term considerations against the composition of the firm's assets and the firm's willingness to accept risk. The ratio of long-term financing to short-term financing at any time is greatly influenced by the financial manager's consideration of the risks and potential payoffs from each financing alternative, and also by the term structure of interest rates.

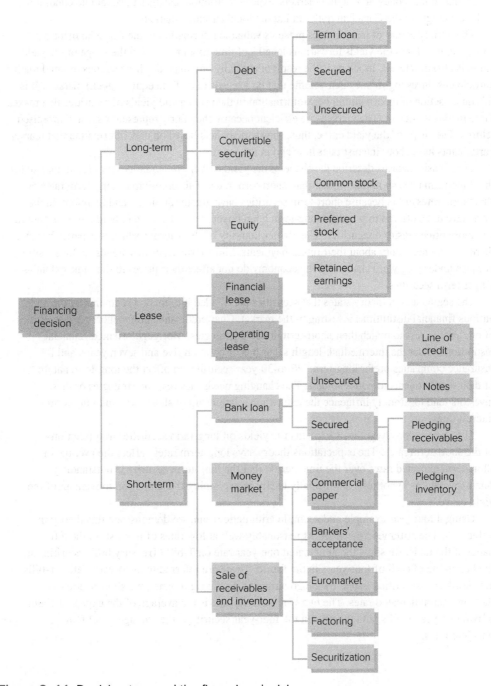

Figure 6–11 Decision tree and the financing decision

LO6 Term Structure of Interest Rates

The term structure of interest rates is often referred to as a yield curve. It shows the interest rate at a specific time for all securities having equal risk but differing maturity dates (term). Therefore, we graph yield (return) against time to maturity. Generally, Government of Canada securities are used to construct yield curves because they have many maturities, and each of the securities has an equally low risk of default. Corporate securities of similar grade (or rating) move in the same direction as government securities but have higher interest rates because of their greater default risk. The yield curves for both corporate and government securities change daily to reflect current competitive conditions in the money and capital markets, expected inflation, changes in economic conditions, and the strength of the Canadian dollar in international currency markets.

The term structure of interest rates presents valuable information to the financial manager. At any time it shows the yields for various lengths of time (maturities), but the shape of the yield curve is also of interest. Its shape is the result of the daily buying and selling actions of bond market participants, investing monies in a volume that far exceeds that of the equity (stock) markets. It is this quick action of incorporating new information in the pricing and yields of securities that makes these markets efficient. The markets are efficient because they fairly represent risks and promised returns. The shape of the yield curve, thus, shows the beliefs based on new information that market participants have about interest rates now and in the future.

Three basic theories describe the shape of the yield curve. The liquidity premium theory states that long-term rates should be higher than short-term rates. This premium of long-term rates over short-term rates exists because short-term securities have greater liquidity, and therefore, higher rates have to be offered to potential long-term bond buyers to entice them to hold these less liquid and more price sensitive securities. The greater liquidity of short-term securities is partly because there is less uncertainty about their future payments. Short-term securities are less price sensitive, because underlying yield changes in the economy do not affect their prices to the same extent as longer-term securities.

The segmentation theory states that securities are divided into market segments by the various financial institutions investing in the market. Chartered banks prefer short-term securities of one year or less to match their short-term lending strategies. Mortgage-oriented financial institutions prefer the intermediate-length securities of between five and seven years, and life insurance companies prefer long-term, 20-to-30-year securities to offset the long-term nature of their commitments to policyholders. The changing needs, desires, and strategies of these investors tend to strongly influence the nature and relationship of short-term and long-term interest rates.

The expectations hypothesis explains the yields on long-term securities as a function of the short-term rates. The expectations theory says long-term rates reflect the average of short-term expected rates over the time period that the long-term security is outstanding. The expectations hypothesis is especially useful in explaining the shape and movement of the yield curve.

Using a four-year example and a simple arithmetic mean, we demonstrate this theory in Table 6–6. The arithmetic mean works reasonably well at low rates of interest. In the left panel of the table, we show the anticipated one-year rate on T-bill (Treasury bill) securities at the beginning of each of four years in the future. These are referred to as forward rates. T-bills are short-term securities issued by the government. In the right panel, we show averages of the one-year anticipated rates. The two-year security rate is the average of the expected yields of two one-year T-bills, and the rate on the four-year security is the average of all four one-year rates.

Table 6–6 The expectations theory

1-yr. T-bill at beginning of yr. 1 = 7%	
1-yr. T-bill at beginning of yr. 2 = 8%	2-yr. security (7% + 8%)/2 = 7.5%
1-yr. T-bill at beginning of yr. 3 = 9%	3-yr. security (7% + 8% + 9%)/3 = 8%
1-yr. T-bill at beginning of yr. 4 = 10%	4-yr. security (7% + 8% + 9% + 10%)/4 = 8.5%

*Exact calculation is
$$[(1.07)(1.08)]^{\frac{1}{2}} - 1 \times 100\% = 7.4988\%$$
$$[(1.07)(1.08)(1.09)]^{\frac{1}{3}} - 1 \times 100\% = 7.997\%$$
$$[(1.07)(1.08)(1.09)(1.10)]^{\frac{1}{4}} - 1 \times 100\% = 8.494\%$$

In this example, the progressively higher rates for two-, three-, and four-year securities represent a reflection of higher anticipated one-year rates in the future. The expectations hypothesis suggests that when long-term rates are much higher than short-term rates, the market is saying that it expects short-term rates to rise. When long-term rates are lower than short-term rates, the market is expecting short-term rates to fall. This theory is useful to financial managers in helping to set expectations for the cost of financing over time and especially in making choices about when to use short-term debt or long-term debt.

All three theories presented have some influence on interest rates. At times, the liquidity premium or segmentation theory dominates the shape of the curve, and at other times, the expectations theory is most important. The financial manager cannot escape making judgments about future developments, and sometimes knowledge of yield curve theories provides a managerial edge for more accurate judgments.

Term Structure Shapes

Figure 6–12 depicts the three common shapes taken by the term structure of interest rates (yield curves) based on government securities. More-risky securities (provincial bonds and corporate bonds of various risks) would lie above these curves in roughly the same shape. The riskier the issuer of the security, the higher the yield curve.

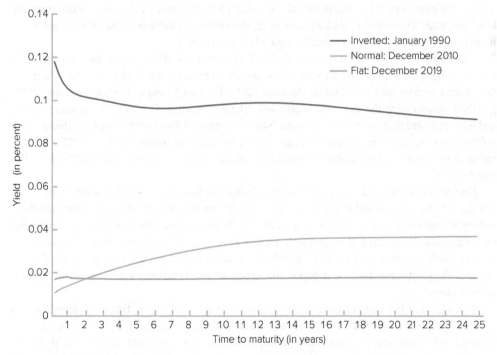

Figure 6–12 Yield curves showing term structure of interest rates
Source: Bank of Canada.

The December 2019 curve, generally referred to as a normal yield curve, is upward-sloping, and the December 2010 term structure is a flat yield curve. The downward-sloping yield curve of January 1990 is referred to as an inverted yield curve, although at much higher yields.

Under economic conditions expected to be positive, we usually see a normal yield curve. However, as signs appear that the economy is slowing down, yield curves usually invert on the expectations that the weaker economy will bring lower inflationary pressures and, thus, lower interest rates. The Bank of Canada generally cooperates in lowering interest rates to help stimulate the economy as it weakens. When the economy is overheating, the Bank of Canada often raises interest rates to slow economic activity and borrowing by adopting a restrictive (or tight money) monetary policy, sometimes bringing on a recession.

Bank of Canada
bankofcanada.ca

In 1990, we had an inverted yield curve at much higher interest rates that foreshadowed a recession and falling interest rates. At certain times in 2019 the yield curve inverted, perhaps suggesting an economic slowdown. However, in 2020 we saw a normal yield curve at very low rates.

Interest rates are influenced by many variables, but inflationary levels have a major influence on the height of the yield curve, and inflationary expectations have influence on its shape. In 1990, inflation was in excess of 5 percent, but by 2000 it had dropped to about 2 percent. This is demonstrated by the higher level of the 1990 yield curve in Figure 6–12. When inflation increases, lenders charge a premium for the purchasing power they will lose when the loan is repaid in cheaper, inflated dollars. Although short-term rates are influenced more by current demands for money than by inflation, long-term rates are greatly affected by the expected rate of inflation over the life of an investment.

Within Canada, inflation and the value of the Canadian dollar are major determinants of interest rates. The relationship between interest rates and the foreign exchange value of the Canadian dollar is covered in Chapter 21, which deals with international finance.

Interest Rate Volatility

In designing working capital policy, the astute financial manager is interested not only in the term structure of interest rates but also in the relative volatility and the historical level of short-term and long-term rates. Figure 6–13 uses long-term corporate bonds and short-term commercial paper to provide insight into interest rate volatility over a long time period.

Short-term rates are much more volatile than long-term rates. As a general rule, short-term rates have been lower than long-term rates, but there have been a number of exceptions. Short-term rates exceeded long-term rates in the early 1980s, for a brief time in 1986, in the early 1990s, and then spiked during the recession of 2007–08. These were all periods of tight monetary policy and were followed by economic slowdowns. Note that although short-term rates have fluctuated wildly about long-term rates, long-term rates have fallen from the historic peak of 1982 as inflation rates have declined from in excess of 12 percent annually to about 2 percent by the 1990s and the 2000s.

How should a financial manager respond to fluctuating interest rates and changing term structures? Managers should always be aware of the greater volatility of short-term rates relative to longer-term rates, so as to not get caught offside. They do not want to be holding a lot of short-term financial obligations that might prove difficult to service if interest rates move up quickly. As financial managers plan investment and financing decisions, they should keep in mind the shape of the yield curve, because it embeds the expectations of market participants about future interest rates.

When interest rates are high, especially with an inverted yield curve, financial managers generally prefer to temporarily borrow short term if funds are available. This is because the inverted yield curve suggests that interest rates, both short- and long-term, will decline in the future. As rates decline, the financial officers try to lock in lower rates with long-term borrowing. Some of these long-term funds are used to reduce short-term debt, and the rest are available for future expansion. Expansion generally requires additional investment in both capital assets (plant and equipment) and in working capital.

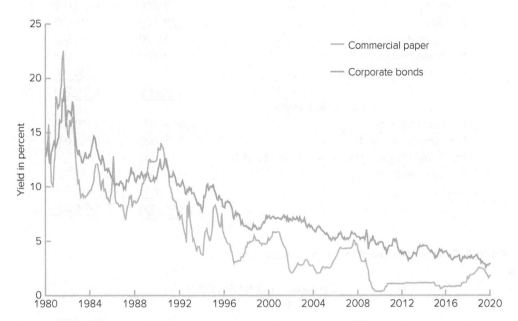

Figure 6–13 Long- and short-term interest rates

Source: www.bank-banque-canada.ca

A DECISION PROCESS

Assume we are comparing alternative financing plans for working capital. As indicated in Table 6–7, $500,000 of working capital (current assets) must be financed for the Edwards Corporation. Under plan A, we finance all our current asset needs with short-term funds, whereas under plan B, we finance only a relatively small portion of working capital with short-term money—relying heavily on long-term funds. In either case, we carry $100,000 of capital assets with long-term financing commitments. As indicated in part 3 of the table, under plan A we finance total needs of $600,000 with $500,000 of short-term financing and $100,000 of long-term financing, whereas with plan B we finance $150,000 short-term and $450,000 long-term.

Plan A carries the lower cost of financing, with interest of 6 percent on $500,000 of the $600,000 required. We show the effect of both plans on bottom-line earnings in Table 6–8.[1] Assuming the firm generates $200,000 in earnings before interest and taxes, plan A provides aftertax earnings of $80,000, but plan B generates only $73,000.

---

[1] Common stock is eliminated from the example to simplify the analysis. If it were included, all of the basic patterns would still hold.

Table 6–7 Alternative financing plans

EDWARDS CORPORATION	Plan A	Plan B
Part 1. Current Assets		
Temporary	$250,000	$ 250,000
Permanent	250,000	250,000
Total current assets.	500,000	500,000
Short-term financing (6%).	500,000	150,000
Long-term financing (10%)	0	350,000
	$500,000	$ 500,000
Part 2. Capital Assets		
Plant and equipment.	$100,000	$ 100,000
Long-term financing (10%)	$100,000	$ 100,000
Part 3. Total Financing (summary of parts 1 and 2)		
Short-term (6%).	$500,000	$ 150,000
Long-term (10%)	100,000	450,000
	$600,000	$ 600,000

Table 6–8 Impact of financing plans on earnings

EDWARDS CORPORATION	
Plan A	
Earnings before interest and taxes	$200,000
Interest (short-term): 6% × $500,000	−30,000
Interest (long-term): 10% × $100,000	−10,000
Earnings before taxes.	160,000
Taxes (50%)	80,000
Earnings after taxes	$ 80,000
Plan B	
Earnings before interest and taxes	$200,000
Interest (short-term): 6% × $150,000	−9,000
Interest (long-term): 10% × $450,000	−45,000
Earnings before taxes.	146,000
Taxes (50%)	73,000
Earnings after taxes	$ 73,000

Note: Long-term financing could also be in the form of equity. Equity financing does not have an explicit cost on the income statement but would impact earnings per share.

Introducing Varying Conditions

Although plan A, employing cheaper short-term sources of financing, appears to provide $7,000 more in return, this is not always the case. During tight money periods, short-term financing may be difficult to find or may carry exorbitant rates.

Furthermore, inadequate financing may mean lost sales or financial embarrassment. For these reasons, the firm may wish to evaluate plans A and B based on differing assumptions about the economy and the money markets.

An Expected Value Approach

The maximization of shareholder wealth has been identified as an important goal of the firm, and management will make many decisions attempting to meet this objective. However, in spite of the best possible planning process, irregular economic conditions may have an adverse impact on the results achieved by the firm. To increase wealth over time, the firm must have more correct decisions than incorrect decisions. Put another way, the firm's average decision should increase firm value.

An expected value approach will identify the possible results for the firm under differing economic conditions, as well as assign a probability to the occurrence of each economic condition. The expected value is then calculated as the average result based on the probable economic conditions. If the firm makes decisions based on the expected value approach, it will sometimes exceed expectations and sometimes not meet expectations, but on average it will have results that add value to the firm.

As an example, let us suggest that past history combined with economic forecasting may indicate an 80 percent probability of normal events and a 20 percent chance of extremely tight money. To determine these probabilities, a firm could use the economic and financial information supplied by financial institutions. The financial institutions, through their economics departments, regularly suggest the future direction of interest rates. The firm could combine these predictions with its knowledge, based on experience, of how interest rates impact on the particular firm. Financial institutions provide market assessments and comments on a daily basis through their websites. We should also be able to use the term structure of interest rates to determine the market's expectations of the direction of future interest rates.

Using plan A, under normal conditions the Edwards Corporation enjoys a $7,000 superior return over plan B (as indicated in Table 6–8). Let us now assume that under disruptive tight money conditions, plan A would provide a $15,000 lower return than plan B, because of high short-term interest rates. These conditions are summarized in Table 6–9, and an expected value of return is computed. The expected value represents the sum of the expected outcomes under the two conditions. We see that even when downside risk is considered, plan A carries a higher expected return of $2,600.

Table 6–9 Expected returns under different economic conditions

EDWARDS CORPORATION						
1. Normal conditions	Expected higher return under plan A vs. plan B		Probability of normal conditions		Expected outcome	
	$7,000	×	0.80	=	+$5,600	
2. Tight money	Expected lower return under plan A vs. plan B		Probability of tight money			
	($15,000)	×	0.20	=	(3,000)	
Expected value of return for plan A versus plan B				=	+$2,600	

For another high-risk firm in the same industry that might suffer $50,000 lower returns during tight money conditions, plan A becomes too dangerous to undertake, as indicated in Table 6–10. Plan A's expected return is now $4,400 less than that of plan B.

Table 6–10 Expected returns for high-risk firm

The Other Corporation						
1. Normal conditions	Expected higher return under plan A vs. plan B		Probability of normal conditions		Expected outcome	
	$7,000	×	0.80	=	+$5,600	
2. Tight money	Expected lower return under plan A vs. plan B		Probability of tight money			
	($50,000)	×	0.20	=	(10,000)	
Expected value of return for plan A versus plan B				=	−$4,400	

SHIFTS IN ASSET STRUCTURE

Thus far our attention has been directed to the risk associated with various financing plans. We have said that short-term financing is generally cheaper, and thus more profitable, but carries a higher risk. The manager faces a risk-return tradeoff. Risk-return analysis must also be carried to the asset side and to the interaction between both sides of the balance sheet. On the asset side, we note that as we proceed down the balance sheet, assets generally become less liquid. Longer-term assets carry greater risks but higher potential returns. Again, the tradeoff. Keep in mind the relationship between both sides of the balance sheet. A firm with heavy risk exposure due to short-term borrowing may compensate in part by carrying highly liquid assets. Conversely, a firm with established long-term debt commitments may choose to carry a heavier component of less liquid, highly profitable assets.

Either through desire or compelling circumstances, business firms have decreased the liquidity of their current asset holdings since the early 1960s. The average current ratio for Canadian non-financial corporations, which was slightly above 2.0:1 in 1960, declined below 1.0:1 by the early 1990s, moving slightly above that later in the decade and into the recent period. The economic difficulties of 2007–08 were followed by a period of greater liquidity for several years. Figure 6–14 shows the current ratio since 1990.

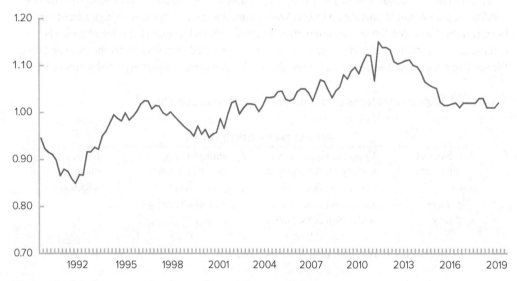

Figure 6–14 Current ratio of non-financial corporations

The increased cost of financing current assets resulting from the general rise in interest rates may be one reason for this decline. The diminishing liquidity can also be traced in part to more sophisticated, profit-oriented financial management, as well as to a better utilization of cash balances via computer. Better control of accounts receivable and inventory positions has allowed for the drop in the current ratio. Less liquidity can also be traced to the long-term effect inflation has had on the corporate balance sheet—forcing greater borrowing to carry more expensive assets—and to decreasing profitability during recessions.

TOWARD AN OPTIMAL POLICY

As previously indicated, the firm should attempt to relate financing patterns to asset liquidity and vice versa. The firm should also consider its financing in relation to the risks it is prepared to face and the potential returns. Table 6–11 presents a number of different working capital

Table 6–11 Current asset liquidity and asset-financing plan

Financing Plan	Asset Liquidity	
	Low Liquidity	High Liquidity
Short-term	1 (risky)	2
	High profit	Moderate profit
	High risk	Moderate risk
Long-term	3	4 (conservative)
	Moderate profit	Low profit
	Moderate risk	Low risk

alternatives. Along the top of the table is asset liquidity and along the side, the type of financing arrangement. The combined impact of the two variables is shown in each of the four panels of the table.

LO7 Each firm must decide how it wishes to tradeoff risk and profitability as it combines asset liquidity and its financing needs. The aggressive, risk-oriented firm in panel 1 of the table borrows short-term and maintains relatively low levels of liquidity, hoping to increase profit. It benefits from low-cost short-term financing and has a greater investment in high-return assets. It does not tie up funds in low-return current assets. The aggressive firm with this risky approach is vulnerable to a credit crunch. Short-term interest rates are more volatile, and funding may temporarily become more expensive or unavailable. At these times, the aggressive firm may have difficulties continuing in business because it does not have the liquidity cushion to sustain itself through the difficult times.

The more conservative firm, following the plan in panel 4, utilizes established long-term financing and maintains a high degree of liquidity. The conservative firm pays more in the long run on its financing and has more money tied up in low-return current assets. Both of these factors reduce its return on assets and equity. However, the conservative firm builds a cushion in the buildup of current assets and by putting long-term financing in place that may allow it to survive market downturns and periods of high interest rates.

In panels 2 and 3 we see more moderate positions in which the firm compensates for short-term financing with highly liquid assets (2) or balances low liquidity with pre-committed, long-term financing (3).

Each financial manager must structure their working capital position and the associated risk-return tradeoff to meet the company's needs. For firms whose cash flow patterns are predictable—typified by the public utilities sector—a low degree of liquidity can be maintained without significant risk increases. Immediate access to capital markets, such as that enjoyed by large, prestigious firms, also allows a greater risk-taking capability. Firms with volatile cash flow patterns, on the other hand, probably should be more conservative by maintaining higher liquidity to meet cash flow slowdowns and by establishing solid longer-term financing. In each case, the ultimate concern must be for maximizing the overall valuation of the firm through a judicious consideration of risk-return options.

In the next two chapters, we examine the various methods for managing the individual components of working capital. In Chapter 7, we consider the techniques for managing cash, marketable securities, receivables, and inventory. In Chapter 8, we look at trade and bank credit and also at other sources of short-term funds.

SUMMARY

1. Working capital management involves the financing and management of the current assets of the firm. A firm's ability to properly manage current assets and the associated liabilities may determine how well it can survive in the short run. The financial manager probably spends the most time on working capital management. (LO1)

2. As sales increase, a firm requires an increasing investment in current assets to support the increased sales. (LO2)

3. Production processes are usually more operationally efficient on a level basis. However, sales volumes are likely to fluctuate over time. Although production and sales should be roughly matched over the long run, the short-term differences will result in the buildup of current assets. If part of this buildup in current assets is permanent, and sales levels continue, financial arrangements should carry longer maturities. This demands more careful financial planning and attention to the firm's liquidity. As assets become less liquid, their risk increases. (LO3)

4. The cash flow cycle of the firm is determined by the inventory holding period plus the collection period less the accounts payable period. (LO4)

5. A hedged approach is an attempt by a financial manager to reduce risk. Hedging attempts to match the maturities of debt obligations to the maturities of assets. Assets should convert to cash as liabilities become payable. (LO5)

6. The astute financial manager must keep an eye on the general cost of borrowing, the term structure of interest rates, and the relative volatility of short- and long-term rates. The term structure relates yields on similar risk obligations to the time until maturity. The shape of the term structure tells us the expectations and demands of market participants in regard to interest rates. (LO6)

7. The firm has a number of risk-return decisions to consider. Though long-term financing provides a safety margin in availability of funds, its higher cost may reduce the profit potential of the firm. On the asset side, carrying highly liquid current assets assures the bill-paying capability of the firm but detracts from profit potential. Each firm must tailor the various risk-return tradeoffs to meet its own needs. The peculiarities of a firm's industry have a major impact on the options open to management. (LO7)

DISCUSSION QUESTIONS

1. Explain how rapidly expanding sales can drain the cash resources of the firm. (LO2)

2. What is the significance to working capital management of matching sales and production? (LO3)

3. How is a cash budget used to help manage current assets? (LO3)

4. "The most appropriate financing pattern would be one in which asset buildup and the length of financing terms are perfectly matched." Discuss the difficulty involved in achieving this financing pattern. (LO5)

5. "By using long-term financing to finance part of temporary current assets, a firm may have less risk but lower returns than a firm with a normal financing plan." Explain the significance of this statement. (LO5)

6. A firm that uses short-term financing methods for a portion of permanent current assets is assuming more risk but expects higher returns than a firm with a normal financing plan. Explain. (LO5)

7.	What does the term structure of interest rates indicate? (LO6)

8.	What are the three theories for describing the shape of the term structure of interest rates (the yield curve)? Briefly describe each theory. (LO6)

9.	What might an inverted yield curve suggest to the financial manager? (LO6)

10.	Discuss macroeconomic factors that would influence the yield curve. (LO6)

11.	Suppose a bond trader believes that interest rates will begin to fall in the near future. Which strategy should the trader adopt? If the trader controls lots of money, what effect will the trader's action have on the yield curve? (LO6)

12.	Discuss the relative volatility of short- and long-term interest rates. (LO7)

13.	What reasons can you give for the changes in corporations' liquidity? (LO1)

INTERNET RESOURCES AND QUESTIONS

The Bank of Canada provides weekly financial statistics, including yields on T-bills and benchmark bonds that can be used to construct current and historical yield curves: bankofcanada.ca

Royal Bank Dominion Securities (rbcds.com) has wealth management services as well as offering:

Interest rate forecasts: rbc.com/economics/economic-reports

TMX with CanDeal provide information on benchmark bond pricing: tmxmoney.com

Bond quotes are difficult to find, although often available it one opens a trading account at a financial institution.

Bloomberg provides a wealth of information including the U.S. yield curve and that of other major industrialized countries: bloomberg.com/markets/rates-bonds/government-bonds/us

1.	Construct the Canadian yield curve using information from the Bank of Canada. Construct the most current yield curve and a yield curve of one year ago.
    a.	How would you describe the yield curves?
    b.	What are your expectations for future interest rates?

2.	Using a site such as Bloomberg, construct current yield curves for Brazil, the United States, Britain, another European country, and Japan on the same chart, using Excel. Label appropriately, including date and source. Identify the similarities and differences in the curves. What do the yield curves suggest about the different economies?

3.	Discuss the predictions for the future trends in interest rates in Canada and identify the factors that are driving interest rate changes. Use a market commentary from a major financial institution.

PROBLEMS

1.	Bondi Beachwear Company expects sales next year to be $750,000. Inventory and accounts receivable will have to be increased by $120,000 to accommodate this sales level. The company has a steady profit margin of 10 percent, with a 30 percent dividend payout. How much external funding will Bondi Beachwear Company have to seek? Assume there is no increase in liabilities other than that which will occur with the external financing.

2. Axle Supply Co. expects sales next year to be $300,000. Inventory and accounts receivable will increase by $60,000 to accommodate this sales level. The company has a steady profit margin of 8 percent, with a 20 percent dividend payout. How much external funding will the firm have to seek? Assume there is no increase in liabilities other than that which will occur with the external financing.

3. Garza Electronics expects to sell 500 units in January, 250 units in February, and 1,000 units in March. January's beginning inventory is 700 units. Expected sales for the whole year are 7,200 units. Garza has decided on a level monthly production schedule of 600 units (7,200 units/12 months = 600 units per month). What is the expected end-of-month inventory for January, February, and March? Show the beginning inventory, production, and sales for each month to arrive at ending inventory.

4. Antonio Banderos & Scarves sells headwear that is very popular in the fall-winter season. Units sold are anticipated as follows:

October.	1,000
November.	2,000
December.	4,000
January.	3,000
	10,000

If seasonal production is used, it is assumed that inventory will directly match sales for each month and there will be no inventory buildup.

The production manager thinks the above assumption is too optimistic and decides to go with level production to avoid being out of merchandise. She will produce the 10,000 items at a level of 2,500 per month.

   a. What is the ending inventory at the end of each month? Compare the units sold to the units produced and keep a running total.

   b. If the inventory costs $5 per unit and will be financed through the bank at 6 percent per annum, what is the monthly financing cost and the total for the four months?

5. Bambino Sporting Goods makes exceptional gloves that sell well in the spring and early summer season. A projection of units sold is as follows:

March	3,000
April.	7,000
May	11,000
June	9,000
	30,000

If seasonal production is used, it is assumed that inventory will directly match sales for each month and there will be no inventory buildup.

The production manager thinks the above assumption is too optimistic and decides to go with level production to avoid being out of merchandise. He will produce the 30,000 items at a level of 7,500 per month.

   a. What is the ending inventory at the end of each month? Compare the units sold to the units produced and keep a running total.

   b. If the inventory costs $20 per unit and will be financed through the bank at 6 percent per annum, what is the monthly financing cost and the total for the four months?

6. Eastern Auto Parts Inc. has 15 percent of its sales paid for in cash and 85 percent on credit. All credit accounts are collected in the following month.

Assume the following sales:

January............	$ 65,000
February...........	55,000
March.............	100,000
April.............	45,000

Sales in December of the prior year were $75,000.

Prepare a cash receipts schedule for January through April.

7. Front Page Video Games Corporation has forecasted the following monthly sales:

January............	$95,000	July...............	$40,000
February..........	88,000	August	40,000
March............	20,000	September	50,000
April.............	20,000	October...........	80,000
May	15,000	November..........	100,000
June	30,000	December..........	118,000
Total sales = $696,000			

The firm sells its Last Spike video game for $5 per unit, and the cost to produce the game is $2 per unit. A level production policy is followed. Each month's production is equal to annual sales (in units) divided by 12.

Of each month's sales, 30 percent are for cash and 70 percent are on account. All accounts receivable are collected in the month after the sale is made.

a. Construct a monthly production and inventory schedule in units. Beginning inventory in January is 20,000 units. (Note: To do part *a*, you should work in terms of units of production and units of sales.)

b. Prepare a monthly schedule of cash receipts. Sales in the December before the planning year were $100,000. Work part *b* using dollars.

c. Determine a cash payments schedule for January through December. The production costs of $2 per unit are paid for in the month in which they occur. Other cash payments, besides those for production costs, are $40,000 per month.

d. Prepare a monthly cash budget for January through December. The beginning cash balance is $5,000, and that is also the minimum desired.

8. Seasonal Products Corporation expects the following monthly sales:

January............	$20,000	July...............	$ 10,000
February..........	15,000	August	14,000
March............	5,000	September	20,000
April.............	3,000	October...........	25,000
May	1,000	November..........	30,000
June	3,000	December..........	22,000
Total sales = $168,000			

Sales are 20 percent for cash in a given month, with the remainder going into accounts receivable. All 80 percent of the credit sales are collected in the month following the sale. Seasonal Products sells all of its goods for $2.00 each and produces them for $1.00 each. Seasonal Products uses level production, and average monthly production is equal to annual production divided by 12.

a. Generate a monthly production and inventory schedule in units. Beginning inventory in January is 5,000 units. (Note: To do part **a,** you should work in terms of units of production and units of sales.)

b. Determine a cash receipts schedule for January through December. Assume dollar sales in the prior December were $15,000. Work using dollars.

c. Determine a cash payments schedule for January through December. The production costs ($1 per unit produced) are paid for in the month in which they occur. Other cash payments, besides those for production costs, are $6,000 per month.

d. Construct a cash budget for January through December. The beginning cash balance is $1,000, and that is also the required minimum.

e. Determine total current assets for each month. (Note: Accounts receivable equal sales minus 20 percent of sales for a given month.)

9. Liz's Health Food Store has estimated monthly financing requirements for the next six months as follows:

January	$8,000	April	$ 8,000
February	2,000	May	9,000
March	3,000	June	4,000

Short-term financing will be utilized for the next six months. Projected annual interest rates are:

January	8.0%	April	15.0%
February	9.0%	May	12.0%
March	12.0%	June	12.0%

a. Compute total dollar interest payments for the six months. To convert an annual rate to a monthly rate, divide by 12.

b. Compute the total dollar interest payments if long-term financing at 12 percent had been utilized throughout the six months. Assume a long-term rate is locked in on an interest-only loan.

10. In the previous problem, what long-term interest rate would represent a break-even point between using short-term financing as described in part **a** and long-term financing? Hint: Divide the interest payments in Problem 8**a** by the amount of total funds provided for the six months and multiply by 12.

11. Gabriel Health Services Ltd. requires $1.5 million in financing over the next two years. The firm can borrow at 5 percent per year over the two years. However, with some economic forecasting, it has been suggested that financing in the first year will be 3.5 percent and 6.25 percent in the second year. Determine the total interest charges under both possibilities. Which action is less costly?

12. Vincent Black Lightning requires $900,000 in financing over the next three years. The firm can borrow the funds for three years at 4.5 percent interest per year. Vincent decides to do forecasting and predicts that if he utilizes short-term financing instead, he will pay 3 percent interest in the first year, 5 percent in the second year, and 7 percent interest in the third year. Determine the total three-year interest cost under each plan. Which plan is less costly?

13. Sauer Food Company has decided to buy a new computer system with an expected life of three years. The cost is $150,000. The company can borrow $150,000 for three years at 10 percent annual interest or for one year at 8 percent annual interest.

How much would Sauer Food Company save in interest over the three-year life of the computer system if the one-year loan is utilized and the loan is rolled over (re-borrowed) each year at the same 8 percent rate? Compare this to the 10 percent, three-year loan. What if interest rates on the 8 percent loan go up to 13 percent in year two and 18 percent in year three? What is the total interest cost now compared to the 10 percent, three-year loan?

14. Nighthawk Steel, a manufacturer of specialized tools, has $4,200,000 in assets.

Temporary current assets...............................	$1,000,000
Permanent current assets	2,000,000
Capital assets	1,200,000
Total assets..	$4,200,000

Short-term rates are 4 percent. Long-term rates are 6.5 percent. (Note that long-term rates imply a return to any equity). Earnings before interest and taxes are $860,000. The tax rate is 25 percent.

If long-term financing is perfectly matched (hedged) with long-term asset needs, and the same is true of short-term financing, what will earnings after taxes be? For an example of perfectly hedged plans, see Figure 6–8.

15. In the previous problem, assume the term structure of interest rates becomes inverted, with short-term rates going to 9 percent and long-term rates 4.5 percentage points lower than short-term rates.

If all other factors in the problem do not change, what will earnings be after taxes? Why has the company benefited?

16. Colter Steel has $4,200,000 in assets. The temporary current assets are in place for nine months and reduce to zero for three months.

Temporary current assets...............................	$1,000,000
Permanent current assets	2,000,000
Capital assets	1,200,000
Total assets..	$4,200,000

Short-term rates are 8 percent. Long-term rates are 13 percent. (Note that long-term rates imply a return to any equity). Earnings before interest and taxes are $996,000. The tax rate is 30 percent.

If long-term financing is perfectly matched (synchronized) with long-term asset needs, and the same is true of short-term financing, what will earnings after taxes be?

17. Currently, Atlas Tours has $5.4 million in assets. This is a peak six-month period. During the other six months temporary current assets drop to $400,000 (for computation purposes still consider these temporary current assets).

Temporary current assets...............................	$1,200,000
Permanent current assets	1,800,000
Capital assets	2,400,000
Total assets..	$5,400,000

Short-term rates are 4 percent. Long-term rates are 5 percent. Annual earnings before interest and taxes are $1,080,000. The tax rate is 38 percent.

a. If the assets are perfectly hedged throughout the year, what will earnings after taxes be?

b. If short-term interest rates increase to 5 percent when assets are at their lowest level, what will earnings after taxes be?

18. Collins Systems Inc. is trying to develop an asset-financing plan. The firm has $300,000 in temporary current assets and $200,000 in permanent current assets. Collins also has $400,000 in capital assets. Assume a tax rate of 40 percent.

    a. Construct two alternative financing plans for Collins. One of the plans should be conservative, with 80 percent of assets financed by long-term sources, and the other should be aggressive, with only 30 percent of assets financed by long-term sources. The current interest rate is 15 percent on long-term funds and 10 percent on short-term financing.

    b. Given that Collins's earnings before interest and taxes are $180,000, calculate earnings after taxes for each of your alternatives.

    c. What would happen if the short- and long-term rates were reversed?

19. Lear Inc. has $800,000 in current assets, $350,000 of which are considered permanent current assets. In addition, the firm has $600,000 invested in capital assets.

    a. Lear wishes to finance all capital assets and half of its permanent current assets with long-term financing costing 10 percent. Short-term financing currently costs 5 percent. Lear's earnings before interest and taxes are $200,000. Determine Lear's earnings after taxes under this financing plan. The tax rate is 30 percent.

    b. As an alternative, Lear might wish to finance all capital assets and permanent current assets plus half of its temporary current assets with long-term financing. The same interest rates apply as in part *a.* Earnings before interest and taxes will be $200,000. What will be Lear's earnings after taxes? The tax rate is 30 percent.

    c. What are some of the risks associated with each of these alternative financing strategies?

20. Date Wireless has the following assets:

Current assets: Temporary	$1,000,000
Permanent	1,000,000
Capital assets	7,000,000
Total	$ 9,000,000

Its operating profit (EBIT) is expected to be $1.0 million. Its tax rate is 40 percent. Shares are valued at $25. Capital structure is either short-term financing at 6 percent or equity. There is no long-term debt.

    a. Calculate expected earnings per share (EPS) if the firm is perfectly hedged.

    b. Calculate expected EPS if it has a capital structure of 40% debt.

    c. Recalculate *a* and *b* if short-term rates go to 11 percent.

21. King Lyon has the following assets:

Current assets	$ 2,500,000
Capital assets	7,500,000
Total	$10,000,000

During 4 months of the year, current assets drop to $1,000,000 (total assets will then be $8,500,000). Its operating profit (EBIT) is expected to be $486,500. Its tax rate is 20 percent. Shares are valued at $17. Its capital structure is short-term financing at 2 percent and long-term financing of 40 percent equity, 60 percent debt at 4 percent.

    a. Calculate expected EPS if the firm is perfectly hedged.

22. Phu Lighters has the following assets:

Current assets	$1,750,000
Capital assets	3,000,000
Total	$4,750,000

During 3 months of the year, current assets drop to $400,000. Its operating profit (EBIT) is expected to be $620,000. Its tax rate is 40 percent. Shares are valued at $10. Its capital structure is short-term financing at 3 percent and long-term financing of 50 percent equity, 50 percent debt at 6 percent.

a. Calculate expected EPS if the firm is perfectly hedged.

b. Calculate expected EPS if Phu is a more aggressive with its capital structure and finances all current assets and 20 percent of its capital assets with short-term loans.

c. Recalculate *a* and *b* if short-term rates go to 8 percent while long-term rates remain the same.

23. Pick a day within the past week and construct a yield curve for that day. Pick a day approximately a year ago and construct a yield curve for that day. How are interest rates different? *The Globe and Mail* or the *National Post* (Financial Post) should be of help in solving this problem. What does the term structure suggest to you as a financial manager?

24. Using the expectations hypothesis theory for the term structure of interest rates, determine the expected return for securities with maturities of two, three, and four years based on the following data. Do an analysis similar to that in Table 6–6.

1-year T-bill at beginning of year 1	4%
1-year T-bill at beginning of year 2	5%
1-year T-bill at beginning of year 3	7%
1-year T-bill at beginning of year 4	9%

25. Using the expectations hypothesis theory for the term structure of interest rates, determine the expected return for securities with maturities of two, three, and four years based on the following data.

1-year T-bill at beginning of year 1	5%
1-year T-bill at beginning of year 2	8%
1-year T-bill at beginning of year 3	7%
1-year T-bill at beginning of year 4	10%

26. The government currently promises a return of 5 percent annually on a one-year bond and 6 percent annually on a two-year bond. What is your expectation for the interest rate you would receive on a one-year government bond one year from now?

27. The following information was available as of the close of business June 1, 20XX, on Government of Canada bonds.

Coupon	Maturity	Price	Yield
5.00%	June 1, 20XX+1	102.35	2.60
10.50%	June 1, 20XX+2	113.91	3.26
8.50%	June 1, 20XX+3	107.41	3.39

Calculate the anticipated one-year interest rate at 20XX+2 (up to June 20XX+3).

28. The following information was available as of the close of business March 1, 20YY, on government of Canada bonds.

Coupon	Maturity	Price	Yield
8.25%	Mar. 1, 20YY+1	102.75	5.78
3.75%	Mar. 1, 20YY+2	95.70	5.85
5.75%	Mar. 1, 20YY+3	98.65	6.22

Calculate the anticipated one-year interest rate for 20YY+2 (up to March 20YY+3).

29. Gary's Pipe and Steel Company expects next year's sales to be $800,000 if the economy is strong, $500,000 if the economy is steady, and $350,000 if the economy is weak. Gary believes there is a 20 percent probability the economy will be strong, a 50 percent probability of a steady economy, and a 30 percent probability of a weak economy. What is the expected level of sales for next year?

30. Sharpe Knife Company expects sales next year to be $1,500,000 if the economy is strong, $800,000 if the economy is steady, and $500,000 if the economy is weak. Mr. Sharpe believes there is a 20 percent probability the economy will be strong, a 50 percent probability of a steady economy, and a 30 percent probability of a weak economy. What is the expected level of sales for the next year?

31. Assume Stratton Health Clubs, Inc., has $3 million in assets. If it goes with a low liquidity plan for the assets, it can earn a return of 20 percent, but with a high liquidity plan, the return will be 13 percent. If the firm goes with a short-term financing plan, the financing costs on the $3 million will be 10 percent; with a long term financing plan, the financing costs on the $3 million will be 12 percent.(Review Table 6–11 for parts *a*, *b*, and *c* of this problem.)

   a. Compute the anticipated return after financing costs on the most aggressive asset-financing mix.

   b. Compute the anticipated return after financing costs on the most conservative asset-financing mix.

   c. Compute the anticipated return after financing costs on the two moderate approaches to the asset-financing mix.

   d. Would you necessarily accept the plan with the highest return after financing costs? Briefly explain.

32. Assume that Atlas Sporting Goods Inc. has $800,000 in assets. If it goes with a low-liquidity plan for the assets, it can earn a return of 15 percent, but with a high-liquidity plan, the return will be 12 percent. If the firm goes with a short-term financing plan, the financing costs on the $800,000 will be 8 percent; with a long-term financing plan, the financing costs on the $800,000 will be 10 percent.

   a. Compute the anticipated return after financing costs on the most aggressive asset-financing mix.

   b. Compute the anticipated return after financing costs on the most conservative asset-financing mix.

   c. Compute the anticipated return after financing costs on the two moderate approaches to the asset-financing mix.

   d. Would you necessarily accept the plan with the highest return after financing costs? Briefly explain.

MINI CASE

Gale Force Corporation

During mid-October 20XX, the top managers of the Gale Force Corporation, a leading manufacturer of kite-surfing equipment, were gathered in the president's conference room reviewing the results of the company's operations during the past fiscal year (which runs from October 1 to September 30).

"Not a bad year, on the whole," remarked the president, 32-year-old Charles (Chuck) Jamison. "Sales were up, profits were up, and our return on equity was a respectable 15 percent. In fact," he continued, "the only dark spot I can find in our whole annual report is the profit-on-sales ratio, which is only 2.25 percent. Seems like we ought to be making more than that, don't you think, Tim?" He looked across the table at the vice-president for finance, Timothy Baggitt, age 28.

"I agree," replied Tim, "and I'm glad you brought it up, because I have a suggestion on how to improve that situation." He leaned forward in his chair as he realized he had captured the interest of the others. "The problem is, we have too many expenses on our income statement that are eating up the profits. Now I've done some checking, and the expenses all seem to be legitimate except for interest expense. We paid over $250,000 last year to the bank just to finance our short-term borrowing. If we could have kept that money instead, our profit-on-sales ratio would have been 4.01 percent, which is higher than that of any other firm in the industry."

"But, Tim, we have to borrow like that," responded Roy ("Pop") Thomas, age 35, the vice-president for production. "After all, our sales are seasonal, with almost all occurring between March and September. Since we don't have much money coming in from October to February, we have to borrow to keep the production line going." "Right," Tim replied, "and it's the production line that's the problem. We produce the same number of products every month, no matter what we expect sales to be. This causes inventory to build up when sales are slow and begin to deplete when sales pick up. That fluctuating inventory causes all sorts of problems, not the least of which is the excessive amount of borrowing we have to do to finance the inventory accumulation." (See Tables 1 through 5 for details of Gale Force's current operations based on equal monthly production.)

Table 1, Part 1 Sales forecast, cash receipts and payments, and cash budget

	October	November	December	January	February	March
Sales Forecast						
Sales (units)	150	75	25	0	0	300
Sales (unit price: $3,000)	$ 450,000	$ 225,000	$ 75,000	0	0	$ 900,000
Cash Receipts Schedule						
50% cash	$ 225,000	$ 112,500	$ 37,500	· 0	0	$ 450,000
50% from prior months sales*	375,000	225,000	112,500	37,500	0	0
Total cash receipts	$ 600,000	$ 337,500	$ 150,000	$ 37,500	0	$ 450,000
Cash Payments Schedule						
Production in units . .	400	400	400	400	400	400
Production costs (each: $2,000)	$ 800,000	$ 800,000	$ 800,000	$ 800,000	$ 800,000	$ 800,000
Overhead	200,000	200,000	200,000	200,000	200,000	200,000
Dividends and interest	0	0	0	0	0	0
Taxes	150,000	0	0	$ 150,000	0	0
Total cash payments	$1,150,000	$1,000,000	$1,000,000	$1,150,000	$1,000,000	$1,000,000
Cash Budget (required minimum balance: $125,000)						
Cash flow	$ –550,000	–662,000	–850,000	–1,112,500	–1,000,000	–550,000
Beginning cash	125,000	125,000	125,000	125,000	125,000	125,000
Cumulative cash balance	–425,000	–537,500	–725,000	–987,500	–875,000	–425,000
Monthly loan or (repayment)	550,000	662,500	850,000	1,112,500	1,000,000	550,000
Cumulative loan	550,000	1,212,500	2,062,500	3,175,000	4,175,000	4,725,000
Ending cash balance .	$ 125,000	$ 125,000	$ 125,000	$ 125,000	$ 125,000	$ 125,000

*Note: September sales assumed to be $750,000.

Table 1, Part 2 Sales forecast, cash receipts and payments, and cash budget

	April	May	June	July	August	September
Sales Forecast						
Sales (units)	500	1,000	1,000	1,000	500	250
Sales (unit price: $3,000)	$ 1,500,000	$ 3,000,000	$ 3,000,000	$ 3,000,000	$1,500,000	$ 750,000
Cash Receipts Schedule						
50% cash	$ 750,000	$ 1,500,000	$ 1,500,000	$ 1,500,000	$ 750,000	$ 375,000
50% from prior month's sales*	450,000	750,000	1,500,000	1,500,000	1,500,000	750,000
Total cash receipts	$ 1,200,000	$ 2,250,000	$ 3,000,000	$ 3,000,000	$2,250,000	$1,125,000
Cash Payments Schedule						
Production in units . . .	400	400	400	400	400	400
Production costs (each: $2,000).	$ 800,000	$ 800,000	$ 800,000	$ 800,000	$ 800,000	$ 800,000
Overhead	200,000	200,000	200,000	200,000	$ 200,000	200,000
Dividends and interest	0	0	0	0	$1,000,000	0
Taxes	$ 150,000	0	0	$ 300,000	0	0
Total cash payments	$ 1,150,000	$ 1,000,000	$ 1,000,000	$ 1,300,000	$2,000,000	$1,000,000
Cash Budget (required minimum balance: $125,000)						
Cash flow	50,000	1,250,000	2,000,000	1,700,000	250,000	125,000
Beginning cash	125,000	125,000	125,000	125,000	400,000	650,000
Cumulative cash balance	175,000	1,375,000	2,125,000	1,825,000	650,000	775,000
Monthly loan or (repayment)	(50,000)	(1,250,000)	(2,000,000)	(1,425,000)	0	0
Cumulative loan	4,675,000	3,425,000	1,425,000	0	0	0
Ending cash balance . .	$ 125,000	$ 125,000	$ 125,000	$ 400,000	$ 650,000	$ 775,000

*Note: September sales assumed to be $750,000.

Table 2 Sales forecast (in units)

First Quarter		Second Quarter		Third Quarter		Fourth Quarter	
October. . . .	150	January.	0	April.	500	July.	1,000
November. .	75	February. . . .	0	May	1,000	August	500
December. .	25	March.	300	June	1,000	September . . .	250

Table 3 Production schedule and inventory(equal monthly production)

	Beginning Inventory	Production This Month	Sales	Ending Inventory	Inventory ($2,000/unit)
October........	400	400	150	650	$1,300,000
November......	650	400	75	975	1,950,000
December......	975	400	25	1,350	2,700,000
January........	1,350	400	0	1,750	3,500,000
February.......	1,750	400	0	2,150	4,300,000
March........	2,150	400	300	2,250	4,500,000
April..........	2,250	400	500	2,150	4,300,000
May	2,150	400	1,000	1,550	3,100,000
June	1,550	400	1,000	950	1,900,000
July..........	950	400	1,000	350	700,000
August	350	400	500	250	500,000
September	250	400	250	400	800,000

Table 4 Total current assets, first year

	Cash	Accounts Receivable*	Inventory	Total Current Assets
October........	$125,000	$ 225,000	$1,300,000	$1,650,000
November......	125,000	112,500	1,950,000	2,187,500
December......	125,000	37,500	2,700,000	2,862,500
January........	125,000	0	3,500,000	3,625,000
February.......	125,000	0	4,300,000	4,425,000
March........	125,000	450,000	4,500,000	5,075,000
April..........	125,000	750,000	4,300,000	5,175,000
May	125,000	1,500,000	3,100,000	4,725,000
June	125,000	1,500,000	1,900,000	3,525,000
July..........	400,000	1,500,000	700,000	2,600,000
August	650,000	750,000	500,000	1,900,000
September	775,000	375,000	800,000	1,950,000

*Equals 50 percent of monthly sales.

Table 5 Cumulative loan balance and interest expense (1% per month)

	October	November	December	January	February	March
Cumulative loan balance............	$ 550,000	$ 1,212,500	$2,062,500	$3,175,000	$4,175,000	$ 4,725,000
Interest expense (12.00%)..........	$ 5,500	$ 12,125	$ 20,625	$ 31,750	$ 41,750	$ 47,250
	April	May	June	July	August	September
Cumulative loan balance............	$4,675,000	$ 3,425,000	$1,425,000	0	0	0
Interest expense (12.00%)..........	$ 46,750	$ 34,250	$ 14,250	0	0	0

"Now, here's my idea," said Tim. "Instead of producing 400 items a month, every month, we match the production schedule with the sales forecast. For example, if we expect to sell 150 windsurfers in October, then we only make 150. That way we avoid borrowing to make the 250 more that we don't expect to sell, anyway. Over the course of an entire year, the savings in interest expense could really add up."

"Hold on, now," Pop responded, feeling that his territory was being threatened. "That kind of scheduling really fouls up things in the shop where it counts. It causes a feast or famine environment—nothing to do for one month, then a deluge the next. It's terrible for the employees, not to mention the supervisors who are trying to run an efficient operation. Your idea may make the income statements look good for now, but the whole company will suffer in the long run."

Chuck intervened. "OK, you guys, calm down. Tim may have a good idea or he may not, but at least it's worth looking into. I propose that you all work up two sets of figures, one assuming level production and one matching production with sales. We'll look at them both and see if Tim's idea really does produce better results. If it does, we'll check it further against the other issues Pop is concerned about and then make a decision on which alternative is better for the firm."

a. Tables 1 through 5 contain the financial information describing the effects of level production on inventory, cash flow, loan balances, and interest expense. Reproduce these tables as if Tim's suggestion were implemented; that is, change the "Production This Month" column in Table 3 from 400 each month to 150, 75, 25, and so on, to match "Sales" in the next column. Then, recompute the remainder of Table 3, and Tables 1, 4, and 5, on the basis of the new production numbers. Beginning inventory is still 400 units. Beginning cash is still $125,000 and that remains the minimum required balance.

b. Given that Gale Force is charged 12 percent annual interest (1 percent a month) on its cumulative loan balance each month (Table 5), how much would Tim's suggestion save in interest expense in a year?

c. Until now we have not considered any inefficiencies that have been introduced as a result of going from level to seasonal production. Assume there is an added expense for each sales dollar of 0.5 percent (0.005). On the basis of this fact and the information computed in part *b,* is seasonal production justified?

Current Asset Management

LEARNING OBJECTIVES

LO1 Extend Chapter 6 concepts of liquidity and risk to current asset management, recognizing that a firm's investment in current assets should achieve an adequate return for its liquidity and risk.

LO2 Examine cash management as the control of receipts and disbursements to minimize nonearning cash balances while providing liquidity, and compare techniques to make cash management more efficient.

LO3 Define the various marketable securities available for investment by the firm, and calculate the yield on these instruments.

LO4 Characterize accounts receivable as an investment resulting from the firm's credit policies, outline the considerations in granting credit, and evaluate a credit decision that changes credit terms to stimulate sales.

LO5 Assess inventory as an investment and apply techniques to reduce the costs of this investment.

The financial manager must carefully allocate resources among the current assets of the firm—cash, marketable securities, accounts receivable, and inventory. In managing cash and marketable securities, the primary concern should be for safety and liquidity, with secondary attention placed on maximizing returns. As we consider accounts receivable and inventory, a stiffer profitability test must be met as liquidity risk increases. The investment level should not be a matter of happenstance or historical determination; it must meet the same return-on-investment criteria applied to any decision. We may need to choose between an increase in inventory, a new plant location, or a major research program. We shall examine the decision techniques that are applied to the various forms of current assets in order to provide an appropriate return while providing timely liquidity for the firm's operations.

LO1 COST-BENEFIT ANALYSIS

We have identified the goal of the firm as the maximization of shareholder wealth but, in practice, this is a demanding objective for the financial manager. Decisions made within the firm that evaluate liquidity, risk, and adequate returns for current assets add to its successes or failures. It is important that each decision consider all the factors that will result from new procedures or projects. Cost-benefit analysis provides a framework to identify all the resultant changes arising from a decision. Some results will be incremental, increasing the firm's value, and some will be decremental, decreasing value. Good value-adding decisions will ensue when the benefits exceed the costs.

Cost-benefit analysis (as demonstrated under the topic "cash management analysis") must consider explicit and implicit costs and benefits. Opportunity costs (benefits) are forgone alternatives. Employee time and effort resulting from a new procedure must be considered they it could have been directed elsewhere if not for the new procedure. Capital that is tied up as a result of a new project could have been earning a return elsewhere in the firm. As we examine and analyze techniques for working capital management, consideration should be given to

* Employee costs for training, implementation, and monitoring
* New technology required
* Capital tied up (or freed up)
* Rates of return on capital
* Timeliness of information provided (whether better or worse)
* Exposure to risk
* Fees or charges

Careful thought and information gathering must be the inputs into cost-benefit analysis. We will use this technique as a foundation for many of the techniques to follow. Several tools can be used by the financial manager to analyze whether a decision will create shareholder value. Common methods to measure value include net present value (NPV), break-even analysis, and sensitivity analysis.

Cost-benefit analysis is first examined in this chapter under the topic of cash management analysis. Furthermore, we often consider cost-benefit analysis on the basis of rates of return (yields) or, alternatively, the cost (interest) of financing in comparison to the amount of capital invested or borrowed for investment.

With an investment, interest or some other form of benefit is earned on the basis of the investment (opportunity cost of having capital tied up). Therefore, the return (return on investment, ROI) is

$$r = \frac{\text{Monies received}}{\text{Net capital tied up}}$$

Returns are most commonly expressed on an annual basis, so we adjust to this time period. For example, if an investment tied up $5,000 with a receipt of $250 after six months, with an adjustment for two six-month periods in a year, the return would be[1]

$$r = \frac{\$250}{\$5,000} \times 2$$
$$= 0.10$$
$$= 10\%$$

The formulas developed in this chapter and in Chapter 8 are derived from this concept.

 FINANCE IN ACTION

Why Are Firms Holding Such High Cash Balances?

In early 2020, corporations around the globe and in the United States reported massive cash balances, although down from the highs of 2017.

Microsoft	$137 billion	49% of assets
Google (Alphabet)	$121 billion	46% of assets
Apple	$ 95 billion	30% of assets
Shell	$ 22 billion	6% of assets
Walmart	$ 9 billion	4% of assets

Non-financial U.S. firms held about $1.6 trillion in cash at this time, representing about 10 percent of assets, which was the highest level since the 1960s. Large amounts had been held outside the United States to avoid high U.S. tax rates, but with lower tax rates in 2017 about $1 trillion has been repatriated. However, much of the repatriated capital was used for significant dividend payouts and share repurchases, rather than investment activity. About 40 percent of the total cash was held by technology firms.

Within Canada, cash holdings were significant, at about 8 percent of assets, although on a smaller absolute scale.

Shopify	$2.6 billion	81% of assets
Suncor	$2.1 billion	2% of assets
Open Text	$1.0 billion	13% of assets
BlackBerry	$0.8 billion	23% of assets
Magna	$0.8 billion	3% of assets

Of note is the higher percentage held by the technology firms, as compared to Suncor, a resource company, or Magna, an auto parts manufacturer. Ongoing R&D activities require large cash commitments as technology changes rapidly,

The financial crisis of 2008 was another "credit crunch" period. The banks severely limited the lines of credit of corporations, the commercial paper market dried up, and banks weren't even lending to each other.

Corporations were more cautious as they were uncertain about the future and fearful of another cash freeze by the banking establishment. The opportunity cost of holding cash balances is not as significant within the current low interest rate environment.

---

[1]The return might be more accurately expressed on an annual effective basis as 10.25%

$$r = \left(1 + \frac{\$250}{\$5,000}\right)^{2} - 1 = 0.1025 = 10.25\%.$$

LO2 CASH MANAGEMENT

Managing cash has become more sophisticated in the new global and electronic age as financial managers try to squeeze every dollar of profit out of their cash management strategies. Despite whatever lifelong teachings you might have learned about the virtues of cash, the corporate manager actively seeks to keep this nonearning asset to a minimum. Generally, the less cash you have the better off you are; however, you still do not want to get caught without cash when you need it. With lower interest rates today and, hence, lower opportunity costs, firms have opted for higher cash balances. The penalties imposed by short-term creditors and bankers when a company runs out of cash may have a lasting impact on relationships. Highly liquid securities or standby lines of credit available through banking arrangements can meet cash needs quickly. Liquidity, a desirable characteristic of financial assets, may be defined as the degree to which a financial asset can be converted into cash quickly and at fair market value.

Minimizing cash balances as well as having accurate knowledge of when cash moves into and out of the company can improve overall corporate profitability. Knowledge of the cash flow cycle, discussed in Chapter 6, can assist in understanding cash management, and the financial forecasting pro formas of Chapter 4 are invaluable tools for identifying the cash requirements of the firm. The small business often runs into difficulties when these cash requirements are not properly identified and appropriate arrangements are not made to provide financing as it is needed.

Reasons for Holding Cash Balances

There might be several reasons for holding cash or highly liquid marketable securities:

- Transactions of an immediate (payroll) or strategic nature (mergers, acquisitions)
- Compensating balances for bank services
- Precautionary balances if bank financing becomes unavailable (cyclical, seasonal, new product—oriented businesses)
- Avoiding taxes by not repatriating cash

COLLECTIONS AND DISBURSEMENTS

Managing a firm's cash inflows and payments is a function with many variables such as float, mail systems, electronic funds transfer mechanisms, lockboxes, international sales, and more. The small business must be on top of these considerations. These are presented in the following section.

Float

Some people are shocked to realize that even the most trusted asset on a corporation's books, cash, may not portray the actual dollars available for use at any given moment. There are, in fact, two cash balances of importance:

- The corporation's recorded amount
- The amount available for use by the corporation at the bank

The difference between the two is float. Float exists as a result of the time lag between when a payment or receipt is recorded in the corporation's ledgers and the eventual acknowledgement that it has altered the corporate bank account.

Canadian Payments
System
bankofcanada.ca

Float arises from payments or receipts that are

- In the mail
- Clearing the banking system
- Being processed
- Slow to be acknowledged by the firm's (bank's) information system

With float, the firm's funds may not be deployed effectively or, conversely, the firm may take advantage of float opportunities. The efficient Canadian banking system with over $170 billion cleared daily provides same-day clearing (unlike the United States' next-day clearing) and has virtually eliminated its contribution to float. Nevertheless, float still remains, but with large volumes of payments and receipts, float time can become fairly predictable, and therefore, can be effectively managed.

Table 7–1 provides an example determining the bank records for usable funds. Perhaps only $800,000 of the deposits (cheques from customers) have been processed and deposited to the firm's account, and only $400,000 of the firm's cheques may have completed a similar cycle. Float will then provide $300,000 in extra short-term funds.

Table 7–1 The use of float to provide funds

	Corporate Books	Bank Books (usable funds) (amounts actually cleared)
Initial amount............	$100,000	$100,000
Deposits...............	+1,000,000	800,000
Cheques................	−900,000	−400,000
Balance................	+$200,000	+$500,000
	+ $300,000 float	

Some companies actually operate with a negative cash balance on the corporate books, knowing that float will carry them through at the bank. Table 7–2 represents the phenomenon known as "playing the float." The firm may write $1.2 million in cheques, estimating that only $800,000 will clear by the end of the week, thus leaving it with surplus funds in its bank account. The negative balance on the corporation's books becomes a positive temporary balance on the bank's books from the float of $200,000. Obviously, float can also work against the firm if cheques going out are being processed more quickly than cheques coming in.

Table 7–2 Playing the float

	Corporate Books	Bank Books (usable funds) (amounts actually cleared)
Initial amount..........	$ 100,000	$ 100,000
Deposits..............	+1,000,000*	+800,000*
Cheques..............	−1,200,000	−800,000
Balance..............	−$100,000	+$100,000
	+ $200,000 float	

*Assumed to remain the same as in Table 7–1.

Improving Collections and Extending Disbursements

A firm must be diligent in collecting monies owed to it, in depositing those monies into a bank account, and in holding on to monies as long as possible, so that the funds can be utilized efficiently by the corporate treasurer. Having monies in a bank account even one day longer can make a significant difference to the firm. Faster collections can be achieved by

- Encouraging customers to pay on a timely basis
- Cutting down on the time monies take to arrive in the firm's possession
- Accounting for and processing monies quickly upon receipt
- Depositing monies quickly into the firm's bank accounts

Once concentrated and administered centrally in the firm's bank accounts, the funds can be more efficiently deployed, because

- Treasury has better control of the funds
- Transaction and administration costs are lower
- Concentrated sums can earn better returns invested in marketable securities (i.e., $100,000 receives a higher rate than 20 × $5,000)

The chartered banks, such as BMO, have numerous services to improve the collection and cheque-posting process. One method is to have customers make payment to the firm's local offices throughout the country, with cheques deposited at a local bank branch. The local branch credits directly to the corporate account in a centralized location. Details of the various deposits will be available to the corporate treasurer by way of bank-produced reports or by viewing the bank accounts directly from a personal computer tied into the bank's system. Such a system reduces the time the customer's cheque is in the mail because of the proximity of the branch offices.

A lockbox system is an alternative to collection at local branch offices (they may not exist) or when customers are scattered across and outside the country. Under this plan, customers forward their cheques to a post office box in one of the cities that serves as a regional data processing centre for the chartered banks. This allows the bank to process the cheques immediately through its computer network and credit the firm's account on a timelier basis. The firm is notified of the deposit and can do its accounting after the funds have already been put to work. The company, thus, retains many of the benefits of regional branch office collections and, with lower cheque processing costs, reduces corporate overhead.

Bank of Montreal Cash Management
bmo.com
(under "business," click "cash management")

On the other side of the ledger, it is important that disbursements be made only when due and not before. This allows a firm to retain the use of these funds for a longer period and to utilize them to increase returns. In Canada, because of the efficiency of the banking system in cheque clearing, any attempt to extend float has little effect. The one opportunity to extend disbursements in Canada may involve mailing cheques from dispersed locations so that the time in the mail might be extended. However, this method may impose extra administration costs and antagonize suppliers.

Electronic Funds Transfer

Today the collection and disbursement of monies is increasingly initiated through the techniques of electronic funds transfer, a system in which funds are moved between and within institutions without the use of a cheque. Through the use of terminal communication between a store and the bank, payment to the store will be automatically and instantly charged against an individual's account at the bank. This is done with the debit card. For the customer, it is a quick and safe way to pay. For the store, it cuts down on cheque handling and nonsufficient funds (NSF) cheques and provides immediate funds settlement. People also spend more. For the banks, it is another chargeable service, and it cuts down on their float.

Many large corporations have computerized cash management systems. For example, a firm may have 55 branch offices and 56 bank branches, one branch for each branch office and a lead bank branch in which the major corporate account is kept. At the end of each day the financial manager can check all the company's bank accounts online. They can then transfer all excess cash balances from each bank branch to the corporate lead bank for overnight investment in money market securities.

Canadian banks have developed sophisticated cash management systems for their clients, which provide real-time payment finality each business day. On the disbursement side, payment can be initiated the same day to almost anywhere in Canada for payroll, pension, or dividend payments. Float time is reduced, accuracy and security are improved, and cheques are eliminated. As for collections, automated same-day bill payments occur for mortgages, insurance premiums, and cable charges through preauthorized cheques, speeding up the collection process.

 FINANCE IN ACTION

Cash Management Systems: The Octopus

In 1998 Hong Kong's subway operator MTR Corporation developed a stored value, debit-like card as a way to pay for transportation throughout the city. A low-range radio transmitter installed in turnstiles or countertops could read the "Octopus" cards through various substances, such as wallets. Today these systems are common worldwide.

Although implemented to reduce costs, this smart card has had a more significant effect by generating revenue for MTR. Because significant balances are held on the Octopus cards at any time, the cash or capital used to establish the stored value on the cards is available to MTR. Positive investment returns can be generated from these monies by effective cash management, in a manner similar to that used by the credit card companies.

Today, 99 percent of Hong Kong residents use Octopus cards, which are accepted across the city for micropayments on items such as newspapers, fast food, or scones at the coffee shop. The card also provides access to buildings and other facilities.

For businesses, Canadian banks offer a range of cash management systems. TD Bank outlines its system at its website (tdcommercialbanking.com). The Bank of Montreal highlights its cash management services on its website (bmo.com).

Q1 Identify other applications for the Octopus card.

Q2 What options do BMO and TD offer for cash management?

octopus.com

Electronic Data Interchange In conjunction with electronic funds transfer, *electronic data interchange (EDI)* is a powerful tool used by businesses. Besides the electronic transfer of funds directly from the bank account of one business to its supplier, remittance information that can update the inventory, accounts receivable, and payables accounts of the trading partners is initiated at the same time without direct involvement of staff. EDI eliminates cheques, float, mail, and processing costs generated by the preparation and posting of documents such as purchase orders, invoices, and receiving reports. These transactions are facilitated through the regional data centres operated by the Canadian Payments System. Some companies will not purchase from suppliers that are not set up to handle EDI transactions.

Today, the vast majority of large companies use computers to initiate money transfers and to receive reports from their banks on lockbox receipts and bank balances, thus allowing them to judge the amount of float available.

Cash Management Analysis

An efficiently maintained cash management program can be an expensive operation. Using a cost-benefit analysis, the expenses of setting up a program must be compared to the benefits that may accrue. Suppose a firm has average daily collections of $2 million and 1.5 days can be saved in the collection process by establishing a sophisticated collection network. Also, through stretching the disbursement schedule by one day, perhaps another $2 million becomes available for alternative uses. The money that could be earned on this freed-up capital represents a significant opportunity benefit to the firm. An example of this process is shown in Figure 7–1.

To complete the example, suppose the bank that sets up the cash management system will charge monthly fees of $15,000, but will also provide you with more timely information worth $40,000 a year to your firm. If the firm is able to earn 4 percent on the funds freed up, is the bank's system worth it?

Benefits		
Freed-up funds $2,000,000 × 1.5 days =..............	$3,000,000	
2,000,000 × 1.0 days =..............	2,000,000	
	$5,000,000	
Opportunity benefit at 4% (interest earned		
on funds freed up)	$5,000,000 × 4%	= $200,000
Value of more timely information		40,000
		$240,000
Costs		
Bank fees	$15,000 × 12	= $180,000
Net benefit....................................		$ 60,000

The new system is worth it!

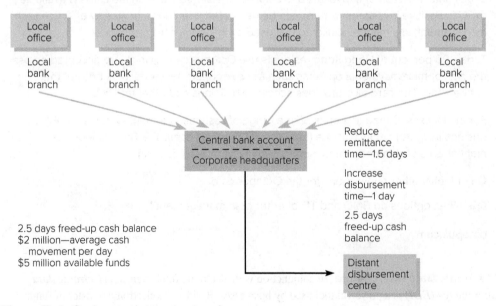

Figure 7–1 Cash management network

International Cash Management

International electronic funds transfer is mainly carried out through SWIFT (swift. com). SWIFT is an acronym for the Society for Worldwide Interbank Financial Telecommunications, which provides round-the-clock international payments between banks—foreign exchange, derivatives and trade transactions, and cash flows due to international securities transactions. There are over 11,000 financial institutions in over 200 countries using SWIFT's secure messaging (SWIFTNET). SWIFT's daily payment messages (payments, securities, treasury, trade) are estimated to be over 32 million.

SWIFT
swift.com

Rigid security standards are enforced. Every message is encrypted (converted to code), and every money transaction is authenticated by another code. These security measures are important to the bank members as well as to SWIFT, which assumes the financial liability for the accuracy, completeness, and confidentiality of transaction instructions from and to the point of connection to member bank circuits. One area of increasing concern has been electronic fraud, and SWIFT uses advanced smart card technology to improve its security system. Additionally, it will automate the process by which banks exchange secret authentication keys with each other.

International cash management has many differences from domestic-based cash management systems. Payment methods differ from country to country. For example, in Poland, Russia, and other eastern European countries, cheques are seldom used due to a preference for cash, but electronic payments are more common than in the United States. International cash management is more complex, because liquidity management involving short-term cash balances and deficits has to be managed across international boundaries and time zones and is subject to the risks of currency fluctuations and interest rate changes in all countries. There are also differences in banking systems, cheque-clearing processes, account balance management, information reporting systems, cultural beliefs, and tax and accounting procedures.

A company may prefer to hold cash balances in one currency rather than another. This might occur either because of future expectations regarding foreign currency rate changes or because of interest rate differentials on short-term investments. In periods when one country's currency has been rising relative to others, financial managers often try to keep as much cash as possible in the country with the strong currency. For example, in the past decade the U.S. dollar was rising relative to most currencies. At that time, the tendency was to try to keep balances in U.S. bank accounts or in U.S.-dollar-denominated bank accounts in foreign banks. The latter are commonly known as Eurodollar deposits. Because of the growth of the international money markets in size and in scope, Eurodollar deposits have become an important aspect of cash management. At the international level, cash managers employ domestic management techniques. Using forecasting devices such as the cash budget and daily cash reports, they collect and invest excess funds, until needed, in Eurodollar money market securities or other appropriate investments in securities denominated in strong currencies. A more in-depth coverage of international cash and asset management is presented in Chapter 21.

LO3 MARKETABLE SECURITIES

The firm may hold excess funds in anticipation of some major cash outlay such as a dividend payment or partial retirement of debt or as a precaution against an unexpected event. Indeed, when cash flow projections are based on expected values, the firm is bound to have shortages and surpluses. When funds are being held for other than immediate transaction purposes, they should be converted from cash into interest-earning marketable securities.[2]

The financial manager, in choosing short-term securities, considers factors such as

- Yield
- Maturity
- Minimum investment required
- Safety
- Marketability
- Transactions costs

Under normal conditions, the longer the maturity period of the security is, the higher the yield will be, as displayed in Figure 7–2. This is evidence of the liquidity premium theory discussed in Chapter 6. However, the financial manager would want to closely match expected cash flows with the maturity schedule of marketable securities. A hedged approach is based to a certain extent on the reliability of the forecasted cash flows.

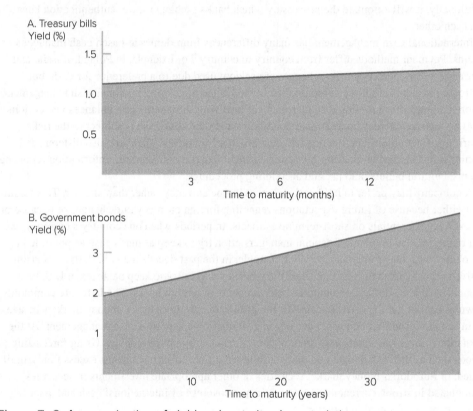

Figure 7–2 An examination of yield and maturity characteristics

The problem in stretching out the maturity of an investment is not that you are legally locked in (generally, you can sell the security when funds are needed) but that you may have to take a loss to convert the security to cash. A $5,000 government bond issued initially at 5 percent, with three years to maturity, may bring only $4,600 if the going interest rate climbs to 8 percent. This risk of price change increases as the maturity date is extended. A complete discussion of interest rate risk is included in Chapter 16.

---

[2]The one possible exception to this principle is found in the practice of holding compensating balances at chartered banks—a topic for discussion in Chapter 8.

Various forms of short-term marketable securities and investments are presented in Table 7–3. These securities are bought and sold in the money market, a wholesale market with daily transactions exceeding the dollar volume of the stock market tenfold. The key characteristics of each investment are delineated along with examples of yields for January 2020 and compared with those at March 1990, when rates were considerably higher.

bankofcanada.ca
bba.org.uk

Table 7–3 Hierarchy of money market instruments and rates (in percent)

Investment	Maturity*	Minimum Amount	Safety	Marketability	Yield Mar. 1990‡	Yield Jan. 2020
Prime rate (best corporate customers)					14.25	3.95
Bank rate (Bank of Canada's rate to banks, dealers).					13.38	1.750
Commercial (corporate) paper.	3 m	100,000	Good	Fair	13.33	1.88
Bankers' acceptances. . . .	3 m	25,000	Good	Good	13.27	1.87
Provincial government Treasury bills	3 m	25,000	Excellent	Excellent	13.18	1.69
Federal government Treasury bills§	3 m	1,000	Excellent	Excellent	13.13	1.64
Overnight repo.	day	100,000	Excellent	Excellent	—	1.7450
Overnight financing rate (call money).	day	100,000	Excellent	Excellent	—	1.7477
Money market deposits. . .	Open	500	Excellent	None	10.15	1.50
Term deposits and GICs. . .	1 year	5,000	Good	None†	12.75	0.10–2.40
Savings accounts (minimums)	Open	None	Excellent	None†	8.75	0.01–2.30

*Many of these securities can be purchased with different maturities than those indicated.
‡Quoted yields are often for wholesale amounts above $1 million.
§In the summer of 1981, 3-month Treasury bills offered yields in excess of 20 percent.
†Though not marketable, these investments are highly liquid and can often be withdrawn without penalty.

Most money market securities are

- Unsecured (no physical asset backing up pledge of payment) promissory notes.
- Highly liquid with high trading volumes.
- In either bearer (ownership resides with individual in possession) or street (investment dealer's name) form. This facilitates ease of trading.
- Short-term (maturity or payback occurs in less than one year) and most commonly issued for periods of 1, 2, 3, or 6 months, or 1 year.
- Traded continuously, producing maturities of any period desired (a 3-month security sold one month later becomes a 2-month security).
- Sold on a discount basis. The instrument is sold at less than the maturity value. The return (considered interest, not a capital gain, by the tax department) is the gain from the discounted price to the maturity value.
- Bought and sold on the basis of their promised yield (price) with the best rates for transactions of $1,000,000 or more. Lower yields accompany lower-sized investments.

Yield Calculations These are calculated on a discount basis, meaning the return received is the difference between the price paid and the maturity value. As an example, suppose a financial security sells at 99.531 of its maturity value, with maturity occurring in 90 days. The annualized yield that would be quoted in the marketplace is given by the formula[3]

$$\frac{100 - P}{P} \times \frac{365}{d} = r \quad \text{(7-1a)}$$

where

P = Discounted price as percentage of maturity value

d = Number of days to maturity

r = Annualized yield

In our example,

$$\frac{100 - 99.531}{99.531} \times \frac{365}{90} = 0.0191 \text{ or } 1.91\%$$

The above calculation does not consider the potential compounding effects on the interest earned (return) after the 90-day period. The yield is expressed as an annual rate that ignores interest earned on interest—in other words, the compounding effects. An *annualized effective yield* calculation considers the compounding and is expressed by the formula

$$\left(1 + \frac{100 - P}{P}\right)^{\frac{365}{d}} - 1 = r \quad \text{(7-1b)}$$

In our example, this is 0.0192, or 1.92 percent. With a hand calculator, this is easy to determine if we identify 100 = FV, −99.531 = PV, 90/365 = N, and 0 = PMT. We then compute I/Y = r.

The Rates and Securities

At the foundation of interest rates in the economy is the rate on one-day money lent between financial institutions to meet temporary cash shortfalls. The banks exchange billions of dollars a day through their clearing systems, and often are left with deficit or surplus positions with the Bank of Canada. This requires them to borrow from each other or large corporations at the overnight rate. The overnight, or call, money rate is the rate at which the major financial institutions lend money to each other for this short period. In other countries the rate may have other names, such as the federal funds rate in the United States but, regardless of its name, there is a strong relationship between the overnight rate and the other short-term interest rates of the marketplace.

---

[3]Formula 7-1a is derived from the basic formula for determining the interest rate earned on an investment, which is $I = Prt (I = 100 − 99.531, P = 99.531, t = 90/365, r =$ to be determined). In the United States, 360 days is used in the calculation.

U.S. Overnight Money Market Rates Soar

In late 2019 overnight money rates in the United States that had been at about 2 percent jumped to over 10 percent. The Federal Reserve quickly pumped over $125 billion into the system and the rates returned to the 2 percent range.

Liquidity was a temporary problem as corporations had committed to buying treasury bonds (to finance the increasing federal debt), paying their quarterly tax bills and the general effort of the Federal Reserve Bank since 2011 of reducing its holdings of bonds by selling them into the market.

Q1 Have short-term U.S. yields soared again lately?

federalreserve.gov

The Bank of Canada sets a target band for overnight money rates as the primary focus of short-term interest rate policy, and acts to maintain rates within this band. By shifting Government of Canada monies, which it controls, between accounts at the Bank of Canada and the financial institutions, the Bank of Canada can change the supply of money in the financial system. The change in the money supply will bring interest rates into the Bank of Canada's desired target range for the overnight rate. This desired target range for the overnight rate is changed infrequently, and with

Bank of Canada
bankofcanada.ca/core-
functions/monetary-policy/
key-interest-rate/

any change, the Bank of Canada will explain its intentions for monetary policy and the reasoning for the change.

The bank rate is the interest rate charged to financial institutions when they borrow (occasionally) from our lender of last resort—the Bank of Canada. The bank rate is set at the upper limit of the overnight rate target band established by the Bank of Canada. The prime rate is the rate charged on loans by the banks to their best customers and is about 1.75 percent (175 basis points) above the bank rate.

From 1980 until early 1996, the bank rate was set based on the average yield of 91-day T-bills sold at the Tuesday auction by the Bank of Canada. However, because the supply and demand forces in the market determined Treasury bill yields, frequent changes occurred in the bank rate. Therefore, the Bank of Canada's desire for interest rates in the economy was not always clear. Today, daily fluctuations of the Treasury bill rate or the overnight rate do not reset the bank rate (see Figure 7–3).

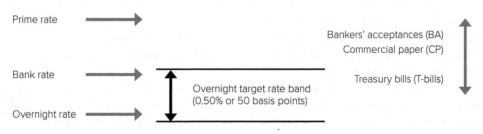

T-bill, BA, and CP rates are short-term rates of somewhat longer maturities, fluctuating within or above the band

Figure 7–3 Money market rate hierarchy

Treasury Bills (T-bills) are obligations of the Government of Canada and are the most liquid and actively traded security. The government is prepared to repurchase them at any time, making T-bills virtually risk free. T-bills are auctioned biweekly, with maturities of 98 days, 182 days, and one year. Although federal government T-bills can be bought at retail in amounts as small as $1,000, the yields on these smaller denominations are substantially less than quoted in the money market.

Canadian provinces, municipalities, and their agencies or Crown corporations also issue short-term securities such as Treasury bills. There is a good secondary market for these securities, and they generally provide a slightly higher return than do Government of Canada T-bills.

Commercial (Corporate) Paper Unsecured promissory notes issued to the public by large business corporations are known as commercial or corporate paper. Many major corporations in Canada issue billions of dollars of commercial paper although its use has dropped noticeably since the financial crisis of 2008. Finance companies such as the mortgage subsidiaries of the major banks and sales finance companies are very active in the commercial paper market, issuing what is commonly referred to as finance company paper. The commercial paper market grew rapidly in Canada with the securitization of assets and as banks have encouraged paper as an alternative to bankers' acceptances, which put the bank at risk.

Bankers' acceptances are securities issued by corporations, with payment guaranteed by a bank, and generally arise from foreign trade. After the financial crisis of 2008 their significance relative to commercial paper grew. They are explored more fully in Chapter 8. The acceptance is a draft drawn on a bank for payment when presented to the bank. Unlike a cheque, a corporation does not have to deposit funds at the bank to cover the draft until the bank has accepted the draft for future payment of the required amount. The holder of the bankers' acceptance may have to wait 30, 60, or 90 days to collect the money, but if desiring cash now, may sell the draft at a discount into the market. There is an active market, including banks themselves, for liquidity needs involving bankers' acceptances.

LIBOR (London Interbank Offered Rate) is the rate offered for currency deposits in the London international banking market that are not subject to national banking requirements. Thus, companies can lend money (i.e., deposit) to banks at that rate. This is essentially a Eurocurrency deposit, although strictly speaking it should be held in Paris or Frankfurt or some other part of Europe. The most common Eurocurrency is the U.S. Eurodollar, which is a U.S. dollar held on deposit by foreign banks that is, in turn, lent out by those banks to anyone seeking dollars. LIBOR is often used as a base lending rate for companies that may borrow at a floating interest rate of LIBOR plus a small premium. The use of LIBOR is discussed further in Chapter 21.

Banks offer alternatives to money market securities, although they are less popular because they are less liquid and pay interest rather than trade at a discount. Bearer deposit notes are transferable from one investor to another. In the United States bearer deposit notes are known as certificates of deposit (CD). Canadian CDs are not transferable. Bank swapped deposits have arisen as Canadian companies take advantage of differences in international short-term interest rates. In a typical case a Canadian company would convert Canadian dollars to U.S. dollars and deposit them in a U.S. bank. Concurrently, the company would execute a futures contract to sell the U.S. dollars for Canadian dollars when the deposit matures. Thus, the company ends up with a hedged U.S. dollar investment. "Hedged" suggests that the investor has no foreign exchange risk. The combination of direct yield and foreign exchange cost or yield may generate a higher return than would a straight deposit in Canada.

The money market is primarily for the wholesale investor, but for the smaller retail investor there are options available. The term deposit or GIC is an investment held at a financial institution. The investor's funds are held on deposit at a specified rate over a given time period (one month to seven years) as evidenced by the certificate received. There is limited liquidity for these investments, as they are not negotiable.

The lowest-yielding investment may well be a *savings account*. Its relative advantages are that it can accommodate small investments and that it can usually be liquidated with no notice. Thus, although not attractive to the large corporations that have other more lucrative options available, the savings account is still a good short-term investment alternative for small businesses and individuals.

For the small investor there is the money market fund, a product that pools the monies of many small investors and invests in a collection of short-term, highly liquid securities. For as little as $500, the investor can have part of the higher-yielding securities with returns only slightly lower to cover management and administrative fees. Some financial institutions also offer accounts that invest in T-bills or other money market securities to allow their customers more attractive deposit returns.

 FINANCE IN ACTION

Treasury Bills, or Commercial Paper, for Liquidity and Safety

As governments reduced debt loads through the 1990s and 2000s, Treasury bills were less available for short-term investment, and commercial paper outstanding grew (Figure 8–3). As investors sought better returns, asset-backed commercial paper (ABCP) or securitizations became quite popular. This financial security was no longer backed by the earning power of well-established companies but by car loans, credit cards, and mortgages. Investors and analysts alike forgot both to exercise due diligence and the lesson that higher returns come with higher risk. By 2007, the security-backed ABCP was in trouble, liquidity was frozen, and yields (if achievable) jumped significantly. This created a crisis of confidence in the world markets.

The three-month Treasury bill issued by federal governments is perhaps the safest and most-liquid investment available. Most major countries offer Treasury bills or something similar. Yields can be compared at financial websites. The different yields are usually a reflection of differences in inflation and monetary policy among countries. A higher rate is not necessarily better if higher inflation reduces the real rate of return.

In early 2020, the following rates were available on three-month government securities:

Canada	1.65%	United States	1.58
Russia	6.06	Britain	0.68
Germany	–0.60	Japan	–0.12

The rates throughout most of the major countries had been quite low, to encourage economic growth. Japan's economy had been slow for several years. Germany is part of the European Economic Union using the euro, a common currency, which requires similar monetary policies and interest rates in the countries of the monetary union. Britain has maintained a separate monetary policy and Russia has higher inflation.

Q1 What are the current rates on three-month T-bills in these countries?

Q2 Has the use of commercial paper recovered?

bloomberg.com/markets/rates-bonds

bankofcanada.ca

Investing.com/rates-bonds

LO4 MANAGEMENT OF ACCOUNTS RECEIVABLE

Despite the expansion of credit via bank credit cards and the creation of finance subsidiaries, a substantial portion of the investment in assets by industrial companies continues to be in accounts receivable. This granting of credit by companies as an alternative to the banks or the capital markets occurs because trade credit facilitates sales. Credit is a part of the complete marketing package presented to a potential customer. It does, however, require careful monitoring and analysis by the financial manager.

Of course, the accounts receivable of one firm is an account payable at another firm.
The smaller firm, in fact, may lack access to the capital markets or to bank financing. Banks may be unwilling to lend to the small firm because the security it can offer is insufficient or the risks are too high and the profit margins too low. Larger firms with higher profit margins on their product, by extending trade credit, in effect provide access for the smaller firm to these financing sources. Remember, the large firm likely supports its accounts receivable position with short-term financing through the banks or the capital markets. Examine Figure 8–1 to see the extent of trade credit financing in Canada.

Trade credit is readily available and convenient. According to Statistics Canada, accounts receivable as a percentage of total assets for nonfinancial corporations in Canada have remained between 10 and 15 percent since 1962. In absolute terms, accounts receivable have risen from $7 billion from the 1960s to 520 billion by 2020.

Accounts Receivable as an Investment

As is true of other current assets, accounts receivable should be thought of as an investment. The level of accounts receivable should not be adjudged too high or too low based on historical standards of industry norms; rather, the test should be whether the level of return we are able to earn from this asset equals or exceeds the potential gain from other commitments. For example, if we allow our customers 10 extra days to clear their accounts, our accounts receivable balance increases—draining funds from marketable securities and perhaps drawing down the inventory level. We must ask whether we are optimizing our return in light of appropriate risk and liquidity considerations.

FINANCE IN ACTION

Receivables, Credit Card Receivables, Securitizations

Loblaw at mid 2020 had about 11 percent of its assets as receivables. $1.0 billion were regular receivables, $2.8 billion were credit card receivables and it had sold $1.5 billion to third-parties as part of its securitization program. A sizable investment in receivables!

Q1 What are Loblaw's current loss provisions for accounts receivable and inventory?

Q1 What do Loblaw's financial statements say about the use of estimates for inventory and accounts receivable?

loblaw.ca
Symbol: L

Suppose a company's annual sales are $10.95 million and the company sells on terms of net 30, meaning customers are expected to pay their bills 30 days after purchase. Therefore,

$$\text{Average daily sales} = \$10.95 \text{ million} \times \frac{1}{365} = \$30,000$$

$$\text{Average accounts receivable} = \$30,000 \times 30 \text{ days} = \$900,000$$

$$\textit{or } \text{Average accounts receivable} = \$10.95 \text{ million} \times \frac{30}{365} = \$900,000$$

If annual credit sales remain at $10.95 million and customers pay in 30 days, on average, the daily accounts receivable balance is $900,000. This is the company's investment as a result of its credit policy.

Notice that if the customers pay 10 days later,

$$\text{Average accounts receivable} = \$10.95 \text{ million} \times \frac{40}{365} = \$1,200,000$$

This is an increased investment of $300,000, on average, every day of the year. That investment could have been in marketable securities as an alternative. If those securities offered a return of 6 percent, the annual opportunity cost of allowing customers to pay 10 days later would be $18,000 ($300,000 × 6%).

An example of a buildup in accounts receivable is presented in Figure 7–4, with supportive financing provided through reducing lower/higher-yielding assets and/or increasing lower-cost liabilities. If accounts receivable are increased for an expected return, they must be supported by bank loans or perhaps a less-significant position in marketable securities. Both have a cost to the firm offset by the return on receivables.

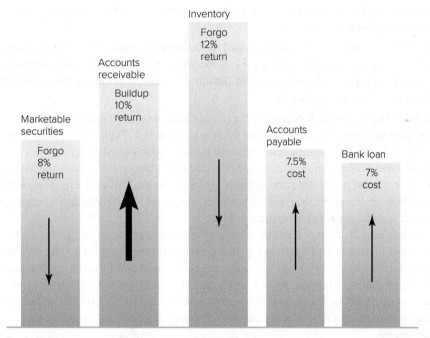

Figure 7–4 Financing growth in accounts receivable

Credit Policy Administration

In the extension of credit, three primary policy variables to consider in conjunction with our profit objective are

1. Credit standards
2. Terms of credit
3. Collection policy

Credit Standards A firm must decide on the degree of credit risk it is prepared to accept. We have seen that large sums of "potential" cash can be invested in accounts receivable. Any receivable that becomes uncollectible affects the firm's success. Accounts receivable are self-liquidating assets. This depends on the ability of a firm's customers to sell their product so the firm granting credit can be paid. The degree of acceptable credit risk is influenced by several factors. These factors include whether the firm is attempting to establish a market, whether the firm is responding to competitive pressures, and the degree of utilization of plant capacity. Auto companies regularly offer credit direct to the ultimate customer to deal with oversupply of cars and to more fully utilize plant capacity.

To establish the degree of credit risk of a potential customer, a firm should develop a credit profile. This profile establishes the customer's strengths and weaknesses. Most importantly, it questions if customers are able to pay and if they can buy enough. Companies that analyze credit risk tend to develop a system in some way related to the *four Cs of credit*.

Character: An analyst attempts to determine the customer's willingness to pay. If things get rough, does the customer go into hiding or attempt to work things out? Clues as to the strength of corporate character come from information on fraudulent activities, legal disputes, union problems, dealings with other suppliers, and even the willingness to supply credit information.

Capacity: The ability to pay is perhaps the most important C. Capacity is built on marketing abilities; experience in the business; the management team; and, overall, the ability to generate profits. To judge a customer's ability to generate profits is a difficult process. Financial ratio analysis can be of considerable assistance, however, as is an investigation of the customer's abilities based on past experience.

Capital: This is a look at assets and net worth. Strong net worth is evidence of past success and a commitment by shareholders to the firm. Growing assets demonstrate an ongoing successful business. In difficult economic times, when its ability to generate profits is diminished, a strong net worth helps a company survive.

Conditions: This is the state of the economy and the industry in general. One's experience and knowledge best help an analyst in getting a fix on conditions. One tries to foresee how existing conditions affect the potential credit customer. How the customer adapts to changing conditions in the marketplace is also a consideration.

The preceding is a simple sketch of the four Cs of credit. An analyst examines information and attempts to determine the potential customer's degree of credit risk. Regardless of the amount of information and analysis, judgments must be made because credit analysis is not an exact science. Firms must strike a balance in their credit policy to ensure that the firm is not exposed to undue risk; however, a credit policy that is too stringent could restrict the firm's capacity to grow and compete. Once the degree of credit risk is established, it must be measured against company policy to determine whether granting credit is acceptable.

The assessment of credit risk and the setting of reasonable credit standards that allow marketing and finance to set objectives together are based on the ability to get information and analyze it. An extensive network of credit information has been developed by credit agencies throughout the country. The most prominent source is Dun & Bradstreet, which provides computer access to information contained in its database of more than 240 million businesses. Information is given on a firm's line of business, financial situation, payment history, and creditworthiness.

Dun & Bradstreet has created statistical models to analyze the risk of a bad debt. Some of the more important variables they put into their model are the age of the company in years, negative public records, total number of employees, facility owned, financial statement data, payment index, percent of satisfactory payment experiences, and the percentage of slow or negative payment experiences. The model is able to predict payment problems and bankruptcy with a high probability 12 months before they occur.

Dun & Bradstreet
Canada
dnb.com/ca-en

Given that the world is doing more and more business on a global scale, the fact that you can track companies around the world on its database is helpful. The companies on the database can be accessed through a D-U-N-S number, which is accepted by the United Nations as a global business identification standard. The Data Universal Number System (D-U-N-S) is a unique nine-digit code assigned by Dun & Bradstreet to each business in its information base. It can be used to track a whole family of companies that are related through ownership. Subsidiaries, divisions, and branches can be tracked to their ultimate parent company at the top of the family pyramid. For example, this tracking ability helps to determine who would ultimately be responsible for a bad debt that occurred in a subsidiary.

Certain industries have also developed their own special credit reporting agencies. Even more important are the local credit bureaus that keep close tabs on day-to-day transactions in a given community.

In addition, information can be gathered from

- Sales reports and visits to the potential customer's place of business
- Customer's financial statements
- Financial institutions
- Other suppliers and industry contacts
- Other credit reporting agencies such as Equifax

Terms of Trade *Terms of trade* refers to the length of time credit is granted and whether a discount is allowed for early payment. The credit period is often set in response to what the competition is doing. Furthermore, significant customers with financial clout may require and receive credit terms that meet their needs.

Equifax
equifax.com

A company may set a different credit period to increase sales or perhaps to make up for product deficiencies. Discounts are usually offered to encourage early payment to address cash flow concerns rather than to stimulate sales. We have already seen how the length of the credit period allowed (not necessarily the stated term) can have a dramatic impact on the level of investment in accounts receivable. Offering the credit terms "2/10, net 30" enables the customer to deduct 2 percent from the face amount of the bill when paying within the first 10 days, but if the discount is not taken, the customer must remit the full amount within 30 days. As later demonstrated in Chapter 8, the annualized cost of not taking a cash discount may be substantial. It is important to recognize that many companies in Canada do not make payments within the agreed payment terms. Keeping this statistic in mind, companies must plan their terms of trade adequately to ensure necessary liquidity.

Collection Policy A third area for consideration under credit policy administration is the collection function. A company must establish collection procedures that get after delinquent accounts in a timely and regular manner. The procedures should be applied consistently with the goal of not only collecting the debt but also maintaining the customer. A number of quantitative measures may be applied to the credit department of the firm.

1. $\text{Average collection period} = \dfrac{\text{Accounts receivable}}{\text{Average daily credit sales}}$

   (See formula 3–4*b* in Chapter 3.) As was discussed in Chapter 6, the average collection period is part of the cash conversion period. An increasing collection period will have implications for financial planning, as it will take longer to turn the accounts receivable investment into cash. When applying this formula, a company must be careful if sales vary throughout the year, as it can give distorted signals. A trend toward a longer collection period could be the result of a predetermined plan to extend credit terms or the consequence of poor credit administration. Management should monitor this measure closely as compared to the collection department's credit terms and industry averages. If the collection period extends beyond these standards, management should seek corrective action, as it is likely that increasing amounts of capital are being tied up unproductively in accounts receivable.

2. Ratio of bad debts to credit sales An increasing ratio may indicate too many weak accounts or an aggressive market expansion policy. On the other hand, too low a ratio may indicate an overly restrictive credit policy that is limiting sales. The standard for this ratio should be past experience and industry averages.

3. Aging of accounts receivables We may wish to determine the amounts of time the various accounts have been on our books. The likelihood of accounts becoming uncollectible increases dramatically the further the account extends beyond its credit terms. Furthermore, older receivables represent less profitable investments. If there is a buildup in receivables beyond our normal credit terms, we may wish to take remedial action. Such a buildup is shown in the following table.

Age of Receivables, June 30, 20XX		
Month of Sales	Age of Account (days)	Amounts
May	0–30	$ 60,000
April......................	31–60	25,000
March.....................	61–90	5,000
February....................	91–120	10,000
Total receivables.............		$100,000

If our normal credit terms are 30 days, we may be doing a poor job of collecting our accounts, with particular attention required on the over-90-day accounts. It is important to examine the nature of the accounts receivable because their characteristics can change quickly due to their rapid turnover.

An Actual Credit Decision

We bring together the various elements of accounts receivable management in a decision about a potential change or implementation of a credit policy. This is done to, it is hoped, improve company performance by comparing the firm's financial situation under the present credit policy with what it would be under the proposed credit policy. Only those financial variables that change are relevant for analysis. Our analysis and decision are good if we improve the wealth of the shareholders. Generally, credit policy changes affect the level of sales by changing credit standards or by changing the length of the credit period. Often, changes are a response to competitive pressures.

For example, let us assume a firm is considering a credit decision to sell to a group of customers that will result in sales increasing from $100,000 to $110,000, an increase of $10,000 in new annual sales. The cost of producing the product is 67 percent of sales, and selling expenses are expected to be 10 percent of sales. Additionally, collection costs are projected at 5 percent of sales, and because the new customers are risky, we forecast 10 percent of the new sales to be uncollectible. Although this is a very high rate of nonpayment, the critical question is, what is the potential contribution of these incremental sales to profitability? These incremental revenues and expenses are fairly easy to identify with the traditional income statement approach.

	Current	Projected
Sales................................	$100,000	$110,000
Cost of goods sold	67,000	73,700
Gross profit margin	33,000	36,300
Selling expenses......................	10,000	11,000
Bad debt expense	10,000	11,000
Collection expense....................	5,000	5,500
Income before interest and taxes..........	$ 8,000	$ 8,800

However, other costs may be more elusive, in particular the opportunity costs that will arise if the firm commits to the new credit policy. A major consideration is the increased investment in accounts receivable and the opportunity cost on the firm's funds tied up in this asset. This cost is often taken from the rate on short-term demand loans, which are sometimes used to finance accounts receivable. If bank financing is used for the incremental investment, this cost would be described fully by an income statement approach. However, the cost of an increased investment in accounts receivable is not always easily identified by such a direct cost. Sometimes, the increased investment is provided by an increased equity contribution, and expected return to the shareholders does not show up on the income statement. The use of an opportunity cost in the analysis captures the broader possibilities for financing the accounts receivable position.

Additionally, our analysis might consider possible investments in inventories or plant or equipment that may result from increased sales. We do not, however, consider them in this example.

In our example, our firm expects its receivables to turn over six times a year, and we assume that the opportunity cost is 15 percent. The analysis, set out below, proceeds on the basis of the incremental revenues and costs that we have identified from selling to the new group of customers, and includes the opportunity cost on the increased investment in accounts receivable. Incremental analysis isolates and identifies only the relevant changes that result from a shift in credit policy.

Accounts receivable arise only on credit sales, and it is the average credit period (when customers actually pay) not the stated credit terms that determine the size of the receivables.

		Summary of Costs/Benefits
Incremental sales	$10,000	
Incremental contribution margin	(100% – 67%)	$ 3,300
Incremental selling expense.	10%	<1,000>
Incremental bad debts (uncollectible)	10%	<1,000>
Incremental collection costs.	5%	<500>
Incremental accounts receivable*.	10,000/6	
(sales/turnover).	= 1,667	
Incremental opportunity cost on investment in accounts receivable.	15% (1,667 × 15% =)	<250>
Total incremental change		$ 550

*We could actually argue that our out-of-pocket commitment to sales is only 67 percent of the $10,000, or $6,700, which is the cost of goods sold. This would indicate a smaller commitment to receivables of $1,117 ($6,700/6). However, does this best capture the opportunity cost of an investment that has changed in substance from inventory to credit with the concurrent change in the profit and equity accounts and their subsequent expectation of return?

Our decision would be to proceed with the new credit policy. Not only have the increased profits and costs been considered in the analysis but, most important from an investor or shareholder perspective, consideration also has been given to the opportunity cost of having funds tied up or invested in accounts receivable. This opportunity cost of funds in our example is a before-tax cost.

This analysis is basically for one time period and assumes that the incremental changes are perpetual. It may neglect considerations such as the time value of money, changes to product life, earlier capital expenditure requirements as increasing sales wear out machinery sooner, and tax changes due to the previously noted considerations.

Another Example of a Credit Decision

Assume that the firm currently has annual sales of $121,667 and collection occurs in 30 days. It is expected that sales will increase to $146,000 if 45 days of credit are extended to customers. Additionally, administration costs are projected to increase by $1,000. Another cost is the expected increase in bad debt expense from 1 to 1.5 percent of sales. The firm has an opportunity cost of capital of 12 percent and its variable costs are 80 percent of sales.

	Current	Projected	Summary
Annual sales.........................	$121,667	$146,000	
Incremental sales		24,333	
Incremental contribution margin (100–80%).........		4,867	$4,867
Incremental administration costs		1,000	<1,000>
Bad debts:			
1%..	1,216		
1.5%......................................		2,190	
Incremental bad debts		974	<974>
Accounts receivable..........................	121,667	146,000	
	× 30/365 =	× 45/365 =	
	10,000	18,000	
Incremental accounts receivable investment		8,000	
Incremental opportunity cost on investment in accounts receivable	12%	960	<960>
Total incremental changes			$1,933

Decision: Implement new credit terms.

On an incremental basis, with consideration given to the investment in accounts receivable, there is positive value added to the firm from changing the credit policy.

LO5 INVENTORY MANAGEMENT

Inventory needs to be financed, and its efficient management can increase a firm's profitability. Just like accounts receivable, inventory can represent a sizable investment by a company. An adequate return is expected on this investment. The amount of inventory is not totally controlled by company management; it also is affected by sales, production, and economic conditions.

A good case study is the automobile industry. Its inventory management is influenced by cyclical sales that are highly sensitive to the economy. Automakers often suffer from inventory buildups when sales decline because adjusting production levels takes time. As the economy slows, the car manufacturers implement buyer incentive programs such as zero percent financing and cash rebates. These programs cut profit margins per car, but generate cash flow and reduce investment expenses associated with holding high inventories. Efforts are made to make the production lines more flexible by running several makes of cars to allow quicker response to changing consumer tastes.

 FINANCE IN ACTION

No Wine Before Its Time

Inventory at Peller Estates, the winery, represents 34 percent of its assets. Based on its cost of goods sold and inventories its turnover ratio is 1.4 times a year or every 264 days (9 months). A slow inventory turnover and a significant investment.

andrewpeller.com
Symbol: ADW.A

Inventory management has been changing. Seeking to reduce the large costs that can be tied up in inventory, companies have been developing ways to control overinvestment. The just-in-time (JIT) process that brings parts to the assembly line just as they are needed has helped to reduce inventories. We have also seen the benefits of online inventory reporting systems that allow management to quickly respond to changing market conditions. Excess inventory buildups do not appear to be as prevalent as in the past.

Inventory is the least liquid of current assets, and it should provide the highest yield to justify investment. Although the financial manager may have direct control over cash management, marketable securities, and accounts receivable, control over inventory policy is generally shared with production management and marketing.

In Chapter 3 we noted the relationship between cost of goods sold and inventory, which was expressed either as the inventory holding period or inventory turnover ratio. This relationship is expressed in the following example:

$$\frac{COGS}{Day} \times \text{Holding period} = \text{Average inventory} \quad \text{(3-5b)}$$

$$\frac{\$1,216,667}{365} \times 30 = \$100,000$$

It can also be expressed as a turnover ratio of 12 (365/30). The average inventory position may fluctuate dramatically above the average if sales of the firm's product vary throughout the year. Also, note how the average inventory and the cost of financing the inventory position will change as the holding period (turnover) or level of sales (and thus COGS) changes.

Level versus Seasonal Production

A manufacturing firm must determine whether a plan of level or seasonal production should be followed. Production scheduling is complicated by uncertain demand and the desire to provide immediate service. Furthermore, inventory buildups may be used to take advantage of quantity discount offers. In addition, an inventory buildup is a hedging technique to deal with anticipated resource shortages or price increases. Level production was discussed in Chapter 6. While level (even) production throughout the year allows for maximum efficiency in the use of labour and machinery, it may result in unnecessarily high inventory buildups before shipment, particularly in a seasonal business. We may have 10,000 bathing suits in stock in November.

If we produce on a seasonal basis, the inventory problem is eliminated, but we then have unused capacity during slack periods. Furthermore, as we shift to maximum operations to meet seasonal needs, we may be forced to pay overtime wages for labour and to sustain other inefficiencies as equipment is overused.

Here we have a classic problem in financial analysis. Are the cost savings from level production sufficient to justify the extra expenditure in carrying inventory? Let us look at a typical case.

	Production	
	Level	Seasonal
Average inventory	$100,000	$70,000
Operating costs—after taxes	50,000	60,000

Though we have to invest $30,000 more in average inventory under level production, we save $10,000 in operating costs. This represents a 33 percent return on investment. If our required rate of return is 10 percent, this would clearly be an acceptable alternative.[4] In any organization, a cost-benefit analysis must be completed based on a sensitivity analysis of projected sales to determine whether a seasonal or level production method is more cost effective. Cost of sales, projected revenue, and labour costs are all variables to be considered through the evaluation.

---

[4] The problem may be further evaluated by using the capital budgeting techniques presented in Chapter 12.

Inventory Policy in Inflation (and Deflation)

While the consumer price index has risen consistently, from 87 in 1995 to 137 by December 2020, the commodity price index has been quite volatile over the same period. From 233 in 2001, it was up to 881 in July 2008, down to 382 in February 2009, 722 in April 2011, 290 in February 2016, and back to 425 by January 2020.

Price increases on nickel and copper were so great in the late 1980s that Inco almost didn't know what to do with the cash flow it was generating. A dividend of over $1 billion was paid to shareholders. Only the most astute inventory manager can hope to prosper in this environment. The problem can be partially controlled by taking moderate inventory positions (that is, not fully committing at one price).

Another way of protecting an inventory position is by use of a futures contract, a hedging technique. A futures contract is an agreement to sell (buy) a commodity at a specific price and on a specific date in the future, regardless of the actual price of the commodity at that future date. Although a company gives up the ability to make a potentially large gain if prices move up, it also avoids a potential loss if prices go down. The advantage to the financial manager is that uncertainty, or risk, is removed, as the manager knows the price that will be received at the future date. Planning can occur with a known cash flow. Futures are traded on organized exchanges that ensure that the contracts are fulfilled.

CME Group
cmegroup.com

Rapid price movements in inventory may also have a major impact on the reported income of the firm, a process described in Chapter 3. A firm using FIFO (first-in, first-out) accounting may experience large inventory profits when old, less expensive inventory is written off against new high prices in the marketplace. The benefits may be transitory, as the process reverses itself when prices decline. Nevertheless, profits that result from holding inventories are subject to tax, if they are carried to the bottom line. This reduces cash flow when increasing costs are being incurred to purchase new inventories. Additionally, escalating financing expenses are required to finance the inflating inventory position, although the actual number of inventory items may remain constant.

The Inventory Decision Model

Substantial research has been devoted to the problem of determining optimum inventory size, order quantity, usage rate, and similar considerations. An entire branch in the field of operations research is dedicated to the subject. We examine a somewhat simple model that is dependent on the certainty of the variables used—in particular, the certainty of steady demand for the product.

In developing an inventory model, we must evaluate the two basic costs associated with inventory: the carrying costs and the ordering costs. Through a careful analysis of both of these variables, we can determine the optimum order size to place to minimize costs.

Carrying Costs Carrying costs include interest on funds tied up in inventory and the cost of warehouse space, insurance premiums, and material handling expenses. There is also an implicit cost associated with the dangers of obsolescence and rapid price change. The larger the order we place, the greater the average inventory we will have on hand, and the higher the carrying cost.

Ordering Costs As a second factor, we must consider the ordering costs and the processing of inventory into stock. If we maintain a relatively low average inventory in stock, we must order many times, and total ordering cost will be high. The opposite patterns associated with the two costs are portrayed in Figure 7–5.

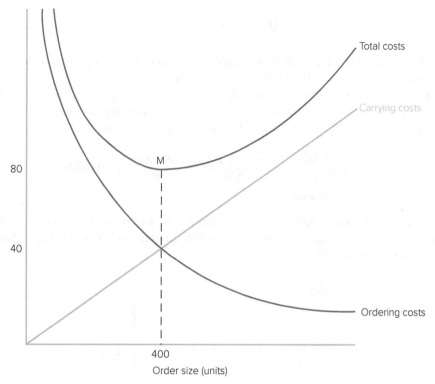

Cost of ordering and carrying inventory ($)

Total costs

Carrying costs

M

80

40

Ordering costs

400

Order size (units)

Figure 7–5 Determining the optimum inventory level

As the order size increases, carrying costs go up because we have more inventory on hand. With larger orders, we will order less frequently and overall ordering costs will go down. The approximate tradeoff between the two can best be judged by examining the total cost curve. At point *M*, we have appropriately played the advantages and disadvantages of the respective costs against each other. With larger orders, carrying costs will be excessive, while at a reduced order size, constant ordering will put us at an undesirably higher point on the ordering cost curve.

The question becomes, how do we mathematically determine the minimum point (*M*) on the total cost curve? Under certain fairly reasonable assumptions (primarily constant usage), we may use the following formula:

$$EOQ = \sqrt{\frac{2SO}{C}} \quad \text{(7–2)}$$

Economic Ordering Quantity The economic ordering quantity, the EOQ, is the amount most advantageous for the firm to order each time. We determine this value, translate it into average inventory size, and determine the minimum total cost amount (*M*). The terms in the EOQ formula are defined as follows:

S = Total sales in units

O = Ordering cost for each order

C = Carrying cost per unit in dollars

Q = Quantity per order

Our total inventory costs are given by the following formula:[5]

$$TC = \frac{SO}{Q} + \frac{CQ}{2} \quad (7\text{--}3)$$

This formula represents total costs as ordering costs times the number of times we order each year (S/Q) plus carrying costs times the average inventory ($Q/2$).

Let us assume we anticipate selling 2,000 units, it will cost us $8 to place each order, and the price per unit is $1, with a 20 percent carrying cost to maintain the average inventory (the carrying charge per unit is $0.20). Substituting these values into our formula, we show

$$EOQ = \sqrt{\frac{2SO}{C}} = \sqrt{\frac{2 \times 2{,}000 \times \$8}{\$0.20}} = \sqrt{\frac{\$32{,}000}{\$0.20}} = \sqrt{160{,}000}$$
$$= 400 \text{ units}$$

The optimum order size is 400 units. On the assumption we use up inventory at a constant rate throughout the year, our average inventory on hand will be 200 units, as indicated in Figure 7–6. Average inventory equals EOQ + 0/2.

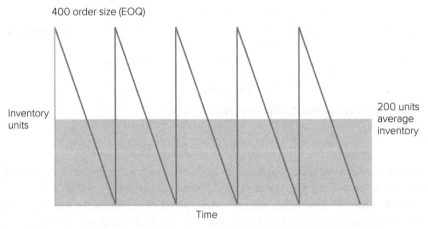

Figure 7–6 Inventory usage pattern

---

[5] To achieve minimum total costs (M), we must take the first derivative and set it equal to zero.

$$\frac{d\text{TC}}{dQ} = \frac{-SO}{Q^2} + \frac{C}{2}$$
$$\frac{-SO}{Q^2} + \frac{C}{2} = 0$$
$$\frac{C}{2} = \frac{SO}{Q^2}$$
$$Q^2 = \frac{2SO}{C}$$
$$Q = \sqrt{\frac{2SO}{C}}$$

We note that minimum costs are achieved in Figure 7–4, where

$$\frac{SO}{Q} = \frac{CQ}{2}$$
$$SO = \frac{CQ^2}{2}$$
$$2SO = CQ^2$$
$$\frac{2SO}{C} = Q^2$$
$$Q = \sqrt{\frac{2SO}{C}}$$

Our total costs with an order size of 400 and an average inventory size of 200 units are computed in Table 7–4.

Table 7–4 Total costs for inventory

1. Ordering costs $= \dfrac{2,000 \text{ order size}}{400 \text{ units}} = 5$ orders

   5 orders at \$8 per order = \$40
2. Carrying costs = Average inventory in units × Carrying cost per unit

   $200 \times \$0.20 = \$40$
3. Order cost \$40

   Carrying cost . . . . $\underline{+40}$

   Total cost \$80

Point **M** on Figure 7–5 can be equated to a total cost of \$80 at an order size of 400 units. At no other order point can we hope to achieve lower costs. The same basic principles of total cost minimization that we have applied to inventory can be applied to other assets as well. For example, we may assume cash has a carrying cost (opportunity cost of lost interest on marketable securities as a result of being in cash) and an ordering cost (transaction costs of shifting in and out of marketable securities) and then work toward determining the optimum level of cash. In each case we are trying to minimize the overall costs and increase profit.

Safety Stock and Stockouts

In our analysis thus far we have assumed that we would use up inventory at a constant rate and that we would receive new inventory when the old level of inventory reached zero. To verify this point, you may wish to reexamine Figure 7–5. We have not specifically considered the problem of being out of stock.

A stockout occurs when a firm is out of a specific inventory item and is unable to sell or deliver the product. The risk of losing sales to a competitor may cause a firm to hold a safety stock to reduce this risk. Although the company may use the EOQ model to determine the optimum order quantity, management cannot always assume the delivery schedules of suppliers will be constant or assure delivery of new inventory when inventory reaches zero. A safety stock guards against late deliveries due to weather, production delays, equipment breakdowns, and the many other things that can go wrong between the placement of an order and its delivery.

A minimum safety stock increases the cost of inventory because the carrying cost rises. This cost should be offset by eliminating lost profits on sales due to stockouts and also by increased profits from unexpected orders that can now be filled.

In the prior example, if a safety stock of 50 units were maintained, the average inventory figure would be 250 units.

$$\text{Average inventory} = \frac{\text{EOQ}}{2} + \text{Safety stock}$$

$$\text{Average inventory} = \frac{400}{2} + 50$$

$$= 200 + 50 = 250$$

The inventory carrying cost now increases to \$50.

$$\text{Carrying costs} = \text{Average inventory in units} \times \text{Carrying cost per unit}$$
$$= 250 \times \$0.20 = \$50$$

The amount of safety stock that a firm carries is likely to be influenced by the predictability of inventory usage and the time period necessary to fill inventory orders. The following discussion indicates safety stock may be reduced in the future.

Just-in-Time Inventory Management

Just-in-time inventory management (JIT) was designed for Toyota by the Japanese firm Shigeo Shingo and found its way to other countries. Just-in-time inventory management is part of a total production concept that often interfaces with a total quality control program. A JIT program has several basic requirements: (1) quality production that continually satisfies customer requirements; (2) close ties between suppliers, manufacturers, and customers; and (3) minimization of the level of inventory.

Usually, suppliers are located near manufacturers that can make orders in small lot sizes because of short delivery times. One side effect has been for manufacturers to reduce their number of suppliers to assure quality as well as to ease the complexity of ordering and delivery. Computerized ordering/inventory tracking systems both on the assembly line and in the supplier's production facility are necessary for JIT to work.

Cost Savings from Lower Inventory Cost savings from lower levels of inventory and reduced financing costs are supposed to be the major benefits of JIT. On average, it is estimated that over the last decade JIT inventory systems have reduced inventory-to-sales ratios by over 10 percent. Some individual cases are more dramatic.

Harley-Davidson reduced its in-process and in-transit inventory by $20 million at a single plant, and General Electric trimmed inventory by 70 percent in 40 plants. In one sense, the manufacturer pushes some of the cost of financing onto the supplier. If the supplier also imposes JIT on its suppliers, these efficiencies work their way down the supplier chain to create a leaner production system for the whole economy.

Other Benefits There are other, not so obvious, cost savings to JIT inventory systems. Because of reduced warehouse space for inventory, some plants in the automotive industry have reduced floor space by 70 percent over the more traditional plants that warehoused inventory. This saves construction costs and reduces overhead expenses for utilities and human resources. The JIT systems have been aided in the last few years by the development of the Internet and electronic data interchange systems (EDI) between suppliers and production and manufacturing departments. EDI reduces rekeying errors and duplication of forms for the accounting and finance functions. Reductions in costs from quality control are often overlooked by financial analysts, because JIT prevents defects rather than detects poor quality; therefore, no cost savings are recognized. One last item is the elimination of waste, which is one of the side benefits of a total quality control system coupled with JIT inventory systems.

It is important to realize that the JIT inventory system is very compatible with the concept of economic ordering quantity. The focus is to balance reduced carrying costs from maintaining less inventory with increased ordering costs. Fortunately, electronic data interchange minimizes the disadvantage of having to place orders more often.

The Downside of JIT Some JIT management systems allow for inventory levels as low as one-hour's worth of parts. The discipline of these levels and the required process has imposed an extraordinary rigour on firms demanding continuous deliveries, and a substantial expenditure on computer systems to coordinate the activity. Nevertheless, when there are significant increases in demand, capacity may not be available to deliver products. While firms strive for a competitive and cost advantage using JIT inventory, the firm must maintain the service levels expected by customers. Therefore, firms usually carry additional inventory to avoid stockouts.

JIT for Money and Inventory Control

Global trade for centuries has relied on the letter of credit to facilitate the exchange of goods in return for money. This method (covered more extensively in Chapter 21) requires numerous paper documents and coordination between banks around the world for funds transfer, and it is often a slow, cumbersome exercise. Infor Nexus and United Parcel Service Inc. have developed Internet-based systems to allow physical goods to move with appropriate documentation and electronic funds transfer occurring at the same time in supply chain management.

The benefit is that money is transferred more quickly, cash flow is increased, and trading activity can increase as there is less time spent on paperwork. With letters of credit, money is often taken from accounts but may take a couple of weeks before it is in the hands of a supplier.

Inventory needs better controls for the fast pace of today's business world. The RFID (radio frequency ID tag), or electronic bar code, is revolutionizing how we track inventory. The cost of each tag has been reduced below 1 cent. RFID technology is required from suppliers by many companies if sales are to occur.

With an RFID system, the goods are continually scanned, providing the firm with information on the inventory status. This increases sales as more accurate stocking patterns allow better JIT processes and reduce costs from the decreased labour expenses of receiving, stocking, and counting goods. Furthermore, theft is reduced. However, RFID requires expenditures on wireless readers, software, and new processes. Additionally, it requires close partnerships with suppliers for common standards in packaging. Overall, it facilitates better control over the firm's inventory investment.

Q1 What do you think of Infor Nexus' "The power of information" media presentation?

Infor Nexus

printronix.com

Tsunami Shuts Down Global Supply Chains

Car companies, using computers and telecommunications networks, coordinate their JIT management system of shipments by air, sea, and land from all parts of the globe. JIT has resulted in efficiencies, reduced inventory investment, and improved quality.

In 2011, the earthquake and tsunami that struck Japan caused widespread damage, including power shortages. The disruptions experienced by Japanese auto parts suppliers and electronics manufacturers, whose parts were required by North American auto manufacturers, caused a two- to four-month slowdown in deliveries, reducing production activities and significantly impacting Canadian GDP. Canadian exports of grains also suffered as Japanese ports were damaged and could not receive deliveries.

The cost of this dependency is lost business when the supply chain is disrupted.

SUMMARY

1. Current assets of the firm entail a sizable investment that must be financed. The concepts of asset growth in relation to sales, hedging, risk, liquidity, and profitability are important as we study current assets. The more liquid an asset, the easier it is to convert that asset to cash, allowing the firm greater flexibility. This flexibility is sacrificed when monies are committed to less-liquid assets. Therefore, we must have higher expectations for the return on those assets; otherwise, the firm will become less efficient. (LO1)

2. In cash management, the primary goal should be to keep the balances as low as possible, consistently, with the notion of maintaining adequate funds for transactions and compensating balances. Cash moves through the firm in a cycle as customers make payments and the firm pays its bills. We try to speed the inflow of funds and defer their outflow in managing the company's float. The increased use of electronic funds transfer systems both domestically and internationally is reducing float and making for timelier collections and disbursements. (LO2)

3. Excess short-term funds may be placed in marketable securities. There is a wide selection of issues, maturities, and yields from which to choose. Safety and liquidity are primary considerations for marketable securities. (LO3)

4. Accounts receivable are an investment of the firm based on its credit policies, and a test of profitability should be applied. Management of accounts receivable calls for determining credit standards and the forms of credit to be offered as well as the development of an effective collection policy. There is no such thing as bad credit—only unprofitable credit extension. Incremental analysis of credit policies highlights the critical variables in determining profitability. (LO4)

5. Inventory is the least liquid of the current assets, so it should provide the highest yield. We recognize three different inventory types: raw materials, work-in-progress, and finished goods inventory. We manage inventory levels through models such as the economic ordering quantity (EOQ) model, which helps us determine the optimum average inventory size that minimizes the total cost of ordering and carrying inventory. The just-in-time inventory management model (JIT) focuses on the minimization of inventory through quality production techniques and close ties between manufacturers and suppliers. The EOQ and JIT models are compatible and can work together in the management of inventory. (LO5)

REVIEW OF FORMULAS

Annualized yield marketplace

$$\frac{100 - P}{P} \times \frac{365}{d} = r \tag{7–1a}$$

Annualized effective yield

$$\left(1 + \frac{100 - P}{P}\right)^{\frac{365}{d}} - 1 = r \tag{7–1b}$$

P = Discounted price as percent of maturity value
d = Number of days to maturity

$$EOQ = \sqrt{\frac{2SO}{C}} \tag{7–2}$$

$$TC = \frac{SO}{Q} + \frac{CQ}{2} \tag{7–3}$$

DISCUSSION QUESTIONS

1. In the management of cash and marketable securities, why should the primary concern be for safety and liquidity rather than profit maximization? (LO1)

2. Define liquidity. (LO1)

3. Why are cash flows of more interest than income to the treasury manager? (LO1)

4. How can a firm operate with a negative cash balance on its corporate books? (LO2)

5. Explain the similarities and differences between lockbox systems and regional collection offices. (LO2)

6. Why would a financial manager want to slow down disbursements? (LO2)

7. Use a financial publication to find the going interest rates for the list of marketable securities in Table 7–3. Which security would you choose for a short-term investment? Why? (LO3)

8. Why are Treasury bills a favourite place for financial managers to invest excess cash? (LO3)

9. Why are U.S. money market rates generally lower than Canadian money market rates on instruments of similar risk? (LO3)

10. Differentiate between the money market and the Eurobond market. (LO3)

11. Explain why the bad debt percentage or any other similar credit-control percentage is not the ultimate measure of success in the management of accounts receivable. What is the key consideration? (LO4)

12. Precisely what does the EOQ formula tell us? What assumption is made about the usage rate for inventory? (LO5)

13. Why might a firm keep a safety stock? What effect is it likely to have on carrying cost of inventory? (LO5)

14. If a firm uses a JIT inventory system, what effect is that likely to have on the number and location of suppliers? (LO5)

INTERNET RESOURCES AND QUESTIONS

The Bank of Canada provides some current and historical money market yields under financial statistics: bankofcanada.ca

The RateHub has current savings rates across Canada: ratehub.ca

Bloomberg and Investing.com provide government yields for several maturities and for several countries: bloomberg.com/markets/rates-bonds and investing.com/rates-bonds

The central banks of several countries maintain sites that are linked through the Federal Reserve of the United States (About the Fed). These sites outline the purpose and function of central banks and maintain historical interest rates: federalreserve.gov

The Department of Finance provides definitions of debt instruments, describes the auction process, and demonstrates how yields and prices are calculated on money market instruments: canada.ca/en/department-finance

The chartered banks provide descriptions of their cash management services. The Bank of Montreal is a good example: bmo.com

1. Provide current yields on four different money market securities in Canada, and from similar securities from the United States, using a site such as the Bank of Canada's. How do the rates compare?

2. Compare yields on 3-month government securities using a site such as Bloomberg or Investing.com. Why are the rates similar or different?

3. List the cash management services provided by a chartered bank.

4. Compare the overnight call rate in Canada and Japan using the Bank of Japan site. Why is there a difference in rates? boj.or.jp/en/

PROBLEMS

1. Porky's Sausage Co. shows the following values on its corporate books.

Corporate Books:	
Initial amount.	$10,000
Deposits	+80,000
Cheques	−50,000
Balance.	$40,000

The initial amount on the bank's books is also $10,000. However, only $70,000 in deposits has been recorded and only $25,000 in cheques have cleared. Fill in the table below and indicate the amount of float.

Bank Books:	
Initial amount.	$10,000
Deposits	_____
Cheques	_____
Balance.	_____
Float.	_____

2. Sheila's Society Clothing Manufacturer has collection centres around the country to speed up cash collections. The company also makes its disbursements from remote disbursement centres, so cheques written by Sheila's take longer to clear the bank. Collection time has been reduced by two and one-half days and disbursement time has been increased by one and one-half days because of these policies. Excess funds are being invested in short-term instruments yielding 6 percent per annum.

   a. If the firm has $4 million per day in collections and $3 million per day in disbursements, how many dollars has the cash management system freed up?

   b. How much can Sheila's earn per year on short-term investments made possible by the freed-up cash?

3. Aurora Electrical Company of Yellowknife ships wind turbines throughout the country. Mr. Beam, the financial manager, has determined that through the establishment of local collection centres around the country, he can speed up the collection of payments by two days. Furthermore, the cash management department of the company's bank has indicated to him that he can defer payments on his accounts by one day without offending suppliers. The bank has a remote disbursement centre in New Brunswick.

   a. If Aurora Electrical Company has $1.5 million per day in collections and $0.8 million per day in disbursements, how many dollars will the cash management system free up?

   b. If Aurora Electrical Company can earn 4 percent per annum on freed-up funds, how much income can be generated?

   c. If the total cost of the system is $125,000, should it be implemented?

4. Megahurtz International Car Rentals has rent-a-car outlets throughout the world. It keeps funds for transaction purposes in many foreign currencies. Assume that in 20XX it held 100,000 *reals* in Brazil worth $42,000. It earned 12 percent interest, but the *real* declined 20 percent against the dollar.

   a. What is the value of its holdings, based on Canadian dollars, at year-end?

   b. What is the value of its holdings, based on Canadian dollars, at year-end if it earned 9 percent and the *real* went up by 10 percent against the dollar?

5. The current cash management system of Low Ash Cat Foods requires five days to collect its daily receipts of $225,000. Now Bank offers to reduce the collection time by four days for an annual fee of $49,000. If the opportunity cost of funds is 6 percent, should Low Ash accept the bank's offer?

6. Leeft Bank offers to reduce the collection time for your company's daily cash receipts by two days with its cash management system. This service will cost you $15,000 per year. Currently, short-term money market rates average 5 percent. If you anticipate annual sales of $46.355 million, would you accept the bank's offer?

7. Your banker has analyzed your company account and has suggested that her bank has a cash management package for you. She suggests that with a concentration banking system, your float can be reduced by three days on average. You, of course, are delighted (you're not sure why), but you do know your average daily collections amount to $305,000. Your opportunity cost of funds is 9 percent. The bank provides this service for $52,500 plus a compensating balance in your current account of $75,000. (A compensating balance is the amount you are required to maintain interest free at that bank.) Is this package worth it? If so, by how much?

8. Ron's chequebook shows a balance of $400. A recent statement from the bank (received last week) shows that all cheques written as of the date of the statement have been paid, except numbers 325 and 326, which were for $35.00 and $58.00, respectively. Since the statement date, cheques 327, 328, and 329 have been written for $22.00, $45.00, and $17.00, respectively.

   There is an 80 percent probability that cheques 325 and 326 have been paid by this time. There is a 50 percent probability that cheques 327, 328, and 329 have been paid.

   a. What is the total value of the five cheques outstanding?

   b. What is the expected value of payments for the five cheques outstanding?

   c. What is the difference between parts *a* and *b*? This represents a type of float.

9. Lett's commercial paper is currently selling at a discount. It sells for 97.29 of par and matures in 120 days.

   a. Calculate its yield as quoted in the market.

   b. Calculate its effective annual yield.

10. Camembert's commercial paper is currently selling at a discount. It sells for 99.16 of par and matures in 83 days.

    a. Calculate its yield as quoted in the market.

    b. Calculate its effective annual yield.

11. A bankers' acceptance is discounted by Canmex Inc. at 98.71 of par. It matures in 60 days.

    a. What is the cost to the company on a nominal basis?

    b. What is the effective annual cost to the company?

12. A 91-day Treasury bill with a face value of $1 million is sold to yield 5.27 percent.

    a. At what price did the T-bill sell if the yield was quoted by the market?

    b. At what price did the T-bill sell if the yield was an effective annual yield?

13. Sanders' Prime Time Lighting Co. has credit sales of $1,875,000 and accounts receivable of $195,205. Compute the value for the average collection period.

14. Oral Roberts Dental Supplies has annual sales of $5,200,000. Ninety percent are on credit. The firm has $559,000 in accounts receivable. Compute the value of the average collection period.

15. Rubble and Flint Stone Quarries has annual credit sales of $3,195,027.50 and an average collection period of 43 days. What is the company's average accounts receivable balance?

16. Darla's Cosmetics had annual credit sales of $1,003,750 and an average collection period of 36 days in 20XX. What was the company's average accounts receivable balance?

17. In the previous problem, if accounts receivable change in 20XY to $138,600, and credit sales increase to $1,204,500, should we assume that the firm has a more or less lenient credit policy?

18. Mervyn's Fine Fashion has an average collection period of 42 days. The accounts receivable balance is $86,302. What is the value of credit sales?

19. Bugle Boy Company has an opportunity cost of funds of 10 percent and a credit policy based on net 45 days. If all of its customers adhere to the stated terms and annual sales increase from $3.96 million to $5.82 million, what will be the increased cost of funds tied up in accounts receivable?

20. Wontaby Ltd. is extending its credit terms from 30 to 45 days. Sales are expected to increase from $4.7 million to $5.8 million as a result. Wontaby finances short-term assets at the bank at a cost of 10 percent annually. Calculate the additional annual financing cost of this change in credit terms.

21. Johnson Electronics is considering extending trade credit to some customers previously considered poor risks. Sales would increase by $100,000 if credit is extended to these new customers. Of the new accounts receivable generated, 10 percent will prove to be uncollectible. Additional collection costs will be 3 percent of sales, and production and selling costs will be 79 percent of sales.
    a. Compute the incremental income before taxes.
    b. What will the firm's incremental return on sales be if these new credit customers are accepted?
    c. If the receivable turnover ratio is 6 to 1, and no other asset buildup is needed to serve the new customers, what will Johnson Electronics' incremental return on new average investment be?

22. Henderson Office Supplies is considering a more liberal credit policy to increase sales, but it expects that 8 percent of the new accounts will be uncollectible. Collection costs are 5 percent of new sales, production costs are 78 percent of sales, and accounts receivable turnover is five times. Assume an increase in sales of $60,000. No other asset buildup will be required to service the new accounts.
    a. What is the level of investment in accounts receivable to support this sales expansion?
    b. What would be Henderson's incremental before-tax return on investment?
    c. Should Henderson liberalize credit if a 25 percent before-tax return is required (opportunity cost of capital)?
       Assume Henderson also needs to increase its level of inventory to support new sales and that inventory turnover is four times.
    d. What would be the total incremental investment in accounts receivable and inventory to support a $60,000 increase in sales?
    e. Given the income determined in part *b* and the investment determined in part *d*, should Henderson extend more liberal credit terms?

23. Comiskey Fence Co. is evaluating extending credit to a new group of customers. Although these customers will provide $180,000 in additional credit sales, 12 percent are likely to be uncollectible. The company will incur $15,700 in additional collection expenses. Production and marketing expenses represent 70 percent of sales. The company has a receivables turnover of five times. No other asset buildup will be required to service the new customers. The firm has a 15 percent desired return on investment.

 a. Should Comiskey extend credit to these customers?

 b. Should credit be extended if 15 percent of the new sales prove uncollectible?

 c. Should credit be extended if the receivables turnover drops to 1.5 and 12 percent of the accounts are uncollectible (as was the case in part *a*)?

24. Reconsider Comiskey Fence. Assume the average collection period is 120 days. All other factors are the same (including 12 percent uncollectible). Should credit be extended?

25. Slow Roll Drum Co. is evaluating the extension of credit to a new group of customers. Although these customers will provide $180,000 in additional credit sales, 12 percent are likely to be uncollectible. The company will also incur $16,200 in additional collection expense. Production and marketing costs represent 72 percent of sales. The firm is in a 34 percent tax bracket. No other asset buildup will be required to service the new customers. The firm has a 10 percent desired return. Assume the average collection period is 120 days.

 a. Compute the return on incremental investment.

 b. Should credit be extended?

26. Apollo Data Systems is considering a promotional campaign that will increase annual credit sales by $600,000. The company will require investments in accounts receivable, inventory, and plant and equipment. The turnover for each is as follows:

Accounts receivable	5 ×
Inventory	8 ×
Plant and equipment	2 ×

All $600,000 of the sales will be collectible. However, collection costs will be 3 percent of sales, and production and selling costs will be 77 percent of sales. The cost to carry inventory will be 6 percent of inventory. Amortization expense on plant and equipment will be 7 percent of plant and equipment. The tax rate is 30 percent.

 a. Compute the investments in accounts receivable, inventory, and plant and equipment based on the turnover ratios. What is the total value of the investment made?

 b. Compute the accounts receivable collection costs and production and selling costs and add the two figures together.

 c. Compute the costs of carrying inventory.

 d. Compute the amortization expense on new plant and equipment.

 e. Add together all the costs in parts *b*, *c*, and *d*.

 f. Subtract the answer from part *e* from the sales figure of $600,000 to arrive at income before taxes. Subtract taxes at a rate of 30 percent to arrive at income after taxes.

 g. Divide the aftertax return figure in part *f* by the total investment figure in part *a*. If the firm has required return on investment of 12 percent, should it undertake the promotional campaign described throughout this problem?

27. In the previous problem, if inventory had been only four times,

 a. What would be the new value for inventory investment?

 b. What would be the return on investment? You need to recompute the total investment and the total costs of the campaign to work toward computing income after taxes. Should the campaign be undertaken?

28. Maddox Resources has credit sales of $180,000 yearly with credit terms of net 30 days, which is also the average collection period. Maddox does not offer a discount for early payment, so its customers take the full 30 days to pay.

    a. What is the average receivables balance? What is the receivables turnover?

    b. If Maddox offered a 2 percent discount for payment in 10 days and every customer took advantage of the new terms, what would the new average receivables balance be? Use the full sales of $180,000 for your calculation of receivables.

    c. If Maddox reduces its bank loans, which cost 12 percent, by the cash generated from reduced receivables, what will be the net gain or loss to the firm? Should it offer the discount?

    d. Assume the new trade terms of 2/10, net 30 will increase sales by 20 percent because the discount makes Maddox price competitive. If Maddox earns 16 percent on sales before discounts, should it offer the discount?

29. Lipto Biomedic has credit sales of $740,000 yearly with credit terms of net 60 days, with an average collection period of 75 days. Lipto does not offer a discount for early payment.

    a. What is the average receivables balance? What is the receivables turnover?

    b. If Lipto offered a 3 percent discount for payment in 10 days and every customer took advantage of the new terms and paid on the tenth day, what would the new average receivables balance be? Use the full sales of $740,000 for your calculation of receivables.

    c. If Lipto reduces its bank loans, which cost 8 percent, by the cash generated from reduced receivables, what will be the net gain or loss to the firm? Should it offer the discount?

    d. Assume the new trade terms of 3/10, net 30 will increase sales by 12 percent because the discount makes Lipto price competitive. If Lipto earns 19 percent on sales before discounts, should it offer the discount?

30. Tobin Fisheries currently sells to its customers on terms of 2/10, net 30. Its average collection period is 15 days, with 80 percent currently taking the discount. All sales are credit sales. Upper management has expressed concern about sluggish sales, and the marketing department would like a more attractive credit package. Next year's sales are projected to be $3.1 million. It has been estimated that with terms of 3/10, net 60, sales next year would jump to $4.2 million and 60 percent of sales would take the discount, but the average collection period would increase to 34 days. Tobin's contribution margin of 5.5 percent would hold with the expansion of sales, as would its short-term financing cost of 10 percent. Should Tobin initiate the change in credit policy?

31. Happy Trail Adventure Products is reevaluating its credit policy. Current terms are 2/10, net 30, resulting in annual sales of 400,000 units. Cash sales that qualify for the discount account for 10 percent of sales, 65 percent qualify for the discount by paying on the 10th day, and the other 25 percent pay, on average, in 40 days. Unit sales price is $24.00 and variable production costs are $21.00 per unit. Bad debts are 1.5 percent of credit sales.

    The new policy of 2/10, net 60 is expected to increase sales by 12 percent annually. Cash sales are expected to remain at 10 percent of sales, but those qualifying for the discount by paying in 10 days would drop to 25 percent; the other 65 percent would, on average, pay in 70 days. It is expected that variable production costs would remain at $21.00 per unit but that bad debt expense would increase to 2 percent of credit sales. Happy Trail's banker would continue to finance working capital requirements at 13 percent. Should the new policy be implemented?

32. Power Play Inc. has seen profits drop acutely because of the economic downturn. To enhance profitability and to preserve cash, Power Play is considering shortening its credit period and eliminating its cash discount. Terms are currently 3/10, net 60 and would be changed to net 30. Currently, 60 percent of customers, on average, pay at the end of the credit period (60 days);

the other 40 percent pay, on average, in 10 days and receive the discount. It is anticipated that under the new policy customers will pay, on average, in 30 days. At present, average monthly sales are $450,000, but they are expected to fall to $400,000 with the tightening of credit. Variable production costs are 78 percent, and bank financing is currently floating at 11 percent. Bad debt losses at 2 percent of sales are expected to drop to 1.75 percent of sales.

a. Should Power Play's credit policy be tightened?

b. What is the average accounts receivable balance under both policies?

c. Discuss the choice of discount rate for this analysis.

33. OB1 Sabres Ltd. has determined that product sales are not what they could be because they have unused capacity. As a result, the company is considering adjusting its marketing strategy. At present, all sales to distributors are on a cash basis, but the competition offers credit terms. Similar credit terms for OB1 Sabres have been suggested. Research suggests that sales in the upcoming year would jump from $4.3 million annually to $5.5 million with credit terms of 2/10, net 30. Furthermore, research estimates that 75 percent of the customers would take the discount and the remainder would pay on average on the 30th day. Inventory turnover would remain at 15 times a year. Cost of goods sold (variable costs) are 75 percent of gross sales. Bad debts are estimated to be .75 percent of credit sales. Credit department expenses would be $50,000 per year plus the salary of two individuals at $35,000 per year each. One of the staff would be reassigned from another division without affecting costs or productivity as that individual is currently redundant in that division. Marketing expenses are 4 percent of gross sales. Bank financing of working capital requirements is at 11 percent. Should OB1 Sabres Ltd. adopt the proposed policy? Show your calculations.

34. First Picked Fruits Inc. is considering two alternatives to stimulate sales. Currently, the policy is net 30 and the average collection period is 40 days, with bad debt losses of 1.25 percent of sales. All sales are credit sales and are expected to be $6.1 million annually under this policy.

Under policy 1, credit terms would be lengthened to 45 days to a select group of new customers, with an expected increase in sales to $6.9 million annually. However, it is expected that the incremental sales would experience bad debt losses of 1.75 percent and that their average collection period would be 50 days. No change would occur in the average collection period or bad debt loss experience on the existing credit sales. Under policy 2, credit terms would be lengthened to 60 days to a select group of new customers (not completely overlapping with the first group). Sales would be expected to rise to $7.2 million annually. Incremental sales expectations would be payment, on average, after 65 days, and bad debt losses of 2 percent. No change would occur in the average collection period or bad debt losses on the original credit sales. First Picked Fruits has an opportunity cost of funds of 16 percent, and its variable costs are 94 percent of sales.

a. Is either alternative advantageous?

b. Any concerns with this analysis as stated?

c. Any theoretical concerns with an apparent one-year time horizon for analysis?

35. Route Canal Shipping Company has the following schedule for aging of accounts receivable:

	AGE OF RECEIVABLES		
	April 20, 20XX		
(1)	(2)	(3)	(4)
Month of Sales	Age of Account	Amounts	Percent of Amount Due
April	0–30	$105,000	_____
March	31–60	60,000	_____
February	61–90	90,000	_____
January	91–120	45,000	_____
Total receivables		$300,000	100%

a. Fill in column (4) for each month.

b. If the firm had $1,440,000 in credit sales over the four-month period, compute the average collection period. Average daily sales should be based on a 120-day period.

c. If the firm likes to see its bills collected in 30 days, should it be satisfied with the average collection period?

d. Disregarding your answer to part *c* and considering the aging schedule for accounts receivable, should the company be satisfied?

e. What additional information does the aging schedule bring to the company that the average collection period may not show?

36. Nowlin Pipe & Steel has expected sales of 72,000 pipes this year, an ordering cost of $6.00 per order, and carrying costs of $2.40 per pipe.

a. What is the economic ordering quantity?

b. How many orders will be placed during the year?

c. What will the average inventory be?

d. What is the total cost of ordering and carrying inventory?

37. Lokerup Alarms expects to sell 100,000 door locks this year. Estimated costs per unit are $1.00 for warehouse space, $2.50 for material handling expenses, $1.25 for interest costs and $3.00 for other carrying costs. Ordering costs are estimated at $38.75 per order.

a. What is the economic ordering quantity?

b. How many orders will be placed during the year?

c. What will the average inventory be?

d. What is the total cost of ordering and carrying inventory?

38. Friendly Home Services expects sales of baskets to be $125,000 this year, an ordering cost of $75.00 per order, and carrying costs of $3.00 per basket. The price of a basket is $25.

a. What is the economic ordering quantity?

b. How many orders will be placed during the year?

c. What will the average inventory be?

d. What is the total cost of ordering and carrying inventory?

39. Fisk Corporation is trying to improve its inventory control system and has installed an online system at its retail stores. Fisk anticipates sales of 75,000 units per year, an ordering cost of $8 per order, and carrying costs of $1.20 per unit.

a. What is the economic ordering quantity?

b. How many orders will be placed during the year?

c. What will the average inventory be?

d. What is the total cost of inventory expected to be?

40. (See previous problem for basic data.) In the second year, Fisk Corporation finds that it can reduce ordering costs to $2 per order, but carrying costs will stay the same at $1.20 per unit.

a. Recompute *a, b, c,* and *d* in the previous problem for the second year.

b. Now compare years one and two and explain what has happened.

41. Higgins Athletic Wear has expected sales of 22,500 units a year, carrying costs of $1.50 per unit, and an ordering cost of $3.00 per order.

a. What is the economic order quantity?

b. What is average inventory? What is the total carrying cost?

c. What is the total inventory cost?

d. Assume an additional 30 units will be required as safety stock. What will the new average inventory be? What will the new total carrying cost be?

42. Joseph Sports Equipment, Inc., is considering a switch to level production. Under level production, cost efficiencies would occur and aftertax costs would decline by $35,000, but inventory would increase by $400,000. Joseph would have to finance the extra inventory at a cost of 10.5 percent.

a. Should the company go ahead and switch to level production?

b. How low would interest rates need to fall before level production would be feasible?

43. Minty Airfresheners Ltd. maintains an inventory of packaged bottles with chemical disinfectants to meet its annual demand for 81,600 packages to service restrooms. Each package costs $4.75, and the order cost is $106.25 per order. Carrying costs have been identified as $1.50 per package. Minty Airfresheners bases its orders on the economic ordering quantity. Recently, the wholesaler of the packages, in an attempt to shift the inventory burden to Minty Airfresheners, has offered a 10 percent discount if orders are placed quarterly. Should the present ordering policy of Minty Airfresheners be changed?

44. Downey Disks is experiencing some inventory control problems. The manager currently orders four times each year with the annual purchase of the inventory costing $200,000. Each inventory item costs $5, ordering costs are $125, and each item costs $2.50 to carry. What is the opportunity cost of the present ordering system as compared to an EOQ ordering system?

45. Bonsay Dance has seen its inventory turnover drop from 12 to 8 times per year with its annual cost of goods sold remaining at $10 million per year. Its financing costs are at 5 percent. How much is this costing Bonsay?

46. Baktoo Basics Ltd. is considering introducing an inventory control system that will increase inventory turnover from 10 to 15 times per year. Its annual cost of goods sold is expected to be $6 million, and its financing costs are at 11 percent. Should Baktoo Basics consider an expenditure of $17,500 on the new control system?

COMPREHENSIVE PROBLEM

47. Bailey Distributing Company sells small appliances to hardware stores throughout the West. Chuck Bailey, the president of the company, is thinking about changing the credit policies offered by the firm to attract customers away from competitors. The current policy calls for a 1/10, net 30, and the new policy would call for a 3/10, net 50. Currently, 40 percent of Bailey customers are taking the discount, and it is anticipated that this number would go up to 50 percent with the new discount policy. It is further anticipated that annual sales would increase from a level of $200,000 to $250,000 as a result of the change in the cash discount policy.

The increased sales would also affect the inventory level carried by Bailey. The average inventory carried by Bailey is based on a determination of an EOQ. Assume unit sales of small appliances will increase from 20,000 to 25,000 units. The ordering cost for each order is $100 and the carrying cost per unit is $1 (these values will not change with the discount). Each unit in inventory has an average cost of $6.50.

Cost of goods sold is equal to 65 percent of net sales, general and administrative expenses are equal to 10 percent of net sales, and interest payments of 12 percent will be necessary only for the increase in the accounts receivable and inventory balances. Taxes will equal 25 percent of before-tax income.

a. Compute the accounts receivable balance before and after the change in the cash discount policy. Use the net sales (Total sales – Cash discounts) to determine the average daily sales and the accounts receivable balances.

b. Determine EOQ before and after the change in the cash discount policy. Translate this into average inventory (in units and dollars) before and after the change in the cash discount policy.

c. Complete an income statement before and after the policy change.

d. Should the new cash discount policy be utilized? Briefly comment.

8

Sources of Short-Term Financing

LEARNING OBJECTIVES

LO1 Characterize trade credit as an important form of short-term financing, and calculate its cost to the firm if a discount is forgone.

LO2 Describe bank loans as self-liquidating, as short-term, and as having their interest cost tied to the prime rate. Also, calculate interest rates under differing conditions.

LO3 Describe commercial paper as a short-term, unsecured promissory note of the firm.

LO4 Review borrowing in foreign markets as a cost-effective alternative for the firm.

LO5 Explain that offering accounts receivable and inventory as collateral may lower the interest costs on a loan.

LO6 Demonstrate the hedging of interest rates to reduce borrowing risk.

In this chapter we examine the cost and availability of various short-term funds, which we record as current liabilities. Attention is focused on trade credit from suppliers, bank loans, corporate promissory notes, foreign borrowing, and loans against receivables and inventory. Although it is often suggested that loans are available only to those who already have money, the objective of this chapter is to demonstrate how required funds could be made available on a short-term basis from the various suppliers of credit.

Figure 8–1 shows the overall profile of various sources and forms of debt in financing nonfinancial Canadian corporations at the end of 2019. Among these Canadian companies, short-term financing made up over 65 percent of the overall total debt. In this chapter we deal with the sources that provide that short-term financing. Chapter 16 explores in depth the longer-term sources of that debt, and Chapter 21 examines the international sources.

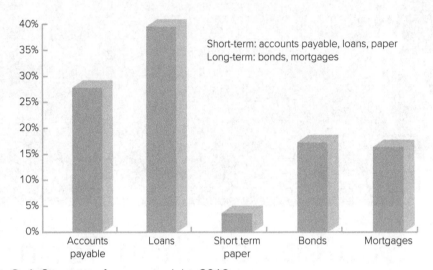

Figure 8–1 Structure of corporate debt, 2019

COST OF FINANCING ALTERNATIVES

For short-term financing, the firm relies on trade credit, bank or government financing, and borrowing in the wholesale money markets by way of commercial paper or LIBOR–based loans (international). With a conservative financing approach (Chapter 6) term loans, leases, bonds, and mortgages may be used. The firm may also finance its current asset positions through factoring or asset securitization.

Regardless of the alternative(s) used, each financing method has a cost that should be effectively compared against the other options. The best manner for comparison is with an annual interest rate. Although several variations and formulas are presented in this chapter, each formula is based on the following concept[1] (similar to the one in Chapter 7):

$$r = \frac{\text{Monies paid}}{\text{Net capital borrowed}} \times \text{Time periods in year}$$

This is a development of the formula $I = Prt$ in which I = interest or monies paid, P = principal or net capital borrowed, r = annual interest rate, and t = time in years. Consider this concept as you examine the formulas in this chapter.

---

[1]The return could be more accurately expressed on an annual effective basis as

$$r = \left(1 + \frac{\text{Monies paid}}{\text{Net capital borrowed}}\right)^{\text{time periods in year}} - 1$$

TRADE CREDIT

LO1 One of the largest providers of short-term credit is usually at the firm's doorstep—the manufacturer or seller of goods and services. This is a true alternative form of borrowing comparable to bank loans, particularly for the small business. About 40 percent of short-term financing is in the form of accounts payable or trade credit. Trade payables are a spontaneous source of funds, growing as the business expands on a seasonal or long-term basis, and contracting in like fashion.

For example, if annual purchases of a company are $7.3 million and are paid on terms of net 30 days, the average accounts payable balance will be $600,000. An expansion in business, and thus purchases, by 20 percent to $8.76 million increases the accounts payable balance to $720,000. This represents an expansion in available credit by $120,000 as long as purchases remain at the higher level. Unlike bank credit, this expansion occurs somewhat painlessly. We see this relationship develop from the accounts payable period ratio examined in Chapter 3 and again used to examine the cash conversion cycle in Chapter 6.

$$\text{Accounts payable period} = \frac{\text{Accounts payable}}{\text{Average daily purchases (COGS)}} \quad \text{3–6b (rearranged)}$$

Annual Purchases		Credit Period/365		Average Accounts	Payable Balance
$7,300,000	×	30/365	=	$600,000	$120,000 increase
$8,760,000	×	30/365	=	$720,000	

Payment Period

Trade credit is extended for 30 to 60 days, although that varies by industry. For example, many suppliers of foodstuffs, such as ice cream, to small retailers give only 10 days to pay. Many firms attempt to stretch the payment period to provide additional short-term financing. This is an acceptable form of financing as long as it is not carried to an abusive extent. Going from a 30- to a 35-day average payment period may be tolerated within the trade, but stretching payments to 65 days might alienate suppliers and cause a diminishing credit rating with D&B Canada and local credit bureaus. A major variable in determining the payment period is the possible existence of a cash discount.

D&B Canada
dnb.com/ca-en/

Going back to our previous example, see how stretching payables to 40 days on annual purchases of $8.76 million increases accounts payable to $960,000, which represents an increase in available credit of $240,000 (additional financing available).

Annual Purchases		Credit Period/365		Average Accounts	Payable Balance
$8,760,000	×	30/365	=	$720,000	$240,000 increase
$8,760,000	×	40/365	=	$960,000	

Cash Discount Policy

A cash discount allows for a reduction in price if payment is made within a specified time period. A 2/10, net 30 cash discount means we can deduct 2 percent if we remit our funds within 10 days after billing, but failing this, we must pay the full amount by the 30th day.

By forgoing a discount the firm has additional financing available on an ongoing basis, but at a cost. **Note: For use of the formula for the cost of forgoing the discount we use the net purchase price. However to be consistent with our ratio calculations, computing additional financing available by forgoing the discount and ease of overall computation we use the gross purchase price.**

The following identifies the use of the formula (8-1) in calculating the cost of forgoing the discount.

On a $100 billing we could pay $98 up to the 10th day or $100 at the end of 30 days. If we fail to take the cash discount, we get to use $98 for 20 more days for a $2 fee. The interest rate on the use of that money is then a whopping 37.24 percent. Note that we first consider the interest cost and then convert this to an annual basis. The standard formula for approximating this interest cost is

The cost of forgoing the discount[2]

$$K_{\text{DIS}} = \frac{d\%}{100\% - d\%} \times \frac{365}{f(\text{date}) - d(\text{date})} \quad \text{(8–1)}$$

$d\%$ = Discount percentage
$f(\text{date})$ = Final payment period
$d(\text{date})$ = Discount period

$$K_{\text{DIS}} = \frac{2\%}{100\% - 2\%} \times \frac{365}{30 - 10} = 37.24\%$$

This formula fails to account for the cumulative effect of being able to earn interest on the interest in each succeeding 20-day period after the first period. The methods and rationale for such compounding are covered in Chapter 9. This can be formulated as

The effective annual cost of forgoing the cash discount

$$i = \left(1 + \frac{2}{98}\right)^{\frac{365}{20}} - 1 = 0.4459$$

PV = (98)	FV = 100
PMT = 0	$N = \dfrac{20}{365}$

$$\boxed{CPT} \ \boxed{I/Y} = 44.59\%.$$

Therefore, the real rate of interest is more like 44.59 percent.

Again, going back to our example of annual purchases of $8.76 million, note that if the discount is taken, the accounts payable balance is $235,200. If not taken, this balance is $705,600. Not taking the discount provides additional credit of $470,400 on an average daily basis. The cost is the discount forgone, which amounts to 2 percent of $8.76 million, or $175,200. This represents an annualized cost of $175,200/$470,400, or 0.3724 (37.24%). This is the result obtained by the formula.

The accounting treatment may call for purchases to be recorded at the net cost with discounts forgone, somewhat like a penalty, and recorded as *purchase discounts lost*. Therefore, we work with the net purchases price.

Annual Purchases		Credit Period/365		Average Accounts		Payable Balance
$8,760,000 × 98%	×	10/365	=	$235,200	}	$470,400 increase
$8,760,000 × 98%	×	30/365	=	$705,600		

Cash discount terms may vary. For example, on a 2/10, net 90 basis, it would cost us only 9.3 percent not to take the discount and to pay the full amount after 90 days.

$$K_{\text{DIS}} = \frac{2\%}{100\% - 2\%} \times \frac{365}{90 - 10} = 9.31\%$$

The compounded rate of interest is 9.66%.

PV = (98)	FV = 100
PMT = 0	$N = \dfrac{80}{365}$

$$\boxed{CPT} \ \boxed{I/Y} = 9.66\%.$$

---

[2]Note the similarity between this formula and formula 7–1*b* and the concept previously examined under "Cost of Financing Alternatives."

In each case, we must ask ourselves whether bypassing the discount and using the money for a longer period is the cheapest means of financing. In the first example, with an approximated cost of 37.24 percent, it probably is not. We would be better off borrowing $98 for 20 days at some lesser rate. For example, at 10 percent interest we would pay $0.54 in interest as opposed to $2 under the cash discount policy.[3] With the 2/10, net 90 arrangement, the cost of missing the discount is only 9.3 percent, and we may choose to let our suppliers carry us for an extra 80 days.

Net Credit Position

In Chapter 2, we defined accounts receivable as a use of funds and accounts payable as a source. The manager should closely watch the relationship between the two to determine the firm's net credit position. If a firm has average daily sales of $5,000 and collects in 30 days, the accounts receivable balance is $150,000. If this is associated with average daily purchases of $4,000 and a 25-day average payment period, the average accounts payable balance is $100,000—indicating $50,000 more in credit extended than received. This is a positive net trade credit position. Changing this situation to an average payment period of 40 days increases the accounts payable to $160,000 ($4,000 × 40). Accounts payable would then exceed accounts receivable by $10,000, thus leaving funds for other needs. Larger firms tend to be net providers of trade credit (relatively high receivables), with smaller firms in the user position (relatively high payables). Anyone who has dealt with the large retail chains knows how carefully they manage their payables, using them as important sources of funds.

 FINANCE IN ACTION

CN Rail Maintains a Negative Trade Credit Position

CN Rail is a major transportation provider in North America. Shippers using CN can access ports on the Atlantic, Pacific, and Gulf coasts. With its attention to financial performance, CN is one of the continent's best-performing transportation companies. It relies heavily on trade credit to finance its operations.

Its balance sheet at the end of 2019 (in millions) showed the following working capital accounts:

Cash & equivalents	$ 782	Accounts payable	$2,127
Accounts		Short-term debt	2,181
receivable	1,242		
Inventory	608		
Other	428		
Total current		Total current	
assets	$3,060	liabilities	$4,308

Its net credit position is a negative $885 ($1,242 − $2,127), which suggests that it is receiving more credit (accounts payable) from suppliers than it is providing to customers (accounts receivable). This is an advantageous manner in which to finance the investment in current assets and an effective use of trade credit. A net credit position should not be confused with the net working capital position, which is current assets less current liabilities and is reflected in the current ratio (Chapter 3).

Q1 What is CN Rail's current net credit position based on the latest quarterly report?

cn.ca
Symbol: CNR

---

[3] Note that $\frac{20}{365} \times 10\% \times \$98 = \$0.54$.

LO2 BANK CREDIT

Banks may provide funds to finance seasonal needs, product-line expansions, long-term growth, and so on. The preferred type of loan from the point of view of most bankers is a self-liquidating loan, the use of which generates cash flows that form a built-in, or automatic, repayment scheme. Although Canadian banks have traditionally lent monies for short-term needs through renewing old loans, many of the 90- or 180-day agreements take on the characteristics of longer-term financing.

Canadian Bankers
Association
cba.ca

Today banking is a full-service operation. The modern banker's function is much broader than merely accepting deposits, making loans, and processing cheques. A banking institution may be providing investment services, a credit card operation, real estate lending, data processing services, trust services, insurance and helpful advice in cash management or international trade. This wide array of services has become possible because of periodic changes in the Bank Act that continually expand the types of operations with which a bank may become involved.

Foreign banks from countries such as Japan, China, Germany, Britain, and the United States do business in Canada as Schedule II and III banks. Banking today is international in scope, with Canadian banks operating in foreign countries with reciprocal banking arrangements. Canada has one of the most competitive and stable banking environments in the world.

Demand Loans and the Prime Rate

Short-term and self-liquidating loans, known as demand loans, are generally repayable at any time by the borrower, or full payment can be "demanded" by the bank at any time. These loans, tied to a prime rate, most often carry a variable interest rate that fluctuates with interest rate levels in the economy. The prime rate is the rate the bank charges its most creditworthy customers, and it is scaled up proportionally to reflect the credit risk of the borrower. In competitive markets, banks may actually charge top customers less than the published prime rate. The average customer can expect to pay 1 or 2 percent above prime, but in tight money periods a speculative borrower may pay 5 or more percentage points over prime. The bank rate is the rate the Bank of Canada charges the chartered banks on loans.

The prime rate, as discussed in Chapter 7, is competitively set by the chartered banks above the Bank of Canada rate. Interest rates are determined by the supply of and demand for money in the marketplace, and these forces naturally cause interest rates to move up and down over time. The prime rate is no exception, and this results in the interest rate charged on demand loans changing on a regular basis. Therefore, if the money supply tightens and interest rates go up, the interest charges on bank loans will become more expensive. Prudent managers factor this cost consideration into their decision to hold current assets that are likely financed to some extent with bank loans.

Bank of Canada
bankofcanada.ca

Figure 8–2 presents the average prime rate from 1972 until 2020 for Canada compared with the United States. Although the period before 1971 does not show up, it should be pointed out that interest rates in the 1950s and early 1960s were relatively stable. After this period, the prime rate has become highly volatile, moving as much as 10 percent in the 12-month period leading up to August 1981 when it hit a high point of 22.75 percent. With lower inflation in the 1990s, the prime rates in both countries came down significantly. Since late 2010, with relatively stable inflation and interest rates, the prime rate in Canada has been at 3.0 percent.

Fees and Compensating Balances

In providing loans and other services, banks will often charge setup, commitment, administration, or review fees. These are usually charged when the loan proceeds are advanced. In effect, the proceeds

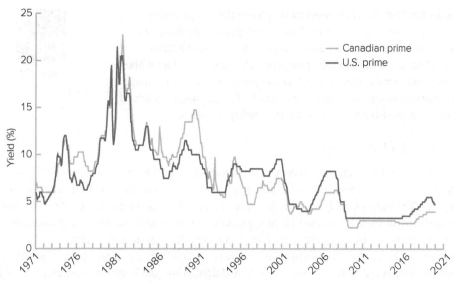

Figure 8–2 Prime interest rate movements

of the loan are reduced by the amount of the fees. For example, a fee of $100 on a loan of $1,000 indicates the firm effectively receives only $900.

An alternative requirement may be that firms or individuals maintain a minimum average account balance in chequing accounts, referred to as a compensating balance, to cover banking costs. The required amount of a compensating balance is usually computed as a percentage of customer loans outstanding or as a percentage of bank commitments toward future loans to a given account. As above, the firm will net only $900 after the $100 compensating balance (assuming it is 10%).

Generally, fees for services or compensating balances are charged by banks on a cost-plus-profit basis as opposed to requiring a compensating balance. In the past, loan rates were "padded" to subsidize other bank services, but with direct costing of each service, loan rates can become very competitive.

Some view the compensating balance requirement as an unusual arrangement. Where else would you walk into a business establishment, buy a shipment of goods, and then be told you could not take 20 percent of the purchase home with you? If you borrowed $100,000, paying 8 percent interest on the full amount with a 20 percent compensating balance requirement, you would be paying $8,000 for the use of $80,000 in funds, or an effective rate of 10 percent.

The amount that must be borrowed to end up with the desired sum of money is simply calculated by taking the needed funds and dividing by $(1 - c)$, where c is the compensating balance expressed as a decimal. Administration fees that must be paid upfront can be considered in the same way as a compensating balance, since the firm does not get full use of the borrowed funds.

For example, if you need $100,000 in funds, you must borrow $125,000 to ensure that the intended amount is available. This would be calculated as follows:

$$\textbf{Amount to be borrowed} = \frac{\textbf{Amount needed}}{(1 - c)}$$

$$\textbf{For this example} = \frac{\$100,000}{(1 - 0.20)} = \$125,000$$

A check on this calculation could be done to see if we actually end up with the use of $100,000:

$ 125,000	Loan
−25,000	20% compensating balance requirement
$ 100,000	Available funds

Under the Bank Act, borrowers must agree to the compensating balance requirement, and Canadian banks must disclose the full cost of the loan, which is increased by the need for a compensating balance. However, banks seem to be making most of their loans these days without the requirement for a compensating balance, preferring instead to charge interest rates consistent with their cost of funds. The emphasis has turned to doing more intensive analysis of the profitability of each loan.

Bank Act
laws-lois.justice.gc.ca/eng/
acts/B-1.01

Maturity Provisions

Bank loans have been traditionally short term in nature (though perhaps renewable). In the past decade there has been a movement to the use of the term loan in which credit is extended for one to seven years. The loan is usually repaid in monthly or quarterly instalments over its life rather than in one single payment. Only superior credit applicants, as measured by working capital strength, potential profitability, and competitive position, can qualify for term-loan financing.

Bankers are hesitant to affix a single interest rate to a term loan. The more common practice is to allow the interest rate to change with market conditions. Thus, the interest rate on a term loan may be tied to the prime rate, and changes (floats) with it. A good customer may have its rate set at prime plus 1 percent, for example. More is said on term loans in Chapter 16 when we discuss longer-term financing.

Cost of Bank Financing

The annual interest rate on a loan is based on the loan amount, the dollar interest paid, the length of the loan, and the method of repayment. Notice how formula 8–2 follows the concept identified earlier in "Cost of Financing Alternatives." It is easy enough to observe that $60 interest on a $1,000 loan for one year would carry a 6 percent interest rate. But what if the same loan were for 120 days? To come to an approximate answer to that question we use this formula.

The annual interest rate

$$R_{ANNUAL} = \frac{I}{P} \times \frac{365}{d} \quad (8\text{--}2)$$

R_{ANNUAL} = Annual rate

I = Interest

P = Principal

d = Days loan is outstanding

$$R_{ANNUAL} = \frac{\$60}{\$1,000} \times \frac{365}{120} = 18.25\%$$

Since we have use of the funds for only 120 days, the annual rate is approximately 18.25 percent. If we considered the accumulation of interest on the interest in the second and third 120-day periods, we would come to an annual interest rate of 19.39 percent.

PV = (1,000)		FV = 1,060
PMT = 0		$N = \frac{120}{365}$
	CPT I/Y = 19.39%.	

To highlight the effect of time, if you borrowed $20 for only 10 days and paid back $21, the effective interest rate would be almost 500 percent.

PV = (20)		FV = 21
PMT = 0		$N = \frac{10}{365}$
	CPT I/Y = 493.48%.	

The time dimension of a loan is not only important but also is the way in which interest is charged. We have assumed interest would be paid when the loan comes due. If the bank deducts the interest in advance (discounted loan), the effective rate of interest will increase. For example, a $1,000, 120-day loan with $60 of interest deducted in advance represents the payment of interest on only $940, or an annual rate of 19.41 percent.

The annual rate on discounted loan

$$R_{\text{DIS}} = \frac{I}{P - I} \times \frac{365}{d} \quad \text{(8–3)}$$

$$R_{\text{DIS}} = \frac{\$60}{\$1,000 - \$60} \times \frac{365}{120} = 0.1941 = 19.41\%$$

The effective annual rate is 20.71 percent. Again, formula 8–3 is derived from the concept developed in "Cost of Financing Alternatives."

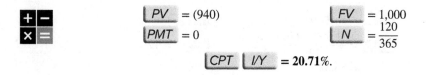

$$
\begin{array}{ll}
\boxed{PV} = (940) & \boxed{FV} = 1,000 \\
\boxed{PMT} = 0 & \boxed{N} = \dfrac{120}{365}
\end{array}
$$

$$\boxed{CPT}\ \boxed{I/Y} = 20.71\%.$$

Interest Costs with Fees or Compensating Balances

If a loan is made with bank fees or compensating balances, the annual interest rate is the stated interest rate divided by $(1 - c)$, where c is the compensating balance expressed as a decimal. Assume 6 percent is the stated annual rate and a 20 percent compensating balance is required.

The annual rate with compensating balances

$$R_{\text{COMP}} = \frac{I}{(1 - c)} \quad \text{(8–4)}$$

$$R_{\text{COMP}} = \frac{6\%}{(1 - 0.2)} = 7.5\%$$

If dollar amounts are used and the stated rate is unknown, formula 8–5 can be used. The assumption is that we are paying $60 interest on a $1,000 loan, but are able to use only $800 of the funds. The loan is for a year.

$$R_{\text{COMP}} = \frac{I}{P - B} \times \frac{365}{d} \quad \text{(8–5)}$$

B = Compensating balance in dollars

$$R_{\text{COMP}} = \frac{\$60}{\$1,000 - \$200} \times \frac{365}{365} = 7.5\%$$

$$
\begin{array}{ll}
\boxed{PV} = (800) & \boxed{FV} = 860 \\
\boxed{PMT} = 0 & \boxed{N} = 1
\end{array}
$$

$$\boxed{CPT}\ \boxed{I/Y} = 7.50\%.$$

Of course, the firm may have ongoing cash needs greater than the compensating balance required. In theory, the compensating balance is supposed to be above and beyond those needs. However, in some cases the compensating balance requirement does not require the firm to have more cash on hand than it otherwise would. In such cases the firm would not use formula 8–4 or 8–5 to adjust the annual rate of the loan.

Rate on Instalment Loans

The most confusing borrowing arrangement to the average bank customer or consumer is the instalment loan. An instalment loan calls for a series of equal payments over the life of the loan. Financial institutions provide these fixed-rate loans for up to several years by matching the required funds with a fixed-rate obligation on funds they have borrowed by way of term deposits. This reduces the financial institution's risk. Though federal legislation prohibits a misrepresentation of interest rates on loans to customers, it would be possible for a loan officer or an overeager salesperson to quote a rate on an instalment loan that is approximately half the true rate.

Assume you borrow $1,000 on a 12-month instalment basis, with regular monthly payments to apply to interest and principal, and the interest requirement is $60. Though it might be suggested that the rate on the loan is 6 percent ($60/$1,000), this is not the case. It is true that you pay a total of $60 in interest, but you do not have the use of $1,000 for one year. Rather, you are paying back the $1,000 on a monthly basis, with an average outstanding loan balance for the year of a little more than $500. The effective annual rate of interest is 11.46 percent.

$$PV = (1,000) \qquad FV = 0$$

$$PMT = \frac{(1,000 + 60)}{12} \qquad N = 12$$

$$= 88.3\overline{3}$$

$$CPT \quad I/Y = 0.9080319\%.$$

This is a monthly effective interest rate and must be converted to an annual effective rate. Multiply by 12 to get an annual nominal rate:

$$\mathbf{0.9080319 \times 12 = 10.896383}$$

For an annual effective rate

$$2nd \quad \{ICONV\}$$

$$NOM = 10.896383 \quad ENTER \quad \uparrow$$

$$C/Y = 12 \quad ENTER \quad \uparrow$$

$$EFF \quad CPT \quad = 11.457$$

or

$$12 \quad 2nd \quad EFF{\rightarrow} \quad 10.896383 = 11.457$$

The formula for compounding the monthly effective rate to an annual rate is

$$\mathbf{(1 + 0.009080319)^{12} - 1 = 0.11457 = 11.457\%}$$

Formula 8–6 can be used for approximating the effective rate of interest on an instalment loan.

$$R_{\text{INSTAL}} = \frac{\textbf{2} \times \textbf{Annual number of payments} \times I}{(\textbf{Total number of payments} + 1) \times P} \quad (8\text{–}6)$$

$$R_{\text{INSTAL}} = \frac{2 \times 12 \times \$60}{13 \times \$1,000} = \frac{\$1,440}{\$13,000} = 11.08\%$$

The Credit Crunch Phenomenon

In 1969–70, 1973–74, 1979–81, 1990–92, 2001, and 2007–08, the economy and financial markets experienced credit shortages. These shortages were the result of the

- Tightening of money supply growth by the Bank of Canada to curb inflation
- Increased risk aversion of bankers and businesses following speculative excesses

Both of these cause a decrease in available funds for lending, triggering higher interest rates. The economy eventually slows from the increased cost of carrying inventory and receivables as well as from the reluctance or inability to invest in capital. This often produces periods of higher unemployment.

The earlier credit shortages came during times of higher inflation and resulted from government action to bring it under control. In 2001, large losses were experienced in the high-tech industry as growth projections fell short, leaving financial institutions with large loan losses, which resulted in restricted lending.

In 2007–08, the worldwide credit crunch came as the security behind asset-backed securities (commercial paper, mortgages, and credit swaps) was called into question. The financial institutions that were heavily invested in these securities suffered large losses, which reduced their capital base (equity) severely to the point of failure, entrenchment (less lending), and reluctance to even lend to other financial institutions. A significant recession occurred. The central banks and governments of the major economic countries provided considerable liquidity to the financial system through a variety of measures (bailouts, lower interest rates, security purchases, takeovers), attempting to avert hardship as credit availability diminished. Recovery from this financial crisis took until about 2014.

Keeping inflation low creates more stable business and economic environments. To deal with credit shortages, it is not appropriate to impose artificial limits on interest rates or credit availability, nor to exert governmental pressure. The market will eventually adjust. Even in 1980 and 1981, as the prime went above 20 percent, funds were available for borrowers, though at a high cost.

Bank of Canada policy since the late 1980s has aimed at maintaining a low rate of inflation and, to a certain extent, at influencing the level of the Canadian dollar on international markets. As a result, monetary policy cannot ignore economic circumstances in the major industrial countries. This is explored in Chapter 21. Borrowed funds, when measured against the rate of inflation, can represent expensive money to financial managers.

FINANCE IN ACTION

Small Business Financing Sources

For the busy small business owner it is often difficult to find sources of financing as sales expand. The Government of Canada through the Business Development Bank of Canada (BDC) provides lots of information and links to many useful sites. How to get financing for a small business, including government assistance programs, is outlined at the government website: bdc.ca.

You may wish to check out the small business loan options available online at many banks, such as the Royal Bank: rbcroyalbank.com

Q1 What are the different sources of financing available?

Q2 What is a business angel?

Annual Percentage Rate

The key cost in bank or financial institution lending is the interest rate charged on a loan. Generally, interest rates or yields are expressed on an annual basis. However, some institutions state interest rates on a monthly or some other time-period basis. Requirements have come into place to reveal interest rates on an annual basis. The annual percentage rate (APR) expresses interest rates on an annual basis. Nevertheless, an APR may be expressed on a nominal basis (simple interest) or effective basis (with compounding). These terms are examined closely at the beginning of Chapter 9.

LO3 FINANCING THROUGH COMMERCIAL PAPER

As an alternative to bank financing, large prestigious firms may issue commercial paper in the wholesale money markets. Commercial paper is a short-term, unsecured promissory note issued to the public, usually in denominations of $100,000 or more. To the borrower, commercial paper usually carries an effective interest rate below that available through borrowing from the banks. Bypassing the bank's function as intermediary, commercial paper allows more direct contact between the borrower and lender of funds without the overhead. Rather than paying interest, commercial paper is sold at a discount from the maturity value, with the depth of the discount determining the rate of return.

It has been suggested that the spread between borrowing and lending rates on large sums is about 2 percent (200 basis points) when funds are passed through an intermediary like a bank. However, the spread drops to about 1/2 percent (50 basis points) when funds are transferred through the wholesale money markets.

As Figure 8–3 indicates, the commercial paper market increased dramatically until the credit crunch of 2007–08, which was brought on by difficulties in the asset-backed paper market. At that time, true security behind asset-backed commercial paper came into question and the market dried up. By 2019, the market had not fully recovered to its previous levels but with regulations on disclosure, particularly related to the asset pools, better credit-rating monitoring, and increased liquidity requirements, it was hoped that an increase in activity would occur. Meanwhile, bank lending increased as an alternative, evidenced in Figure 8-1. The increase before the crunch of 2007–08 was the result of

- Lower borrowing rates for qualified firms compared to bank rates
- The improved ability of corporations to raise short-term funds (over 200 firms active)
- A decrease in government borrowing (shorter supply of T-bills)
- Higher costs to borrowers for bankers' acceptances (bank reserve requirements)
- The development of asset-backed commercial paper

Commercial paper can be classified thus:

- *Finance or direct paper*, issued by finance companies (Household Finance Corporation, Ford Credit, Dell Financial Services) primarily to institutional investors such as pension funds, insurance companies, and money market mutual funds to fund their ordinary course of business.

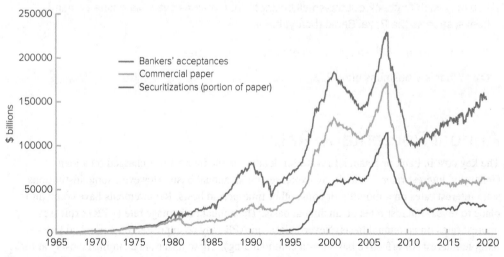

Figure 8–3 Corporate short-term paper outstanding

- *Dealer paper*, sold by industrial or utility firms using an intermediate dealer network to distribute their paper, and often issuing it to fund seasonal fluctuations in inventory or accounts receivable.
- *Asset-backed (ABCP)*, which has the security (or lack thereof), of short-term assets (receivables) such as car loans, mortgages, and credit card receipts that have been stripped from the originating firm into a new legal entity or trust. Note the dramatic increase in ABCP since introduced in the mid-1990s (as a portion of commercial paper) as lenders have sought greater safety in their investments.

Traditionally, commercial paper is just that. A paper certificate is issued to the lender to signify the lender's claim to be repaid. This certificate could be lost, stolen, misplaced, or damaged, and in rare cases, someone could fail to cash it in at maturity. Although the investments are fairly sound, there is increasing clearing and settlement risk from the increased volume of transactions in the money markets. The Canadian Depository for Securities Ltd. (CDS) has established an online, real-time national clearing house for money market securities. CDS is owned by the banks, investment dealers, and trust companies and provides a similar service for equity market transactions. Paper certificates are held by CDS as the underlying security, but subsequent transactions will involve electronic transfers and a book-entry ledger. The use of computer-based electronic issuing methods lowers costs, simplifies administration, increases security, and links the lender or lender's bank and the issuing company. Bank lines of credit, call loans, and security loans will be tied into the system to produce net fund positions for companies. Better service and increased liquidity will result from this new clearing mechanism.

Canadian Depository for Securities
cds.ca

Advantages of Commercial Paper

Commercial paper is an attractive alternative to short-term bank financing, because

- Generally, it is cheaper (funds are raised in the wholesale market).
- Compensating balances are not required (although banks offer standby lines of credit).
- It is prestigious to float paper in a somewhat exclusive market.
- Asset-backed paper can free up a firm's balance sheet. (Assets are sold into a separate legal entity, a trust, and the firm receives cash).

As is indicated in Figure 8–4, the rate differential with prime is generally between 0.5 and 2 percent. However, in 1982 during a tight credit period, the differential in the U.S. market reached 5 percent.

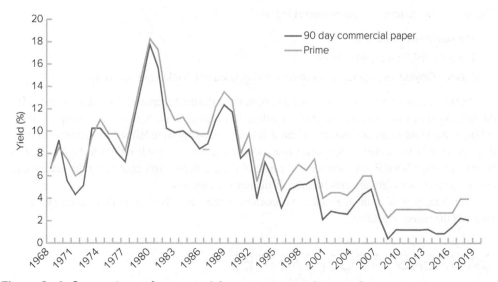

Figure 8–4 Comparison of commercial paper rate to prime rate*

*Average interest rate at December 31.

Limitations on the Issuance of Commercial Paper

The risks in the commercial paper market include

- The possibility of default
- The potential for a liquidity freeze
- A lack of loyalty or ongoing commitment (as opposed to a banking relationship)

Defaults in commercial paper have ranged from the Atlantic Acceptance Corporation in 1965; through Olympia and York, the Mercantile Bank and Confederation Life Insurance Company in the 1980s; to the winding up of Coventree Capital in 2007–08. Many were left holding unsecured IOUs that could not be liquidated as the market froze. Despite investment-grade ratings as high as R1 (low) by the Dominion Bond Rating Service at the time of default, these firms could not raise additional capital to meet their commitments because of financial difficulties.

Therefore, lines of credit at a bank are important in protecting the firm against adverse turns of events in the money markets.

BANKERS' ACCEPTANCES

Figure 8–3 displays the significant role played by bankers' acceptances in short-term debt financing in recent years, particularly as commercial paper lost its appeal. The use of bankers' acceptances has remained steady. Their main use has been to finance inventories of finished goods in transit to the buyers. As you can imagine, companies engaged in foreign trade find this form of financing especially helpful given the long lead times involved.

In the 1990s banks began to encourage companies to enter the commercial paper market rather than use bankers' acceptances to borrow short-term funds. To comply with international banking regulations, Canadian banks set aside reserves to cover contingent liabilities such as bankers' acceptances. This made it more expensive for banks to guarantee them, and they were less willing to do so. The banks' new growth market for financing has been asset-based securities.

As an example of a bankers' acceptance, a Canadian company is importing machinery from a German manufacturer, and agrees to pay in 180 days. The Canadian company arranges a letter of credit with a Canadian bank. Under the letter of credit, the bank agrees to accept a draft drawn by the German company on the Canadian importer. Hence, the term "bankers' acceptance" is used to signify the accepted draft once it has been sent by the exporter to the importer's bank. By accepting the draft, the bank has substituted its creditworthiness for that of the customer. If the bank is one of our major banks, the draft becomes a highly marketable money market instrument. This means that the German manufacturer does not have to hold the draft until the due date, but, rather, it can sell it in the money market at a discount from its face value. The discount allows the buyer of the bankers' acceptance to realize a return for holding the acceptance until the 180-day payment period is up.

LO4 FOREIGN BORROWING

An increasing source of funds for Canadian firms has been the large Eurocurrency market. Loans from foreign banks denominated in U.S. dollars (the most common currency) are called Eurodollar loans at LIBOR rates and are usually short term to intermediate term in maturity. Many multinational corporations have found cheaper ways of borrowing in foreign markets, either directly or through foreign subsidiaries at very favourable interest rates. The companies then convert the borrowed foreign currency to dollars, which are then sent to Canada to be used by the parent company. There is, however, foreign exchange exposure risk associated with these loans. This can be offset if the loan is balanced or hedged with foreign currency revenue streams. Eurodollar loans are also available in Canadian dollars; thus, foreign exchange risk is avoided while allowing Canadian firms to access capital from markets beyond our borders. This topic is given greater coverage in Chapter 21.

FINANCE IN ACTION

Manipulating the Eurodollar Loan Market

Eurodollar loan interest rates are currently based on LIBOR, the most utilized base rate in the world. LIBOR is the rate banks lend to each other and it is set every day by Thomson Reuters from estimated rates forwarded from participating banks. Loans tied to LIBOR are estimated to be at least $500 trillion.

In 2012, brokers of several investment banks conspired to fix the rates sent to Thomson Reuters. Activity such as this reduces confidence in the financial markets, resulting in decreased economic activity. Two banks, alone, paid fines of over $2 billion based on the actions of their traders. More fines followed.

The Bank of England has stated that sterling LIBOR will cease to exist after 2021 because of its manipulation during the financial crisis of 2008.

Q1 What will replace sterling LIBOR? Will it be SONIA?

USE OF COLLATERAL IN SHORT-TERM FINANCING

Almost any firm would prefer to borrow on an unsecured (no-collateral) basis, but if the borrower's credit rating is too low or its need for funds is too great, the lending institution requires that certain assets be pledged. A secured credit arrangement might help the borrower to obtain funds that would otherwise be unavailable.

LO5 Furthermore, a secured loan is often available at a lower rate of interest because of the increased protection afforded the lender. Regardless of whether or not the loan is secured, the borrower has the ability to negotiate the conditions, reporting requirements, and rate of interest charged on the loan. The banks are in competition and will often lower their stated interest rate to attract or maintain business.

In any loan, the lender's primary concern, however, is whether the borrower's capacity to generate cash flow is sufficient to liquidate the loan as it comes due. Few lenders would make a loan strictly on the basis of collateral. Collateral is merely a stopgap device to protect the lender when all else fails. The bank or finance company is in business to collect interest, not to repossess and resell assets.

Though a number of different assets may be pledged, we direct our attention to accounts receivable and inventory. The authority to assign accounts receivable as security on a loan comes under provincial legislation. Section 178 of the Bank Act covers inventories of manufactured goods as loan collateral. It gives banks the ability to take possession of, to look after, and to sell the inventories, if required.

Lines of Credit Credit lines are usually established on a year-to-year basis between a bank and its customer. This allows the firm to finance temporary cash needs. The line of credit is an agreement whereby the bank sets out the maximum amount it allows the firm to owe it at any one time. The amount of the line depends on an assessment of the firm's creditworthiness. Major considerations are the management capabilities of the firm, its profitability, and its net worth position. The line of credit is usually evidenced by a letter from the bank. However, the letter does not legally bind the bank to extend credit to the customer on demand. If the creditworthiness of the customer were to change or if the market were to become tight for funds, the bank might refuse to lend money under the line of credit agreement. In practice, however, a bank would be very reluctant not to honour its commitments under lines of credit.

Arranging lines of credit is an important role of the financial manager. Credit lines are available at floating interest rates tied into the prime rate. The best customers are able to get prime, which may be in Canadian funds, in U.S. funds, or at a LIBOR rate.

Revolving Credit Agreements The basic differences between the revolving credit agreement and the lines of credit are that the revolving credits are usually for periods longer than one year, and they usually involve a fee calculated as a fraction of the unused portion of the credit. Technically, because they are for periods longer than one year, revolving credits are generally classed as intermediate rather than short-term financing.

Transaction Loans Sometimes a borrower needs a loan to fund one particular project. In such cases a line of credit or a revolving credit agreement would not make sense. The bank might finance a company to finish work on a piece of machinery that is to be delivered on contract to a large customer. When the machine is delivered and paid for, the firm would repay its debt to the bank.

ACCOUNTS RECEIVABLE FINANCING

Accounts receivable financing may include pledging receivables as collateral for a loan or an outright sale (factoring receivables). Receivables financing is popular because it permits borrowing to be tied directly to the level of asset expansion at any time. As the level of accounts receivable goes up, we are able to borrow more.

A drawback is that this is a relatively expensive method of acquiring funds, so it must be carefully compared to other forms of credit. Accounts receivable represent valuable short-term assets, and they should be committed only where the appropriate circumstances exist. An ill-advised accounts receivable financing plan may exclude the firm from a less expensive bank term loan. Next we investigate more closely the characteristics and the costs associated with the pledging and selling of receivables.

Pledging Accounts Receivable

The lending institution generally stipulates which of the accounts receivable are of sufficient quality to serve as collateral for a loan. For example, banks generally do not accept accounts receivable more than 90 days old. The firm may borrow up to 75 percent of the value of the acceptable collateral from a bank. The loan percentage depends on the financial strength of the borrowing firm and on the credit risk of its accounts. The lender has full recourse against the borrower in the event any of the accounts go bad. The interest rate in a receivables borrowing arrangement is generally 1 to 3 percent in excess of the prime rate.

The interest is computed against the loan balance outstanding, a figure that may change quite frequently, as indicated in Table 8–1. In the illustration, interest is assumed to be 12 percent annually, or approximately 1 percent per month. In month 1, the firm can borrow $6,000 against $10,000 in acceptable receivables and must pay $60 in interest. Similar values are developed for succeeding months.

Table 8–1 Receivable loan balance

	Month 1	Month 2	Month 3	Month 4
Total accounts receivable	$11,000	$15,100	$19,400	$16,300
Acceptable receivables (to bank) . . .	10,000	14,000	18,000	15,000
Loan balance (60%)	6,000	8,400	10,800	9,000
Interest—1% per month	60	84	108	90

Additionally, the bank will require the firm to report regularly on its accounts receivable position and will likely establish other requirements covering insurance, withdrawal of funds, and obtaining of additional debt.

Factoring Receivables

A firm may be able to sell its receivables to a factoring company. Factoring companies primarily deal only with companies that produce physical products rather than service companies. They may provide accounts receivable management alone or combined with receivables-based financing.

The factoring company may be used as a direct substitute for the firm's accounts receivable department. The client firm sells its product and sends a copy of the invoice to the factor, which then takes over collection responsibility. The factor keeps track of payments, sends follow-up notices to late payers, and usually provides a credit guarantee for collection. Rates for this management service, including the credit guarantee, are 1 to 2 percent per month. Thus, although the factor's service is not cheap, the client firm may save on bad debt expenses as well as administrative costs related to managing collections.

Factoring companies also provide financing based on receivables as collateral. The factor will advance a proportion of the value of receivables, sometimes as much as 80 to 90 percent. Accounts receivable effectively are purchased by a factoring company at a discount to the face value of invoices depending on their size and the estimated time to collection. If the factoring company cannot collect a receivable purchased on a recourse basis, it retains the right to return the receivable to the company that sold it for payment.

Consider, as an illustration, a case where a factor administers all of a client's receivables and advances 80 percent of their value as an operating loan. If $100,000 a month is processed at a 1 percent commission, and a 12 percent annual borrowing rate (based on a discount basis) is charged on the loan, the total cost of the borrowing is calculated as approximately 24 percent on an **annual** basis.

1.0%	Commission
<u>1.0%</u>	Interest for one month (12% annual/12)
2.0%	Total fee monthly
2.0%	Monthly × 12 = 24% annual rate

The important part of the factoring analysis, however, is to determine what portion of the cost relates to the administration and credit guarantee service and to determine if that is reasonable. If the equivalent cost of a secured loan from the bank was also 12 percent, the company would have to determine if the commission costs of 1 percent per month, or $12,000 per year, are justified by administrative and credit loss savings. For example, if the firm estimated that factoring would save $10,000 in credit-checking and clerical costs as well as avoid a 1/2 percent bad debt experience, the estimated savings would be $16,000 per year versus a cost of $12,000.

$10,000	Administrative cost savings
<u>$ 6,000</u>	Bad debt savings ($100,000 × 0.005 × 12)
$16,000	

Choosing to factor its receivables would therefore be a sound financial decision.

Asset-backed Securities

Accounts receivable financing is the sale of receivables by large firms in public offerings arranged by securities dealers. Although factoring has long been one way of selling receivables, public offerings of securities backed by receivables as collateral gained respectability when General Motors Acceptance Corporation (GMAC) made a public offering of $500 million of asset-backed securities in December 1985.

These asset-backed securities are nothing more than the sale of receivables through public offerings. In former years, companies that sold receivables were viewed as short of cash, financially shaky, or in some sort of financial trouble. However, there had been growing acceptance of this form of financing in Canada, until 2007 when it was found that many of the assets backing these securities were suspect. There have been asset-backed security offerings based on car loans and credit card receivables, but the offerings backed by sub-prime mortgages to individuals with credit difficulties caused a financial crisis by 2007. Figure 8-3 shows the increasing use of asset-backed commercial paper.

The public offerings of asset-backed securities have ranged from commercial paper with a short term to maturity to five-year term notes. Asset-backed commercial paper trades at 5 to 50 basis points above bankers' acceptances.

Credit Cards, Music, Beer, and Travel

Figure 8-3 shows the significant growth in the use of asset-backed securities since the early 1990s. About half of commercial paper issued in now asset-backed.

One of the first, in November 1991, was by Sears Canada Receivables Trust (SCRT), formed to buy accounts receivable (credit card balances) from Sears Canada. Commercial paper and debentures were issued to provide financing for the trust. Credit card receivables have a low default rate and this asset-backed paper offered very good security to investors. In fact, SCRT received a better credit rating than Sears Canada itself. Sears is now gone.

Rock singer David Bowie raised US$55 million in 1997 at a 7.9 percent interest rate over 15 years by securitizing future royalties from over 300 songs that he had written. Originally getting a Aaa rating from Moody's, the Bowie Bond was downgraded to a Baa3 (almost junk) when music streaming developed. Nevertheless the Bowie Bonds were all paid off.

In 1999, Punch Taverns, a U.K. pub company, issued over £300 million of securitized credit notes using the cash flow from its pubs as collateral. Many thought the cash flow stream to be quite reliable, and Punch Taverns received an A credit rating.

However, in 2007, asset-backed securities financing dropped significantly as a credit crunch developed and the yield differential above T-bills (see Finance in Action box in Chapter 1) soared . Paper had been collateralized with mortgages to individuals who did not have the means to repay (check out NINJA loans) unless housing prices increased indefinitely. Housing prices fell. The asset-backed commercial paper (ABCP) had no liquidity. Some blamed the Bowie Bond and other asset-backed securities based on "esoteric" assets.

The market has come back after 2007–08. In 2014 Miramax issued $250 million of securities at 3.04% on its file library including *Pulp Fiction* and the *English Patient*. In 2017 Dumiao issued Renminbi 245 million (about $48 million Canadian) of asset-backed securities based on instalment payment receivables related to travel commitments established on its online platform, Qunar. These securities were offered on the Shanghai Stock Exchange.

Q1 With Spotify and Apple Music, will the cash flow streams from music royalties be as lucrative in the future?

Q1 Can you find an "esoteric" asset-backed security? How about a dirty laundry bond?

One of the benefits to the issuer is that it trades future cash flows for immediate cash. The asset-backed security is likely to carry a high credit rating of AA or better, even when the issuing firm may have a low credit rating. This allows the issuing firm to acquire lower-cost funds than it could with a bank loan or a bond offering. Even though this short-term market is still relatively small by money market standards, it does provide an important avenue for corporate liquidity and short-term financing.

There are also several problems facing the public sale of receivables. Computer systems need to be upgraded to service securities and to handle the paperwork that is needed to keep track of the loans for the investors in the

Dominion Bond
Rating Service
dbrs.com

securities. A second consideration for the buyer of these securities is the probability that the receivable will actually be paid. Even though the loss rates on loans were about one-half of 1 percent in the 1980s, bad debts can be much higher during recessions. During a serious recession, or a credit meltdown such as that of 2007–08, the owners of the asset-backed securities might find themselves without the promised cash flows as people can't make payments on their receivables. To counteract these fears, many issuers set up a loan-loss reserve fund to partially insure against the possibility of a loss.

INVENTORY FINANCING

We may also borrow against inventory to acquire funds. The extent to which inventory financing may be employed is based on the liquidity or marketability of the pledged goods, their associated price stability, and the perishability of the product. Another significant factor is the degree of physical control that can be exercised over the product by the lender. We can relate some of these factors to the stages of inventory production and the nature of lender control.

Stages of Production

Raw materials and finished goods are likely to provide the best collateral, whereas goods in process may qualify for only a small percentage loan. For a firm holding widely traded raw materials such as lumber, metals, grain, cotton, and wool, a loan of 70 to 80 percent is possible. The lender may have to place only a few quick phone calls to dispose of the goods at market value if the borrower fails to repay the loan. For standardized finished goods, such as tires, canned goods, and building products, the same principle would apply. On the other hand, goods in process, representing altered but unfinished raw materials, may qualify for a loan of only one-quarter their value or less.

Nature of Lender Control

The methods for controlling pledged inventory go from the simple to the complex, providing ever-greater assurances to the lender but progressively higher administrative costs.

Blanket Inventory Liens The simplest method is a blanket inventory lien in which the lender has a general claim against the inventory of the borrower. Specific items are not identified or tagged, and there is no physical control.

Trust Receipts A trust receipt is an instrument acknowledging that the borrower holds the inventory and proceeds from sales in trust for the lender. Each item is carefully marked and specified by serial number. When sold, the proceeds are transferred to the lender, and the trust receipt is cancelled. Also known as *floor planning*, this financing device is very popular among auto and industrial equipment dealers and in the television and home appliance industries. Although it provides tighter control than does the blanket inventory lien, it still does not give the lender direct control over inventory—only a better and more legally enforceable system of tracing the goods.

Warehousing Under this arrangement, goods are physically identified, segregated, and stored under the direction of an independent warehousing company. The firm issues a warehouse receipt to the lender, and goods can be moved only with the lender's approval.

The goods may be stored on the premises of the warehousing firm, an arrangement known as public warehousing, or on the borrower's premises under a field warehousing agreement. When field warehousing is utilized, an independent warehousing company still exercises control over inventory.

Appraisal of Inventory Control Devices

Although the more structured methods of inventory financing appear somewhat restrictive, they are well accepted in certain industries. For example, field warehousing is popular in grain storage and food canning. Well-maintained control measures do involve substantial administrative expenses, and they raise the overall costs of borrowing. The costs of inventory financing may run 15 percent or higher. As is true of accounts receivable financing, the extension of funds is well synchronized with the need.

HEDGING TO REDUCE BORROWING RISK

LO6 Those firms that need to borrow funds or to lend funds for the continuing operations of their firm are exposed to the risk of interest rate changes. One way to partially reduce that risk is through interest rate hedging activities in the financial futures market. Hedging means to engage in a transaction that partially or fully reduces a prior risk exposure. The financial futures market is set up to allow for the trading of a financial instrument at a future time. This instrument is separate from the firm's requirement, through a business transaction, to borrow or lend funds at a fixed rate at some time in the future. Chapter 19 further discusses the futures market.

Let us suppose it is January 2022, and a firm will be required to borrow funds for equipment sometime between now and June 2022 at a fixed rate of interest and for an extended period of time. This exposes the firm to the risk that interest rates might go up in the future, forcing it to pay higher interest rates than the current market rates. To hedge this risk, the firm might sell a Canadian government bond future contract that is to be closed out in June 2022, through the financial futures market. The sale price of this contract is established by the initial January transaction. A subsequent purchase of a June 2022 contract at a currently unknown price will be necessary to close out the transaction.

In the futures market you do not physically deliver the goods (in this case the government bond). What you do is execute a later transaction that reverses your initial position. Thus, if you initially sell a futures contract, you later buy a contract that covers your initial sale. If you initially buy a futures contract, the opposite is true, and you later sell a contract that covers your initial purchase position.

In the case of selling a Canadian government bond futures contract, the subsequent pattern of interest rates determines whether the futures contract is profitable or not. If interest rates go up, Canadian government bond prices go down and you can buy a subsequent contract at a lower price than the sales value that you originally established. The result is a profitable transaction that can be used to offset the higher costs the firm will incur when borrowing to pay for its equipment. Note the following example:

Sale price, June government bond contract* (sale occurs in January 2022)	$95,000
Purchase price, June 2022 government bond contract (the purchase occurs in June 2022).	90,000
Profit on futures contract.	$ 5,000

*Only a small percentage of the actual dollars involved must be invested to initiate the contract. This is known as a *margin*.

The reason government bond prices went down is because, as previously mentioned, interest rates and bond prices move in opposite directions, and interest rates went up. If the reverse was true and bond prices had increased with lower interest rates, the futures contract would show a loss. The firm, however, would be able to borrow at more desirable lower rates of interest, so once again the firm is covered, or hedged. The lesson to be learned from this example is that rising interest rates can mean profits in the financial futures market if you initially sell a contract and later buy it back. This can offset higher interest rates on borrowed funds that might be required in the future course of business.

The financial futures market can be used to partially or fully hedge against almost any financial event. In addition to the Government of Canada bond future, there is the bankers' acceptance future, which is used to hedge short-term interest rates. Both of these contracts are available through the Montreal Exchange. The level of activity in these futures is minimal when compared to the financial futures available in the United States, where, besides Treasury bonds, trades may be initiated in Treasury bills, certificates of deposit, GNMA certificates,[4] and many other instruments.

CME Group
cmegroup.com

---

[4]GNMA stands for the Government National Mortgage Association, also known as Ginnie Mae.

Montreal Exchange Opts for Futures

Canada's oldest stock exchange was the Montreal Exchange, but after combining with the Toronto Stock Exchange it has since concentrated on derivatives trading.

The Montreal Futures Exchange (m-x.ca) has carved out a strong niche in derivatives that offer a means for firms to hedge their interest rate risk. The bankers' acceptance future (BAX) and bond futures on 2-, 5-, 10-, and 30-year Government of Canada bonds have proved quite popular. In fact, they have nicely withstood a challenge from the CME Group (cmegroup.com) the world's largest futures and options exchange. The CME Group offers futures and options contracts on a variety of interest rates.

Hedgers use the BAX offered by the Montreal Exchange (Bourse de Montreal). Under quotes for the BAX contracts at the Montreal Exchange the open-interest position is given. This gives an idea of the contract's liquidity.

Many Canadian companies with global business engage in hedging activities. The company's latest financial statements will identify hedging activities in the notes, perhaps listed under derivative instruments.

Q1 What is the trading unit of the BAX?

Q2 When is the open interest of the first BAX to expire?

SUMMARY

1. The easiest access to short-term financing is through trade credit provided by suppliers as a natural outgrowth of the buying and reselling of goods. Larger firms tend to be net providers of trade credit, whereas smaller firms are net users. Firms that do not take advantage of discounts in order to provide themselves with additional financing may find it quite expensive. (LO1)

2. Bank financing is usually in the form of short-term, self-liquidating loans. A financially strong customer is offered the prime, or lowest, rate with the rates to other accounts scaled up appropriately. Economic factors cause the prime to change frequently, and thus the interest rate on loans changes as well. Short-term loans are usually on a demand basis, which allows the amount outstanding to move up and down based on business conditions. Compensating balances and discount loans change the actual interest rate stated. (LO2)

3. An alternative to bank credit for the large, prestigious firm is the use of commercial paper. Though generally issued at a rate below prime, it is an impersonal means of financing that may dry up during difficult financing periods. (LO3)

4. Firms are also turning to foreign sources of funds, either through the Eurodollar market or through borrowing foreign currency directly. These markets represent alternative sources of capital often at cheaper rates, but they may introduce foreign exchange risk. (LO4)

5. By using a secured form of financing, the firm ties its borrowing requirements directly to its asset buildup. We may pledge our accounts receivable as collateral or sell them outright, as well as borrow against inventory. Though secured-asset financing devices may be expensive, they may fit the credit needs of the firm, particularly those of a small firm that cannot qualify for premium bank financing or the commercial paper market. (LO5)

6. The financial manager may wish to consider the use of hedging through the financial futures market. The consequences of rapid interest rate changes can be reduced through participation in the financial futures market. (LO6)

REVIEW OF FORMULAS

The cost of forgoing the discount

$$K_{DIS} = \frac{d\%}{100\% - d\%} \times \frac{365}{f(\text{date}) - d(\text{date})} \qquad (8\text{--}1)$$

$d\%$ = Discount percentage
$f(\text{date})$ = Final payment period
$d(\text{date})$ = Discount period

$$\text{Amount to be borrowed} = \frac{\text{Amount needed}}{(1 - c)}$$

c is compensating balance requirement expressed as a decimal.

$$R_{ANNUAL} = \frac{I}{P} \times \frac{365}{d} \qquad (8\text{--}2)$$

R_{ANNUAL} = Annual rate
I = Interest
P = Principal
d = Days loan is outstanding

Annual rate on discounted loan

$$R_{DIS} = \frac{I}{P - I} \times \frac{365}{d} \qquad (8\text{--}3)$$

Annual rate with compensating balances

$$R_{COMP} = \frac{I}{(1-c)} \qquad (8\text{–}4)$$

c is compensating balance requirement expressed as a decimal.

$$R_{COMP} = \frac{I}{(P-B)} \times \frac{365}{d} \qquad (8\text{–}5)$$

B = Compensating balance in $

$$R_{INSTAL} = \frac{2 \times \text{Annual number of payments} \times I}{(\text{Total number of payments} + 1) \times P} \qquad (8\text{–}6)$$

DISCUSSION QUESTIONS

1. Under which circumstances would it be advisable to borrow money to take a cash discount? (LO1)

2. Discuss the relative use of credit between large and small firms. Which group is generally in the net creditor position? Why? (LO1)

3. What is the prime interest rate? How does the average bank customer fare in regard to the prime interest rate? Are companies ever allowed by banks to borrow at less than prime? (LO2)

4. What advantages do compensating balances have for banks? Are the advantages to banks necessarily disadvantages to corporations? (LO2)

5. A borrower is often confronted with a stated interest rate and an effective interest rate. What is the difference, and which one should the financial manager recognize as the true cost of borrowing? (LO2)

6. Commercial paper may show up on corporate balance sheets as either a current asset or a current liability. Explain this statement. (LO3)

7. What are the advantages of commercial paper in comparison with bank borrowing at the prime rate? What are the disadvantages? (LO3)

8. What is the major advantage of a bankers' acceptance? (LO3, LO4)

9. Discuss the major types of collateralized short-term loans. (LO5)

10. What is an asset-backed public offering? (LO5)

11. What is meant by hedging in the financial futures market to offset interest rate risks? (LO6)

12. What is the difference between pledging and factoring accounts receivable? (LO5)

INTERNET RESOURCES AND QUESTIONS

The Canadian exchange for interest rate futures is the Montreal Exchange. It includes a history of the exchange and specifications for the bankers' acceptances and government bond contracts: m-x.ca

The CME Group is the world's largest derivatives exchange. It lists a variety of interest rate products: cmegroup.com

1. Identify the Canadian dollar interest rate futures contracts, including the contract size and how settlement prices are determined, available on the Montreal Exchange.

2. Compare interest rates on secured and unsecured lines of credit at Canadian financial institutions.

PROBLEMS

1.   Compute the cost of not taking the following trade discounts:

   a.   1/10, net 20

   b.   2/15, net 30

   c.   2/10, net 45

   d.   3/10, net 180

2.   To finance additional inventory, Arbutus Ltd. is considering forgoing the cash discount on all of its purchases currently offered on terms of 2/10, net 45. No payments will be stretched. Annual purchases are $9.21 million.

   a.   Calculate the additional financing available to Arbutus Ltd. by forgoing the cash discount.

   b.   Calculate the annual cost of forgoing the cash discount.

3.   S. Pumpkins has an average inventory of $630,000, with an annual turnover rate of eight times. The average accounts receivable balance is $520,250, and customers pay on average in 30 days. S. Pumpkins pays accounts in 45 days.

   a.   Calculate S. Pumpkins' average accounts payable balance.

   b.   Calculate its annual sales.

4.   Paul Promptly is a very cautious businessman. His suppliers offer trade credit terms of 3/10, net 70. Mr. Promptly never takes the discount offered, but he pays his suppliers in 60 days rather than the 70 days allowed so that he is sure the payments are never late. What is Mr. Promptly's cost of not taking the cash discount?

5.   Little Kimi Clothiers can borrow from its bank at 6 percent to take a cash discount. The terms of the cash discount are 2/15 net 90. Should the firm borrow the funds?

6.   Chris Angle can borrow from its bank at 8 percent to take a cash discount. The terms of the cash discount are 1/10 net 60. Should Chris borrow the funds?

7.   The average price on 91-day Treasury bills at a recent Tuesday auction was 98.671 with maturity value 100. Calculate the T-bill's annualized yield.

8.   The average price on 182-day Treasury bills was 98.097 with maturity value at 100. Calculate the T-bill's annualized yield.

9.   McGriff Dog Food Company normally takes 20 days to pay for average daily credit purchases of $9,000. Its average daily sales are $10,000 and it collects accounts in 25 days.

   a.   What is its net credit position?

   b.   If the firm stretches its average payment period from 20 days to 32 days (and all else remains the same), what is the firm's new net credit position?

10.   Sampson Orange Juice Company normally takes 30 days to pay for its average daily credit purchases of $7,500. Its average daily sales are $9,000, and it collects its accounts in 34 days.

   a.   What is its net credit position?

   b.   If the firm extends its average payment period from 30 days to 45 days (and all else remains the same), what is the firm's new net credit position? Has it improved its cash flow?

11.   Your bank will lend you $2,000 for 45 days at a cost of $25 interest. What is your annual rate of interest? What is your effective annual rate?

12.   A pawnshop will lend you $3,000 for 50 days at a cost of $45 interest. What is your annual rate of interest? What is your effective annual rate?

13.   Dr. Painkiller is going to borrow $3,000 for one year at 8 percent interest. What is the annual rate of interest if the loan is discounted?

14. Marty Not is going to borrow $8,000 for 120 days and pay $215 in interest. What is the annual rate of interest if the loan is discounted?

15. Talmud Book Company borrows $16,000 for 30 days at 9 percent interest. What is the dollar cost of the loan?

16. Dr. Ruth is going to borrow $5,000 to help write a book. The loan is for one year and the money can either be borrowed at the prime rate or the LIBOR rate. Assume the prime rate is 6 percent and LIBOR 1.5 percent less. Also assume there will be a $40 transaction fee with LIBOR. What loan has the lower annual interest cost?

17. Gulliver Travel Agencies thinks interest rates in Europe are low. The firm borrows euros at 9 percent for one year. During this time period the dollar falls 14 percent against the euro. What is the annual interest rate on the loan for one year?

18. Maxim Air Filters Inc. plans to borrow $300,000 for one year. Northeast National Bank will lend the money at 10 percent interest and requires a compensating balance of 20 percent. What is the annual rate of interest?

19. Computer Graphics Company requires $250,000 to complete a project.
    a. With a compensating balance requirement of 20 percent, how much will the firm need to borrow?
    b. Given your answer to part *a* and a stated interest rate of 10 percent on the total amount borrowed, what is the annual rate on the $250,000 actually being used?

20. Carey Company is borrowing $200,000 for one year at 12 percent from Second National Bank. The bank requires a 20 percent compensating balance. What is the annual rate of interest? What would the annual rate be if Carey were required to make 12 equal monthly payments to retire the loan? The principal, as used in formula 8–6, refers to funds the firm can effectively utilize.

21. Randall Corporation plans to borrow $200,000 for one year at 8 percent from the Dominion Trust Company. There is a 20 percent compensating balance requirement. Randall keeps minimum transaction balances of $10,000 in the normal course of business. This idle cash counts toward meeting the compensating balance requirement. What is the annual rate of interest?

22. The treasurer of Brandon Blue Sox is seeking a $20,000 loan for 180 days from the Brandon Credit Union. The stated interest rate is 10 percent and there is a 15 percent compensating balance requirement. The treasurer always keeps a minimum of $1,500 in the firm's chequing account. These funds could count toward meeting any compensating balance requirements. What is the annual rate of interest on this loan?

23. Tucker Drilling Corp. plans to borrow $200,000. Northern Dominion Bank will lend the money at one-half of a percentage point over the prime rate of 8 percent and requires an administration fee of 2 percent. There is a 20 percent compensating balance requirement. What is the annual rate of interest?

24. Your company plans to borrow $5 million for 12 months, and your banker gives you a stated rate of 8 percent interest. You would like to know the annual rate of interest for the following types of loans. (Each of the following parts stands alone.)
    a. Simple 8 percent interest with a 10 percent compensating balance
    b. Discounted interest
    c. An instalment loan (12 payments)
    d. Discounted interest with a 1 percent administration fee

25. If you borrow $4,000 at $500 interest for one year, what is your annual interest cost for the following payment plan?

    a. Annual payment

    b. Semiannual payments

    c. Quarterly payments

    d. Monthly payments

26. Vroom Motorcycle Company is borrowing $30,000 from First Prairie Bank. The total interest charge is $9,000. The loan will be paid by making equal monthly payments for the next three years. What is the annual rate of interest on this instalment loan?

27. Morrisette Records' commercial paper is currently selling at 98.512 percent of maturity value; it matures in 75 days. What annualized yield is it offering to investors?

28. CO2 Coals' commercial paper is currently selling at 99.123 percent of maturity value; it matures in 51 days. What annualized yield is it offering to investors?

29. Calculate the cost of discounting a $100,000 bankers' acceptance if it is due in 90 days and is sold at $97,915. Ignore bank fees.

30. Blue Grass Filters requires additional financing. Currently, it pays for all purchases on the discount date under terms of 2/15, net 75. Its banker will lend funds at 11 percent.

    a. Should Blue Grass Filters obtain funding from the bank or by forgoing the cash discount?

    b. Assuming the bank is the cheaper alternative, why might Blue Grass Filters still choose to forgo the cash discount to obtain financing?

31. The Reynolds Company buys from its suppliers on terms of 2/10, net 40. Reynolds has not been utilizing the discount offered and has been taking 55 days to pay its bills. The suppliers seem to accept this payment pattern, and Reynolds' credit rating has not been hurt.

    Mr. Duke, Reynolds Company's vice-president, has suggested that the company begin to take the discount offered. Mr. Duke proposes the company borrow from its bank at a stated rate of 14 percent. The bank requires a 20 percent compensating balance on these loans. Current account balances would not be available to meet any of this required compensating balance. Do you agree with Mr. Duke's proposal?

32. In the previous problem, if the compensating balance requirement were 10 percent instead of 20 percent, would you change your answer? Do the appropriate calculation.

33. Burt's Department Store needs $300,000 to take a cash discount of 3/10, net 70. A banker will loan the money for 60 days at an interest cost of $8,100.

    a. What is the annual rate on the bank loan?

    b. How much would it cost (in percentage terms) if Burt's did not take the cash discount and paid the bill in 70 days instead of 10 days?

    c. Should Burt's borrow the money to take the discount?

    d. If the banker requires a 20 percent compensating balance, how much must Burt's borrow to end up with the $300,000?

    e. What would be the interest rate in part *d* if the interest charge for 60 days were $10,125? Should Burt's borrow with the 20 percent compensating balance? (There are no funds to count against the compensating balance requirement.)

34. Neveready Flashlights Inc. needs $300,000 to take a cash discount of 2/10, net 70. A banker will loan the money for 60 days at an interest cost of $5,500.

   a. What is the annual rate on the bank loan?

   b. How much would it cost (in percentage terms) if the firm did not take the cash discount, but paid the bill in 70 days instead of 10 days?

   c. Should the firm borrow the money to take the discount?

   d. If the banker requires a 15 percent compensating balance, how much must the firm borrow to end up with the $300,000?

   e. What would be the effective interest rate in part *d* if the interest charge for 60 days were $6,850? Should the firm borrow with the 20 percent compensating balance? (The firm has no funds to count against the compensating balance requirement.)

35. Rockford Filing Ltd. requires $1 million in financing for a 45-day period. Three alternatives are being considered. Which alternative should be selected?

   a. Establish a line of credit with the bank at an interest rate of 10 percent. The bank will charge an annual commitment fee of 1 percent to establish the line of credit.

   b. Forgo trade discounts from suppliers on terms of 2/15, net 60.

   c. Issue commercial paper for 45 days at a discount of 1.25 percent.

36. Bernie's Macs requires $600,000 in financing for a 60-day period. Three alternatives are being considered. Which alternative should be selected?

   a. Establish a line of credit with the bank at an interest rate of 7 percent. The bank will require an annual commitment fee of $4,750 to establish the line of credit.

   b. Forgo trade discounts from suppliers on terms of 2/30, net 90.

   c. Issue commercial paper for 60 days at a discount of 1.91 percent.

37. Rapier Fencing requires $750,000 in financing for a 60-day period. Three alternatives are being considered. Which alternative should be selected?

   a. Establish a line of credit with the bank at an interest rate of 6 percent payable on a discounted basis.

   b. Forgo trade discounts from suppliers on terms of 1.5/10, net 70.

   c. Issue commercial paper for 60 days sold at a discounted price of 98.8 percent of maturity value.

38. Macco Bakers requires $500,000 in financing for a 90-day period. Three alternatives are being considered. Which alternative should be selected?

   a. Establish a line of credit with the bank at an interest rate of 8 percent. The bank will charge a fee of $5,000 to establish the line of credit.

   b. Forgo trade discounts from suppliers on terms of 2/10, net 100.

   c. Issue commercial paper for 90 days at a discount of 2.05 percent.

39. Ajax Box Company is negotiating with two banks for a $100,000 loan. Midland Bank requires a 20 percent compensating balance, discounts the loan, and wants to be paid back in four quarterly payments. Central Bank requires a 10 percent compensating balance and does not discount the loan, but it wants to be paid back in 12 monthly instalments. The stated rate at both banks is 8 percent. Compensating balances and any discounts will be subtracted from the $100,000 in determining the available funds in part *a.*

   a. Which loan should Ajax accept?

   b. Recompute the annual cost of interest, assuming Ajax ordinarily maintains $20,000 at each bank in deposits that will serve as compensating balances.

   c. How much did the compensating balances inflate the percentage interest costs? Does your choice of banks change if the assumption in part *b* is correct?

40. Marla Maple Sugar Company sells to the 12 accounts listed below.

Account	Receivable Balance Outstanding	Average Age of the Account over the Last Year
A	$ 60,000	28
B	120,000	43
C	70,000	10
D	20,000	52
E	50,000	42
F	220,000	34
G	30,000	16
H	300,000	65
I	40,000	33
J	90,000	50
K	210,000	14
L	60,000	35

Trump Financial Corporation will lend 90 percent against account balances that have averaged 30 days or less; 80 percent for account balances between 31 and 40 days; and 70 percent for account balances between 41 and 45 days. Customers that take over 45 days to pay their bills are not considered as adequate accounts for a loan.

The current prime rate is 10 percent, and Trump Financial Corporation charges 5 percent over prime to Marla Maple Sugar Company as its annual loan rate.

a. Determine the maximum loan for which Marla Maple Sugar Company could qualify.

b. Determine how much one month's interest expense would be on the loan balance determined in part *a*.

41. Towers Arcades currently borrows $560,000 per month from its bank on the strength of receivables, which average $800,000 per month. Credit terms are net 30. The bank's interest rate is 10 percent annually, with an additional charge of .5 percent to process the accounts receivable used as security. The processing charge is based not on the loan amount but on the dollar value of the underlying receivables pledged as collateral.

Towers has an offer from a factoring company to buy all of its receivables without recourse for a fee of 2 percent of the value of the receivables purchased. The factoring firm is prepared to lend Towers Arcades $560,000 per month at an interest rate of 11 percent. The factoring company would eliminate Tower's credit department expense, including bad debts costs, of $15,000 a month. Should Towers Arcades switch to the factoring company?

42. The treasurer for Thornton Pipe and Steel Company wishes to use financial futures to hedge her interest rate exposure. She will sell five Canadian bond futures contracts at $105,000 per contract. It is July and the contracts must be closed out in December of this year. Long-term interest rates are currently 7.4 percent. If they increase to 8.5 percent, assume the value of the contracts will go down by 10 percent. Also, if interest rates do increase by 1.1 percentage points, assume the firm will have additional interest expense on its business loans and other commitments of $60,800. This expense, of course, is separate from the futures contract.

a. What will be the profit or loss on the futures contract if interest rates go to 8.5 percent?

b. Explain why a profit or loss occurred on the futures contracts.

c. After considering the hedging in part *a,* what is the net cost to the firm of the increased interest expense of $60,800? What percent of this increased cost did the treasurer effectively hedge away?

d. Indicate whether there would be a profit or loss on the futures contracts if interest rates went down.

MINI CASE

Fresh & Fruity Foods

Fresh & Fruity Foods is a mail-order company operating out of a winery near Summerland, British Columbia. The company specializes in sending British Columbian specialties to catalogue customers nationwide. Sales are seasonal, with most occurring in November and December—when people select Fresh & Fruity's Famous Fruit Fantasy boxes as Christmas gifts. Although seasonal, the company's sales are fairly predictable, because the bulk of Fresh & Fruity's customers are regulars who purchase year after year. The company has also managed to smooth out its sales somewhat by offering incentives, such as the Fruit of the Month Club, which encourages customers to buy throughout the year.

The nature of the mail-order business is such that most of Fresh & Fruity's sales are on credit; therefore, the company has historically had a high accounts receivable balance relative to sales. It has also historically been short of cash; forcing it to delay payments to suppliers as long as possible (its average time to pay accounts in 20XX was 67 days).

In January 20XY, Tom Appleby and Alice Plummer, the president and treasurer of Fresh & Fruity, respectively, were discussing the cash flow problem over lunch. "You know, Tom," Alice said as she sliced a piece of avocado, "I was reading the other day about a company called Kringle's Candles & Ornaments, and it occurred to me that we're a lot like them. Most of our assets are current ones, like their accounts receivable and inventory, and over half of ours are financed just like theirs, by current liabilities—that is, accounts payable." She paused for a sip of chardonnay, and continued, "They got around their cash flow problems by issuing long-term debt, which took the pressure off their current obligations. I've been looking at that for our company, too. But then I got to thinking, there's another way that's a good deal easier and would produce results just as quickly."

"Oh? And what's that?" Tom replied, his interest captured.

"All we have to do," she said, "is to reduce our accounts receivable balance. That will help reduce our accounts payable balance, since, as our customers begin paying us earlier, we can, in turn, pay our suppliers earlier. If we could get enough customers to pay us right away, we could even pay some of the suppliers in time to take advantage of the 2 percent discount they offer for payments within 10 days." (Fresh & Fruity's suppliers operated on a 2/10, net 60 basis.) "That would increase our net income and free up even more cash to take advantage of even more discounts!" She looked excited at the prospect.

"Sounds great, but how do we get people to pay us earlier?" Tom inquired, doubtfully.

"Easy," Alice continued. "Up to now we've been giving them incentives to pay later. Remember our 'Buy Now, No Payments for Two Months' program? Well, a lot of our customers use it, and it's caused our accounts receivable balance to run way up. So what we have to do now is give them incentives to pay earlier. What I propose is to cancel the buy now/pay later plan, and instead offer a 10 percent discount to everyone who pays with their order."

"But won't that cause our revenues to drop?" Tom asked, again still doubtful.

"Yes, but the drop will be offset by even more new customers who will come in to take advantage of the discount. I figure the net effect on sales will be just about zero, but our accounts receivable balance could be cut in half! Now here's a kicker I just thought of. After we've reduced our accounts receivable balance as far as practical, I'd like to look into the possibility of reducing our accounts payable still further by replacing them with a bank loan. The effective rate of interest that we pay by not taking our suppliers' discounts is, after all, pretty high. So what I'd like to do is take out a loan once a year of a sufficient size that would enable us to take all the discounts our suppliers offer. The interest that we'll pay on the loan is bound to be less than what we pay in discounts lost—so we'll see another gain in earnings on our income statement. In fact, these two initiatives together might have a really significant impact!"

"You've convinced me," Tom said. "Let's go back to the office and run some figures to see what happens!"

Assume that Alice Plummer's first initiative to offer a 10 percent discount was to be implemented, and the company's average collection period would drop to 32 days. As a result of Alice's first initiative, Fresh & Fruity would be able to take advantage of the 2 percent discount on one-third of its purchases. Fresh & Fruity can obtain an 8 percent loan for one year.

Prepare a report outlining the costs and benefits of the various alternatives. (Guided questions are available in the instructor's manual.) Include recommendations.

Fresh & Fruity Foods Inc.
Income Statement
For year ending December 31, 20XX

Revenue from sales:

Gross sales (credit).............................		$1,179,000

Cost of goods sold:

Beginning inventory.............................		$ 141,000
Purchases	$969,000	
Less: cash discounts.........................	0	
Net purchases..............................		969,000
Goods available for sale.......................		1,110,000
Less: Ending inventory		79,557
Cost of goods sold		1,030,443
Gross profit		148,557
Selling and administrative expenses		73,000
Earnings before interest and tax....................		75,557
Interest expense		0
Earnings before tax		75,557
Income taxes @ 33%.............................		24,934
Net income......................................		$ 50,623

Fresh & Fruity Foods Inc.
Balance Sheet
As of December 31, 20XX

Assets:

Cash	$ 3,560	
Accounts receivable...............................	209,686	
Inventory	79,557	
Total current assets................................		$292,803
Property, plant, and equipment, net		11,430
Total assets.......................................		$304,233

Liabilities and equity:

Accounts payable.................................	$180,633	
Notes payable (bank loans)	0	
Total current liabilities.............................		$180,633
Long-term debt		0
Total liabilities....................................		180,633
Common stock...................................	96,600	
Retained earnings................................	27,000	
Total equity		123,600
Total liabilities and equity		$304,233

Selected ratios:

Return on sales....................................	4.29%
Return on equity....................................	40.96%
Inventory turnover	14.82
Receivables turnover	5.62
Average payment period	67

CHAPTER

9

The Time Value of Money

LEARNING OBJECTIVES

LO1 Explain the concept of the time value of money.

LO2 Calculate present values, future values, and annuities based on the number of time periods involved and the going interest rate.

LO3 Calculate yield based on the time relationships between cash flows.

Establishing the value of assets (capital budgeting) that produce cash flows for future periods is a major consideration of finance. Estimating the cash flows, determining returns required by investors, considering the risks involved, and placing a current price (present worth) on these cash flows are significant endeavours. Both the cost of capital and the capital asset pricing model will assist us in this endeavour, as will the financial markets.

Capital Growth

Manhattan Island was purchased in 1624 for what appeared to be the ridiculously low figure of 60 guilders or about $24. But was it really ridiculous? Reinvested at an annual interest rate of 6 percent until 2020, it would be worth $299 billion (no taxes), an amount sufficient to repurchase most of New York City. Investing the $24 at 7.5 percent compounded annually, would produce over $81 trillion—an astronomical amount. However, at 4 percent it would have grown to only $150 million. The sale price in 1624 may have been an appropriate value for the land.

This is a dramatic example of the time value of money. Money, or "capital," has an opportunity cost related to time. Money received today is considered more valuable than the same money received at some time in the future, because today the money could be spent or, alternatively, invested at some interest rate to earn additional money. The investor/lender essentially requires that a financial "rent" be paid on their funds as current dollars are set aside today in anticipation of higher returns in the future.

The time value of money applies to many decisions. Understanding the effective rate on a business loan, the mortgage payment in a real estate transaction, or the value of an investment is dependent on understanding the time value of money. The mathematical concepts and calculations of the time value of money are developed in this chapter through several methods (your choice):

- Financial calculators (Appendix E for additional guidance on calculator functions)
- Tables (Appendixes A through D)
- Mathematical formulas

A calculator, set of tables, or computer are equivalent tools for time value calculations. However, to fully understand and be able to calculate values and interest rates, the student must visualize the timing patterns of the cash flows. This will provide the basis for solid financial decision making that will increase shareholder or investor value.

Visualization

A time line to identify expected cash flows and when they will occur is a helpful visualization technique to simplify a problem. Common to all time-value-of-money calculations are five variables. These are represented below on a time line:

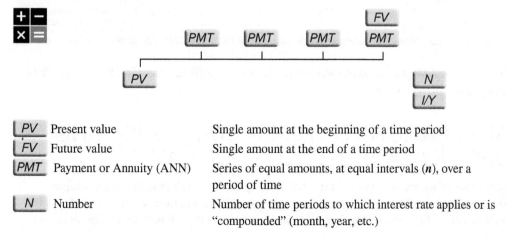

PV	Present value	Single amount at the beginning of a time period
FV	Future value	Single amount at the end of a time period
PMT	Payment or Annuity (ANN)	Series of equal amounts, at equal intervals (n), over a period of time
N	Number	Number of time periods to which interest rate applies or is "compounded" (month, year, etc.)

| I/Y | Interest rate (in %) | Interest, or rate of return, per period or per compounding period (n) |
| CPT | Compute (or **COMP**) | Initiates computation of one of the time value variables |

Calculator

A business calculator can capture any cash flow or series of cash flows over a period of time and be used to evaluate their value at a particular time (usually the present) or the relationship between the different cash flows expressed as an interest or rate of return. All business calculators have five keys corresponding to the variables identified on the above time line.

Additionally, calculators have a "begin" (BGN) or (DUE) key, which is used when cash flows occur at the beginning of a time period, such as with leases. Normally, tables (as in our appendices) or calculators assume that any cash flows occur at the end of time periods.

The +/− sign used for a cash flow will also be important for proper results. Calculators may vary in their "thinking," but there are some general considerations. It is helpful to think in terms of whether the investor (borrower) is receiving or paying out capital. For example, if an investor purchases an investment this is an outflow (negative cash flow) from which the investor expects inflows in the future (positive cash flows). The inputs for your calculation should reflect this consideration to achieve the appropriate answer.

Spreadsheet

An electronic spreadsheet can also be utilized for these calculations, especially when we want to repeat them with different variables.

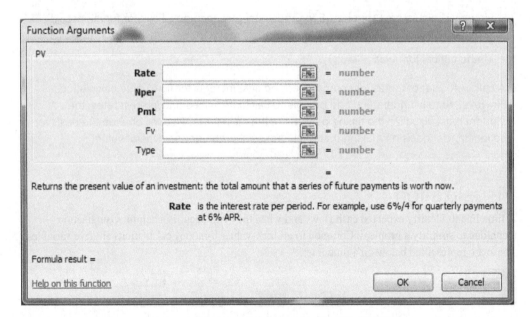

Type: A (1) achieves a result as one would with the BGN or DUE calculator key. Rate: is the *I/Y* key (as a percent) of the calculator.

APPLICATION TO THE CAPITAL BUDGETING DECISION AND THE COST OF CAPITAL

Time-value-of-money concepts and the calculations (present values and yields) of this chapter form the foundation for two of the most important considerations in finance and, ultimately, for the decisions of the firm. The *capital budgeting decision* involves the commitment (or not) of capital for an extended period of time and, therefore, focuses on the time value of money in today's terms (present value). The **capital structure decision**, which involves the appropriate mix of debt and equity for the firm, determines the **cost of capital** that is often used (with some adjustments) as the discount rate (yield) to evaluate the financial decisions of the firm.

Capital budgeting is essentially a cost-benefit analysis in that the costs (capital for new plant, equipment, or products) provide benefits (cash flows and earnings) over several future time periods. Decisions and analysis must evaluate whether the future benefits from these projects are sufficient to justify the current outlays. The mathematical tools of the time value of money are the first step toward making capital allocation decisions. This technique allows the evaluation of the present worth of these future benefits on the same terms as the current capital cost outlays.

LO1 To equate values that occur at different points in time in time-value-of-money calculations, a discount rate is required. The discount rate is also referred to as an interest rate, rate of return, yield, opportunity cost, or the cost of capital. It specifies a relationship between a value or series of values tomorrow and a value today (effectively, the future values are discounted). The interest rate or yield (cost) is the evaluation yardstick, often determined from the firm's cost of capital, which is employed to determine value and provide criteria in the acceptance or rejection of an investment proposal.

The Right Yardstick

From our Manhattan Island example, the choice of an appropriate discount rate, 6 or 7.5 percent, produces a significant difference in value, $200 billion versus $49 trillion. However, at 1 percent it would have amounted to only $1,186 ($56,000 at 2 percent). With no banks to pay interest, the $24 worth of trinkets was probably a good deal.

When working with the time-value-of-money, only values that are specified at the same time can be added or subtracted. (Doing otherwise is a common mistake.) The formulas and concepts to apply time-value-of-money considerations are now developed.

 FINANCE IN ACTION

Greece: Like Theseus Lifting the Boulder of Debt

In 2014, Greece had a debt level (approximately US$425 billion) of about 170 percent of GDP (approximately US$250 billion). Many were expressing concerns about its solvency, although the economy appeared to be on the road to recovery.

By 2020 national debt to GDP was 180 percent in Greece although Japan's ratio was 235 percent. The difference was most of Japanese debt was owed within the country. U.S. debt was 106 percent of GDP and Canada's was 88 percent, with provincial government debt included.

The time value of money reveals that the significance of Greece's debt load was overestimated in 2014. About half of the debt required no interest payments for 10 years. Greek bonds at that time called for a 5.8 percent interest rate over 10 years. In present value terms, this debt was worth about $121 billion, not $213 billion, effectively reducing the debt load to about $333 billion, or about 133 percent of GDP. Still significant but less severe!

By extending the maturities and lowering interest rates (sometimes to zero) on its debt, Greece was working to make its debt manageable. The time value of money helps us to identify the real value or cost of the debt.

Q1 What is the Greek debt situation today? How does its debt compare to other countries?

LO2 FUTURE VALUE (COMPOUND VALUE)— SINGLE AMOUNT

A future value is a measure of an amount that is allowed to grow at a given interest rate over a time period. The future value is also referred to as the compound value. Assume an investor has $1,000 and wishes to know its worth after four years if it grows at 10 percent per year. Each year the investor is credited with the interest earned so that, in subsequent years, interest is earned on interest. This is known as compounding, and the more frequently it occurs, the higher the future value. At the end of the first year, the investor will have $1,000 × 1.10, or $1,100. By the end of year two, the $1,100 will have grown to $1,210 ($1,100 × 1.10). The four-year pattern is indicated below.

1st year..............	$1,000 × 1.10 = $1,100
2nd year	$1,100 × 1.10 = $1,210
3rd year	$1,210 × 1.10 = $1,331
4th year..............	$1,331 × 1.10 = $1,464

After the fourth year, the investor has accumulated $1,464. Because compounding problems often cover a long time period, a more generalized formula is necessary to describe the compounding procedure. We shall let

$$FV = \text{Future value}$$
$$PV = \text{Present value}$$
$$i = \text{Interest rate}$$
$$n = \text{Number of periods}$$

The formula is[1]

$$FV = PV(1 + i)^n \quad \text{(9–1)}$$

In this case, PV = $1,000, i = 10 percent, and n = 4, so we have

$$FV = \$1,000(1.10)^4 = \$1,464$$

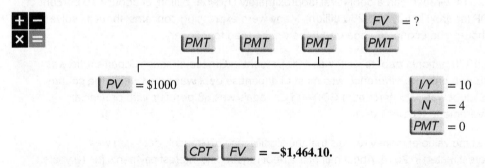

$$\boxed{CPT} \; \boxed{FV} = -\$1,464.10.$$

With the known variables input into the calculator, we compute FV = −$1,464.10. The result is negative (dependent on calculator) to indicate that $1,464.10 must be given up in the future to receive $1,000 today, or vice versa. We will often ignore the negative sign in our illustrations, as the meaning should be clear.

---

[1] All formulas are developed at the end of this chapter, in Appendix 9A.

The term $(1.10)^1$ is found to equal 1.464 by multiplying 1.10 by itself four times (the fourth power) or by using logarithms. Using an interest rate table, such as presented at the back of the text in Appendix A, can also reveal the future value of a dollar. With $n = 4$ and $i = 10$ percent, the value is also found to be 1.464.

The table also tells us the amount that $1 would grow to if it was invested for any number of periods at a given interest rate. We multiply this factor times any other amount to determine the future value.

In determining the future value, we will change our formula from $FV = PV(1 + i)^n$ to

$$FV = PV \times FV_{IF}$$
$$FV = 1,000 \times 1.464 = 1,464$$

where FV_{IF} equals the interest factor found in the table.

As another example, suppose $10,000 was invested for 10 years at 8 percent. The future value would be

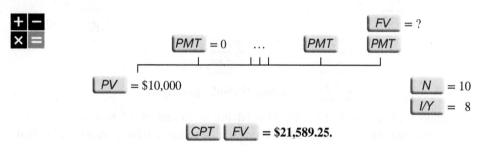

$$\boxed{CPT} \; \boxed{FV} = \$21,589.25.$$

ANNUAL INTEREST RATES—EFFECTIVE AND NOMINAL

Interest rates are most commonly expressed on an annual basis and we will accept that convention unless specified otherwise. However, it is not always clear whether or not an expressed interest rate has incorporated the effects of compounding. Again, unless specified otherwise, we will assume that compounding effects are included in an expressed interest rate. However, we should be able to adjust interest rates for compounding effects.

In the previous future value example, the investor earned an annual rate of interest of 10 percent. If we had simply multiplied the 10 percent annual rate of interest by the four years the monies were invested, we would get a 40 percent rate of return. This would be a return of $400. However, we would have missed the compounding effects of interest on interest. The 40 percent rate of return is referred to as a nominal rate of interest, an interest rate that does not capture the effects of compounding. Generally, at the end of a period of time, often a year, the investor receives interest and can reinvest it, along with the original investment, for another year. The investor will earn interest on interest as well as on the original investment.

In our example, after four years of reinvestment, $464 in interest was earned. Over the four-year period, this represents a 46.4 percent rate of return. This is the effective rate of interest, an interest rate that includes any compounding effects. An effective rate of interest is more informative because we can calculate the actual interest earned or, if we are borrowing, the actual cost of the loan.

When compounding is called for, a formula to calculate the effective rate of interest can be developed. At the end of the first compounding period, the return on the original investment plus the interest earned is given by the principal (1.00), representing 100 percent of the investment, and the interest rate (0.10) added together (1.00 + 0.10 = 1.10). This suggests 110 percent of the original investment value. This value is then raised to an exponent (4) representing the number of compounding periods. The original principal (1.00), which does not represent any return of interest, is then subtracted to isolate the effective interest rate or return of 46.4%. To demonstrate the increasing value of the investment (principal plus interest),

$$1.00 \times (1 + i) = (1 + i)^1$$
$$(1 + i)^1 \times (1 + i) = (1 + i)^1$$
$$(1 + i)^1 \times (1 + i) = (1 + i)^1$$
$$(1 + i)^1 \times (1 + i) = (1 + i)^1$$

Note the similarity to the future-value development in the previous section.

By formula, the effective interest rate is

$$(1 + i)^{n-1} = \textbf{Effective interest rate} \quad \textbf{(9–2)}$$

$$i = \text{Interest rate per compounding period}$$

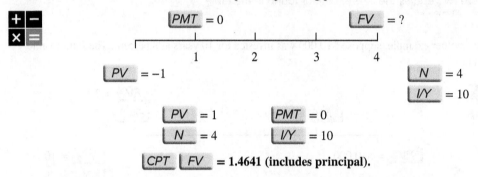

If we multiply our future value of 1.4641 by the original investment of $1,000 we get the value of $1,464.10, the same amount as derived in the previous section on future values. The $464.10 is 46.4 percent of the $1,000.

Interest rates are usually expressed as annual rates, but not all annual rates are equal. Quite often annual rates of interest are expressed as nominal rates and do not include the compounding effects that may be in effect. For example, an institution may quote a rate of 10 percent, compounded quarterly. Each quarter an investor will receive 2.5 percent on the investment. By formula,

$$(1 + i/m)^m - 1 = \textbf{Effective annual interest rate}$$

where

$$m = \text{Number of compounding periods per year}$$

For this example,

$$(1 + 0.10/4)^4 - 1 = 0.1038, \text{ or } 10.38\%$$

PV	= (1)	FV	= 1.025
PMT	= 0	N	= $\frac{1}{4}$

CPT I/Y = 10.38%

To find the accumulated future value with compounding,

PV	= −1	PMT	= 0
N	= 4	I/Y	= $\frac{10}{4}$

CPT FV = 1.1038 (includes principal).

The calculator will convert nominal annual interest rates to effective annual interest rates. Effective annual rates will be larger than nominal annual rates.

4 |2nd| |EFF→| 10 = 10.38
or
|2nd| {ICONV}
NOM = 10 |ENTER|
C/Y = 4 |ENTER|
EFF *CPT* = **10.38**

 FINANCE IN ACTION

Starting Salaries 50 Years from Now—Will $533,001 Be Enough?

The answer is probably yes if inflation averages 4 percent over the next 50 years. Over the last 50 years the inflation rate was about 4 percent range, so $533,001 might allow a postsecondary graduate to pay their bills in 50 years if inflation rates stay about the same. The $533,001 is based on a starting salary of $75,000 today and the future value of a dollar for 50 periods at 4 percent. Of course, $75,000 may be too low for some majors and too high for others.

Inflation in Canada actually was as high as 12.7 percent in 1981, although it has averaged slightly less than 2 percent since 2000. This has been the target of the Bank of Canada. Conversely, there were declining prices during the depression of the 1930s. Suppose inflation averaged 6 percent over the next 50 years; then, it would require $1,381,512 to replace a $75,000 salary today. At 10 percent inflation, the graduate would need to ask an employer for a starting salary of $8,804,314 in 50 years to be as well off as their predecessor of today. However, at 2 percent the salary would be only $201,869. Those in more popular majors would probably not take a penny under $8.8 million if inflation was 10 percent. Although 10 percent inflation seems high for Canada, in some countries it might be a happy occurrence, although worldwide inflation in 2019 was about 3.4 percent. In 2008, Zimbabwe's inflation rate exceeded 1 million percent, but was down to a more modest 170 percent in 2019. In 2019 Venezuela's inflation rate approached 300,000 percent annually.

The intent of this discussion is to demonstrate the effect of the time value of money. So far, all of the discussion has been forward looking. Now let's look back. How much would one of your grandparents have had to make 50 years ago to equal a $75,000 salary today, assuming a 4 percent rate of inflation? The answer is $10,553. The Bank of Canada's inflation target and the core inflation rate are provided at its website.

Q1 What is the latest inflation rate?

Q2 In 50 years, with this inflation rate, what will be equivalent to $100,000 today?

bankofcanada.ca

It is important that we distinguish between nominal and effective interest rates because, over time, they can represent a significant difference in the time value of money. Effective interest rates that include compounding effects give accurate results and allow us to better compare interest rates from different investments.

PRESENT VALUE (DISCOUNTED VALUE)—SINGLE AMOUNT

A present value, the opposite of a future value, is today's worth of a future amount. The concept of present value is that a sum payable in the future is worth less today than the stated amount.

Earlier, we determined that the future value of $1,000 for four periods at 10 percent was $1,464. We could reverse the process to state that $1,464 received four years into the future, with a 10 percent interest or discount rate, is worth only $1,000 today—its present value. The relationship is depicted in Figure 9–1.

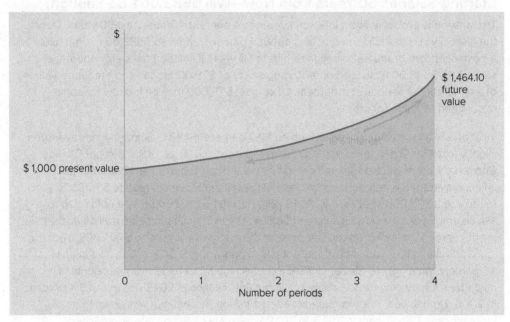

Figure 9–1 Relationship of present value and future value

The formula for present value is derived from the original formula for future value.

$$FV = PV(1 + i)^n \quad \textbf{Future value}$$

$$PV = FV\left[\frac{1}{(1+i)^n}\right] = FV(1 + i)^{-n} \quad \textbf{Present value} \quad (9\text{–}3)$$

$\boxed{FV} = -\$1,464.10$

$\boxed{PV} = ?$

$\boxed{I/Y} = 10$

$\boxed{N} = 4$

$\boxed{PMT} = 0$

$\boxed{CPT}\ \boxed{PV} = \$1,000.$

An inheritance of $50,000 might be expected 15 years from today at a time when interest rates for longer periods are 6 percent. The present value would be

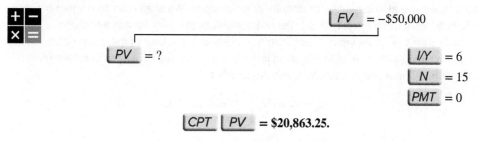

$$\boxed{FV} = -\$50,000$$

$$\boxed{PV} = ?$$

$$\boxed{I/Y} = 6$$
$$\boxed{N} = 15$$
$$\boxed{PMT} = 0$$

$$\boxed{CPT} \ \boxed{PV} = \$20,863.25.$$

FUTURE VALUE (CUMULATIVE FUTURE VALUE)—ANNUITY

An annuity may be defined as a series of consecutive payments or receipts of equal amount (generally assumed to occur at the end of each period). The future value of an annuity (FV_A) is a measure of the amount to which a series of consecutive payments grow, at a given interest rate over a time period.

If we invest $1,000 at the end of each year for four years and our funds grow at 10 percent, we find the future value of the annuity (Figure 9–2) to be $4,641. In a sense, we find the future value for each payment and then total them.

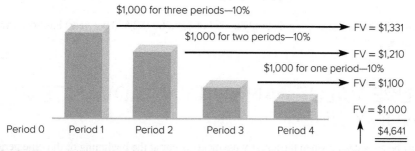

$1,000 for three periods—10% → FV = $1,331
$1,000 for two periods—10% → FV = $1,210
$1,000 for one period—10% → FV = $1,100
FV = $1,000

Period 0   Period 1   Period 2   Period 3   Period 4 $4,641

Figure 9–2 Compounding process for annuity

Although this is a four-period annuity, the first $1,000 comes at the end of the first period and has but three periods to run, the second $1,000 at the end of the second period, with two periods remaining—and so on down to the last $1,000 at the end of the fourth period. The final payment (period 4) is not compounded at all.

We shall let A = Series of equal payments. This will be PMT on most calculators. The formula for the future value of an annuity is as follows:

$$FV_A = A \left[\frac{(1+i)^n - 1}{i} \right] \quad \text{(9–4a)}$$

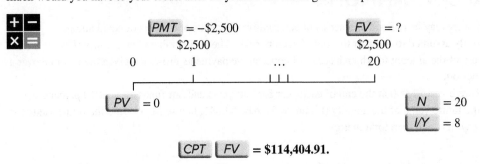

$$\boxed{PMT} = -\$1{,}000 \qquad\qquad \boxed{FV} = ?$$

| | $\$1,000$ | $\$1,000$ | $\$1,000$ | $\$1,000$ |

0   1   2   3   4

$\boxed{PV} = 0$

$\boxed{I/Y} = 10$

$\boxed{N} = 4$

$$\boxed{CPT} \ \boxed{FV} = \$4{,}641.00.$$

Suppose a wealthy relative offered to set aside \$2,500 a year for you for the next 20 years; how much would you have to your credit after 20 years if the funds grew at 8 percent?

$$\boxed{PMT} = -\$2{,}500 \qquad\qquad \boxed{FV} = ?$$

$\$2,500$ … $\$2,500$

0   1   …   20

$\boxed{PV} = 0$

$\boxed{N} = 20$

$\boxed{I/Y} = 8$

$$\boxed{CPT} \ \boxed{FV} = \$114{,}404.91.$$

A rather tidy sum, considering that only a total of \$50,000 (\$2,500 per year) has been invested over the 20 years.

FUTURE VALUE—ANNUITY IN ADVANCE (ANNUITY DUE)

There may be an occasion when the annuity payments occur at the beginning of the time period instead of the end, as we have assumed to this point. These earlier payments increase the future value because the payments have a longer time to earn interest. An annuity in advance places payments at the beginning of each period. This is also referred to as an annuity due. Some older calculators use this term rather than a "Begin" key. Annuity in advance tables are available, but a financial calculator handles the problem easily.

We shall let A_{BGN} = Series of equal payments at the beginning of each period.

The formula for the future value of an annuity (in advance) is as follows:

$$\textbf{(In advance) FV}_A = A_{\text{BGN}}\left[\frac{(1+i)^{n+1}-(1+i)}{i}\right] \quad \text{(9--4b)}$$

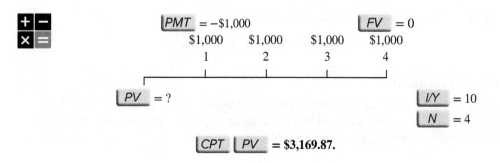

$\text{PMT} = -\$1{,}000$ $\text{FV} = ?$

| | $1,000 | $1,000 | $1,000 | $1,000 | |
| 0 | 1 | 2 | 3 | 4 |

$\text{PV} = 0$ $I/Y = 10$

$N = 4$

BGN key on (DUE key)

$$\text{CPT} \quad \text{FV} = \$5{,}105.10.$$

Also note that (in advance) $\text{FV}_A = \text{FV}_A \times (1+i)$.

Comparing to the calculation for formula 9--4a we obtain

$$\$5{,}105.10 = \$4{,}641 \times [1 + 0.10]$$

Tables (optional)

We note that this result could be obtained with the tables (Appendix C) with $n = 5$. This gives the factor 6.105, which is reduced by 1.000 to take account of the payment that does not occur at $t = 4$.

PRESENT VALUE (CUMULATIVE PRESENT VALUE)—ANNUITY

The present value of an annuity is today's worth of a series of consecutive payments, at a given interest rate over a time period. Each individual payment is discounted back to the present and then all of the discounted payments are added up, determining the present value of an annuity.

The formula for the present value of an annuity is as follows:

$$\text{PV}_A = A\left[\frac{1 - \dfrac{1}{(1+i)^n}}{i}\right] = A\left[\frac{1 - (1+i)^{-n}}{i}\right] \quad \text{(9--5a)}$$

An investment pays $1,000 a year for four years at a discount, or interest, rate of 10 percent. The present value of this annuity would be

$\text{PMT} = -\$1{,}000$ $\text{FV} = 0$

| | $1,000 | $1,000 | $1,000 | $1,000 |
| | 1 | 2 | 3 | 4 |

$\text{PV} = ?$ $I/Y = 10$

$N = 4$

$$\text{CPT} \quad \text{PV} = \$3{,}169.87.$$

A debt requires payment of $700 a year for 12 years at a discount, or interest, rate of 5 percent. The present value of this annuity would be

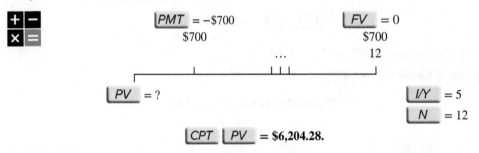

$PMT = -\$700$ $FV = 0$

$$CPT \quad PV = \$6,204.28.$$

PRESENT VALUE—ANNUITY IN ADVANCE

We may want to determine the value of an annuity when the first contribution is made immediately. Calculations follow as compared to the previous annuity, with the contributions at the end of each time period.

The formula for the present value of an annuity (in advance) or annuity due is as follows:

$$\textbf{(In advance) } PV_A = A_{BGN}\left[\frac{(1 + i) - \dfrac{1}{(1 + i)^{n-1}}}{i}\right] = A_{BGN}\left[\frac{(1 + i) - (1 + i)^{-n+1}}{i}\right] \quad \textbf{(9–5b)}$$

$PMT = -\$1,000$ $FV = 0$

$\$1,000$	$\$1,000$	$\$1,000$	$\$1,000$	0
0	1	2	3	4

$PV = ?$

$I/Y = 10$
$N = 4$
BGN key on (DUE key)

$$CPT \quad PV = \$3,486.85.$$

Also, note that (in advance) $PV_A = PV_A \times (1 + i)$.

Comparing to the calculation for formula 9–5a we obtain

$$\textbf{\$3,486.85 = \$3,169.87 \times [1 + .10]}$$

DETERMINING THE ANNUITY VALUE

In our prior discussion of annuities, we assumed the unknown variable was the future value or the present value—with specific information available on the annuity value (*A*), the interest rate, and the number of periods or years. In certain cases, our emphasis may shift to solving for one of these other values (on the assumption that future value or present value is given). For now we will concentrate on determining an unknown annuity rate.

Annuity Equalling a Future Value (Sinking-Fund Value)

Assuming we wish to accumulate $4,641 after four years at a 10 percent interest rate, how much must be set aside at the end of each of the four periods?

The formula for an annuity equal to a future value is as follows:

$$A = \text{FV}_A \left[\frac{i}{(1 + i)^n - 1} \right] \quad (9\text{–}6a)$$

PMT = ?				FV = −$4,641
	?	?	?	?
0	1	2	3	4

PV = 0

I/Y = 10
N = 4

CPT PMT = $1,000.

The solution is the exact reverse of that previously presented under the discussion of the future value of an annuity.

Tables (optional)

Or we could take the previously developed statement for the future value of an annuity and solve for *A*.

$$\text{FV}_A = A \times \text{FV}_{\text{IFA}}$$

$$A = \frac{\text{FV}_A}{\text{FV}_{\text{IFA}}}$$

The future value of an annuity is given as $4,641, and FV_{IFA} may be determined from Appendix C. Whenever you are working with an annuity problem relating to future value, you employ Appendix C, regardless of the variable that is unknown. For *n* = 4, and *i* = 10 percent, FV_{IFA} is 4.641. Thus, *A* equals $1,000.

$$A = \frac{\text{FV}_A}{\text{FV}_{\text{IFA}}} = \frac{\$4,641}{4.641} = \$1.000$$

As a second example, assume the director of the Women's Tennis Association must set aside an equal amount for each of the next 10 years to accumulate $100,000 in retirement funds, and that the return on deposited funds is 6 percent.

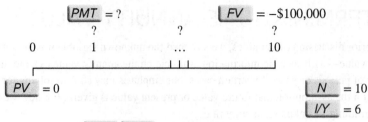

$$PMT = ?$$ $$FV = -\$100{,}000$$

	?	?	?
0	1	...	10

$$PV = 0$$

$$N = 10$$
$$I/Y = 6$$

$$CPT \quad PMT = \$7{,}586.80.$$

The formula for an annuity in advance equalling a future value is as follows:

$$A_{\text{BGN}} = \text{FV}_A \left[\frac{i}{(1+i)^{n+1} - (1+i)} \right] \qquad \text{(9–6b)}$$

For the same example as above, the required payment or annuity would be \$7,157.35. With the annuity in advance a smaller payment is required annually.

Annuity Equalling a Present Value (Capital Recovery Value)

In this instance, we assume that you know the present value and wish to determine what size annuity can be equated to that amount. Suppose your wealthy uncle presents you with \$10,000 now to help you get through the next four years of college or university. If you are able to earn 6 percent on deposited funds, how much can you withdraw at the end of each year for four years? We need to know the value of an annuity equal to a given present value.

The formula for an annuity equal to a present value is as follows:

$$A = \text{PV}_A \left[\frac{i}{1 - \dfrac{1}{(1+i)^n}} \right] = \text{PV}_A \left[\frac{i}{1 - (1+i)^{-n}} \right] \qquad \text{(9–7a)}$$

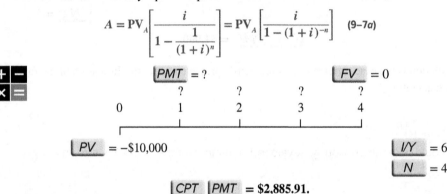

$$PMT = ?$$ $$FV = 0$$

	?	?	?	?
0	1	2	3	4

$$PV = -\$10{,}000$$

$$I/Y = 6$$
$$N = 4$$

$$CPT \quad PMT = \$2{,}885.91.$$

> **Tables (optional)**
>
> We can take the previously developed statement for the present value of an annuity and reverse it to solve for A.
>
> $$PV_A = A \times PV_{\text{IFA}}$$
>
> $$A = \frac{PV_A}{PV_{\text{IFA}}}$$
>
> The appropriate table is Appendix D (present value of an annuity). We determine an answer of \$2,886.
>
> $$A = \frac{PV_A}{PV_{\text{IFA}}} \ (n = 4,\ i = 6\%)$$
>
> $$A = \frac{\$10{,}000}{3.465} = \$2{,}886$$

The flow of funds would follow the pattern in Table 9–1. Annual interest is based on the beginning balance for each year.

Table 9–1 Relationship of Present Value to Annuity (rounding differences)

Year	Beginning Balance	Annual Interest (6 percent)	Annual Withdrawal	Ending Balance
1	$10,000.00	$600.00	$2,885.91	$7,714.09
2	7,714.09	462.85	2,885.91	5,291.03
3	5,291.03	317.46	2,885.91	2,722.58
4	2,722.58	163.35	2,885.91	0

The formula for an annuity in advance equalling a present value is as follows:

$$A_{BGN} = PV_A \left[\frac{i}{(1+i) - \dfrac{1}{(1+i)^{n-1}}} \right] = PV_A \left[\frac{i}{(1+i) - (1+i)^{-n+1}} \right] \quad (9\text{–}7b)$$

For the same example as above (formula 9–7a), the available payment or annuity would be $2,722.56, suggesting a lower annual payment, although received sooner.

The same process can be used to indicate necessary repayments on a loan. Suppose a homeowner signs a $40,000 mortgage to be repaid over 20 years at 8 percent interest. How much must they pay annually to eventually liquidate the loan? In other words, what annuity paid over 20 years is the equivalent of a $40,000 present value with an 8 percent interest rate? This assumes payments in arrears (9–7a).

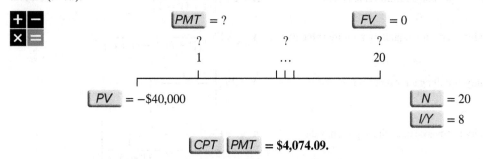

$$\boxed{PMT} = ? \qquad\qquad \boxed{FV} = 0$$

$$\boxed{PV} = -\$40,000 \qquad \boxed{N} = 20 \qquad \boxed{I/Y} = 8$$

$$\boxed{CPT}\ \boxed{PMT} = \$4,074.09.$$

Part of the payment to the mortgage company will go toward the payment of interest, with the remainder applied to debt reduction, as indicated in Table 9–2.

Table 9–2 Payoff table for loan (amortization table)

	1	2	3	4	(1 – 4)
Period	Beginning Balance	Annual Payment	Annual Interest (8 percent)	Repayment on Principal	Ending Balance
1	$40,000	$4,074	$3,200	$ 874	$39,126
2	39,126	4,074	3,130	944	38,182
3	38,182	4,074	3,055	1,019	37,163

If this same process is followed over 20 years, the balance will be reduced to zero. The student might note that the homeowner will pay over $41,000 of **interest** during the term of the loan, as indicated below.

Total payments ($4,074 for 20 years)	$ 81,480
Repayment of principal	−40,000
Payments applied to interest	$ 41,480

FORMULA SUMMARY

In our discussion thus far, we have considered the following time-value-of-money problems with our calculator, by formula, or with tables. In each case we knew three or four variables and solved for an unknown.

	Formula	Appendix
Future value—single amount (9–1)	$FV = PV(1 + i)^n$	A
Present value—single amount (9–3)	$PV = FV\left[\dfrac{1}{(1 + i)^n}\right]$	B
Future value—annuity (9–4a)	$FV_A = A\left[\dfrac{(1 + i)^n - 1}{i}\right]$	C
Future value—annuity in advance (9–4b)	$FV_A = A_{BGN}\left[\dfrac{(1 + i)^{n+1} - (1 + i)}{i}\right]$	—
Present value—annuity (9–5a)	$PV_A = A_{BGN}\left[\dfrac{1 - \dfrac{1}{(1 + i)^n}}{i}\right]$	D
Present value—annuity in advance (9–5b)	$PV_A = A\left[\dfrac{(1 + i) - \dfrac{1}{(1 + i)^{n-1}}}{i}\right]$	—
Annuity equalling a future value (9–6a)	$A = FV_A\left[\dfrac{i}{(1 + i)^n - 1}\right]$	C
Annuity in advance equalling a future value (9–6b)	$A_{BGN} = FV_A\left[\dfrac{i}{(1 + i)^{n+1} - (1 + i)}\right]$	—
Annuity equalling a present value (9–7a)	$A = PV_A\left[\dfrac{i}{1 - \dfrac{1}{(1 + i)^n}}\right]$	D
Annuity in advance equalling a present value (9–7b)	$A_{BGN} = PV_A\left[\dfrac{i}{(1 + i) - \dfrac{1}{(1 + i)^{n-1}}}\right]$	—

LO3 DETERMINING THE YIELD ON AN INVESTMENT

We will follow the prior procedure once again, but now the unknown variable will be i, the interest rate, yield, or return on the investment. Yield is a measure equating values across different time periods.

Yield—Present Value of a Single Amount

An investment producing $1,464 after four years has a present value of $1,000. What is the interest rate, or yield, on the investment?

The *I/Y* can also be used to determine the growth rate of an investment or pattern of payments over time.

The formula is as follows:

$$i = \left(\frac{FV}{PV}\right)^{\frac{1}{n}} - 1 \quad (9\text{–}8)$$

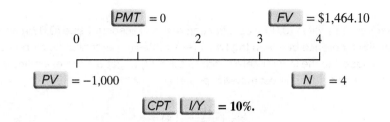

$$PMT = 0 \qquad\qquad FV = \$1,464.10$$

```
   0      1      2      3      4
```

$$PV = -1,000 \qquad\qquad N = 4$$

$$CPT \quad I/Y = 10\%.$$

Tables (optional)

We can also use the basic formula for the present value of a single amount and rearrange the terms.

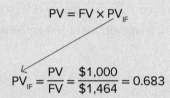

$$PV = FV \times PV_{IF}$$

$$PV_{IF} = \frac{PV}{FV} = \frac{\$1,000}{\$1,464} = 0.683$$

The determination of PV_{IF} does not give us the final answer, but it scales down the problem so that we may ascertain the answer from Appendix B. A portion of Appendix B is reproduced below.

Periods	1%	2%	3%	4%	5%	6%	8%	10%
2	0.980	0.961	0.943	0.925	0.907	0.890	0.857	0.826
3	0.971	0.942	0.915	0.889	0.864	0.840	0.794	0.751
4	0.961	0.924	0.888	0.855	0.823	0.792	0.735	0.683

Read down the left-hand column of the table until you have located the number of periods in question (in this case $n = 4$), and read across the table for $n = 4$ until you have located the computed value of PV_{IF} from above. We see that for $n = 4$ and PV_{IF} equal to 0.683, the interest rate, or yield, is 10 percent. This is the rate that will equate \$1,464 received in four years to \$1,000 today.

If a PV_{IF} value does not fall under a given interest rate, an approximation is possible. For example, with $n = 3$ and $PV_{IF} = 0.861$, 5 percent may be suggested as an approximate answer.

Interpolation may also be used to find a more precise answer. In the above example, we write out the two PV_{IF} values between which the designated PV_{IF} (0.861) falls and take the difference between the two.

PV_{IF} at 5%	0.864
PV_{IF} at 6%	0.840
	0.024

We then find the difference between the PV_{IF} value at the lowest interest rate and the designated PV_{IF} value.

PV_{IF} at 5%	0.864
PV_{IF} designated	0.861
	0.003

We next express this value (0.003) as a fraction of the preceding value (0.024) and multiply by the difference between the two interest rates (6 percent minus 5 percent). The value is added to the lower interest rate (5 percent) to get a more exact answer of 5.125 percent rather than the estimated 5 percent.

$$5\% + \frac{0.003}{0.024}(1\%) =$$

$$5\% + 0.125(1\%) =$$

$$5\% + 0.125\% = 5.125\%$$

Yield—Present Value of an Annuity

Assuming a $10,000 investment will produce $1,490 a year for the next 10 years, what is the yield on the investment?

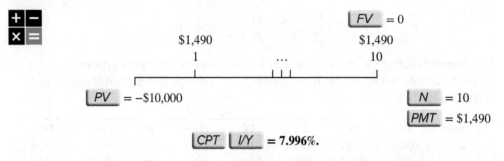

$$\boxed{PV} = -\$10,000 \qquad \boxed{N} = 10$$
$$\boxed{PMT} = \$1,490$$

$$\boxed{CPT}\ \boxed{I/Y} = 7.996\%.$$

Tables (optional)

Let's look at the present value of an annuity. Take the basic formula for the present value of an annuity, and rearrange the terms.

$$PV_A = A \times PV_{IF}$$

$$PV_{IFA} = \frac{PV_A}{FV}$$

The appropriate table is Appendix D (the present value of an annuity of $1).

$$PV_{IFA} = \frac{PV_A}{A} = \frac{\$10,000}{\$1,490} = 6.711$$

If the student will flip to Appendix D and read across the columns for $n = 10$ periods, they will see that the yield is 8 percent.

The same type of approximated or interpolated yield that applied to a single amount can also be applied to an annuity when necessary.

SPECIAL CONSIDERATIONS IN TIME VALUE ANALYSIS

We have assumed that interest was compounded or discounted on an annual basis. This assumption will now be relaxed. Contractual arrangements, such as an instalment purchase agreement or a corporate bond contract, may call for semiannual, quarterly, or monthly compounding periods. The adjustment to the normal formula is simple. To determine **n**, multiply the number of years by the number of compounding periods during the year. The factor for **i** is then determined by dividing the quoted annual interest rate by the number of compounding periods.

Case 1: Find the future value of a $1,000 investment after five years at 8 percent annual interest, compounded semiannually.

$$PMT = 0 \qquad FV = ?$$

0   5

$PV = -1,000$ Years = 5 $N = 10$

$$I/Y = \frac{8}{2} = 4\% \text{ per compounding period}$$

$CPT \quad FV = \$1,480.24.$

> ## Tables (optional)
>
> Since the problem calls for the future value of a single amount, the formula is $FV = PV \times FV_{IF}$. Using Appendix A for $n = 10$ and $i = 4$ percent, the answer is $1,480.
>
> $$FV = PV \times FV_{IF}$$
> $$FV = \$1,000 \times 1.480 = \$1,480$$

Case 2: Find the present value of 20 quarterly payments of $2,000 each to be received over the next five years. The stated interest rate is 8 percent per annum. The problem calls for the present value of an annuity.

$$FV = 0$$

$2,000 \quad \ldots \quad \$2,000$

0        $\ldots$ 5

$PV = ?$ Years = 5 $N = 20$

$$I/Y = 8/4 = 2\% \text{ per compounding period}$$

$$PMT = -\$2,000$$

$CPT \quad PV = \$32,702.87.$

> ## Tables (optional)
>
> We again follow the same procedure as in Case 1 in regard to *n* and *i*.
>
> $$PV_A = A \times PV_{IFA}(n = 20, i = 2\%)$$
> $$\text{(from Appendix D)}$$
> $$PV_A = \$2,000 \times 16.351 = \$32,702$$

Patterns of Payment

Time-value-of-money problems may evolve around a number of different payment or receipt patterns. Not every situation will involve a single amount or an annuity. For example, a contract may call for the payment of a different amount each year over a three-year period. To determine present value, each payment is discounted to the present and then summed. (Assume 8 percent discount rate.)

1.	$1,000	PV = $ 926
2.	2,000	PV = 1,715
3.	3,000	PV = 2,381
		$5,022

A more involved problem might include a combination of single amounts and an annuity. If the annuity will be paid at some time in the future, it is referred to as a deferred annuity, and it requires special treatment. Assume the same problem as above, but with an annuity of $1,000 that will be paid at the end of each year from the fourth through the eighth year. With a discount rate of 8 percent, what is the present value of the cash flows?

1.	$1,000	
2.	2,000	Present value = $5,022
3.	3,000	
4.	1,000	
5.	1,000	
6.	1,000	Five-year annuity
7.	1,000	
8.	1,000	

We know that the present value of the first three payments is $5,022, but what about the annuity? Let's diagram the five annuity payments.

Present value					A_1 $1,000	A_2 $1,000	A_3 $1,000	A_4 $1,000	A_5 $1,000
0	1	2	3		4	5	6	7	8

FV = 0 PMT = $1,000

N = 5 I/Y = 8

CPT PV = $3,992.71.

However, this result is discounted only to the beginning of the first stated period of an annuity—in this case the beginning of the fourth year, as diagrammed below.

				Beginning of fourth period				
Present value			$3,993	A_1 $1,000	A_2 $1,000	A_3 $1,000	A_4 $1,000	A_5 $1,000
0	1*	2	3	4	5	6	7	8

*Each number represents the end of the period; for example, 4 represents the end of the fourth period.

The $3,993 must finally be discounted back to the present. Since this single amount falls at the beginning of the fourth period—in effect, the equivalent of the end of the third period—we discount back for three periods at the stated 8 percent interest rate.

FV = $3,992.71 PMT = 0

N = 3 I/Y = 8

CPT PV = $3,169.54.

Therefore, this pattern of uneven payments is worth (present worth) $3,170. The last step in the discounting process is shown below.

				End of the third period—beginning of the fourth period				
$3,170 Present value		$3,993 (single amount)		A_1 $1,000	A_2 $1,000	A_3 $1,000	A_4 $1,000	A_5 $1,000
0	1	2	3	4	5	6	7	8

Calculator To calculate the present value of uneven cash flows, calculators have special function keys requiring the net present value concept. This is discussed in Appendix E.

Perpetuities

A perpetuity is an annuity or a series of payments that has no end date and seemingly goes on forever.

Equal Payments The formula for a perpetual annuity is as follows (payments at end of period):

$$PV = \frac{A}{i} = \frac{PMT}{i} \quad \text{(9–9)}$$

Assuming the receipt of $100 payment a year forever with an annual interest rate of 5 percent, the present value is

$$PV = \frac{\$100}{0.05} = \$2,000$$

If we assume a very large number for the number of periods (n), say 1,000, the calculator can be used in place of the formula.

$FV = 0$ $PMT = \$100$

$N = 1,000$ $I/Y = 5$

CPT $PV = \$2,000.$

Growing Payments The formula for a perpetual annuity growing at a constant rate (g) is as follows (payments at end of period):

$$PV = \frac{A_1}{i - g} \quad \text{(9–10)}$$

Assuming the receipt of a first payment of $100, growing at 3 percent annually forever and with an annual interest rate of 5 percent, the present value is

$$PV = \frac{\$100}{0.05 - 0.03} = \$5,000$$

If we assume a very large number for the number of periods (n) the calculator can be used in place of the formula.

$FV = 0$ $PMT = \$100$

$N = 1,000$ $I/Y = 5 - 3 = 2$

CPT $PV = \$5,000.$

Growing Annuity (with End Date)

The formula for an annuity growing at a constant rate (g) for a limited period of time (n) is as follows (payments at end of period):

$$PV_n = A_1 \left(\frac{1}{i-g}\right)\left[1 - \left(\frac{i+g}{1+i}\right)^n\right] \quad (9\text{-}11)$$

Assuming the receipt of a first payment of $100, growing at 3 percent annually for 10 years and with an annual interest rate of 5 percent, the present value is

$$PV = \$100\left(\frac{1}{0.05-0.03}\right)\left[1 - \left(\frac{1+0.03}{1+0.05}\right)^{10}\right]$$
$$= \$100(50)[1 - 0.8250481] = \$874.76$$

CANADIAN MORTGAGES

In Canada it is common to have mortgages that have interest compounded semiannually, with payments made monthly. The potential problem with blended payments of principal and interest made on a monthly basis is that the interest is being paid before it is actually due. Calculations must acknowledge the early payment of interest. We cannot just divide the semiannual interest rate by six. To adjust, we must calculate a monthly effective interest rate that, when compounded over a six-month period, is equivalent to the semiannual effective interest rate. It is with this monthly effective interest rate that we calculate the monthly payment.

Say the interest rate offered at the bank is 8 percent annually. Therefore, the rate for six months is 4 percent (8/2). We now need a rate that, when compounded six times, will equal 4 percent; by formula $(1 + i)^1 = 1.04$. Solving for i gives us 0.6558 percent.

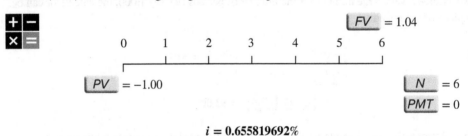

$$i = 0.655819692\%$$

Also with EFF→ (dependent on calculator)

$$6 \boxed{\text{2nd}} \boxed{\text{EFF→}} 4 = 3.9349174 \quad \textbf{(6-month equivalent)}$$

$$\left(\begin{array}{c}\textbf{number of payment periods} \\ \textbf{in compounding period}\end{array}\right)\left(\frac{\textbf{six-month}}{\textbf{Interest rate}}\right)$$

Then divide by 6:

$$\frac{3.9349174}{6} = .6558196 \text{ \% (monthly effective interest rate)}$$

We begin with 1, and six months later it is 1.04. We have determined the interest rate for one of the six periods, a monthly effective interest rate.

Now we can calculate the monthly payment on the mortgage. Suppose the mortgage is for $80,000, to be paid off over 20 years at our interest rate of 8 percent annually.

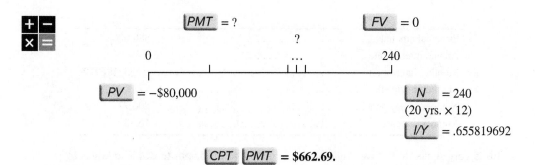

$$\boxed{PMT} = ? \qquad\qquad \boxed{FV} = 0$$

$$?$$

$$0 \qquad\qquad \dots \qquad\qquad 240$$

$$\boxed{PV} = -\$80{,}000 \qquad\qquad \boxed{N} = 240$$
$$(20 \text{ yrs.} \times 12)$$
$$\boxed{I/Y} = .655819692$$

$$\boxed{CPT}\ \boxed{PMT} = \textbf{\$662.69.}$$

With this calculation, the outstanding principal is the present value (PV) of the remaining payments.

FINANCE IN ACTION

Is a Weekly Mortgage a Good Idea?

The banks often promote the weekly mortgage as a great way to pay off your mortgage early. It is suggested that you can reduce the time to pay off a mortgage by perhaps four to five years, depending on circumstances. However, do these claims identify the complete picture?

We have noted that a mortgage for $80,000 paid monthly over 20 years at an 8 percent interest rate would require a monthly payment of $662.69. If you were to pay weekly, the bank would likely take that monthly payment and divide by four to represent the weeks in a month. The weekly payment will therefore be $165.67. Some banks do identify this as an accelerated payment schedule.

Principal amount	$80,000
Annual interest rate	8%
Weekly interest rate	0.15096273%*
Weekly payment	$165.67
Number of payments	865.48
Number of years	16.64

$*\left(1 + \dfrac{0.08}{2}\right)^{26} -1 \times 100\%$ For 26 weeks in a six-month period.

Sounds great until the situation is examined more closely. With weekly payments a mortgagee is actually making an extra monthly payment each year.

Weekly	$52 \times \$165.67 = \$8{,}614.84$
Monthly	$12 \times \$662.69 = \underline{7{,}952.28}$
Extra payment	$ 662.56

Presumably, if a homeowner can afford $8,614.84 as weekly payments over one year, the homeowner could pay the same amount as monthly payments. In that case the monthly payment would be $717.90.

Principal amount	$80,000
Annual interest rate	8%
Monthly interest rate	0.655819691%
Monthly payment	$717.90
Number of payments	200.77
Number of years	16.73

This is very similar to the weekly plan. So what is a homeowner to do? The key is to match your cash inflows with your cash outflows. A mortgage is the major obligation (outflow) for most people, and salary the major inflow. If the homeowner is paid monthly, take out a monthly mortgage! If the homeowner is paid weekly, take out a weekly mortgage! Otherwise, cash flows to the household will be inefficiently allocated. The homeowner with a weekly mortgage, but monthly pay, would be forced to save money from each pay to meet the weekly obligation or, even worse, to borrow until the next monthly pay period. The best strategy for the homeowner is to determine the largest payment out of each pay that can be afforded and to match the amortization period and payment period to that payment.

A FINAL NOTE

The key foundation tool of financial management is the ability to understand and to calculate the time value of money. Value is determined by the ability to generate cash flows. The time value of money allows us to properly value cash flows that occur at different points in time. Therefore, it is essential that the student of finance be able to comfortably handle the problems of this chapter.

SUMMARY

1. The time value of money suggests that a dollar today is worth more than a dollar tomorrow. Alternatively, a dollar invested today will grow to a larger value tomorrow. Through the discounting technique, that dollar tomorrow is equated (discounted) to a value today. Discounting values to a common time period allows for comparison. (LO1)

2.,3. In working a time-value-of-money problem, the student should determine, first, whether the problem deals with future value, present value or yield and, second, whether a single sum or an annuity is involved. The major calculations in Chapter 9 are summarized below in case a calculator is not used. (LO2) (LO3)

REVIEW OF FORMULAS

A. *Future value of a single amount.*

Formula: $FV = PV(1+i)^n$ (9–1)

Appendix A

When to use: In determining the future value for a single amount.

Sample problem: You invest $1,000 for four years at 10 percent interest. What is the value at the end of the fourth year?

B. *Effective interest rate.*

Formula: $(1+i)^n - 1 = $ Effective interest rate   (9–2)

When to use: In determining an interest rate that captures interest compounding.

C. *Present value of a single amount.*

Formula: $PV = FV\left[\dfrac{1}{(1+i)^n}\right] = FV(1+i)^{-n}$ (9–3)

Appendix B

When to use: In determining the present value of an amount to be received in the future.

Sample problem: You will receive $1,000 after four years at a discount rate of 10 percent. How much is this worth today?

D. *Future value of an annuity.*

Formula: $FV_A = A\left[\dfrac{(1+i)^n - 1}{i}\right]$ (9–4a)

Appendix C

When to use: In determining the future value of a series of consecutive, equal payments (an annuity).

Sample problem: You will receive $1,000 at the end of each period for four periods.

What is the accumulated value (future worth) at the end of the fourth period if money grows at 10 percent?

When the payments are at the beginning of each period:

Formula: $FV_A = A_{BGN}\left[\dfrac{(1+i)^{n+1} - (1+i)}{i}\right]$ (9–4b)

E. Present value of an annuity.

Formula: $PV_A = A \left[\dfrac{1 - \dfrac{1}{(1+i)^n}}{i} \right] = A \left[\dfrac{1 - (1+i)^n}{i} \right]$ (9–5a)

Appendix D

When to use: In determining the present worth of an annuity.

Sample problem: You will receive $1,000 at the end of each period for four years. At a discount rate of 10 percent, what is the current worth?

When the payments are at the beginning of each period:

Formula: $PV_A = A_{BGN} \left[\dfrac{(1+i) - \dfrac{1}{(1+i)^{n-1}}}{i} \right] = A_{BGN} \left[\dfrac{(1+i) - (1+i)^{-n+1}}{i} \right]$ (9–5b)

F. Annuity equalling a future value.

Formula: $A = FV_A \left[\dfrac{i}{(1+i)^n - 1} \right]$ (9–6a)

Appendix C

When to use: In determining the size of an annuity that will equal a future value.

Sample problem: You need $1,000 after four periods. With an interest rate of 10 percent, how much must be set aside at the end of each period to accumulate this amount?

When the payments are at the beginning of each period:

Formula: $A_{BGN} = FV_A \left[\dfrac{i}{(1+i)^{n+1} - (1+i)} \right]$ (9–6b)

G. Annuity equalling a present value.

Formula: $A = PV_A \left[\dfrac{i}{1 - \dfrac{1}{(1+i)^n}} \right] = PV_A \left[\dfrac{i}{1 - (1+i)^{-n}} \right]$ (9–7a)

Appendix D

When to use: In determining the size of an annuity equal to a given present value.

Sample problems:

a. What four-year annuity is the equivalent of $1,000 today with an interest rate of 10 percent?

b. You deposit $1,000 today and wish to withdraw funds equally over four years. How much can you withdraw at the end of each year if funds earn 10 percent?

c. You borrow $1,000 for four years at 10 percent interest. How much must be repaid at the end of each year?

When the payments are at the beginning of each period:

Formula: $A_{BGN} = PV_A \left[\dfrac{i}{(1+i) - \dfrac{1}{(1+i)^{n-1}}} \right] = PV_A \left[\dfrac{i}{(1+i) - (1+i)^{-n+1}} \right]$ (9–7b)

H. Determining the yield on an investment.

Formulas	Tables
a. $i = \left(\dfrac{FV}{PV}\right)^{\frac{1}{n}} - 1$ (9–8)	Appendix B Yield—present value of a single amount
b. Interpolation required	Appendix D Yield—present value of an annuity

When to use: In determining the interest rate (i) that will equate an investment with future benefits.

Sample problem: You invest $1,000 now, and the funds are expected to increase to $1,360 after four periods.

What is the yield on the investment?

I. Less than annual compounding periods.

Semiannual	Multiply $n \times 2$	Divide i by 2	Then use normal formula
Quarterly	Multiply $n \times 4$	Divide i by 4	
Monthly	Multiply $n \times 12$	Divide i by 12	

When to use: If the compounding period is more (or perhaps less) frequent than once a year.

Sample problem: You invest $1,000 compounded semiannually at 8 percent per annum over four years.

Determine the future value.

J. Patterns of payment—deferred annuity.

Formulas	Tables
$PV_A = A\left[\dfrac{1 - \dfrac{1}{(1+i)^n}}{i}\right] = A\left[\dfrac{1 - (1+i)^{-n}}{i}\right]$	Appendix D
$PV = FV\left[\dfrac{1}{(1+i)^n}\right] = FV(1+i)^{-n}$	Appendix B

When to use: If an annuity begins in the future.

Sample problem: You will receive $1,000 per period, starting at the end of the fourth period and running through the end of the eighth period. With a discount rate of 8 percent, determine the present value.

K. Perpetuity.

Formula: $PV = \dfrac{A}{i} = \dfrac{PMT}{i}$ (9–9)

L. Perpetuity growing at a constant rate (g).

Formula: $PV = \dfrac{A_1}{i - g}$ (9–10)

M. Growing annuity (with end date).

Formula: $PV_n = A_1\left(\dfrac{1}{i - g}\right)\left[1 - \left(\dfrac{1+g}{1+i}\right)^n\right]$ (9–11)

Use a time line to set up the problem.

Use $\boxed{I/Y}$ =, $\boxed{N}$ =, $\boxed{PV}$ =, $\boxed{FV}$ =, $\boxed{PMT}$ = .

Input the known values for the above, including a zero if necessary (this ensures memory is cleared). Calculate the unknown value.

The student is encouraged to work on the many problems found at the end of the chapter.

DISCUSSION QUESTIONS

1. How is the future value (Appendix A) related to the present value of a single sum (Appendix B)? (LO2)

2. How is the present value of a single sum (Appendix B) related to the present value of an annuity (Appendix D)? (LO2)

3. Why does money have a time value? (LO1)

4. Does inflation have anything to do with making a dollar today worth more than a dollar tomorrow? (LO1)

5. Adjust the annual formula for a future value of a single amount at 12 percent for 10 years to a semiannual compounding formula. What are the interest factors (FV_{IF}) for the two assumptions? Why are they different? (LO2)

6. If, as an investor, you had a choice of daily, monthly, or quarterly compounding, which would you choose? Why? (LO3)

7. What is a deferred annuity? (LO2)

8. List five different financial applications of the time value of money. (LO1, LO2)

9. Discuss why the compounding of interest within a tax-sheltered plan is so effective, as opposed to paying taxes each year. (LO1)

INTERNET RESOURCES AND QUESTIONS

The Financial Consumer Agency of Canada under the Government of Canada protects rights and provides financial education for consumers. It has a website with several financial tools for time value calculations, including a mortgage calculator.

www.canada.ca/en/services/finance/tools.html

The Bank of America provides a mortgage calculator for U.S. mortgages: www.bankofamerica.com/mortgage/mortgage-calculator

The Canadian banks have sites that have mortgage calculators. The Royal Bank calculator has a breakdown for weekly and biweekly accelerated mortgage payments: rbcroyalbank.com/mortgages/index.html

The Bank of Montreal site, under tools and calculators, has a mortgage calculator: bmo.com/main/personal/mortgages/calculators#

1. Problems 59 to 62 in this chapter include mortgage calculations. After you have completed these problems, use a mortgage calculator such as the one available at a site listed above to redo the calculations. Are the results the same, and, if not, why is there a difference?

2. Redo the above calculations using a mortgage calculator from a U.S. financial institution. Why is there a difference in the numbers calculated?

PROBLEMS

1. What is the present value of
   a. $8,000 in 10 years at 6 percent?
   b. $16,000 in 5 years at 12 percent?
   c. $25,000 in 15 years at 8 percent?
   d. $1,000 in 40 years at 20 percent?

2. You will receive $6,800 three years from now. The discount rate is 10 percent.

   a. What is the value of your investment two years from now?

   b. What is the value of your investment one year from now?

   c. What is the value of your investment today?

3. If you invest $12,000 today, how much will you have

   a. in 6 years at 7 percent?

   b. in 15 years at 12 percent?

   c. in 25 years at 10 percent?

   d. in 25 years at 10 percent (compounded semiannually)?

4. You invest $3,000 for three years at 12 percent.

   a. What is the value of your investment after one year?

   b. What is the value of your investment after two years?

   c. What is the value of your investment after three years?

   d. What is the future value of $3,000 in 3 years at 12 percent interest?

5. How much would you have to invest today to receive

   a. $12,000 in 6 years at 12 percent?

   b. $15,000 in 15 years at 8 percent?

   c. $5,000 each year for 10 years at 8 percent?

   d. $5,000 each year, at the beginning, for 10 years at 8 percent?

   e. $50,000 each year for 50 years at 7 percent?

   f. $50,000 each year for 50 years, at the beginning, at 7 percent?

6. If you invest $8,000 per period for the following number of periods, how much would you have?

   a. 10 years at 5 percent

   b. 20 years at 9 percent

   c. 35 periods at 11 percent

7. Rework the previous problem, assuming that the $8,000 per period is received at the beginning of each year. (Annuity in advance)

8. You invest a single amount of $20,000 for 6 years at 7 percent. At the end of 6 years you take the proceeds and invest them for 8 years at 10 percent. How much will you have after 14 years?

9. Delia has a choice between $30,000 in 50 years or $650 today. If long-term rates are 8 percent, what should be her choice?

10. "Red" Herring will receive $11,000 a year for the next 18 years as a result of his patent. At present, 9 percent is an appropriate discount rate.

    a. Should he be willing to sell out his future rights now for $100,000?

    b. Would he be willing to sell his future rights now for $100,000, if the payments will be made at the beginning of each year?

11. Phil Goode will receive $175,000 in 50 years. Sounds great! However if current interest rates suggested for discounting are 14 percent, what is the present worth of his future "pot of gold"?

12. Carrie Tune will receive $18,000 a year for the next 20 years as payment for a song she has just written. If a present 10 percent discount rate is applied,

    a. Should she be willing to sell out her future rights now for $160,000?

    b. Would she be willing to sell her future rights now for $160,000, if the payments will be made at the beginning of each year?

13. George Penny will receive $32,250 for the next 10 years as a payment for a slogan he coined. Currently a 6 percent discount rate is appropriate.

    a. Should he be willing to sell his future rights now for $240,000?

    b. Should he be willing to sell his future rights now for $240,000, if payments will be made at the beginning of the year?

14. The Epic Contest awards $10,000,000. It will be paid over the next 50 years at the rate of $250,000 per year with the first payment today. With a discount rate of 9 percent, what is the present value of this prize?

15. Joan Lucky won the $80 million lottery. She is to receive $1 million a year for the next 50 years plus an additional lump-sum payment of $30 million after 50 years. The discount rate is 12 percent. What is the current value of her winnings?

16. Larry Doby invests $50,000 in a mint condition 1952 "Rocket" Richard Topps hockey card. He expects the card to increase in value 8 percent per year for the next five years. How much will his card be worth after five years?

17. Dr. Sisters has been secretly depositing $10,500 in her savings account every December starting in 2009. Her account earns 6 percent compounded annually. How much did she have in December 2021? (Assume a deposit is made in the last year) Make sure to carefully count the years.

18. At a growth (interest) rate of 8 percent annually, how long will it take for a sum to double? To triple? Select the year that is closest to the correct answer.

19. If you owe $30,000 at the end of seven years, how much should your creditor accept in payment immediately if she could earn 11 percent on her money?

20. Jack Hammer invests in a stock that will pay dividends of $2.00 at the end of the first year; $2.20 at the end of the second year; and $2.40 at the end of the third year. Also at the end of the third year he believes he will be able to sell the stock for $33. What is the present value of these future benefits if a discount rate of 11 percent is applied?

21. S. Ken Flint retired as president of Colour Tile Company, but he is currently on a consulting contract for $45,000 per year for the next 10 years.

    a. If Mr. Flint's opportunity cost (potential return) is 10 percent, what is the present value of his consulting contract?

    b. Assuming Mr. Flint will not retire for two more years and will not start to receive his 10 payments until the end of the third year, what would be the value of his deferred annuity?

    c. Recalculate part *a* assuming the contract stipulates that payments are to be made at the beginning of each year.

22. Cousin Berta invested $100,000 10 years ago at 12 percent, compounded quarterly.

    a. How much has she accumulated?

    b. What is her effective annual interest rate (rate of return)?

23. Determine the amount of money in a savings account at the end of five years, given an initial deposit of $3,000 and an 8 percent annual interest rate when interest is compounded (a) annually, (b) semiannually, and (c) quarterly. Calculate the effective annual interest rate of each compounding possibility.

24. Joe Macro wishes to have accumulated $60,000 10 years from today by making an equal annual deposit into an account that pays 10 percent, compounded quarterly.

    a. What is the effective annual interest rate?

    b. How large an annual deposit is required to meet Joe's objective?

    c. How large an annual deposit is required if the deposits are made at the beginning of each year?

25. Sally Gravita has received a settlement from an insurance company that will pay her $23,500 annually for 12 years. Current interest rates are 8 percent, compounded semiannually.

    a. What is the effective annual interest rate?

    b. How much is the present worth of Sally's settlement?

    c. How much is the present worth of Sally's settlement if payments are made at the beginning of each year?

26. Your grandfather has offered you a choice of one of the three following alternatives: $5,000 now; $1,000 a year for eight years; or $12,000 at the end of eight years. Assuming you could earn 11 percent annually, which alternative would you choose? If you could earn 12 percent annually, would you still choose the same alternative?

27. You need $23,000 at the end of 7 years, and your only investment outlet is a 9 percent long-term certificate of deposit (compounded annually). With the certificate of deposit, you make an initial investment at the beginning of the first year.

    a. What single payment could be made at the beginning of the first year to achieve this objective?

    b. What amount could you invest at the end of each year annually for 7 years to achieve this same objective?

28. Carol Travis started a paper route on January 1, 2020. Every three months, she deposits $500 in her bank account, which earns 4 percent annually but is compounded quarterly. On December 31, 2023, she used the entire balance in her bank account to invest in a contract that pays 9 percent annually. How much will she have on December 31, 2026?

29. On January 1, 2016, Charley Dow bought 1,000 shares of stock at $12 per share. On December 31, 2018, he sold the stock for $18 per share. What was his annual rate of return?

30. April Wine bought 425 shares of stock at $5.50 per share. Four years later she sold the stock for $21 per share. What was her annual growth rate (rate of return, ROR) for her capital?

31. Al Counsel purchased 357 shares of Eco-Survival Tours on July 1, 2016 for $5.00 per share. Find his annual rate of return if he sold the stock

    a. On June 30, 2017, for $6.00 per share.

    b. On December 31, 2019, for $10.92 per share.

    c. On June 30, 2022, for $8.39 per share.

32. John Foresight has just invested $8,370 for his son (age one). The money will be used for his son's education 17 years from now. He calculates that he will need $90,000 for his son's education by the time the boy goes to school. What rate of return will Mr. Foresight need to achieve this goal?

33. Chris Seals has just given an insurance company $56,521. In return, she will receive an annuity of $7,500 for 12 years.

    a. At what rate of return must the insurance company invest this $56,521 to make the annual payments?

    b. What rate of return is required if the annuity is payable at the beginning of each year?

34. Mr. G. Day has approached his bank about a loan. He expects to receive $30,000 in three years and $85,000 nine years from now. These funds will be applied against the loan as they are received. The bank suggests that interest rates will be 9 percent for the next five years and 7 percent in subsequent years. Calculate the maximum amount Mr. G. Day can borrow.

35. Ms. R. Emm has purchased land for $90,000 in cash today and another $45,000 four years from today. Interest rates over a four-year period are currently 8 percent, compounded semiannually. Calculate the cash value of the property.

36. Count Crow wishes to have a large celebration eight years from today costing $150,000. Currently, he has an investment of $625,000 in a financial institution earning 7.5 percent interest annually. Count Crow also wishes to receive an annual payment from his investment over this period at the beginning of each year starting today. Calculate how much of an annual payment the Count can expect.

37. Graham Bell has just retired after 30 years with the telephone company. His total pension funds have an accumulated value of $300,000, and his life expectancy is 16 more years. His pension fund manager assumes he can earn a 7 percent return on his assets. What will be his yearly annuity for the next 16 years?

38. River Babylon, an archaeology professor, invests $65,000 in a parcel of land that is expected to increase in value by 8 percent per year for the next five years. He will take the proceeds and provide himself with a 12-year annuity. Assuming a 9 percent interest rate, how much will this annuity be?

39. Una Day is planning to retire in 20 years, at which time she hopes to have accumulated enough money to receive an annuity of $12,000 a year for 25 years of retirement. During her pre-retirement period she expects to earn 8 percent annually, while during retirement she expects to earn 10 percent annually on her money. What annual contributions to this retirement fund are required for Una to achieve her objective and sleep well at night?

40. Louisa and Bart are twins, aged 20. Advanced for their age in some respects, they were both working and also planning their financial future. Both felt they could commit $5,000 per year for their retirement expected at age 65.

    However, Louisa planned to start right away on her commitment by investing $5,000 per year in her tax-free savings account for the next 15 years and then make no further commitment to this account until she reached retirement at age 65 (thirty years). She would leave her money in the tax-free account, accumulating interest during this 30-year period.

    Bart, on the other hand, was going to spend freely for the next 15 years and then make his commitment of $5,000 per year to the tax-free savings account for the following 30 years, until his retirement at age 65.

    a. How much would Louisa and Bart have in their tax-free retirement account if yields (interest rates) are 10 percent throughout their lifetime?

    b. How much would Louisa and Bart have in their tax-free retirement account if yields (interest rates) are 3 percent throughout their lifetime?

41. You wish to retire after 30 years, at which time you want to have accumulated enough money to receive an annuity of $55,000 a year for 18 years of retirement. During the period before retirement, you can earn 9 percent annually, while after retirement you can earn 7 percent on your money.

    a. What annual contributions to the retirement fund will allow you to receive the $55,000 annually?

    b. What annual contributions are required if the contributions are made at the beginning of each year?

42. Your retirement planning suggests a goal of $57,000 a year in today's dollars for 30 years of retirement. Retirement will begin 35 years from today, at which time you will expect your first annuity payment. Inflation between now and retirement is expected to be 4 percent annually (do not consider inflation during retirement). The anticipated yield over the pre-retirement

period is 7 percent annually, and 8 percent per annum is anticipated during retirement. Calculate how much you should set aside each year between now and retirement to achieve your goal. (Ignore taxes.)

43. For your retirement you would like to receive $75,000 a year in today's dollars for a period of 25 years. A problem, of course, is that you expect inflation to average 2.5 percent a year for the next 33 years until your retirement. (Inflation will not be a concern during retirement.) Interest rates (borrowing rates equal lending rates in this perfect market without taxes) are expected to be 7 percent until retirement and 5 percent during retirement. Your first retirement annuity is to be received 33 years from today, and your first contribution to your retirement will be at the end of this year and will be made 33 times. You will also require $125,000 (do not inflate) from your retirement funds in 17 years for a sabbatical that you are planning. Calculate the equal annual (33) contributions to your retirement fund required for this all to happen.

44. Del Monty will receive the following payments at the end of the next three years: $2,000, $3,500, and $4,500. Then from the end of the fourth year through the end of the tenth year, he will receive an annuity of $5,000 per year. At a discount rate of 9 percent, what is the present value of these future benefits?

45. Bridget Jones has a contract in which she will receive the following payments for the next five years: $1,000, $2,000, $3,000, $4,000, $5,000. She will then receive an annuity of $8,500 a year from the end of the sixth year through the end of the fifteenth year. The appropriate discount rate is 14 percent. If she is offered a buyout of the contract for $30,000, should she do it?

46. Darla White has just purchased an annuity to begin payment at the end of 2024 (that is the date of the first payment). Assume it is now the beginning of 2021. The annuity is for $12,000 per year and is designed to last 8 years. If the interest rate for this problem is 11 percent, what is the most she should have paid for the annuity?

47. Emphatically Square and heirs will receive $1,000 a year forever with a long-term annual expected interest rate of 7 percent. What is the current worth of this annuity?

48. Forever College will provide a scholarship of $7,500 a year forever with a long-term annual expected interest rate of 6 percent. What is the current worth of this annuity?

49. On second thought, Emphatically Square and heirs will receive $1,000 a year forever that will grow by 3 percent annually. The long-term annual expected interest rate is 7 percent. What is the current worth of this annuity?

50. On third thought, Forever College will provide a scholarship of $7,500 a year forever, growing in value by 2 percent per year. The long-term annual expected interest rate is 6 percent. What is the current worth of this annuity?

51. On fourth thought, Emphatically Square and heirs will receive $1,000 a year for only 25 years, but it will grow by 3 percent annually. The long-term annual expected interest rate is 7 percent. What is the current worth of this annuity?

52. On fifth thought, Forever College will provide a scholarship of $7,500 a year for only 30 years, growing in value by 2 percent per year. The long-term annual expected interest rate is 6 percent. What is the current worth of this annuity?

53. For your retirement you would like to receive the equivalent of $90,000 a year in today's dollars for a period of 30 years. You expect inflation to average 3 percent a year for the next 70 years. Yields (borrowing rates equal lending rates in this perfect market without taxes) are expected to be 5 percent until retirement and 4 percent during retirement. Your first retirement annuity is to be received 40 years from today and your first contribution to your retirement will be at the end of this year and will be made 40 times. You will also require $250,000 (do not inflate) from your retirement funds in 10 years for an anniversary bash that you are planning. Calculate the equal annual (40) contributions to your retirement fund required for this all to happen.

54. If you borrow $9,725 and are required to pay back the loan in five equal annual instalments of $2,500, what is the interest rate associated with the loan?

55. Sarah Adia owes $15,000 now. A lender will carry the debt for three more years at 8 percent interest. That is, in this particular case, the amount owed will go up by 8 percent per year for three years. The lender then will require that Sarah pay off the loan over the next 5 years at 9 percent interest. What will her annual payment be?

56. If your uncle borrows $50,000 from the bank at 10 percent interest over the eight-year life of the loan, what equal annual payments must be made to discharge the loan, plus pay the bank its required rate of interest (round to the nearest dollar)? How much of his first payment will be applied to interest? To principal? How much of his second payment will be applied to each?

57. Jim Thomas borrows $70,000 at 12 percent interest toward the purchase of a home. His mortgage is for 30 years.
    a. How much will his annual payments be? (Although home payments are usually on a monthly basis, we shall do our analysis on an annual basis for ease of computation. We get a reasonably accurate answer.)
    b. How much interest will he pay over the life of the loan?
    c. How much should he be willing to pay to get out of a 12 percent mortgage and into a 10 percent mortgage with 30 years remaining on the mortgage? Assume current interest rates are 10 percent. Carefully consider the time value of money. Disregard taxes.

58. Larry Davis borrows $80,000 at 14 percent interest toward the purchase of a home. His mortgage is for 25 years.
    a. How much will his annual payments be? (Although home payments are usually on a monthly basis, we shall do our analysis on an annual basis for ease of computation. We will get a reasonably accurate answer.)
    b. How much interest will he pay over the life of the loan?
    c. How much should he be willing to pay to get out of a 14 percent mortgage and into a 10 percent mortgage with 25 years remaining on the mortgage? Assume current interest rates (yields) are 10 percent.

59. Peter Piper has applied for a mortgage of $120,000. Interest is computed at 8.5 percent compounded semiannually. The mortgage will be paid off over 20 years.
    a. Calculate Peter's monthly payment.
    b. Calculate Peter's weekly payment.
    c. Calculate Peter's biweekly (every 2nd week) payment.

60. Ocean Spray has applied for a mortgage of $200,000. Interest is computed at 4.5 percent compounded semiannually. The mortgage will be paid off over 25 years.
    a. Calculate Ocean's monthly payment.
    b. Calculate Ocean's weekly payment.
    c. Calculate Ocean's biweekly (every 2nd week) payment.

61. Bing and Monica Cherrie require a mortgage of $145,000 and can afford monthly payments of $1,150 on the mortgage. Current interest rates are 4 percent compounded semiannually. How long should the Cherries select to pay off the mortgage (the amortization period)?

62. Deidre Hall can afford monthly payments of $690 on a mortgage. Current mortgage rates are 3.5 percent, compounded semiannually. The longest period over which a mortgage can be amortized is 25 years. What size mortgage can Deidre afford?

63. Your younger sister, Barbara, will start college in five years. She has just informed your parents that she wants to go to Eastern University, which will cost $15,000 per year for four years (assumed to come at the end of each year). Anticipating Barbara's ambitions, your parents started investing $2,000 per year five years ago and will continue to do so for five more years. How much more will your parents have to invest each year for the next five years to have the necessary funds for Barbara's education? Use 10 percent as the appropriate interest rate throughout this problem (for discounting or compounding).

64. Barbara (from the previous problem) is now 18 years old (five years have passed), and she wants to get married instead of going to school. Your parents have accumulated the necessary funds for her education.

    Instead of her schooling, your parents are paying $7,000 for her upcoming wedding and plan to take a year-end vacation costing $4,000 per year for the next three years.

    How much will your parents have at the end of three years to help you with graduate school, which you will start then? You plan to work on a master's and perhaps a Ph.D. If graduate school costs $12,850 per year, approximately how long will you be able to stay in school based on these funds? Use 10 percent as the appropriate interest rate throughout this problem.

65. You are chairperson of the investment fund for Middle Hockey League. You are asked to set up a fund of quarterly payments to be compounded quarterly to accumulate a sum of $250,000 after 10 years at an 8 percent annual rate (40 payments). The first payment into the fund is to occur three months from today, and the last payment is to take place at the end of the tenth year.

    a. Determine how much the quarterly payment should be. (Round to whole numbers.) On the day after the sixteenth payment is made (the beginning of the fourth year) the interest rate goes up to a 12 percent annual rate, and you can earn a 12 percent annual rate on funds that have been accumulated as well as all future payments into the fund. Interest is to be compounded quarterly on all funds.

    b. Determine how much the revised quarterly payments should be after this rate change (there are 24 payments and compounding dates). The next payment will be in the fourth quarter of the fourth year. (Round all values to whole numbers.)

COMPREHENSIVE PROBLEM

66. Dr. Harold Wolf of Medical Research Corporations (MRC) was thrilled with the response he received from drug companies for his latest discovery, a unique electronic stimulator that reduces the pain from arthritis. The process had not yet passed the rigorous federal testing from Health Canada and was still in the early stages of development, but the interest was intense. He received three offers, described below, for the discovery. An appropriate discount rate for this decision is 10 percent.

    Offer I $1,000,000 now plus $200,000 from years 6 through 15. Also, if the product had over $100 million in cumulative sales by the end of year 15, he would receive an additional $3,000,000 at that time. Dr. Wolf thought there was a 70 percent probability this would happen.

    Offer II   Thirty percent of the buyer's gross profit on the product for the next four years. The buyer in this case was Zhay Pharmaceutical. Zhay's gross profit margin was 60 percent. Year 1 sales are projected to be $2 million and then expected to grow by 40 percent per year.

    Offer III A trust fund would be set up for the next 8 years. At the end of that period Dr. Wolf would receive the proceeds. The trust fund called for semiannual payments for the next 8 years of $200,000. Payments would start immediately (beginning).

    Determine the present value of each offer and select the best offer.

MINI CASE

Allison Boone, M.D.

Allison Boone had been practising medicine for seven years. Her specialty was neurology. She had received her bachelor's degree in chemistry from the University of Toronto and her M.D. from McMaster University. She did her residency at Toronto General Hospital. Allison practised neurology in a clinic with three other doctors in Toronto.

Her husband, Samuel L. Boone, held an administrative position at the Toronto Dominion Bank. Allison and Samuel had been married for five years and were the parents of young twin sons, Todd and Trey. They lived in the Beaches area in a beautiful four-room house overlooking Lake Ontario.

Allison normally left for work at 7:30 a.m. and closed her office at 5:30 p.m. to return home. On Tuesday, July 6, 20XX, at 5:15 p.m., she received an emergency call from Toronto General Hospital and immediately went to the hospital to help a patient who had suffered serious brain damage. By the time she had administered aid and helped prepare the patient for surgery it was 11:00 p.m.

On her way home along Lakeshore Boulevard, she was confronted head-on by a drunken driver going over 110 kilometres an hour. A crash was inevitable, and Allison and the other driver were killed instantly. The drunken driver was making a late delivery for Wayland Frozen Foods Inc.

Legal Considerations

The families of both drivers were devastated by the news of the accident. After the funeral and explaining the situation to the children, Samuel Boone knew he must seek legal redress for his family's enormous loss. Following interviews with a number of lawyers, he decided to hire Sloan Whitaker.

Whitaker was with a Toronto law firm (Hanson, Whitaker, and Thomason) that specialized in plaintiff's lawsuits. He had been in practice for over 20 years since graduating from Osgoode Law School.

When Whitaker began his investigation on behalf of Samuel Boone and his family, he was surprised to find out the driver of the delivery vehicle had a prior record of alcohol abuse and that Wayland Frozen Foods Inc. had knowledge of the problem when it hired him. It appears the driver was a relative of the owner, and at the time of employment he revealed what he termed "a past alcoholic problem that was now under control." In any event, he was acting as an employee for Wayland Frozen Foods in using its truck to make a business-related delivery at the time of the accident. The fact that he was speeding and intoxicated at the time of the impact only increased the legal exposure for Wayland Frozen Foods.

After much negotiating with the law firm that represented Wayland Frozen Foods (and its insurance company), Whitaker received three proposals for an out-of-court settlement to be paid to Allison Boone's family. The intent of the proposals was to replace the future earnings of Allison Boone, less any of the earnings she would have personally needed for her normal living requirements. Also, the value that she provided for her family as a wife and mother, quite aside from her earning power, had to be considered. Finally, there was the issue of punitive damages that Wayland Frozen Foods was exposed to as a result of letting an unqualified driver operate its truck. If the case went to court, there was no telling how much a jury might assign to this last factor.

The three proposals are listed below. An actuarial table indicated that Allison, age 37 at the time of the accident, had an anticipated life expectancy of 40 more years.

Proposal 1   Pay the family of Allison Boone $300,000 a year for the next 20 years, and $500,000 a year for the remaining 20 years.

Proposal 2   Pay the family a lump-sum payment of $5 million today.

Proposal 3   Pay the family of Allison Boone a relatively small amount of $50,000 a year for the next 40 years, but also guarantee them a final payment of $75 million at the end of 40 years.

In order to analyze the present value of these three proposals, Whitaker called on a financial expert to do the analysis. You will aid in the process.

a. Using a current long-term interest rate, recommend a proposal to the Boone family. Justify your choice of discount rate.

b. Now assume that a discount rate of 11 percent is used. Which of the three alternatives provides the highest present value?

c. Explain why the change in outcome takes place between part *a* and part *b*.

d. If Whitaker thinks punitive damages are likely to be $4 million in a jury trial, should he be more likely to settle out of court or go before a jury?

APPENDIX 9A

Derivation of Time-Value-of-Money Formulas

Formula 9–1 (Future value)

$$FV_1 = PV + iPV \qquad\qquad\qquad = PV(1 + i)$$
$$FV_2 = PV(1 + i) + iPV(1 + i) \qquad = PV(1 + i) \times (1 + i) \quad = PV(1 + i)^2$$
$$FV_3 = PV(1 + i)^2 + iPV(1 + i)^2 \qquad = PV(1 + i)^2 \times (1 + i) \quad = PV(1 + i)^3$$
$$FV_n = PV(1 + i)^{n-1} + iPV(1 + i)^{n-1} = PV(1 + i)^{n-1} \times (1 + i) = PV(1 + i)^n$$
$$FV = PV(1 + i)^n$$

Formula 9–3 (Present value)

$$FV = PV(1 + i)^n \qquad\qquad PV = FV \times \left[\frac{1}{(1 + i)^n}\right]$$

Formula 9–4a (Future value—annuity)

$$FV_1 = A + 0 \qquad\qquad\qquad\qquad = A$$
$$FV_2 = A + A + Ai \qquad\qquad\qquad = A + A(1 + i)$$
$$FV_3 = A + [A + A(1 + i)] + i[A + A(1 + i)] = A + [A + A(1 + i)](1 + i)$$
$$\quad = A + A(1 + i) + A(1 + i)^2$$
$$FV_4 = A + A + A(1 + i) + A(1 + i)^2 + i[A + A(1 + i) + A(1 + i)^2]$$
$$\quad = A + A(1 + i) + A(1 + i)^2 + A(1 + i)^3$$
$$FV_A = A + A(1 + i) + A(1 + i)^2 + A(1 + i)^3 + \cdots + A(1 + i)^{n-1}$$

To get the sum of this geometric series, multiply by $(1 + i)$ and deduct the original equation.

$$FV_A(1 + i) = A(1 + i) + A(1 + i)^2 + A(1 + i)^3 + \cdots + A(1 + i)^{n-1} + A(1 + i)^n$$
$$\underline{-FV_A \qquad -A + A(1 + i) + A(1 + i)^2 + A(1 + i)^3 + \cdots + A(1 + i)^{n-1}}$$
$$FV_A(1 + i) - FV_A = A(1 + i)^n - A$$
$$FV_A + iFV_A - FV_A = A(1 + i)^n - A$$
$$iFV_A = A[(1 + i)^n - 1]$$
$$FV_A = \left[\frac{A(1 + i)^n - 1}{i}\right]$$

Formula 9–4b (Future value—annuity in advance)

$FV_1 = A + iA = A(1 + i)$

$FV_2 = A + iA + A(1 + i) + i[A(1 + i)] = A(1 + i) + (1 + i)[A(1 + i)] = A(1 + i) + A(1 + i)^2$

$FV_3 = A + iA + A(1 + i) + A(1 + i)^2 + i[A(1 + i)] + A(1 + i)^2]$

$\quad = A(1 + i) + A(1 + i)^2 + A(1 + i)^3$

$FV_A = A(1 + i) + A(1 + i)^2 + A(1 + i)^3 + \cdots + A(1 + i)^n$

To get the sum of this geometric series, multiply by $(1 + i)$ and deduct the original equation.

$FV_A(1 + i) = A(1 + i)^2 + A(1 + i)^3 + A(1 + i)^4 + \cdots + A(1 + i)^n + A(1 + i)^{n+1}$

$\underline{-FV_A \qquad -A(1 + i) + A(1 + i)^2 + A(1 + i)^3 + A(1 + i)^4 + \cdots + A(1 + i)^n}$

$\qquad FV_A(1 + i) - FV_A = A(1 + i)^{n+1} - A(1 + i)$

$\qquad FV_A + iFV_A - FV_A = A(1 + i)^{n+1} - A(1 + i)$

$\qquad iFV_A = A[(1 + i)^{n+1} - (1 + i)]$

$$FV_A = A_{BGN}\left[\frac{(1 + i)^{n+1} - (1 + i)}{i}\right]$$

Formula 9–5a (Present value of an annuity)

$PV_1 = A(1 + i)^{-1}$

$PV_2 = A(1 + i)^{-1} + A(1 + i)^{-2}$

$PV_3 = A(1 + i)^{-1} + A(1 + i)^{-2} + A(1 + i)^{-3}$

$PV_n = A(1 + i)^{-1} + A(1 + i)^{-2} + A(1 + i)^{-3} + \cdots + A(1 + i)^{-n}$

To get the sum of this geometric series, multiply by $(1 + i)$ and deduct the original equation.

$PV_n(1 + i) = A(1 + i)^0 + A(1 + i)^{-1} + A(1 + i)^{-2} + A(1 + i)^{-3} + \cdots + A(1 + i)^{-(n-1)}$

$\underline{-PV_n \qquad -A(1 + i)^{-1} + A(1 + i)^{-2} + A(1 + i)^{-3} + \cdots + A(1 + i)^{-n}}$

$\qquad PV_n(1 + i) - PV_n = A - A(1 + i)^{-n}$

$\qquad PV_n + iPV_n - PV_n = A[1 - (1 + i)^{-n}]$

$\qquad iPV_n = A[1 - (1 + i)^{-n}]$

$$PV_A = A\left[\frac{1 - \dfrac{1}{(1 + i)^n}}{i}\right]$$

Formula 9–5b (Present value of an annuity in advance)

$PV_1 = A$

$PV_2 = A + A(1 + i)^{-1}$

$PV_3 = A + A(1 + i)^{-1} + A(1 + i)^{-2}$

$PV_n = A + A(1 + i)^{-1} + A(1 + i)^{-2} + \cdots + A(1 + i)^{-(n-1)}$

To get the sum of this geometric series, multiply by $(1 + i)$ and deduct the original equation.

$PV_n(1 + i) = A(1 + i) + A(1 + i)^0 + A(1 + i)^{-1} + A(1 + i)^{-2} + \cdots + A(1 + i)^{-(n-2)}$

$\underline{-PV_n \qquad -A + A(1 + i)^{-1} + A(1 + i)^{-2} + \cdots + A(1 + i)^{-(n-1)}}$

$\qquad PV_n(1 + i) - PV_n = A(1 + i) - A(1 + i)^{-(n-1)}$

$\qquad PV_n + iPV_n - PV_n = A[(1 + i) - (1 + i)^{-(n-1)}]$

$\qquad iPV_n = A[(1 + i) - (1 + i)^{-(n-1)}]$

$$PV_A = A_{BGN}\left[\frac{(1 + i) - \dfrac{1}{(1 + i)^{n-1}}}{i}\right]$$

Formula 9–6a (Annuity equalling a future value)

$$FV_A = A\left[\frac{(1+i)^n - 1}{i}\right] \qquad\qquad A = FV_A\left[\frac{i}{(1+i)^n - 1}\right] \quad \text{(9–4a)}$$

Formula 9–6b (Annuity in advance equalling a future value)

$$FV_A = A_{BGN}\left[\frac{(1+i)^{n+1} - (1+i)}{i}\right] \qquad A_{BGN} = FV_A\left[\frac{i}{(1+i)^{n+1} - (1+i)}\right] \quad \text{(9–4b)}$$

Formula 9–7a (Annuity equalling a present value)

$$PV_A = A\left[\frac{1 - \dfrac{1}{(1+i)^n}}{i}\right] \qquad\qquad A = PV_A\left[\frac{i}{1 - \dfrac{1}{(1+i)^n}}\right] \quad \text{(9–5a)}$$

Formula 9–7b (Annuity in advance equalling a present value)

$$PV_A = A_{BGN}\left[\frac{(1+i) - \dfrac{1}{(1+i)^{n-1}}}{i}\right] \qquad A_{BGN} = PV_A\left[\frac{i}{1 + i - \dfrac{1}{(1+i)^{n-1}}}\right] \quad \text{(9–5b)}$$

Formula 9–9 (Perpetual annuity)

$$PV_\infty = A(1+i)^{-1} + A(1+i)^{-2} + A(1+i)^{-3} + \cdots (n \to \infty)$$

To get the sum of this geometric series, multiply by $(1 + i)$ and deduct the original equation.

$$PV_\infty(1+i) = A(1+i)^0 + A(1+i)^{-1} + A(1+i)^{-2} + A(1+i)^{-3} + \cdots (n \to \infty)$$
$$\underline{-PV_n \qquad -A(1+i)^{-1} + A(1+i)^{-2} + A(1+i)^{-3} + \cdots (n \to \infty)}$$

$$PV_\infty(1+i) - PV_\infty = A$$
$$PV_\infty + iPV_\infty - PV_\infty = A$$
$$iPV_\infty = A$$
$$PV = \frac{A}{i}$$

Formula 9–10 (Perpetual growing annuity)

$$PV_\infty = A_0(1+i)^{-1}(1+g)^1 + A_0(1+i)^{-2}(1+g)^2 + A_0(1+i)^{-3}(1+g)^3 + \cdots (n \to \infty)$$

To get the sum of this geometric series, multiply by $(1 + i)(1 + g)^{-1}$ and deduct the original equation.

$$PV_\infty(1+i)(1+g)^{-1} = A_0(1+i)^0(1+g)^0 + A_0(1+i)^{-1}(1+g)^1 + A_0(1+i)^{-2}(1+g)^2 + \cdots (n \to \infty)$$
$$\underline{-PV_\infty \qquad\qquad -A_0(1+i)^{-1}(1+g)^1 + A_0(1+i)^{-2}(1+g)^2 + A_0(1+i)^{-3}(1+g)^3 + \cdots (n \to \infty)}$$

$$PV_\infty(1+i)(1+g)^{-1} - PV_\infty = A_0$$
$$PV_\infty[(1+i)(1+g)^{-1} - 1] = A_0$$
$$PV_\infty[(1+i)(1+g)^{-1} - 1(1+g)(1+g)^{-1}] = A_0$$
$$PV_\infty[[(1+i) - (1+g)](1+g)^{-1}] = A_0$$
$$PV_\infty[i - g] = A_0(1+g)^1$$
$$PV_\infty[i - g] = A_1$$
$$PV = \frac{A_1}{i - g}$$

The formula is valid provided that $i > g$.

Formula 9–11 (Growing annuity for a limited period)

$$PV_n = A_0(1 + i)^{-1}(1 + g)^1 + A_0(1 + i)^{-2}(1 + g)^2 + A_0(1 + i)^{-3}(1 + g)^3 + \cdots + A_0(1 + i)^{-n}(1 + g)^n$$

To get the sum of this geometric series, multiply by $(1 + i)(1 + g)^{-1}$ and deduct the original equation.

$$PV_n(1 + i)(1 + g)^{-1} = A_0(1 + i)^0(1 + g)^0 + A_0(1 + i)^{-1}(1 + g)^1 + A_0(1 + i)^{-2}(1 + g)^2 + \cdots + A_0(1 + i)^{-(n-1)}(1 + g)^{(n-1)}$$

$$-PV_n \qquad\qquad -A_0(1 + i)^{-1}(1 + g)^1 + A_0(1 + i)^{-2}(1 + g)^2 + A_0(1 + i)^{-3}(1 + g)^3 + \cdots + A_0(1 + i)^{-n}(1 + g)^n$$

$$PV_n(1 + i)(1 + g)^{-1} - PV_n = A_0 - A_0(1 + i)^{-n}(1 + g)^n$$

$$PV_n[(1 + i)(1 + g)^{-1} - 1] = A_0[1 - (1 + i)^{-n}(1 + g)^n]$$

$$PV_n[(1 + i)(1 + g)^{-1} - 1(1 + g)(1 + g)^{-1}] = A_0[1 - (1 + i)^{-n}(1 + g)^n]$$

$$PV_n[[(1 + i) - (1 + g)](1 + g)^{-1}] = A_0[1 - (1 + i)^{-n}(1 + g)^n]$$

$$PV_n[i - g](1 + g)^{-1} = A_0[1 - (1 + i)^{-n}(1 + g)^n]$$

$$PV_n = A_0[i - g]^{-1}(1 + g)[1 - (1 + i)^{-n}(1 + g)^n]$$

$$PV_n = A_1[i - g]^{-1}[1 - (1 + i)^{-n}(1 + g)^n]$$

$$PV_n = A_1\left(\frac{1}{i - g}\right)\left[1 - \left(\frac{1 + g}{1 + i}\right)^n\right]$$

10

Valuation and Rates of Return

LEARNING OBJECTIVES

LO1 Describe the valuation of a financial asset as based on the present value of future cash flows.

LO2 Propose that the required rate of return in valuing an asset is based on the risk involved.

LO3 Assess the current value (price) of bonds, preferred shares (perpetuals), and common shares based on the future benefits (cash flows).

LO4 Evaluate the yields on financial claims based on the relationship between current price and future expected cash flows.

LO5 Describe the use of a price-earnings ratio to determine value.

Chapter 9 considered the basic principles of the time value of money. In this chapter we extend this concept to determine how financial assets (bonds, preferred stock, and common stock) are valued and how investors establish the rates of return they require for investing in these assets. The following chapter uses the material from this chapter to determine the overall cost of financing to the firm. For the corporation to attract funds it must pay the rates of return (yields) demanded by the providers of capital (bondholders and shareholders). These costs of corporate financing (capital) are collectively the firm's cost of capital, which is employed in Chapters 12 and 13 to analyze whether or not a project is an acceptable investment (the capital budgeting decision). This development is depicted in Figure 10–1.

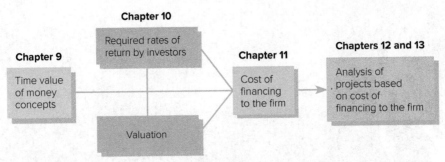

Figure 10–1 The relationship between time value of money, required return, cost of financing, and investment decisions

Financial calculators are used to work the problems in this chapter. Your answer will be slightly different if it is determined using the tables. Whether you use tables, calculators, or computers to do these calculations, you must firmly comprehend the concept behind present value analysis to be successful.

LO1 VALUATION CONCEPTS

In our market-based or mixed capitalistic system, the value of an asset is ultimately determined by what someone else is prepared to pay for it at the moment. When financial assets trade on a regular basis in well-developed financial markets, current values are easily determined. In less well-developed markets (thin markets) or where markets do not exist at all, we require other objective measures for determining value.

What someone is prepared to pay for a financial asset (or security) is referred to as its market value. The financial assets that we study in this chapter often trade in financial markets, where their prices change minute by minute. Thus, market values change regularly.

A financial asset (capital), as contrasted to a real asset, is basically a claim against a firm, government, or individual for future expected cash flows. Its current or market value can therefore be seen as deriving from future expected benefits and the return that investors expect from those benefits. With new information, investors change their expectations about future cash payouts and their required rates of return from securities. Prices will be bid up or down according to interpretations of this new information as the financial assets are exchanged between investors.

FINANCE IN ACTION

Covid-19: A Challenge to Value

In early 2020 the financial markets nosedived on fears created by the Coronavirus pandemic. Within a month financial markets around the globe had fallen by over 30 percent. By September the markets are mostly recovered and NASDAQ, the technology exchange, had done particularly well.

Valuation of a financial asset based on these concepts can also be seen as the present value of those future anticipated cash flows derived using an appropriate discount rate. This is our "time value of money" concept. In well-developed financial markets, the present value of a financial asset's future expected cash flows should be equal to its market value. In "thin" or nonexistent markets we will often rely on present value techniques for valuating a financial security.

Throughout the balance of this chapter, concepts of valuation are applied to corporate bonds, preferred stock, and common stock. Although we describe the basic characteristics of each form of security as part of the valuation discussion, extended discussion of each security is deferred until Chapters 16 and 17.

LO2 Yield

The market-determined required rate of return is the discount rate used for the "time value" calculations, and depends on the market's perceived level of risk associated with an individual security. Required or expected rates of returns on investments are referred to as yields. Sometimes the yield is called an interest rate, but "interest rate" more appropriately refers to fixed payments and may be only part of the total return, or yield, on an investment. Capital is allocated to companies by the market and investors based on estimates of risk, efficiency, and expected returns—which are based to some degree on past performance. The reward to the manager for the efficient use of capital is a lower required return demanded by investors compared to competing companies that do not manage their financial resources as well.

Bombardier, Inc.
bombardier.com
RBC Royal Bank
rbc.com

Required rates of return are competitively determined among the many companies seeking financial capital. For example, the Royal Bank, due to its low financial risk, reasonable return, and strong market position in banking, is likely to raise debt or equity capital at a significantly lower cost than Bombardier, which has a much more volatile business environment. Investors are willing to accept a lower return for a lower risk, and vice versa.

The required rate of return is usually envisioned over the length of time the investor expects to own or hold the financial security. Thus, the yield to maturity, or discount rate, is the rate of return required by investors over that period. The investor allows three basic factors to influence their required rate of return.

Bank of Canada
bankofcanada.ca

1. The Required Real Rate of Return This is the rate of return that the investor demands for giving up current use of the funds on a non-inflation-adjusted basis. It is the financial rent the investor charges for using their funds for one year, five years, or any given time period. Historically, the real rate of return demanded by investors has been about 2 to 3 percent. Throughout the 1980s and early 1990s, the real rate of return was much higher—5 to 7 percent. Today, we are back to the more long-term historical norm.

2. Inflation Premium In addition to the real rate of return, the investor requires a premium to compensate for the eroding effect of inflation on the value of the dollar. It would hardly satisfy an investor to have a 3 percent total rate of return in a 5 percent inflationary economy. Under such circumstances, the lender (investor) would be paying the borrower 2 percent (in purchasing power) for use of the funds. This would be irrational. No one wishes to *pay* another party to use their funds. The inflation premium added to the real rate of return ensures that this does not happen. The size of the inflation premium is based on the investor's expectations about future inflation. Through the 1980s the inflation premium was 4 to 5 percent. In the late 1970s it was in excess of 10 percent. Since 2000 the annual inflation rate has been slightly less than 2 percent.

If one combines the real rate of return and the inflation premium, the risk-free rate of return is determined. This is the rate that compensates the investor for the current use of their funds and for the loss in purchasing power due to inflation but not for taking risks. The risk-free rate of return is often considered to be the yield on Government of Canada Treasury bills. As an example, if the real rate of return was 3 percent and the inflation premium was 4 percent, we would say the risk-free rate of return was 7 percent.[1]

In Chapter 6 we examined the term structure of interest rates by looking at the yields for various maturities of Government of Canada securities. We discovered first that because of a liquidity preference to deal with uncertainty, longer-term rates are higher than short-term rates. Second, a yield curve is a reflection of the expectations of investors as to what they believe interest rates, or yields, will be in the future. Those expectations are formulated by many factors, including inflationary expectations, government monetary policy, government fiscal policies (in particular, the upward pressure on interest rates created by the demands of debt financing), and the influences on Canadian interest rates from the global financial community.

3. Risk Premium We must now add the risk premium to the risk-free rate of return. This is a premium associated with the special risks of a given investment. Of primary interest to us are two types of risks: business risk and financial risk (explored in Chapter 5). Business risk relates to the possible inability of the firm to hold its competitive position and maintain stability and growth in its earnings. We can relate this to the firm's capital assets and operating leverage. Financial risk relates to the possible inability of the firm to meet its debt obligations as they come due. This relates to the firm's capital structure and the maturity of its financial obligations. This is the financial leverage we examined in Chapter 5. From an investor's viewpoint, we often speak of different risks such as

Default risk: that the firm will not be able to meet its payment obligations as promised

Liquidity risk: that there is a weak market for a firm's securities, making it difficult to sell them on short notice

Maturity risk: that the value of the security will fluctuate due to the time until final payment

Whatever the label, risk concerns add to the required rate of return.

In addition to these two forms of risk, the risk premium is greater or less for different investments. For example, because bonds possess a contractual obligation for the firm to pay interest and repay principal to bondholders, they are considered less risky than common stock, where no such obligation exists. On the other hand, common stock carries the potential for unlimited return when the corporation is very profitable.

The risk premium of an investment may range from as low as zero on a very short-term Canadian government-backed security to 10 to 15 percent on a gold mining expedition. Typical risk premiums range from 2 to 6 percent. On the corporate bonds of a somewhat risky firm we might suggest a risk premium of 3 percent. If we add this risk premium to the two components of the risk-free rate of return, we arrive at an overall required rate of return of 10 percent.

---

[1] Actually, a slightly more accurate representation would be

$$\text{Risk-free rate} = (1 + \text{Real rate of return})(1 + \text{Inflation premium}) - 1$$

We would show

$$(1.03)(1.04) - 1 = 0.0712 = 7.12 \text{ percent}$$

+ Real rate of return.	3%
+ Inflation premium	4
= Risk-free rate	7%
+ Risk premium	3
= Required rate of return	10%

In this instance, we assume that we are evaluating the required return on a bond issued by a firm. If the security had been the common stock of the same firm, the risk premium might have been 5 to 6 percent, thus making the required rate of return 12 to 13 percent.

As we conclude this section, please recall that the required rate of return is effectively identical to the yield expected by investors. The required rates of return and their components are common to the valuation of all financial securities.

LO3 VALUATION OF BONDS

A bond represents a long-term debt owed by a firm (or government) to an investor (bondholder) that obligates it to make regular interest (or coupon) payments and then a final lump-sum payment at a future date (maturity). This is one of the ways a firm hopes to raise long-term capital to invest in revenue-generating assets. A bond is usually outstanding for several years from the date it is originally sold (issued) to the final payment at maturity. During this time the bond may be traded many times in the financial markets among investors, and its price will fluctuate based on the prevailing supply and demand factors.

A bond contractually promises a stream of annuity payments (known as *interest* or *coupon*) and a final payment (known as *maturity,* or *face* or *par value*). Generally, the maturity value is $1,000, or multiples thereof. In its most common form, the maturity value and coupon payments of a bond are fixed (cannot change) by contract over the term of the bond.

Investors will value these future expected cash flows to determine the current price of the bond. The discount factor used to determine the price or present value is called the yield to maturity (Y). Yield, therefore, is the relationship between the price investors are prepared to pay and future expected cash flows—in this case, the coupon payments and the maturity value. The value of Y is determined in the bond markets and represents the required rate of return demanded by investors on a bond of a given risk and maturity. *Yield to maturity and the interest (or coupon) rate are not the same thing*.

Over time, the market will evaluate different economic factors and a new yield, or required rate of return, will be demanded on the bond. Because the coupon payments and maturity values are fixed, the price of the bond will move up or down as these benefits become more or less desirable. Bond prices change constantly in the financial markets. Therefore, the price of a bond, discounted by the current yield to maturity (**Y**), is equal to the sum of

- The present value of regular interest payments and
- The present value of the maturity value

This relationship can be expressed graphically as follows:

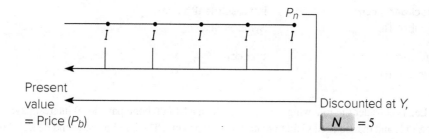

Where

$$P_b = \text{Price of the bond}$$
$$I_t = \text{Interest payments}$$
$$P_n = \text{Principal payment at maturity}$$
$$t = \text{Number corresponding to a period; running from 1 to } n$$
$$N = \text{Total number of periods}$$
$$Y = \text{Yield to maturity (or required rate of return)}$$

With a calculator:

$$P_b = \boxed{PV} \qquad I_t = \boxed{PMT}$$
$$N = \boxed{N} \qquad Y = \boxed{I/Y}$$
$$P_n = \boxed{FV}$$

FINANCE IN ACTION

Market Yields and Market Values

The financial markets offer a wide range of yields, for the most part based on the risk of the investment. The risk of the investment generally centres on whether the investor is likely to receive the promised future payments, be they interest, dividend payments, or capital gains.

Although we speak of required rates of return, we must remember that no future returns are certain and can only be "expected." In January 2020, a range of yields included

Treasury bills (one-month)	1.73%
10-year government bond	1.57
10-year corporate bond	2.64
Dividend yield (S&P/TSX Composite)	2.99
Price-earnings ratio (S&P/TSX Composite Index)	18.69×

A roller coaster of expected and realized returns has been exhibited by BlackBerry, formerly known as Research In Motion (RIM). It rose from a market share value of $4.5 billion in mid-2006 to almost $80 billion in mid-2008, surpassing the value of the Royal Bank. BlackBerry was worth less than $5 billion by early 2020. During that same period, the Royal Bank value rose fairly steadily from $59 to $154 billion.

The same could be said for Bausch Health, formerly Valient Pharmaceuticals, which rose to a capitalization of $122 billion in July 2015 (Royal Bank $108 billion at this time) but in early 2020 was worth $14 billion.

Share prices usually reflect the market's belief in a firm's ability to generate revenues and profits.

Q1 What are current yields in the marketplace?

Q2 What are the current equity value and revenue of BlackBerry and the Royal Bank?

blackberry.com
Symbol: BB

ir.bauschhealth.com
Symbol: BHC

rbc.com
Symbol: RY

tmx.com

Let us consider the following example in which a $1,000 bond pays $100 interest payments for 20 periods and the required yield to maturity is 10 percent. The bond price would be as follows:

From our graphical representation,

$$P_n = \boxed{FV} = \$1{,}000$$
$$I = \boxed{PMT} = \$100$$
$$\boxed{N} = 20$$
$$Y = \boxed{I/Y} = 10$$
$$P_b = \boxed{CPT}\ \boxed{PV} = -\$1{,}000.$$

This relationship can also be expressed mathematically, using the same notation, by the following formula:

$$P_b = \sum_{t=1}^{n}\frac{I_t}{(1+Y)^t} + \frac{P_n}{(1+Y)^n} \quad \text{(10–1)}$$

Using the same example as above,

$$P_b = \sum_{t=1}^{20}\frac{\$100}{(1+0.10)^t} + \frac{\$1{,}000}{(1+0.10)^{20}} = \$1{,}000$$

Tables (optional)

We could use present value tables. Take the present value of the interest payments (Appendix D) and then add this value to the present value of the principal payment at maturity (Appendix B).

(PV_A) Present value of interest payments......................	$ 851.40
(PV) Present value of principal payment at maturity.............	149.00
Total present value, or price, of the bond	$1,000.40

The price of the bond in this case is essentially the same as its par, or stated, value to be received at maturity of $1,000. This is because the annual interest rate is 10 percent (the annual interest payment of $100 divided by $1,000), and the yield to maturity, or discount rate, is also 10 percent. When the interest rate on the bond and the yield to maturity are equal, the bond trades at par value.

TIME AND YIELD TO MATURITY—IMPACT ON BOND VALUATION

Let us now examine the conditions in the market that cause the yield to maturity to change, and the subsequent effect on the price of a bond.

LO4 Increase in Inflation Premium

Although other factors will cause the required rate of return to change almost continually, inflation tends to be a major factor. For example, assume that the inflation premium, from our previous example, goes up from 4 to 6 percent while all else remains constant. The required rate of return would now become 12 percent.

+ Real rate of return.....................................	3%
+ Inflation premium	6
= Risk-free rate	9%
+ Risk premium..	3
= Required rate of return...............................	12%

This increase in the required rate of return, or yield to maturity, on the bond causes its price to change. Of course, the required rate of return on all other financial assets also goes up proportionately. A bond that pays only 10 percent interest when the required rate of return (yield to maturity) is 12 percent has its price fall below its former value of approximately $1,000. The new price of the bond, $850.61, is computed as follows:

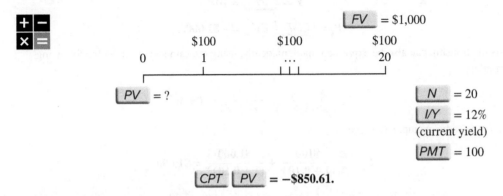

A purchaser of this bond, selling at this *discount* price, still receives a 12 percent return, but it consists of interest and capital appreciation with the maturity payment.

Spreadsheet: Bond value

	A	B	C	D	E	F	G
1	rate	%I/Y	12%		"=+PV(C1,C2,C3,C4,)		
2	nper	N	20		"= PV(rate, nper,(pmt),(fv),[type])		
3	pmt	PMT	-$100		$850.61		
4	fv	FV	-$1,000				
5					"=+RATE(12,20,-100,-1000)		
6					"= rate(rate, nper,(pmt),(fv),[type])		
7					$850.61		

Tables (optional)

Total Present Value

(PV_A) Present value of interest payments (Appendix D)	$746.90
(PV) Present value of principal payment at maturity (Appendix B)	104.00
Total present value, or price, of the bond	$850.90

In this example, we assumed that increasing inflation caused the required rate of return (yield to maturity) to go up and the bond price to fall by approximately $150. The same effect would occur if the business risk increased or if the demanded level for the *real* rate of return became higher.

Decrease in Inflation Premium

Of course, the opposite effect would happen if the required rate of return went down because of lower inflation, less risk, or other factors. Let's assume that the inflation premium declines and the required rate of return (yield to maturity) goes down to 8 percent. The 20-year bond with the 10 percent interest rate would now sell for $1,196.36.

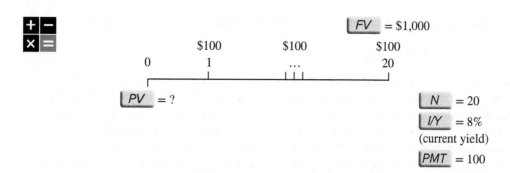

CPT PV = **−$1,196.36.**

A purchaser of this bond, selling at this premium price, will receive an 8 percent return, but it consists of higher interest and a capital loss with the maturity payment.

Tables (optional)

Total Present Value

(PV_A) Present value of interest payments (Appendix D).........................	$ 981.80
(PV) Present value of principal payment at maturity (Appendix B)	215.00
Total present value, or price, of the bond	$1,196.80

The price of the bond has now risen $196.36 above par value. This is certainly in line with the expected result, because the bond is paying 10 percent interest when the required yield in the market is only 8 percent. The 2 percent differential on a $1,000 par value bond represents $20 per year. The investor receives this differential for the next 20 years. The present value of $20 for the next 20 years at the current market rate of interest of 8 percent is $196.36. This explains why the bond is trading at $196.36 over its stated, or par, value.

The further the yield to maturity on a bond falls away from the stated interest rate on the bond, the greater the price change effect is. This is illustrated in Table 10–1 for the 10 percent interest rate, 20-year bonds discussed in this chapter. Also, note the inverse relationship between price and yield. As required yield increases, price decreases, and as yield decreases, price increases.

Table 10–1 Bond price sensitivity to yield to maturity

(10 percent interest payment, 20 years to maturity)	
Yield to Maturity	**Bond Price**
2%...........................	$2,308.11
4.............................	1,815.42
6.............................	1,458.80
7.............................	1,317.82
8.............................	1,196.36
9.............................	1,091.29
10............................	1,000.00
11............................	920.37
12............................	850.61
13............................	789.26
14............................	735.07
16............................	644.27
20............................	513.04
25............................	406.92

Clearly, different yields to maturity have a significant impact on the price of a bond.[2]

Time to Maturity

The impact of a change in yield to maturity on valuation is also affected by the remaining time to maturity. The effect of a bond paying 2 percent more or less than the going rate of interest is much greater for a 20-year bond than it is for a 1-year bond. In the latter case, the investor gains or gives up only $20 for one year. That is not the same as having this differential for an extended time. Let's once again return to the 10 percent interest rate bond and show the effect of a 2 percent decrease or increase in yield to maturity for varying *times* to maturity. The values are shown in Table 10–2 and graphed in Figure 10–2. The upper part of the figure shows how the amount (premium) above

Table 10–2 Bond price sensitivity to time to maturity changes

Time period in years (of 10 percent coupon bond)	Bond price with 8 percent yield to maturity	Bond price with 12 percent yield to maturity
0	$1,000.00	$1,000.00
1	1,018.52	982.14
5	1,079.85	927.90
10	1,134.20	887.00
15	1,171.19	863.78
20	1,196.36	850.61
25	1,213.50	843.14
30	1,225.16	838.90

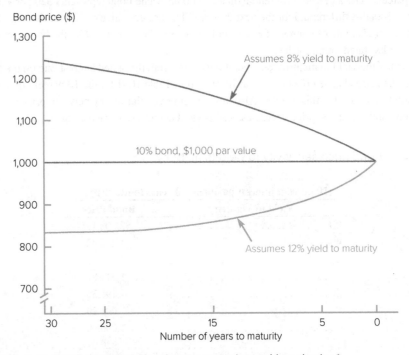

Figure 10–2 Relationship between time to maturity and bond price*

*The relationship in the graph is not symmetrical in nature.

---

[2]Observe that the impact of a decrease or increase in interest rates is not equal. For example, a 2 percent decrease in interest rates produces a $196.36 gain in the bond price, and an increase of 2 percent causes a $149.39 loss. Although price movements are not symmetrical around the price of the bond when the time dimension is the maturity date of the bond, they are symmetrical around the duration of the bond. The duration represents the weighted average time period to recapture the interest and principal on the bond.

par value is reduced as the number of years to maturity becomes smaller and smaller. The figure should be read from left to right. The lower part shows how the amount (discount) below par value is reduced with progressively fewer years to maturity. Clearly, the longer the maturity the greater the impact of changes in yield.

Determining Yield to Maturity from the Bond Price

Recall from Chapter 6 that our discussion of the term structure of interest rates revealed an investor preference for liquidity. This resulted in higher required yields for longer-term maturities, all other things being equal. The preference for liquidity can be explained by the impact of yield changes on longer-term maturities, in that they experience greater price fluctuations for a given yield change. This subjects the holder of a longer-term security to greater risk and, therefore, a higher expected yield is required.

Until now we have used yield to maturity as well as other factors, such as the interest rate on the bond and number of years to maturity, to determine the price of the bond. We now assume we know the price of the bond, the interest rate on the bond, and the years to maturity, and we wish to determine the yield to maturity. Once we have computed this value, we have determined the rate of return investors are demanding in the marketplace to provide for inflation, risk, and other factors.

We could use formula 10–1, but it looks complicated.

$$P_b = \sum_{t=1}^{n} \frac{I_t}{(1 + Y)^t} + \frac{P_n}{(1 + Y)^n}$$

We determine the value of Y, the yield to maturity, that equates the interest payments (I_t) and the principal payment (P_n) to the price of the bond (P_b). This is similar to the calculations to determine yield in the previous chapter. It is most easily performed with a business calculator.

Assume a 15-year bond pays $110 per year (11 percent) in interest and $1,000 after 15 years in principal repayment. The current price of the bond is $932.89.

 FINANCE IN ACTION

The Ups and Downs of Bond Yields and Prices

Government and corporate bonds trade (prices change) in the markets among investors. Investors are promised a fixed semiannual coupon payment and the face value, or par value, on the maturity of the bond. Since these cash flows are fixed, it is the price of bonds in the markets that must change to reflect investor expectations about the future and required rates of return. The daily dollar trading in bonds exceeds stock market trading by about 10 times.

Let's examine the price changes on government bonds. Between June and December of 1982, long-term bond yields dropped from 16.48 to 11.92 percent. A 20-year bond with a 12 percent coupon rate would have increased in price over this period from $740 to $1,006, a 36 percent return or 72 percent on an annualized basis. These opportunities do not occur very often, however.

In 2008, it was a different story, with GMAC corporate bonds that were used to finance a variety of activities including troublesome automobile leases and residential mortgages. Dominion Bond Rating Service lowered GMAC's bond rating from investment grade at BBB to junk bond status of B in several steps from October 2007 to June 2008. It was considered riskier. GMAC 5.45 percent bonds maturing December 2009 fell from $1,002.60 to $834.40 between February and August 2008. The promised yield (if realized) rose from 5.45 to 21 percent. Any takers?

By 2020, bond yields sat at quite low yields with risk on the upside. If inflation pushed yields higher, bond prices would fall, reducing year-over-year returns on bond investments.

The German Government in late 2019 sold 30-year bonds (bunds) totalling 824 million euros with a 0 percent coupon that yielded a negative 0.11 percent. German bonds are paid annually (if at all).

Bond quotes are expressed as follows:

Issuer	Coupon	Maturity Date	Price	Yield	Yield Change
Canada	2.750	2048-Dec-01	126.066	1.63	+1.627

The price is expressed as a percentage of maturity value of $1,000 due December 1, 2048 (or as value per $100 of maturity value). The coupon rate is annual interest, $27.50, (calculated on the maturity value) that the issuer is obligated to pay, usually every six months ($13.75). The yield is the current expected return.

Getting bond quotes is difficult, unless one has an investment account with a financial institution, but some information can be obtained if one is persistent. Benchmark bond quotes are available at TMXMoney. Limited live quotes are available at Perimeter Financial (pfin.ca).

Q1 What are the current price and yield to maturity of Government of Canada bonds of different maturities?

Q2 What are the current price and yield to maturity of two corporate bonds of similar maturities?

We wish to determine the yield to maturity, or discount rate, that equates future flows with the current price.[3]

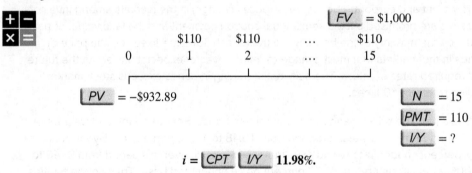

$$i = \boxed{CPT} \ \boxed{I/Y} \ 11.98\%.$$

---

[3] An approximate yield formula is given by

$$\text{Approximate yield to maturity } (Y') = \frac{\text{Annual interest payment} + \dfrac{\text{Principal payment} - \text{Price of the bond}}{\text{Number of years to maturity}}}{0.6 \text{ (Price of the bond)} + 0.4 \text{ (Principal payment)}}$$

This formula is recommended by Gabriel A. Hawawini and Ashok Vora, "Yield Approximations: A Historical Perspective," *Journal of Finance 37* (March 1982), pp. 145–56. It tends to provide the best approximation.

Semiannual Interest and Bond Prices

Until now, in our bond analysis we have been considering examples where interest was paid annually. However, most bonds in Canada and the United States pay interest semiannually. This is not the case in countries such as Germany. Thus, a 10 percent interest rate bond may actually pay $50 twice a year instead of $100 annually. To make the conversion from an annual to semiannual analysis, we follow three steps.

Deutsche Bundesbank
bundesbank.de

1. Divide the annual interest rate by two.
2. Multiply the number of years by two.
3. Divide the annual yield to maturity by two.

Assume a 10 percent, $1,000 par value bond has a maturity of 20 years. The annual yield to maturity is 12 percent. In following the preceding three steps, we would show,

1. 10%/2 = 5% semiannual interest rate; therefore, 5% × $1,000 = $50 semiannual interest
2. 20 × 2 = 40 periods to maturity
3. 12%/2 = 6% yield to maturity, expressed on a semiannual basis

In computing the price of the bond issued, on a semiannual analysis, we show

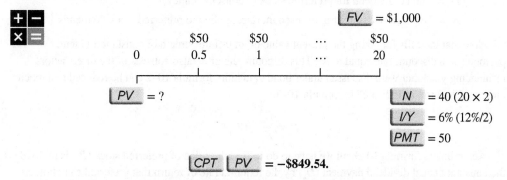

The answer of PV = $849.54 is slightly below that which we found previously for the same bond, assuming an annual interest rate ($850.61). In terms of accuracy, the semiannual analysis is a

more acceptable method. As is true in many finance texts, the annual interest rate approach is given first for ease of presentation, and then the semiannual basis is given. In the problems at the end of the chapter, you will be asked to do problems on both an annual and semiannual interest payment basis.

Tables (optional)

Total Present Value

(PV_A) Present value of interest payments (Appendix D)	$752.30
(PV) Present value of principal payment at maturity (Appendix B)	97.00
Total present value, or price, of the bond	$849.30

VALUATION OF PREFERRED STOCK

Preferred stock represents a long-term interest by an investor in a firm. This is another way that a firm hopes to raise long-term capital to invest in its revenue-generating assets. A preferred share, although considered an equity financial asset, is a hybrid security that has neither the ownership privileges of common stock nor the legally enforceable provisions of debt. Preferreds offer regular fixed payments (usually quarterly or every three months) as a dividend, but do not have the binding contractual obligation to pay interest as on debt. Generally, preferred stock is a perpetuity, meaning it has no maturity date.

Preferreds are valued in the market on the basis of the expected stream of dividend payments and without any principal payment since there is no ending life. If preferred stock had a maturity date, the analysis would be similar to that for bonds. Preferred stock dividends carry a higher order of precedence than common stock dividends as to payment. To value a perpetuity such as preferred stock, we first consider the formula

$$P_p = \frac{D_p}{(1 + K_p)^1} + \frac{D_p}{(1 + K_p)^2} + \frac{D_p}{(1 + K_p)^3} + \cdots + \frac{D_p}{(1 + K_p)^n} + \cdots \ (n \rightarrow \infty) \quad \text{(10–2)}$$

Represented graphically as

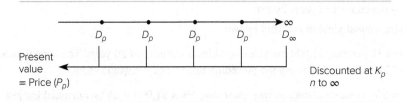

Where

P_p = Price of preferred stock

D_p = Annual dividend for preferred stock (a constant value)

K_p = Required rate of return, or discount rate, applied to preferred stock dividends

Note that the calls for taking the present value of an infinite stream of constant dividend payments at a discount rate equal to K_p. This discount rate of K_p also consists of the three factors influencing yield that were discussed under bond valuation. formula 10–2 can be reduced to a much more usable form, as indicated in formula 10–3.

$$P_p = \frac{D_p}{K_p} \quad \text{(10–3)}$$

According to formula 10–3, all we have to do to find the price of preferred stock (P_p) is to divide the constant annual dividend payment (D_p) by the required rate of return that preferred shareholders are demanding (K_p). For example, if the annual dividend were $10 and the shareholder required a 10 percent rate of return, the price of preferred stock would be $100.

$$P_p = \frac{D_p}{K_p} = \frac{\$10}{0.10} = \$100$$

We could achieve the same with a calculator using a large number, such as 1,000, for N.

I/Y = 10%	FV = 0
PMT = $10	N = 1,000

CPT PV = −$100.

As was true in our bond valuation analysis, if the rate of return required by security holders changes, the value of the financial asset (in this case, preferred stock) changes. You may also recall that the longer the life of an investment, the greater the impact of a change in required rate of return. It is one thing to be locked into a low-paying security for one year when the rate goes up; it is quite another to be locked in for 10 or 20 years. With preferred stock, you have a *perpetual* security, so the impact is at a maximum. Assume in the prior example that because of higher inflation or increased business risk, K_p (the required rate of return) increases to 12 percent. The new value for the preferred stock shares then becomes

$$P_p = \frac{D_p}{K_p} = \frac{\$10}{0.12} = \$83.33$$

If the required rate of return were reduced to 8 percent, the opposite effect would occur. The preferred stock price would be recomputed as

$$P_p = \frac{D_p}{K_p} = \frac{\$10}{0.08} = \$125$$

It is not surprising that preferred stock is now trading well above its original price of $100. It is still offering a $10 dividend (10 percent of original offering price of $100), while the market is demanding only an 8 percent yield. To match the $10 dividend with the 8 percent rate of return, the market price will advance to $125.

Determining the Required Rate of Return (Yield) from the Market Price

In our analysis of preferred stock, we have used the value of the annual dividend (D_p) and the required rate of return (K_p) to solve for the price of preferred stock (P_p). We could change our analysis to solve for the required rate of return (K_p) as the unknown, given that we knew the annual dividend (D_p) and the preferred stock price (P_p). We take formula 10–3 and rewrite it as formula 10–4, where the unknown is the required rate of return (K_p).

$$P_p = \frac{D_p}{K_p} \quad \text{(reverse the position of } K_p \text{ and } P_p) \quad \text{(10–3)}$$

$$K_p = \frac{D_p}{P_p} \quad \text{(10–4)}$$

Using formula 10–4, if the annual preferred dividend (D_p) is $10 and the price of preferred stock (P_p) is $100, the required rate of return (yield) would be 10 percent.

$$K_p = \frac{D_p}{P_p} = \frac{\$10}{\$100} = 10\%$$

If the price goes up to $130, the yield will be only 7.69 percent.

$$K_p = \frac{\$10}{\$130} = 7.69\%$$

We see that the rise in market price causes quite a decline in the yield.

VALUATION OF COMMON STOCK

Common stock also represents a long-term investment in a firm, again as a means of raising long-term capital for the firm's operations. It represents an ownership interest referred to as equity and entitles a common shareholder to the firm's profits after all contractual obligations (wages, interest) are satisfied. The value of a common share to the shareholder is the claim on these residual earnings of the firm. These earnings can be retained and reinvested in the firm's operations or paid out as dividends.

Investors place value on common shares based on the firm's ability to generate cash flow or earnings and the risks attached to those expected earnings. These earnings will eventually flow to the shareholder as dividends in current periods or at some time in the future, possibly as a liquidating dividend at the end of the corporation's life. Therefore, a share of common stock can be valued based on the present value of

- An expected stream of future dividends (dividend valuation model)
- The expected future earnings (price/earnings model)

Shareholders will be influenced by a change in earnings, a change in the risks faced by the firm, or other variables, but the ultimate value of any holding rests with the distribution of earnings in the form of dividend payments. Though the shareholder may benefit from the retention and reinvestment of earnings by the corporation, at some point the earnings must be translated into cash flow for the shareholder.

A stock valuation model based on future expected dividends can be stated as

$$P_0 = \frac{D_1}{(1 + K_e)^1} + \frac{D_2}{(1 + K_e)^2} + \frac{D_3}{(1 + K_e)^3} + \cdots + \frac{D_n}{(1 + K_e)^n} + \cdots \ (n \to \infty) \quad \text{(10–5)}$$

where

P_0 = Price of the stock today

D = Dividend for each year

K_e = Required rate of return for common stock (discount rate)

With modification, this dividend valuation model formula, for shares, is generally applied to three different circumstances:

1. No growth in dividends
2. Constant growth in dividends
3. Variable growth in dividends (Appendix 10B)

No Growth in Dividends

Under the no-growth circumstance, common stock is similar to preferred stock. The common stock pays a constant dividend each year. For that reason we merely translate the terms in formula 10–4, which applies to preferred stock, to apply to common stock. This is shown as new formula 10–6.

$$P_0 = \frac{D_1}{K_e} \quad \text{(10–6)}$$

Where

P_0 = Price of common stock today

D_1 = Current annual common stock dividend (a constant value) $(D_1 = D_2 = D_3 \ldots D_\infty)$

K_e = Required rate of return for common stock

Assume D_0 = $1.86 and K_e = 12 percent; the price of stock would be $15.50.

$$P_0 = \frac{\$1.86}{0.12} = \$15.50$$

A no-growth policy for common stock dividends does not hold much appeal for investors and so is seen infrequently in the real world.

Constant Growth in Dividends

A firm that increases dividends at a constant rate is a more likely circumstance. Perhaps a firm decides to increase its dividends by 5 or 7 percent per year. Under such a circumstance, formula 10–5 converts to formula 10–7.

$$P_0 = \frac{D_0(1+g)^1}{(1+K_e)^1} + \frac{D_0(1+g)^2}{(1+K_e)^2} + \frac{D_0(1+g)^3}{(1+K_e)^3} + \cdots + \frac{D_0(1+g)^n}{(1+K_e)^n} + \cdots (n \to \infty) \quad \text{(10–7)}$$

Represented graphically as

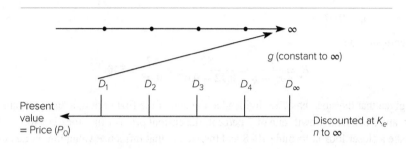

Where

P_0 = Price of common stock today

$D_0(1+g)^1$ = Dividend in year 1, D_1

$D_0(1+g)^2$ = Dividend in year 2, D_2, and so on

g = Constant growth rate in dividends

K_e = Required rate of return for common stock (discount rate)

In other words, the current price of the stock is the present value of the future stream of dividends growing at a constant rate. If we can anticipate the growth pattern of future dividends and determine the discount rate, we can ascertain the price of the stock.

For example, assume the following information:

D_0 = Latest 12-month dividend (assume $1.87)

D_1 = First year, $2 (growth rate, 7%)

D_2 = Second year, $2.14 (growth rate, 7%)

D_3 = Third year, $2.29 (growth rate, 7%) etc.

K_e = Required rate of return (discount rate), 12%

Then

$$P_0 = \frac{\$2}{(1.12)^1} + \frac{\$2.14}{(1.12)^2} + \frac{\$2.29}{(1.12)^3} + \cdots + \frac{\$2(1.07)^n}{(1.12)^n} + \cdots (n \to \infty)$$

To find the price of the stock, we take the present value of each year's dividend. This is no small task when the formula calls for us to take the present value of an *infinite* stream of growing dividends. Fortunately, formula 10–7 can be compressed into a much more usable form if two circumstances are satisfied.

1. The dividend growth rate (g) must be constant forever.
2. The discount rate (K_e) must exceed the growth rate (g).

These assumptions are usually made to reduce the complications in the analytical process. They then allow us to reduce or rewrite formula 10–7 as formula 10–8. Formula 10–8 is the basic formula for finding the value of common stock and is referred to as the dividend valuation model.

$$P_0 = \frac{D_1}{K_e - g} \quad \text{(10–8)}$$

This is an extremely easy formula to use in which[4]

P_0 = Price of the stock today

D_1 = Dividend at the end of the first year (or period)

K_e = Required rate of return (discount rate)

g = Constant growth rate in dividends

Based on the current example,

$D_1 = \$2$

$K_e = 0.12$

$g = 0.07$

P_0 is computed as

$$P_0 = \frac{D_1}{K_e - g} = \frac{\$2}{0.12 - 0.07} = \frac{\$2}{0.05} = \$40$$

Thus, given that the stock has a $2 dividend at the end of the first period, a discount rate of 12 percent, and a constant growth rate of 7 percent, the current price of the stock is $40.

Let's take a closer look at formula 10–8 and the factors that influence valuation. For example, what is the anticipated effect on valuation if K_e (the required rate of return, or discount rate) increases as a result of inflation or increased risk? Intuitively, we would expect the stock price to decline if investors demand a higher return and the dividend and growth rate remain the same. This is precisely what happens.

If D_1 remains at $2 and the growth rate ($g$) is 7 percent but K_e increases from 12 percent to 14 percent, using formula 10–8, the price of the common stock would now be $28.57. This is considerably lower than its earlier value of $40.

$$P_0 = \frac{D_1}{K_e - g} = \frac{\$2}{0.14 - 0.07} = \frac{\$2}{0.07} = \$28.57$$

Similarly, if the growth rate (g) increases and D_1 and K_e remain constant, the stock price can be expected to increase. Assume $D_1 = \$2$, K_e is set at its earlier level of 12 percent, and g increases from 7 percent to 9 percent. Using formula 10–8 once again, the new price of the stock would be $66.67.

$$P_0 = \frac{D_1}{K_e - g} = \frac{\$2}{0.12 - 0.09} = \frac{\$2}{0.03} = \$66.67$$

We should not be surprised to see that an increasing growth rate has enhanced the value of the stock.

---

[4]To derive this relationship we multiply both sides of formula 10–7 by $\dfrac{(1 + K_e)}{(1 + g)}$ and subtract formula 10–7 from the product. The result is

$$\frac{P_0(1 + K_e)}{(1 + g)} - P_0 = D_0$$

$$P_0 \left[\frac{1 + K_e}{1 + g} - 1 \right] = D_0$$

Therefore,

$$P_0 \left[\frac{(1 + K_e) - (1 + g)}{1 + g} \right] = D_0$$

$$P_0(K_e - g) = D_0(1 + g)$$

$$P_0 = \frac{D_1}{K_e - g}$$

Determining the Inputs for the Dividend Valuation Model

Our model for valuation based on future dividends seems reasonable, but where do we find the numbers for the model that allow us to determine the share price? Our Finance in Action box demonstrates. Dividends are fairly accessible, if they are paid, and are found in annual reports or at various investment sites. An appropriate required return for the common shares (K_e) can be estimated using CAPM, examined further in Appendix 11A, or by using the current yield for long-term Government of Canada bonds to which a risk premium is added, based on the riskiness of the common shares. This yield to maturity concept is discussed earlier in this chapter.

 FINANCE IN ACTION

Estimating Value with the Dividend Capitalization Model

Historical earnings are available in annual reports and accessible on company websites or at the SEDAR site (sedar.com) for publicly traded companies. Several investment sites provide earnings estimates for Canadian companies, although the information is often in U.S. dollars (look carefully). An example is reuters.com/companies

We will estimate the share value of the Royal Bank of Canada (RY) using the dividend capitalization model as of January 2020.

D_0 = $4.20 (dividends available at TMXMoney site)
K_e = 7.68%
   6% (for risk) plus 1.68% (Government of Canada long-term bond rate from Bank of Canada site (bankofcanada.ca))

g = 3.54 (1-year earnings growth from TD research, extrapolated to dividends)

$$D_1 = D_0 \times (1 + g)$$
$$= \$4.20 \times (1.0354)$$
$$= \$4.35$$

$$P_0 = \frac{D_1}{K_e - g} = \frac{\$4.35}{0.0768 - 0.0354} = \$105.07$$

The actual price of Royal Bank shares at this time was $106.55. This may suggest the shares are slightly overpriced, or we should revisit the inputs to our model.

With the same methodology, the dividend capitalization model, you should be able to calculate a value for a Royal Bank's share today.

Q1 Can you suggest any reasons for a difference between the market share price and the model's share value?

tmx.com
Symbol: RY

It is the value for growth (g) that will require some effort on our part. This is the long-run growth rate for the firm. What we can do is examine the historical growth rate of the firm and project it into the future, adjusting for any micro (firm-related) or macro (overall economy) factors that we believe will cause the growth rate to change. New technologies, changing government regulations, economic slowdowns, and external shocks such as wars are some of the events that might alter our growth estimates.

The historical growth rates are best estimated from dividends, but we could also use the growth in earnings per share, revenues per share, or cash flow per share if one or the other of these items is not readily available. We might also use an alternative entry if there is possible distortion of one or more of the historical growth rates. In fact, determining the growth rates for all of these entries would give us a broader picture of the probable growth rate for the firm.

If, for example, the earnings per share figure five years ago was $1.50 and the last reported earnings per share was $2.10, the historical growth rate would be 7 percent.

PV = (1.50) FV = 2.10

PMT = 0 N = 5

CPT I/Y = **6.96% (round to 7 percent).**

Stock Valuation Based on Future Stock Value The discussion of stock valuation to this point has related to the concept of the present value of future dividends. This is a valid concept, but suppose we wish to approach the issue from a slightly different viewpoint. Assume we are going to buy a stock and hold it for three years and then sell it. We wish to know the present value of our investment. This is somewhat like the bond valuation analysis. We receive a dividend for three years (D_1, D_2, D_3) and then a price (payment) for the stock at the end of three years (P_3). What is the present value of the benefits? What we do is add the present value of three years of dividends and the present value of the stock price after three years. Assuming a constant growth dividend analysis, the stock price after three years is simply the present value of all future dividends after the third year (from the fourth year on). Thus, the current price of the stock in this case is nothing other than the present value of the first three dividends, plus the present value of all future dividends (which is equivalent to the stock price after the third year). Saying the price of the stock is the present value of all future dividends is also the equivalent of saying it is the present value of a dividend stream for a number of years plus the present value of the price of the stock after that time period. The appropriate formula is still $P_0 = D_1/(K_e - g)$, which we have been using throughout this part of the chapter.

Determining the Required Rate of Return from the Market Price

In our analysis of common stock, we have used the first year's dividend (D_1), the required rate of return (K_e), and the growth rate (g) to solve for the stock price (P_0) based on formula 10–8.

We could change the analysis to solve for the required rate of return (K_e) as the unknown, given that we know the first year's dividend (D_1), the stock price (P_0), and the growth rate (g). We take formula 10–8 and algebraically rearrange it to provide formula 10–9.

$$P_0 = \frac{D_1}{K_e - g} \quad \text{(10–8)}$$

$$K_e = \frac{D_1}{P_0} + g \quad \text{(10–9)}$$

This formula allows us to compute the required return (K_e) from the investment. Returning to the basic data from the common stock example,

K_e = Required rate of return (to be solved)

D_1 = Dividend at the end of the first year $2

P_0 = Price of the stock today $40

g = Constant growth rate 0.07

$$K_e = \frac{\$2}{\$40} + 0.07 = 0.05 + 0.07 = 0.12 = 12\%$$

In this instance, we would say that the shareholder demands a 12 percent return on the common stock investment. Of particular interest are the individual parts of the formula for K_e that we have been discussing. Let's write out formula 10–9 again.

$$K_e = \frac{\text{First year's dividend}}{\text{Common stock price}} \left(\frac{D_1}{P_0}\right) + \text{Growth } (g)$$

The first term represents the dividend yield the shareholder receives, and the second term represents the anticipated growth in dividends, earnings, and stock price. Though we have been describing the growth rate primarily in terms of dividends, it is assumed that the earnings and stock price also grow at that same rate over the long term if all else holds constant. Observe that the preceding formula represents a total return concept. The shareholder is receiving a current dividend plus anticipated growth in the future. If the dividend yield is low, the growth rate must be high to provide the necessary return. Conversely, if the growth rate is low, a high dividend yield is expected. The concepts of dividend yield and growth are clearly interrelated.

LO5 The Price-Earnings Ratio Concept and Valuation

In Chapter 2 we introduced the concept of the price-earnings ratio (P/E). The price-earnings ratio represents a multiplier applied to current earnings to determine the value of a share of stock in the market. It is considered a pragmatic, everyday approach to valuation. If a stock has earnings per share of $3 and a P/E ratio of 12 times, it carries a market value of $36. Another company with the same earnings but a P/E ratio of 15 times enjoys a market price of $45.

The price-earnings ratio is influenced by the earnings and sales growth of the firm, the risk (or volatility in performance), the debt-equity structure of the firm, the dividend policy, the quality of management, and a number of other factors. Firms that have bright expectations for the future tend to trade at high P/E ratios, but the opposite is true of low P/E firms. It is because of those future expectations of earnings that one should be careful in applying historical P/E ratios to current earnings.

FINANCE IN ACTION

Valuation of Small Businesses

The value of a small business takes on importance when the business is sold as part of a divorce settlement, for estate purposes, or when the owner wishes to retire. Unlike a firm trading in the public securities market, there is no ready market for a local bookstore, a bowling alley, or an accountant's practice. Lower liquidity decreases the value assigned the business.

Another factor affecting value is the importance of a key person in the operation of the business. If the founder of the business is critical to its functioning, the goodwill established by the owner will often diminish after they depart, resulting in declining cash flows and a loss of value.

Earnings of a small business are often lower than those of a publicly traded company. The owners of small businesses often intermingle personal and business expenses. Family use of cars, health insurance, travel, and so on, may be charged as business expenses even when Canada Revenue Agency tries to restrict the practice. Furthermore, small, private businesses try to report earnings that are as low as possible to minimize taxes. Publicly traded companies report quarterly, often attempting to show ever-increasing profits to boost share prices. Analysts will carefully examine the earnings reports of the small business, making necessary adjustments that may increase the stated earnings.

The average small business may sell at some multiple of average adjusted earnings for the previous three years. Sale prices on comparable businesses are also considered in the valuation. Accountants and financial analysts with experience in similar business valuations can be of immense help.

In January 2020, the average P/E for the top 300 companies of the Toronto Stock Exchange (the S&P/TSX Composite Index) almost 19 to 1. There is often a large variation among firms, based on their future earnings expectations and earnings at that moment. P/E ratios are reported only for common shares, which have a claim on the earnings, and only when earnings are positive.

Toronto Stock Exchange
tmx.com
The Globe and Mail
theglobeandmail.com

Price-earnings ratios can be looked up in many financial newspapers (theglobeandmail.com) and at several other websites, such as investcom .com or tmxmoney.com. The typical information is displayed in Table 10–3.

Table 10–3 An example of stock quotations, January 2020

	Open	High	Low	Close	Year high	Year low	Volume	EPS	P/E	Div	Yield
Royal Bank (RY)	106.50	106.75	106.26	106.55	109.68	97.30	4.2 m	8.75	12.2	3.48	3.60
Descartes (DSG)	60.13	60.72	60.10	60.38	60.72	38.21	0.07 m	0.54	112.3	0	0

The P/E ratio is determined by dividing the closing price by the latest reported earnings.
The yield is determined by dividing the current dividend (quarterly × 4) by the closing price.
Other columns show the open, high, and low prices for the day; the volume of shares traded; and the high and low prices for the year.
The company stock ticker symbols used by the Toronto Stock Exchange for identification are also shown.

The P/E ratio represents an easily understood, pragmatic approach to valuation that is widely used by stockbrokers and individual investors. The dividend valuation approach (based on the present value of dividends) we have been using throughout the chapter is more theoretically sound and is likely to be used by sophisticated financial analysts. To some extent, the two concepts can be brought together. A stock that has a high required rate of return (K_e) because of its risky nature generally has a low P/E ratio. Similarly, a stock with a high expected growth rate (g) normally has a high P/E ratio. In the first example, both methods provide a low valuation, while in the latter case both methods provide a high valuation.

Variable Growth in Dividends

In the discussion of common stock valuation, we have considered procedures for firms that had no growth in dividends and for firms that had a constant growth. Most of the discussion and literature in finance assumes a constant growth dividend model. However, there is also a third case, and that is one of variable growth in dividends. The most common variable growth model is one in which the firm experiences very rapid or supernormal growth for a number of years and then levels off to more normal, constant growth. This is modelled in Appendix 10B. The supernormal growth pattern is often experienced by firms in emerging industries, such as in the early days of electronics or microcomputers.

In evaluating a firm with an initial pattern of supernormal growth, we first take the present value of dividends during the exceptional growth period. We then determine the price of the stock at the end of the supernormal growth period by taking the present value of the normal, constant dividends that follow the supernormal growth period. We discount this price to the present and add it to the present value of the supernormal dividends. This gives us the current price of the stock. A numerical example of a supernormal growth rate evaluation model is presented in Appendix 10B.

Finally, in the discussion of common stock valuation models, readers may ask about the valuation of companies that currently pay no dividends. Since virtually all of our discussion has been based on values associated with dividends, how can this no-dividend circumstance be handled? One approach is to assume that even for the firm that pays no current dividends, at some point in the future shareholders will be rewarded with cash dividends. We then take the present value of their deferred dividends.

A second approach to valuing a firm that pays no cash dividend is to take the present value of earnings per share for a number of periods and add that to the present value of the last earnings per share, valued as a perpetuity. The discount rate applied to future earnings is generally higher than the discount rate applied to future dividends.

FINANCE IN ACTION

Diamonds, Nickel, Gold, or Software—for Value?

Share prices for several Canadian companies represent fascinating examples of valuation based on future expected cash flows that were highly speculative.

In 1991, Dia Met Minerals Ltd. shares traded at $0.26, and the firm's equity value was less than $2 million. In 1992, the shares traded as high as $60, and the equity in Dia Met was worth $600 million. Dia Met Minerals had little in the way of hard assets and had never paid a dividend. Investors had bid up the share price on the basis of the promised future cash flows. Quality diamonds had been discovered in the Northwest Territories. By 1999, mining production began to generate cash flows from those diamonds, and today Canada is a world leader in diamond production. Dia Met was acquired by BHP Ltd., a company that trades on the Australian Stock Exchange.

As a result of the rush to find diamonds in Canada, another company, Diamond Fields Resources Inc., was formed to locate diamonds, and for $450,000 it sponsored two prospectors. Near Voisey's Bay, Labrador, they found one of the world's richest deposits of nickel, copper, and cobalt. In the fall of 1994, Diamond Fields stock traded for $3.55, and by 1996 it was trading at over $160 per share (adjusted for stock splits). Inco purchased Diamond Fields for $4.3 billion, even though no full-scale mining had begun. The value, established by Inco bidding in the securities market, was based on the promised returns from this rich mineral deposit in the future. In 1996, nickel sold at about $3.80 per pound, and the future looked bright; but by 1998 nickel sold for less than $2 per pound, and Voisey's Bay was mothballed. By 2006, Inco was acquired by CVRD, becoming Vale Inco, and in 2007 nickel was priced above $22 a pound.

Shares in the company Bre-X soared in value from a few dollars in early 1995 to over $240 by mid-1996 on the basis of reports that it had discovered one of the largest world gold finds in the wilds of Borneo. Value was established on the possibility of future earnings. However, by 1997 it was apparent that Bre-X was a hoax, and the shares plunged in value to almost nothing.

Investors become excited about future potential revenues that may, they hope, result in profits. Internet companies created a "bubble" in share prices for high-tech companies through 1999 and 2000 on the belief that revenues and profits would continue to climb. Nortel soared to a value of $350 billion but within two years of that was worth only $3 billion. In 2009, Nortel sought bankruptcy protection. Some suggested that the Internet, with its effect on the economy, had changed valuation standards. Similarly, BlackBerry increased in value from $4.5 to $80 billion between 2006 and 2008, only to fall back to $5 billion by 2020.

Q1 To what extent is Vale Inco developing Voisey's Bay?

Q2 How have the share prices of Vale (Inco), BHP, and BB performed over the last year?

vale.com	**asx.com.au**	**blackberry.com**
Symbol: VALE (NYSE)	Symbol: BHP	Symbol: BB

SUMMARY AND REVIEW OF FORMULAS

1. The primary emphasis in this chapter is on valuation of financial assets: bonds, preferred stock, and common stock. Regardless of the security being analyzed, valuation is normally based on the concept of determining the present value of future cash flows. Thus, we draw on many of the time-value-of-money techniques developed in Chapter 9. (LO1)

2. Inherent in the valuation process is a determination of the rate of return demanded by investors. The rate of return is also referred to as the discount rate, or yield to maturity. We note that the required rate of return is composed of a real rate of return, an inflation premium, and a risk premium based on the uncertainty of the future expected cash flows. When we have identified the rate of return required by investors, we have also identified what it will cost the corporation to raise new capital. (LO2)

3., 4. In the section below, we specifically review the valuation techniques (price and yield) associated with bonds, preferred stock, and common stock. (LO3) (LO4)

Bonds

The price, or current value, of a bond is equal to the present value of interest payments (I_t) over the life of the bond plus the present value of the principal payment (P_n) at maturity. The discount rate used in the analytical process is the yield to maturity (Y). The yield to maturity (required rate of return) is determined in the marketplace by factors such as the real rate of return, an inflation premium, and a risk premium.

The formula for bond valuation was presented as formula 10–1.

$$P_b = \sum_{t=1}^{n} \frac{I_t}{(1 + Y)^t} + \frac{P_n}{(1 + Y)^n} \quad \text{(10–1)}$$

Bonds fit the pattern described by the above graphical representation. Usually, we are concerned with determining the current price of the bond or its yield. The other variables are likely known.

> **Tables (optional)** We say the present value of interest payments is
>
> $$PV_A = A \times PVI_{IFA} \, (n = \underline{\hspace{1cm}}, i = \underline{\hspace{1cm}}) \quad \text{(Appendix D)}$$
>
> Whereas the present value of the principal payment at maturity is
>
> $$PV = FV \times PV_{IF} \, (n = \underline{\hspace{1cm}}, i = \underline{\hspace{1cm}}) \quad \text{(Appendix B)}$$
>
> Adding these two values together gives us the price of the bond. We may use annual or semiannual analysis.
>
> The value of the bond is strongly influenced by the relationship of the yield to maturity in the market to the interest rate on the bond and also the length of time to maturity.
>
> If we know the price of the bond, the size of the interest payments, and the maturity of the bond, we can solve for the yield to maturity, as discussed in Appendix 10A.

Preferred Stock

In determining the value of preferred stock, we are taking the present value of an infinite stream of level dividend payments. This would be a tedious process if it were not for the fact that the mathematical calculations can be compressed into a simple formula. The appropriate formula is

$$P_p = \frac{D_p}{K_p} \quad \text{(10-3)}$$

According to this formula, to find the preferred stock price (P_p) we take the constant annual dividend payment (D_p) and divide this value by the rate of return that preferred shareholders are demanding (K_p).

If, on the other hand, we know the price of the preferred stock and the constant annual dividend payment, we can solve for the required rate of return on preferred stock as

$$K_p = \frac{D_p}{P_p} \quad \text{(10-4)}$$

Common Stock

The value of common stock is also based on the concept of the present value of an expected stream of future dividends. Unlike preferred stock, the dividends are not necessarily level. The firm and shareholders may experience

1. No growth in dividends

2. Constant growth in dividends

3. Variable or supernormal growth in dividends

It is the second circumstance that receives most of the attention in the financial literature. If a firm has constant growth (g) in dividends (D) and the required rate of return (K_e) exceeds the growth rate, formula 10-8 can be utilized.

$$P_0 = \frac{D_1}{K_e - g} \quad \text{(10-8)}$$

In using this formula, all we need to know is the value of the dividend at the end of the first year, the required rate of return, and the discount rate. Most of our valuation calculations with common stock utilize formula 10-8.

If we need to know the required rate of return (K_e) for common stock, formula 10-9 can be employed.

$$K_e = \frac{D_1}{P_0} + g \quad \text{(10-9)}$$

The first term represents the dividend yield on the stock, and the second term represents the growth rate. Together they provide the total return demanded by the investor.

5. The price-earnings ratio represents a multiplier applied to earnings to determine share price. It is an easy rule of thumb used to determine value, but it does not incorporate the dynamics of the other models, including future expected cash flows and today's required rate of return. (LO5)

DISCUSSION QUESTIONS

1. How is valuation of financial assets by investors related to the cost of financing (cost of capital) for the firm? (LO1)

2. How is valuation of any financial asset related to future cash flows? (LO2)

3. Why might investors demand a lower rate of return for an investment in BCE as compared to Air Canada? (LO2)

4. What are the three factors that influence the required rate of return by investors? (LO2)

5. What is meant by real rate of return? (LO2)

6. If inflationary expectations increase, what is likely to happen to the yield to maturity on bonds in the marketplace? What is also likely to happen to the price of bonds? (LO2, LO4)

7. Why is the remaining time to maturity an important factor in evaluating the impact of a change in yield to maturity on bond prices? (LO4)

8. These valuation models are based on investors' required rates of return and their reflection in the prices of the assets. Does the change in price always occur according to the model? (LO2)

9. What three adjustments have to be made in going from annual to semiannual bond analysis? (LO3)

10. Why is a change in required yield for preferred stock likely to have a greater impact on price than a change in required yield for bonds? (LO3)

11. What type of dividend pattern for common stock is similar to the dividend payment for preferred stock? (LO1)

12. What two conditions must be met to go from formula 10–7 to formula 10–8 in using the dividend valuation model? (LO5)

$$P_0 = \frac{D_1}{K_e - g} \quad (10\text{–}8)$$

13. What two components make up the required rate of return on common stock? (LO5)

14. What factors might influence a firm's price-earnings ratio? (LO5)

15. How does a firm's price-earnings ratio relate to K_e? To g? (LO5)

16. How is the supernormal growth pattern likely to vary from the more normal, constant growth pattern? (LO3)

17. What approaches can be taken in valuing a firm's stock when there is no cash dividend payment? (LO3)

INTERNET RESOURCES AND QUESTIONS

The Globe and Mail has daily share prices, dividend yields, and price-earnings ratios (Investing): globeandmail.com

Perimeter Financial provides some information on Canadian fixed income securities: pfin.ca

Reuters provides considerable information on common shares (stocks: search): reuters.com/finance/markets

The Toronto Stock Exchange (TMX) site includes information on listed stocks that include daily and yearly high and low prices, opening prices, volume, EPS, P/E ratios, and dividend yields: tmxmoney.com

The Government of Canada Finance Department provides a technical guide on determining bond prices and yields, as well as definitions of various government bonds: fin.gc.ca

The Bank of Canada provides current money market and long-term bond yields:
bankofcanada.ca

1. What is the price and yield of Government of Canada bonds of 1, 2, 5, 10, and 30 years?

2. Find the price-earnings ratio and dividend yield for today for the following corporations: Encana (ECA), Imperial Oil (IMO), Molson Coors (TPX.A), OpenText (OTEX), and Royal Bank Preferred (RY.PR.J). Discuss the reasons for differences in the ratios among these securities.

PROBLEMS

1. The Wild Rose Company has $1,000 par value (maturity value) bonds outstanding at 9 percent interest. The bonds will mature in 20 years with annual payments. Compute the current price of the bonds if the present yield to maturity is

    a. 6 percent

    b. 8 percent

    c. 12 percent

2. Midland Oil has $1,000 par value (maturity value) bonds outstanding at 8 percent interest. The bonds will mature in 25 years with annual payments. Compute the current price of the bonds if the present yield to maturity is

    a. 7 percent

    b. 10 percent

    c. 13 percent

3. Exodus Limousine Company has $1,000 par value bonds outstanding at 10 percent interest. The bonds will mature in 50 years with annual payments. Compute the current price of the bonds if the current yield to maturity is

    a. 5 percent

    b. 15 percent

4. Referring back to the previous problem, part *b*, what percent of the total bond value does the repayment of principal represent?

5. Applied Software has a $1,000 par value bond outstanding that pays 12 percent interest with annual payments. The current yield to maturity on such bonds in the market is 7 percent. Compute the price of the bonds for these maturity dates

    a. 30 years

    b. 15 years

    c. 1 year

6. The Victoria Telephone Company has a $1,000 par value bond outstanding that pays 5 percent interest with annual payments. The current yield to maturity on such bonds in the market is 8 percent. Compute the price of the bonds for these maturity dates:

    a. 30 years

    b. 15 years

    c. 1 year

7. For the previous problem, graph the relationship in a manner similar to the top half of Figure 10–2. Also explain why the pattern of price change occurs.

8. A Sunfish bond is paying 10 percent interest for 20 years on a semiannual basis. Assume interest rates in the market (yield to maturity) decline from 12 percent to 8 percent:

   a. What is the bond price at 12 percent?

   b. What is the bond price at 8 percent?

   c. What would be the percentage return on an investment bought when rates were 12 percent and sold when rates are 8 percent?

9. For the same Sunfish bond (as in the problem above) assume interest rates in the market (yield to maturity) increase from 6 to 12 percent.

   a. What is the bond price at 6 percent?

   b. What is the bond price at 14 percent?

   c. What would be the percentage return on an investment bought when rates were 6 percent and sold when rates are 14 percent?

10. Ron Rhodes calls his broker to inquire about purchasing a bond of Golden Years Recreation Corporation. His broker quotes a price of $1,170. Ron is concerned that the bond might be overpriced based on the facts involved. The $1,000 par value bond pays 13 percent annual interest payable semiannually, and has 18 years remaining until maturity. The current yield to maturity on similar bonds is 11 percent. Compute the new price of the bond and comment on whether you think it is overpriced in the marketplace.

11. The Vinny Cartier Company issued bonds at $1,000 per bond. The bonds had a 25-year life when issued, with semiannual payments at the then annual rate of 12 percent. This return was in line with required returns by bondholders at that point, as described below:

Real rate of return..................................	3%
Inflation premium	6
Risk premium	3
Total return	12%

   Assume that ten years later the inflation premium is 3 percent, the risk premium has declined to 2 percent and both are appropriately reflected in the required return (or yield to maturity) of the bonds. The bonds have 15 years remaining until maturity. Compute the new price of the bond.

12. Martin Shipping Lines issued bonds 10 years ago at $1,000 per bond. The bonds had a 30-year life when issued, with semiannual payments at the then annual rate of 10 percent. This return was in line with required returns by bondholders at that point, as described below:

Real rate of return..................................	2%
Inflation premium	4
Risk premium	4
Total return	10%

   Assume that today the inflation premium is only 2 percent and is appropriately reflected in the required return (or yield to maturity) of the bonds. Compute the new price of the bond.

13. Lance Whittingham IV specializes in buying deep discount bonds. These represent bonds that are trading at well below par value. He has his eye on a bond issued by the Leisure Time Corporation. The $1,000 par value bond with semiannual payments has 4 percent annual interest and has 16 years remaining to maturity. The current yield to maturity on similar bonds is 10 percent.

   a. What is the current price of the bonds?

   b. By what percent will the price of the bonds increase between now and maturity?

   c. What is the annual compound rate of growth in the value of the bonds? (An approximate answer is acceptable.)

14. Bonds issued by the Coleman Manufacturing Company have a par value of $1,000, which is also the amount of principal to be paid at maturity. The bonds are currently selling for $850. They have 10 years to maturity. Annual interest is 9 percent ($90), paid semiannually. Compute the yield to maturity.

15. Bonds issued by the Tyler Food Chain have a par value of $1,000, are selling for $1,080, and have 20 years remaining to maturity. Annual interest payment is 12.5 percent ($125), paid semiannually. Compute the yield to maturity.

16. Ann Nichols is considering a bond investment in the Southwest Technology Company. The $1,000 bonds have a quoted annual interest rate of 8 percent, and the interest is paid semiannually. The yield to maturity on the bonds is 10 percent annually. There are 25 years to maturity. Compute the price of the bonds.

17. You are called in as a financial analyst to appraise the bonds of the Holtz Corporation. The $1,000 par value bonds have a quoted annual interest rate of 14 percent, paid semiannually. The yield to maturity on the bonds is 12 percent annually. There are 15 years to maturity.

    a. Compute the price of the bonds.

    b. With 10 years remaining to maturity, if yield to maturity goes down substantially to 8 percent, what will be the new price of the bonds?

    c. With a price of $858 what is the yield to maturity if the bond has 10 years to maturity?

18. Douglas bonds mature in 10 years and have an annual coupon rate of 10.5 percent with semiannual payments. The $1,000 par value bond currently trades at $1,105 in the market. Compute the annual yield to maturity on the Douglas bond.

19. A $1,000 par value bond has a 6 percent coupon, which is paid on a semiannual basis. It matures in either 1 year or 20 years. Current yields on similar bonds are either 4 percent or 8 percent.

    a. Calculate the price of the bond for the four possibilities.

    b. What is the relationship between price and yield?

    c. What is the relationship between bond price changes and time to maturity?

20. A preferred share of Hilton Chocolate Company pays an annual dividend of $6. It has a required rate of return of 8 percent. Compute the price of a preferred share.

21. Airdrie Lanes preferred shares pay an annual dividend of $1.20, payable on a quarterly basis. Current yields of similar risk preferred shares are 3 percent. What is the price of each preferred share?

22. X-Tech issued preferred shares many years ago. They carry a fixed dividend of $5 per share. With the passage of time, yields have soared from the original 5 percent to 12 percent (yield is the same as required rate of return).

    a. What was the original issue price?

    b. What is the current value of a X-Tech preferred share?

    c. If the yield on the Preferred Stock Index declines, how will the price of these preferred shares be affected?

23. The Quaid Brothers Corporation has preferred shares outstanding that pay an annual dividend of $12. Each has a price of $108. What is the required rate of return (yield) on the preferred stock?

24. B2Y Solutions has preferred shares outstanding that pay an annual dividend of $3, payable quarterly. Each has a price of $75.00. What is the required rate of return (yield) on the preferred stock?

25. Stagnant Iron and Steel Co. currently pays a $4.20 annual cash dividend (D_0). It plans to maintain the dividend at this level for the foreseeable future, as no future growth is anticipated. If the required rate of return by common shareholders (K_e) is 12 percent, what is the price of each common share?

26. Allied Coal will pay a common share dividend of $3.40 at the end of the year (D_1). The required return on common shares (K_e) is 14 percent. The firm has a constant growth rate (g) of 8 percent. Compute the current price of the shares (P_0).

27. Husky Kennels will pay a quarterly common share dividend of $0.20 at the end of the next quarter. The required return on common shares is 8 percent and the firm has a constant growth rate of 3 percent. Compute the price of a common share of Husky.

28. Friedman Steel Company will pay a dividend of $1.50 per share in the next 12 months (D_1). The required rate of return (K_e) is 10 percent and the constant growth rate is 5 percent.

    a. Compute P_0.

    (For the remaining questions in this problem, all variables remain the same except the one specifically changed. Each question is independent of the others.)

    b. Assume K_e, the required rate of return, goes up to 12 percent, what will be the new value of P_0?

    c. Assume the growth rate (g) goes up to 7 percent, what will be the new value of P_0?

    d. Assume D_1 is $2, what will be the new value of P_0?

29. The Fleming Corporation paid a dividend of $4 last year. Over the next 12 months, the dividend is expected to grow at 8 percent, which is the constant growth rate for the firm. The new dividend after 12 months will represent D_1. The required rate of return is 13 percent. Compute the price of a common share.

30. Rick's Department Stores has had the following pattern of earnings per share over the last five years:

Year	Earnings per Share
20XU	$4.00
20XV	4.20
20XW	4.41
20XX	4.63
20XY	4.86

    The earnings per share have grown at a constant rate (on a rounded basis) and will continue to do so in the future. Dividends represent 40 percent of earnings.

    a. Project earnings and dividends for the next year (20XZ). Round all values in this problem to two places to the right of the decimal point.

    b. If the required rate of return is 13 percent, what is the anticipated share price at the beginning of 20XZ?

31. Just Tin Coatings has had the following pattern of earnings per share over the last five years:

Year	Earnings per Share
20XU	$2.00
20XV	2.18
20XW	2.28
20XX	2.42
20XY	2.62

    The earnings per share have grown over this period and will continue to do so in the future in the same general fashion. Dividends represent 30 percent of earnings.

    a. Project earnings and dividends for the next year (20XZ). Round all values in this problem to two places to the right of the decimal point.

    b. If the required rate of return is 12 percent, what is the anticipated share price at the beginning of 20XZ?

32. Freudian Slips has just paid a dividend of $2.12 for the year and it is expected to grow at 6 percent per year. With a current share price of $54.50, what is Freudian's required (expected) rate of return?

33. A firm will pay a $4.00 dividend at the end of year one, has a share price of $50, and a constant growth rate of 5 percent. Compute the required (expected) rate of return.

34. Triple Peaks Playhouse will pay a quarterly dividend of $0.40 at the end of the next quarter. It has common share price of $32.00 and a constant growth rate of 4 percent. Compute the required rate of return.

35. A firm pays a $1.50 dividend at the end of year one. It has a share price of $60 ($P_0$) and a constant growth rate (g) of 9 percent.

   a. Compute the required (expected) rate of return (K_e). Also indicate whether each of the following changes would make the required rate of return (K_e) go up or down.

   (In each question below, assume only one variable changes at a time. No actual numbers are necessary.)

   b. The dividend payment increases.

   c. The expected growth rate increases.

   d. The stock price increases.

36. Hunter Petroleum Corporation paid a $2 dividend last year. The dividend is expected to grow at a constant rate of 5 percent forever. The required rate of return is 12 percent (this will also serve as the discount rate in this problem). Round all values to three places to the right of the decimal point where appropriate.

   a. Compute the anticipated value of the dividends for the next three years. That is, compute D_1, D_2, and D_3; for example, D_1 is $2.10 ($2.00 × 1.05). Round all values throughout this problem to three places to the right of the decimal point.

   b. Discount each of these dividends back to the present at a discount rate of 12 percent and then sum them.

   c. Compute the price of the stock at the end of the third year (P_3).

$$P_3 = \frac{D_4}{K_e - g}$$

   (D_4 is equal to D_3 times 1.05)

   d. After you have computed P_3, discount it back to the present at a discount rate of 12 percent for three years.

   e. Add together the answers in parts *b* and *d* to get P_0, the current value of the stock. This answer represents the present value of the first three periods of dividends, plus the present value of the price of the stock after three periods (which, in turn, represents the value of all future dividends).

   f. Use formula 10–8 to show that it will provide approximately the same answer as part *e*.

$$P_0 = \frac{D_1}{K_e - g} \quad \text{(10–8)}$$

   For formula 10–8, use D_1 = $2.10, K_e = 12 percent, and g = 5 percent. (The slight difference between the answers to parts *e* and *f* is due to rounding.)

37. You have been examining three firms in the telecommunications business. You have identified the following P/E ratios for the companies.

   a. Which firm appears to be the best value on the P/E ratio alone?

Graham	18
Ted	34
Showus	21

   b. Why do you suppose that Ted has the highest P/E ratio?

(And for more fun and review, do these valuation problems.)

38. What is the value of a common share that has just paid a dividend of $2.25, is expecting an indefinite annual growth rate of 5 percent, and requires a return of 17 percent based on perceived market risks?

39. Calculate the price of a bond originally issued six years ago that pays semiannual interest at the rate of 12 percent and matures in nine years at $1,000. The market currently requires an 8 percent return for a bond of this risk.

40. The Tahitian Lottery has promised an annual stipend of $75,000, forever, and permanent residency on Tahiti. Assuming interest rates of 6 percent, how much must the Tahitian authorities set aside today to guarantee this stipend?

41. A bond just purchased pays annual interest of 10 percent. In seven years it matures at its face value of $25,000. What price was paid if current yields on a bond of this risk are 8.5 percent?

42. Burrito Bell issued a series of $1,000 bonds eight years ago with an annual coupon rate of $100. The bonds mature 12 years from now. If an investor requires a 6 percent return on this investment, what would be the price of a Burrito Bell bond?

43. Current yields are 9 percent on a preferred share that pays a perpetual annual dividend of $6.00. What is the appropriate price of one preferred share?

44. With an anticipated dividend of $1.20, continual annual growth of 8 percent, and a market expectation of a 19 percent yield, at what price would a common share sell?

45. You wish to invest $175,000 in a 12-year annuity. Current yields over the same time to maturity are 8 percent. What could you expect as an annual payment?

46. You have purchased a preferred share that promises a $3.00 dividend. If you expect a 14 percent yield, what price did you pay for the preferred?

47. Waterman Company has had a fantastic growth of 22 percent per year, but this growth rate is expected to fall to 6 percent in the near future and then continue at that rate for a long time. Shareholders expect a 17 percent annual rate of return and a dividend of $0.75 next year. What is the share price of Waterman's common stock?

48. Lou Spence bought a stock seven years ago for $15.00 a share. If it is now selling for $42.39 a share, what is the stock's compound annual growth rate? (No dividends were paid.)

49. You are interested in receiving a true yield on a government bond investment of 8 percent. Your broker suggests a 20-year issue with 12 years to maturity, an original coupon rate of 10 percent, payable semiannually, and a face value of $10,000. The bond has had its coupons stripped, so you won't receive the coupon payments. What price will you pay?

50. A national financial institution is currently offering $50,000 a year for life as a special promotion. Current inflation is 2 percent a year, and the real rate of return is assumed to be 3 percent. One could suggest that this financial institution would receive a 2 percent premium for the risk inherent in its long-term investments. Assuming you will live forever, how much will this promise cost the financial institution today when you win?

51. Thunderbay Ltd. has a 20-year bond outstanding that matures in 14 years. The annual coupon rate is 11 percent, paid semiannually. Current annual nominal yields for bonds of similar risk are 9 percent. What is the price of this bond?

52. Royal Blue Bonds were purchased nine years ago at $1,000, with a 13 percent annual coupon. Today they are sold for $1,215. Assuming the coupons were reinvested at 9 percent, what was the annual yield actually received?

53. Baffin College has an endowment that pays one lucky student $7,500 a year forever; of course, it is a different student each year. Long-term yields are 10 percent.

    a. How much is currently required to fund the endowment?

    b. If the endowment will not commence until five years from today, how much is required?

54. Clear Water Records has its preferred shares trading at $31 with an annual dividend of $1.55, paid out quarterly. What is its annual yield?

55. Kris P. Bacon is considering purchasing a Bitz bond with semiannual payments having an annual coupon rate fixed at 7 percent. Its face value of $1,000 is payable in 8 years and the bond trades at $1,203.67. What is the expected yield on the Bitz bond?

56. Miller Timepieces has a timeless growth rate of 5 percent. It expects to pay a quarterly dividend of $0.35 at the end this quarter. The common shares are currently priced at $46.67 in the market. What is its projected rate of return (yield)?

COMPREHENSIVE PROBLEM

57. Allie Reynolds, the chief financial officer of Healthy Products Inc., has been asked to do an evaluation of Fibre Cereal Inc. by the president, Gail Martinez. Healthy Products was planning a joint venture with Fibre Cereal (privately traded) and Gail and Allie needed a better feel for what Fibre's stock is worth because there is interest in buying the firm at some time in the future. Fibre Cereal paid a dividend at the end of year one of $1.20 out of earnings of $2.45 (payout almost 49 percent), with an anticipated growth rate of 10 percent; the required rate of return is 13 percent.

    a. What is the value of a share based on the dividend valuation model?

    b. Indicate that the value computed in part *a* is correct by showing the values of D_1, D_2, and D_3 and the anticipated share price at the end of year three, as present values. Then sum the computations.

    c. As an alternative measure, examine the value of the firm based on the price-earnings (P/E) ratio times earnings per share. The anticipated P/E ratio can be estimated by taking the average of five publicly traded food industry companies. The P/E ratios were as follows during the time period under analysis:

	P/E ratio
Del Monte	12
General Mills	15
Maple Leaf	14
Kellogg	22
Kraft	17

    d. If, in computing the industry average P/E, it is decided to weight Kellogg by 40 percent and the other four firms by 15 percent each, what would be the new weighted average industry P/E? (Kellogg is more similar to Fibre.) What will be the new suggested share price? (Earnings per share remain at $2.45.)

    e. By what percent will the share price change as a result of using the weighted average industry P/E in part *d* as compared to part *c*?

MINI CASE

Gilbert Enterprises

Tom Gilbert, founder and chair of the board of Gilbert Enterprises, could not believe his eyes as he read the quote about his firm in *The Globe and Mail*. The stock had closed at $35.25, down $3.75 for the week. He called his vice-president of finance, Jane Arnold, and they agreed to meet on Saturday morning at 9 a.m. for breakfast.

When Jane arrived, they reviewed the stock's performance for the past few months. Although the stock opened the year (20XX) at $28.50 per share, it had reached a high of $50 in March, but had steadily slid in value to its current level of $35.25 in mid-May. Tom and Jane both thought the stock was undervalued in the marketplace and were seriously considering an announcement that the firm was going to repurchase up to one million of its own shares in the open market beginning on June 1, 20XX. They thought this would send a message to investors that the market had placed the stock at an unrealistically low level.

Before taking any action, they decided to consult with their investment banking representative, Albert Roth, senior vice-president at the investment firm of Baker, Green, and Roth. Roth had aided the firm in initially selling its stock to the public ("going public") five years ago, and was quite familiar with its operations. Although he was surprised to receive their call during an early Saturday morning round of golf at the country club, he promised to get back to them in the next few days with his recommendation on a stock repurchase.

Gilbert Enterprises was the third-largest firm in the auto parts replacement industry, specializing in brake parts, power transmissions, batteries, cables, and other products related to used automobiles. Although most of the auto industry advertising relates to flashy new cars, Albert Roth knew that the auto parts replacement industry was becoming increasingly important.

His research indicated that the average age of an automobile life had reached eight years in 20XX, up from a mere 6.8 years from 10 years previously. Why? New vehicle price increases had far surpassed the rise in consumer income. People are forced to keep their old cars longer whether they want to or not. Furthermore, environmental legislation mandated more emission inspections and maintenance programs. Consumers were being forced to spend more money to update older automobiles to meet these standards.

Gilbert Enterprises had the most advanced just-in-time (JIT) inventory management system in the industry. For that reason, Albert Roth believed the firm would enjoy supernormal growth, beyond industry standards, for the next three years. His best estimate was that a 15 percent growth rate during that time period was entirely reasonable. After that time span, a more normal growth rate of 6 percent was expected. Current dividends were 1.20 per share, and he decided to use a discount or required rate of return of 10 percent.

He discussed this approach with his partners, and although they generally agreed, they suggested that he also consider a more traditional approach of comparing the firm's P/E ratio to other firms in the industry. P/E data along with other information are shown in Table 1 for Gilbert Enterprises and three other firms in the industry.

Table 1 Comparative data for auto parts replacement firms

	Gilbert Enterprises	Reliance Parts	Standard Auto	Allied Motors
Annual growth in EPS (past five years).....	12.0%	8.0%	7.0%	9.0%
Return on shareholders' equity	18.0%	25.3%	14.0%	15.3%
Return on total assets...................	12.1%	8.1%	10.5%	9.8%
Debt to total assets.....................	33.0%	68.0%	25.0%	36.0%
Market value..........................	$35.25	$70.50	$24.25	$46.75
Book value............................	$16.40	$50.25	$19.50	$50.75
Replacement value.....................	$43.50	$68.75	$26.00	$37.50
Dividend yield........................	3.40%	2.18%	5.26%	3.12%
P/E ratio..............................	16.8	24.1	14.2	18.1

What recommendation would you suggest that Albert Roth make? Do you suggest the firm is under- or overvalued?

APPENDIX 10A

The Bond Yield to Maturity Using Interpolation

As demonstrated in the body of the chapter, this calculation is much easier and more accurate if a financial calculator is used. However, here we use a numerical example to demonstrate this process. Assume a 20-year bond pays $118 per year (11.8 percent) in interest and $1,000 after 20 years in principal repayment. The current price of the bond is $1,085. We wish to determine the yield to maturity, or discount rate, that equates the future flows with the current price.

Because the bond is trading above par value at $1,085, we can assume the yield to maturity must be below the quoted interest rate of 12 percent (the yield to maturity would be the full 12 percent at a bond price of $1,000). As a first approximation, we try 10 percent. Annual analysis is used.

Present Value of Interest Payments

$PV_A = A \times PV_{IFA} \ (n = 20, i = 10\%) \quad$ (Appendix D)

$PV_A = \$118 \times 8.514 = \$1,004.65$

Present Value of Principal Payment at Maturity

$PV = FV \times PV_{IF} \ (n = 20, i = 10\%) \quad$ (Appendix B)

$PV = \$1,000 \times 0.149 = \$149$

Total Present Value

Present value of interest payments........................	$1,004.65
Present value of principal payment at maturity..............	149.00
Total present value, or price, of the bond	$1,153.65

The discount rate of 10 percent gives us too high a present value in comparison to the current bond price of $1,085. Let's try a higher discount rate to get a lower price. We will use 11 percent.

Present Value of Interest Payments

$PV_A = A \times PV_{IFA}(n = 20, i = 11\%) \quad$ (Appendix D)

$PV_A = \$118 \times 7.963 = \$939.63$

Present Value of Principal Payment at Maturity

$PV = FV \times PV_{IF} \ (n = 20, i = 11\%) \quad$ (Appendix B)

$PV = \$1,000 \times 0.124 = \$124$

Total Present Value

Present value of interest payments........................	$ 939.63
Present value of principal payment at maturity..............	124.00
Total present value, or price, of the bond	$1,063.63

The discount rate of 11 percent gives us a value slightly lower than the bond price of $1,085. The rate for the bond must fall between 10 and 11 percent. Using linear interpolation, the answer is 10.76 percent.

$1,153.65	PV @ 10%	$1,153.65	PV @ 10%
1,063.63	PV @ 11%	1,085.00	bond price
$ 90.02		$ 68.65	

$$10\% + \frac{\$68.65}{\$90.02}\,(1\%) = 10\% + 0.76(1\%) = 10.76\%$$

PROBLEMS

1. Bonds issued by the Peabody Corporation have a par value of $1,000, are selling for $890, and have 18 years to maturity. The annual interest payment is 8 percent. Find yield to maturity by combining the trial-and-error approach with interpolation, as shown in this appendix. (Use an assumption of annual interest payments.)

2. Bonds issued by the Bullwinkle Corporation have a par value of $1,000, are selling for $1,100, and have seven years to maturity. The annual interest payment is 9 percent, payable semiannually. Find yield to maturity by combining the trial-and-error approach with interpolation, as shown in this appendix.

APPENDIX 10B

Valuation of a Supernormal Growth Firm

The formula for the valuation of a supernormal growth firm is

$$P_0 = \sum_{t=1}^{n} \frac{D_t}{(1 + K_e)^t} + P_n \left(\frac{1}{1 + K_e} \right)^n \quad \text{(10B–1)}$$

(Supernormal   (After supernormal
growth period)   growth period)

Represented graphically as

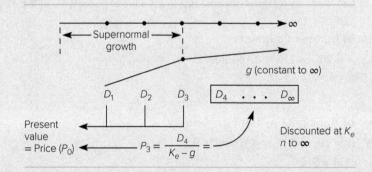

The formula is not difficult to use. The first term calls for determining the present value of the dividends using the supernormal growth period. The second term calls for computing the present value of the future stock price as determined at the end of the supernormal growth period. If we add the two together, we arrive at the current stock price. We are adding together the two benefits the shareholder will receive: (1) a future stream of dividends during the supernormal growth period and (2) the future stock price.

Let's assume that the firm paid a dividend over the last 12 months of $1.67; this represents the current dividend rate. Dividends are expected to grow by 20 percent per year over the supernormal growth period (*n*) of three years. They will then grow at a normal constant rate (*g*) of 5 percent.

The required rate of return (discount rate) as represented by K_e is 9 percent. We first find the present value of the dividends during the supernormal growth period.

1. **Present Value of Supernormal Dividends**

    $D_0 = \$1.67$. We allow the value to grow at 20 percent per year over the three years of supernormal growth.

    $D_1 = D_0 (1 + 0.20) = \$1.67 (1.20) = \$2.00$
    $D_2 = D_1 (1 + 0.20) = \$2.00 (1.20) = \$2.40$
    $D_3 = D_2 (1 + 0.20) = \$2.40 (1.20) = \$2.88$

    We then discount these values back at 9 percent to find the present value of dividends during the supernormal growth period.

	Supernormal Dividends	Present Value of Dividends during the Supernormal Period ($K_e = 9\%$)
D_1	$2.00	$1.83
D_2	2.40	2.02
D_3	2.88	2.22
		$6.07

The present value of the supernormal dividends is $6.07. We now turn to the future stock price.

2. **Present Value of Future Stock Price**

    We first find the future stock price at the end of the supernormal growth period. This is found by taking the present value of the dividends that will be growing at a normal, constant rate after the supernormal period. This will begin *after* the third (and last) period of supernormal growth. Since after the supernormal growth period the firm is growing at a normal, constant rate ($g = 5$ percent) and K_e (the discount rate) of 9 percent exceeds the new, constant growth rate of 5 percent, we have fulfilled the two conditions for using the constant dividend growth model after three years. That is, we can apply formula 10–8 (without subscripts for now).

$$P = \frac{D}{K_e - g}$$

In this case, however, D is really the dividend at the end of the fourth period, because this phase of the analysis starts at the beginning of the fourth period, and D is as of the end of the first period of analysis in the formula. Also, the price we are solving for now is the price at the beginning of the fourth period, which is the same concept as the price at the end of the third period (P_3).

We thus say

$$P_3 = \frac{D_4}{K_e - g} \quad \text{(10B–2)}$$

D_4 is equal to the previously determined value for D_3 of $2.88 moved forward one period at the constant growth rate of 5 percent.

$$D_4 = \$2.88(1.05) = \$3.02$$

Also,

$$K_e = 0.09 \text{ discount rate (required rate of return)}$$
$$g = 0.05 \text{ constant growth rate}$$

$$P_3 = \frac{D_4}{K_e - g} = \frac{\$3.02}{0.09 - 0.05} = \frac{\$3.02}{0.04} = \$75.50$$

This is the value of the stock at the end of the third period. We discount this value back to the present.

Stock Price After Three Years	Present Value of Future Price ($K_e = 9\%$)
$75.50	$58.30

The present value of the future stock price (P_3) of $75.50 is $58.30.

By adding together the answers in part 1 and part 2 of this appendix, we arrive at the total present value, or price, of the supernormal growth stock.

1. Present value of dividends during the normal growth period	$ 6.07
2. Present value of the future stock price..................................	58.30
Total present value, or price..	$64.37

The process we have just completed is presented in Figure 10B–1. Students who wish to develop skills in growth analysis should work the problems at the end of this appendix.

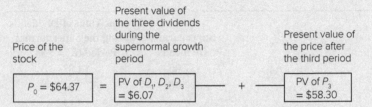

Figure 10B–1 Stock valuation under supernormal growth analysis

REVIEW OF FORMULAS

1. $P_0 = \sum_{t=1}^{n} \dfrac{D_t}{(1 + K_e)^t} + P_n \left(\dfrac{1}{1 + K_e} \right)^n$ (10B-1)

2. $P_3 = \dfrac{D_4}{K_e - g}$ (10B-2)

PROBLEMS

1. Surgical Supplies Corporation paid a dividend of $1.12 over the last 12 months. The dividend is expected to grow at a rate of 25 percent over the next three years (supernormal growth). It will then grow at a normal, constant rate of 7 percent for the foreseeable future. The required rate of return is 12 percent (this will also serve as the discount rate).

    a. Compute the anticipated value of the dividends for the next three years (D_1, D_2, and D_3).

    b. Discount each of these dividends back to the present at a discount rate of 12 percent and then sum them.

    c. Compute the price of the stock at the end of the third year (P_3). (Review Appendix 10B for the definition of D_4.)

    d. After you have computed P_3, discount it back to the present at a discount rate of 12 percent for three years.

    e. Add together the answers in parts *b* and *d* to get the current value of the stock. (This answer represents the present value of the first three periods of dividends plus the present value of the price of the stock after three periods.)

2. You are considering investing in Black Tie Co., a holding enterprise that will pay a dividend of $2.00, which will increase by 12 percent each year over the following three years and then grow at an annual rate of 5 percent indefinitely. You expect a 22 percent return on your invested capital. What price would you pay for a share in this company?

3. Ninja Co. will pay a dividend of $5.00, which will increase by 9 percent each year over the following three years and then grow at an annual rate of 6 percent forever. You expect a 16 percent return on your invested capital. What price would you pay for a share in this company?

4. Sleepy Ltd. expects its present $1.25 dividend (just paid) to grow by 20 percent over the next three years, after which it will remain the same with no growth, forever. If an investor requires a return of 16 percent for investing in Sleepy, what would be its current price?

5. Clarinet Inc. has an expected yield of 18 percent. It anticipates paying the same dividend of $1.10 for four more years, after which the dividend will grow at 7 percent a year indefinitely. Based on the dividend valuation (capitalization) model, at what price should Clarinet currently sell?

6. March Hair Ltd. just paid a dividend of $1.80, which it expects to be $2.90 next year and $4.00 the next year. After that time, the dividend will likely decline to 5 percent per year, forever. With required rates of return at 14 percent, what should investors pay for March Hair?

CHAPTER 11

Cost of Capital

LEARNING OBJECTIVES

LO1 Explain that the cost of capital represents the overall cost of financing to the firm.

LO2 Define the cost of capital as the discount rate normally used to analyze an investment. It is an evaluation tool.

LO3 Construct the cost of capital based on the various valuation techniques from Chapter 10 as applied to bonds, preferred stocks, and common shares.

LO4 Examine how a firm attempts to find a minimum cost of capital by varying the mix of its sources of financing.

LO5 Apply the marginal cost of capital concept.

Determining an appropriate discount rate to value future cash flows is one of the most important considerations in finance and in business. The analysis process will directly affect decisions and the future strategic direction of firms and individuals.

Suppose a young doctor is rendered incapable of practising medicine due to an auto accident in the last year of her residency. In a subsequent legal action, the court determines that the best approximation of her future earning potential before the accident was $100,000 a year for the next 30 years. If her lawyer argues for a 5 percent discount rate, the settlement value becomes $1,537,300, while the insurance company's argument for a 12 percent rate becomes $805,500. The difference is not trivial.

For a firm to decide whether expected future inflows justify a current investment, we evaluate with an appropriately selected discount rate. This evaluation yardstick determines whether an investment proposal is acceptable or not acceptable in maximizing shareholders' wealth. This chapter sets out the concepts, methods, and procedures for making that determination.

The minimal acceptable return for capital invested today, to receive benefits in the future, should be what it costs us to acquire the funds for investment. If the firm's cost of funds is 12 percent, projects of the same risk as the average of the firm's existing assets must be tested to make sure they earn at least 12 percent. By using this as the discount rate, we can decide whether we can reasonably expect to earn the financial cost of doing business. The 12 percent discount rate would not be appropriate for considering projects that exhibit different risks than the average of the existing assets of the firm.

LO1 THE OVERALL CONCEPT

Decisions made by the financial manager are aimed at increasing shareholder value and should be judged against a cost of capital standard. A firm's cost of capital is

- A composite of the various costs of the borrowed or assembled financings
- Determined by the components of its capital structure (debt and equity)
- Based on the costs (or yields) currently demanded by investors in the financial markets

Funds (capital) will be invested in the firm's assets to produce future cash flows. The present value (benefit) of these cash flows should be compared in value against the cost of acquiring the assets. This comparison requires a discount rate or a cost of capital. The cost of capital is the tool used to evaluate (discount) future cash flows and assign a value to them. It is the standard that will satisfy shareholders.

To illustrate this concept, examine two projects of equal risk:

- A plant superintendent wishes to purchase a conveyor system (8 percent rate of return (ROR))
  – borrowing funds at 6 percent (aftertax cost)
- A division manager suggests the development of a new digital component for one of the company's products (14 percent ROR)
  – selling common shares at an effective cost of 15 percent

Judging each investment against the specific means of financing used to fund it runs the risk of making investment selection decisions arbitrary and inconsistent. If projects and financing are matched in this way, the project with the lower return would be accepted and the project with the higher return would be rejected.

If stock and debt are sold in equal proportions, the average cost of financing would be

$$0.5 \times 0.06 = 0.03$$
$$0.5 \times 0.15 = \underline{0.075}$$
$$\text{Overall} = 0.105 = 10.5\%$$

We would now reject the 8 percent conveyor system and accept the 14 percent component project. This would be a rational and consistent decision.

Though an investment financed by low-cost debt might appear acceptable at first glance, the use of debt might increase the overall risk to the firm (as discussed in Chapter 5), eventually making all forms of financing more expensive. Therefore, the general conclusion has been that each project must be measured against the overall cost of funds to the firm.

LO2 The use of the cost of capital to analyze investment projects, as determined with the Baker Corporation example below, rests on two important assumptions:

- The capital structure of the firm will be the same as that currently in place.
- Investment proposals analyzed are of the same risk as the firm's current investments.

If the financial leverage (capital structure) of the firm is altered, the risks to the investors from holding debt or equity will change. Investors will then require different rates of return and, as these required rates of return are the firm's costs of financing, the firm's cost of capital must be revised.

If new proposals are riskier than the current investments of the firm, investors, through their debt or equity holdings, will expect and demand higher returns from their investments, and the cost of capital calculation must be revised upward accordingly. Otherwise, projects might be accepted that do not satisfy the risk and return preferences of investors, thus causing the firm value to drop.

The determination of cost of capital can best be understood by examining the capital structure of a hypothetical firm, the Baker Corporation, in Table 11–1. Note that the aftertax costs of the individual sources of financing are determined, weights are then assigned to each, and finally, a weighted average cost is determined. The relevant costs are those related to new funds that might be raised in future financings rather than the costs of funds raised to fund investments in the past. The remainder of the chapter examines each of these procedural steps.

Table 11–1 Cost of capital—Baker Corporation

		Cost (after tax)	Weights	Weighted Cost
Debt	K_d	6.55%	30%	1.97%
Preferred stock	K_p	10.94	10	1.09
Common equity (retained earnings).	K_e	12.00	60	7.20
Weighted average cost of capital	K_a			10.26%

Each element in the capital structure (on the right side of the balance sheet) has an explicit or opportunity cost associated with it, herein referred to by the symbol **K**. Although all liabilities have some cost associated with them, we usually determine only the cost of longer-term liabilities for simplicity in a cost of capital calculation. Nevertheless, current liabilities can sometimes be significant in the capital structure of a firm.

FINANCE IN ACTION

Capital Availability for Small Business

The options for raising capital in a small business are limited because the full scope of the capital market is not available to the smaller firm. Investors and the investment dealers that put together financing packages in the capital markets shy away from the small business because of the risks perceived in a small business and because the amount of capital required is limited. Capital markets operate as wholesale markets, and require financing deals of a sufficient size to achieve economies of scale. Small business risks may relate only to a lack of understanding of the business by the capital markets, but nevertheless, the small business owner will likely have to raise capital elsewhere.

Debt financing is generally limited to bank operating loans that are used to support liquid current assets and term loans secured by capital assets. The cost of these loans is often several percentage points above the prime rate, unless special government or bank programs are available.

As for equity, options are personal savings, love money (from family and good friends), government assistance, and venture capital funding. The sale of shares (equity) in the capital markets is pretty well impossible in the startup phase of the business. Money from "angels" or venture capital firms is also difficult to access in the firm, on the expectations of rates of return of between 25 to 40 percent annually. Family and friends may have similar expectations.

Canada's Venture Capital and Private Equity Association (CVCA) is a significant source of information on the venture capital business in Canada.

Considering the higher debt costs and the high expectations for equity returns by investors, the cost of capital in the small business will be substantial. This places a significant demand on the returns that need to be achieved by the business. Cost of capital is used to evaluate the desirability of capital investment projects by the firm.

Q1 What are the financing options available to the small firm from Small Business BC?

Q2 Can you describe two recent venture capital deals as well as the amounts involved?

smallbusinessbc.ca/growing-a-business

cvca.ca

 FINANCE IN ACTION

Double Double with that Capital!

In 2006, Tim Hortons wanted to raise additional capital for its operations by going to the public financial markets. Capital can be raised through securities issued as bonds, preferreds, or common equity. In this instance, common shares were sold to the public at $27 per share to raise approximately $775 million.

To raise capital successfully in the public capital markets, the services of investment firms (as underwriters), lawyers, accountants, and others are required. The firm pays these experts for raising, or floating, the capital on their behalf. This reduces the proceeds received by the firm from the amount paid by the public. These flotation costs increase the cost of raising capital.

Out of the approximately $775 million worth of common equity sold to the public, the investment firms received fees of approximately $47 million. Other expenses incurred by the issue amounted to $12.25 million.

Therefore, the flotation costs of this issue were approximately 7.6 percent (59.25/775) of the price paid by the public. As the public based their expectation of a return on the price they paid, the flotation expenses increased Tim Hortons' cost of the issue.

By the end of 2014 Tim Hortons had merged with Burger King and was bought by Restaurant Brands International (QSP on TSX).

Q1 What are the flotation costs of Freshii's subordinated voting share issue of early 2017? (Search the SEDAR site.)

sedar.com

LO3 This cost is directly related to the valuation concepts developed in the previous chapter. The cost of a security is a function of how the security is valued in the marketplace by investors. Once we decide on the proper method for valuing a particular security, the mathematics involved are relatively simple. In Chapter 10, we examined the valuation techniques for financial assets. Let us now examine how the various components of the capital structure might be calculated by a firm's financial analyst.

COST OF DEBT

The cost of debt is measured by the interest rate, or yield, that would have to be paid to bondholders to persuade them to buy bonds. The present market-determined yield that we have seen in the term structure of interest rates is a reflection of future interest rate expectations. This is an appropriate yield to use, because the investment proposals to be evaluated will be successful or not successful in the future as well. A simple case might involve our being able to sell $1,000 bonds, paying $100 in annual interest for $1,000. Our cost of debt would, thus, be 10 percent. Of course, the computation becomes a little more difficult if our $1,000 bonds sell for an amount more or less than $1,000. If this is the case, we could use the yield-to-maturity techniques discussed in Chapter 10.

For example, assume Baker Corporation is preparing to issue new debt. To determine the likely cost of the new debt in the marketplace, the firm computes the yield on its currently outstanding debt. This is not the rate at which the old debt was issued; it is the rate that investors are demanding today. Assume the debt issue pays $100 per year in interest, has a 20-year life, and is currently selling for $940.

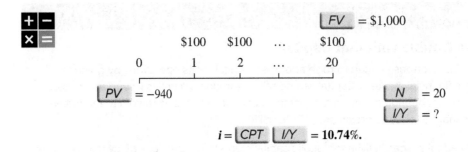

Spreadsheet: Yield to Maturity Calculation

	A	B	C	D	E	F	G	H
1	nper	N	20		"= +RATE(C1,C2,C3,C4,)			
2	pmt	PMT	$100		"= rate(nper,(pmt),(pv),fv,[type], [guess])			
3	pv	PV	-$940		10.74%			
4	fv	FV	$1,000					
5					"= +RATE(20,100,-940,1000)			
6					"= rate(nper,(pmt),(pv),fv,[type], [guess])			
7					10.74%			

In many cases, we do not have to compute the yield to maturity. It is available from other sources, such as the financial pages of various daily and weekly newspapers, from one of the larger investment dealers that deal in bond trading, or from several websites. The type of information available for a sample of outstanding bonds in early 2020 is presented in Table 11–2.

In 2020 if the firm were BMO, for example, the financial manager could observe that debt maturing in 2026 would have a yield to maturity of 2.06 percent. This is true even though the debt was originally issued at a yield close to 2.70 percent, the established coupon rate. The financial manager should also observe that lower-rated bonds typically offer the investing public a higher rate of return. TELUS, with an BBB (high) rating, had a yield of 3.71 percent, whereas Hydro One, with a similar maturity and an A (high) rating, offered the yield of 2.84 percent. Greece's financial problems were not as severe as in 2012 and reflected yields (although at a higher level) of the EEC.

Hydro One
hydroone.com

Table 11–2 Sample bond information

Issuer	Interest Payable	Maturity	Price	Yield	Rating (AAA = lowest risk)
Canada	1.00%	June 2027	96.49	1.51	AAA
Canada	4.00	June 2041	141.78	1.67	AAA
BMO	2.70	Dec. 2026	104.11	2.06	AA
Hydro One	4.39	Sept. 2041	125.04	2.84	A (high)
Suncor	3.00	Sept. 2026	104.14	2.32	A (low)
Suncor	5.39	Mar. 2037	128.76	3.20	A (low)
TELUS	4.40	Oct. 2042	110.63	3.71	BBB (high)
Greece		10 years		1.40	BB (low)
Brazil		10 years		6.77	BB (low)

Note: Pricing for January 2020. Greece's 10-year bond, with a CCC rating in Feb. 2012, had a suggested yield of 36%.

Adjustments With the bond's yield to maturity determined by calculation or by going to the current published market yields (or it is given) we must adjust the yield for

- Tax considerations (interest payments are a tax-deductible expense)
- Flotation costs (costs incurred to sell new debt)

The yield to maturity indicates how much the corporation has to pay on a before-tax basis and does not consider the costs the firm will incur to sell new debt.

Since interest is tax deductible, the true cost of the bond is less than the interest paid because the government is picking up part of the cost by allowing the firm to reduce taxes. The aftertax cost of debt (with a simplifying assumption) is the yield to maturity times one minus the tax rate. This is presented as formula 11–1a.

$$K_d = Y(1 - T) \quad \text{(11–1a)}$$

Where

$$K_d = \text{Cost of debt}$$
$$Y = \text{Yield (or yield to maturity)}$$
$$T = \text{Tax rate}$$

Earlier, we determined that current yield on existing debt for Baker Corporation was 10.74 percent. Assuming that new debt can be issued at the same going market rate and that the firm is in a 39 percent tax bracket, the aftertax cost of debt would be 6.55 percent.[1]

$$K_d = Y(1 - T)$$
$$= 10.74\% (1 - .39)$$
$$= 10.74\% (.61)$$
$$= 6.55\%$$

Observe in Table 11–1, column 1, that the aftertax cost of debt for Baker Corporation is the 6.55 percent that we have just computed.

---

[1] More accurately, we could use a time-line development to compute the aftertax yield with a present value calculation. We would adjust the initial proceeds by the flotation costs and by the present value of the tax savings resulting from the flotation costs over the first five years of the bond's life. The annual interest payments would be included at one minus the tax rate. The final payment on the debt would be included in the calculation as a future value. This would have only a minor impact on the final cost of debt. For example, a 20-year bond $K_d = 6.83\%$ (PV = –970, PMT = 65.51, FV = 1,000, $N = 20$, compute $I/Y = 6.83$).

The aftertax cost of debt to the firm should also consider all selling and distribution costs, known as flotation costs. These costs are usually quite small, and they are often bypassed in some types of loans. To explicitly include flotation costs we would have[2]

$$K_d = \frac{Y(1-T)}{1-F} \quad \text{(11–1b)}$$

Where

$$F = \text{Flotation, or selling, cost (after tax)}$$

The flotation cost (F) in this formula is expressed as a percentage of the funds raised. Therefore, $1 - F$ will also be a percentage, equal to net proceeds (P_n) received by the firm as a percentage of gross proceeds raised from the public. The difference is absorbed by investment dealers, accountants, lawyers, and others. With flotation costs typically in the 2 to 10 percent range for a bond issue, the firm will net over 90 percent of the funds invested by the bondholders. The bondholder's expected yield will be based on the amount they have invested and not on what the firm has received. Thus, flotation costs increase the cost of the debt to the firm.

Expressed alternatively, a bond issue (with a $1,000 face value) with net aftertax proceeds to the firm of $970 can be said to have net proceeds ($1 - F$) of 97 percent ($970/$1,000), or flotation costs of 3 percent ($30/$1,000).

If flotation costs had been 3 percent of proceeds or, in other words, if the firm netted $970 on a $1,000 bond with the seller of the bonds, known as the investment dealer or underwriter, receiving $30, then the following adjustment would be made:

$$K_d = \frac{Y(1-T)}{1-F} = \frac{10.74\%(1-0.39)}{1-0.03} = \frac{6.55\%}{0.97} = 6.75\%$$

We will continue our example with 6.55 percent, without the flotation cost adjustment.

 FINANCE IN ACTION

Debt Costs Around the Globe

A corporation needing long-term debt financing usually looks first in its own backyard; that is, in the country where it will invest the capital. However, multinational corporations will carefully investigate global interest rates to find those that are the most cost effective. A risk of borrowing in a foreign country is the likelihood that exchange rates will change before the debt is paid back. This may make the debt cost far greater than anticipated.

In January 2020, the following long-term interest rates were demanded in capital markets for government securities with 10 years to maturity. Top-rated corporations would expect to pay 1 to 2 percent above these rates.

Canada	1.56%
Australia	1.17
Brazil	6.77
Germany	−0.22
Greece	1.40
Japan	−0.01
Britain	0.63
U.S	1.82

Notice the generally low rates as inflationary pressures were not much in evidence. Indeed there were some deflationary pressures. Low rates and, in fact, negative yields

---

[2] Actually, the rate might be slightly higher to reflect that generally yields are lower for bonds trading at a discount from par ($940 in this case) because of potential tax advantages and higher leverage potential. This is not really a major issue in this case.

COST OF PREFERRED STOCK

The cost of preferred stock is similar to the cost of debt in that a constant annual payment is made, but it is dissimilar in that there is no maturity date on which a principal payment must be made. Thus, the determination of the yield on preferred stock is simpler than determining the yield on debt. However, one must examine the actual preferreds quite closely for the attached bells and whistles, as they may actually have maturity dates that make their valuation similar to bonds. Yield is determined by dividing the annual dividend by the current price (this process was discussed in Chapter 10).

$$K_p = \frac{D_p}{P_p} \quad \text{(10–3)}$$

The rate of return to preferred shareholders is also the annual cost to the corporation for a preferred stock issue, with a slight alteration to account for flotation costs. There is no downward tax adjustment $(1 - T)$ because a preferred stock dividend, unlike debt interest payments, is not a tax-deductible expense. The formula is, however, adjusted as we did with debt by dividing the preferred yield by $1 - F$, which is effectively the net proceeds of a new issue expressed as a percentage of gross proceeds. The cost of preferred stock is expressed as[3]

$$K_p = \frac{D_p/P_p}{(1 - F)} \quad \text{(11–2a)}$$

Where

K_p = Cost of preferred stock

D_p = Annual dividend on preferred stock

P_p = Price of preferred stock

F = Flotation, or selling, costs

For Baker Corporation, the annual dividend is $10.50, the preferred stock price is $100, and the flotation, or selling, costs are estimated at $4. The flotation costs of $4 received by the underwriter are 4 percent ($4/$100) of the price paid investors ($100). The firm nets $96 or 96 percent ($96/$100).

The calculation of preferred cost becomes

$$K_p = \frac{D_p/P_p}{1 - F} = \frac{\$10.50/\$100}{1 - 0.04} = \frac{0.1050}{0.96} = 0.1094 = 10.94\%$$

The same result will be obtained by dividing the dividend payment by the price or proceeds received by the firm after flotation costs ($P_n = P_p - F$), because the valuation formula is a perpetuity.

---

[3]Note that in Chapter 10, K_p was presented with no adjustment for flotation charges. Some may wish to formally change the formula with an additional subscript to indicate the flotation cost adjustment, K_{pn}.

A new share of preferred stock with a selling cost (flotation cost) produces proceeds to the firm equal to the selling price in the market minus the flotation cost ($96). Therefore, the cost of preferred stock can also be presented as

$$K_p = \frac{D_p}{P_p - F} \quad \text{(11–2b)}$$

The effective cost of preferred shares becomes

$$K_p = \frac{D_p}{P - F} = \frac{\$10.50}{\$100 - \$4} = \frac{\$10.50}{\$96} = 0.1094 = 10.94\%$$

Carefully examine the similarity of these two formulas before referring back to Table 11–1, column 1, where we find that 10.94 percent is the cost of preferred stock in the Baker Corporation example.

COST OF COMMON EQUITY

Determining the cost of common equity in the capital structure is a more involved task than for debt or preferred shares. Those instruments are simpler because a stated coupon or dividend rate is in evidence. The required yields of investors in common equity are not as clear. Dividends may be paid but investors also have a claim on residual earnings (after expenses, debt costs, taxes, and preferred dividends). This may result in increased dividend payments and/or increases in share prices, which lead to capital gains.

Common stock costs cannot simply be based on the out-of-pocket cost cash dividend. This is the dividend yield, which is the current year's dividend divided by the market price.

$$\text{Dividend yield} = \frac{\text{Current dividend}}{\text{Market price}}$$

The "Dividend Yields" Finance in Action box shows common dividend yields of about 2 to 5 percent for better dividend-paying stocks and generally less than the preferred yields. If new common stock were thought to be so cheap, firms would have no need to issue other securities and could profitably finance projects that earned these meager returns. On the other hand, who would invest in a corporation with such inadequate yields?

Furthermore, though new financing capital raised by debt and preferreds will always come from the markets and, thus, incur flotation costs, this may not happen with common equity. This is because common equity comes from two sources. Internally generated funds are produced from the residual claim on earnings of common shares (recorded as retained earnings), and externally generated funds come from the issue of new shares (recorded as common shares). New shares issues will incur flotation expenses, raising the cost of common equity.

 FINANCE IN ACTION

Dividend Yields

Dividend yields are often a focus of investor sentiment after the market has gone through a period of upheaval. Cash flow by way of regular quarterly dividend payments—in other words, "A bird in the hand . . ."—is somewhat reassuring to investors.

However, investors have often focused on the speculative potential of firms hoping for capital gains as share prices soared. Then they fall! With low interest rates at the banks and caution toward speculative investments, high-dividend-paying stocks increasingly become popular if backed by solid earnings power. Of course, to attract investors' monies, firms are required to offer healthy dividend yields. Preferreds generally have a higher dividend yield as, unlike common, they do not have a claim on future earnings growth. In January 2020 the following dividend yields were available to investors:

	Common Shares		Preferred Shares	
	Symbol	Yield	Symbol	Yield
BMO	BMO	4.08%	BMO.PR.E	5.78%
BCE Inc	BCE	5.10	BCE.PR.E	6.16
TransAlta	TA	1.83	TA.PR.J	6.81

These yields can be found daily on the pages of *The Globe and Mail* or the *Financial Post*. They can also be found at the TSX website (tmxmoney.com).

Q1 What are the current dividend yields required by the market for these companies?

Q2 Do any dividend yields on common shares exceed the preferreds?

The determination of the yield required by investors for common share investments (becoming the cost of equity financing, with some adjustments) is difficult in practice because the future payments to shareholders have greater uncertainty than with bonds or preferreds. Two valuation models have been developed to determine the return required by common equity investors:

- *Dividend model*, which is based on dividends to be paid and their growth over time
- *Capital asset pricing model (CAPM)*, which is based on a relationship between risk and return

It is unlikely that both models, in practice, will provide the same result because of the many assumptions and variables that must be determined. Nevertheless, they should produce similar results, and using two models can improve the accuracy in estimating the expected returns from common equity as each model acts as a check on the other.

In determining the cost of common equity we consider the following:

- Will internal or external funds be required (with a possible adjustment for flotation costs)?
- Will the dividend valuation model, CAPM, or an average of both be used to determine the yield and, thus, cost to the firm?

Valuation Approach (Dividend Model)

The cost of common stock is a function of the pricing and performance demands of current and future shareholders. An appropriate approach is to develop a model for valuing common stock that is dependent on the required return demanded from it. Investors receive their return from dividends and the increase in share price. Our dividend valuation model (or dividend capitalization model) uses both components to derive a cost of equity capital.

In Chapter 10, the constant dividend growth model yielded the following relationship between stock price and demanded return:

$$P_0 = \frac{D_1}{K_e - g} \quad \text{(10–8)}$$

Where

P_0 = Price of the stock today

D_1 = Dividend at the end of the first year (or period)

K_e = Required rate of return/cost of equity

g = Constant growth rate in dividends

We then found we could rearrange the terms in the to solve for *formula K_e* instead of P_0. This was presented in formula 10–9 and, once again, here as formula 11–3.

$$K_e = \frac{D_1}{P_0} + g \quad \text{(11–3)}$$

The required rate of return (K_e) is equal to the dividend at the end of the first year (D_1), divided by the price of the stock today (P_0), plus a constant growth rate (g). Although the growth rate applies directly to dividends, it must also apply to earnings over the long term. The formula's assumption that there is a constant relationship between earnings per share and dividends per share (i.e., a constant payout ratio) ensures the ability to sustain the growth in dividend payments.

In the Baker Corporation example, the expected dividend for this year is $2, the current stock price is $40, and the dividends have been and are expected to continue to grow at a rate of 7 percent. Given that information, we would calculate K_e to be equal to 12 percent.

$$K_e = \frac{D_1}{P_0} + g = \frac{\$2}{\$40} + 7\% = 5\% + 7\% = 12\%$$

This result assumes shareholders expect to receive a 5 percent return on their investment by way of dividends and a 7 percent return by way of an increase in the price of their shares. Thus, they are investing in this stock on the basis that they demand and expect to receive a 12 percent return on their investment.

Cost of Retained Earnings

Up to this point, we have discussed the cost (required return) of common stock equity capital in a general sense. These funds can be supplied by

Statistics Canada
statcan.ca

- Purchasers of new shares of common stock (external)
- Income kept in the firm as retained earnings (internal)

In 2019, Statistics Canada reported Canadian nonfinancial corporations as having $0.9 trillion of their historical equity financing as retained earnings and $1.7 trillion as common share issues.[4] Retained earnings form an important source of ownership or equity capital investment funds.

Retained earnings represent

- Past and present earnings of the firm (reinvested)
- Minus previously distributed dividends

Retained earnings, by law, belong to common shareholders. They represent a source of equity capital supplied by the current shareholders. But just because the firm did not have to go to the market to raise new funds does not mean these internally generated funds are free.

There is an opportunity cost involved as the funds could be paid out as dividends to the current shareholders, who could then redeploy them by buying other stocks, bonds, real estate, and so forth. The expected rate of return on these alternative investments becomes the opportunity cost of not having paid out the earnings in dividends. It seems reasonable to assume shareholders could earn a return equivalent to that provided by their present investment in the firm (on an equal-risk basis).[5] This is represented by $D_1/P_0 + g$.

Computing the cost of retained earnings takes us back to where we began our discussion of the cost of common stock. The cost of retained earnings is equivalent to the rate of return on the firm's

---

[4] This represents the most recent published data (July 2019). Statistics Canada, *Quarterly balance sheet and income statement, by industry,* Table: 33-10-0007-01.

[5] Chapter 14, in dealing with the concept of efficient markets, provides more insight as to why this assumption is reasonable.

common stock. This is the opportunity cost. Thus, we say the cost of common equity in the form of retained earnings is equal to the required rate of return on the firm's stock.[6]

$$K_e = \frac{D_1}{P_0} + g \quad \text{(11–3)}$$

Thus, K_e represents not only the required return on common stock as previously defined but also the cost of equity in the form of retained earnings. It is a symbol with double significance.

The cost of common equity in the form of retained earnings for Baker Corporation is equal to 12 percent, the previously calculated required rate of return of shareholders. Please refer back to Table 11–1 and observe in column 1 that 12 percent is the value we have used for common equity.

Cost of New Common Stock

Let's now consider the other source of equity capital, new common stock. If we are issuing **new** common stock, we must pay a slightly higher return than K_e, which represents the required rate of return of **present** shareholders. The higher return is needed to cover the distribution costs of the new securities. If the required return for current shareholders was 12 percent and shares were quoted to the public at $40, a new distribution of securities would need to earn slightly more than 12 percent to compensate for sales commissions and other expenses. The corporation does not receive the full $40 because of these costs. The formula for K_e is restated as K_n (the cost of new common stock) to reflect this requirement.

Common stock

$$K_e = \frac{D_1}{P_0} + g$$

New common stock

$$K_n = \left(\frac{D_1}{P_0} + g\right)\frac{P_0}{P_n} \text{ or } K_n = \frac{\frac{D_1}{P_0} + g}{1 - F} \quad \text{(11–4)}$$

The only new term is P_n (net proceeds received on a new share issue after flotation costs and any underpricing of the share price).

If net proceeds are expressed as a percentage we can divide K_e by the net proceeds to get K_n.
Assume

$$D_1 = \$2$$
$$P_0 = \$40$$
$$F = \$4$$
$$g = 7\%$$

$$P_n = P_0 - F$$
$$= \$40 - \$4$$
$$= \$36$$

Then

$$K_n = \left(\frac{\$2}{\$40} + 7\%\right)\left(\frac{\$40}{\$36}\right)$$
$$= (5\% + 7\%)(1.111) = 13.33\%$$

---

[6]One could make the seemingly logical suggestion that this is not a perfectly equivalent relationship. For example, if shareholders receive a distribution of retained earnings in the form of dividends, they may have to pay taxes on the dividends before they can reinvest them in equivalent yield investments. Additionally, the shareholder may incur brokerage costs in the process. For these reasons, one might suggest that the opportunity cost of retained earnings is less than the rate of return on the firm's common stock. The current majority view, however, is that the appropriate cost for retained earnings is equal to the rate of return on the firm's common stock. The strongest argument for this equality position is that for a publicly traded company, a firm always has the option of buying back some of its shares in the market. Given that this is so, it is assured a return of K_e. Thus, the firm should never make an alternative investment that has an expected equity return of less than K_e. Nevertheless, students may wish to look into the minority view as well. In the event a tax adjustment is made, the cost of retained earnings can be represented as $K_r = K_e(1 - t_r)$, where K_r is the cost of retained earnings, K_e is the required return on common stock, and t_r is the average shareholder marginal tax rate on dividend income.

The cost of new common stock to the Baker Corporation is 13.3 percent. This value is used more extensively later in the chapter. New common stock was not included in the original assumed capital structure for the Baker Corporation presented in Table 11–1.

The flotation costs in this example are 10 percent of proceeds, as the firm will net $36 on a $40 common share with the seller of the shares, the underwriter, receiving $4 ($4/$40 = .10 = 10%). The calculation would then be

$$K_n = \frac{\dfrac{D_1}{P_0} + g}{1 - F} = \frac{\dfrac{\$2}{\$10} + .07}{1 - .10} = \frac{.12}{.90} = 0.1333 = 13.33\%$$

The flotation cost adjustment applies to the complete formula for K_n. It is the required return of investors, which is increased to determine the cost to the firm when flotation costs are considered and investors base their expectations on what they pay, not what the firm receives.

CAPM for the Required Return on Common Stock

An alternative model for calculating the required return on common stock is represented by the capital asset pricing model (CAPM). The attributes of this model are covered in Appendix 11A, so we consider it only briefly at this point. Some proclaim the capital asset pricing model as an important advance in our attempts at common stock valuation, but others suggest that it is not a valid description of how the real world operates.

The model is based on a risk-return relationship for determining the required rate of return for common equity or, indeed, any capital asset. The model follows from the discussion in Chapter 10 on yield to maturity, in which an expected return is developed as follows:

Required return = Risk-free rate + Risk premium

This can be presented graphically as a linear relationship between the required rate of return (K_j) and a measure of risk (β) for the firm's business. Greater risk in a firm's business operations requires a greater rate of return for common shareholders.

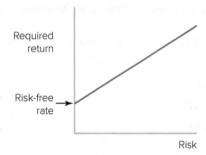

The CAPM develops the risk premium from the relationship between a share's returns and the returns of the stock market as a whole. Under CAPM, the required return for common stock (or other investments) expressed as a cost to the firm can be described by the following formula:

$$K_j = R_f + \beta_j(R_m - R_f) \quad \text{(11–5)}$$

Where

- K_j = Required return on common stock or the cost of equity.
- R_f = Risk-free rate of return; often taken as equivalent to the current rate on short-term Government of Canada Treasury bills.
- β_j = Beta coefficient. The beta measures the historical volatility (risk) of an individual stock's (j) return relative to a stock market index. A beta greater than one indicates greater volatility (as measured by price movements) than the market; the reverse would be true for a beta less than one.
- R_m = Return in the market as measured by an appropriate index.

A flotation cost adjustment can be achieved, for new equity, by adjusting the formula by

$$K_{jn} = \frac{K_j}{1 - F} \text{ or } K_{jn} = K_j\left(\frac{P_0}{P_n}\right) \quad \text{(11–6)}$$

Where

K_{jn} = Cost of new equity (CAPM)

P_0 = Current price

P_n = Net proceeds received on a new share issue after flotation costs (and any underpricing of the share price)

 FINANCE IN ACTION

Canadian Utilities, Return on Common Equity, and Cost of Capital

Canadian Utilities (CU) is primarily a holding company for power generation, utilities management, and energy services. By 2020, it had assets exceeding $22 billion and revenues of about $4.4 billion. Although nonregulated subsidiaries have played a role in the sector, and deregulation has occurred in the energy business, Canadian Utilities still has 86 percent of earnings subject to government regulation. Its subsidiary companies must appear before the Alberta Utilities Commission (AUC) and foreign government bodies to determine the cost of service rates. These rates become the charges customers pay for their gas.

To determine the cost of service rates, each utility prepares for an intensive hearing to establish the cost of financing the utility's operation, its WACC (weighted average cost of capital). Often, there are divergent views on the costs of the various components of the firm's capital structure, a fair rate of return, and indeed, the nature of the capital structure itself. These costs and structure are debated in an attempt to reach consensus on the firm's cost of capital. In early 2020, Canadian Utilities had the following:

Capital Structure	Book Value
Accounts payable	2%
Other liabilities	25
Long-term debt	41
Preferreds	7
Common equity	25

Its profits are restrained by AUC and foreign regulatory body decisions, which established CU's return on equity for 2020 in the 7.21 to 8.75 percent range. Furthermore, the common equity ratio within the capital structure had a stated acceptable percentage.

Regulatory matters are discussed in the management discussion and analysis of the financial statements.

Q1 Have recent AUB decisions impacted CU's return on common equity?

Q2 What is the rating on CU's commercial paper, debentures, and preferred shares?

canadianutilities.com
Symbol: CU

dbrsmorningstar.com

standardandpoors.com

In the Baker Corporation example, the following values might apply:

$$R_f = 9\%$$
$$R_m = 11\%$$
$$\beta_j = 1.5$$

Based on formula 11–4, K_j would then equal

$$K_j = 9\% + 1.5(11\% - 9\%) = 9\% + 1.5(2\%)$$
$$= 9\% + 3\% = 12\%$$

In this case, we have structured the data so that K_j (the required return under the CAPM) would equal K_e (the required return under the dividend valuation model). In both cases, the computations lead to a 12 percent estimate as the cost of common equity. In real life, the two models rarely give exactly the same estimate. Nevertheless, both models are attempting to determine the same thing—the expected, or required, return of investors.

For now, we use the dividend valuation model; that is, $K_e = D_1/P_0 + g$. Those who wish to study the capital asset pricing model further are referred to Appendix 11A.

With flotation costs ($P_0 = \$40$, $F = \$4$)

$$K_{jn} = K_j \left(\frac{P_0}{P_n} \right) = 12\% \left(\frac{\$40}{\$36} \right) = 13.33\%$$

Or

$$K_{jn} = \frac{K_j}{1 - F} = \frac{12\%}{1 - 0.10} = 13.33\%$$

Overview of Common Stock Costs

For those of you who are suffering from an overexposure to K's in the computation of cost of common stock, let us recap. We have to consider which model to use to establish the investor's required return on common equity and then determine whether or not flotation costs will be required.

Dividend Valuation or Dividend Capitalization Model:

Internally generated (retained earnings)

$$K_e = \frac{D_1}{P_0} + g$$

Externally generated (new common stock)

$$K_n = \frac{\frac{D_1}{P_0} + g}{1 - F} \qquad \text{or} \qquad K_n = \left(\frac{D_1}{P_0} + g \right) \frac{P_0}{P_n}$$

Capital Asset Pricing Model (CAPM):

Internally generated (retained earnings)

$$K_j = R_f + \beta_j(R_m - R_f)$$

Externally generated (new common stock)

$$K_{jn} = \left(\frac{K_j}{1 - F} \right) \qquad \text{or} \qquad K_{jn} = K_j \left(\frac{P_0}{P_n} \right)$$

OPTIMAL CAPITAL STRUCTURE—
WEIGHTING COSTS

Having established the techniques for computing the cost of the various elements in the capital structure, we must now discuss methods of assigning weights to these costs to determine our weighted average cost of capital. We attempt to weight capital components in accordance with our desire to achieve a minimum overall cost of capital. That will be the optimum capital structure because at that point the value of shareholders' wealth is maximized. For purposes of this discussion, Table 11–1 (cost of capital for the Baker Corporation) is reproduced here.

		Cost(after tax)	Weights	WeightedCost
Debt	K_d	6.55%	30%	1.97%
Preferred stock	K_p	10.94	10	1.09
Common equity (retained earnings).	K_e	12.00	60	7.20
Weighted average cost of capital	K_a			10.26%

By formula the weighted average cost of capital (WACC) is

$$K_a = \left(\frac{V_d}{V_a}\right)K_d + \left(\frac{V_p}{V_a}\right)K_p + \left(\frac{V_e}{V_a}\right)K_e \quad \text{(11–7)}$$

V = Value of components (subscripts) of capital structure (expressed as market value)

How does the firm decide on the appropriate weights for debt, preferred stock, and common stock financing? In other words, why not use all debt for future financing since the preceding chart indicates that it is substantially cheaper than the alternatives? The use of debt beyond a reasonable point will probably greatly increase the firm's financial risk and thereby drive up the costs of all sources of financing. For a more complete discussion of the theory related to this point, please see Appendix 11B.

One way for us to explore this critical point is to assume that you plan to start your own company and are considering the following three different capital structures. For ease of presentation, only debt and equity (common stock) are being considered. As it happens, the costs of the components in the capital structure change each time you vary the proposed debt-equity mix (weights).

Financial Plan A:	Cost (after tax)	Weights	Weighted Cost
Debt	6.5%	20%	1.3%
Equity.	12.0	80	9.6
			10.9%
Financial Plan B:			
Debt	7.0%	40%	2.8%
Equity.	12.5	60	7.5
			10.3%
Financial Plan C:			
Debt	9.0%	60%	5.4%
Equity.	15.0	40	6.0
			11.4%

We see that the firm can reduce the cost of capital by including more debt financing as we consider plan B versus plan A. Beyond a point, however, the continued use of debt becomes unattractive, causing increases in the costs of the various sources of financing that more than offset the benefit of substituting cheaper debt for more expensive equity. In our example, that point seems to occur somewhere around the debt-equity mix represented by plan B. Traditional financial theory maintains that there is a U-shaped cost of capital curve relative to debt-equity mixes for the firm, as illustrated in Figure 11–1. In this illustration, the optimum capital structure occurs at a 40 percent debt-to-equity ratio.

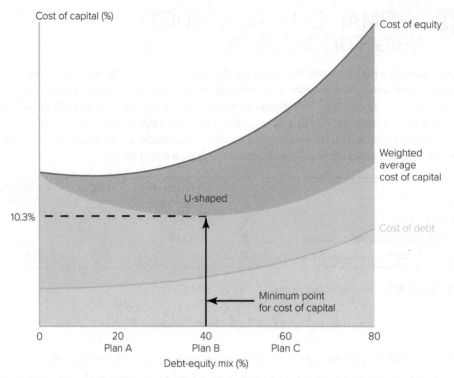

Figure 11–1 Cost of capital curve

Most firms use 40 to 70 percent total debt (total debt/total assets) in their capital structure without exceeding norms acceptable to creditors and investors. Distinctions should be made, however, between firms that carry high or low business risks. As discussed in Chapter 5, a growth firm in a reasonably stable industry can afford to absorb more debt than its counterparts in cyclical industries. Examples of debt used by companies in various industries are presented in Table 11–3.

Table 11–3 Debt (total) to total assets, early 2020

Selected Companies with Industry Designation	Symbol	Debt/Assets Percent
Air Canada (airlines)	AC	85
Bank of Montreal (financials)	BMO	94
Canadian Tire (consumer retail)	CTC	75
Descartes (software)	DSG	18
Encana (energy)	ECA	51
Loblaw (consumer staples)	L	60
Melcor (real estate)	MRD	47
Nutrien (fertilizers)	POT	46
Shopify (e-commerce software)	SHOP	7
Teck (mining)	TECK.B	42
West Fraser (forest products)	WFT	40

In determining the appropriate capital mix, the firm generally begins with its present capital structure and ascertains whether that structure is optimal. If it is not, subsequent financing should carry the firm toward a financing mix deemed more desirable. Note that only the costs of new or incremental financing should be considered. The historical costs of financing to the firm are not relevant except to the extent that they provide clues as to what future financing costs are likely to be.

Market Value Weightings

Toronto Stock
Exchange
tmx.com

To calculate the cost of capital, we weight each component of the capital structure based on how the corporation will raise funds in the future (presumably its optimal capital structure) and it is with that capital structure mix that new investments must find their success. If the firm is to be successful, the new investments must achieve a rate of return equal to the overall cost of the financing used. Past costs are not relevant. Unless the corporation has calculated its optimal capital structure, we presume that the present structure will be maintained and is appropriate for cost of capital calculations.

These ratios were calculated as follows: 1 − (equity/total assets) from the latest balance sheet available at each company's website. Company sites can be accessed through the TSX site under listed companies. Please note that these are based on book values not market values.

1. What are the latest debt ratios for the above companies?
2. Compare the book value of equity of these companies with their market capitalization.

However, the present capital structure should be based on the market value of debt and equity. It should not be based on book values from the financial statements. Why? Remember that the cost of funding for each component in the capital structure is based on the expectations of investors for the returns they require from the corporation. In Chapter 6, we discovered that expectations about the future are part of today's interest rates (the expectations hypothesis) and that the returns expected by investors from their investment are based on what they have at stake—the market value of their investment.

Suppose an investor purchased shares in a corporation several years ago for $1,000 and those shares are now worth $10,000. (Book value = $1,000, market value = $10,000). If that investor expected the investment to generate a 12 percent return over the next year, by way of dividends or a capital gain from an increasing share price, $1,200 would be expected based on the market value, and not $120 based on the book value. Therefore, investors have the market value of their investment at stake at any time and this is what determines their required rates of return and the costs of financing to the firm.

If there is an active market for the securities of the corporation, such as the Toronto Stock Exchange, it is easy to identify their market value. The market value will be available in the newspaper or by calling an investment dealer. Without an active market for a firm's securities we must use the present value models from Chapter 10 to determine market value.

Present value models are employed to revalue the debt, preferreds, and common equity of the firm's financial statements from their book value to market value. The historically based book values and the financial footnotes should disclose information for each of these components of the capital structure to identify the cash flows (future values, payments, time periods) needed for the present value models.

Furthermore, to calculate the current market values of each component of the capital structure we will need discount rates. We will use the current yields (interest rates) from the market. Current yields on securities of similar risk are found in newspapers, on many websites, and from investment dealers. Table 11–2 illustrates how these yields are found.

Calculating Market Value Weightings

From the financial statements (often historically based) with the accompanying notes, the following is determined:

- Debt: 20 years to maturity, annual coupon rate of 16 percent, current yield 12 percent
- Preferreds: Dividend rate of 7 percent, current yield 10 percent
- Common shares: 1 million shares outstanding, currently trading at $8 per share in the market

The capital structure is as follows:

	Book Value	Book Value Weightings	Market Value	Market Value Weightings
Debt	$2,000,000	0.29	$ 2,597,555	0.23
Preferreds	1,000,000	0.14	700,000	0.06
Common stock	1,000,000	0.14 ⎫	8,000,000	0.71
Retained earnings	3,000,000	0.43 ⎬		
	$7,000,000	1.00	$11,297,555	1.00

The debt's market value was calculated using the maturity value, or future value, of $2 million; annual payments of $320,000 (16% of $2,000,000); and a period of 20 years, all identified from the financial statements. The discount rate applied to determine the present value of the debt was 12 percent, which is the current yield on debt. Interest payments, by contract, are based on the maturity value.

FV = $2,000,000 PMT = $320,000

N = 20 I/Y = 12

PV = ?

CPT PV = **$2,597,555.**

The preferreds' market value was calculated by using the formula

$$P_p = \frac{D_p}{K_p} \quad \text{(10–3)}$$

With

D_p = $70,000 (7% of $1,000,000)

K_p = 10%, the current yield on the preferreds

Notice that for the market value of equity, the accounting categories of common stock and retained earnings are combined into equity. The investors' market value of shares at $8 represents both equity accounts. Therefore, the value of equity is $8 times the 1 million shares outstanding, or $8 million.

The market value weightings would now be combined with the costs of the various components, as in Table 11–1, to derive the cost of capital. Today, when the capital markets are highly dynamic and often unforgiving, it is essential that the financial manager base decision making on the market value of assets and evaluate those assets with the current yields or costs of the various components of the capital structure. Nowhere is this more important than in making capital investment decisions based on a discount rate derived from a cost of capital calculation.

CAPITAL ACQUISITION AND INVESTMENT DECISION MAKING

So far, the various costs of financial capital and the optimum capital structure have been discussed. Financial capital consists of bonds, preferred stock, and common equity. These forms of financial capital appear on the corporate balance sheet under liabilities and equity. The money raised by selling these securities, along with the earnings retained in the firm, is invested in the real capital of the firm, the long-term productive assets of plant and equipment.

Long-term funds are usually invested in long-term assets, with several asset-financing mixes possible over the business cycle. Obviously, a firm wants to provide all of the necessary financing at the lowest possible cost. This generally leads the financial manager to attempt to sell common stock when prices are relatively high, to minimize the cost of equity.[7] The financial manager also wants to

---

[7]In Chapter 14 we discuss the rationality of such market timing in more detail.

sell debt at low interest rates. Since there is short-term and long-term debt, the manager needs to know how interest rates move over the business cycle and when to use short-term versus long-term debt.

Thus, the task is for the firm to find a balance between debt and equity that achieves its minimum cost of capital. Although we discussed minimizing the overall cost of capital K_a at a single debt-to-equity ratio, firms seem, in reality, to operate within a relevant range of debt to equity before they become penalized with a higher overall cost because of increased risk.

Figure 11–2 shows a theoretical cost of capital curve at three different points. As we move from time period t to time period $t + 2$, falling interest rates and rising stock prices cause a downward shift in K_a. This graph illuminates two basic points: (1) the firm wants to keep its debt-to-equity ratio between x and y at all times, and (2) the firm would rather finance its long-term needs at K_{at+2} than at K_{at}. Corporations do have some leeway in the money and capital markets such that it is not uncommon for the debt-to-equity ratio to fluctuate between x and y over a business cycle. Note, however, that the firm at point y has lost the flexibility of increasing its debt-to-equity ratio without incurring the penalty of higher capital costs.

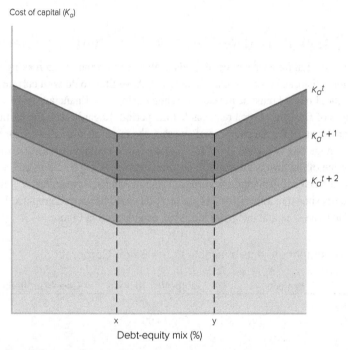

Figure 11–2 Cost of capital over time

only if the return exceeds the cost. So what's the big deal? The "big deal" is that it is one thing for managers of corporations to understand the concept, but it is quite another for them to implement it. Often companies do not properly measure the cost of capital or are incorrectly focused on growth rather than shareholder wealth. Joel M. Stern and G. Bennett Stewart III, as developers of the EVA concept, maintain that they can teach corporate managers a program that ensures the return on capital exceeds the cost. In the process, shareholder wealth is maximized.

The value of the EVA technique is that it focuses the organization on creating value for the shareholders and it is an extension of the cost of capital concept examined in the chapter.

Q1 What does the Stern Stewart Institute provide today?

sternstewartinstitute.com

Cost of Capital in the Capital Budgeting Decision

The current cost of capital for each source of funds is always important when making a capital budgeting decision. Historical costs for past funding may have little to do with current costs against which future potential returns must be measured. When raising new financial capital, a company taps the various sources of financing over a reasonable time period. Regardless of the particular source of funds the company is using for the purchase of an asset, the required rate of return, or discount rate, is the weighted average cost of capital (WACC). As long as the company earns its cost of capital, the common share value of the firm is maintained, since shareholders' expectations are being met. For example, assume the Baker Corporation was considering making an investment in eight projects with the returns and costs shown in Table 11–4. These projects could be viewed graphically and merged with the WACC to make a capital budgeting decision, as indicated in Figure 11–3.

Table 11–4 Investment projects available to the Baker Corporation

Projects	Expected Returns	Cost ($ millions)
A.	16.00%	$10
B.	14.00	5
C.	13.50	4
D.	11.80	20
E.	10.40	11
F.	9.50	20
G.	8.60	15
H.	7.00	10
		$95

Notice that the Baker Corporation is contemplating $95 million in projects. Given that the WACC is 10.26 percent, however, it should choose only projects A through E, or $50 million in new assets. Selecting assets F, G, and H would probably reduce the market value of the common stock because these projects do not provide a return equal to the overall costs of raising funds. We cannot forget that using the WACC assumes that the Baker Corporation is in its optimum capital structure range and will employ that structure in the future. Furthermore, when using the cost of capital to evaluate capital projects, we are assuming those projects will not adjust the risk complexion of the corporation. If they do, investors will change their required rates of return, and the cost of capital as calculated will be inappropriate.

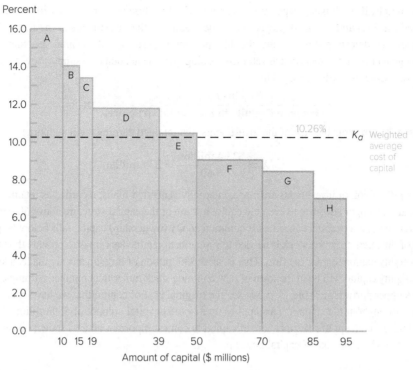

Figure 11–3 Cost of capital and investment projects for the Baker Corporation

THE MARGINAL COST OF CAPITAL

Nothing guarantees the Baker Corporation that its component cost of capital will stay constant for as much money as it wants to raise, even if a given capital structure is maintained. If a large amount of financing is desired, the market may demand a higher cost of capital for each extra increment of funds desired. The point is analogous to the fact that you may be able to go to your relatives and best friends and raise funds for an investment at 10 percent. After exhausting the lending or investing power of those closest to you, and you have to look to other sources, your marginal cost of capital will probably go up. (As background for this discussion, the cost of capital table for the Baker Corporation is reproduced again.)

		Cost (after tax)	Weights	Weighted Cost
Debt	K_d	6.55%	30%	1.97%
Preferred stock	K_p	10.94	10	1.09
Common equity (retained earnings).	K_e	12.00	60	7.20
WACC	K_a			10.26%

We need to review the nature of the firm's capital structure to explain the concept of marginal cost of capital as it applies to the firm. Note that 60 percent of the firm's capital is in the form of common equity. This equity (ownership) capital is represented initially by share capital and subsequently by share capital and retained earnings. Management has learned through experience that 60 percent is the amount of equity capital the firm must maintain to keep a balance acceptable to security holders, between fixed income securities and ownership interest. However, depending on how quickly the firm's capital needs expand, the growth in internally generated funds that are recorded as retained earnings may not be enough to support the investment needs of the firm and maintain a balanced capital structure.

For example, if the Baker Corporation generates $23.4 million in earnings, it will be recorded as retained earnings and will be deployed with other capital in the investments of the firm.[8] Since management has determined that equity should represent 60 percent of the capital structure, these internally generated funds recorded as retained earnings will be adequate to support investments of $39 million. More formally, we say that

$$X = \frac{\text{Retained earnings}}{\text{Percent of equity in the capital structure}} \quad \text{(11–8)}$$

(Where X represents the size of the investments that retained earnings will support.)

$$X = \frac{\$23.4 \text{ million}}{0.60} = \$39 \text{ million}$$

Once $39 million of investments are made, internally generated funds, recorded as retained earnings, are no longer adequate to keep the equity portion of the capital structure above 60 percent. Lenders and investors become concerned if common equity (ownership) capital falls below 60 percent. Because of this, **new** common stock is needed to supplement retained earnings to provide the 60 percent common equity component for the firm. That is, after $39 million of investments are made, additional common equity capital will be in the form of new common stock rather than retained earnings.

In the upper portion of Table 11–5, we see the original cost of capital that we have been discussing throughout the chapter. This applies up to a total capital amount of $39 million. After $39 million, the concept of marginal cost of capital becomes important and, as shown on the lower portion of the table, the cost of capital goes up.

Table 11–5 Cost of capital for different amounts of financing

		Cost (after tax)	Weights	Weighted Cost
First $39 million:				
Debt	K_d	6.55%	.30	1.97%
Preferred	K_p	10.94	.10	1.09
Common equity*	K_e	12.00	.60	7.20
				$K_a = 10.26\%$
Next $11 million:				
Debt	K_d	6.55%	.30	1.97%
Preferred	K_p	10.94	.10	1.09
Common equity†	K_n	13.33	.60	8.00
				$K_{mc} = 11.06\%$

*Retained earnings
†New common equity

In the lower portion of the table, K_{mc} represents the **marginal** cost of capital, which becomes 11.06 percent after $39 million. The cost of capital increases for capital above $39 million because the invested common equity is now in the form of new common stock rather than retained earnings. The overall cost becomes slightly more for the additional funding because of flotation costs (**F**). The cost of new common stock was shown earlier in the chapter as formula 11–6. In this circumstance, it is calculated

$$K_n = \left(\frac{D_1}{P_0} + g\right)\left(\frac{P_0}{P_n}\right) = \left(\frac{\$2}{\$40} + 7\%\right)\left(\frac{\$40}{\$36}\right)$$

$$= 13.33\%$$

---

[8]This basic concept, known as *sustainable growth rate,* is an important one for the student or practitioner of finance to grasp. Too often, managers have assumed that as long as their firms were profitable, they could continue to grow as quickly as possible. Rude awakenings sometimes followed when banks refused to advance any more loans to the cash-strapped firms. The formula for determining the internally sustainable growth rate of the firm is discussed in Chapter 4. Assuming the firm's debt ratio is optimal, the rest of the balance sheet can grow no faster than the equity portion.

The flotation cost (F) of $4.00 reduces the net share proceeds (P_n) to $36 and makes the cost of new common stock 13.33 percent. This is higher than the 12 percent cost of retained earnings we have been using and, therefore, causes the increase in the marginal cost of capital.

To carry the example a bit further, let us assume the cost of debt of 6.55 percent applies to the first $15 million of debt the firm raises. After that, the aftertax cost of debt rises to 7.9 percent because of the need to tap more expensive sources. Since debt represents 30 percent of the capital structure for the Baker Corporation, the cheaper form of debt is available to support the capital structure up to $50 million. We derive the $50 million by using this formula

$$Z = \frac{\text{Amount of lower} - \text{cost debt}}{\text{Percent of debt in the capital structure}} \quad \text{(11–9)}$$

(Where Z represents the size of the investments in which lower-cost debt can be utilized.)

$$Z = \frac{\$15 \text{ million}}{0.30}$$
$$= \$50 \text{ million}$$

After the first $50 million of capital is raised, lower-cost debt is no longer available to make up 30 percent of the capital structure. After $50 million in total financing, the aftertax cost of debt goes up to the previously specified 7.9 percent. The marginal cost of capital for over $50 million in financing is shown in Table 11–6.

Table 11–6 Cost of capital for increasing amounts of financing

		Cost (after tax)	Weights	Weighted Cost
Over $50 million:				
Debt (higher cost)	K_d	7.90%	.30	2.37%
Preferred.	K_p	10.94	.10	1.09
Common equity				
(new common stock)	K_n	13.33	.60	8.00
				$K_{mc} = 11.46\%$

This increase in the cost of debt causes another rise in the marginal cost of capital (K_{mc}) to 11.46 percent after $50 million of financing. Observe that the capital structure with over $50 million of financing reflects both the increase in the cost of debt and the continued exclusive use of new common stock to represent additional common equity capital.

We could carry on this process by next considering at what point an increase in the cost of preferred stock would be demanded by investors, or at what points the costs of debt or new common stock increase as more and more capital is required. For now, however, it is important that you merely understand the basic process and can think it through when the details of an actual situation are at hand.

To summarize then, we have calculated that the Baker Corporation has a basic weighted average cost of capital of 10.26 percent. This chapter was devoted to demonstrating the development of that value. Table 11–1 presented it originally. We found, however, that as the firm's investment plans required it to substantially expand its capital structure, the weighted average cost of capital increased. This process demonstrated the concept of marginal cost of capital. The first increase, or break point, occurred at $39 million. At that point, the marginal cost of capital went up to 11.06 percent as a result of having to raise new common stock (in other words, we passed the firm's sustainable growth rate). The second increase in the cost of capital occurred when the total required capital structure passed $50 million. Beyond there, the marginal cost of capital increased to 11.46 percent as a result of the need to utilize more expensive sources of debt. These marginal changes are summarized as

Amount of Financing	Marginal Cost of Capital
0–$39 million.....................	10.26%
$39–50 million.....................	11.06
Over $50 million	11.46

Remember that this discussion of marginal cost of capital is highly dependent on the investment opportunities available to the firm and, in turn, has a great effect on them. Figure 11–3 showed the estimated returns from investment for projects A through H. Figure 11–4 reproduces the returns originally shown in Figure 11–3 and includes the concept of marginal cost of capital. Observe that the marginal cost of capital (dotted lines) increases even as the marginal returns (straight lines) decrease.

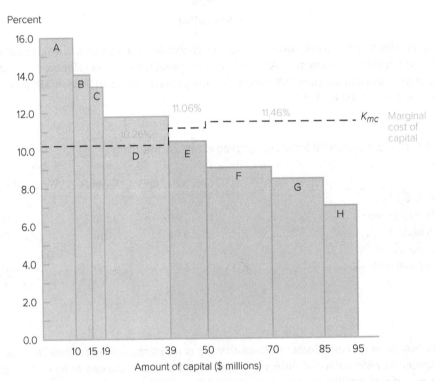

Figure 11–4 Marginal cost of capital and Baker Corporation investment alternatives

In the earlier, Figure 11–3, presentation, the Baker Corporation seemed justified in choosing projects A through E, representing capital expenditures of $50 million. Figure 11–4 represents a more sophisticated consideration of the investment alternatives and, as such, tells a slightly different story. Because of the increasing marginal cost of capital, the returns exceed the cost of capital for only the first $39 million of projects. This means that only projects A through D are deemed acceptable.

For most of our discussion of capital budgeting decisions in the next chapter, we assume we are operating at the original marginal cost of capital before substantially increasing the capital structure. This means that most of our decisions are made based on the initial weighted average cost of capital. Such an approach is generally acceptable, but it is up to the astute financial analyst to realize when this will not be the case. If there seem to be very real financing consequences involved with taking on marginal projects, they must consider them.

SUMMARY

1. The cost of capital is determined by computing the costs from the various sources of financings and weighting them in proportion to their expected representation in future financings. As such, it is the overall cost of financing of the firm at the present time based on expectations of the future. (LO1)

2. The cost of capital is a critical component in the valuation of a firm and its future prospects. An investment is expected to generate cash flows in the future. To evaluate the worth of these cash flows, we want to discount them to the present and compare their value with the investment cost. By using the cost of capital as the discount rate, we suggest that the cash flows are valued on the basis of the financing required to make the investment that will produce those cash flows. The cost of capital is used under the assumption that the investment evaluated is of the same risk as the average investment of the firm. It is important to realize that the cost of capital is a concept used as an evaluation tool to analyze investment proposals. (LO2)

3. A cost of capital calculation requires the determination of the appropriate weightings of the components of the firm's capital structure and the current costs of those components. We saw how to determine the weightings based on the market value of the existing capital structure. The cost of each component in the capital structure is closely associated with the valuation of that source. For debt and preferred stock, the cost is directly related to the current yield determined by investors, with the cost of debt reduced downward to reflect the tax-deductibility of interest costs.

   For common stock, the cost of retained earnings (K_e) is the current dividend yield on the security plus the anticipated future rate of growth in dividends. Minor adjustments must be made to the formula to determine the cost of new common stock issues. A summary of the Baker Corporation's capital costs, as developed throughout the chapter, is presented in Table 11–7. (LO3)

Table 11–7 Cost of components in the capital structure

1. Cost of debt	$K_d = \text{Yield} (1 - T) = 6.55\%$	Yield = 10.74% T = Corporate tax rate, 39.0%
2. Cost of preferred stock	$K_p = \dfrac{D_p}{P_p - F} = 10.94\%$	D_p = Preferred dividend, $10.50 P_p = Price of preferred stock, $100 F = Flotation costs, $4.00
3. Cost of common equity (retained earnings)	$K_e = \dfrac{D_1}{P_0} + g = 12.0\%$	D_1 = First-year common dividend, $2.00 P_0 = Price of common stock, $40.00 g = Growth rate, 7.0%
4. Cost of new common stock	$K_n = \left(\dfrac{D_1}{P_0} + g\right)\left(\dfrac{P_0}{P_n}\right) = 13.33\%$	Same as above, with F = Flotation costs of $4, P_n = $36

4. The weights for each of the elements in the capital structure should be chosen with a view to minimizing the overall cost of capital. Although debt is usually the cheapest form of financing, excessive use of debt may increase the financial risk of the firm and drive up the costs of all sources of financing. The wise financial manager attempts to ascertain which level of debt will result in the lowest overall cost of capital. That level of debt defines the optimum capital structure. Once the optimum capital structure has been established, the weighted average cost of capital is used as the discount rate in converting future cash flows to their present value. The major decision rule, then, is to determine if an investment proposal will earn at least the cost of the firm's financing. Investments that earn more than that cost increase the value of the firm or create value. (LO4)

5. The marginal cost of capital is important in considering what happens to a firm's cost of capital as it tries to finance large requirements for funds. At first the company uses up its access to retained earnings, with the cost of financing rising as higher-cost, new common stock is substituted for retained earnings. Common stock is needed to maintain the optimum capital structure (i.e., the appropriate debt-to-equity ratio). Needs for larger amounts of financial capital can also cause the costs of the individual means of financing to rise by raising the interest rates the firm must pay or by depressing the price of the stock because more is offered for sale than the market wants to absorb at the old price. The marginal cost of capital is the cost of the next dollar of financing required based on the presumption that the next dollar comes from a weighted mix of the optimal financing sources. (LO5)

REVIEW OF FORMULAS

Subscripts: d = debt, p = preferred, e = common equity (dividend model), j = common equity (CAPM).

K = Cost of, or required return from, the various sources of capital

V = Value of components (subscripts) of capital structure (expressed as market value)

Y = Yield (expected investor yields form basis for various costs of capital, aftertax and flotation adjustments)

T = Corporate tax rate

F = Flotation costs (as a percentage of gross proceeds: may be actual dollar cost)

P = Market price of share or stock

n = Subscript added to: K to indicate net cost after flotation costs P to indicate net price after flotation costs and price discounts (new issue)

D = Annual dividend

D_1 = Dividend at the end of a period (usually one year)

g = Dividend growth rate (infinite)

R_f = Risk-free rate

β_j = Beta coefficient (measure of risk)

R_m = Return in the market as measured by an appropriate index

1. Cost of debt

$$K_d = Y(1 - T) \qquad (11\text{--}1a)$$

$$K_d = \frac{Y(1 - T)}{1 - F} \qquad (11\text{--}1b)$$

2. Cost of preferred stock

$$K_p = \frac{D_p / P_p}{1 - F} \qquad (11\text{--}2a)$$

$$K_p = \frac{D_p}{P_p - F} \ (F \text{ as cost}) \qquad (11\text{--}2b)$$

3. Cost of common equity

Dividend model:

$$K_e = \frac{D_1}{P_0} + g \ \text{ (retained earnings)} \qquad (11\text{--}3)$$

$$K_n = \frac{\dfrac{D_1}{P_0} + g}{1 - F} \text{ or } K_n = \left(\frac{D_1}{P_0} + g\right)\frac{P_0}{P_n} \text{ (new common equity)} \qquad (11\text{--}4)$$

CAPM:

$$K_j = R_f + \beta_j(R_m - R_f) \text{ (retained earnings)} \qquad (11\text{--}5)$$

$$K_{jn} = \frac{K_j}{1 - F} \quad \text{or} \quad K_{jn} = K_j\left(\frac{P_0}{P_n}\right) \text{ (new common equity)} \qquad (11\text{--}6)$$

$$K_a = \left(\frac{V_d}{V_a}\right)K_d + \left(\frac{V_p}{V_a}\right)K_p + \left(\frac{V_e}{V_a}\right)K_e \text{ (weighted average cost of capital)} \qquad (11\text{--}7)$$

4. $$X\left(\frac{\text{Size of the investments that}}{\text{retained earnings will support}}\right) = \frac{\text{Retained earnings}}{\text{\% of equity in the capital structure}} \qquad (11\text{--}8)$$

5. $$Z\left(\frac{\text{Size of the investments that}}{\text{lower} - \text{cost debt will support}}\right) = \frac{\text{Amount of lower} - \text{cost debt}}{\text{\% of debt in the capital structure}} \qquad (11\text{--}9)$$

DISCUSSION QUESTIONS

1. Why do we use the overall cost of capital for investment decisions even when an investment will be funded by only one source of capital (e.g., debt)? (LO1)

2. How does the cost of a source of capital relate to the valuation concepts presented in Chapter 10? (LO2)

3. In computing the cost of capital, do we use the historical costs of existing debt and equity or the current costs as determined in the market? Why? (LO3)

4. Why is the cost of debt less than the cost of preferred stock if both securities are priced to yield 10 percent in the market? (LO3)

5. What are the two sources of equity (ownership) capital for the firm? (LO3)

6. Explain why retained earnings has an opportunity cost associated with it. (LO3)

7. Why is the cost of retained earnings the equivalent of the firm's own required rate of return on common stock (K_e)? (LO3)

8. Why is the cost of new common stock (K_n) higher than the cost of retained earnings (K_e)? (LO3)

9. How are the weights determined to arrive at the optimal weighted average cost of capital? (LO4)

10. Explain the traditional, U-shaped approach to the cost of capital. (LO4)

11. Identify other variables (ratios) besides the debt-to-equity ratio that influence a company's cost of capital. You may wish to refer to Chapter 3 for possibilities. (LO4)

12. It has often been said that if the company can't earn a rate of return greater than the cost of capital, it should not make investments. Explain. (LO2)

13. What effect would inflation have on a company's cost of capital? (*Hint:* Think about how inflation influences interest rates, stock prices, corporate profits, and growth.) (LO3)

14. What is the concept of marginal cost of capital? (LO5)

15. What limitations are there in using the dividend valuation model to determine the cost of equity capital? (LO3)

16. What is the justification for using market value weightings rather than book value weightings? (LO4)

INTERNET RESOURCES AND QUESTIONS

Two Canadian sites rate and grade debt. The ratings determine the spread corporations pay above Government of Canada securities:

standardandpoors.com
dbrsmorningstar.com

Canadian bank investment sites, the Bank of Canada, and IIROC (Investment Industry Regulatory Organization of Canada) identify current yields on bond issues: iiroc.ca

The TSX identifies current pricing on preferreds and common stock, including P/E ratios and dividend yields: tmxmoney.com

Betas and other useful share information are available on many Canadian companies at Reuters: reuters.com

1. Calculate the cost of capital for a corporation listed on one of the major exchanges in Canada. Use current pricing on debt and equity from the sites identified above, and use the latest filed financial statement of the selected company. The financial statements will be available at sedar.com.

2. Update the information included in Table 11–2. Have any of the ratings changed? Can you suggest why the ratings have changed?

3. Find the betas, P/E ratios, and dividend yields for the companies listed in Table 11–2. What do they tell you about the relative risk of the companies?

PROBLEMS

1. Recently, Hertz Pain Relievers bought a massage machine that provided a return of 8 percent. It was financed by debt costing 7 percent. In August, Mr. Hertz came up with a heating compound that had a return of 14 percent. The chief financial officer, Mr. R. Ental, told him it was impractical because it would require the issuance of common stock at a cost of 16 percent to finance the purchase. Is the company following an appropriate approach to using its cost of capital?

2. Royal Petroleum Co. can buy a piece of equipment that is anticipated to provide a 9 percent return and can be financed at 6 percent with debt. Later in the year, the firm turns down an opportunity to buy a new machine that would yield a 16 percent return but would cost 18 percent to finance through common equity. Assume debt and common equity each represent 50 percent of the firm's capital structure at 6 percent cost of debt and 18 percent cost of equity.

   a. Compute the weighted average cost of capital.

   b. Which project(s) should be accepted?

3. Pogo Stick Co can issue debt yielding 9 percent. The company is paying at a 25 percent tax rate. What is the aftertax cost of debt?

4. A brilliant young scientist is killed in a plane crash. It is anticipated that he could have earned $240,000 a year for the next 50 years. The attorney for the plaintiff's estate argues that the lost income should be discounted back to the present at 4 percent. The lawyer for the defendant's insurance company argues for a discount rate of 8 percent. What is the difference between the present value of the settlement at 4 percent and 8 percent? Compute each one separately.

5. Calculate the aftertax cost of debt under each of the following conditions.

	Yield	Corporate Tax Rate
a	8.0%	22%
b	14.0%	36%
c	11.5%	42%

6. Calculate the aftertax cost of debt under each of the following conditions.

	Yield	Corporate Tax Rate
a	8.0%	18%
b	12.0%	34%
c	10.6%	15%

7. Calculate the aftertax cost of debt on a bond issue yielding 10 percent. The issuing company pays tax at a rate of 34 percent and will incur distribution costs of 1 percent on this bond issue.

8. The Goodsmith Charitable Foundation, which is tax-exempt, issued debt last year at 9 percent to help finance a new playground facility in Vancouver. This year the cost of debt is 25 percent higher; that is, firms that paid 11 percent for debt last year will be paying 13.75 percent this year.

   a. If the Goodsmith Charitable Foundation borrowed money this year, what would be the aftertax cost of debt, based on its cost last year and the 25 percent increase?

   b. If the receipts of the foundation were found to be taxable by CRA (at a rate of 30 percent because of involvement in political activities), what would be the aftertax cost of debt?

9. Waste Disposal Systems has an aftertax cost of debt of 6 percent. With a tax rate of 33 percent, what can you assume the yield is on the debt?

10. Octopus Transit has a $1,000 par value bond outstanding with 10 years to maturity. The bond carries an annual interest payment of $75, payable semiannually, and is currently selling for $1,092. Octopus is in a 35 percent tax bracket. The firm wishes to know what the aftertax cost of a new bond issue is likely to be. The yield to maturity on the new issue will be the same as the yield to maturity on the old issue because the risk and maturity date will be similar.

    a. Compute the yield to maturity on the old issue and use this as the yield for the new issue.

    b. Make the appropriate tax adjustment to determine the aftertax cost of debt.

11. Russell Container Company has a $1,000 par value bond outstanding with 20 years to maturity. The bond carries an annual interest payment of $95, and is currently selling for $920. Russell is in a 25 percent tax bracket. The firm wishes to know what the aftertax cost of a new bond issue is likely to be. The yield to maturity on the new issue will be the same as the yield to maturity on the old issue because the risk and maturity date will be similar.

    a. Compute the yield to maturity on the old issue and use this as the yield for the new issue.

    b. Make the appropriate tax adjustment to determine the aftertax cost of debt.

12. For Russell Container Company, described in the previous problem, assume the yield on the bonds goes up by one percentage point and that the tax rate is now 34 percent.

    a. What is the new aftertax cost of debt?

    b. Has the aftertax cost of debt gone up or down from the previous problem? Explain why.

13. Terrier Company is in a 40 percent tax bracket and has a bond outstanding that yields 10 percent to maturity.

    a. What is Terrier's aftertax cost of debt?

    b. Assume that the yield on the bond goes down by 1 percentage point, and due to tax reform, the corporate tax rate falls to 25 percent. What is Terrier's new aftertax cost of debt?

    c. Has the aftertax cost of debt gone up or down from part *a* to part *b*? Explain why.

14. Suncor is planning to issue debt that will mature in the year 2037. In many respects the issue is similar to currently outstanding debt of the corporation. Using Table 11–2 in the chapter, identify

    a. The yield to maturity on similarly outstanding debt for the firm, in terms of maturity.

    b. Assume that because the new debt will be issued at par, the required yield to maturity will be 0.15 percent higher than the value determined in part *a*. Add this factor to the answer in **a**. (New issues at par sometimes require a slightly higher yield than old issues that are trading below par. There is less leverage and fewer tax advantages.)

    c.   If the firm is in a 25 percent tax bracket, what is the aftertax cost of debt?

15.   Schuss Inc. can sell preferred shares for $60 with an estimated flotation cost of $3.00. The preferred stock is anticipated to pay $7 per share in dividends.

    a.   Compute the cost of preferred stock for Schuss Inc.

    b.   Do we need to make a tax adjustment for the issuing firm?

16.   The Meredith Company issued $100 par value preferred shares 10 years ago. The shares provided an 8 percent yield at the time of issue. Each preferred share is now selling for $75. What is the current yield or cost of preferred stock? (Disregard flotation costs.)

17.   Radio Gaga can issue preferred shares at $25 with an annual dividend of $1.50. Flotation expenses of a new issue will be 5 percent. What is the cost of a preferred share issue?

18.   The treasurer of Sutton Security Systems is asked to compute the cost of fixed income securities for her corporation. Even before making the calculations, she assumes the aftertax cost of debt is at least 2 percent less than that for preferred stock. Based on the following facts, is she correct?

    Debt can be issued at a yield of 10.5 percent, and the corporate tax rate is 34 percent. Preferred shares will be priced at $50 and pay a dividend of $4.40. The flotation cost on the preferred stock is $2.00.

19.   Ellington Electronics wants you to calculate its cost of common stock. During the next 12 months, the company expects to pay dividends (D_1) of $1.50 per share, and the current price of its common stock is $30 per share. The expected growth rate is 8 percent.

    a.   Compute the cost of retained earnings (K_e).

    b.   If a $2 flotation cost is involved, compute the cost of new common stock (K_n).

20.   Compute K_e and K_n under the following circumstances:

    a. $D_1 = \$4.60$; $P_0 = \$60$; $g = 6\%$; $F = \$4.00$.

    b. $D_1 = \$0.25$; $P_0 = \$20$; $g = 10\%$; $F = \$1.50$.

    c. E_1 (earnings at the end of period one) = $6; payout ratio equals 30 percent; $P_0 = \$25$; $g = 4.5\%$; $F = \$2$.

    d. D_0 (dividend at the beginning of the first period) = $3; growth rate for dividends and earnings (g) = 7%; $P_0 = \$42$; $F = \$3.00$.

21.   Sam's Fine Garments sells jackets and sports coats in suburban malls throughout the country. Business has been good, as indicated by the six-year growth in earnings per share. The earnings have grown from $1.00 to $1.87.

    a.   Determine the compound annual rate of growth in earnings ($n = 6$).

    b.   Based on the growth rate determined in part **a**, project earnings for next year (E_1). Round to two places to the right of the decimal point.

    c.   Assume the dividend payout ratio is 40 percent. Compute D_1. Round to two places to the right of the decimal point.

    d.   The current price of the stock is $15. Using the growth rate (g) from part **a** and D_1 from part **c**, compute K_e.

    e.   If the flotation cost is $1.75, compute the cost of new common stock (K_n).

22.   The Tyler Oil Company's capital structure is as follows:

Debt	35%
Preferred stock	15
Common equity	50

The aftertax cost of debt is 7 percent; the cost of preferred stock is 10 percent; and the cost of common equity (in the form of retained earnings) is 13 percent.

Calculate Tyler Oil Company's weighted average cost of capital in a manner similar to Table 11–1.

23. As an alternative to the capital structure shown in the previous problem for Tyler Oil Company, an outside consultant has suggested the following modifications.

Debt	60%
Preferred stock	5
Common equity	35

Under this new and more debt-oriented arrangement, the aftertax cost of debt is 8.8 percent, the cost of preferred stock is 10.5 percent, and the cost of common equity (in the form of retained earnings) is 15.5 percent.

Recalculate Tyler's weighted average cost of capital. Which plan is optimal in terms of minimizing the weighted average cost of capital?

24. Given the following information, calculate the weighted average cost of capital for Genex Corporation. Line up the calculations in the order shown in Table 11–1.

Percent of Capital Structure:	
Debt	35%
Preferred stock	10
Common equity	55
Additional Information:	
Bond coupon rate	13%
Bond yield	11%
Dividend, expected common	$3.00
Dividend, preferred	$10.00
Price, common	$50.00
Price, preferred	$98.00
Flotation cost, preferred	$5.50
Corporate growth rate	8%
Corporate tax rate	30%

25. Given the following information, calculate the weighted average cost of capital for Hadley Corporation. Line up the calculations in the order shown in Table 11–1.

Percent of Capital Structure:	
Debt	30%
Preferred stock	10
Common equity	60
Additional Information:	
Corporate tax rate	34%
Dividend, preferred	$9.00
Dividend, expected common	$3.50
Price, preferred	$102.00
Corporate growth rate	6%
Bond yield	7%
Flotation cost, preferred	$3.20
Price, common	$70.00

26. Given the following information, calculate the weighted average cost of capital for Puppet Corporation.

Percent of Capital Structure:	
Debt	55%
Preferred stock	5
Common equity	40
Additional Information:	
Bond coupon rate	8.5%
Bond yield	7%
Bond flotation cost	2%
Dividend, expected common	$1.50
Price, common	$30.00
Dividend, preferred	5%
Flotation cost, preferred	3%
Flotation cost, common	4%
Corporate growth rate	6%
Corporate tax rate	35%

a. Calculate the cost of capital assuming use of internally generated funds.

b. Calculate the cost of capital assuming use of externally generated funds.

c. Why is there a difference? Why does only common equity change?

27. Valvano Publishing Company is trying to calculate its cost of capital for use in a capital budgeting decision. Mr. Washburn, the vice-president of finance, has given you the following information and asked you to compute the weighted average cost of capital.

The company currently has outstanding a bond with an 11 percent coupon rate and a convertible bond with a 7.1 percent rate. The firm has been informed by its investment dealer, Dean, Smith, and Company, that bonds of equal risk and credit rating are now selling to yield 13 percent. The common stock has a price of $45 and an expected dividend (D_1) of $2.52 per share. The firm's historical growth rate of earnings and dividends per share has been 14.5 percent, but security analysts on Bay Street expect this growth to slow to 11 percent in the future. The preferred stock is selling at $50 per share and carries a dividend of $5.50 per share. The corporate tax rate is 34 percent. The flotation costs are 3 percent of the selling price for preferred stock.

The optimum capital structure for the firm seems to be 35 percent debt, 10 percent preferred stock, and 55 percent common equity in the form of retained earnings.

Compute the cost of capital for the individual components in the capital structure, and then calculate the weighted average cost of capital.

28. McNabb Construction Company is trying to calculate its cost of capital for use in making a capital budgeting decision. Mr. Reid, the vice-president of finance, has given you the following information and has asked you to compute the weighted average cost of capital.

The company currently has an outstanding bond with a 9.5 percent coupon rate and another bond with a 7.8 percent rate. The firm has been informed by its investment dealer that bonds of equal risk and credit ratings are now selling to yield 10.5 percent. The common stock has a price of $98.44 and an expected dividend (D_1) of $3.15 per share. The historical growth pattern (g) for dividends is as follows:

$2.00
2.24
2.51
2.81

a. Compute the historical growth rate, round it to the nearest whole number, and use it for **g**.

The preferred stock is selling at $90 per share and pays a dividend of $8.50 per share. The corporate tax rate is 30 percent. The flotation cost is 2 percent of the selling price for preferred stock. The optimum capital structure for the firm is 30 percent debt, 10 percent preferred stock, and 60 percent common equity in the form of retained earnings.

b. Compute the cost of capital for the individual components in the capital structure, and then calculate the weighted average cost of capital.

29. Western Electric Utility Company faces increasing needs for capital. Fortunately, it has an A (low) credit rating. The corporate tax rate is 25 percent. Western's treasurer is trying to determine the corporation's current weighted average cost of capital to assess the profitability of capital budgeting projects. Historically, the corporation's earnings and dividends per share have increased at about a 6 percent annual rate.

Western Electric's common stock is selling at $60 per share, and the company will pay a $4.50 per share dividend (D_1). The company's $100 preferred stock has been yielding 9 percent in the current market. Flotation costs for the company have been estimated by its investment dealer to be $1.50 for preferred stock. The company's optimum capital structure is 40 percent debt, 10 percent preferred stock, and 50 percent common equity in the form of retained earnings. Refer to the table below on bond issues for comparative yields on bonds of equal risks to Western Electric, maturing in 2038. Compute the values for parts **a**, **b**, **c**, and **d** from the information given.

Data on Bond Issues			
Issue	Rating	Price	Yield to Maturity
Utilities:			
Bell Canada 6.17%, 2037............	BBB (high)	133.21	3.56
Epcor 6.65%, 2038................	A (low)	154.19	2.84
Hydro One 6.03%, 2039............	A (high)	128.91	2.76
Industrials:			
Loblaw 5.90%, 2036	BBB	130.81	3.39
Suncor 5.39, 2037	A (low)	128.76	3.20

a. Cost of debt, K_d

b. Cost of preferred stock, K_p

c. Cost of common equity in the form of retained earnings, K_e

d. Weighted average cost of capital

30. Eaton International Corporation has the following capital structure:

	Cost (after tax)	Weightings	Weighted Cost
Debt	7.1%	25%	1.78%
Preferred stock (K_p)	8.6	10	.86
Common equity (K_e)			
(retained earnings)	14.1	65	9.17
Total:			
Weighted average cost of capital (K_a) ...			11.81%

a. If the firm has $19.5 million in retained earnings, at what size capital structure will the firm run out of retained earnings?

b. The 7.1 percent cost of debt referred to above applied only to the first $14 million of debt. After that the cost of debt will go up. At what size capital structure will there be a change in the cost of debt?

31. The Nolan Corporation finds that it is necessary to determine its marginal cost of capital. Nolan's current capital structure calls for 45 percent debt, 15 percent preferred stock, and

40 percent common equity. Initially common equity will be in the form of retained earnings (K_e) and then new common stock (K_n). The costs of the various sources of financing are as follows: debt, 5.6 percent; preferred stock, 9.0 percent; retained earnings, 12.0 percent; and new common stock, 13.2 percent.

a. What is the initial weighted average cost of capital? (Include debt, preferred stock, and common equity in the form of retained earnings, K_e.)

b. If the firm has $12 million in retained earnings, at what size of investment will the firm run out of retained earnings?

c. What will the marginal cost of capital be immediately after that point? (Equity will remain at 40 percent of the capital structure, but it will all be in the form of new common stock, K_n.)

d. The 5.6 percent cost of debt referred to above applies only to the first $18 million of debt. After that the cost of debt will be 7.2 percent. At what size of investment will there be a change in the cost of debt?

e. What will the marginal cost of capital be immediately after that point? (Consider the facts in both parts *c* and *d*.)

32. The Evans Corporation finds that it is necessary to determine its marginal cost of capital. Evans' current capital structure calls for 30 percent debt, 10 percent preferred stock, and 60 percent common equity. Initially, common equity will be in the form of retained earnings (K_e) and then new common stock (K_n). The costs of the various sources of financing are as follows: debt, 6.2 percent; preferred stock, 9.4 percent; retained earnings, 12 percent; and new common stock, 13.4 percent.

a. What is the initial weighted average cost of capital? (Include debt, preferred stock, and common equity in the form of retained earnings, K_e.)

b. If the firm has $20 million in retained earnings, at what size of investment will the firm run out of retained earnings?

c. What will the marginal cost of capital be immediately after that point? (Equity will remain at 60 percent of the capital structure, but it will all be in the form of new common stock, K_n.)

d. The 6.2 percent cost of debt referred to above applies only to the first $36 million of debt. After that, the cost of debt will be 7.8 percent. At what size of investment will there be a change in the cost of debt?

e. What will the marginal cost of capital be immediately after that point? (Consider the facts in both parts *c* and *d*.)

33. Eaton Electronic Company's treasurer uses both the capital asset pricing model and the dividend valuation model to compute the cost of common equity (also referred to as the required rate of return for common equity).

Assume the following:

$R_f = 7\%$, $K_m = 10\%$, $\beta_j = 1.6$, $D_1 = \$0.70$, $P_0 = \$19$, $g = 8\%$

a. Compute K_j (required rate of return on common equity based on the capital asset pricing model).

b. Compute K_e (required rate of return on common equity based on the dividend valuation model).

COMPREHENSIVE PROBLEMS

34. Medical Research Corporation is expanding its research and production capacity to introduce a new line of products. Current plans call for the expenditure of $100 million on four projects of equal size ($25 million) but with different returns. Project A is in blood clotting proteins

and has an expected return of 18 percent. Project B relates to a hepatitis vaccine and carries a potential return of 14 percent. Project C, dealing with a cardiovascular compound, is expected to earn 11.8 percent, and Project D, an investment in orthopedic implants, is expected to show a 10.9 percent return.

The firm has $15 million in retained earnings. After a capital structure with $15 million in retained earnings is reached (in which retained earnings represent 60 percent of the financing), all additional equity financing must come in the form of new common stock.

Common stock is selling for $25.00 per share, and underwriting costs are estimated at $3.00 if new shares are issued. Dividends for the next year will be $0.90 per share (D1), and earnings and dividends have grown consistently at 11 percent per year.

The yield on comparative bonds has been hovering at 11 percent. The investment dealer believes the first $20 million of bonds could be sold to yield 11 percent, while additional debt might require a 2 percent premium and be marketed to yield 13 percent. The corporate tax rate is 30 percent. Debt represents 40 percent of the capital structure.

a. Based on the two sources of financing, what is the initial weighted average cost of capital? (Use K_d and K_e.)

b. At what size capital structure will the firm run out of retained earnings?

c. What will the marginal cost of capital be immediately after that point?

d. At what size capital structure will there be a change in the cost of debt?

e. What will the marginal cost of capital be immediately after that point?

f. Based on the information about potential returns on investments in the first paragraph and information on marginal cost of capital (in parts *a*, *c*, and *e*), how large a capital investment budget should the firm use?

g. Graph the answer determined in part *f*.

35. Masco Oil and Gas Company is a very large company with common stock listed on the Toronto Stock Exchange and bonds traded over the counter. As of the current balance sheet, it has three bond issues outstanding:

$150 million of 10% series	2027
$ 50 million of 7% series	2029
$ 75 million of 5% series	2036

The vice-president of finance is planning to sell $75 million of bonds next year to replace the debt due to expire. Present market yields on similar BB-rated bonds are 12.1 percent. Masco also has $90 million of 7.5 percent, non-callable preferred stock outstanding, and it has no intentions of selling any more preferred stock in the future. The preferred stock is currently priced at $80.00 per share, and its dividend per share is $7.80.

The company has had very volatile earnings, but its dividends per share have had a very stable growth rate of 8 percent, and this will continue. The expected dividend (D1) is $1.90 per share, and the common stock is selling for $40.00 per share. The company's investment dealer has quoted the following flotation costs to Masco: $2.50 per share for preferred stock and $2.20 per share for common stock.

On the advice of its investment dealer, Masco has kept its debt at 50 percent of assets and its equity at 50 percent. Masco sees no need to sell either common or preferred stock in the foreseeable future as it generates enough internal funds for its investment needs when these funds are combined with debt financing. Masco's corporate tax rate is 40 percent.

Compute the cost of capital for the following:

a. Bond (debt) (K_d)

b. Preferred stock (K_p)

c. Common equity in the form of retained earnings (K_e)

d. New common stock (K_n)

e. Weighted average cost of capital

36. River Runs Ltd. has the following right-hand side of its balance sheet:

Debt: 8% coupon, 12 years to maturity	$ 10,000,000
Preferred shares: 6% dividend	2,000,000
Common shares: 1,000,000 outstanding	1,000,000
Retained earnings	6,000,000
	$19,000,000

New debt could be issued to yield 12 percent, with flotation costs netting the firm $965 on each $1,000 bond. Preferred shares would require a current yield of 10 percent, with aftertax flotation costs of 4 percent. Common shares currently trade at $11, but new shares would be discounted to $10.50 to encourage sales. Aftertax flotation costs on new common shares would be 5 percent. The anticipated dividend growth rate is 12 percent. The expected dividend is $0.75.

River Runs Ltd. has a 40 percent tax rate and would require new share capital to fund new investments.

a. Based on market value weightings, calculate River's weighted average cost of capital.

37. Island Capital has the following capital structure:

Bonds	$20,000,000
Perpetuals (preferred shares)	4,000,000
Common shares	20,000,000
Retained earnings	19,500,000
	$63,500,000

The existing bonds have a coupon rate of 8 percent with 18 years left to maturity, but current yields on these bonds are 11 percent. Flotation costs of $25.00 per $1,000 bond would be expected on a new issue.

The existing perpetuals have a $25.00 par value and an annual dividend rate of 9 percent. New perpetuals could be issued at a $50.00 par value with an 8 percent yield. Flotation costs would be 3 percent.

There are four million common shares outstanding that currently trade at $18.00 per share and expect to pay a dividend next year of $1.75 that will continue to grow at 7 percent per annum for the foreseeable future. New shares could be issued at $17.50 and would require flotation expenses of 5 percent of proceeds.

Island's tax rate is 39 percent, and it is expected that internally generated funds will be sufficient to fund capital projects in the near future.

a. Compute Island Capital's current cost of capital with market value weightings.

b. How would the cost of capital calculation change if new shares are required to fund the equity component of the capital structure?

38. Trois-Rivières Manufacturing has 10,000 bonds (face value of $1,000 each) with a 10 percent coupon maturing in 8 years. Its preferreds (100,000 shares) have a face value of $25 and pay a 7.5 percent dividend, and it has 600,000 common shares outstanding. Retained earnings are reported at $4,500,000.

During the last five years, Trois-Rivières Manufacturing has enjoyed steady growth, with common stock dividends growing from $0.80 to $1.23 (just recently paid). The common share price currently trades at $15.00. If new shares were issued at $15.00, they would require flotation expenses of 7 percent of proceeds.

The preferred shares currently trade at $26.50, and any new issue would require flotation expenses of 5 percent of price to investors.

The bonds currently pay interest semiannually and are trading at a price that yields a nominal 12 percent annual rate (12.36 effective annual rate). Flotation costs of new debt would be 4 percent of proceeds.

Trois-Rivières' tax rate is 38 percent, and equity financing would require a new share issue.

a. Calculate the weighted average cost of capital of Trois-Rivières Manufacturing.

39. Murchie's is considering diversification by way of acquisition to reduce its reliance on its volatile core business. Mad Max, the CEO, has asked for your calculation of a discount rate to be used to analyze the potential acquisition targets. The following information has been assembled.

Long-term bonds	$10,000,000
Subordinated perpetual bonds	2,000,000
Common shares	2,062,500
Retained earnings.	937,500
	$15,000,000

The yield on 98-day Treasury bills is 7.38 percent. Long-term debt has 15 years to maturity and has a coupon rate of 12 percent paid semiannually. Currently the bonds are trading at a premium of 15 percent to face value. A new debt issue would incur flotation costs of 3 percent of the issue price.

The perpetual bonds were issued at a yield of 9 percent but currently are trading to yield 12 percent. The flotation costs of a new issue would be 4 percent.

There are 750,000 common shares outstanding, currently priced at $4.50. Murchie's, with a beta of 1.7, is planning a dividend of $0.10. Future growth is suggested at a compound annualized rate of 15 percent. A new issue of common shares would net the firm $4.10 per share. Murchie's tax rate is 43 percent. Internally generated funds will not be sufficient to fund future expansion plans.

a. Calculate Murchie's weighted average cost of capital.

b. Calculate Murchie's weighted average cost of capital if it has negative income for tax purposes.

c. Comment on the appropriateness of Murchie's present capital structure.

d. Comment on the use of the weighted average cost of capital as calculated to analyze the suggested acquisitions.

APPENDIX 11A

Cost of Capital and the Capital Asset Pricing Model

The work of Harry Markowitz, examined in Chapter 13, highlights the importance of thinking of investments, their returns, and their risks in a portfolio context. The risk of an investment is not so much its individual risk but the risk it adds to a portfolio, or collection of assets. Individual, or unique, risks tend to disappear (they cancel each other out) within a portfolio. However, some risk still remains, and it is this risk that is of interest as it will shape the value that investors or shareholders place on assets. William Sharpe and others developed a model that focused on the risk that cannot be diversified away, which suggests that the nondiversifiable risk will determine the pricing of assets in an efficient market. Efficient markets are examined in Chapter 14.

The Capital Asset Pricing Model

The capital asset pricing model (CAPM) relates the risk-return tradeoffs of individual assets to market returns. It suggests the expected return of an asset based on the asset's risk that cannot be diversified away. Common stock returns over time have generally been used to test this model, since stock prices are widely available and efficiently priced, as are market indexes of stock performance. In theory, the CAPM encompasses all assets, but in practice it is difficult to measure returns on all types of assets or to find an all-encompassing market index. For our purposes, we use common stock returns to explain the model, and occasionally we generalize to other assets.

The basic form of the CAPM is a linear relationship between returns on individual stocks and stock market returns over time. By using least squares regression analysis, the return on an individual stock, K_j, is expressed in formula 11A–1.

$$K_j = \alpha + \beta_j R_m + e \quad \text{(11A–1)}$$

Where

K_j = Return on individual common stock of a company
α = Alpha, the intercept on the y-axis
β_j = Beta, the coefficient of stock (j)
R_m = Return on the stock market (an index of stock returns is used, usually the S&P/TSX Composite Index)
e = Error term of the regression formula

As indicated in Table 11A–1 and Figure 11A–1, this formula uses historical data to generate the alpha coefficient (α) and the beta coefficient (β_j), a measurement of the return performance of a given stock versus the return performance of the market. Assume we want to calculate a beta for Parts Associates Inc. (PAI), and we have the performance data for that company and the market shown in the table. The relationship between PAI and the market appears graphically in the figure.

Table 11A–1 Performance of PAI and the market

Year	Rate of Return on Stock	
	PAI	Market
1..............................	12.0%	10.0%
2..............................	16.0	18.0
3..............................	20.0	16.0
4..............................	16.0	10.0
5..............................	6.0	8.0
Mean return....................	**14.0%**	**12.4%**
Standard deviation..............	**4.73%**	**3.87%**

The alpha term in Figure 11A–1 of 2.8 percent is the y-intercept of the linear regression. It is the expected return on PAI stock if returns on the market are zero. However, if the returns on the market are expected to approximate the historical rate of 12.4 percent, the expected return on PAI would be $K_j = 2.8 + 0.9(12.4) = 14.0$ percent. This maintains the historical relationship. If the returns on the market are expected to rise to 18 percent next year, expected return on PAI would be $K_j = 2.8 + 0.9(18.0) = 19$ percent.

The error term (e) is useful in determining the degree of confidence we would have in estimates of returns based on the regression line. From the historical data, it is evident that not all observations lie on the regression line, and yet we propose to use the relationship that it suggests to predict return expectations in the future. On the basis of the historical observations that do not fit on the line, the error terms, we can express the likelihood that our predicted returns are within an acceptable range of the prediction. Statistically, this involves calculating the standard error of the estimate.

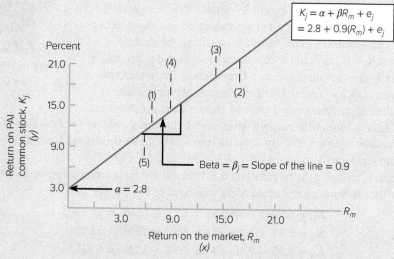

$$K_j = \alpha + \beta R_m + e_j$$
$$= 2.8 + 0.9(R_m) + e_j$$

Figure 11A–1 Linear regression of returns between PAI and the market

As the CAPM is developed, our focus will be on the beta term. If we plot only excess returns—that is, asset and market returns above the risk-free rate of return—it is found that alpha is not significantly different from zero. In addition, our expectation for the error term is also zero. In a diversified portfolio, the error terms tend to offset each other.

Notice that we are talking in terms of expectations. The CAPM is an expectational (*ex ante*) model, and there is no guarantee that historical data will reoccur. One area of empirical testing involves the stability and predictability of the beta coefficient based on historical data. Research has indicated that betas are more useful in a portfolio context (for groupings of stocks) because the betas of individual stocks are less stable from period to period than portfolio betas. In addition, research indicates betas of individual common stocks have a tendency to approach 1.0 over time.

The Security Market Line

The capital asset pricing model evolved from formula 11A–1 into a risk premium model where the basic assumption is that investors expected to take more risk must be compensated by larger expected returns. Investors should also not accept returns that are less than they can get from a riskless asset. For CAPM purposes, it is assumed that short-term government Treasury bills may be considered a riskless asset.[9] When viewed in this context, an investor must achieve an extra return above that obtainable from a Treasury bill to induce the assumption of more risk. This brings us to the more common and theoretically useful model:

$$K_j = R_f + \beta_j(R_m - R_f) \quad \text{(11A–2)}$$

Where

R_f = Risk-free rate of return

β_j = Beta coefficient from formula 11A–1

R_m = Return on the market index

$R_m - R_f$ = Premium or excess return of the market versus the risk-free rate (since the market is riskier than R_f, the assumption is that the expected R_m will be greater than R_f)

$\beta_j(R_m - R_f)$ = Expected return above the risk-free rate for the stock of company j, given the level of risk

The model centres on beta, the coefficient of the premium demanded by an investor to invest in an individual stock. For each individual security, beta measures the sensitivity (volatility) of the security's return to the market. By definition, the market has a beta of 1.0, so if an individual company's beta is 1.0, it can expect to have returns as volatile as the market and total returns equal

---

[9]A number of studies have also indicated that longer-term government securities may appropriately represent R_f (the risk-free rate).

to the market. A company with a beta of 2.0 would be twice as volatile as the market and would be expected to generate more returns, whereas a company with a beta of 0.5 would be half as volatile as the market.

Ibbotson SBBI Classic
Yearbook
duffandphelps.com

The term $(R_m - R_f)$ indicates common stock is expected to generate a rate of return higher than the return on a Treasury bill. This makes sense, since common stock has more risk. In fact, research by Roger Ibbotson shows that this risk premium over the last 83 years is close to 6.5 percent on average, but exhibits a wide standard deviation.[10] In the actual application of the CAPM to cost of capital, companies often use this historical risk premium in their calculations. In our example, we use 6.5 percent to represent the expected $(R_m - R_f)$.

For example, assuming the risk-free rate is 5.5 percent and the market risk premium $(R_m - R_f)$ is 6.5 percent, the following returns would occur with betas of 2.0, 1.0, and 0.5:

$$K_2 = 5.5\% + 2.0(6.5\%) = 5.5\% + 13.0\% = 18.5\%$$
$$K_1 = 5.5\% + 1.0(6.5\%) = 5.5\% + 6.5\% = 12.0\%$$
$$K_{.5} = 5.5\% + 0.5(6.5\%) = 5.5\% + 3.25\% = 8.75\%$$

 FINANCE IN ACTION

Risks and Returns

In early 2020 the following betas were reported for three companies listed on the Toronto Stock Exchange (TSX).

Telus (T).	0.61
Shopify (SHOP).	0.92
Teck (TECK.B)	1.42

These betas give us a sense of the performance we should expect from each of the companies. We measure performance based on changes in the company's market share price. Telus would be least sensitive to market movements, whereas Teck, a world leader in resource production, would be most sensitive to market movements. In an up market, Teck's share price would be expected to outperform the two other companies. This would, however, be appropriate, given that with a higher beta Teck would be riskier. In a down market, Teck would be expected to underperform the other companies.

A portfolio with equal value weightings of the three stocks would have a beta of 0.98 (0.61 × 0.33 + 0.92 × 0.33 + 1.42 × 0.33). This portfolio, with virtually the same beta, would be expected to perform similarly to the market, which has a beta of 1. A portfolio beta would be a more reliable estimate of performance because, through the benefits of diversification, the individual risks of each company would be reduced. Although beta measures risk in relation to the market fairly well, it does not capture the individual risk of a company's performance (the error term in formula 11A–1).

In constructing an individual's portfolio of investments, betas can be used (and are by investment managers) to assemble a collection of stocks. Betas would be used to construct a portfolio based on an investor's attitude toward risk and expected returns. Higher-beta portfolios would expect greater returns, but with greater risks.

Q1 What are the current betas of these companies?

Q2 Can you find any Canadian companies with higher betas?

reuters.com/finance/markets

---

[10]Ibbotson, *SBBI Classic Yearbook, Stocks, Bonds, Bills and Inflation: 2013* (Chicago, IL: Morningstar, 2013).

The beta term measures the riskiness of an investment relative to the market. To outperform the market, one would have to assume more risk by selecting assets with betas greater than 1.0. Another way of looking at the risk-return tradeoff would be that if less risk than the market is desired, an investor would choose assets with a beta of less than 1.0. Beta is a good measure of a stock's risk when the stock is combined into a portfolio, and therefore, it has some bearing on the assets a company acquires for its portfolio of real capital.

In Figure 11A–1, individual stock returns were compared to market returns, and the beta from formula 11A–1 was shown. From formula 11A–2, the risk premium model, a generalized risk-return graph called the security market line (SML) can be constructed that identifies the risk-return tradeoff of any common stock (asset) relative to the company's beta. This is shown in Figure 11A–2.

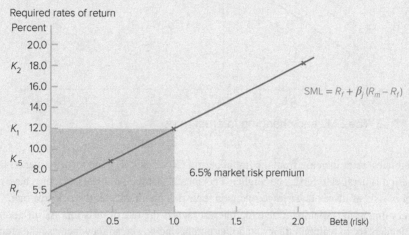

Figure 11A–2 The security market line (SML)

The required return for all securities can be expressed as the risk-free rate plus a premium for risk. Thus, we see that a stock with a beta of 1.0 would have a risk premium of 6.5 percent added to the risk-free rate of interest, 5.5 percent, to provide a required return of 12 percent. Since a beta of 1.0 implies risk equal to the stock market, the return is also at the overall market rate. If the beta is 2.0, twice the market risk premium of 6.5 percent must be earned, and we add 13 percent to the risk-free rate of 5.5 percent to determine the required return of 18.5 percent. For a beta of 0.5, the required return is 8.75 percent.

Cost of Capital Considerations

When calculating the cost of capital for common stock, remember that K_e is equal to the expected total return from the dividend yield and capital gains.

$$K_e = \frac{D_1}{P_0} + g$$

K_e is the return required by investors based on expectations of future dividends and growth. The SML provides the same information but in a market-related risk-return model. As required returns rise, prices must fall to adjust to the new equilibrium return level, and as required returns fall, prices rise. Stock markets are generally efficient, and when stock prices are in equilibrium, the K_e derived from the dividend model is equal to K_j derived from the SML. However, just as with the dividend valuation model we had to allow for flotation costs on a new share issue, we must do the same for the CAPM. We adjust K_j by multiplying by P_0/P_n.

The SML helps us to identify several circumstances that can cause the cost of capital to change. Figure 11–2 examined required rates of returns over time with changing interest rates and stock prices. Figure 11A–3 does basically the same thing, only through the SML format.

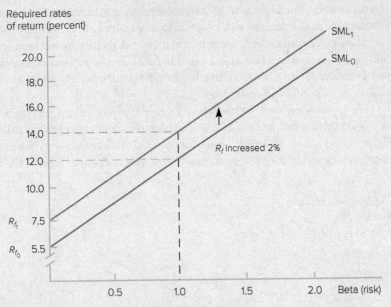

Figure 11A–3 The SML and changing interest rates

When interest rates increase from the initial period (R_{f_1} versus R_{f_0}), the security market line in the next period is parallel to SML_0, but higher. This means that required rates of return have risen for every level of risk, as investors desire to maintain their risk premium over the risk-free rate.

One very important variable influencing interest rates is the rate of inflation. As inflation increases, lenders try to maintain their real dollar purchasing power, so they increase the required interest rates to offset inflation. The risk-free rate can be thought of as

$$R_f = RR + IP$$

Where

RR = The real rate of return on a riskless government security when inflation is zero
IP = An inflation premium that compensates lenders (investors) for loss of purchasing power

An upward shift in the SML indicates that the prices of all assets shift downward as interest rates move up. In Chapter 10, this was demonstrated in the discussion showing that when market interest rates went up, bond prices adjusted downward to make up for the lower coupon rate (interest payment) on the old bonds.

Another factor affecting the cost of capital is a change in risk preferences by investors. As investors become more pessimistic about the economy, they require larger premiums for assuming risks. Even though the historical average market risk premium may be close to 6.5 percent, this is not stable, and investors' changing attitudes can have a big impact on the market risk premium. A more risk-averse attitude shows up in higher required stock returns and lower stock prices. For example, if investors raise their market risk premium to 8 percent, the rates of return from the original formulas increase as follows:

$$K_2 = 5.5\% + 2.0\,(8.0\%) = 5.5\% + 16.0\% = 21.5\%$$
$$K_1 = 5.5\% + 1.0\,(8.0\%) = 5.5\% + 8.0\% = 13.5\%$$
$$K_{.5} = 5.5\% + 0.5\,(8.0\%) = 5.5\% + 4.0\% = 9.5\%$$

The change in the market risk premium causes the required market return (beta = 1.00) to be 13.5 percent instead of the 12 percent, from Figure 11A–2. Any asset riskier than the market would have a larger increase in the required return. For example, a stock with a beta of 2.0 would need to generate a 21.5 percent return, instead of the 18.5 percent in the figure. The overall shape of the new security market line (SML_1) is shown in Figure 11A–4. Note the higher slope for SML_1, in comparison to SML_0.

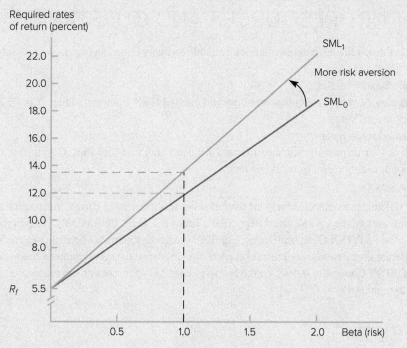

Figure 11A–4 The SML and changing investor expectations

In many instances, rising interest rates and pessimistic investors go hand in hand, so the SML may change its slope and intercept at the same time. This combined effect would cause both severe drops in the prices of risky assets and much larger required rates of return for such assets.

The capital asset pricing model and the SML have been presented to further your understanding of market-related events that affect the firm's cost of capital, such as market returns and risk, changing interest rates, and changing risk preferences.

Although the capital asset pricing model has received criticism because of the difficulties of dealing with the betas of individual securities and because of the problems involved in consistently constructing the appropriate slope of the SML to represent reality, it provides some interesting insights into risk-return measurement.

REVIEW OF FORMULAS

1.
$$K_j = \alpha + \beta_j R_m + e \qquad \text{(11A–1)}$$

2.
$$K_j = R_f + \beta_j(R_m - R_f) \qquad \text{(11A–2)}$$

DISCUSSION QUESTIONS

11A–1. How does the capital asset pricing model help explain changing costs of capital? (LO2)

11A–2. Why does K_e approximate K_j, or why does $D_1/(P_0 - g)$ approximate $R_f + \beta_j(R_m - R_f)$? (LO3)

11A–3. How does the SML react to changes in the rate of interest, changes in the rate of inflation, and changing investor expectations? (LO1, LO3)

11A–4. If an individual stock lay above the SML, what would be an appropriate investment strategy? Why? (LO2)

11A–5. Why would an efficient market be an important assumption for the development of the CAPM? (LO1)

11A–6. Why do you think the CAPM is or is not useful to the financial manager? (LO2)

INTERNET RESOURCES AND QUESTIONS

Betas and other useful share information are available on many Canadian companies at Reuters (search):

reuters.com/finance/markets

BigCharts provides historical quotes on stocks and the S&P/TSX Composite Index (CA:GSPTSE) going back several years:

bigcharts.marketwatch.com

The Bank of Canada provides some current and historical yields on securities. Government of Canada bonds can represent the risk-free rate:

bankofcanada.ca

11A–1. Calculate the expected yield for the following securities using current information and the framework of the CAPM: BlackBerry (BB), Teck (TECK.B), CNR (CNR), Nutrien (NTR), and the S&P/TSX Composite Index. The TSX (tmxmoney.com) has betas as well, although different than Reuters. For the market portfolio, determine the average annual return on the S&P/TSX Composite Index over the last five years. Do your results seem reasonable in today's market?

PROBLEMS

1. Assume $R_f = 4$ percent and $R_m = 8$ percent. Compute K_j for the following betas, using formula 11A–2.

    a. 0.7

    b. 1.4

    c. 1.7

2. For the preceding problem, assume an increase in interest rates changes R_f to 7.0 percent; also assume that the market premium $(R_m - R_f)$ changes to 6.5 percent.

    a. Compute K_j for the three betas of 0.7, 1.4, and 1.7.

3. The risk-free interest rate on one-year debt is 7 percent and the return on the market is expected to be 13 percent. A stock with a beta of 1.2 pays no dividends over the next year. If it is currently priced at $15.00, what will its price be at the end of the year?

4. Currently, Treasury bills yield 4.75 percent and the market prices risk at 6.90 percent. You have invested in a stock efficiently priced by the CAPM with a beta of 1.15 that will pay an expected dividend of $1.80 in one year. If the stock expects no capital appreciation in value over the next year, compute its current price.

5. You have invested in a stock with some systematic risk. It has a beta of 1.05. The current anticipated market portfolio return for the upcoming year is 16 percent, and the anticipated market risk premium is 7 percent. Calculate the expected yield on this stock based on the CAPM.

6. The risk-free rate is projected to be 2.5 percent for the upcoming year. Investor expectations concerning the market portfolio reveal expected excess returns of 6 percent during the same period. You have been holding Cranberry Dream's shares with a beta of 1.75.

    a. What would be Cranberry Dream's anticipated return based on the SML?

    b. If your analysis reveals an expected return of 11 percent, what investment strategy would you suggest? Justify and fully explain your position.

    And now for some WACC (weighted average cost of capital) calculations using the CAPM for the cost of equity.

7. Austen Sensibles Ltd. has the following capital structure, which it expects to maintain into the foreseeable future:

Debt	35%
Preferreds	10%
Common stock	35%
Retained earnings	20%

Current yields on similar risk bonds are 11 percent. Flotation costs would be negligible and can be ignored for calculation purposes.

New preferred shares are currently being considered and are expected to be offered at $100.00 with a dividend of 8 percent. Flotation costs would be 5 percent.

Austen has a beta of 0.9. Currently, Treasury bills are yielding 8.5 percent for one year, and the market portfolio (the S&P/TSX Composite Index) is expected to yield 16 percent over the next year.

Austen has a tax rate of 44 percent and expects internally generated funds to be sufficient to fund new investments.

a. Calculate the cost of capital of Austen Sensibles Ltd.

8. Huron Ltd. has the following capital structure:

16% Debentures, due in 14 years	$30,000,000
Preferreds (8% dividend, 40,000 shares)	3,000,000
Common shares: 3,600,000 outstanding	7,200,000
Retained earnings	5,600,000
Foreign currency translation	2,200,000
	$48,000,000

In today's capital markets, a company with risk characteristics similar to Huron's would be subject to the following yields:

- Bank prime rate is 7 percent.
- The average yield on 91 day T-bills is 5 percent.
- Debentures would require a yield of 9.5 percent. Flotation costs aftertax would be 4 percent.
- Preferreds would require a yield of 6.5 percent. Flotation costs aftertax would be 5 percent.
- The market portfolio is anticipated to yield 13 percent over the next year.
- Huron's historical beta is 1.25.

Huron's shares currently trade at $15.50. A new issue would net $15.00, including aftertax flotation costs. Internally generated funds will be sufficient to fund Huron's upcoming enterprises. Huron's tax rate is 40 percent.

a. Calculate Huron Ltd.'s cost of capital.

b. A major new investor in Huron is concerned with the possible rejection of viable business proposals based on the calculations just performed. The shareholder suggests that Huron can borrow at prime plus 1 percent and that should be good enough as a discount rate. Prepare a reply to the shareholder. (A "Yes, sir" or "No, ma'am" is not a correct answer.)

9. Orbit Corp. has the following balance sheet:

Cash	$ 500,000	Demand loans at prime + 1%	$ 3,000,000
A/R	2,500,000	Subordinated debentures	
Inventory	4,000,000	8% coupon, 12 years to maturity	12,000,000
Land	15,000,000	Preferred issue 6%	7,000,000
Equipment	20,000,000	Common stock: 5,000,000	
		shares outstanding	5,000,000
		Retained earnings	15,000,000
	$42,000,000		$42,000,000

Today's market is subject to different supply and demand factors and underlying economic events than when Orbit's capital structure was put in place. This has been translated into the following current yields, which are demanded by the marketplace for a company exhibiting the same risk characteristics as Orbit Corp.:

- The bank's prime rate is now 9.5 percent. The average yield on 91-day T-bills is now 8.5 percent.

- Subordinated debentures would now demand 12 percent; the underwriter would float them for 5 percent of par.

- Preferreds would now call for a stated yield of 11 percent. The underwriters would take 6 percent of issue price for their fee.

- Orbit's stock currently trades on the market at $25. Flotation costs would be 8 percent of the current market price.

This high-growth stock, 12 percent per year, pays no dividends but it has been determined to have a beta of 1.7. A well-diversified market portfolio of stocks would yield excess returns of 9 percent above the risk-free rate of interest in the foreseeable future.

Retained earnings will be insufficient to contribute the equity portion of funding of new investments. Orbit's tax rate is 23 percent.

a. Calculate Orbit's cost of capital.

b. Would you suggest that Orbit consider paying a small dividend?

c. Explain how Orbit might improve its capital structure. Justify your position.

APPENDIX 11B

Capital Structure Theory and Modigliani and Miller

The foundation supporting cost of capital theories was primarily developed by Professors Modigliani and Miller in the late 1950s and mid-1960s.[11] They actually went through an evolutionary process in which they proposed many different theories and conclusions about cost of capital.

Nobel Prize
nobelprize.org

However, before we discuss Modigliani and Miller, we briefly touch on the work of David Durand in the early 1950s, which was the first written attempt to describe the effect of financial leverage on cost of capital and valuation. Professor Durand described three different theories of cost of capital: the net income approach, the net operating income (NOI) approach, and the traditional approach.[12]

Net Income Approach

Under the net income (NI) approach, it is assumed that the firm can raise all the funds it desires at a constant cost of equity and debt. Since debt tends to have a lower cost than equity, the more debt utilized, the lower the overall cost of capital and the higher the evaluation of the firm, as indicated in Figure 11B–1.

Under this approach, the firm would be foolish not to use 100 percent debt to minimize cost of capital and maximize valuation. However, the assumption of constant cost of all forms of financing regardless of the level of utilization has been severely challenged by practitioners.

---

[11]Franco Modigliani and Merton H. Miller, "The Cost of Capital, Corporation Finance and the Theory of Investment," *American Economic Review,* June 1958, and "Taxes and the Cost of Capital: A Correction," *American Economic Review,* June 1963, pp. 433–43.

[12]See David Durand, "Costs of Debt and Equity Funds for Business: Trends and Problems of Measurement," *Conference on Research in Business Finance,* National Bureau of Economic Research, New York, 1952.

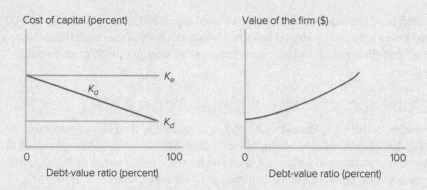

K_e = Cost of equity; K_d = Cost of debt; K_a = Cost of capital.

Value is the market value of the firm.

Figure 11B–1 Net income (NI) approach

Net Operating Income Approach

A second approach covered by Professor Durand was the net operating income (NOI) approach. Under this proposition, the low cost of debt is assumed to remain constant with greater debt utilization, but the cost of equity increases to such an extent that the cost of capital remains unchanged. Essentially, only operating income matters, and how you finance it makes no difference in terms of cost of capital or valuation. In Figure 11B–2 we see the effects of the NOI approach.

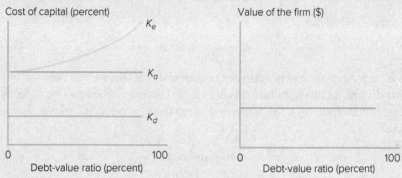

Figure 11B–2 Net operating income (NOI) approach

Finally, Professor Durand described the traditional approach to cost of capital, which lies somewhere between the net income approach and the net operating income approach. In the traditional approach, there are benefits from increased debt utilization, but only up to a point. After that point, the cost of capital begins to turn up and the valuation of the firm begins to turn down. A graphical representation of the traditional approach is seen in Figure 11B–3.

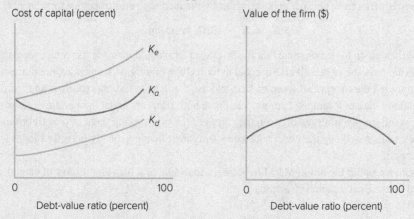

Figure 11B–3 Traditional approach as described by Durand

The student will perhaps realize that the traditional approach described by Durand in 1952 is similar to what is accepted today (as described in the main body of the chapter), but the many theories of Modigliani and Miller had a major impact as we went from 1952 to the currently existing theory.

Modigliani and Miller's Initial Approach

The approaches described by Durand were largely unsupported by theories and mathematical proofs. The major contribution by Modigliani and Miller (M&M) was to add economic and financial theories to naive assumptions. Although it is beyond the scope of this text to go through all the various mathematical proofs of M&M, their basic positions are presented.

Under the initial M&M approach, it is assumed that the value of the firm and its cost of capital are independent of the means of financing that occurs. This is similar to the NOI approach described by Durand, but the rationale or mechanism for arriving at this conclusion is different.

M&M stipulate that the value of the firm equals the following:

$$V = \frac{\text{EBIT}}{K_a} \quad \text{(11B–1)}$$

Where

$$V = \text{Value}$$
$$EBIT = \text{Earnings before interest and taxes}$$
$$K_a = \text{Cost of capital}$$

They further stipulate that

$$K_a = K_{eu} \quad \text{(11B–2)}$$

Where K_{eu} represents the cost of equity for an unlevered firm (one with no debt).

But what if a firm decides to include debt in its capital structure? Then the cost of equity for this leveraged firm increases by a risk premium to compensate for the additional risk associated with the debt.

$$K_{eL} = K_{eu} + \text{Risk premium}$$
$$K_{eL} = K_{eu} + (K_{eu} - I)(D/S) \quad \text{(11B–3)}$$

K_{eL} represents the cost of equity to the leveraged firm, I is the interest rate on the debt, D is the amount of debt financing, S is the amount of stock (equity) financing. The actual symbols aren't important for our purposes. The important point to observe in formula 11B–3 is that a risk premium is associated with the cost of equity financing (K_e) when leverage is involved.

M&M thus say a firm cannot reduce the cost of capital or increase the valuation of the firm, because any benefits from cheaper debt are offset by the increased cost of equity financing. That is,

$$K_{eL} = K_{eu} + \text{Risk premium}$$

M&M then go on to demonstrate that if a leveraged firm could increase its value over another firm not using leverage (when all else is equal in terms of operating performance), then investors would simply sell the overpriced leverage firm and use homemade leverage (borrow on their own) to buy the underpriced, unleveraged firm's stock. Since both firms are equal in operating performance, investors would simply arbitrage between the values of the two to bring them into equilibrium (sell the overpriced firm and buy the underpriced one using their own personally borrowed funds as part of the process).

In summary, under the initial M&M hypothesis, the value of a firm and its cost of capital are unaffected by the firm's capital structure.

Modigliani and Miller with the Introduction of Corporate Taxes

As is true of many economic models, M&M made a number of assumptions in their initial theory of cost of capital that tended to simplify the analysis. The most critical simplifying assumption was to ignore the impact of corporate taxes on the cost of capital to the firm. (Durand made similar simplifying assumptions.) Once M&M began to consider the effect of taxes, their whole outlook changed. Because interest on debt is a tax-deductible expense, the tax effect greatly reduces the cost of debt and the associated cost of capital. Furthermore, with a reduced cost of capital, there is an increased valuation for the firm.

A key adjustment to a basic valuation formula is that

$$V_L = V_U + TD \quad \text{(11B-4)}$$

Formula 11B–4 says the value of a leveraged firm (V_L) is equal to the value of an unleveraged firm (V_U), plus an amount equal to the corporate tax rate (T) times the amount of debt (D) the firm has. If an unleveraged firm has a value of $1,000,000 ($V_U$), then a leveraged firm with $400,000 in debt and a tax rate of 34 percent will have a value of $1,136,000.

$$
\begin{aligned}
V_L &= V_U + TD \\
&= \$1,000,000 + 0.34\,(\$400,000) \\
&= \$1,000,000 + \$136,000 \\
&= \$1,136,000
\end{aligned}
$$

A firm with $600,000 in debt has a value of $1,204,000, and so on.

$$
\begin{aligned}
V_L &= V_U + TD \\
&= \$1,000,000 + 0.34\,(\$600,000) \\
&= \$1,000,000 + \$204,000 \\
&= \$1,204,000
\end{aligned}
$$

Graphically, we are led to the positions presented in Figure 11B–4.

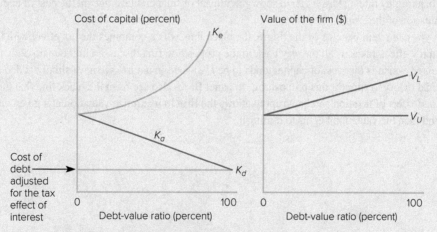

Figure 11B–4 Modigliani and Miller with corporate taxes

As can be seen in the figure, once corporate taxes are introduced, it is assumed that every increment of debt reduces the cost of capital, eventually down to the cost of debt itself. Furthermore, the more debt a firm has, the higher its valuation.[13]

---

[13]The only constraint to this proposition is that the amount of debt cannot exceed the amount of assets.

Under the second version of M&M, every firm should be 100 percent (perhaps 99.9%) financed by debt to lower its cost of capital and increase its valuation. With corporate taxes our cost of equity capital becomes

$$K_{eL} = K_{eu} + (K_{eu} - 1)(D/S)(1 - T) \quad \text{(11B–5)}$$

Modigliani and Miller with Bankruptcy Considerations

Since no firm or investor in the real world operates on the basis of the just-described M&M hypothesis, there must be some missing variables. One of the disadvantages of heavy borrowing is that the firm may eventually go bankrupt (a topic discussed in Appendix 16A). A firm that does not borrow has **no** such threat. Other things being equal, the threat of bankruptcy increases as the amount of borrowing increases.

When bankruptcy occurs, the firm may be forced to sell assets at a fraction of their value. Furthermore, there are likely to be substantial legal fees, court costs, and administrative expenses. Even if a firm does not go bankrupt but is on the verge of bankruptcy, customers may hesitate to do business with the firm. Suppliers may demand advanced payments, and so on.

Also, as a firm increases the amount of debt it has, there are likely to be restrictive covenants or provisions in debt agreements that hinder the normal operations of the firm (the current ratio must be at a given level or no new projects can be undertaken without lender approval).

All of these bankruptcy-related considerations have an implicit cost. If the potential cost of bankruptcy were $10 million, then the probability of that bankruptcy must also be considered. Of course, if the firm has no debt, then the probability of bankruptcy is zero and the obvious cost is zero. If the firm has 50 percent debt, there may be a 10 percent probability of bankruptcy and the expected cost is $1 million ($10,000,000 × 10%). Finally, with 90 percent debt, there may be a 25 percent probability of bankruptcy and the expected cost is $2.5 million ($10,000,000 × 25%). Once these expected costs of bankruptcy are present valued, they must be deducted from the current, unadjusted value of the firm to determine true value. Similarly, the expected value of the threat of future bankruptcy also tends to increase the cost of capital to the firm as progressively more debt is utilized.

In Figure 11B–5, we combine the effect of the corporate tax advantage (M&M II) with the effect of the bankruptcy threat (M&M III) to show the impact of financial leverage on the cost of capital and valuation of the firm.

As you can see in panel A of the figure, the black line, which combines the tax effect with the bankruptcy effect, takes us all the way back to the proposition first discussed in the main body of the chapter, which is that cost of capital tends to be U-shaped in nature. We have simply added some additional theory to support this proposition. In panel B, we also see from the black line that the combined effect of taxation and bankruptcy allows the firm to maximize valuation at a given debt level and then the valuation begins to diminish.

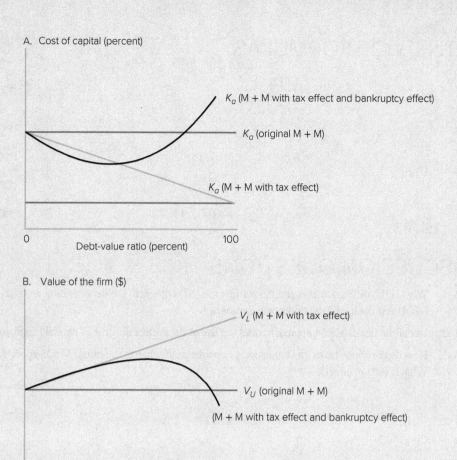

A. Cost of capital (percent)

K_a (M + M with tax effect and bankruptcy effect)

K_a (original M + M)

K_a (M + M with tax effect)

0

Debt-value ratio (percent)

100

B. Value of the firm ($)

V_L (M + M with tax effect)

V_U (original M + M)

(M + M with tax effect and bankruptcy effect)

0

Debt-value ratio (percent)

100

Figure 11B–5 Combined impact of the corporate tax effect and bankruptcy effect on valuation and cost of capital

The Miller Model

As if to temporarily confuse an already settled issue, Professor Miller announced at the annual meeting of the American Finance Association in 1976 that he was rejecting his own latest version of the M&M hypothesis (M&M III, as indicated by the black lines in Figure 11B–5).[14] His new premise was that he had considered corporate taxes but not personal taxes in the earlier M&M models. He suggested that, when one began considering personal taxes in the process, share ownership had substantial advantages over debt ownership. Why? Because, at the time, gains from share ownership were potentially taxed at a much lower rate than interest income, due to the capital gains component that was part of the anticipated return to shareholders. Long-term capital gains have traditionally been taxed at a rate lower than other income. Miller said that once you factored all tax considerations (corporate and personal) into the analysis, there was not an overall advantage to debt utilization to the firm, and therefore, the cost of capital was unaffected by the capital structure of the firm.

Subsequent research has partially taken issue with Professor Miller. We can somewhat safely return to the U-shaped approach generally described in the chapter and in this appendix.

---

[14]Merton H. Miller, "Debt and Taxes," *Journal of Finance,* May 1977, pp. 261–75.

REVIEW OF FORMULAS

1. $$V = \frac{\text{EBIT}}{K_a}$$ (11B–1)

2. $$K_a = K_{eu}$$ (11B–2)

3. $$K_{eL} = K_{eu} + (K_{eu} - I)(D/S)$$ (11B–3)

4. $$V_L = V_U + TD$$ (11B–4)

5. $$K_{eL} = K_{eu} + (K_{eu} - 1)(D/S)(1 - T)$$ (11B–5)

DISCUSSION QUESTIONS

11B–1. What is the difference between the net income (NI) approach, the net operating income (NOI) approach, and the traditional approach?

11B–2. Under the initial M&M approach, does the use of debt affect the cost of capital? Explain.

11B–3. How do corporate taxes and bankruptcy considerations change the initial M&M approach? What is the net effect?

12

The Capital Budgeting Decision

LEARNING OBJECTIVES

LO1   Define capital budgeting decisions as long-run investment decisions.

LO2   Explain that cash flows rather than accounting earnings are evaluated in the capital budgeting decision.

LO3   Evaluate investments by the average accounting return, the payback period, the net present value, the internal rate of return, and the profitability index.

LO4   Appraise the use of the cost of capital as the discount rate in capital budgeting analysis.

LO5   Integrate the cash flows that result from an investment decision, including the aftertax operating benefits and the tax shield benefits of capital cost allowance (amortization).

LO6   Perform net present value analysis to assist in the decision-making process concerning long-run investments.

LO1 One of the most significant decisions that the management of a firm will ever have to make concerns capital investment. Capital budgeting decisions are important as they usually involve the long-term commitment of a firm's resources and because a large amount of capital is usually involved; management is setting the firm into a strategic direction that is difficult to change. A decision to build a new plant, develop a new technology, purchase another company, or expand into a foreign market may influence the performance of the firm over the next decade or more. A bad decision can lead to great financial stress and even bankruptcy for a firm.

The capital budgeting decision involves the planning of expenditures for a project with a life of at least one year and usually considerably longer. In general, the capital expenditure decision requires extensive planning to ensure that engineering and marketing information is available, product design is completed, necessary patents are acquired, production costs are fully understood, and the capital markets are tapped for the necessary funds. Throughout this chapter, we use the techniques developed in our discussion of the time value of money to equate future cash flows to present ones. The firm's cost of capital is used as the basic discount rate.

One problem that a manager faces is that as the time horizon moves further into the future, uncertainty becomes a greater hazard. The manager is uncertain about annual costs and inflows, product life, interest rates, economic conditions, and technological change.

The personal computer industry experiences rapid change and risk mixed with significant capital investment. In 1976, the Apple 1 was introduced with 8K of RAM. As others entered the personal computing market, it has rapidly transformed communication and informational technologies. Today a flash drive can have 2 TB (terabyte) of memory. Many technology companies have risen on great dreams and then failed when their promised cash flows did not materialize. Similarly, the development of the oil sands in northern Alberta has involved the commitment of billions of dollars to projects subject to the volatile uncertainty in the price of oil and environmental concerns.

Capital budgeting analyzes long-run investment decisions (new projects, replacements, diversification into new areas) while considering the impact of uncertainty. Canadian tax law and development will impact capital budgeting decisions significantly and must be considered.

ADMINISTRATIVE CONSIDERATIONS

A good capital budgeting program requires that a number of steps be taken in the decision-making process.

1. Search and discovery of investment opportunities
2. Collection of data
3. Evaluation of alternatives and decision making
4. Plan implementation
5. Ongoing reevaluation and adjustment

The search for new opportunities is the least emphasized, though perhaps the most important, of the five steps. Although it is outside the scope of this book to suggest procedures for developing an organization that is conducive to innovation and creative thinking, the marginal return of such an organization is likely to be high (and a high marginal return is the essence of capital budgeting).

The collection of data should go beyond engineering data and market surveys. It must attempt to identify possible important events and capture the relative likelihood of their occurrence. The probabilities of increases or slumps in product demand may be evaluated from statistical analysis, but other outcomes may have to be estimated subjectively. The likely competitive reaction of other industry participants to any new investment by a firm is an important element to be considered in this analysis. The collection of data, however, is not a perfect process. Eventually a decision must be made based on the best available data. Although more information collection is possible, the cost becomes too high when compared to the marginal benefit.

After all data have been collected and evaluated, the final decision must be made. Generally, determinations involving relatively small amounts are made at the department or division level, whereas major expenditures can be approved only by top management. Once a plan is developed and implemented, constant monitoring of the results of a given decision may indicate that a whole new set of probabilities must be developed based on actual experience. This may cause an initial decision to then be reevaluated and perhaps reversed. This process is outlined in Figure 12–1.

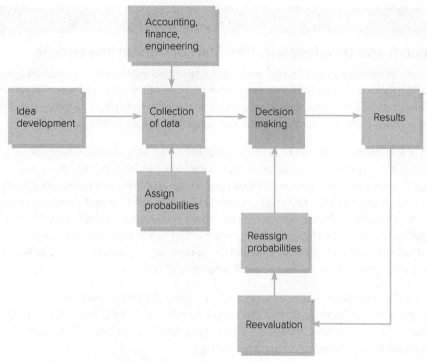

Figure 12–1 Capital budgeting procedures

THE NOTION OF RESULTANT CASH FLOWS

Capital budgeting is about investment decisions and the value that those investment decisions can create for the firm. In most cases the investment decisions will produce benefits and costs to the firm over several time periods. Those benefits and costs for the most part can be identified as cash flows. Furthermore, the investments will likely entail the commitment of a substantial amount of capital.

From an analytical standpoint, the task in capital budgeting is to identify the amount and timing of all the resultant cash flows stemming from a possible investment decision. By the term *resultant cash flows* we mean those incremental cash flows (inflows) and decremental cash flows (outflows) that occur only if we decide to make a given capital investment. Those cash flows that would continue to be generated by the firm regardless of the investment decision are irrelevant for the investment analysis. Furthermore, expenses that have already been incurred, sunk costs, are irrelevant to the decision process as the capital budgeting process looks forward, not back.

Once the resultant cash flows have been identified, it is necessary to value them. The use of the discounting techniques explored in Chapter 9 is the best method to equate the resultant cash flows to present values for comparison with the cost of the investment. The choice of an appropriate discount rate based on the risk of the project will be an important consideration.

Let us suppose we are considering the replacement of an older machine with a new one. The cost of the new machine would be a decremental cash flow, but any money we received on the sale of the old machine would be an incremental cash flow. Alternatively, we could consider the net cash flow of the investment, which would be the cost of the new machine minus the resale value of the old one. If the same operator, at the same wage, were required to operate either machine, the machine operator's wages would not be a resultant cash flow and, therefore, would be ignored in the analysis. If, on the other hand, the new machine required a more skilled operator at a higher wage, the difference in operators' wages would be the resultant cash flow.

The relevant, or resultant, cash flows should be included in the analysis at market value and should include any opportunity costs or benefits that may not be explicitly stated. This may take the form of an alternative decision embedded in the major decision under analysis. For example, we might consider the value of building on a property we own. There will be no cash flow resulting from using the property, but there is the opportunity cost of not selling the property at today's value. That cost should form part of an analysis.

 FINANCE IN ACTION

Relevance?

Rupert is considering an extension to his house to accommodate his growing home business. There will be new equipment, additional furniture, and a larger inventory. He has an existing mortgage and the bank would be willing to advance the required funds for the extension. The bank also would be willing to provide an operating loan for working capital requirements based on his accounts receivable position. Alternatively, Rupert could rent space in a nearby office complex instead of the extension. What are the relevant considerations for this investment?

As is sometimes the case, there are really two investment choices:

- Home extension versus rental of office space
- Business expansion

Q1 Are there any other considerations that have been missed?

Current Cash Flows	Future Cash Flows
Cash flows are identified as inflows (+) or outflows (−)	
Home: Capital cost of extension −	Increased value of home (less capital gains tax) + (only related to extension)
Rent space:	Repairs and maintenance −
	Increased heat, power, cleaning −
	Rent (other costs as not covered) −
Irrelevant: Financing costs (included in initial cost)	
Business-related revenues, expenses, investments (would occur anyway)	
Business: Increased inventory investment −	Increased revenues +
Furniture investment −	Increased expenses −
Rent or build option (above) −	Recovery of inventory investment +
	Salvage value of furniture +
Irrelevant: Preexisting costs and revenues (or those that would occur anyway)	

Identification of the resultant cash flows attached to a particular capital budgeting decision is a critical task and requires careful thought and judgment on the part of the capital budgeting analyst. It may be helpful to conceptualize the appropriate resultant cash flows by developing a time line. Much of the rest of this chapter is devoted to considering methods of identifying the timing and amounts of all resultant cash flows.

LO2 ACCOUNTING FLOWS VERSUS CASH FLOWS

In capital budgeting decisions, the emphasis is on cash flow rather than reported income. Accounting assigns the costs of an asset to those periods during which the asset provides economic benefit to the firm. However, to analyze a capital investment proposal, we often have to be able to translate accounting profit figures into actual cash flows, in order that we can apply time-value-of-money techniques to the timing of those cash flows. The presence of many working capital accounts attests to the difference between accounting flows and cash flows.

One of the most important differences between accounting profits and the timing of cash flows relates to amortization.[1] Amortization does not represent an actual expenditure of current funds and it is added back to profit to determine the amount of cash flow generated in the current period. We should distinguish between

- Amortization expensed in the financial statements (noncash flow)
- Capital cost allowance (CCA) allowed for tax purposes (cash flow consequence)

CCA will affect cash flows by reducing taxable income, thus creating tax savings, which have a value to a project and the firm. This effect (identified in Chapter 2) will be explored later in this chapter.

Table 12–1 illustrates the effect of adding back amortization to the accounting profit to arrive at the actual cash flow. Alston Corporation has $50,000 of new equipment amortized on a straight-line basis over 10 years ($5,000 per year). The firm has $20,000 in earnings before amortization and taxes and is in a 25 percent tax bracket. The firm shows $11,250 in earnings after taxes to which the noncash deduction of $5,000 in amortization is added to determine cash flow of $16,250.

Table 12–1 Cash flow for Alston Corporation

Earnings before amortization and taxes (EBAT) (cash flow)	$20,000
Amortization (noncash expense)	5,000
Earnings before taxes	15,000
Taxes (cash outflow) 25%	3,750
Earnings after taxes	11,250
Amortization	+5,000
Cash flow	$16,250
Alternative method of cash flow calculation	
Cash inflow (EBAT)	$20,000
Cash outflow (taxes)	−3,750
Cash flow	$16,250

An even more dramatic illustration of the difference between accounting and cash flow is provided by the situation shown in Table 12–2. That table demonstrates what would happen if the amortization expense for Alston had been $20,000 rather than $5,000. Net earnings before and after taxes would have been zero, but the company ends the year with $20,000 more in the bank than it had at the beginning.

Table 12–2 Revised cash flow for Alston Corporation

EBAT	$20,000
Amortization	20,000
Earnings before taxes	0
Taxes	0
Earnings after taxes	0
Amortization	+20,000
Cash flow	$20,000

---

[1] Chapter 2 explores amortization in further detail. It notes that amortization is not a new source of funds (except as tax savings), but represents a noncash expense. Furthermore, it is noted that *amortization* is a generic term to represent the loss of utility in capital assets. Past practice suggested the use of the term *depreciation* for tangible assets, amortization for intangible assets, and depletion for natural resource assets. The use of these terms by corporations is still common.

To the capital budgeting specialist, the concentration on cash flow rather than accounting figures seems obvious. It is sometimes harder for practising managers to consider cash flows and ignore the effects reported in the historical cost accounting statements. Publicly traded firms are constantly scrutinized by security analysts and market participants to anticipate the next quarterly earnings. Share prices may drop dramatically if earnings are lower than they projected, even if by a small amount.

Consider these two investment proposals, with next year's anticipated results:

- A, with zero aftertax earnings and $100,000 in cash flow
- B, with no amortization, having $50,000 in both aftertax earnings and cash flow

Although a capital budgeting analysis indicates that proposal A is a superior investment, there may be more consideration given to reported aftertax earnings than to cash flow, and proposal B may be selected. This type of understandable sensitivity to earnings among managers leads to periodic criticism of the short-term focus of decisions rather than the longer-term economic benefits. However, after the tax person cometh, it is the coin in our pockets, not the accountant's income, that matters.

Be sensitive, therefore, to the concessions to short-term pressures that are sometimes made by top executives. Some observers have held that modern financial decision-making tools reinforce this tendency. Nevertheless, in the material that follows, the emphasis is on the use of proper evaluation techniques aimed at identifying the best economic choice and, therefore, at providing long-term wealth maximization.

 FINANCE IN ACTION

Cash Flow Mobility

An overriding objective of investors is to buy into firms with commercial potential. In the wireless age, products and services might not provide an adequate return in themselves, but their use may increase cash flows to mobility networks that can justify the investments. Furthermore, in the fast-paced high-technology business, investments are important to keep firms "in the game."

AirIQ, which is listed on the TSX, provides GPS services used by vehicle and trucking fleets to locate their vehicles across North America, determine their speeds, unlock their doors, and perform many other functions from a central location. AirIQ began in 1997 with an idea. It received some initial funding from the National Research Council, then from a subsidiary of Bell Canada Enterprises (BCE), and also from the public through listing on the TSX. Its history as a startup operation is highlighted on its website.

Q1 How has AirIQ continued in business when it has a significant accumulated deficit? Has it broadened its business?

airiq.com
Symbol: IQ

LO3 METHODS OF EVALUATING INVESTMENT PROPOSALS

Five methods for evaluating capital expenditures are considered, along with the shortcomings and advantages of each.

1. Average accounting return (AAR)
2. Payback period (PP)
3. Net present value (NPV)
4. Internal rate of return (IRR)
5. Profitability index (PI)

The average accounting return (AAR) and payback period methods are widely used even though each method has some serious theoretical shortcomings. The net present value (NPV) and internal rate of return (IRR) methods are more comprehensive, and one or the other should be applied to most situations. The profitability index (PI) can be used in ranking from the most to least desirable project and is really a variation of the NPV method.

Ryan and Ryan revealed in their 2002 paper that the NPV method had become the preferred financial analysis method among the Fortune 1000 companies, although the other techniques were identified as well. The paper also provides a good summary of other studies of usage over the years.[2]

Average Accounting Return

The average accounting return (AAR) is a simple evaluation technique for investment projects, given by the following formula:

$$\frac{\textbf{Average earnings after tax}}{\textbf{Average book value}}$$

Let us suppose that an investment project has the following projected earnings and amortized cost for the capital asset over the next four years. The asset can be purchased for $30,000 and is expected to last four years, at which time it would have no value. Therefore, it is amortized on a straight-line basis over that period.

	Earnings After Tax	Amortized Capital Asset
Capital cost		$30,000
Year 1	$2,000	22,500
Year 2	4,000	15,000
Year 3	8,000	7,500
Year 4	2,000	0
Average*	16,000/4 = $4,000	75,000/5 = 15,000
Average accounting return	$4,000/15,000 = 26.7%	

*$16,000 = $2,000 + $4,000 + $8,000 + $2,000
$75,000 = $30,000 + $22,500 + $15,000 + $7,500
Average amortization also by ($30,000 − $0)/2 = $15,000

The average accounting return is fairly easy to calculate and makes use of information readily prepared by the accounting conventions. In this example, the average earnings after tax for the four years is $4,000, and this is divided by the average investment of $15,000. This gives an AAR of 26.7 percent.

Firms frequently calculate the AAR, but it has serious flaws. We have noted earlier that asset value comes from the amount and timing of cash flows. The AAR method for evaluating investments is flawed because

- Accounting earnings, not cash flows, are used.
- All earnings are given equal treatment. (The $2,000 in the first and fourth years receive the same value. This is not correct based on the time value of money.)
- Book values establish the value of the investment, not market values.
- No objective evaluation yardstick is suggested, such as the cost of capital used by the NPV and IRR methods.

Establishing Cash Flows

To examine the next four approaches to capital budgeting analysis, consider a situation in which the cash flow patterns of two investments are estimated. We are called on to select between Investment A and Investment B, both requiring an initial capital investment of $10,000 (an outflow). The resultant, and in this case incremental, aftertax cash flows for these investments are shown in Table 12–3.

---

[2]Ryan, P.A. and Ryan, G.P., "Capital Budgeting Practices of the Fortune 1000: How Have Things Changed?" *Journal of Business and Management*, Volume 8, Number 4, Winter 2002.

Table 12-3 Investment alternatives

| | Net Cash Inflows (of a $10,000 investment) | |
Year	Investment A	Investment B
1	$5,000	$1,500
2	5,000	2,000
3	2,000	2,500
4		5,000
5		5,000

Payback calculations:

A: $5,000 + $5,000 = $10,000 (2 years)

B: $1,500 + $2,000 + $2,500 + 0.8 ($5,000) = $10,000 (3.8 years)

To arrive at the aftertax cash flows of Table 12–3, we must begin with revenues and include consideration of tax-allowable amortization (capital cost allowance) and taxes. In our example, both investments qualify for a 20 percent CCA rate. CCA is discussed in detail later in the chapter, where the calculation of the tax-allowable amortization for this machine is calculated (in Table 12–9). The relevant tax rate is 40 percent. Note that the net cash flow increment is calculated by subtracting any additional taxes incurred from the increased revenue. Column 5 is the resultant cash flow that is produced for each investment in Table 12–3.

| | Net Operating Cash Flows (on a $10,000 net capital outlay) Investment A | | | | |
| | (1) | (2) | (3) | (4) | (5) |
Year	Increased Revenue	Increased CCA	Increased Taxable Income	Increased Taxes (@ 40%)	Increased Cash Flow (1) – (4)
1	$7,667	$1,000	$6,667	$2,667	$5,000
2	7,133	1,800	5,333	2,133	5,000
3	2,373	1,440	933	373	2,000

| | Net Operating Cash Flows (on a $10,000 net capital outlay) Investment B | | | | |
| | (1) | (2) | (3) | (4) | (5) |
Year	Increased Revenue	Increased CCA	Increased Taxable Income	Increased Taxes (@ 40%)	Increased Cash Flow (1) – (4)
1	$1,833	$1,000	$ 833	$ 333	$1,500
2	2,133	1,800	333	133	2,000
3	3,207	1,440	1,767	707	2,500
4	7,565	1,152	6,413	2,565	5,000
5	7,719	922	6,797	2,719	5,000

Payback Period

The payback period (PP) method simply computes the time required to recoup the initial investment. We can examine Table 12–3.

For Investment A, the $10,000 is recovered in two years—the payback period. Investment B takes somewhat longer and the $10,000 is recovered during the fourth year. Only $4,000 of the fourth year's $5,000 is required for full recovery, which we suggest occurs 0.8 (4,000/5,000) of the way through the year—a payback of 3.8 years.

In using the payback period to select Investment A, two important considerations are ignored. First, there is no consideration of the amount of cash flow generated after the initial investment is recaptured. The $2,000 in Year 3 for Investment A is ignored, as is the $5,000 in Year 5 for Investment B.

Even if the $5,000 inflow in Year 5 were $50,000, it would have no effect on the decision. Therefore, the payback period places a premium on liquidity and tends to emphasize the shorter time horizon. Second, the method fails to consider the time value of money.

If we had two possible $10,000 investments with the following inflow patterns, the payback period would rank them equally.

Year	Early Returns	Late Returns
1	$9,000	$1,000
2	1,000	9,000
3	1,000	1,000

Although both investments have a payback period of two years, the first alternative is clearly superior, because the $9,000 comes in the first year rather than the second. We could overcome this drawback by developing a discounted payback method.

The payback period has some features that help to explain its use by corporate management:

- Easy to understand
- Heavy emphasis on liquidity (recoup initial investment quickly, in 3 to 5 years, or it will not qualify)
- Provides an initial view of an investment's risk

A rapid payback may be particularly important to firms in industries characterized by rapid technological developments or other sources of uncertainty. This is particularly relevant in a small business. Given that some decisions may be justifiable only on the basis of cash flow estimates far in the future (and therefore relatively more uncertain), managers often opt for the decisions with the more predictable cash flow estimates.

The payback period method fails to definitively discern the optimum, or best, economic solution to a capital budgeting problem:

- It ignores cash flows beyond the payback period (concentrating only on the initial years).
- It does not employ time-value-of-money concepts (although a discounted payback can be determined).

The payback period method may fail to accept projects that can add substantial value to the firm. This is unlike the more comprehensive and more theoretically correct capital budgeting methods that will value all possible cash flows.

Net Present Value

The net present value (NPV) of an investment discounts all the cash inflows over the life of the investment to determine whether they equal or exceed the required investment. If the present value of the inflows less the initial capital outflow is positive, value is added to the firm. The basic discount rate is usually the cost of capital to the firm.

If we once again evaluate investments A and B from Table 12–3, using an assumed cost of capital or a discount rate of 10 percent, we arrive at the following figures for net present value:

Investment A

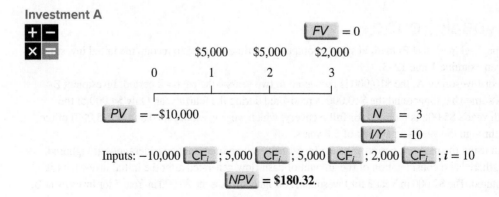

Investment B

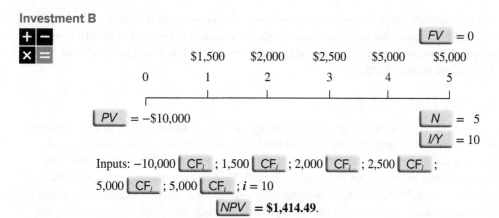

Inputs: $-10{,}000 \; \boxed{CF_i} \; ; \; 1{,}500 \; \boxed{CF_i} \; ; \; 2{,}000 \; \boxed{CF_i} \; ; \; 2{,}500 \; \boxed{CF_i} \; ;$

$5{,}000 \; \boxed{CF_i} \; ; \; 5{,}000 \; \boxed{CF_i} \; ; \; i = 10$

$\boxed{NPV} = \$1{,}414.49.$

Spreadsheet function = NPV (cell for discount rate, cell for cash flow in 1st time period: cell for cash flow in final time period) + cell for initial time zero cash flow

i.e., = NPV (B1, D4:H4) + C4

Do not include time zero cash flows within formula.

Spreadsheet Screen Shot

	A	B	C	D	E	F	G	H
1	Discount rate	10.00%						
2	Year		0	1	2	3	4	5
3								
4			-10,000	1,500	2,000	2,500	5,000	5,000
5								
6	NPV	1,414.49						
7		`= NPV(B1,D4:H4)+C4`						
8		`= NPV(rate, value1, value2, …) + time zero value`						

		$10,000 Investment, 10 Percent Discount Rate					
Year	**Investment A**			**Year**	**Investment B**		
1	$5,000	PV =	$ 4,545	1	$1,500	PV =	$ 1,364
2	5,000	PV =	4,132	2	2,000	PV =	1,653
3	2,000	PV =	1,503	3	2,500	PV =	1,878
			$10,180	4	5,000	PV =	3,415
				5	5,000	PV =	3,105
							$11,415

Present value of inflows.........	$10,180	Present value of inflows.........	$11,415
Present value of outflows........	10,000	Present value of outflows........	10,000
Net present value	$ 180	Net present value	$ 1,415

Even though both proposals have a positive NPV and, thus, are acceptable, Investment B has a considerably higher net present value than Investment A. Investment B will add the most value to the firm today. This is a different conclusion than suggested by the payback period. NPV is a superior method because it

- Includes all cash flows
- Utilizes time-value-of-money concepts
- Utilizes an objective evaluation tool (the cost of capital)
- Can employ more than one discount rate (unlike the IRR method)

The IRR method, which also incorporates the time value of money in its analysis, is a special case of the NPV method. For theoretical reasons, the NPV method is preferred to the IRR method. Additionally, more complex problems can be handled with the NPV method more easily than with the IRR, without technical problems.

Internal Rate of Return

The internal rate of return (IRR) calls for determining the yield on an investment; that is, calculating the discount rate that equates the cash outflows (cost) of an investment with the subsequent cash inflows. It is that discount rate that produces an NPV of zero. We believe the NPV method is the superior evaluation technique, but some still prefer IRR. This may be because yield sometimes appears more comprehensible than the absolute value derived from the NPV analysis. We are more used to seeing rates of return, interest rates, and yields in our daily lives, and these seem to equate with the IRR. The IRR calculation requires a trial-and-error or interpolation procedure to determine a discount rate. This is true for a calculator or a computer, although they can perform the procedure fairly quickly.

The simplest case would be an investment of $100 that provides $120 after one year, or a 20 percent internal rate of return. For more complicated situations we must use the techniques developed in Chapter 9. For example, a $1,000 investment returning an annuity of $244 per year for five years provides an internal rate of return of 7.02 percent.

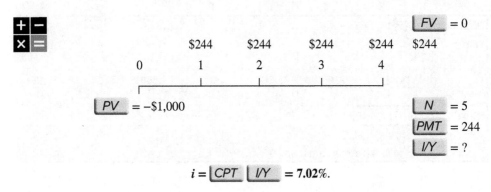

$i = \boxed{CPT} \boxed{I/Y} = 7.02\%.$

Tables (optional)

1. First divide the investment (present value) by the annuity.

$$\frac{\text{Investment}}{\text{Annuity}} = \frac{\$1,000}{\$244} = 4.1(PV_{IFA})$$

2. Then proceed to Appendix D (present value of an annuity). The factor of 4.1 for five years indicates a yield of 7 percent.

If an uneven cash inflow is involved, the process becomes somewhat more complicated, particularly when using tables.

Let us again evaluate the two investment alternatives in Table 12–3, only this time using the internal rate of return to rank the two projects. Neither proposal represents a precise annuity stream. We begin with Investment A, which qualifies for a 20 percent CCA rate for income tax–allowable amortization. Tax-allowable amortization for this machine is discussed later in the chapter and is calculated in Table 12–9. The relevant tax rate is 40 percent. Net cash flow increment is calculated by subtracting any additional taxes incurred from the increased revenue. Column 5 is the cash flow produced earlier for Investment A in Table 12–3. We set out to determine the discount rate equating the future increased cash flows with the initial investment.

Year	(1) Increased Revenue	(2) Increased CCA	(3) Increased Taxable Income	(4) Increased Taxes (@ 40%)	(5) Increased Cash Flow (1) – (4)
1	$7,667	$1,000	$6,667	$2,667	$5,000
2	7,133	1,800	5,333	2,133	5,000
3	2,373	1,440	933	373	2,000

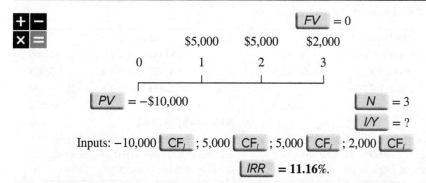

Inputs: $-10,000$ CF$_I$; 5,000 CF$_I$; 5,000 CF$_I$; 2,000 CF$_I$

IRR = **11.16%**.

Spreadsheet function = IRR (cell for cash flow at time zero; cell for cash flow in final time period; cell for discount rate as guess) i.e., = IRR (C3:F3)

Spreadsheet Screen Shot

	A	B	C	D	E	F
1	Year		0	1	2	3
2						
3			-10,000	5,000	5,000	2,000
4						
5	IRR	11.16%				
6		" = IRR(C3:F3)				
7		" = IRR(**values, [guess]**)				

Tables (optional)

1. To find a beginning value to start our first trial, average the inflows as if we were really getting an annuity.

$$
\begin{aligned}
\$\ 5,000 \\
5,000 \\
\underline{2,000} \\
\$12,000 \div 3 = \$4,000
\end{aligned}
$$

2. Then, divide the investment by the "assumed" annuity value in step 1.

$$\frac{\text{Investment}}{\text{Annuity}} = \frac{\$10,000}{\$4,000} = 2.5 \ (\text{PV}_{IFA})$$

3. Proceed to Appendix D to arrive at a *first approximation* of the internal rate of return, using

$$(\text{PV}_{IFA}) \text{ factor} = 2.5$$
$$n \text{ (period)} = 3$$

The factor lies between 9 and 10 percent. This is only a first approximation—our actual answer will be closer to 10 percent or higher, because our method of average cash flows theoretically moved receipts from the first two years into the last year. This averaging understates the actual internal rate of return. The same method would overstate the IRR for Investment B because it would move cash from the last two years into the first three years. Since we know that cash flows in the early years are worth more and increase our return, we can usually gauge whether our first approximation is overstated or understated.

4. Next, enter into a trial-and-error process to arrive at an answer. Because these cash flows are uneven, unlike an annuity, we need to use Appendix B. We begin with 10 percent and then try 12 percent.

Year	10 Percent		Year	12 Percent	
1	$5,000 × 0.909 =	$ 4,545	1	$5,000 × 0.893 =	$4,465
2	5,000 × 0.826 =	4,130	2	5,000 × 0.797 =	3,985
3	2,000 × 0.751 =	1,502	3	2,000 × 0.712 =	1,424
		$10,177			$9,874

NPV = $177 (high)

At 10 percent, the present value of the inflows exceeds $10,000—thus, we use a higher discount rate.

NPV = −$126 (low)

At 12 percent, the present value of the inflows is less than $10,000—therefore, the discount rate is too high.

The answer must lie between 10 percent and 12 percent, indicating an approximate answer of 11 percent.

If we want to be more accurate, the results can be *interpolated*. Because the internal rate of return is determined when the present value of the inflows (PV_I) equals the present value of the outflows (PV_O), we need to find a discount rate that equates the PV_I to the cost of $10,000 ($PV_O$), where NPV = 0. The total difference in present values between 10 percent and 12 percent is $303.

$10,177	PV_I @ 10%	$10,177	PV_I @ 10%
9,874	PV_I @ 12%	10,000	(cost)
$ 303		$ 177	

The solution at 10 percent is $177 away from $10,000. Actually, the solution is ($177/$303) percent of the way between 10 and 12 percent. Because there is a 2 percent difference between the two rates used to evaluate the cash inflows, we need to multiply the fraction by 2 percent and then add our answer to 10 percent for the final answer of

$$10\% + (\$177/\$303)(2\%) = 11.17\% \text{ IRR}$$

Note that this answer is not as accurate as the calculator, due to rounding. The calculator is more accurate.

For Investment B the same process yields an answer of 14.33 percent (you may wish to confirm this by calculating the 14.33%).

Year	(1) Increased Revenue	(2) Increased CCA	(3) Increased Taxable Income	(4) Increased Taxes (@ 40%)	(5) Increased Cash Flow (1) − (4)
1	$1,833	$1,000	$ 833	$ 333	$1,500
2	2,133	1,800	333	133	2,000
3	3,207	1,440	1,767	707	2,500
4	7,565	1,152	6,413	2,565	5,000
5	7,719	922	6,797	2,719	5,000

The use of the internal rate of return method calls for the prudent selection of Investment B, with an IRR of 14.33 percent, in preference to Investment A with an IRR of 11.16 percent. The final selection of any investment under the IRR method depends on the yield exceeding some minimum cost standard, usually based on the cost of capital to the firm. Again, in this example, with a cost of capital of 10 percent, both investments would be acceptable.

This conclusion is the same one reached with the NPV method. Under most circumstances, the NPV and IRR methods suggest the same conclusion, and the subsequent discussion is restricted to these two approaches.

The IRR method, like the NPV method,
- Includes all cash flows
- Utilizes time-value-of-money concepts
- Utilizes an objective evaluation tool (usually the cost of capital)

However, it is not as effective a method as the NPV, because to use it,
- Cumbersome trial and error or interpolation is required
- It may inappropriately suggest an incorrect decision between mutually exclusive projects
- Multiple discount rates can result, causing confusion (discussed later under selection strategy)
- Unlike the NPV, more than one discount rate for different time periods cannot be utilized

An adjustment to the above investment calculations is in order. Under the Canadian tax system, amortization for tax purposes is called *capital cost allowance, or CCA*. On many capital items, CCA is calculated on a declining-balance method. If this applies to the investments in question, the calculations of internal rate of return and net present value become more complicated because the value of the CCA tax shield may continue at ever-diminishing amounts well past the economic life of the asset. For simplicity, we have ignored the value of tax savings past Year 3 for Investment A and Year 5 for B. Since there are leftover tax savings in these examples, however, the true internal rates of return and net present values are slightly higher than those calculated. The handling of declining balance, CCA tax shields in capital budgeting decision making is discussed later in this chapter.

Profitability Index

The profitability index (PI) is the ratio of cash inflows to cash outflows in present value terms. It is an alternative presentation of the NPV method and is used to place returns from different size investments onto a common measuring standard.

$$\text{(PI) Profitability index} = \frac{\text{Present value of the inflows}}{\text{Present value of the outflows}}$$

Using the information from the NPV analysis, we find for Investment A that the PI is 1.0180 ($10,180/$10,000), and for B it is 1.1414 ($11,414/$10,000). As both investments have a profitability index greater than 1, they will add value to the firm because in each case the present value of cash inflows exceeds the initial capital investment (cash outflow). Furthermore, Investment B has a higher relative value than A, based on the size of the investment, which in this example is the same for both investments.

 FINANCE IN ACTION

Capital Budgeting Practices Utilized by Smaller, Privately Held Businesses

Although the techniques described in this chapter are intended to be used by the modern, sophisticated financial manager, not everyone uses them. Surveys of large firms show usage of discounted cash flow techniques (NPV and IRR) and usage of the weighted average cost of capital. These are essential tools for today's financial manager. (Refer to note 2.)

Studies of smaller privately held firms reveal that although increasing numbers of these firms use discounted cash flow methods, many used the payback period or another simple approach.

There are perhaps two reasons large firms use the more sophisticated and theoretically correct techniques, whereas smaller firms do not employ them to the same extent. The first is that the small business owner is likely to be less familiar with the discounted cash flow techniques. Although the small business owner likely understands the time-value-of-money concept and applies it in a general fashion, they are unlikely equipped with the time or knowledge to apply the detailed techniques and inputs required by discounted cash flow analysis. The small business owner's skills are more likely to be in designing products, meeting customer's demands, and hiring and satisfying employees.

The second reason may be because small business owners spend more time with bankers than with shareholders or bondholders. When approaching a banker for a loan for capital investments, the owner must be prepared to demonstrate the capacity to repay the loan within a set period of time rather than show the investment's NPV or IRR. The payback period is often the maturity period the bank will allow for the loan.

Summary of Evaluation Methods

A summary of the results and various conclusions reached under the four capital budgeting methods based on cash flows is presented in Table 12–4.

Table 12–4 Capital budgeting results

	Investment A	Investment B	Selection
Payback period	2 years	3.8 years	Quickest payback: A
Net present value	$180	$ 1,414	Highest net present value: B
Internal rate of return	11.16%	14.33%	Highest yield: B
Profitability index	1.0180	1.1414	Highest relative profitability: B

LO4 SELECTION STRATEGY

The NPV, IRR, and PI methods must have the profitability based on the time value of money equal or exceed the cost of capital for the project to be potentially acceptable. If profitability in these methods exceeds the cost of the investment, value will be added to the firm. These methods are similar and generally lead to the same decision. The PI, it should be noted, is really only a variation of the NPV method.

The IRR and NPV methods are clearly superior to the payback period and the average accounting return (AAR) methods, because they evaluate all the resultant cash flows from an investment decision and employ the time value of money. Furthermore, the acceptance of an investment when using the IRR and NPV methods is determined by the cost of capital. This is an objective criterion

[2]Ryan, P.A. and Ryan, G.P., "Capital Budgeting Practices of the Fortune 1000: How Have Things Changed?" *Journal of Business and Management*, Volume 8, Number 4, Winter 2002.

determined in the financial markets. The payback period and AAR methods fail to produce such an objective yardstick upon which to accept or reject an individual project.

However, the IRR method does have some flaws when compared to the NPV method, which may produce unclear results. These flaws are discussed below under mutually exclusive projects, the discounting consideration, and multiple internal rates. These explain why the NPV is a better methodology. The NPV method can also handle more complex problems that require more than one discount rate. The nature of the IRR method is that there can be only one discount rate.

Mutually Exclusive Projects

If investments are mutually exclusive, the selection of one alternative precludes the selection of any other alternative. As we will see below, under certain circumstances of mutual exclusivity the IRR method will suggest a different decision than the NPV.

To illustrate mutually exclusive projects, let us assume we are going to build a specialized assembly plant in central Canada. Four cities are under consideration, only one of which will be picked. In this situation, we select the alternative with the highest acceptable yield or the highest net present value and disregard all others. Even if certain locations provide a marginal return in excess of the cost of capital, they may be rejected. In the following table, the possible alternatives are presented.

Mutually Exclusive Alternatives	IRR	Net Present Value (thousands)
Oakville...............................	15%	$300
Sarnia	12	200
Ottawa................................	11	100
Cost of capital	**10**	—
Windsor...............................	9	(100)

Among the mutually exclusive alternatives, only Oakville would be selected. Of course, if the alternatives were not a mutually exclusive need for multiple specialized plants, we would accept all of the alternatives that provided a return in excess of our cost of capital. Only Windsor would then be rejected.

Applying this logic to Investments A and B in the prior discussion and assuming a cost of capital of 10 percent, only Investment B would be accepted if the alternatives were mutually exclusive, but both would clearly qualify if they were not mutually exclusive.

	Investment A	Investment B	Accepted If Mutually Exclusive	Accepted If Not Mutually Exclusive
Internal rate of return	11.16%	14.33%	B	A, B
Net present value	$180	$1,414	B	A, B

The discussion to this point has assumed the internal rate of return and net present value methods call for the same decision. Although this is generally true, there are exceptions. Two rules may be stated:

1. Both methods accept or reject the same investments based on minimum return or cost of capital criteria. If an investment has a positive net present value, it also has a yield in excess of the cost of capital.

2. In certain limited cases, however, the two methods may give different answers in selecting the best investment from a range of acceptable alternatives. This will be demonstrated later after the net present value profile is presented.

Discounting Consideration

The methodology for the internal rate of return discounts all cash flows from the future to the present at the same discount rate. The IRR is the discount rate that makes the present value of those cash flows equal to the initial investment or, in other words, produces an NPV of zero. However, with our knowledge of the term structure of interest rates and our later study of risk, we should wonder whether the same discount rate is appropriate over time and whether the same discount should be applied to cash flows of a differing nature. Table 12–5 demonstrates the use of different discount rates for different time periods with the NPV method. Fortunately, the NPV methodology allows us to handle these considerations if they are appropriate to the analysis. This makes the NPV method of discounted cash flow analysis more flexible than the IRR method.

Table 12–5 Internal rate of return and net present value ($10,000 investment)

Investment A (11.16% IRR)			Investment A			
Year	Cash flow		Year	Cash flow		
1	$5,000 →		1	$5,000 →	10%	
2	5,000 →		2	5,000 →	11%	
3	2,000 →	Discounted at 11.16%	3	2,000 →	12%	Discounted at various rates if desired
	NPV = 0			NPV = $27		

The IRR methodology suggests that all cash flows throughout the term of a project are reinvested within the firm at the IRR. This reinvestment assumption, particularly at higher IRRs, may be unrealistic. The NPV assumes reinvestment at the cost of capital for some consistency across projects. As examined later, the NPV method may employ a different discount rate (or different discount rates for different periods) as appropriate.

Modified Internal Rate of Return

A methodology that combines the reinvestment assumption of the net present value method (cost of capital) with the internal rate of return is termed the modified internal rate of return (MIRR). The method determines the discount rate that will equate the future value of inflows, each growing at the cost of capital with the initial investment.

As an example, assume an initial investment of $10,000 will produce the following inflows:

Year	Inflows
1	$6,000
2	5,000
3	2,850

The cost of capital is 10 percent.
The future value of the inflows is determined.

Future Values at End of Year 3, Discount Rate at 10%			
		Periods of Growth	Future Value
Year 1.........................	$6,000	2	$ 7,260
Year 2.........................	5,000	1	5,500
Year 3.........................	2,850	0	2,850
Total future value...............			$15,610

With a present value of $10,000 and a future value of $15,610, the yield, or MIRR, is 16 percent. The conventional IRR would have been 20.87 percent.

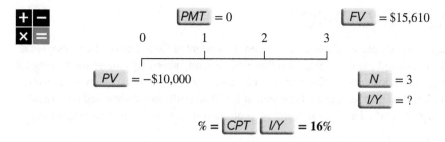

$$\% = \boxed{CPT} \; \boxed{I/Y} = 16\%$$

The MIRR, using the more realistic assumption of reinvestment at the cost of capital, gives a more conservative, perhaps better, answer. However, the traditional IRR has a wider usage and will be employed as a methodology in this text, unless otherwise specified.

Multiple Internal Rates

It is possible with the IRR method to have more than one discount rate that equates the future cash flows and the initial investment, depending on the pattern of cash flows. For example, suppose an investment has the following pattern of cash flows.

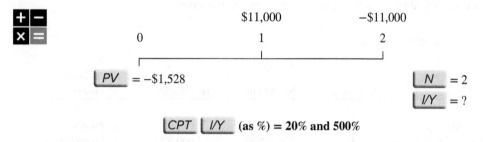

$$\boxed{CPT} \; \boxed{I/Y} \; \text{(as \%)} = 20\% \text{ and } 500\%$$

The present value of the cash flows in Years 1 and 2 is shown in Table 12–6. The pattern of cash flows is what one might find on an environmentally sensitive project where rehabilitation costs have to be incurred at the end of the project. The project would have an initial capital investment (cash outflow) to start the project, followed by positive cash flows, and finally a negative cash flow. This occurs when the project can no longer yield positive profits and the firm is then obligated to incur costs (cash outflow) to restore the property to its original condition.

Table 12–6 Multiple IRRs

	Cash Flow	@ 20%	@ 500%
0	−1,528	−1,528	−1,528
1	11,000	9,167	1,833
2	−11,000	−7,639	−305
NPV		0	0

We are left with a dilemma when we calculate the IRR in this example. Both 20 percent and 500 percent are correct because they produce an NPV equal to zero, but which IRR should be used to decide whether or not to proceed with the project? With the NPV method and an acceptable discount rate employed in the calculations, we can easily decide if the project is worthwhile. It turns out in our example that any discount rate between 20 percent and 500 percent produces a positive NPV. However, if our cost of capital is 15 percent, the NPV would be negative and the project would not add value to the firm. The IRRs of 20 percent or 500 percent would suggest that this would be a worthwhile project. Thus, the NPV method gives a better decision rule under these circumstances.

It turns out that there can be as many IRRs as there are changes of sign from positive to negative in the cash flows. This flaw in the IRR method could lead to incorrect decisions, or at best, vague results. The NPV method handles this situation well and produces a clear result.

CAPITAL RATIONING

At times, management may place a dollar constraint on the amount of funds that can be invested in a given period. This is capital rationing. The executive planning committee may emerge from a lengthy capital budgeting session to announce that only $5 million may be spent on new capital projects this year. Although $5 million may represent a large sum, it is still an artificially determined constraint and not the product of marginal analysis in which all projects with positive net present values are accepted.

Perhaps a management team may adopt a posture of capital rationing because it fears the risks attached to rapid growth strategies or because it is hesitant to use external sources of financing. However, in a purely theoretical sense, capital rationing hinders a firm from maximizing value.

If capital budgeting analysis is performed correctly, risk will be captured in the discount rate (cost of capital) used to evaluate an investment. Then, if the NPV is positive, the investment, with appropriate consideration for risk, will add value to the firm. With capital rationing as indicated in Table 12–7, acceptable projects must be ranked, and only those with the highest positive NPV are accepted. Under capital rationing, only projects A through C, calling for $5 million in investment, will be accepted. Although projects D and E have returns exceeding the cost of funds, as evidenced by a positive NPV, they will not be accepted under capital rationing.

Table 12–7 Capital rationing

	Project	Investment	Total Investment	Net Present Value
Capital	A	$2,000,000		$400,000
rationing	B	2,000,000		380,000
solution →	C	1,000,000	$5,000,000	150,000
	D	1,000,000		100,000
Best →	E	800,000	6,800,000	40,000
solution	F	800,000		(30,000)

Why would experienced managers impose a capital constraint? Besides the periodic reluctance to go to external sources for funding, many times the reason probably derives from one or two other sources. External sources of funding expose management to greater scrutiny by the impersonal capital markets, and may dilute control of the firm from the issue of more shares. Use of the PI may be useful under capital rationing constraints.

 FINANCE IN ACTION

Strategies: Right or Wrong?

Canada's important but cyclical resource industries are faced with decisions regarding large capital investments to modernize or expand their operations. Often massive projects are envisioned, sometimes constructed, and become operative just as the demand for their product has declined, exposing the firms to declining revenues despite the increased costs created by the new investments.

In 1996, Inco (vale.com/Canada), one of Canada's most significant mining companies, purchased a rich nickel deposit at Voisey's Bay, Labrador, for $4.3 billion. As nickel prices dropped, the project was mothballed. In 2002, Inco committed to developing a mine and processing plant for $700 million. The first concentrate was expected in 2006, with nickel prices jumping upward. In 2005, Inco took over its rival Falconbridge, but a year later Inco became a subsidiary, of Vale S.A. (formerly Companhia Vale do Rio Doce) from Brazil, selling for $19.4 billion. Nickel prices continued to move up and then back down. Nevertheless, Vale Inco planned over $14 billion in capital expenditures for 2009.

Another mining company, Teck, made a massive investment in Fording Coal Trust in 2008, shortly before the financial crisis, which put severe strains on the company. Teck recovered significantly only to mothball its massive Frontier oil sands mine development in 2020, amidst plunging oil prices.

The business of Vale Inco and Teck, with tangible assets like nickel, is quite different from the knowledge assets of the information age as represented by companies such as Shopify or BlackBerry.

In 2014, Enbridge received approval from the joint review panel of the federal government to proceed with the $6.5 billion Northern Gateway pipeline. Environmental concerns, vocal opposition, and appeasement of First Nations interests led to the end of the project in 2016. In a similar vein, Kinder Morgan sought to expand capacity on its Trans Canada Pipeline System to the southern BC coast. In 2018 Kinder Morgan sold its stake in the expansion to the federal government for $4.5 billion, citing continuing delays.

Q1 How has the share price of Vale (NYSE: VALE) performed in recent years?

Q2 Has Vale Inco maintained its heavy capital expenditure program?

Q3 How has Teck (TCK.B) done since its acquisition of Fording Coal in 2008?

Q4 What happened to the Trans Mountain pipeline project?

nyse.com   **tmx.com**

In some cases the concern is with how many new projects the current management team can oversee at one time. In other words, the constraint being imposed is actually one related to available management talent, even though it is presented as a restriction on the amount of capital available. Thus, although the projects might look good under the assumption that their implementation will be supervised by experienced company managers, they are less attractive if additional new managers must be employed.

Another case relates to industries where the experience with forecasting future demand has been so unsuccessful that management deliberately funds new projects in relation to cash near at hand. This has often been the situation with Canada's forest products industry, which accounts for a significant portion of the jobs, GDP, and export earnings in the country. This latter form of capital rationing is really a qualitative way of dealing with high levels of uncertainty. A variation on the forecasting problem

Canadian Institute
of Forestry
cif-ifc.org

is upper management's experience with capital budgeting analysis in which estimated cash flows are biased in an upward direction to promote certain projects. To limit the "rigging" of acceptable projects, management rations capital.

NET PRESENT VALUE PROFILE

An interesting way to summarize the characteristics of an investment is through the use of the net present value profile. The profile allows us to graphically portray the NPV of a project at different discount rates. Let's apply the profile to the investments we have been discussing. The projects are summarized again:

	Aftertax Cash Inflows (of a $10,000 investment)	
Year	Investment A	Investment B
1	$5,000	$1,500
2	5,000	2,000
3	2,000	2,500
4		5,000
5		5,000

To apply the net present value profile, you need to know *three* characteristics about an investment:

1. *The NPV at a zero discount rate.* That is easy to determine. With no discount rate, the present values and future values are the same. For Investment A, the net present value would be $2,000 ($5,000 + $5,000 + $2,000 − $10,000). For Investment B, the answer is $6,000 ($1,500 + $2,000 + $2,500 + $5,000 + $5,000 − $10,000).

2. *The NPV as determined by a normal discount rate* (such as the cost of capital). For these two investments, we used a discount rate of 10 percent. As was summarized in Table 12–4 earlier, the net present values for the two investments at that discount rate were $180 for Investment A and $1,414 for B.

3. *The IRR for the investments.* Once again referring to Table 12–4, we see the IRR is 11.16 percent for Investment A and 14.33 percent for B. Also realize that the IRR is the discount rate that allows the project to have a net present value of zero. This characteristic becomes more important when we present our graphic display.

We summarize the information about discount rates and net present values for each investment below and graphically in Figure 12–2.

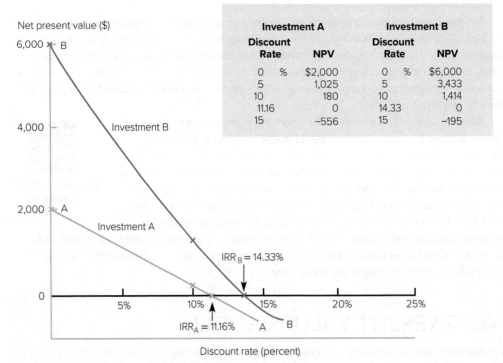

Investment A		Investment B	
Discount Rate	NPV	Discount Rate	NPV
0 %	$2,000	0 %	$6,000
5	1,025	5	3,433
10	180	10	1,414
11.16	0	14.33	0
15	−556	15	−195

Figure 12–2 Net present value profile

Investment A		Investment B	
Discount rate	Net Present Value	Discount rate	Net Present Value
0	$2,000	0	$6,000
10%	180	10%	1,414
11.16% (IRR)	0	14.33% (IRR)	0

Note that in Figure 12–2 we have graphed the three points for each investment. Investment A shows a $2,000 NPV at a zero discount rate, a $180 NPV at a 10 percent discount rate, and a zero NPV at an 11.16 percent discount rate. We then connected the points. The same procedure was applied to Investment B. The reader can also visually approximate what the NPV for the investment projects would be at other discount rates (such as 5 percent).

In the preceding example, the NPV of Investment B was superior to A at every point. This is not always the case in comparing projects. To illustrate, let's introduce a new project, Investment C, and then compare it with Investment B.

Characteristics of Investment C

Investment C ($10,000 investment)	
Year	Aftertax Cash Inflows
1	$9,000
2	3,000
3	1,200

1. The NPV at a zero discount rate for this project is $3,200 ($9,000 + 3,000 + 1,200 – 10,000).

2. The NPV at a 10 percent discount rate is $1,563.

3. The IRR is 22.49 percent.

You might compute these values for yourself, but that is not necessary at this point.

Comparing Investment B to Investment C in Figure 12–3, we observe that at low discount rates, Investment B has a higher NPV than C. However, at high discount rates, Investment C has a higher

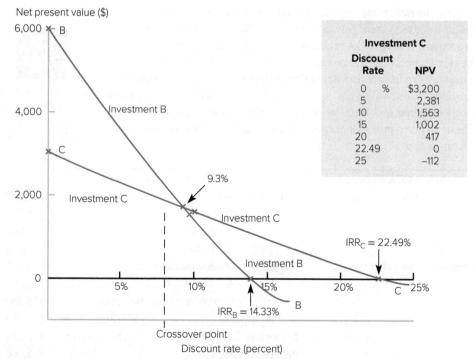

Figure 12–3 Net present value profile with crossover

NPV than B. The actual crossover point is at approximately 9.3 percent. That is to say, if you had to choose between Investments B and C, your answer would depend on the discount rate. At low rates (below 9.3 percent), you would opt for Investment B. At higher rates (above 9.3 percent), you would select Investment C. Since the cost of capital is presumed to be 10 percent, you would probably prefer Investment C (remember, though, that the cost of capital can change).

Why does Investment B do well compared to Investment C at low discount rates, and relatively poorly compared to Investment C at high discount rates? This difference is related to the timing of inflows. Let's examine the inflows.

	Cash Inflows (of a $10,000 investment)	
Year	Investment B	Investment C
1	$1,500	$9,000
2	2,000	3,000
3	2,500	1,200
4	5,000	
5	5,000	

Investment B has heavy late inflows ($5,000 in both the fourth and fifth years), and these are more strongly penalized by high discount rates. Investment C has extremely high early inflows that are less affected by high discount rates than are later flows.

As previously mentioned in the chapter, if the investments are not mutually exclusive and capital is not being rationed, we would probably accept both Investment B and C at discount rates below 14.33 percent. Below that discount rate they both have positive net present values. On the other hand, if we can select only one, the decision may well turn on the choice of a discount rate. Observe in Figure 12–3 that at a discount rate of 5 percent, we would select Investment B, at 10 percent we would select Investment C, and so on, because the NPV is greater. The net present value profile helps us make such decisions. This also suggests that the NPV method is superior to the IRR method when projects are mutually exclusive.

CAPITAL COST ALLOWANCE

To analyze the anticipated cash flow patterns under any investment proposal, we have to know how to consider the effects of tax-allowable amortization on our cash flow estimates. Although financial accounting entries for amortization have no cash flow effects, tax-allowable amortization expenses do. The Income Tax Act of Canada lays out a system of allocating amortization, called capital cost allowance (CCA), that reduces the tax payable for profitable firms and, therefore, is important in estimating the cash flow effects of proposed project investments. CCA creates tax shields or tax savings.

As an example:

CCA classes of the Income Tax Act
cra-arc.gc.ca/tx/bsnss/ tpcs/slprtnr/rprtng/cptl/ clsss-eng.html

Before CCA Expense		After CCA Expense	
Income (cash flow)	$12,000	Income (cash flow)	$12,000
		CCA	5,000
		Taxable income	7,000
Tax @ 25%...................	3,000	Tax @ 25%...................	1,750
Income (cash flow) after taxes......	$ 9,000	Income after taxes	$ 5,250
		Add back CCA.................	5,000
		Income/cash flow after taxes	$10,250
		Aftertax expense .... $5,000 (1 − T) =	$ 3,750
		Tax savings.................... $5,000 (T) =	$ 1,250
		Before-tax expense	$ 5,000

For tax-deductible CCA purposes, assets are divided into a number of classes, each of which is assigned a CCA rate. All of the assets of a given class form what is called an asset pool. To calculate the tax shield resulting from capital cost allowance, most of the asset classes call for declining-balance CCA. A sampling of CCA classes (subject to the declining-balance rule), their accompanying CCA rates, and some of the items that might be assigned to a particular class are included in Table 12–8.

Table 12–8 Some declining-balance CCA classes

Class	Rate	Assets
Class 1	4%	Bridges, buildings, dams
Class 3	5	Windmills, telegraph poles
Class 6	10	Greenhouses, hangars, wood jetties
Class 7	15	Boats, ships, canoes
Class 8	20	Most machinery, radio communications equipment
Class 9	25	Aircraft
Class 10	30	Automobile equipment, computer hardware, feature films
Class 12	100	Cutlery, television commercials, computer software
Class 16	40	Taxicabs, autos for short-term rental, video games (coin)
Class 17	8	Roads, parking lots, storage area
Class 30	40	Telecommunications satellites and spacecraft
Class 33	15	Timber resource property
Class 42	12	Fibre optic cable
Class 50	55	Computer equipment and systems

Of the CCA classes, some of the larger amounts involving capital investment projects often fall under Class 1 (buildings) and Class 8 (machinery). Table 12–9 calculates the CCA for the assets (Class 8) involved in Investments A and B considered earlier in this chapter.

Table 12–9 Capital cost allowance for Investment A or B

Year 1:
Net original cost $10,000
Less: CCA 1/2($10,000 × 0.20) 1,000
UCC* . . . . $ 9,000
Year 2:
Less: CCA ($9,000 × 0.20) 1,800
UCC . . . . $ 7,200
Year 3:
Less: CCA ($7,200 × 0.20) 1,440
UCC . . . . $ 5,760
Year 4:
Less: CCA ($5,760 × 0.20) 1,152
UCC . . . . $ 4,608
Year n:
UCC (for Year n − 1) . . . .
Less: CCA (UCC in Year n − 1 × 0.20) . . . .
Equals: UCC (for Year n) . . . .

*UCC (Undepreciated capital cost), half rate in first year $UCC_n = (1 - \frac{d}{2})(1 - d)^{n-1}$

Note that under the *half-rate rule*, for most assets, only half the normal CCA is allowed as a tax-deductible expense in the year of acquisition. This rule does not apply to some Class 12 assets, normally written off 100 percent in the first year. Property in Classes 14 and 15 (see Table 12–11) is also exempt from the half-rate rule because of the depletion nature of those allowances.

Once an asset has been assigned to a given CCA pool, CCA is calculated on the undepreciated capital cost (UCC) of the pool of assets rather than on a single individual asset. What we have just calculated is the maximum CCA a firm can deduct for a given year. There may be circumstances where a firm would want to claim less than the maximum allowable CCA. For example, if the firm were in a loss situation and expected to be for many years hence, it might decide that taking the maximum CCA allowable might only reduce the tax shield available in the future while there is no income to shield from tax currently.[3]

Addition and Disposal of Assets

When an asset is purchased, its purchase price is added to the pool. When an asset is sold, on the other hand, the lower of the sale price or its original cost is deducted, unless netted out against a concurrent purchase. A pool can have CCA applied to it forever as long as there is at least one asset in it. If an asset is sold for more than its original cost, the difference is treated as a capital gain for tax purposes.

A capital gain for tax purposes is the difference between the purchase price of an asset and its sale price, assuming the price has gone up and the asset was not held primarily for resale as part of doing business. In that case, it would be considered as income. For tax purposes, only 50 percent of a capital gain, known as the taxable capital gain, is added to taxable income for the year. Tax is then paid on the increased amount of taxable income.

---

[3] The carryover rule is forward seven or back three years to be applied against taxable income. Thus, the consideration to delay or not to delay CCA expenses is not a straightforward one, although the option to carry losses back makes delay a less likely choice.

Assume Firm XYZ chose to buy Investment A in Year 1 and then also bought Investment B in Year 2. This is our example from Table 12–3, with both investments costing $10,000. Assume also that these are the only assets in Class 8. The UCC balance for Class 8 assets at the end of Year 3 would then be $12,960 (from Table 12–9 we see it would include $5,760 from A and $7,200 from B).

Suppose that in Year 4, XYZ sells both of the assets in Class 8, after which no assets remain in that pool. The liquidation of the pool could give rise to a number of different tax effects depending on the amounts for which the assets were sold. (See Table 12–10.)

Table 12–10 Liquidation of asset pool

	Outcome 1	Outcome 2	Outcome 3	Outcome 4
Year 3:				
UCC....................	$12,960	$12,960	$12,960	$12,960
Year 4:				
Sale price—A.............	5,000	7,000	7,500	12,000*
Sale price—B.............	5,000	5,960	7,500	7,200
Balance in pool	$ 2,960	$ 0	$ (2,040)	$ (4,240)
Capital gain	$ 0	$ 0	$ 0	$ 2,000
Tax consequences (@ 25%)				
Positive values are tax savings:				
From CCA pool	$ 735	$ 0	$ (510)	$ (1,060)
From capital gain	$ 0	$ 0	$ 0	$ (250)
	$ 735	$ 0	$ (510)	$ (1,310)

*Only original cost of $10,000 is deducted from pool; excess of $2,000 is capital gain.

Under Outcome 1, the pool has a leftover balance of $2,960, as the resale value of the assets declined more quickly than allowed for under the CCA schedule. That leftover balance is called a terminal loss and is tax-deductible in Year 4, creating a tax savings. Under Outcome 2, the amount realized on the sale of the assets is equal to the previous UCC, and the pool balance is zero, leaving no need for further adjustment. In Outcome 3, the sale price exceeds the UCC. More CCA was taken than the difference between the purchase and resale prices. The $2,040 is added to revenue in Year 4, creating taxes payable, and is termed recapture. Outcome 4 generates both a capital gain of $2,000 on the resale of A and recapture of $4,240 to eliminate the negative balance that would still be left in the pool after accounting for the capital gain.

Straight-Line CCA Classes

Some classes of capital items are not subject to rules of declining balance, but rather may be amortized for tax purposes on a straight-line basis. Table 12–11 lists some examples of classes subject to straight-line CCA.

Table 12–11 Straight-line CCA classes

Class 13.......	Certain leasehold improvements (to be amortized over the life of the lease)
Class 14.......	Certain patents, franchises, or licences for a limited period (to be amortized over the life of the asset)
Class 15.......	Woods assets (amortized depending on the amount cut in the year)

Investment Tax Credit

The investment tax credit (ITC) was originally a temporary measure that various governments have adjusted over time to include expenditures on scientific research, transportation equipment, film production, and other selected properties. Besides being used to encourage expansion of the types of businesses favoured by government policymakers, the ITC has been used to encourage investment in certain geographical regions. ITCs available in 2020 include the following:

Qualified Property, Scientific Research & Experimental Development Expenditures:	
CCPC (Canadian-controlled private corporation)	35%
Other corporations and for expenditures above $500,000	15
Qualified property in selected areas and certain activities	10
Journalism employees (maximums)	25
Mineral exploration	15
Apprenticeship job creation (maximums)	10

Unlike the CCA tax shield that reduces taxable income and then taxes indirectly, ITCs, by reducing taxes otherwise payable, represent direct dollar cash flow. Under certain conditions, where a corporation is not in a position to pay taxes, there is a provision for a cash refund.[4] For simplicity, the method of present value analysis that we use assumes that all cash flows related to tax consequences occur at the end of each appropriate year.

Canada Revenue Agency
canada.ca/en/revenue-agency.html

In the case of a new $100,000 machine (Class 8) bought by a profitable firm with a 25 percent tax rate, the first-year cash flow effect generated by tax savings or tax shield would be

$$\frac{1}{2}(20\% \times \$100,000) \times 25\% = \$2,500$$

This cash flow effect occurs at the end of the year.

If this machine qualified as a scientific research expenditure in Alberta, it would be eligible for a 20 percent ITC. Taxes would first be reduced by $20,000 (20% × $100,000). An ITC, however,

---

[4] Section 127.1 of the Income Tax Act.

reduces the amount available for CCA in the year following acquisition by the amount of the credit, which in this case is $20,000. Therefore, the UCC in the second year before CCA is taken would be

$$\$100,000 - \left[\frac{1}{2}(20\% \times \$100,000)\right] - \$20,000 = \$70,000$$

In addition, the scientific research expenditure is fully deductible as an expense. The corporation is therefore entitled to the full write-off of the expense and the ITC.

To summarize, the ITC produces a direct cash flow and a reduction in the CCA pool in the year following acquisition.

LO5 COMBINING CCA WITH CASH FLOW ANALYSIS

Capital cost allowance, by reducing taxes payable, affects a project's cash flows. Consider the following example. A firm is deciding on the acquisition of two new delivery vans for its fleet:

- Tax rate is 25 percent.
- Two new vans cost $30,000 total (Table 12–8, CCA Class 10 rate = 30 percent).
- An old van will be sold for $500 (because of purchase of new vans).
- Asset pool has UCC of $52,000 before purchase and sale.

The asset pool becomes $81,500, but the incremental change of relevance is $29,500. What was in the pool before continues regardless of the decision.

Beginning UCC	$52,000
Additions to the pool	30,000
Dispositions from the pool.	500
UCC	$81,500

In the current year, the maximum allowable CCA in respect to automobile equipment would be

$$[\textbf{Beginning UCC} + \frac{1}{2}(\textbf{Additions} - \textbf{Dispositions})] \times \textbf{CCA rate}$$

This is the amount that will have an effect on cash flow. Table 12–12 demonstrates the change in the CCA tax shield available in the first few years.

Table 12–12 Capital cost allowance for vans

Year	Beginning UCC Effect	CCA Calculation	Change in CCA Available
1	$29,500 ($81,500 − $52,000)	$\frac{1}{2}\left[29,500 \times 0.30\right]$	$4,425
2	25,075	25,075 × 0.30	7,523
3	17,552	17,552 × 0.30	5,266
4	12,286	12,286 × 0.30	3,686
5	8,600	8,600 × 0.30	2,580

After Year 1, we have created a steadily declining balance in perpetuity as long as the asset pool continues to exist. For the investment decision analysis, we need to calculate the present value of the tax savings resulting from the yearly allowable capital allowance expense, or in other words, the CCA tax shield. Given how the CCA system operates, we must provide the present value of a perpetual CCA tax shield. The general formula to account for the tax shield effect can be developed, then, as[5]

$$\frac{C_{pv} d T_c}{r + d}$$

Where

C_{pv} = Change in capital cost pool resulting from acquiring the asset, as a present value
d = CCA rate for the asset class
T_c = Corporate tax rate
r = Discount rate

In adjusting this formula for the half-rate rule, we obtain

$$\frac{C_{pv} d T_c}{r + d} \times \frac{1 + 0.5r}{1 + r}$$

One further complication to the present value calculation must be included to make it complete. In the normal course of events, we would expect at some time in the future to sell or salvage those two vans. An asset sold must be subtracted from the UCC of the asset pool. We would expect to have other values still in the Class 10 CCA pool. Therefore, we would realize a cash inflow on the sale of the vans but lose the CCA tax shield associated with that value in future years. This causes a need to adjust the CCA tax shield formula as follows to take into account the estimated timing and amount of the salvage value:

$$\text{PV of CCA tax shield} = [C_{pv} - S_{pv}] \left(\frac{d T_c}{r + d} \right) \left(\frac{1 + 0.5r}{1 + r} \right) \quad \text{(12–1)}$$

Where

S_{pv} = Change in capital cost pool resulting from the salvage value, as a present value
n = Number of years in the future we intend to sell the asset

If we examine formula 12–1 we note three components. Within the square brackets is the present value of all changes in the CCA pool as a result of an investment decision, including any additions and deletions. These changes, assuming an asset pool remains open, will affect tax savings on a declining-balance basis forever, and this is handled by the term in the first round brackets following the square brackets. The final round bracket adjusts for the half-rate rule. What the formula achieves, in a somewhat simplified manner,[6] is the present value of tax savings from all resultant changes in a CCA pool from an investment decision.

Applying or not applying the half-rate rule to the CCA salvage value effects should not have a material effect on the NPV of a project and should not be the critical basis for any investment decision. We opt for a ***simplified three-step formula*** in which all changes in the asset pool (including ITC

---

[5]The development is exactly the same as for the dividend growth model derived in Chapter 10. The major conceptual difference is only that g (growth rate) is negative. Thus,

$$PV = \frac{C_1 d T_c}{(1 + r)^1} + \frac{C_1 (1 - d)^1 T_c}{(1 + r)^2} + \frac{C_1 (1 - d)^2 T_c}{(1 + r)^3} + \cdots$$

$$= \frac{C_1 d T_c}{r - (-d)} = \frac{C_1 d T_c}{r + d}$$

[6]Some prefer not to apply the half-rate rule to the CCA effects from a salvage value. This is because the half-rate rule does not apply to salvage if an asset is sold by itself. If, however, an asset is disposed of in the same year as another asset (same class) is purchased, only the net difference (new asset price − disposal value) is added to the asset pool. The half-rate rule will apply only to the net difference, ***so there is no cash flow effect from the salvage value within the asset pool because it is netted away***. The S_{pv} could be dropped from the equation completely. The CCA formula is developed on the assumption that the asset pool continues (this makes the formula work), which for consistency suggests that this netting will occur. Some suggest that it is most appropriate to take CCA tax shields as if they occur at time zero. The formula is then

$$PV = \frac{C d T_c}{r + d} \left(1 + \frac{r}{2}\right) - \frac{1}{(1 + r)^n} \left(\frac{S d T_c}{r + d}\right) \left(1 + \frac{r}{2}\right)$$

See G. A. Sick and G. A. Mumey, "The Timing of Cash Flows and Related Taxes," *Financial Management* 19, no. 4 (December 1990), pp. 14–15.

perhaps) are determined, the perpetual tax shield formula is applied, and then there is adjustment for the half-rate rule. Tax experts can argue over possible cash flow timing effects several years in the future.

In the case of the proposed van purchases (net $29,500), if we expected to sell them after four years' usage at an estimated value of $4,000, and if the company's estimated cost of capital was 12 percent, the present value of the CCA tax shield from the vans would be

$$PV = [\$29,500_{pv} - \$4,000_{pv}(n = 4, r = 12\%)]\left(\frac{0.30 \times 0.25}{0.12 + 0.30}\right)\left(\frac{1 + .5(0.12)}{1 + 0.12}\right)$$

$$= [\$29,500 - \$2,542](0.17857)(0.94643)$$

$$= \$26,958(0.169005)$$

$$= \$4,556$$

The estimated value of $4,000 for the two vans in four years is referred to as the *salvage value*. This is the estimated market value at that time. The vans would probably be able to generate cash flows beyond the four years, but our analysis would require the value of those cash flows. We perhaps make a rather simplifying assumption by suggesting the salvage value captures the present value of the cash flows beyond the fourth year.

 FINANCE IN ACTION

Continual Capital Budgeting

In the 1970s, the development of the vast tar sands of northern Alberta commenced on a large scale. This region has reserves of oil to rival any deposit in the world. The problem, and hence the cost of, recovering the oil is that it is mixed with sticky tar sand, unlike the oil from conventional oil sites.

Syncrude Canada Ltd. was a joint venture formed in 1964 by governments and private-sector oil companies to extract oil from these sands. With the increasing oil prices of the 1970s, the capital budgeting numbers on full-scale development of the tar sands looked good. Even with the high costs of extracting the oil and the huge initial capital costs, the expectation of future oil prices suggested that this would be a profitable venture.

Syncrude was built in the 1970s for $2.3 billion. Its first barrel of oil in 1978 cost $30, and by 1999 its unit cost of a barrel of oil had declined to $11 Canadian. Syncrude persisted by "de-bottlenecking" the production process and reducing its cost structure by way of continual capital budgeting projects reaching billions of dollars annually. R&D expenditures annually exceed $75 million. In 2019 per barrel costs were $33.

Today, Syncrude is the largest source of oil in Canada, producing over 350,000 barrels of synthetic sweet light oil daily. Over the years there have been challenges, but significant capital expenditures persisted. Oil prices dropped as low as $10 a barrel in the 1980s, and were in the low $30s in 2020 (WCS—Western Canadian Select). More recently with limited pipeline capacity there have been difficulties getting oil to markets. Furthermore, the carbon footprint of the oil sands is under continual scrutiny.

The draglines of the past have been replaced with the massive trucks of today as Syncrude continues massive capital expenditures. The economic impact is felt throughout Canada. Suncor owns almost 60 percent of Syncrude.

Q1 What are Syncrude's (or Suncor's) current production and operating costs per barrel of oil? Compare to current oil prices.

Q2 What are the current capital expenditures at the oil sands projects of Suncor?

syncrude.ca   **suncor.com**   **oilsandsmagazine.com**

A Decision

Analysis requires that all future cash flows resulting from the purchase and use of the vans (including the CCA tax shield effect) more than offset the initial cost. Additional information for the investment decision includes

- Additional $33,000 per year in extra sales
- Additional $16,000 per year in extra operating costs
- Salvage value of $4,000 as already identified

All this is summarized in Table 12–13 on a NPV basis. On the basis of this financial analysis, the investment in the vans clearly creates value. However, there may be other effects of this decision that have not been quantified or are difficult to quantify. For example, the addition of the two vans may implicitly reduce the amount of time a supervisor spends on their present duties. Management should then factor in any additional overall company effects against the favourable result of the information already included.

Table 12–13 Net present value of resultant cash flows at 12%

		Investment in Vans			
Year	Cash Flow	Amount	$(1 - t)$	Aftertax Cash Flow	Present Value
0	Purchase vans	–$30,000	—		–$30,000
0	Sell old van	500	—		500
1–4	Operating	33,000 – 16,000 = 17,000	0.75	$12,750	38,726
4	Salvage	4,000	—		2,542
Present value of CCA tax shields ($30,000 – $500 – $2,542)(0.169005)*					4,556
NPV of resultant cash flows and initial investment					$ 16,324

*This number is from our calculation using formula 12–1.

IRR Solution

For IRR analysis we can use the framework we have employed for the NPV analysis. Our purpose, however, is to find the discount rate that reduces the NPV to zero. This will involve trial and error complicated by the CCA formula in particular, because the IRR is part of the formula as r.

Since our NPV is fairly large, let us try 35 percent as our discount rate (see Table 12–14). We are very close to an NPV of zero; close enough for significance. Normal calculator functions will not work because the cash flow related to CCA, unlike the other cash flows, changes with each new discount rate. If the NPV was significantly different from zero we would continue with trial and error.

Table 12–14 IRR solution framework using 35%

		Investment in Vans			
Year	Cash Flow	Amount	$(1 - t)$	Aftertax Cash Flow	Present Value
0	Purchase vans	–$30,000	—		–30,000
0	Sell old van	500	—		500
1–4	Operating	17,000	0.75	$12,750	25,461
4	Salvage	4,000	—		1,204
Present value of CCA tax shields					

$$[\$30,000 - \$500 - \$1,204]\left(\frac{0.30 \times 0.25}{0.35 + 0.30}\right)\left(\frac{1 + .5(0.35)}{1 + 0.35}\right)$$

= $28,296(0.115385)(0.87037)					2,842
Present value of resultant cash flows and initial investment					$ <7>

LO6 COMPREHENSIVE INVESTMENT ANALYSIS (NPV)

Investment analysis can involve the consideration of new projects or technologies, expansions of existing or new businesses, or the replacement of existing equipment or technologies. Engineers are constantly faced with examining new technology for possible increases in operational efficiencies. Any analysis requires focus on the resultant changes from a possible decision.

The replacement decisions, for example, can be analyzed by using a total analysis of both the old and the new machines or by using a differential analysis. We use the differential approach, which emphasizes the changes in cash flow between using the old and the new machines.

The Dalton Corporation is considering replacing its old (two years) computer:

- Old computer cost $100,000 (CCA rate of 45 percent).
- Current market value of old computer is $40,000.
- New computer's cost is $150,000 (CCA rate also 45 percent).
- Investment tax credit (ITC) of 15 percent is available.
- Cost savings estimated at $20,000 to $45,000 per year over five years.
- Salvage value of new computer $30,000, old zero, in five years.
- Tax rate is 25 percent; cost of capital is 14 percent.

Table 12–15 determines the initial investment cost. Tax shield effects (lost or gained) on a capital sale or purchase are considered in our CCA tax shield formula. The formula requires us only to identify the present value of the changes in the CCA pool.

Table 12–15 Net price of the new computer

Price of the new computer	$150,000
– Investment tax credit (15%) or $22,500	19,737*
Net price of new computer.	130,263
– Cash inflow from sale of old computer.	40,000
Net cost of new computer	$ 90,263

*Our assumption about cash flows (revenues, expenses) and tax-initiated cash flows is that they occur at the end of the year. Therefore, the tax credit of $22,500 is discounted one year. The CCA pool is affected in the year after acquisition. The CCA tax shield formula is constructed assuming tax savings effects occur at the end of the year.

Our next considerations:

- The cash flow effects related to tax shield benefits
- Operating benefits (and/or costs)
- Other resultant costs such as working capital adjustments
- Salvage values

Incremental CCA Tax Savings (Shields)

If the replacement decision is taken, we note three changes in the UCC. In the first year, the net increase would be $110,000 ($150,000 – $40,000). In the second year, a decrease of $22,500 would result from the ITC. The half-rate rule does not apply to the change due to the ITC. In the fifth year, the UCC would decrease by $30,000 as a result of the salvage value. The present value of the CCA tax shield using formula 12–1 takes care of the net first-year investment and the salvage value.

$$\text{PV} = \left[\$110,000_{pv} - \$30,000_{pv}\left(n = 5, r = 14\%\right)\right]\left(\frac{(0.45)(0.25)}{0.14 + 0.45}\right)\left(\frac{1 + 0.5(0.14)}{1 + 0.14}\right)$$
$$= [\$110,000 - \$15,581](0.19068)(0.93860)$$
$$= \$16,898$$

Chapter 12: The Capital Budgeting Decision   **449**

However, some CCA tax shield is lost from the second year forward due to the ITC. This effect is handled by using formula 12–1 (without the half-rate rule) and discounting the result back one year.

$$PV = -\left[\$22,500_{pv}\left(n = 1, r = 14\%\right)\right]\left(\frac{(0.45)(0.25)}{0.14 + 0.45}\right)$$

$$= -[\$19,737(0.19068)]$$

$$= -\$3,763$$

In total, the present value of the CCA tax shield is $13,135 ($16,898 – $3,763), and is included in Table 12–16, the summary of this investment decision.

Table 12–16 Differential analysis of new computer

Year	Cash Flow	Amount	(1 – Tax rate)	Aftertax Cash Flow	Present Value (@ 14%)
0	New computer	–90,263	—	—	–$90,263
0	Working capital investment	–5,000	—	—	–5,000
1	Cost savings	20,000	0.75	15,000	13,158
2	Cost savings	38,000	0.75	28,500	21,930
3	Cost savings	40,000	0.75	30,000	20,249
4	Cost savings	45,000	0.75	33,750	19,983
5	Cost savings	45,000	0.75	33,750	17,529*
5	Salvage	30,000	—	—	15,581
5	Working capital recovery	5,000	—	—	2,597
Present value of CCA tax shield benefits . . . (from calculation)					13,135
Net present value					$28,895

*The present value of all the cost savings may be handled in one output from the calculator, particularly if it is an annuity.

Cost Savings

The second type of benefit that requires consideration relates to the cost savings that can be realized by installing the new computer. As previously stated, these are estimated at between $20,000 and $45,000 per year over the next five years. The aftertax benefits are summarized in Table 12–16, where the cost savings are multiplied by one minus the tax rate to calculate the value of the savings on an aftertax basis. The cost savings are combined with the other resultant costs and benefits of the computer installation in Table 12–16.

Other Resultant Costs

In any analysis, all changes that are a result of an investment decision must be considered to correctly determine the value of an investment. One change that should not be overlooked is a change in working capital. In Chapters 6 and 7, it was pointed out that often with increasing sales a firm finds it has more capital tied up in accounts receivable, inventory, and other current assets. These current assets support the new sales level.

A benefit of many new investments is the increased level of sales that can be obtained, and it is likely that incremental increases in working capital will result from new investments. This working capital investment resulting from the decision to invest in a new project must be considered in the analysis as a resultant cost. Of course, when the project ends, through salvage of equipment or for other reasons, the working capital position would be unwound, resulting in a positive cash flow to the project.

In our computer example, we will suppose that as a result of this investment decision the firm will increase its investment in working capital by $5,000. Notice in Table 12–16 that a negative cash flow occurs at time 0, and a positive cash flow occurs when the project ends in Year 5. The working capital recovered in Year 5 in present value terms is worth only $2,597. The working capital investment during the length of the project will cost the firm $2,403 ($5,000 –$2,597).

In practice, projects are ongoing, and working capital positions will continue in support of the next project. However, for analysis purposes, we should isolate and assign resultant cash flows properly to each project in order to make correct decisions. The ongoing working capital position now is related to the next project. The best analysis comes when we think of a project with a clear beginning and a definitive end.

According to the estimates used in this investment analysis and presented in Table 12–16, the NPV is positive. Thus, the purchase of the new computer can be recommended on the basis of the financial analysis. The company will be better off by $28,895 today if the new computer is put into use. There may be other costs attached to this decision that have not yet been quantified. If so, the fact that the financial analysis thus far revealed a positive NPV should not dissuade management from analyzing whether there will be other costs (or benefits) that have not been included in this analysis. The analysis would be aided by the development of a time line.

One can extend this analysis to evaluate investment decisions that don't involve replacement of equipment. If the analysis is used to evaluate mutually exclusive projects of different lifetimes, caution should be exercised. It is important that projects be analyzed over the same period to ensure equal treatment.

DISCOUNTED CASH FLOW MODELS— THE DIFFICULTIES

Although, conceptually, the discounted cash flow models, the NPV, and IRR are straightforward and theoretically strong, in practice they encounter some problems. Both models require the estimation of future expected cash flows and the selection of an appropriate opportunity cost of capital or discount rate, as per the following model

$$PV = \sum_{n=1}^{k} \frac{CF_n}{(1 + r)^n}$$

Where

PV = Present or market value

CF = Resultant aftertax cash flows

r = Discount rate appropriate to project's risk

There can be difficulties and mistakes in estimating the future expected cash flows. Projects may entail the use of new products or technologies where there is no past data on which to base future projections. For those projects that have past results, practitioners often just extrapolate, assuming trends will continue as they have in the past. New economic and societal developments are not considered. Furthermore, there is often bias built into estimates by those who want to see a project accepted, and therefore, the cash flow projections become overly optimistic. As well, cash flow projections may not properly reflect the influence of inflation in boosting the nominal value of the cash flows over time. In preparing the resultant cash flows from a proposed project, analysts may fail to identify all the relevant cash flows. Effects on other product lines, opportunity costs, and the possible benefits to future projects are often missed in the preparation of the discounted cash flow analysis.

Determining the discount rate is also problematic. Theoretically, it should be the rate that is equated with the risk of the project under consideration. How is that rate determined in practice? Several models have been developed to assist us in this task, and this question of risk is explored further in Chapter 13. However, in the end, there must be a judgment call based on knowledge and experience. The use of the cost of capital has been developed in Chapter 11, but we have learned that there are many inputs into the cost of capital calculation that call for estimation. The cost of capital relies on well-developed, efficient capital markets to establish the cost components of the capital structure. These markets may not always be efficient or available. The market costs based on current yields capture anticipated inflation, and therefore, the cash flows must capture the same assumptions about inflation, as mentioned above. In addition, the risk of the cash flows may vary over time, and this would suggest the use of different discount rates. The NPV method can handle this adjustment, unlike the IRR method, but it adds to the complexity of the analysis.

Finally, management must be convinced that the decisions suggested by cash flow analysis produce value by increasing share prices. Management may feel that discounted cash flow analysis does not capture all of the benefits produced by a project. Projects that have a negative NPV may be accepted to produce a better image for the company, to effect fairer treatment of employees, or for the development of new technologies and competencies for the corporation. Often, these considerations cannot be captured by NPV analysis but will add value to the company. Additionally, negative NPV projects may be accepted because management's focus may be more on goals such as increasing earnings per share, the book rate of return, or market share. These goals do not always increase shareholder value, but they may increase the benefits paid to management or look good in the financial press.

On the other hand, capital projects that may have positive values may not be initiated because of government restrictions, capital market failures (lack of funding), or the scope of the project may be beyond management's capabilities or control.

When NPV analysis suggests that a project can add value to the firm, we should examine the results carefully. In an efficient market, which is discussed further in Chapter 14, it is stated that all transactions should have an NPV equal to zero. If this is the case, how could our analysis produce a positive NPV? Either we have a competitive advantage over other corporations or we have made a mistake in the analysis. Positive values suggested by NPV analysis portray a wealth shift within society to new projects, technologies, companies, and entrepreneurs with ideas.

SUGGESTED CONSIDERATIONS FOR NPV ANALYSIS

1. Identify events along a time line. Also note relevant variables such as the discount rate, CCA rate, tax rate, and time period.
2. Identify cash flows, not income, and on an aftertax basis.
3. Present individual sources of cash flows one at a time. Each cash flow identified along your time line is to be brought to the same point, time 0, and then summed to determine the NPV. Cash flows that appear as annuities can be handled in one calculation. Capital items are best handled by the CCA formula, which deals with the cash flow and the tax consequences separately.
4. Interest costs should not be identified as cash flows because they are already considered in the discount rate used, the cost of capital. To include the interest costs and their tax consequences in the cash flows would amount to double counting.
5. Include all resultant costs and benefits. This is perhaps the most important and difficult step. Take time to think! As a result of the decision being considered, what will change for the firm? Consider additional staffing, the effect on other divisions of the organization, and the required buildup in working capital to support the decision under consideration. Include all opportunity costs and ignore costs already incurred, because nothing can be done about those costs now. For example, land already owned has had its original cost already spent, but if we use the land in a project under consideration we forgo the opportunity of selling it and receiving the proceeds.
6. Use market values for the cash flows. The land mentioned in point 5 should be entered into the analysis at the market value forgone if the land is used in the project rather than sold.
7. Consider risk. This is discussed in Chapter 13.

SUMMARY

1. The capital budgeting decision involves the planning of expenditures for a project with a life of at least one year and usually considerably longer. Although top management is often anxious about the impact of decisions on short-term reported income, the planning of capital expenditures dictates adopting a longer time horizon. Although effective short-term decisions allow the firm to continue in operation for the long term, effective long-term decisions have the greatest effect on shareholder wealth. (LO1)

2. Cash flows and their timing are important for capital budgeting analysis because we are using the time value of money. When we receive the cash is important. Accounting income that includes accruals and does not consider opportunity costs fails in the important decision-making framework of identifying the timing of cash flows and opportunity costs. (LO2)

3. Five methods are used to analyze capital investment proposals: AAR, payback period, NPV, IRR, and the PI. The first two methods, although widely used, have serious theoretical flaws. The latter methods, because they consider the timing and overall amount of cash flows, are more complete methods for assessing capital budgeting decisions. Under certain circumstances, the NPV method is superior to the IRR.

   Investment alternatives may be classified as either mutually exclusive or not mutually exclusive. If they are mutually exclusive, the selection of one alternative precludes the selection of all other alternatives, and projects with a positive NPV may be eliminated. The same may also be true under capital rationing, a method under which management determines the maximum amount that can be invested in any one time period. (LO3)

4. The cost of capital is used as the discount rate for analyzing an investment under the assumption that the investment is of the same risk as the average collection of current investments owned by the firm. This seems somewhat unlikely, but the cost of capital is a good starting point in determining the discount rate to be used in the analysis.

   Although capital budgeting techniques are economically rational by design, the combination of future uncertainty and information complexity means that decision inputs are highly dependent on managerial judgment. Projects with large initial investments, with long time horizons, and facing a high degree of future uncertainty are particularly difficult to justify using capital budgeting or any other analytical technique. In Chapter 13 we examine how differing levels of risk can be factored into the capital budgeting decision-making process. (LO4)

5. A capital budgeting decision will likely have a major impact on the firm. Therefore, careful consideration should be given to all the costs and benefits that will result from a decision to proceed with an investment. The NPV analysis suggests that the moment a decision is made to proceed with an investment having a positive NPV, the wealth of the shareholders is increased by the amount of that NPV. All incremental cash flows should be identified.

   Tax considerations are also a major factor in capital budgeting decisions. In this chapter we have considered the effects of tax-allowable amortization (CCA) and investment tax credits (ITC) in relation to the analysis. At this time in Canada, the tax system is being used to attempt to encourage investment in some of the less-affluent regions of the country and also to attempt to channel investments toward R&D. (LO5)

6. NPV analysis is best performed by carefully developing the cash flows that will likely result from an investment decision before proceeding to the calculations. (LO6)

REVIEW OF FORMULAS

$$\text{PV of CCA tax shield} = \left[C_{pv} - S_{pv} \right] \left(\frac{dT_c}{r + d} \right) \left(\frac{1 + 0.5r}{1 + r} \right)$$

(12–1)

Where

C_{pv} = Change in capital cost pool resulting from acquiring the present value

S_{pv} = Change in capital cost pool resulting from the salvage value, as a present value

r = Discount rate

d = CCA rate for the asset class

T_c = Corporate tax rate

n = Number of years in the future we intend to sell the asset

DISCUSSION QUESTIONS

1. What are the important administrative considerations in the capital budgeting process? (LO1)

2. Why does capital budgeting rely for analysis on cash flows rather than net income effects? (LO2)

3. What are the weaknesses of the payback period? Why do many managers use it? (LO3)

4. What is normally used as the discount rate under the NPV method? Why? (LO4)

5. What does the term *mutually exclusive investments* mean? (LO3)

6. If a corporation has projects that will earn more than the cost of capital, should it ration capital? (LO4)

7. What is the NPV profile? What three points (characteristics) should be determined to create the profile? (LO3)

8. What else, besides the forecast IRR and NPV, might top management consider in making capital budgeting decisions? (LO6)

9. Generally, what effect does the CCA system have on the timing of CCA tax shield benefits? (LO5)

10. What is the ITC? How does it affect the capital budgeting decision? (LO5)

11. How would you modify your capital budgeting analysis (NPV methodology) to account for expected inflation? (LO5)

12. What implications does an efficient market (Chapter 14) have for NPV calculations? (LO6)

13. How does the MIRR include concepts from both the traditional IRR and the NPV method? (LO3)

INTERNET RESOURCES

Information on ITCs and CCA is available at Canada Revenue Agency: canada.ca/en/revenue-agency

or in the Income Tax Act: laws-lois.justice.gc.ca/eng/acts/I-3.3/

PROBLEMS

1. Assume Primus Corporation has earnings before amortization and taxes of $90,000, amortization of $40,000, and a 30 percent tax bracket. Compute its cash flow using the following format:

Earnings before amortization and taxes	_____
Amortization	_____
Earnings before taxes	_____
Taxes @ 30%	_____
Earnings after taxes	_____
Amortization	_____
Cash flow	_____

2. Assume a corporation has earnings before amortization and taxes (EBAT) of $100,000 and amortization of $50,000, and it has a 34 percent tax rate. Compute its cash flow.

3. a. In the previous problem, how much would cash flow be if there was only $10,000 in amortization? All other factors are the same.

   b. How much cash flow is lost due to the reduced amortization between problems 2 and 3a?

4. Blink 281 Corporation is considering an investment that will cost $120,000 and last for five years. The investment will be amortized on a straight-line basis over that period. Earnings generated by the investment before amortization and taxes over this period are as follows:

Year 1	$35,000
Year 2	37,000
Year 3	41,000
Year 4	45,000
Year 5	50,000

   Blink 281 Corporation has a tax rate of 25 percent.

   a. What is the AAR of this project?

   b. Should this project be accepted? What criteria would you use to accept or decline the project?

   c. What are the problems with this type of analysis?

5. Assume Secundus Corporation has earnings before amortization and taxes of $440,000 and amortization of $140,000.

   a. If it is in a 35 percent tax bracket, compute its cash flow.

   b. If it is in a 20 percent tax bracket, compute its cash flow.

6. Assume a firm has EBAT of $200,000, and no amortization. It is in a 25 percent tax bracket.

   a. Compute its cash flow.

   b. Assume it has $200,000 in amortization. Recompute its cash flow.

   c. How large a cash flow benefit did the amortization provide?

7. Al Quick, president of a Toronto Stock Exchange–listed firm, is very short term oriented and interested in the immediate consequences of his decisions. Assume Mr. Quick is considering a project that will provide an increase of $2 million in cash flow because of favourable tax consequences but carries a two-cent decline in earnings per share because of a write-off against first quarter earnings. What decision might Mr. Quick make?

8. Pluto Corporation is considering an investment that will cost $210,000 and last for three years. The investment will be amortized on a straight-line basis over that period. Earnings generated by the investment before amortization and taxes over this period are as follows:

Year 1	$110,000
Year 2	120,000
Year 3	150,000

   Pluto Corporation has a tax rate of 25 percent. What is the AAR of this project?

9. Assume a $250,000 investment and the following cash flows for two alternatives:

Year	Product X	Product Y
1	$90,000	$50,000
2	90,000	80,000
3	60,000	60,000
4	20,000	70,000

Which of the alternatives would you select under the payback method?

10. Assume a $50,000 investment and the following cash flows for two alternatives:

Year	Investment X	Investment Y
1	$10,000	$20,000
2	11,000	25,000
3	13,000	15,000
4	16,000	—
5	30,000	—

Which of the alternatives would you select under the payback method?

11. Referring to the previous problem, if the inflow in the fifth year for Investment X were $30,000,000 instead of $30,000, would your answer change under the payback method?

12. Referring to problem 10, analyze the two investment alternatives under the net present value method using a 15 percent discount rate. Would your answer change?

13. The Short-Line Railroad is considering a $100,000 investment in either of two companies. The cash flows are as follows:

Year	Electric Co.	Water Works
1	$70,000	$15,000
2	15,000	15,000
3	15,000	70,000
4–10	10,000	10,000

a. Using the payback method, what decision should be made?

b. Explain why the answer in part a can be misleading.

14. Britney Javelin Company is considering two investments, both of which cost $15,000. The cash flows are as follows:

Year	Project A	Project B
1	$8,100	$ 6,750
2	5,400	4,050
3	4,050	10,800

a. Which of the two projects should be chosen based on the payback method?

b. Which of the two projects should be chosen based on the NPV method? Assume a cost of capital of 7 percent.

c. Should a firm normally have more confidence in answer *a* or answer *b*?

15. A firm buys a new piece of equipment for $24,907 and will receive a cash flow of $4,500 per year for eight years. What is the IRR?

16. Hand Salsa buys a new piece of equipment for $11,778 and will receive a cash flow of $2,000 per year for 10 years. What is the IRR?

17. King's Department Store is considering the purchase of a new machine at a cost of $13,869. The machine will provide $3,000 per year in cash flow for six years. King's cost of capital is 12 percent. Using the IRR method, evaluate this project and indicate whether it should be undertaken.

18. Elgin Restaurant Supplies is analyzing the purchase of a manufacturing machine that will cost $20,000. The annual cash inflows are as follows.

Year	Cash Flow
1	$10,000
2	9,000
3	6,500

a. Determine the IRR.

b. With a cost of capital of 12 percent, should the machine be purchased?

c. With information from part *b*, compute the PI.

19. Altman Hydraulic Corporation will invest $160,000 in a project that will produce the following cash flows. The cost of capital is 11 percent. Should the project be undertaken? (Some projects may incur negative cash flows in later years, such as a mining project that may have to restore lands to their original condition after extracting the ore and when positive cash flows dwindle.)

Year	Cash Flow
1	$ 54,000
2	66,000
3	(60,000)
4	57,000
5	120,000

20. Hamilton Control Systems will invest $90,000 in a temporary project that will generate the following cash inflows:

Year	Cash Flow
1	$23,000
2	38,000
3	60,000

The firm will also be required to spend $15,000 to close the project at the end of the three years. If the cost of capital is 10 percent, should the investment be undertaken? Use the NPV method.

21. Twelve Inch Toes Corp. will invest $175,000 in a project that will not begin to produce returns until the third year. From the end of the third year until the end of the tenth year (8 periods), the annual cash flow will be $43,000. If the cost of capital is 11 percent, should this project be undertaken?

22. Helmsdale Excursions is considering investing $250,000 in a project that will begin to produce returns in the fourth year. From the end of the fourth year until the end of the twelfth year (9 periods), the annual aftertax cash flow will be $50,000. If the cost of capital is 8 percent, should this project be undertaken?

23. DeBarry Corporation makes an investment of $50,000 that yields the following cash flows:

Year	Cash Flow
1	$10,000
2	10,000
3	16,000
4	18,000
5	20,000

a. What is the present value with a 9 percent discount rate (cost of capital)?

b. What is the IRR?

c. In this problem would you make the same decision in parts *a* and *b*?

24. The Green Goddess Company is considering the purchase of a new machine that would increase the speed of manufacturing tires and save money. The net cost of the new machine is $45,000. The annual cash flows have the following projections.

Year	Cash Flow
1	$15,000
2	20,000
3	25,000
4	10,000
5	5,000

a. If the cost of capital is 10 percent, what is the NPV?

b. What is the IRR?

c. Should the project be accepted? Why?

25. You are asked to evaluate the following two projects for Boring Corporation using the NPV method combined with the PI approach. Which project would you select? Use a discount rate of 10 percent.

Project X (DVDs of the weather reports) ($10,000 investment)		Project Y (slow-motion replays of commercials) ($30,000 investment)	
Year	Cash Flow	Year	Cash Flow
1	$5,000	1	$ 15,000
2	3,000	2	8,000
3	4,000	3	9,000
4	3,600	4	11,000

26. Turner Video will invest $48,500 in a project. The firm's discount rate (cost of capital) is 9 percent. The investment will provide the following inflows:

1	$10,000
2	12,000
3	16,000
4	20,000
5	24,000

The IRR is 14 percent.

a. If reinvestment is assumed at the cost of capital rate used by the NPV method, what will be the total value of the inflows after five years? (Assume the inflows come at the end of each year.)

b. If the reinvestment is assumed at the IRR, what will be the total value of the inflows after five years?

c. Generally, is one reinvestment assumption likely to be better than another?

27. The Last Century Corporation uses the MIRR. The firm has a cost of capital of 7 percent. The project being analyzed has a $25,000 initial investment and is expected to produce the following cash flows:

Year	Cash Flow
1	$12,000
2	10,000
3	7,200

a. What is the MIRR?

b. What is the traditional IRR? Why is there a difference?

28. Music Box Records uses the MIRR. The firm has a cost of capital of 10 percent. The project being analyzed has a $39,000 initial investment and is expected to produce the following cash flows:

Year	Cash Flow
1	$16,000
2	12,300
3	15,100

a. What is the MIRR?

b. What is the traditional IRR? Why is there a difference?

29. The Caffeine Coffee Company uses the MIRR. The firm has a cost of capital of 12 percent. The project being analyzed has a $27,000 initial investment and is expected to produce the following cash flows:

Year	Cash Flow
1	$15,000
2	12,000
3	9,000

a. What is the MIRR?

b. What is the traditional IRR? Why is there a difference?

30. The Suboptimal Glass Company uses a process of capital rationing in its decision making. The firm's cost of capital is 13 percent. It will invest only $60,000 this year. It has determined the IRR for each of the following projects:

Project	Project Size	Internal Rate of Return
A	$10,000	15%
B	30,000	14
C	25,000	16.5
D	10,000	17
E	10,000	23
F	20,000	11
G	15,000	16

a. Pick out the projects that the firm should accept.

b. If projects D and E are mutually exclusive, how would that affect your overall answer? That is, which projects would you accept in spending the $60,000?

31. Keller Construction is considering two new investments. Project E calls for the purchase of earth-moving equipment. Project H represents the investment in a hydraulic lift. Keller wishes to use a NPV profile in comparing the projects. The investment and cash flow patterns are as follows:

Project E ($20,000 investment)		Project H ($20,000 investment)	
Year	Cash Flow	Year	Cash Flow
1	$ 5,000	1	$16,000
2	6,000	2	5,000
3	7,000	3	4,000
4	10,000		

a. Determine the NPV of the projects based on a zero discount rate.

b. Determine the NPV of the projects based on a 9 percent discount rate.

c. The IRR on Project E is 13.23 percent, and the IRR on Project H is 16.29 percent. Graph a NPV profile for the two investments, similar to Figure 12–3. (Use a scale up to $8,000 on the vertical axis, with $2,000 increments. Use a scale up to 20 percent on the horizontal axis, with 5 percent increments.)

d. If the two projects are not mutually exclusive, what would your acceptance or rejection decision be if the cost of capital (discount rate) is 10 percent? (Use the NPV profile for your decision; no actual numbers are necessary.)

e. If the two projects are mutually exclusive (the selection of one precludes the selection of the other), what would be your decision if the cost of capital is (1) 6 percent, (2) 13 percent, (3) 18 percent? Use the NPV profile for your answer.

32. Luft Watch Company is considering an investment of $15,000, which produces the following inflows:

Year	Cash Flow
1	$8,000
2	7,000
3	4,000

You are going to use the NPV profile to approximate the value for the IRR. Please follow these steps:

a. Determine the NPV of the project based on a zero discount rate.

b. Determine the NPV of the project based on a 10 percent discount rate.

c. Determine the NPV of the project based on a 20 percent discount rate (it will be negative).

d. Draw a NPV profile for the investment. Observe the discount rate at which the NPV is zero. This is an approximation of the IRR on the project.

e. Compute the IRR. Compare your answers in parts *d* and *e*.

33. XYZ Corporation has decided to sell one of its windmills for $5 million. This building is part of the Class 3 (5 percent) CCA pool, and XYZ had it built five years ago at a cost of $4.5 million. XYZ's tax rate is 25 percent. XYZ uses 12 percent as its cost of capital.

a. If the Class 3 UCC at the start of the year in question was $12 million (and this was the only disposal), what would be the tax consequences of the sale of the windmill?

b. If the Class 3 UCC at the start of the year of the sale was $4 million, what would be the tax effect of the sale?

c. If the UCC at the start of the year was $6 million and this was the last windmill in the pool, what would be the tax effects?

34. A $95,000 investment is to be amortized for tax purposes using the maximum CCA available.

a. If the investment represents a fleet of automobiles for a telephone utility, what will be the allowable CCA rate?

b. How much will the addition of the automobiles increase the allowable dollar CCA in Year 1? in Year 2?

c. If the investment had been for machinery, what difference would that have made in the CCA rate allowed?

d. What difference will it make when the cars are scrapped for next to nothing after five years? (The company's autos tend to accumulate very high mileage, and the company has adopted the practice of giving them away to interested employees when their usefulness to the company ceases.)

35. Coastal Shipping Corporation has decided to sell one of its vessels for $1 million. This vessel is part of the Class 7 (15 percent) CCA pool, and Coastal had it built three years ago at a cost of $1.2 million. Coastal's tax rate is 25 percent. Coastal uses 10 percent as its cost of capital.

    a. If the Class 7 UCC at the start of the year in question was $2 million (and this was the only disposal), what would be the tax consequences of the sale of the vessel?

    b. If the Class 7 UCC at the start of the year of the sale was $0.8 million, what would be the tax effect of the sale?

    c. If the UCC at the start of the year was $0.6 million and this was the last vessel in the pool, what would be the tax effects?

36. Nexus Corp. has made a $1,500,000 investment that is to be amortized for tax purposes using the maximum CCA available.

    a. If the investment represents an aircraft, what will be the allowable CCA rate?

    b. How much will the addition of the aircraft increase the allowable dollar CCA in Year 1? in Year 2?

    c. If the investment had been for a hangar for the aircraft, what difference would that have made in the CCA rate allowed?

    d. What will be the tax consequences when the aircraft is scrapped for $200,000 after 10 years?

37. The Thorpe Corporation will purchase a $50,000 piece of production machinery with an estimated useful life of five years. The new machine is expected to allow an increase in sales of $80,000 per year, while increased incremental costs amount to $45,000 per year. The firm is in a 25 percent income tax bracket. Complete the following table to determine the first-year cash flow effect of the investment.

Increased sales	_____
Increased costs	_____
EBAT	_____
Amortization	_____
Earnings before taxes	_____
Taxes	_____
Earnings after taxes	_____
Amortization	_____
Net cash flow	_____

38. Acme Auto Parts Ltd. has gained approval for an eligible scientific research and experimental development on Cape Breton Island and is intending to invest $1.7 million.

    a. Assuming the tax rules governing ITCs and CCA remain the same as represented in this chapter, compute the ITC available to Acme.

    b. What will be the original capital cost base for CCA purposes?

    c. Compute the present value of the ITC and CCA combined (Acme uses 10 percent as its discount rate). Acme's tax rate is 22 percent.

39. Follett Enterprises has purchased three greenhouses over the past five years, but today it sold them all for $500,000. Five years ago, Follett purchased the first greenhouse for $300,000, two years later it purchased the second for $250,000, and last year it purchased one for $400,000. Follett Enterprises has a marginal tax rate of 30 percent. CCA on greenhouses is 10 percent.

    a. Calculate the tax shields and any taxes payable to Follett on an annual basis over the five-year period resulting from these investments.

    b. Assuming the asset pool continues, calculate the tax shields on an annual basis over the five-year period.

    c. Calculate the present value of the tax shields and any taxes payable under the assumptions of part *a* and *b*. Calculate the present value of the CCA tax shields with formula 12–1 and compare your results. Follett's cost of capital is 14 percent.

40. The Elite Car Rental Corporation is contemplating expanding its short-term rental fleet by 30 automobiles at a cost of $900,000. It expects to keep the autos for only two years and to sell them at the end of that period for 60 percent, on average, of what they cost. The plan is to generate $21,000 of incremental revenue per additional auto in each year of operation. The controller estimates that other costs will amount to 20 cents per kilometre on an average of 40,000 kilometres per car per year. She also estimates that the new business will require an investment of $10,000 in additional working capital. The firm is in a 30 percent tax bracket and uses 12 percent as a cost of capital. Should Elite purchase the automobiles? Do all of the necessary calculations to substantiate your recommendation.

41. Albert I. Stein Ltd. is considering the investment of $75,000 in a new machine that will allow it to do research on developing a new microchip for use in video games. The machine will be assigned to CCA Class 8. The firm is considered a Canadian-controlled private corporation eligible for the small business tax deduction. (The tax rate is, therefore, 15 percent.) A 20 percent ITC is available.

    If the machine is purchased, Stein expects to be able to develop a new product for the video game market that would be ready for sale about two years after the machine is purchased. This new product is anticipated to provide new revenues of $121,000 per year for the seven years after introduction, and to have associated expenses of $90,000 per year for the first five of those years and $105,000 for the last two. Other development costs associated with the new product in the initial two years are estimated at $17,500 per year. The firm's controller estimates its cost of capital at 13 percent and that $0.10 in additional working capital is required for every $1.00 in extra sales.

    Should Albert I. Stein Ltd. purchase the new machine? Do all relevant calculations to support your recommendation.

42. Pierce Labs, located in Gaspe Bay, purchased a radio communication system three years ago for $310,000. It has a potential buyer for the system that is willing to pay $85,000. A new system will cost $390,000 and is eligible for a 15 percent ITC.

    It is estimated the new system would provide the following stream of cost savings over the next five years:

Year	Cost Savings
1	$99,000
2	88,000
3	77,000
4	66,000
5	55,000

    The tax rate is 30 percent, and the estimated cost of capital is 12 percent. Should the new system be purchased?

COMPREHENSIVE PROBLEMS

43. On graduating from college, Steven MacLean joined the financial analysis section of a large Canadian industrial concern, Ontario Corporation. Soon after, MacLean was assigned to help in the financial analysis of a proposed acquisition by Ontario of a firm in a business unlike any of Ontario's traditional businesses. After a month of searching, MacLean had assembled the following additional information:

    a.

TARGET FIRM
Balance Sheet at 12/31/XX (000s)

Cash	$ 150	Current liabilities	$ 150
Accounts receivable	400		
Inventory	600	Long-term debt	750
Net capital assets	2,100	Equity	2,350
Total	$3,250		$3,250

b. Target Firm's sales for 20XX had been $3.5 million, and because it was operating at full capacity, it looked as if all classes of assets would increase at a pace directly proportional to any increase in sales.

c. The interest rate on Target's long-term debt was 12.5 percent with annual interest payments being made at the end of each year.

d. MacLean recommended the long-term debt be maintained after the acquisition.

e. At the end of 20XX, Target had two million shares outstanding, which had traded recently at prices around $1.50 per share.

f. The following estimates of sales and earnings before interest and taxes were the most reliable MacLean had come across:

Year	Annual Sales (millions)	Annual EBIT
1	$3.7	$650,000
2	4.0	700,000
3	4.1	720,000
4	4.2	720,000
5	4.0	690,000
6–10	4.3	700,000

In arriving at EBIT, amortization expenses of $140,000 per year had been deducted.

g. Expenditures on capital assets would be necessary to allow for growth and to replace worn-out equipment. MacLean estimated that $200,000 per year would be required in years 1–5, with $80,000 per year thereafter.

h. The income tax rate for both firms was expected to remain at 30 percent.

i. Ontario Corporation used 13 percent as its cost of equity and had a weighted average cost of capital of 11 percent.

Compute the price MacLean should recommend that Ontario Corporation offer to pay for each of Target Firm's shares.

44. Signs for Fields Machinery Ltd. is considering the replacement of some technologically obsolete machinery with the purchase of a new machine for $72,000. Although the older machine has no market value, it could be expected to perform the required operation for another 10 years. The older machine has an unamortized capital cost of $27,000.

The new machine with the latest in technological advances will perform essentially the same operations as the older machine but will effect cost savings of $17,500 per year in labour and materials. The new machine is also estimated to last 10 years, at which time it could be salvaged for $11,500. To install the new machine will cost $7,000.

Signs for Fields has a tax rate of 30 percent, and its cost of capital is 15 percent. For accounting purposes, it uses straight-line amortization, and for tax purposes its CCA is 20 percent.

a. Should Signs for Fields Machinery purchase the new machine?

b. If the old machine has a current salvage value of $9,000, should Signs for Fields purchase the new machine?

c. Calculate the IRR and PI for part *a*.

45. M and C Hammer Machinery Ltd. is considering the replacement of some worn machinery with a new machine costing $54,000. The older machine has no market value but could continue to perform the required operation for another 10 years. The older machine has an unamortized capital cost of $20,000.

The new machine will perform essentially the same operations as the older machine but will effect cost savings of $15,000 per year in labour and materials. The new machine is also estimated to last 10 years, at which time it could be salvaged for $8,000. To install the new machine will cost $5,000.

M and C Hammer has a tax rate of 30 percent, and its cost of capital is 14 percent. Its capital cost allowance is 20 percent.

   a. Should M and C Hammer Machinery purchase the new machine?

   b. If the old machine has a current market value of $7,000, should M and C Hammer purchase the new machine?

   c. Calculate the IRR and PI for part *a*.

46. Helmsdale Improvements Ltd. is evaluating the replacement of an older machine. There are two possible replacements under consideration—the OuOu and the Major OuOu. The existing machine was purchased a few years ago for $32,000 and currently has a book value of $8,500. If sold today, it would probably be worth $4,500.

The OuOu machine has a price tag of $50,000 and expected annual operating costs of $19,500. It could do the required job for seven years, at which time it could be sold for a projected $6,000.

The Major OuOu machine is a little pricier at $69,000, but its expected annual operating costs are only $13,000. After seven years it could be sold for approximately $8,000.

The existing machine is currently a Class 10 asset for CCA purposes, with a 30 percent rate. Either of the new machines would join the same asset pool. Improvements Ltd. has a tax rate of 25 percent and its cost of capital is 14 percent.

Which new machine would you recommend Helmsdale Improvements Ltd. purchase?

47. The Jagged Pill Ltd. has placed a $60,000 nonrefundable deposit on a new venture. The deposit can be expensed immediately. This has entitled Jagged Pill to additional information (of a trade-secret variety) and allows Jagged Pill to purchase a unique machine for an additional $525,000.

From the information revealed, it is projected that the expected life of the machine and this venture is eight years. At that time, the machine could be salvaged for an estimated $30,000. An additional capital upgrading of the machine costing $105,000 is anticipated in four years.

Projected annual cash flows before taxes and amortization for the venture are $165,000. If purchased, this unique machine will join the ongoing Class 8 pool with a CCA rate of 20 percent.

Jagged Pill's corporate tax rate is 25 percent. Its cost of capital is 13 percent.

   a. Calculate the NPV for this new venture.

   b. Calculate the IRR for this new venture.

   c. Calculate the PI of this new venture.

   d. Should Jagged Pill proceed with the new venture and equipment purchase?

48. Good T. has been considering a special investment for some time. This project will require an immediate capital expenditure of $2 million for required equipment. Good T. will house the equipment in an unused warehouse. Good T. has no other intended use for the warehouse but is aware that it could be rented out at $100,000 a year. Good T. will also use equipment purchased a year ago for $750,000 (current market value: $525,000) that was not ready for use and therefore had not been capitalized for the purposes of tax-related amortization. Cash flow before taxes and amortization is expected to be $650,000 a year for six years, at which time it will increase to $750,000 a year until the end of Year 12. At that time all of the equipment that

has been used can be salvaged for a mere $50,000. Additional working capital requirements related to this new equipment will be $75,000.

New equipment (and equipment previously purchased) CCA rate	30%
Tax rate	39%
Cost of capital	14%

a. Should Good T. proceed with the new project?

b. If Good T's cost of capital was not constant over the life of the project, how could this be handled within your analysis?

49. Torch Concerts Ltd. is considering acquiring a vacant lot adjacent to one of its centres. The lot would be used for parking during special events at the nearby Sports and Convention Centre and for other short-term projects. The primary purpose would be to hold the land as an investment. It is projected that in seven years, the land will be worth $700,000—a large gain from its present price of $325,000.

Purchase of the vacant lot would require an immediate investment of $60,000 in working capital, but this would help generate an estimated $50,000 a year in cash flow before amortization and taxes.

Torch has a corporate tax rate of 25 percent, and its cost of capital is at 15 percent. Amortization for tax purposes on concert centres is 20 percent. Taxable capital gains are 50 percent of the capital gain and would be payable one year after the sale of the land. Should Torch Concerts acquire the vacant lot?

50. Clueless Company, a successful business enterprise, is considering a new capital project with a degree of risk 50 percent higher than its normal business ventures. The new project would involve an investment of $375,000 in new equipment that would generate annual cash flow revenues of $200,000 over the 15 years of the project. Annual cash flow expenses over the same period would be $85,000. The product made on the new equipment would be sold on terms of net 60 (with working capital implications). Expenses would not be on credit. At the end of the project, the equipment could be sold for scrap and would recover $15,000 for Clueless.

The Clueless Company has a tax rate of 30 percent and its cost of capital is 12 percent. The CCA rate on the new equipment would be 30 percent. Should Clueless proceed with the new project?

51. Quixotic Enterprises is about to embark on another venture. Poncho Sanchos, the faithful financial analyst, once again will examine the viability of this venture after 31 failures.

A number of windmills are to be constructed on the southern frontier to generate electricity. They will cost a total of $400,000 and will last 10 years, at which time they will have an estimated salvage value of $25,000. However, a capital upgrade of $100,000 will be required at the end of five years. An inventory of parts (working capital) amounting to $10,000 will be required during the term of the venture and will be housed in a warehouse that is currently not being used, but which has been used for Quixotic's previous ventures. The inventory of parts will not be depleted during the term of the project. The warehouse could be rented out at $5,000 per year.

This enterprise is expected to generate revenues of $150,000 a year for 10 years. The federal experts on wind will impose their new tax on the wind, and that will cost the venture $7,500 a year. This new tax will be a deduction for income tax purposes and will be known as the BWT (Big Wind Tax).

Tax rate	25%
CCA rate	5%
Cost of capital	20%

a. Calculate the NPV of this venture.

b. Calculate the IRR of this venture.

c. Calculate the PI of this venture.

d. Should Quixotic dream the impossible dream?

52. J. Letterman Ltd. is considering the replacement of one of its older machines that is still capable of doing the job but is considerably inefficient. A new machine costing $210,000 will reduce annual operating costs from $75,000 per year to $42,500 per year. The new machine will last 10 years and will be amortized for tax purposes at 30 percent. The older machine has a book value of $46,500 and a CCA rate of 30 percent. The older machine could be sold for $32,500 today. In 10 years the older machine could be scrapped for $12,000, whereas the new machine would still be worth $50,000.

Also, the older machine requires a spare parts inventory (not eligible for tax-related amortization) of $10,000 that is not required by the newer machine. J. Letterman's tax rate is 28 percent, and its cost of capital is 12 percent. Would you advise Letterman to replace the older machine?

53. Midnight Oil and Gas is considering building a pipeline from a remote source of gas with only a 10-year supply of reserves. This qualifies the pipeline for a CCA rate of 20 percent rather than the normal 4 percent. The pipeline will cost $1 million; accompanying buildings will cost another $200,000. The buildings are Class 1 with a CCA rate of 4 percent.

Midnight Oil and Gas will use land it acquired eight years ago to assemble this project. The land was purchased for $500,000, and it is now worth $2 million. Annual cash flows before amortization from the pipeline and taxes for the 10-year period are estimated at $625,000.

In 10 years the buildings and pipeline will be worthless, but the land will be worth $4.5 million. Environmental clean-up costs at the end of the project are expected to be $1.2 million.

Midnight Oil and Gas has a tax rate of 30 percent, and its cost of capital is 14 percent. Capital gains are taxed at 50 percent of the gain. Should Midnight Oil and Gas build the pipeline?

54. Investigation and a reasonable amount of footwork brought the following information to the attention of April Kehg, executive assistant to the board of Swiss Ventures Inc. She, with your able assistance, will prepare a proposal to submit to the board under the heading "the St. Bernard Venture."

Capital outlays on the project are expected to occur over the next two years, and the project, which will produce widgets for the wireless communication business, will be a unique entity to the Swiss Ventures family of projects. An immediate outlay of $600,000 will be required for the land to house the specialized building that will be constructed over the next year. Final payment on the building will amount to $1.1 million inclusive and will be due in exactly one year. Payment for the machinery to produce the widgets will amount to $175,000 and will be due after the initial test period, which will take to the end of the second year.

After the testing period, cash flows will begin in the third year. It is assumed that the revenues and expenses will be acknowledged at the end of each year. Beginning in the third year, revenues are expected to amount to $875,000 until the twelfth year. Expenses are projected at $325,000 to the twelfth year from the third year. These estimates are the averages of estimates obtained from the marketing staff and the production department. The expected values have been determined through preliminary work by Kehg.

In 12 years everything will end, as the market for the widget will be gone. The building will be scrapped for $225,000, and the machinery will be sold for $50,000. It is anticipated that the land will appreciate in value by 9 percent a year.

The following additional information is available:

CCA rate: building	4%
machinery	30%
Corporate tax rate	30%
Cost of capital	15%
Capital gain	50% of gain taxable

Would you recommend proceeding with the St. Bernard Venture?

55. Marceline Enterprises is considering an expansion to its amusement park. The cost of this expansion is pegged at $1 million but will require additional capital expenditures of $200,000 every three years. In nine years it is expected that the expansion, which will be separated from the existing amusement park, can be sold for $150,000. Amusement parks belong to CCA Class 37, with a CCA rate of 15 percent.

Along with the capital investment, Marceline expects to increase its working capital requirements by 5 percent of any capital investment during the period of this investment.

Operating cash flows for the entire operation are expected to increase by $250,000 in each of the first two years, by $325,000 in each of the following three years, and by $375,000 for the final four years.

Marceline Enterprises has a corporate tax rate of 25 percent and at the current time its cost of capital is 11 percent.

Should it proceed with the investment? Show your analysis.

MINI CASE

Aerocomp Corporation

As she headed toward her boss's office, Emily Hamilton, chief operating officer for the Aerocomp Corporation—a computer services firm that specialized in airborne support—wished she could remember more of the training in financial theory that she had been exposed to in college. Emily had just completed summarizing the financial aspects of four capital investment projects that were open to Aerocomp during the coming year, and she was faced with the task of recommending which should be selected. What concerned her was the knowledge that her boss, Kay Marsh, a "street smart" chief executive, with no background in financial theory, would immediately favour the project that promised the highest gain in reported net income. Emily knew that selecting projects purely on that basis would be incorrect, but she wasn't sure of her ability to convince Kay, who tended to assume financiers thought up fancy methods just to show how smart they were.

As she prepared to enter Kay's office, Emily pulled her summary sheets from her briefcase and quickly reviewed the details of the four projects, all of which she considered to be equally risky.

A. A proposal to add a jet to the company's fleet. The plane was only six years old and was considered a good buy at $300,000. In return, the plane would bring over $600,000 in additional revenue during the next five years with only about $56,000 in operating costs. (See Table 1 for details.)

Table 1 Financial analysis of project A: Add a twin-jet to the company's fleet

	Initial Expenditures	Year 1	Year 2	Year 3	Year 4	Year 5
Net cost of new plane..............	$300,000					
Additional revenue.................		$ 43,000	$76,800	$112,300	$225,000	$168,750
Additional operating costs		11,250	11,250	11,250	11,250	11,250
Amortization		45,000	66,000	63,000	63,000	63,000
Net increase in income..............		(13,250)	(450)	38,050	150,750	94,500
Less: Tax at 33%		0	0	12,557	49,748	31,185
Increase in aftertax income		$($13,250)	($450)	$ 25,494	$101,003	$ 63,315
Add back amortization..............		$ 45,000	$66,000	$ 63000	$ 63,000	$ 3,000
Net change in cash flow.............	($300,000)	31,750	65,550	88,494	164,003	126,315

B. A proposal to diversify into copy machines. The franchise was to cost $700,000, which would be amortized over a 40-year period. The new business was expected to generate over $1.4 million in sales over the next five years, and over $800,000 in aftertax earnings. (See Table 2 for details.)

Table 2 Financial analysis of project B: Diversify into copy machines

	Initial Expenditures	Year 1	Year 2	Year 3	Year 4	Year 5
Net cost of new franchise..........	$700,000					
Additional revenue...............		$87,500	$175,000	$262,500	$393,750	$525,000
Additional operating costs		26,250	26,250	26,250	26,250	26,250
Amortization.....................		17,500	17,500	17,500	17,500	17,500
Net increase in income............		43,750	131,250	218,750	350,000	481,250
Less: Tax at 33%		14,438	43,313	72,188	115,500	158,813
Increase in aftertax income		$29,313	$ 87,938	$146,563	$234,500	$322,438
Add back amortization............		$17,500	$ 17,500	$ 17,500	$ 17,500	$ 17,500
Net change in cash flow...........	(700,000)	46,813	105,438	164,063	252,000	339,938

C. A proposal to buy a helicopter. The machine was expensive and, counting additional training and licensing requirements, would cost $40,000 a year to operate. However, the versatility that the helicopter was expected to provide would generate over $1.5 million in additional revenue, and it would give the company access to a wider market as well. (See Table 3 for details.)

Table 3 Financial analysis of project C: Add a helicopter to the company's fleet

	Initial Expenditures	Year 1	Year 2	Year 3	Year 4	Year 5
Net cost of helicopter.............	$800,000					
Additional revenue...............		$ 100,000	$ 200,000	$300,000	$450,000	$600,000
Additional operating costs		40,000	40,000	40,000	40,000	40,000
Amortization		120,000	176,000	168,000	168,000	168,000
Net increase in income............		(60,000)	(16,000)	92,000	242,000	392,000
Less: Tax at 33%		0	0	30,360	79,860	129,360
Increase in aftertax income		($60,000)	($16,000)	$ 61,640	$162,140	$262,640
Add back amortization............		$ 120,000	$ 176,000	$168,000	$168,000	$168,000
Net change in cash flow...........	(800,000)	60,000	160,000	229,640	330,140	430,640

D.   A proposal to begin operating a fleet of trucks. Ten could be bought for only $51,000 each, and the additional business would bring in almost $700,000 in new sales in the first two years alone. (See Table 4 for details.)

Table 4 Financial analysis of project D: Add fleet of trucks

	Initial Expenditures	Year 1	Year 2	Year 3	Year 4	Year 5
Net cost of new trucks	$510,000					
Additional revenue.		$382,500	$325,125	$ 89,250	$ 76,500	$ 51,000
Additional operating costs		19,125	19,125	25,500	31,875	38,250
Amortization		76,500	112,200	107,100	107,100	107,100
Net increase in income.		286,875	193,800	(43,350)	(62,475)	(94,350)
Less: Tax at 33%		94,669	63,954	0	0	0
Increase in aftertax income		$192,206	$129,846	($43,350)	($62,475)	($94,350)
Add back amortization.		$ 76,500	$112,200	$ 107,100	$ 107,100	$ 107,100
Net change in cash flow.	(510,000)	268,706	242,046	63,750	44,625	12,750

In her mind, Emily quickly went over the evaluation methods she had used in the past: payback period, internal rate of return, and net present value. Emily knew that Kay would add a fourth, size of reported earnings, but she hoped she could talk Kay out of using it this time. Emily herself favoured the NPV method, but she had always had a tough time getting Kay to understand it.

One additional constraint that Emily had to deal with was Kay's insistence that no outside financing be used this year. Kay was worried that the company was growing too fast and had piled up enough debt for the time being. She was also against a stock issue for fear of diluting earnings and her control over the firm.

As a result of Kay's prohibition of outside financing, the size of the capital budget this year was limited to $800,000, which meant that only one of the four projects under consideration could be chosen. Emily wasn't too happy about that, either, but she had decided to accept it for now and concentrate on selecting the best of the four.

As she closed her briefcase and walked toward Kay's door, Emily reminded herself to have patience; Kay might not trust financial analysis, but she would listen to sensible arguments. Emily only hoped her financial analysis sounded sensible!

a.   Refer to Tables 1 through 4. Add up the total increase in aftertax income for each project. Given what you know about Kay Marsh, to which project do you think she will be attracted?

b.   Compute the payback period, IRR, and NPV of all four alternatives based on cash flow. Use 10 percent for the cost of capital in your calculations. For the payback period, merely indicate the year in which the cash flow equals or exceeds the initial investment. You do not have to compute midyear points.

c.   i.   According to the payback method, which project should be selected?
     ii. What is the chief disadvantage of this method?
     iii. Why would anyone want to use this method?

d.   i.   According to the IRR method, which project should be chosen?
     ii. What is the major disadvantage of the IRR method that occurs when high IRR projects are selected?
     iii. Can you think of another disadvantage of the IRR method?
     iv. If Kay had not put a limit on the size of the capital budget, would the IRR method allow acceptance of all four alternatives? If not, which one(s) would be rejected and why?

e. i. According to the NPV method, which project should be chosen? How does this differ from the answer under the IRR?

ii. If Kay had not put a limit on the size of the capital budget, under the NPV method which projects would be accepted? Do the NPV and IRR both reject the same project(s)? Why?

iii. Given all the facts of the case, are you more likely to select project A or C?

f. i. According to the PI method, which project should be chosen?

ii. Does your answer conflict with the NPV method? Why? Which method suggests the best project?

MINI CASE

Galaxy Systems Inc.

As the three division managers of Galaxy Systems Inc. entered the central headquarters meeting room, each felt under pressure. They were there to meet with Marlene Davidson, the senior vice-president of finance.

Marlene, a CA who had spent seven years with KPMG before being recruited by Galaxy Systems, was a strong believer in implementing the latest techniques in corporate financial management.

She maintained that there should not be one figure for cost of capital that was uniformly applied throughout the corporation. Although the current figure of 12 percent was well documented, she intended to propose that different types of investments utilize different discount rates. Her first inclination was to suggest that the nature of the project be the controlling factor in determining the discount rate. The riskier the project, the higher the discount rate required. For example, repair to old machinery might carry a discount rate of 6 percent; a new product, 12 percent; and investments in foreign markets, 20 percent. This was a well-accepted method that she had used a number of times while on consulting assignments at KPMG.

When she discussed this approach with Joe Halstead, the CEO of Galaxy Systems, he said the risk-adjusted discount rate made a lot of sense to him. He went on to say that management as well as shareholders tended to be risk-averse, and therefore, higher-risk projects should meet tougher return standards.

However, in the case of Galaxy Systems, Joe suggested they consider a slightly different approach. He maintained that his company was made up of three distinctly different businesses and that each business should have its own imputed rate to be used as its discount rate.

The three divisions were (1) the airline parts manufacturing division, (2) the auto airbags production division, and (3) the aerospace division. The latter division built modern missile and control systems and jet fighter planes under contract with the U.S. Defense Department.

Joe maintained that each division had a risk dimension that was uniquely its own. He asked Marlene about a strategy to measure risk exposure for each division. She suggested that there were two major approaches to do this.

A. Find comparable public companies in the industry each division was in and look up their betas. The higher the average beta for a given industry, the more risk the comparable companies in that industry had. Divisions that were in industries with higher average betas have higher required rates of return.

B. A second approach would not rely on betas for comparable companies to the division, but rather would utilize internal data for that division. The more volatile the division's annual earnings were, relative to the company's annual earnings, the riskier the division and the higher the required rate of return.

The Meeting

CEO Joe Halstead liked these ideas and suggested that Marlene present them to the division managers. After the usual social patter following their arrival at central headquarters, Marlene laid her ideas on the table. At first, the division managers seemed somewhat shocked at her proposals. Marlene had not realized the extent that "empire building" had developed over the years. The three division managers clearly were apprehensive about what discount rate (sometimes referred to as a hurdle rate) would be assigned to their divisions.

The head of the airline parts manufacturing division argued against the use of the betas of publicly traded companies to determine risk. He said there were very few companies that were exclusively engaged in the manufacturing of airline parts. Most of his competitors were subsidiaries of other large companies such as McDonnell Douglas or Raytheon, which were involved in numerous activities. He argued that using the betas of such multi-industry firms and applying them to his division to determine risk would be unfair.

The head of the auto airbags production division had another concern. His three plants were all located in Ontario, and the province had tough environmental laws. About one out of every five investments in his division was mandatory under provincial law.

Finally, the head of the aerospace division said that risk should not be the key variable for determining the divisional discount rates. He suggested that the key consideration in determining the discount rate should be the perceived importance of the division to the corporation. He said, "Galaxy Systems was founded as an aerospace company and our future should be tied to our heritage." Approximately 40 percent of Galaxy Systems' revenues and earnings were currently tied to the aerospace division, and the other two divisions split the remainder of sales and income almost evenly (30/30).

The Initial Decision

After receiving the input from her boss and the three division heads, Marlene decided to go with the following system. The weighted average cost of capital of 12 percent for the entire corporation would be the starting point for the corporation.

The airline parts manufacturing division would continue to use 12 percent as its discount rate.

Because firms comparable to the auto airbags production division had an average beta of 0.8 and the division itself had less-variable earnings from year to year than the corporation, it would be assigned a discount rate of 10 percent.

The head of the aerospace division was displeased to be assigned a discount rate of 15 percent. Marlene justified the high hurdle rate on the basis of an average beta of 1.55 in the aerospace industry and the highly risky business of dealing with various governments. Contracts were based on politics, a hard risk to quantify.

The risk-free rate of return was currently 6 percent and the expected premium for market risk was 5.5 percent.

The CCA rate on all equipment required for the capital investments is 20 percent. The firm's tax rate is 40 percent.

Application of Divisional Hurdle Rates

The application of the new system got its first test when the auto airbags production division and the aerospace division simultaneously submitted four proposals.

Proposal A. The auto airbags production division submitted a proposal for a new airbag model that would cost $3,050,000 to develop. The anticipated revenue stream for the next 10 years was $720,000 per year.

Proposal B. The aerospace division proposed the development of new radar surveillance equipment. The anticipated cost was $3,100,000. The anticipated revenue stream for this project was $750,000 per year for the next 10 years.

Proposal C. This was a second proposal from the auto airbags production division. It called for special equipment to be used in the disposal of environmentally harmful waste material created in the manufacturing process. The equipment cost $225,000 and was expected to provide cost savings of $30,000 per year for 15 years.

Proposal D. This was a second proposal from the aerospace division. It called for the development of a new form of a microelectric control system that could be used for fighter jets that were still in the design stage at another aerospace company. If the other aerospace company was successful in the development of the fighter jets, they would be sold to underdeveloped countries in various sectors of the world. The cost to produce the microelectric control system was $1,700,000 and the best-guess estimate was that the investment would return $500,000 a year for the next eight years.

a.   Which proposals should be accepted or rejected? Use an appropriate divisional discount rate. Do you agree with the discount rates assigned by Marlene Davidson?

b.   What subjective elements might override or influence any of the answers determined by quantitative analysis?

c.   Assume the head of the aerospace division asked for a second review on the new radar surveillance equipment (proposal B). He maintains that the numbers presented in proposal B are correct, but he wants you, the analyst, to know that $300,000 has already been spent on the initial research on this project. (It's not included in the $3,100,000.) He suggests that this might influence your decision. What should be your response?

Risk and Capital Budgeting

LEARNING OBJECTIVES

LO1 Describe the concept of risk based on the uncertainty of future cash flows.

LO2 Characterize most investors as risk averse.

LO3 Analyze risk as standard deviation, coefficient of variation, or beta.

LO4 Integrate the basic methodology of risk-adjusted discount rates for dealing with risk in capital budgeting analysis.

LO5 Describe and apply the techniques of certainty equivalents, simulation models, sensitivity analysis, and decision trees to help assess risk.

LO6 Assess how a project's risk may be considered in a portfolio context.

No one area is more essential to financial decision making than the evaluation and management of risk. The price of a firm's stock is strongly influenced by the amount of risk investors perceive as inherent in the firm's operations. We are constantly trying to achieve the appropriate mix between profitability and risk to satisfy those with a stake in the affairs of the firm and to realize the goal of wealth maximization for shareholders.

Our valuation models are built on future expected cash flows and the rate at which we discount those expectations to the present. The discount rate is based on the market's perception of the risks inherent in those cash flows. In Chapter 12, we often used the cost of capital as the discount rate in our analysis, but it was based on the assumption that the project under consideration had the same risk as the firm. This was a strong assumption!

The difficulty is not in finding viable investment alternatives but in determining where we want to be on the risk-return scale. Would we prefer a 30 percent potential return on a new product in Russia or a safe 8 percent return on an extension of our current product line in our home territory? The question can be answered only in terms of profitability, the risk position of the firm, and the disposition toward risk of both management and shareholders. In this chapter, we examine additional definitions of *risk*, its measurement, its incorporation into the *capital budgeting* process, and the basic tenets of portfolio theory.

RISK IN VALUATION

As we consider risk our focus should be on these questions:

- How do we characterize risk?
  - Uncertainty, not fixed
  - Variation and standard deviation
- How do we reduce risk?
  - Hedging, knowledge, insurance, derivatives, diversification
- Can we compose a relationship between risk and return?
  - Beta from the capital asset pricing model (CAPM)

LO1 Risk suggests the chance of peril or of loss, but here may also be the possibility of great gain. With greater loss or gain comes greater risk. Risk may be defined in terms of the variability of possible outcomes from a given investment. A Government of Canada Treasury bill is relatively certain and there is no variability—hence, there is no risk. On the other hand, a gold-mining expedition in the deepest wilds of Borneo suggests a great variability of possible outcomes and this project would be quite risky. There is considerable uncertainty.[1]

In Figure 13–1, three investments have different possible outcomes, each centred on the same value ($20,000). When we evaluate cash flows that are expected in the future, they represent an average of several possibilities. When using evaluation techniques, such as those used in Chapter 12 which consider expected values, we may miss this important information.

---

[1] We use the term *uncertainty* in its normal sense, rather than in the more formalized sense in which it is sometimes used in decision theory to indicate that insufficient evidence is available to estimate a probability distribution.

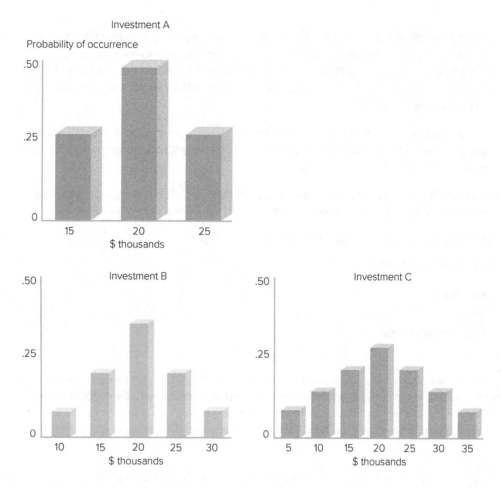

Figure 13–1 Variability and risk

The Risky Skies and Beyond

In early 1996, WestJet Airlines Ltd., with equity invested by successful Albertan oil and gas entrepreneurs and the Ontario Teachers' Pension Plan Board, became a western-based Canadian discount airline. This was despite evidence that in the United States and Canada nine out of ten cut-rate airlines failed.

Southwest Airlines of the United States was the model for success that WestJet would follow, achieving a profit for over 25 years by keeping operating costs well below the major carriers and by increasing passenger traffic on carefully selected short-haul routes.

WestJet has been a success since its beginning, but several airlines have failed since including Canada 3000, Roots Air, Jetsgo, Harmony Airlines, Zoom Airlines, and Canjet.

WestJet began by purchasing three 22-year-old Boeing 737s for $15 million and flying to five destinations. In 1999 it had sold shares to the public at a price of $2.96 (adjusted for three 3-for-2 stock splits since). By 2019, WestJet operated 180 planes, with plans to expand to about 193 by 2027. Besides flying to numerous sites across North America, by 2020 WestJet flew to 110 destinations worldwide. It had introduced Swoop, an ultra low-cost carrier, as its other operations expanded.

In our example, each investment is expected to return $20,000, as this is the average of the possible outcomes. Note, however, that as we move from Investment A to Investment C, the dispersion of possible outcomes widens, or the variability (risk) increases. Because you may gain or lose the most in Investment C, it is considered the riskiest of the three. Therefore, the greater the dispersion, the greater the risk.

LO2 THE CONCEPT OF RISK AVERSION

A basic assumption in financial theory is that most investors and managers are risk averse—that is, for a given situation they would prefer relative certainty to uncertainty. They wish to avoid risk. In Figure 13–1, therefore, they would prefer Investment A over Investments B and C, despite the fact that all three investments have the same expected value of $20,000. You are probably risk averse too. Assume you have saved $3,000 for your last year in college and are challenged to flip a coin, double or nothing. Heads, you end up with $6,000; tails, you are broke. You would probably stay with your certain $3,000.

This is not to say that investors or businesspeople are unwilling to take risks, but rather that they require a higher expected value, or return, for risky investments. In Figure 13–2, we compare a low-risk proposal with an expected value of $20,000 to a high-risk proposal with an expected value of $30,000. The higher-risk project exhibits a greater dispersion of returns. The higher expected return may well compensate investors for absorbing greater risk.

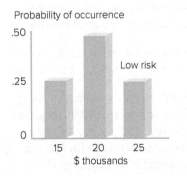
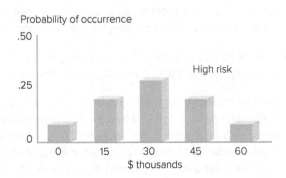

Figure 13–2 Risk-return trade-off

LO3 ACTUAL MEASUREMENT OF RISK

A number of basic statistical devices may be employed to measure the extent of risk inherent in any given situation. Assume we are examining an investment with the probability of possible outcomes shown in Table 13–1.

Table 13–1 Probability distribution of outcomes

Outcome	Probability of Outcome	Assumptions
$300	.2	Pessimistic
600	.6	Moderately successful
900	.2	Optimistic

Probabilities such as those in this table are generally based on some combination of past experience, industry ratios and trends, interviews with company executives, and sophisticated simulation techniques. The probability values may be easy to estimate for the introduction of a mechanical stamping process for which the manufacturer has 10 years of past data, but they are difficult to assess for a new product in a foreign market. In forecasted results for capital projects, new products tend to realize significantly less than the forecasted returns, sales expansion projects realize most of what is forecasted, and cost reduction projects tend to realize more than their forecasted returns. Because of the difficulty of estimating future results, it is important to analyze carefully the range and probability of possible outcomes.

With the data before us, we compute two important statistical measures—the expected value and the standard deviation. The expected value is a weighted average of the outcomes times their probabilities.

$$\overline{D}(\text{expected value}) = \sum DP \quad \text{(13–1)}$$

$$
\begin{array}{ccc}
D & P & DP \\
300 \times 0.2 = & & \$\ 60 \\
600 \times 0.6 = & & 360 \\
900 \times 0.2 = & & 180 \\
\hline
& & \$600 = \sum DP
\end{array}
$$

The expected value is $600. We then compute the standard deviation—the measure of dispersion, or variability, around the expected value. The formula for the standard deviation is quite simple:

$$\sigma(\text{standard deviation}) = \sqrt{\sum (D - \overline{D})^2 P} \quad \text{(13–2)}$$

These steps should be followed:

Step 1: Subtract the expected value ($\overline{D}$) from each outcome $(D)\,(D - \overline{D})$			Step 2: Square	Step 3: Multiply by P and sum		Step 4: Determine the square root
D	$\overline{D}$	$(D - \overline{D})$	$(D - \overline{D})^2$	P	$(D - \overline{D})^2 P$	
300	$-\ 600 =$	$-\ 300$	90,000	$\times\ 0.20 =$	18,000	
600	$-\ 600 =$	0	0	$\times\ 0.60 =$	0	
900	$-\ 600 =$	300	90,000	$\times\ 0.20 =$	18,000	
					36,000	$\sqrt{36,000} = \$190$

The standard deviation of $190 gives us a rough average measure of how far each of the three estimated possible outcomes falls away from the expected value. Generally, the larger the standard

Bankers: Are They Risk Averse?

Risk and its management are a major preoccupation for bankers. They do not like uncertainty and try to "hedge" or protect themselves against losses. However, we sometimes see banks experience huge losses, despite their careful lending practices. In 2008, we saw large bank failures and government bailouts to prevent other bank failures. Since the financial recession of 2008–09, heavier regulation requirements have been placed upon financial institutions.

How do bankers deal with risk in a world of increasing volatility and competition brought on by the deregulation of the financial markets? In the past, bankers learned to deal with liquidity risk (not having enough cash on hand) and credit risk (the chance that a borrower might experience cash flow problems) within rules set in the 1930s. To deal with liquidity risk, lines of credit were established with central banks and with other commercial banks. By diversifying their loans, not lending too much to one borrower, and matching the maturities of their loans and deposits (hedging), the banks dealt with credit risk.

However, by the 1970s new risks appeared. The banks had begun to do a significant amount of their business outside Canada, and the world had entered an era of floating exchange rates. With inflation and market shocks such as the oil crisis, exchange rates fluctuated dramatically, exposing the banks and their clients to large risks. To deal with the exchange rate volatility, the banks developed forward markets in which exchange rates could be set in advance.

In the 1980s, the markets had become increasingly sophisticated and interrelated. Disintermediation occurred as large corporate clients moved funds to the wholesale markets to find better returns. As loans and deposits became mismatched, banks began the "securitization" of their assets. This allowed the banks to sell loans that no longer fit appropriately within their portfolio.

To reduce other risks, the banks also entered the derivative markets that had developed to pre-fix the prices on such items as interest, exchange rates, and credit risk. Today this is a huge market as reported by the Bank for International Settlements (bis.org).

The bank failures and bailouts of 2008 resulted from and exacerbated a liquidity crisis. Investors lost faith in our economic structures and a global recession resulted. Financial institutions had lost sight of due diligence in advancing loans toward mortgage-backed securities and other credit-related derivatives that even the bankers did not understand well. Furthermore, banks became over-leveraged (loans to capital base) so that losses significantly reduced the bank's equity, putting the whole enterprise in jeopardy (see Chapter 5).

By 2020 banks were concerned with compliance issues brought into play after 2008. These new regulations, higher capital requirements, risks in their IT systems, the separation of functions, and the quality of their assets hindered their ability to compete globally, while they are regulated locally, to a large extent. For banks there is a trade-off between control and flexibility.

Q1 Why would disintermediation increase risk to investors?

Q1 What is the size of the derivatives market?

bis.org

deviation (or spread of possible outcomes), the greater the risk, as indicated in Figure 13–3, where we compare the standard deviation of three investments with the same expected value of $600. However, the dispersion of possible outcomes is different for each investment. The investment with the greater standard deviation would be considered the riskiest.

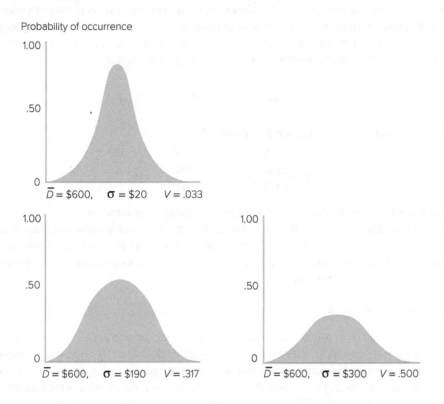

Figure 13–3 Probability distribution with differing degrees of risk

If the expected values of the investments were quite different (such as $600 versus $6,000), a direct comparison of the standard deviations for each distribution would not be very helpful in measuring risk. This is because standard deviation is measured in the same scale as the expected value for each investment. The same standard deviation is much more significant on $600 than on $6,000. Figure 13–4 shows this comparison.

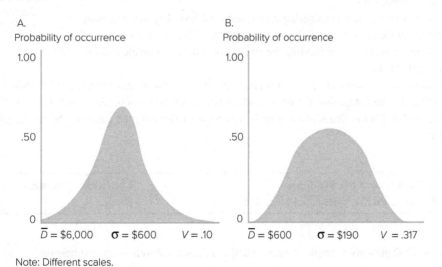

Note: Different scales.

Figure 13–4 Relationship of risk to discount rate

Note that the investment in panel A of Figure 13–4 appears to have a high standard deviation—but not when related to the expected value of the distribution. A standard deviation of $600 on an investment with an expected value of $6,000 may indicate less risk than a standard deviation of $190 on an investment with an expected value of only $600.

We can eliminate the size difficulty by developing a third measure, the coefficient of variation (V), which allows for a comparable scale across different investments. This rather imposing term calls for nothing more difficult than dividing the standard deviation of an investment by the expected value. Generally, the larger the coefficient of variation, the greater the risk.

$$\text{Coefficient of variation } (V) = \frac{\sigma}{D} \quad \text{(13–3)}$$

For the investments in panels A and B of Figure 13–4, we show

$$\begin{array}{cc} \textbf{A} & \textbf{B} \\ V = \dfrac{600}{6,000} = 0.10 & V = \dfrac{190}{600} = 0.317 \end{array}$$

We have correctly identified the second investment as carrying the greater risk.

The standard deviation and coefficient of variation of an investment measure its unique risk—that is, the risk of the investment based only on its possible outcomes. However, an investment is not usually undertaken in isolation, and it may be worth considering its interrelationships with the possible outcomes of other investments.

Risk in a Portfolio

Beta (β), as discussed in Appendix 11A, is developed in the context of portfolios of common stock in which there is significant diversification. A regression line (formula 11A–1) $K_j = \alpha + \beta Rm + e$ suggests the relationship between an individual stock's return and the market return. In a portfolio of stocks, the error terms (e) are diversified away, leaving beta (β). Beta measures the volatility of returns on an individual stock relative to a stock market index of returns (covariance of stock with market/variance of market), such as the Toronto Stock Exchange (S&P/TSX Composite) stock index.[2]

Historically, stock market indexes, such as the S&P/TSX Composite, which are representative of the market portfolio, achieve annual returns in the range of 5 to 7 percent above the risk-free rate of return over the long term. These returns are compensation for the greater volatility or risk experienced from day to day from these investments.

Toronto Stock
Exchange
tmx.com

Beta may be useful in considering investments and how they relate to other investments of the firm, particularly in the context of a diversified collection of assets. In this context, we are limiting the concept of risk to systematic risk or market-related risk.

A common stock with a beta of 1.0 is said to be of equal risk with the market. Stocks with betas greater than 1.0 are riskier than the market, whereas stocks with betas of less than 1.0 are less risky than the market. For the financial manager it is important to identify the nature of the risk faced by the firm.

Total risk (unique risk significant)	→	Coefficient of variation
Market-related risk (systematic) when diversified	→	Beta

Table 13–2 presents a sample of betas calculated for several well-known companies.

---

[2] Other market measures may also be utilized.

Table 13–2 Betas, January 2020

Company Name	Beta
BlackBerry (BB)	1.35
Bombardier (BBD.B)	2.06
Canadian Tire (CTC)	0.36
Canopy (WEED)	3.77
Nutrien (NTR)	0.95
Power Corp. (POW)	0.97
Royal Bank (RY)	1.03
Teck (TECK.B)	2.32
Telus (T)	0.60

*Betas for several Canadian companies are available at a couple of websites. Update the above betas. Why have the betas changed and why are they not the same at each site?
†Check out the Stern site for industry betas (thanks to Aswath Damodaran).

Earlier, we developed other measures that helped gauge the risk that firms experience in their operations. They may not be as sophisticated as standard deviation or beta, but they provide a measure of risk. These measures included

- Debt utilization and liquidity ratios (Chapter 3)
- Operating and financial leverage (Chapter 5)
- Payback period (Chapter 12)

RISK AND THE CAPITAL BUDGETING PROCESS

How can risk analysis be used effectively in the capital budgeting process? In Chapter 12 we made no explicit distinction between risky and nonrisky events.[3] We showed the amount of the investment and the annual returns—making no comment about the riskiness or likelihood of achieving these returns. We know that enlightened investors and managers need further information. A $1,400 investment that produces certain returns of $600 a year for three years is not the same as a $1,400 investment that produces returns with an expected value of $600 for three years but has a high coefficient of variation. Investors, being risk averse by nature, apply a stiffer test to the second investment.

Remember that the capital budgeting process involves estimating future cash flows and that each estimate of those cash flows is the average of many possibilities. The more dispersed those possibilities, the greater the risk of the investment proposal. Our task is to consider the risk in our capital budgeting analysis. Many techniques have been developed to assist in gaining a better appreciation and understanding of the risks inherent in investment projects available to the firm. We now describe briefly some of these techniques.

LO4 Risk-adjusted Discount Rate

A favoured approach to adjusting for risk is to use different risk-adjusted discount rates for proposals with different risk levels. A project that carries a normal amount of risk and does not change the overall risk composure of the firm should be discounted at the firm's cost of capital. Investments

---

[3] Our assumption was that the risk factor could be considered constant for various investments.

carrying greater than normal risk should be discounted at a higher rate, and so on. Figure 13–5 shows a possible risk/discount rate trade-off scheme. In that figure, risk is measured by the coefficient of variation (V). Higher discount rates will make future expected cash flows worth less today, but of course, that is generally how we value riskier cash flows.

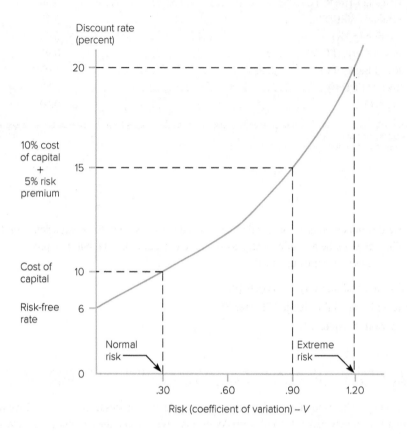

Figure 13–5 Relationship of risk to discount rate

In Figure 13–5, the normal risk for the firm is represented by a coefficient of variation of 0.30. An investment with this risk would be discounted at the firm's normal cost of capital of 10 percent. As the firm selects riskier projects with, for example, a V of 0.90, a risk premium of 5 percent is added for this increase in V of 0.60, from 0.30 to 0.90. If the company selects a project with a coefficient of variation of 1.20, it adds another 5 percent risk premium for this additional V of 0.30, from 0.90 to 1.20. Notice that the same risk premium of 5 percent was added for a smaller increase in risk. This is an example of being increasingly risk averse at higher levels of risk and potential return.

Another method for adjusting the discount rate to account for differing risk is to use the capital asset pricing model. By identifying the beta of a particular proposal and with knowledge of the capital markets, we can determine the required return on the proposal given its risk. There are difficulties with the model, but it does provide a framework for adjusting discount rates based on risk.

Increasing Risk over Time

Our ability to forecast accurately diminishes as we forecast further in time. As the time horizon becomes longer, more uncertainty enters the forecast.

Syncrude (discussed in the "Continual Capital Budgeting" Finance in Action box in Chapter 12) has been a Canadian success story while adapting to widely fluctuating forecasts in oil prices. In 1972, the price of oil was below US$2 a barrel, but with the formation of OPEC prices rapidly increased to above $10 a barrel. Syncrude, one year later, began billions of dollars of capital construction and by the end of the decade, as prices approached $36 a barrel, produced its first barrel of oil. At the time, predictions were for oil to reach $100 a barrel within a few years, but by 1986 the price had dropped back to just over $10 a barrel. By 2008, oil prices exceeded $140 a barrel, but within a very short time they were under $40. In 2014, oil prices were again above $100 per barrel and below $50 per barrel in 2020.

Syncrude
syncrude.ca

These unexpected events create a higher standard deviation in cash flow estimates and increase the risk associated with long-lived projects. Figure 13–6 depicts the relationship between risk and time.

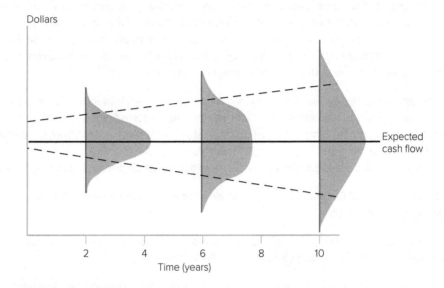

Figure 13–6 Risk over time

Even though a forecast of cash flows shows a constant expected value, Figure 13–6 shows that the range of outcomes and probabilities increases as we move from Year 2 to Year 10. The standard deviations increase for each forecast of cash flow. If cash flows were forecast as easily for each period, all distributions would look like the first one for Year 2. However, as later expected cash flows are more uncertain and exhibit increasing standard deviations, there is greater risk in the longer-term cash flows forecasts than in the near-term forecasts.

Both the time value of money and risk are included in a risk-adjusted discount rate. The nature of discounting as a compounding process is such that cash flows further out in time do bear greater risk. This is consistent with the notion that later cash flows should bear more risk. However, it could be suggested that risk lessens as a project continues because the firm has become more knowledgeable about its operation and the cash flows are more predictable. Certainty equivalents and decision trees help us to address this consideration.

 FINANCE IN ACTION

Financial Crisis 2008, U.S. Government Default 2011, Crimea Conflict 2014, and Brexit 2020: How Do You Get a Risk Reading?

Risk was re-priced in the financial markets in 2008. Major concerns with exotic derivatives, subprime mortgages, excessive debt, lax regulatory standards, transparency (information openness), and handsome salaries to financial executives who did not seem to bear downside risk, all contributed to a crisis of confidence in the markets, a tightening of credit, and institutional failure. In 2011, risk was re-priced again as default on debt obligations by the U.S. Government became a possibility. The continuing Brexit developments have caused instability in the financial markets. How does one read the risks developing or measure risks around the world?

How might we determine a risk-adjusted discount rate for evaluating an investment in Russia? Russia has abundant natural resources (oil and gold) and a well-educated population (98% literacy rate), but has high inflation, erratic GDP growth, and extremely an volatile stock market, and close to nonexistent shareholders' rights. S&P's ratings (standardandpoors.com/home/en/us) (categories) for sovereign debt might help us to establish a discount rate.

The yield spread (difference) between government securities and commercial bank yields or other corporate yields can reveal the market's perceptions of risk. In Canada, the spread between 1-month Treasury bills and prime corporate paper is usually in the 20- to 30-basis-point range (100 basis points equal 1%). In 2008, it jumped well above 100 basis points as identified at the Bank of Canada (bankofcanada.ca).

Another differential closely watched is the yield spread between 3-month U.S. Treasury bills (treasury.gov/resource-center/data-chart-center/interest-rates/Pages/TextView.aspx?data=yield) and the 3-month LIBOR (global-rates.com/interest-rates/libor/libor.aspx). In 2008, this spread jumped from about 30 basis points to well over 300 basis points. One can also observe this spread at the Bloomberg site (bloomberg.com/markets/rates-bonds).

The Chicago Board of Options Exchange has developed a volatility index (VIX) based on risk at the NYSE (cboe.com).

Aswath Damodaran at NYU provides risk premiums for countries around the world. (pages.stern.nyu.edu/~adamodar/New_Home_Page/data.html).

Q1 How does Russia's credit rating compare to Argentina's? To India's? To Mexico's? And what are their risk premiums as reported at Damodaran's NYU site?

Q2 Track the Canadian 1-month T-bill rate to the 1-month prime corporate paper rate over two years. How has the spread narrowed or widened? Why?

Qualitative Measures

Rather than relate the discount rate—or required return—to the coefficient of variation or the beta, management may wish to set up risk classes based on qualitative considerations. Examples are presented in Table 13–3. Once again we are assigning the discount rate according to the perceived risk.[4]

Table 13–3 Probability distribution of outcomes

	Discount Rate
Low or no risk (repair to old machinery).................	6%
Moderate risk (new equipment).........................	8
Normal risk (addition to normal product line)...............	10
Risky (new product in related market)....................	12
High risk (completely new market)......................	16
Highest risk (new product in foreign market)..............	20

---

[4] Throughout all of this, note the difficulty implied for managers trying to gain approval for "new" ideas with long development time horizons. Considering Canada's relatively inferior position with respect to most new technologies, its relatively high manufacturing costs, its need to depend on selling into foreign markets, and the purported risk-averseness of the Canadian people, you have the very definition of a serious impediment to investment for the long-term development of the Canadian industrial economy.

Example—Risk-adjusted Discount Rate In Chapter 12 we compared two $10,000 investment alternatives and indicated that each had a positive net present value (at a 10 percent cost of capital). That analysis is reproduced in Table 13–4.

Table 13–4 Capital budgeting analysis

Year	Investment A (10% discount rate)		Year	Investment B (10% discount rate)	
1	$5,000	$ 4,545	1	$1,500	$ 1,364
2	5,000	4,132	2	2,000	1,653
3	2,000	1,503	3	2,500	1,878
		$10,180	4	5,000	3,415
			5	5,000	3,105
					$11,415
Present value of inflows.....		$10,180	Present value of inflows.....		$11,415
Investment		10,000	Investment		10,000
Net present value		$ 180	Net present value		$ 1,415

Though both proposals are acceptable, if they were mutually exclusive, only Investment B would be undertaken. But what if we add a risk dimension to the problem? Assume Investment A calls for an addition to the normal product line and is assigned a discount rate of 10 percent. Further, assume Investment B represents a new product in a foreign market and must carry a 20 percent discount rate to adjust for the large risk component. This risk adjustment by way of the discount rate as suggested in Table 13–3 accounts for the greater uncertainty in the estimated cash flows for project B. As indicated in Table 13–5, our answers are reversed; Investment A is now the only acceptable alternative.

Table 13–5 Capital budgeting decision adjusted for risk

Year	Investment A (10% discount rate)		Year	Greater Risk Investment B (20% discount rate)	
1	$5,000	$ 4,545	1	$1,500	$ 1,250
2	5,000	4,132	2	2,000	1,389
3	2,000	1,503	3	2,500	1,447
		$10,180	4	5,000	2,411
			5	5,000	2,009
					$ 8,506
Present value of inflows.....		$10,180	Present value of inflows.....		$ 8,506
Investment		10,000	Investment		10,000
Net present value		$ 180	Net present value		$ (1,494)

Other methods besides the risk-adjusted discount rate are also used to evaluate risk in the capital budgeting process. The spectrum runs from a seat-of-the-pants executive preference approach to sophisticated computer-based statistical analysis. All methods, however, include a common approach—they must recognize the riskiness of a given investment proposal and make an appropriate adjustment for risk.

LO5 CERTAINTY EQUIVALENTS

The certainty equivalent approach adjusts each cash flow according to its probability distribution to a value that is equal on the basis of having no inherent risk and is, therefore, certain. In effect, a decision maker would be indifferent between choosing the risky cash flow and the certain cash flow. The certain cash flows would be smaller because of the risk aversion of individuals. These adjusted cash flows would then be discounted at the risk-free discount rate or, effectively, on the basis of the time value of money alone.

In practice, the expected value for a given year is multiplied by a percentage figure indicating the degree of certainty and then translated back to the present at a risk-free discount rate (less than the cost of capital). Items with a high degree of certainty might be multiplied by 100 percent, less certain items by 75 percent, and so on down the scale. This approach is difficult to apply, because it calls for certainty equivalents for each distribution of possible outcomes and depends on the individual decision maker's attitude toward risk.

For example, we might establish that the final decision maker for the firm values uncertain cash flows in the following manner:

Year of Uncertain Cash Flow	Value as Certain Cash Flow
1	85%
2	80%
3	65%

The company's cost of capital is 13 percent, and the risk-free rate of return is 5 percent. A proposal costing $1,100 has the following pattern of cash flows and certainty equivalents:

Year	Cash Flow	Certainty Equivalent	
1	$ 500	$ 425	(500 × 85%)
2	600	480	(600 × 80%)
3	800	520	(800 × 65%)

The net present value (NPV) of this proposal using certainty equivalents and the risk-free rate (5 percent) for discount purposes is $189.

Year	Certainty Equivalent	Present Value
0	− $1,100	− $1,100
1	425	405
2	480	435
3	520	449
		NPV = $189

Risk has been considered and a positive NPV has been achieved, so this would be an acceptable proposal.

COMPUTER SIMULATION MODELS

Computers make it possible to simulate various economic and financial outcomes using a large number of variables. Thus, simulation is one way of dealing with the uncertainty involved in forecasting the outcomes of capital budgeting projects or other types of decisions. A Monte Carlo simulation model uses random variables for inputs. By programming the computer to randomly select inputs from probability distributions, the outcomes generated by a simulation are distributed about a mean; thus, instead of generating one return or net present value, a range of outcomes with standard deviations is provided. A simulation model relies on repetition of the same random process as many as several hundred times. Because the inputs are representative of what one might encounter in the real world, many possible combinations of returns are generated.

One of the benefits of simulation is its ability to test various possible combinations of events. This sensitivity testing allows the planner to ask "what if" questions, such as What will happen to the returns on this project if oil prices go up? Go down? What effect will a 5 percent increase in interest rates have on the net present value of this project? The analyst can use the simulation process to test possible changes in economic policy, sales levels, inflation, or any other variable included in the modelling process. Some simulation models are driven by sales forecasts with assumptions to derive income statements and balance sheets. Others generate probability acceptance curves for capital budgeting decisions by informing the analyst about the probabilities of having a positive net present value.

Crystal Ball software
oracle.com/us/products/
applications/crystalball/

For example, each distribution in Figure 13–7 would have a value picked randomly and used for one simulation. The simulation would be run many times, each time selecting a new random variable to generate the final probability distribution for the net present value (at the bottom). For that probability distribution, the expected values are on the horizontal axis and the probability of occurrence is plotted on the vertical axis. The outcomes also indicate something about the riskiness of the project, which is indicated by the overall dispersion.

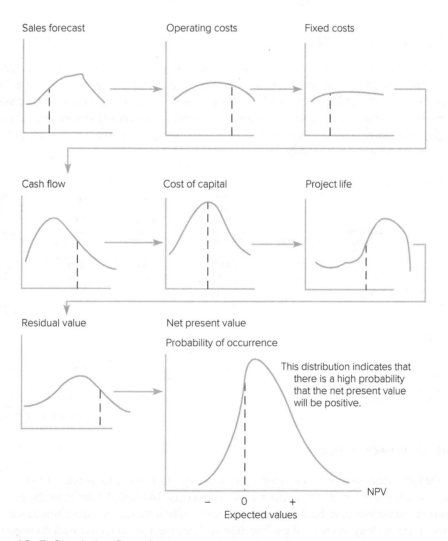

Figure 13–7 Simulation flow chart

SENSITIVITY ANALYSIS

Another method for employing the power of the computer is known as sensitivity analysis. However, it is not as complex, nor as expensive, as the Monte Carlo simulation. Sensitivity analysis sets up the project analysis with the methodology developed in Chapter 12, but with the intent of changing one variable at a time. The resulting impact on the NPV of the project and, ultimately, our decision is observed. We thus determine the variables to which the project's success is sensitive. Identifying these variables may suggest further research to more closely define their expected values. Through sensitivity analysis we can observe the different results possible if the project is implemented.

Sensitivity analysis is not without its problems. Variables generally do not change in isolation but tend to be related. For example, if the discount rate decreases, it likely reflects lower inflation rates, and lower inflation rates would likely affect our cash flow projections. We have to be careful with the results when one variable at a time is changed without considering the impact on the other variables in the analysis.

Also, sensitivity analysis determines only the impact a variation in a particular variable will have on the project. It does not identify the probability of that variation. We do not truly identify risk in sensitivity analysis. We might conclude that an adverse result rules out accepting a project, even though the probability of that result is quite small. It is, therefore, important that we consider the probabilities of variations in the key variables. With the aid of computers, one also must be careful to plan the output of sensitivity analysis, because it is easy to generate lots of meaningless paper.

DECISION TREES

Decision trees lay out the sequence of decisions that can be made and present a tabular or graphical comparison that resembles the branches of a tree and highlights the differences between investment choices. Figure 13–8 examines a semiconductor firm's consideration of two choices: (A) expanding the production of semiconductors for sale to computer manufacturers, or (B) forward integrating into the highly competitive home computer market. The cost of both projects would be the same, $60 million, but the NPV and risk are different.

	(1) Expected Sales	(2) Probability	(3) Present Value of Cash Flow from Sales ($ millions)	(4) Initial Cost ($ millions)	(5) NPV (3) − (4) ($ millions)	(6) Expected NPV (2) × (5) ($ millions)
Expand semiconductor capacity	High	.50	$100	$60	$40	$20.00
	Moderate	.25	75	60	15	3.75
	Low	.25	40	60	(20)	(5.00)
A						Expected NPV = $18.75
Start						
B						
Enter home computer market	High	.20	$200	$60	$140	$28.00
	Moderate	.50	75	60	15	7.50
	Low	.30	25	60	(35)	(10.50)
						Expected NPV = $25.00

Figure 13–8 Decision trees

If the firm expanded its semiconductor capacity (project A), it would be assured of some demand, so a high likelihood of a positive rate of return exists. The market demand for these products is volatile over time, but long-run growth seems to be a reasonable expectation as the emphasis on technology increases. If the firm expanded into the home computer market (project B), it would face stiff competition from many existing firms. It stands to lose more money under low expected sales conditions than under option A, but it will make more under high expected sales conditions. Even though project B has a higher expected NPV than project A, its extra risk makes for a difficult choice. Clearly, more analysis would have to be done before management made the final choice between these two projects. Nevertheless, the decision tree has identified critical areas where managerial judgment must be exercised.

LO6 THE PORTFOLIO EFFECT

Up to this point we have examined the risk in individual investments by measuring standard deviation and the coefficient of variation for the expected benefits. However, we should consider the impact of a given investment on the overall risk of the firm—the portfolio effect.[5]

For example, we might undertake a particular investment in the consumer products industry that appears to carry a high degree of risk, but if our primary business is the manufacture of electronic components for industrial use, that investment may actually diminish the overall risk exposure of the firm. This may occur because electronic component sales generally expand when the economy does well and falter in a recession. The consumer products industry often reacts in the opposite fashion—performing poorly in boom periods and reacting well relative to other industries in recessionary periods. By investing in the consumer products industry, an electronic components manufacturer could actually smooth out the cyclical fluctuations inherent in its business and reduce overall risk exposure.

Harry Markowitz
nobelprize.org/
search/?s=markowitz

As is indicated in Figure 13–9, the risk reduction phenomenon is demonstrated by a less dispersed probability distribution. We say that the standard deviation for the entire company (the portfolio of investments) has been reduced.

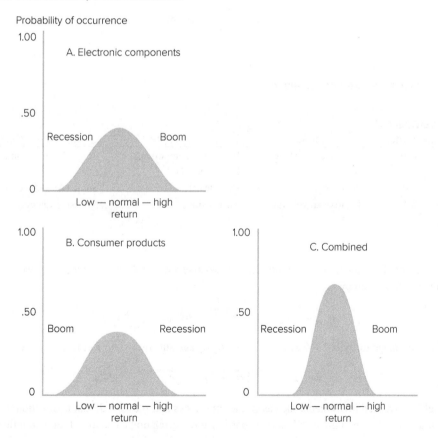

Figure 13–9 Portfolio considerations in evaluating risk

---

[5]Here the portfolio of investments refers to plant, equipment, new products, and so forth, rather than stocks and bonds.

Portfolio Risk

When two or more investments (A and B) are put together, they form a portfolio, and we are interested in the portfolio's return (expected value) and its risk (standard deviation). Whether a given investment changes the overall risk of the firm depends on its relationships to other investments. The expected value calculation is a straightforward weighted average:

$$\overline{D}_p = \sum x_i \overline{D}_i \quad \text{(13–4)}$$

Where

$$x_i = \% \text{ weighting in the portfolio of each investment}$$
$$\overline{D}_i = \text{Expected value of each investment}$$

Standard deviation for a portfolio is somewhat more complicated, as it requires the variance of the individual investments and their relationship with each other, based on their expected pattern of cash flows over time. This relationship of how two investments move together is measured by covariance.

$$\text{Cov}_{AB} = \sum P(D - \overline{D}_i)(F - \overline{F}_i) \quad \text{(13–5)}$$

D and F represent the range of expected outcomes for the investments.

Covariance is brought to a standardized scale known as the coefficient of correlation when divided by the standard deviations of the two investments. Do not confuse the coefficient of correlation with the coefficient of variation. The coefficient of correlation will range from -1 to $+1$. Examples are presented in Table 13–6. The formula is

$$\rho_{AB} = \frac{\text{Cov}_{AB}}{\sigma_A \sigma_B} \quad \text{(13–6)}$$

Table 13–6 Measures of correlation

Coefficient of Correlation	Condition	Example	Impact on Risk
-1	Negative correlation	Electronic components, food products	Large risk reduction
0	No correlation	Beer, textiles	Some risk reduction
$+1$	Positive correlation	Two airlines	No risk reduction

The standard deviation of a portfolio (AB) of two assets requires two variances and two covariances. It is given by

$$\sigma_{AB} = \sqrt{x_A^2 \sigma_A^2 + x_B^2 \sigma_B^2 + 2\,\text{Cov}_{AB}\,x_A x_B} \quad \text{(13–7)}$$

If we rearrange formula 13–6 as $\text{Cov}_{AB} = \rho_{AB}\,\sigma_A\,\sigma_B$ and substitute into formula 13–7, we get

$$\sigma_{AB} = \sqrt{x_A^2 \sigma_A^2 + x_B^2 \sigma_B^2 + 2\rho_{AB}\,\sigma_A \sigma_B\,x_A x_B} \quad \text{(13–8)}$$

Highly correlated investments such as two airline stocks that move in the same direction in good times as well as bad times will have a coefficient of correlation close to $+1$, and do little or nothing to diversify away risk. Projects moving in opposite directions, such as consumer products and electronic components, will likely be negatively correlated with a coefficient of correlation approaching -1, and provide a high degree of risk reduction. Examining formula 13–8 reveals that a reduced correlation coefficient, particularly a negative value, will lower the standard deviation of the portfolio. This is how risk reduction occurs.

Projects that are totally uncorrelated provide some overall reduction in portfolio risk, though not as much as negatively correlated investments. For example, if a beer manufacturer purchases a textile firm, the projects are neither positively nor negatively correlated, but the purchase reduces the overall risk of the firm simply through the law of large numbers. If you have enough unrelated projects going on at one time, good and bad events will probably even out.

We observe that as we add investments to a portfolio the risk of the portfolio or its standard deviation calculation becomes more complex. With three investments, there are three variance terms and six covariance terms; with four investments, there are four variances and 12 covariances; and so on. Two important conclusions come out of this portfolio work:

- Covariance becomes more significant in a portfolio than variance.
  - An individual investment might be quite risky itself, but it may reduce a portfolio's risk (standard deviation) if it has a negative coefficient of correlation with the other investments.
- In a portfolio with less than perfectly correlated investments, risk is reduced.

  - Unsystematic or unique risk is eliminated (to a large extent).
  - Systematic risk thus properly describes the risk-return relationship (leading to the CAPM).
  - Investors will price assets on systematic risk if diversification can be achieved.

 FINANCE IN ACTION

Diversification: Go by Country or by Corporation

In the last number of years, Canadian investors have increasingly sought to diversify their stock holdings by investing abroad. Decreased restrictions on our ability to invest overseas and a growing awareness that we can improve our returns by investing outside Canada have led to this trend. Canada represents only about 2 percent of the world's capital markets.

International diversification has meant including investments in various countries around the globe whose economies are not highly correlated. However, as the world becomes increasingly integrated we are observing that the global economy is increasingly correlated. In other words, countries tend to move through expansions and recessions together; therefore, less diversification occurs. One only has to look at Europe. At one time it was important to diversify across several currencies; however, some of those currencies no longer exist.

Instead, we may be able to achieve effective diversification by investing in globally based companies such as Microsoft or Nokia that have already achieved international diversification. We can then supplement our portfolios with companies that are subject to unique local events. We could think of entertainment and travel companies, or utilities subject to local deregulation activities.

Regardless of our choice, as the world becomes increasingly integrated through trading patterns and cultural "sameness," it will become harder to find investments that can effectively diversify risk.

An Example of Portfolio Risk Reduction

In the real world, very few investment combinations take on values as extreme as -1 or $+1$ or, for that matter, exactly 0. The more likely case is a point somewhere in between, such as $-.2$ negative correlation or $+.3$ positive correlation, as indicated along the continuum in Figure 13–10.

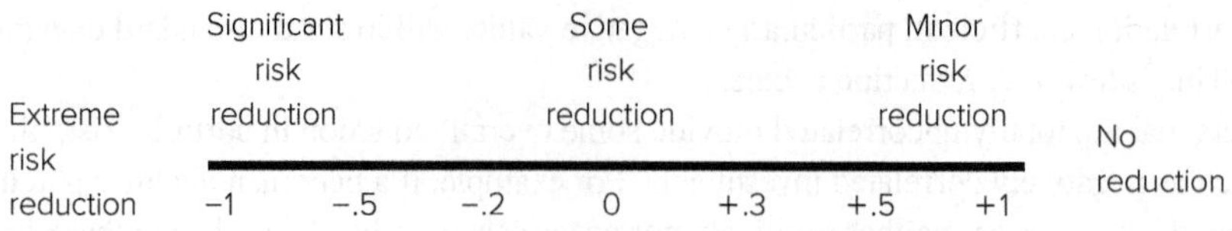

	Significant risk reduction		Some risk reduction		Minor risk reduction		
Extreme risk reduction							No reduction	
	−1	−.5	−.2	0	+.3	+.5	+1	

Figure 13–10 Levels of risk reduction as measured by the coefficient of correlation

The fact that risk can be reduced by combining risky assets with low or negatively correlated assets can be seen by the example of Conglomerate Inc. Conglomerate has fairly average returns and standard deviations of returns. The company is considering the purchase of two separate but large companies with sales and assets equal to its own. Management is struggling with the decision, since both companies have a 14 percent rate of return, which is 2 percent higher than that of Conglomerate, and they have the same standard deviation of returns as that of Conglomerate, at 2.83 percent. This information is presented in the first three columns of Table 13–7.

Table 13–7 Rates of return for Conglomerate Inc. and two merger candidates

Year	(1) Conglomerate Inc.	(2) Positive Correlation Inc. +1.0	(3) Negative Correlation Inc. −.9	(1) + (2) Conglomerate Inc. + Positive Correlation Inc.	(1) + (3) Conglomerate Inc. + Negative Correlation Inc.
1	14%	16%	10%	15%	12%
2	10	12	16	11	13
3	8	10	18	9	13
4	12	14	14	13	13
5	16	18	12	17	14
Mean return	12%	14%	14%	13%	13%
Standard deviation of returns (σ)*	2.83%	2.83%	2.83%	2.83%	.63%
Correlation coefficients with Conglomerate, Inc				+1.0	−.9

*Technically, the calculation of the standard deviation is based on whether we are dealing with a population or a sample. For a sample, an adjustment is made to get an unbiased estimate.

Because management desires to reduce risk (σ) and to increase returns at the same time, it decides to analyze the results of each combination.[6]

These combinations are shown in the last two columns in the table. A combination with Positive Correlation Inc. increases the mean return to 13 percent but maintains the same standard deviation of returns (no risk reduction). Why? This occurs because the coefficient of correlation is +1.0 and no diversification benefits are achieved. A combination with Negative Correlation Inc. also increases the mean return to 13 percent, but it reduces the standard deviation of returns to 0.63 percent, a significant reduction in risk. This occurs because of the offsetting relationship of returns between the two companies, as evidenced by the coefficient of correlation of −.9. When one company has high returns, the other has low returns, and vice versa.

Using our formulas for an equally weighted portfolio of Conglomerate Inc. (C) and Negative Correlation Inc. (N), we can connect with Table 13–7.

The expected value: $\overline{D}_p = \sum x_i \overline{D}_i$ (13–4)

$$0.13 = 0.5(0.12) + 0.5(0.14)$$

---

[6]In Chapter 20, you evaluate a merger situation in which there is no increase in earnings, only a reduction in the standard deviation. Because the lower risk may mean a higher price-earnings ratio, this could be beneficial.

The covariance: $\text{Cov}_{CN} = \sum P(D - \overline{D}_i)(F - \overline{F}_i)$ (13–5)

$$\text{Cov}_{CN} = 0.2(0.14-0.12)(0.10-0.14) + 0.2(0.10-0.12)(0.16-0.14)$$
$$+ 0.2(0.08-0.12)(0.18-0.14) + 0.2(0.12-0.12)(0.14-0.14)$$
$$+ 0.2(0.16-0.12)(0.12-0.14)$$
$$\text{Cov}_{CN} = -0.00072 \text{ or } -0.072\%$$

The coefficient correlation: $\rho_{CN} = \dfrac{\text{Cov}_{CN}}{\sigma_C \sigma_N}$ (13–6)

$$\rho_{CN} = \frac{-0.00072}{(0.0283)(0.0283)} = -0.9$$

The portfolio standard deviation: $\sigma_{CN} = \sqrt{x_C^2 \sigma_C^2 + x_N^2 \sigma_N^2 + 2\,\text{Cov}_{CN} x_C x_N}$ (13–7)

$$\sigma_{CN} = \sqrt{0.5_C^2(0.0283)_C^2 + 0.5_N^2(0.0283) + 2(-0.00072)_{CN}(0.5)_C(0.5)_N}$$
$$\sigma_{CN} = 0.0063 = 0.63\%$$

Or

$$\sigma_{CN} = \sqrt{x_C^2 \sigma_C^2 + x_N^2 \sigma_N^2 + 2\rho_{CN}\sigma_C \sigma_N x_C x_N}$$ (13–8)

$$\sigma_{CN} = \sqrt{0.5_C^2(0.0283)_C^2 + 0.5_N^2(0.0283) + 2(-0.9)_{CN}(0.0283)_C(0.0283)_N(0.5)_C(0.5)_N}$$
$$\sigma_{CN} = 0.0063 = 0.63\%$$

FINANCE IN ACTION

Diversifying Product Lines

Nadir operated a retail business that sold silver jewellery in a large Canadian city. His firm had several outlets in malls across the city. He was careful buying his inventories because decreased sales could have a dramatic impact on the business. Despite slowdowns in the economy at times, his business did reasonably well.

Jewellery is a fashion statement subject to quick change. In order to reduce his risk due to changing customer tastes, Nadir diversified some of his risk by buying product from around the globe. The Middle East, Europe, and Southeast Asia represented sources of his varied product. The silver jewellery produced in the different countries was unique to the different cultures and allowed Nadir to meet the changing needs and desires of customers. This variety allowed Nadir to not only diversify some of his product risk but also visit several exotic locations.

Evaluation of Combinations

The firm should evaluate all possible combinations of projects, determining which provides the best tradeoff between risk and return. In Figure 13–11, we see a number of alternatives that might be available to a given firm. Each point represents a combination of different possible investments. For example, point F might represent a semiconductor manufacturer combining three different semiconductors, two calculators, and two unrelated products. In choosing between the various points or combinations, management should have two primary objectives:

1. Achieve the highest possible return at a given risk level.
2. Allow the lowest possible risk at a given return level.

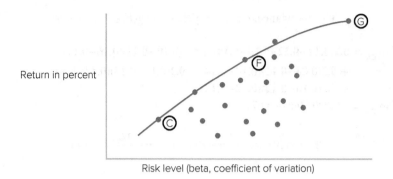

Figure 13–11 Risk–return tradeoffs

All the best opportunities fall along line CFG. Each point on the line satisfies the two objectives of the firm. Any point to the right or below the line is less desirable than any point on the line.

After we have developed our best risk-return line, known in the financial literature as the efficient frontier, we must determine where on the line our firm should be. There is no universally correct answer. To the extent that we are willing to take large risks for superior returns, we would opt for some point on the upper portion of the line—such as G. A more conservative selection might be C or F.

Combining assets with less than perfect positive correlation reduces risk. This is the benefit of diversification. However, we might want to question whether diversification is useful at the firm level. If investors already hold diversified portfolios, might the firm's attempts at diversification only duplicate the investors' actions? Perhaps the firm should stick to what it knows best and let investors achieve diversification through the marketplace.

In recent years, several corporations have announced divestitures and a return to concentrating on the business they know best. This followed a period in which corporate diversification seemed to be the thing to do.

THE SHARE PRICE EFFECT

The firm must be sensitive to the wishes and demands of shareholders. To the extent that unnecessary or undesirable risks are taken, a higher discount rate and lower valuation will probably be assigned to the shares in the market. Higher profits, resulting from risky ventures, could have a result opposite from that intended. In raising the coefficient of variation or beta we could be lowering the overall valuation of the firm.

The aversion of investors to unpredictability (and the associated risk) is confirmed by observing the relative valuation given to cyclical stocks versus highly predictable growth stocks in the market. Metals, autos, and housing stocks generally trade at earnings multipliers well below those for industries with level, predictable performance, such as drugs, soft drinks, and even alcohol or cigarettes. Each company must carefully analyze its own situation to determine the appropriate trade-off between risk and return. The changing desires and objectives of investors tend to make the task somewhat more difficult.

SUMMARY

1. Risk may be defined as the variability of the potential outcomes from an investment. The less predictable the outcomes are, the greater the risk. (LO1)

2. Both management and investors tend to be risk averse; that is, other things being equal, they would prefer to take less risk rather than greater risk. (LO2)

3. Standard deviation is the statistical measure that defines risk. The coefficient of variation is the standard deviation divided by the expected value; it brings the same scale to our statistical measures of risk. (LO3)

4. The most commonly employed method to adjust for risk in the capital budgeting process is to alter the discount rate on the basis of the perceived risk level. High-risk projects carry a risk premium, producing a discount rate well in excess of the average cost of capital. The CAPM may prove helpful in establishing the appropriate discount rate according to the risk inherent in a project. (LO4)

5. In assessing the risk components of a given project, management may employ several techniques. Certainty equivalents adjust cash flows rather than the discount rate and use a risk-free discount rate. Simulation models can be quite elaborate. They generate probabilities of possible outcomes. Sensitivity analysis examines the impact on a project of changing one variable at a time. Decision trees model the possible outcomes from an investment and highlight dependencies between sequential events. (LO5)

6. Management must consider not only the risk inherent in a given project but also the impact of a new project on the overall risk of the firm (the portfolio effect). Negatively correlated projects have the most favourable effect on smoothing out business cycle fluctuations. The firm may wish to consider all combinations and variations of possible projects and to select only those that provide a total risk-return trade-off consistent with its goals. (LO6)

REVIEW OF FORMULAS

D is outcome.
P is probability of outcome.
$\overline{D}$ is expected value.
σ is standard deviation.

1.
$$\overline{D}(\text{expected value}) = \sum DP \qquad (13\text{--}1)$$

2.
$$\sigma(\text{standard deviation}) = \sqrt{\sum(D - \overline{D})^2 P} \qquad (13\text{--}2)$$

3.
$$V(\text{coefficient of variation }) = \frac{\sigma}{\overline{D}} \qquad (13\text{--}3)$$

x_i = % weighting in the portfolio of each investment
D and F: Range of expected outcomes for the investments
ρ_{AB} = Coefficient of correlation between two investments

$$\overline{D}_p = \sum x_i \overline{D}_i \qquad (13\text{--}4)$$

$$\text{Cov}_{AB} = \sum P(D - \overline{D}_i)(F - \overline{F}_i) \qquad (13\text{--}5)$$

$$\rho_{AB} = \frac{\text{Cov}_{AB}}{\sigma_A \sigma_B} \qquad (13\text{--}6)$$

$$\sigma_{AB} = \sqrt{x_A^2 \sigma_A^2 + x_B^2 \sigma_B^2 + 2\,\text{Cov}_{AB} x_A x_B} \qquad (13\text{--}7)$$

$$\sigma_{AB} = \sqrt{x_A^2 \sigma_A^2 + x_B^2 \sigma_B^2 + 2\rho_{AB} \sigma_A \sigma_B x_A x_B} \qquad (13\text{--}8)$$

DISCUSSION QUESTIONS

1. If corporate managers are risk averse, does this mean they will not take risks? Explain. (LO2)

2. Discuss the concept of risk and how it might be measured. (LO1 LO3)

3. When is the coefficient of variation a better measure of risk than the standard deviation? (LO3)

4. Explain how the concept of risk can be incorporated into the capital budgeting process. (LO4)

5. If risk is to be analyzed in a qualitative way, place the following investment decisions in order from the lowest risk to the highest risk: (LO4)
   a. New equipment
   b. Completely new market
   c. Repair of old machinery
   d. New product in a foreign market
   e. New product in a related market
   f. Addition to a product line

6. Assume a company whose performance is highly correlated with the general economy is evaluating six projects, of which two are positively correlated with the economy, two are negatively correlated, and two are not correlated with it at all. Which two projects would you select to minimize the company's overall risk? (LO6)

7. Why use certainty equivalents in a capital budgeting analysis? (LO5)

8. What is the purpose of using simulation analysis? (LO5)

9. Why must one be careful when using sensitivity analysis? (LO5)

10. Why might an analyst set up a decision tree in attempting to make a decision? (LO5)

11. Assume a firm has several hundred possible investments and wants to analyze the risk-return trade-off for portfolios of 20 projects. How should it proceed with the evaluation? (LO6)

12. Explain the effect of the risk-return trade-off on the market value of common stock. (LO4)

13. From a corporate perspective is unique risk (σ) or beta risk (β) the more important consideration? Does it matter? (LO3)

INTERNET RESOURCES AND QUESTIONS

Oracle and Vanguard are software companies that develop and market decision-analysis tools. Demos are available on a free trial basis. Included are a Monte Carlo simulation model and a time-series forecasting model. The demos give a sense of the models required in risk analysis:

oracle.com

vanguardsw.com

1. Using the Standard & Poor's website, as well as Damodaran's NYU website, and your knowledge of the components of yield to maturity from Chapter 10, construct an appropriate discount rate for an investment (for a known technology) from a Canadian viewpoint in the following countries: Finland, Estonia, Chile, and Ecuador.

   standardandpoors.com

   bankofcanada.ca

   pages.stern.nyu.edu

PROBLEMS

1. Assume that you are risk adverse and have the following three choices. Which project would you select? Compute the coefficient of variation for each choice.

	Expected Value	Standard Deviation
A	$1,800	$ 900
B	2,000	1,400
C	1,500	500

2. Pabst Dental Supplies is evaluating the introduction of a new product. The possible levels of unit sales and the probabilities of occurrence are given.

Possible Market Reaction	Sales in Units	Probabilities
Low response.............................	20	.10
Moderate response........................	40	.20
High response............................	65	.40
Very high response.......................	80	.30

a. What is the expected value of unit sales for the new product?

b. What is the standard deviation of unit sales?

3. Northern Wind Power, a new age energy company, is considering the introduction of a product intended to use wind as an energy-producing device. The possible levels of unit sales and the probabilities of occurrence are given.

Acceptance Potential	Sales in Units	Probabilities
Low	50	.10
Moderate	70	.40
Strong..................................	90	.20
Very strong.	140	.30

a. What is the expected value of unit sales for the new product?

b. What is the standard deviation of unit sales?

4. Monarch King Size Beds Ltd. is evaluating a new promotional campaign that could increase sales. Possible outcomes and probabilities of the outcomes are shown below. Compute the coefficient of variation.

Possible Outcomes	Additional Sales in Units	Probabilities
Ineffective campaign	20	.20
Normal response	30	.50
Extremely effective......................	70	.30

5. Sam Sung is evaluating a new advertising program that could increase electronic sales. Possible outcomes and probabilities of the outcomes are shown below. Compute the coefficient of variation.

Possible Outcomes	Additional Sales in Units	Probabilities
Ineffective campaign	80	.30
Normal response	124	.50
Extremely effective	340	.20

6. Five investment alternatives have the following returns and standard deviations of returns.

Alternative	Returns: Expected Value	Standard Deviation
A	$ 1,000	$200
B	3,000	300
C	3,000	400
D	5,000	700
E	10,000	900

Rank the five alternatives from lowest risk to highest risk using the coefficient of variation.

7. In the previous problem, if you were to choose between Alternative B and C only, would you need to use the coefficient of variation? Why?

8. Another five investment alternatives have the following returns and standard deviations of returns.

Alternative	Returns: Expected Value	Standard Deviation
A	$ 1,200	$ 300
B	800	600
C	5,000	450
D	1,000	430
E	60,000	13,200

Rank the five alternatives from lowest risk to highest risk using the coefficient of variation.

9. Digital Technology wishes to determine its coefficient of variation as a company over time. The firm projects the following data (in millions of dollars).

Year	Profits: Expected Value	Standard Deviation
1	180	54
2	240	104
3	300	166
4	400	260

a. Compute the coefficient of variation (V) for each time period.

b. Does the risk (V) appear to be increasing over a period of time? If so, why might this be the case?

10. Ted Fears is highly risk adverse while Sonny Outlook actually enjoys taking a risk.

a. Which of the four investments should Tom choose and why?

b. Which of the four investments should Sonny choose and why?

Investments	Returns: Expected Value	Standard Deviation
Buy stocks	$ 7,000	$ 4,000
Buy bonds	5,000	1,560
Buy commodities.	12,000	15,100
Buy options	8,000	8,850

11. Tim Trepid is highly risk adverse while Mike Macho actually enjoys taking a risk.

a. Which of the four investments should Tim choose and why?

b. Which of the four investments should Mike choose and why?

Investments	Returns: Expected Value	Standard Deviation
Buy shares	$ 9,140	$ 6,140
Buy bonds	7,680	2,560
Buy futures.	19,100	26,700
Buy real estate	17,700	18,200

12. Tomcat Oil Company was set up to take large risks and is willing to take the largest risk possible. HiC Construction Company is more typical of the average corporation and is risk averse.

   a. Which of the following four projects should Tomcat Oil Company choose and why?

   b. Which of the following four projects should HiC Construction Company choose and why?

Projects	Returns: Expected Value	Standard Deviation
A	$183,400	$ 96,600
B	471,800	282,100
C	61,600	75,600
D	87,500	144,900

13. Possible outcomes for three investment alternatives and their probabilities of occurrence are given below.

	Alternative 1		Alternative 2		Alternative 3	
	Outcomes	Probability	Outcomes	Probability	Outcomes	Probability
Failure	$ 50	.2	$ 90	.3	$ 80	.4
Acceptable	80	.4	160	.5	200	.5
Successful	120	.4	200	.2	400	.1

Rank the three alternatives in terms of risk.

14. Mary Beth Clothes is considering opening an additional suburban outlet. An aftertax cash flow of $100 per day (expected value) is projected for each of the two locations being evaluated. Which of these sites would you select based on the distribution of these cash flows (use the coefficient of variation as your measure of risk):

Site A		Site B	
Probability	Cash Flows	Probability	Cash Flows
.20	$ 50	.10	$ 20
.30	100	.20	50
.30	110	.40	100
.20	135	.20	150
		.10	180
Expected value	$100	Expected value	$100

15. Waste Industries is evaluating a $70,000 project with the following cash flows.

Years	Cash Flows
1	$11,000
2	16,000
3	21,000
4	24,000
5	30,000

The coefficient of variation is 0.847.

Based on the following table of risk-adjusted discount rates, should the project be undertaken? An NPV calculation is appropriate.

Coefficient of Variation	Discount Rate
0.00–0.25	6%
0.26–0.50	8
0.51–0.75	10
0.76–1.00	14
1.01–1.25	20

16. Western Dynamite Company is evaluating two new methods of blowing up buildings for commercial purposes over the next five years. Method 1 (implosion) is relatively low in risk for this business and will carry a 10 percent discount rate. Method 2 (explosion) is less expensive to perform, but it is more dangerous and will require a higher discount rate of 15 percent. Either method will require an initial capital outlay of $100,000. The inflows from projected business over the next five years are given below. Which method should be selected using NPV analysis?

Years	Product 1	Product 2
1	$25,000	$28,000
2	30,000	32,000
3	38,000	39,000
4	31,000	33,000
5	19,000	25,000

17. Debby's Dance Studios is considering the purchase of new sound equipment that will enhance the popularity of its aerobics dancing. The equipment will cost $20,900. Debby is not sure how many members the new equipment will attract, but she estimates that her increased annual cash flows for each of the next five years will have the following probability distribution. Debby's cost of capital is 15 percent.

Probability	Cash Flow
.1	$ 4,570
.3	5,550
.4	7,400
.2	9,930

a. What is the expected cash flow?

b. What are the expected NPV?

c. Should Debby buy the new equipment?

18. Larry's Athletic Lounge is considering an expansion program to increase the sophistication of the exercise equipment. The equipment will cost $20,000 and has an estimated life of five years. Larry is not sure how many members the new equipment will attract, but he estimates that his increased annual cash flows for each of the next five years will have the following probability distribution. Larry's cost of capital is 14 percent.

Probability	Cash Flow
.2	$ 2,400
.4	4,800
.3	6,000
.1	7,200

a. What is the expected cash flow?

b. What are the expected NPV and IRR?

c. Should Larry buy the new equipment?

19. Silverado Mining Company is analyzing the purchase of two silver mines. Only one investment will be made. The Yukon mine will cost $2 million, which will produce $400,000 per year in Years 5 through 15 and $800,000 per year in Years 16 through 25. The Labrador mine will cost $2.4 million and will produce $300,000 per year for the next 25 years. The cost of capital is 10 percent.

a. Which investment should be made?

b. If the Yukon mine justifies an extra 5 percent premium over the normal cost of capital because of its riskiness and relative uncertainty of flows, does the investment decision change?

20. Mr. John Backster, a retired executive, desires to invest a portion of his assets in rental property. He has narrowed his choices to two apartment complexes, Windy Acres and Hillcrest Apartments. The anticipated annual cash inflows from each are as follows:

Windy Acres		Hillcrest Apartments	
Yearly aftertax cash inflow	Probability	Yearly aftertax cash inflow	Probability
$10,000	.1	$15,000	.2
15,000	.2	25,000	.3
30,000	.4	35,000	.4
45,000	.2	45,000	.1
50,000	.1		

a. Find the expected value of the cash flow for each apartment complex.

b. What is the coefficient of variation for each apartment complex?

c. Which apartment complex has more risk?

21. Referring to the previous problem, Mr. Backster is likely to hold the apartment complex of his choice for about 10 years and will use this period for decision-making purposes. Either apartment can be purchased for $100,000. Mr. Backster uses a risk-adjusted discount rate approach when evaluating investments. His scale is related to the coefficient of variation (for other types of investments, he also considers other measures).

Coefficient of Variation	Discount Rate	
0–0.35	12%	
0.35–0.40	14	(cost of capital)
0.40–0.50	16	
Over 0.50	not considered	

a. Compute the risk-adjusted net present value for Wrigley Village and Crosley Square using cash flow figures from the previous problem.

b. Which investment should Mr. Backster accept if the two investments are mutually exclusive? If the investments are not mutually exclusive and no capital rationing is involved, how would your decision be affected?

22. Wardrobe Clothing Manufacturers is preparing a strategy for the fall season. One strategy is to go to a highly imaginative, new, four-gold-button sports coat. The all-wool product would be available for males and females. A second option would be to produce a traditional blue blazer line. The marketing research department has determined that the four-gold-button and traditional blue blazer lines offer the following probabilities of outcomes and related cash flows:

	New Coat		Blue Blazer	
Expected Sales	Probability	Present Value of Cash Flows from Sales	Probability	Present Value of Cash Flows from Sales
Fantastic..........	.4	$240,000	.2	$120,000
Moderate	.2	180,000	.6	75,000
Dismal	.4	0	.2	55,000

The initial cost to get into the new coat line is $100,000 in designs, equipment, and inventory. To enter the blue blazer line the initial cost in designs, inventory, and equipment is $60,000.

a. Diagram a complete decision tree of the possible outcomes similar to Figure 13–8. Take the analysis all the way through the process of computing expected NPV for each investment.

b. Given the analysis in part *a*, would you automatically make the investment indicated?

23. When returns from a project can be assumed to be normally distributed, such as those shown in Figure 13–6 (represented by a symmetrical, bell-shaped curve), the areas under the curve can be determined from statistical tables based on standard deviations. For example, 68.26 percent of the distribution will fall within one standard deviation of the expected value (D + 1σ). Similarly, 95.44 percent will fall within two standard deviations (D ± 2σ), and so on. An abbreviated table of areas under the normal curve is shown here.

Number of σs from Expected Value	+ or −	+ and −
0.5	0.1915	0.3830
1.0	0.3413	0.6826
1.5	0.4332	0.8664
1.96	0.4750	0.9500
2.0	0.4772	0.9544

Assume Project A has an expected value of $30,000 and a standard deviation (σ) of $6,000.

a. What is the probability the outcome will be between $24,000 and $36,000?

b. What is the probability the outcome will be between $21,000 and $39,000?

c. What is the probability the outcome will be greater than $18,000?

d. What is the probability the outcome will be less than $41,760?

e. What is the probability the outcome will be less than $27,000 or greater than $39,000?

24. The Caribou Pipeline Company projects a pattern of inflows from the investment shown in the following table. The inflows are spread over time to reflect delayed benefits. Each year is independent of the others.

Year 1		Year 5		Year 10	
Cash inflow	Probability	Cash inflow	Probability	Cash inflow	Probability
65	.20	50	.25	40	.30
80	.60	80	.50	80	.40
95	.20	110	.25	120	.30

The expected value for all three years is $80.

a. Compute the standard deviation for each of the three years.

b. Diagram the expected values and standard deviations for each of the three years in a manner similar to Figure 13–6.

c. Assuming a 6 percent and 12 percent discount rate, complete the table for present value factors.

d. Is the increasing risk over time, as diagrammed in part *b*, consistent with the larger differences in PV_{IF}s over time as computed in part *c*?

e. Assume the initial investment is $135. What is the net present value of the expected values of $80 for the investment at a 12 percent discount rate? Should the investment be accepted?

Year	PV_{IF} 6 percent	PV_{IF} 12 percent	Difference
1	0.943	0.893	0.050
5	_____	_____	_____
10	_____	_____	_____

25. Gifford Western Wear makes blue jeans and cowboy shirts. It has seven manufacturing outlets in British Columbia and Alberta. It is seeking to diversify its business and lower its risk. It is examining three companies—a toy company, a boot company, and a highly exclusive jewellery

store chain. Each of these companies can be bought at the same multiple of earnings. The following represents information about all the companies.

Company	Correlation with Gifford Western Wear	Sales ($ millions)	Average Earnings ($ millions)	Standard Deviation in Earnings ($ millions)
Gifford Western Wear	+1.0	$150	$10	$3
Toy Company	0.2	150	10	6
Boot Company	0.9	150	10	5
Jewellery Company	−0.6	150	10	7

a. What would happen to Gifford Western Wear's portfolio risk return if it bought Toy Company? Boot Company? or Jewellery Company? Pay particular attention to the first column of correlation data.

26. Treynor Pie Co. is a food company specializing in high-calorie snack foods. It is seeking to diversify its food business and lower its risks. It is examining three companies—a gourmet restaurant chain, a baby food company, and a nutritional products firm. Each of these companies can be bought at the same multiple of earnings. The following table represents information about all the companies:

Company	Correlation with Treynor Pie Company	Sales ($ millions)	Expected Earnings ($ millions)	Standard Deviation in Earnings ($ millions)
Treynor Pie Company	+1.0	$126	$10	$4.0
Gourmet restaurant	+0.4	63	9	1.4
Baby food company	+0.3	52	5	1.6
Nutritional products company	−0.7	77	7	3.2

a. Based on the coefficient of correlation, which company is the least risky? Which company is the most risky?

b. Discuss which of the acquisition candidates is most likely to reduce Treynor Pie Company's risk. Explain why.

27. Transoceanic Airlines is examining a resort motel chain to add to its operations. Before the acquisition, the normal expected outcomes for the firm were as follows:

	Outcomes ($ millions)	Probability
Recession..................................	$30	.30
Normal economy	50	.40
Strong economy..........................	70	.30

After the acquisition the expected outcomes for the firm would be

	Outcomes ($ millions)	Probability
Recession..................................	$ 10	.30
Normal economy	50	.40
Strong economy..........................	100	.30

a. Compute the expected value, standard deviation, and coefficient of variation before the acquisition. After the acquisition these values are as follows:

Expected value..	53.0 ($ millions)
Standard deviation	34.9 ($ millions)
Coefficient of variation	.658

b. Comment on whether this acquisition appears desirable to you.

c. Do you think the firm's share price is likely to go up as a result of this acquisition?

d. If the firm was interested in reducing its risk exposure, which of the following three industries would you advise it to consider for an acquisition? Briefly comment on your answer.

    i. Major travel agency

    ii. Oil company

    iii. Gambling casino

28. Jimmy has the following two investments in his portfolio:

Investment	Expected Return	Standard Deviation	Beta	% Weighting
D	18%	5.2%	1.25	40%
E	14%	4.1	0.94	60

a. Which investment is riskier by itself and in a portfolio sense?

b. What is the expected return of the portfolio?

c. With a correlation coefficient of +0.55, what is the standard deviation of the portfolio?

d. What is the beta of the portfolio?

e. What is the significance of the results, in parts *a* through *d*?

29. Astrid has the following two investments in her portfolio:

Investment	Expected Return	Standard Deviation	Beta	% Weighting
M	12%	3.1%	1.40	55%
N	19%	3.9	0.85	45

a. Which investment is riskier by itself and in a portfolio sense?

b. What is the expected return of the portfolio?

c. With a correlation coefficient of +0.30, what is the standard deviation of the portfolio?

d. What is the beta of the portfolio?

e. What is the significance of the results in parts *a* through *d*?

30. Sheila Goodman recently received her MBA from the Harvard Business School. She has joined the family business, Goodman Software Products Inc., as vice-president of finance.

She believes in adjusting projects for risk. Her father is somewhat skeptical but agrees to go along with her. Her approach is somewhat different than the risk-adjusted discount rate approach, but achieves the same objective.

She suggests that the inflows for each year of a project be adjusted downward for lack of certainty and then be discounted back at a risk-free rate. The theory is that the adjustment penalty makes the inflows the equivalent of riskless inflows, and therefore a risk-free rate is justified.

A table showing the possible coefficient of variation for an inflow and the associated adjustment factor is shown next:

Coefficient of Variation	Adjustment Factor
0–0.25	0.90
0.26–0.50	0.80
0.51–0.75	0.70
0.76–1.00	0.60
1.01–1.25	0.50

Assume a $184,000 project provides the following inflows with the associated coefficients of variation for each year:

Year	Inflow	Coefficient of Variation
1	$32,000	0.12
2	59,500	0.28
3	79,900	0.45
4	59,200	0.79
5	65,600	1.15

a. Fill in the following table:

b. If the risk-free rate is 5 percent, should this $184,000 project be accepted? Compute the net present value of the adjusted inflows.

Year	Inflow	Coefficient of Variation	Adjustment Factor	Adjusted Inflow
1	$32,000	0.12	___	___
2	59,500	0.28	___	___
3	79,900	0.45	___	___
4	59,200	0.79	___	___
5	65,600	1.15	___	___

31. Mr. Boone is looking at a number of different types of investments for his portfolio. He identifies eight possible investments.

	Return	Risk
A	10%	1.5%
B	11	3.0
C	13	3.5
D	13	4.0
E	14	4.0
F	14	5.0
G	15	5.5
H	17	7.0

a. Graph the data in a manner similar to Figure 13–11.

b. Draw a curved line representing the efficient frontier.

c. What two objectives do points on the efficient frontier satisfy?

d. Is there one point on the efficient frontier that is best for all investors?

COMPREHENSIVE PROBLEMS

32. The Roaring River Utility Company is a very stable billion-dollar company with a sales growth of about 5 percent per year in good or bad economic conditions. Because of this stability (a coefficient of correlation with the economy of +.3, and a standard deviation of sales of about 5 percent from the mean), Ms. Electra, the vice-president of finance, thinks the company could absorb a small risky company that could add quite a bit of return without increasing the company's risk very much. She is trying to decide which of the two companies Roaring River will buy, using the figures below. Roaring River's cost of capital is 10 percent.

Computer Whiz Company (cost $75 million)		Atlantic Micro-Technology Company (AMT) (cost $75 million)	
Probability	Aftertax Cash Flow for 10 years ($ millions)	Probability	Aftertax Cash Flow for 10 Years ($ millions)
.3	$ 6	.2	$ (1)
.3	10	.2	3
.2	16	.2	10
.2	25	.3	25
		.1	31

a. What is the expected cash flow from both companies?

b. Which company has the lower coefficient of variation?

c. Compute the NPV of each company.

d. Which company would you pick based on NPVs?

e. Would you change your mind if you added the risk dimensions to the problem? Explain.

f. What if Computer Whiz had a correlation coefficient with the economy of +0.5 and AMT had one of −0.1? Which of the companies would give you the best portfolio effects for risk reduction?

g. What might be the effect of the acquisitions on the market value of Roaring River Utility Company's shares?

33. Ace Trucking Company is considering buying 50 new diesel trucks that are 15 percent more fuel-efficient than the ones the firm is now using. Mr. King, the president, has found that the company uses an average of 30 million litres of diesel fuel per year at a price of $1.08 per litre. If he can cut fuel consumption by 15 percent, he will save $4,860,000 per year.

Mr. King assumes the price of diesel fuel is an external market force he cannot control, and any increased costs of fuel will be passed on to the shipper through higher rates. If this is true, then fuel efficiency would save more money as the price of diesel fuel rises (at $1.215 per litre, he would save $5,467,500 in total if he buys the new trucks).

Mr. King has come up with two possible forecasts as shown below—each of which he believes has about a 50 percent chance of coming true. Under assumption one, diesel prices will stay relatively low; under assumption two, diesel prices will rise considerably.

Fifty new trucks will cost Ace Trucking $13.25 million. They will qualify for a 30 percent CCA. The firm has a tax rate of 30 percent and a cost of capital of 11 percent.

a. First, compute the yearly expected costs of diesel fuel for both assumption one (relatively low diesel prices) and assumption two (high diesel prices) from the forecasts below.

Forecast for assumption one:

Forecast for assumption two:

b. What will be the dollar savings in diesel expenses for each year for assumption one and for assumption two?

c. Find the increased cash flow after taxes for both forecasts.

d. Compute the NPV of the truck purchases for each fuel forecast assumption and the combined net present value (that is, weight the NPVs by .5).

e. If you were Mr. King, would you go ahead with this capital investment?

f. How sensitive to fuel prices is this capital investment?

Probability	Price of Diesel Fuel per Litre		
(same for each year)	Year 1	Year 2	Year 3
.1	$0.68	$0.81	$0.95
.2	0.81	0.95	1.08
.3	0.95	1.08	1.22
.2	1.08	1.22	1.35
.2	1.22	1.35	1.49

Probability	Price of Diesel Fuel per Litre		
(same for each year)	Year 1	Year 2	Year 3
.1	$1.22	$1.35	$1.76
.3	1.35	1.49	2.03
.4	1.76	2.03	2.43
.2	2.03	2.30	2.70

34. Indigo Ltd. is faced with three investment proposals with the following information:

Project	Cost	Cash Flow (10 years)	Beta
A	$ 200,000	$ 37,000	1.6
B	160,000	27,500	1.1
C	180,000	27,000	.5

The cash flow is after tax and includes the tax savings on CCA. Indigo has a cost of capital of 10 percent, the market portfolio is expected to earn 11 percent, and the risk-free rate is 3 percent.

a. Which projects would you recommend based on analysis using the firm's cost of capital? Show your analysis.

b. Which projects would you recommend based on the individual risk of each project? Show your analysis.

35. Fine Winehouse is analyzing an investment very different from its current investments. The initial investment would be $500,000 with current liabilities increasing by $30,000. The anticipated revenues have been estimated at $150,000 a year for the six years of the project's life. At the end of six years any remaining equipment would be salvaged for $55,000. Fine Winehouse has a tax rate of 28 percent, and the appropriate CCA rate for this capital project is 30 percent. Currently, the firm has 50 percent debt and 50 percent equity in its capital structure based on market values. It plans to maintain this capital structure in the foreseeable future. The existing shareholders expect a return of 15 percent on their investment, and new debt would require an 8 percent yield. The market risk premium is 7 percent, and the risk-free rate is 2.9 percent. The betas of firms in the wine house business with capital structures similar to Fine Winehouse's have revealed an average industry beta of 1.3.

a. Calculate the two possible discount rates to analyze the Winehouse investment.

b. Justify the choice of one of the discount rates.

c. Should Fine Winehouse proceed with the investment? Show your analysis.

36. Sam McGee, the financial analyst in the service of Labarge Ltd., is investigating the Midnight Sun project that is quite unlike any of its existing projects. It would require an initial investment of $320,000 and the probable increase in current assets would be 15 percent of this initial investment. The anticipated revenues have been estimated at $90,000 a year for three years, followed by revenues of $115,000 for the remaining four years of the project's life. At the end of seven years, any remaining equipment would be salvaged for $25,000. Labarge Ltd. has a tax rate of 38 percent, and the appropriate CCA rate for this

capital project is 30 percent. Currently, the firm has 44 percent debt and 56 percent equity in its capital structure, based on market values. It plans to maintain this capital structure in the foreseeable future. The existing shareholders expect a return of 15 percent on their investment, and new debt would require a 9.53 percent yield. The market risk premium is 8 percent, and the risk-free rate is 3 percent. Sam McGee has examined the betas of firms in the Midnight Sun business, with capital structures similar to that of Labarge Ltd., and this has revealed an average beta of 1.5 for these firms.

a. Calculate the two possible discount rates to analyze the Midnight Sun project.

b. Justify the choice of one of the discount rates.

c. Should Labarge Ltd. proceed with the Midnight Sun project? Show your analysis.

d. How would analysis and decision change if the average beta determined from similar businesses was 2.0 and was based on their equity rather than the overall firm?

MINI CASE

Churchill's Muffins Ltd.

Instead of taking a job with a large company on graduation, John Churchill had started his own chain of muffin shops. The menu featured different varieties of freshly baked muffins, along with coffee and cookies. It also included a soup and sandwich luncheon special, and some fancy pies and pastries.

The first Churchill's opened in Toronto in six years ago. Because Churchill's family had owned a bakery, he had grown up in the old-style bakery business and was aware that it was a dying industry. On the other hand, his summer work for the bakery division of a large supermarket had alerted him to the potential for a muffin-based food concept. Financing for the startup was provided from the proceeds of a mortgage his parents took out on their previously debt-free home, plus $400,000 from James Henson, a local businessman who had great faith in Churchill's abilities. The outside investor's $400,000 had come in the form of $100,000 in common equity and $300,000 in 12 percent preferred shares. John, James, and John's father, Henry, each had a third of the voting power in the corporation. John was concerned about his parents' house being at risk.

After six years, 79 restaurants were in operation across the country, 30 owned by the company and 49 owned by franchisees. In addition, two company and four franchisee stores were under construction. The balance sheet as of December 31, 20XX, is shown in Exhibit 1.

Churchill's Muffins Ltd.
Balance Sheet as of December 31, 20XX

Assets

Current assets:

Cash	$ 345	
Accounts receivable	425	
Inventory	320	
Other current assets	900	$ 1,990

Plant and equipment:

Buildings	5,100	
Leasehold improvements	2,942	
Restaurant equipment.	3,992	
Motor vehicles	498	
Office equipment	430	
Lease rights	210	
	13,172	
Less: Accumulated amortization	3,450	9,722
Land.	3,655	
Construction in progress	433	
Other assets	522	4,610
		$16,322

Liabilities and Shareholders' Equity

Current liabilities:

Notes payable to banks.	$ 550	
Accounts payable.	2,755	
Taxes payable.	534	
Accrued liabilities	987	
Current portion, term debt	799	$ 5,625
Long-term debt, over one year		7,585

Deferred:

Income taxes	332	
Franchise fees.	1,238	1,570

Shareholders' equity:

Preferred stock	300	
Common stock	300	
Retained earnings.	942	1,542
		$16,322

Exhibit 1 Balance sheet

Each of the shops was built to the same specifications for exterior style and interior decor; each had seating for 30. Many customers ate their purchases in their cars or elsewhere. The buildings were located on approximately one-third of a hectare of land and were designed with parking for 20 to 25 cars. All of the restaurants featured the same menu.

Franchisee agreements generally provided the option of operating a specified number of Churchill's outlets in a defined geographical area. Each new location required an initial payment of $20,000, and an additional royalty of 6 percent of sales was paid to corporate. Franchisees were required to spend at least 1 percent of sales on local advertising. All store managers and company trainees were required to attend a three-week training program in Toronto that covered all aspects of restaurant operations.

Churchill's was planning to start construction on another four new company-owned restaurants during 20XY. Although the exact size of these had not been determined, John Churchill believed a bigger size with capacity for 50 persons versus the current 30 would be more profitable.

The company faced at least the following two choices—going with their standard units or going to the larger size. The initial cost for the four smaller shops would be $1.6 million in total, but it would be $3 million for the larger shops. Probabilities were estimated at 30 percent for high demand, 40 percent for medium demand, and 30 percent for low demand. Historically, Churchill had used a higher estimated probability of low demand for company stores than for franchisees' stores, based on experience. The present values of the two proposals are given in Table 1.

Table 1 Present value of cash flows

| Restaurant Size | Level of Demand | Outcomes (NPV) | |
		Company	Franchise
Standard	High	$1,450,000	$ 520,000
	Medium	630,000	300,000
	Low	(200,000)	150,000
Expanded	High	3,812,000	1,040,000
	Medium	740,000	540,000
	Low	(900,000)	(150,000)

Churchill knew this decision facing the company was critical. Although the returns attached to the larger shops seemed more attractive than with the smaller shops, he wondered if the risks were justified.

MINI CASE

Phillips Toy Company

The Phillips Toy Company was considering the advisability of adding a new product line. Ike Barnes, a marketing major who had joined the company right out of business school three years previously, was in charge of new product development. Ike knew that since the founding of the company 18 years ago, sales had grown from $150,000 per year to almost $40 million by 20XX. Although the firm had started out manufacturing toy trucks, it had diversified into items such as puzzles, stuffed animals, miniature trains, and board games.

By late 20XX, however, the need to generate additional new product lines was becoming evident, as sales had been flat for the past three years and expected 20XX profit actually looked as if it might be 5 percent or so less than 20XW's $2 million. After doing a market analysis of possible product additions, Ike decided that the hockey card market was a booming area for potential new and profitable sales. Hockey cards were popular not only among youngsters but also among adults trying to recapture some of their youthful experiences.

In evaluating the market potential, Ike determined that there was no way he could predict the market penetration potential for a new set of hockey cards. The sales for the set, which would be called Hockey Legends, would depend on the quality of the final product as well as the effectiveness of the promotional activities. There was also the danger of errors when the set was initially issued. With approximately 400 cards in the set, there could be incorrect scoring statistics, ages, and so forth. When Johnson & Smith introduced its new set 11 years ago, the cards were highly criticized by collectors because of numerous factual errors. Ike hoped to avoid this problem for the Hockey Legends set. He intended to hire people experienced in the sports card or publishing business to identify potential problems at an early stage.

Ike knew that, over the years, Phillips had developed a manual for evaluating capital budgeting projects. As a first step, in conjunction with the sales manager, Ike predicted anticipated sales over the next six years. Although he thought this too short a time period to evaluate the full potential of the project, he had no choice but to go along with company policy. He decided to start by projecting a wide range for potential sales in 20XY, the first year in which there would be sales. He then assigned probabilities to the outcomes as shown in Table 1.

Table 1 Projected first year's sales

Assumption	Sales	Probability
Pessimistic	$1,100,000	.25
Normal	2,000,000	.40
Optimistic	3,750,000	.20
Highly optimistic	4,500,000	.15

Ike's intention was to determine the expected value for sales for the first year and then project a 20 percent growth rate for the next three years, and 10 percent for the final two years of the forecast period. Operating expenses were expected to average approximately 70 percent of sales. The primary investment to be made was in printing and production equipment, which would fall into Class 8 for CCA purposes. The equipment was forecast to cost $2.8 million and represented virtually the total capital investment for the business, except for about $200,000 in working capital.

Ike looked into the capital budgeting manual to determine the appropriate discount rate, as he had seen a number of different ones used throughout the company. The manual stated that the discount rate was to be based on the coefficient of variation of the first year's sales projections, based on the categories shown in Table 2. Ike was a little concerned that these categories and rates had been struck a few years earlier when interest rates were generally a couple of percentage points higher, and he wondered if that should make any difference.

Table 2 Discount rate determination

Coefficient of Variation	Appropriate Discount Rate
0–.20	8%
.21–.40	10
.41–.60	14
.61–.80	16
Over .80	20

Ike knew top management was eager for him to present a business plan that would be approved and implemented soon. Thus, he was interested in calling his assistants together to get the analysis done immediately so it could be presented, along with a recommendation, at the next meeting of the executive committee.

CHAPTER

14

Capital Markets

LEARNING OBJECTIVES

LO1 Define primary, secondary, money, and capital markets.

LO2 Outline the primary participants raising funds in the capital markets.

LO3 Characterize the Canadian economy as three major sectors allocating funds among themselves.

LO4 Outline the organization of the securities markets.

LO5 Assess the concept of market efficiency and its benefits to the economic system.

LO6 Examine the changing financial regulatory environment.

Raising capital in an appropriate mix (capital structure) is another major consideration of finance. Understanding Canadian and international financial markets, the process of raising capital, and the features of debt and equity are important knowledge bases for the financial manager. Will the investor prefer dividends or reinvestment in the firm? Derivatives can be an exotic means of raising capital or used to reduce the firm's risk in volatile financial markets.

FINANCE MANAGEMENT

Raising Money

Our market-based financial system has developed because of private enterprise and the accumulation of wealth or capital. The study of financial management suggests the pursuit of shareholder wealth as the goal of the firm, with wealth evidenced by the financial claims that individuals have against real assets (capital) and the ability of those assets to generate cash flows. Financial claims are represented by the financial assets (capital) issued by businesses and governments as debt or equity securities.

Capital or security markets facilitate the accumulation of capital by providing opportunities for investors and borrowers to get together. Security instruments are bought and sold in markets around the globe based on their promised risks and returns, with intense competition to raise funds. Investors use the markets to provide future income.

Capital moves quickly in today's markets, seeking out the best returns while minimizing risks. The changes brought on by the European Common Market (central bank, common currency, free trade agreements, sovereign debt problems, and Brexit); growing emerging markets; and the rise of Chinese capitalism increase the competition for funds on a global scale. As the mobility of capital increases, it is incumbent on governments and regulatory agencies to ensure the fair operation of the security markets. When investors perceive that the markets are unfair and financial investments do not properly reflect the risks and returns, then capital accumulation is inhibited.

LO1 THE STRUCTURE

Security markets consist of the new financial securities that are issued by businesses or governments and those securities currently outstanding (not yet matured) that trade among investors on a minute-by-minute basis. When a security is first issued there is a cash flow to the firm or government with the expectation of future cash flows by way of interest payments, dividends, or capital gains back to the investor. This is the primary market. It is innovative in its creation of financial instruments to meet the needs of investors.

Subsequently, securities that have been issued are bought and sold among investors. At this time there is no further cash flow into the firm although the obligation remains for future payments to the new investors. This trading of financial securities occurs in the secondary market. The trading occurs as investors seek to

- Adjust investment portfolios to meet their needs (returns, appropriate risks, cash flows)
- Determine the current value of financial assets
- Provide liquidity

Without secondary markets and the ability to sell financial instruments before maturity, it would be more difficult to raise funds in the primary markets.

Markets are generally separated into short-term and long-term components. The short-term markets that sell and trade fixed income securities with maturities of one year or less are referred to as money markets. The securities most commonly traded in these markets are government Treasury bills, government bonds with maturities of less than three years, commercial paper, bankers' acceptances, and negotiable certificates of deposit. These were previously discussed under working capital in Chapter 7.

The long-term markets are called capital markets and consist of securities having maturities greater than one year. The most common corporate securities in this category are bonds, common stock, preferred stock, and convertible securities. These securities are found on the firm's balance sheet under the designation of long-term liabilities and equities. Taken together with the retained earnings, these long-term securities make up the firm's capital structure. Capital markets are further split into the bond (debt) and stock (equity) markets.

In examining the size and efficiency of financial markets, we want to distinguish between

- The value of securities outstanding (the stock of wealth)
- The trading activity of the market (a measure of its liquidity)

Figure 14–1 identifies the value of financial securities outstanding in the Canadian markets. Although the bond and stock markets on this basis are at about ten times larger than the money market, securities in the money market tend to be more actively traded. Trading activities will be examined later in this chapter. The influence of the mobility of capital is seen in Figure 14–1 by the Canadian-issued securities held by foreigners, particularly in the bond market.

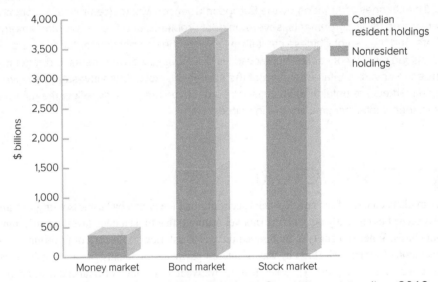

Figure 14–1 Canadian money and capital markets: Securities outstanding, 2019

Canadian securities markets are small but significant within the world capital markets. Figure 14–2 identifies the relative size of the Toronto Stock Exchange (TSX) among the top equity exchanges in the world. With the removal of barriers to the free flow of worldwide capital as it seeks the best risk-return opportunities in the global economy, the Canadian securities markets are influenced, sometimes dramatically, by events in other financial markets.

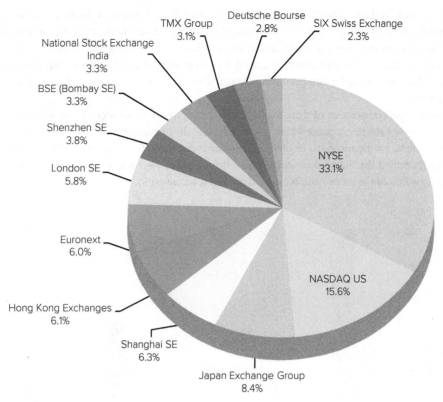

Figure 14–2 Market capitalization (value) of top 13 equity markets (approximately 81% of world capital markets)

In the following chapters of Part 5, we will look at how the capital markets are organized, regulated, and integrated into the corporate and economic system of Canada. We will also see how corporate securities are sold by investment dealers as firms develop their capital structure and examine the rights, contractual obligations, and unique features of each type of security within that capital structure.

FINANCE IN ACTION

Markets in Action

Many websites provide a view to the trading activity of the financial markets. These sites usually provide (close to) real-time quotes on financial securities. Although equity markets (auction markets) are well served with many websites, the bond markets (over-the-counter markets) are not so transparent and it is difficult to get comprehensive real-time quotes. Below are a couple of sites to get a flavour of these markets.

To view the action in the bond markets go to iiroc.ca or tmxmoney.com

To view the action in the equity markets go to tmx.com.

LO2 COMPETITION FOR FUNDS IN THE CAPITAL MARKETS

To put corporate securities into perspective, it is necessary to look at the other securities available in the capital markets, within Canada and globally. Federal governments, provincial governments, and local municipalities all compete with one another for a limited supply of financial capital, with the capital markets serving as a way of allocating the available capital to the most efficient users. The ultimate investor chooses among many kinds of securities of differing maturities, both corporate and noncorporate. The investor generally does this so as to maximize the return for any given level of risk. Thus, the expected return from the universe of securities acts as an allocating mechanism in the markets.

The size and composition of these markets reflect the growth of our society's wealth, the changing roles of the participants within our society, and the increasing role of the international capital markets. Furthermore, the changes in these financial markets reveal new challenges for the management of the financial resources of the firm. Figures 14–3 and 14–4 show the size and composition of the money and bond markets over a recent period.

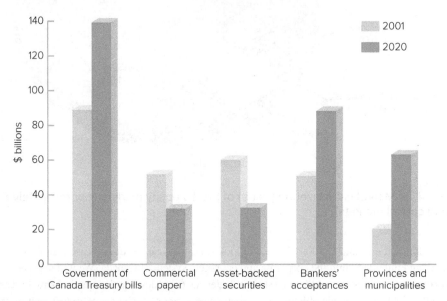

Figure 14–3 Canadian money market: Securities outstanding

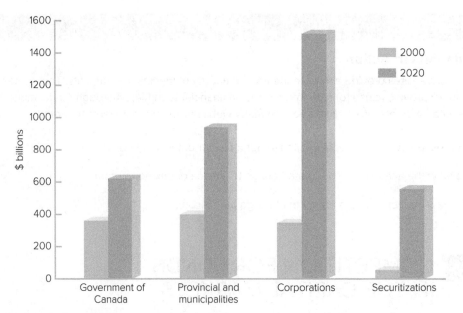

Figure 14–4 Canadian bond market: Securities outstanding ($ Can. and foreign currencies)

In Figure 14–3 the money market shows the significance for Government of Canada Treasury bills financing short-term government borrowing requirements and reflects the competition among investors for these risk-free investments. Recently, there has been a decrease in issues of commercial paper and asset-backed securities resulting from a loss of confidence after the credit/liquidity crisis of 2008. Safer bankers' acceptances have shown an increase in issues outstanding. For the financial manager, investments in short-term marketable securities require careful scrutiny while assuming more risk, with the limited availability of risk-free Treasury bills as governments pay down debt. There will be cautious use of asset-backed securities for short-term financing needs.

The bond market, illustrated in Figure 14–4, shows a healthy increase over the past decade. While federal and provincial bond debt outstanding has shown some increases, we should observe a rather significant increase in corporate debt by way of bonds and securitizations as business takes on a more significant role in the economy. The shift to longer-term securities and toward corporate securities is causing structural changes in the capital markets. As less government debt is available there have been concerns about liquidity in the markets, and bondholders must come to grips with the risks of buying increased corporate obligations. The trend toward securitization, discussed in Chapter 7, is notably in evidence.

The Canadian equity market, represented primarily by the Toronto Stock Exchange (TSX or TMX), as identified in Figure 14–1, is roughly the same size of the bond market in market value terms, based on outstanding obligations of capitalization.

Figure 14–5 illustrates the use of capital markets beyond Canada, primarily in the United States, for raising funds. Bonds outstanding in foreign currencies have grown dramatically for Canadian corporations. The Canadian bond market represents only about 2 percent of the world bond market while the U.S. market represents over 40 percent. Therefore, the Canadian financial manager must be familiar with these markets as they represent larger pools of capital, greater liquidity, and often lower yields to the firm when raising funds.

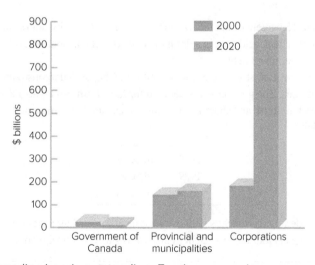

Figure 14–5 Canadian bonds outstanding: Foreign currencies

GOVERNMENT SECURITIES

Government of Canada Securities

In accordance with government fiscal policy, the Bank of Canada manages the federal government's debt to balance budgetary inflows and outflows. When deficits are incurred, the government can sell short-term or long-term securities to finance the shortfall.

The federal government has been a significant borrower in the capital and money markets. Annual deficits add to the federal debt, which by early 2020

Bank of Canada
bankofcanada.ca

stood at about $700 billion. The government had to go to the bond markets regularly either to roll over maturing debt or to finance revenue shortfalls. After 1998, the move again to budget surpluses shifted government funding to the net reduction of debt outstanding, although this has again reversed with the large budget shortfalls following the financial crisis of 2008. The federal government debt of 2020 represented about 31 percent of GDP, whereas in the 1990s it had exceeded 70 percent. Canada's federal debt is less significant than many other countries such as the United States.

The biweekly auction of Treasury bills also plays an important role in government finances. However, with the lower interest rates of the 1990s, the government has returned to a greater reliance on longer-term financing. Treasury bills outstanding are not as significant and with lower availability there have been instances of liquidity problems in the money markets.

 FINANCE IN ACTION

Bond Auctions

The Government of Canada, through its agent the Bank of Canada (bankofcanada.ca), holds auctions on a scheduled basis to sell its bonds through investment dealers into the market. These auctions allocate bonds to the dealers that offer to pay the best price. Bids are submitted electronically and in secret by 12:30 EST on the date of the auction. This is one of the ways in which the government funds its capital requirements. The Bank of Canada (under bonds—results) gives details of the latest bond auction.

Q1 What is the average price and yield of the latest Government of Canada bond auction?

In 2008, less than 15 percent of the federal debt position was held by nonresidents. The payment of interest on the nonresident-held debt is a drain of funds out of Canada. By 2020, nonresidents held about 32 percent of government debt.

The discussion of the term structure of interest rates in Chapter 6 demonstrated the volatile nature of short-term rates. The government's demand for long-term capital also depends on the relationship between long-term and short-term interest rates and this is indicated in the average term to maturity on its debt:

1979	10 years
1989	4 years
2020	6 years

The size of the federal government's debt causes concern regarding instability and uncertainty in both the money and the capital markets. Debt in 2020 was stated before Covid-19.

1997:	$588 billion	68% of GDP	Nonresident holdings	26%
2008:	$458 billion	29% of GDP	Nonresident holdings	14%
2020:	$700 billion	31% of GDP	Nonresident holdings	32%

Provincial and Municipal Government Bonds

The provinces, municipalities, and Crown corporations are important borrowers in the bond markets with the provinces doing the vast majority of borrowing for this group. In 2020, they had a total accumulated debt of approximately $700 billion, of which about 20 percent was denominated in foreign currencies. Historically, the provinces have borrowed mainly long term to fund capital projects, but during the 1990s they became active in the short-term market as well. Together, the provinces and federal government owe about 70 percent of GDP.

As seen in Figure 14–5, the provinces, municipalities, and certain Crown corporations borrow actively in the foreign markets, and in many years, foreign borrowings are larger than domestic financings. In some years provincial funding was greater in capital markets outside Canada, primarily the United States.

Municipal bonds make up a small portion of the bond market. Some of these new financings occur abroad. Because most municipal debentures are relatively illiquid, they tend to be purchased mainly by institutions.

Historically, provincial and municipal bonds have been a significant component of the long-term securities market in Canada, although in recent years the federal government has become a dominant player. The provinces continue to go abroad for much of their financing needs.

CORPORATE SECURITIES

Corporate Bonds

The corporate bond has been an important element of Canadian markets with the overall balance between raising new capital via stock or bond issues volatile, as seen in Figure 14–6. In most years bond financings dominate, while in other years equity issues are as significant. In stronger equity markets with higher share prices, management is more enthusiastic about issuing stock.

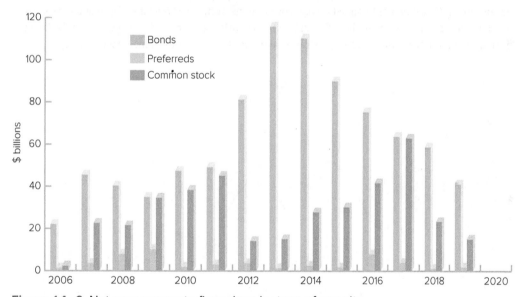

Figure 14–6 Net new corporate financings by type of security

Preferred Stock

Figure 14–6 shows that preferred stock is a source of corporate financing in Canada, although far less significant than bonds or common shares. Preferred stock financings have a role in balancing the capital structure of the corporation.

Preferred share funding in Canada is more significant than in the United States due to the differences in the tax treatment of corporate dividends, as well as the use of a holding company to control ownership of several Canadian companies at the same time. In both countries, interest payments are tax-deductible to a corporation, while dividends are not. Regulated public utilities, which can pass the tax disadvantage of preferred shares versus debt on to the customer, are the major issuers of preferred shares in the United States. In Canada, dividend income is generally not taxable when paid from one Canadian corporation to another. A dividend tax credit is accorded to individual investors and is examined further in Chapter 18. The tax advantage of debt over preferred share financing is thus erased in certain circumstances and is reduced in most others.

Common Stock

The sale of common stock has been significant during buoyant markets, particularly during the 1990s, although bond financings for corporations have been more significant. When the total long-term funding activity, including that by governments, in the Canadian capital markets is considered, common stock financing is a much smaller proportion. Stock financing outside Canada has become increasingly significant and in some years represents 25 percent of new funds raised. This is a concern as it represents a threat to the Canadian capital markets by decreasing their level of activity and lowering the liquidity of financial securities.

CORPORATE FINANCING IN GENERAL

The year-to-year variance in common stock versus debt issuance, as shown in Figure 14–6, is striking. In 2013, $115 billion of net new financings were done with debt (bonds), whereas common shares issues reached a peak of $63 billion in 2017. Total net new issues of debt and equity securities vary greatly, reaching a low of about $26 billion in 2002, a difficult year, and approximately $140 billion in 2014 through.

A large issue of debt may be followed by a large amount of equity at the next financing in order to keep the debt-to-equity ratio in an appropriate range. This does not explain, however, general trends by the whole population of firms toward debt or equity. Figure 14–7 illustrates debt-to-equity ratios among Canadian nonfinancial private corporations from the 1960s. It shows that the debt-to-book-equity ratio rose through the 1970s and 1980s as inflation increased. However, with the lower inflation of the 1990s, lower debt-equity ratios returned. Chapter 11 examined debt capacity.

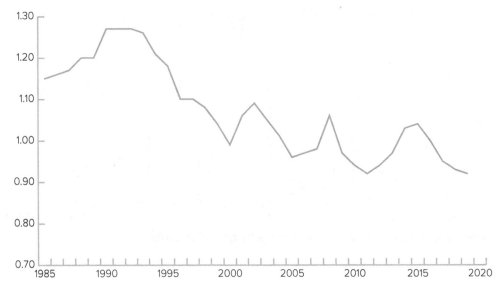

Figure 14–7 Debt-to-equity ratios for nonfinancial private corporations

New financings tend to anticipate and then find realization in a sluggish economy. With an increase in the economy's health, corporations again return to the capital markets.

Low stock market values make managers reluctant to sell shares in their own firms even though they may be eager to buy shares of other firms. However, when the stock market assigns higher share valuations, corporate management will rebuild corporate balance sheets by issuing equity to achieve more normal debt-to-equity ratios. This suggests that managers attempt to time their issues of common stock.

At least two observations on this behaviour should be of interest to students of financial management. First, an increased market value for a firm's shares increases its capacity to incur debt, yet firms substitute equity for debt on their balance sheets at that time. Second, managers seem to believe equity is expensive when stock markets are low by historic standards (and vice versa). This implies that they have some notion of the stock market, generally, underpricing and overpricing equity rather than placing a rational value on it at all points in time.

Internal Versus External Sources of Funds

Although corporations raise a significant amount of long-term financing externally by using bonds, preferred stock, and common stock, funds generated and retained from ongoing operations are at least an equally important source of funds to the corporation. These internally generated funds are generally designated as retained earnings and accounting expense amounts for amortization and other noncash items. In the previous discussion of the cost of capital in Chapter 11, the cost of retained earnings was considered, whereas Chapter 12 demonstrated how the capital budgeting decision is significantly affected by the noncash nature of amortization charges.

Figure 14–8 shows the funding sources of nonfinancial corporations over a recent period. Internally generated funds consisting of retained earnings and capital consumption allowance (tax allowed amortization) generated between 60 and 80 percent of the firm's funding needs. Nevertheless, the external funding amounts were not insignificant and highlight the development of the capital markets.

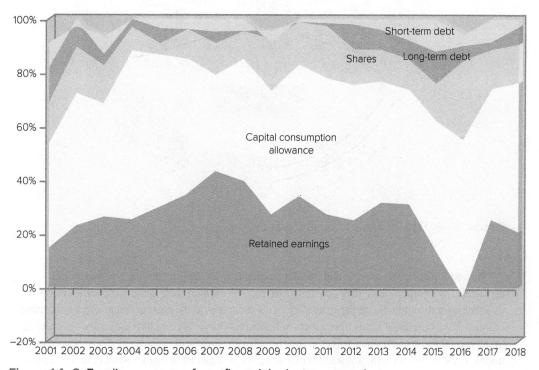

Figure 14–8 Funding sources of non-financial private corporations

The ability to reinvest internally generated funds to some extent insulates managerial decision making from the scrutiny of objective outside analysts. External financing requires increased disclosure of the firm's operations and its plans to the capital markets. Revealing details of a planned competitive strategy might deprive a firm of the benefits of a unique industrial initiative. Furthermore, managers may make fewer risky investment decisions if they have to approach external sources for each investment. Such non-decisions coupled with the flotation costs of external financing would be costly.

Firms that have limited investment opportunities in traditional businesses may look elsewhere to invest internally generated funds rather than pay them out to shareholders.

LO3 THE SUPPLY OF CAPITAL FUNDS

In a three-sector economy consisting of business, government, and households, the major supplier of funds for investment is the household sector. As we have seen in a previous discussion of competition for funds, corporations and governments have traditionally been net demanders of funds. Figure 14–9 diagrams the flow of funds through our basic three-sector economy.

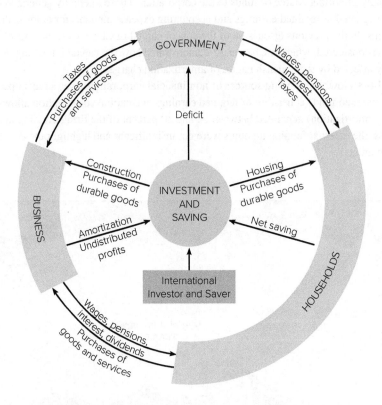

Figure 14–9 Flow of funds through the economy

As households receive wages and transfer payments from the government and wages and dividends from corporations, they generally save some portion of their income. A well-developed financial system will facilitate the funnelling of these savings to the most efficient users or borrowers of funds. This transfer of funds from savers to borrowers can be accomplished directly by investing in the capital markets. Alternatively, a saver of funds can invest with a financial intermediary, or middle person, who, in turn, invests the collected pool of funds from many investors in the capital markets. This is known as *indirect investment*.

The types of financial intermediaries that channel funds into the capital markets are specialized and diverse. The major intermediaries and their total assets are seen in Figure 14–10. Although the banks dominate the other intermediaries, increasingly pension and mutual funds play a vital and growing role in the capital markets. These financial intermediaries help make the flow of funds from one sector of the economy to another very efficient and competitive. They are able to assemble vast pools of funds and, through risk management techniques such as diversification and hedging, reduce risk. Also, because they can generate economies of scale, the cost of funds is lowered, and the efficient allocation of funds to the best users is accomplished at the lowest cost. The international saver and investor has become a critical supplier of funds to the Canadian capital markets.

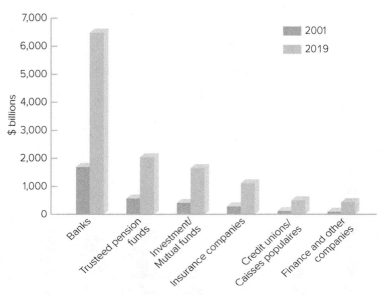

Figure 14–10 Total assets of financial intermediaries

By 2020, nonresidents had supplied $2.4 trillion of portfolio investment to Canada in the money and capital markets. Canadians supplied about $2.4 trillion to the international markets. With direct investments, Canada's net international position was about $700 billion in our favour. Earlier, Figure 14–1 showed the portion of outstanding capital market obligations held by nonresidents. Interestingly, Canadians held about $1.8 trillion in foreign stocks, versus the $0.8 trillion that nonresidents held of Canadian stocks. However, nonresidents held about $1.5 trillion in Canadian bonds versus $589 billion of foreign bonds held by Canadians. With equity investments generally achieving higher returns than debt obligations, this suggests a positive result for Canada.

The financial intermediary is very important in this three-sector economy. The intermediary is a key element in the allocation and reallocation of capital. Our economy could not possibly have developed to the extent that it has without this ability to move vast sums of capital efficiently. The ability to get a loan or to have numerous investment options is the product of a sophisticated financial environment.

The Role of the Security Markets

Security or capital markets exist to facilitate the direct transfer of capital among households, corporations, and governments. Initially, securities or financial claims are issued by borrowers to raise funds, and these securities are sold through the primary markets. If well-developed securities or secondary markets are not available where the trading of securities takes place, the initial sale of securities will be made more difficult. The capital markets are generally divided into the money, bond, and stock markets, with each market offering a certain type of security. The volume of trading in each of these markets is shown in Figure 14–11. We should contrast the volume of trading with the actual dollar value of securities outstanding in each market as was shown in Figure 14–1. Although trading volumes in the money and bond markets are far greater than in the equity markets, the outstanding value of equity securities is larger than money market obligations and as significant as in the bond market.

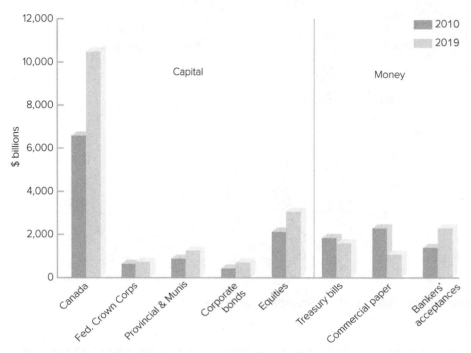

Figure 14–11 Secondary markets: annual value of trading

Trading volumes have increased over the 12-year period, although they dipped during the financial recession of 2007–08. Observe the shifts in trading volumes among the different instruments.

After a security is sold initially as an original offering, it then trades in its appropriate market among all kinds of investors. This trading activity is known as secondary trading since funds flow only among investors and the original borrower gets no further funds when these securities are traded. Secondary trading is vitally important as it provides liquidity for investors and keeps prices competitive among alternative security investments. Furthermore, it is because a well-developed secondary market exists that securities are easier to issue in the first place.

 FINANCE IN ACTION

Moving to the "Show"

The TSX Venture Exchange is Canada's junior equity market. CNSX Markets operates the Canadian Securities Exchange (CSE) for entrepreneurial companies. Both assist smaller firms in accessing capital through public offerings of securities.

During 2019, the Venture Exchange raised over $4.2 billion by way of more than 1,500 financings. There had been 139 new listings. By providing a secondary market where continual trading in these junior securities can take place, these exchanges assist in capital formation within Canada.

In 2019 there were 15 companies that graduated from the TSX Venture Exchange to the senior TSX. As they gained more experience with being a public company and their financial positions improved, these firms wanted to move to an exchange that offered greater liquidity and more prestige. The TSX Venture Exchange provides information on the requirements to go public. (MIG report)

Q1 What is the market capitalization for the TSX Venture Exchange versus the TSX?

Q2 Identify companies that have moved from the junior to the senior exchange.

tmx.com

Security markets provide liquidity in two ways. They enable corporations to raise funds by selling new issues of securities rapidly and at competitive prices, and they allow the investor who purchases securities to sell them with relative ease and speed and thereby to turn a paper asset into cash at will. Ask yourself the question, would I buy securities if there were no place to sell them? You would probably think twice before committing funds to an illiquid investment. It follows that without markets, corporations and governmental units would not be able to raise the large amounts of capital necessary for economic growth. Therefore, the presence and efficient management of security markets in Canada is vitally important to individuals, corporations, and governments alike.

LO4 THE ORGANIZATION OF THE SECURITY MARKETS

The competitive structure and organization of the security markets will continue to evolve, influenced by technological advancements, increased sophistication of market participants, rules of regulatory bodies, and the globalization of the capital markets. We will briefly examine the current organization of the markets and identify the significant trends and developments of the last few years. As indicated earlier, the capital markets often distinguish between the primary markets, in which financial securities are first sold or underwritten, and the secondary markets, in which securities are traded among investors on a regular basis. Secondary market trading activity is further divided between organized exchanges and over-the-counter markets.

The Organized Exchanges

An organized stock exchange is a regulated marketplace where buyers and sellers of securities come together to trade securities in a single location. This can be on the "floor" of an exchange such as the New York Stock Exchange, or via an electronic trading environment such as the Toronto Stock Exchange, or an Electronic Communication Network (ECN) such as TSX Alpha Exchange. Bidding by open cry of quotes has disappeared from most exchanges, although the price offering and acceptance process between buyers and sellers allows us to characterize this as an auction market.

Exchanges facilitate the trading of common shares, preferred shares, some bonds, rights, warrants, options, futures, and commodities that meet the exchange's listing requirements. Buyers and sellers of securities conduct their trades through brokers who act as their agents. The brokers are registered members of the exchange by virtue of having purchased a "seat," and are often part of a broadly based investment dealer organization. Dealers are distinguished from brokers in that dealers own inventories of securities and act as wholesalers. They seek a balance between supply and demand, expecting to produce a profit by holding the securities until a higher price can be obtained.

Organized exchanges usually are sanctioned by securities commissions, which are the regulatory bodies in society. The Income Tax Act, for RRSP purposes, requires that securities be traded on organized exchanges. Key components of a good, organized exchange include

- **Fair prices:** Established by "auction," or a competitive bidding process, allowing equal access to information contained in share prices
- **Transparency:** Provided by the widest range of information (including pricing and trading volumes)
- **Liquidity:** Available by ease of buying and selling on a timely basis
- **Integrity:** Inspired by confidence in corporate governance of listed firms; reliable accounting information; and strict, efficient regulation

These components help establish an exchange's ability to raise external capital for the firm.

Each exchange has its own governing body whose job it is to do the administration and policy setting for the exchange. Each governing body is made up of permanent officers of the exchange, members of the brokerage community, and individuals representing the community outside the brokerage industry. The exchange is also under the jurisdiction of a securities commission formed by the provincial government (in Canada's case).

Canadian Exchanges Today most stock trading in Canada, particularly by value, takes place through the Toronto Stock Exchange (TSX) (tmx.com), which generally trades the securities of larger firms (senior). A lower value of trading in the securities of junior and early stage firms occurs through the TSX Venture Exchange, owned by the TMX Group. The TMX also operates Shorcan Brokers and CanDeal for fixed income securities (with six Canadian bank dealers); NEX for listed companies below TSX Venture listing standards; the Montreal Exchange for derivative securities; and the Boston Options Exchange (BOX) for equity options. TMX Group also operates CDS (Canadian Depository for Securities) for clearing, depository, and settlement services as well as CDCC (Canadian Derivatives Clearing Corporation) a clearing house for derivatives.

Toronto Stock Exchange
tmx.com

In 2004, the Canadian Securities Exchange (CSE) (thecse.com) was recognized formally as a stock exchange to trade the securities of emerging/entrepreneurial companies and it hoped to trade securities from the OTC market. Today Alpha, NEO and Nasdaq Canada are also recognized stock exchanges. The Bourse de Montréal (ME) (m-x.ca) specializing in derivative securities is now part of the TSX. The Intercontinental Exchange operates ICE NGX out of Calgary providing electronic trading for the natural gas and electricity markets. These last two exchanges will be examined in Chapter 19.

Stock exchanges set minimum standards for earnings, assets, shares outstanding, and trading volumes for the companies of all securities listed on the exchange. The TSX accounts for about 54 percent of the share volume of trading in listed stocks in Canada. There are about 1,600 companies listed on the TSX, with a total quoted market value of over $3 trillion. The TSX Venture Exchange has a similar number of firms listed but with a market value of only $50 billion.

Over 100 firms with trading privileges are represented on the TSX, which is established by purchasing a "seat" on the exchange, becoming a member of a self-regulatory organization (SRO) (iiroc.ca), establishing a CDS clearing account (cds.ca), and having electronic access to the TSX and/ or TSX Venture Trading Engine.

The TSX became one of the world's first publicly traded exchanges (X) and earns its profits from fees for listing (yearly fees for each company), from trading (each trade of the brokers), and from data services.

Markets are often represented by an index that suggests the value and changing values of the exchange. The S&P/TSX Composite Index is an average of approximately 250 securities listed on the Toronto Stock Exchange and is weighted based on the market capitalization (number of shares outstanding × price) of the firms represented by the securities. The other commonly followed index is the Dow Jones Industrial Average (DJIA), which represents the New York Stock Exchange. However, it samples only the 30 "best" firms in the United States and is weighted only on the price of those shares. This represents a market-weighted versus a price-weighted index.

Alternative Trading Systems Also known as Electronic Communication Networks (ECNs), alternative trading systems (ATS) are exchanges that use the Internet to electronically match buy and sell orders automatically, although without a match there is no market made as in an organized exchange. These systems or networks have the sanction of securities commissions, and participants include retail and institutional investors, brokers, and dealers. ATS may provide

- Lower trading costs by creating better execution
- More price transparency
- "After hours" trading
- Anonymity and reduced information leakage

Competing ATS in Canada that have captured 38 percent of share trading volume by value include Alpha, operated by TMX, making it the dominant player by trading value. Several other ATS operate in Canada as well (Lynx (LYNX), Liquidnet (LIQUIDNET), Omega (OMEGA) and TriAct (MATCH NOW), Instinet (ICX)). The Ontario Securities Commission (OSC) oversees these marketplaces (osc.gov.on.ca/en/Marketplaces_index.htm).

Foreign Exchanges As the industrialized world has grown, capital markets around the globe have grown in sophistication and size. The world's major exchanges, based on trading activity (liquidity) not outstanding value, are shown in Figure 14–12. Capital is not only available to large corporations in many markets, but also capital flows between markets can have significant effects on a nation's economy. There are over 60 regulated securities exchanges worldwide. The New York Stock Exchange (NYSE) (nyse.com) is the largest in the world by value traded, at about 27 percent, whereas the Toronto Stock Exchange ranks thirteenth on this basis, although on market value it ranks eleventh. However, the Canadian equity market represents only about 3 percent of the world's capital market. There are ongoing trends to amalgamate world exchanges across international boundaries.

NYSE
nyse.com
Euronext
euronext.com
World Federation
of Exchanges
world-exchanges.org

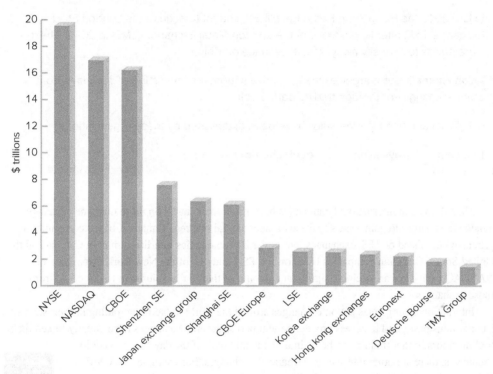

Figure 14–12 World equity markets (top 13): Annual value traded 2019 (approximately 90% of world total)

FINANCE IN ACTION

Going Global!

With growing international trading integration, large capital movements seeking better returns, and standardization in accounting standards coming with IFRS, there has been pressure for consolidation among the world's financial exchanges. Financial firms must have a global presence. Leading up to the financial crisis of 2008, CME Group acquired CBOT (Chicago Board of Trade, for futures and options) and NYMEX (New York Mercantile Exchange), creating the world's largest exchange for derivative and commodity products. The NYSE acquired Euronext of the Netherlands, the largest stock exchange in Europe, in 2007 and then spun it off in 2014.

After a respite, acquisition consolidations returned in late 2010. The Singapore Exchange made a bid for ASX (the Australian Exchange), which was rejected by the Australian

Many Canadian international companies have listed their shares on more than one exchange outside the country to gain access to these broader capital markets. Canadian-based companies are primarily interlisted on U.S. exchanges, with over 200 companies interlisted in both Canada and the United States. Canadian companies listed on the TSX and one of the New York, American, or NASDAQ exchanges are seeing a significant amount of their daily volume in trades come from those exchanges.

International companies list on exchanges around the world to facilitate trading in their shares on a continuous basis, and to access broader capital pools. Several exchanges have already linked their trading floors so that trading can be maintained at all hours of the day. Besides equity exchanges, there are other international financial exchanges. For example, the CME Group, which specializes in metals, foreign exchange currencies, and interest rate futures contracts, has instituted 24-hour computer trading by linking with Reuters Holding PLC. This system, called Globex, enables customers around the world to trade futures and options products when their own exchange is closed.

CME Group
cmegroup.com

The Over-the-Counter Markets

Investment dealers maintain large inventories of securities and facilitate trading activity in the over-the-counter (OTC) market, a market for securities that are not listed on an exchange as they have not met the listing requirements. There is no central location for the OTC market; instead, a network of brokers and dealers is linked by computer display terminals, telephones, and teletypes. Although the organized exchanges trade by auction, the OTC market carries out trading by negotiation.

Many dealers who hold inventories of securities or brokers who facilitate trades establish prices, thus making markets in the securities. With the advent of a centralized computer to keep track of all trades and prices, potential traders have up-to-the-minute price information on all competing traders. This creates competitive pricing. However, there are no listing requirements in the OTC market even if prices are available from an electronic quote system.

Historically, trading in bonds and other fixed income securities in Canada has occurred in the OTC market. This market has traditionally been somewhat reluctant to reveal much information about these trades between dealers. The Investment Dealers Association and the Toronto Stock Exchange (TMX) have established CanDeal (candeal.ca), an electronic trading system that will report in real time the pricing on debt inventories of the major institutions. These institutions provide liquidity to the debt markets. It is hoped that as this information becomes more available it will allow these markets to become more transparent to investors.

CanDeal
candeal.ca

Challenges for the Canadian Exchanges

The Canadian capital markets face several challenges. In raising capital, corporations seek the most competitive market to ensure the least expensive sources of capital. That often means looking beyond Canada's borders, often to the capital markets of the United States. Figure 14–13 identifies the holdings of Canadians abroad and of foreigners in Canada in the capital markets. Well-functioning capital markets require secondary markets with good trading volumes to ensure that prices are fair and reliable. To address this threat from U.S. markets, the Canadian markets have coordinated their efforts and specialized. The TSX, as the senior equities exchange, is seeking links with other global markets to allow 24-hour trading, and has allowed the trading of interlisted stocks in both Canadian and U.S. dollars.

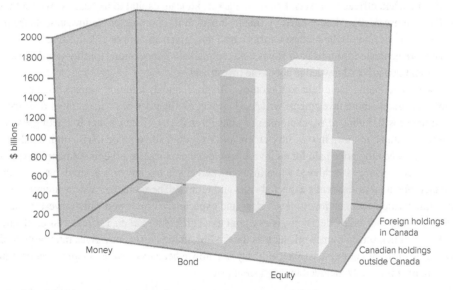

Figure 14–13 Money and capital market investments, 2019

In comparison to the New York markets, the secondary markets in Canada are thin, with fewer buyers and sellers. This condition makes it difficult to carry out large transactions without a significant price effect. The U.S. markets have more participants, a broader range of securities, and investors with greater willingness to take risks. Dealers have played a much larger role in the organized exchanges, acting as specialists that make markets in given stocks. This has meant that a seller generally would have to give up shares at a lower price, on the TSX versus the NYSE, to make them marketable. The extremely liquid markets in the United States have tended to attract business away from Canadian markets. To reduce this relatively higher price of liquidity, the Toronto Stock Exchange has been urging a larger role for dealers acting as principals rather than brokers in stock trading.

Another threat to the Canadian exchanges is common share trading that takes place in the "upstairs rooms" of the investment dealers. This "upstairs trading" of investment dealers refers to the practice of dealers matching large trades in shares between institutional investors through their own trading floors, without first putting the trade to the competitive pricing of the stock exchange. However, the TSX has established an electronic call market for the Canadian markets to counteract upstairs trading. With this system, institutional investors are able to trade large blocks of shares through a computer that matches buy and sell orders without disrupting prices, and since orders quickly go through the TSX's books it is hoped that all investors will receive the best available prices.

As identified in the Finance in Action box, "Going Global!" the other threat to Canadian securities markets is the ongoing worldwide consolidation of exchanges and the interlisting of securities.

The concern with these challenges is that the Canadian stock exchanges may become irrelevant in the execution of trading and the pricing of securities. This will weaken their regulatory role and their function of providing efficient markets with fair prices. It is probably safe to say that over the next decade securities markets will become more competitive as computer systems are employed to do more and more of the trading and as innovations are found that make the secondary markets more liquid. The Investment Industry Association of Canada, through its website, identifies the key issues that challenge the Canadian capital markets.

LO5 MARKET EFFICIENCY

This chapter has discussed the capital markets that allocate monies from those who save to those who borrow. Capital is employed to increase the productive capacity and, thus, the wealth of our society. It has been suggested that competitive and efficient markets accomplish this beneficial allocation of capital. However, we have not yet given criteria to judge whether the Canadian securities markets are competitive and efficient markets. Efficient markets allocate capital to its best use without undue costs. The best use of capital as defined by finance refers to its commitment to investments from which we expect to achieve the highest returns based on a given amount of risk. Returns from an investment are generated from its cash flows, and the market's expectations for those cash flows are derived from the market's knowledge about the investment.

In a well-functioning capital market, monies will move quickly into investments that promise superior returns, and those investments will rise in price. As the price of an investment rises its expected return will diminish. We explored this concept in Part 4, "The Capital Budgeting Process." Capital will continue to move into an investment and its price will continue to rise until a balance is achieved between the price paid for an investment and the returns that the investment is expected to generate. That balance is achieved when investors perceive a fair return is offered, based on the known facts about an investment's expected risks and returns. Therefore, the wide availability of relevant information about an investment's risks and expected returns, upon which investors can base their buying and selling decisions, is essential to an efficient market. Those decisions determine price! Within a risk-return framework such as the CAPM, market efficiency gives rationality to the pricing mechanism of our markets. We could say that all we need to know about an investment in an efficient market is already included in the current price.

FINANCE IN ACTION

Listing Requirements

For the shares of a corporation to be traded on an exchange, the corporation must meet certain requirements and be accepted by the board of governors of the exchange. Listing requirements differ from exchange to exchange, although the more senior exchanges tend to have tougher listing requirements and are more stringent on the disclosure of "material" information. These disclosure requirements impose greater reporting costs on the firm, in addition to higher listing and maintenance fees required by the exchange.

Corporations desiring to be listed on exchanges have decided that public availability of the stock on an exchange benefits their shareholders. The benefits occur either by providing liquidity to owners or by allowing the company a more viable means for raising external capital for growth and expansion. In return, the company must disclose information about the company and any proposed transactions in a timely manner.

The exchanges have the authority to withdraw a listed security's trading or listing privileges either temporarily or permanently. Such actions would be taken to protect the interests of the investors or at the request of the company in respect to its own securities.

Q1 What are the listings requirements on the TSX versus the Venture Exchange?

Q2 What are the listing fees on the Canadian exchanges as well as Nasdaq?

tmx.com

nasdaq.com

 FINANCE IN ACTION

Do Financial Statements Tell the Truth?

As one of the largest bankruptcies in American history, Enron highlighted investor concern for the "truth" in published financial statements. Apparently, Enron did not disclose the full extent of its liabilities when entering into highly leveraged partnership deals. These statements had been signed off by accounting firms but were eventually called into question. The concern was that many firms and their accountants were aggressively interpreting the rules of disclosure in reporting their financial results.

Valeant Pharmaceuticals of Laval, Quebec, in 2015 was the most valuable company in Canada, shortly before its share price plunged 90 percent. Controversy over drug pricing and Valeant's reporting of "non-GAAP" financial statements led to its investigation by the SEC in the United States. Today Valeant has "re-branded" as Bausch Health.

When investors question the integrity of financial statements, there is the possibility that all information that could be known is not available to the investing public, despite a system of regulatory safeguards. If this occurs, market inefficiencies can develop and then investing would no longer be a fair game. Of concern is that investors having lost some faith in the proper functioning of the capital markets are less willing to invest. This, in turn, will slow capital formation and the pace of economic activity.

The Sarbanes-Oxley Act of 2002, which requires greater scrutiny and reporting of financial results as well as makes corporate executives legally accountable for financial statement accuracy, has imposed greater costs on firms. The Dodd-Frank Act of 2010, for financial regulatory reform, was enacted in response to the financial crisis of 2008.

Q1 By manipulating financial statements, do firms harm the capital markets?

Q2 What are the key provisions of the Dodd-Frank Act?

Q3 How has Bausch Health (Valeant) performed recently and has it revised its accounting practices?

bauschhealth.com

sec.gov

osc.gov.on.ca

Criteria of Efficiency

There are several concepts of market efficiency, and there are many degrees of efficiency, depending on which market we are discussing. Markets in general are efficient when (1) prices adjust rapidly to new information, (2) there is a continuous market in which each successive trade is made at a price close to the previous price (the faster the price responds to new information and the smaller the differences in price changes, the more efficient the market), and (3) the market can absorb large dollar amounts of securities without destabilizing the price. The New York Stock Exchange (NYSE) is the world's most efficient capital market on these criteria, while the Toronto Stock Exchange also appears quite efficient. Let us examine the TSX on these criteria.

After the rapid market reversals of 2001 (tech bubble) and 2008 (financial/liquidity crisis) many would argue that a "bubble" and speculative mentality (greed) had been at play in the markets, although to a large extent the markets were reacting to the weakening economies and the disclosure of numerous questionable and misunderstood investments. Our earlier discussions on the valuation of securities suggested that the market set the current price of a security by the discounting of future expected cash flows. With dramatically decreased profit expectations for companies, investors reduced the present value of expected future cash flows from their equity investments and responded accordingly by selling shares. This new information was quickly reflected in the value of the securities on the exchanges.

If we examine the TSX, we find that almost 99 percent of all the volume traded is within a few cents cents of its previous trade. These small price changes suggest a deep, continuous market and one that is reasonably efficient. Prices are now based on one-cent increments.

 FINANCE IN ACTION

Do Mutual Funds Achieve Superior Returns?

If the markets are not efficient, inasmuch as they do not fully incorporate all available information into share prices in a timely manner, it is possible that those who are "in the know" can exploit the market's inefficiency. This would mean that by developing a trading strategy based on patterns of stock return predictability, an investor should be able to "beat the market." Who would be more in the know than the managers of mutual funds? It is their task to uncover private information by which they can readjust the portfolio of stocks in a mutual fund to take advantage of this new knowledge before the rest of the market.

In a study in 1968, Michael Jensen concluded that mutual funds, after expenses, did worse than randomly selected portfolios of stocks. But there was some evidence in the 1980s, from various studies, that some mutual funds did achieve superior returns. However, in a study that spanned the period 1971 to 1991, Burton G. Malkiel reported in the *Journal of Finance* that mutual funds underperformed the market. His conclusion, based on U.S. markets, was that an investor could do best by purchasing a mutual fund with low management fees and which invested only in a basket of stocks such as S&P/TSX Composite Index. This index fund would do better than a fund that is actively managed. The active manager who trades back and forth between different sectors of the market would probably achieve returns less than the index, would generate excess transaction fees, and would trigger more tax burden for the investor.

On the other hand, we have seen instances where a large buyer of securities has significantly moved the values on the Toronto market, which has had a destabilizing effect. This has occurred because of the size of the transaction in relation to the total volume of the entire market. The impact of a large buy order is much more significant in the Toronto market as compared to one in the much larger New York market. This indicates market inefficiency.

Markets are more efficient as certain characteristics become more in evidence. These characteristics serve to improve the quality of information available to investors. In efficient markets there are many buyers and sellers of securities making numerous trades that reflect their perceptions of new information, as it becomes available. This level of activity creates liquidity in the market. Efficient markets also have a great deal of analysis performed and published on the securities that are traded. Thus, more information becomes available to be reflected in the price of securities. Furthermore, an efficient market is well regulated with high standards for the disclosure of information, to ensure that all market participants have the same information available to them at the same time.

A key variable affecting efficiency is the certainty of the income stream. As price movements are less volatile with more certain income streams, investors are more willing to purchase the securities. Fixed income securities, with known maturities, have reasonably efficient markets. The most efficient market is that for Government of Canada securities. The vast majority of trades in the bond market are with Government of Canada bonds, and in the money markets it is Government of Canada Treasury bills. This is changing as the government retires more of these securities. Corporate bond markets are somewhat efficient but less so than government bond markets. A question still widely debated and researched by academics is whether markets for common stock are truly efficient.

The Efficient Market Hypothesis

If stock markets are efficient, it is very difficult for investors to select portfolios of common stocks that can outperform the stock market in general. That is because all relevant and available information would already be reflected in the stock prices. Share prices move up and down quickly as new information is learned. With market efficiency, share prices reflect the true value of a company's equity.

In the terminology of capital budgeting, purchases and sales of stocks in an efficient market are zero-NPV transactions. An investor receives only the going return for an investment based on its risk. The investor does not receive an abnormal return. An abnormal return would be a return above (or below) what the capital market suggests is fair for the risk of an investment. Furthermore, in an efficient market, since all relevant information is reflected in security prices, the same investor has no need to pay for expensive information.

This concept of market efficiency is called the ***efficient market hypothesis***, and it has been stated in three forms, which have been designated the weak, semistrong, and strong forms. The efficient market hypothesis was developed after research suggested that the markets followed a random walk. Researchers had been seeking to discover cycles in stock market movements but were unable to find any patterns. A random walk is the noncorrelation of future price movements with past price movements. It is what we should expect from efficient markets where new information is rapidly reflected in prices and new information arrives randomly. New information must arrive randomly, as it cannot be known ahead of time. The three forms of market efficiency are grades as to the degree of market efficiency. All three forms refer to the nature of information that is included in the price of a security.

Eugene Fama
chicagobooth.edu
(search "Eugene Fama")

The first level of efficiency, the weak form, simply states that prices reflect all of the information contained in the past price history. This implies that past price information is unrelated to future prices, so attempting to extrapolate trends generates no additional gains to investors. This noncorrelation of future price movements with past price movements has been referred to as a random walk and has received much empirical validation. Despite such empirical validation of the random walk theory of stock price movements, some analysts chart past price movements in the belief that the patterns suggest future price movements. These people are known as ***technical analysts***.

The second level of efficiency is the semistrong form. It states that prices reflect all public information, such as announcements of company earnings forecasts. Most of the research in this area focuses on changes in public information and on the measurement of how rapidly prices converge to a new equilibrium after the release of new information. This research has concluded that this information is rapidly reflected in the stock price.

A third level of efficiency, the strong form, states that all information, both private and public, is immediately reflected in stock prices. Under this form of market efficiency, efficient markets should prevent insiders and large institutions from being able to make profits in excess of the market in general. A number of analyses of the portfolio performance of mutual fund managers have shown that this group of investors does no better than the market as a whole. Other research on the buying patterns of insiders has tended to show that strong form market efficiency does not exist.

Much research in recent years had focused on the measurement of market efficiency. Researchers have generally accepted that markets such as the NYSE and, to a lesser extent, the Toronto Stock Exchange are efficient. They search for abnormalities where some sort of trading rule or market strategy can consistently earn an investor above-normal profits. When these inefficiencies are discovered, the researchers generally seek reasons why abnormal profits can be achieved and do not suggest that the market is inefficient. Some abnormalities have been found related to small-firm portfolios, certain days of the week, or the so-called **January effect**. Research has, in some cases, tended to show that abnormally high profits can be earned during January. The abnormal profits are usually attributed to incomplete or poorly distributed information. However, once this information is given on the six o'clock news, as has been done in recent years, the abnormal profit opportunities usually disappear. Disseminating this information makes the market more efficient.

As communications systems advance, information is being disseminated more quickly and accurately. The Internet brings information directly to investors, quickly bypassing investment brokers and advisors. Furthermore, securities laws are forcing fuller disclosure of inside corporate data. The research has shown that our capital markets generally function well. Disclosure of more and better information, therefore, should be digested and reflected in stock prices, allowing for even better valuations.

 FINANCE IN ACTION

Be Careful What You Say and How You Say It!

One of the obligations of a publicly traded company is that it disclose any material changes in its prospects. This usually involves a press release or a public conference, often done over the Internet.

In the era of "fake news" one has to be especially diligent. When Tesla announced that there was to be a delay in delivery for new reservations on its all-electric sedan, Model 3, CNBC misinterpreted this as a delay for a year on the delivery of all vehicles. The share price immediately dropped. Telsa's announced revenue for 2019 was up, but a close look through the financial statements revealed that sales were down significantly in the United States at a time when competitors were entering the market.

As a result of hacking of the AP site, a fake tweet about President Obama being injured in an explosion dropped share values in the market by $130 billion in a matter of seconds in 2013.

In September 2008, the share price of UAL Corp. (United Airlines) dropped 76 percent in a matter of minutes on news of pending bankruptcy in the midst of great market uncertainty. Trading was stopped for over an hour. But the shares soon popped back up to where they had begun that day. The story happened to again make the newswires six years after it was first reported and a panicky market and automated trading by computers weren't able to discern its correctness.

Q1 What is UAL Corp.'s current share price? How has UAL done in the wake of the Covid-19 pandemic?

united.com
Symbol: UAL

The belief—or nonbelief—in market efficiency is important to those who participate in the financial markets. The efficient market hypothesis suggests that the purchase and sale of financial assets is a fair game in which participants receive an appropriate return based on risk. This means there are no big winners or big losers. For the financial manager, it suggests that prices in the market should be accepted as true reflections of value. If the manager believes otherwise, there should be a strong reason as to why the markets do not reflect the manager's beliefs.

It is likely that in certain markets, prices may not fully reflect all available information. This is what drives analysts, investors, and fund managers to change their portfolios to take advantage of new information before other market participants do. Their buying and selling provides the market with liquidity and to a large extent ensures that prices reflect the new information. The market may be efficient for the general population. Those who study and track it on a regular basis may find it inefficient at times, allowing them to profit from their effort and research.

LO6 SECURITIES REGULATION

Well-functioning capital markets are important for our economic system. Fairness, transparency, liquidity, competitiveness, and efficiency have been suggested as key aspects for good capital markets. Regulation of these markets helps to develop and nurture these key aspects. The securities markets are regulated by the securities commissions and self-regulated by the organized exchanges and trade organizations. As well, there are several other bodies that have an impact on the operation of the markets.

Good regulation requires a system that establishes strong

- Enforcement of rules and standards with effective penalties for abuses
- Financial reporting to provide timely, reliable, and relevant information
- Disclosure of material events that impact on a firm's performance to provide transparency
- Audit procedures to ensure appropriate conduct of the firm's managers
- Independent corporate governance to protect the interests of interested stakeholders

Regulation of the securities industry is a provincial responsibility, with each province and territory having its own securities commission. These commissions provide oversight through the Canadian Securities Administrators (CSA). However, most provinces adopt the regulations of the Ontario Securities Commission (OSC), as most companies are listed and trade on the Toronto Stock Exchange. The securities commission oversees the activities of the self-regulatory securities bodies (IIROC and exchanges). The general exception to that uniformity of provincial approach is Quebec. There have been attempts to have the federal government regulate the securities business to cut down on bureaucratic overlap and present a uniform Canadian capital market.

Canadian Securities
Administrators
securities-administrators.ca

Ontario Securities
Commission
osc.gov.on.ca

Stock exchanges are to a great extent self-regulating, providing rules for investment firms and the firms traded on the exchange. They impose listing requirements, demand regular financial statements, demand notice of material changes in corporate affairs, establish trading rules to protect the public, and enact special rules to govern takeover bids exercised through the exchanges.

The Investment Industry Regulatory Organization of Canada (IIROC), which oversees the investment dealers and the trading activity, is an important player in the self-regulation of securities markets. The investment dealers have set up the Canadian Investors Protection Fund (CIPF) (cipf.ca) to reimburse clients in case of a member firm's failure, to monitor the ethics of clients' conduct, and to set up courses of instruction for securities industry employees. Firms are generally integrated, offering institutional and retail services or offering full service or discount brokerage services. Full-service brokerage offers investors investment advice and research, whereas a discount brokerage relies on investors performing their own research and basically provides only services to buy and sell securities.

Investment Industry
Regulatory Organization
of Canada
iiroc.ca

Reporting a firm's financial activities requires generally accepted accounting principles (GAAP), being replaced by CAS (which is based on IFRS). The accounting standards are set down by the Chartered Professional Accountants of Canada and their handbook (cpacanada.ca) as developed by their Accounting Standards Board (ASB). The accountants are now overseen by the Canadian Public Accountability Board (CPAB). All financial reports of publicly traded securities must be filed electronically and are accessible to the public at SEDAR (sedar.com).

Regulation of the capital markets is also dependent on having a knowledgeable public. Educational programs within the securities business are available through several venues but in particular there is the Canadian Securities Institute (CSI) (csi.ca). Its program is required or highly recommended for most participants in the industry.

The basic structural foundation of the whole financial sector in Canada has evolved from the four pillars of finance; banks, trust companies, insurance companies, and securities dealers. The reasoning of legislators suggested that separation of these functions would diversify the financial system and prevent its possible collapse if these functions were too closely entwined. However, with legislative change and a growing sophistication in the marketplace this separation of the four sectors has been significantly eroded. Today, the larger financial institutions provide all these services. Savings deposits are insured up to $100,000 through the Canadian Deposit Insurance Corporation (CDIC) (cdic.ca).

Canadian Bankers
Association
cba.ca

Financial institutions (federally chartered) and administered pension plans report to the Office of the Superintendent of Financial Institutions (OSFI) (osfi-bsif.gc.ca). Furthermore, the Bank of Canada sets rules for sales practices and the auction of government debt, which forms a large portion of the over-the-counter markets.

Another hallmark of the financial sector has been restrictions on nonresident ownership. This was ostensibly to safeguard investors and depositors, as regulators would have more control over Canadian residents. Banking restrictions have been aimed at preventing one individual or group from buying control for the same reason. These restrictions have been questioned as financial institutions seek access to larger capital pools from around the globe.

The policing of fraudulent or unfair practices has been a major concern of these regulatory bodies since the 1930s. After the market crash of 1929, regulations were implemented requiring traded securities to be registered with adequate disclosure of information (including financial statements), providing penalties for insider trading and requiring the registration of organized exchanges. After the market failures as the new century began, further regulations were developed to

- Hold chief officers of a firm responsible for the accuracy of the financial statements
- Provide for independent auditors and boards of directors
- Restrict the accounting activities of audit firms in conflict-of-interest situations
- Implement new accounting standards to handle the expensing of stock options, disclosure of off-balance-sheet financial exposures, and the treatment of derivative securities

There is still a need for a coordinated approach between the federal and provincial governments to deal with the rapidly changing financial environment. While considering more competition and less concentration of power and decision making, recognition will be given to the need for operational effectiveness in the global financial market. The country's investment industry needs financial muscle to compete with the investment goliaths of the United States and other countries, not only in Canada but also abroad.

We will see more one-stop financial service institutions at the retail level especially, but they will be regulated carefully to prevent conflicts of interest. Financial institutions will lend funds to firms and they will take equity positions in firms by holding securities as investment bankers for their own account. More fee income will be generated by arranging financing for corporations directly with savers rather than acting as intermediaries. There will be a global influence on our financial institutions but there will also be more institutions that find a regional or product niche.

 FINANCE IN ACTION

The Regulatory Environment

The Investment Industry Regulatory Organization of Canada (IIROC) provides surveillance, investigation, and enforcement services to the organized exchanges of Canada.

SUMMARY

1. Money markets refer to the wholesale trading of financial assets with less than one year to maturity. The capital markets, comprising the equity, bond, and mortgage markets, are of longer terms to maturity. A primary market is where a security is first issued, and there is a cash flow to the firm or government. The trading of financial securities occurs in secondary markets. (LO1)

2. In capital and money markets, corporations compete for funds not only among themselves but also with government units of all kinds. Corporations account for only about one-third of all funds raised in the Canadian capital market. Nonresidents have become significant holders of Canadian financial assets. Canadian corporations and governments increasingly seek funds from outside Canada. Both bonds and stocks are important sources of funding for the corporation, although their use shows wide variation from year to year. (LO2)

3. The three-sector economy consists of households, corporations, and governmental units, and funds flow through the capital markets from suppliers of funds to the ultimate users. This process is highly dependent on the efficiency of the financial institutions that act as intermediaries in channelling the funds to the most productive users. (LO3)

4. Security markets are divided into organized exchanges and over-the-counter markets. Brokers act as agents for stock exchange transactions, and dealers make markets over the counter at their own risk as owners of the securities they trade. The Toronto Stock Exchange is Canada's senior organized stock exchange. Although the OTC market for shares is not significant in Canada, corporate bond trades and trades in municipal, provincial, and federal government securities are transacted in significant amounts over the counter. (LO4)

5. Throughout this chapter we have tried to present the concept of efficient markets doing an important job in allocating financial capital. We find the existing markets struggling to provide liquidity for both the corporation and the investor while they adjust efficiently to new information. Because of the laws governing the markets, much information is available for investors, and this in itself creates more competitive prices. Moreover, there are few cases of fraud and manipulation. In the future we expect even more efficient markets, with expanded roles for the investment dealers aimed at increasing liquidity for secondary trading. (LO5)

6. The financial environment in Canada is changing rapidly. Traditionally we have had the four pillars of banks, trusts, insurance, and securities, but those pillars have faded. Although governments continue to be concerned about potential conflicts of interest, they have allowed the move toward one-stop financial services. Financial institutions will grow larger to compete effectively in the global financial market. There will be closer links between commercial banking that has tended to take only loan positions and investment banking that takes equity positions in corporations requiring funding. (LO6)

DISCUSSION QUESTIONS

1. Name the major competitors for funds in the capital markets. (LO3)

2. How does the economy influence the amount of funds raised by the federal government in the long-term markets? (LO2)

3. Discuss the average maturity of the federal government's marketable interest-bearing public debt and the implications for the money and capital markets if the present trend continues. (LO2)

4. What implications are there for the capital markets as the federal government reduces/increases its accumulated debt? (LO2)

5. What has been the composition of long-term financing by corporations over the past decade? (LO2)

6. Comment on the use of external versus internal sources of funds by corporations. (LO2)

7. Explain the role of financial intermediaries in the flow of funds through the economy. (LO4)

8. Discuss the importance of security markets for both the corporation and the shareholder or bondholder. (LO4)

9. What is the difference between organized exchanges and over-the-counter markets? (LO4)

10. Why does the Toronto Stock Exchange have listing requirements? What are the major requirements? How do they compare with the listing requirements of the other exchanges? (LO4)

11. How would you define efficient securities markets? (LO5)

12. The efficient market hypothesis is interpreted in a weak form, a semistrong form, and a strong form. How can we differentiate its various forms? (LO5)

13. What is meant by abnormal profits? (LO5)

14. Discuss the characteristics that would make a market efficient. (LO5)

15. Discuss tests you would develop to prove market inefficiencies. (LO5)

16. Why do we have the four pillars of finance concept in Canada? (LO6)

17. What are the implications of the changing regulations governing the Canadian securities industry? (LO6)

18. Discuss the changes currently occurring in Canada's financial and regulatory environment. (LO6)

INTERNET RESOURCES AND QUESTIONS

Market information about the history of exchanges, listing requirements, and quotes on securities is available at the exchange websites:

tmx.com

m-x.ca

nyse.com

nasdaq.com

Market information on the bond market:

iiroc.ca

cbonds.com/countries/Canada-bond

tmxmoney.com/en/market_activity/candeal.html

For securities and exchange commissions:

osc.gov.on.ca   Ontario

sec.gov   United States

iosco.org   International Organization of Securities Commissions

For worldwide stock exchanges, see the World Federation of Exchanges:

world-exchanges.org

1. Identify the listing costs of the various exchanges in Canada and the United States.

    a. Does it make sense to have so many exchanges in Canada?

    b. Why might a firm prefer to list on NASDAQ rather than the NYSE?

    c. Why might a Canadian firm prefer to list on the NYSE rather than the Toronto Stock Exchange?

2. Find the amount and type of protection afforded investors through the Canadian Investor Protection Fund (cipf.ca) as compared to the Canadian Deposit Insurance Corporation (cdic.ca).

15

Investment Underwriting

LEARNING OBJECTIVES

LO1 Characterize investment dealers as intermediaries between corporations and governments in need of funds and the investing public.

LO2 Classify the various roles of investment dealers.

LO3 Outline the distribution process, the allocation of securities among syndicate participants, and the calculation of the spread as cost or a return.

LO4 Analyze the dealer's role in pricing corporate securities. Evaluate the influence of issued securities on earnings per share and market share price.

LO5 Appraise the pros and cons of going public versus going private when raising funds.

LO6 Describe a leveraged buyout.

In Chapter 15 we examine the role of the investment dealer in finding capital, the advantages and disadvantages of selling securities to the public, and the private placement of securities with insurance companies, pension funds, and other lenders.

THE INVESTMENT INDUSTRY

The term ***investment dealer*** tends to be a Canadian term, whereas Americans use ***investment banker*** for a securities corporation that generally performs the same functions. Although we will concentrate on the investment dealer's underwriting function, we should identify the scope of the dealer's activities. One may hear the terms ***investment house, securities house, brokerage,*** or ***dealer*** used interchangeably; they are generally the same. But there is an important distinction between the dealer and the broker functions, although the same firms often perform both functions.

An investment dealer acts as a true intermediary, buying securities on its own behalf and taking the risk that it can resell the securities at a profit. This means that a dealer, through its trading desks, will take significant positions in financial assets of the money markets, bond markets, and equity markets. The corporate financing function, or underwriting, is a function of the primary market and is the focus of this chapter.

Brokers act as agents, receiving a commission by acting for a buyer or seller of securities. The trading function is conducted in the secondary markets and was a focus of Chapter 14. Brokerage is a commission-based function at the retail level for individual investors (discount and full-service) and at the wholesale level for institutions. In 2020 there were 171 investment dealer firms in Canada (100 at the retail level).

Investment Industry
Association of Canada
iiac.ca

Additionally, dealers will have a department to give advice and plan merger and acquisition activities (M&A), sometimes taking capital positions. There will be a management services department to manage client capital and a department that carries on research related to the capital markets, analyzing the economy and specific financial securities.

The so-called corporate finance fraternity within the investment dealer community has long been thought of as an elite group, with memberships in country clubs, yacht clubs, and other such venerable institutions. Although still lucrative, competition has become the new way of doing business. Even the fittest must merge to survive, while others are forced to drop out of the game. Today, the Canadian chartered banks and large foreign investment banking firms dominate the securities business. Approved professionals in the securities business—approximately 30,000 in Canada—can be compensated well, are well trained, and work long and hard hours because of the increasingly competitive environment.

LO1 THE ROLE OF THE INVESTMENT DEALER

The investment dealer, or underwriter, is the one link between the corporation in need of funds and the investor. Although we identified, in Figure 14–8, the significance of internally generated profits and cash flows, the firm also has a need for external funds to invest in receivables, inventories, and capital assets. The capital markets, where these funds may be available, are impersonal and highly specialized. They impose requirements on the firm as to the disclosure of information and the costs associated with that disclosure.

This is where the investment dealer can assist the firm. As a middleperson, the investment dealer is responsible for designing and packaging a security offering and selling the securities to the public. This is an important function that assists in capital formation and the creation of financial securities. With global competition in the capital markets, investment firms must be nimble, aggressive, and innovative. They need the backing of substantial capital themselves to take on the risks required in this business. This is why, as identified in Table 15-1, Canada's largest investment dealers are primarily owned by the big banks.

Table 15–1 Canada's largest investment dealers

RBC Dominion Securities
Scotia Capital
BMO Nesbitt Burns
TD Securities
CIBC World Markets
National Bank Financial
Canaccord Genuity Capital
Optimum Group
GMP Capital

LO2 Enumeration of Functions

The investment dealer plays a number of key roles in the distribution of securities.

Underwriter The underwriting function involves the purchase of a new issue of securities from an issuer at an agreed price. As underwriter, the investment dealer assumes the risk of reselling the securities to those sectors of the economy with excess funds. Usually, the underwriter is a group of investment dealers that share the task of selling the issue. Often, their risk is reduced by an "out clause" that allows them to back away from selling the securities if the market drops suddenly.

The underwriting function has increasingly included the bought deal. With this process, one dealer assumes all the risk and operates over a shorter time period. The dealer purchases the whole issue from well-established firms that qualify for the short-time filing procedures with the securities commission by way of a short-form prospectus. The dealer sells it either publicly or privately but usually to customers who have expressed a solid interest in the issue. Of some concern has been the potential exclusion of the retail client in these quick, prepackaged bought deals. Today, the bought deal is often being done on an overnight basis, and thus the underwriting fees can be reduced significantly because the risk to the underwriter has been reduced.

By giving a firm commitment to purchase the securities from the corporation, the dealer is said to underwrite any risks that might be associated with a new issue. The trend to the bought deal is also partially responsible for the increased need for capital in the investment business. Therefore, we have seen mergers and the entry of the large banks into the investment business. While the risk may be fairly low in handling a bond offering for the Royal Bank in a stable market, such may not be the case in selling the shares of a lesser-known firm in a very volatile market environment.

Though the public offerings of most large, well-established firms usually require the investment dealers to assume the risk of distribution, issues for relatively unknown corporations are still handled on a best efforts or commission basis. These investment offerings are also referred to as a marketed deal and often involve a "roadshow" where management of the firm must make presentations about the company across the country with the assistance of the underwriters. This practice is more common in the United States, even for the largest firms.

An issue of securities by a corporation that adds to its securities already outstanding in the public hands is referred to as a seasoned offering. The first time securities are offered for sale to the public is referred to as an initial public offering (IPO).

Market Maker During distribution and later, the investment dealer may become a market maker in a given security—that is, engaging in the buying and selling of the security to ensure a liquid market. By maintaining an inventory in various securities, the dealer stands ready to buy and sell securities even if a buyer and seller are not available at the same time. A well-functioning secondary market enhances the attractiveness of securities by providing liquidity. The dealer may also provide research on the firm to encourage active investor interest.

Advisor The investment dealer may advise clients on a continuing basis about the securities to be sold, whether a foreign issue would be appropriate; the number of shares or units for distribution; the pricing, including special features; and the timing of the sale. A company considering a stock issuance to the public may be persuaded, in counsel with an investment dealer, to borrow the funds from an insurance company or, if stock is to be sold, to wait for two more quarters of earnings before going to the market. The investment dealer also provides important advisory services in the area of mergers and acquisitions, leveraged buyouts, and corporate restructuring.

Agency Functions The investment dealer may act as an agent for a corporation that wishes to place its securities privately with an insurance company, a pension fund, or a wealthy individual. In this instance the investment dealer shops around among potential investors and negotiates the best possible deal for the corporation. It may also serve as an agent in merger and acquisition transactions. Because of the many critical roles the investment dealer plays, it may be requested to have a representative sit on the board of directors of the client company.

FINANCE IN ACTION

To Market! To Market!

In 2014, Descartes issued $128,250,000 in common shares at a public issue price of $13.50 with an underwriting fee of $0.6075 per share, for a spread of 4.50 percent. The underwriters would earn $5.8 million. Other expenses were $0.7 million for total flotation costs of a little over 5 percent. This was a secondary issue.

New issues of equities listed on the TSX can be found by visiting the TSX website (tmx.com) and searching new company listings and IPOs. Details on an issue can then be found in a *prospectus* produced by the company and its underwriters, and these are available at the SEDAR site (sedar.com). Search the database for public companies under "New Prospectuses."

The prospectus represents the public announcement of a new security issue.

Q1 What annual return would an investor have earned (ignoring dividends) if they purchased these shares in 2014?

Q1 What are the details (as above) of two recent issues of securities (debt and/or equity)?

Symbol: DSG

THE DISTRIBUTION PROCESS

The actual distribution process requires the active participation of a number of parties. The principal, or managing investment dealer, usually calls on other investment houses to share the burden of risk and to aid in the distribution. To this end, they form an underwriting syndicate, composed of as few as 2 or as many as 100 investment houses. This is also referred to as the banking group because they are on the hook for the financing of the issue. In Figure 15–1, we see a typical case in which a hypothetical firm, the Maxwell Corporation, wishes to issue 250,000 additional shares of stock, with CIBC World Markets as the managing underwriter and an underwriting syndicate of 15 firms.

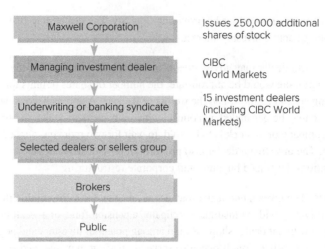

Maxwell Corporation	Issues 250,000 additional shares of stock
Managing investment dealer	CIBC World Markets
Underwriting or banking syndicate	15 investment dealers (including CIBC World Markets)
Selected dealers or sellers group	
Brokers	
Public	

Figure 15–1 Distribution process for an investment deal

The managing investment dealer also helps prepare a prospectus for the corporation issuing the securities. The governing bodies of securities exchanges require full disclosure of all relevant information on publicly traded securities. A prospectus must be prepared for any issue of securities. It includes audited financial statements, information on the firm's operations and history, the major shareholders, and other relevant information. The securities body that examines the prospectus does not pass judgment on the advisability of an investment in the securities offered to the public. It does, however, ensure that adequate information is contained in the prospectus to allow an investor to make an informed decision.

If a corporation already has publicly traded shares outstanding with a market value in excess of $75 million, it may be able to shorten the time and effort required for preparation by filing a short-form prospectus. A corporation that has filed annual and interim financial statements for at least three years can focus its attention on the specific security offering. Matters of price, the features of the security, and the use of the proceeds of the issue are the important considerations. This process is known as the prompt offering qualification system (POP) and has greatly assisted the bought deal. Putting the full prospectus or POP together is an important role of the managing investment dealer.

The banking or underwriting syndicate purchases shares from the Maxwell Corporation and distributes them through channels to the selected dealers or selling group. Although the selling group can purchase the securities at a discount, the group is not financially responsible for underwriting of the issue beyond its own purchases. Syndicate members act as wholesalers in distributing the shares to brokers and dealers who eventually sell the shares to the public. Large investment houses are usually vertically integrated, acting as underwriter-dealer-broker and capturing more fees and commissions.

The Spread

The underwriting spread represents the total compensation available to those who participate in the distribution process. As an example, examine the initial public issue of 2 million shares of Softwood Timber Company.

Public (retail) Price	Underwriter's Price	Differential (spread)
$20.50	$19.3725	$1.1275
$41,000,000	$38,745,000	$2,255,000

The spread (differential between public price and proceeds to issuing company) is often calculated as a percentage based on the price to the public. In this example it would be

$$Spread = \frac{\$1.1275}{\$20.50} = 0.055 = 5.5\%$$

This spread is the flotation cost adjustment introduced in Chapter 11 within the cost of capital calculations. Generally, there are additional costs to the issue (listing fees, legal, audit, other), increasing the flotation expense.

In this example, if the firm had required $41,000,000 they would have had to issue 2,116,402 shares (ignoring other flotation expenses):

$$\text{Number of shares required} = \frac{\textbf{Monies required}}{\textbf{Net proceeds per share}} = \frac{\$41,000,000}{\$19.3725} = 2,116,403$$

However, the return to the underwriter or cost to the firm is based on the price they pay (or receive) for the securities after underwriting costs are deducted. In this example the return (cost) would be

$$\text{Return (cost)} = \frac{\$1.1275}{\$19.3725} = 0.0582 = 5.82\%$$

The further down the dealer is in the distribution process, the higher the price the investment firm must pay for shares. The managing underwriter pays $19.3725, whereas dealers in the selling group syndicate pay $20. This also means that a dealer, by reselling as far down the distribution chain as it can, stands to make a higher profit. If, for example, the managing underwriter resells a volume of shares to a member of the selling group syndicate, it earns $0.6275 per share; for each share the managing underwriter resells directly to the public, it makes $1.1275. This will also alter the return the investment firm receives.

Underwriting, in this sample, represents a total spread of $1.1275, or 5.5 percent, of the offering price. In general, the larger the dollar value of an issue, the smaller the spread as a percentage of the offering price. The underwriting compensation on debt securities will range from about 0.5 percent for larger issues to over 7 percent for smaller issues. On equity issues the spread will range from about 2.25 percent to over 11 percent.

There are two components to flotation costs: the underwriting compensation (spread) and the additional out-of-pocket expenses such as printing and legal costs. Out-of-pocket expenses will range from about 0.3 percent to over 7 percent for either type of issue. Both the underwriting and other expenses of issuing new securities, which can be substantial for a smaller issue, are referred to as the flotation cost.

For the Softwood Timber Company issue, the company's direct issue expenses were estimated at $275,000, or about two-thirds of 1 percent of the total issue proceeds. Thus, the total flotation costs for the issue were just over 6 percent of the total proceeds.

Figure 15–2 and the resultant calculations assume the shares are sold at their offering price of $20.50. If adverse market conditions arise before the distribution is completed or if the issue is mispriced relative to the prices of other competing securities, it may have to be sold for a lesser amount. In these situations the actual realized commissions of the underwriting group are less than the amounts originally planned.

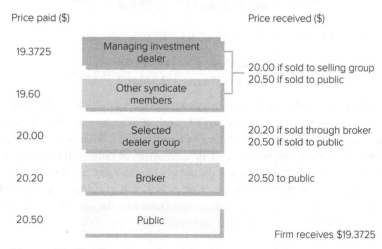

Figure 15–2 Allocation of underwriting spread

PRICING THE SECURITY

Because the syndicate members purchase the stock for redistribution in the marketing channels, they must be careful about the pricing of the stock. When a stock is sold to the public for the first time (i.e., when the firm is going public), the managing investment dealer does an in-depth analysis of the company to determine its value. The study includes an analysis of the firm's industry, financial characteristics, and anticipated earnings and dividend-paying capability.

Based on appropriate valuation techniques that include the formulas from Chapter 10, a tentative price is assigned and compared to that commanded by the common shares of similar firms in a given industry. If the industry's average price-earnings ratio is 10, for example, the issue price should probably not be set far above this norm. Besides the fundamental valuation and the industry comparison, the anticipated public demand for the new issue is a major factor in pricing.

Rather than new issues, however, the majority of common stock flotations handled by investment dealers are additional issues of stocks or bonds for companies already trading publicly in the secondary markets. In such cases, the price is generally set at a level slightly below the current market price for the company's common stock. This process, known as underpricing, helps create a receptive market for the securities, thereby reducing somewhat the pricing risk borne by the underwriting syndicate.

At times an investment dealer handles large blocks of securities for existing shareholders. Because the number of shares may be too large to trade in normal channels, the investment dealer manages the issue and prices the stock below current prices to the public. Such a process of selling the shares of an existing shareholder is known as a secondary offering, in contrast to a primary offering in which corporate securities are sold directly by the corporation.

Dilution

The actual or perceived dilutive effect on shares currently outstanding is a problem facing companies when they issue additional securities. In the case of the Maxwell Corporation, the issuance of 250,000 new shares may represent a 10 percent increment to the 2.5 million shares currently in existence. Let us suppose that earnings are currently $5 million and the capital raised from the public issue will eventually generate additional earnings of $775,000. We will calculate three EPS figures:

1. Before the issue

$$EPS = \frac{\text{Earnings}}{\text{Number of shares}} = \frac{\$5,000,000}{2,500,000} = \$2$$

2. After initial issue

$$EPS = \frac{\text{Earnings}}{\text{Number of shares}} = \frac{\$5,000,000}{2,750,000} = \$1.82$$

3. After the issue, when capital raised impacts to increase earnings

$$EPS = \frac{\text{Earnings}}{\text{Number of shares}} = \frac{\$5,775,000}{2,750,000} = \$2.10$$

The proceeds from the sale of new shares may well be expected to provide the increased earnings necessary to bring earnings back to or to surpass $2 per share as in our example. Although financial theory dictates that a new equity issue should not be undertaken if it diminishes the overall wealth of current shareholders, there may be a time lag in the recovery of earnings per share as a result of the increased shares outstanding, especially if the proceeds are invested in a relatively new business development. For this reason, there may be a temporary weakness in a stock when an issue of additional shares is proposed. In most cases, this is overcome with the passage of time as the wisdom of management's financial decision making is demonstrated.

Market Stabilization

Another problem may set in when the actual public distribution begins—namely, unanticipated weakness in the stock or bond market. Since the sales group has made a firm commitment to purchase stock at a given price for redistribution, it is essential that the price of the stock remain relatively strong. If, in the Softwood Timber Company situation, syndicate members were committed to purchasing the stock at $19.60 or better, they could be in trouble if the sales price fell to $19 or $18. The managing investment dealer or underwriter is generally responsible for stabilizing the offering during the distribution period and may accomplish this by repurchasing securities as the market price moves below the initial public offering price. This is market stabilization.

The period of stabilization usually lasts two or three days after the initial offering, but it may extend up to 30 days for difficult-to-distribute securities. In a very poor market environment, stabilization may be virtually impossible to achieve. Investment dealers may be forced to take substantial losses due to deteriorating stock prices.

Aftermarket

The investment dealer is also interested in how well the underwritten security behaves after the distribution period, as its ultimate reputation rests on bringing strong securities to the market. This is particularly true for initial public offerings.

Research has indicated that initial public offerings tend to do well in the immediate aftermarket: one day as well as several months after issue show excess returns (movement in the price of the stock above and beyond the market). This seems to be true worldwide. However, initial offerings underperform in the first few years after the immediate aftermarket.

The managing underwriter may underprice the issue initially to ensure a successful offering, and therefore the value often jumps after the issue first goes public. The efficiency of the market eventually takes hold, so sustained long-term performance is very much dependent on the quality of the issue and the market conditions at play.

THE SECURITIES INDUSTRY IN CANADA

Dramatic changes in the investment business in Canada have occurred due to the deregulation of the industry in the 1980s, internationalization of the capital markets, and technological advances. Besides the underwriting function, the investment firms have expanded their corporate finance, merger/acquisition advisory service, derivatives, and bond trading activities. In some cases as the markets gain in efficiency, the investment firms are consolidating and focusing their activities on those functions in which they have a competitive advantage.

Traditionally, in Canada banks looked after the short-term funding needs of businesses, investment dealers took care of long-term funding, and the insurance business acted to reduce risk exposure. In 1987, the federal government began to dismantle the framework that separated these functions, and this allowed the banks fuller participation in investment dealer and insurance activities. The Canadian banks moved quickly, buying up existing investment dealers or setting up their own investment houses and eventually producing solid returns on these investments.

Although there are over 100 investment firms in the securities industry, there are only a handful of dominant players. The difficulty that the investment firms of Canada face is a limited capital base. A solid capital base is required in an era when investment firms must risk large amounts of capital to compete by way of the bought deal. Canadian securities firms in capabilities and expertise rank favourably with any investment firm in the world.

One key trend has been a movement toward the integration of services. Large investment firms have moved to combine their banking and investment trading operations with the aid of computerized trading systems. Immense trading floors combine the trading operations of the equity, debt, money, and forward markets. Specialized sections for derivatives and corporate banking have been set up in New York, the world's largest financial market. Derivatives present an alternative to the risk-reduction capabilities of the insurance business. Our concern with these trading activities is

Reshaping America's Securities Business

In 2008, the world dealt with the most dramatic financial crisis since the Depression and the bank failures of the 1930s. The securities business was reshaped in ways somewhat similar to the reorganization of investment dealers in Canada in the 1990s. The securities firms in the United States suddenly needed the capital base provided by banking institutions with their more carefully regulated environment and access to more stable funding from retail deposits.

The major investment bankers got into financial difficulties by expanding credit beyond appropriate bounds. They increased their leverage (sometimes in excess of 40 times equity) based on surging property values in the subprime mortgage business and accepted questionable credit instruments. There was a lack of effective oversight by the regulatory bodies.

In 2007, Bear Stearns was acquired by JP Morgan Chase in a forced sale. In September 2008, Lehman Brothers, in business for 158 years, filed for the largest bankruptcy (over $600 billion) in history, and the dominos continued to fall. Merrill Lynch was acquired by Bank of America, while Goldman Sachs (goldmansachs.com) and Morgan Stanley became bank holding companies. Furthermore, the governments in the United States and several European countries began to take equity positions in the banks and their newly acquired investment arms.

Today, investment firms require an international presence, either through ownership interests or partnerships, to properly serve their clients. Although competing globally, the investment forms are often subject to local financial regulation, complicating their administrative operations.

The Dodd-Frank Wall Street Reform and Consumer Protection Act of 2010 further reshaped the financial landscape (sec.gov/about/laws/wallstreetreform-cpa.pdf).

By 2017 under the Trump administration there began a move to once again deregulate the securities business.

Q1 Check out the Goldman Sachs "Conservation Fund."

goldmansachs.com   Symbol: GS

---

that they bypass the traditional exchange-based trading floors that provide for transparency of trades. To ensure market efficiency, it is important that information on the prices of executed trades be widely available to all participants in the markets.

Another trend in the investment industry in Canada has been the movement to global trading units. With growing international trade investment, dealers have expanded to other countries, following their clients. Canadian investment dealers operate in the large capital markets of the world, raising capital for Canadian governments and corporations. Often the debt issues of the provinces and other borrowers are sold in the Euromarkets and the U.S markets. Figures 14–1 and 14–5 illustrate the large amounts of funding raised abroad. These international markets, besides offering access to large capital pools, have highly skilled professionals and more services than the Canadian markets and provide greater liquidity for the securities. This all translates into cost savings.

Canadian banks have also moved to create North American discount brokerage services with the purchases of U.S. firms. This is a result of the dramatic increase in participation in the capital markets by the retail investor.

The globalization of the capital markets is also leading to 24-hour trading in many financial assets. Trading desks of the large firms already pass their "book" of securities from Toronto to Tokyo to London and back to Toronto so that clients can adjust their portfolios of financial assets at any time. The demands of the worldwide competitive capital markets are leading Canadian investment firms to integrate and specialize in the services in which they enjoy the best advantage. Sometimes this can best be done in Canadian capital markets, and sometimes it can best be done in other capital markets around the globe.

UNDERWRITING ACTIVITY IN CANADA

Corporate issues of debt and equity underwritten in 2010 and 2018 are presented in Figure 15–3. Totals had recovered from the weak markets in the early 2000s and 2008, with debt the more significant underwriting activity. Income trusts and asset-backed securities saw a substantial decline in underwriting activity because of difficulties experienced with these securities in 2008. In Chapter 14, we observed that equity and debt issues switch places as the dominant source of funding from year to year.

Underwriting activity often involves a bought deal where the investment dealer is at risk financially to ensure the placement of funds by the borrower. A bought deal often does not involve a syndicate, which increases the investment dealer's risk exposure. Concern has also been expressed that the bought deal may exclude the retail customer from participating in the initial offering of securities.

In 2018, securities firms received their revenue as follows: from commissions, 35 percent; investment banking, 21 percent; secondary market trading, 22 percent; interest, 13 percent; and other, 9 percent. The Investment Industry Association of Canada (iiac.ca) publishes the latest breakdown of revenues and expenses for the securities industry.

As activity in Canadian markets becomes more open to international competition, and as more activity becomes centred on the large markets of New York, London, and Tokyo, the needs for size and efficiency strike many Canadian securities firms as being paramount.

Size Criteria for Going Public

Although there are no prescribed or official size criteria for approaching public markets, the well-informed corporate financial officer of a private company should have some feel for what their options are. Can a company with $10 million in sales even consider a public offering?

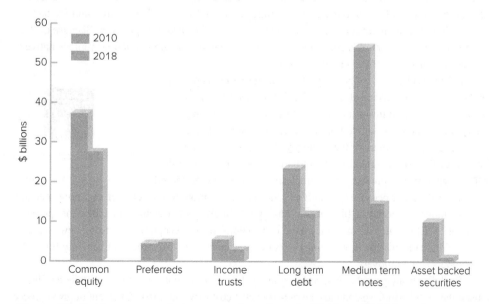

Figure 15–3 New corporate issues underwritten in 2010 and 2018, in Canada

In the United States, the most prestigious investment houses tend to concentrate on underwriting large companies. Because of the absolute difference in size of American versus Canadian investment firms, it is not surprising that even the largest of Canadian firms are often involved in relatively small securities issues.

LO5 PUBLIC VERSUS PRIVATE FINANCING

Our discussion to this point has assumed that the firm was distributing stocks or bonds in the public markets (through the organized exchanges or over the counter, as explained in Chapter 14). However, many companies, by choice or circumstance, prefer to remain private, restricting their financial activities to direct negotiations with bankers, insurance companies, and so forth. Let us evaluate the advantages and the disadvantages of public versus private financing and then explore the avenues open to a privately financed firm.

Advantages of Being Public

First, the corporation may tap the security markets for a greater amount of funds by selling securities directly to the public through a public placement. With millions of individual shareholders in the country, combined with hundreds of institutional investors, the greatest pool of funds is channelled toward publicly traded securities. Furthermore, the attendant prestige of a public security may be helpful in bank negotiations, executive recruitment, and the marketing of products.

Second, shareholders of a heretofore private corporation may also sell part of their holdings if the corporation decides to go public. The shareholder is able to achieve a higher degree of liquidity and to diversify their portfolio. A publicly traded stock with an established price may also be helpful for estate-planning purposes.

Finally, going public allows the firm to play the merger game, using marketable securities for the purchase of other firms. The high visibility of a public offering may even make the firm a potential recipient of attractive offers for its own securities. This may not be viewed as an advantage by firms that do not wish to be acquired.

Disadvantages of Being Public

The company must make all information available to the public through a securities commission filing. Not only is this tedious, time consuming, and expensive, but also important corporate information on profit margins and product lines must be divulged. For Canadian firms that are also listed on the New York Stock Exchange, the filings required by the U.S. Securities and Exchange Commission are even more extensive than those required by Canadian regulators. Because of the need to provide information, a company president must become a public relations representative to all interested members of the securities industry.

Another disadvantage of being public is the tremendous pressure for short-term performance placed on the firm by security analysts and large institutional investors. Quarter-to-quarter earnings reports can become more important to top management than providing a long-run stewardship plan for the company. A capital budgeting decision calling for the selection of alternative A—carrying a million dollars higher net present value than alternative B—may be discarded

New York Stock Exchange
nyse.com

in favour of the latter because alternative B adds two cents more to next quarter's earnings per share.

In a number of cases, the blessings of having a publicly quoted security may become quite the opposite. Although a security may have had an enthusiastic reception in a strong new issues market, a dramatic erosion in value may later occur, causing embarrassment and anxiety for shareholders and employers.

A final disadvantage is the high cost of going public. For example, for issues of under a million dollars, the underwriting spread plus the out-of-pocket cost may run up to 18 percent of gross proceeds.

Are Capital Markets Becoming More Private?

Since the last millennium the number of public companies in Canada and the United States has declined by about half. IPOs in the United States, which had reached 700 in 1996, fell to about 100 by 2017.

Large private equity capital pools have accumulated vast sums. In 2019 it is estimated that $800 billion was raised globally and about $600 billion of that was invested in private ventures. These are the capital polls that have access to new exciting and high return investments.

Large corporations have used their large cash resources to buy back stock at record levels. Stock buybacks approached $1 trillion for 2019 in the United States, exceeding corporate free cash flow. Again, the public capital markers shrink.

All this suggests that the average investor has a decreased opportunity to participate in the capital formation of new ventures. IPOs aren't the beginning for new capital ideas but the point when early investors want to get out as the rates of return decline and stabilize.

Venture Capital

Venture capital is a subset of private equity financing. Startup companies and established companies undergoing substantial change in their operations generally have a difficult time securing financing from conventional lenders, and the capital markets are not willing to provide financing. Private equity companies (cvca.ca) may be willing to advance equity funds to a high-risk firm in the hopes that the firm can eventually go public with an IPO (see the Finance in Action, "IPOs Can Be a Mystery"), providing a substantial return to the venture capital company. The venture capital firms will often provide business advice by sitting on the board of the startup firms. An angel is a wealthy individual who may also provide seed money for startup companies. Generally, venture capital is directed toward technology firms. The Business Development Bank provides information and funding to startup companies (bdc.ca).

INITIAL PUBLIC OFFERINGS

When a corporation first sells shares to the public and is, thus, no longer a private company, it has initiated an initial public offering (IPO). Generally a firm requires about $100 million in revenue to consider an IPO. Firms seem more likely to bring an IPO to market when it is "hot"; that is, when share prices are moving upward in value and there is a lot of investor interest in the stock market. The IPO market dried up considerably in the weak equity markets of 2001 and 2008. Figure 15–3 identifies that "seasoned" issues—that is, issues that add to company shares already outstanding—are more significant in dollar value than IPOs.

The price performance of IPOs subsequent to the initial listing shows considerable volatility of returns. This is what should be expected of these newly listed companies that are offering shares to the public for the first time. These companies have not yet been subject to intense public scrutiny. As a publicly traded company, there are certain disclosure requirements demanded by the securities commission, resulting in more information being available to investors. As this previously unknown information is revealed about these companies, their share prices exhibit volatility.

There is evidence of underpricing of IPOs as the first-day performance shows abnormal or excessive returns. However, over a longer period of 3 to 5 years, IPOs tend to exhibit poor performance returns. It should also be noted that the costs associated with IPOs appear to be quite high.

PRIVATE PLACEMENT

Private placement refers to the selling of securities directly to insurance companies, pension funds, and wealthy individuals rather than through the security markets. The financing device may be employed by a growing firm that wishes to avoid or defer an initial public stock offering, or by a publicly traded company that wishes to incorporate private funds into its financing package. The relative importance of private versus public placement over the past decade is indicated in Figure 15–4. New equity raised privately through the facilities of the TSX represented slightly under 12 percent of all equity raised.

The advantages of private placement are worthy of note. There is no lengthy, expensive registration process with the securities commissions. The firm also has considerably greater flexibility in negotiating with one or a handful of insurance companies, pension funds, or bankers than is possible in a public offering. Because there is no securities registration or underwriting, the initial costs of a private placement may be considerably lower than those of a public issue. However,

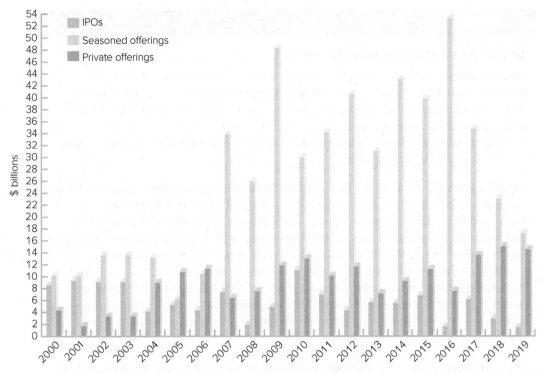

Figure 15–4 New equity financing, Toronto Stock Exchanges, 2000–2019

on an interest-bearing security, the interest rate is usually higher to compensate the investor for holding a less-liquid obligation.

LO6 Going Private and Leveraged Buyouts

Companies owned by shareholders and traded in the securities markets are said to have gone "public" as they are subject to the rules of these publicly regulated institutions. "Private" companies, generally held by a limited number of shareholders, cannot be traded in the securities markets but are not subject to the reporting requirements of the public capital markets.

Confusion in the use of these terms is multiplied when crown corporations owned by our governments or their agencies, and thus the general public, are referred to as "public" corporations, whereas corporations held by shareholders are "private" corporations. We will leave these references to the press.

Throughout the years, a number of firms gave up their public listings to go private. Management figured they could save several hundred thousand dollars a year in annual report expenses, legal and auditing fees, and security analysts' meetings—a significant amount for a small company.

Large corporations not only go private to save several hundred thousand dollars but also may have a long-term strategy in mind. Management may desire to manage for the long term without the short-term performance demands related to reported profits that the stock market places on corporations. Private firms do not have to please analysts with short-term performance. Some corporations that go private are resold to the public in the up markets after some restructuring activities.

There are basically two ways to accomplish going private. A publicly owned company can be purchased by a private company, or the company can repurchase all publicly traded shares from the shareholders. Both methods have been popular and can be accomplished through the use of leveraged buyouts. In a leveraged buyout, the management or some other investor group borrows the needed cash to repurchase all the shares of the company. After the repurchase, the company often exists with a lot of debt and heavy interest expense.

Leverage Imposes Heavy Burdens!

Leveraged buyout activity is limited in Canada. There are perhaps two reasons for this. First, Canadian corporations are not as widely held as U.S. corporations, and only a few entities dominate our market. Second, being more resource based, Canadian corporations are much more susceptible to cyclical swings in the economy. In a leveraged buyout with heavy debt loads, stability in the generation of cash flow to meet interest payments is very important.

Over the years, there have been examples of Canadian divisions of foreign multinationals taken private by managers and investors. There is also the infamous takeover of Federated Stores for $6.6 billion and then Allied Stores for $5 billion in the late 1980s by Campeau Corporation of Toronto. Both purchases were almost completely financed with borrowed money. With increasing interest rates and a slowdown in activity in retail department stores in the late 1980s, Campeau could not service the debt it had accumulated on these leveraged buyouts, despite a large selloff of assets. Federated Stores and Allied Stores were forced to declare a form of bankruptcy protection known as Chapter 11, and Campeau Corporation went bankrupt. Campeau serves to emphasize the risks in the leveraged buyout game.

More recently in 2006, Fortress Investment Group acquired Intrawest, owner of Whistler Blackcomb, in a $2.8 billion leveraged buyout. Subsequently, in the midst of the 2010 Vancouver Olympics, Fortress ran into financial difficulties from the large lingering debt load complicated by an economic downturn. There was also the proposed $52 billion leveraged buyout of BCE by the Ontario Teachers' Pension Plan in 2008. It failed when the creditworthiness of the bonds of Bell Canada, a BCE subsidiary, were questioned due to the large interest obligations required.

Onex Corporation, a private equity firm within Canada, exists largely as a specialist in this field. In recent years Onex has had to take larger equity positions as extreme leverage is no longer as attractive as in the past. In 2019 Onex took WestJet private in a $3.5 billion private equity deal.

Q1 Research and elaborate on why the Ontario Teachers' buyout failed.

Q2 Does Onex provide a good return to its investors?

Symbol: OCX

Some analysts express concern that the borrowing is done at banks rather than through the scrutiny of the "public" securities markets. They also claim that there may be a misdirection of capital into nonproductive activities (leveraged buyouts) instead of the capital formation for new ventures and products. Also, when a large firm goes private, common stock outstanding tends to disappear, leaving fewer investment choices for investors.

Usually, management of the private company must sell assets to reduce the debt load, and a corporate restructuring occurs wherein divisions and products are sold and assets are redeployed into new, higher-return areas. As specialists in the valuation of assets, investment dealers try to determine the "breakup value" of a large company. This is its value if all of its divisions were divided and sold separately. Over the long run, these strategies can be rewarding, and these companies may again become publicly owned.

Onex Corporation
onex.com

Mergers, Acquisitions, and Privatization

Investment dealers are key players in the mergers and acquisitions (M&As) that take place each year. They provide investment advice, calculate values, and assist in strategy development for these activities.

Investment dealers also provide services in privatization deals. The process of privatization by investment dealers involves selling of property previously held by governments by way of "public" share offerings. There has been a significant worldwide trend away from government ownership of business enterprises toward capital formation from the private companies and a greater reliance on the capitalist system. This has been seen in not only the former communist states of Eastern Europe and Asia but also the mixed capitalist states of the West. Britain began the process in the 1980s with the sale of British Telecom for over $25 billion, followed by Japan's sale of Nippon Telephone and Telegraph (NTT) for $80 billion. Canadian examples of this trend include Petro-Canada and CN Rail. Furthermore, this trend is demonstrated by the shift away from government financings toward corporate financings, as exhibited in Figures 14–3 and 14–4.

SUMMARY

1. The role of the investment dealer is critical to the distribution of securities in the Canadian economy. The investment dealer serves as an underwriter, or risk taker, by purchasing the securities from the issuing corporation or government and redistributing them to the public. (LO1)

2. The dealer may act as underwriter, market maker, advisor (mergers, acquisitions, leveraged buyouts, and hostile takeover attempts), and agent for firms in securities matters. Underwriting requires assistance in the pricing and the features of a financial security. Dealers also maintain large inventories of securities, helping to maintain liquid markets. (LO2)

3. Underwriting syndicates that usually assume the risk of a successful sale (or issue) include the banking group that underwrites the issue, and the selling group, and will also utilize brokers that assume no risk. The spread is the difference between the price the managing underwriter pays the corporation or government and the price expected from the public. Spread is calculated on the price to the public (this is a cost). Spread is also calculated based on the price paid by a member of the underwriting syndicate (this is their return). The greater the risk taken by the dealer, the greater will be the spread. The dealer can help sell a new issue on a best-efforts basis. Alternatively, the dealer may assume all of the risk with a bought deal. (LO3)

4. Estimation of market prices uses the formulas and concepts developed in Chapter 10. New issues of securities often result in dilution of earnings per share. The dealer may continue to maintain a market in the distributed securities long after they have been sold to the public. (LO4)

5. Securities can be sold in the public markets as initial public offerings (IPOs) or as "seasoned" issues. Going public may give the corporation and major shareholders greater access to funds as well as additional prestige, but these advantages may quickly disappear in a down market. The corporation must also open its books to the public and orient itself to the supposed short-term emphasis of investors. Private placement—or the direct distribution of securities to large insurance companies, pension funds, and wealthy individuals—may bypass the rigours of securities commission registration and allow more flexibility in the terms of an issue. Large companies at times have gone private through leveraged buyouts to avoid the rigours of public scrutiny and to add value to the firm. Some have become public again, realizing substantial gains. (LO5)

6. A leveraged buyout occurs when an acquiring firm purchases all the equity in a target firm, generally using the assets of the target firm as collateral for the funds required for the takeover. After acquisition, the targeted firm has many of its assets sold to pay off debt, the operations of

the firm are rationalized including layoffs, and a great deal of debt is added to the capital structure of the acquired firm. Though much of the debt used in leveraged buyouts comes from the banking industry, only the public markets can meet the vast capital needs of Canadian corporations. Leveraged buyouts provide a mechanism for former subsidiaries of foreign multinationals to become controlled by Canadian investors, who were often the subsidiary managers. (LO6)

REVIEW OF FORMULAS

Please refer to the review of formulas page in Chapter 10.

DISCUSSION QUESTIONS

1. In what way is an investment dealer a risk taker? (LO2)

2. What is the purpose of market stabilization activities during the distribution process? (LO4)

3. Discuss how an underwriting syndicate decreases risk for each underwriter and at the same time facilitates the distribution process. (LO3)

4. Discuss the reason for the differences between underwriting spreads for stocks and those for bonds. (LO3)

5. Explain how the price-earnings ratio is related to the pricing of a new security issue and the dilution effect. (LO4)

6. Comment on the market performance of companies going public, both immediately after the offering has been made and some time later. Relate this to research that has been done in this area. (LO4)

7. Discuss key changes going on in the investment dealer-brokerage community. Also, who are some of the new participants in the industry? (LO1)

8. Discuss the benefits accruing to a company traded in the public securities market. (LO5)

9. What are some reasons a corporation may prefer to remain privately held? (LO5)

10. If a company wished to raise capital by way of a private placement, where would it look for funds? (LO5)

11. How does a leveraged buyout work? What does the debt structure of the firm normally look like after a leveraged buyout? What might be done to reduce the debt? (LO6)

12. What effect does a leveraged buyout have on the future strategic choices open to the company's management? (LO6)

13. Comment on whether you believe leveraged buyouts are good for an economy. (LO6)

INTERNET RESOURCES AND QUESTIONS

To identify recent listings, including IPOs on stock exchanges, try the listed companies' section of the exchanges: tmx.com

The self-regulating body for investment dealers is the Investment Industry Regulatory Organization of Canada: iiroc.ca

The SEDAR site provides recent press releases and prospectus information: sedar.com

1. Select three IPOs that have come to market in the last three months and indicate the following:
    a. Issue price
    b. Gross proceeds
    c. Net proceeds

d. The reasons for the difference between gross and net proceeds

e. The reasons for raising the capital

PROBLEMS

1. Midas and Company is the managing investment dealer for a major new underwriting. The price of the stock to the managing investment dealer is $15 per share. Other syndicate members may buy at $15.25. The price to the selected dealer group is $15.60, with a price to the brokers of $16.00. The price to the public is $16.50.

    a. If Midas and Company sells its shares to the dealer group, what will be its percentage return?

    b. If Midas and Company performs the dealers' function also and sells to brokers, what will be its percentage return?

    c. If Midas and Company fully integrates its operation and sells directly to the public, what will be its percentage return?

2. Walton and Company is the managing investment dealer for a major new underwriting. The price of the stock to the investment dealer is $18 per share. Other syndicate members may buy at $18.25. The price to the selected dealer group is $18.80, with a price to the brokers of $19.20. The price to the public is $19.50.

    a. If Walton and Company sells its shares to the dealer group, what will be the percentage return?

    b. If Walton and Company performs the dealers' function also and sells to brokers, what will be its percentage return?

    c. If Walton and Company fully integrates its operation and sells directly to the public, what will be its percentage return?

3. The Canadian Loonie Company needs to raise $40 million. The investment dealer Wayne and Shuster will handle the transaction.

    a. If stock is utilized, 2 million shares will be sold to the public at $20.95 per share. The corporation will receive a net price of $20 per share. What is the percentage of underwriting spread per share?

    b. If bonds are utilized, slightly over 40,000 bonds will be sold to the public at $1,001 per bond. The corporation will receive a net price of $998 per bond. What is the percentage of underwriting spread per bond?

    c. Which alternative has the larger percentage of spread? Is this the normal relationship between the two types of issues?

4. Solar Energy Corp. has $5 million in earnings with 2 million shares outstanding. Investment bankers think the stock can justify a P/E ratio of 18. If the underwriting spread is 5 percent, what should be the price to the public? What would the firm net?

5. Tiger Golf Supplies has $15 million in earnings with 4 million shares outstanding. Its investment banker thinks the stock should trade at a P/E ratio of 22. If there is an underwriting spread of 2.8 percent, what should be the price to the public? What would the firm net?

6. Assume Gum Shoe Detective Agency is thinking about three different size offerings for the issuance of additional shares.

Size of Offer	Public Price	Net to Corporation
$1.5 million	$40	$35.80
$5.5 million	$40	$36.90
$20.0 million	$40	$38.45

What is the percentage underwriting spread for each size offering? What principle does this demonstrate?

7. Power Temporaries Inc. has earnings of $4,500,000 with 1,800,000 shares outstanding before a public distribution. Four hundred thousand shares will be included in the sale, of which 250,000 are new corporate shares and 150,000 are shares currently owned by Julie Lipner, the founder and CEO. The 150,000 shares that Julie is selling are referred to as a secondary offering and all proceeds will go to her.

    a. What were the corporation's earnings per share before the offering?

    b. What are the corporation's earnings per share expected to be after the offering?

8. New Brunswick Timber Company currently has 5 million shares of stock outstanding and will report earnings of $9 million in the current year. The company is considering the issuance of 1 million additional shares that will net $40 per share to the corporation.

    a. What is the immediate dilution potential for this new stock issue?

    b. Assume the New Brunswick Timber Company can earn 11 percent on the proceeds of the stock issue in time to include it in the current year's results. Should the new issue be undertaken based on earnings per share?

9. The Hamilton Company currently has 4 million shares of stock outstanding and will report earnings of $6 million in the current year. The company is considering the issuance of 1 million additional shares of stock that will net $30 per share to the corporation.

    a. What is the immediate dilution potential for this new share issue?

    b. Assume the Hamilton Company can earn 10.5 percent on the proceeds of the share issue in time to include it in the current year's results. Should the new issue be undertaken based on earnings per share?

10. In the previous problem, if the 1 million additional shares can be issued only at $23 per share and the company can earn 6.0 percent on the proceeds, should the new issue be undertaken based on earnings per share?

11. The Carma S. Diego Travellers Corp. has 10 million shares of stock outstanding at a current market price of $10. It is considering a new share offering that will net it $9 a share on 1 million shares. Earnings this year are expected to be $18 million.

    a. What is the immediate dilution potential for this new share issue?

    b. Assume Carma S. Diego Travellers Corp. can earn 12 percent on the proceeds of the share issue and these can be realized with this year's results. Should the new issue be undertaken based on earnings per share? Can you suggest why or why not?

    c. If the 1 million additional shares can be issued to net $16 per share and the company can earn 12 percent on the proceeds, should the new issue be undertaken based on earnings per share?

12. Macho Tool Company is going public at $50 net per share to the company. There also are founding shareholders that are selling part of their shares at the same price. Prior to the offering, the firm had $48 million in earnings divided over 12 million shares. The public offering will be for 6 million shares; 4 million will be new corporate shares and 2 million will be shares currently owned by the founding shareholders.

    a. What is the immediate dilution based on the new corporate shares that are being offered?

    b. If the stock has a P/E of 20 immediately after the offering, what will be the share price?

    c. Should the founding shareholders be pleased with the $50 they received for their shares?

13. Trump Card Co. will issue stock at a retail (public) price of $32. The company will receive $29.20 per share.

    a. What is the spread on the issue in percentage terms?

    b. If the firm demands receiving a new price only $2.20 below the public price suggested in part a, what will the spread be in percentage terms?

    c. To hold the spread down to 2.5 percent based on the public price in part a, what net amount should Trump Card Co. receive?

14. Winston Sporting Goods is considering a public offering of common shares. Its investment dealer has informed the company that the retail price will be $18 per share for 600,000 shares. The company will receive $16.50 per share and will incur $150,000 in registration, accounting, and printing fees.

    a. What is the spread on this issue in percentage terms?

    b. What are the total expenses of the issue as a percentage of total value (at retail)?

    c. If the firm wants to net $18 million from this issue, how many shares must be sold?

15. DUR Semiconductors will issue stock at a retail (public) price of $18. The company will receive $16.55 per share.

    a. What is the spread on the issue in percentage terms?

    b. If DUR Semiconductors demands receiving a net price only $0.85 below the public price suggested in part a, what will the spread be in percentage terms?

    c. To hold the spread down to 3 percent based on the public price in part a, what net amount should DUR Semiconductors receive?

16. Becker Brothers is the managing underwriter for a 1 million share issue by Jay's Hamburger Heaven. Becker Brothers is "handling" 10 percent of the issue. Its price is $25, and the price to the public is $26.40. Becker also provides the market stabilization function. During the issuance, the market for the stock turned soft, and Becker was forced to repurchase 40,000 shares in the open market at an average price of $25.75. It later sold the shares at an average value of $23. Compute Becker Brothers' overall gain or loss from managing the issue.

17. Ashley Homebuilding is about to go public. The investment firm of Blake, Webber, and Company is attempting to price the issue. The home building industry generally trades at a 20 percent discount below the P/E ratio on the S&P/TSX Composite Index. Assume that index currently has a P/E ratio of 15. The firm can be compared to the home building industry as follows:

	Ashley	Home Building Industry
Growth rate in earnings per share.....	12 percent	10 percent
Consistency of performance.........	Increased earnings 4 out of 5 years	Increased earnings 3 out of 5 years
Debt to total assets...............	55 percent	40 percent
Turnover of product..............	Slightly below average	Average
Quality of management	High	Average

Assume, in assessing the initial P/E ratio, the investment dealer will first determine the appropriate industry P/E based on the S&P/TSX Composite Index. Then a half point will be added to the P/E ratio for each case in which Ashley Homebuilding is superior to the industry norm, and a half point will be deducted for an inferior comparison. On this basis, what should be the initial P/E for the firm?

18. The investment firm of A. Einstein & Co. will use a dividend valuation model to appraise the shares of the Modern Physics Corporation. Dividends (D_1) at the end of the current year will be $1.44. The growth rate ($g$) is 8 percent and the discount rate (K_e) is 12 percent.

    a. What should be the price of the stock to the public? (Refer to Chapter 10.)

    b. If there is a 6 percent total underwriting spread on the stock, how much will the issuing corporation receive?

    c. If the issuing corporation requires a net price of $34.50 (proceeds to the corporation) and there is a 6 percent underwriting spread, what should be the price of the stock to the public?

19. The investment dealer of Saskatchewan Cloud Inc. uses a dividend valuation model to appraise the shares of Lambert Aerospace Company. Dividends (D_1) at the end of the current year will be $1.20. The growth rate ($g$) is 7 percent and the discount rate (K_e) is 12 percent.

    a. What should be the price of the stock to the public?

b. If there is a 6 percent total underwriting spread on the stock, how much will the issuing corporation receive?

c. If the issuing corporation requires a net price of $23.50 (proceeds to the corporation) and there is a 6 percent underwriting spread, what should be the price of the stock to the public?

20. The Landry Corporation needs to raise $1 million of debt on a 25-year issue. If it places the bonds privately, the interest rate will be 11 percent, and $30,000 in out-of-pocket costs will be incurred. For a public issue, the interest rate will be 10 percent, and the underwriting spread will be 4 percent. There will be $100,000 in out-of-pocket costs.

Assume interest on the debt is paid semiannually, and the debt will be outstanding for the full 25 years, at which time it will be repaid.

Which plan offers the higher net present value? For each plan, compare the net amount of funds initially available—inflow—to the present value of future payments of interest and principal to determine net present value. Assume the stated discount rate is 12 percent annually, but use 6 percent semiannually throughout the analysis. (Disregard taxes.)

21. Midland Corporation has a net income of $15 million and 6 million shares outstanding. Its common stock is currently selling for $40 per share. Midland plans to sell common stock to set up a major new production facility with a net cost of $21,660,000. The production facility will not produce a profit for one year, and then it is expected to earn a 15 percent return on the investment. Wood and Gundy, an investment dealer, plans to sell the issue to the public for $38 per share, with a spread of 5 percent.

a. How many shares of stock must be sold to net $21,660,000? (Note: No out-of-pocket costs must be considered in this problem.)

b. Why is the investment dealer selling the shares at less than its current market price?

c. What are the EPS and the P/E ratio before the issue (based on a stock price of $40)? What will be the price per share immediately after the sale of stock if the P/E stays constant? (based on including the additional shares computed in part a).

d. Compute the EPS and the price (P/E stays constant) after the new production facility begins to produce a profit.

e. Are the shareholders better off because of the sale of shares and the resultant investment? What other financing strategy could the company have tried to increase EPS?

22. The Presley Corporation is about to go public. It currently has aftertax earnings of $7,500,000 and 2,500,000 shares are owned by the present shareholders (the Presley family). The new public issue will represent 600,000 new shares. The new shares will be priced to the public at $20 per share, with a 5 percent spread on the offering price. There will also be $200,000 in out-of-pocket costs to the corporation.

a. Compute the net proceeds to the Presley Corporation.

b. Compute the EPS immediately before the stock issue.

c. Compute the EPS immediately after the stock issue.

d. Determine what rate of return must be earned on the net proceeds to the corporation so that there will not be a dilution in EPS during the year of going public.

e. Determine what rate of return must be earned on the proceeds to the corporation so that there will be a 5 percent increase in EPS during the year of going public.

23. Tyson Works is about to go public. It currently has aftertax earnings of $4,500,000, and 300,000 shares are owned by the present shareholders. The new public issue will represent 400,000 new shares. The new shares will be priced to the public at $15 per share with a 4 percent spread on the offering price. There will also be $160,000 in out-of-pocket costs to the corporation.

a. Compute the net proceeds to the Tyson Works.

b. Compute the earnings per share immediately before the stock issue.

c. Compute the earnings per share immediately after the stock issue.

d. Determine what rate of return must be earned on the net proceeds to the corporation so that there will not be a dilution in earnings per share during the year of going public.

e. Determine what rate of return must be earned on the proceeds to the corporation so that there will be a 10 percent increase in earnings per share during the year of going public.

24. Northern Airlines is about to go public. It currently has aftertax earnings of $6,000,000, and 4,000,000 shares are owned by the present shareholders. The new public issue will represent 300,000 new shares. The new shares will be priced to the public at $18 per share, with a 4 percent spread on the offering price. There will also be $100,000 in out-of-pocket costs to the corporation.

a. Compute the net proceeds to the Northern Airlines.

b. Compute the EPS immediately before the stock issue.

c. Compute the EPS immediately after the stock issue.

d. Determine what rate of return must be earned on the net proceeds to the corporation so that there will not be a dilution in EPS during the year of going public.

e. Determine what rate of return must be earned on the proceeds to the corporation so that there will be a 10 percent increase in EPS during the year of going public.

25. I.B. Michaels has a chance to participate in a new public offering by Hi-Tech Microcomputers. His broker informs him demand for the 500,000 shares to be issued is very strong. His broker's firm is assigned 15,000 shares in the distribution and will allow Michaels, a relatively good customer, 1.5 percent of its 15,000 share allocation.

The initial offering price is $30 per share. There is a strong aftermarket, and the stock goes to $33 one week after issue. After the first full month after issue, Michaels is pleased to observe his shares are selling for $34.75. He is content to place his shares in a lockbox and eventually use their anticipated increased value to help send his son to college many years in the future. However, one year after the distribution, he looks up the shares in *The Globe and Mail* and finds that they are trading at $28.75.

a. Compute the total dollar profit or loss on Michael's shares one week, one month, and one year after the purchase. In each case, compute the profit or loss against the initial purchase price.

b. Also compute this percentage gain or loss from the initial $30 price and compare this to the results that might be expected in an investment of this nature based on prior research. Assume the overall stock market was basically unchanged during the period of observation.

c. Why might a new public issue be expected to have a strong aftermarket?

26. The management of Webster Labs decided to go private in 2003 by buying all 3 million outstanding shares at $18.50 per share. By 2005, management had restructured the company by selling the petroleum research division for $16 million, the fibre technology division for $9.5 million, and the synthetic products division for $20 million.

Because these divisions had been only marginally profitable, Webster Labs is a stronger company after the restructuring. Webster Labs is now able to concentrate exclusively on the contract research and will generate earnings per share of $1.50 this year. Investment dealers have contacted the firm and indicated that, if it returned to the public market, the 3 million shares it purchased to go private could now be reissued to the public at a P/E ratio of 14 times earnings per share.

a. What was the initial total cost to Webster Labs to go private?

b. What is the total value to the company from (1) the proceeds of the divisions that were sold, and (2) the current value of the 3 million shares (based on current earnings and an anticipated P/E of 14)?

c. What is the percentage return to the management of Webster Labs from the restructuring? Use answers from parts a and b to determine this value.

COMPREHENSIVE PROBLEM

27. The Anton Corporation, a manufacturer of radar control equipment, is planning to sell its shares to the general public for the first time. The firm's investment dealer is working with the Anton Corporation in determining a number of items. Information on the Anton Corporation follows:

ANTON CORPORATION
Income Statement
For the year ending Dec. 31, 20XX

Sales (all on credit)	$22,428,000
Cost of goods sold	16,228,000
Gross profit	6,200,000
Selling and administrative expenses	2,659,400
Operating profit	3,540,600
Interest expense	370,600
Net income before tax	3,170,000
Taxes	1,442,000
Net income	$ 1,728,000

Balance Sheet
As of December 31, 20XX

Assets

Cash	$ 150,000
Marketable securities	100,000
Accounts receivable	2,000,000
Inventory	3,800,000
Total current assets	6,050,000
Net plant and equipment	6,750,000
Total assets	$12,800,000

Liabilities and Shareholders' Equity

Accounts payable	$ 1,000,000
Notes payable	1,200,000
Total current liabilities	2,200,000
Long-term liabilities	2,380,000
Total liabilities	4,580,000

Shareholders' equity

Common stock (1,200,000 shares)	4,000,000
Retained earnings	4,220,000
Total shareholders' equity	8,220,000
Total liabilities and shareholders' equity	$12,800,000

a. Assume that 500,000 new corporate shares will be issued to the general public. What will EPS be immediately after public offering? (Round to two places to the right of the decimal point.) Based on the P/E ratio of 10, what will be the initial price of the stock? Use EPS after the distribution in the calculation.

b. Assuming an underwriting spread of 7 percent and out-of-pocket costs of $150,000, what will be the net proceeds to the corporation?

c. What return must the corporation earn on the net proceeds to equal the EPS before the offering? How does this compare with current return on the total assets on the balance sheet?

d. Now assume that, of the initial 500,000 share distribution, 250,000 shares belong to current shareholders and 250,000 are new corporate shares, and these will be added to the 1.2 million corporate shares currently outstanding. What will EPS be immediately after the public offering? What will be the initial market price of the stock? Assume a P/E ratio of 10 and use EPS after the distribution in the calculation.

e. Assuming an underwriting spread of 7 percent and out-of-pocket costs of $150,000, what will be the net proceeds to the corporation?

f. What return must the corporation now earn on the net proceeds to equal EPS before the offering? How does this compare with current return on the total assets on the balance sheet?

MINI CASE
Robert Boyle & Associates Inc.

On a Saturday afternoon in May 20XY, Robert Boyle and his wife Janet were sitting on the porch of their house on Salt Spring Island, British Columbia, watching the fog roll in. The couple frequently spent weekends on the island, when the demands of Robert's business and Janet's teaching job would permit. Robert was the president of Robert Boyle & Associates, a closely held real estate investment trust (REIT) located in Vancouver. From a small office there, Robert had been managing the development of shopping centres for a little over eight years. Robert conducted most of the business himself, and the "associates," a group of about 40 friends, family members, and business colleagues, provided most of the financing. The trust had been quite successful, and today it owned two shopping centres, which produced rental income in 20XX of almost $6 million. (See Tables 1 and 2 for Boyle & Associates' financial statements for 20XX.)

Table 1

Robert Boyle & Associates
Income Statement
For the Year Ending 20XX
(in millions)

Loan income	$ 0.240
Rental income	5.992
Other income	0.168
Total income	6.400
Amortization	0.920
General and administrative expense	0.435
Operating income	5.045
Interest expense	0.945
Net income	$ 4.100
Dividend paid	$ 4.100

Note: Boyle & Associates qualifies as a REIT, so it pays no income tax.

Table 2

Robert Boyle & Associates
Balance Sheet
As of December 31, 20XX
(in millions)

Assets	
Cash and equivalents	$ 2.100
Land development and construction loans	2.000
Property owned, net of amortization	16.000
Other assets	0.900
Total assets	$21.000
Liabilities and Equity	
Bank borrowings	$ 2.000
Mortgages on property	7.000
Other liabilities	0.550
Total liabilities	9.550
Common stock	11.550
Retained earnings	0.000
Total equity	11.550
Total liabilities and equity	$21.000

"You know, Janet," Bob said wistfully, "we ought to move out here permanently. There's just no comparison between life here and on the mainland."

"You get no argument from me," Janet replied. "I've been telling you that ever since we bought this house."

"You could develop real estate just as easily from here as in the city, you know. Which reminds me, what's the latest on the Salt Spring Centre project? You've been quiet about it for about a week now." Janet referred to a proposal Robert had made a few months ago to build the first shopping centre on Salt Spring Island.

Robert sighed. "Well, it's on the back burner right now for lack of financing. I'm convinced that it would make us a lot of money; but, the trouble is, it will take a lot of money to get it built—about $10 million, in fact, and that's more than we've ever had to raise before."

"Oh, come on," Janet said. (She had always been an active participant in the business.) "You've built two shopping centres so far, and didn't have any trouble getting the money for them. Why don't you just borrow some more?"

"Too much borrowed already, I'm afraid," Robert replied. "Our debt-to-assets ratio is quite a bit over the average for REITs now, and our investment dealer says that another loan, or even a bond issue, would be quite expensive in terms of interest cost." (See Table 3 for comparisons between Boyle & Associates and a sample of other REITs.)

Table 3 Industry data and comparisons (in millions)

Company	Total Revenue	Net Income	Number of Shares	Long-Term Debt	Total Equity
JKL Realty Trust	$4.3	$2.6	1.423	$3.1	$ 24.0
UVW REIT	7.8	1.5	2.500	21.2	12.3
Cousins Properties Inc.	52.5	29.6	17.165	14.1	110.7
Bradley REIT.	7.1	1.3	3.360	11.0	6.8
Mortgage Growth Investors Inc. .	14.0	9.9	7.730	19.8	123.9
Dial REIT (newly established). . .	—	—	1.736	10.3	31.3
Average of companies listed	14.3	7.5	5.653	13.3	51.5
Robert Boyle & Associates	6.4	4.1	4.000	9.5	11.6

Company	Total Assets	Earnings per Share	Dividend per Share	Book Value per Share
JKL Realty Trust	$ 27.1	$ 1.83	$ 1.75	$ 16.84
UVW REIT	33.5	0.60	0.57	4.92
Cousins Properties Inc.	124.8	1.72	1.64	6.45
Bradley REIT.	17.8	0.39	0.37	2.01
Mortgage Growth Investors Inc. .	143.7	1.28	1.23	16.03
Dial REIT (newly established). . .	41.6	—	1.64	18.02
Average of companies listed	64.7	0.97	1.20	10.71
Robert Boyle and Associates	21.0	1.03	0.98	2.89

Company	ROE	ROA	Debt to Assets	Asset Turnover	Net Profit Margin
JKL Realty Trust	10.8%	9.6%	0.11	0.16	60.5%
UVW REIT	12.2	4.5	0.63	0.23	19.2
Cousins Properties Inc.	26.7	23.7	0.11	0.42	56.4
Bradley REIT.	19.2	7.3	0.62	0.40	18.3
Mortgage Growth Investors Inc. .	8.0	6.9	0.14	0.10	70.9
Dial REIT (newly established). . .	—	—	0.25	—	—
Average of companies listed	12.8	8.7	0.31	0.22	37.5
Robert Boyle and Associates	35.5	19.5	0.45	0.30	64.1

	5-Year EPS Growth	Dividend Yield	P/E Ratio	Recent	Share Price
JKL Realty Trust	1.1%	11.7%	8.2	$15.00	
UVW REIT	8.1	5.8	16.3	9.75	
Cousins Properties Inc.	2.9	9.8	9.7	16.75	
Bradley REIT.	12.3	2.8	34.2	13.25	
Mortgage Growth Investors Inc. . . .	7.1	6.2	15.5	19.88	
Dial REIT (newly established).	—	8.5	—	19.25	
Average of companies listed	5.3	7.5	14.0	15.65	
Robert Boyle and Associates	9.7				

"Well, what about the shareholders?" Janet insisted. "Can't they contribute some more equity money?" (Boyle & Associates' 40 existing shareholders held 4 million shares with a book value of $2.89 each.)

Robert responded with a smile. "You know the answer to that already," he said. "You and I are the biggest shareholders. But even if all 40 shareholders put in an equal amount it would cost each of us $250,000. You and I don't have that kind of cash, and I'm sure the rest of the shareholders don't either."

"Well, then," Janet continued unperturbed, "you need some more shareholders. Why don't you sell shares to the public? I'm sure it would be a great success once people knew what the company's plans were."

"Yes, that's what our investment dealer said, too," Robert replied. "But I have some reservations. For instance, look at the dilution effect. You know, to qualify as a REIT and, therefore, to pay no income tax at the corporate level, we pay out 100 percent of earnings every year as dividends. Anything that affects earnings per share, then, affects the shareholders' dividends. If we issue a whole lot of new shares, earnings per share will be diluted severely, and the existing shareholders will be most unhappy!"

"But Robert," Janet said, "aren't you ignoring the money you will make on the proceeds of the shares issue? It seems to me that the income from the investment ought to more than offset the initial dilution, producing even more earnings—and dividends—than before. Surely the shareholders will see that."

"Maybe so," Robert said, "but that's not the only problem. Suppose, for example, that the whole shopping centre deal falls through?" (It was not certain at this time that the residents and government authorities on Salt Spring would approve the project.) "If it does, the price of our company's shares, now publicly traded, will surely fall, to the dismay and embarrassment of us all. You know, managing a publicly traded company is not at all like managing a private one. The pressure for short-term performance is terrific. If I don't produce, I'll be voted out of office at the next shareholders' meeting."

"And that's another thing," Robert continued, warming up, "shareholders' meetings. Look what you have to go through as a publicly traded company: shareholders' meetings, annual reports, BC Securities Commission filings, disclosure notices, regulators poking around; why, the administrative tasks alone will require a couple of full-time people! Besides that, look at the cost of the issue itself. The investment dealer will take a cut of about 6.5 percent of the issue, and we'll have to pay about $60,000 out-of-pocket for legal and accounting fees and printing expenses. I bet we'd have to issue almost $11 million in shares just to get $10 million in cash. Pretty expensive!"

"Yes, that's so," Janet agreed. "But even so, the benefits might outweigh the costs. One thing you haven't mentioned is the increase in liquidity for the company's shares you would get if they were publicly traded. You know most of our existing shareholders have been with us for the whole eight years, and they have quite a bit of money tied up in this one basket. How can they diversify their portfolios or sell their holdings outright? I bet they'd love to see the shares publicly traded in the market with an established price."

"All right, you may have a point," Robert conceded. "Tell you what; I'll write a letter to our existing shareholders outlining the pros and cons, and ask them to respond with recommendations. If the prevailing sentiment is to go public, we'll do it, and if it's not, we won't. In the end, though, the whole discussion may depend on how badly we want to build the Salt Spring Centre. If we want it, we'll probably have to go public to build it."

"I knew you would have it all figured out," Janet said, approvingly. "Now, how about a martini?"

a. Refer to Table 3 for comparisons between Boyle & Associates and other REITs. Note the industry average P/E ratio. The investment dealer will set Boyle's P/E ratio based on how the company compares to the industry average in six areas: return on equity, return on assets, debt to assets, asset turnover, net profit margin, and five-year earnings per share growth. The investment dealer will start with the industry average P/E, and will add one-half point for each of the areas in which Boyle is superior to the industry, and will subtract one-half point for each area in which Boyle is inferior to the industry. After tabulating the results, the investment dealer will subtract one point for good measure to ensure the issue presents an attractive opportunity. On this basis, what will the dealer determine to be the proper P/E ratio for Boyle & Associates?

b. Considering that the dealer's spread will be 6.5 percent of the total issue size, and Boyle will have to pay $60,000 out-of-pocket expenses, what is the total issue size necessary to yield $10 million in cash to the company?

c. Assume 699,029 shares will be sold at a public price of $15.45 to provide approximately $10.8 million. What dollar return on the net proceeds of the offering must Boyle & Associates earn to bring earnings per share up to what it was before the offering ($1.03)? After you compute the dollar return on the net proceeds, convert this to a ratio (percentage of net proceeds). Compare this answer to Boyle's return on assets in 20XX (Table 3). Based on the company's performance in 20XX, do you think the required return can be earned?

d. If half of Boyle's associates decide to sell their existing shares in addition to the initial offering, how many total shares will have to be issued by the company to yield $10 million in cash to the company?

e. Summarize the pros and cons of Boyle & Associates going public. Based on Robert Boyle's letter, would you recommend going public or not? What would be the major reason affecting your opinion?

Long-Term Debt and Lease Financing

LEARNING OBJECTIVES

LO1 Identify and describe the key features of long-term debt.

LO2 Differentiate bond yields and prices as influenced by how corporations and governments are rated by bond rating services.

LO3 Analyze the decision of whether or not to call in (refund the obligation) and reissue debt, when interest rates have declined.

LO4 Outline some of the features of innovative forms of raising long-term financing, including zero-coupon rate bonds, floating-rate bonds, and real return bonds.

LO5 Outline the characteristics of long-term lease financing that make it an alternative form of long-term financing.

LO6 Analyze a lease versus borrow-to-purchase decision.

Shakespeare's advice, "Neither a borrower nor a lender be," hardly applies to corporate financial management. The virtues and drawbacks of debt usage were considered in Chapter 5 and in Chapter 11. One can only surmise that today's financial managers, although sometimes cautious in assuming debt, nevertheless find debt financing an essential component of the firm's capital structure. The corporate sector has regularly shown a willingness to increase debt financing through bonds, as identified in Figure 14–4.

In Chapter 16, we consider the diverse features of long-term debt instruments. These features and the creditworthiness of the issuing corporation have a direct influence on the important measure of return for bonds, which is the yield to maturity. Creditworthiness is examined through credit rating firms. Furthermore, the analytical framework for the cost-benefit decision to call back or refund an existing bond issue is examined.

Lease financing is considered as a special case of long-term or intermediate debt financing. Particular attention is given to the accounting rules that affect leasing and the decision analysis for examining a lease versus borrow-to-purchase decision. A well-run business will make prudent use of both long-term debt and leases in its capital structure. Both are necessary to help build the capital needed for a firm's growth.

THE SIGNIFICANT ROLE OF DEBT

Expansion of the economy pressures corporations to raise significant amounts of borrowed capital to facilitate their own growth. This continuously expanded level of borrowing has forced those evaluating the quality of corporate bond issues to reevaluate the benchmarks used to judge capital adequacy. The borrowing quality of the average corporation has changed over time, but the increased efficiencies of the modern corporation that we have examined in earlier chapters have allowed for sharper margins to service debt.

Figure 16–1 attempts to capture the effects of this extra borrowing on the safety margin of pretax, pre-interest earnings (operating and non-operating) over interest charges, referred to as interest coverage or times interest earned. This is formula 3–12 from Chapter 3. From over four times interest earned in the early 1970s, the average interest coverage ratio steadily declined for Canadian nonfinancial corporations until it reached 0.9 times in the final quarter of 1991, rebounding to over 3.5 times by 2020. Coupled with the increase in their cash reserves, this is evidence of the more conservative nature of corporations in our recent period.

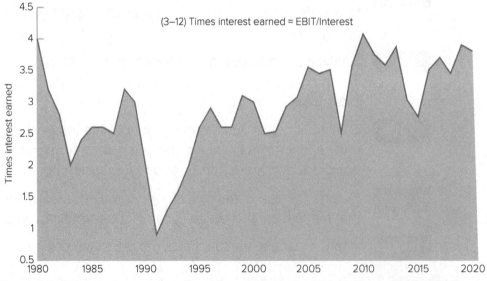

Figure 16–1 Interest coverage—Canadian nonfinancial corporations, 1980–2020

When the interest-paying capability of corporate borrowers declines, it is not uncommon for large and small corporations to default on their obligations, resulting in the reorganization or liquidation of the firm's assets. In these situations, the debt contract dictates the relative bargaining positions of the lenders and the borrowing corporation in the reorganization or liquidation efforts.

LO1 THE DEBT CONTRACT

The corporate bond represents the basic long-term debt instrument for most large corporations. The bond agreement specifies basic items such as the par value, the coupon rate, and the maturity date. These features are important in establishing value for the bond.

Par Value (Face Value)

The initial value of the bond is its par value (face value) and the bond is initially sold at close to this value. This value is fixed and does not change. Most corporate bonds are traded in $1,000 units. The par value is also known as the maturity value.

Coupon Rate

The actual interest rate on the bond is its coupon rate, usually payable in semiannual instalments. This is a contractual payment and does not change. To the extent that interest rates or yields in the market go above or below the coupon rate, the market price on the bond will trade at a discount or premium.

These are the market values of $1,000 face value bonds trading in January 2020, when market-demanded yields were between 1.35 and 2.65 percent for these maturities of investment grade bonds:

Table 16–1 Coupon rates, yields, and pricing

Issuer	Coupon Rate	Price	Maturity	YTM
Trans Canada Pipelines	5.650	1,246.55	June 2029	2.65
Hydro One	5.000	1,463.36	Oct. 2046	2.58
Enbridge	2.990	1,033.65	Oct. 2029	2.59
CIBC	1.900	995.88	Apr. 2021	1.35

Maturity Date

The final date on which repayment of the bond principal is due is the maturity date. The par or face value is due on this date.

The bond agreement is supplemented by a much longer document termed a bond indenture. The indenture, often containing over 100 pages of complicated legal wording, covers every detail surrounding the bond issue, including restrictions on the corporation, collateral pledged, methods of repayment, and procedures for initiating claims against the corporation. An independent trustee (for example, RBC Royal Trust) is appointed by the corporation to administer the bond indenture provisions under the guidelines of the trust acts of the individual provinces.

www.

RBC Royal Trust
royaltrust
.rbcwealthmanagement.com

Trusts listed
cdic.ca

(click "members")

Restrictive Covenants

To prevent weakening the claims that debt holders have against the assets or cash flows of a borrowing firm, certain promises, or covenants, are made by the firm in the indenture. These covenants to some degree limit the flexibility of management in running the firm but are meant to protect the investment of the debt holder.

Negative Pledge A common covenant that limits the securing of subsequent debt ahead of debt already outstanding, and may also limit additional borrowing, is referred to as a negative pledge.

Minimum Ratios Restrictions may also require maintaining minimum ratios, such as debt to equity, working capital, and dividend payout ratios.

For example, at the beginning of the new millennium Bombardier (bombardier.com) took write-downs of assets as it implemented new accounting guidelines on how it would expense research and development costs on its airplanes. This dramatically increased Bombardier's debt to equity ratios, requiring it to implement $1 billion in asset sales to avoid technical bankruptcy by violating some of its covenants. The saga continues in 2020.

Security Provisions

A secured claim is one in which specific assets are pledged to bondholders in the event of default.
- Under a mortgage agreement, real property (plant and equipment) is pledged as security for the loan. A mortgage may be senior or junior in nature, with the former requiring satisfaction of claims before payment is given to the latter.
- The after-acquired property clause requires that any new property be placed under the original mortgage.
- Generally, the greater the protection offered a given class of bondholders, the lower the risk assumed and the lower the interest rate received.
- Only infrequently are pledged assets actually sold and the proceeds distributed to bondholders. Typically, the defaulting corporation is reorganized, and existing claims are partially satisfied by issuing new securities to the participating parties. The stronger and better-secured the initial claim is, the higher the quality of the new security to be received in exchange. Existing management may be terminated and held legally responsible for any imprudent actions that led to failure to meet obligations.

Unsecured Debt

The term debenture usually refers to a long-term, unsecured corporate bond. Among the major participants in debenture offerings are prestigious firms such as Bell Canada Enterprises (BCE) and Royal Bank. Because of the legal problems associated with specific asset claims in a secured bond offering, the trend is decidedly toward unsecured debt—allowing the bondholder a general claim against the corporation rather than a specific lien against an asset. Even unsecured debt may be divided between high-ranking and subordinated debt.

The Royal Bank of Canada
rbcroyalbank.com

- A subordinated debenture is an unsecured bond in which payment to the holder occurs only after designated senior debenture holders are satisfied (see Figure 16–2). For a further discussion of payment of claims and the hierarchy of obligations, see Appendix 16A, which also covers bankruptcy considerations.
- A junk bond is a bond rated below investment grade (BB or below) from ratings agencies; though not in default, it is of questionable quality and speculative with higher yields than top-quality corporate debt. High-yield securities are easier to sell in the more developed and greater-risk-taking U.S. capital market. Junk bonds have developed to some extent in Canada as investors seek higher yields, especially with the decrease in income trusts. Nevertheless, the Canadian market is thin for junk bonds.

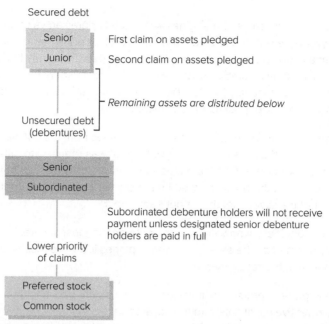

Figure 16–2 Priority of claims

 FINANCE IN ACTION

Don't Forget to Read the Fine Print

Although bond indentures are scrutinized by organizations such as the Canadian Bond Investors Association (bondinvestors.ca) we should be diligent in examining these legal documents that sometimes are several hundred pages in length.

In late 2014, Enbridge moved $17 billion in cash-generating assets to its Income Fund to allow an increase of 33 percent in the dividend to shareholders. This weakened the protection afforded bondholders, which immediately drove down the value of Enbridge bonds. Tim Hortons and Valeant initiated similar maneuvres to fund growth for the benefit of shareholders.

In 2008–09 we suffered the most severe financial recession since the 1930s. The TSX took until 2014 to return to the same value it had before the financial crisis. The crisis stemmed from lending on the basis of what had become inferior debt obligations. What had once been well-secured investments gradually eroded to become securities backed by almost-worthless assets.

Initially, mortgage-backed securities (MBS) and collateralized debt obligations (CDO) were investments or securities backed by diversified assets that produced regular and safe cash flows from obligations such as car payments and credit card receipts. However, adventurous financial institutions began to replace the well-secured assets with less-diversified and less-creditworthy assets. MBS began to place subprime mortgages in their collection of assets. These subprime mortgages were granted to individuals with poor credit ratings. These were NINJA loans (No Income, No Job, No Assets). People forgot to check the fine print and to examine the assets held to back these securities. The market failed spectacularly.

This was not the first time investors got carried away and forgot to check the fine print. In 1987, Continental Airlines (eventually acquired by Delta Airlines) issued $350 million in bonds secured by planes and spare engines with a total appraised value of $467 million. Bonds of this type were referred to as equipment bonds, or equipment trust certificates. With equipment as collateral for protection, if there was default, money had been lent at a rate lower than on unsecured bonds of equal risk. Bondholders found out after Continental declared bankruptcy in 1990 that Continental had put its oldest and least salable planes into the asset pool used as collateral.

The bond indenture allowed Continental to remove planes from the collateral pool and sell them to raise cash. If planes were sold, Continental was required to either replace the planes or buy back bonds. Continental bought back its risky class of bonds that were selling at a discount, not the bonds backed by the planes as collateral. Continental took more money out of the asset pool than it put back into it.

The first-class bondholders, who were supposed to be the most secure, found themselves unprotected by the asset pool. Those planes left were mostly old models that had very little value in the resale market.

Covenants are in place to protect the investor when times are bad, and thus one should not overlook permissive covenants with the hope of squeezing out a slightly higher interest rate. The investor may be trading off significant protection for very little "extra" return.

Q1 What court cases are of interest to the Canadian Bond Investors Association?

Q2 Has the market for MBS and CDOs recovered?

Methods of Repayment

Historically, some Canadian and British government bond issues were perpetual in nature. In the case of one unusual U.S. issue, West Shore Railroad, 4 percent bonds are not scheduled to mature until 2361 (almost 350 years into the future). Nevertheless, most bonds have some orderly or preplanned system of repayment with various provisions.

Single-Sum Payment Single-sum payments allow bonds to be paid off with one simple payment at maturity.

Serial Payments Bonds may be paid off in instalments, or serial payments, over the life of the issue. Each bond has its own predetermined date of maturity and receives interest only to that point. Although the total issue may span 20 years, 15 or 20 maturity dates may be assigned specific dollar amounts.

Sinking-Fund Provision Under a sinking-fund provision, semiannual or annual contributions are made by the corporation into a fund administered by the trustee for purposes of debt retirement. The trustee takes the proceeds and goes into the market to purchase bonds from willing sellers. If no willing sellers are available, a lottery system is used among outstanding bondholders.

Conversion At the option of the bondholder, bonds can be converted into common stock (an action called conversion). The mechanics of convertible bond trading are discussed at length in Chapter 19.

Call Feature A call provision allows the corporation to call in or force in the debt issue before maturity with a premium over par value of 5 to 10 percent. Bonds with a call feature are redeemable issues.

- A corporation may decide to call in outstanding debt issues when interest rates on new securities are considerably lower than those on previously issued debt to reduce interest expense.
- Modern call provisions usually do not take effect until the bond has been outstanding at least five to ten years in order to allow an original investor to reap some reward in case bonds were purchased before a general decrease in interest rates.
- Generally, the call premium declines over time, usually by 1/2 to 1 percent per year after the call period begins.

 FINANCE IN ACTION

Junk or High-Yield Bonds?

In Canada, bonds rated below triple B (BBB) by the bond rating services are not considered investment grade by many pension funds and other institutional buyers. Although the press prefers to call bonds rated below investment grade "junk bonds," the investment dealers that trade in these securities like to use the term "high-yield bonds" or "debt." The DBRS Morningstar (dbrs.com) and S&P (standardandpoors.com) rate bonds in Canada.

A below-investment-grade market has been established in Canada for companies that do not have the ratings or stable cash flow of a bank or utility company. Companies have tended to use the U.S. market for its breadth and greater liquidity. The Canadian high-yield market, at $10 billion, pales beside the U.S. market of $1 trillion.

Portfolio managers such as Deans Knight Capital Management (deansknight.com) invest significant amounts in high-yielding debt for institutional investors. Investment firms offer limited high-yield securities to individual investors. Many high-yield mutual funds, which can be identified through the Globefund website, are offered in the Canadian marketplace. The Royal Bank, for instance, offers a high-yield investment fund, with over 80 percent invested in U.S securities.

With many TSX listings ranking below investment grade, there is a large market for junk bonds that can offer an above-average return to investors. The following 2020 issues exhibit high yields compared to government debt yields of about 1.30 percent at the time.

	YTM	Rating	Maturity (years)	Yield to Maturity
TransAlta	6.50%	BB +	20	5.84%
Sobeys	5.79	BB +	16	3.82
Bombardier	7.35	B −	6	6.96

Q1 What are the holdings of a high-yield bond (mutual) fund? (At the Globefund site, use the Fund Screener.)

Q2 Can you identify three junk bonds and their yields on the basis of one of the bond rating sites?

Q3 Are the companies listed above still rated "junk"?

theglobeandmail.com/globe-investor
standardandpoors.com

LO2 BOND PRICES, YIELDS, AND RATINGS

The financial manager must be sensitive to interest rate changes and price movements in the bond market. The treasurer's interpretation of market conditions influences the timing of new issues, the coupon rate offered, the maturity date, and the necessity for a call provision.

The price of a bond is inversely related to current interest rates. During the period 1977 to 1982, the market interest rate on outstanding 30-year, AAA corporate bonds went from 9.5 percent to 18.3 percent, and the average price of such existing bonds dropped about 48 percent. Imagine the disillusionment of a conservative investor during that period as $1,000, 9.5 percent, top-quality bonds declined, and were quoted at $525.[1] It is small consolation to the bondholder who has many decades to wait while their capital is tied up making below-market returns. The longer the life of the issue, the greater the influence is of interest rate changes on the price of the bond.[2] The same process works in reverse if interest rates go down. The value of a 30-year, $1,000 bond initially issued to yield 18.3 percent would rise to $1,800 if interest rates declined to 9.5 percent (assuming the bond is not callable). There have been tremendous returns on bonds, particularly when yields declined in late 1982. An illustration of interest-rate effects on bond prices is presented in Table 16–2 for a bond paying 12 percent interest. Observe that years to maturity as well as market interest rates have a strong influence on bond prices.

Table 16–2 Interest rates and bond prices (the bond pays 12% interest, semiannually)

Years to Maturity	Rate in the Market				
	8%	10%	12%	14%	16%
1	$1,037.72	$1,018.59	$1,000	$981.92	$964.33
15	1,345.84	1,153.72	1,000	875.91	774.84
25	1,429.64	1,182.56	1,000	861.99	755.33

Note: This table is based on semiannual interest payments, with annualized interest rates.

FINANCE IN ACTION

The Prospectus

When securities that are issued will be publicly traded, provincial securities commissions require that the details of this financial asset, whether it is debt or equity (or something in between), be disclosed to investors. This is done by way of developing a prospectus (short or long form) and by filing an electronic version of the prospectus with SEDAR (System for Electronic Document Analysis and Retrieval) (sedar.com). SEDAR is operated by the Canadian Securities Administrators (CSA) and the Canadian Depository for Securities (CDS).

Recent and historical documents can be viewed at SEDAR with a search of the database for public companies.

Q1 What are the features of a recently issued debt security? Include information on the following: private or public placement, coupon rate, maturity date, underwriting spread, currency, security, redemption feature, and any special features.

sedar.com

---

[1] Bond prices are generally quoted as a percentage of original par value. In this case, the quote would be read 52.5.

[2] This is known as Malkiel's second theory of bonds. It is completely true only when the coupon rate of the bond is equal to or greater than the original discount rate.

Over the past couple of decades, long-term interest rates have shown a definite downward trend from the high-inflation era of the late 1970s and early 1980s, as Figure 16–3 illustrates. As we observed in Chapter 14, there has been a definite trend toward longer-term maturities in the last number of years as firms try to lock in the lower interest rates. At the same time, firms have broadened their debt structure with money market instruments and medium-term notes. Corporate yields would be higher than those for the government.

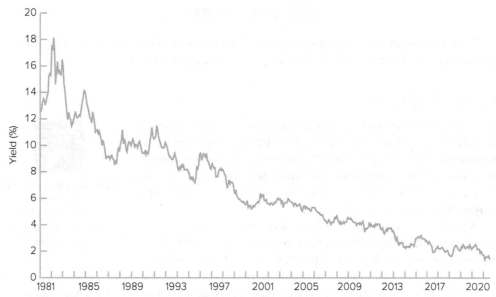

Figure 16–3 Long-term yields on government bonds

Bond Yields

Bond yields are quoted on three different bases: coupon rate, current yield, and yield to maturity. To illustrate, we apply each to a $1,000 par value bond paying $100 per year interest for 10 years and currently selling in the market for $900.

Coupon Rate (nominal yield) Stated interest payment divided by the par value is the coupon rate. Generally, the coupon rate is fixed under the terms of the indenture.

$$\frac{\textbf{Annual interest payment}}{\textbf{Par (maturity) value}} = \frac{\$100}{\$1,000} = .10 = 10\%$$

Current Yield The stated interest payment divided by the current price of the bond gives the current yield. The current yield is focused on the short term and does not consider the time to maturity.

$$\frac{\textbf{Annual interest payment}}{\textbf{Market price value}} = \frac{\$100}{\$900} = .1111 = 11.11\%$$

Yield to Maturity The interest rate that equates future interest payments and the payment at maturity to the current market price is the yield to maturity (YTM). This represents the concept of the internal rate of return. Although the yield to maturity has its flaws, it is the most instructive yield calculation.

In our illustration, we determine an internal rate of 11.75 percent. This is the discount rate, which we call the yield (Y), which equates the annual interest payments of $100 for 10 years and the final payment of $1,000 to the current price of $900.

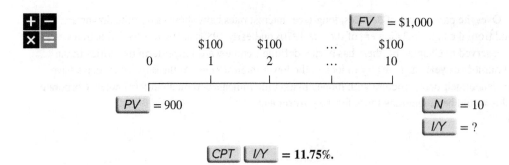

$$CPT \quad I/Y = 11.75\%.$$

When financial analysts speak of bond yields, the general assumption is that they are speaking of yield to maturity. This is deemed to be the most significant measure of return.

Bond Ratings

Bond rating services provide a somewhat objective assessment of the investment quality of securities. In Canada, DBRS Morningstar and Standard and Poor's from the United States provide independent ratings. In the United States, Moody's Investor Service performs a similar service. Issuing corporations and investors alike pay close attention to the ratings assigned by bond rating services.

A bond receives ratings on the basis of the corporation's management, its ability to make interest payments, consistency of performance, size, working capital position, financial ratios, and a number of other factors. In a manner similar to financial analysis of Chapter 3, the rating service calculates ratios such as profit margins, coverage ratios, debt to equity, and total liabilities to equity. There is also a close examination of the debt indenture to identify the protection afforded the debt holder.

The rating systems of DBRS Morningstar and Standard and Poor's are outlined below:

High (+), medium, and low (–) modifiers are also added to each of the ranges to make the rating even more precise.

Dominion Bond Rating Service
dbrsmorningstar.com

Standard and Poor's
standardandpoors.com

	Description
AAA	Highest quality
AA	
A	
BBB	
BB	Speculative or medium quality
B	
CCC	
D	Default

A higher rating indicates a lower amount of risk. The higher the rating assigned a given issue, the lower the interest payments required to satisfy potential investors. A major corporation may be able to issue a bond with a considerably lower yield to maturity because it is rated AA by the DBRS Morningstar, but a smaller, riskier firm may qualify for only a BB or lower rating and be forced to pay a higher rate, as noted in Table 16–3. The yield spread between higher- and lower-rated bonds varies with economic conditions. If investors are pessimistic about the economy, they might accept as much as 3 percent less to hold high-quality securities, though in normal times the spread might be only 1 percent.

Table 16–3 Outstanding debt issues, January 2020

Rating/Issuer	Coupon	Maturity Date	Price	Yield to Maturity
AAA				
Government of Canada	2.50	June 1, 2024	105.40	1.20
Government of Canada	5.75	June 1, 2029	139.02	1.27
Government of Canada	2.75	June 1, 2048	132.97	1.36
AA (Low)				
Province of Ontario	2.35	June 1, 2024	108.57	1.52
A (low)				
TransCanada Pipeline	5.65	June 20, 2029	124.66	2.65
TransCanada Pipeline	4.35	June 6, 2046	116.84	3.38
BBB (High)				
Telus	3.30	May 2, 2029	106.44	2.51
Telus	4.40	Jan. 29, 2046	115.49	3.49
BB (High)				
TransAlta	6.90	Nov. 15, 2030	114.23	5.16
B (Low)				
Bombardier	7.35	Dec. 22, 2026	102.10	6.96

Do these securities still have the same ratings and yields? Check out bond ratings at dbrsmorningstar.com, standardandpoors.com. Check out yields at cbonds.com/countries/Canada-bond.

Examining Actual Bond Offerings

Recall that the true return on a bond issue is measured by yield to maturity (the last column of Table 16–3). Generally, lower-rated bonds and longer-term maturities offered higher yields.

Bond issues are often quoted by how many basis points they trade above Government of Canada issues. For example, the Government of Ontario bond rated AA and maturing in 2024 was trading 32 basis points above a comparable Canada issue, while the Bombardier bond maturing in 2026 and rated B low (less than investment grade) was trading 576 basis points higher than the Canada bond.

Bonds that trade at a discount are often more desirable (because of capital gains possibilities) and, therefore, have somewhat lower yields. Both services have websites that outline the criteria for each category more completely.

 FINANCE IN ACTION

Before the Fall

Before Enron filed for the biggest corporate bankruptcy in U.S. history, it was negotiating to be bought out and merged with Dynegy Inc. Until October 2001, Enron had a solid bond rating from both Standard and Poor's and Moody's bond rating services. However, in November 2001, both bond rating organizations lowered Enron's bond rating to junk bond status. This violation of bond indenture covenants immediately resulted in $3.9 billion of debt becoming due and payable.

The Dynegy deal was abandoned, partly as a result of the lower rating, and Enron shortly thereafter filed for protection under Chapter 11 of the U.S. Bankruptcy Code. Although the rating services claimed they were looking at bondholder protection with the downgrade, their announcements came only after the markets had already dramatically decreased the value of Enron stock. Were the rating services providing valuable insight into the market or reflecting what the market already knew?

LO3 THE REFUNDING DECISION

When interest rates decline, a firm may decide to refund a bond issue to reduce interest expense on borrowing. It is made feasible by the call provision that enables a corporation to buy back bonds at close to par rather than at high market values when interest rates are declining. The decline in long-term interest rates over the past couple of decades has provided a good environment for refunding.

Because bond indenture agreements in Canada normally contain the financial advantage clause, refunding of high-cost debt has been more infrequent than one would expect.[3] Dofasco's call in July 1986 of its 17 percent debentures, issued in 1982 and due in 1997, thus had particular significance in the investment community. Before the call, each $1,000 worth of these bonds traded for $1,250. The day after the call announcement they were worth $1,113, precisely the redemption value. The investment community was not pleased and took issue with Dofasco's call. Bond indentures were rewritten thereafter.

Besides refunding an issue to achieve a lower interest rate, the corporation may want to remove restrictive covenants in the bond indenture, reissue new debt with a longer term than the issue currently outstanding, or reorder the firm's capital structure.

Dofasco
dofasco.arcelormittal.com

A Capital Budgeting Problem

The refunding decision involves the following, and an example appears below:
- Costs (outflows)—financing costs related to redeeming and reissuing securities.
- Benefits (inflows)—savings in annual interest costs and some tax savings.
- Aftertax cost of new debt—as the appropriate discount rate.

The task of an analyst is to determine whether or not the refunding of bonds will add to the value of the firm.

Since the savings from a refunding decision are certain—unlike the savings from most other capital budgeting decisions—the aftertax cost of new debt is used as the discount rate rather than the more generalized cost of capital.[4] In this case then, the aftertax cost of new debt is 10 percent × (1 − tax rate), or 6 percent (10 × (1 − .25)).

---

[3] This clause states that borrowers cannot use money raised more cheaply to finance the redemption of high-cost debt.
[4] A minority opinion would be that there is sufficient similarity between the bond refunding decision and other capital budgeting decisions to disallow any specialized treatment. Also note that although the bondholders must still bear some risk of default, for which they are compensated, the corporation assumes no risk.

Refunding Example

	Old Issue	New Issue
Size.	$10,000,000	$10,000,000
Interest rate.	10.5%	8%
Total life.	25 years	20 years
Remaining life	20 years	20 years
Call premium	10%	—
Underwriting costs.	$125,000	$200,000
Other issue costs	25,000	30,000
Overlap period	1 month $\left(\dfrac{1}{12}\right)$	
Short-term yield.	3.5%	
Tax bracket. 25%		
Discount rate 6%		

8% (1 − .25) = 6%, the aftertax borrowing rate for new issue

Step A—Costs (outflow considerations)

1. **Payment of call premium.** The first cost is the 10 percent call premium on $10 million, or $1 million. This prepayment penalty is necessary to call in the original issue. Because it is considered a capital item, the $1 million cash expenditure will cost $1 million on an aftertax basis.[5]

Net cost of call premium	$1,000,000

2. **Borrowing expenses on the new issue.** The second cost is the $200,000 underwriting cost of the new issue and the $30,000 in other expenses. The actual aftertax costs of these expenses is somewhat less because their payment is tax deductible. Expenses related to the borrowing of money or issuing of shares, such as printing and advertising costs, legal and accounting expenses, filing fees, and underwriting commissions (the investment dealer's fee), are deductible for tax purposes.

These financing expenses are considered capital in nature and, for tax purposes, must be amortized over five years on a straight-line basis (20 percent per year). If the debt is repaid, any undeducted balance of these borrowing costs is deductible in the year the debt is fully repaid, unless the repayment is part of a refinancing. Therefore, in a refunding decision, unamortized borrowing costs on the old issue must be expensed on the original amortization schedule.

In our example, equal deductions of $46,000 ($230,000/5) a year will occur over the next five years. The tax savings from a noncash write-off are equal to the amount times the tax rate. For a company in a 25 percent tax bracket, $46,000 of annual tax deductions will provide $11,500 ($46,000 × 0.25) of tax savings each year for the next five years. The present value of the annual tax savings is

Calculator computation: $48,442

 $\boxed{N} = 5; \boxed{I/Y} = 6\%, \boxed{PMT} = 11,500, \boxed{FV} = 0$

The net borrowing costs (underwriting and other flotation expenses) of the reissue equal the actual expenditure less the present value of the future tax savings.

Actual expenditure.	$230,000
Less: PV of future tax savings	48,442
Net cost of borrowing costs	$181,558

---

[5]This is unlike the situation in the United States, where the call premium is tax deductible.

3. ***Duplicate interest during overlap period.*** An overlap period generally occurs because the new bonds must be sold before the old ones are redeemed. During this period, the company is responsible for paying interest on the old outstanding bond issue. To offset this expense, the company can temporarily invest the proceeds of the new bond issue in short-term securities until they are used to pay off the old bond issue.

In this example, we allow one month as an estimate of the overlap period, although it could be longer. Interest paid is a tax-deductible expense, whereas interest earned is taxable. The net cash flow effect of having to continue paying interest on the old issue during the overlap period is the difference between what is paid on the old issue and what is earned on the new (10.5% versus 3.5% in this case):

$$0.105 \times \frac{1}{12} \times \$10,000,000 \times (1 - 0.25) \dots\dots\dots\dots\dots\dots \quad \$65,625$$

$$0.035 \times \frac{1}{12} \times \$10,000,000 \times (1 - 0.25) \dots\dots\dots\dots\dots\dots \quad \underline{21,875}$$

$$\$43,750$$

The firm will not likely earn interest on the full $10 million because the underwriter pays the firm a reduced amount after the underwriting fees. We use $10 million for ease of calculation.

Step B—Benefits (inflow considerations) The major inflows in the refunding decision are related to the reduction of annual interest expense.

4. ***Aftertax cost savings in lower interest rates.*** The corporation enjoys a 1.875 aftertax percentage point drop in interest rates ($10.5\% - 8.0\% = 2.5 \times [1 - 0.25]$), on $10 million of bonds if it refunds the bond issue:

$10.5\% \times \$10,000,000 \times (1 - 0.25) \dots\dots\dots\dots\dots\dots\dots\dots$	\$787,500
$8.0\% \times \$10,000,000 \times (1 - 0.25) \dots\dots\dots\dots\dots\dots\dots\dots$	600,000
Aftertax savings$\dots\dots\dots\dots\dots\dots\dots\dots\dots\dots\dots\dots\dots\dots\dots\dots$	\$187,500
Or $1.875\% \times \$10,000,000$ (the same) $\dots\dots\dots\dots\dots\dots\dots\dots$	\$187,500

Applying a 6 percent discount rate for a 20-year annuity,

$$PMT = \$187,500; \quad N = 20; \quad I/Y = 6\%; \quad FV = 0$$

$$CPT \quad PV = \$2,150,610$$

Present value of cost savings in lower interest rates: $2,150,610.

The borrowing expenses of the old issue, the underwriting, and other costs are irrelevant for the decision analysis on a refunding decision.

Step C—Net Present Value We now compare our outflows and our inflows.

Costs (outflows)	
1. Net cost of call premium $\dots\dots\dots\dots\dots\dots\dots\dots\dots\dots\dots\dots$	\$1,000,000
2. Net cost of borrowing expenses on new issue $\dots\dots\dots\dots\dots$	181,558
3. Duplicate interest during overlap period $\dots\dots\dots\dots\dots\dots$	43,750
Present value of costs	\$1,225,308
Benefits (inflows)	
4. Aftertax cost savings in lower interest rates $\dots\dots\dots\dots\dots$	\$2,150,610
Present value of benefits $\dots\dots\dots\dots\dots\dots\dots\dots\dots\dots\dots\dots$	\$2,150,610
Net present value $\dots\dots\dots\dots\dots\dots\dots\dots\dots\dots\dots\dots\dots\dots$	\$ 925,302

The refunding decision has a positive net present value, suggesting that interest rates have dropped sufficiently to favour refunding. The only question is, will interest rates go lower—indicating an even better time for refunding? This is a consideration all firms must face, and there is no easy answer.

A number of other factors may complicate the problem. For example, the overlapping time period in the refunding procedure when both issues are outstanding and the firm is paying double interest could be longer than one month. If the bonds were issued at a discount, the difference between the redemption value and the amount the company received for the bond would be tax deductible in the year of redemption.

Note that the discount rate for a refunding decision is the aftertax cost of the new debt.

LO4 OTHER FORMS OF BOND FINANCING

As interest rates continued to show increasing volatility in the 1980s, innovative forms of bond financing were presented to the market.

Zero-Coupon Bond

- With a zero-coupon bond, there is no interest payment; the bonds are sold at a deep discount from face value.
- The return to the investor is the difference between the investor's cost and the face value received at the end of the life of the bond.
- The zero-coupon bond has had limited appeal in Canada, particularly after an unfavourable tax ruling late in 1991. However, the Bank of Canada publishes information on zero-coupon bonds based on government securities that have been stripped of their coupons—strip bonds (bankofcanada.ca/rates/interest-rates/bond-yield-curves).

Strip Bond

- A strip bond is arranged by an investment dealer and is based on government securities and, more recently, on corporate bonds.
- The actual coupons and the face value of the security are sold separately with differing maturities to suit the investor. The securities are sold at a fraction of face value and are ultimately redeemed at full value.
- The investor receives no interest but a fixed return on the initial investment. There is no need to be concerned about reinvesting coupon payments at possibly lower rates of return.

FINANCE IN ACTION

Selling Redeemable Debentures

In February 2020 AGI or Ag Growth International (AFN), a global leader in planning, engineering, and manufacturing equipment solutions in the agricultural business, announced an issue of 5.25 percent unsecured debentures due December 31, 2026, in the amount of $85 million. These debentures were redeemable after December 2021 at 103.9375 percent of the principal amount. Thereafter the redemption price declined yearly. Details of these and other redemptions can be found at sedar.com.

Back in July 2014, Cameco planned on redeeming its 4.7 percent $300 million issue of debentures. They were to be redeemed at $1,039.96 for each $1,000 debenture. The redemption price was established at 0.22 percent above the Government of Canada bond of similar maturity (at the time, about 1 year with a yield of 0.97 percent). Cameco was going to issue 10-year bonds at a coupon rate of 4.19 percent for $500 million at the same time.

Q1 Did the Cameco redemption and issue of new bonds make financial sense?

Symbols: CCO, AFN

- The major drawback is that the difference in value between the purchase price and the maturity must be amortized on a straight-line basis as interest income over the number of years to maturity, and tax must be paid annually on this interest income, even though the bondholder does not have a cash return until maturity.
- Strip bonds are favoured by institutes with tax-exempt or deferred status, and by those likely to more precisely match their assets (the bonds) with their future liabilities.
- The prices of strip bonds tend to be highly volatile when there are changes in interest rates, due to the fact there is no annual interest payment to modify the effects of interest rate changes in the marketplace.

Strip Bond Illustrated

An investor desires an 8 percent yield or return for a 10-year investment. The investment dealer locates a Government of Canada bond that matures in 10 years, strips the coupons or semiannual payments from the bond (to sell to other clients), and agrees to sell the face or maturity value of the bond to the investor for $463.19. In 10 years the investor collects $1,000. (Larger multiples of the $1,000 bond are possible.) The investor has realized a holding period or true yield to maturity (YTM) of 8 percent, without the risk of having to reinvest the coupons at lower interest rates.

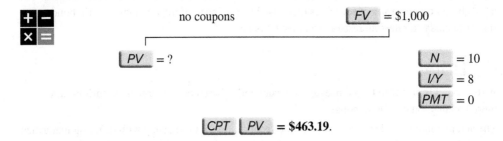

Floating-Rate Bond

- Floating-rate bonds, popular in European capital markets, allow the interest rate paid on the bond to change with market conditions (usually monthly or quarterly). The interest rate is usually tied to some overall market rate, such as the yield on Treasury bills or the prime rate. Thus, a bond that was initially issued to pay 6 percent may lower the interest payments to 4 percent during some years and raise them to 9 percent in others.
- The investor has a constant (or almost constant) market value for the security, even though interest rates vary. The one exception that can cause a change to this principle is that floating-rate bonds often have broad limits that interest payments cannot exceed.

 FINANCE IN ACTION

Strips or Real Returns

A strip bond has only a single payment. The coupons and residual (principal or face value) of an original bond are separated and sold individually. By purchasing one of the parts there is no need to worry about reinvesting the coupon payments as they come due.

- For example, the interest rate on a 6 percent initial offering may not be allowed to go over 13 percent or below 4 percent. If long-term interest rates dictated an interest payment of 15 percent, the payment would still remain at 13 percent. This could cause some short-term loss in market value. To date, floating-rate bonds have been relatively free of this problem.

- Floating-rate bonds still represent a relatively small percentage of the total market of new debt offerings.

Real Return Bond

- The real return bond adjusts the principal amount on the basis of inflationary changes.

In November 1991, the government issued Canada's first real return bond. The bond would provide a real yield of 4.25 percent above the inflation rate as measured by the Canadian consumer price index (CPI). A coupon payment of 4.25 percent was paid semiannually on the adjusted principal.

Real return bonds
bankofcanada.ca/markets/
government-securities-
auctions/real-return-bonds

Revenue Bond

- The revenue bond is based on an enterprise that generates a dependable stream of cash flow, and this, rather than the firm's assets, is the security for investors.

- The revenue bond was introduced to the Canadian market in 1996.

NAV Canada, with RBC Dominion Securities as lead underwriter, issued $3 billion in revenue bonds to assist in the purchase of the air traffic control network from Transport Canada. With no competition allowed, the ability to set rates, a surcharge on all airline tickets, and a levy on foreign aircraft over Canadian skies, cash flow to NAV Canada would seem assured. NAV Canada has since issued several well-received revenue bonds.

The Forest Bond for Sustainability

In late 2016 the first Forest bond was issued by the International Finance Corporation (IFC), a member of the World Bank Group. Investors could be repaid in either carbon credits or cash. The issue raised $152 million to assist in development and prevent deforestation in developing countries. The five-year bond with a 1.56 percent annual US dollar coupon was listed on the London Stock Exchange.

ifc.org

EUROBOND MARKET

- A Eurobond is a bond issued and traded outside the country, payable in currency that is not legal tender of the trading country.

    An example might be a bond of a Canadian corporation that is payable in U.S. dollars and sold in London, Paris, Tokyo, or Singapore.

- International investment dealer syndicates place Eurobonds all over the world. These issues allow corporations to tap the resources of this large market of funds. Although these issues in euros carry exchange risk, an issue in Canadian dollars in the Euromarket would not be subject to exchange rate fluctuations.

- *Eurocurrencies* are units of currency deposited in banks outside the country issuing the currencies. Of such deposits, the U.S. Eurodollar is the most prevalent.

- Disclosure requirements in the Eurobond market are less demanding than those of Canadian domestic regulatory agencies.

- Investors in Eurobonds are generally not able to rely on bond rating agencies, though Moody's and S&P's have been rating selected Eurobond issues for a fee.

Moody's
moodys.com/Pages/default_
ca.aspx

CORPORATE DEBT FOR THE MEDIUM TERM
Term Loans

- The term loan is advanced against capital asset security.
- The term loan is not payable on demand.
- The choice of lenders for term loans in Canada is wide and includes banks, trust companies, life insurance companies, credit unions and caisses populaires, specialized equipment lenders, the Business Development Bank of Canada, pension funds, and term lending specialists such as Commercial Capital Corporation.
- Funding that often includes equity participation is available from venture capitalists and from "angels"—wealthy individuals looking for good growth prospects in a company.
- The length of time on a term loan is generally three to ten years.
- The interest rate charged is often floating (e.g., prime plus 1.5 percent), although lenders sometimes, depending on economic and market circumstances, fix the rate for the full term of the loan.
- Principal and interest repayments are usually made monthly or quarterly, with a balloon payment of principal required at the end of the term.

Business Development
Bank of Canada
bdc.ca/en

    Figure 16–4 provides a sample of a credit offer from a term lender to a potential borrower. Take special note of the legal covenants governing the credit as extended.

Term Loan Offer: Acme Company Limited

We are pleased to make the following offer to finance:

BORROWER:	Acme Company Limited
LENDER:	XYZ Insurance Company of Canada
AMOUNT:	$3,000,000
REPAYMENT:	$25,000 per month, including principal and interest, to liquidate in 10 years. Subject to adjustment to reflect changes in Prime Lending Rate.
INTEREST:	Prime (average of five largest banks) + 1½%, payable monthly or fixed-rate option at rates for 1-, 2-, 3-, or 5-year term as set from time to time.
SECURITY:	A first fixed charge on all land, buildings, and equipment. A first floating charge on all other assets subject only to the bank charge on accounts receivable and inventory.
LEGAL COVENANTS:	1. Annual audited financial statements provided to XYZ Insurance within 90 days after fiscal year-end. 2. Quarterly financial statements to be provided within 30 days of quarter-end. 3. Net worth of the borrower including capital, retained earnings, and shareholders' loans is not to fall below $2,000,000 during the term of the loan. 4. Debt/equity ratio is not to exceed 2:1. 5. Working capital ratio is not to be less than 1.5:1. 6. Capital expenditures are not to exceed $500,000 in any fiscal year without XYZ's approval. 7. Management salaries and bonuses are not to exceed $750,000 per annum without XYZ's approval. 8. An annual list of capital assets is to be provided.

Figure 16–4 Sample credit offer

Operating Loans

- The operating loan is generally advanced based on current asset security.
- The operating loan is payable on demand.

Medium-Term Notes

- Medium-term notes (MTNs) are of three to maybe ten years' duration.
- MTNs can be issued by companies that have already filed a "shelf prospectus" with the appropriate securities commissions. This process allows companies to bring further securities to market on the basis of information already filed with the commission.
- The advantage of an MTN to a company is that it can issue the notes and receive settlement in about five days, as against the two weeks normally required by a public issue with full prospectus.
- The MTN can be issued for as little as several million dollars, which makes it more flexible as a funding vehicle compared to the larger public bond issues.
- Investment dealers act only as agents to the company and receive a spread on the issue above government bonds.

This market began in the 1980s when the big car companies issued 3- to 5-year commercial paper by way of the shelf prospectus. The market is still developing and is somewhat "illiquid," as the term notes are generally sold to specific buyers and the MTNs do not trade frequently.

MORTGAGE FINANCING

There are various sources of debt financing for the financial manager to consider, depending on the needs of the firm. The overall objective is to obtain the required funds at the lowest overall cost. Rates and criteria are different for residential compared to commercial mortgages due to risk differences. This type of financing is secured by real property.

Criteria for Approval

Similar to other forms of loans, the lender considers the following information to approve the mortgage:
* Security for the loan (appraised value of the land and building)
* Ability of the firm to make payments (net income per income statement)
* Risk of default on payments (credit report from independent source)

The higher the value of the property being mortgaged, the greater the amount that can be approved based on the lender's LTV (loan-to-value ratio). Mortgages for factories, plazas, office complexes, and other commercial real estate are about 3 percent higher than residential mortgages and usually require application and arranging fees payable to the lender. There may also be fees to the mortgage broker to package the information to satisfy the lender's criteria.

Generally, the aftertax cost of mortgage financing is lower than other forms of debt because of the lower risk offered by the solid security of real estate over the long term.

Application Requirements

Normally, lenders require the following to evaluate a mortgage application:
* Current and projected financial statements, especially past and projected cash flows
* Application fees, either fixed amount or percentage of the loan amount
* Credit report from an independent reporting agency
* Formal appraisal of the property being mortgaged, by qualified appraisers
* Environmental reports (usually phase 1 and 2) by a qualified independent company

The costs for the above reports are the responsibility of the applicant, whether or not the loan is approved. These financing costs are tax deductible over a 5-year period at 20 percent per year.

Mortgage Term and Amortization

The various mortgage lenders include chartered banks, foreign banks, BDC (Business Development Bank), trust and insurance companies, venture capital, and various private lenders. Unlike residential mortgages, the rates and terms vary depending on the applicant's credit status, the quality and use of the property, and whether it is a first or second mortgage on the property.

The term of the mortgage is the period of time to maturity, usually 6 months to 10 years, whereby the balance of the loan is payable to the lender. The amortization period, usually 25 years, is the period of time required to pay out the loan by making periodic, usually monthly, blended payments of principal and interest throughout the amortization period. Lenders usually provide a computerized "amortization schedule" that divides the monthly payments between interest and the principal reduction amount.

Almost all companies that own real estate will mortgage the property since it is usually the lowest cost of debt financing and helps to lower the overall cost of capital.

ASSET-BACKED SECURITIES

- With asset-backed securities, current assets of a firm (receivables) are sold into a trust from which an investor receives the cash flow as the receivable payments are made.
- The firm gets immediate capital in exchange for its assets rolled into a trust, and frees up its capital tied up in these current assets.
- The investor receives a steady return as the receivables (or other assets) are collected.
- Asset-backed securities can be of a more medium term.

There is a permanent nature to current assets, and this suggests hedged financing of a longer term as well. Credit card asset-backed securities (ABS), although individually turning over balances on a short-term basis, are replenished by other credit users and generally have a 2- to 7-year life span. Car loan ABS are based on auto and truck loans of 3 to 5 years, and mortgage-backed securities have become quite popular, paying a regular return of principal and interest to the investor. With the use of an investment dealer to access capital and a trust to ensure payment to investors, firms can unlock their capital tied up in medium-term assets.

Unfortunately, the financial crisis of 2008 was precipitated by asset-backed security trusts that held very questionable securities. The underlying securities, primarily mortgages, were held on properties that had lost their value and ultimately required mortgage payments by individuals who could not afford the payments. This emphasized the financial lesson that assets must ultimately provide a sustainable cash flow.

ADVANTAGES AND DISADVANTAGES OF DEBT

The financial manager must consider whether debt contributes to or detracts from the firm's operations. In certain industries, such as airlines, very heavy debt utilization is a way of life, whereas in other industries (drugs, photographic equipment) reliance is placed on other forms of capital.

Advantages of Debt	Disadvantages of Debt
• The financial obligation is clearly specified and is of a fixed nature (with the exception of floating-rate bonds).	• Interest and principal payment obligations are set by contract and must be met regardless of the economic position of the firm.
• In an inflationary economy, debt may be paid back with cheaper dollars with declined purchasing power.	• Bond indenture agreements may place burdensome restrictions on the firm to maintain financial ratios. Bondholders may take virtual control of the firm if important indenture provisions are not met.
• The use of debt, to the extent that it does not strain the risk position of the firm, may lower the cost of capital to the firm with its low aftertax cost.	• Utilized beyond a given point, debt may depress outstanding common stock values.
• Interest payments are tax deductible.	

LO5 LEASING AS A FORM OF DEBT

When a corporation contracts to lease an oil tanker or a computer and signs a noncancellable, long-term agreement, the transaction has all the characteristics of a debt obligation.

The Chartered Professional Accountants (CPA) require that certain types of leases must be shown as long-term obligations on the financial statements of the firm. At one time, lease obligations could merely be divulged in footnotes to financial statements, and large lease obligations did not have to be included in the debt structure (except for the upcoming payment). Consider the case of firm ABC, whose balance sheet is shown in Table 16–4. A footnote to the financial statements might have indicated a lease obligation of $12 million a year for the next 15 years, with a present value of $100 million. Under current practice, this information has been moved directly to the balance sheet, as indicated in Table 16–5.

Table 16–4

Balance Sheet (in $ millions)			
Current assets...............	$ 50	Current liabilities.............	$ 50
Capital assets	150	Long-term liabilities	50
		Total liabilities.............	$100
		Shareholders' equity...........	100
		Total liabilities and	
Total assets..................	$200	shareholders' equity.........	$200

Table 16–5

Revised Balance Sheet (in $ millions)			
Current assets.................	$ 50	Current liabilities..............	$ 50
Capital assets	150	Long-term liabilities	50
Leased property under		Obligation under	
capital lease*	100	capital lease*	100
		Total liabilities...............	$200
		Shareholders' equity............	100
		Total liabilities and	
Total assets....................	$300	shareholders' equity...........	$300

*New categories.

We see that both a new asset and a new liability have been created, as indicated by the asterisks. The essence of this treatment is that a long-term, noncancellable lease is tantamount to purchasing the asset with borrowed funds, and this should be reflected on the balance sheet. Note that between the original balance sheet (Table 16–4) and the revised balance sheet (Table 16–5), the total-debt-to-total-assets ratio has gone from 50 percent to 66.7 percent, even though the effect on the firm's credit rating or share price may be minimal.

$$\text{Original} \quad \frac{\text{Total debt}}{\text{Total assets}} = \frac{\$100 \text{ million}}{\$200 \text{ million}} = 50\%$$

$$\text{Revised} \quad \frac{\text{Total debt}}{\text{Total assets}} = \frac{\$200 \text{ million}}{\$300 \text{ million}} = 66.7\%$$

To the extent that the financial markets are efficient, the information was already known by analysts who took the data from footnotes or other sources and made their own adjustments. Nevertheless, corporate financial officers fought long, hard, and unsuccessfully to keep the lease obligation off the balance sheet. They seem to be much less convinced about the efficiency of the marketplace than are financial theorists.

 FINANCE IN ACTION

Sale and Leaseback if Firm is under Duress

In 2017 SNC-Lavalin sold its Montreal headquarters for $170 million and leased it back for 20 years, confirming its commitment to Canada despite increasing operations in Europe and the Middle East. Later scandals damaged SNC-Lavalin's prospects considerably.

Capital Lease Versus Operating Lease

Not all leases must be capitalized (present value) and placed on the balance sheet. Only under circumstances in which substantially all the benefits and risks of ownership are transferred in a lease is this treatment necessary. Under these circumstances, we have a capital (or finance) lease. Identification as a capital lease and the attendant financial treatment are required whenever any one of the four following conditions is present:

1. The arrangement transfers ownership of the property to the lessee (the leasing party) by the end of the lease term.
2. The lease contains a bargain purchase price at the end of the lease. The option price has to be sufficiently low so exercise of the option appears reasonably certain.
3. The lease term is equal to 75 percent or more of the estimated life of the leased property.
4. The present value of the minimum lease payments equals 90 percent or more of the fair value of the lease property at the inception of the lease.[6]

Canadian Finance and
Leasing Association
cfla-acfl.ca

There is close similarity between a capital lease and borrowing to purchase an asset for financial reporting purposes.

*   The capital lease calls not only for present valuing the lease obligation on the balance sheet, but also for treating the arrangement for income statement purposes as if it were somewhat similar to a purchase-borrowing arrangement.
*   Under a capital lease, the asset account shown in Table 16–5 as "Leased property under capital lease" is amortized, or written off, over the life of the lease with an annual expense deduction. Also the liability account shown in the table as "Obligation under capital lease" is written off through regular amortization, with an implied interest expense on the remaining balance.
*   For financial reporting purposes, the annual deductions are amortization of the asset plus implied interest expense on the remaining present value of the liability.
*   Capital leases include oil drilling equipment, airplanes, rail equipment, certain forms of real estate, and other long-term assets.
*   It represents the greatest volume of leasing obligations.

---

[6]The discount rate used for this test is the leasing firm's new cost of borrowing or the lessor's (the firm that owns the asset) implied rate of return under the lease. The lower of the two must be used when both are known.

An operating lease is a lease that does ***not*** meet any of the four capital lease criteria.

- An operating lease is usually short term, and often cancellable at the option of the lessee.
- The lessor (the owner of the asset) may provide for the maintenance and upkeep of the asset.
- An operating lease does not require the capitalization, or presentation, of the full obligation on the balance sheet.
- Operating leases are used most frequently with assets such as automobiles and office equipment.
- An operating lease usually calls for an annual expense deduction equal to the lease payment, with no specific amortization.

Besides a straightforward direct lease, in which a firm acquires the use of an asset offered in general to the market by a lessor, there are also sale-and-leaseback arrangements and leveraged leases.

Sale and Leaseback Under a sale-and-leaseback arrangement, a firm would sell an asset it already owns to another party. It would then lease the asset back from that party, as in the Leasing in and out of Fashion! Finance in Action box.

Leveraged Leases In leveraged leases, three parties are involved: a lessee, a lessor, and a lender. The asset is generally financed by an equity investment by the lessor (often about 20%) and a loan to the lessor from a financial institution for the remainder. Leveraged leasing is common where the asset in question requires a large capital outlay.

Advantages of Leasing

Why is leasing so popular? In the United States it has emerged as a trillion dollar industry, with firms such as Clark Equipment, GE Capital, and U.S. Leasing International providing an enormous amount of financing. Although industry figures for the Canadian leasing market are not publicly tabulated, the Canadian market is significant but less spectacular. There are approximately 100 lessors in the Canadian equipment leasing business. The banks are major players in the car leasing business in which as many cars are now leased as purchased.

Major reasons for the popularity of leasing include the following:

1. The lessee may lack sufficient funds or the credit capability to purchase the asset from a manufacturer that is willing, however, to accept a lease agreement or to arrange a lease obligation with a third party.
2. The provisions of a lease obligation may be substantially less restrictive than those of a bond indenture.
3. There may be no down payment requirement, as would generally be the case in the purchase of an asset (leasing allows for a larger indirect loan).
4. The lessor may possess particular expertise in a given industry—allowing for expert product selection, maintenance, and eventual resale. Through this process the negative effects of obsolescence may be lessened.
5. Creditor claims on certain types of leases, such as real estate, are restricted in bankruptcy and reorganization proceedings. Leases on chattels (non-real-estate items) have no such limitation.

 FINANCE IN ACTION

Leasing in and out of Fashion!

Over the years, a lessor's ability to claim capital cost allowance (CCA) has been limited. Tax-exempt institutions at times entered into sale-and-leaseback arrangements, which traded off CCA for lower rental payments. For cash-strapped institutions such as universities and colleges, this was a viable means of freeing up much-needed capital. The University of Ottawa actually sold its entire library collection and then leased it back.

There are also some tax factors to be considered. Where one party to a lease is in a higher tax bracket than the other party, certain tax advantages, such as an investment tax credit, may be better utilized. For example, a wealthy party may purchase an asset and take an investment tax credit then lease the asset to another party in a lower tax bracket for actual use. Also, lease payments on the use of land are tax deductible, whereas land ownership does not allow a similar deduction for amortization. Note that to be treated as a legitimate lease contract for tax purposes, the Canada Revenue Agency requires that lease payments not include an excess amount, implying the lessee is purchasing the underlying asset on an instalment basis.

Canada Revenue Agency
canada.ca/en/revenue-agency.html

Finally, a firm may wish to engage in a sale-and-leaseback arrangement to provide it with an infusion of capital while allowing it to continue to use the asset. Even though the dollar costs of a leasing arrangement are often higher than the dollar costs of owning an asset, the advantages just cited may outweigh the direct cost factors.

LO6 LEASE-VERSUS-PURCHASE DECISION

Corporations and individuals are often faced with the decision as to whether to purchase an asset or to enter into a lease arrangement to allow the use of the asset without the large capital commitment.

The classic lease-versus-purchase decision does not fit most capital leasing decisions anymore because of the similar financial accounting and tax treatment accorded to a capital lease and borrowing to purchase. An exception may occur when land is part of the lease arrangement. Furthermore, the classic lease-versus-purchase decision is still appropriate for the operating lease, and this is where we concentrate our analysis.

Our example of financing an asset worth $5,000 (stated obligations):

- $5,000 borrowed and amortized over 5 years at 10% interest: –$1,319
- Lease over 5 years, annual lease payment (beginning of year): –$1,295

Year	0	1	2	3	4	5
Lease obligations	$1,295	$1,295	$1,295	$1,295	$1,295	
Loan obligations		$1,319	$1,319	$1,319	$1,319	$1,319

The purchaser of the asset would be entitled to deduct interest charges on the loan, effecting a tax shield, and be able to claim capital cost allowance (CCA). The asset may also have salvage value. The lease payments are deductible for tax purposes, effecting a tax savings.

In the analysis of the lease-versus-borrow decision, we are looking at a type of capital budgeting problem. Besides determining the appropriate cash flows, it is important to discount the future expected cash flows to the present at a proper discount rate. Because the costs associated with both leasing and borrowing are contractual and certain, we use the aftertax cost of new debt as the discount rate rather than the cost of capital used in most capital budgeting decisions. The aftertax cost of debt is a lower discount rate, representing greater certainty in the cash flow stream.

However, if a salvage value is relevant in a lease-versus-borrow decision, we usually discount it at the higher cost of capital to acknowledge the greater uncertainty in its estimation. All other cash flows in the analysis are relatively more certain than the salvage value. Therefore, these cash flows are discounted at the lower discount rate, the aftertax borrowing rate.

Let us first analyze the costs and benefits of borrowing to purchase. This is laid out in Table 16–6. The loan payments (column 1) are costs, and the tax shields on the interest portion of the loan payments are benefits. To determine the interest payments, we could set up an amortization schedule to separate the annual payment into the interest and principal components. The interest portion has been identified and then multiplied by the tax rate to determine the tax shields (column 3). The tax shields have been deducted from the annual loan payment (column 4) to determine the aftertax cost of the loan. Finally, we have calculated the present value of the aftertax costs at a discount rate of 6 percent (column 5). The 6 percent is the aftertax cost of borrowing. It was computed by multiplying the interest rate of 10 percent by (1 – Tax rate): [10% (1 – 0.4) = 6%].

Table 16–6 Net present value of borrow-purchase

Year	(1) Payment	(2) Loan Interest	(3) Interest Tax Shield (2) × 0.4	(4) Aftertax Cost of (1) + (3)	(5) Present Value at 6%
1	($1,319)	$500*	$200	($1,119)	($1,056)
2	(1,319)	418	167	(1,152)	(1,025)
3	(1,319)	328	131	(1,188)	(997)
4	(1,319)	229	92	(1,227)	(972)
5	(1,319)	120	48	(1,271)	(950)
					(5,000)

*$5,000 × 10% = $500.

Notice that the present value of the aftertax cost of the annual loan payments is $5,000, which equals the cost of the asset and the original amount of the loan. This is always the case when the aftertax borrowing rate is used as the discount rate. From a calculation standpoint, this means we may avoid setting up an amortization schedule. The amount borrowed will equal the present value of the loan payments plus the tax savings on the interest portion of the loan payment.

The next task is to calculate the CCA tax shield. In this example the asset falls into CCA Class 8, which allows a 20 percent CCA deduction. Thus, using formula 12–1, the present value (PV) of the CCA tax shield (assuming a zero salvage value) would be

$$\text{PV of CCA tax shield} = \frac{CdT}{r+d}\left[\frac{1+0.5r}{1+r}\right]$$
$$= \frac{\$5,000 \times 0.20 \times 0.40}{0.06+0.20}\left[\frac{1+0.03}{1+0.6}\right]$$
$$= \$1,495$$

The CCA tax shield has been included in Table 16–7. The total cost of the loan alternative is $3,505. If we had a salvage value on the asset, this could be included as an additional line of the table.

Table 16–7 Net present value of operating lease outflows

Year	Tax Payment	Shield	Aftertax Cost of Leasing	Present Value at 6%
0	($1,295)	$ 0	($1,295)	($1,295)
1	(1,295)	518	(777)	(733)
2	(1,295)	518	(777)	(692)
3	(1,295)	518	(777)	(652)
4	(1,295)	518	(777)	(615)
5	0	518	518	387
				($3,600)

We can use the calculator and simplify this process:

0–4 Lease payments

PMT(BGN) = (1,295), $N = 5$, $I/Y = 6\%$, FV = 0 . . . .   (5,782)

1–5 Tax savings

PMT(END) = 518, $N = 5$, $I/Y = 6\%$, FV = 0   2,182

PV of leasing . . . .   (3,600)

We can summarize the cash outflows from borrow to purchase as

Cost of asset	(5,000)
PV of CCA shield	1,495
PV of borrowing	(3,505)

Next, we analyze the cash outflows from leasing. To consider the time value of money, we have discounted the annual values in the borrowing alternative at an interest rate of 6 percent, the aftertax cost of debt to the firm. To treat the analysis of each financing alternative equally we must use the same discount rate for the cash flows of the leasing alternative. The net present value (NPV) calculation for the operating lease option is shown in Table 16–7.

Note the adjustments in the table for the timing of the cash flows related to the lease payments and tax shields on the lease payments. Though the lease payments are generally made at the start of the year, the tax deductions related to them can be claimed only over the year for which the payment applies.

The borrow-to-purchase alternative has a lower present value of aftertax costs ($3,505 as against $3,600) that would appear to make it the more desirable alternative.

The NPV of borrow to purchase is $95. However, many of the previously discussed qualitative factors that support leasing must also be considered in the decision-making process.

Table 16–8 Summary of lease versus borrow-to-purchase analysis

Borrow-to-Purchase Alternative	
Cost of asset	(5,000)
PV of CCA shield	1,495
PV of borrowing	(3,505)
Operating Lease Alternative	
0–4 Lease payments	
PMT(BGN) = (1,295), $N = 5$, $I/Y = 6\%$, FV = 0	(5,782)
1–5 Tax savings	
PMT(END) = 518, $N = 5$, $I/Y = 6\%$, FV = 0	2,182
PV of leasing	(3,600)
NPV of borrow to purchase	$95

SUMMARY

1. The use of debt financing by corporations has grown rapidly since the 1960s, and the degree to which earnings are sufficient to cover interest payments has deteriorated. Corporate bonds may be secured by a lien on a specific asset or may carry an unsecured designation, indicating that the bondholder possesses a general claim against the corporation. A special discussion of the hierarchy of claims for firms in financial distress is presented in Appendix 16A. Long-term debt may have sinking-fund provisions, a call feature, or conversion provisions that cause the debt to be repaid or converted to equity before maturity.Qualcomm® Snapdragon™ 730G with Octa-core†† (LO1)

2. Bond prices and yields are inversely related. The yields on which corporate and government bonds are evaluated are generally based on the level of interest rates in the economy and particularly by the inflation rate. More specifically, the yield required on an issue is based on its rating as determined by one of the bond rating services. The rating is determined by the rating agency's analysis of the corporation or government's ability to pay its financial commitments. (LO2)

3. During periodic cyclical downturns in interest rates, corporations have an opportunity for refunding debt if the issue has a call provision. This allows the replacement of high interest rate bonds with lower interest rate bonds. This is a capital budgeting decision in which the financial manager must consider whether the savings in lower aftertax interest payments will compensate for the additional costs of calling the old issue and selling a new one. The discount rate for this analysis is the aftertax borrowing rate on the new issue. (LO3)

4. Innovative forms of raising long-term debt are attempts to serve a market that is not completely satisfied by the current offerings. New types of debt can meet the needs of both the investor and the issuer and earn healthy returns to the innovators. (LO4)

5. The long-term, noncancellable lease should be considered as a special debt form available to the corporation. It is capitalized on the balance sheet to represent both a debt and an asset account and is amortized on a regular basis. Leasing offers a means of financing in which lessor expertise and other financial benefits can be imparted to the lessee (leasing party). (LO5)

6. A lease versus borrow-to-purchase decision for an operating lease requires careful consideration of all cash flows, including loan and lease payments, tax shields from interest payments and CCA, and any salvage value. The appropriate discount rate is the aftertax cost of debt. (LO6)

DISCUSSION QUESTIONS

1. Corporate debt has expanded significantly since the 1980s. What has been the effect on interest coverage? (LO1)

2. What are some basic features of bond agreements? (LO1)

3. What is the difference between a bond agreement and a bond indenture? (LO1)

4. Discuss the relationship between the coupon rate (original interest rate at time of issue) on a bond and its security provisions. (LO2)

5. Take the following list of securities and arrange them in order of their priority of claims: (LO1)

Preferred stock	Senior debentures	Subordinated debenture
Senior secured debt	Common stock	Junior secured debt

6. Which method of bond repayment reduces debt and increases the amount of common stock outstanding? (LO1)

7. What is the purpose of serial repayments and sinking funds? (LO1)

8. Under which circumstances would a call on a bond be exercised by a corporation? What is the purpose of a deferred call? (LO1, LO4)

9. Discuss the relationship between bond prices and interest rates. What effect do changing interest rates have on the price of long-term bonds versus short-term bonds? (LO2)

10. What is the difference between the following yields: coupon rate, current yield, yield to maturity? (LO2)

11. How does the bond rating affect the interest rate paid by a corporation on its bonds? (LO2)

12. Bonds of different risk classes have a spread between their interest rates. Is this spread always the same? Why? (LO2)

13. Use Table 16–3 to answer the following questions. (LO2)

    a. Why would the TransCanada Pipeline 4.35 percent bond have a higher yield to maturity than the Telus 3.30 percent bond?

    b. What do you suggest is the spread above Government of Canada bonds for a medium-term (2029) bond of TransCanada Pipeline of a similar maturity. Why the difference?

14. Explain how the bond refunding problem is similar to a capital budgeting decision. (LO3)

15. What cost of capital is generally used in evaluating a bond refunding decision? Why? (LO3)

16. Discuss the advantages and disadvantages of debt. (LO1)

17. Explain how the zero-coupon rate bond, or stripped bond, provides return to the investor. What are the advantages to the corporation? (LO4)

18. Explain how floating-rate bonds can save the investor from potential embarrassments in portfolio valuation. (LO4)

19. What is a Eurobond? (LO4)

20. What do we mean by capitalizing lease payments? (LO5)

21. Explain the close parallel between a capital lease and the borrow-purchase decision from the viewpoint of both the balance sheet and the income statement. (LO6)

22. In the lease-versus-purchase decision, why is the discount rate the aftertax cost of debt? (LO6)

INTERNET RESOURCES

Bond ratings and the criteria for bond ratings on Canadian, U.S., and international sovereign debt securities are available at several sites:
dbrsmorningstar.com
moodys.com
standardandpoors.com

Historical yields for a broad selection of Canadian and U.S. bonds are available at the Bank of Canada site:
bankofcanada.ca

The current pricing and yield to maturity on bonds is available at several sites:
iiroc.ca (bond quotes)
bloomberg.com (markets, rates and bonds)
cbonds.com/countries/Canada-bond

Eurobond information and pricing is available at the Swiss Exchange site: six-group.com/exchanges/index.html

Prospectus information on new debt securities is available at SEDAR (System for Electronic Document Analysis and Retrieval), a subsidiary of the Canadian Depository for Securities: sedar.com

PROBLEMS

(Assume the par value of the bonds in the following problems is $1,000 unless otherwise specified.)

1. The Garland Corporation has a bond outstanding with a $90 annual interest with semiannual payment, a market price of $820, and a maturity date in 10 years. Find the following:
    a. The coupon rate (nominal yield).
    b. The current yield.
    c. The yield to maturity.
    d. The yield an investor would realize if coupon payments were reinvested at 6 percent (holding period return).

2. Preston Corporation has a bond outstanding with a $70 annual interest with a semiannual coupon payment, a market price of $1,068, and a maturity date in 7 years. Find the following:
    a. The coupon rate (nominal yield).
    b. The current yield.
    c. The yield to maturity.
    d. The yield an investor would realize if coupon payments were reinvested at 9 percent.

3. Myra Breck must choose between two bonds:

    Bond A pays $100 annual interest with semiannual payment and has a market value of $800. It has 10 years to maturity.

    Bond B pays $100 annual interest with semiannual payment and has a market value of $900. It has 2 years to maturity.
    a. Compute the current yield on both bonds.
    b. Which bond should she select based on your answer to part *a*?
    c. A drawback of current yield is that it does not consider the total life of the bond. What is the yield to maturity on these bonds?
    d. Has your answer changed between parts *b* and *c* of this question?

4. Bill Board must choose between two bonds:

    Bond A pays $90 annual interest with semiannual payment and has a market value of $850. It has 10 years to maturity.

    Bond B pays $80 annual interest with semiannual payment and has a market value of $900. It has 2 years to maturity.
    a. Compute the current yield on both bonds.
    b. Which bond should he select based on your answer to part *a*?
    c. A drawback of current yield is that it does not consider the total life of the bond. What is the yield to maturity on these bonds?
    d. Has your answer changed between parts *b* and *c* of this question?

5. Match the yield to maturity in column 2 with the appropriate debt security in column 1.

(1)	(2)
Debenture	6.85%
Secured debt	8.20%
Subordinated debenture	7.76%

6. The Milken Investment Fund buys 90 bonds of the Levine Corporation through its broker. The bonds pay 11 percent annual interest. The yield to maturity (market rate of interest) is 14 percent. The bonds have a 20-year maturity. Using an assumption of semiannual interest payments,

    a. Compute the price of a bond.

    b. Compute the total value of the 90 bonds.

7. Lee, Braun and James Company pays a 12 percent coupon rate on debentures due in 20 years. The current yield to maturity on bonds of similar risk is 10 percent. The bonds are currently callable at $1,060. The theoretical value of the bonds will be equal to the present value of the expected cash flow from the bonds. This is the normal definition we use.

    a. Find the theoretical market value of the bonds using semiannual analysis.

    b. Do you think the bonds will sell for the price you arrived at in part *a*? Why?

8. The yield to maturity for 15-year bonds is as follows for four different bond rating categories.

AAA	6.4%	A	7.0%
AA	6.6	BBB	7.2

    The bonds of Falter Corporation were rated as AA and issued at par a few weeks ago. The bonds have just been downgraded to A. Determine the new price of the bonds, assuming a 15-year maturity and semiannual interest payments.

9. The 20-year A-rated bonds of Polly Cracker Company were initially issued at a 10 percent yield (paid semiannually). After 5 years, the bonds have been upgraded to AA. Such bonds are currently yielding 8 percent (semiannual compounding). Determine the price of a Polly Cracker bond.

10. A previously issued, A-rated 20-year industrial bond provides a return one-quarter higher than the prime interest rate of 9 percent. Previously issued public utility bonds provide a yield of one-half of a percentage point higher than previously issued industrial bonds of equal quality. Finally, new issues of public utility bonds, rated A, pay three-eighths of a percentage point more than previously issued public utility bonds. What should the interest rate be on a newly issued A-rated public utility bond?

11. A 10-year, $1,000 par value strip bond is to be issued to yield 8 percent.

    a. What should be the initial price of the bond?

    b. If immediately upon issue, interest rates dropped to 6 percent, what would be the value of the strip bond?

    c. If immediately upon issue, interest rates increased to 10 percent, what would be the value of the strip bond?

12. What is the effective yield to maturity on a strip bond that sells for $376.89 and will mature in 20 years?

13. Millennium Bonds were sold six years ago with a 10 percent, 25-year maturity, $1,000 par value, and a floating-rate covenant. If rates on similar risk bonds are currently yielding 7 percent, what is your estimate as to the bond's value?

14. Rap Stars was a bond outstanding with a 6 percent annual coupon paid semi-annually that is redeemable by the firm at a 5 percent premium to face (maturity) value, The bond will mature in 8 years. Current yields in the marketplace for a bond with Rap Stars rating are 3.5 percent. What is the suggested current price of this Rap Star bond?

15. It was 12 years ago that Anchor Corporation borrowed $6,000,000. Since then, cumulative inflation has been 80 percent (a compound rate of approximately 5 percent per year).

    a. When the firm repays the original $6,000,000 loan this year, what will be the effective purchasing power of the $6,000,000?

    b. To maintain the original $6,000,000 purchasing power, how much should the lender be repaid?

    c. If the lender knows he will receive only $6,000,000 in payment after 12 years, how might he be or she compensated for the loss in purchasing power? A descriptive answer is acceptable.

16. A $1,000 par value bond was issued 15 years ago at a 14 percent coupon rate, paid semiannually. It currently has 10 years remaining to maturity. Interest rates on similar debt obligations are now 8 percent.

    a. What is the current price of the bond?

    b. Assume Igor Sharp bought the bond three years ago, when it had a price of $1,025. What is his dollar profit based on the bond's current price?

    c. Further assume Igor Sharp paid 20 percent of the purchase price in cash and borrowed the rest (known as buying on margin). Igor used the interest payments from the bond to cover the interest costs on the loan. How much of the purchase price of $1,025 did Igor Sharp pay in cash?

    d. What is Igor's percentage return on his cash investment? Divide the answer to part *b* by the answer to part *c*.

    e. Explain why his return is so high.

17. A $1,000 par value bond was issued 25 years ago at an 8 percent coupon rate. It currently has 15 years remaining to maturity. Interest rates on similar debt obligations are now 14 percent.

    a. Compute the current price of the bond using an assumption of semiannual payments.

    b. If Mr. Mitchell initially bought the bond at par value, what is his percentage loss (or gain)?

    c. Now assume Mrs. Gordon buys the bond at its current market value and holds it to maturity; what will be her percentage return?

    d. Although the same dollar amounts are involved in parts *b* and *c*, explain why the percentage gain is larger than the percentage loss.

18. The Wagner Corporation has a $20 million bond obligation outstanding, which it is considering refunding. Though the bonds were initially issued at 9 percent, the interest rates on similar issues have declined to 7.5 percent. The bonds were originally issued for 20 years and have 16 years remaining. The new issue would be for 16 years. There is an 8 percent call premium on the old issue. The underwriting cost on the new $20 million issue is $525,000, and the underwriting cost on the old issue was $400,000. The company is in a 30 percent tax bracket, and it will allow an overlap period of one month (1/12 of the year). Treasury bills currently yield 3 percent. Should the old issue be refunded with new debt?

19. Delta Corporation has a $30 million bond obligation outstanding, which it is considering refunding. Though the bonds were initially issued at 7 percent, the interest rates on similar issues have declined to 4.6 percent. The bonds were originally issued for 10 years and have 6 years remaining. The new issue would be for 6 years. There is a 5 percent call premium on the old issue. The underwriting cost on the new $30,000,000 issue is $600,000, and the underwriting cost on the old issue was $750,000. The company is in a 25 percent tax bracket,

and it will allow a overlap period of one month. Treasury bills currently yield 1 percent. Should the old issue be refunded with new debt?

20. The Harding Corporation has $50 million of bonds outstanding that were issued at a coupon rate of 10.25 percent seven years ago. Interest rates have fallen to 9 percent. Preston Alter, the vice-president of finance, does not expect rates to fall any further. The bonds have 18 years left to maturity, and Preston would like to refund the bonds with a new issue of equal amount also having 18 years to maturity. The Harding Corporation has a tax rate of 25 percent. The underwriting cost on the old issue was 2.5 percent of the total bond value. The underwriting cost on the new issue will be 1.8 percent of the total bond value. The original bond indenture contained a five-year protection against a call, with an 8 percent call premium starting in the sixth year and scheduled to decline by one-half percent each year thereafter (consider the bond to be seven years old for purposes of computing the premium). Should the Harding Corporation refund the old issue?

21. In the previous problem, what would be the aftertax cost of the call premium at the end of year 13 (in dollar value)?

22. Providence Industries has an outstanding debenture of $25 million that was issued when flotation costs could be expensed immediately. It carries a coupon rate of 10 percent and has 15 years to maturity. Currently, similar risk bonds are yielding 9 percent over a 15-year period, and Providence is wondering if a refunding would be economically sound. The existing debenture has a call premium of 5 percent at present. It is estimated that a new issue would require underwriting costs of $470,000 and other costs of $80,000. No overlap period would be required. Providence Industries has a tax rate of 25 percent. Its cost of capital is 16 percent.

    a. Should Providence Industries refund the old issue? Show your calculations.

    b. Discuss your choice of discount rate.

    c. Suppose the refunding was not justified economically. What other reasons might Providence have for refunding the old issue?

23. United Oui Stand Ltd. has a bond outstanding that carries a 9 percent coupon rate paid annually. Current bond yields are 7 percent. It has $40 million outstanding and 10 years left to maturity. A new issue would require $1 million for flotation costs, and the existing issue has written off all its flotation expenses. An overlap period of 30 days would be anticipated, during which money market rates would be 3 percent. United Oui Stand Ltd. has a tax rate of 25 percent. The call premium on the outstanding issue is currently at 7 percent.

    a. Calculate if refunding would be justified.

    b. Compute the price of a bond in the market, if there was no call provision. How does this compare to the call price?

24. Daedulus Wings has had several successful years in the airline business and had received recognition from many quarters for flying higher, further, and cheaper than the competition. Its financial state of affairs has not been as successful. The new vice-president of finance is reviewing some debentures that carry fairly high semiannual payments.

    The vice-president notes in particular a bond issue that was issued 8 years ago with 15 years to maturity at an annual rate of 12 percent, payable semiannually. It has a call provision at a premium of 8 percent above par value. The bond issue has $50 million outstanding.

    Current long-term interest rates are 7.5 percent, payable on a semiannual basis and short-term rates are 3 percent. If the old bonds are called, the vice-president will require an overlap period of one-half a month. Wings has a tax rate of 35 percent. Underwriting and other financing expenses will be $1 million.

    Should the old issue be refunded and replaced with a debt issue with a comparable maturity? Show your calculations.

25. Webber Musicals Corporation is considering replacing its $2 million preferred share issue because market yields have declined. The existing preferreds carry a dividend of $5 per share, which is a rate of 10 percent on the par value. Current market yields on Webber preferreds are estimated to be 7 percent. Webber preferreds are currently trading at $71.43. Flotation expenses on a new preferred issue would be $160,000. Webber's tax rate is 28 percent. There is no call provision. Should Webber Musicals consider replacing its existing preferred shares? Show your calculations.

26. The Richmond Corporation has just signed a 144-month lease on an asset with an 18-year life. The minimum lease payments are $3,000 per month ($36,000 per year) and are to be discounted back to the present at an 8 percent annual discount rate. The estimated fair value of the property is $290,000. Should the lease be recorded as a capital lease or an operating lease?

27. The Ellis Corporation has heavy lease commitments. A new vice-president wants the lease obligations footnoted in the balance sheet as follows:

ELLIS CORPORATION ($ millions)			
Current assets...............	$ 50	Current liabilities.............	$ 10
Capital assets	50	Long-term liabilities	30
		Total liabilities...............	40
		Shareholders' equity...........	60
Total assets.................	$100	Total liabilities and equity	$100

The footnotes would state that the company had $10 million in annual capital lease obligations over the next 20 years.

a. Discount these annual lease obligations back to the present at a 6 percent discount rate (round to the nearest million dollars).

b. Construct a revised balance sheet that includes lease obligations, as in Table 16–6.

c. Compute total debt to total assets on the original and revised balance sheets.

d. Compute total debt to equity on the original and revised balance sheets.

e. In an efficient capital market environment, should the consequences of the CICA recommendation, as viewed in the answers to parts *c* and *d*, change stock prices and credit ratings?

f. Comment on management's perception of market efficiency (the viewpoint of the financial officer).

28. The Hegan Corporation plans to lease a $900,000 asset to the Doby Corporation. The lease will be for 10 years.

a. If the Hegan Corporation desires a 10 percent return on its investment, how much should the lease payments be?

b. If the Hegan Corporation is able to generate $130,000 in immediate tax shield benefits from the asset to be purchased for the lease arrangement and will pass the benefits along to the Doby Corporation in the form of lower lease payments, how much should the revised lease payments be? Continue to assume the Hegan Corporation desires a 10 percent return on the 10-year lease.

29. Omni Enterprises is considering whether to borrow funds and purchase an asset or to lease the asset under an operating lease arrangement. If it purchases the asset, the cost will be $10,000. It can borrow funds for four years at 12 percent interest. The asset will qualify for a 25 percent CCA. Assume a tax rate of 35 percent.

The other alternative is to sign two operating leases, one with payments of $2,600 for the first two years and the other with payments of $4,600 for the last two years. In your analysis, round all values to the nearest dollar. The leases would be treated as operating leases.

a. Compute the aftertax cost of the lease for the four years.

b. Compute the annual payment for the loan.

c. Compute the amortization schedule for the loan. (Disregard a small difference from a zero balance at the end of the loan. It is due to rounding.)

d. Determine the cash flow effect of the CCA.

e. Compute the aftertax cost of the borrow-purchase alternative.

f. Compute the present value of the aftertax cost of the two alternatives.

g. If the objective is to minimize the present value of aftertax costs, which alternative should be selected?

30. Kumquat Farms Ltd. has decided to acquire a kumquat picking machine. The cost of the picking machine is $45,000, and it has an economic life of 10 years. At the end of seven years, the market (salvage) value is estimated to be $11,000. Seven years is the time horizon for analysis.

The owner of Kumquat Farms Ltd. has discussed this acquisition with his financial services conglomerate. It has agreed to lend him the purchase price at 10 percent per year, payable in equal blended payments at the end of each year, for seven years.

An alternative method of financing the equipment would be to lease it from the local leasing store. Annual lease payments, payable at the beginning of each of the next seven years, would be $7,750. This would be considered an operating lease.

The equipment has a CCA of 20 percent. The benefits of any tax shields are realized at the end of each year. The company's tax rate is 25 percent. Kumquat Farms' cost of capital is 16 percent. Should Kumquat Farms Ltd. lease or buy the picking machine? Show all calculations.

31. I2C Beams Ltd., a manufacturer of lighted hockey pucks, is negotiating with the Hat Trick Company to purchase or to lease a machine that produces red-lighted pucks. The machine would cost $140,000. In five years the machine would have an estimated salvage value of $35,000. Its useful economic life is nine years.

I2C Beams can borrow funds at 9 percent from its Playoff Bank and has a tax rate of 25 percent. The capital cost rate on this machine is 30 percent, and I2C Beam's cost of capital is 14 percent. Lease payments would be at the beginning of each year, and tax savings would occur at the end of each year. Lease payments would be $29,000 over a five-year term.

Should I2C Beams Ltd. lease or borrow to purchase the machine? Show your calculations. We note that of all the cash flows, the salvage value has the greatest uncertainty. We recognize this by discounting the salvage value at a higher discount rate—the cost of capital.

32. Orwell Futures has decided to acquire a travelling machine. Its cost is $75,000. In five years it can be salvaged for $25,000. Friendly Loansharks has agreed to advance funds for the entire purchase price at 9 percent per annum payable in equal instalments at the end of each year over the five years.

As an alternative, the machine could be leased over the five years from the manufacturer, Ageless Ventures, with annual lease payments of $15,800 payable at the beginning of each year.

Orwell Futures' tax rate is 25 percent. Its cost of capital is 15 percent, and its tax shields are realized at the end of the year. Travelling machines have a CCA rate of 30 percent. If the machine is owned, annual maintenance costs will be $750. Should Orwell Futures lease or buy its machine? Show all calculations.

33. Dan Teasin's Furs and Coats Ltd. has decided to acquire a cooling machine. Its cost is $50,000. In five years it can be salvaged for $15,000. The Cloister Bank has agreed to advance funds for the entire purchase price at 8 percent per annum payable in equal instalments at the end of each year over the five years.

As an alternative, the machine could be leased over the five years from the manufacturer, Snowbird Ltd., with annual lease payments of $10,000 payable at the beginning of each year.

Dan Teasin's tax rate is 20 percent. Its cost of capital is 15 percent, and its tax shields are realized at the end of the year. Cooling machines have a CCA rate of 20 percent. If the machine is owned, annual maintenance costs will be $500. Should Dan Teasin's lease or buy its machine? Show all calculations.

34. Koss Leasing requires a 14 percent return on its investments. It is prepared to lease you a truck for two years, provided that it can achieve this return. The lease payments are to be made at the beginning of the year. The truck, which has a useful economic life of six years, cost Koss $60,000. Its estimated value in two years is $17,000. The CCA rate is 30 percent, and Koss's tax rate is 25 percent.

Calculate the annual lease payment required by Koss Leasing.

MINI CASE
Leland Industries

Leland Industries is one of the country's largest producers of bakery and snack goods, with operations primarily located in central Canada. Over the last 10 years, Leland had been one of the most efficient bakeries in the country, with a 10-year average sales growth of 9.8 percent and an average return on equity of 16.8 percent. Management goals for the company include 10 percent earnings growth per year, and an average return of 16.8 percent on equity over time.

Late in 20XX, Leland reached an agreement with a major food chain to provide private-label bakery services in addition to its own products that are sold to Loblaw, Safeway, and many other grocery stores. The new private-label program had significant startup costs, including new packaging techniques and the addition of 250 sales routes.

Al Oliver, the vice-president of finance, believed in maintaining a balanced capital structure, and since a one million common share issue totalling $25 million in value had been offered earlier in the year, he thought this was a good time to go to the debt market. Previously, the firm's debt issues had been privately placed with insurance companies and pension funds, but Al believed this was an appropriate time to approach the public markets based on the company's recent strong performance.

He called his investment dealer and was told that the rating the firm received from S&P and DBRS Morningstar would be a key variable in determining the interest rate that would be paid on the debt issue. Leland Industries intended to issue $20 million of new debt.

A comparison of Leland Industries to other bakeries is shown in Table 1. The other five firms all had issued debt publicly according to Ben Gilbert, who was Leland Industries' major contact at the investment dealing firm of Gilbert, Rollins, and Ross.

As an alternative to a straight bond issue, Ben suggested that the firm consider issuing floating-rate or even zero-coupon rate bonds. He said the principal advantage to the floating-rate bonds was that they could be issued at 1¼ percent below the going market rate for straight debt issues. Al was pleasantly surprised to hear this, and asked his investment dealer what the catch was; he had heard many times that "there is no such thing as a free lunch." His investment dealer explained that with a floating-rate bond the problem of interest rate changes was shifted from the borrower to the lender. To quote Ben:

> Normally the risk of changes in yield to maturity is a burden or opportunity that bondholders must consider. If yields go up, bond prices of existing bonds go down, and the opposite is true if rates decline. There is a risk, and many investors do not like this risk. With a

Table 1 Bond ratings of comparative firms

International Bakeries

Debt to total assets....................	30%	Bond price..........................	$1,100
Times interest earned.................	7.1 ×	Annual interest......................	10.35%
Fixed charge coverage	5.0 ×	Maturity............................	25 years
Current ratio........................	3.1 ×	Par value (principal payment)	$1,000
Return on shareholders equity	22%		
Rating............................	AA (high)		

Gates Bakeries

Debt to total assets....................	42%	Bond price..........................	$920
Times interest earned.................	5.5 ×	Annual interest......................	9.45%
Fixed charge coverage	4.2 ×	Maturity............................	20 years
Current ratio........................	2.3 ×	Par value (principal payment)	$1,000
Return on shareholders equity	17.1%		
Rating............................	A (high)		

Prairie Products

Debt to total assets....................	65%	Bond price..........................	$1,150
Times interest earned.................	2.0 ×	Annual interest......................	15.75%
Fixed charge coverage	1.7 ×	Maturity............................	15 years
Current ratio........................	1.2 ×	Par value (principal payment)	$1,000
Return on shareholders equity	7%		
Rating............................	B (low)		

Dyer Pastries

Debt to total assets....................	35%	Bond price..........................	$1,060
Times interest earned.................	6.0 ×	Annual interest......................	10.30%
Fixed charge coverage	3.6 ×	Maturity............................	20 years
Current ratio........................	2.8 ×	Par value (principal payment)	$1,000
Return on shareholders equity	19%		
Rating............................	AA (low)		

Nolan Bread

Debt to total assets....................	47%	Bond price..........................	$950
Times interest earned.................	4.9 ×	Annual interest......................	10.30%
Fixed charge coverage	3.8 ×	Maturity............................	25 years
Current ratio........................	2.1 ×	Par value (principal payment)	$1,000
Return on shareholders equity	15%		
Rating............................	A (medium)		

Leland Industries*

Debt to total assets....................	44%
Times interest earned.................	5.7 ×
Fixed charge coverage	3.7 ×
Current ratio........................	2.0 ×
Return on shareholders equity	16.8%
Rating: To be determined..............	

*The first three ratios for Leland Industries assume the impact of the new bond issue. Of course, these are approximations. The bond rating agencies require such information.

floating-rate bond the interest rate that the investor directly receives changes with market conditions and therefore the bond tends to trade at its initial par value. For example, if a bond were issued at 9 percent interest for 20 years and market rates went to 13 percent, a floating-rate bond would adjust its payment up to 13 percent, and the market value would remain at $1,000. On a straight bond issue the interest rate would remain at 9 percent, and because it is 4 percent below the market, the bond price would drop to the $700 range.

Al quickly perceived that with a floating-rate bond he could pay 1 1/4 percent lower interest than with a fixed-rate bond, but that in future years he could not predict what his interest rates would be.

He was pretty turned off by the whole idea until his investment dealer suggested that the futures and options experts at Gilbert, Rollins, and Ross could hedge this risk at a probable aftertax cost of about $120,000 per year. While he was making this point, Ben gave Al a copy of *Foundations of Financial Management* by Block, Hirt, Danielsen, and Short, suggesting that he review the material on hedging at the end of Chapter 8 and in Chapter 19. Al knew that he must make a decision about the benefits and costs of floating-rate bonds.

Before the discussion was over, Al was presented with one last option. It was possible the firm might wish to issue zero-coupon rate bonds. Because no interest was paid on an annual basis and the only gain to the investor came in the form of capital appreciation, Al initially liked the idea. However, he remembered the "no free lunch" argument and asked Ben what drawbacks there might be to this type of issue. Ben responded:

> Well, Al, since you are not paying annual interest or retiring any part of the issue during its life, there can be greater risk, which may mean there is a lower rating on the issue. You, of course, know what that means in terms of a higher required yield on the bond issue.

Al thought he would need to put some numbers to zero-coupon bonds as well as many of the other items that Ben brought up. He called his young assistant in for some help.

a. Compute the yield to maturity and the aftertax cost of debt for the bonds of the other firms. Assume a tax rate of 35 percent for the firms.

b. Based on the data in Table 1, which rating and cost of debt do you think is most likely for Leland Industries?

c. If the bonds of Leland Industries carried a requirement that 5 percent of the bonds outstanding be retired each year, what would be the total amount of bonds outstanding after the third year? What would be the aftertax dollar cost of interest payments on this sum? Assume a 10 percent interest rate.

d. From a strictly dollars-and-cents viewpoint, does the floating-rate bond with the hedging approach appear to be viable?

e. Assume the zero-coupon rate bonds would be issued at a yield of ¾ of 1 percent above a regular bond issue for 20 years. What will be the initial price of a $1,000 bond? How many bonds must be issued to raise $20 million? What is the danger in issuing the zero-coupon rate bonds?

MINI CASE

Warner Motor Oil Co.

Gina Thomas was concerned about the effect that high interest expenses were having on the bottom-line reported profits of Warner Motor Oil Co. Since joining the company three years ago as vice-president of finance, she noticed that operating profits appeared to be improving each year, but that earnings after interest and taxes were declining because of high interest charges.

Because interest rates had finally started declining after a steady increase, she thought it was time to consider the possibility of refunding a bond issue. As she explained to her boss, Sam Rosen, refunding meant calling in a bond that had been issued at a high interest rate and replacing it with a new bond that was similar in most respects but carried a lower interest rate. Bond refunding was feasible only in a period of declining interest rates. Sam, who had been the CEO of the company for the last seven years, understood the general concept, but he still had some questions.

He said to Gina, "If interest rates are going down, bond prices are certain to be going up. Won't that make it quite expensive to buy in outstanding issues so that we can replace them with new issues?" Gina had a quick and direct answer. "No, and the reason is that the old issues have a call provision associated with them." A call provision allows the firm to call in bonds at slightly over par (usually 8 to 10 percent above par) regardless of what the market price is.

Gina thought if she could present a specific example to Sam he would have a better feel for the bond refunding process. She proposed to call in an 11.50 percent $30,000,000 issue that was scheduled to mature in 20 years. The bonds had been issued in 20XS, and since it was now 20XX the bonds had 15 years remaining to maturity. It was Gina's intent to replace the bonds with a new $30,000,000 issue that would have the same maturity date 15 years into the future as that of the original 20XS issue. Based on advice from the firm's investment firm, Walston and Sons, the bonds could be issued at a rate of 10 percent. Joe Walston, a senior partner in the investment firm, further indicated that the underwriting cost on the new issue would be 2.8 percent of the $30,000,000 amount involved.

Before she could do her analysis, Gina needed to accumulate information on the old 11.50 percent bond issue that she was proposing to refund. The original bond indenture indicated that the bonds had an 8 percent call premium, and that the bonds could be called anytime after five years. Gina explained to Sam that the bondholders were protected from having their bonds called in for the first five years after issue, but that the bonds were fair game after that. Furthermore, from the sixth through the 13th year, the call premium went down by 1 percent per year. By the 14th year after issue, there was no call premium and the corporation could merely call in the bonds at par. Since in this case five years had passed, the call premium would be exactly 8 percent.

Gina checked with the chief accountant and found out that the underwriting cost on the old issue had initially been $400,000. The firm was currently paying taxes at a rate of 30 percent.

Outline the considerations in whether or not to refund this bond issue. What must Gina present to Sam? Will Gina achieve her original objective?

APPENDIX 16A
Financial Alternatives for Distressed Firms

Although we have consistently considered businesses as going concerns throughout this book, we have also spoken of the risks (and securities premiums for such risks) associated with failure. For example, we stated that during uncertain economic times, a large, financially secure firm might be able to raise debt capital as much as 3 percentage points more cheaply than a medium-sized firm, even if the latter is well managed. Such a differential recognizes the fact that the smaller firm may more quickly find itself in financial distress under adverse market circumstances.

A firm may be in financial distress because of technical insolvency or bankruptcy. Insolvency refers to a firm's inability to generate enough cash to pay its bills as they come due. Thus, a firm may be technically insolvent even though it has a positive net worth; there simply may not be sufficient liquid assets to meet current obligations. In other circumstances, the fair market value of a firm's assets are less than its total liabilities—in other words, the firm has a negative net worth. In such a case, either management or the creditors may judge that the best remedy possible is liquidation of the firm. Under the Bankruptcy and Insolvency Act, then, either management or creditors can initiate legal action to have the firm declared bankrupt and have the firm's assets liquidated. Generally, the term **financial failure** covers the gamut of circumstances from technical insolvency to the declaration of legal bankruptcy.

There are firms that do not fit into either of these categories but are still suffering from extreme financial difficulties. Perhaps they are rapidly approaching a situation in which they cannot pay their bills or where concerns over net worth deterioration may lead to bankruptcy proceedings.

Firms suffering from technical insolvency or negative net worth may participate in out-of-court settlements or in-court formal bankruptcy proceedings. Out-of-court settlements, where possible, allow the firm and its creditors to bypass certain lengthy and expensive legal proceedings. It follows, however, that if an agreement cannot be reached on a voluntary basis between a firm and its creditors, in-court procedures are necessary.

www.

Bankruptcy and
Insolvency Act
laws-lois.justice.gc.ca/eng/
acts/B-3/index.html

Out-of-Court Settlements

Out-of-court settlements may take many forms. Four alternatives are examined. The first is an extension in which creditors agree to allow the firm more time to meet its financial obligations. A new repayment schedule is developed subject to the acceptance of the creditors.

A second alternative is a composition, under which creditors agree to accept a fractional settlement of their original claim. They may be willing to do this because they believe the firm is unable to meet its total obligations, and they wish to avoid formal bankruptcy procedures. In the case of either a proposed extension or a composition, some creditors may not agree to go along with the arrangements. If their claims are relatively small, major creditors may allow them to be paid off immediately and in full to hold the agreement together. If their claims are large, no out-of-court settlement may be possible and formal bankruptcy proceedings may be necessary.

A third out-of-court settlement may take the form of a creditor committee established to run the business. Here, the parties involved judge that management can no longer effectively conduct the affairs of the firm. Once the creditors' claims have been partially or fully settled, a new management team may be brought in to replace the creditor committee. The outgoing management may be willing to accept the imposition of a creditor committee only when formal bankruptcy proceedings appear likely and they wish to avoid that stigma. There are also circumstances in which creditors are unwilling to form such a committee because they fear lawsuits from other dissatisfied creditors or from common or preferred shareholders.

A fourth out-of-court settlement is an assignment, in which liquidation of assets occurs without going through formal court action. To effect an assignment, creditors must agree on liquidation values and the relative priority of claims. This is not easy.

In actuality, there may be combinations of two or more of the just described out-of-court procedures. For example, there may be an extension as well as a composition, or a creditor committee may help to establish one or more of the alternatives.

In-Court Settlements

Proposal for an Arrangement under the Bankruptcy and Insolvency Act

In November 1992 the revision of the Bankruptcy Act of 1949 came into law as the Bankruptcy and Insolvency Act. The most significant revisions concerned the source of proposals for reorganizing a firm in order to save the firm and jobs. In recent years, larger corporations, unlike smaller firms, were able to escape bankruptcy under the Companies Creditors Arrangement Act, which dated from the 1930s. The revised Bankruptcy and Insolvency Act tries to legislate and simplify the provisions that restrict the secured creditors' rights in order to save the firm.

Proposals to reorganize the firm can now come from the bankrupt firm, the trustee in bankruptcy, the liquidator, or the receiver, but not the creditors. This is significant because under the previous legislation, the proposal had to come from the bankrupt or insolvent firm. In recent memory, Westar Mining could not put forward a proposal to save the company because the directors resigned, fearing certain liabilities. Under the new legislation, a proposal could now come from another source.

A proposal begins with a notice of intention, which allows a stay of proceedings against all creditors, including the secured creditors, for 30 days while a proposal for reorganization is prepared. Extensions of 45 days at a time are possible if the courts believe progress is being made. Because no one wins in a bankruptcy, a proposal allows a firm time to submit a plan to creditors.

The key to the revised legislation is that the secured creditors can now be part of the restructuring. The company in difficulty must keep the creditors informed of issues such as cash flow while attempting to develop a proposal in everyone's interest. Creditors are organized into classes based on their similarity of claims, and two-thirds of the creditors by value in each class as well as a majority of the creditors voting must accept the proposal. When Olympia & York sought to satisfy creditors, there were over 30 creditor classes. If accepted by the creditors, the proposal must then be ratified by the court. Ratification depends on a judgment that the plan is fair, equitable, and feasible.

An internal reorganization calls for an evaluation of current management and its operating policies. If current management is shown to be incompetent, it will probably be discharged and replaced by new management. An evaluation and possible redesign of the current capital structure is also necessary. If the firm is top heavy with debt (as is normally the case), alternative securities such as preferred or common stock may replace part of the debt.[7] Any restructuring must be fair to all parties involved.

Therefore, under a recapitalization, each of the old security holders must swap its old securities for new ones, the amount of which is determined by a current market valuation of the firm. Under what is called the absolute priority rule, all senior claims on asset value must be settled in full before any value can be given to a junior claimant. Thus, a bondholder must be awarded the full face value of their bond in a new security before preferred or common shareholders can receive any new securities. A simple example might clarify this a bit (see Table 16A–1).

Table 16A-1 Debt restructuring

Company A Capital Structure (book value) Before Reorganization:	
Bonds...	$20 million
Subordinated debentures	12 million
Preferred stock......................................	4 million
Common stock.......................................	25 million
Total capital	$61 million

Company A Capital Structure After Reorganization:	
Bonds...	$10 million
Income bonds.......................................	10 million
Common stock.......................................	20 million
Total capital	$40 million*

*$40 million would be the estimated market evaluation of these securities.

In this example, the former bondholders and preferred shareholders would receive new securities covering the full value of their former holdings for a total of $36 million, whereas the shareholders would receive only the residual, or $4 million worth of securities. The bondholders and preferred shareholders, however, would receive different securities than held previously. This is because the former bonds and debentures were a regular commitment of funds, helping to create a cash flow strain on the corporation. Now there is a smaller commitment to interest payments but a promise of dividends if the company can improve its profits and cash flow. In the example, the former shareholders would have only 25 percent of the outstanding common shares in the restructured company. It is easy to imagine a corporate reorganization where there would be no residual value left for the common shareholders (such would happen in this case if the market value of the securities at the time of reorganization were pegged at $36 million or less).

An external reorganization in which a merger partner is found for the firm may also be considered. The surviving firm must be deemed strong enough to carry out the financial and management obligations of the joint entities. Old creditors and shareholders may be asked to make concessions to ensure that a feasible arrangement is established. Their motivation to do so would be that they hope to come out further ahead than if such a reorganization were not undertaken. Ideally, the firm should be merged with a strong firm in its own industry, although this is not always possible. The Canadian banking industry found such a need to merge weaker firms with stronger firms within the industry in the mid-1980s.

Liquidation

A liquidation, or selloff, of assets may be recommended when an internal or external reorganization does not appear possible or when it is determined that the assets of the firm are worth more in liquidation than through a reorganization. Priority of claims becomes extremely important in a liquidation, because it is unlikely that all parties will be fully satisfied in their demands.

---

[7] Another possibility is the income bond on which interest is payable only if the firm makes money.

Secured creditors generally seize the assets on which they have a lien. If, on liquidation, the secured creditors realize less than their secured claims, they become normal unsecured creditors for the unsettled balance remaining.

After the claims of secured creditors are settled, the priority of claims in a bankruptcy liquidation is as follows:

1. Cost of administering the bankruptcy procedures (lawyers get in line first).

2. Wages and salaries due employees up to a maximum of $2,000 per worker.

3. Outstanding source deductions.

4. Rent in arrears within certain prescribed limits.

5. Claims for prior judgments lodged against the bankrupt.

6. Certain other claims of the Crown.

7. General or unsecured creditors are next in line. Examples of claims in this category are those held by debenture (unsecured bond) holders, trade creditors, bankers who have made unsecured loans, and the Crown. There may be senior and subordinated positions within category 7, indicating that subordinated debtholders must turn over their claims to senior debtholders until complete restitution is made to the higher-ranked category. Subordinated debenture holders may keep the balance if anything is left after that payment.

8. Preferred shareholders.

9. Common shareholders.

 FINANCE IN ACTION

Survival: Failure

Algoma Steel of Sault Ste. Marie, Ontario (algoma.com), sought protection under the Companies Creditors Arrangement Act (CCAA) in October 2001. Bondholders with a first mortgage, employees, and unsecured creditors all had significant interests in the rearrangement of the company's capital structure and its survival. So did the City of Sault Ste. Marie, where Algoma is an important employer.

In February 2002, Algoma came out of bankruptcy protection as a restructured company. It survives to this day.

In 2004, both Air Canada (aircanada.com) and Stelco (stelco.com) were under the protection of the Companies Creditors Arrangement Act (CCAA), trying to successfully restructure. They both hoped to emerge as stronger companies.

Air Canada came out of bankruptcy protection and operates successfully today.

In 2006 Stelco came out of bankruptcy, and share prices jumped from an established $5.50 to $19.49 the first day. In August 2007 it was bought by U.S. Steel. However by 2014 U.S. Steel again placed Stelco under protection of the CCAA. Bedrock Industries (bi15.com) purchased Stelco from U.S. Steel.

By 2018 Stelco was once again restructured as Stelco Holdings Inc. Stelco then began to trade publicly. Important players in the restructuring were the unions and the members they represented because of significant pension and retiree benefit liabilities.

Q1 How has Stelco (STLC) performed after the CCAA protection of 2018?

Under the revised Bankruptcy and Insolvency Act, creditors that have supplied goods to a bankrupt company can repossess those goods for up to 30 days. The 30 days do not include when a stay of proceedings is in force.

Let us examine a typical situation to determine "who" should receive "what" under a liquidation in bankruptcy. Assume the Mitchell Corporation has a book value and liquidation value as shown in Table 16A–2. Liabilities and shareholders' claims are also presented.

Table 16A-2 Financial data for the Mitchell Corporation

Assets	Book Value	Liquidation Value
Accounts receivable.	$ 200,000	$160,000
Inventory	410,000	240,000
Machinery and equipment	240,000	100,000
Building and plant	450,000	200,000
	$1,300,000	$700,000
Liabilities and Shareholders' Claims		
Liabilities:		
Accounts payable.	$ 300,000	
First lien, secured by machinery and equipment*	200,000	
Senior unsecured debt	400,000	
Subordinated debentures	200,000	
Total liabilities.	1,100,000	
Shareholders' Claims:		
Preferred stock.	50,000	
Common stock.	150,000	
Total shareholders' claims.	200,000	
Total liabilities and shareholders' claims.	$1,300,000	

*A lien represents a potential claim against property. The lien holder has a secured interest in the property.

We see that the liquidation value of the assets is far less than the book value ($700,000 versus $1,300,000). Also, the liquidation value of the assets will not cover the total value of liabilities ($700,000 versus $1,100,000). Since all liability claims will be met, it is evident that lower-ranked preferred shareholders and common shareholders will receive nothing.

Before a specific allocation is made to the creditors (those with liability claims), the three highest priority levels in bankruptcy must first be covered. That would include the cost of administering the proceedings, allowable past wages due to workers, and overdue taxes. For the Mitchell Corporation, we shall assume these total $100,000. Since the liquidation value of assets was $700,000 this would leave $600,000 to cover creditor demands, as indicated in the left-hand column of Table 16A–3.

Table 16A-3 Asset values and claims

Balance Sheet		Creditor Claims	
Asset values in liquidation.	$ 700,000	Accounts payable.	$ 300,000
Administrative costs, wages, and taxes.	−100,000	First lien, secured by machinery and equipment.	200,000
Remaining asset values	$ 600,000	Senior unsecured debt	400,000
		Subordinated debentures	200,000
		Total liabilities.	$1,100,000

Before we attempt to allocate the values in the left-hand column of this table to the right-hand column, we must first identify any creditor claims that are secured by the pledge of a specific asset. In the present case, there is a first lien on the machinery and equipment of $200,000. Referring back to Table 16A–2, we observe that the machinery and equipment has a liquidation value of only $100,000. The secured debtholders will receive $100,000, with the balance of their claim placed in the same category as the unsecured debtholders. In Table 16A–4 we show asset values available for unsatisfied secured claims and unsecured debt (top portion) and the extent of the remaining claims (bottom portion).

Table 16A-4 Asset values available for unsatisfied secured claims and unsecured debtholders—and their remaining claims

Asset Values:	
Asset values in liquidation..................................	$ 700,000
Administrative costs, wages, and taxes	100,000
Remaining asset values	600,000
Payment to secured creditors.............................	−100,000
Amount available to unsatisfied secured claims and unsecured debt......................................	$ 500,000
Remaining Claims of Unsatisfied Secured Debt and Unsecured Debt:	
Secured debt (unsatisfied first lien)........................	$ 100,000
Accounts payable.......................................	300,000
Senior unsecured debt	400,000
Subordinated debentures	200,000
	$1,000,000

In comparing the available asset values and claims in this table, it appears that the settlement on the remaining claims should be at a 50 percent rate ($500,000/$1,000,000). The allocation will occur in the manner presented in Table 16A–5.

Table 16A-5 Allocation procedures for unsatisfied secured claims and unsecured debt

(1) Category	(2) Amount of Claim	(3) Initial Allocation (50%)	(4) Amount Received
Secured debt (unsatisfied 1st lien).......	$ 100,000	$ 50,000	$ 50,000
Accounts payable....................	300,000	150,000	150,000
Senior unsecured debt	400,000	200,000	300,000
Subordinated debentures..............	200,000	100,000	0
	$1,000,000	$500,000	$500,000

Each category receives 50 percent as its initial allocation. However, the subordinated debenture holders must transfer their $100,000 initial allocation to the senior debtholders in recognition of their preferential position. The secured debtholders and those having accounts payable claims are not part of the senior-subordinated arrangement and thus hold their initial positions.

Finally, in Table 16A–6, we show the total amounts of claims, the amount received, and the percent of the claim that was satisfied.

Table 16A-6 Payments and percent of claims

(1) Category	(2) Total Amount of Claim	(3) Amount Received	(4) Percent of Claim Satisfied
Secured debt (1st lien)	$200,000	$150,000	75%
Accounts payable....................	300,000	150,000	50
Senior unsecured debt	400,000	300,000	75
Subordinated debentures	200,000	0	0

The $150,000 in column 3 for secured debt represents the $100,000 from the sale of machinery and $50,000 from the allocation process in Table 16A–5. The secured debtholders and senior unsecured debtholders come out on top in terms of percent of claim satisfied (it is coincidental that they are equal). Furthermore, the subordinated debtholders and, as previously mentioned, the preferred and common shareholders receive nothing. Naturally, allocations in bankruptcy will vary from circumstance to circumstance. Working problem 16A–1 below will help to reinforce many of the liquidation procedure concepts discussed in this section.

DISCUSSION QUESTIONS

16A–1. What is the difference between technical insolvency and bankruptcy?

16A–2. What are four out-of-court settlements? Briefly describe each.

16A–3. What is the difference between an internal reorganization and an external reorganization under formal bankruptcy procedures?

16A–4. What are the first three priority items under liquidation in bankruptcy after the claims of secured creditors are settled?

PROBLEM

16A–1. The trustee in the bankruptcy settlement for Immobile Homes lists the following book values and liquidation values for the assets of the corporation. Liabilities and shareholders' claims are also shown.

	Book Value	Liquidation Value
Assets		
Accounts receivable.	$1,000,000	$ 700,000
Inventory	1,100,000	600,000
Machinery and equipment	800,000	400,000
Building and plant	3,000,000	1,800,000
Total assets.	$5,900,000	$3,500,000
Liabilities and Shareholders' Claims		
Liabilities:		
Accounts payable.	$2,000,000	
First lien, secured by machinery and equipment	650,000	
Senior unsecured debt	1,300,000	
Subordinated debentures	1,450,000	
Total liabilities.	5,400,000	
Shareholders' claims:		
Preferred stock	100,000	
Common stock	400,000	
Total shareholders' claims	500,000	
Total liabilities and shareholders' claims.	$5,900,000	

a. Compute the difference between the liquidation value of the assets and the liabilities.

b. Based on the answer to part **a**, will preferred stock or common stock participate in the distribution?

c. Given that the administrative costs of bankruptcy, workers' allowable wages, and unpaid taxes add up to $400,000, what is the total of remaining asset value available to cover secured and unsecured claims? (Wages and taxes owed totalled $50,000.)

d. After the machinery and equipment is sold to partially cover the first lien secured claim, how much will be available from the remaining asset liquidation values to cover unsatisfied secured claims and unsecured debt?

e. List the remaining asset claims of unsatisfied secured debt holders and unsecured debt holders in a manner similar to that shown at the bottom portion of Table 16A–4.

f. Compute a ratio of your answers in part *d* and part *e*. This will indicate the initial allocation ratio.

g. List the remaining claims (unsatisfied secured and unsecured) and make an initial allocation and final allocation similar to that shown in Table 16A–5. Subordinated debenture holders may keep the balance after full payment is made to senior debt holders.

h. Show the relationship of amount received to total amount of claim in a similar fashion to that of Table 16A–6. (Remember to use the sales [liquidation] value for machinery and equipment plus the allocation amount in part *g* to arrive at the total received on secured debt.)

CHAPTER

17

Common and Preferred Stock Financing

LEARNING OBJECTIVES

LO1 Outline the rights of shareholders as owners of the corporation.

LO2 Briefly describe cumulative voting as a method to potentially give minority shareholders representation on the board of directors. Calculate the number of shares required to elect a director.

LO3 Characterize a rights offering as a method used to raise funds for the firm and calculate values of rights, shares, and shareholder wealth during the rights-offering process.

LO4 Describe poison pills and other provisions that make it difficult for outsiders to gain control of the corporation against management wishes.

LO5 Characterize preferred shares as a type of security somewhere between debt and common stock.

LO6 Calculate the different tax treatment and resulting aftertax income from preferred dividends as compared to bond interest.

LO7 Differentiate the features of various securities in a risk–return framework.

Equity financing is as significant as debt financing for Canadian firms based on securities outstanding, as we observed in Figure 14–1. The nature of new corporate issues underwritten in 2010 and 2018, as highlighted in Figure 15–3, reveals equity issues relative to debt issues. Common equity, preferred stock, and income trusts (based on ownership) are very important components of capital formation in our country. Common equity also encompasses retained earnings, which are significant.

Common stock represents the ultimate ownership of the firm, whether it is in the form of all outstanding shares of a closely held corporation or one share out of the over one billion shares of the Royal Bank. The control of the company is legally in the hands of the common shareholder, although practically it is wielded by management on an everyday basis. Furthermore, recent court decisions in Canada have emphasized the fair treatment of all stakeholders in the firm.

Approximately half of Canadians own shares directly or indirectly through mutual and pension funds, as noted in Figure 14–10. Only home ownership has greater participation among Canadians, at over 63 percent, as an investment. This significant participation among Canadians in the equity markets can be attributed to increasing share prices over the years, growing investment in mutual funds, a more sophisticated investing public, increased investment by women, and growing affluence. Investors increasingly scrutinize the share price performance of Canadian and foreign firms, seeking the higher returns promised from equity investments as compared to the lower interest rates of debt securities or savings accounts.

The management of publicly traded corporations is increasingly sensitive not only to discerning investors but also to the large institutional shareholders (mutual and pension funds) that hold significant equity positions in firms and execute the majority of daily trading. Some investment dealers specialize in dealing exclusively with institutional accounts, particularly those dealers that have a foreign parent company. Institutional investors are supplanting a select group of Canadian families as the dominant players in the financial markets.

Preferred stock represents a hybrid security, combining the fixed payment (dividend) feature of debt with a limited claim on earnings, similar to common stock. The preferred shareholder does not have the same ownership interest in the firm as the common shareholder, but they do have a priority claim to dividends superior to that of the common shareholder, although ranking behind debt holders.

As was discussed in Chapter 14, preferred stock has been a minor but significant method by which Canadian corporations have raised funds to balance their capital structure. Preferred stock deserves more than the passing mention it is sometimes accorded.

Income trusts represent a form of equity financing that frees up the capital structure of the firm by establishing a separate legal entity. The trust controls "former" company assets that generate a stream of cash flows and in exchange for the sale of these assets the firm receives a capital injection. Additionally, the firm usually continues to manage the assets for fees. These investment vehicles, primarily real estate assets known as REITs, have unitholders that are like shareholders with a claim on the trust's cash flows. The cash flows are fairly stable and significant because they are formed based on mature business assets.

As with bonds, our interest in common equity, preferred shares, and income trusts extends to their claim on the expected income streams that might be generated by the firm. This is ultimately the source of the value that investors will place on these equity investments in the marketplace.

Why Change Your Company and Share Name?

As the following examples identify some corporations feel the need to re-brand themselves with a name change. These companies have experienced difficult times or are industries that have fallen out of favour.

The markets remain skeptical that a simple name change will reverse difficulties. True corporate value comes from the firm's assets and their ability to generate cash flow, that is unlikely to be altered by cosmetic changes.

Former name	Current name (2020)
Encana	Ovintiv (OVV)
RIM	BlackBerry (BB)
Valeant (formerly Biovail)	Bausch Health (BHC)
TransCanada Corporation	TC Energy (TRP)
Google	Alphabet (GOOG)
Philip Morris	Altria (MO)

LO1 COMMON SHAREHOLDERS' CLAIM TO INCOME

All income that is not paid out to creditors or preferred shareholders automatically belongs to common shareholders. They have a residual claim to income, regardless of whether these funds are paid out in dividends or retained in the corporation. Take, for example, a firm that earns $10 million before capital costs and pays $1 million in interest to bondholders and a like amount in dividends to preferred shareholders. Ignoring tax savings on interest payments for the moment, the firm will then have $8 million available for common shareholders. Perhaps half of these funds will be paid out as common stock dividends. The balance will be reinvested in the business for the benefit of shareholders, with the hope of providing even greater income, dividends, and price appreciation in the future.

Realize, though, that the common shareholder does not have a legal or enforceable claim to dividends. Whereas a bondholder may force the corporation into bankruptcy for failure to make interest payments, common shareholders must accept circumstances as they are or attempt to change management if they desire a new dividend policy.

The Voting Right

Occasionally, a company has more than one class of common stock outstanding, a dual-class share structure, with the different shares carrying different rights and privileges. As owners of the firm, common shareholders have the right to cast ballots, or by way of proxy, to vote for the board of directors and on all other major issues. Over 100 firms listed on the Toronto Stock Exchange have a second class of common share with unusual voting rights. While Bombardier Class B common shares have the same dividend as the Class A shares, the Class A shares have 10 votes for each share, and the Class B shares have a subordinated voting right. This allows the founding family to maintain ownership control. As the Class A shares have greater voting power, they tend to trade at a premium to the Class B shares.

There may also be nonvoting stock. Canadian Tire became a well-publicized example of the potential dangers of nonvoting shares. In 1986 a play was made by the franchised dealers to gain control of Canadian Tire by tendering an offer to purchase a significant number of the voting shares. The voting shares soared in value to over $160 per share as compared to the nonvoting shares that traded at about $13, as no offer was made for the nonvoting shares.

A provision of the Class A Canadian Tire nonvoting shares, supposedly in place to protect the rights of the nonvoting shareholders, was circumvented with the tender offer. However, the Ontario Securities Commission (OSC) in a decision later backed by the Supreme Court of Ontario, declared that the deal was abusive because it was artificial in form, contrived only to circumvent a **coattail provision** and confound the justifiable expectations of investors. The coattail provision was there to provide that the nonvoting shareholders would become equal voting shareholders and receive the same share price as voting shareholders if there was to be an effective change in controlling ownership of Canadian Tire. Shortly after this case the Toronto Stock Exchange adopted new regulations to protect nonvoting shareholders in corporate takeovers.

Canadian Tire
investors.canadiantire.ca

Although the different classes of common stock may at times have different voting rights, they do have a vote. Bondholders and preferred shareholders, on the other hand, may vote only when a violation of their corporate agreements exists. The most common case of this is when a specified number (often two years' worth) of periodic dividends have been omitted on preferred shares. In that situation, the preferred shareholders often acquire voting privileges.

The most important voting matter is the election of the board of directors. As indicated in Chapter 1, the board has primary responsibility for the stewardship of the corporation. If illegal or imprudent decisions are made, the board members can be held legally liable to injured parties. Additionally, corporate directors serve on important subcommittees of the company and, in this manner, have a direct effect on corporate affairs. Examples of board committees include the audit committee, the long-range financial planning committee, and the compensation committee. Selection of a new chief executive officer, sometimes following a decision to prematurely remove the old one, is probably the board's single most important duty.

Election of the members of the board of directors may occur through the familiar majority voting system or by a cumulative voting method.

Majority Voting

- Any group of shareholders owning more than 50 percent of the common stock may elect all of the directors.

Cumulative Voting

- A shareholder gets one vote for each share of stock they own times one vote for each director to be elected.
- The shareholder may then accumulate votes in favour of a specified number of directors.
- It is possible for those who hold less than a 50 percent interest to elect board members.

LO2 Cumulative Voting Example

In a firm with 10,000 shares outstanding, you own 1,001 shares, and nine directors are to be elected. Your total number of votes under a cumulative system would be

Number of shares owned	1,001
Number of directors to be elected	9
Number of votes	9,009

Now let us consider the situation where you cast all of your ballots for only one director of your choice. With nine directors to be elected, there is no way you can be stopped from creating one of the nine highest vote-getters. Since you own 1,001 shares, the maximum number of shares a majority interest could control would be 8,999. This would entitle that group to 80,991 votes.

Number of shares owned (majority)	8,999
Number of directors to be elected	9
Number of votes (majority)	80,991

These 80,991 votes cannot be spread thinly enough over nine candidates to stop you from electing your one director. For example, if they are spread evenly over nine choices, each of the majority's directorial picks will receive 8,999 votes, but your choice will receive 9,009 votes. Because the top nine vote-getters are elected, your candidate will claim a director position.

To determine the number of shares needed to elect a given number of directors under cumulative voting, the following formula is used:

$$\text{Shares required} = \frac{\left(\begin{array}{c}\text{Number of} \\ \text{directors desired}\end{array} \times \begin{array}{c}\text{Total number of} \\ \text{shares outstanding}\end{array}\right)}{\left(\begin{array}{c}\text{Total number of directors} \\ \text{to be elected}\end{array} + 1\right)} + 1 \quad \text{(17–1)}$$

The formula reaffirms that in the previous instance, 1,001 shares would elect one director.

$$\frac{1 \times 10,000}{9 + 1} + 1 = \frac{10,000}{10} + 1 = 1,001$$

If three director positions out of nine were desired, 3,001 shares would be necessary.

$$\frac{3 \times 10,000}{9 + 1} + 1 = \frac{30,000}{10} + 1 = 3,001$$

It thus turns out that with approximately 30 percent of the outstanding shares, a minority interest can control one-third of the board. If a majority rule instead of a cumulative voting system were used, a minority interest would be able to elect no one. A group controlling 5,001 out of 10,000 outstanding shares could elect each and every director.

The following is a restatement of the proposition: If the number of minority shares outstanding under cumulative voting is known, we can determine how many directors those minority shares can elect by use of the formula

$$\begin{array}{c}\text{Number of directors} \\ \text{that can be elected}\end{array} = \frac{\left(\begin{array}{c}\text{Shares} \\ \text{owned}\end{array} - 1\right) \times \left(\begin{array}{c}\text{Total number of} \\ \text{directors to be elected}\end{array} + 1\right)}{\text{(Total number of shares outstanding)}} \quad \text{(17–2)}$$

Plugging 3,001 into the formula yields

$$\frac{(3,001 - 1)(9 + 1)}{10,000} = \frac{3,000(10)}{10,000} = 3$$

If the formula yields an uneven result, such as 3.1 or 3.7, the fractional amount is irrelevant. This means all results between 3 and 4 from the application of the formula indicate that three directors can be elected.

Although cumulative voting may give minority interests an opportunity to elect a representative to the board of directors, there is no requirement in Canada that directors must be chosen by cumulative voting, although federal and some provincial statutes provide for it. In the United States, 22 states require cumulative voting in preference to majority rule, 18 consider it permissible as part of the corporate charter, and only 10 states make no judgment on the advisability of its use.

 FINANCE IN ACTION

A Claim to Income and a Right to Vote?

Common equity represents ownership of the firm and should entitle shareholders to cash flows generated, after paying contractual obligations, and should have an equal vote in the direction of the firm. However, there are many examples of dual-class shares within Canada.

The drawback of these shares is that the general shareholders' voice is not heard and nepotism may be experienced. The advantage may be that the firm can take a longer-term view and some suggest that dual class shares may outperform the general market.

A common method of thwarting the ambitions of the minority is to stagger the terms of directors so only a few are elected each year. If the nine directors referred to earlier were elected three per year, a minority interest would then require 2,501 shares to elect a single board member.

$$\frac{1 \times 10,000}{3 + 1} + 1 = 2,501$$

In such a case, a minority holder controlling 25 percent of the shares could be denied board representation.

THE RIGHT TO PURCHASE NEW SHARES

In addition to a claim to residual income and the right to choose the directors, the common shareholders may also enjoy a privileged position in the offering of new securities. If the corporate charter contains a pre-emptive right provision, holders of common stock must be given the first option to purchase new shares. Even when the corporate charter does not provide a pre-emptive right clause, new issues of common shares are usually offered first to existing shareholders.

The pre-emptive right provision ensures that management cannot subvert the position of present shareholders by selling shares to outside interests without first offering them to current shareholders. If such protection were not afforded, a 20 percent shareholder might find their interest reduced to 10 percent by a major distribution of new shares to outsiders. Not only would voting rights be diluted, but also proportionate claims to corporate earnings would also be similarly reduced.

LO3 The Use of Rights in Financing

Corporations sometimes raise equity capital by means of rights offerings. Rights offerings allow the current shareholders the privilege of purchasing new shares at a favourable price (subscription price). Each shareholder gets one right for each share held and requires one or more rights to acquire a new share at the favourable price. Current shareholders are a built-in market for raising capital at a cost below that of underwriting a new issue. An investment dealer will likely assist in a rights offering for a fee.

Let us examine how a rights offering would work for the mythical Walton Corporation, which is in need of some capital funding.

Walton Corporation

Market share price (P_o)	$40
Shares outstanding	9 million
Equity market value	$360 million
Required capital funds	$30 million
Subscription price (discounted)	$30
New shares required (S)	1 million

Each old shareholder receives one right for each share of stock owned and may combine a specified number of rights plus $30 cash to buy a new share of stock. The discounted subscription price is meant to encourage the success of the rights offering. A share issue through the markets would have a much smaller discount. In a rights offering the following questions must be considered:

1. How many rights should be necessary to purchase one new share of stock?
2. What is the monetary value of these rights?

Rights Required Since nine million shares are currently outstanding, nine million rights will be issued. However, only one million new shares are required to be issued to raise the $30 million. The ratio of old to new shares is 9 to 1. On this basis, the old shareholder is able to combine nine rights plus $30 cash to purchase one new share of stock.

This means that a shareholder with 90 shares of stock would receive 90 rights that could be applied toward the purchase of 10 new shares of stock at $30 apiece. As is discussed later in this chapter, shareholders may choose to sell their rights rather than exercise them by purchasing new shares.

Monetary Value of a Right Anything that contributes to the privilege of purchasing a higher-priced stock for $30 per share obviously has a market value. The following two-step analysis aids in determining that value.

Nine old shares, previously worth $40 per share, bestow the capability of buying one new share for $30. This means we end up with a total market value of $390 spread over 10 shares. Therefore, on completion of the rights offering, the value of a share would theoretically equal $39, if all else remains the same and all rights are utilized.

Nine old shares sold at $40 each	$360
One new share to sell at $30	30
Total value of 10 shares	$390
Average value of one share	$ 39

Thus, the rights offering entitles the holder to buy for $30 a share that should carry a value of $39. With a differential between the anticipated price and the subscription price of $9 and nine rights required to participate in the purchase of one share, the value of a right becomes $1.

Average value per share	$39
Subscription price	30
Differential	$ 9
Rights required to buy one share	9
Value of a right ($9/9 shares)	$ 1

The period during which rights may be bought, sold, or exercised is usually four to six weeks after what is termed the ex-rights date. This date, along with the other dates during the offering process, is outlined in Figure 17–1. The rights are issued in the same way dividends are paid. On what is called the **record date,** the company's books of record are closed, and all common shareholders listed on that date receive rights. Shares go ex-rights two business days prior to the record date. Investors buying the shares on or after the ex-rights date receive no rights. Between the date of the rights issue announcement and the ex-rights date, the stock is referred to as cum-rights or rights-on, bestowing on any purchaser of the stock the right to subscribe to the new issue. The following example summarizes the timing:

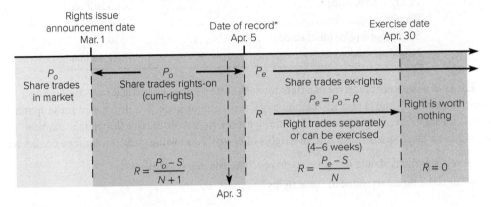

Figure 17–1 Timeline during rights offering

*For administrative purposes, the share trades ex-rights one business day in advance of the announced date.

	Value of Stock	Value of Right
March 1–April 3: Stock trades cum-rights....................	$40	$1 (of the $40)
April 4: Stock trades ex-rights............................	39	1
April 5: Date of record..................................	39	1
April 30: End of subscription period.......................	39	—

Upon reaching the ex-right period, the price of the shares decreases by the theoretical intrinsic value of the detached right. The remaining value ($39) is the value of the share ex-rights. Though there is a time period remaining between the ex-rights date (April 4) and the end of the subscription period, the market immediately discounts the expected future dilution. Thus, the ex-rights value precisely reflects the same value as can be expected when the new, underpriced $30 stock issue is sold.

The formula for the value of the right when the stock is trading cum-rights or rights-on is

$$R = \frac{P_o - S}{N + 1} \quad \text{(17–3)}$$

Where

P_o = Market value cum rights

S = Subscription price

N = Number of rights required to purchase a new share of stock

In the above example,

$$R = \frac{\$40 - \$30}{9 + 1} = \frac{\$10}{10} = 1$$

Using formula 17–3 we determined that the value of a right in the Walton Corporation offering was $1. An alternative formula giving precisely the same answer is

$$R = \frac{P_e - S}{N} \quad \text{(17–4)}$$

The only new term is P_e, the market value of the stock when shares are trading ex-rights. The calculation becomes

$$R = \frac{\$39 - \$30}{9} = \frac{\$9}{9} = 1$$

It is important to realize that rights seldom sell at their theoretical, intrinsic value, due to buying and selling costs and also because imbalances in demand and supply may develop. For example, there may be great enthusiasm for the new issue, causing the market value of the right to exceed the initial theoretical value (perhaps the right will trade for $1.75).

Effect of Rights on Shareholders' Position

At first glance, a rights offering appears to bring great benefits to shareholders. But is this really the case? Does a shareholder really benefit from being able to buy a stock that is initially $40 (and later $39) for $30? Don't answer too quickly!

Think of it this way. Assume 100 people own shares of stock in a corporation and they decide to have the corporation sell new shares to themselves at 25 percent below current value. It cannot really make sense that they can enhance their wealth by selling their own product more cheaply to themselves. What is gained by purchasing inexpensive new shares has to be lost by diluting the value of existing outstanding shares.

Rights Offering: No Wealth Increase

Take the case of Shareholder A, who owns nine shares of Walton Corporation before the rights offering and also has $30 in cash. His holdings would appear as follows:

Nine old shares at $40	$360
Cash	30
Total value	$390

If he receives and exercises nine rights to buy one new share at $30, his portfolio contains

Ten shares at $39 (diluted value)	$390
Cash	0
Total value	$390

He is no better off. A second alternative would be for him to sell his rights in the market and stay with his position of owning only nine shares and holding cash.

Nine shares at $39 (diluted value)	$351
Proceeds from sale of rights	9
Cash	30
Total value	$390

As indicated, whether he chooses to exercise his rights or not, the stock still goes down to a lower value (others are still diluting). Once again, his overall value remains constant. The value received for the rights ($9) exactly equals the extent of dilution in the value of the original nine shares.

 FINANCE IN ACTION

Funds for a Small Business

Smaller businesses often have working capital needs. Publicly traded companies will sometimes go to the markets to raise these funds through a rights offering. This was the purpose of International Frontier Resources when it sought to raise approximately $695,000 in late 2019.

Advanced Proteome Therapeutics Corp. in June 2017 had sought $935,847 to cover its working capital deficiency by way of a rights offering to existing shareholders, hoping to raise about $1,900,000. Four (4) rights and $0.06 would get you one (1) new common

It would be foolish for the shareholder to throw away the rights as worthless securities. They would then suffer the pains of dilution without the offsetting gain from the sale of the rights.

Nine shares at $39 (diluted value)	$351
Cash	30
Total value	$381

Empirical evidence indicates that this careless activity occurs 1 to 2 percent of the time.

Desirable Features of Rights Offerings

The student may ask, "If the shareholder is no better off in terms of total valuation, why undertake a rights offering?" There are a number of possible advantages.

By giving current shareholders a first option to purchase new shares, we protect their current position in regard to voting rights and claims to earnings. Of equal importance, the use of a rights offering gives the firm a built-in market for new security issues. Because of this built-in base, distribution costs are likely to be considerably lower than under a straight public issue in which investment dealers must underwrite the full risk of distribution. Investment dealers may assist in a rights offering but with a lower expected fee.

Additionally, a rights offering may generate more interest in the market than would a straight public issue. There is a market not only for the stock, but also for the rights. Because the subscription price is normally set 15 to 25 percent below current value, there is the false appearance of a bargain, creating further interest in the offering.

American Depositary Receipts (ADRs)

Since foreign companies want to tap into the world's largest capital market, the United States, they need to offer securities for sale in the United States that can be traded by investors and have the same liquidity features as U.S. securities.

 FINANCE IN ACTION

ADRs or Shares?

In 2020, over 500 foreign companies were listed on the New York Stock Exchange (NYSE) in order to access the world's largest and most liquid capital market. The majority of these foreign companies are traded as American depositary receipts (ADRs) or global

American depositary receipts (ADRs) are certificates that have a legal claim on an ownership interest in a foreign company's common stock. The shares of the foreign company are purchased and put in trust in a foreign branch of a New York bank. The bank, in turn, receives and can issue depositary receipts to the American shareholders of the foreign firm. ADRs allow foreign shares to be traded in the United States much like a common stock. Dividends are paid in dollars and are more easily collected than if the actual shares of the foreign stock were owned. ADRs are considered to be more liquid, less expensive, and easier to trade than a foreign company's stock bought directly on that country's exchange. BNY Mellon has a good listing of depositary receipts.

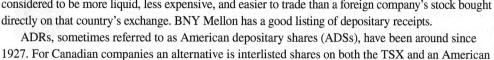

BNY Mellon
adrbnymellon.com

ADRs, sometimes referred to as American depositary shares (ADSs), have been around since 1927. For Canadian companies an alternative is interlisted shares on both the TSX and an American exchange, to access the capital of both markets.

LO4 Poison Pills

During the 1980s, a new wrinkle was added to the meaning of rights when firms began receiving merger and acquisition proposals from companies interested in acquiring voting control of the firm. Management of companies considered potential takeover targets began to develop defensive tactics in fending off these unwanted mergers. One widely used strategy was called the poison pill. Other techniques are discussed in Chapter 20.

 FINANCE IN ACTION

Fewer Pills to Swallow

In 2013, the securities administrators put out a discussion paper suggesting target firms be given more time to resist hostile takeovers. This would (perhaps) permit directors to extract greater value for the shareholders, fulfilling their fiduciary duty. The Ontario Securities Commission (osc.gov.on.ca), along with other provincial jurisdictions, extended the minimum time for a bid to remain outstanding from 35 days to 115 days, and bids would require that a minimum of more than 50 percent of all outstanding target securities be tendered.

Since the changes, the number of tender offers that have degenerated into hostile takeover attempts and the triggering of poison pill provisions has been muted.

Most poison pills have a trigger point. When a potential buyer accumulates a given percentage of the common stock, the other shareholders receive rights to purchase additional shares from the company, generally at very low prices. These new shares may have special privileges not available to shareholders that have acquired the large block of shares. If the rights are exercised by shareholders, this increases the total shares outstanding and dilutes the potential buyer's ownership percentage, making it more expensive to complete the acquisition.

Poison pill strategies often are put in place without a shareholders' vote. In 1988, Inco Ltd. (Vale) was the first Canadian corporation to introduce a poison pill. Inco's poison pill gave its directors the ability to initiate a rights offering when a hostile buyer acquired more than 20 percent of the company's stock. The rights offering allowed shareholders other than the shareholder with the large share holding to purchase additional shares at half price. Many suggest that poison pills lower the potential for maximizing shareholder value by discouraging potential high takeover bids. Attempts by other companies to introduce poison pills have sometimes been overridden by disgruntled shareholders.

Vale
vale.com/canada

LO5 PREFERRED STOCK

Between bonds and common stocks is an intermediate, or hybrid, form of security known as preferred stock. Preferred shareholders are entitled to receive a stipulated dividend and generally must receive the dividend before the payment of dividends to common shareholders.

Bondholders	←Preferred Shareholders→	Common Shareholders
• Creditors of the firm	• Entitled to receive stipulated dividends before common shareholders	• Owners of the firm
• Contractual claim against the corporation for the payment of interest		• Entitled to the corporation's residual income
	• Cumulative dividends	
• Can force the corporations into bankruptcy if interest payments are not made	• May forgo dividends if deemed necessary	• Right to vote

For example, XYZ Corporation might receive $100 per share for a new issue of preferred stock on which it specifies $6 as the annual dividend. Under normal circumstances, the corporation would pay the $6 per share dividend. Let us assume it also has $1,000 bonds carrying 7 percent interest and shares of common stock with a market value of $50, normally paying a $1 cash dividend.

The 7 percent interest must be paid on the bonds. The $6 preferred dividend has to be paid before the $1 dividend on common, but both may be waived without threat of bankruptcy. Common shareholders are the last in line to receive payment, but their potential participation in earnings is unlimited. They may not receive the $1 dividend this year but may receive much larger dividends in the future. On the other hand, the preferred shareholder's dividend remains at $6.

LO6 Justification for Preferred Stock

Because preferred stock has few unique characteristics, why might the corporation choose to issue it and, equally importantly, why are investors willing to purchase the security?

One reason corporations issue preferred stock is to achieve a balance in their capital structures. It is a means of expanding the capital base of the firm without diluting the common stock ownership position or incurring contractual debt obligations. Firms that are heavy users of debt, such as public utilities and capital goods producers, may go to preferred stock to balance their sources of financing. Canadian banks became more frequent issuers of preferreds when perpetual preferred shares were counted as part of the capital in tests of the banks' capital adequacy under the Bank Act, revised in 1980.

Even in these cases there may be a drawback. Although interest payments on debt are tax-deductible, preferred stock dividends are not. The interest cost on 5 percent debt may be only 3 to 3.5 percent on an aftertax-cost basis, whereas the aftertax cost on 5 percent preferred stock would be the stated amount. A firm issuing the preferred stock may be willing to pay the higher aftertax cost to assure investors that it has a balanced capital structure, thereby lowering the costs of the other sources of funds in the capital structure.

Some dividend yields on preferreds can be quite attractive to an investor.

Investor Interest Primary purchasers of preferred stock are corporate investors, insurance companies, and pension funds. To the corporate investor, preferred stock offers a very attractive advantage over bonds. In many cases the tax law provides that any corporation that receives either preferred or common dividends from another corporation may receive those dividends tax free. For the individual investor, the preferred dividend offers the advantage of the dividend tax credit, which reduces the amount of tax payable on dividend income. By contrast, the interest on bonds is usually taxable to the recipient.

Because of this tax consideration, it is not surprising that corporations are able to issue preferred stock at a slightly lower pre-tax yield than debt.

Bond versus Preferred example	
Debenture (unsecured bond)	
Yield...	6.71%
Preferred	
Yield...	6.35%

On a before-tax basis, the bond offers the higher yield, and yet it is a less risky investment. Let us examine the aftertax yields.

Assuming the investor is in the top tax bracket of the province of Alberta, we will use the top marginal tax rates as identified in Table 2–13. Examining aftertax yields:

Before-tax *debenture* yield.........................	6.71%
Combined marginal tax rate (48%)	(3.22)
Aftertax debenture yield	3.49%
Before-tax *preferred* yield	6.35
Combined marginal tax rate (31.71%)...............	(2.01)
Aftertax preferred yield	4.34%

Summary of Tax Considerations Tax considerations work in two opposing directions.

- The aftertax cost of debt is cheaper than preferred stock to the issuing corporation because interest is tax-deductible to the payer. (This is true even though the quoted rate may be higher.)
- Generally, the receipt of preferred dividends is more valuable than corporate bond interest to the (corporate) recipient because the dividend is exempt from taxation.
- For the individual taxpayer, the dividend tax credit reduces the amount of tax payable as compared to that payable on interest income.

Some of the large holding companies that are such important players in Canadian capital markets quite naturally make extensive use of preferred share offerings because of the tax and capital structure effects combined. Some analysts have believed that the intricate use of preferred financings has allowed holding companies to report extra-large profits and minimize taxes, all while financing expansion. For example, a company with pre-tax profit of $10 million would pay about $5 million in tax. The company, it is claimed, could do much better by borrowing substantial sums to buy preferred shares. It could, for example, borrow $100 million at 10 percent. That would create an annual expense of $10 million, reducing the ordinary income to zero. Using the borrowed money to buy $100 million of preferred shares yielding about $7.5 million in dividends would increase the company's end profit by a whopping 50 percent.

 FINANCE IN ACTION

Preferred Yields During Covid-19 Pandemic

In March 2020 the financial markets were severely shocked with concerns for the economic impact of the coronavirus pandemic. Meanwhile, the yields on preferred shares of top Canadian corporations, such as the banks, which had been swept up in the downdraft of the equity markets offered significant yields on preferred shares. Debt securities offered only meager yields. Would it be worthwhile to take the risk of investing in preferreds?

Bank of Montreal (BMO.PR.E).	9.327%
Royal Bank (RY.PR.Z).	6.875%

Provisions Associated with Preferred Stock

A preferred stock issue contains a number of stipulations and provisions that define the shareholder's claim to income and assets.

1. **Cumulative dividends.** Most preferred stock issues have a cumulative claim to dividends. That is, if preferred stock dividends are not paid in any one year, they accumulate and must be paid in total before common shareholders can receive dividends. If preferred stock carries a $2 cash dividend and the company does not pay dividends for three years, preferred shareholders must receive the full $6 before common shareholders can receive anything.

   The cumulative dividend feature makes a corporation very cognizant of its obligation to preferred shareholders. When a financially troubled corporation has missed a number of dividend payments under a cumulative arrangement, there may be a financial recapitalization of the corporation in which preferred shareholders receive new securities in place of the dividend arrearage. Assume the corporation has now missed five years of dividends under a $2-per-year obligation and still remains in a poor cash position. Preferred shareholders may be offered $10 or more in new common stock for forgiveness of the missed dividend payments. Preferred shareholders may be willing to cooperate to keep the corporation financially viable.

2. **Conversion feature.** Similarly to certain forms of debt, preferred stock may be convertible into common shares at the option of the holder. One new wrinkle on convertible preferreds is the use of

convertible exchangeable preferreds that allow the company to force conversion from convertible preferred stock into convertible debt. This can be used to allow the company to change preferred dividends into tax-deductible interest payments when it is to the company's advantage to do so.

Convertibility is discussed at length in Chapter 19. In Canada, about 25 percent of preferred share issues carry a conversion feature, versus about 40 percent in U.S. markets.

3. **Call feature.** Preferred stock, like debt, may be callable or "redeemable." That is, the corporation may retire the security before maturity at some small premium over par. This, of course, accrues to the advantage of the corporation and to the disadvantage of the preferred shareholder. A preferred issue carrying a call feature is accorded a slightly higher yield than a similar issue without this provision.

4. **Retractable feature.** A preferred share containing a provision that allows redemption of the shares at the option of the shareholder has a retractable feature. This provision creates advantages and disadvantages for the company and shareholder in just the opposite direction as does the call provision.

5. **Participation provision.** A small percentage of preferred stock issues are participating; that is, they may participate over and above the quoted yield when the corporation is enjoying a particularly good year. For example, the participation provision may provide that once the common stock dividend equals the preferred stock dividend, the two classes of securities may share equally in additional payouts.

6. **Floating rate.** Some shares are floating-rate preferred stock that has plus or minus a percentage from the selected money market rate such as the prime or an average bankers' acceptance rate. Often, preferred shares paying a fixed return are set to convert to a floating-rate return in the near future. Thus, the issuing firms have protected themselves from being locked into a fixed-rate security in perpetuity—as have the investors.

7. **Par value.** As with common shares, federally incorporated companies issue no-par-value preferreds. However, many balance sheets still show par value preferred shares issued before the Canada Business Corporations Act was amended to disallow their issue.

Despite preferreds no longer having a par value, corporations still may use a similar term. They may refer to the "stated value" per share in establishing the redeemable and dividend features.

8. **Dutch auction preferred stock.** Dutch auction preferred stock is similar to floating-rate preferred stock, but it is a short-term instrument. The security matures every seven weeks and is sold (reauctioned) at a subsequent bidding. The concept of Dutch auction means the stock is issued to the bidder willing to accept the lowest yield and then to the next lowest bidder, and so on until all the preferred stock is sold. This is much like the Treasury bill auctions held by the Bank of Canada. This auction process at short-term intervals allows investors to keep up with the changing interest rates in the short-term market. Some corporate investors like Dutch auction preferred stock because it allows them to invest at short-term rates and take advantage of the tax benefits available to them with preferred stock investments. Chartered banks have been big buyers of auction preferreds.

INCOME TRUSTS

Income trusts allow a firm to raise additional capital for its ongoing operations by selling off its mature assets into a new operating company. Generally, it is these mature assets that generate stable and strong cash flows. The new operating company is financed by a combination of subordinated debt and share equity held in an income trust, managed by a trustee. In turn the income trust is financed by an equity investment of investors or unitholders, as opposed to shareholders in a company.

Unlike preferred or common stock, income trusts are not identified as a liability or equity on the firm's balance sheet because the mature assets are sold into the new operating company. However, the additional financing can improve the firm's capital structure and the original firm, by managing the new operating company, can generate a good income.

Income trusts were developed as an investment to provide high returns (yields) for the investor because of their tax efficiency and the strong cash flows generated by the mature assets. Today's income trusts in Canada are taxed similarly to corporations. As a result, the number of income trusts that exceeded 200 in 2006 have dropped by more than half, with REITs (real estate, with tax advantages maintained) the dominant type.

The new operating company holding the mature assets is financed with the right mix of debt and equity in its capital structure to minimize its corporate taxes. Interest paid on the debt, dividends from the equity, and some return of capital "flow through" to the income trust. The income trust, which pays no taxes, thus provides a higher cash distribution on a monthly or quarterly basis to unitholders, who pay the required taxes at the individual's marginal tax rate.

 FINANCE IN ACTION

The Fall of Income Trusts

Enerplus Resources Fund royalty trust was the first established trust in Canada, in 1985. After that many trusts, such as the Boston Pizza Royalties and Big Rock Brewery, enjoyed tax-free status while passing on higher cash distributions to unitholders.

In September 2005, the federal government claimed income trusts had cost hundreds of millions of dollars in lost taxes, and they had diverted monies away from more entrepreneurial ventures toward established "sunset" businesses.

On October 31, 2006, Finance Minister Jim Flaherty clipped the wings of income trusts with the announcement of new tax rules. With the exception of real estate income trusts and mutual fund investment trusts, income trusts formed after this date would be subject to taxation in the same way as corporations. Unitholders would be eligible for dividend tax credits equating to dividends paid by a corporation. Income trusts formed on or before the date were allowed a phasing-out period until 2011.

Both Enerplus and Big Rock converted back to regular stock companies but many income trusts remain, such as Boston Pizza Royalties. Several income trusts remain listed on the TSX. (tmx.com)

Q1 How have these trusts or now shares performed over the last several years?

tmx.com   **Symbol: ERF   BR   BPF.UN**

Income trusts represent a complicated structure that allows the strong cash flows of mature assets to flow to investors in a tax-efficient manner. Furthermore, these strong cash flows are not derailed by the other assets of a firm that may not be producing similar strong and stable cash flows. The firm gains by improving its financing capabilities. The market for income trusts is a recent development.

In March 1999, as part of Suncor's ongoing expansion of its oil sands plant in Fort McMurray, northern Alberta, a long-term power agreement was reached with TransAlta Utilities. TransAlta would build a $315 million facility to supply power to the Suncor plant. For both companies, the expansion in capital assets required funding from the capital markets.

Through its investment dealer at the time, Merrill Lynch, Suncor announced the sale of Canadian Originated Preferred Securities (COPrS), raising $240 million. In its prospectus, Suncor labelled these securities as junior, subordinated debentures. The securities were to pay interest at 9.05 percent a year for 49 years; almost forever. They were, however, redeemable after five years, at par.

These newly named securities had features similar to bonds and to preferred shares. The features were set to appeal to the demands of the investment community, and a clever name would assist in their sale. After that initial offering, "income trusts" secured by the revenue streams of various businesses became all the rage. Some of the more interesting income trusts included

- A&W Revenue Royalties Income Fund units (AW.UN) based on "burger" sales
- BMO BOaTS secured by first mortgages
- Yellow Pages Income Fund (YLO.UN)
- Sleep Country Canada Income Fund (Z.UN)
- Big Rock Brewery Income Trust (BR.UN)

Concerns were expressed that income trusts distorted capital distribution in the economy. Rather than having firms reinvest cash flows into productive assets, the cash flows from mature businesses are flowing into the hands of investors. The question became, did they reinvest or engage in current consumption? The government acted to limit certain income trusts.

LO7 COMPARING FEATURES OF COMMON AND PREFERRED STOCK AND DEBT

Table 17–1 compares the characteristics of common stock, preferred stock, and bonds. Consider carefully the comparative advantages and disadvantages of each.

Table 17–1 Features of alternative security issues

	Common Stock	Preferred Stock	Bonds
1. Ownership and control of the firm	Belongs to common shareholders through voting rights and residual claim to income	Limited rights when dividends are missed	Limited rights under default in interest payments
2. Obligation to provide return	None	Must receive payment before common shareholder	Contractual obligation
3. Claim to assets in bankruptcy	Lowest claim of any security holder	Bondholders and creditors must be satisfied first	Highest claim
4. Cost of distribution	Highest	Moderate	Lowest
5. Risk–return tradeoff	Highest risk, highest return (at least in theory)	Moderate risk, moderate return	Lowest risk, moderate return
6. Tax status of payment by corporation	Not deductible	Not deductible	Tax-deductible cost = Interest payment $\times$ (1 − tax rate)
7. Tax status of payment to recipient	Dividend to other corporation usually tax-exempt Special tax treatment with dividend tax credit	Same as common stock	Interest usually fully taxable

In terms of the risk-return relationships embodied in these three classes of securities (as well as in the other investments discussed in Chapter 7), we might expect the risk-return pattern depicted in Figure 17–2. The lowest return is obtained from savings accounts, and the highest return and risk are generally associated with common stock. In between, we note that short-term instruments generally, though not always, provide lower returns than longer-term instruments. We also observe that government securities pay lower returns than issues originated by corporations because of the lower

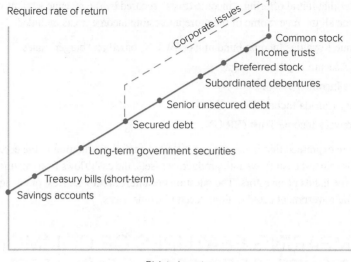

Figure 17–2 Risk and expected return for various security classes

risk involved. Preferred stock as a hybrid form of security may appear to pay a lower return than other long-term debt instruments because of the tax-exempt status of preferred stock dividends to corporate purchasers or because of the dividend tax credit available to individual investors. When the risk-return relationship is expressed on an aftertax basis, we do see preferreds somewhere between debentures and common stock.

Next, we observe increasingly high return requirements on debt, based on the presence or absence of security provisions and the priority of claims on unsecured debt. At the top of the scale is common stock. Because of its lowest priority of claim in the corporation and its volatile price movement, it has the highest demanded return.

Although extensive research studies have tended to validate these general patterns, short-term or even intermediate-term reversals have occurred, in which investments with lower risk have outperformed investments at the higher end of the risk scale.[1]

[1] Ibbotson Associates, *Stocks, Bonds, Bills and Inflation: 2009 Yearbook* (Chicago: Ibbotson Associates Capital Management Research Center, 2007).

SUMMARY

1. Common stock ownership carries three primary rights or privileges. First, there is a residual claim to income. All funds not paid out to other classes of securities automatically belong to the common shareholder; the firm may then choose to pay out these residual funds in dividends or to reinvest them for the benefit of common shareholders. Different classes of shares may carry the right to differing dividend amounts. There can also be cases where dividends on a particular class of stock are tied to the performance of a subsidiary company.

   Because common shareholders are the ultimate owners of the firm, they alone have the privilege of voting (except under default or other unusual conditions). The major voting choice for the shareholders is in electing the members of the firm's board of directors. There may be more than one class of stock whose voting rights differ. In Canada there are many examples of stock with different voting rights. The general purpose of such stock is to allow a company to raise additional equity capital without diluting the controlling ownership of a current group of shareholders. Many of the nonvoting issues contain a so-called *coattail clause* allowing for the participation of their holders in any premium paid by an acquirer for the voting shares. (LO1)

2. To expand the role of minority shareholders, corporations may use a system of cumulative voting in which each shareholder has voting power equal to the number of shares owned times the number of directors to be elected. By cumulating votes for a small number of selected directors, minority shareholders are sometimes able to have representation on the board. (LO2)

3. Common shareholders may also enjoy a first option to purchase new shares. This privilege is extended through the procedure known as a rights offering. A shareholder receives one right for each share of stock owned and may combine a certain number of rights, plus cash, to purchase a new share. Although the cash or subscription price is usually somewhat below the current market price, the shareholder neither gains nor loses through the process. (LO3)

4. Poison pills are provisions established by a firm to prevent a hostile takeover. They usually provide for an extensive dilution in ownership if shares are acquired by an unwelcome firm in an attempt to take over the company. A poison pill makes it very expensive for the unwelcome firm to complete the takeover unless the unwelcome firm is prepared to negotiate with the management of a firm being pursued. (LO4)

5. A hybrid, or intermediate, security falling between debt and common stock is preferred stock. Preferred shareholders are entitled to receive a stipulated dividend and must receive this dividend before any payment is made to common shareholders. Preferred dividends usually accumulate if they are not paid in a given year. Preferred shareholders cannot, however, initiate bankruptcy proceedings nor seek legal redress if nonpayment occurs. Recent court decisions have strengthened the position of preferred shareholders during corporate reorganizations. (LO5)

6. Preferred shares pay dividends that are subject to special provisions under the Income Tax Act. The effect is to make dividends more attractive than interest to the investor, other things being equal. Therefore, when comparing returns offered on preferreds and bonds, it is appropriate to look at aftertax yields. (LO6)

7. Common stock, preferred stock, bonds, and other securities (income trusts) tend to receive returns over the long term in accordance with risk, with corporate issues generally paying a higher return than government securities. (LO7)

REVIEW OF FORMULAS

1. Shares required

$$\text{Shares required} = \frac{\left(\substack{\text{Number of} \\ \text{directors desired}} \times \substack{\text{Total number of} \\ \text{shares outstanding}}\right)}{\left(\substack{\text{Total number of} \\ \text{directors to be elected}} + 1\right)} + 1 \qquad (17\text{--}1)$$

2. Number of directors

$$\text{Number of directors that can be elected} = \frac{\left(\dfrac{\text{Shares owned}}{}-1\right) \times \left(\dfrac{\text{Total number of directors to be elected}}{}+1\right)}{(\text{Total number of shares outstanding})}$$ (17–2)

3. $$R = \frac{P_o - S}{N + 1}$$ (17–3)

   R = Value of a right
   P_o = Market value of the stock-rights-on (stock carries a right)
   S = Subscription price
   N = Number of rights required to purchase a new share of stock

4. $$R = \frac{P_e - S}{N}$$ (17–4)

   P_e is the market value of stock-ex-rights (stock no longer carries a right).

DISCUSSION QUESTIONS

1. Why has corporate management become increasingly sensitive to the desires of large institutional investors? (LO1, LO4)

2. What is the difference in dividend payments between Bombardier and TELUS nonvoting shares and their voting common shares? How do you explain the difference in their trading values? (LO1)

3. Why do corporations use special categories in issuing common stock? (LO1)

4. What are the possible disadvantages, from an investor's point of view, of being able to buy only nonvoting shares in a given company? What do you think of the increased tendency among Canadian companies to issue large amounts of nonvoting shares? (LO1, LO4)

5. What is the purpose of cumulative voting? Are there any disadvantages to management? (LO2)

6. Why has preferred stock been a much more popular source of funds for corporations in Canada than in the United States? (LO5)

7. How does the pre-emptive right protect shareholders from dilution? (LO3)

8. If common shareholders are the owners of the company, why do they have only the last claim on assets and only a residual claim on income? (LO1)

9. During a rights offering the underlying stock is said to sell rights-on and ex-rights. Explain the meaning of these terms and their significance to current shareholders and potential shareholders. (LO3)

10. Why might management use a poison pill strategy? (LO4)

11. Preferred stock is often referred to as a hybrid security. Why? (LO5)

12. If preferred stock is riskier than bonds, why has preferred stock had lower yields than bonds in recent years? (LO5)

13. Why is the cumulative feature of preferred stock particularly important to preferred shareholders? (LO5)

14. A small amount of preferred stock is participating. What would your reaction be if someone said common stock is also participating? (LO5)

15. What is an advantage of floating-rate preferred stock for the risk-averse investor? What is an advantage for the issuing corporation? (LO5)

16. Speculate on whether it would be easier to buy control, in general, of a company listed on the TSX or one listed on the NYSE. Which situation strikes you as being better in this regard? (LO1, LO4)

17. What features of income trusts make them an attractive investment? Why do corporations set up income trusts? (LO6)

18. Put an X by the security that has the feature best related to the following considerations. You may wish to refer to Table 17–1. (LO7)

	Common Stock	Preferred Stock	Bonds
a. Ownership and control of the firm	_____	_____	_____
b. Obligation to provide return	_____	_____	_____
c. Claims to assets in bankruptcy	_____	_____	_____
d. High cost of distribution	_____	_____	_____
e. Highest return	_____	_____	_____
f. Highest risk	_____	_____	_____

INTERNET RESOURCES AND QUESTIONS

Websites for researching preferred and common stocks are numerous. Many are free, but the best information is available only for a fee.

Canadian companies file news releases, financial statements, and other relevant information with SEDAR (System for Electronic Document Analysis and Retrieval):
sedar.com

The TSX Toronto Stock Exchange site will connect to a company's website, which often has annual reports available:
tmx.com

Research on Canadian companies is available at Investcom, Zacks, GlobeInvestor, and Reuters:
investcom.com
zacks.com
theglobeandmail.com/globe-investor
reuters.com

Canadian companies listed on U.S. exchanges are likely to have research available at the U.S. Yahoo site:
finance.yahoo.com

BigCharts permits the graphing of Canadian stocks and market indexes shown with a "ca" prefix:
bigcharts.marketwatch.com

1. The major banks and TransCanada Pipelines usually have several outstanding preferred share issues.
    a. Identify for two preferred issues: the current price, yield, and any special features. A visit to the company's website and annual report will likely be required to identify any special features.
    b. Compare the above yields to the yield on corporate bonds.

2. Identify the latest filings at SEDAR. What are the features of any preferred offerings? Are there many trust offerings?

PROBLEMS

1. Folic Acid Inc. has $20 million in earnings, pays $2.75 million in interest to bondholders and $1.80 million in dividends to preferred shareholders.
    a. What are the common shareholders' residual claims to earnings?
    b. What are the common shareholders' legal, enforceable claims to dividends?

2.   Diploma Mills has $30 million in earnings, pays $4.25 million in interest to bondholders and $2.95 million in dividends to preferred shareholders.

   a.   What are the common shareholders' residual claims to earnings?

   b.   What are the common shareholders' legal, enforceable claims to the dividends?

3.   Anita Job owns 507 shares in the Rapid Employment Company (a firm that provides temporary work). There are 11 directors to be elected. Twenty-one thousand shares are outstanding. The firm has adopted cumulative voting.

   a.   How many total votes can be cast?

   b.   How many votes does Anita Job control?

   c.   What percentage of the total votes does she control?

4.   Katie Homes and Garden Co. has 10,640,000 shares outstanding. Shares are currently selling at $52 per share. If an unfriendly outside group acquired 25 percent of the shares, existing shareholders will be able to buy new shares at 30 percent below the currently existing share price.

   a.   How many shares must the unfriendly outside group acquire for the poison pill to go into effect?

   b.   What will be the new purchase price for the existing shareholders?

5.   Michael Meyers wishes to know how many shares are necessary to elect 5 directors out of the 14 directors up for election in the Austin Power Company. There are 150,000 shares outstanding and cumulative voting is used.

6.   Mr. R.C. Cola owns 7,001 shares of Softdrinks Inc. There are 10 seats on the company board of directors, and the company has a total of 77,000 shares outstanding. Softdrinks Inc. utilizes cumulative voting.

   Can Mr. Cola elect himself to the board when the vote to elect 10 directors is held next week?

7.   Boston Fishery has been experiencing declining earnings but has just announced a 50 percent salary increase for its top executives. A dissident group of shareholders wants to oust the existing board of directors. There are currently 11 directors and 60,000 shares of stock outstanding. Mr. Bass, the president of the company, has the full support of the existing board. The dissident shareholders control proxies for 20,001 shares. Mr. Bass is worried about losing his job.

   a.   Under cumulative voting procedures, how many directors can the dissident shareholders elect with the proxies they now hold? How many directors could they elect under majority rule with these proxies?

   b.   How many shares (or proxies) are needed to elect six directors under cumulative voting?

8.   Midland Petroleum is holding a shareholders meeting next month. Ms. Ramsay is the president of the company and has the support of the existing board of directors. All 11 members of the board are up for reelection. Mr. Tbone Pickens is a dissident shareholder. He controls proxies for 40,001 shares. Ms. Ramsay and her friends on the board control 60,001 shares. Other shareholders, whose loyalties are unknown, will be voting the remaining 19,998 shares. The company uses cumulative voting.

   a.   How many directors can Mr. Pickens be sure of electing?

   b.   How many directors can Ms. Ramsay and her friends be sure of electing?

   c.   How many directors could Mr. Pickens elect if he obtains all the proxies for the uncommitted votes? Will he control the board?

9.   In the previous problem, if nine directors were to be elected, and Ms. Ramsay and her friends had 60,001 shares and Mr. Pickens had 40,001 shares plus half the uncommitted votes, how many directors could Mr. Pickens elect?

10. Mr. Frost controls proxies for 32,000 of the 60,000 outstanding shares of Express Frozen Foods Inc. Mr. Cooke heads a dissident group that controls the remaining 28,000 shares. There are seven board members to be elected and cumulative voting applies. Frost does not understand the cumulative voting and plans to cast 90,000 of his 224,000 votes for his brother, Jack. His remaining votes will be spread evenly for three other candidates.

    How many directors can Cooke elect if Frost acts as described above? Use logical numerical analysis rather than a set formula to answer the question.

11. Macho Iron Works was established 16 years ago. Four years later, the company went public. At that time, Fred Macho, the original owner, decided to establish two classes of stock. The first represents Class A founders' stock and is entitled to 10 votes per share. The normally traded common stock, designated as Class B, is entitled to one vote per share. This year, Mr. I.M. Meek was considering purchasing shares in Macho Iron Work. While he knew founders' shares were not present in many companies, he decided to buy the shares anyway because of a new high-technology melting process the company had developed.

    Of the 1,500,000 total shares currently outstanding, the original founder's family owns 62,635 shares. What is the percentage of the founder's family votes compared to the Class B votes?

12. Grantland Rice Co. has issued rights to its shareholders. The subscription price is $45, and 4 rights are needed along with the subscription price to buy one of the new shares. The stock is selling for $55 rights-on.

    a. What would be the value of one right?

    b. If the stock goes ex-rights, what would be the new share price?

13. Redirect Energy Corporation has issued rights to its shareholders. The subscription price is $25, and four rights are needed along with the subscription price to buy one of the new shares. The stock is selling for $30 rights-on.

    a. What would be the value of one right?

    b. If the stock goes ex-rights, what would be the new share price?

14. Prime Direct Corporation has issued rights to its shareholders. The subscription price is $20.00, and three rights are needed along with the subscription price to buy one of the new shares. The stock is selling for $25.00 rights-on.

    a. What would be the value of one right?

    b. If the stock goes ex-rights, what would be the new share price?

15. Harmon Candy Co. has announced a rights offering for its shareholders. Cindy Barr owns 500 shares of Harmon Candy stock. Five rights plus $62 cash are needed to buy one of the new shares. The stock is currently selling for $70 rights-on.

    a. What is the value of a right?

    b. How many of the new shares could Cindy buy if she exercised all her rights? How much cash would this require?

    c. Cindy doesn't know if she wants to exercise her rights or sell them. What alternative would have the most beneficial effect on her wealth?

16. Skyway Airlines has announced a rights offering for its shareholders. Harold Post owns 800 shares of Skyway Airlines stock. Four rights plus $60 cash are needed to buy one of the new shares. The stock is currently selling for $72 rights-on.

    a. What is the value of a right?

    b. How many of the new shares could Harold buy if he exercised all his rights? How much cash would this require?

    c. Harold doesn't know if he wants to exercise his rights or sell them. What alternative would have the most beneficial effect on his wealth?

17. Todd Winningham IV has $4,000 to invest. He has been looking at Gallagher Tennis Clubs Inc. common stock. Gallagher has issued a rights offering to its common shareholders. Six rights plus $38 cash will buy one new share. Gallagher's stock is selling for $50 ex-rights.

a. How many rights could Todd buy with his $4,000? Alternatively, how many shares could he buy with the same $4,000 at $50 per share?

b. If Todd invests his $4,000 in Gallagher rights and the price of Barton shares rise to $59 per share ex-rights, what would be his dollar profit on the rights? (First compute profits per right.)

c. If Todd invests his $4,000 in Gallagher shares and the price of a share rises to $59 ex-rights, what would be his total dollar profit?

d. What would be the answer to part **b** if the price of a Gallagher share price falls to $30 ex-rights instead of rising to $59?

e. What would be the answer to part **c** if the price of a Gallagher share falls to $30 ex-rights?

18. Mr. and Mrs. Anderson own five shares of Magic Tricks Corporation's common stock. The market value of the stock is $60. They also have $48 in cash. They have just received word of a rights offering. One new share of stock can be purchased at $48 for each five shares currently owned (based on five rights).

a. What is the value of a right?

b. What is the value of the Andersons' portfolio before the rights offering? (Portfolio in this question represents stock plus cash.)

c. If the Andersons participate in the rights offering, what will be the value of their portfolio, based on the diluted value (ex-rights) of the stock?

d. If they sell their five rights but keep their stock at its diluted value and hold on to their cash, what will be the value of their portfolio?

19. Smelly Kat Industries, a public company, wishes to raise $25 million for product line expansion. Because the existing shareholders are excited by the company's prospects, a rights offering will be used to raise the necessary capital. Each of the 5 million shareholders will receive one right. The subscription price is $25.00 per share, and the market price of the existing shares is currently $30.00. Calculate the value of a right at the present time.

20. Delovely Productions Limited wants to raise $42 million for shows. A rights offering will be used to raise the necessary capital from existing shareholders. Each of the six million shareholders will receive one right. The subscription price is $14 per share, and the market price of the existing shares is currently $17. Calculate the value of a right at the present time.

21. Walker Machine Tools has five million shares of common stock outstanding. The current market price of Walker common stock is $42 per share rights-on. The company's net income this year is $15 million. A rights offering has been announced in which 500,000 new shares will be sold at $36.50 per share. The subscription price of $36.50 plus 10 rights is needed to buy one of the new shares.

a. What are the EPS and P/E ratio before the new shares are sold via the rights offering?

b. What would be the EPS immediately after the rights offering? What would be the P/E ratio immediately after the rights offering? (Assume there is no change in the market value of the common stock, except for the change that occurs when the stock begins trading ex-rights.)

22. The Shelton Corporation has some excess cash that it would like to invest in marketable securities for a long-term hold. Its vice-president of finance is considering three investments (Shelton Corporation is in a 25 percent tax bracket). Which one should he select based on aftertax return: (a) Government bonds at a 3 percent yield; (b) corporate bonds at a 6 percent yield; or (c) preferred stock at a 5 percent yield?

23. National Health Corporation (NHC) has a cumulative preferred stock issue outstanding, which has a stated annual dividend of $9 per share. The company has been losing money and has not paid preferred dividends for the last five years. There are 300,000 shares of preferred stock outstanding and 600,000 shares of common stock.

   a. How much is the company behind in preferred dividends?

   b. If NHC earns $11,000,000 in the coming year after taxes and before dividends, and this is all paid out to the preferred shareholders, how much will the company be in arrears (behind in payments)? Keep in mind that the coming year would represent the sixth year.

   c. How much, if any, would be available in common stock dividends in the coming year if $11,000,000 is earned as explained in part *b*?

24. Osmond Dental Products is four years in arrears on cumulative preferred stock dividends. There are 850,000 preferred shares outstanding, and the annual dividend is $6.50 per share. The vice-president of finance sees no real hope of paying the dividends in arrears. She is devising a plan to compensate the preferred shareholders for 90 percent of the dividends in arrears.

   a. How much should the compensation be?

   b. Osmond will compensate the preferred shareholders in the form of bonds paying 12 percent interest in a market environment in which the going rate of interest is 14 percent. The bonds will have a 15-year maturity. Indicate the market value of a $1,000 par value bond.

   c. Based on market value, how many bonds must be issued to provide the compensation determined in part *a*?

25. Enterprise Storage Company has 400,000 shares of cumulative preferred stock outstanding, which has a stated dividend of $4.75. It is six years in arrears in its dividend payments.

   a. How much in total dollars is the company behind in its payments?

   b. The firm proposes to offer new common shares to the preferred shareholders to wipe out the deficit. The common stock will pay the following dividends over the next four years:

D_1	$1.25
D_2	1.50
D_3	1.75
D_4	2.00

    The company anticipates earnings per share after four years will be $4.05 with a P/E ratio of 12.

    The common stock will be valued as the present value of future dividends plus the present value of the future stock price after four years. The discount rate used by the investment dealer is 10 percent. What is the calculated value of the common stock?

   c. How many shares of common stock must be issued at the value computed in part *b* to eliminate the deficit (arrears) computed in part *a*?

26. The treasurer of Garcia Mexican Food Restaurants (a corporation) currently has $100,000 invested in preferred stock yielding 7.5 percent. He appreciates the tax advantages of preferred stock and is considering buying $100,000 more with borrowed funds. The cost of the borrowed funds is 9.5 percent. He suggests this proposal to his board of directors. The directors are somewhat concerned by the fact that the treasurer is paying 2 percent more for funds than he is earning. The firm is in a 25 percent tax bracket.

   a. Compute the amount of the aftertax income from the additional preferred stock if it is purchased.

   b. Compute the aftertax borrowing cost to purchase the additional preferred stock. That is, multiply the interest cost times $(1 - t)$.

c. Should the treasurer proceed with his proposal?

d. If interest rates and dividend yields in the market go up six months after a decision to purchase is made, what impact will this have on the outcome?

27. Referring back to the original information in the previous problem, if the yield on the $100,000 of preferred stock is still 7.5 percent and the borrowing cost remains 9.5 percent, but the tax rate is only 20 percent, is this a feasible investment?

28. Hailey Transmission has two classes of preferred stock: floating-rate preferred stock and straight (normal) preferred stock. Both issues have a par value of $100. The floating-rate preferred stock pays an annual dividend yield of 7 percent, and the straight preferred stock pays 8 percent. Since the issuance of the two securities, interest rates have gone up by 3 percent for each issue. Both securities will pay their year-end dividend today.

a. What is the price of the floating-rate preferred stock likely to be?

b. What is the price of the straight preferred stock likely to be?

COMPREHENSIVE PROBLEMS

29. The Crandall Corporation currently has 100,000 shares outstanding that are selling at $50 per share. It needs to raise $900,000. Net income after taxes is $500,000. Its vice-president of finance and its investment dealer have decided on a rights offering, but they are not sure how much to discount the subscription price from the current market value. Discounts of 10 percent, 20 percent, and 40 percent have been suggested. Common stock is the sole means of financing for the Crandall Corporation.

a. For each discount, determine the subscription price, the number of shares to be issued, and the number of rights required to purchase one share. (Round to one place after the decimal point where necessary.)

b. Determine the value of one right under each of the plans. (Round to two places after the decimal point.)

c. Compute the EPS before and immediately after the rights offering under a 10 percent discount from the subscription price.

d. By what percentage has the number of shares outstanding increased?

e. Shareholder X had 100 shares before the rights offering and participated by buying 20 new shares. Compute his total claim to earnings both before and after the rights offering; that is, multiply shares by the EPS figures computed in part **c.**

f. Should shareholder X be satisfied with this claim over a longer period of time?

30. Snyder Meat Packing Co. is a small firm that has been very profitable over the past five years and has also exhibited a strong earnings growth trend. Mr. Snyder owns 35 percent of the three million shares of common stock outstanding, but he is nevertheless worried about being taken over by a larger firm in the future. He has read some articles in the *Financial Post* about techniques used to discourage forced mergers and takeovers. The firm currently uses majority voting for nine directors. Mr. Snyder wonders which of the following proposals would make it easier for him to reject a takeover bid.

a. What would be the effect of cumulative voting?

b. What would be accomplished if shareholders could vote for only one-third of the directors every year (staggered terms)?

c. Should Mr. Snyder reduce or increase the number of directors? Does the answer to this question depend on majority rule or cumulative voting?

31. Dr. Robert Grossman founded Electro Cardio Systems Inc. (ECS), nine years ago. The principal purpose of the firm was to engage in research and development of heart

pump devices. Although the firm did not show a profit until year four, by this last year it reported aftertax earnings of $1.2 million. The company had gone public six years ago, three years after it started at $10.00 a share. Investors were initially interested in buying the stock because of its future prospects. By year-end last year, the stock was trading at $42.00 per share because the firm had made good on its promise to produce life-saving heart pumps and, in the process, was now making reasonable earnings. With 850,000 shares outstanding EPS were $1.41.

Dr. Grossman and the members of the board of directors were initially pleased when another firm, Parker Medical Products, began buying their stock. John Parker, the chairman and CEO of Parker Medical Products, was thought to be a shrewd investor, and the fact that his firm bought 50,000 shares of ECS was taken as an affirmation of the success of the heart pump research firm. However, when Parker bought the next 50,000 shares, Dr. Grossman and members of the board of directors of ECS became concerned that Parker and his firm might be trying to take over ECS.

Upon talking to his attorney, Dr. Grossman was reminded that ECS had a poison pill provision that took effect when any outside investor accumulated 25 percent or more of the shares outstanding. Current shareholders, excluding the potential takeover company, were given the privilege of buying up to 500,000 new shares of ECS at 80 percent of current market value. Thus, new shares were restricted to friendly interests. The attorney also found that Dr. Grossman and "friendly" members of the board of directors currently owned 175,000 shares of ECS.

a. How many more shares would Parker Medical Products need to purchase before the poison pill provision went into effect? Given the current price of ECS stock of $42.00, what would be the cost to Parker to get up to that level?

b. ECS's ultimate fear was that Parker Medical Products would gain over a 50 percent interest in its shares outstanding. What would be the additional cost to Parker to get to 50 percent (plus 1 share) of the stock outstanding of ECS at the current market price of ECS stock? In answering this question, assume Parker had previously accumulated the 25 percent position discussed in part *a.*

c. Now assume that Parker exceeds the number of shares you computed in part *b* and gets all the way up to accumulating 625,000 shares of ECS. Under the poison pill provision, how many shares must "friendly" shareholders purchase to thwart a takeover attempt by Parker? What will be the total cost? Keep in mind that friendly interests already own 175,000 shares of ECS and to maintain control they must own one more share than Parker.

d. Would you say the poison pill is an effective deterrent in this case? Is the poison pill in the best interest of the general shareholders (those not associated with the company)?

MINI CASE

Alpha Biogenetics

Alpha Biogenetics was founded 13 years ago by Steve Menger, PhD, M.D. At the time, the company consisted of little more than a one-room laboratory, Dr. Menger, and a lab assistant. However, Dr. Menger's outstanding research attracted the attention of the Scientific Venture Capital Fund, and by 20XT the venture capital fund had contributed $4 million in so-called "risk capital" funding. The financial support of the fund along with the work of Dr. Menger and other scientists who joined the company allowed Alpha Biogenetics to develop potential leading-edge drugs in the areas of growth hormones, microgenes, and glycosylation inhibitors.

In the year 20XT, the company achieved its first profit of $1,600,000 and made a public offering of 2 million new shares at a price of $9.60 per share. At the same time, the Scientific Venture Capital Fund sold the 1.2 million shares it had received for its capital contributions, also at $9.60 per share. In the parlance of investment banking, the venture capitalist "cashed in its position."

Between the 2 million new shares sold by the firm and the 1.2 million old shares sold by the venture capitalist, 3.2 million shares were put in the hands of the public. At the same time, Dr. Menger held one million shares, three other PhDs working for the company had 600,000 shares in total, and Ami Barnes, the chief financial officer, owned 200,000 shares. Altogether, the insiders owned 1.8 million shares, or 36 percent of the total of 5 million shares outstanding.

Outside shares	3.2 million	(64%)
Insider shares	1.8 million	(36%)
Shares outstanding	5.0 million	(100%)

By 20XX, total earnings had increased to $4,800,000, and the stock price was $33.60. Also, many of the firm's products were well received in the biotech community.

However, there was one problem that troubled Dr. Menger and the other inside investors. They had control of only a minority interest of 36 percent of the shares outstanding. If an unfriendly takeover offer were to be made, they could be voted out of control of the company. In the early stages of the company's development, this was an unlikely event, but such was no longer the case. The company now had products that others in the biotech industry, such as Biogen, Cygnus, and Genentech might wish to acquire through a takeover. Most of these firms had their own high-quality scientists who could quickly relate to the products being developed by Dr. Menger and Alpha Biogenetics.

Dr. Menger was particularly concerned because the year 20XY was not likely to be as good as prior ones and could make the company's shareholders a little less happy with its performance. Management was about to settle a lawsuit against the firm, which could have adverse consequences in the year 20XY. Also, two of the firm's major clients were encountering severe financial difficulties and certain write-offs related to this were inevitable in the year 20XY.

Dr. Menger expressed his concern to Bill Larson, who was a partner in the investment banking firm of Caruthers, Larson, and Rosen. Bill had been heavily involved in the initial public offering in 20XT of Alpha Biogenetics, when his firm was the lead underwriter.

In response to Dr. Menger's concerns about an unfriendly takeover, Bill suggested the possibility of a poison pill. He said that poison pill provisions were used by many public corporations to thwart potentially unfriendly takeovers.

Poison pills could take many different forms, but Bill suggested that the controlling inside shareholders be allowed to purchase up to 1,500,000 new shares in the firm at 70 percent of current market value if an outside group acquired 25 percent or more of the current shares outstanding. This provision could discourage a potential takeover offer, as we shall see. Furthermore, Bill explained that poison pills do not require the approval of shareholders to implement as is true of other forms of anti-takeover amendments.

At the firm's 20XX annual meeting held in the second week of March 20XY, Dr. Menger discussed the firm's financial performance for 20XX as well as seven other items on the agenda, including the election of members of the board of directors, the approval of the firm's auditors from Deloitte & Touche, and the announcement of the poison pill provision that the firm planned to implement in the next two months.

Dr. Menger was somewhat surprised at the strong reaction that he got on the latter item. An institutional shareholder that represented the Ontario Public Employees Retirement System (OPERS) said her multi-billion-dollar pension fund was really turned off by poison pill provisions and that other large institutional investors felt the same way. She said that the role of corporate management was to maximize shareholder wealth, and anti-takeover provisions, such as poison pills, tended to discourage tender offers to purchase firms at premiums over current market value.

She further stated that poison pills tended to protect current management against the threat of being displaced and, therefore, gave them a feeling of security that sometimes led to poor decisions and encouraged unusually high compensation packages and even potential laziness.

There was a hush in the room after her remarks. Dr. Menger felt compelled to answer her charges and stated that the poison pill provision was not intended to protect poor performance but was being put into place to provide a sense of permanency to the current management. He said that if management became overly concerned with job security and short-term quarter-to-quarter performance, they would not take a long-term perspective that was essential to building a company for the future. As an example, he suggested that R&D expenditures might be cut back to beef up a quarterly earnings report.

He also said that a sense of security and permanency allowed the company to compete for top-notch scientists and managers who otherwise would be hesitant to give up their current positions to go to a company that was a takeover target.

Bill Larson, the firm's investment banker, also got into the discussion. He said that although in certain instances poison pills thwarted potential shareholder value-maximizing offers, in other cases they had the opposite effect. Because the company was protected against capricious or minimal takeover offers, companies that wanted to acquire firms with poison pill provisions tended to offer a premium price well above the average offer. This was necessary because the firm could easily deflect a normal offer.

As Dr. Menger took all these comments in, he decided to have one last meeting with his executive committee on the topic of implementing a poison pill provision.

a. What were the EPS and P/E ratio in the year that the firm went public (20XT)?

b. Assuming a 5 percent underwriting spread, and $120,000 in out-of-pocket costs, what were the net proceeds to the corporation?

c. What rate of return did the Scientific Venture Capital Fund earn on its $4 million investment? Does this appear to be reasonable?

d. What were EPS in 20XX? Based on the share price of $33.60, what was the P/E ratio?

e. Under the poison pill provision, how much would it cost an unfriendly outside party to acquire 25 percent of the shares outstanding at the 20XX share price?

f. Now assume an unfriendly outside party acquired all the shares not owned by the inside control group. How many shares must the inside control group buy from the corporation to maintain its majority position? What would be the total dollar cost?

g. Based on the pro and con arguments made at the annual meeting, do you think that poison pills are in the best interests of shareholders?

Dividend Policy and Retained Earnings

LEARNING OBJECTIVES

LO1 Justify management's decision criteria as to whether internally generated funds should be reinvested or paid out as dividends.

LO2 Describe a dividend payment as a passive or active decision based on investor preference and the informational content of dividends. Calculate dividend payout ratios and dividend yields.

LO3 Outline the many factors to be considered in dividend policy. Calculate aftertax income from dividends and calculate share prices based on earnings multiples.

LO4 Outline the life cycle and growth of dividends.

LO5 Outline dividend payment procedures.

LO6 Distinguish the effect of stock splits and stock dividends on the position of the shareholders. Calculate the changes in the balance sheet that result.

LO7 Discuss the reasons for a share repurchase.

LO8 Explain a dividend reinvestment plan.

Owners of successful small businesses must continually decide what to do with the profits their firms have generated. One option is to reinvest in the business—purchasing new plant and equipment, expanding inventory, and perhaps hiring new employees. Another alternative is to withdraw the funds from the business and invest them elsewhere. Prospective uses might include buying other stocks and bonds, purchasing a second business, or perhaps spending a lost weekend in Las Vegas.

A corporation and its shareholders face exactly the same type of decision. Should funds associated with profits of the corporation be reinvested in assets of the business or be paid to shareholders in the form of dividends or through share repurchases?

FINANCE IN ACTION

Dividends/Repurchases or Reinvestment

Profit reinvestment or distribution to shareholders seems to go through cycles brought on by economic turns or new government policies.

In 2012 there were significant special dividends in the United States in anticipation of tax increases in 2013. Costco paid a special dividend of $7 per share, totalling over $3 billion.

After the U.S. tax cuts of 2017, which slashed corporate tax rates from 35 to 21 percent, corporations repatriated vast amounts of capital from overseas. Although in some cases reinvestment occurred, almost $1 trillion was returned to shareholders by share buybacks. Apple, besides increasing its dividend, had bought back about $200 billion in shares by 2020.

Then the Covid-19 pandemic struck in 2020, drying up corporate cash flow and forcing corporations to cut back on dividends and share repurchases. That cash paid out in the previous few years would have come in handy!

The same pattern of economic circumstances reversing has been seen in the firms. In 1989, Inco Ltd. paid a special dividend of US$10 per share, for a total cash payout of US$1.1 billion. The regular dividend over the previous six years had been $0.20 annually. The day the dividend was paid, Inco's share price fell by US$10.

Inco had cash surpluses from significant increases in nickel prices. Inco management decided not to reinvest and returned capital to shareholders. The shareholders and the market responded well to the dividend payment. Yet a couple of years later it did not have the capital resources to develop its discovery of its large iron ore deposit in Labrador. Inco has since been bought by Vale Corporation.

In early 2014, Sears Canada paid a special dividend of $5.00 per share, for a total payout of $500 million, after selling properties worth over $300 million. It had paid special dividends in 2010 and 2012 as well. Share prices jumped on the original announcement, despite losses on operations. Sears wasn't reinvesting in its operations nor adapting to the changing retail market. In 2017 it filed for bankruptcy protection.

Q1 If shareholders responded well to the special dividend, why did Inco's share price fall by about US$10?

Q2 Are special dividends an appropriate alternative to reinvestment strategies? Why or why not?

Q3 Why has Apple been increasing dividends and buying back shares?

investor.apple.com
tmx.com
Symbol: AAPL, VALE

DIVIDEND THEORIES

LO1 The Marginal Principle of Retained Earnings

With focus on long-term strategy, corporate directors should theoretically ask, "How can we make the best use of company funds?" The rate of return the corporation can achieve through reinvestment (retained earnings) for the benefit of shareholders must be compared to what shareholders could earn if the funds were paid to them in dividends. This is known as the marginal principle of retained earnings. Each potential project to be financed by reinvestment of internally generated funds must provide a higher rate of return than the shareholder could achieve alone. The return on reinvested funds will be obtained by the capital appreciation of the share price. This is the opportunity cost of using shareholder funds, and if the firm cannot achieve the required rate of return on reinvested earnings, they should be paid out to shareholders, usually as dividends.

Residual Theory

The marginal principle of retained earnings suggests that dividends are a passive decision variable. They are to be paid out only if the corporation cannot make better use of the funds for the benefit of shareholders. The active decision variable is retained earnings, based on reinvestment. Management decides how much retained earnings will be spent for internal corporate needs, and the residual (the amount left after internal expenditures) is paid out to the shareholders in cash dividends. This is the residual theory of dividends.

This concept parallels the idea of free cash flow discussed in Chapter 2. For example,

Cash flow from operations............................	$1,000,000
Less: Capital investments (+ NPVs)	600,000
Residual: Dividends	400,000

An Incomplete Theory

The problem with the residual theory of dividends is that we have not given recognition to how shareholders feel about receiving dividends. If the shareholders' only concern is with achieving the highest return on their investment, either in the form of corporate retained earnings remaining in the business or as current dividends paid out, then there is no issue. But if shareholders have a preference for current funds over retained earnings, then our theory is incomplete. The issue is not only whether investment of retained earnings or dividends provides the highest return, but also how shareholders react to the two alternatives.

Some researchers maintain that shareholders are indifferent to the division of funds between retained earnings and dividends[1] (holding investment opportunities constant), but others disagree.[2] Though there is no conclusive proof one way or the other, the judgment of most researchers is that investors have some preference between dividends and retained earnings. Certainly, most financial managers believe investors have a preference as evidenced by the dividend-paying records of firms.

Arguments for the Irrelevance of Dividends

- Dividend policy is irrelevant to the valuation of the firm, in perfect markets.
- Assuming there are no costs to producing one's own dividend, shareholders are indifferent to when dividends are paid as they can achieve the same result on their own. A firm may pay a final liquidating dividend.

---

[1] Merton H. Miller and Franco Modigliani, "Dividend Policy, Growth and Valuation of Shares," *Journal of Business* 34 (October 1961), pp. 411–33. Under conditions of perfect capital markets with an absence of taxes and flotation costs, it is argued that the sum of discounted value per share after dividend payments equals the total valuation before dividend payments.

[2] Myron J. Gordon, "Optimum Investment and Financing Policy," *Journal of Finance* 18 (May 1963), pp. 264–77; and John Lintmer, "Dividends, Earnings, Leverage, Stock Prices, and the Supply of Capital to the Corporation," *Review of Economics and Statistics* 44 (August 1962), pp. 243–69.

Figure 18–1 establishes homemade dividends as an argument to suggest investor indifference to the timing of dividend payments. The scenario:

- Shareholder owns 100 shares
- Year 1 expected dividend of $5 per share
- Year 2 liquidating dividend of $5 per share (no value left in the firm)
- Expected rate of return on investment is 16.25 percent
- Therefore the share is valued at $8 (Part A)

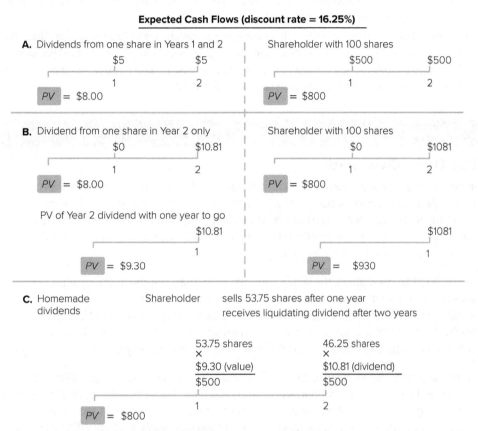

Figure 18–1 Homemade dividends

If the Year 1 dividend is omitted and reinvested at the 16.25 percent return expected by shareholders, the shares are valued at the same $8. In Year 2, the firm will pay a dividend consisting of the original liquidating dividend of $5 plus $5.81 ($5 × 1.1625). The present value of $10.81 two years from the present at 16.25 percent is $8. If the first dividend is omitted, the value of the $10.81 with one year to go is $9.30 (Part B).

However, the shareholder with 100 shares may value an annual cash flow of $500 ($5 × 100) and might not want the dividend at Year 1 delayed. The homemade dividend argument suggests that this investor can still have the desired cash flow of $500. The shares at the end of Year 1 (if the dividend is not paid) will be worth $930 ($9.30 × 100) on the basis of the present worth of their liquidating value of $1,081 ($10.81 × 100). By selling 53.75 shares, the shareholder can realize $500 ($9.30 × 53.75), which is the same as would have been received if the $5 dividend had been paid.

In the second year, the investor will also receive $500 ($10.81 × 46.25) from the dividend of $10.81 on the remaining 46.25 shares that are still held. Figure 18–1 shows the effect of selling some shares in Year 1 and receiving the liquidating dividend on the remaining shares.

Cash flow received from an equity investment by selling shares is referred to as a "homemade dividend."

Arguments for the Relevance of Dividends

The primary contention in arguing for the relevance of dividend policy is that shareholders' needs and preferences go beyond the marginal principle of retained earnings. The issue is not only who can best utilize the funds (the corporation or the shareholders), but also what are shareholders' preferences.

- Dividend payouts are relevant because they resolve uncertainty in the minds of investors. Though earnings reinvested in the business theoretically belong to common shareholders, there is still an air of uncertainty about their eventual translation into dividends.

- Shareholders apply a higher discount rate (K_e) to yield a lower valuation to funds retained in the business as opposed to those that are paid out.[3]

- Dividends have information content. In essence, the corporation is telling the shareholder, "We are having a good year, and we wish to share the benefits with you." If the dividend per share is raised, then the information content of the dividend increase is quite positive, while a reduction in the dividend generally has negative informational content.

 FINANCE IN ACTION

Pay Those Dividends!

In late 2019 Dorel Industries of Montreal, a maker of Schwinn and Cannondale bikes, suspended its dividend. Subsequently, its share price dropped by about 30 percent. Dorel stated that its cash flow would be significantly impacted by the U.S. increase in tariffs on Chinese goods. A significant portion of Dorel's business was selling product sourced from China to American retail chains.

In mid-2017 Home Capital, the largest non-bank mortgage lender in the country, suffered a "run on the non-bank" with up to 95 percent of its high interest deposits being withdrawn. Its dividend was suspended to preserve liquidity. Share prices dropped to $5.00. Then one of the world's wealthiest investors, Warren Buffett, provided a $2 billion line of credit and $400 million of equity. Share prices have since recovered.

TransCanada Pipelines, now TC Energy, became the poster firm for the pitfall of cutting dividends. Its share price dropped significantly after the dividend was reduced in 1999, even though management maintained that the cut would allow TransCanada to refocus the corporate strategy and to reinvest in worthy capital projects. Investors did not buy it at the time, but as management demonstrated effective capital decisions, the share price responded well through the generally weak markets of the early 2000s.

Interestingly, TELUS also cut its dividend in late 2001 to redeploy the monies into capital projects, and the market responded favourably to the news. In this case, the market saw the wisdom of reinvesting the capital. Charts of a firm's performance can be viewed through the TSX website (tsx.com).

Investors waffle on whether or not they value reinvestment in capital projects or higher dividend payouts, especially after disappointing earnings results, poor investments, or questionable business practices. Some suggest that a dividend payout prevents management from investing in marginal projects.

In the wake of the oil spill crisis of 2010, British Petroleum (BP) suspended its quarterly dividend of $2.6 billion to assist in the compensation for victims of its oil disaster. The announcement was the first time the company had suspended dividends.

---

[3] See Note 2.

In practice, it appears that most corporations adhere to the following logic. First, investment opportunities relative to a required return (marginal analysis) are determined. This is then tempered by some subjective notion of shareholders' desires. Corporations with unusual growth prospects and high rates of return on internal investments generally pay a relatively low dividend (perhaps for its informational content). For the more mature firm, an analysis of both investment opportunities and shareholder preferences may indicate a higher rate of payout is necessary.

DIVIDENDS IN PRACTICE

LO2 Dividend Payouts

Dividend policies of selected major Canadian corporations are presented in Table 18–1, over a recent 10-year period. The payout ratio is the dividend as a percentage of earnings. The Bank of Montreal, which has maintained an uninterrupted dividend since 1829, had an average payout ratio of about 50 percent over the period. Its dividend policy appears to be a relatively consistent percentage of earnings. Canadian Tire, with steadily increasing earnings, has maintained a payout ratio of around 25 percent.

Bank of Montreal
bmo.com

Table 18–1 Earnings and dividends of selected Canadian corporations

	Ten-Year	2019	2018	2017	2016	2015	2014	2013	2012	2011	2010
Bank of Montreal											
Earnings (total)	$67.74	$9.66	$8.17	$7.93	$6.94	$6.59	$6.44	$6.27	$6.15	$4.84	$4.75
Dividends (total)	$29.37	$4.06	$3.78	$3.56	$3.40	$3.24	$3.08	$2.94	$2.80	$2.80	$2.80
Payout ratio (average)	48%	42%	46%	45%	49%	49%	48%	47%	46%	58%	59%
Canadian Tire											
Earnings	$83.62	$12.58	$10.64	$10.67	$9.22	$8.61	$7.59	$6.91	$6.13	$5.71	$5.56
Dividends	$21.81	$4.25	$3.74	$2.85	$2.30	$2.10	$1.88	$1.40	$1.25	$1.13	$0.91
Payout ratio	26%	34%	35%	27%	25%	24%	25%	20%	20%	20%	16%
Air Canada											
Earnings	$16.79	$5.44	$0.60	$7.31	$3.10	$3.10	$1.03	$0.34	$0.02	−$0.51	−$0.91
Dividends	$0.00	$0.00	$0.00	$0.00	$0.00	$0.00	$0.00	$0.00	$0.00	$0.00	$0.00
Payout ratio	0%	0%	0%	0%	0%	0%	0%	0%	0%	0%	0%
BCE Inc.											
Earnings	$30.30	$3.37	$3.10	$3.11	$3.33	$2.98	$2.97	$2.54	$3.17	$2.88	$2.85
Dividends	$25.24	$3.17	$3.02	$2.87	$2.73	$2.60	$2.47	$2.33	$2.22	$2.05	$1.78
Payout ratio	83%	94%	97%	92%	82%	87%	83%	92%	70%	71%	62%
Suncor											
Earnings	$16.62	$1.86	$2.02	$2.68	$0.27	−$1.38	$1.84	$2.60	$1.79	$2.67	$2.27
Dividends	$9.78	$1.68	$1.44	$1.28	$1.16	$1.14	$1.02	$0.73	$0.50	$0.43	$0.40
Payout ratio	59%	90%	71%	48%	430%	n.a.	55%	28%	28%	16%	18%

Even where earnings per share have declined, the continuance of historical dividend patterns is important. Dofasco had paid a dividend every year since 1937 until losses in the early 1990s caused it to miss its 1993 dividend. Dividends were reinstated and Dofasco grew significantly through the 1990s and early 2000s. In 2006, Dofasco became a subsidiary of ArcelorMittal.

BCE, on the other hand, had increased its dividend each year for 20 years until 1995. Changing technology increased the company's capital expenditures in the late 1990s, the Nortel spinoff in 2000 cut its dividend, and the financial crisis of 2008 had an impact. Since then BCE has returned to annual increases in its dividend payout. Suncor has followed a similar pattern during this 10-year period.

At the other end of the spectrum, Air Canada has had strong growth after its time in bankruptcy but has not yet paid dividends. The company has required large amounts of capital to fund its business. Air Canada has had its ups and downs over the years, and the Covid-19 pandemic of 2020 will affect the company significantly.

Dividend Yields

In 2020, fewer than 50 companies on the Toronto Stock Exchange had maintained dividends for over 25 years, down from almost 100 in 1980. Of the over 1,500 companies listed on the exchange, about half paid a dividend. The dividend yield (dividends/market share price) for the S&P/TSX Composite companies has been approximately 3 percent over an extended period of time. In 2020 depressed share prices had significantly increased dividend yields.

Table 18–2 displays the dividend yields for selected Canadian companies. Remember, dividends are not taxed as heavily as interest income. Holding companies, utilities, and banks generally offer the highest dividend yields.

Table 18–2 Dividend yields on selected common shares, March 2020 (distorted by Covid-19 pandemic impact on share prices)

Company	Current	Symbol
Inter Pipeline	20.17%	IPL
Power Corp.	8.43	POW
BCE	6.55	BCE
National Bank	6.13	NA
TC Energy	5.83	TRP

Dividend Stability

In considering shareholders' desires in dividend policy, a primary factor is the maintenance of stability in dividend payments. Thus, corporate management must not only ask, "How many profitable investments do we have this year?" but also, "What has been the pattern of dividend payments in the last few years?" Though earnings may change from year to year, the dollar amount of cash dividends tends to be much more stable, increasing in value only as new permanent levels of income are achieved while resisting any downward adjustment. Note in Figure 18–2 the stable dividends and the considerably greater volatility of earnings for Canadian corporations. During the early 1990s, and again in 2001, as earnings dipped, dividends were greater than earnings.

Investors seem to have a psychological disposition toward a dividend payment pattern that is stable and predictable. For them, it resolves some uncertainty about the firm's operations and the investors are prepared to reward the firm with higher share prices. To the investor this predictability has value. In the last number of years, increased dividends and stability in the payment of dividends have again become valued highly in the capital markets. Increased dividend yields have been observed and income trusts with high dividend yields have been popular.

By maintaining a record of relatively stable dividends, corporate management hopes to lower the discount rate (K_e) applied to future dividends of the firm. A higher share price lowers the cost of capital. The operative assumption appears to be that a shareholder would much prefer to receive

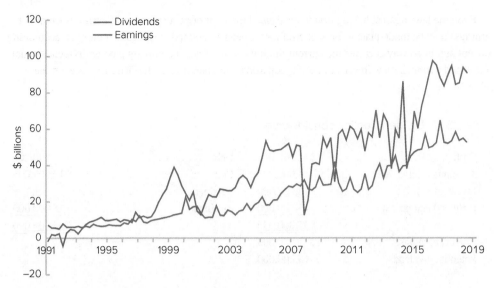

Figure 18–2 Corporate earnings and dividends (all industries)

$1 per year for three years rather than 75 cents for the first year, $1.50 for the second year, and 75 cents for the third year—for the same $3 total.

We temper our theory of marginal analysis of retained earnings to include a notion of shareholder preference, with the emphasis on dividend stability. The dividend payout patterns in Table 18–1 and Figure 18–2 seem to demonstrate this consideration.

LO3 OTHER FACTORS INFLUENCING DIVIDEND POLICY

Corporate management must also consider the legal basis of dividends, the cash flow position of the firm, and the corporation's access to capital markets. Other factors that must be considered include management's desire for control and the tax and financial position of shareholders.

Legal Rules

Canadian firms are not permitted to pay dividends that would impair the initial capital contributions to the firm. For this reason, dividends may be distributed only from past and current earnings. To pay dividends in excess of this amount would mean the corporation is returning to investors their original capital contributions (raiding the capital). If the ABC Company has the following statement of net worth, the maximum dividend payment possible would be $20 million.

Common stock (1 million shares)	$10,000,000
Retained earnings.	20,000,000
Net worth	$30,000,000

Why all the concern about impairing permanent capital? Since the firm is going to pay dividends only to those who contributed capital in the first place, what is the problem? There is no abuse to the shareholders, but what about the creditors? They have extended credit on the assumption that a given capital base would remain intact throughout the life of the loan. Though they may not object to the payment of dividends from past and current earnings, they must have the protection of keeping contributed capital in place.[4]

---

[4] Of course, on liquidation of the corporation, the contributed capital to the firm may be returned to common shareholders after creditor obligations are met. Normally, shareholders who need to recoup all or part of their contributed capital sell their shares to someone else.

Even the laws against having dividends exceed the total of past and current earnings (retained earnings) may be inadequate to protect creditors. Because retained earnings is merely an accounting concept and in no way certifies the current liquidity of the firm, a company paying dividends equal to retained earnings may, in certain cases, jeopardize the operation of the firm. Let us examine Table 18–3.

Table 18–3 Dividend policy considerations

Cash	$ 1,000,000	Debt	$10,000,000
Accounts receivable	4,000,000	Common stock	10,000,000
Inventory	15,000,000	Retained	
Plant and equipment	15,000,000	earnings	15,000,000
	$35,000,000		$35,000,000
Current earnings	$ 1,500,000		
Potential dividends	15,000,000		

Theoretically, management could pay up to $15 million in dividends by selling assets even though current earnings are only $1.5 million. In most cases, such frivolous action would not be taken, but the mere possibility encourages creditors to closely watch the balance sheets of corporate debtors and, at times, to impose additional limits on dividend payments as a condition for the granting of credit.

Company directors are also prohibited from declaring dividends when the company is insolvent or when the payment of dividends would make the company insolvent. Both legal insolvency (liabilities exceeding assets) and technical insolvency (inability to pay creditors) are included. This restriction is meant to prevent troubled firms from acting to the advantage of shareholders at the obvious expense of creditors. Furthermore, a corporation may be prevented from paying dividends if the conditions under bond indentures or loan provisions are not fulfilled. Debtholders are not eager to see their security position weakened by cash payouts if the corporation doesn't perform to certain expectations.

Cash Position of the Firm

Not only do retained earnings fail to portray the liquidity position of the firm, but there are also limitations to the use of current earnings to indicate liquidity. As described in Chapter 4, a growth firm producing the greatest gains in earnings may be in the poorest cash position. As sales and earnings expand rapidly, there is an accompanying buildup in receivables and inventory that may far outstrip cash flow generated through earnings. Note that the cash balance in Table 18–3 represents only two-thirds of current earnings of $1.5 million. A firm must do a complete analysis of funds available before establishing a dividend policy.

For the small business owner, their cash position may be relevant. Does the owner desire the cash for personal reasons, and what are the tax consequences relative to salary? This decision can seem somewhat arbitrary as compared to a broadly based decision process.

Access to Capital Markets

The medium-to-large-size firm with a good record of performance may have relatively easy access to the financial markets. A company in such a position may be willing to pay dividends now, knowing it can sell new stock or bonds in the future if funds are needed. Some corporations may even issue debt or stock now and use part of the proceeds to ensure the maintenance of current dividends. Though this policy seems at variance with the concept of a dividend as a reward, management may justify its action on the basis of maintaining stable dividends. It should be clear that larger firms have sufficient ease of entry to the capital markets to modify their dividend policy in this regard. Many firms may actually defer the payment of dividends because they know they will have difficulty in going to the capital markets for more funds.

Desire for Control

Management must also consider the effect of the dividend policy on its collective ability to maintain control. The directors and officers of a small, closely held firm may be hesitant to pay any dividends for fear of diluting the cash position of the firm and forcing the owners to look to outside investors for financing. The funds may be available through venture capital sources that wish to have a large say in corporate operations.

On the other hand, a larger firm with a broad base of shareholders may face a different type of threat in regard to dividend policy. Shareholders, spoiled by a past record of dividend payments, may demand the ouster of management if dividends are withheld.

Tax Position of Shareholders

The tax rates applicable to dividend income have been subject to change over the years, and this trend will likely continue. However, the payment of a cash dividend is generally taxable to the recipient, with some feeling the burden more heavily than others. To the wealthy individual, dividend income in 2020 could have attracted a net tax of up to 28.33 to 42.61 percent, dependent on the province or territory. A medium-income taxpayer, making roughly $90,000 in taxable income, would have paid 3.4 to 23.28 percent on dividend income. In the case of the corporate recipient, the dividend payment would probably have been tax-exempt. In addition, dividends to the many large institutional investors that own so much of the common equity in the market are also usually tax-exempt.

The dividend tax credit is meant to adjust for the fact that the corporation has already paid tax on the income on which the dividend was based. To adjust for this double taxation, the dividend paid is grossed up and taxes are calculated and then reduced by a dividend tax credit. Provincial taxes are calculated in a similar manner to federal taxes. Overall, the effect on the investor is to have dividend income preferable to interest income, other things being equal. This was identified in Table 2–13. Take, for example, a case where taxes must be computed on a $1,000 dividend payment to an individual, living in Alberta, whose combined federal and provincial marginal tax bracket is 2020's top rate of 31.71 percent (for dividends).

Sample Calculation of Tax on Individual Dividend Receipt (2020)	
Dividend received	$1,000
Gross-up (38%)	380
Taxable amount	1,380
Federal tax (at 33%)	455
Less: Federal tax credit (15.0198% of $1,380)	207
Federal tax payable	248
Provincial tax payable (15% of $1,380)	207
Provincial tax credit (10% of $1,380)	138
Provincial tax payable	69
Total taxes payable	317
Net dividend ($1,000 − $317)	$ 683

The preceding is merely meant to show the nature of the dividend tax credit. Each taxpayer must make their own calculation in relation to the rules that exist for the year in question. Table 2–13 shows the top and middle combined marginal tax rates in all provinces.

For the individual, the Income Tax Act taxes capital gains at an effective rate of one-half of the individual's normal tax rate. Thus, an individual in a top tax bracket in Alberta would pay $240 tax on $1,000 of capital gains and $480 on interest income (based on Table 2–13).

Because of differences among investors' tax rates and risk preferences, certain investor preferences for dividends versus capital gains have been observed in the market. This investor behaviour is called the clientele effect. Investors in high marginal tax brackets usually prefer companies that reinvest most of their earnings, thus creating more growth in earnings and stock prices. The returns from such investments will be in the form of capital gains, which are taxed at low rates or not at all. Investors in lower tax brackets have traditionally had a preference for dividends since the tax penalty is small at lower marginal tax rates and they also receive regular returns on their investment. The clientele effect then can be used to explain the advantages of a stable dividend policy that makes investors more certain about the type and timing of their returns.

LO4 LIFE CYCLE GROWTH AND DIVIDENDS

One of the major influences on dividends is the corporate growth rate in sales and the subsequent return on assets. Figure 18–3 shows a corporate life cycle and the corresponding dividend policy that is most likely to be found at each stage.

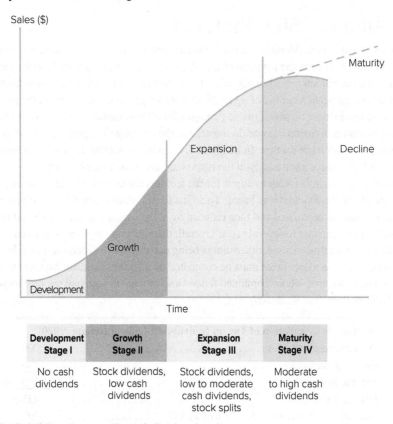

Development Stage I	Growth Stage II	Expansion Stage III	Maturity Stage IV
No cash dividends	Stock dividends, low cash dividends	Stock dividends, low to moderate cash dividends, stock splits	Moderate to high cash dividends

Figure 18–3 Life cycle growth and dividend policy

Stage I

A small firm pays no dividends because it needs all of its profits (if there are any) for reinvestment in new productive assets. If the firm is successful in the marketplace, the demand for its products will create growth in sales, earnings, and assets, and the firm will move into Stage II.

Stage II

The firm has numerous projects that add value. The projects have positive NPVs (Chapter 12), and the returns on the projects exceed shareholder expected rates of return (opportunity costs). Sales and returns on assets will be growing at an increasing rate, and earnings will still be reinvested.

- Early on, stock dividends (distribution of additional shares) may be instituted.
- Later, low cash dividends may be started to inform investors that the firm is profitable but cash is still needed for continued growth and investment. At this stage, careful financial forecasting (Chapter 4) is required. The large demand for funds will likely send the firm to the capital markets (Chapter 14) as internal funds are not usually sufficient to meet the growth demands.

Microsoft's Life Cycle

From the time it went public in 1987 until 2003, Microsoft did not pay dividends to its shareholders. It reinvested funds into the company, accumulating huge amounts of cash reserves by the new millennium. Shareholders saw stock (share) splits but no dividends. A small, semiannual dividend began in 2003 as cash flow continued to accumulate in significant amounts.

In July 2004, Microsoft announced a special dividend of $3 per share for a total payout of $32 billion, a buyback of outstanding shares totalling $30 billion, and an adjustment toward a regular quarterly dividend ($0.08 per share).

Since 2004, Microsoft has paid out regular and increasing dividends. By 2020 the annual dividend was $2.04, about 40 percent of earnings. Microsoft continued to hold large cash and marketable securities positions (about $134 billion).

Q1 How has Microsoft's stage in the life cycle (with evidence) changed over time?

Q2 What is Microsoft's current cash position? Is it appropriate?

microsoft.com/investor/default.aspx
Symbol: MSFT (NASDAQ)

Stage III

The expansion of sales continues, but at a decreasing rate, and returns on investment may decline as more competition enters the market and tries to take away the firm's market share. During this period, the firm is more and more capable of paying cash dividends, as the asset expansion rate slows and external funds become more readily available. Stock dividends and stock splits are still common in the expansion phase, and the dividend payout ratio usually increases from a low level of 5 to 15 percent of earnings to a moderate level of 25 to 40 percent of earnings.

Stage IV

At maturity, the firm maintains a stable growth rate in sales similar to that of the economy as a whole, and when risk premiums are considered, its return on assets level out to those of the industry and the economy. In unfortunate cases, firms suffer declines in sales if product innovation and diversification have not occurred over the years. In Stage IV, assuming maturity rather than decline, dividends might range from 40 to 60 percent of earnings. These percentages differ from industry to industry depending on the individual characteristics of the company, such as operating and financial leverage and the volatility of sales and earnings over the business cycle.

In a general sense, the life cycle of the firm relates to the theory and practice of dividend policy. When opportunities are good the marginal principle of retained earnings applies, but as growth slows and dividends begin, investors expect the dividends to continue for various reasons. Management at this point tries to stabilize the dividend payout.

LO5 DIVIDEND PAYMENT PROCEDURES

Now that we have examined the many factors that influence dividend policy, let us track the actual procedures for announcing and paying a dividend. Though dividends are quoted on an annual basis, the payments actually occur quarterly throughout the year.

An example of the dividend timeline occurs when a company board of directors declares a quarterly dividend:

- Declaration date   December 3, 2019
- Amount $0.90 per share
- Record date   Monday February 3, 2020
- Ex-dividend date   Friday January 31, 2020
- Payment date   February 26, 2020

The common dividend of $0.90 suggested shareholders could expect to receive $3.60 per year in dividends. With the share price at 92.50 on December 3, we calculate the annual dividend yield to be 3.9 percent ($3.60/$92.50).

As illustrated in Figure 18–4, four key dates are associated with the declaration of a quarterly dividend: the dividend declaration date, the ex-dividend date, the dividend record date, and the dividend payment date.

| Declaration date | Ex-dividend date | Record date | Payment date |
| December 3 | January 31 | February 3 | February 26 |

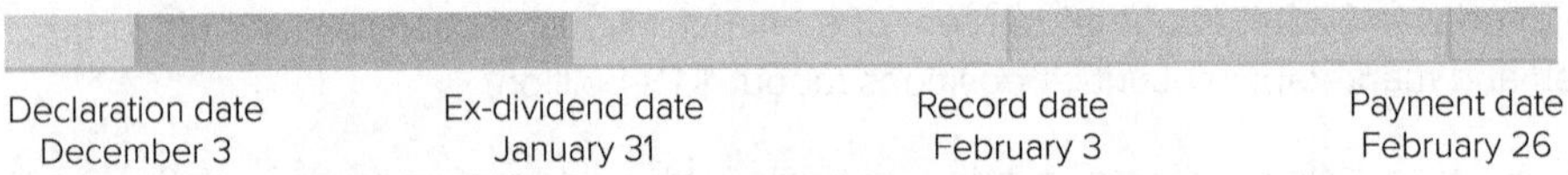

Figure 18–4 Dividend payment timeline

- On the dividend declaration date, a firm's board of directors announces the next dividend.
- The ex-dividend date is the one business day before the dividend record date. If you bought the stock on the ex-dividend date or later, your name eventually is transferred to the corporate books, but you have bought the stock without the right to receive the quarterly dividend. The previous shareholder would receive the dividend payment. Thus, if you bought the shares on January 31, you would not receive the dividend on February 26.
- The dividend record date is when the firm determines who is entitled to receive a cash dividend on that date.
- The dividend payment date is the date monies would be sent out to the entitled shareholders.

Investors are very conscious of the date on which the stock goes ex-dividend, and the value of the stock should go down by exactly the value of the dividend on the ex-dividend date (all other things being equal). This is because the dividend represents cash that will leave the firm. Studies have shown, however, that the price of the shares does not quite drop by the amount of the dividend. The reason has been attributed to tax considerations. If investors are indifferent between dividends and retention of earnings for capital gains, the share price should drop by the aftertax value of the dividend.

LO6 STOCK DIVIDEND

A stock dividend represents a distribution of additional shares to common shareholders. The typical size of such a dividend is 10 percent or less of the current amount of stock outstanding. In the case of a 10 percent stock dividend, a shareholder with 100 shares would receive 10 new shares in the form of a stock dividend. Larger distributions of 20 to 25 percent or more are usually considered to be stock splits, which are discussed later in this chapter.

Accounting Considerations for a Stock Dividend

Assume that before the declaration of a stock dividend, the XYZ Corporation has the net worth position indicated in Table 18–4.

If a 10 percent stock dividend is declared, the shares outstanding will increase by 100,000 (10 percent of 1 million shares). An accounting transfer will occur between retained earnings and the common stock account based on the market value of the stock dividend. If the stock is selling for $15 per share, we assign $1.5 million to common stock. The net worth position of XYZ after the transfer is shown in Table 18–5. In effect, retained earnings are capitalized.

Table 18–4 XYZ Corporation's financial position before stock dividend

Capital Accounts	
Common stock (1 million shares issued)......................	$15,000,000
Retained earnings..	15,000,000
Net worth...	$30,000,000

Table 18–5 XYZ Corporation's financial position after stock dividend

Capital Accounts	
Common stock (1.1 million shares issued)	$16,500,000
Retained earnings..	13,500,000
Net worth...	$30,000,000

Value to the Investor

Is a stock dividend of real value to the investor? When a stock dividend is declared, the asset base of the company remains the same, and the investor's proportionate ownership in the business is unchanged. The investor merely has more paper.

The same is true in the corporate setting. In the case of the XYZ Corporation, shown in Tables 18–4 and 18–5, we assumed that 1 million shares were outstanding before the stock dividend and that 1.1 million shares were outstanding afterward. Now let us assume the corporation had aftertax earnings of $6.6 million. Without the stock dividend, earnings per share would be $6.60, and with the dividend, would be $6.

$$\text{Earnings per share} = \frac{\text{Earnings after tax}}{\text{Shares outstanding}}$$

Without stock dividend:

$$= \frac{\$6.6 \text{ million}}{1 \text{ million shares}} = \$6.60$$

With stock dividend:

$$= \frac{\$6.6 \text{ million}}{1.1 \text{ million shares}} = \$6 \text{ (10\% decline)}$$

Earnings per share have gone down by exactly the same percentage that shares outstanding increased. For further illustration, assuming Shareholder A had 10 shares before the stock dividend and 11 afterward, what is the total claim to earnings? As expected, they remain the same at $66.

$$\text{Claims to earnings} = \text{Shares} \times \text{Earnings per share}$$

Without stock dividend:

$$10 \times \$6.60 = \$66$$

With stock dividend:

$$11 \times \$6 = \$66$$

Taking the analogy one step further, assuming the stock sold at 20 times earnings before and after the stock dividend, what is the total market value of the portfolio in each case?

$$\text{Total market value} = \text{Shares} \times (\text{Price/earnings ratio} \times \text{Earnings per share})$$

Without stock dividend:

$$10 \times (20 \times \$6.60) = 10 \times \$132 = \$1,320$$

With stock dividend:

$$11 \times (20 \times \$6) = 11 \times \$120 = \$1,320$$

The total market value is unchanged. Note that if the shareholder sells the 11th share to acquire cash, his stock portfolio is worth $120 less than it was worth before the stock dividend.

Under the federal income tax legislation that became effective May 23, 1985, stock dividends declared and paid after that date are treated as regular dividends. Previously, no tax was payable on stock dividends. This change in the tax law makes stock dividends less attractive to some shareholders than previously, and it has had a negative effect on the number of stock dividends declared.

Possible Value of Stock Dividends

There are limited circumstances under which a stock dividend may be of value. If at the time a stock dividend is declared the cash dividend per share remains constant, the shareholder receives greater total cash dividends. Assume the annual cash dividend for the XYZ Corporation remains $1 per share even though earnings per share decline from $6.60 to $6. In this instance, a shareholder moving from 10 to 11 shares as the result of a stock dividend has a $1 increase in total dividends. The overall value of their portfolio may then increase in response to larger dividends.

Use of Stock Dividends

Stock dividends are most frequently used by growth companies as a form of information content in explaining the retention of funds for reinvestment purposes. This was indicated in the discussion of the life cycle of the firm earlier in the chapter. A corporation president may state, "Instead of doing more in the way of cash dividends, we are providing a stock dividend. The funds remaining in the corporation will be used for highly profitable investment opportunities." The market reaction to such an approach may be neutral or slightly positive.

A second use of stock dividends may be to camouflage the inability of the corporation to pay cash dividends and to try to cover up the ineffectiveness of the firm's operations in generating cash flow. The president may proclaim, "Though we are unable to pay cash dividends, we wish to reward you with a 15 percent stock dividend." Well-informed investors are likely to think little of a management that uses such a strategy.

STOCK SPLITS

A stock split is similar to a stock dividend, only more shares are distributed. For example, a two-for-one stock split would double the number of shares outstanding. In general, distributions increasing the number of shares outstanding by more than 20 to 25 percent are handled as stock splits.

The accounting treatment for a stock split is somewhat different from that for a stock dividend in that there is no transfer of funds from retained earnings to the capital accounts. There is, instead, a proportionate increase in the number of shares outstanding. For example, a two-for-one stock split for the XYZ Corporation would necessitate the statement adjustments shown in Table 18–6.

Table 18–6 XYZ Corporation before and after stock split

Before	
Common stock (1 million shares issued)	$15,000,000
Retained earnings	15,000,000
Total shareholders' equity	$30,000,000
After	
Common stock (2 million shares issued)	$15,000,000
Retained earnings	15,000,000
Total shareholders' equity	$30,000,000

In this case, all adjustments are in the common stock account. Because the number of shares is doubled, the market price of the stock should drop by half. The financial literature contains much discussion about the effect of a split on overall stock value. The consensus seems to be that stock splits do not seem to add any real value to share prices.

The primary purpose of a stock split is to lower the price of a security into a more popular trading range. A stock selling for over $50 per share may be excluded from consideration by many small investors because they generally must purchase shares in lots of 100. Stronger companies that have witnessed substantial growth in market share price usually initiate splits. Once again, the evidence suggests that the price of a stock is no hindrance to its popularity, and a stock split does not add value to the company's shares.

For example, one share of Berkshire Hathaway (BRK.A), controlled by Warren Buffett, one of the world's wealthiest individuals, traded on the New York Exchange at a price above $271,000 ($347,000 before the Coronavirus slump) in March 2020. It is the large institutional investors that drive market prices, and share price does not appear to matter to these investors. Buffett maintained that share splits do not add value and were attractive only to speculators. However, in 1996, he decided to split some of the original Class A shares into 30 Class B shares, each with 1/200th the vote of a Class A share. He did this to counter unit investment trusts that had been set up to offer smaller investors a "piece" of Berkshire Hathaway. Buffett was concerned that investors would have to incur fees and commissions when investing in these unit trusts.

Berkshire Hathaway
berkshirehathaway.com

FINANCE IN ACTION

Microsoft and Stock Splits and Its Life Cycle

In 2020, Microsoft common stock had a total market capitalization of over US$1 trillion.

You might wonder how the small investor in Microsoft has fared. If an investor had bought 100 shares of common stock in Microsoft on September 1, 1987, at the market price of $1.58 per share, the investor would have spent $158 plus broker commissions. Over the years no dividends were paid until 2003 but the share split many times.

When a stock splits, its share price is adjusted accordingly. For example, if an investor has 100 shares of a $20 stock and the company splits the stock 2 for 1, the investor now has 200 shares selling at $10 per share. In the case of Microsoft, the shares had split nine times between September 1987 and February 2003. The table below illustrates how stock splits had worked for Microsoft. If you had purchased 100 shares of Microsoft in September 1987 for $158 you would have had 28,800 shares worth $718,848 in 2003.

Microsoft began paying dividends for the first time in 2003 when its share price was about $25. At the time it had about $40 billion in cash, suggesting that it was not reinvesting in solid capital projects. A first dividend or dividend increase is not always a good sign as it may indicate slower growth for the company and lower capital appreciation of the share price for investors. Microsoft was entering the later stages of its life cycle.

Stock splits have become less common in recent years as the small investor has utilized ETFs to a larger extent.

Q1 Have Microsoft shares split since 2004?

Q2 What is the current share price? The market capitalization? The share value of the original 100 shares (including dividends per share since 2003?

microsoft.com/investor/default.aspx
Symbol: MSFT (NASDAQ)

Stock Split	Amount	Number of Shares	Share Price	Value
2/14/03	2 for 1	28,800	$24.96	US$718,848
3/12/99	2 for 1	14,400		
2/20/98	2 for 1	7,200		
12/6/96	2 for 1	3,600		
5/20/94	2 for 1	1,800		
6/12/92	3 for 2	900		
6/26/91	3 for 2	600		
4/13/90	2 for 1	400		
9/18/87	2 for 1	200		
	Purchase	100	$ 1.58	$158

REPURCHASE OF STOCK AS AN ALTERNATIVE TO DIVIDENDS

LO7

A firm with excess cash and inadequate investment opportunities may choose to repurchase its own shares in the market rather than pay a cash dividend. For this reason, the stock repurchase decision may be thought of as an alternative to the payment of cash dividends.

We show that the benefits to the shareholder are equal under either alternative, at least in theory. For purposes of study, assume the Morgan Corporation's financial position may be described by the data in Table 18–7.

Table 18–7 Financial data of Morgan Corporation

Earnings after taxes	$3,000,000
Shares.	1,000,000
Earnings per share	$3
P/E ratio (assuming excess cash leaves company).	10
Market price per share	$30
Excess cash	$2,000,000

The firm has $2 million in excess cash, and it wishes to compare the value to shareholders of a $2 cash dividend (on the million shares outstanding) as opposed to spending the funds to repurchase shares in the market. If the cash dividend is paid, the shareholder would have $30 in stock and the $2 cash dividend. On the other hand, the $2 million may be used to repurchase shares at slightly over market value (to induce sale).[5] The overall benefit to shareholders is that earnings per share go up as the number of shares outstanding is decreased. If the P/E ratio of the stock remains constant, then the price of the stock should also go up. If a purchase price of $32 is used to induce sale, then 62,500 shares would be purchased.

$$\frac{\text{Excess funds}}{\text{Purchase price per share}} = \frac{\$2,000,000}{\$32} = 62,500 \text{ shares}$$

Total shares outstanding are reduced to 937,500 (1,000,000 − 62,500). Revised earnings per share for the Morgan Corporation become

$$\frac{\text{Earnings after taxes}}{\text{Shares}} = \frac{\$3,000,000}{937,500} = \$3.20$$

---

[5] To derive the desired equality between the two alternatives, the purchase price for the new shares should equal the current market price plus the proposed cash dividend under the first alternative ($30 + $2 = $32).

Since the P/E ratio for the stock is 10, the market value of the stock should go to $32.00. Thus, we see that the consequences of the two alternatives are presumed to be the same.

(1) Funds Used for Cash Dividend		(2) Funds Used to Repurchase Stock	
Market value per share..............	$30	Market value per share..............	$32
Cash dividend per share............	2		
	$32		

In either instance, the total value is presumed to be $32. Theoretically, the shareholder would be indifferent with respect to the two alternatives. This changes somewhat, however, when taxes and transaction costs are brought into the decision-making process. Let us first look at taxes. Though the cash dividend is immediately taxed in Alternative 1, the gain in Alternative 2 may be untaxed as a capital gain. Furthermore, if there is to be a capital gains tax incurred, it is delayed until the stock is sold. From a tax viewpoint, the repurchase of shares may provide maximum benefits.

On the other hand, one can argue that dividends put cash in the shareholders' hands without any transaction costs. If the company is buying back significant amounts of its shares, it has to pay some premium above $30 to induce enough shareholders to sell. Also, there will be transaction costs in managing and executing the buybacks. Finally, the remaining shareholders have to incur transaction costs if they want to realize the equivalent of the cash dividend in cash.

Other Reasons for Repurchase

- The Morgan Corporation believes their shares are selling at bargain basement prices, which would be a contradiction of the efficient market hypothesis (Chapter 14). By repurchasing shares the corporation is able to maintain a constant demand for its own securities and to perhaps stave off further price erosion, at least temporarily. Corporate management believes that the announcement of a repurchase reassures investors of the value of their investment.

- Reacquired shares may also be useful for employee stock options or as part of a tender offer in a merger or acquisition.

- Firms also often reacquire part of their shares as a protective device against being taken over by others. As the equity value of a firm decreases relative to the value of its physical assets, outsiders may attempt to gain control of the firm by using the value of the physical assets to finance the purchase of the equity. To reduce the availability of their companies to these highly leveraged buyouts, the managements of potential takeover targets often take on debt to buy back some of their stock. Greater debt in a target company makes a takeover less attractive.

- Corporations may have strategic goals for the organization that may be adversely impacted by the number of shares outstanding. As an example, firms may begin to repurchase shares in their own stock for the purpose of creating a tighter ownership holding within the company. An organization considering making themselves a merger or acquisition target would have considerable interest in ensuring shares are less widely held. The benefit of a tighter ownership structure allows a buyout process to possibly be less contested among remaining shareholders. By repurchasing more of its shares the firm holds more of the ownership and has greater control over the offer.

- Some evidence exists for superior returns on shares after repurchase. It is suggested that management is conveying new information about future expected earnings when a repurchase announcement is made. With improved results in the following months, the share price shows increasing value.

There is one caveat for firms that continually repurchase their own shares. Some analysts may view the action as a noncreative use of funds. The analysts may ask, "Why aren't the funds being used to develop new products or to modernize plant and equipment?" Thus, it is important that management carefully communicates the reasons for the repurchase decision to analysts and shareholders—such as the fact that the stock is a great bargain at its current price.

Timing the Buyback

From 2017 to 2020 repurchases were significant in the United States. Capital was being repatriated from overseas because of lower tax rates. Although there was some reinvestment of capital by firms, there was a concern that share buybacks were large and taking capital out of the capital markets. This was significant in early 2020 when many firms found they had cash flow problems from the market downturn inflicted by the Covid-19 pandemic.

Share buybacks are one way firms can return cash to their investors at a time when investment alternatives do not appear attractive. Buybacks are also announced to shore up share prices and produce tax-deferred returns to some shareholders.

In June 2017 Bank of Montreal announced a buyback or repurchase program for 4 million shares over the following month.

Great Canadian Gaming Corporation cancelled a $350 million share buyback program in March 2020, as it suspended operations in its 25 facilities across Canada due to Covid-19. It needed the cash.

Information on buybacks can be found at the SEDAR website (sedar.com) with an "issuer bid circular" search, or perhaps a "press release" search.

Q1 Find a recent buyback announcement. What are the details of the offer?

Symbols: BMO, GC

LO8 DIVIDEND REINVESTMENT PLANS

During the 1970s, many companies started dividend reinvestment plans (DRIPs) for their shareholders. These plans take various forms, but basically they provide the investor with an opportunity to buy additional shares of stock with the cash dividend paid by the company. Over 100 companies listed on the Toronto Stock Exchange offer DRIPs on their capital stock. Participation in these plans is voluntary. Search a firm's stock ticker symbol to identify if a DRIP is in place: ca. dividendinvestor.com

Some firms permit discounts to share value on DRIPs but these are becoming less common. Nevertheless, the shareholder that participates in a DRIP even at the market price benefits by saving on brokerage commissions and administrative costs. Furthermore, this disciplined method for reinvesting the returns from the share investment utilizes the compounding principle of earning returns on returns over time. A shareholder may also be allowed to add cash payments of up to $1,000 per quarter to their dividend payments to buy more shares at the reduced rate. With a dividend reinvestment plan, the company is the beneficiary of increased cash flow since dividends paid are returned to it for reinvestment.

Reinvesting dividends makes a significant difference to an investor's accumulated capital over a lifetime.

SUMMARY

1. The first consideration in establishing a dividend policy is the firm's ability to reinvest the funds generated by the business versus the shareholder's ability to invest those funds elsewhere. The firm's need for earnings retention and growth is represented in the life cycle growth curve. (LO1)

2. The theory of highest return for internally generated funds must be tempered by a consideration of shareholders' preferences. Shareholders may be given a greater payout than the optimum determined by rational analysis to resolve their uncertainty about the future (i.e., for informational purposes). This would seem to be supported by the evidence of firms continuing to pay dividends despite the fact that earnings have declined dramatically. Dividend increases appear to have a positive impact on share value. (LO2)

3. Shareholders may prefer a greater than normal retention to defer the income tax obligation associated with cash dividends. Another important consideration in establishing a dividend policy may be the shareholders' desire for steady dividend payments. Lesser factors influencing dividend policy are legal rules relating to maximum payment, the cash position of the firm, and the firm's access to capital markets. One must also consider the desire for control by corporate management and shareholders. (LO3)

4. The life cycle of a firm entails a growth phase with expanding opportunities requiring lots of cash; thus no or minimal dividends are paid. As the growth rate fades and excessive cash flow is generated, the firm begins to return capital to shareholders by way of dividends. (LO4)

5. After a dividend is declared, the ex-dividend date, the record date, and the payment date are important. (LO5)

6. An alternative (or a supplement) to cash dividends may be the use of stock dividends and stock splits. Though neither of these financing devices directly changes the intrinsic value of the shareholder position, they may provide communication to shareholders and bring the share price into a more acceptable trading range. A stock dividend may take on some actual value when total cash dividends are allowed to increase. Nevertheless, the alert investor watches for abuses of stock dividends—situations in which the corporation indicates that something of great value is occurring when, in fact, the new shares created merely represent the same proportionate interest for each shareholder. (LO6)

7. The decision to repurchase shares may be thought of as an alternative to the payment of a cash dividend. Decreasing shares outstanding causes earnings per share, and perhaps the market price, to go up. The increase in the market price may be equated to the size of the cash dividend forgone. (LO7)

8. Many firms are now offering shareholders the option of reinvesting cash dividends in the company's common stock. Cash-short companies have been using DRIPs to raise external funds. Other companies simply provide a service to shareholders by allowing them to purchase shares in the market for low transaction costs. (LO8)

DISCUSSION QUESTIONS

1. How does the marginal principle of retained earnings relate to the returns a shareholder may make in other investments? (LO1, LO2)

2. Discuss the difference between a passive and an active dividend policy. (LO2)

3. In general, how does the shareholder feel about the relevance of dividends? (LO1)

4. Explain the relationship between a company's growth possibilities and its dividend policy. (LO4)

5. Discuss the major factors that may influence the firm's willingness and ability to pay dividends. (LO3)

6. If you buy a stock on the ex-dividend date, will you receive the upcoming quarterly dividend? (LO5)

7. Describe the importance of shareholder tax rates in setting dividend policy. (LO3)

8. How is a stock split versus a stock dividend treated on the financial statements of a corporation? (LO6)

9. Why might a stock dividend or a stock split be of limited value to an investor? (LO6)

10. Does it make sense for a corporation to repurchase its own stock? Explain. (LO7)

11. How does the life cycle curve explain the relationship between corporate growth and residual dividend theory? (LO4)

12. Why might an investor prefer capital gains to dividends? (LO3)

13. What advantages to the corporation and the shareholder do dividend reinvestment plans offer? (LO8)

14. Discuss a corporate repurchase announcement on the basis of market efficiency (Chapter 14). (LO7)

15. What impact does a repurchase have on a firm's capital structure? Will it increase the value of the shares in the firm? (LO7)

16. Inco Ltd. paid a special dividend of US$10 a share in 1989. What was the purpose? By returning over $1 billion in total to shareholders, what was management saying to the investment community? (LO1)

17. Why do corporate executives consider a stable dividend policy important? (LO3)

18. If a company in which you hold shares decided to increase its dividend would that increase your expected returns from this investment? (LO1, LO2)

INTERNET RESOURCES AND QUESTIONS

The Toronto Stock Exchange site provides common and preferred share prices, P/E ratios, latest earnings, and dividend yields:
tmx.com

Dividend Investor provides dividend information for firms if a stock market ticker symbol is provided.
ca.dividendinvestor.com

Recent filings under securities legislation, including dividend payment announcements, are available from the System for Electronic Document Analysis and Retrieval (SEDAR), owned by the Canadian Depository for Securities (CDS):
sedar.com

The Reuters website provides share pricing, P/E ratios, earnings per share (EPS), and dividend yields:
reuters.com/finance/markets

1. Update the selected dividend yields from Table 18–2. Comment on any changes and possible reasons for the increase or decrease in yields.

2. Determine earnings and dividends for the last five years for Royal Bank, TC Energy, and Teck in a manner similar to Table 18–1. Comment on the dividend patterns and the possible reasons for these patterns.

3. Compare the dividend yields on the common and preferred shares of the TD Bank and TransAlta Utilities. Why is there a difference in yields?

PROBLEMS

1. Omni Telecom is trying to decide whether to increase its cash dividend or use the funds to increase its future growth rate. It will use the dividend valuation model (Chapter 10) for purposes of analysis. The current values are the following:

   $D_0 = \$1.50$ $K_e = 10\%$ $g = 4\%$

   Under Plan A, the dividend (D_1) will be increased to $1.80 with K_e and g unchanged.

   Under Plan B, the dividend (D_1) will remain at $1.50, K_e will remain unchanged, but g will increase to 6%.

   a. Compute the current price under Plan A.

   b. Compute the current price under Plan B.

   c. Which plan produced the higher value? Suggest why this occurred.

2. Roget's Search Engine Limited plans to pay dividends of $2.00, $3.50, and then a liquidating dividend of $20.25 over the next three years. If investors expect a 10 percent return on their investment, what is the value of the company today?

3. Suppose Roget's Search Engine, from the previous problem, decides to forgo the dividend payments in Years 1 and 2 and instead reinvests the funds in additional projects available to the firm. Demonstrate whether or not the suspension of dividends is appropriate under the following assumptions:

   a. Reinvested funds earn 8 percent.

   b. Reinvested funds earn 10 percent.

   c. Reinvested funds earn 12 percent.

4. Gallagher Parades reported EPS of $3.00 and paid $0.75 in dividends. What is the payout ratio?

5. Sewell Enterprises earned $160 million last year and retained $100 million. What is the payout ratio?

6. Auction.com earned $420 million last year and had a 35 percent payout ratio. How much did the firm add to its retained earnings?

7. Ronstadt Drum Company earned $710 million last year and paid out 25 percent of earnings in dividends.

   a. By how much did the company's retained earnings increase?

   b. With 85 million shares outstanding and a share price of $40, what was the dividend yield?

8. Springsteen Music Company earned $820 million last year and paid out 20 percent of earnings in dividends.

   a. By how much did the company's retained earnings increase?

   b. With 100 million shares outstanding and a share price of $50, what is the dividend yield?

9. The stock of the Pills Berry Corporation is currently selling at $60.00 per share. The firm pays a dividend of $1.80 per share.

   a. What is the annual dividend yield?

   b. If the firm has a payout rate of 50 percent, what is the firm's P/E ratio?

10. The stock of Raptor BB Ranch is currently selling at $25.00 per share. The firm pays a dividend of $1.25 per share.

    a. What is the annual dividend yield?

    b. If the firm has a payout ratio of 50 percent, what is the firm's P/E ratio?

11. The shares of Ynot Development Company sell for $22.50. The firm has a P/E ratio of 15, and 20 percent of earnings are paid out in dividends. What is the dividend yield?

12. The shares of Chretien Golf Links Limited sell for $50.00. The firm has a P/E ratio of 20, and 30 percent of earnings are paid out in dividends. What is the dividend yield?

13. The Channel Weather News is selling for $32.00 the day before the stock goes ex-dividend. The annual dividend yield is 4 percent, and the dividends are paid quarterly. Based solely on the impact of the cash dividend, by how much should the share price change on the ex-dividend date? What is the suggested new price of a share?

14. Peabody Mining Company's common stock is selling for $50.00 the day before the stock goes ex-dividend. The annual dividend yield is 5.6 percent, and dividends are distributed quarterly. Based solely on the impact of the cash dividend, by how much should the stock go down on the ex-dividend date? What is the suggested new price of the stock?

15. Planetary Travel Co. has $240,000,000 in shareholders' equity. Eighty million dollars is listed as common stock and the balance is in retained earnings. The firm has $500,000,000 in total assets and 2 percent of this value is in cash. Earnings for the year are $40,000,000 and are included in retained earnings.
    a. What is the legal limit on current dividends?
    b. What is the practical limit based on liquidity?
    c. If the company pays out the amount in part *b,* what is the dividend payout ratio?

16. In doing a five-year analysis of future dividends, Newell Labs Inc. is considering the following two plans. The values represent dividends per share.

Year	Plan A	Plan B
1	$2.50	$ .80
2	2.55	3.30
3	2.50	0.35
4	2.65	2.80
5	2.65	6.60

    a. How much, in total dividends per share, will be paid under each plan over the five years?
    b. Ms. Carter, the vice-president of finance, suggests that shareholders often prefer a stable dividend policy to a highly variable one. She will assume shareholders apply a lower discount rate to dividends that are stable. The discount rate to be used for Plan A is 10 percent; the discount rate for Plan B is 12 percent. Which plan will provide the higher present value for the future dividends?

17. The following companies have different financial statistics. What dividend policies would you recommend for them? Explain your reasons.

	Turtle Co.	Hare Corp.
Growth rate in sales and earnings	5%	20%
Cash as a percentage of total assets	15%	2%

18. Goren Bridge Construction Co. has two important shareholders: Ms. Queen and the Ace Corporation. Ms. Queen is in a 31 percent combined marginal tax bracket, while the Ace Corporation is in a 36 percent combined marginal bracket.
    a. If Ms. Queen receives $3.80 in cash dividends, how much in taxes (per share) will she pay?
    b. If the Ace Corporation receives $3.80 in cash dividends, how much in taxes (per share) will it pay?

19. Below are the EPS and the dividends per share of three companies.

Alpha Co.		Beta Co.		Delta Co.	
EPS	DPS	EPS	DPS	EPS	DPS
$4.00	$2.00	$4.00	$2.00	$4.00	$2.00
4.20	2.10	4.20	2.00	4.20	1.50
4.80	2.40	4.80	2.00	4.80	2.00
5.60	2.80	5.60	2.00	5.60	3.00
6.00	3.00	6.00	2.30	6.00	2.00

a. What are the payout ratios for each company on an annual basis?

b. Can you explain some of the reasons for such differences in payout patterns?

c. Which company would you prefer to own as a shareholder? (Assume the bottom row is the most recent year's data.) Why? What other kinds of information would you want before you invested your money?

20. A financial analyst is attempting to assess the future dividend policy of Interactive Technology by examining its life cycle. She anticipates no payout of earnings in the form of cash dividends during the developmental stage, (I). During the growth stage, (II), she anticipates 10 percent of earnings will be distributed as dividends. As the firm progresses to the expansion stage, (III), the payout will go up to 40 percent, and eventually reach 60 percent during the maturity stage, (IV).

a. Assuming EPS will be as follows during each of the four stages, indicate the cash dividend per share (if any) during each stage.

Stage I	$0.20
Stage II.	2.00
Stage III.	2.80
Stage IV	3.00

b. Assume in Stage IV that an investor owns 425 shares and is in a 31.33 percent marginal combined tax bracket for dividends. What will be the investor's aftertax income from the cash dividend?

c. In what two stages is the firm most likely to utilize stock dividends or stock splits?

21. Squash Delight Inc. had the following balance sheet:

Assets	
Cash	$ 100,000
Accounts receivable	300,000
Capital assets	600,000
Total assets.	$1,000,000

Liabilities	
Accounts payable	$ 150,000
Notes payable	50,000
Common stock 100,000 shares	300,000
Retained earnings.	500,000
	$1,000,000

The firm has a market price of $10 a share.

a. Show the effect on the equity account(s) of a two-for-one stock split.

b. Show the effect on the equity account of a 10 percent stock dividend. Part *b* is separate from part *a*. In part *b* do not assume the stock split has taken place.

c. Based on the balance in retained earnings, which of the two dividend plans is more restrictive on future cash dividends?

22. Sun Energy Company has the following capital section in its balance sheet. Its stock is currently selling for $5 per share.

Common stock (100,000 shares)	$200,000
Retained earnings...............................	200,000
	$400,000

The firm intends to first declare a 10 percent stock dividend and then pay a $0.30 cash dividend (which also causes a reduction of retained earnings). Show the capital section of the balance sheet after the first transaction and then after the second transaction.

23. Philips Rock and Mud is trying to determine the maximum amount of cash dividends it can pay this year. Assume its balance sheet is as follows:

Assets	
Cash	$ 312,500
Accounts receivable.............................	800,000
Capital assets	987,500
Total assets.................................	$2,100,000
Liabilities and Shareholders' Equity	
Accounts payable...............................	$445,000
Long-term notes payable	280,000
Common stock (250,000 shares)	500,000
Retained earnings...............................	875,000
Total liabilities and shareholders' equity............	$2,100,000

a. From a legal perspective, what is the maximum amount of dividends per share the firm could pay? Is this realistic?

b. In terms of cash availability, what is the maximum amount of dividends per share the firm could pay?

c. Assume the firm earned a 16 percent return on shareholders' equity. If the board wishes to pay out 60 percent of earnings in the form of dividends, how much will dividends per share be?

24. The Adams Corporation has earnings of $750,000, with 300,000 shares outstanding. Its P/E ratio is 8. The firm is holding $400,000 of funds to invest or pay out in dividends. If the funds are retained, the aftertax return on investment will be 15 percent, and this will add to present earnings. The 15 percent is the normal return anticipated for the corporation, and the P/E ratio would remain unchanged. If the funds are paid out in the form of dividends, the P/E ratio will increase by 10 percent, because the shareholders in this corporation have a preference for dividends over retained earnings. Which plan will maximize the market value of the stock?

25. The Vinson Corporation has earnings of $500,000 with 250,000 shares outstanding. Its P/E ratio is 20. The firm is holding $300,000 of funds to invest or pay out in dividends. If the funds are retained, the aftertax return on investment will be 18 percent, and this will add to present earnings. The 18 percent is the normal return anticipated for the corporation, and the P/E ratio would remain unchanged. If the funds are paid out in the form of dividends, the P/E ratio will increase by 10 percent because the shareholders in this corporation have a preference for dividends over retained earnings. Which plan will maximize the market value of the stock?

26. Omni Telecom is trying to decide whether to increase its cash dividend immediately or use the fund to increase its future growth rate. It will use the dividend valuation model originally presented in Chapter 10 for purposes of analysis.

D_0 is currently $2.00, Ke is 10 percent, and g is 5 percent.

Under Plan A, D_0 would be immediately increased to $2.20 and Ke and g will remain unchanged.

Under Plan D, D_0 will remain at $2.00 but g will go up to 6 percent and Ke will remain unchanged.

a. Compute the price of the stock today under Plan A.

b. Compute price of the stock today under Plan B.

c. Which plan will produce the higher value?

27. Wilson Pharmaceuticals has done very well in the stock market during the last three years. Its stock has risen from $45 per share to $70 per share. Its P/E ratio is 20. Its current statement of net worth is

Common stock (4 million shares issued;	
10 million shares authorized).....................	$ 55,000,000
Retained earnings...............................	45,000,000
Net worth	$100,000,000

a. What changes would occur in the statement of net worth after a two-for-one stock split?

b. What would the statement of net worth look like after a three-for-one stock split?

c. Assume Wilson earned $14 million. What would its EPS be before and after the two-for-one stock split?

d. What would the price per share be before and after the two-for-one and the three-for-one stock splits? (Assume the P/E ratio of 20 stays the same.)

e. Should a stock split change the P/E ratio for Wilson?

28. Vegas Products sells marked playing cards to blackjack dealers. It has not paid a dividend in many years but is currently contemplating some kind of dividend. The capital accounts for the firm are

Common stock (200,000 shares)	$5,000,000
Retained earnings...............................	5,000,000
Net worth	$10,000,000

The company's stock is selling for $40 per share, and it earned $400,000 during the year with 200,000 shares outstanding, indicating a P/E ratio of 20.

a. What adjustments would have to be made to the capital accounts for a 10 percent stock dividend?

b. What adjustments would be made to EPS and the share price? (Assume the P/E ratio remains constant.)

c. How many shares would an investor end up with if they originally had 100 shares?

d. What is the investor's total investment worth before and after the stock dividend if the P/E ratio remains constant? (There may be a small difference due to rounding.)

e. Has Vegas Products pulled a magic trick, or has it given the investor something of value? Explain.

29. Matrix Corp Inc. is considering a 15 percent stock dividend. The capital accounts are as follows:

Common stock (4,000,000 shares).................	$ 40,000,000
Retained earnings...............................	60,000,000
Net worth	$100,000,000

The company's stock is selling for $40 per share. The company had total earnings of $12,000,000 with 4,000,000 shares outstanding and EPS were $3.00. The firm has a P/E ratio of 13.33.

a. What adjustments would have to be made to the equity accounts for a 15 percent stock dividend? Show the new capital accounts.

b. What adjustments would be made to EPS and the share price? (Assume the P/E ratio remains constant.)

c. How many shares would an investor have if they originally had 100?

d. What is the investor's total investment worth before and after the stock dividend if the P/E ratio remains constant? (There may be a slight difference due to rounding.)

e. Assume Mr. Neo, the president of Matrix Corp., wishes to benefit the shareholder by keeping the cash dividend at a previous level of $1.05 in spite of the fact that the shareholders now have 15 percent more shares. Because the cash dividend is not reduced, the share price is assumed to remain at $40.

   What is an investor's total investment worth after the stock dividend if she had 100 shares before the stock dividend?

   Under the scenario described in part *e,* is the investor better off?

f. As a final question, what is the dividend yield on the shares under the scenario described in part *e*?

30. Worst Buy Company has had a lot of complaints from customers of late and its stock price is now only $2 per share. It plans to employ a one-for-five reverse stock split to increase the share value. Assume Dean Smith owns 140 shares.

   a. How many shares will he own after the reverse stock split?

   b. What is the anticipated share price after the reverse stock split?

   c. Because investors often have a negative reaction to reverse stock splits, assume the shares go up to only 80 percent of the value computed in part *b.* What will be the share price?

   d. How has the value of Dean Smith's holdings changed from before the reverse stock split to after the reverse stock split (based on the share value computed in part *c*)?

31. The Belton Corporation has $5 million in earnings after taxes and 1 million shares outstanding. The stock trades at a P/E of 10. The firm has $4 million in excess cash.

   a. Compute the current price of the stock.

   b. If the $4 million is used to pay dividends, how much will dividends per share be?

   c. If the $4 million is used to repurchase shares in the market at a premium price of $54 per share, how many shares will be reacquired? (Round to the nearest share.)

   d. What will be the new EPS?

   e. If the P/E remains constant, what will be the new price of the securities? By how much, in terms of dollars, did the repurchase increase the share price?

   f. Has the shareholder's total wealth changed as a result of the stock repurchase as opposed to the cash dividend?

   g. From the shareholder's perspective, is there any major tax advantage to tendering one's shares versus the receipt of cash dividends?

   h. What are some other reasons a corporation may wish to repurchase its own shares in the market?

32. This problem compares the aftertax income on a $35,000 investment for the following two investors resident in Ontario and two possible investments. Table 2–13 will be of assistance. Rudy Hill earns within the mid marginal tax bracket. This is his only investment. Grace Valley is in the top marginal tax bracket. This is her only investment. Investment A provides $2,800 in dividends and no capital gains. Investment B provides no dividends but $2,800 of capital gains.

   a. Calculate the aftertax return for Hill in Investment A and Investment B.

   b. Calculate the aftertax return for Valley in Investment A and Investment B.

c. Indicate the difference in aftertax income between the two investors in Investment A.

d. Indicate the difference in aftertax income between the two investors in Investment B.

e. In the answers to parts **c** and **d,** why is there a smaller difference between the answers for one investment than for the other?

33. The Hastings Sugar Corporation has the following pattern of net income each year and associated capital expenditure projects for which the firm can earn a higher return than the shareholders could earn if the funds were paid out in the form of dividends.

Year	Net Income	Profitable Capital Expenditure
1	$10 million	$ 7 million
2	15 million	11 million
3	9 million	6 million
4	12 million	7 million
5	14 million	8 million

The Hasting Corporation has 2 million shares outstanding. (Note: The following questions are separate from each other.)

a. If the marginal principle of retained earnings is applied, how much in total cash dividends will be paid over the five years?

b. If the firm simply uses a payout ratio of 40 percent of net income, how much in total cash dividends will be paid?

c. If the firm pays a 10 percent stock dividend in Years 2 through 5 and also pays a cash dividend of $2.40 per share for each of the five years, how much in total dividends will be paid?

d. Assume that the payout ratio in each year is to be 30 percent of net income and that the firm will pay a 20 percent stock dividend in Years 2 through 5. How much will dividends per share for each year be?

COMPREHENSIVE PROBLEM

34. Lyle Communications had finally arrived at the point where it had a sufficient excess cash flow of $2.4 million to consider paying a dividend. It had 2 million shares outstanding and was considering paying a cash dividend of $1.20 per share. The firm's total earnings were $8 million, providing $4 in EPS. Lyle Communications shares traded in the market at $64.

However, Liz Crocker, the chief financial officer, was not sure that paying the cash dividend was the best route to go. She had recently read a number of articles in *The Globe and Mail* about the advantages of stock repurchases and, before she made a recommendation to the board of directors, she decided to do a few calculations.

a. What is the firm's P/E ratio?

b. If the firm paid the cash dividend, what would be its dividend yield and dividend payout per share?

c. If a shareholder held 100 shares and received the cash dividend, what would be the total value of the shareholder's portfolio?

d. Assume that instead of paying the cash dividend, the firm used the $2.4 million of excess funds to purchase shares at $65.20, slightly over the current market price. How many shares could be repurchased? (Round to the nearest share.)

e. What would be the new EPS under the share repurchase alternative?

f. If the P/E ratio stayed the same under the share repurchase alternative, what would be the share value? What would be the value of the shareholder's portfolio, which included 100 shares?

MINI CASE

Montgomery Corporation

In January, the board of directors of the Montgomery Corporation, one of Canada's largest retail store chains, was having its regularly scheduled meeting to establish and declare the next quarterly dividend. (Statements for the firm and industry are shown in Tables 1 and 2.) However, this meeting wasn't so regular. One of the directors, Sidney Mobler, who was also a vice-president in the company and chief financial officer, had brought a guest: Don Jackson, a financial analyst. Don had spent a considerable amount of time in the finance department and more than a few hours in Sidney's office developing a proposal concerning the company's dividend policy. He had finally persuaded Sidney to allow him to present his idea to the board.

Table 1 Selected financial data, Montgomery Corporation (in $ millions, except per-share data)

	20XR	20XS	20XT	20XU	20XV	20XW	20XX
Sales	$27,357.4	$30,019.8	$35,882.9	$38,828.0	$40,715.3	$44,281.5	$48,000.0
Net income	$ 650.1	$ 861.2	$1,342.2	$1,454.8	$1,303.3	$1,351.3	$1,700.0
Amount to preferred dividends	—	—	—	$ 16.7	$ 21.5	$16.8	$ 22.6
Amount to common dividends	$ 429.1	$ 476.3	$ 537.0	$ 630.8	$ 639.0	$ 648.3	$ 725.4
Amount to retained earnings	$ 221.0	$ 384.9	$ 805.2	$ 807.3	$ 642.8	$ 686.2	$ 952.0
Common shares outstanding	347.9	351.4	354.6	361.6	363.1	376.6	378.0
EPS (on average common shares)	$ 1.96	$ 2.46	$ 3.80	$ 4.06	$ 3.60	$ 3.65	$ 4.51
DPS (on average common shares)	$ 1.36	$ 1.36	$ 1.48	$ 1.70	$ 1.76	$ 1.76	$ 1.96
Payout ratio (DPS/EPS)*	69.4%	55.3%	38.9%	41.8%	48.9%	48.2%	43.5%
Total retained earnings	$7,041.2	$7,426.1	$8,231.3	$9,038.6	$9,681.4	$10,367.6	$11,319.6
Cash balance	$1,170.7	$1,307.6	$1,502.5	$1,765.0	$2,357.2	$ 2,984.4	$ 3,235.0

*DPS (dividends per share)/EPS (earnings per share).

Table 2 Selected financial data, other retail chains

	20XR	20XS	20XT	20XU	20XV	20XW	20XX
Ears Department Stores							
EPS	$0.69	$0.93	$1.38	$1.82	$2.29	$2.35	$2.50
DPS	$0.05	$0.05	$0.08	$0.09	$0.10	$0.12	$0.13
Payout ratio	7.2%	5.4%	5.8%	4.9%	4.4%	5.1%	5.2%
The Lake							
EPS	$0.38	$0.61	$0.81	$1.10	$0.95	$0.23	$0.30
DPS	$0.09	$0.11	$0.13	$0.17	$0.20	$0.20	$0.20
Payout ratio	23.7%	18.0%	16.0%	15.0%	21.1%	87.0%	66.7%
Price One Inc.							
EPS	$0.10	$0.19	$0.37	$0.51	$0.80	$1.21	$1.40
DPS	$0.01	$0.02	$0.04	$0.08	$0.11	$0.16	$0.24
Payout ratio	10.0%	10.5%	10.8%	15.7%	13.8%	13.2%	17.1%
Ureka							
EPS	$0.35	$0.38	$0.54	$0.55	$0.66	$0.91	$1.10
DPS	$0.06	$0.06	$0.07	$0.10	$0.11	$0.13	$0.18
Payout ratio	17.1%	15.8%	13.0%	18.2%	16.7%	14.3%	16.4%
Sporty							
EPS	$2.75	$2.94	$3.13	$2.91	$2.66	$3.53	$4.70
DPS	$0.92	$1.00	$1.08	$1.18	$1.18	$1.24	$1.48
Payout ratio	33.5%	34.0%	34.5%	40.5%	44.4%	35.1%	31.5%
National Wheels							
EPS	$0.16	$0.23	$0.35	$0.48	$0.58	$0.80	$1.10
DPS	$0.02	$0.02	$0.04	$0.05	$0.07	$0.09	$0.12
Payout ratio	12.5%	8.7%	11.4%	10.4%	12.1%	11.3%	10.9%

Note: DPS refers to dividends per share; EPS refers to earnings per share.

"Ladies and gentlemen," Don began, after being introduced by Sidney, "I'll skip the preliminaries and get right to the point. I think that Montgomery's dividend policy is not in the best interests of our shareholders."

Observing the rather chilly stares from around the room, he hastened on: "Now, I don't mean we have a bad policy or anything like that; it's just that I think we could do an even better job of increasing our shareholders' wealth with a few small changes." He paused for effect. "Let me explain. Up to now our policy has been to pay a constant dividend every year, increasing it occasionally to reflect the company's growth in sales and income. The problem is, that policy takes no account of the investment opportunities that the company has from year to year. In other words, this year we will use most of our net income to pay the same, or a greater, dividend than last year, even though there might be company investments available that would pay a much greater return if we committed the funds to the firm's investments instead. In effect, our shareholders are being shortchanged: they will realize perhaps a 6 percent yield on their investment as a result of receiving the dividend, when they could realize a 12 percent or higher return as a result of the company's return on its investments. I see this as a serious shortcoming in our management of the shareholders' funds."

"Now, fortunately, correcting this situation is not difficult. All we have to do is adopt what is called a *residual* dividend policy. That is, each year we would allocate money from income to those capital spending projects for which the return—that is, IRR—is greater than our cost of capital. Any money that is not so used in the capital budget would be paid out to the shareholders in the form of dividends. In this way we would ensure that the shareholders' money is working the hardest way it can for them."

Clarence Autry, who was also on the board of directors of the Canadian Pacific and no stranger to the world of corporate finance, broke in. "Young man," he said dryly, "your proposal ignores reality. It's not whether the shareholders are theoretically better off that counts; it's what they want that counts. You cannot tell the shareholders you're doing what's best for them by cutting the dividend; the dividend is what they want. Not only is that dividend sure money in their pockets now, but the fact that it's the same size as last time, or even higher, is a signal to them that their company is doing well and will continue to do so in the future. These decisions can't always be made on the basis of good-looking formulas from the back room, you know."

Barbara Reynolds, who was the head of the directors' auditing committee, and somewhat of an accounting expert, agreed with Clarence. "That's a good point, and one that's well recognized by our competitors too. If you check, I don't think you'll find a single one of them that's cut their dividend in the last six years, even though their net income may have declined significantly. Furthermore, the whole argument is meaningless anyway, because the dividend is not really competing with the capital budget for funds. We don't turn away profitable projects in favour of paying the dividend. If there are worthy projects in which we want to invest, and we would rather use our available cash to pay the dividend, then we seek financing for the investments from outside sources. In a way, we can have our cake and eat it too." She chuckled, pleased at the analogy.

Don, however, was not to be intimidated. "Yes, ma'am, what you say is true," he replied, "and I would respond that our competitors are not treating their shareholders fairly, either. Furthermore, we do seek outside financing occasionally for large projects, but there are two problems associated with doing it routinely, as you suggest. First, it might be viewed as borrowing, or issuing stock, to pay the dividend, which would cast the company in a very poor light. Second, it's more expensive to finance from outside sources than from inside due to the fees charged by the investment dealers. Therefore, I believe we should exhaust our inside sources of financing before turning to the outside."

Barbara stood her ground. "That's all very well, but it's still not necessary to cut the dividend in order to fund the capital budget. As a last resort, if the company's cash balances were about to be drawn down too low, we could always declare a stock dividend instead of a cash dividend."

"Ladies, gentlemen," Chairman Edward Asking intervened, "your comments are all very perceptive, but we must move on to the business at hand. All in favour of changing to a residual dividend policy, please raise your hand."

a.   Refer to Table 1. Would you say that Montgomery's policy up to now has been to pay a constant dividend, with occasional increases as the company grows?

b. Refer to Table 2. What type of dividend policies would you say are being practised by Montgomery's competitors in the retailing industry? Do you think that any firms are following a residual dividend policy?

c. Calculate the expected return to the common shareholders under the firm's present policy, given an expected dividend next year of $2.10 and a growth rate of 7.1 percent. Montgomery's stock currently sells for $35.

d. Assume that if Don's proposal were adopted, next year's dividend would be zero but earning growth would rise to 14 percent. What will be the expected return to the shareholders (assuming the other factors are held constant)?

e. Is the size of the capital budget limited by the amount of net income, as Don implies? What is the maximum size that the capital budget can be in 20XY without selling assets or seeking outside financing?

f. Don says the cost of the outside financing is more expensive than the cost of internal financing due to the flotation costs charged by investment dealers. Given the data you have, what would you say is the firm's cost of internal equity financing?

g. Assume Montgomery can sell bonds priced to yield 13 percent. What is the firm's aftertax cost of debt? (The tax rate is 25 percent.)

h. Given the cost of debt and the cost of internal equity financing, why doesn't Montgomery just borrow the total amount needed to fund the capital budget and the dividend as well?

i. Do you go along with Clarence's comment that it's what the shareholders want, not their total rate of return, that counts? Why or why not?

j. Barbara suggests that if cash is needed for the capital budget, a stock dividend could be substituted for the cash dividend. Do you agree? How do you think the shareholders would react? Regardless of their reaction, is the stock dividend an equivalent substitute for the cash dividend?

k. After all is said and done, do you think the firm's dividend policy matters? If so, what do you think Montgomery's policy should be?

Derivative Securities

LEARNING OBJECTIVES

LO1 Distinguish between and outline the uses of forwards, futures, and options.

LO2 Calculate the hedge on futures and the value of call and put options.

LO3 Characterize the securities offered by a corporation that are convertible into common shares at the option of the investor and are a means of raising funds.

LO4 Calculate the conversion value of a convertible security.

LO5 Examine the benefits of a convertible security, including a fixed rate of return and the potential for capital appreciation.

LO6 Describe warrants and compare them to convertible securities.

LO7 Calculate the intrinsic value and the speculative premium on a warrant.

LO8 Show how convertible securities and warrants affect earnings per share as reported on the income statement.

Finance is the study of value. Expected cash flows and their risks determine the value of an asset. Throughout the history of trade and commerce there have been attempts to control the cash flows and the risks faced by an enterprise in an uncertain world. Often contracts, establishing the price of commodities before their future exchange, were used to better facilitate the trading of goods and services. These contracts were the beginning of what we today call derivatives. Derivatives give the holder the right to buy or sell a particular commodity or asset, at an established price, at some time in the future. The price is guaranteed.

Changing prices of commodities, foreign exchange, and interest rates lead to a great deal of uncertainty in the trading of goods and services. Derivatives can help to lessen the uncertainty in a trade relationship. Hedging, or risk reduction, occurs because a derivative allows a purchaser to lock in a price before the actual transaction takes place. The benefit of risk reduction is that it will likely encourage increased trade.

The ultimate value of these financial assets, securities, or contracts comes from or is "derived" from the particular asset to which they lay claim. The right to buy or sell a particular asset (a derivative) becomes more or less valuable as the asset changes in price. Derivatives, which have a limited life, vary in price to a far greater extent than the particular asset from which they derive their value.

Derivatives have often been the most highly publicized areas of finance because of the spectacular losses experienced by some speculators. These speculators, in their use of derivatives, have increased not only their expected return (loss) but also the risk of their investments. Many, however, do not use derivatives to increase risks and potential rewards. If deployed properly, derivatives can be used to reduce the risk and the pattern of cash flows that companies experience from price changes.

Numerous financial markets offer for sale a wide variety of contracts to purchase or sell various assets at a predetermined and fixed price at some time in the future. The "derivatives" contracts are forwards, futures, and options. These contracts convey the right to purchase or sell things such as currencies, Treasury bills, market indexes, crude oil, orange juice, and shares in corporations, allowing financial managers ways to control their risks.

Investors look for investment options providing downside protection as well as capital appreciation potential. To satisfy investor demands, corporations have issued derivatives, usually options, to raise money for corporate endeavours. Convertible securities, warrants, and rights (studied in Chapter 17) are options that offer the investor in these securities the ability to purchase, or to convert to, common shares of the corporation. These innovative securities give the investor the right to obtain common shares at a fixed (exercise) price, and this right becomes valuable when the market price of the shares exceeds the fixed price. Convertibles, rights, and warrants trade in organized auction and over-the-counter markets.

Convertibles, warrants, and rights take on many of the same characteristics as these derivatives, as they are valued similarly, and they also trade in financial markets. Options issued by corporations are different from derivatives because their purpose is to raise funds for the corporation in an innovative way.

The other derivatives are offered in financial markets as side bets on the future price direction of certain assets and have no direct influence on the valuation of a corporation. These derivatives, known as forwards, futures, and options, are not issued by the corporation but by the market itself to facilitate the altering of the cash flows and risks faced in business transactions.

In this chapter we will very briefly explore derivatives for risk reduction purposes, and then examine convertible securities and warrants issued by corporations.

LO1 FORWARDS

The most basic of derivative contracts are forwards, which have been around since Greek and Roman times. Forwards are customized contracts that fix the price of some commodity for delivery at a specified place and a specified time in the future. These contracts are customized because the amount of the contract and the date of delivery (known as the settlement date) are negotiated between the two parties to the contract. These derivatives are not liquid and are not traded on exchanges because of their specific nature.

The advantage of forward contracts to the two parties involved is that by fixing the price and date for future delivery of a commodity they have removed a large portion of the uncertainty surrounding a future transaction. With forwards, no payment is due until the future agreed-upon date. In some cases a good-faith deposit, or other similar security, is required at the time the contract is written.

Today's derivative markets trace their beginnings to Chicago. In the middle of the 19th century the produce from the American Midwest passed through Chicago on its way to the rest of the world. In the fall, vast amounts of grain and other produce arrived at the port for shipment all at once. Prices fell drastically with the huge supply, and later jumped when the supply was minimal. The volatility in prices was unsettling to both the producers and users of the produce. An opportunity was presented to the merchants of Chicago to develop the city as an important centre. By introducing forward contracts, they could fix the price that farmers would receive for their produce and the price users of the produce would be required to pay. Increased trade would be encouraged when both parties could reliably predict their revenues and costs based on a fixed price. The merchants of Chicago would gain from introducing the forwards, guaranteeing the contracts, and building storage facilities. Chicago has since evolved into the world's largest exchange for futures and options.

Perhaps the most common forward market in Canada is the market for currencies provided by banks. Over 30 percent of Canada's GDP is based on foreign trade, and therefore dealing in foreign currencies is a major factor in many businesses. Foreign currency hedging with forwards, futures, and options is illustrated in Chapter 21.

To illustrate the use of a forward we will employ the Finance in Action box entitled "Derivatives for Bob's Farming Operation."

 FINANCE IN ACTION

The Derivatives Market

For many, the derivatives markets are used to "hedge," or reduce, the risk on commercial transactions. Financial institutions or the organized exchanges facilitate trade by matching up participants on both sides of a transaction. We can think of the derivatives markets as a big insurance clearing house.

The Bank of International Settlements (BIS) reports on the world derivatives market in the OTC (over-the-counter) market and on organized exchanges. In 2019, the derivatives contracts traded through the OTC market had an outstanding value of US$640 trillion. If these contracts could not be fulfilled, the cost would have been $15 trillion. The market is huge! The market is dominated by interest rate contracts, although currency contracts are quite significant in the OTC market.

In the organized exchanges, futures contracts totalled $35 trillion and options trading $61 trillion, mostly for interest rates and in U.S dollars.

OTC Market			
	Interest rate contracts	80%	(38% US$, 26% euros)
	Currency contracts	15	(44% US$, 15% euros)
	Other (equities, credit, commodities)	5	
		100%	

Nevertheless, besides facilitating risk reduction, some terrific losses have occurred in the derivatives markets as a result of the speculation by "rogue" traders who have taken a position on the direction that prices of commodities or interest rates might move and have been wrong.

Barings Bank, which eventually failed, lost $1.4 billion in 1995 on options and futures derived from the value of the Nikkei (Tokyo Stock Exchange) index. Sumitomo Corporation lost at least $2.6 billion, acknowledged in 1996, from purchases of derivatives in the copper market. In 2009, Morgan Stanley lost over $9 billion in credit default swaps.

In 1998, Long-Term Capital Management (LTCM) was bailed out to the tune of $4.6 billion by the Federal Reserve that feared its failure might destabilize the world's financial markets. LTCM had apparently borrowed well over $100 billion to speculate in interest rate derivatives. The fund's speculation was proved wrong. It is interesting that one of the directors of LTCM was Myron Scholes, the Nobel laureate who developed the famous option-pricing model.

In Canada, a $6.6 billion derivatives loss came from Amaranth in 2006 from betting on gas futures. Initially, the bets had worked when Hurricane Katrina struck the Gulf refineries, but the bets soured when the following summer and winter temperatures were warmer than expected.

These are dramatic stories and should not override the value that derivatives can bring in risk reduction if deployed properly. It is worth remembering that derivatives are a zero-sum game. On the other side of the ledger from those who have suffered large losses are those who have gained the same large amounts. However, economic activity and the depth of the capital markets are enhanced by the risk reduction (hedging) that derivatives afford corporations.

Q1 Why would you think the U.S. dollar dominates foreign exchange contracts, whereas interest rate contracts are equally split between euros and the U.S. dollar?

Q2 What trends in its latest report does the BIS note in the OTC derivatives market?

Q3 What derivatives players are featured in *The Big Short*?

bis.org

A forward will be used to hedge Bob's risk of price fluctuations on his corn crop. In early May, as Bob sows his crop, he agrees to sell his corn to a Lethbridge distiller, at an agreed price and for September delivery. The agreed price is $3.79 a bushel to be paid by the distillery on delivery in September. Bob could wait until September, but is exposed to a fair amount of uncertainty (or risk) as to the price of corn at that time. Based on corn prices over the last year, corn could sell for $4.40 a bushel (1 bushel = 0.35 hectolitres), which would be fortunate, or it could sell for $3.50, which would be unfortunate. In May corn sells for $3.75 in the cash market.

 FINANCE IN ACTION

Derivatives for Bob's Farming Operation

Bob farms in southern Alberta, growing about 500,000 bushels of corn each year. Most of his crop is sold to the distilleries in Lethbridge to produce liquor. With a little bit of flavouring, distilled corn can produce rum, rye, gin, and many of our favourite alcohols. There are many risks in farming, besides the weather. Bob knows fairly closely his costs of growing the corn, but with the volatile grain markets he is unsure what his crop will earn when sold for cash in the fall.

An average acre in southern Alberta with heavy irrigation produces fewer than 100 bushels of corn per acre compared to over 200 in Iowa, where little irrigation or fertilization are required. It's tough competition! Iowa, of course, sets the standard, and corn is bought and sold based on U.S. dollars. Corn also is the basis for the pricing of the other grains. Bob may employ one of several techniques to reduce the risk he faces on the price of his corn crop. He may employ forwards, futures, options, and/or insurance programs.

	Corn Price (US$)	Cash Received
Forward		
Agreed delivery of 500,000 bushels	$3.79	US$1,895,000 guaranteed
Could be.	4.40	US$2,200,000 possible
or	3.50	US$1,750,000 possible

By entering into a forward contract with the distillery, Bob has the responsibility to deliver 500,000 bushels of corn in September and in return will receive US$1,895,000 regardless of the price of corn at that time. The advantage of entering into the forward contract is that Bob knows exactly what his revenues will be and can determine if it is worth planting his crop. By waiting to sell the corn in September, Bob is exposed to a great deal of uncertainty. Forward contracts are often customized as to the exact amount and exact date required by the two parties. This exact matching of Bob's crop commodity (asset) with a forward contract (liability) is known as hedging. Perfect hedges are possible in the forward market, but they are difficult to achieve in future markets.

Forward contracts can be executed on any commodity, but the most common are foreign exchange or interest rate contracts. Usually, these are contracted with financial institutions, which act as brokers. The financial institution enters into a forward contract with one party to buy, let us say, a given amount of foreign currency at an agreed future date. Simultaneously, the financial institution enters into another forward contract to sell a similar amount of foreign currency to another party, also at that future date. The financial institution has little risk and is hedged. Moreover, it likely makes a profit by buying at one price and selling at a higher price.

FUTURES

Futures are similar to forward contracts, except that they are available through financial markets. Futures are standardized contracts that fix the price of some commodity for delivery at a specified place and a specified time in the future. Futures are generally available on commodities, interest rates, market indexes, and currencies. They allow for flexibility in delivery, as the underlying asset can be delivered any time during the month of expiry. The standardization of the contract produces contracts that are available only in set amounts or multiples thereof, only for certain months, and may require delivery of a specific quality of asset. For example, on the Chicago Mercantile Exchange the Canadian dollar is available only in multiples of $100,000 and only for the months of March, June, September, and December. In dealing in commodities such as wheat, only a specified grade of wheat is acceptable for delivery. With bond futures, the specified underlying asset is a bond of a minimum given maturity.

A Brief History of Derivatives

	Ancient Greece, Rome, and medieval trade fairs showed evidence of forward contracting for the delivery of commodities. Lacked standardization of contracts and an active marketplace.
15th century	London, Bruges, Antwerp, Amsterdam trading centres • Forward contracts in use.
1571	Royal Exchange of London (London International Financial Futures and Options Exchange) • Commodity exchange.
1634–38	Tulip Bulb Craze • Call options on tulip bulbs. Option holder had the right to purchase next year's bulbs at today's prices, at a premium of 20 percent.
1848	Chicago Board of Trade/Chicago Board Option Exchange • Local grain merchants provided marketplace to sell commodities, reducing price volatility. This prompted investment in storage facilities, transportation networks, performance bonds (margins) to overcome defaults, and warehouse receipts issued by a clearing office to satisfy forward contracts. Thereafter, forward contracts could be settled through the clearing office by buying and selling contracts for the same month.
1869	Royal Exchange of London • The Suez Canal was completed, reducing the shipping and delivery times to three months. The forward contract on tin was set at three months.
1887	Winnipeg Grain and Produce Exchange (Winnipeg Commodity Exchange, WCE) • Futures contracts for farm produce made available.
1971	International Money Market (IMM) (part of Chicago Mercantile Exchange (CME)) • Foreign currency futures introduced in response to freely floating exchange rates.
1973	Black-Scholes model for European call and put options introduced.
1973	Chicago Board Options Exchange (CBOE) • Standardized listed options on stocks.
1974	Montreal Stock Exchange (ME) • Stock, interest rate (1979) options and futures introduced.
1975	Chicago Board of Trade (CBOT) • Interest rate futures to hedge volatile interest rates.
1981	Chicago Board of Trade (CBOT) • Eurodollar future introduced as first cash-settled contract.
1982	Kansas City Board of Trade • Stock index futures introduced on Value Line Index.
1983	New York Mercantile Exchange (NYMEX) • Stock index futures introduced.
1984	Chicago Board Options Exchange (CBOE) • Options available on stock indexes, followed by interest rate options in 1989, LEAPS (long-term) in 1990, and FLEX (flexible exchange options on indexes) available in 1993.
1999	Chicago Mercantile Exchange (CME) • Temperature-related futures (HDD, CDD) are announced.
2000	CME demutualizes and markets begin to integrate and merge.
2007–08	CME Group formed, combining CME, CBOT, NYMEX, COMEX. NYSE/Euronext merger brings in LIFFE. Large losses by Morgan Stanley, AIG, and JP Morgan (2012) on credit default swaps.
2010	Dodd-Frank legislation calls for increased transparency in derivatives markets, bringing them into exchanges.

| 2013 | Intercontinental Exchange (ICE) purchases NYSE-Euronext. |
| 2017 | Deutsche Bank ($170 million), Barclays ($94 million), and HSBC ($45 million) settle lawsuits for conspiring to manipulate the European Interbank Offered Rate (Euribor) and related derivatives. |

cboe.com   sgx.com   m-x.ca/accueil_en.php
cmegroup.com   theice.com   nseindia.com

 FINANCE IN ACTION

Go Forward with Energy, Hogs, or Currency

Forwards are a risk management tool to lock in the prices on commercial transactions for some time in the future. They are customized products developed by individual firms to suit the needs of their customers. These forward contracts, although generally similar in the basics, have unique features and economic influences that require a strong understanding of each forward's risks and rewards. Futures are similar to forwards but are standardized and sell on organized exchanges.

With deregulation of the energy markets, forward contracts on the price of power were instituted by Ontario Power Generation (OPG), which is in the business of the generation and sale of electricity to customers. The ICE (NGX) now provides futures on natural gas and electricity.

Ontario Pork provides a similar service, in another product, to hog producers. Examine these contracts at ontariopork.on.ca. Futures hog pricing is also available at the CME Group.

Perhaps the best-developed forward market is on currency forwards. These markets tend to be dominated by the banking industry, but there are some other players in the market.

One player in the market is OFX. Forward rate quotes are available at the UBC Sauder website (fx.sauder.ubc.ca).

Q1 How is the forward rate determined on currencies, according to Canadian Forex?

CME Group   **cmegroup.com**

Futures exchanges trace their modern development to the middle of the 19th century. The forward markets at the Royal Exchange of London and the Chicago Board of Trade began to develop standardized contracts. These became known as futures. The three-month contract, standard on all futures exchanges today, was instituted at the Royal Exchange in 1869. The three-month period was the result of the opening of the Suez Canal; shipping times from suppliers throughout the British Empire now became reliable and achievable in less than three months.

The Chicago Board of Trade, one part of the CME Group, established performance bonds (margins) held by third parties to overcome the defaults that often occurred on forward contracts. To satisfy contract deliveries, a seller had to deliver the underlying asset to a warehouse, and a receipt was issued by a clearing office. When this practice was well established, contracts could be settled through the clearing office by buying and selling contracts for the same month. An actual physical exchange of the asset did not have to take place! Today over 90 percent of futures contracts are satisfied with no actual delivery of the asset to the futures exchange. The contract is closed out in Chicago and the actual delivery of the underlying asset occurs locally. The standardization of contracts and the establishment of procedures have ensured reliable markets with liquidity where traders can establish future prices for assets.

To examine how a futures contract works, let us return to our example of Bob, the farmer in southern Alberta, who sells his corn crop of 500,000 bushels each fall. Bob sold his corn crop to a Lethbridge distiller by way of a forward contract. However, let us suppose that Bob does not have a firm contract and needs to sell his corn crop to the general market.

With standardized futures contracts, there is unlikely to be one that exactly covers the amount of the underlying asset required or is deliverable on the exact date the asset is required or available. Futures expire on the third Friday of a given month, and it is usually best to select the future with the closest expiry date after the asset is required or available.

In our example, outlined below, a standardized contract happens to cover the underlying asset and delivery date completely, but that is rarely the case. The forward contract results are noted for comparison.

	Corn Price (US$)	Cash Received (US$)
Forward (from previous section)		
Agreed delivery of 500,000 bushels	$3.79	$1,895,000 guaranteed
In September		
Sell corn at		
Cash (spot) rate	3.50	$1,750,000
Close out future		
Future (September expiry)		
Sold at	3.78	$1,890,000
Purchase at	3.52	$1,760,000
Gain (loss) on future	0.26	$ 130,000
Total revenues with cash market and future.		**$1,880,000**

In May, through the CME Group, Bob purchases a contract to sell corn at an agreed price of US$3.78 a bushel for 500,000 bushels. The futures market allows a participant to buy (go long) or to sell (go short) at the quoted future price. Bob has gone short and is obligated to deliver 500,000 bushels of corn by September or close out his contract. With the forward contract Bob is locked in, but the future contract allows Bob to sell the contract back to the market before it expires.

In September, Bob will deliver his corn to a local buyer, as he does not want to deliver his corn to Chicago. He will receive the September cash price, which in our example is US$3.50 a bushel. This is less than his expectation of $3.78 based on the futures contract that he purchased in May. However, the September futures contract is trading at US$3.52 in Chicago when it is September. Since Bob already has a future contract to sell at $3.78, he now purchases a contract to buy at $3.52. The contracts now offset each other, and the market credits Bob with the gain or loss. In this example, Bob has earned $130,000, which can be added to monies received in the cash market for total revenues of US$1,880,000.

CME Group
cmegroup.com

Bob has not done as well as in the forward market because of transportation cost considerations between Chicago and southern Alberta. This is why the future contract price in Chicago and the cash price in Alberta are slightly different in September. The key to the future contract is that the price of corn is locked in close to a predicted price and there will be no large surprises. The futures market also gives participants the liquidity to move out of a contractual position at their convenience, at prices that are competitively determined. If corn had moved in the opposite direction in this example, the cash market would have presented a gain to Bob, but he would have suffered a loss on the future contract.

When a futures contract is purchased, a small margin deposit is required. This is a small percentage of the overall contract amount, such as 5 percent. Each day, as the future contract moves in price, the profit or loss is marked to market. This means that the margin deposit is debited or credited. If the margin deposit begins to be depleted, a further margin deposit may be required. In Bob's case, he contracted to sell at US$3.78 a bushel. If the September contract moved to $3.80, Bob is out some money and $10,000 ($0.02 × 500,000) will be debited from his margin account.

This futures example does not identify an important risk to Bob. What would happen in a bad crop year if Bob is able to produce only 167,000 bushels of corn, a worst-case scenario? Bob will have to purchase 333,000 bushels of corn in the market to deliver under his contract or close out the contract. It is likely that if Bob has had a crop failure there has been a general failure, and corn prices will be sky-high. Purchasing the corn in the cash market will be very expensive, or alternatively, closing out the futures contract by purchasing a contract to buy will incur a large loss. How can Bob protect against this possible outcome? In May, Bob could have purchased options to buy 333,000 bushels of corn. This would act as insurance.

LO2 OPTIONS

Although options have been in existence for a long time, their modern development on financial exchanges can also be traced to the middle of the 19th century. Options are similar to futures. Options are standardized contracts that fix the price of some commodity for delivery at a specified place and a specified time in the future. Unlike futures and forwards, options can expire. The holder of an option can exercise the option, sell it, or let it expire. In 1973, the Black-Scholes model for pricing European call and put options was introduced, and the Chicago Board Options Exchange (CBOE) listed standardized options on stocks. Today, there are options available on stocks, market indexes, currencies, interest rates, and numerous commodities.

There are some key terms to understanding options (See also Figure 19–1 and Figure 19–2):

- *Call option* gives the holder the right to *buy* an underlying asset at a preset price.

- *Put option* gives the holder the right to *sell* an underlying asset.

Chicago Board Options Exchange
cboe.com

- *Underlying asset* is the commodity, currency, bond, stock, or other asset that is deliverable under the option contract.

- *Exercise or strike price* is the preset price at which the underlying security can be bought or sold, based on the price contracted for under the option. The exercise price is not the same as the current market price of the underlying asset.

- *Premium* is the price at which an option is bought or sold in the market. If you purchase an option, the price you pay is called a premium.

- *Intrinsic value* is the minimum value of an option.

- *Speculative (time value) premium* is the difference between the market price of an option (premium) and its intrinsic value.

Call option
Derivatives market clearinghouse

Call option purchaser
Holder

Call option seller
Writer

Put option
Derivatives market clearinghouse

Put option purchaser
Holder

Put option seller
Writer

Figure 19–1 Option participants

As an example, we might purchase a call (put) option, which gives us the right to buy (sell) 5,000 bushels of corn (the underlying asset) at a fixed price of US$2.30 (the exercise price) any time until the third Friday in September. This price would be set even if corn fell to US$1.60 or rose to US$3 in the cash markets. For this option, we might pay $0.14 a bushel or US$700 ($0.14 × 5,000 bushels). The US$700 is called the premium. When we purchase an option, another party sells it. The seller of an option is called the writer and is under an obligation, if the option is exercised.

- **Call option writer** is obligated to **sell** the underlying asset, at the preset price, to the option holder if the option is exercised.
- **Put option writer** is obligated to **buy** the underlying asset, at the preset price, from the option holder if the option is exercised.
- The exchange (such as the CBOE) acts as a clearinghouse, executing contracts to ensure that they are honoured. This requires separate contacts with both the purchaser and seller of an option.
- The Montreal Options Exchange provides an options calculator for practising with options valuation. (m-x.ca/accueil_en.php)

Call Option

Let us examine a call option on the shares of a company. In February, shares in Walter P. Company trade at $25. Call options are available on organized exchanges, independent of the company shares. On one such exchange, a May call option on Walter P. Company is being sold, with an exercise price of $24. This gives the holder the right to Walter P. Company shares at the exercise price of $24 per share up to May. One call option gives the right to buy one share, but options are usually purchased in multiples of 100. There is no obligation to buy.

This call option would have a minimum or intrinsic value of $1 ($25 − $24), because at a minimum we can exercise the option to buy shares worth $25 for only $24. Experience tells us that options almost always trade above the intrinsic value by a speculative premium. Therefore, in our example the option's market price or premium is $2.50 (picked arbitrarily for this example). The speculative premium is $1.50 ($2.50 − $1). For $2.50 the purchaser of the call option can purchase a share of Walter P. Company for $24 until May.

The call option pricing relationships are illustrated in Figure 19–2. The illustration shows that the actual market price of the option (the premium) is greater than the intrinsic value at all values.

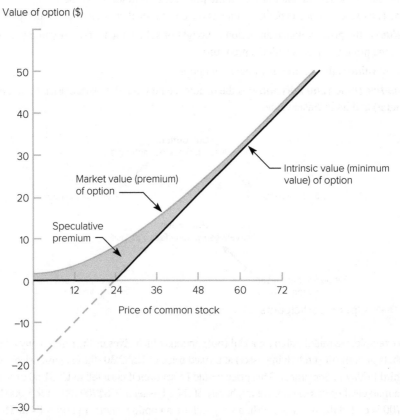

Figure 19–2 Market price relationships for a call option

		Share Price Increases To:	Gain
Share price	$25.00	$50.00	$50 – $25 ÷ $25 = 100%
Call option @ $24.00 for May			
Intrinsic value of the option	$25.00 – $24.00 = $ 1.00	$50.00 – $24.00 = $26.00	
Speculative premium	$ 1.50	$ 0.75 (arbitrary pick)	
Premium (market price of call)	$ 2.50	$26.75	$26.75 – $2.50 ÷ $2.50 = 970%
		Share Price Decreases To:	Loss
Shares	$25.00	$12.50	$12.50 – $25 ÷ $25 = –50%
Call option @ $24.00 for May		$12.50 – $24.00 = $ 0.00	
Speculative premium		$ 0.25 (arbitrary pick)	
Premium (market price of call)	$ 2.50	$ 0.25	$0.25 – $2.50 ÷ $2.50 = –90%

Also, the intrinsic value is zero until the market price of the underlying share rises above the exercise price of $24.

In the illustration above, we see what can happen as the underlying share price moves up or down. If the share price moves up to $50, the call option on the share at the fixed price of $24 will be worth $26.75, including the speculative premium. However, if the share price moves down, the option almost becomes worthless. The potential gain or loss on the call option is much greater than the gain or loss on the shares by themselves. Figure 19–1 also illustrates the relationships in this example.

The size of a speculative premium in the markets will be determined by

1. **The time to expiry of the option.** A longer time to expiry gives a greater time for the underlying asset to rise in price.

2. **The volatility of the underlying share (asset).** An asset that has larger price changes stands a greater chance of having a significant price increase. This has value to the option investor.

3. **The opportunity cost of funds.** At a higher opportunity cost of funds it is more advantageous for an investor to be holding the option, at a lower cash outlay, than the actual share. This has value to the option investor.

When an investor sees value in a characteristic of an option, the speculative premium will increase. The relationships between intrinsic value, market value of an option, and the underlying share (asset) value are illustrated in Figure 19–1. The actual market price of an option is always greater than the intrinsic value. The intrinsic value is zero until the market price of the underlying shares rises above the exercise price of $24.

Put Option

Now let us examine a put option on the stock of Walter P. Company. Shares in Walter P. Company in February trade at $25. On organized exchanges independent of the company shares, a May put option is available at the exercise price of $27. This gives the holder the right to **sell** Walter P. Company shares at an exercise price of $27 per share up to May. There is no obligation to sell.

This put option would have a minimum, or intrinsic, value of $2 ($27 – $25), because we can exercise the option to sell shares at $27 that are worth only $25. Experience again tells us that options almost always trade above the intrinsic value by a speculative premium. Therefore, in our example the option's market price is $3 (picked arbitrarily for this example). The speculative premium is $1. For $3 the purchaser of the put option can sell a share of Walter P. Company for $27 until May.

The put option pricing relationships are illustrated in Figure 19–3. The illustration shows that the actual market price of the option (the premium) is greater than its intrinsic value at all values. Also, the intrinsic value is zero until the market price of the underlying share falls below the exercise price of $27.

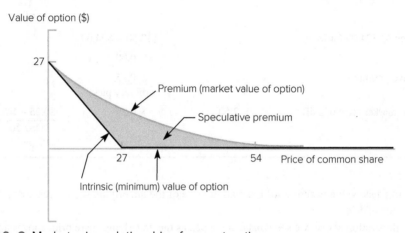

Figure 19–3 Market price relationships for a put option

In the illustration, we see what can happen as the underlying share price moves up or down. If the share price moves down to $12.50, the put option on the share at the fixed price of $27 will be worth $15, including the speculative premium. However, if the share price moves up to $50, the option almost becomes worthless because of the put option holder's right to sell a $50 share at $27.

The size of a speculative premium will be determined, as it was for call options, by the time to expiry of the option, the volatility of the underlying share (asset), and the opportunity cost of funds. As the first two factors increase, so will the speculative premium on a put option. The speculative premium of a put option will fall as the opportunity cost increases.

Put options are often used to hedge or reduce the risk of holding an asset. In the above example, if a share of Walter P. Company were held as well as put, notice what happens. If the share price goes up, the investor gains big on the shares but loses $2.75 on the put. However, if the share price goes down, the loss of $12.50 on the share is offset by the gain of $12 on the put option. The put option can be thought of as insurance protecting against a drop in the price of the stock, with the price of the option the premium on the insurance.

		Share Price Increases To:	Gain
Share price	$25.00	$50.00	$50 − $25 over $25 = 100%

The gain is shown as:

$$\frac{\$50 - \$25}{\$25} = 100\%$$

Put option @ $27.00 for May

		Share Price Increases To:	
Intrinsic value of the option	$27.00 − $25.00 = $ 2.00	$27.00 − $50.00 = $ 0.00	
Speculative premium	$ 1.00	$ 0.25 (arbitrary pick)	
Premium (market price of put)	$ 3.00	$ 0.25	$0.25 − $3 over $3 = −92%

$$\frac{\$0.25 - \$3}{\$3} = -92\%$$

		Share Price Decreases To:	Loss
Shares	$25.00	$12.50	$12.50 − $25 over $25 = −50%

$$\frac{\$12.50 - \$25}{\$25} = -50\%$$

Put option @ $27.00 for May

		Share Price Decreases To:	
Put option @ $27.00 for May		$27.00 − $12.50 = $14.50	
Speculative premium		$ 0.50 (arbitrary pick)	
Premium (market price of call)	$ 3.050	$15.00	$15 − $3 over $3 = 400%

$$\frac{\$15 - \$3}{\$3} = 400\%$$

OPTIONS VERSUS FUTURES

Both options and futures have a limited life, are standardized, and are guaranteed by the market acting as a clearinghouse. Differences relate to the pattern of cash flows experienced:

Options

- Require a larger up-front payment with speculative premium
- Involve limited risk—the maximum potential loss is the purchase price
- Can have delivery anytime
- Are most useful when used in conjunction with a potential business contract; if the contract falls through, the option does not have to be exercised

Futures

- Require a small margin deposit, credited or debited (marked to market) daily as the current futures price moves up or down from the original contracted future price
- Can have delivery only in the delivery month

Options Issued by Corporations

To raise capital for the corporation, options are sometimes issued, as they may better meet the investment objectives of securities investors. Rights, convertible securities, and warrants are types of options issued by corporations, and they confer on the holder the right to acquire shares in the corporation for a preset price and up to a preset date. Once these corporate options are issued they usually trade on organized or over-the-counter exchanges until their expiry. Their value is determined in much the same way as call options.

FINANCE IN ACTION

Weather Derivatives

Weather derivatives are offered in the over-the-counter market to lay off, or hedge, the risk companies face from adverse weather conditions. Risk would be handled through the market rather than a specific insurance carrier. In 1999, the Chicago Mercantile Exchange began offering temperature-related futures and options based on the temperature being above or below a given value. Details on weather futures can be found at the CME website.

Warm temperatures, for example, can have an effect on ski areas; the revenues generated by utility companies; or, if the temperatures are quite warm, the costs of running air conditioners. Likewise, cool temperatures can have an effect on business costs. Weather options and futures can reduce the risks companies face if weather conditions are different from the expected. These derivatives can compensate for losses incurred that result from the abnormal weather.

Q1 What is a "degree day" as used for a weather derivative?

cmegroup.com

LO3 CONVERTIBLE SECURITIES

A convertible security is a bond or share of preferred stock that can be converted, at the option of the holder, into common stock. Thus, the owner has a fixed-income security that can be transferred to a common stock interest if and when the affairs of the firm indicate that such a conversion is desirable. For purposes of discussion we refer to convertible bonds (debentures), although the same principles apply to convertible preferred stock. These securities are sold by corporations to raise capital.

When a convertible debenture is initially issued, a conversion ratio to common stock is specified. The ratio indicates the number of shares of common stock to which the debenture may be converted. The conversion ratio may also be expressed as a conversion price. To arrive at the conversion price, we divide the face value of the bond by the conversion ratio.

LO4   **Face value = Conversion price × Conversion ratio**   **(19–1)**

The Williams Company

$10 million of convertible debentures

Maturity in 25 years

Coupon rate 6%

Current yield on pure bond (no conversion features) of similar risk is 8%.

Each $1,000 bond is convertible into 20 shares (conversion ratio) of common stock.

The conversion ratio is 20 and the conversion price is $50.

$1,000. . . . . = 20 × $50 (with formula 19–1)

Common share price . . . . = $45

Conversion value . . . . = $45 × 20 = $900

Convertible debenture market price. . . . . = $1,010

Conversion premium . . . . = $1,010 − $900 = $110

Pure bond value . . . . = $785.18

Premium over pure bond value. . . . . = $1,010 − $785.18 = $224.82

LO5 Value of the Convertible Bond

Convertible bonds have a minimum value determined by their value either as equity or as debt. The conversion privilege gives an equity value based on the share price. This conversion value is produced from the common share price times the number of shares received (conversion ratio) on conversion. For a bond (or debenture) of the Williams Company, this is $900 ($45 × 20). Convertible bonds will initially sell for close to par, or face value, ($1,000). If the Williams bond sells for $1,010 (assumed) and the conversion value is $900, there is a $110 conversion premium, representing the dollar difference between market value of the convertible bond and its conversion value. The extent of the conversion premium is influenced by the expectations of future performance of the common stock.

If the price of the common stock really takes off and goes to $60 per share, the conversion privilege becomes quite valuable. The bond, which is convertible into 20 shares, will go up to at least $1,200 and perhaps more. You do not have to convert to common shares immediately but may enjoy the price appreciation of the convertible in concert with the common shares.

Convertible bonds also have debt value. If the common share price drops to $25, we find that the value of the convertible bond will not fall all the way to $500 (20 × $25 per share). This is because the convertible still has value as an interest-bearing security. A pure or straight debt issue (no conversion feature) of similar maturity (25 years) and quality with an 8 percent yield has a pure bond value of $785.18.[1] The convertible will not fall below this value.[2] With a market price of $1,010, the premium over the pure bond value is $224.82 ($1,010 − $785.18).

Thus, a convertible bond has a floor value determined by its value as either equity or debt. On the other hand, it has upside potential (with some downside protection) and will, therefore, trade at a premium to the higher of its conversion value or pure bond value.

The price pattern for the Williams convertible bond is depicted in Figure 19–4. We see the effect on the convertible bond price as the common stock price, shown along the horizontal axis, is assumed

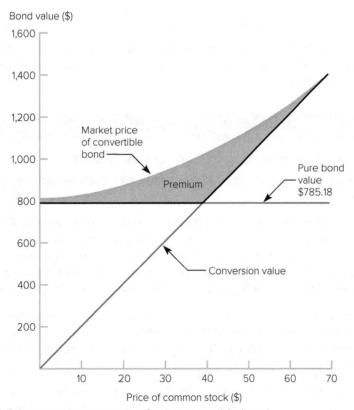

Figure 19–4 Price movement pattern for a convertible bond

---

[1]Based on the discounting procedures of Chapter 10, with semiannual coupon payments.
[2]The floor value can change if interest rates in the market change. For now we assume they are constant.

to change. When the common stock price is very low, the convertible trades above the pure bond value. As the common stock price moves to higher levels, the convertible bond trades at a premium to its conversion value. It always seems to trade at a premium to one of these "floor" values.

Is This Fool's Gold?

Have we repealed the old risk-return tradeoff principle—the idea that to get superior returns we must take larger than normal risks? With convertible bonds, we appear to limit our risk while maximizing our return potential. Although there is some truth to this statement, there are many qualifications.

- **Limited downside protection.** When convertible debentures begin going up in value, the floor's protection can become meaningless. In the case of the Williams Company, the floor is at $785.18. An investor who bought the convertible bond at $1,200 would be exposed to $414.82 in potential losses (hardly adequate protection for a true risk averter). If interest rates in the market rise, the floor price, or pure bond value, could fall, creating more downside risk.

- **Below market-rate interest.** The interest rate on convertibles is significantly below that for instruments in a similar risk class at time of issue.

- **Premium payment.** The premium payment is a cost forgone in purchasing additional shares to garner a profit in case share price goes up.

- **Possible call provision attachment.** A call provision can give the corporation the option of redeeming the bonds at a specified price above par ($1,000) in the future.

None of these negatives is meant to detract from the fact that convertibles carry some inherently attractive features if they are purchased with investor objectives in mind. If the investor wants downside protection, they should search out convertible bonds trading below par, perhaps within 10 to 15 percent of the floor value. Though a fairly large move in the stock may be necessary to generate upside profit, the investor has the desired protection and some hope for capital appreciation.

Advantages and Disadvantages to the Corporation

Having established the fundamental characteristics of the convertible security from the investor's viewpoint, let us now examine the factors a corporate financial officer must consider in weighing the advisability of a convertible offer for the firm.

 FINANCE IN ACTION

Financing With or Investing in Convertible Securities

Innergex Renewable Energy Inc. (INE: TSX) develops and operates hydro, wind, and solar energy.

In late 2019 the company raised $125 million in capital by issuing convertible unsecured subordinated debentures with a 4.65 percent coupon, conversion price of $22.90, conversion ratio of 43.6681, and maturity of October 2026. They were redeemable at par after October 2022. In 2019 the share price was about $16 at the time of issue. Why would the convertible bond trade primarily as a fixed-income security (pure bond value)?

At the same time Innergex called for the redemption of its 4.25 percent convertible debentures that has a maturity date of October 2020. Their conversion price was $15. There was $100 million outstanding. Should an investor have accepted the call at par value ($1,000) or converted?

In May 2019 Tesla (TSLA: Nasdaq) issued $1.35 billion of convertible bonds to mature in 2024. They had a coupon rate of 2 percent and a conversion ratio of 3.2276 shares. In March of 2020, during the Covid-19 pandemic, Tesla shares were trading at about $519. Why would the convertible bond trad primarily as an equity security and at what approximate price?

Advantages

- Interest paid on convertible issues is lower than that paid on a straight debt instrument.
- Convertible feature acts as a sweetener that allows smaller corporations access to the bond market.
- Convertible debentures are attractive to a corporation that believes its stock is currently undervalued.

Recall that in the case of the Williams Company, $1,000 bonds were convertible into 20 shares of common stock at a conversion price of $50. Since the common stock had a current price of $45 and new shares of stock might be sold at only $44, the corporation effectively received $6 over current market price, assuming future conversion.[3]

Disadvantages

- If stock price rises above the conversion price, the firm could raise the capital needed by issuing fewer shares than those sold from the conversion of the securities.

For example, if a firm needs $10 million in funds and offers straight stock now at a net price of $44, it must issue 227,272 shares. With a convertible price of $50, the number of shares potentially issued is only 200,000 shares. Finally, if no convertible bonds are issued now and the stock goes up to $60, only 166,667 shares will be required.

- Corporations must consider the accounting treatment accorded to convertibles.
- Proper procedure ensures that there is a dilution effect on earnings per share when convertible securities are issued.
- In addition, management should consider the potential reduction in voting power after conversion occurs.
- A call provision must be established at issue in order for the company to force security holders to convert the securities to common stock.

Forcing Conversion

We know that when the value of the common stock goes up, the convertible security moves in a similar fashion. Convertible debentures may go up substantially in value if the share value increases and the debenture will trade primarily as equity. However, the holder of a convertible bond has no immediate incentive to convert to common because of the interest payments, unless the company calls the bond.

At the time of issue, a corporation establishes a future privilege for calling in the bond at some percent above par value. Thus, the $1,000 debenture is redeemable at an amount greater than $1,000. Most bonds have a 5 to 10 percent call premium, often declining as the bond gets closer to maturity. If a corporation wishes to force conversion when the conversion value rises above the call price, it merely announces that it will call the issue at the call price. Bondholders have the choice between converting to shares of stock or accepting the call price. All rational bondholders take the shares if they have a higher value. The term forced conversion is derived from the fact that in such a situation, the bondholder has no choice but to convert.

Conversion may also be encouraged through a step-up in the conversion price over time. At the end of specified time periods the bond is convertible into a decreasing number of shares. Thus, there is a strong inducement to convert rather than accept an adjustment to a higher conversion price and a lower conversion ratio. The effectiveness of this step-up provision in forcing conversion depends on positive share price performance.

---

[3] There is always a bit of underpricing to ensure the success of a new offering.

Accounting Considerations with Convertibles

Convertible securities, warrants (long-term options to buy stock), and other dilutive securities may generate additional common stock in the future and therefore the potential effect of the diluted earnings per share should be considered. Let us examine the unadjusted (for conversion) financial statements of the XYZ Corporation in Table 19–1.

Table 19–1 XYZ Corporation

1. *Condensed balance sheet:*

4.5% convertible debentures (10,000 debentures of $1,000 convertible into 40 shares per bond, or a total of 400,000 shares)	$10,000,000
Shareholders' equity	
Common stock (1 million shares)	10,000,000
Retained earnings.	20,000,000
Liabilities and shareholders' equity.	$40,000,000

2. *Condensed income statement:*

Earnings before interest and taxes	$ 2,450,000
Interest (4.5% of $10 million)	450,000
Earnings before taxes.	2,000,000
Taxes (25%)	500,000
Earnings after taxes	$ 1,500,000

3. *Earnings per share:*

$$\frac{\text{Earnings after taxes}}{\text{Shares of common outstanding}} = \frac{\$1,500,000}{1,000,000} = \$1.50 \text{ (basic)}$$

4. *Diluted earnings per share:*

$$\frac{\text{Adjusted aftertax earnings}}{\text{Shares outstanding + Shares from conversion}} = \frac{\overset{\text{Reported earnings}}{\$1,500,000} + \overset{\text{Interest savings}}{\$225,000}}{1,000,000 + 400,000}$$

$$= \frac{\$1,725,000}{1,400,000} = \$1.23/\text{share}$$

An analyst would hardly be satisfied in accepting the unadjusted earnings per share (EPS) figure of $1 for the XYZ Corporation. In computing EPS, we have not accounted for the 400,000 additional shares of common stock that could be created by converting the bonds.

How then do we make this full disclosure? According to the Chartered Professional Accountants Canada (CPA), we need to compute EPS as if the common shares related to conversions had actually been issued at the beginning of the accounting period.

CPA Canada
cpacanada.ca

$$\text{Diluted earnings per share} = \frac{\text{Adjusted aftertax earnings}}{\text{Shares outstanding + Shares from conversion}} \quad (19\text{--}2)$$

Earnings must be redefined to add the costs related to the convertible securities to the numerator of the EPS ratio. Thus, the adjustment would include adding dividends paid on convertible preferred shares, interest (after tax) on convertible debt, and appropriate adjustments on the cash that would have been received had warrants, rights, and options been exercised. The denominator in the ratio includes common shares outstanding, the common share equivalent of all convertible preferred shares and bonds, the common shares that would be issued if all outstanding rights to purchase common shares were exercised, and the common shares that would be issued if all outstanding warrants and other options were exercised. Cash received from the potential exercise of a warrant or option is used to reduce the number of shares outstanding. Conversions that result in a higher EPS or lower loss per share (i.e., antidilutive) are ignored.

We get new EPS for the XYZ Corporation by assuming that 400,000 new shares would have been created from potential conversion while, at the same time, allowing for the reduction in interest payments that would have occurred as a result of the conversion of the debt to common stock. Since before-tax interest payments on the convertibles are $450,000 annually for the XYZ Corporation, the aftertax cost is about $225,000. The assumption is that had conversion occurred at the beginning of the year, this aftertax interest cost would have been saved, augmenting the reported income by $225,000. Thus, diluted earnings per share for XYZ Corporation become $1.23.

$$\text{Diluted earnings per share} = \frac{\text{Adjusted aftertax earnings}}{\text{Shares outstanding } + \text{ Shares from conversion}}$$

$$= \frac{\overset{\text{Reported}}{\underset{\text{earnings}}{\$1,500,000}} + \overset{\text{Interest}}{\underset{\text{savings}}{\$225,000}}}{1,000,000 + 400,000} = \frac{\$1,725,000}{1,400,000} = \$1.23/\text{share}$$

The result of calculating the diluted earnings per share amount is a reduction of 18 percent from the (basic) earnings per share. The new figure is the one that would be used by a sophisticated investor in analyzing the value of a common share of XYZ Corporation.

Some Final Comments on Convertible Securities

While convertible debentures in the U.S. market are of such importance that they encourage much investor activity and research, in Canada they account for a small percentage of capital market activity. Nevertheless, there are a number of ETFs (such as Blackrock's CVD: TSX) that hold a diversified portfolio of convertible securities.

LO6 WARRANTS

A warrant is an option to buy a stated number of shares of stock at a specified price over a given time period. We can find numerous warrants listed on the Toronto Stock Exchange (TSX) and the Venture Exchange (TSX-V) with the suffix –WT, after the share symbol. Warrants are favoured by small businesses and are issued more frequently on the Venture Exchange. The warrants issued on the Venture Exchange tend to expire in a shorter time.

FINANCE IN ACTION

Preferreds with Options

Preferred issues tend to round out the capital structure of many Canadian firms, especially banks and utilities. In theory, preferreds are perpetual securities with cumulative or non-cumulative dividends, usually on a quarterly basis. They are fixed income securities.

However, on closer examination, most preferreds have some sort of option for the benefit of the issuer and/or the holder. Many preferreds have a reset option by which the firm can change the coupon rate on a predetermined basis. They also have an option available to the holder to convert to a floating rate coupon or the reverse if the preferred already has a floating rate. Some also have the option to convert the preferred in a common share.

Healthy yields are available on the preferred shares on an aftertax basis (dividend tax credit) when compared to bond yields.

Preferreds are listed on the TSX with "PR" added after the company's share symbol and can be found on various websites. To find the options available on preferred issue, the footnotes to the financial statements of the company, under share capital, can be useful.

Q1 Can you find current outstanding convertible preferred shares?

Q2 Why do the BCE preferreds seem to come in pairs (i.e., the S/T series?

cibc.com
bce.ca

Issue; Dividend	Rating	Conversion Value	Market Value	Preferred Yield	Common Yield
CIBC(CM.PR.P); $0.2443	P-3(High)	n/a	$11.65	8.39%	4.73%
BCE(BCE.PR.M); $0.1727	P-2(low)	n/a	$10.85	6.37%	4.85%

Table 19–2 shows three issues listed on the TSX. The Resverlogix warrants entitled the holder to buy one share of common stock for $2.05 until June 2021. As Resverlogix common shares traded above the exercise price, there is a positive intrinsic, or minimum, value for these warrants. The Spark Power warrant had no intrinsic value but still trades at a positive value as there is a possibility that its common shares will rise in value before August 2023.

Table 19–2 Relationships determining warrant prices, March 2020

(1) Firm	(2) Warrant Price	(3) Share Price	(4) Exercise Price	(5) Intrinsic Value (3) – (4)	(6) Speculative Premium (2) – (5)	(7) Expiry Date
Spark Power (SPG. WT.TO)	0.08	1.80	3.75	0	0.08	Aug. 2023
Resverlogix Corp. (RVX.WT.TO)	2.87	3.45	2.05	1.40	1.47	June 2021
Enwave (ENW.WT.V)	1.70	2.36	1.50	0.86	0.84	Nov. 2022

Traditionally, warrants were issued as a sweetener in a bond offering, making the issue of the debt feasible when it might not otherwise be so. More recently, warrants have been issued in conjunction with preferred share issues, common share issues, and even as a standalone fundraising issue. When warrants are attached to another security issue, such as a bond, the combination of bond and attached warrants is called a unit. Warrants are usually detachable from the other security in the unit and often trade on the Toronto Stock Exchange or its venture exchange. After warrants are exercised, the other security to which they were attached remains in existence.

Because a warrant is dependent on the market movement of the underlying common stock and has no "security value" as such, it is highly speculative. If the common stock of the firm is volatile, the value of the warrants may change dramatically. There is a high degree of risk entailed in investing in warrants. Warrants are popular with companies that are young and growing, with companies in some financial difficulty, and with the Canadian chartered banks.

LO7 Valuation of Warrants

Because the value of a warrant is closely tied to the underlying stock price, we can develop a formula for the intrinsic value of a warrant.

$$I = (M - E) \times N \quad \text{(19–3)}$$

Where

I = Intrinsic value of a warrant
M = Market value of common stock
E = Exercise price (or strike price) of a warrant
N = Number of shares each warrant entitles the holder to purchase

Using the data from Table 19–2, we see that Resverlogix's common shares were trading at $3.45 in March 2020. Each warrant carried with it the right to purchase one share of Resverlogix's common stock at the exercise price, or strike price, of $2.05 per share until June 2021. Using formula 19–3, the intrinsic (or minimum) value was $1.40, or ($3.45 − $2.05) × 1. Since the warrant had over a year to run and was an effective vehicle for speculative trading, it was selling at $2.87 per warrant. This was $1.47 more than its intrinsic value. Investors were willing to pay a premium because a small percentage gain in the share price could generate large percentage increases in the warrant price. Formula 19–4 demonstrates the calculation of the speculative premium.

$$S = W - I \quad \text{(19–4)}$$

Where

S = Speculative premium
W = Warrant price
I = Intrinsic value

For Resverlogix, we use the formula to show the indicated speculative premium of $1.47.

$$\$1.47 = \$2.87 - \$1.40$$

Even if Resverlogix were trading at less than the $2.05 exercise price, the warrant might still have some value in the market. Speculators might purchase the warrant in the hope that the common stock would increase sufficiently in the future to make the option provision valuable.

As an example, the warrant of Spark Power in Table 19–2 was selling at $0.08, even though the share price was $1.95 below the exercise price. Notice that the intrinsic (minimum) value of Spark Power is zero and is not negative when the market price is less than the exercise price. A warrant cannot have a negative intrinsic value. If the share price of Spark Power should surpass a price of $1.80 before August 2023, then the warrant would command a positive intrinsic value.

www.

Resverlogix
resverlogix.com

Since a lot can happen in the time before the warrant expires, investors are prepared to pay a speculative premium for Spark Power.

The typical relationship between the warrant price and the intrinsic value of a warrant is depicted in Figure 19–5. We assume that the warrant entitles the holder to purchase one new share of common stock at $20. Note that although the intrinsic value of the warrant is negative at a common stock price between $0 and $20, the warrant still carries some value in the market. Also, observe that the difference between the market price of the warrant and its intrinsic value is diminished at the upper ranges of value. Two reasons may be offered for the declining premium.

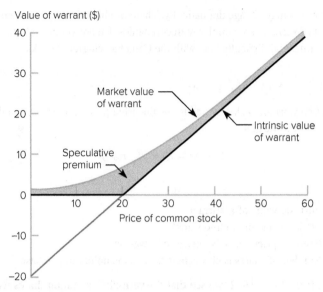

Figure 19–5 Market price relationships for a warrant

First, the speculator loses the ability to use leverage to generate high returns as the price of the stock goes up. When the price of the stock is relatively low, say $25, and the warrant is in the $5 range, a $10 movement in stock could mean a 200 percent gain in the value of the warrants, as indicated in the left-hand panel of Table 19–3.

At the upper levels of stock value, much of this leverage is lost. At a stock value of $50 and a warrant value of approximately $30, a $10 movement in the stock would produce only a 33 percent gain in the warrant, as indicated in the right panel of Table 19–3.

Table 19–3 Leverage in valuing warrants

Low Stock Price	High Stock Price
Stock price, $25; warrant price,	Stock price, $50; warrant price,
$5* + $10 movement in stock price	$30 + $10 movement in stock price
New warrant price, $15 ($10 gain)	New warrant price, $40 ($10 gain)
Percentage gain/in warrant	Percentage gain/in warrant
$= \dfrac{\$10}{\$5} \times 100 = 200\%$	$= \dfrac{\$10}{\$30} \times 100 = 33\%$

*The warrant price would be greater than $5 because of the speculative premium. Nevertheless, we use $5 for ease of computation.

Another reason speculators pay a very low premium at higher stock prices is that there is less downside protection. A warrant selling at $30 when the stock price is $50 is more vulnerable to downside movement than is a $5 to $10 warrant when the stock is in the $20 range.

Use of Warrants in Corporate Finance

Let us consider for a moment the suitability of warrants for corporate financing purposes. As previously discussed, warrants may allow for the issuance of debt under difficult circumstances. Though a straight debt issue may not be acceptable or may be accepted only at very high interest rates, the same security may be well received because of the inclusion of detachable warrants. Warrants may also be included as an add-on in a merger or acquisition agreement. For example, a firm might offer $20 million cash plus 10,000 warrants in exchange for all of the outstanding shares of the acquisition target.

The use of warrants has traditionally been associated with aggressive high-flying firms such as real estate investment trusts, airlines, and conglomerates. A perusal of the daily stock quotations reveals that warrants are a popular investment security issued by firms ranging from chartered banks to speculative mining companies.

Despite their popularity, warrants may not be as desirable as convertible securities as a financing device for creating new common stock. A corporation with convertible debentures outstanding may force the conversion of debt to common stock through a call, while no similar device is available to the firm with warrants. The only possible inducement for causing an early exercise of the warrant might be a step-up in option price, whereby the warrant holder may pay a progressively higher option price if they do not exercise by a given date.

The capital structure of the firm after the exercise of a warrant is somewhat different from that created after the conversion of a debenture. In the case of a warrant, the original debt outstanding remains in existence after the detachable warrant is exercised, whereas the conversion of a debenture extinguishes the former debt obligation.

LO8 Accounting Considerations with Warrants

As with convertible securities, the potential dilutive effect of warrants must be considered. All warrants are included in computing diluted earnings per share through the Treasury stock method (*CPA Canada Handbook—Accounting,* Section 3500). In the fully diluted earnings per share calculation, the accountant must recognize the weighted average number of common shares that would result from the exercise of all warrants at the beginning of the period and the proceeds used to buy back common shares at the average market price for the period. The basic and diluted earnings per share calculations are now similar to U.S. and International GAAP.

COMPARISONS OF RIGHTS, WARRANTS, AND CONVERTIBLES

In Chapter 17, we discussed common shareholders' right to purchase new shares. While rights, warrants, and convertibles all entitle individual investors to purchase new common shares, we can differentiate these financial instruments from the following perspectives listed in Table 19–4.

Table 19–4 Distinguishing rights, warrants, and convertible securities

	Rights	Warrants	Convertible Securities
Issuer	Issued by corporations; pre-emptive right.	Issued privately by corporations; attached to bonds, preferred shares, common shares or as a standalone issue. Used as sweeteners.	Issued by corporations; can be convertible bonds or preferred shares.
Exercise price and market price at time of issue	Subscription price < market price at time of issue	Exercise price > market price at time of issue	Conversion price > market price at time of issue
Time frame	Short	Long	Long
Dilution to existing shareholders	May help prevent dilution of ownership and voting power.	Yes. New shares are issued when exercised.	Yes. New shares are issued when converted.
Capital structural change when exercised	Corporation's equity increases while debt remains the same. No wealth effect on individuals if rights are exercised or sold.	Corporations' equity increases, while debt remains the same.	Corporation's debt is reduced, while equity increases when bonds are converted; delayed equity financing.

SUMMARY

1. Forwards, futures, and options are derivatives that can be used for speculative investment or, more importantly, to hedge a transaction. Derivatives increase or decrease risk. (LO1)

2. Convertible securities are options issued by the corporation as an alternative way to raise funds. Bonds and preferred shares may have a feature that allows conversion to common shares. The option to convert to common shares rests with the investor up to a certain date. (LO2)

3. Each security offers downside protection and upside potential. The holder has a fixed-income security that will not go below a minimum amount because of the interest or dividend payment feature, and at the same time they have a security that is potentially convertible to common stock. If the common stock goes up in value, the convertible security appreciates as well. From a corporate viewpoint the firm may force conversion to common stock through a call feature and thus achieve a balanced capital structure. Interest rates on convertibles are usually lower than those on straight debt issues. The same is true for dividends on convertible preferred shares. (LO3)

4. The conversion value is the equity value determined by the current market price multiplied by the number of shares received on conversion. (LO4)

5. A convertible security has value as a debt instrument (fixed interest return) and as equity (capital appreciation). (LO5)

6. A warrant is an option to buy a stated number of shares of stock at a specified price over a given time period. The warrant has a large potential for appreciation if the stock goes up in value. Traditionally, warrants have been used primarily as sweeteners for debt instruments or as add-ons in merger tender offers. Their use as investment vehicles in recent years has become quite extensive. When warrants are exercised, the basic debt instrument to which they may have been attached is not eliminated, as is the case for a convertible debenture. (LO6)

7. A warrant has an intrinsic value but trades above that value until the exercise date. This is known as the speculative premium. (LO7)

8. The potential dilutive effect of warrants and convertible securities is an important consideration in computing EPS. (LO8)

REVIEW OF FORMULAS

1. Face value = Conversion price × Conversion ratio   (19–1)

2. Diluted earnings per share = $\dfrac{\text{Adjusted aftertax earnings}}{\text{Shares outstanding} + \text{Shares from conversion}}$ (19–2)

3. Intrinsic value of a warrant $I = (M - E) \times N$ (19–3)

   Where

   I = Intrinsic value of a warrant
   M = Market value of common stock
   E = Exercise price (or strike price) of a warrant
   N = Number of shares each warrant entitles the holder to purchase

4. Speculative premium of a warrant $S = W - I$ (19–4)

   Where

   S = Speculative premium
   W = Warrant price
   I = Intrinsic value

DISCUSSION QUESTIONS

1. What is the difference between forwards, futures, and options? (LO1)

2. How can a company force conversion of a convertible bond? (LO4, LO5)

3. What are the basic advantages to the corporation of issuing convertible securities? (LO5)

4. Explain the difference between basic EPS and fully diluted EPS. (LO8)

5. Why, in the case of a convertible preferred share, are investors willing to pay a premium over the theoretical value (pure preferred value or conversion value)? (LO4)

6. Why is it said that convertible securities have a floor price? (LO4)

7. Find the price of two convertible securities in a newspaper. (LO4, LO5)
   a. Explain what factors cause their prices to be different from their par values.
   b. What will happen to their value if long-term interest rates decline?

8. What is meant by a step-up in the conversion price? (LO4, LO5)

9. Which adjustments to aftertax earnings are necessary to compute EPS when convertible preferred shares are outstanding? When warrants are outstanding? (LO8)

10. Explain how convertible bonds and warrants are similar and different. (LO6)

11. Explain why warrants generally are issued and why they are used in corporate finance. (LO6, LO7)

12. Why do warrants sell above their intrinsic values? (LO7)

13. Which factors determine the size of the speculative premium on a warrant? (LO7)

14. Investigate and explain put warrants. (LO7)

INTERNET RESOURCES AND QUESTIONS

Links to international futures and options exchanges can be found at: world-exchanges.org

The Globe and Mail, under Report on Business, provides exchange rates for major currencies: theglobeandmail.com/investing/market/currencies

The various futures and options exchanges have informative websites. The sites explain derivatives, list the types of contracts available, and in some cases provide pricing on the derivatives:

Key U.S. sites:	Canadian site:	International sites:
cboe.com	m-x.ca/accueil_en.php	lme.com
cmegroup.com		sgx.com
		theice.com

The Sauder School of Business provides extensive exchange rate information including forward rates: fx.sauder.ubc.ca

The Chicago Mercantile Exchange (CME) Group provides quotes for cash prices, futures settlement prices, and option settlement prices: cmegroup.com

The Toronto Stock Exchange provides quotes for shares and warrants: tmx.com

1. Global Surf and Turf has purchased software from a European manufacturer, with payment due three months from today. The payment due is 265,000 euros. Hedge this liability with a forward contract. How much will Surf and Turf pay in three months in Canadian dollars? How much would they have to pay today?

2. You expect to have 25,000 bushels of wheat for sale in the fall and you would like to hedge your risk of price fluctuations through the CME Group.

   a. Identify today's date and find the cash price for Chicago #2 hard winter wheat.

   b. Identify the settle price on a futures contract to sell your wheat in the fall. Assume you enter into a futures contract for 25,000 bushels of wheat.

   c. Assume the price of wheat in the cash market, in your region of the country, in the fall is US$12 a bushel above the spot price. Without delivering your wheat to Chicago, close out the futures contract and calculate your gains, losses, and net receipts on the 25,000 bushels of wheat.

   d. Assume the price of wheat in the cash market, in your region of the country, in the fall is US$8 a bushel below the spot price. Without delivering your wheat to Chicago, close out the futures contract and calculate your gains, losses, and net receipts on the 25,000 bushels of wheat.

3. You manufacture silver jewellery for sale to local retail outlets. This upcoming spring you will require 5,000 ounces of silver and you would like to hedge your risk of price fluctuations through the CME Group.

   a. Identify today's date and find the cash price for spot silver.

   b. Identify the settle price on a futures contract to buy your silver in the spring. Assume you enter into a futures contract for 5,000 ounces of silver.

   c. Assume the price of silver in the cash market, in your region of the country, in the fall is US$50 an ounce above the spot price. Without taking delivery of your silver through the Chicago Exchange, close out the futures contract and calculate your gains, losses, and net receipts on the 5,000 ounces of silver.

   d. Assume the price of silver in the cash market, in your region of the country in the fall, is US$35 an ounce below the spot price. Without taking delivery of your silver through the Chicago Exchange, close out the futures contract and calculate your gains, losses, and net receipts on the 5,000 ounces of silver.

4. You provide light sweet crude oil (WTI) for several refineries in eastern Canada. This upcoming summer you will require 30,000 barrels and you would like to hedge your risk of price fluctuations through the CME Group.

   a. Identify today's date and find the cash price for light sweet crude oil.

   b. Identify the settle price on a futures contract to buy your oil in the summer. Assume you enter into a futures contract for 30,000 barrels of crude oil.

   c. Assume the price of crude oil in the cash market in the summer is US$110 a barrel above the spot price. Without taking delivery of your sweet crude oil through the CME Group, close out the futures contract and calculate your gains, losses, and net receipts on the 30,000 barrels of oil.

   d. Assume the price of crude oil in the cash market in the summer is US$60 a barrel below the spot price. Without taking delivery of your sweet crude oil through the CME Group, close out the futures contract and calculate your gains, losses, and net receipts on the 30,000 barrels of oil.

5. The following companies are listed on the Toronto Stock Exchange (TSX): Bombardier, Bank of Montreal, Teck, and Suncor. All four companies also have listed call options through the Montreal Exchange (M-X).

   a. Identify today's date and the current share price for each company.

   b. Identify the price of the call option that expires in two months for each company, at the first strike price above the current market price of the common shares.

   c. Calculate the intrinsic value and the speculative premium of each call option.

6. Bombardier, Bank of Montreal, Teck, and Suncor also have listed put options available through the M-X.

   a. Identify today's date and the current share price for each company.

   b. Identify the price of the put option that expires in three months for each company, at the first strike price below the current market price of the common shares.

   c. Calculate the intrinsic value and the speculative premium of each put option.

PROBLEMS

1. Giffen Forest Products has sold lumber to the British company Bulldog Builders, with payment due six months from today. The payment due is £155,000. The Canadian dollar and British pound rate is 1.7275 and the six-month C$/£ forward rate is 1.7083. Hedge this liability with a forward contract. How much will Giffen Forest Products receive in six months in Canadian dollars? How much would they have to pay today?

2. You farm in Alberta and expect to have 1,000 tonnes of canola for sale in the fall. You would like to hedge your risk of price fluctuations through the Chicago Mercantile Exchange. Today is early March, and the cash price for canola is C$450 per tonne. The settle price on a futures contract to sell your canola in November is C$436 per tonne. Assume you enter into a futures contract to deliver 1,000 tonnes of canola.

   a. Assume the price of canola in the cash market, in Alberta, in November is C$475 per tonne. Without delivering your canola to Chicago, close out the futures contract and calculate your gains, losses, and net receipts on the 1,000 tonnes of canola.

   b. Assume the price of canola in the cash market, in Alberta, in November is C$400 per tonne. Without delivering your canola to Chicago, close out the futures contract and calculate your gains, losses, and net receipts on the 1,000 tonnes of canola.

3. You manufacture gold jewellery for sale to local retail outlets. This upcoming fall you will require 500 troy ounces of gold (1 troy ounce = 31.103 grams) and you would like to hedge your risk of price fluctuations through CME Group (NYMEX, COMEX). Today's (April) price of gold is US$1,582 per ounce. The settle price on a futures contract to buy gold in August is US$1,595 per ounce. Assume you enter into a futures contract for 500 troy ounces of gold.

   a. Assume the price of gold in the cash market, in your region of the country, in August is US$1,950 an ounce. Without taking delivery of your gold through the New York Exchange, close out the futures contract and calculate your gains, losses, and net payments on the 500 ounces of gold.

   b. Assume the price of gold in the cash market, in your region of the country, in August is US$1,225 an ounce. Without taking delivery of your gold through the New York Exchange, close out the futures contract and calculate your gains, losses, and net payments on the 500 ounces of gold.

4. The following companies' shares and options trade at the identified prices. The options have a July expiry and the identified strike prices.

	Share Price	Call Option Price	Put Option Price	
Abracadabra	$58.85	$13.30	$2.95	Strike at $50
Cinder	45.10	2.40	2.30	Strike at $45
I-invest	8.01	1.70	1.50	Strike at $ 8
Tomato	39.87	2.85	2.70	Strike at $40

a. Calculate the intrinsic (minimum) value and the speculative premium on the call option of each company.

b. Calculate the intrinsic value and the speculative premium on the put option of each company.

c. If the share price of Abracadabra goes to $70, calculate the price of the call and put options if both have a speculative premium of $0.50.

d. If the share price of Abracadabra goes to $45, calculate the price of the call and put options if both have a speculative premium of $1.25.

5. DNA Labs Inc. has a $1,000 convertible bond outstanding that can be converted into 40 shares of common stock. The common stock is currently selling for $26.75 a share, and the convertible bond is selling for $1,118.50.

a. What is the conversion value of the bond?

b. What is the conversion premium?

c. What is the conversion price?

6. Kepon Trucking Company has a $1,000 par value convertible bond outstanding that can be converted into 200 shares of common stock. The common stock is currently selling for $4.50 a share, and the convertible bond is selling for $990.

a. What is the conversion value of the bond?

b. What is the conversion premium?

c. What is the conversion price?

7. The bonds of Stein Co. have a conversion premium of $35. Their conversion price is $20. The common stock price is $18.50. The bond maturity value is $1,000. What is the price of the convertible bonds?

8. The bonds of Goniff Bank & Trust have a conversion premium of $90. Their conversion price is $12.50. The common stock price is $10.25. The bond maturity value is $1,000. What is the price of the convertible bonds?

9. Sherwood Forest Products has a convertible bond quoted in the bond market at 95. (Bond quotes represent percentage of par value. Thus, 70 represents $700, 80 represents $800, and so on.) The bond matures in 10 years and carries a coupon rate of 6.5 percent. The conversion ratio is 25, and the common stock is currently selling for $35 per share on the TSX. The bond maturity value is $1,000.

a. Compute the conversion premium.

b. At what price does a common share need to sell for the conversion value to be equal to the current bond price?

10. Hughes Technology has a convertible bond outstanding, trading in the marketplace at $935. The par value is $1,000, the coupon rate is 5 percent, and the bond matures in 15 years. The conversion ratio is 40, and the company's common stock is selling for $21.00 per share. Interest is paid semiannually.

a. What is the conversion value?

b. If similar bonds, which are not convertible, are currently yielding 6 percent, what is the pure bond value of this convertible bond? (Use semiannual analysis as described in Chapter 10.)

11. Hamilton Steel Company has a convertible bond outstanding, trading in the marketplace at $930. The par value is $1,000, the coupon rate is 8 percent, and the bond matures in 25 years. The conversion price is $50, and the company's common stock is selling for $44 per share. Interest is paid semiannually.

a. What is the conversion value?

b. If similar bonds, which are not convertible, are currently yielding 10 percent, what is the pure bond value of this convertible bond? (Use semiannual analysis as described in Chapter 10.)

c. What is the conversion premium?

12. In the previous problem, if the interest rates on similar bonds, which are not convertible, go up from 10 to 12 percent, what will the new pure bond value be for Hamilton Steel Company bonds? Assume the Hamilton Steel Company bonds have the same coupon rate of 8 percent as described in the previous problem and that 25 years remain to maturity. Use semiannual analysis.

13. Western Pipeline Inc. has been very successful in the last five years. Its $1,000 par value convertible bonds have a conversion ratio of 28. The bonds have a quoted interest rate of 5 percent a year, paid semiannually. The firm's common stock is currently selling for $43.50 per share. The current bond price has a conversion premium of $10.00 over the conversion value.

    a. What is the current price of the bond?

    b. What is the current yield on the bond?

    c. What is the yield to maturity on the bond if it has seven years to maturity?

    d. If the common stock price goes down to $22.50 and the conversion premium goes up to $100, what will be the new yield to maturity on the bond?

14. Standard Olive Company of British Columbia has a convertible bond outstanding with a coupon rate of 9 percent payable semiannually, and a maturity date of 15 years. The bond maturity value is $1,000. It is rated A, and competitive nonconvertible bonds of the same risk class carry a 10 percent return. The conversion ratio is 25. Currently, the common stock is selling for $30 per share on the Venture Exchange.

    a. What is the conversion price?

    b. What is the conversion value?

    c. Compute the pure bond value. (Use semiannual analysis.)

    d. Draw a graph that includes the floor price and the conversion value but not the convertible bond price. For the stock price on the horizontal axis, use 10, 20, 30, 40, 50, and 60.

    e. Which will influence the bond price more—the pure bond value (floor value) or the conversion value?

15. Swift Shoe has convertible bonds outstanding that are callable at $1,080. The bonds are convertible into 22 shares of common stock. The stock is currently selling for $59.25 per share.

    a. If the firm announces that it is going to call the bonds at $1,080, what action are bondholders likely to take and why?

    b. Assume that instead of the call feature, the firm has the right to drop the conversion ratio from 22 down to 20 after 5 years and down to 18 after 10 years. If the bonds have been outstanding for 4 years and 11 months, what will the price of the bonds be if the stock price is $60? Assume the bonds carry no conversion premium.

    c. Further assume that you anticipate in two months that the common stock price will be up to $63.50. Considering the conversion feature, should you convert now or continue to hold the bond for at least two more months?

16. Vernon Glass Company has $20 million in 10 percent convertible bonds outstanding. The conversion ratio is 50, the share price is $19, and the bond matures in 10 years. The bonds are currently selling at a conversion premium of $70 over their conversion value.

    If the price of the common shares rises to $25 on this date next year, what would your rate of return be if you bought a convertible bond today and sold it in one year? Assume that in one year the conversion premium has shrunk from $70 to $15.

17. Tulsa Drilling Company has $1 million in 11 percent convertible bonds outstanding. Each bond has $1,000 par value. The conversion ratio is 40, the stock price is $32, and the bonds mature in 10 years. The bonds are currently selling at a conversion premium of $70 over the conversion value.

  a. If the price of Tulsa Drilling Company common stock rises to $42 on this date next year, what would your rate of return be if you bought a convertible bond today and sold it in one year? Assume that on this date next year, the conversion premium has shrunk from $70 to $20.

  b. Assume the yield on similar nonconvertible bonds has fallen to 8 percent at the time of sale. What would the pure bond value be at that point? (Use semiannual analysis). Would the pure bond value have a significant effect on valuation then?

18. Manpower Electric Company has 7 percent convertible bonds outstanding. Each bond has a $1,000 par value. The conversion ratio is 25, the stock price is $38, and the bonds mature in 16 years.

  a. What is the conversion value of the bond?

  b. Assume that after one year the common share price falls to $27.50. What is the conversion value of the bond?

  c. Also, assume that after one year interest rates go up to 10 percent on similar bonds. There are 15 years left to maturity. What is the pure value of the bond? Use semiannual analysis.

  d. Will the conversion value of the bond (part *b*) or the pure value of the bond (part *c*) have a stronger influence on its price in the market?

  e. If the bond trades in the market at its pure bond value, what would be the conversion premium (stated as a percentage of the conversion value)?

19. B.C. Fisheries Ltd. has convertible preferred shares outstanding currently trading at $31.00. The preferreds pay an annual dividend of $2.00 and have a redeemable feature effective in two years. It is rated Pfd-2, and competitive nonconvertible preferreds of the same risk class carry an 8 percent return. The conversion ratio is 1.25. The common stock is selling for $24.00 per share on the TSX Venture Exchange and pays an annual dividend of $0.60.

  a. What is the conversion value of the preferreds?

  b. What is the dividend yield on the preferreds?

  c. What is the dividend yield on the common shares?

  d. Why would an investor not switch to another higher yielding preferred share?

  e. Why would an investor not convert to common shares?

20. Hanson Toy Co. has warrants outstanding that allow the holder to purchase 1.5 shares of stock per warrant at $22 per share (option price). The common stock is currently selling for $28, while the warrant is selling for $12.25 per share.

  a. What is the intrinsic (minimum) value of this warrant?

  b. What is the speculative premium on this warrant?

  c. What should happen to the speculative premium as the expiration date approaches?

21. Spring Fields has warrants outstanding that allow the holder to purchase one common share at $17 per share (option price). The common stock is currently selling for $21. The warrant is selling for $6.

  a. What is the intrinsic (minimum) value of this warrant?

  b. What is the speculative premium on this warrant?

22. Preston Toy Co. has warrants outstanding that allow the holder to purchase one common share at $22 per share (option price). The common stock is currently selling for $28. The warrant is selling for $10.50.

  a. What is the intrinsic (minimum) value of this warrant?

  b. What is the speculative premium on this warrant?

23. Sleepless Night Ltd.'s warrant is priced at a speculative premium of $3.00 to its intrinsic (minimum) value. Each warrant entitles the holder to purchase one share in Sleepless Night Ltd. for a total cost of $10.00. Sleepless Night shares currently trade in the market for $16.25 each. What is the current price of a Sleepless Night warrant?

24. You can buy a warrant for $4.00 that gives you the option to buy one share of common stock at $14.50 per share. The stock is currently selling at $12.00 per share.
    a. What is the intrinsic (minimum) value of the warrant?
    b. What is the speculative premium on the warrant?
    c. If the share price rises to $21.75 per share and the warrant sells at its intrinsic value plus a speculative premium of $1.00, what will be the percentage increase in the share price and the warrant price if you bought a share and the warrant at the prices stated above, $12 and $4.00?

25. The warrants of Slowbus Transportation Corporation allow the holder to buy a share of stock at $17.50 and are selling for $2.75. The share price is currently $15.00. To what price must the share go for the warrant purchaser to at least be assured of breaking even?

26. The warrants of Integra Life Sciences allow the holder to buy a share of stock at $11.75 and are selling for $2.85. The share price is currently $8.50. To what price must the share price go for the warrant purchaser to at least be assured of breaking even?

27. Assume you can buy a warrant for $5 that gives you the option to buy one share of common stock at $15 per share. The stock is currently selling at $18 per share.
    a. What is the intrinsic (minimum) value of the warrant?
    b. What is the speculative premium on the warrant?
    c. If the stock rises to $27 per share and the warrant sells at its theoretical value without a premium, what will be the percentage increase in the stock price and the warrant price if you bought the stock and the warrant at the prices stated above? Explain this relationship.

28. The Manning Investment Company bought 100 Cable Corp. warrants one year ago and would like to exercise them today. The warrants were purchased for $30 each, and they expire when trading ends today (assume there is no speculative premium left). Cable Corp. common stock is selling today for $60 per share. The option price is $36, and each warrant entitles the holder to purchase two shares of stock, each at the option price.
    a. If the warrants are exercised today, what would be the Manning Investment Company's dollar profit or loss?
    b. What is the Manning Investment Company's percentage rate of return?

29. Assume in the previous problem that Cable Corp. common stock was selling for $50 per share when the Manning Investment Company bought the warrants.
    a. What was the intrinsic (minimum) value of a warrant at that time?
    b. What was the speculative premium per warrant when the warrants were purchased?
    c. What would the Manning Investment Company's total dollar profit or loss have been had it invested the $3,000 directly in Cable Corp.'s common shares one year ago at $50 and sold them today at $60?
    d. What would the percentage rate of return be on this common stock investment? Compare this to the rate of return on the warrant investment computed in the previous problem, part **b**.

30. Mr. John Hailey has $1,000 to invest in the market. He is considering buying 50 shares of the Comet Airlines at $20 per share. His broker suggests that he may wish to consider purchasing warrants instead. The warrants are selling for $5, and each warrant allows him to purchase one share of Comet Airlines common stock at $18 per share.

a. How many warrants can Mr. Hailey purchase for the same $1,000?

b. If the price of the stock goes to $30, what would be his total dollar and percentage return on the shares?

c. At the time the shares go to $30, the speculative premium on the warrant goes to zero (though the intrinsic value of the warrant goes up). What would be Mr. Hailey's total dollar and percentage return on the warrant?

d. Assuming the speculative premium remains $3.50 over the intrinsic value, how far would the price of the stock have to fall before the warrant has no value?

31. Hughes Technology has net income of $450,000 in the current fiscal year. There are 100,000 shares of common stock outstanding along with convertible bonds, which have a total face value of $1,200,000. The $1,200,000 is represented by 1,200 different $1,000 bonds. Each $1,000 bond pays 6 percent interest and was issued when the average A-bond yield was 10 percent. The conversion ratio is 20. The firm is in a 34 percent tax bracket. Calculate Hughes's EPS.

32. Using information from the previous problem, assume the average A-bond yield was 8 percent instead of 10 percent at the time the convertible bonds were issued. All other facts are the same.

a. What are the basic EPS for Hughes Technology?

b. Indicate the value for fully diluted earnings per share.

33. Meyers Business Systems has two million shares of stock outstanding. It also has two convertible bond issues outstanding with terms as follows:

A. 9 percent convertible, 2028	$12,000,000
B. 10 percent convertible, 2029	$15,000,000

The issue with the 9 percent coupon rate was first sold when average A bonds were yielding 12 percent, and it is convertible into 300,000 shares. The issue with the 10 percent coupon rate was first sold when average A bonds were yielding 15.5 percent, and it is convertible into 400,000 shares. Earnings after taxes are $4 million and the tax rate is 50 percent.

a. Compute both basic and diluted earnings per share for Meyers.

b. Now assume Meyers also has warrants outstanding, which allow the holder to buy 100,000 shares of stock at $20 per share. The stock is currently selling for $40 per share. Compute basic EPS considering the possible impact of both the warrants and convertibles. The firm's rate of return is 20 percent.

COMPREHENSIVE PROBLEM

34. United Technology Corporation (UTC) has $40 million of convertible bonds outstanding (40,000 bonds at $1,000 par value) with a coupon rate of 11 percent. Interest rates are currently 8 percent for bonds of equal risk. The bonds were originally sold when the average BBB rate was 12 percent, and they have 15 years left to maturity. The bonds may be called at a 9 percent premium over par as well as be converted into 30 shares of common stock. The tax rate for the company is 25 percent.

The firm's common stock is currently selling for $41 per share, and it pays a dividend of $3.50. The expected income for the company is $38 million, with 6 million shares of common stock currently outstanding.

Thoroughly analyze this bond and determine whether IMS should call the bond at the 9 percent call premium. In your analysis, consider the following:

a. The effect of the call on basic and fully diluted earnings per share and the common stock price (assume the call forces conversion).

b. The consequences of your decision on financing flexibility.

c. The net change in cash outflows to the company.

d. If the bond is called, will the shareholders take the call price or the 30 shares of common stock?

e. Assuming the bondholders could have converted the bond into common stock whenever they desired, would you as a bondholder have waited for the company to call your bond and thereby force a decision on your part? Explain.

MINI CASE
Hamilton Products

Andre Weatherby, an aspiring artist, had just sold his fifth painting of the year and now had $5,000 in cash to invest. His first inclination was to place his money in a CDIC-insured savings account, but he was disappointed to find out that his annual return would be less than 2 percent.

Knowing little about investment alternatives, Andre knew he must seek advice from a pro. He recalled that at his 10-year high school reunion he had run into Carol Upshaw, a University of Saskatchewan finance major, who was now a stockbroker with Dominion Securities.

Early Monday morning Andre called Carol and she said she would be able to provide him with help. During the course of their conversation, Andre indicated that he wanted to invest his funds in a stock or bond that provided a good annual return and also had the potential to increase in value. Beyond that, he was able to stipulate little else.

Carol considered a number of alternatives but decided on Hamilton Products. She was particularly interested in the firm's convertible securities, which paid 6.5 percent annual interest and were also convertible in 27 shares of common stock. The bonds had a maturity date 20 years in the future. She explained to Andre that he would not only receive a good annual return but also could enjoy appreciation in value if the common stock did well.

The bonds were to be issued at a par value of $1,000 on the day that Andre called. The common stock of Hamilton Products was currently selling for $32.75 per share. Straight, nonconvertible bonds of equal risk and maturity to those of Hamilton Products were currently yielding 8 percent. Carol said that because the bonds paid 6.5 percent interest, they should hold up well in value even if the stock did poorly. The initial pure bond price value was $853.17.

Hamilton Products produced hot asphalt and ready-mixed concrete and was located in Vancouver, British Columbia. Plans called for $12 billion for highway and mass transit projects over the next six years. Although the design and approval of new projects was taking longer than expected, by late 20XX competitive bidding on projects was starting and Hamilton Products stood to be a major winner in the process. For this reason Carol thought the firm's share price could well increase in the future.

Andre decided to buy the convertible bonds. Since his expertise was in painting and not investing, he wanted to get back to his main endeavour as quickly as possible.

Fortunately, the stock did well over the next two years, increasing in value to $45.50. The bonds also increased in value to $1,250.

It was at this point that Carol called Andre and warned him that a major provincial investigation into highway construction contracts might be undertaken by a subcommittee of the B.C. legislature. She thought Hamilton Products could be a target of the investigation and suggested that he take his profits and look elsewhere for an investment.

However, Andre was now intrigued by his high returns and decided to hold onto his bonds (somewhat to Carol's disappointment). As it turned out, Hamilton Products was found in violation of provincial regulations on a number of major contracts and the share price plummeted to $29.75 per share in the next year. During the same time period, a combination of a downgrading of the firm's credit rating and an increase in interest rates caused the yield on straight, nonconvertible bonds of those of equal risk and maturity to Hamilton Products to go to 10 percent. Hamilton Product's bonds had 17 years remaining to maturity.

Although Andre was disappointed in the drop in the firm's common stock price, he thought he could take some comfort in the fact that the convertible bonds were an interest-paying security, which gave them a basic value below which they normally would not fall.

a. At the time that Andre purchased the bonds, what was the conversion value? What was the conversion premium?

b. When the bonds got up to $1,250, what was the conversion premium?

c. Assume there is a conversion premium of $98 when the common stock price fell to $29.75. What is the price of the convertible bond?

d. What is the pure bond value after interest rates have gone up to 10 percent? The yield to maturity (required rate of return) is 10 percent and there are 17 years left to maturity. The bonds are continuing to make annual interest payments of 6.5 percent ($65). The principal payment at maturity is $1,000.

e. How much comfort should Andre take in the pure bond value computed in part *d*?

CHAPTER

20

External Growth through Mergers

LEARNING OBJECTIVES

LO1 Explain some defensive measures taken to avoid an unfriendly takeover.

LO2 Analyze the motives for mergers and divestitures, including financial considerations and the desire to increase operating efficiency. Also, perform an NPV analysis for a merger proposal.

LO3 Explain acquisition through cash purchases or by one company exchanging its shares for another company's shares.

LO4 Evaluate the impact of the merger on earnings per share and share value.

LO5 Characterize the diversification benefits of a merger.

LO6 Outline the reasons for using a holding company.

The risks and opportunities of mergers, divestitures, and international investment are increasingly important in our competitive and interconnected business world. We can reinforce the valuation techniques and risk considerations learned in earlier chapters as we examine these topics.

THE INTERNATIONAL AND CANADIAN MERGER ENVIRONMENT

Low interest rates, changing regulations, intense competition, evolving technology, and strong capital markets or the aftermath of economic meltdowns are reasons suggested for merger activity.

Mergers of the 1960s and 1970s were motivated by the desire to create conglomerates that would benefit from diversification, whereas the mergers of the 1980s, as leveraged buyouts, were attempts to achieve financing gains. The merger wave that ended in 1989 saw RJR Nabisco (*Barbarians at the Gate*) acquired for $30 billion.

Strategic global positioning seemed the focus of the mergers of the 1990s and 2000s to create trading dominance. The communications, entertainment, financial services, pharmaceuticals, consumer goods, and transportation industries were experiencing major structural changes, with convergence the focus of many business associations. The telecommunications industry received more attention than any other in the late 1990s with the convergence of voice, electronic, and visual mediums. The deals of the late 1990s occurred as the capital markets reached historic highs on the strength of solid earnings and low interest rates.

The mergers after the financial crisis of 2008 were driven by the large cash hoards acquired by corporations, historically low interest rates, depressed share prices, and the globalization of markets. Attempted mergers, such as the NYSE Euronext–Deutsche Börse stock market merger and the Potash Corporation (PotashCorp) acquisition by BHP Billiton, were increasingly subject to regulatory reviews and denial as the resultant firms tended to dominate their respective markets or evoke nationalistic concerns. BHP Billiton proposed the acquisition of Rio Tinto in 2008 for $165 billion (inflation adjusted) before falling commodity prices made the acquisition unattractive.

Nutrien (former PotashCorp.)
nutrien.com

In the years following the Covid-19 pandemic expect mergers that will create challenges for many corporations.

Corporate divestitures are a significant component of merger activities. A divestiture is the sale or spinoff of a subsidiary or a division. Divestiture activity is attributed to different reasons: corporate strategies refocusing on core businesses, companies rationalizing their business to take advantage of the global marketplace, and perceptions that valuations of some

Table 20–1 Largest mergers and acquisitions (2020)

	Buyer	Acquired Company	Value, US $ Billions (inflation adj.)	Year
1	Vodaphone Airtouch	Mannesmann	$310	1999
2	America Online	Time Warner	245	2000
3	Pfizer	Warner Lambert	172	2000
4	Verizon Communications	Verizon Wireless	143	2013
5	Dow Chemical	Dupont	140	2015
6	United Technologies	Raytheon	122	2019
7	T Mobile	Sprint	122	2018
8	Exxon Corp	Mobil Corp	121	1998
9	RFS Holdings	ABN-Amro	121	2007
10	Anheuser-Busch	SAB Miller	115	2015
11	Glaxo Wellcome	SmithKline Beecham	113	2001

assets are high. The global trend of merger activity recently has been to solidify market share in a company's core business.

During the late 1970s and early 1980s, the divestiture thrust of many large foreign-based companies led to a number of leveraged buyouts of Canadian operations. The 1980 implementation of the National Energy Policy, the provisions of which favoured Canadian-owned energy companies, also led to the sale of Canadian oil and gas operations by foreign companies. For example, Dome Petroleum's purchase of Hudson's Bay Oil and Gas from U.S.–based Conoco was a key ingredient in one of the most interesting and nearly disastrous sagas in Canadian corporate history. Additionally, Petro-Canada, created as a federal Crown corporation in 1976, bought five oil companies for $6.5 billion. However, by 1995, majority ownership of Petro-Canada was in private hands as the federal government sold off its interest.

In the mid-1990s, the federal government played a large part in the acquisitions and divestitures market, with the sale of CN Rail, Petro-Canada, and Canada's air traffic control system to Nav Canada. Table 20–2 highlights the largest Canadian mergers and acquisitions.

Table 20–2 Largest mergers and acquisitions by Canadian companies

	Buyer	Acquired Company	Value, C$ Billions	Year
1	Rio Tinto	Alcan	43.9	2007
2	Agrium	Potash	36.0	2018
3	Enbridge	Spectra Energy	32.8	2017
4	Inco	Vale	19.9	2006
5	Falconbridge	Xstrata	19.2	2006
6	Suncor Energy	Petro-Canada	19.2	2009
7	CNOOC	Nexen	19.0	2013
8	Manulife Financial	John Hancock	18.9	2004
9	Thomson	Reuters	18.2	2007

Canada! Part of the Action

In late 2019 MDA, builder of the Canadarm, returned to Canadian ownership with its purchase for $1 billion by Northern Private Capital (backing from Jim Balsillie of BlackBerry and Jim Risley of Clearwater FineFoods). MDA, a world-class space technology company, built satellites, space robotics, and space infrastructure.

When fortunes changed in the Canadian oil patch, Cenovus acquired oil sand and conventional natural gas assets of ConocoPhillips for $18 billion in 2017, while TC Energy acquired Columbia Pipeline for $10 billion in 2016. Enbridge merged with Spectra Energy in 2017 to create the largest energy infrastructure company in North America.

By 2018 PotashCorp had merged with Agrium to form a new company Nutriem (NRT: TO), a fertilizer powerhouse worth $36 billion. Potash had been the subject of a 2010 takeover bid by BHP Billiton. The Canadian government had blocked the bid, suggesting the deal did not have a net benefit to Canada. Similarly, a LSE–TSX stock market merger of 2011 was abandoned after investor and regulatory roadblocks developed.

Another energy company, Encana, had split into two companies in 2008: Encana and Cenovus Energy. Encana had resulted from the previous merger of Alberta Energy (AEC) and PanCanadian Energy (PCE) in 2002. PCE had once been part of the Canadian Pacific Railway conglomerate. In 2019 Encana relocated to the United States and was renamed Ovindiv.

Pension plans have become players in acquisition activity. In 2008, the Ontario Teachers' Pension Plan had its attempt to acquire BCE for $50 billion thwarted by the market meltdown and bond indenture problems.

Early 2002 had seen Molson (molsoncoors.com) buy Kaiser, Brazil's second-largest brewer. However, by 2004 Molson had merged with Coors as worldwide consolidation of the beer business continued. Labatt already had been lost to Interbrew (Stella Artois), and subsequently to Anheuser-Busch InBev (ab-inbev.com), the world's largest brewer. The brewing industry in Canada continued to change as Sleeman Breweries Ltd. was acquired in a $400 million deal by Sapporo Breweries Ltd. of Japan in 2006. Sleeman was the last of the three large breweries in Canada to be acquired by foreign owners.

Consolidation in the retail business was in evidence in 2014 due to increased competition from the United States. Loblaw acquired Shoppers for $13 billion, uniting the two biggest chains in their respective markets, and Sobeys (Empire Company) acquired Safeway for $6 billion. There were subsequent store closures in 2014.

All this activity was rationalizing the marketplace with a global and North American focus. Canadian firms were there to compete. Mergers seemed to be focused on establishing a global presence in a core business, but this strategy sometimes fell afoul of the regulatory authorities of the world, which were concerned with market dominance and decreased competition. Merged companies were often required to sell some assets, thus presenting opportunities for more junior companies.

Q1 Is this merger activity beneficial to Canadians?

Q2 What were the barriers to the BCE and LSE/TSX takeovers?

tmx.com

bce.ca

Symbols: NRT, BCE, OVV, L, EMP.A

NEGOTIATED VERSUS TENDERED OFFERS

Although as the new millennium started mergers were negotiated in a friendly atmosphere between officers and directors of the participating corporations, this is not always the case. Product lines, quality of assets, and future growth prospects were discussed, and eventually an exchange ratio was hammered out and presented to the investment community and the financial press. In the previous decade, unfriendly takeover attempts had been a common occurrence.

If the potential buyer cannot come to agreement on merger terms with the potential seller's management and board of directors, there are still two alternatives available. First, the potential buyer can ask the seller's shareholders for the right to vote their shares at the company's next annual meeting. This gives rise to what is known as a **proxy fight**, as management and the potential buyers vie for the right to vote a majority of the shareholders' shares.

LO1 Second, rather than engage in a lengthy and expensive proxy fight, the potential buyer can elect to make a tender offer through a stock exchange directly to the target company's shareholders. If the tender offer is lucrative enough to attract over 50 percent of the voting stock, the buyer gains control and can conclude the merger.

A takeover tender offer, in which a company attempts to acquire a target firm against its will, may please the company's shareholders, but its management faces the dangers of seeing the company going down the wrong path in a merger and perhaps of their being personally ousted. To avoid an unfriendly takeover, management may institute one or more of several takeover defences. These defensive tactics are sometimes referred to as "applying shark repellent." In many cases the tactics serve only to increase the cost of the takeover without preventing it. These tactics include the following:

1. Turn to a white knight. A white knight is the term for a friendly company that agrees to bid a higher price for the targeted company and cooperate with the existing management in achieving a takeover that management believes is in the firm's (and management's) best interests.

2. Selling crown jewels. The targeted company may sell a prized division or asset of the company, making the takeover less attractive to the buyer.

3. A targeted repurchase of shares. The targeted company agrees to pay a premium to the acquiring company for the shares already purchased to have them discontinue the acquisition. This is sometimes referred to as **greenmail**.

4. Voting in golden parachutes. These are contracts that pay existing management rather large sums of money if the company is taken over and they lose their jobs. Although golden parachutes may make the takeover more expensive, they probably best serve management.

5. Taking on more debt. By going to the capital markets and raising additional debt and perhaps buying back shares, paying large dividends, or purchasing new assets, the targeted firm becomes more expensive to acquire and thus less attractive.

6. Adopting a poison pill. These are also known as shareholders' rights plans. Inco adopted the first Canadian company protection plan. If a potential acquirer buys 20 percent or more of Inco's equity and cannot reach an agreement with the board of directors, the plan would allow other Inco shareholders, but not the potential acquirer, to buy newly issued shares at half-price. This makes the takeover very expensive. Proponents of this practice claim such protection against creeping takeovers is justified because management should be spending its time running the company rather than watching over its shoulder for whoever might be planning to try to take over the company. These plans have drawn criticism from some large investment managers.

Although a given takeover bid may not appeal to management, it may still entice shareholders. The bidding may get so high that shareholders demand action. The desire of management to maintain the status quo and institute defensive tactics can come into conflict with the objective of shareholder wealth maximization, as was discussed in Chapter 1.

The proliferation of nonvoting shares in Canada may complicate a given takeover situation. In many cases there are clauses in the corporation's bylaws that attempt to include the nonvoting equity holders in the premium stock pricing generated by a takeover bid. This is generally done by stipulating that a tender offer, aimed at securing voting control, must include an offer to purchase the nonvoting shares as well as the voting. As we noted in Chapter 17 in the Canadian Tire case, these clauses are sometimes open to varying interpretation. In the situations where there are no provisions for inclusion of the nonvoting shareholders in a control takeover bid, the nonvoting shareholder loses the opportunity to make substantial gains if the firm is taken over.

The Domino Effect of Merger Activity

An attempt by one company to buy control of another often leads to a series of mergers, with the chain of merger activity often beginning in another country. Often, these domino effects come in merger waves when it is suggested that it is cheaper to acquire other companies than to expand through new product development or the purchase of new plant and equipment. This is often the result of depressed share prices.

The interwoven nature of Canadian and U.S. merger activity and the unfriendly takeover was classically illustrated in the 1980s with an attempted takeover of Gulf Oil. To fend off T. Boone Pickens's unfriendly takeover attempt, Gulf's management arranged to have the company bought by *white knight* Chevron (formerly Standard Oil of California) for a record (at the time) of US$13.3 billion. To reduce the financial strain imposed by the large purchase price, Chevron had Gulf Oil sell its shares of Gulf Canada for $2.8 billion (Canadian) to the Olympia & York Corporation of Canada.

However, the chain of interrelated mergers did not stop there. To raise the financing for the deal, Olympia & York sold to Gulf Canada its stake in Abitibi-Price, one of Canada's largest forest products companies, for $1.2 billion. To raise the capital for the Abitibi-Price acquisition, Gulf Canada sold a portion of its assets to Petro-Canada for $890 million, to Ultramar for $120 million, and to Norcen Energy for $300 million. Declining oil prices led Gulf Canada to make a successful unsolicited takeover bid for Hiram Walker Resources in an attempt to diversify away from an overdependence on oil and gas. The price tag on that takeover was $3.3 billion. After being taken over by Gulf, Walker then sold its ownership of Home Oil to Interprovincial Pipeline for $1.1 billion. This one chain of interrelated events demonstrates not only the linked nature of the U.S. and Canadian merger markets but also the intricacies of the financial arrangements of large merger transactions.

Although hostile takeovers in Canada are much less prevalent than in the United States because of fewer widely held companies, they still occur. By swallowing a so-called *poison pill,* a takeover target contrives to have more debt and/or less liquid assets to become less attractive to the would-be acquirer. In the Hiram Walker situation, the acquisition target made a deal to sell its *crown jewel*—its liquor distilling operations—to Allied-Lyons of Britain for $2.6 billion. Allied-Lyons at the time was fending off an unfriendly takeover attempt by Elders Ltd. of Australia. The *shark repellent* strategy adopted by Hiram Walker did not fend off Gulf Oil, but it did increase the overall costs of the transaction and make the final prize less valuable to the buyer.

One rule for avoiding being targeted as a takeover candidate is to never get caught with a large cash position. A firm with large cash balances serves as an ideal target for a leveraged buyout. The acquiring company is able to negotiate a bank loan based on the target company's assets and then go into the marketplace to make a cash tender offer. Firms with strong asset or market positions and low earnings are also prime takeover targets.

Foreign Acquisitions

Today, firms from Canada and other countries are quite willing to purchase major U.S. firms. An infamous example occurred in the late 1980s when Robert Campeau of Toronto executed successful bids of $4.9 billion for Allied Stores and $6.6 billion for Federated Department Stores in the United States. Campeau's stated objective was to diversify his company's dependence on the Canadian real estate market. Purchases of retail chains are popular because of the so-called hidden asset value of real estate worth more than its stated book value. Hudson Bay Company became a takeover target in 2017 because of its real estate assets in the United States. Allied and Federated filed for Chapter 11 bankruptcy in the United States, and in 1990 Campeau Corporation failed in Canada. Campeau had expanded too fast with merger candidates that were too expensive.

In 1995 Seagram, a Canadian company, sold an interest in DuPont for over $12 billion and bought its interest in MCA for almost $8 billion from a Japanese firm. Both DuPont and MCA were U.S. firms. In 1998 Seagram purchased the record producer Polygram, a British firm, for $15.6 billion and then in 2000 agreed to a $50 billion merger with the French media and entertainment corporation Vivendi.

Vivendi
vivendi.com

 FINANCE IN ACTION

Let's Make a Deal

The year 2019 saw merger and acquisition activity in the cannabis trade with Aurora and Canopy getting involved. WestJet went private when purchased by Onex. TD Ameritrade was purchased by Charles Schwab, Cineplex by the United Kingdom's Cineworld, and the Stars Group by Flutter Entertainment, also from the United Kingdom (appropriate that online gambling made a deal).

In 2013, there were some concerns relating to acquisitions of Canadian companies by sovereign (state-owned) companies. Nexen was acquired by CNOOC (China) for $19 billion and Progress Energy by Petronas (Malaysia) for $5.5 billion.

In late 2013, the Canadian Securities Administrators (CSA) proposed new rules to allow the boards of companies more discretion in fending off hostile takeovers, allowing more time for shareholders to consider an offer and to fulfill a board's fiduciary obligations.

When OpenText (OTC) made a hostile takeover bid for all the common shares of Accelio Corporation (LIO) at $2.75 per share in 2002, Accelio sought out Adobe Systems as a white knight and received a more attractive offer. Takeover bid circulars detailing takeover offers such as this are posted at the SEDAR website (sedar.com). (Search the database for public companies under "takeover bid circular.")

Q1 What are the details of a recently announced takeover bid?

Q2 Does the takeover bid of question 1 make financial sense? Why or why not?

Q3 What are the concerns about foreign takeovers of Canadian companies?

 FINANCE IN ACTION

No to Foreign Acquisition! Or Maybe!

Generally, there has been a willingness to allow foreign investment in Canada and takeovers of Canadian firms. There have also been notable exceptions.

In 2017 the Canadian government approved the takeover of Norsat International by Hytera Communications Corp. of China, despite national security concerns both in Canada and the United States. Norsat manufactures radio transceivers and radio systems used by Canada's NATO partners.

Yet in 2018 the government blocked the sale of Aecon Group to a Chinese government–backed company for security reasons.

The attempt by BHP Billiton of Australia to acquire PotashCorp in 2010 was also turned down as it was not deemed a net benefit to Canada. PotashCorp eventually merged with Agrium to become Nutrien.

Government Regulation of Takeovers

The absolute size of the recent merger deals listed in Tables 20–1 and 20–2 and the corporate concentration they imply has caused concern. Unlike in the United States, where fears of undue corporate concentration have been entrenched in antitrust laws since the beginning of the 20th century, Canadians have generally been unconcerned about high concentration levels of corporate power. However, on June 19, 1986, the Competition Act came into force, replacing the toothless Combines Investigation Act. In 75 years there had not been one successful prosecution of a contested merger under the Combines Act.

The competition law makes a merger or acquisition illegal if it "lessens competition substantially in a given market." Charges under the new act are civil rather than criminal, which increases the chances of a conviction if, in fact, competition will be seriously impaired by a merger. In the late 1990s, we saw the federal government prevent merger activity in the banking industry on fears of decreased competition and increasing concentration of power.

If Canadians have been generally unconcerned about corporate concentration, the same cannot be said about foreign ownership. Canadian nationalists made this a major political issue during the 1960s, which led to the establishment of the Foreign Investment Review Agency (FIRA) under the Foreign Investment Review Act by the early 1970s. Under the watchful eye of FIRA, virtually no large takeovers of Canadian firms by foreigners occurred. FIRA was replaced by the Investment Canada Act (ICA) in 1985, however, in an attempt to make Canada a more hospitable place for foreign capital.

Since that time there have been significant takeovers of Canadian firms, particularly in the resource industries. Investment Canada does, however, require some evidence that the takeover of a Canadian company by a foreign entity will result in a net gain for Canada as a whole.

LO2 MOTIVES FOR BUSINESS COMBINATIONS

In Canada, there is no specific definition of what constitutes a merger. In contrast, the term in the United States denotes the acquisition of one company by another followed by the liquidation of the acquired company into the acquiring company. Such rarely happens in Canada. Instead, the acquirer usually buys a majority, sometimes all, of the voting shares of the selling company, but both remain as separate legal entities after the acquisition. This normal situation in Canada is commonly referred to by both the merger and acquisition labels.

The term amalgamation does, however, have a precise legal definition in Canada. An amalgamation is a statutory combination under one of the provincial corporations or companies acts, the Canada Corporations Act, or the Canada Business Corporations Act. In this chapter, we use the word **merger** to connote any transaction by which two or more companies are combined, either under a statutory amalgamation or just by ownership.

Financial Motives

The financial motives for mergers are a key consideration.

Portfolio Effect As discussed in Chapter 13, a merger allows the acquiring firm to enjoy a potentially desirable portfolio effect by achieving risk reduction while perhaps maintaining the firm's rate of return. If two firms that benefit from opposite phases of the business cycle combine, their variability in performance may be reduced. Risk-averse investors may then discount the future expected performance of the merged firm at a lower rate and thus assign it a higher valuation than was assigned to the separate firms. The same point can be made in regard to multinational mergers. Through merger, a firm that has holdings in diverse economic and political climates can enjoy some reduction in the risks that derive from foreign exchange translation, government politics, military takeovers, and localized recessions.

Although the portfolio diversification effect of a merger is intellectually appealing, with each firm becoming a mini internal capital market unto itself, the practicalities of the situation can become quite complicated. One of the major forces of merger activity in the mid to late 1960s was the desire for diversification. A lesson learned from the frenzied takeover strategies of many conglomerates of that time is that too much diversification can strain the managerial capabilities of a firm, even one with excellent management talent.

Evidence of the lack of success of some mergers is the fact that many of the acquisitions we see involve the sale of a previously acquired subsidiary by one company to another. For example, after undertaking a diversification strategy for decades, Canadian Pacific initiated a divestiture program that eventually resulted in its split into five separate companies. Divestiture programs are usually undertaken either to reduce the debt incurred under the old acquisition strategies or to redeploy assets consistent with new corporate strategies. This seems to have been the case in the early 1990s as corporations attempted to deal with the more competitive and demanding conditions of the international marketplace. The stock market reaction to divestitures may actually be positive when it can be shown that management is freeing itself from an unwanted or unprofitable division.[1]

Access to Capital A merger can create *improved financing posture* as a result of expansion in size. Larger firms may enjoy greater access to financial markets and, thus, be in a better position to raise debt and equity capital. Such firms may also be able to attract larger and more prestigious investment bankers to handle future financing.

Greater financing capability may also be inherent in the merger itself. This is likely to be the case if the acquired firm has a strong cash position or a low debt-equity ratio that can be used to expand borrowing by the acquiring company.

One of the popular acquisition devices in the 1980s, and to some extent since, has been the leveraged buyout. As discussed in Chapter 15, leveraged buyouts result when either existing management or an outsider makes an offer to go private by retiring all the shares of the company. The buying group borrows the necessary money, using the assets of the acquired firm as collateral. The buying group then repurchases all of the shares and expects to retire the debt over time with the cash flow from operations or the sale of corporate assets.

Tax Loss Carry-Forward A tax loss carry-forward might be available in a merger if one of the firms has previously sustained a tax loss. An operating loss may be carried forward up to 20 years, but not back, by the acquiring company. In any event, a tax loss carry-forward must be used up as quickly as possible when there are offsetting profits. In the 1980s Amoco was motivated to purchase Dome Petroleum with its substantial losses because the tax loss carry-forward provided significant value to Amoco as the acquiring company. Tax losses approximated $2 billion.

As an example of tax loss benefits, assume firm A acquires firm B, which has a $220,000 tax loss carry-forward. We look at firm A's financial position before and after the merger. Based on the carry-forward, the company can reduce its total taxes from $75,000 to $20,000, and thus it could pay $55,000 for the carry-forward alone (this is on a nondiscounted basis). The tax shield value of a carry-forward is equal to the loss involved times the tax rate ($220,000 × 25% = $55,000).

	20XX	20XY	20XZ	Total Values
Firm A (without merger)				
Before-tax income	$ 100,000	$ 100,000	$ 100,000	$300,000
Taxes (25%)	25,000	25,000	25,000	75,000
Income available to shareholders.	$ 75,000	$ 75,000	$ 75,000	$225,000
Firm A (with merger and associated tax benefits)				
Before-tax income	$ 100,000	$ 100,000	$ 100,000	$300,000
Tax loss carry-forward.	100,000	100,000	20,000	
Net taxable income.	0	0	80,000	
Taxes (25%)	0	0	20,000	20,000
Cash flow effect to shareholders	$ 100,000	$ 100,000	$ 60,000	$280,000

---

[1] J. Fred Weston, "Divestitures: Mistakes or Learning," *Journal of Applied Corporate Finance* 4 (Summer 1989), pp. 68–76.

As would be expected, income available to shareholders has gone up by a like amount ($280,000 − $225,000 = $55,000). Of course, firm B's anticipated operating gains and losses for future years must also be considered in arriving at a purchase price.

Synergistic Effect Perhaps the greatest management motive for a merger is the possible synergistic effect. Synergy is said to occur when the whole is greater than the sum of the parts. This "2 + 2 = 5" effect may be the result of eliminating overlapping functions in production and marketing as well as meshing various engineering and administrative capabilities. The increased cash flows from greater efficiencies suggested will add value. In planning mergers, however, there is often a tendency to overestimate the possible synergistic benefits that might accrue.

Nonfinancial Motives

The nonfinancial motives for mergers and consolidations include the desire to expand management and marketing capabilities as well as the acquisition of new products.

Management Desires Companies that are in traditional lines of business may attempt to expand into more dynamic industries to upgrade their image. Edgar Bronfman Jr. of Seagram thought the entertainment business more dynamic than chemicals, but eventually sold to the even bigger Vivendi of France.

This also suggests that the desire of management for size and influence may impact decision making when mergers are considered. This may conflict with what is best for the shareholder, which is the topic of agency theory identified in Chapter 1.

Marketing Expansion Although mergers may be directed toward either horizontal integration (the acquisition of competitors) or vertical integration (the acquisition of buyers or sellers of goods and services to the company), the new competition laws should preclude the substantial elimination of competition. For this reason, mergers may become more directed toward companies in allied but not directly related fields. The pure conglomerate merger of firms with totally unrelated firms is still undertaken but after more careful deliberation than in the past. The trend in the new millennium seems to be toward convergence, or the focusing of the corporation on related businesses on a global scale. Mergers seem to be creating corporations with substantial international operations.

Acquiring Technology Of increasing importance is the acquisition of technology and related patents, particularly in the communications industry. Apple's purchase of Nortel's patent division and Google's acquisition of Motorola seemed to some extent motivated by the desire to control patents in order to avoid lawsuits, as well as the continual need to expand the knowledge base in this field.

Motives of Selling Shareholders

Most of our discussion has revolved around the motives of the acquiring firm that initiates a merger. Likewise, the selling shareholders' motives are important. They may be motivated by a desire to receive the acquiring company's shares, which may have greater acceptability or activity in the marketplace than the stock they hold. Also, when cash is offered instead of shares, the selling shareholders gain an opportunity to diversify their holdings into many new investments. As we discuss later in the chapter, the selling shareholders generally receive an attractive price for their stock that may well exceed its current market or book value. An exchange offer may represent an opportunity to get a value approaching the replacement costs for their assets in an inflationary environment.

To encourage the support of officers of the selling company, who may also be shareholders, the officers may receive attractive postmerger management contracts as well as directorships in the acquiring firm. In some circumstances, they may be allowed to operate the company as a highly autonomous subsidiary after the merger (though this is probably the exception). This is most likely to happen when the acquiring firm is in a different business and is not likely to try to integrate the acquired company into the operating system of its new parent.

A final motive of the selling shareholders may simply be the bias against smaller businesses that has developed in this country and around the world. Real clout in the financial markets may dictate being part of a larger organization. These motives should not be taken as evidence that all or even most officers or directors of smaller firms wish to sell—a matter that we examine further when we discuss negotiated offers versus takeover attempts.

LO3 TERMS OF EXCHANGE

In determining the price to be paid for a potential acquisition, a number of factors are considered, including earnings, dividends, and growth potential. We divide our analysis of merger terms of exchange between cash purchases and stock-for-stock exchanges, in which the acquiring company trades stock rather than pays cash for the acquired firm. A good merger is beneficial to both firms. The terms of exchange allow us to reexamine the valuation models of Chapter 10, the cost of capital in Chapter 11, and capital budgeting from Chapter 12.

Cash Purchases

The cash purchase of another company can be viewed within the context of a capital budgeting decision. Instead of purchasing new plant or machinery, the purchaser has opted to acquire a *going concern*. For example, assume the Invest Corporation is analyzing the acquisition of the Sell Corporation for $1 million. The Sell Corporation has expected cash flow (aftertax earnings plus amortization) of $100,000 per year for the next five years and $150,000 per year for the 6th through the 20th years. Furthermore, the synergistic benefit of the merger (in this case, combining production facilities) should reduce operating costs by $10,000 per year. Finally, the Sell Corporation has a $50,000 tax loss carry-forward that can be used immediately by the Invest Corporation. Assuming a 25 percent tax rate, the $50,000 loss carry-forward will generate $12,500 extra in aftertax profits immediately. The Invest Corporation has a 10 percent cost of capital, and this is assumed to remain stable with the merger. Our analysis is as follows:

Cash Outflow:			
Purchase price			$1,000,000
Less: Tax shield benefit from tax loss carry-forward ($50,000 × 25%)			
(PV would be $11,354)			12,500
Net cash outflow			$ 987,500
Cash inflows:			
Years 1–5:	$ 100,000	operating cash inflow	
	10,000	synergistic benefit	
	$ 110,000	annual cash inflow	
Present value of $110,000			$ 416,987
Years 6–20:	$ 150,000	operating cash flow	
	10,000	synergistic benefit	
	$ 160,000	annual cash inflow	
Present value of $ 160,000			755,644
Total present value of cash inflows			$1,172,631

The present value for the first five years is based on $N = 5$, $\%I/Y = 10$ percent. For the 6th through the 20th years, we determine the present value $N = 15$, $\%I/Y = 10$ percent, and then "present value" the lump sum five years with $N = 5$, $\%I/Y = 10$ percent.

The net present value of the investment is

Total present value of inflows	$ 1,172,631
Net cash outflow	987,500
Net present value	$ 185,131

The IRR is 12.51 percent, which exceeds the 10 percent cost of capital.

The acquisition appears to represent a desirable alternative for the expenditure of cash with a positive net present value of $185,131. The market environment of the late 1990s presented opportunities in which firms could be purchased at a value below the replacement costs of their assets and thus represented a potentially desirable capital investment.

LO4 Stock-for-Stock Exchange

On a stock-for-stock exchange, we use a somewhat different analytical approach, emphasizing the earnings per share effect of exchanging securities (and ultimately the market valuation of those earnings). The analysis is primarily from the viewpoint of the acquiring firm. The shareholders of the acquired firm are concerned mainly about the initial price they are paid for their shares and about the outlook for the acquiring firm.

Assume Expand Corporation is considering the acquisition of Small Corporation. Significant financial information on the firms before the merger is provided in Table 20–3.

Table 20–3 Financial data on potential merging firms

	Small Corporation	Expand Corporation
Total earnings.	$200,000	$500,000
Shares of stock outstanding	50,000	200,000
EPS.	$4.00	$2.50
P/E ratio	7.5×	12×
Market price per share	$30.00	$30.00

We begin our analysis with the assumption that one share of Expand Corporation ($30) will be traded for one share of Small Corporation ($30). In actuality, Small Corporation will probably demand more than $30 per share because the acquired firm usually gets some premium over the current market value. Later, we consider the effect of paying such a premium.

If 50,000 new shares of Expand Corporation are traded in exchange for all the old shares of Small Corporation, Expand Corporation then has 250,000 shares outstanding. At the same time, its claim to earnings will go to $700,000 when the two firms are combined. Postmerger earnings per share will be $2.80 for the Expand Corporation, as indicated in Table 20–4.

Table 20–4 Postmerger earnings per share

Total earnings: Small ($200,000) + Expand ($500,000).	$700,000
Shares outstanding in surviving corporation:	
Old (200,000) + New (50,000)	250,000
New EPS for Expand Corporation $= \dfrac{\$700,000}{250,000} = \$2.80$	

A number of observations are worthy of note. First, the earnings per share of Expand Corporation have increased as a result of the merger, rising from $2.50 to $2.80. This has occurred because Expand Corporation's P/E ratio was higher than that of Small Corporation at the time of the merger (12 versus 7.5). *Whenever a firm acquires another entity whose P/E ratio is lower than its own, there is an immediate increase in earnings per share*. The P/E ratio comparison is an important variable to be considered.

However, it is unlikely that Small Corporation will give up its shares at the current market value of $30 per share. If we assume Expand Corporation is willing to pay the shareholders of Small Corporation $48 worth of stock for each share of its stock outstanding, things will change. Expand will now be paying 12 times Small Corporation's earnings ($48/$4), which is equal to the current P/E ratio of Expand Corporation. Under these circumstances there will be no change in postmerger earnings per share for Expand Corporation.

Endless possibilities can occur in mergers based on stock-for-stock exchanges. Even if the acquiring company increases its immediate earnings per share as a result of the merger, the impact on long-term growth should be examined. Furthermore, the increased number of shareholders and the possible dilution effects should also be considered.

Shareholders may be concerned about trading or maintaining parity in dividends per share rather than with the impact on earnings per share. The acquiring company may offer fixed-income securities as well as common stock to satisfy the shareholders of the acquired company.

MARKET VALUE MAXIMIZATION

The ultimate test of a merger lies in the concept of market value maximization. We must try to assess how shareholders (present and potential) will view the merger and how they will price the merged firm's shares in the marketplace. Thus, we must consider not only the immediate impact on earnings per share but also the effect on the surviving firm's postmerger P/E ratio. Although a merger with Small Corporation, as suggested, increases Expand Corporation's earnings per share from $2.50 to $2.80, there may be a decrease in Expand Corporation's postmerger P/E ratio because of a slowing of the expected growth rate and/or an increase in its risk of the new firm. All the financial factors must be brought together to determine the potential impact on shareholder values in the new firm. The techniques of Chapter 12 should be of assistance in determining the value that may be created.

LO5 Portfolio Effect

Inherent in all of our discussions is the importance of the merger's portfolio effect on the risk-return posture of the firm. This is an extension of the Chapter 13 discussion. The reduction or increase in risk may influence the share market value and, thus, P/E ratio as much as the change in the growth rate. To the extent that we are diminishing the overall risk of the firm with a merger, the market value of the firm may increase even if the potential earnings growth is unchanged. Business risk reduction may be achieved by acquiring another firm that is influenced by business cycle conditions in opposite ways from their influence on our own firm, while financial risk reduction may be achieved by restructuring our postmerger financial arrangements to include less debt.

Perhaps Expand Corporation is diversifying from a heavy manufacturing industry into the real estate/housing industry. Although heavy manufacturing industries move with the general business cycle, the real estate/housing industry tends to be countercyclical. Even though the expected value of earnings per share may remain relatively constant as a result of the merger, the standard deviation of possible outcomes may decline as a result of risk reduction through diversification, as is indicated in Figure 20–1.

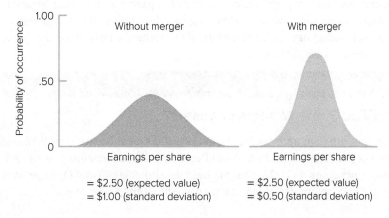

Figure 20–1 Risk reduction portfolio benefits

We see that the expected value of the earnings per share has remained constant in this instance, but the standard deviation has gone down. Because there is less risk in the corporation, the investor may be willing to assign a higher valuation, thus increasing the P/E ratio.

Like synergy, however, countercyclical effects are hard to capture, as the relationships of different businesses to the general business cycle change somewhat over time. In addition, some have argued persuasively that it is more efficient for the shareholder to diversify their portfolio than it is for an individual firm to do so. An associated irony is that, because diversified companies are so difficult for analysts to understand in their totality, they often command a lower P/E than the average of those that would have been assigned to the individual parts. This is one of the reasons that diversified companies, such as Canadian Pacific, in the late 1980s and again in 2001, went through divestment of their numerous businesses.

ACCOUNTING CONSIDERATIONS IN MERGERS AND ACQUISITIONS

The role of financial accounting has been of great significance in the area of mergers and acquisitions. When a price substantially above book value is paid for a potential acquisition, goodwill may be created above fair market value on the balance sheet of the acquiring firm. The value of the acquired assets is established at their fair market value.

A merger is treated on the books of the acquiring firm as a purchase of assets.[2] Under a purchase of assets, any excess of the purchase price over the fair market value of assets must be recorded as goodwill. In the *CPA Canada Handbook,* Section 3064, the amortization of goodwill is not permitted, although if the fair value of the goodwill drops, the loss in value is to be recognized on the income statement. Those assets classified as intangible in a business combination such as a merger are to be amortized over their useful life. For tax purposes, 75 percent of goodwill can be considered an eligible capital expenditure, which has a 7 percent CCA rate. This will create tax savings as the eligible capital expenditure is expensed.

There are potential benefits to a corporation in offering share purchases rather than nonequity compensation (cash, bonds, preferred stock, and so on). A share purchase more readily qualifies a merger for a tax-free exchange under Sections 85(1) or 87(4) of the Income Tax Act. Under a tax-free exchange, the shareholders of the acquired firm may defer any capital gains taxes until the newly acquired shares have been sold. Thus, there would be no immediate tax for trading a share of stock in a corporation that was purchased 10 years ago at $5 for $100 in an acquiring corporation stock. When the stock is sold, the tax is recognized. If the tender offer were for cash, there would be an immediate tax obligation.

Why is a cash offer popular? Shareholders of acquired firms at times have been disenchanted with the performance of acquiring companies' shares and, at times, with the stock market in general. For this reason they wanted to take cash, pay tax, and invest in a new, diversified set of investments. Acquiring corporations went along with the cash tender offer pattern to satisfy the demands of selling shareholders. Strong stock markets and the large purchase prices allow for the return to share issues. The bust in the technology market at the turn of the millennium has shown the dangers in accepting stock instead of cash in mergers.

 FINANCE IN ACTION

Are Diversified Firms Winners or Losers?

A generation ago, the corporate conglomerate was thought to be the ideal business model. Firms such as Brascan and Canadian Pacific owned subsidiaries that were in widely different industries. In 2005, Brascan became Brookfield Asset Management. The advantages of the conglomerate organization were thought to be many.

[2] See Section 1582 of the *CPA Canada Handbook.*

But wait a minute! Don't run out and buy stock in a conglomerate just yet. Research has shown that a single-line business tends to have higher operating profitability than the subsidiary of a conglomerate in the same industry. This is due to greater focus. A conglomerate may represent a "jack of all trades, master of none."

Also, a failing business cannot have a value below zero if operated on its own, but it may have a negative value if it is part of an otherwise profitable conglomerate. There, its losses can continue to eat into the profits and value of the nonrelated divisions.

What about stock market performance? How do conglomerates compare to single-industry firms in terms of providing returns to investors? There are enough studies on this topic to fill a midsize university's library. The results of hundreds of studies are pretty much a draw.

What is not a draw is the overall value assigned to conglomerates versus single-industry firms. There is a diversification discount of 13 percent to 15 percent on average.[3] Furthermore, the more unrelated the divisions, the greater the discount.

Q1 Is diversification worthwhile in the pursuit of shareholder wealth maximization, from the firm's perspective? from an investor's perspective?

brookfield.com

Symbol: BAM.A

By using cash instead of stock, a corporation may diminish the perceived dilutive effect of a merger. If Small Corporation had been acquired for straight cash by Expand Corporation, no new shares are issued and earnings per share go up proportionately by the amount of new aftertax earnings. This latter argument tends to be weakened by recognition of the fact that cash tendered in a merger has a substantial capital cost associated with it and, furthermore, that new shares of stock may later have to be authorized and sold to finance the cash drain.

PREMIUM OFFERS AND STOCK PRICE MOVEMENTS

Premiums seem to range from 5 to 50 percent over market value in a merger or acquisition with an average of about 30 percent. These high merger premiums may be related to market values for securities in general. To the extent that replacement value exceeds market value, a high premium over market value may be justified. In addition, the motivation of the acquiring company in making the purchase was sometimes not to turn around a poor performer but to take advantage of the superior market or product position of the acquired company.

Researchers into takeover activity have found that acquirees have superior price performance on a risk-adjusted basis. It is not surprising that a company that is offered a large premium over its current market value has a major upside movement. For the investor, however, much of the upward price movement may occur before the public announcement of the merger offer. Even if the share price increases further toward the offer price after the public announcement, it generally occurs quickly, emphasizing the efficiency of the markets based on public information.

ARBs (arbitrageurs), who specialize in merger situations, have the strategy to purchase the stock of the acquisition candidate in the hope of being bought out at a higher tender offer price. They accumulate stock below the offer price, hoping the merger will go through at that price or

---

[3] P.G. Berger and E. Ofek (1996) "Bustup Takeovers of Value-destroying Diversified Firms," *Journal of Finance,* Volume 51(4): 1175–1200; and O.A. Lamont and C. Polk (2002),"The Diversification Discount: Cash Flows Versus Returns," *Journal of Finance,* Volume 56(5): 1693–1721.

even higher. The ARBs often become allies of acquiring companies because their profits (and their avoidance of losses) are dependent on the merger's actual completion.

In a stock-for-stock exchange, an ARB may attempt to lock in its profit position by buying the stock of the acquisition candidate at a lower price and, at the same time, short-selling the stock of the acquirer at a higher price. A short sell is a current sale of stock that is not owned, with the intention of acquiring the stock in the future to close out the position. When the merger is consummated, the ARB will trade the acquiree's stock for a share of the acquiring company's stock and use the stock to cover the short position. Thus, the selling price is pre-established at the high price, and the buy price is pre-established at a lower price. Even if the acquiring company's stock goes up or down from $40 after the merger has been announced, the sale price and profit spread have been established. The ARB as short seller will lose if the merger does not go forward.

The only problem with any merger-related investment strategy is that the merger may be called off. In that case the merger candidate's stock, which shot up, will likely fall back and the Johnny-come-lately investor will lose money.

All this information on price movement patterns has significance to corporate financial managers, who must understand and react to the motivations of investors. For example, once the ARBs have established their investment position, they will do everything possible to see that the merger goes through. This, at a minimum, will include voting all their shares in favour of a merger. On a more active basis, it may encompass a strategy of influencing other large shareholders, and it could ultimately include an attempt to discredit the management of a target company in the eyes of the shareholders.

 FINANCE IN ACTION

Refocusing Strategies

Diversification at one time had been a key goal of many large corporations and they expanded into many varied lines of business. Many found the experience less than successful. Some have suggested that there is little need for the firm to diversify if its shareholders already own a diversified share portfolio. Instead, the firm should concentrate on what it knows best, perhaps on a global scale.

We see a new trend as business and government attempt to direct their energies on a simpler and more focused line of business. In Canada, the federal government shed Petro-Canada and CN Rail. Ontario sold off SkyDome. Alberta sold off TELUS in the mid-1990s.

For corporations, we have seen BCE spin off Nortel (what a great move) and Canadian Pacific split into five separate companies (see Chapter 3). Brookfield (formerly Brascan) has tried to simplify its vast holdings along five asset classes even though it continues to hold many firms. Quebecor is another vast empire with numerous interwoven firms, but whether these are in printing, TV, magazine publishing, the Internet (canoe.ca), or newspapers, the common theme is communications. These various media are converging, and this is the focus of Quebecor's operations.

Q1 What are the asset classes for the operations of Brookfield?

Symbol: BAM.A

MERGERS AND THE MARKET FOR CORPORATE CONTROL

The high level of corporate merger activity is sometimes justified by the proposition that a competitive market for corporate control is an effective brake on any tendency for agent managers to diverge from striving to maximize shareholder wealth. However, to the extent that activity in this so-called market for corporate control creates financial value for shareholders, there have been studies where results suggest that all of the excess value is transferred to the selling shareholders.

Although the evidence seems to support the general conclusion that the shareholders of acquired companies realize substantial excess returns when a merger occurs, studies suggest that the shareholders of bidder firms realize negligible excess returns on takeovers. Because the bidding firms in the U.S. situation are generally much larger than the acquired firms and because the bidding firms' corporate strategies are often based on active acquisition programs, however, those research results are at least partially muddied by measurement problems. In effect, the expectation of its making attractive acquisitions may be already discounted in the company's normal share price.

A study of Canadian merger activity between 1964 and 1983 came to what may be a significantly different conclusion in regard to the sharing of the abnormal returns between buyer and seller.[4] As Figure 20–2 shows, the data from that study revealed that, consistently with U.S.–based studies, target firms received higher abnormal returns on average than did the bidder firms. Unlike the U.S. studies, however, the bidder firms did receive significant abnormal returns on average. In addition, the figure indicates that there were generally higher abnormal returns in cases where the mergers were related, especially for the acquirees.

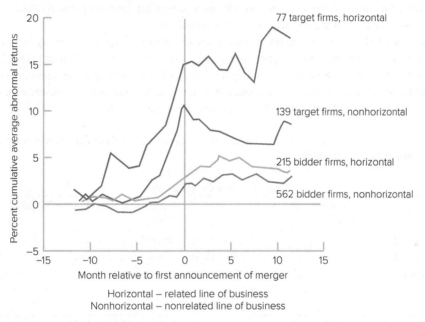

Figure 20–2 Abnormal returns relative to merger announcements

Thus, the evidence to this point seems to imply there may be some overall benefit to merger activity. In many cases, if value is actually created, it can be attributed to a new management team changing the status quo. This may be particularly appropriate in a company where the previous management had become too wedded to investing in the traditional industry regardless of whether or not the cost of capital was higher than the potential returns. Whether or not the buyer gets some of the value created by the merger is still a question requiring further research.

LO6 HOLDING COMPANIES

The holding company or conglomerate has been declining in prominence in the Canadian economy. A holding company is one that has control over one or more other firms. Power Corporation (POW), Onex (OCX), and Brookfield (BAM.A) have been significant Canadian holding companies. To establish voting control, the holding company may sometimes own less than a majority interest, but

---

[4]B. Espen Eckbo, "Mergers and the Market for Corporate Control: The Canadian Evidence," *Canadian Journal of Economics* 19, no. 2 (May 1986), pp. 236–260.

it is still able to determine policy as a result of widely spread minority interests among the other shareholders.

The advantage of the holding company was that it seemed to afford opportunities for leverage. It allowed effective corporate control with minimal equity investments. Assume Giant Holding Corporation (GHC) has the investment interests in companies A, B, and C shown in Table 20–5. Assume also that GHC has effective voting control of the three companies because of the widely dispersed interests of these companies' other owners. It owns 20 percent of the equity of company A, 37.5 percent of company B, and 25 percent of company C. Through these interlocking positions, Giant Holding Corporation controls $420 million in assets (the combined assets of the three companies), with only $20 million of common stock equity in its own firm. Its equity-to-assets controlled ratio is 4.8 percent ($20 million/$420 million). If we really want to get creative, we can assume another holding company has control of Giant Holding Corporation with only a small investment in it, thus creating additional levels of ownership.

The holding company device also benefits from the isolation of the legal risks of the firms. Theoretically, if company C loses money, this will not legally affect the other firms, because company C is a separate legal entity with separate shareholders.

The fact that dividends paid from one Canadian corporation to another are generally free of tax makes the holding company form of organization much more common in Canada than in the United States, where those dividends would be partially taxable. In Canada, holding companies have often placed their investments in subsidiary companies in preferred rather than common shares as the dividends paid on preferred tend to be higher than those on common stock.

Table 20–5 Assets, liabilities, and owners' equity of Giant Holding Corporation and related companies (in $ millions)

Giant Holding Corporation			
Assets		**Liabilities and Shareholders' Equity**	
Common shareholdings:			
Company A	$ 10	Long-term debt	$ 15
Company B	15	Preferred stock	10
Company C	20	Common stock equity	20
	$ 45		$ 45
Company A			
Assets		**Liabilities and Shareholders' Equity**	
Current assets	$ 50	Current liabilities	$ 20
Plant and equipment	50	Long-term debt	30
	$ 100	Common stock equity	50
			$100
Company B			
Assets		**Liabilities and Shareholders' Equity**	
Current assets	$ 60	Current liabilities	$ 10
Plant and equipment	60	Long-term debt	70
	$ 120	Common stock equity	40
			$120
Company C			
Assets		**Liabilities and Shareholders' Equity**	
Current assets	$ 80	Current liabilities	$20
Plant and equipment	120	Long-term debt	100
	$ 200	Common stock equity	80
			$200

Drawbacks

Leverage is a two-edged sword. Poor returns are magnified in a pyramided corporate structure with heavy debt commitments. Although companies A, B, and C are separate legal entities that cannot force the bankruptcy of another, there can still be a disastrous indirect chain effect. For example, if company A has a bad year, it may be unable to pay dividends to the holding company, which in turn may be unable to pay interest on the $15 million it has in long-term debt. The more complicated the arrangement, the more vulnerable the operation is to reversals.

The complicated administrative policies and procedures of a holding company are also worthy of note. With multiple managements, boards of directors, dividend policies, and reporting systems, the expenses are high and the opportunities for problems are substantial.

Furthermore, investors do not easily understand the structure of holding companies and this tends to depress the share price. This is part of the reason we have seen the breakup of large conglomerates at the turn of the millennium. As indicated in the earlier Finance in Action box "Are Diversified Firms Winners or Losers?" there apparently is a discounted value placed on conglomerates by the financial markets.

SUMMARY

1. An unsolicited tender offer for a target company is generally considered hostile. Offers are often made at values well in excess of the current market price, and management of the target company becomes trapped in the agency dilemma of maintaining its current position versus agreeing to the wishes of the acquiring company, and even the target company's own shareholders. To prevent takeovers, defensive measures include poison pills, shareholders' rights plans, targeted repurchase of shares, selling of crown jewels, and welcoming white knights. (LO1)

2. Corporations may seek external growth through mergers to achieve risk reduction, to improve access to the financial markets through increased size, or to obtain tax loss carry-forward benefits. A merger may also expand the marketing and management capabilities of the firm and allow for new product development. Although some mergers promise synergistic benefits (the $2 + 2 = 5$ effect), these can be elusive, with initial expectations exceeding subsequent realities. Recently, as the economic environment has become more competitive and demanding, we have seen corporations refocus on their core business. Furthermore, many corporations may not realize the expected benefits of diversification. (LO2)

3. The cash purchase of another corporation takes on many of the characteristics of a classic capital budgeting decision. In a stock-for-stock exchange, there is often a tradeoff between an immediate increase in earnings per share and current dilution to achieve faster growth. If a firm buys another firm with a P/E ratio lower than its own, there is an immediate increase in earnings per share. However, long-term earnings growth prospects must also be considered. The ultimate objective of a merger, as is true of any financial decision, is shareholder wealth maximization, and the immediate and delayed effects of the merger must be evaluated in this context. (LO3)

4. The accounting considerations in a merger are also important. Where the purchase price exceeds the book value of the acquired firm (after postmerger asset value adjustments based on fair market value), goodwill may be created. Mergers must be accounted for as purchases of assets with the attendant possibility of creating goodwill. (LO4)

5. Diversification by combining entities with different patterns of cash flows reduces the variability of the overall cash flows. This should reduce risk and the attractiveness of the combined entity. Unfortunately for corporations, diversification has not always added the expected benefits, and in some cases, it has added unexpected management problems brought on by unfamiliarity with the new business. The benefits of diversification may be best achieved at the investor level. (LO5)

6. The holding company is viewed as a means of accumulating large asset control with a minimum equity investment through leveraging the investment. The holding company is declining in significance. The drawbacks of holding companies have been seen in their discounted share prices. (LO6)

DISCUSSION QUESTIONS

1. Briefly discuss three significant features of the merger movement of the past few decades. (LO2)

2. Is risk reduction in the firm's portfolio of undertakings likely to be best achieved through horizontal integration, vertical integration, or conglomerate-type acquisitions? (LO2)

3. If a firm wishes to achieve immediate appreciation in EPS as a result of a merger, how can this be best accomplished in terms of exchange variables? What is a possible drawback to this approach in terms of long-range considerations? (LO3)

4. What are the purchase of assets accounting treatments of a merger? What is the effect of including goodwill? (LO3)

5. Suggest synergy that might occur in mergers in the financial services or in the energy sectors. (LO2)

6. Generally, a shareholder of the selling corporation demands a higher price if cash consideration is tendered. Explain why this might be the case. (LO3)

7. Explain how the weak stock market of the late 1970s served as an impetus to the merger wave of the late 1970s and 1980s. Did this happen again in the wake of the 2008–09 financial recession? (LO2)

8. It is possible for the postmerger P/E ratio to move in a direction opposite to that of the immediate postmerger EPS. Explain why this could happen. (LO4)

9. Explain why unusually high premiums have sometimes been paid in the merger movement. (LO2)

10. Suggest some ways firms have tried to avoid being takeover targets. (LO1)

11. Why do management and shareholders often have divergent viewpoints about the desirability of a takeover? (LO2, LO5)

12. How can the ordinary investor benefit from a possible merger? What is the danger of investing in a proposed merger target? Explain. (LO2)

13. How does a merger ARB benefit from a possible merger? What is the danger in being a merger ARB? Explain. (LO1, LO2)

14. Compare the use of leverage in a holding company to the concept of operating and financial leverage explained in Chapter 5. Does a holding company have any tax complications related to dividends? (LO6)

15. Why has the United States been traditionally concerned about corporate concentration arising from merger activity, whereas Canada's concern has been much more with foreign ownership? (LO6)

INTERNET RESOURCES AND QUESTIONS

Mergers, acquisitions, and divestitures occur with increasing frequency in the financial markets. News services, public filings, company websites, and share price activity are the best sources for this information.

News services:	reuters.com
	canoe.com
	theglobeandmail.com
	newswire.ca
Public securities filings:	sedar.com
Company websites:	tmx.com
Share price charting:	bigcharts.marketwatch.com (For search of TSX firms use "ca:" prefix)

1. Using a recent news report, identify a potential or accomplished merger or acquisition.
   a. Comment on why the merger was proposed.
   b. Was the merger a friendly or hostile takeover?
   c. What share price was set on each company for the proposed takeover? Was the merger an exchange of shares or was it a cash offer?
   d. What relevant information was filed with the securities commission?
   e. Chart the price performance of both parties to the merger, for a reasonable period before and after the announcement date of the proposed merger. Comment on how the shares in each company performed over this period.
   f. Do you believe the merger is positive for the shareholders of the companies involved? Was the takeover positive for other stakeholders?

PROBLEMS

1. The Charles Corporation desires to expand. It is considering a cash purchase of Atlas Enterprises for $2,000,000. The Atlas Corporation has a $600,000 tax loss carry-forward that could be used immediately by the Charles Corporation, which is paying taxes at the rate of 25 percent. Atlas will provide $260,000 per year in cash flow (aftertax income plus CCA) for the next 20 years. If the Charles Corporation has a cost of capital of 12 percent, should the merger be undertaken?

2. The Wayne Corporation desires to expand. It is considering a cash purchase of the Gretz Corporation, a company in a similar business, for $3 million. The Gretz Corporation has a $600,000 tax loss carry-forward that could be used immediately by the Wayne Corporation, which is paying taxes at the rate of 40 percent. The Gretz Corporation is projected to provide $380,000 per year in available cash flows for the next 20 years. If the Wayne Corporation considers its cost of capital as 11 percent, should it pursue the Gretz merger?

3. Assume the Arrow Corporation is considering the acquisition of Failure Unlimited. The latter has a $400,000 tax loss carry-forward. Projected earnings for the Arrow Corporation are as follows:

    a. How much will the total taxes of Arrow Corporation be reduced as a result of the tax loss carry-forward?

    b. How much will the total income available to shareholders be for the three years if the acquisition occurs?

	20XX	20XY	20XZ	Total
Before-tax income	$ 160,000	$200,000	$320,000	$680,000
Taxes (25%)	40,000	50,000	80,000	170,000
Income available to shareholders. . . .	$ 120,000	$150,000	$240,000	$510,000

4. J & J Enterprises is considering a cash acquisition of Patterson Steel Company for $4,000,000. Patterson will provide the following pattern of cash inflows and synergistic benefits for the next 20 years. There is no tax loss carry-forward.

	Years		
	1–5	6–15	16–20
Cash inflow (aftertax)	$440,000	$600,000	$800,000
Synergistic benefits (aftertax) . . .	$ 40,000	$ 60,000	$ 70,000

    The cost of capital for the acquiring firm is 12 percent. Should the merger be undertaken?

5. Worldwide Scientific Equipment is considering a cash acquisition of Medical Labs for $1.6 million. Medical Labs will provide the following pattern of cash inflows and synergistic benefits for the next 25 years. There is no tax loss carryforward.

	Years		
	1–5	6–15	16–25
Cash inflow (aftertax)	$150,000	$170,000	$210,000
Synergistic benefits (aftertax) . . .	$ 20,000	$ 30,000	$ 50,000

    The cost of capital for the acquiring firm is 11 percent. Should the merger be undertaken?

6. McGraw Trucking Company is considering a cash acquisition of Hill Storage Company for $3 million. Hill Storage will provide the following pattern of cash inflows and synergistic benefits for the next 20 years. There is no tax loss carry-forward.

	Years		
	1–5	6–15	16–20
Cash inflow (aftertax)	$200,000	$240,000	$320,000
Synergistic benefits (aftertax) . .	$ 30,000	$ 50,000	$ 90,000

    The cost of capital for the acquiring firm is 9 percent. Should the merger be undertaken?

7. Assume the following financial data for the Wolf Corporation and Lamb Enterprises.

	Wolf Corporation	Lamb Enterprises
Total earnings.....................	$125,000	$500,000
Number of shares of stock outstanding ..	100,000	500,000
EPS...............................	$1.25	$1.00
P/E ratio	16 ×	20 ×
Market price per share	$20.00	$20.00

a. If all the shares of the Wolf Corporation are exchanged for shares of the Lamb Enterprises on a share-for-share basis, what will be postmerger EPS for Lamb Enterprises? Use an approach similar to Table 20–4.

b. Explain why the EPS of Lamb Enterprises changed.

c. Can we necessarily assume that Lamb Enterprises is better or worse off?

8. The Jeter Corporation is considering acquiring the A-Rod Corporation. The data for the two companies are as follows:

	A-Rod Corporation	Jeter Corporation
Total earnings.....................	$1,000,000	$4,000,000
Number of shares of stock outstanding ...	400,000	2,000,000
EPS...............................	$2.50	$2.00
P/E ratio	12	15
Market price per share	$30	$30

a. The Jeter Corp. is going to give A-Rod Corp. a 60 percent premium over A-Rod Corp.'s current market value. What price will it pay?

b. At the price computed in part *a,* what is the total market value of A-Rod Corp.? (Use number of A-Rod Corp. shares times price).

c. At the price computed in part *a,* what is the P/E ratio Jeter Corp. is assigning to A-Rod Corp.?

d. How many shares must Jeter Corp. issue to buy the A-Rod Corp. at the total value computed in part *b*? (Keep in mind Jeter Corp.'s price per share is $30).

e. Given the answer to part *d,* how many shares will Jeter Corp. have after the merger?

f. Add together the total earnings of both corporations and divide by the total number of shares computed in part *e.* What are the new postmerger EPS?

g. Why has Jeter Corp.'s EPS gone down?

h. How can Jeter Corp.'s hope to overcome this dilution?

9. Dr. Payne helped start Surgical Inc. 15 years ago. At the time, he purchased 200,000 shares of stock at one dollar per share. In 20XX, he has the opportunity to sell his interest in the company to Medical Technology for $40 a share. His marginal tax rate would be 28 percent.

a. If he sells his interest, what will be the value for before-tax profit, taxes, and aftertax profit? No capital gain exemptions have been used.

b. Assume, instead of cash, he accepts stock valued at $40 per share. He holds the stock for five years and then sells it for $72.50 (the stock pays no cash dividends). What will be the value for before-tax profit, taxes, and aftertax profit?

c. Using an 11 percent discount rate, compare the aftertax profit figure in part *b* to part *a.*

10. Lindbergh Airlines is planning to make an offer for Flight Simulators Inc. The shares of Flight Simulators are currently selling for $30 per share.

a. If the tender offer is planned at a premium of 60 percent over market price, what will be the offered share price for Flight Simulators?

b. Suppose before the offer is actually announced the share price of Flight Simulators rises to $42 because of strong merger rumours. If you buy the shares at that price and the merger goes through at the price computed in part **a,** calculate your percentage gain.

c. There is always the possibility that the merger will be called off after it is announced and the shares will fall to their original price. Calculate your loss if this occurs and you bought at $42.

d. If there is a 75 percent probability that the merger will go proceed and only a 25 percent chance that it will be called off, does this appear to be a good investment? Assume your purchase price was $42.

11. A merger between Minnie Corporation and Mickey Corporation is under consideration. The financial information for these firms is as follows:

	Minnie Corporation	Mickey Corporation
Total earnings...................	$800,000	$ 1,600,000
Number of shares of stock outstanding	200,000	800,000
EPS...........................	$4	$2
P/E ratio......................	10 ×	20 ×
Market price per share............	$40	$40

a. On a share-for-share exchange basis, what will be the postmerger EPS?

b. If Mickey Corporation pays a 25 percent premium over the market value of Minnie Corporation, how many shares will be issued?

c. With the 25 percent premium, what will be the postmerger EPS?

12. In the case of the Minnie and Mickey merger described in the previous problem, assume a 100 percent premium will be paid and there is a 25 percent synergistic benefit to total earnings from the merger. Will the postmerger earnings go up or down, based on your calculations?

13. Assume the Shelton Corporation is considering the acquisition of Cook Inc. The expected EPS for the Shelton Corporation will be $3.00 with or without the merger. However, the standard deviation of the earnings will decrease from $1.89 to $1.20 with the merger because the two firms are negatively correlated.

a. Compute the coefficient of variation for the Shelton Corporation before and after the merger (consult Chapter 13 to review statistical concepts if necessary).

b. Discuss the possible impact on Shelton's postmerger P/E ratio, assuming investors are risk averse.

14. General Meter is considering two mergers. The first is with Firm A in its own volatile industry; the second is a merger with Firm B in an industry that moves in the opposite direction (and will tend to level out performance due to negative correlation).

General Meter Merger with Firm A		General Meter Merger with Firm B	
Possible Earnings ($ in millions)	Probability	Possible Earnings ($ in millions)	Probability
$40	.30	$10	.25
50	.40	50	.50
60	.30	90	.25

a. Compute the mean, standard deviation, and coefficient of variation for both investments. (Consult Chapter 13 to review statistical concepts if necessary.)

b. Assuming investors are risk averse, which alternatives can be expected to bring the higher valuation?

15. Wright Aerospace is considering the acquisition of Columbus Shipping Corporation. The book value of the Columbus Shipping Corporation is $30 million, and Wright Aerospace is willing to pay $90 million in cash and preferred stock. No upward adjustment of asset values is anticipated. Wright Aerospace Corporation has 2 million shares outstanding. A purchase of assets financial treatment will be used.

a. How much will the annual amortization be?

b. Is any tax benefit involved?

c. Explain how the recording of goodwill could have been avoided.

16. Ontario Corporation, a holding company, has investments in three other firms. Values are expressed in millions of dollars.

EASTERN CORPORATION

Assets		Liabilities and Shareholders' Equity	
Current assets...............	$ 80	Current liabilities.............	$ 40
Plant and equipment..........	120	Long-term debt	40
		Common equity	120
	$200		$200

CENTRAL CORPORATION

Assets		Liabilities and Shareholders' Equity	
Current assets...............	$100	Current liabilities.............	$30
Plant and equipment..........	200	Long-term debt	70
		Common equity	200
	$300		$300

WESTERN CORPORATION

Assets		Liabilities and Shareholders' Equity	
Current assets...............	$100	Current liabilities.............	$ 90
Plant and equipment..........	200	Long-term debt	110
		Common equity	100
	$300		$300

The Ontario Corporation has voting control of the three other corporations with the following investment interests in each: 25 percent of the equity in Eastern Corporation, 20 percent of the equity in Central Corporation, and 10 percent of the equity in the Western Corporation.

Ontario Corporation's long-term debt is equal to 30 percent of its assets; its preferred stock is equal to 20 percent; and its common stock is equal to 50 percent.

a. Fill in the following table for Ontario Corporation:

Assets		Liabilities and Shareholders' Equity	
Common shareholdings:			
Eastern Corporation...........	_____	Long-term debt	_____
Central Corporation...........	_____	Preferred stock...............	_____
Western Corporation	_____	Common equity	_____
Total.....................	_____	Total.....................	_____

b. Compute the percentage of Ontario Corporation's common equity to the total holding company assets in the three corporations.

MINI CASE

National Brands vs. A-1 Holdings

It was 5:30 Friday afternoon, January 22, 20XX. Bill Hall, the chairman and CEO of National Brands Inc. was clearing up the last of the papers on his desk and was looking forward to a relaxing weekend. It had been a good week. The company's annual results were in, and they showed that 20XW had been the best year in the company's history. Sales and net income were up over 8 percent from last year, and there was over $1.1 billion in the cash and equivalents account to invest in the coming year.

The phone rang. It was Maria Ortiz, his secretary. "Did you hear the latest on the newswire?" Maria asked.

"No, what's up?" Bill replied, with a suspicious feeling that his evening wasn't going to be so relaxing after all.

"Kelly O'Brien, head of A-1 Holdings, just announced that he's bought 5 percent of our outstanding shares, and now he's making a tender offer for all of the rest at $55."

"I knew it!" Bill spat out. "He was in here just a few weeks ago, talking about whether we would sell the company to him. We turned down his offer because we want to stay independent, and he left after implying that we weren't looking out for our shareholders. He's got some plan to restructure the company around a six-member board of directors instead of the 15 we have now. Now he's trying to do it anyway, whether we like it or not!"

"Looks like it," Maria agreed. "So what do you think we should do?"

"OK, contact Tom Straw, the chief operating officer and Doris Faraday in finance, and tell them to get up here for a meeting right away," Bill directed. "Oh, and have Stan Lindner from public relations come, too; we're sure to have a press release about this, and—oh, wait—call my wife and tell her I won't be home until late tonight."

After about half an hour, those who Bill had called for began arriving, armed with pencils, papers, and calculators in anticipation of the coming session. Bill, in the meantime, had managed to compile some financial data about A-1 Holdings, which he had summarized on a sheet of paper along with like data about his own company, National Brands, for comparison (see Table 1). He passed the sheet around among the others.

Table 1 Selected financial data

	National Brands	A-1 Holdings
Total earnings expected in the coming year. .	$ 500,000,000	$ 192,000,000
Number of shares outstanding	113,640,000	61,800,000
EPS.	$4.40	$3.11
P/E ratio	10.9	4.2
Market price.	$47.88	$13.00
Book value per share	$26.84	$6.39
Growth rate before merger.	8.53%	19.61%
Liquid assets (cash and equivalent)	$1,153,000,000	$1,736,800,000
Total assets.	$5,160,300,000	$2,294,500,000
Total debt	$2,110,300,000	$1,899,500,000
Total equity	$3,050,000,000	$395,000,000
Dividend-payout ratio	48.0%	0.0%

"OK, let's start with what we know," Bill led off. "A-1 already has 5 percent of our outstanding shares, and it is making a bid for the rest at $55, or 7.875 over market."

"I hate to be the devil's advocate," Stan said, thinking of the 25,000 shares he owned personally, "but that sounds like a pretty fair offer. What will happen if he succeeds?"

"Most of us will be out of a job, and this company will become just another card in Kelly O'Brien's poker hand," Bill said acidly. "Our employees deserve better than that, so let's talk about what we can do to keep it from happening."

"What about a poison pill?" Tom suggested. "We could take out a fair-sized loan based on our heavy cash position, and A-1 would have a tough time absorbing it—just look at the amount of debt they're carrying now!"

"That would probably work, but it's not very good for us, either," Stan agreed. He was still thinking about the $7 a share profit to be made in a buyout. "So how about someone else? You know, a white knight who would top A-1's offer but would keep the structure of the company substantially the same as it is now."

"I don't know who we could ask," Bill said, "and besides that, the basic problem would probably still occur—we would lose our status as an independent entity."

Doris had been working on some figures on her pad, and she spoke up now. "There's another alternative," she said, "that I'm surprised you all haven't mentioned, given the financial status of the two companies."

"What, what?" Bill said. "Don't keep us in suspense!"

"It's the Pacman defence," she continued, unruffled. "What we do is launch a tender offer of our own for all of A-1's outstanding stock. If it's successful, we not only thwart the takeover attempt but also gain a new business in the bargain."

"Didn't Martin Marietta try that with Bendix back in 1989?" Bill asked. "As I recall, it didn't turn out very well for them."

"You're right; it didn't," Doris agreed, "and no one else has tried it since. But just comparing the numbers here between National and A-1, I think it might work out quite well for us. I've been doing some calculating here, and I think an offer to A-1's shareholders of $17 a share would be accepted, and we could conclude the whole affair rather quickly."

"I'm interested." Bill said. "Tell you what: Put your finance staff on it over the weekend and have them work up the proposal formally. Get the legal and accounting people to help you too. In the meantime, Stan, tip off the news media that we will have an announcement of our own shortly and draft up a public notice for A-1's shares at $17 each. Don't release it yet, but be ready to on Monday. Oh, and be sure to include in it that I said the deal will not cause any dilution of National's EPS. One last thing; Doris, draft an open letter to our shareholders for my signature, explaining what's happening and reassuring them that we will keep their company intact and prosperous."

"Any questions? If not, let's get on it. Mr. O'Brien is about to get a surprise!"

a. (i) A-1 is offering $55 a share for National's stock. How much total cash will it have to raise to buy the company? (The remaining 95 percent?)

   (ii) Assume A-1 plans to borrow the money needed to make the purchase. If A-1 uses the amount of liquid assets currently on hand at National to offset the amount it needs to borrow, what is the net amount it will have to borrow?

   (iii) Assuming A-1 does borrow the amount you determined in (2) above, what will A-1's total debt be after the purchase is completed? In making your calculation, consider all forms of debt that the combined firm will have. Now compute A-1's debt-to-equity ratio (A-1's equity will not increase). Given this ratio, do you think it is likely that A-1 will be able to obtain the necessary debt financing?

   (iv) Suppose instead that A-1 decides to issue stock to raise the money needed for the purchase (i.e., the amount you computed in (2) above will be raised through a stock issue instead of by borrowing). How many shares of A-1 stock will have to be issued? (Assume the price at which it will be issued is $13 and disregard flotation costs.)

(v) If A-1 raises the money by issuing new shares of its stock, what will A-1's EPS be after the purchase is complete and the earnings are combined?

(vi) Do you think A-1's shareholders will be happy if this deal goes through? What about the current National shareholders?

b. (i) If National employs the Pacman defence and tries to buy A-1 for $17 a share, how much will the total dollar price be?

(ii) If National wants to finance the purchase by issuing stock, and it plans to use the amount of liquid assets on hand at A-1 to offset the amount of stock that needs to be issued, what will the total dollar price be? (Assume they will be issued at $47.88 and disregard flotation costs.)

(iii) What will be National's debt-to-equity ratio after the purchase is complete? (Assume it was completed per your calculations in part *b* (2) above.) Note that National's total equity will not increase since no new shares are issued.

(iv) Suppose, instead, that National decides to first use A-1's liquid assets to pay down most of A-1's debt. How many shares of National at $47.88 will have to be issued? Use the cost figure from your answer to part *b* (1).

(v) What will the new National's EPS be, assuming the deal is completed per your calculations in part *b* (4) above?

(vi) Is Bill Hall correct in his statement that National's EPS will not be diluted as a result of the purchase of A-1?

c. If National's P/E does not change following the purchase of A-1, what will its stock price be? Is it likely that National's P/E will remain at 10.9? Or do you think it will rise or fall?

d. (i) Do you think National's Pacman defence will be successful? Or do you think A-1 will succeed in buying out National?

(ii) Do you think that National's shareholders are better off as a result of A-1's attack and National's Pacman defence (assuming it succeeds)?

(iii) Do you think Kelly O'Brien, head of A-1, should be viewed as a "good guy," whose action will produce more efficient companies, or a "bad guy," who is a destroyer of traditional values and employees' careers?

CHAPTER

21

International Financial Management

LEARNING OBJECTIVES

LO1 Identify and then analyze reasons for a foreign investment decision.

LO2 Examine the effects of exchange and political risk on the foreign investment decision.

LO3 Assess the effects of exchange rates on the firm's profitability and cash flow.

LO4 Characterize the factors influencing exchange rates.

LO5 Utilize spot, cross, and forward exchange rates and compute forward premiums and discounts.

LO6 Evaluate techniques to hedge or reduce foreign exchange risk.

LO7 Explain the purposes and nature of the multinational operations of the corporation.

LO8 Outline potential ways to finance international operations.

The political systems that emerged from World War II contributed to the establishment of trade relations between nations and the sustained growth of the world economy. The United States became the dominant player in the world economy, with the U.S. dollar used as the reserve currency. Meanwhile, the European nations formed the European Common Market in an effort to promote better trade relations among themselves, and today the Common Market rivals the might of the U.S. market. In the East, the rise of Japan, China, and other Asian countries has added significant players to the world economy. Today, the U.S. economy is not as dominant. In recent years, the United States has incurred enormous trade deficits and external debt, which has initiated tremendous capital flows and placed great demands on the world financial markets.

THE SCOPE

The examination of international financial management will focus on money flows due to trade and capital flows related to investment. International business operations, by their very nature, are often complex and risky, and require special understanding. Such an understanding is important whether you work for a multinational firm, a large bank, or a major brokerage firm, or are just involved in managing your own personal financial affairs.

Foreign exchange rates, the factors influencing these rates, and strategies for dealing with currencies add to the risks of the firm as money flows across borders. Furthermore, political and economic risk intensifies, as do the complexities of international financing through the global capital markets as the firm invests in other countries.

Trade

Nations today are dependent on one another for many valuable and scarce resources. This growing interdependence necessitates the development of sound international business relations. It is virtually impossible for any country to isolate itself from the influence of international developments in an integrated world economy, and today capitalism seems part of every economy, including the Chinese economy.

To a greater extent than most other industrialized economies, Canada is truly open to the forces of world trade. The significance of international business operations becomes more apparent if we look at the importance of foreign trade relative to the size of the Canadian economy. Figures 21–1 and 21–2 show the world's top merchandise exporters and importers. Canada exports over

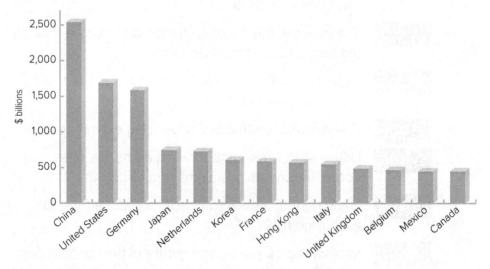

Figure 21–1 World's leading merchandise exporters, 2018

Top 13 represent 58% of world total of $19.5 trillion.

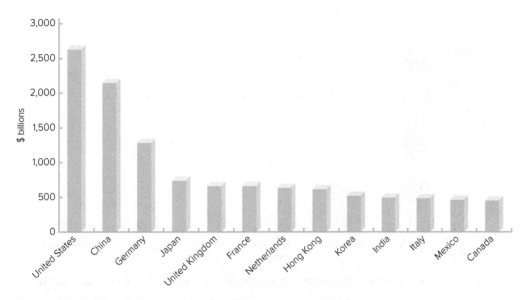

Figure 21–2 World's leading merchandise importers, 2018

Top 13 represent 60% of world total of $19.9 trillion. Commercial services add $5.5 trillion.

30 percent out of its total production of goods and services. In comparison, the United States, a major player in international trade by any absolute measure, exports just over 10 percent of its domestic production.

The importance of access to U.S. markets for Canadian economic success is demonstrated by Figure 21–3. In exports and imports, trade with the United States dwarfs our trade with other regions of the world. Canada's strong trade ties with the United States, combined with Canada's physically large but economically small domestic market, have led to trade agreements such as the North American Free Trade Agreement (NAFTA). This agreement has opened up opportunities for truly competitive Canadian enterprises, while threatening the viability of others not able to match international levels of efficiency. In 2020 NAFTA was revised as CUSMA in Canada and USMCA with some changes. Many Canadian companies derive a significant amount of their revenue from worldwide sources.

International trade and financial transactions, which are subject to currency exchange risk, are identified in the current account of Canada's international balance of payments, as shown in Figure 21–4. Transfers included inheritances and personal remittances.

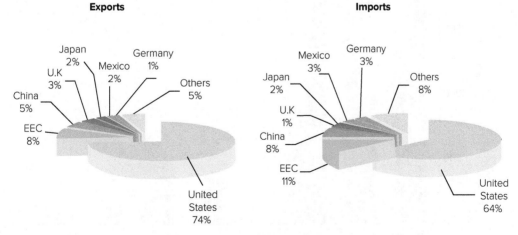

Figure 21–3 Canada's 2019 merchandise exports and imports by region

Note: Merchandise; Exports $640 billion, imports $664 billion, GDP $2.3 trillion.

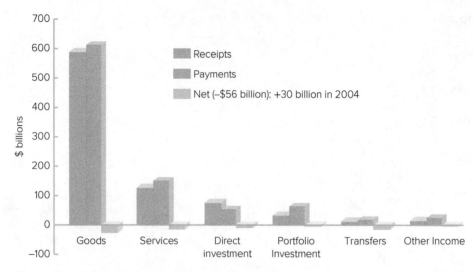

Figure 21–4 Canada's international balance of payments, current account, 2018

From Figure 21–4, we note the substantial flows on goods trade and that in 2018 Canada had a deficit (exports exceeded imports) while we have to go back to 2004 for a surplus. The current account surplus or deficit will play a part in determining exchange rates.

The international balance of payments attempts to record all the transactions that occur between Canada and the rest of the world over one year. The other portion of the balance of payments, the capital account, records direct investment and investment in financial securities, to be viewed shortly. These investments from the capital account show up as interest on the debts of Canadians in the current account.

Capital Investment

Foreign investments by Canadians are significant in the capital and real asset markets, as seen in Figure 21–5. Direct investment in foreign enterprises accounts is the largest component of this

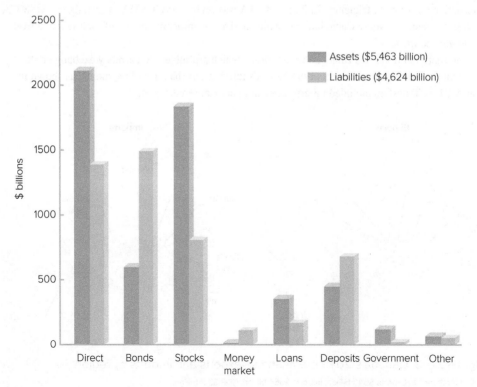

Figure 21–5 Canada's international investment position, third quarter 2019

investment, although there is a significant portfolio investment held directly in stocks and, to a lesser extent, in bonds. This portfolio investment has become larger as individual Canadians seek to diversify their holdings internationally. Figure 21–6 shows the primary recipients of Canadian investment (direct and portfolio) abroad, in particular the United States, our largest trading partner. Foreign investment in Canada is dominated by direct investment and by the bond portfolio.

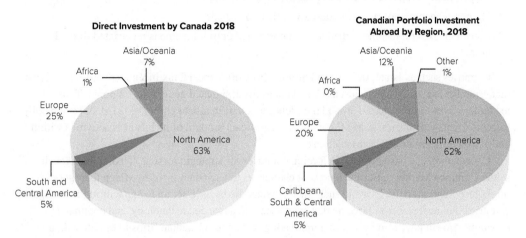

Figure 21–6 Canada's investment abroad, 2018 (assets)

Figure 21–7 documents that the United States dominates foreign portfolio investment in Canada. This foreign domination of ownership in important sectors of the Canadian economy has been blamed for many ills, not the least of which is the failure of our firms to invest heavily in new product research and development. Furthermore, it raises concerns over Canada's dependence on one market in the global context.

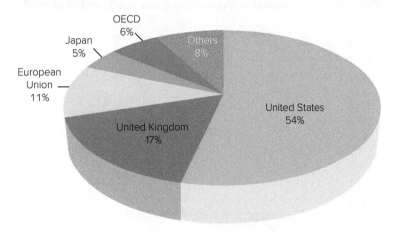

Figure 21–7 Portfolio (debt) investment in Canada, November 2019

LO1 Reasons for Capital Investment

Despite higher risks, foreign capital investments are undertaken for reasons that include

- Higher potential returns
- Strategic advantages
- Broader diversification possibilities

The average rate of return for foreign investment is often higher than the rate of return on domestic investments. This is perhaps the major reason Canadian firms expand their operations outside Canada's borders. Foreign investments offer higher rates of return for several reasons:

- Resource availability and ease of exploitation lower production costs.
- Significantly lower wages result in lower production costs.
- Larger, more concentrated markets produce better revenues.
- Corporate income tax rates are often lower than in Canada.
- Canadian taxes on income earned may be postponed until it income is repatriated (brought home).

Countries such as Israel, Ireland, and South Africa offer special tax incentives for foreign firms that establish operations there (just as Canada does for designated geographic regions). Today, technology is easily transferred around the globe, so a multinational corporation (MNC) can readily relocate to many countries. A MNC conducts a significant amount of its business activities within and across different political jurisdictions.

Canadian MNCs have invested in foreign countries for strategic reasons. Trading blocs such as the Common Market in Europe represent challenges to Canadian firms by which their goods might face import tariffs. To avoid such trade barriers, firms have set up manufacturing in foreign countries. Political stability, large market size, access to advanced technology, and continued economic growth have also been prime motivating factors for Canadian firms to establish their operations in the United States. The decision to invest in a foreign country by a firm operating in an oligopolistic industry is also motivated by strategic considerations. When a competitor undertakes a direct foreign investment, other companies quickly follow with defensive investments in the same foreign country.

Many academics believe international diversification of risks is also an important motivation for direct foreign investment. The basic premise of portfolio theory in finance is that an investor can reduce the risk level of a portfolio by combining those investments whose returns are less than perfectly positively correlated. Figure 21–8, comparing single-country and multicountry investment portfolios, implies that further reduction in investment risk can be achieved by diversifying across

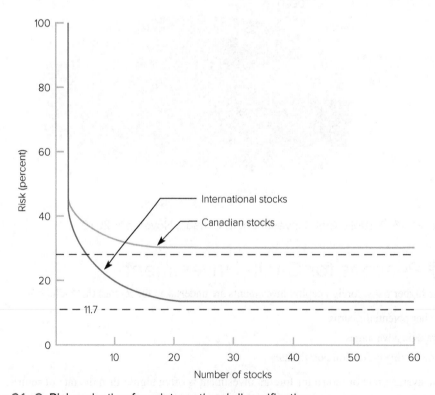

Figure 21–8 Risk reduction from international diversification

national boundaries. International stocks in the figure show a consistently lower percentage of risk compared to any given number of Canadian stocks in a portfolio. It is argued, however, that institutional and political constraints, language barriers, and lack of adequate information on foreign investments prevent investors from diversifying across nations. However, multinational firms, through their unique position around the world, can derive the benefits of international diversification. This is due, at least partially, to their ability to operate as an efficient internal capital market, bypassing the many frictions that exist among and within nation-based capital, managerial, and technology markets.

LO2 THE RISKS

The risks of international financial management include foreign exchange risk, exchange rate (economic and translations) exposure, and political risk.

Foreign Exchange Risk

When conducting business internationally, corporations or investors inevitably must deal with more than one currency. To accommodate the free-trading Western nations, the international monetary system established a freely floating rate system to replace the rigid, fixed exchange rate system. For the most part, the new system proved its agility and resilience during the most turbulent years of oil price hikes and hyperinflation of the 1970s and 1980s. The free market exchange rates responded and adjusted well to these adverse conditions. Consequently, exchange rates fluctuated over a much wider range than they had in the past. The increased volatility of exchange markets forced many multinational firms, importers, and exporters to pay more attention to the function of foreign exchange risk management.

Since most foreign currency values fluctuate from time to time, the monetary value of an international transaction or investment, measured in either the seller's or the buyer's currency, is likely to change over time. As a result, the value of an investment or the expected receipt (payment) of funds from a commercial transaction will be more or less than the value originally established.

Figure 21–9 illustrates the volatility of the Canadian dollar in relation to the U.S. dollar from 2007 through 2020.

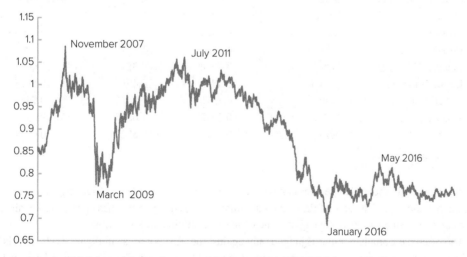

Figure 21–9 $U.S. per $Cdn: January 2007 to February 2020

Exchange Rates

Suppose that in February you were planning a visit to Europe in the summer. The number of euros you would obtain for C$10,000 depends on the exchange rate at the time you offered your Canadian dollars for sale. The relationship between the values of two currencies is known as the foreign exchange rate.

The exchange rates were: 0.6370 euros/Can$	March 2020	
0.5792 euros/Can$.	July 2020	

You would have received 6,370 euros in March but only 5,792 in July. That 578 euros difference would mean a much better time in the bars (if they opened from the Covid-19 pandemic)!

The exchange rate between Canadian dollars and euros can be quoted from a Canadian or European perspective. The March 2017 rate of 0.6370 euros/Can$ is the same as 1.5699 Can$/euro (1/0.6370).

Exchange rates
fx.sauder.ubc.ca

The Globe and Mail and the *Financial Post* publish exchange rates for the major currencies daily. The Bank of Canada is another reliable source. A good website for quotes is available at the Sauder School of Business. Table 21–1 illustrates the currencies of a number of countries and their exchange rates relative to the Canadian dollar. This table lists the number of units (or fractions thereof) of a foreign currency that one could purchase with one Canadian dollar (foreign currency units/$) on a particular day in the month indicated. Foreign exchange rates change from minute to minute and from day to day.

Table 21–1 Selected currencies and exchange rates (number of foreign currency units you can purchase with one Canadian dollar)

Country	Currency Unit	April 1996	October 2008	January 2020
Australia.	dollar	0.9361	1.2329	1.1457
Brazil	real	0.7340	1.7286	3.3467
China	renminbi	6.1200	5.5586	5.2056
Denmark.	kroner	4.2735	4.7103	5.0636
India	rupee	25.1572	40.112	53.996
Jamaica.	dollar	27.8200	57.823	102.260
Japan.	yen	78.6782	79.239	80.580
Mexico	peso	5.4540	10.503	14.717
South Africa.	rand	3.1348	8.1301	11.671
Sudan	dinars	110.000	n.a.	4,077.960
Sweden.	krona	4.9261	6.2422	7.2202
Switzerland	franc	0.8984	0.9240	0.7199
Russia.	ruble	4.9283	21.887	50.000
Thailand	baht	18.6518	28.329	23.468
United Kingdom.	pound	0.4842	0.4986	0.5817
United States	dollar	0.7346	0.8125	0.7447
Venezuela.	bolivar	0.2612	1.6606	55,199.69
Europe	euro	0.5915*	0.6322	0.6772

*Euro estimated

The changes in the exchange rates can be readily noticed in this table by observing what $1 Canadian could buy. The value of the Canadian dollar—its exchange rate—has appreciated against most currencies since 1996, except against the Chinese renminbi and Swiss franc.

Too often the Canadian dollar is judged only against the U.S. dollar, as in Figure 21–9. This is likely because of how closely our economy is tied to the U.S. economy. Some currencies have such severe devaluations due to high inflation rates that they rename their currencies and start over again.

LO3 Exchange Rate Exposure

Exposure refers to the amount by which the value of assets and liabilities may vary due to fluctuations in the exchange rate. This exposure to a change in value may actually be realized or it may not. As shareholders and financial managers, our concern should be how exposure to exchange rate fluctuations affects the value of shareholders' equity.

Economic exposure identifies the market value of assets and liabilities denominated in foreign currencies that is subject to change in economic value because of fluctuations in exchange rates. This economic exposure is a measure of concern to financial practitioners, but it is sometimes difficult to measure. Foreign exchange risk refers to the possible change in value of foreign exchange rates. Importers, exporters, investors, and MNCs are all exposed to foreign exchange risk. The foreign exchange risk impacts on the economic exposure of a multinational company in foreign countries. We identify foreign exchange risk as accounting or translation exposure, and as transaction exposure.

Accounting or translation exposure is the amount of loss or gain resulting from the treatment of foreign investments in the parent company's books, based on the accounting rules established by the parent company's government. In Canada, these rules are spelled out in the *CPA Canada Handbook*, Section 1650, which identifies the foreign operation as integrated or self-sustaining.

The *Handbook* recommendations for an integrated operation's exposure suggest its transactions be captured as if they had been performed by the parent company. Under the recommended temporal method, the value of capital assets and liabilities normally carried at historical cost would not be retranslated each time a balance sheet is prepared. Monetary items are translated at the rate of exchange in effect on the balance sheet date, which will show up in net income immediately, although under certain circumstances there is provision to amortize the gain or loss. The temporal method best approximates economic exposure and value change.

 FINANCE IN ACTION

The Birth and Perhaps Death of a Currency—the Euro!

The dream of a united Europe with one currency existed from the 1950s. On January 4, 1999, the dream of a single currency became a reality as the European Economic and Monetary Union (EMU) came into effect. A new common currency, the euro, became the legal currency for 11 countries (Germany, France, Italy, Austria, the Netherlands, Spain, Portugal, Finland, Belgium, Ireland, and Luxembourg). These countries used their traditional currencies, such as the German deutschemark, Italian lira, and French franc, alongside the euro until 2002. Then the euro became the only legal currency in the countries of the EMU, with currency notes and coins available. Over the weekend prior to its debut, the banks of Europe reprogrammed their computers to handle all future transactions in euros. All electronic payments, bank transactions, and stock and bond market trades are now recorded in euros. Travel in Europe is much easier using one currency. (Britain and Denmark chose not to join the EMU.) Today, 19 countries use the euro as their currency.

This monetary union exerts pressure for common monetary policy through the European Central Bank and creates a more uniform economic policy across the region. In fact, to join the EMU, individual countries have to achieve targeted goals on budget deficits and inflation rates. The new currency reduces the cost of doing business in many ways. One very tangible way is the elimination of exchange rates between these currencies. Hedging activities between currencies are no longer necessary. Of course, foreign trading between Canada and the other members of the EMU still requires hedging the Canadian dollar against the euro.

The Euro Zone represents a larger exporting presence than the United States. The euro is somewhat a rival to the U.S. dollar as a world reserve currency. However, after the worldwide financial problems that began in 2008, the euro was under stress. Bailouts had to be initiated for Portugal, Ireland, and then Greece. The governments of these countries had incurred significant debt and were running large deficits in violation of agreements to maintain their financial situation within certain limits.

Many felt these countries should default on their debt and be dropped from the Euro Zone. Austerity in government programs was severe with many suggesting that countries such as Greece would have been better off by devaluing their own currency (if they had one) and having the economy self- correct by this mechanism.

By 2020, there was renewed strength in the European economy, although Britain was preparing to leave (Brexit) the European Common Market and the effects of Covid-19 were yet to be determined.

Q1 What is the current exchange rate of the euro to the C$, £ British, and US$?

ecb.europa.eu

 FINANCE IN ACTION

Whiskey Is Risky! So Is Trade in a Frightened World!

Argentina, sub-Saharan Africa, India, Thailand, and South Africa are emerging markets. Their public finances are often stretched, their financial markets not well developed, and they exist in an increasingly divided world revisiting barriers to trade. How will they fare in the aftermath of the Covid-19 pandemic?

India opened its market to foreign distillers in the mid-1990s. This represented a tremendous growth potential and wonderful investment opportunity for worldwide distillery companies such as Seagram of Canada.

However, Seagram was not fully prepared for the differences of the Indian market. Although the company bottled its scotch whiskey in India, the company was still subject to a 400·percent duty on the product. Furthermore, the local product that used molasses rather than grain sold for $7 compared to Seagram's price of $40 a bottle. To prevent tampering, which was a widespread Indian practice, Seagram had to use special caps on its bottles. The bottles themselves were superior and, therefore, more expensive than locally used bottles.

Complicating Seagram's cash flow considerations was the evaporation rate ("the angel's share") in India due to the high heat, which took 8 percent of the whiskey annually versus 2 percent in Canada. Furthermore, India is a federation of states, many with different laws. Seagram was required to produce different labels in 18 states, four states had announced prohibition, and there was a nationwide ban on advertising.

The subcontinent of India presents many varied cultural and political risks. India is the world's most populous free market democracy but it suffers from corruption and government inefficiencies. Fortunately, a little "dram" could put things in a better perspective. Seagram's liquor business was sold to Pernod Ricard and Diageo in 2000.

seagram

A self-sustaining operation's exposure, it is suggested, is best captured by its net investment or equity position. Under the current rate method, all assets and liabilities denominated in foreign currency are converted at the rate of exchange in effect on the date of balance sheet preparation. A gain or loss should be reported in a separate category of shareholders' equity. The effect of this method is to restate equity based on changes in the exchange rate. However, this may not represent economic exposure. For example, a declining exchange rate may not make a foreign capital asset less valuable because the prices of products produced with the asset can be increased in step with the exchange rate, particularly if the product is sold on the world market. The exception to reporting a self-sustaining operation with the current rate method is when there is extreme inflation in a foreign country and, therefore, devaluation of its currency. In this case, the reported value of an equity investment would quickly disappear, although that is not likely the true situation. Overall, the impact of the accounting exposure on reported earnings of multinational firms resulting from the translation of a foreign subsidiary's balance sheet may be substantial. However, it is often an unrealized gain or loss.

Transaction exposure is identified as the foreign exchange gains and losses resulting from international transactions that are realized when foreign funds are converted to Canadian dollars. These gains or losses, because they are realized, will be reflected in the corporation's income statement and do represent a real loss or gain in economic value. As a consequence of these transactional gains and losses, the volatility of reported earnings per share increases. Hedging techniques can be used to minimize this transaction exposure by fixing the value for the foreign currency transaction.

Political Risk

Besides exchange exposure, political risk should also be carefully evaluated before direct investment in foreign countries:

- The government may change several times during the foreign firm's tenure in that country, and the new government may not be as friendly or as cooperative as the previous administration.
- An unfriendly government may impose foreign exchange restrictions, or the foreign ownership share may be limited to a set percentage of the total.
- Repatriation (transfer) of a subsidiary's profit to the parent company may be blocked, at least temporarily.
- The government may even expropriate (take over) the foreign subsidiary's assets.

The multinational company may experience a sizable loss of income and/or property as a result of this political interference. Executives from Sherritt International have been banned from entering the United States because American senators did not like Sherritt investing in Cuba. Brascan, now Brookfield, a dominant Canadian holding company conglomerate described in Chapter 20, had 89 percent of its assets in Brazil in 1977. However, the nationalization of its 83 percent interest in Light Serviços de Eletricidade by the Brazilian government in 1978 provided the impetus for Brookfield to refocus its investments on Canada. In 2011, Venezuela moved to nationalize gold companies, including Canadian interests. In 2020 Canadian resource companies are active in over 100 countries with over half their assets abroad.

Sherritt International
sherritt.com

Companies use different methods for assessing political risk. Some hire consultants to provide them with a political risk analysis. Others form their own advisory committees (little foreign affairs departments) consisting of top-level managers from headquarters and foreign subsidiaries. After ascertaining the country's political risk level, the multinational firm can use one of the following strategies to guard against such risk:

1. ***Establish a joint venture with a local entrepreneur.*** By bringing a local partner into the deal, the MNC not only limits its financial exposure but also minimizes anti-foreign feelings. It may also enhance its chances of commercial success by including a partner that knows the culture intimately.

2. ***Enter into a joint venture, preferably with firms from other countries.*** For example, Suncor might pursue an oil production operation in Africa in association with Royal Dutch Petroleum and Nigerian National Petroleum as partners. A foreign government is more hesitant to antagonize partner-firms of many nationalities at the same time.

3. ***Obtain insurance in advance against such risks when the perceived political risk level is high.*** Export Development Corporation (EDC), a federal government agency, sells insurance policies to qualified firms. This agency can insure against losses due to expropriation, war, revolution, or any resulting impossibility of repatriating revenues or capital. Many firms have used this service over the years. Private insurance companies such as Lloyds of London, American International Group Inc. (AIG), and others issue similar policies to cover political risk. Political risk umbrella policies do not come cheap. Coverage for projects in fairly safe countries can cost anywhere from 0.3 percent to 12 percent of the insured values per year. They are more expensive or unavailable in troubled countries. EDC's rates are lower than those of private insurers, and its policies extend for 20 years, as against three years or less for private insurance policies.

EXCHANGE RATE MANAGEMENT

LO4 Factors Influencing Exchange Rates

The present international monetary system consists of a mixture of freely floating exchange rates and fixed rates. The currencies of Canada's major trading partners are traded in free markets. In such a market, the supply of and demand for those currencies determines the exchange rate between two currencies. This activity, however, is subject to intervention by many countries' central banks. Factors that tend to increase the supply or decrease the demand schedule for a given currency bring down the value of that currency in foreign exchange markets. Similarly, the factors that tend to decrease the supply or increase the demand for a currency raise the value of that currency. Fundamental factors such as inflation, interest rates, foreign trade balances, and government policies are important in explaining both the short-term and long-term fluctuations of a currency value.

Inflation When the inflation rate between two countries is different, the exchange rate adjusts to correspond to the relative purchasing powers of the countries. Suppose apples are the commodity of value in Canada and China. If it takes $1 to buy an apple in Toronto and 5.2056 renminbi to buy the similar apple in Shanghai, then the rate of exchange between the Canadian dollar and renminbi is renminbi 5.2056/$1 or $0.1921/renminbi. If the price of an apple doubles in Toronto while the price in Shanghai remains the same, the purchasing power of a dollar in Toronto drops 50 percent. Consequently, you can exchange $1 for only 2.6028 renminbi in foreign currency markets (or now receive $0.3842, or double the previous rate, per renminbi). This means currency exchange rates tend to vary inversely with their respective purchasing powers to provide the same or similar purchasing power in each country. This is called the purchasing power parity theory. Purchasing power parity is based on the "law of one price." Identical goods should be priced the same, after adjusting for the exchange rate differential. Otherwise, there is an incentive to buy in one country and sell in another at a profit. Such action will drive the price of the identical goods toward each other.

Interest Rates All else being equal, the value of a currency offering a higher interest rate will appreciate relative to the foreign currency. If investors could earn 3 percent interest per year in Canada and 5 percent per year in Britain, they would prefer to invest in Britain, provided the inflation rate and perceived risk is the same in both countries. As investors sell Canadian dollars to buy British pounds, the value of the pound appreciates relative to the dollar. At the same time, the increased demand for British securities also tends to reduce the interest rate differential between the United Kingdom and Canada. Thus, interest rates and exchange rates adjust until the foreign exchange market and the money market reach equilibrium. This interplay between interest rate differentials and exchange rates is called the interest rate parity theory. Interest rate parity suggests that the interest rate paid (charged) on similar-risk financial instruments should be the same through the forward exchange rate. The forward exchange rate is the exchange rate at which monies can be exchanged when the financial instrument matures. This is demonstrated in the Finance in Action box discussing interest rates.

FINANCE IN ACTION

Interest Rates in Other Countries: Are They a Deal?

At one time, an investor could have earned 4.85 percent in Canada or 0.21 percent in Japan for 90 days with the purchase of a deposit through a major bank. Suppose a Japanese firm had 100,000,000 yen in excess funds for 90 days and was looking to achieve a return on its monies. One could suggest that a draft backed by a Canadian bank would have comparable risk to a draft guaranteed by a Japanese bank. And besides, the Canadian bank's deposit rate looked more attractive!

To invest in a Canadian deposit, the Japanese firm at the time would have had to convert its funds to Canadian dollars at the spot rate (C$1/114.10 yen). This would have allowed an investment of C$876,424 ($100,000,000/114.10). Over 90 days this investment would earn C$10,481 ($876,424 × 0.0485 × 90/365). The firm would have C$886,905. With the 90 days now up, the Japanese firm would require the funds for its operation, so these funds would be converted back into Japanese yen.

The firm could wait until the 90 days were up and then convert the Canadian dollars back into Japanese yen, but that would expose the firm to uncertainty as to what the exchange rate would be in 90 days. To remove this foreign exchange risk, the Japanese firm could lock in the exchange rate it would receive in 90 days with a forward contract. The forward rate at the time was 112.81 yen to the Canadian dollar. This would give the Japanese firm 100,051,753 yen.

The Japanese firm would, therefore, achieve a return of 0.21 percent on its funds (51,753 yen/100,000,000 yen × 365/90). This return is identical to what the Japanese firm could have earned by investing in the Japanese deposit. This example was constructed using rates found daily in major business newspapers. It demonstrates interest rate parity and the connection among spot rates, forward rates, and interest rates between countries. If we found that the return achieved in Canada on a similar risk investment was different from what was available in Japan, the return difference would not last for long. Investors would move their money to take advantage of the better return, and the movement of large sums of money would cause the exchange rates and available interest rates on deposits to adjust. This would ensure the relationship found in our example remains close.

Interest rate parity should always make this example work. You can use forward rates available through the *The Globe and Mail* or the UBC Sauder site, and the rates on government bonds available through Bloomberg, to reconstruct this example with current rates.

Q1 Demonstrate, at this time, interest rate parity through the forward rate between Canada and Britain or Canada and the United States. Does the theory still hold?

fx.sauder.ubc.ca   bloomberg.com   theglobeandmail.com

Balance of Payments Surplus in the balance of payments appreciates the value of the currency while continuous deficits in the balance of payments depress the value of a currency. The term *balance of payments* refers to a system of government accounts that catalogues the flow of economic transactions between the residents of a given country and the residents of all other countries. The balance of payments statement for Canada is prepared by Statistics Canada. Figure 21–4 showed Canada's balance of payments in 2018. The statement resembles the funds flow statement presented in Chapter 2 and keeps track of the country's exports and imports as well as the flow of capital and gifts. When a country sells (exports) more goods and services to foreign countries than it purchases (imports) from abroad, it has a surplus in its balance of trade. Japan, for example, through its aggressive competition in world markets, exports far more goods than it imports and has been enjoying large trade surpluses for many years. Since the foreigners who buy Japanese goods are expected to pay their bills in yen, the demand for yen and its value has increased in foreign currency markets. On the other hand, continuous deficits in the balance of payments depress the value of a currency because such deficits would increase the supply of that currency relative to the demand.

Government Policies Monetary and fiscal policies also affect the currency value in foreign exchange markets. A national government may, through its central bank, intervene in the foreign exchange market, buying and selling currencies as it sees fit to support the value of its currency relative to others. Sometimes, a given country may deliberately pursue a policy of maintaining an undervalued currency to promote cheap exports. At times, some nations affect the foreign exchange rate indirectly by restricting the flow of funds into and out of the country. Expansionary monetary policy and excessive government spending are primary causes of inflation; continual use of such policies eventually reduces the value of the country's currency. In the Canadian example, a rapid expansion of the money supply in the late 1970s and increasingly large government deficits caused a substantial decline in our foreign exchange rate from US$1.05 in 1976 to a low of US$0.69 in 1986. The Canadian dollar fell against the U.S. dollar to an all-time low of just under $0.62 in early 2002, rebounded to $1.09 in 2007, fell to $0.80 in early 2009, back up over $1.06 in July 2011, and down to $0.69 in March 2020.

Other Factors Other factors may also affect the demand for a country's currency and its exchange rate. A pronounced and extended stock market rally in a country attracts investment capital from other countries, thus creating a huge demand by foreigners for that country's currency. This increased demand tends to increase the value of that currency. The huge capital flows into the United States, which has been seen as the best place to invest over the last decade, have contributed to the rise in its currency's value against most world currencies. Similarly, a significant drop in demand for a country's principal exports worldwide is expected to result in a corresponding decline in the value of its currency. A precipitous drop in gold prices caused the South African rand to drop in value during the early 1980s.

Political turmoil within a country has often been responsible for driving capital out of a country into more stable countries. A mass exodus of capital, due to the fear of political risk, undermines the value of a country's currency in the foreign exchange market. During the 2014 Scottish separation referendum there was concern about a possible exodus of capital, which would weaken the economy. If widespread labour strikes appear to weaken the nation's economy, they also have a depressing influence on its currency value.

The Canadian dollar also seems to be perceived as a play on commodity prices because of the influence natural resources have on our economy. As the world economy slows and/or the demand for commodities declines, leading to declines in their prices, the Canadian dollar falls in value against the U.S. dollar. The U.S. dollar is considered a currency more broadly based on a manufacturing/service economy.

Although a wide variety of factors influencing exchange rates have been discussed, a few words of caution are in order. All of these variables do not necessarily influence all currencies to the same degree. Some factors may have an overriding influence on one currency's value, but their influence on another currency may be negligible at that time. In other words, exchange rates are partially measures of our confidence in the future performance of a particular economy. An event that may destroy our confidence in one economy's future may not do so in another.

LO5 Spot Rates and Forward Rates

When you look into a major financial newspaper, you discover that two exchange rates exist simultaneously for most major currencies—the spot rate and the forward rate. The spot rate for a currency is the exchange rate at which the currency is traded for immediate delivery. For example, you might walk into the local branch of TD Canada Trust and ask for euros. The banker will indicate the rate at which the euro is selling, say euro 0.674/$. If you are satisfied with the rate, you buy 674 euros with $1,000 and walk out the door. This is a spot market transaction at the retail level.

The trading of currencies for future delivery is called a forward market transaction. Suppose Suncor expects to receive 20 million euros from a French customer 90 days (October) from now (July). Given the recent volatility in foreign exchange markets, it is not certain what these euros will be worth in dollars 90 days from today. To eliminate this uncertainty, the treasurer at Suncor calls a bank and offers to sell 20 million euros for Canadian dollars 90 days from now. In their negotiation, the two parties may agree on an exchange rate of euro 0.7184/$, which is $1.3920/euro. Because the exchange rate is established for future delivery, it is a forward rate. After 90 days, Suncor delivers 20 million euros to the bank and receives $27.84 million.

Suncor
suncor.com

The difference between spot and forward exchange rates, expressed in dollars per unit of foreign currency, may be seen in the following example, in July.

Rates	Japanese Yen ($/yen)	British Pound (£) ($/£)
Spot	0.012030	1.7510
30-day forward	0.012053	1.7473
90-day forward	0.012097	1.7396
180-day forward	0.012174	1.7288

The forward exchange rate of a currency is generally slightly different from the spot rate prevailing at that time. Since the forward rate deals with a future time, the expectations regarding the future value of that currency are reflected in the forward rate. Forward rates may be greater than the current spot rate (trade at a premium) or less than the current spot rate (trade at a discount). In July, forward rates on the Japanese yen were at a premium in relation to the spot rate, while the forward rates for the British pound were at a discount from the spot rate. This means on that day the participants in the foreign exchange market expected the yen to appreciate relative to the Canadian dollar in the near-term future, while they expected the British pound to depreciate against the dollar. The size of the premium or discount gives a hint as to the degree to which market participants expect the currency to appreciate (depreciate). The premium or discount also reflects the time value of money and the degree to which interest rates in each country differ. In this example, interest rates are lower in Japan and higher in Britain.

It is very common to express the discount or premium as an annualized percentage deviation from the spot rate. The percentage discount or premium is computed with the following formula:

$$\text{Forward premium (discount)} = \frac{\text{Forward} - \text{Spot}}{\text{Spot}} \times \frac{12}{\text{Contract length (months)}} \quad \text{(21–1)}$$

For example, in July, the 90-day forward contract in yen was selling at a 2.23 percent premium:

$$\frac{0.012097 - 0.012030}{0.012030} \times \frac{12}{3} = 0.0223 = 2.23\%$$

While the 90-day forward contract in pounds was trading at a 2.61 percent discount:

$$\frac{1.7396 - 1.7510}{1.7510} \times \frac{12}{3} = -0.0260 = -2.60\%$$

The spot and forward transactions occur in what is called the over-the-counter market. Foreign currency dealers (usually large commercial banks or investment dealers) and their customers (importers, exporters, investors, multinational firms, etc.) negotiate the exchange rate, the length of the forward contract, and the commission in a mutually agreeable fashion. Although the length of a typical forward contract may generally vary between one month and six months, contracts for longer maturities are not uncommon. The dealers, however, may require higher returns for longer contracts.

Cross Rates

Quite often, exchange rates for different currencies are expressed only in terms of a dominant currency, such as the U.S. dollar. In Canada, exchange rates are likely to be expressed only in terms of the Canadian dollar. If currency quotations were in Canadian dollars only, we would have to make some further calculations if we were interested in the exchange rate between currencies that did not involve the Canadian dollar. This exchange rate is achieved by calculating a cross rate, an exchange rate calculated for two currencies by relating each currency to a common currency.

For example, in July, the Japanese yen was selling for $0.012030 Canadian and the British pound was selling for $1.7510 Canadian. Therefore, the British pound was 145.55 times more expensive than the Japanese yen (1.7510/0.012030). The cross rate between the yen and the pound was, therefore, 145.55 yen/£. The inverse was that the yen was 1/145.55 the value of the pound. The cross rate between the pound and the yen was 0.006870 £/yen (0.012030/1.7510).

Alternatively, we could determine the cross rate, knowing that $1 Canadian will buy 83.1255 yen (1/0.012030), and a pound will purchase $1.7510. Thus, £1 gets 1.7510 times the 83.1255 yen per dollar, which equals 145.55 yen for £1 (1.7510 × 83.1255).

	Canadian Dollar	Japanese Yen	British Pound
Canadian dollar	—	0.012030	1.7510
Japanese yen	83.1255	—	145.55
British pound	0.5711	0.004912	—

Cross currency rates are available daily in the *National Post* and *The Globe and Mail*.

LO6 Hedging (Risk Reduction) Techniques

Flows of money from one country to another create foreign exchange risk due to the regular changes in the value of currencies in relation to each other. Earlier this was identified as transaction exposure. There are several hedging techniques available, at a cost, to reduce foreign exchange risk.

We identify four hedging techniques and use the spot and forward rates identified earlier.

1. Hedging in the forward exchange market
2. Hedging in the money market
3. Hedging in the currency futures market
4. Hedging in the options market

To see how to employ the hedging, or covering, techniques, we can identify a transaction where a firm is exposed to foreign exchange risk. Suppose a British fertilizer company purchases potash from Nutrien of Canada for £1.5 million in July, and Nutrien is promised the payment in British pounds in 90 days. Nutrien is now exposed to foreign exchange risk by agreeing to receive the payment in a foreign currency in the future. It is up to Nutrien to find a way to hedge, or reduce, this exposure, if it (or its receiver) so desires. An alternative transaction could be where the British fertilizer company agrees to pay $2,626,500 Canadian in 90 days. The British company in this situation has the transaction exposure, and that can also be hedged.

Forward Exchange Market Hedge One simple method to hedge the exposure is in the forward exchange market. The forward exchange market is controlled in Canada by six of the major banks. Forward exchange traders are prepared to guarantee today, by contract, an exchange rate (buy or sell) for many currencies, based on settlement on some future date. No matter what the actual exchange rate is on that future date, the forward traders will live up to their contract.

To establish forward cover, Nutrien would sell a forward contract in July to deliver the £1.5 million, 90 days from then, in exchange for C$2,609,400 million (based on a 90-day forward rate of 1.7396). In October, Nutrien receives payment from the British company and delivers the £1.5 million to the bank that signed the contract. In return, the bank delivers C$2,609,400 million to Nutrien. Regardless of what happened to the value of the British pound in the interim, Nutrien is guaranteed the funds. Nutrien has hedged and eliminated its foreign exchange risk. In contrast, if the sale had been invoiced in Canadian dollars, the British company, not Nutrien, would have been exposed to the exchange risk.

Nutrien
nutrien.com

Money Market Hedge A second way to eliminate transaction exposure in this example is to borrow money in British pounds, converting them to Canadian dollars immediately. When the accounts receivable from the sale are collected three months later, the loan is cleared with the proceeds. This strategy consists of Nutrien taking the following steps in July:

1. Borrow £1,482,779 (£1,500,000/1.01161370 = £1,482,779) at the British rate of 4.71 percent per year for three months. Nutrien borrows less than the full amount of £1,500,000 in recognition of the fact that interest must be paid on the loan. The annual rate of 4.71 percent interest translates into 1.161370 percent for 90 days. To arrive at the size of the loan required today, the £1,500,000 is divided by 1.01161370.

2. Convert the British pounds into Canadian dollars in the spot market (1.7510). Receipt is C$2,596,346 (1,482,779 × 1.7510).

3. Invest the C$2,596,346 in Canada for the 90 days. Canadian interest rates at 2.04 percent annually or 0.503014 percent quarterly are lower than British rates. The investment available in 90 days, to compare with the forward, is $2,609,406 (2,596,346 × 1.00503014).

Then, in October (90 days later),

1. Receive the payment, £1,500,000, from British Fertilizer Company.
2. Clear the loan with the proceeds from that payment.

The money market hedge basically calls for matching the exposed asset (accounts receivable) with a liability (loan payable) in the same currency. Some firms prefer this money market hedge because of the earlier availability of funds this method provides.

Currency Futures Market Hedge Transaction exposure associated with a foreign currency can also be covered in the currency futures market. The International Monetary Market (IMM) of the Chicago Mercantile Exchange is the world's largest currency futures exchange. Although the futures market and forward market are similar in concept, they differ in their operations.

To keep our example simple, we will assume that there is a currency futures contract between Canadian dollars and British pounds. In reality, Nutrien would have to complete two futures contracts on the Chicago exchange, first by selling pounds for U.S. dollars and second by buying Canadian dollars with the U.S. dollars. Furthermore, as examined in Chapter 19, the futures market has standardized contracts, as to date and amount, which makes it difficult to hedge a position completely. Currency futures usually expire in March, June, September, and December. A hedge may be able to cover most of the exposure but would not be perfect. The advantage of the currency hedge would be the liquidity of a market, which gives the flexibility of closing out the contracts early if it suits Nutrien.

For Nutrien, an expectation must be set for what the exchange rate will be in October. A good choice is the rate at which the pound (or dollar) is currently trading in the forward or futures market. This becomes the target rate to be hedged. Nutrien then enters into a futures contract to sell £1.5 million (M) in October. When October comes around and Nutrien receives the £1.5M, it will convert to Canadian dollars in the cash (spot) market and close out the future contract by buying pounds. In the futures market, contracts are generally closed out for cash and delivery is not taken of the underlying commodity, in this case a currency.

Date	Futures Market	
July	Expectation £1.5M at $1.7360/£ = $2.604M	Sells £1.5M for Dec. delivery at $1.7360/£ = $2.604M
	Spot Market	
October	Sells £1.5M at $1.6695/£ = $2.504M	Buys £1.5M at $1.6695/£ = $2.504M
	Loss = $0.100M	Gain = $0.100M

 FINANCE IN ACTION

Devaluation and Deflation

Nigeria devalued its currency, the naira, by 15 percent in early 2020. The naira was pegged at 306 to the US dollar before it was reset at 360 to the dollar. Over 90 percent of Nigeria's foreign exchange was from oil sales. The combination of weakened oil prices and the Covid-19 pandemic forced the hand of Nigeria's central bank.

In 2002, two equally troubling concerns were exhibited in the world's financial and foreign exchange markets. Both were putting downward pressure on certain currencies.

In Japan, interest rates hovered around zero percent in the short term. The Japanese economy had stagnated during the 1990s and since that period has shown little or no growth. Declining values in the stock and real estate markets had put downward pressure on prices. Some products did not increase in price for over 20 years. Would you consider this a problem? However, through this period unemployment remained at low levels.

The banks were struggling with numerous bad loans. Combined, these factors suggested that holding cash was not so bad an idea. The aging population, with fixed capital resources, was happy to see declining prices. The result was that Japan was forced to deal with deflationary pressures that were placing severe strain on the economy. Furthermore, with deflationary pressures the value of the yen was declining, which was a concern to many trading nations.

In Argentina, three years of recession and government excesses led to the biggest default on debt in history. The government was forced to devalue the peso by 40 percent overnight. Tough economic measures were called for in an economy that already had unemployment rates nearing 20 percent. Cash was unavailable to many and some of Argentina's major cities took to issuing their own currencies to provide the means for the exchange of goods and services to occur.

In early 2016 Argentina went on a floating exchange rate, resulting in an effective 30 percent devaluation in its currency. Inflation continues to hover around 40 percent per year.

Q1 How has the value of the Nigerian naira fared in recent years?

Q2 How has Argentina's currency (the peso) and its inflation rate performed in the last few years?

fx.sauder.ubc.ca

What would happen if, while Nutrien was waiting for its receivable, the pound dropped in value relative to the Canadian dollar? If Nutrien remained unhedged, it would have lost $100,000 based on its expectation for the exchange rate in October. By hedging in the futures market, Nutrien would reduce the loss to nil. A $100,000 gain in the futures market would cancel out the $100,000 loss in the spot market. In an actual situation, there would be some small gain or loss because of the inability to hedge the full exposure due to the standardization of contracts to the amount and date of expiry. It is unlikely that the spot and future markets would quote the same rate when there is still time to expiry.

Options Market Hedge The options market for currencies is primarily available on the Chicago Mercantile Exchange. An option on currencies gives the purchaser the right to buy (call) or to sell (put) the foreign currency at an agreed-upon exchange rate up to a predetermined date, if the purchaser is so inclined. An option gives a right but not an obligation to the purchaser. For this right, the purchaser pays a fee called a premium.

Again, to keep our example simple we will assume that there is a currency options contract between Canadian dollars and British pounds. Furthermore, we will assume an option is available for the size of the contract (£1.5) (nonstandard amounts are unavailable), and a nonstandard option price (£1.7360, the expected rate) for the month of October.

Nutrien would purchase an option (put) to sell £1.5 million in October at a fixed price of (£1.7360/$). For a price (the premium) of perhaps $0.015 per pound, Nutrien could purchase the option for a total cost of $22,500. The option would give Nutrien protection if the pound dropped in value but would also allow Nutrien to gain if the pound appreciated in value. If the pound appreciated, Nutrien would sell the pounds in the cash (spot) market and let the option expire, receiving more on the transaction than expected. If the pound dropped in value, Nutrien would also sell pounds in the cash (spot) market, losing money based on its expectation, but this would be offset by selling the option, which would have increased in value. In the latter case Nutrien has hedged its exposure for a price.

Hedging is not the only means companies have for protecting themselves against foreign exchange risk. Over the years, multinational companies have developed elaborate foreign asset management programs that involve strategies such as switching cash and other current assets into strong currencies while piling up debt and other liabilities in depreciating currencies. Companies also encourage the quick collection of bills in weak currencies by offering sizable discounts, while extending liberal credit in strong currencies.

LO7 THE MULTINATIONAL CORPORATION

The focus of international financial management has been the multinational corporation (MNC). One might ask, just what is a MNC? Some definitions of a multinational corporation require that a minimum percentage (often 30 percent or more) of a firm's business activities be carried on outside its national borders. For purposes of our discussion, however, a firm doing business across its national borders is considered a multinational enterprise. Four of the several forms that such multinational corporations can take are briefly examined.

Exporter

An MNC could produce a product domestically and export some of that production to one or more foreign markets. This is generally considered the least risky method of going international—reaping the benefits of foreign demand without committing any long-term investment to a foreign country.

Licensing Agreement

A firm with exporting operations may get into trouble when a foreign government imposes or substantially raises an import tariff to a level at which the exporter cannot compete effectively with the local domestic manufacturers. The foreign government may even ban all imports into the country at times. When this happens, the exporting firm may grant a license to an independent local producer to use the firm's technology in return for a license fee or a royalty. In essence, then, the MNC exports technology rather than the product to that foreign country. Another advantage of licensing over straight export arises when some adaptation of the product for local preference is desirable.

Joint Venture

As an alternative to licensing, the MNC may establish a joint venture with a local foreign manufacturer. The legal, political, and economic environments around the globe are more conducive to the joint venture arrangement than any of the other modes of operations. Many countries permit foreign multinationals to carry out business in their countries only if they have a local partner with a substantial ownership interest. Such regulations explain why Ford did not set up operations in China in the 1950s, or Coca-Cola in India. Historical evidence also suggests that a joint venture with a local entrepreneur exposes the firm to the least amount of political risk. Consequently, this form of business is preferred by many business firms and by foreign governments as well.

Fully Owned Foreign Subsidiary

Although the joint venture form is desirable for many reasons, it may be hard to find a willing and cooperative local entrepreneur with sufficient capital to participate. In addition, as mentioned earlier, some multinationals have had policies prohibiting joint ventures. Under these conditions the MNC may have to set up foreign operations alone. For political reasons, however, a wholly owned foreign subsidiary is becoming more of a rarity. During the remainder of this chapter, we use the term *foreign affiliate* to refer to either a joint venture or a fully owned subsidiary.

The environment faced by the MNC is riskier and more complex than that of the domestic economy. Differences in rates of taxation, financial market structure, local administrative practices, social customs, and cultural mores must all be dealt with by the MNC. The attraction of international finance is that with increased risk comes the possibility of increased returns. The major risks that the firm must contend with are foreign exchange fluctuations and political interference.

LO8 FINANCING INTERNATIONAL BUSINESS OPERATIONS

When the parties to an international transaction are well known to each other and the countries involved are politically stable, sales are generally made on credit, as is customary in domestic business operations. If the foreign importer is relatively new and/or the political environment is volatile, the possibility of nonpayment by the importer is worrisome for the exporter. To reduce the risk of nonpayment, an exporter generally requests that the importer furnish a letter of credit. The importer's bank normally issues the letter of credit in which the bank promises to subsequently pay the money for the merchandise.

For example, assume Canadian Western Farms (CWF) is negotiating with a South Korean trading company to export soybean meal. The two parties agree on price, method of shipment, timing of shipment, destination point, and so forth. Once the basic terms of sale have been agreed to, the South Korean trading company (importer) applies for a letter of credit from its commercial bank in Seoul. The Korean bank, if it so desires, issues such a letter of credit, which specifies in detail all of the steps that must be completed by the Canadian exporter before payment is made. If CWF complies with all specifications in the letter of credit and submits to the Korean bank the proper documentation to prove it has done so, the Korean bank guarantees the payment on the due date. On that date, the Canadian firm is paid by the Korean bank, not by the buyer of the goods. All of the credit risk to the exporter is absorbed by the importer's bank, which is in a good position to evaluate the creditworthiness of the importing firm.

The exporter that requires cash payment or a letter of credit from foreign buyers of marginal credit standing is likely to lose orders to competitors. Instead of risking the loss of business,

Canadian firms can find an alternative way to reduce the risk of nonpayment by foreign customers. This alternative method consists of obtaining export credit insurance. The insurance policy provides assurance to the exporter that should the foreign customer default on payment, the insurance company will pay for the shipment. The Export Development Corporation (EDC), an agency of the Canadian federal government, provides this kind of insurance to exporting firms.

Export Development Corporation
edc.ca

Funding of Transactions

Assistance in the funding of foreign transactions may take many forms.

Export Development Corporation The EDC is a federal agency that facilitates the financing of Canadian exports by offering the following:

- Protection for the exporter by insuring 90 percent of the value of export sales.
- Guarantees on loans made by financial institutions to foreign purchasers of Canadian products.
- Financing for projects when no commercial credit is available. In these cases the Canadian supplier receives payment from the proceeds of the loan to the foreign buyer. Such capital goods might include communications equipment, heavy machinery especially for use in energy-related projects, radar systems, and the like.

Loans from the Parent Company or a Sister Affiliate In addition to contributing equity capital, the parent company often provides loans of varying maturities to its foreign affiliate.

- Direct loans from the parent to the foreign subsidiary. These loans are rarely extended because of foreign exchange risk, political risk, and tax treatment.
- Indirect loan arrangements through an intermediary to a foreign affiliate.
  - *Parallel loans.* Figure 21–10 depicts a typical parallel loan arrangement. A Canadian firm wanting to lend funds to its Dutch affiliate locates a Dutch parent firm that wants to transfer funds to its Canadian affiliate. Avoiding the exchange markets, the Canadian parent lends dollars to the Dutch affiliate in Canada, while the Dutch parent lends euros to the Canadian affiliate in the Netherlands. At maturity, the two loans would be repaid to the original lenders. Notice that neither loan carries any foreign exchange risk. In essence, both parent firms are providing indirect loans to their affiliates.
  - *Fronting loans.* A fronting loan is simply a parent's loan to its foreign subsidiary channelled through a financial intermediary, usually a large international bank. A schematic of a fronting loan is shown in Figure 21–11. In the example, the Canadian parent company deposits funds in an Amsterdam bank and the bank in turn lends the same amount to its affiliate in the

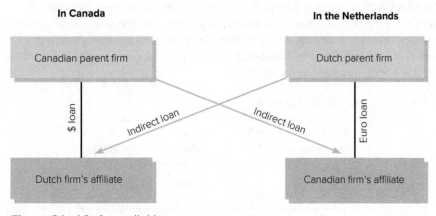

Figure 21–10 A parallel loan arrangement

Figure 21–11 A fronting loan arrangement

Netherlands. In this manner, the bank fronts for the parent by extending a risk-free (fully collateralized) loan to the foreign affiliate. In the event of political turmoil, the foreign government is more likely to allow the Canadian subsidiary to repay the loan to a large international bank than to allow the same affiliate to repay the loan to its parent company. Thus, the parent company reduces its political risk.

Even though the parent company would prefer that its foreign subsidiary maintain its own financial arrangements, many banks are apprehensive about lending to a foreign affiliate without a parent guarantee. A large portion of bank lending to foreign affiliates is based on some sort of a guarantee by the parent firm. Usually, because of its multinational reputation, the parent company has a better credit rating than its foreign affiliates. The lender advances funds on the basis of the parent's creditworthiness even though the affiliate is expected to pay back the loan. The terms of a parent guarantee may vary greatly, depending on the closeness of the parent–affiliate ties, the parent–lender relations, and the home country's legal jurisdiction.

Eurocurrency Loans A Eurocurrency is a unit of currency held on deposit in a bank outside the country issuing the currency. The origins of the Eurocurrency market date back to the 1960s, when interest rate ceilings in the United States provided a disincentive for American corporations to repatriate revenues generated abroad. Thus, American companies deposited U.S. dollar funds with banks outside the United States.

- The Eurocurrency market is a significant part of world credit markets that provides short-term loans for multinational firms and their foreign affiliates.
- The lower costs and greater credit availability of the Eurocurrency market are major attractions for borrowing.

 FINANCE IN ACTION

Rating the Countries

Most governments of the world issue debt securities to fund the projects and programs they deem appropriate for their country. Buyers of these debt securities will require a yield that reflects the risk investors perceive for each country's ability to meet its payment obligations. Considerations will be given to how well the government manages the economy and the overall financial wealth of the country. Inflation rates, unemployment, total government debt, and the annual deficit will all be factors in rating the debt securities of each government. Standard & Poor's rating service out of New York rates the bond issues of many sovereign governments.

A sampling from early 2020 follows:

Canada	AAA	Spain	A
United States	AA+	India	BBB–
Britain	AA	South Africa	BB
Israel	AA–	Nigeria	B–
Japan	A+	Argentina	CCC-

These ratings give us an idea of the risk faced in the countries rated. A rating of AAA is of exceptional quality, AA is excellent, A is good, BBB is adequate, BB is questionable, B is poor, and CCC is very poor. Therefore, the ratings may suggest a discount rate appropriate for the risk of an investment in that particular country. A "plus" or "minus" sign slightly modifies the rating. Of course, these are government ratings; any corporate ratings within a country would in all likelihood be lower due to higher risk, suggesting a higher discount rate.

Q1 What is the current rating of these countries?

moodys.com
standardandpoors.com

The lower borrowing costs in the Eurocurrency market are attributed to the smaller overhead costs for lending banks given the huge size of transactions, the creditworthiness of borrowing corporations and nations, and the absence of reserve or capital requirements on the part of the lending institution. These currency transactions are outside the regulatory control of the domestic financial regulators.

- The lending rate for borrowers in the Eurocurrency market is based on the London Interbank Offered Rate (LIBOR). Interest rates on loans are calculated by adding premiums to this basic rate. These premiums are usually between 0.25 percent to 0.50 percent depending on the customer, the length of the loan period, and the size of the loan.

  Although the rates in the Eurocurrency market tend to be cheaper than domestic rates in either Canada or the United States, the LIBOR rate tends to be more volatile than the banks' prime rates because of the volatility of supply and demand in the Eurocurrency market.

- Lending in the Eurocurrency market is almost exclusively done by commercial banks.

  Large Eurocurrency loans, especially if they are for any extended time period, are often syndicated by a group of participating banks. Eurocurrency loans with maturities greater than one year are known as **Eurocredits**. The loan agreement is put together by a lead bank known as the **manager**, which historically has usually been one of the largest U.S., European, or Canadian banks. The manager charges the borrower a once-and-for-all fee or commission of 0.25 percent to 1 percent of the loan value. A portion of this fee is kept by the lead bank, and the remainder is shared by all the participating banks. The aim of forming a syndicate is to diversify the risk, which would be too large for any single bank to handle by itself.

Eurobond Market When long-term funds are needed, borrowing in the Eurobond market has become an important alternative for leading MNCs.

- Eurobond issues are sold simultaneously in several different national capital markets, but they are denominated in a currency different from that of the nation in which the bonds are issued. Although the U.S. dollar dominates this market, the euro is expected to become a significant rival currency.

- Eurobond issues are underwritten by an international syndicate of banks and securities firms. Eurobonds of longer than seven years in maturity generally have a sinking-fund provision.

- Disclosure requirements in the Eurobond market are much less stringent than those required by the securities commissions in Canada and the United States. Furthermore, the registration costs in the Eurobond market are generally lower than those charged in Canada and the United States.

- The Eurobond market offers tax flexibility for borrowers and investors alike. Because most Eurobonds are issued by a fully owned offshore finance subsidiary in a tax-haven country such as Luxembourg, no withholding taxes on interest are paid. Historically, many wealthy investors bought Eurobonds through Swiss bank accounts so that their interest income could be kept anonymous.

Nevertheless, a caveat may be in order with respect to the effective cost of borrowing in the Eurobond market. When a multinational firm borrows by floating a foreign currency–denominated debt issue on a long-term basis, it creates transaction exposure, a kind of foreign exchange risk. If the foreign currency appreciates in value during the bond's life, the cost of servicing the debt could be prohibitively high. Thus, currency selection for denominating Eurobond issues must be made with extreme care and foresight. To lessen the impact of foreign exchange risk, some recently issued Eurobond issues have been denominated in multi-currency units.

International Equity Markets To avoid nationalistic reactions to wholly owned foreign subsidiaries, multinational firms such as Unilever, Daimler, General Motors, Bombardier, and Apple sell shares to worldwide shareholders. It is also believed that widespread foreign ownership of the firm's common stock encourages the loyalty of foreign shareholders and employees toward the firm. Thus, selling common stock to residents of foreign countries is not only an important financing strategy but also a risk-minimizing strategy for many MNCs.

Nasdaq
nasdaq.com

- To attract investors from all over the world, reputable multinational firms list their shares on major stock exchanges around the world. Many Canadian companies are listed on the New York Stock Exchange and on NASDAQ.
- Many foreign corporations such as Siemens, Honda, BP, Volvo, and the like accommodate American investors by issuing American Depository Receipts (ADRs). All of the American-owned shares of a foreign company are placed in trust in a New York bank. In turn, the bank issues its depository receipts to the American shareholders and maintains a shareholder ledger on these receipts, thus enabling the holders of ADRs to sell or otherwise transfer them as easily as they transfer any American company shares. Most ADRs trade in the over-the-counter market, although a few are listed on the New York Stock Exchange. ADR prices tend to move parallel with the prices of the underlying securities in their home markets.

The world equity markets are consolidating through mergers and cooperative arrangements (e.g., Deutsche Börse with a stake in Bombay Exchange).

This international exposure also brings an additional responsibility for the MNC to understand the preferences and needs of heterogeneous groups of investors of various nationalities. The MNC may have to print and circulate its annual financial statements in many languages. Some foreign investors are more risk averse than their counterparts in North America, preferring dividend income to less certain capital gains. Common stock ownership among individuals in countries such as Japan and Norway is insignificant, with financial institutions holding substantial amounts of common stock issues.

Institutional practices around the globe also vary significantly when it comes to issuing new securities. Unlike the Canadian situation, commercial banks in many European countries have long played a dominant role in the securities business. They underwrite stock issues, manage portfolios, vote the stock they hold in trust accounts, and hold directorships on company boards. In Germany, the banks also run an over-the-counter market in many stocks. Canadian banks have recently been allowed to own securities subsidiaries that underwrite stock issues and manage portfolios.

The International Finance Corporation Whenever a multinational company has difficulty raising equity capital due to lack of adequate private risk capital in a foreign country, the firm may explore the possibility of selling partial ownership to the International Finance Corporation (IFC). The IFC, a unit of the World Bank Group, was established in 1956 and is owned by the member countries of the World Bank. Its objective is to further economic development by promoting private enterprises in these countries. The profitability of a project and its potential benefit to the host country's economy are the two criteria the IFC uses to decide whether or not to assist a venture. The IFC participates in private enterprise through either buying equity shares of a business or providing long-term loans, or a combination of the two, for up to 25 percent of the total capital.

International Finance Corporation
ifc.org

The IFC expects the other partners to assume managerial responsibility, and it does not exercise its voting rights as a shareholder. The IFC helps finance new ventures as well as the expansion of existing ones in a variety of industries. Once the venture is well established, the IFC sells its investment position to private investors to free up its capital.

GLOBAL CASH MANAGEMENT

The issues discussed in this chapter directly affect how the MNC would organize its finance function and how it should manage its funds globally. The multinational finance function can be organized with (1) each subsidiary completely decentralized, (2) all finance functions centralized at parent headquarters, or (3) a mix of centralization and decentralization. Because of government restrictions of funds flows, differing rates of inflation, and volatile exchange rates, global cash management involves a number of tradeoffs and explicit decisions. The considerations in any such system include a method for

1. Estimating the levels of local and corporate cash needs at given times
2. Creating the ability to withdraw cash from the subsidiary and centralize it
3. Deciding how to reallocate cash once it has been centralized

Although any such system is highly dependent on a good information system, it is easy to underestimate the difficulties in language problems, technical problems in operating in many countries, local resistance to losing resources, and government regulations restricting multinational cash flows.

Once local needs have been allowed for, a decision is made as to whether or not to have the local manager invest excess funds or have them remitted to the parent's central cash pool. To centralize cash, a dividend paid from the subsidiary to the parent is often the most straightforward method. Outright government restrictions on dividends, exchange controls, capital investment requirements, withholding taxes, or other problems, however, usually complicate the decision. Given high rates of inflation and devaluations that occur in some countries, the parent must often develop approaches such as revaluing capital assets because foreign governments restrict the amount of cash that can be taken out as dividends to some percentage of invested capital.

When dividends are not the best way to move cash from the subsidiary to the parent, other ways include management fees, sales commissions, royalties, and repayment of principal and interest on loans. In addition, transfer pricing of components and finished products moving from the parent to subsidiary or among subsidiaries from different countries can be used to manage the flows of cash internationally. However, the setting of transfer prices is affected by so many other company and environmental considerations, such as performance measures of subsidiary managements or country taxation rates, that cash management considerations tend often not to be major determinants of transfer pricing policy. The obvious attractiveness of using transfer pricing is that, unlike dividends, transfer prices are not subject to withholding taxes or many other restrictions.

SUMMARY

1. Although discounted cash flow analysis is applied to screen the projects in the initial stages, strategic considerations and political risk are often the overriding factors in reaching the final decision. One of the most important differences between domestic and international investments is that the information on foreign investments is generally less complete and often less accurate. Therefore, analyzing a foreign investment proposal is more difficult than analyzing a domestic investment project. (LO1)

2. Multinational companies have made billions of dollars worth of direct investments in foreign countries over the years. Lower production costs overseas, tax deferral provisions, strategic advantages, and benefits of international diversification are some of the motivational factors behind the flow of direct investment between nations. Foreign direct investments are usually quite large, and many of them are exposed to political risk. (LO2)

3. International business transactions are denominated in foreign currencies. The rate at which one currency unit is converted into another is called the exchange rate. In today's global monetary system, the exchange rates of major currencies are fluctuating rather freely. These freely floating exchange rates expose multinational business firms to foreign exchange risk. To deal with this foreign currency exposure effectively, the financial executive of an MNC must understand foreign exchange rates and how they are determined. (LO3)

4. Foreign exchange rates are influenced by differences in inflation rates among countries, differences in interest rates, governmental policies, and the expectations of the participants in the foreign exchange markets. (LO4)

5. A spot rate is the exchange rate one receives for immediate delivery of the foreign currency. A forward exchange rate is the exchange rate fixed today by contract for the delivery of the foreign currency at a fixed date in the future. (LO5)

6. The international financial manager can reduce the firm's foreign currency exposure by hedging in the forward exchange market, the money markets, the currency futures market, or the options market. (LO6)

7. When a domestic business firm crosses its national borders to do business in other countries, it enters a riskier and more complex environment. A multinational firm is exposed to foreign exchange risk and political risk in addition to the usual business and financial risks. In general, international business operations have been more profitable than domestic operations, and this higher profitability is one factor that motivates business firms to go overseas. International operations account for a significant proportion of the earnings for many North American firms. Multinational firms have played a major role in promoting economic development and international trade for several decades. Canada has been the site of large multinational investments. Canadian firms are investing significant sums in other countries, most notably in the United States. The multinational firm can operate in a foreign jurisdiction as an exporter, through a licensing agreement, a joint venture, or by way of a fully owned subsidiary. (LO7)

8. Financing international trade and investment is another important area of international finance that one must understand in order to raise funds at the lowest cost possible. The multinational firm has access to both the domestic and foreign capital markets. The Export Development Corporation aids in financing Canadian exports to foreign countries. Borrowing in the Eurobond markets may appear less expensive at times, but the effect of foreign exchange risk on debt-servicing cost must be weighed carefully before borrowing in these markets. Floating common stock in foreign capital markets is another viable financing alternative for many multinational companies. The International Finance Corporation, which is a subsidiary of the World Bank, also provides debt capital and equity capital to qualified firms. These alternative

sources of financing may significantly differ with respect to cost, terms, and conditions. Therefore, the financial executive must carefully locate and use the proper means to finance international business operations. (LO8)

REVIEW OF FORMULAS

1. $\text{Forward premium (discount)} = \dfrac{\text{Forward} - \text{Spot}}{\text{Spot}} \times \dfrac{12}{\underset{\text{length}}{\text{Contract}} (\text{month})}$

(21–1)

DISCUSSION QUESTIONS

1. What risks do foreign affiliates of a multinational firm face in today's business world? (LO2)

2. What are allegations sometimes made against foreign affiliates of multinational firms and against the multinational firms themselves? (LO2)

3. List the factors that affect the value of a currency in foreign exchange markets. (LO4)

4. Explain how exports and imports tend to influence the value of a currency. (LO4)

5. Differentiate between the spot exchange rate and the forward exchange rate. (LO5)

6. What is meant by translation exposure in terms of foreign exchange risk? (LO3)

7. Which factors influence a Canadian business firm to look into expanding in international markets? (LO1)

8. Which procedures would you recommend for a multinational company in studying exposure to political risk? Which actual strategies can be used to guard against such risk? (LO6)

9. What factors beyond the normal domestic analysis go into a financial feasibility study for a multinational firm? (LO3)

10. What is a letter of credit? (LO8)

11. What are the differences between a parallel loan and a fronting loan? (LO8)

12. What is LIBOR? How does it compare to the Canadian banks' domestic prime rates? (LO8)

13. What is the danger or concern in floating a Eurobond issue? (LO8)

14. What are ADRs? (LO8)

15. Should multinational firms dictate debt ratio limits and dividend payouts to their foreign affiliates? (LO7)

INTERNET RESOURCES AND QUESTIONS

Daily foreign exchange rates on over 200 currencies and historical rates on over 60 currencies, including the ability to plot historical price trends, are available at this University of British Columbia site:
fx.sauder.ubc.ca

Daily settlement prices on currency futures and options for several currencies are available at the Chicago Mercantile Exchange site. There is also a free hookup to live quotes:
cmegroup.com

Bond ratings on the debt of numerous governments are available at two sites:
moodys.com standardandpoors.com

1. Explain the functions of the Export Development Corporation (EDC) and the International Finance Corporation (IFC). Further information is available at edc.ca and ifc.org.

2. Find the current exchange rate, the rate one year ago, and the rate three years ago in relation to *a* and *b*.

    a. The Canadian dollar on the following currencies: Bahamian dollar, Czech koruna, Chilean peso, Egyptian pound, and Indian rupee. Which currencies have appreciated?

    b. The British pound on the following currencies: Bahamian dollar, Czech koruna, Chilean peso, Egyptian pound, and Indian rupee. Which currencies have appreciated?

    c. Plot the exchange rate movement of the British pound against the Egyptian pound over the last year.

3. For yesterday's date, find the settle price for a currency future on the Chicago Mercantile Exchange for the next three traded months for the following currencies: Canadian dollar, euro, British pound, Brazilian real, and Russian ruble. Which currencies are expected to depreciate in value in relation to the U.S. dollar?

4. For yesterday's date find the last price for a currency call option and put option on the Chicago Mercantile Exchange for the next traded month, with an option price slightly above the current spot price for the following currencies: Canadian dollar, euro, British pound, Brazilian real, and Russian ruble. Which currencies are expected to depreciate in value in relation to the U.S. dollar?

PROBLEMS

1. Using the foreign exchange rates for January 2020, presented in Table 21–1, determine the number of Canadian dollars required to buy the following amounts of foreign currencies:

    a. 10,000 euros

    b. 2,000 rupees

    c. 100,000 yen

    d. 5,000 Swiss francs

    e. 20,000 Swedish krona

    f. 50,000 baht

2. Obtain and recalculate the currency exchanges of problem 1 at today's rates. How do these figures compare to those obtained in that problem? Has the dollar strengthened or weakened against these securities? Identify *a* or *b* as your source.

    a. Use a recent edition of the *Financial Post:* financialpost.com/markets/currencies/index.html.

    b. Use fx.sauder.ubc.ca/data.html.

3. Suppose following spot and forward rates for the euro ($/euro) were reported:

Spot	1.4767
30-day forward	1.4765
90-day forward	1.4761
180-day forward	1.4773

    a. Was the euro selling at a discount or premium in the forward market?

    b. What was the 30-day forward premium (or discount)?

    c. What was the 180-day forward premium (or discount)?

d. Suppose you executed a 90-day forward contract to exchange 100,000 euros into Canadian dollars. How many dollars would you get 90 days hence?

e. Assume a French bank entered into a 180-day forward contract with TD Bank to buy $100,000. How many euros will the French bank deliver in six months to get the Canadian dollars?

4. Suppose an Egyptian pound is selling for $0.0719 and a Jordanian dinar is selling for $1.8932. What is the exchange rate (cross rate) of the Egyptian pound to the Jordanian dinar? That is, how many Egyptian pounds are equal to a Jordanian dinar?

5. Suppose a Mexican peso is selling for $0.0682 and a Brazilian real is selling for $0.3017. What is the exchange rate (cross rate) of the Mexican peso to the Brazilian real? That is, how many Mexican pesos are equal to a Brazilian real?

6. Suppose a Thai baht is selling for $0.03280 and a Panamanian balboa is selling for $1.3404. What is the exchange rate (cross rate) of the Thai baht to the Panamanian balboa? That is, how many Thai baht are equal to the Panamanian balboa?

7. From the base price level of 100 in 1974, Swiss and Canadian price levels in 2017 stood at 200 and 362, respectively. If the 1974 $/Sf exchange rate was $0.40/Sf, what should the exchange rate be in 2020?

8. In the previous problem, if Canada had somehow managed no inflation since 1974, what should the exchange rate be in 2020, using the purchasing power parity theory?

9. From the base price level of 100 in 1996, Russian and Canadian price levels in 2020 stood at 1,500 and 150, respectively. If the 1996 $/ruble exchange rate was $0.20/1 ruble, what should be the exchange rate in 2020?

10. An investor in Canada bought a one-year New Zealand security valued at 120,000 New Zealand dollars. The Canadian dollar equivalent was $100,000. The New Zealand security earned 8 percent during the year, but the New Zealand dollar depreciated 3 cents against the Canadian dollar during the time period ($0.8333/NZD to $0.8033/NZD). After transferring the funds back to Canada, what was the investor's return on her $100,000?

11. A French investor buys 300 shares of Teck for $4,500 ($15 per share). Over the course of a year, Teck goes up by $2.75.

a. If there is a 10 percent gain in the value of the dollar versus the euro, what will be the total percentage return to the French investor?

b. Now assume the stock increases by $3.50 but the dollar decreases by 10 percent versus the euro. What will be the total percentage return to the French investor?

12. A Canadian investor buys 200 shares of Macrohard for $12,200 ($61.00 per share). Over the course of a year, Macrohard shares decline by $3.00.

a. If there is a 4 percent gain in the value of the U.S. dollar versus the Canadian dollar, what will be the total percentage return to the Canadian investor?

b. Now assume the stock declines by $6.00, but the U.S. dollar decreases by 2 percent versus the Canadian dollar. What will be the total percentage return to the Canadian investor?

13. Saturn Industries sells its products under a licensing agreement to many parts of the globe. Under the terms of an agreement reached with a German company, a payment for Saturn's services is due in one year for 1 million euros. There is some concern over the value of the euro in one year, as the Canadian dollar has been strengthening.

The spot rate is 1.3805 Canadian dollars for one euro, but the one-year forward rate is 1.3676 Canadian dollars for one euro. Currently, interest rates are 3 percent in Canada and 4 percent in Germany for one year. There is also a belief within the firm that the spot rate in one year will be 1.3825 because the euro is due to get stronger.

a. Outline the various options available to Saturn Industries to handle its foreign exchange exposure.

b. Make a recommendation.

14. Royal Minty of Britain has purchased 10,000 ounces of silver from Silver Products at US$16.60, payable in 180 days. The current spot rate is 1.8127 ($US/£) and the 180-day forward is 1.7863. The CEO at Royal Minty suggests that the spot rate in six months time will be 1.7915.

    Interest rates in Britain are currently 4.70 percent for 180 days and 1.15 percent in the United States.

    a. Outline the various options available to Royal Minty to handle its foreign exchange exposure.

    b. Make a recommendation.

15. Nickel Plains of Canada has purchased 500,000 pounds of nickel from Coin Ltd. at US$6.96, payable in 90 days. The current spot rate is 1.3404 (C$/US$) and the 90-day forward is 1.3421. The vice-president of finance at Nickel Plains suggests that the spot rate in three months' time will be 1.3333. Interest rates in Canada are currently 2 percent for 90 days and 1.6 percent in the United States.

    a. Outline the various options available to Nickel Plains to handle its foreign exchange exposure.

    b. Make a recommendation.

16. Weese R. Grains of Canada has sold 5,000 tonnes of wheat to Pete's Apasta Company of Italy at 110 euros per tonne and payable in one year. The current spot rate is 1.3805 (C$/euro) and the 1-year forward is 1.3676. The financial analyst at Weese R. suggests that the spot rate in one year will be 1.3485. Interest rates in Canada are currently 3.40 percent for 1 year and 3.77 percent in Italy.

    a. Outline the various options available to Weese R. Grains to handle its foreign exchange exposure.

    b. Make a recommendation.

17. You are the vice-president of finance for Exploratory Resources, headquartered in Calgary. In January 2012, your firm's American subsidiary obtained a six-month loan of $1 million (U.S.) from a bank in Calgary to finance the acquisition of an oil-producing property in Oklahoma. The loan will also be repaid in U.S. dollars. At the time of the loan, the spot exchange rate was US$1.0125/C$ and the U.S. currency was selling at a premium in the forward market. The June 2012 futures contract (face value = $100,000 per contract) was quoted at US$1.0107.

    a. Explain how the Calgary bank could lose on this transaction.

    b. How much is the bank expected to lose/gain due to foreign exchange risk?

    c. If there is a $100 total brokerage commission per contract, would you still recommend that the bank hedge in the currency futures market?

18. Campbell Electronics Corporation has a wholly owned foreign subsidiary in Jamaica. The subsidiary earns $5 million per year before taxes in Jamaica. The foreign income tax rate is 20 percent. Campbell's subsidiary repatriates the entire aftertax profit in the form of dividends to the parent corporation. The Canadian corporate tax rate is 25 percent of foreign earnings before taxes.

    Disregarding any problems associated with exchange rates, complete the following table:

Before-tax earnings	_____
Foreign income tax @ 20%	_____
Earnings after foreign income taxes.	_____
Dividends repatriated.	_____
Gross Canadian taxes.	_____
Foreign tax credit.	_____
Net Canadian taxes payable	_____
Aftertax cash flow	_____

APPENDIX 21A

Cash Flow Analysis and the Foreign Investment Decision

Direct foreign investments are often relatively large. As we mentioned previously, these investments are exposed to some extraordinary risks, such as foreign exchange fluctuations and political interference, which are nonexistent for domestic investments. Therefore, the final decision is often made by the board of directors after considering the financial feasibility and the strategic importance of the proposed investment. Financial feasibility analysis for foreign investments is basically conducted in the same manner as it is for domestic capital budgets. Certain important differences exist, however, in the treatment of foreign tax credits, foreign exchange risk, and remittance of cash flows. To see how these are handled in foreign investment analysis, let us consider a hypothetical illustration.

Q Systems Inc., a Quebec-based manufacturer of word processing equipment, is considering the establishment of a manufacturing plant in Salaysia, a country in Southeast Asia. The Salaysian plant will be a wholly owned subsidiary of Q Systems, and its estimated cost is 90 million ringgits (2 ringgits = $1). Based on the exchange rate between ringgits and dollars, the cost in dollars is $45 million. In addition to selling in the local Salaysian market, the proposed subsidiary is expected to export its word processors to the neighbouring markets in Singapore, Hong Kong, and Thailand. Table 21A–1 shows expected revenues and operating costs. The country's investment climate, which reflects the foreign exchange and political risks, is rated BBB (considered fairly safe) by a leading Asian business journal.

Table 21A-1 Cash flow analysis of a foreign investment

	Projected Cash Flows (millions ringgits unless otherwise stated)					
	Year 1	Year 2	Year 3	Year 4	Year 5	Year 6
Revenues	45.00	50.00	55.00	60.00	65.00	70.00
– Operating expenses....................	28.00	30.00	30.00	32.00	35.00	35.00
– Amortization.........................	10.00	10.00	10.00	10.00	10.00	10.00
Earnings before Salaysian taxes............	7.00	10.00	15.00	18.00	20.00	25.00
– Salaysian income tax (25%)	1.75	2.50	3.75	4.50	5.00	6.25
Earnings after foreign income taxes.........	5.25	7.50	11.25	13.50	15.00	18.75
= Dividends repatriated..................	5.25	7.50	11.25	13.50	15.00	18.75
Gross Canadian taxes (46% of foreign earnings before taxes)	3.22	4.60	6.90	8.28	9.20	11.50
– Foreign tax credit	1.75	2.50	3.75	4.50	5.00	6.25
Net Canadian taxes payable	1.47	2.10	3.15	3.78	4.20	5.25
Aftertax dividend received by Q Systems	3.78	5.40	8.10	9.72	10.80	13.50
Exchange rate (ringgits/$)	2.00	2.04	2.08	2.12	2.16	2.21
Aftertax dividend (C$)....................	1.89	2.65	3.89	4.58	5.00	6.11
PV of dividends ($) (at 20%)..............	1.58 +	1.84 +	2.25 +	2.21 +	2.01 +	2.05 = $11.94

After considering the investment climate and the nature of the industry, Q Systems has set a target rate of return of 20 percent for this foreign investment. Salaysia has a 25 percent corporate income tax rate and has waived the withholding tax on dividends repatriated (forwarded) to the parent company. A dividend payout ratio of 100 percent is intended for the foreign subsidiary. Q Systems' marginal tax rate is 30 percent. It was agreed by Q Systems and the Salaysian government that the subsidiary will be sold to a Salaysian entrepreneur after six years for an estimated 30 million ringgits. The plant will be amortized over a period of six years using the straight-line method. The cash flows generated through amortization cannot be remitted to the parent company until the subsidiary is sold to the local private entrepreneur six years from now. The Salaysian government requires the subsidiary to invest the amortization-generated cash flows in local government bonds yielding an aftertax rate of 15 percent. The amortization cash flows thus compounded and accumulated can be returned to Q Systems when the project is terminated. Although the value of ringgits in the foreign exchange market has remained fairly stable for the past three years, the projected budget deficits and trade deficits of Salaysia are likely—according to a consultant hired by Q Systems—to result in a gradual devaluation of ringgits against the Canadian dollar at the rate of 2 percent per year for the next six years.

Note that the analysis in Table 21A–1 is primarily done in terms of ringgits. Expenses (operating, amortization, and Salaysian income taxes) are subtracted from revenues to arrive at earnings after foreign income taxes. These earnings are then repatriated (forwarded) to Q Systems in the form of dividends. Dividends repatriated thus begin at 5.25 ringgits (in millions) in Year 1 and increase to 18.75 ringgits in Year 6. The next item, gross Canadian taxes, refers to the unadjusted Canadian tax obligation. Dividends received from a foreign subsidiary, unlike those received from a Canadian subsidiary, are fully taxable. In the case of Q Systems, this rate is equal to 46 percent of foreign earnings before taxes (earnings before Salaysian taxes).[1] For example, gross Canadian taxes in the first year are equal to

Earnings before Salaysian taxes	$7.00
46% of foreign pretax earnings	46%
Gross Canadian taxes	$3.22

From gross Canadian taxes, Q Systems may take a foreign tax credit equal to the amount of Salaysian income tax paid. Gross Canadian taxes minus this foreign tax credit are equal to net Canadian taxes payable. Finally, aftertax dividends received by Q Systems are equal to dividends repatriated minus Canadian taxes payable. In the first year, the values are

Dividends repatriated	$5.25
Less: Net Canadian taxes payable	1.47
Aftertax dividends received by Q	$3.78

The figures for aftertax dividends received by Q Systems are all stated in ringgits. These ringgits are now converted into dollars. The initial exchange rate is 2.00 ringgits per dollar, and this will go up by 2 percent per year.[2] For the first year, 3.78 million ringgits will be translated into $1.89 million. Aftertax dividends in Canadian dollars grow from $1.89 million in Year 1 to $6.11 million in Year 6. The last row of Table 21A–1 shows the present value of these dividends at a 20 percent discount rate. The *total* present value of estimated aftertax dividends to be received by Q Systems adds up to $11.94 million. We know that repatriated dividends will be just one part of the cash flow. The second part consists of amortization-generated cash flow accumulated and reinvested in Salaysian government bonds at 15 percent per year.

The compound value of reinvested amortization cash flows (10 million ringgits per year) is

10 million ringgits = 87.54 millon ringgits after six years
$$N = 6, \; I/Y = 15\%$$

---

[1] If foreign earnings had not been repatriated, there is a possibility that this tax obligation would not be due.

[2] The 2 percent appreciation means the dollar is equal to an increasing amount of ringgits each year. The dollar is appreciating relative to ringgits, and ringgits are depreciating relative to the dollar. Since Q Systems' earnings are in ringgits, they are being converted at a less desirable rate each year. Q Systems may eventually decide to hedge its foreign exchange risk exposure.

These 87.54 million ringgits must next be translated into dollars and then discounted back to the present. Since the exchange rate is forecast at 2.21 ringgits per dollar in the sixth year (third line from the bottom in Table 21A–1), the dollar equivalent of 87.54 million ringgits becomes

87.54 million ringgits ÷ 2.21 = $39.61 million

The $39.61 million can now be discounted back to the present for six years at 20 percent.

$$\underline{\frac{\$39.61 \text{ million}}{= \$13.27 \text{ million}}} \qquad N = 6, \, I/Y = 20\%$$

The final benefit to be received is the 30 million ringgits when the plant is sold six years from now. We first convert this to dollars and then take the present value.

30 million ringgits ÷ 2.21 = $13.57 million

The present value of $13.57 million after six years at 20 percent is

$$\underline{\frac{\$13.57 \text{ million}}{= \$ \, 4.55 \text{ million}}} \qquad N = 6, \, I/Y = 20\%$$

The present value of all cash inflows in dollars is equal to

Present value of dividends	$11.94 million
Present value of repatriated amortization	13.27
Present value of plant sale	4.55
Total value of inflows	$29.76 million

The cost of the project was initially specified as 90 million ringgits, or $45 million. Thus, we see the total present value of inflows in dollars is less than the cost, and the project has a negative net present value.

Total present value of inflows	$29.76 million
Cost	45.00
Net present value	$ −15.24 million

The project is not acceptable on the basis of net present value criteria. However, before such a recommendation is made to the board of directors, the financial analyst must reconsider the project and assess its strategic importance for the firm. One must debate whether or not the specific foreign project is consistent with the firm's overall long-term goals. If the firm wants to use this foreign project as a base for its future marketing of small computers in this part of the world, then the negative net present value should not be the only factor in making the decision. As a next step, the analyst considers any special circumstances of a nonroutine nature that may have led the firm to consider this foreign investment. For example, if Q Systems' North American domestic market share is eroding, a new market penetration like the one under consideration may be part of a much larger decision that is crucial for the firm's future.[3]

---

[3] The impact of the 20 percent discount rate should also be considered. At discount rates commonly applied to conventional domestic investments, often closer to 10 percent, the project would be accepted on a net present value basis.

PROBLEMS

21A–1. The Office Automation Corporation is considering a foreign investment. The initial cash outlay will be $10 million. The current foreign exchange rate is 2 francs = $1. Thus, the investment in foreign currency will be 20 million francs. The assets have a useful life of five years and no expected salvage value. The firm is allowed a straight-line method of amortization. Sales are expected to be 20 million francs and operating cash expenses 10 million francs every year for five years. The foreign income tax rate is 25 percent. The foreign subsidiary will repatriate all aftertax profits to Office Automation in the form of dividends. Furthermore, the amortized cash flows (equal to each year's amortization) will be repatriated during the same year they accrue to the foreign subsidiary. The applicable cost of capital that reflects the riskiness of the cash flows is 16 percent. The Canadian tax rate is 40 percent of foreign earnings before taxes.

a. Should the Office Automation Corporation undertake the investment, if the foreign exchange rate is expected to remain constant during the five-year period?

b. Should Office Automation undertake the investment if the foreign exchange rate is expected to be as follows?

Year 0..	$1 = 2.0 francs
Year 1..	$1 = 2.2 francs
Year 2..	$1 = 2.4 francs
Year 3..	$1 = 2.7 francs
Year 4..	$1 = 2.9 francs
Year 5..	$1 = 3.2 francs

APPENDICES

APPENDIX A

Future Value of $1, FV_{IF}, $FV = PV(1 + i)^n$

Period						Percent					
	1%	2%	3%	4%	5%	6%	7%	8%	9%	10%	11%
1	1.010	1.020	1.030	1.040	1.050	1.060	1.070	1.080	1.090	1.100	1.110
2	1.020	1.040	1.061	1.082	1.103	1.124	1.145	1.166	1.188	1.210	1.232
3	1.030	1.061	1.093	1.125	1.158	1.191	1.225	1.260	1.295	1.331	1.368
4	1.041	1.082	1.126	1.170	1.216	1.262	1.311	1.360	1.412	1.464	1.518
5	1.051	1.104	1.159	1.217	1.276	1.338	1.403	1.469	1.539	1.611	1.685
6	1.062	1.126	1.194	1.265	1.340	1.419	1.501	1.587	1.677	1.772	1.870
7	1.072	1.149	1.230	1.316	1.407	1.504	1.606	1.714	1.828	1.949	2.076
8	1.083	1.172	1.267	1.369	1.477	1.594	1.718	1.851	1.993	2.144	2.305
9	1.094	1.195	1.305	1.423	1.551	1.689	1.838	1.999	2.172	2.358	2.558
10	1.105	1.219	1.344	1.480	1.629	1.791	1.967	2.159	2.367	2.594	2.839
11	1.116	1.243	1.384	1.539	1.710	1.898	2.105	2.332	2.580	2.853	3.152
12	1.127	1.268	1.426	1.601	1.796	2.012	2.252	2.518	2.813	3.138	3.498
13	1.138	1.294	1.469	1.665	1.886	2.133	2.410	2.720	3.066	3.452	3.883
14	1.149	1.319	1.513	1.732	1.980	2.261	2.579	2.937	3.342	3.797	4.310
15	1.161	1.346	1.558	1.801	2.079	2.397	2.759	3.172	3.642	4.177	4.785
16	1.173	1.373	1.605	1.873	2.183	2.540	2.952	3.426	3.970	4.595	5.311
17	1.184	1.400	1.653	1.948	2.292	2.693	3.159	3.700	4.328	5.054	5.895
18	1.196	1.428	1.702	2.026	2.407	2.854	3.380	3.996	4.717	5.560	6.544
19	1.208	1.457	1.754	2.107	2.527	3.026	3.617	4.316	5.142	6.116	7.263
20	1.220	1.486	1.806	2.191	2.653	3.207	3.870	4.661	5.604	6.727	8.062
25	1.282	1.641	2.094	2.666	3.386	4.292	5.427	6.848	8.623	10.835	13.585
30	1.348	1.811	2.427	3.243	4.322	5.743	7.612	10.063	13.268	17.449	22.892
40	1.489	2.208	3.262	4.801	7.040	10.286	14.974	21.725	31.409	45.259	65.001
50	1.645	2.692	4.384	7.107	11.467	18.420	29.457	46.902	74.358	117.39	184.57

Period	12%	13%	14%	15%	16%	17%	18%	19%	20%	25%	30%
1	1.120	1.130	1.140	1.150	1.160	1.170	1.180	1.190	1.200	1.250	1.300
2	1.254	1.277	1.300	1.323	1.346	1.369	1.392	1.416	1.440	1.563	1.690
3	1.405	1.443	1.482	1.521	1.561	1.602	1.643	1.685	1.728	1.953	2.197
4	1.574	1.630	1.689	1.749	1.811	1.874	1.939	2.005	2.074	2.441	2.856
5	1.762	1.842	1.925	2.011	2.100	2.192	2.288	2.386	2.488	3.052	3.713
6	1.974	2.082	2.195	2.313	2.436	2.565	2.700	2.840	2.986	3.815	4.827
7	2.211	2.353	2.502	2.660	2.826	3.001	3.185	3.379	3.583	4.768	6.276
8	2.476	2.658	2.853	3.059	3.278	3.511	3.759	4.021	4.300	5.960	8.157
9	2.773	3.004	3.252	3.518	3.803	4.108	4.435	4.785	5.160	7.451	10.604
10	3.106	3.395	3.707	4.046	4.411	4.807	5.234	5.696	6.192	9.313	13.786
11	3.479	3.836	4.226	4.652	5.117	5.624	6.176	6.777	7.430	11.642	17.922
12	3.896	4.335	4.818	5.350	5.936	6.580	7.288	8.064	8.916	14.552	23.298
13	4.363	4.898	5.492	6.153	6.886	7.699	8.599	9.596	10.699	18.190	30.288
14	4.887	5.535	6.261	7.076	7.988	9.007	10.147	11.420	12.839	22.737	39.374
15	5.474	6.254	7.138	8.137	9.266	10.539	11.974	13.590	15.407	28.422	51.186
16	6.130	7.067	8.137	9.358	10.748	12.330	14.129	16.172	18.488	35.527	66.542
17	6.866	7.986	9.276	10.761	12.468	14.426	16.672	19.244	22.186	44.409	86.504
18	7.690	9.024	10.575	12.375	14.463	16.879	19.673	22.091	26.623	55.511	112.46
19	8.613	10.197	12.056	14.232	16.777	19.748	23.214	27.252	31.948	69.389	146.19
20	9.646	11.523	13.743	16.367	19.461	23.106	27.393	32.429	38.338	86.736	190.05
25	17.000	21.231	26.462	32.919	40.874	50.658	62.669	77.388	95.396	264.70	705.64
30	29.960	39.116	50.950	66.212	85.850	111.07	143.37	184.68	237.38	807.79	2,620.0
40	93.051	132.78	188.88	267.86	378.72	533.87	750.38	1,051.7	1,469.8	7,523.2	36,119.
50	289.00	450.74	700.23	1,083.7	1,670.7	2,566.2	3,927.4	5,988.9	9,100.4	70,065.	497,929.

Note: Factor calculation with calculator.

Set PV = 1   Set PMT = 0

Select N = number of required periods

Select I/Y = required interest rate

COMP PV = ?

Excel Spreadsheet

=FV (i, n, 0, PV, 0)

i = Decimal or % 0 in 3rd position for PMT

PV as 1

1 = For beginning of period (5th position)

APPENDIX B

Present Value of $1, PV_{IF} $PV = FV \left[\dfrac{1}{(1+i)^n} \right] = FV(1+i)^{-n}$

Period	1%	2%	3%	4%	5%	6%	7%	8%	9%	10%	11%
1	0.990	0.980	0.971	0.962	0.952	0.943	0.935	0.926	0.917	0.909	0.901
2	0.980	0.961	0.943	0.925	0.907	0.890	0.873	0.857	0.842	0.826	0.812
3	0.971	0.942	0.915	0.889	0.864	0.840	0.816	0.794	0.772	0.751	0.731
4	0.961	0.924	0.885	0.855	0.823	0.792	0.763	0.735	0.708	0.683	0.659
5	0.951	0.906	0.863	0.822	0.784	0.747	0.713	0.681	0.650	0.621	0.593
6	0.942	0.888	0.837	0.790	0.746	0.705	0.666	0.630	0.596	0.564	0.535
7	0.933	0.871	0.813	0.760	0.711	0.665	0.623	0.583	0.547	0.513	0.482
8	0.923	0.853	0.789	0.731	0.677	0.627	0.582	0.540	0.502	0.467	0.434
9	0.914	0.837	0.766	0.703	0.645	0.592	0.544	0.500	0.460	0.424	0.391
10	0.905	0.820	0.744	0.676	0.614	0.558	0.508	0.463	0.422	0.386	0.352
11	0.896	0.804	0.722	0.650	0.585	0.527	0.475	0.429	0.388	0.350	0.317
12	0.887	0.788	0.701	0.625	0.557	0.497	0.444	0.397	0.356	0.319	0.286
13	0.879	0.773	0.681	0.601	0.530	0.469	0.415	0.368	0.326	0.290	0.258
14	0.870	0.758	0.661	0.577	0.505	0.442	0.388	0.340	0.299	0.263	0.232
15	0.861	0.743	0.642	0.555	0.481	0.417	0.362	0.315	0.275	0.239	0.209
16	0.853	0.728	0.623	0.534	0.458	0.394	0.339	0.292	0.252	0.218	0.188
17	0.844	0.714	0.605	0.513	0.436	0.371	0.317	0.270	0.231	0.198	0.170
18	0.836	0.700	0.587	0.494	0.416	0.350	0.296	0.250	0.212	0.180	0.153
19	0.828	0.686	0.570	0.475	0.396	0.331	0.277	0.232	0.194	0.164	0.138
20	0.820	0.673	0.554	0.456	0.377	0.312	0.258	0.215	0.178	0.149	0.124
25	0.780	0.610	0.478	0.375	0.295	0.233	0.184	0.146	0.116	0.092	0.074
30	0.742	0.552	0.412	0.308	0.231	0.174	0.131	0.099	0.075	0.057	0.044
40	0.672	0.453	0.307	0.208	0.142	0.097	0.067	0.046	0.032	0.022	0.015
50	0.608	0.372	0.228	0.141	0.087	0.054	0.034	0.021	0.013	0.009	0.005

Percent

Percent

Period	12%	13%	14%	15%	16%	17%	18%	19%	20%	25%	30%	35%	40%	50%
1	0.893	0.885	0.877	0.870	0.862	0.855	0.847	0.840	0.833	0.800	0.769	0.741	0.714	0.667
2	0.797	0.783	0.769	0.756	0.743	0.731	0.718	0.706	0.694	0.640	0.592	0.549	0.510	0.444
3	0.712	0.693	0.675	0.658	0.641	0.624	0.609	0.593	0.579	0.512	0.455	0.406	0.364	0.296
4	0.636	0.613	0.592	0.572	0.552	0.534	0.515	0.499	0.482	0.410	0.350	0.301	0.260	0.198
5	0.567	0.543	0.519	0.497	0.476	0.456	0.437	0.419	0.402	0.320	0.269	0.223	0.186	0.132
6	0.507	0.480	0.456	0.432	0.410	0.390	0.370	0.352	0.335	0.262	0.207	0.165	0.133	0.088
7	0.452	0.425	0.400	0.376	0.354	0.333	0.314	0.296	0.279	0.210	0.159	0.122	0.095	0.059
8	0.404	0.376	0.351	0.327	0.305	0.285	0.266	0.249	0.233	0.168	0.123	0.091	0.068	0.039
9	0.361	0.333	0.300	0.284	0.263	0.243	0.225	0.209	0.194	0.134	0.094	0.067	0.048	0.026
10	0.322	0.295	0.270	0.247	0.227	0.208	0.191	0.176	0.162	0.107	0.073	0.050	0.035	0.017
11	0.287	0.261	0.237	0.215	0.195	0.178	0.162	0.148	0.135	0.086	0.056	0.037	0.025	0.012
12	0.257	0.231	0.208	0.187	0.168	0.152	0.137	0.124	0.112	0.069	0.043	0.027	0.018	0.008
13	0.229	0.204	0.182	0.163	0.145	0.130	0.116	0.104	0.093	0.055	0.033	0.020	0.013	0.005
14	0.205	0.181	0.160	0.141	0.125	0.111	0.099	0.088	0.078	0.044	0.025	0.015	0.009	0.003
15	0.183	0.160	0.140	0.123	0.108	0.095	0.084	0.074	0.065	0.035	0.020	0.011	0.006	0.002
16	0.163	0.141	0.123	0.107	0.093	0.081	0.071	0.062	0.054	0.028	0.015	0.008	0.005	0.002
17	0.146	0.125	0.108	0.093	0.080	0.069	0.060	0.052	0.045	0.023	0.012	0.006	0.003	0.001
18	0.130	0.111	0.095	0.081	0.069	0.059	0.051	0.044	0.038	0.018	0.009	0.005	0.002	0.001
19	0.116	0.098	0.083	0.070	0.060	0.051	0.043	0.037	0.031	0.014	0.007	0.003	0.002	
20	0.104	0.087	0.073	0.061	0.051	0.043	0.037	0.031	0.026	0.012	0.005	0.002	0.001	
25	0.059	0.047	0.038	0.030	0.024	0.020	0.016	0.013	0.010	0.004	0.001	0.001	0	
30	0.033	0.026	0.020	0.015	0.012	0.009	0.007	0.005	0.004	0.001	0	0	0	0
40	0.011	0.008	0.005	0.004	0.003	0.002	0.001	0.001	0.001	0	0	0	0	0
50	0.003	0.002	0.001	0.001	0.001	0	0	0	0	0	0	0	0	0

Note: Factor calculation with calculator.

Set FV = 1   Set PMT = 0

Select N = number of required periods

Select I/Y = required interest rate

COMP PV = ?

Excel Spreadsheet

=PV (i, n, 0, FV, 0)

i = Decimal or %

0 in 3rd position for payment

FV as 1

1 = For beginning of period (5th position)

APPENDIX C

Future Value of an Annuity of $1, FV_{IFA} $FV_A = A\left[\dfrac{(1+i)^n - 1}{i}\right]$

Percent

Period	1%	2%	3%	4%	5%	6%	7%	8%	9%	10%	11%
1	1.000	1.000	1.000	1.000	1.000	1.000	1.000	1.000	1.000	1.000	1.000
2	2.010	2.020	2.030	2.040	2.050	2.060	2.070	2.080	2.090	2.100	2.110
3	3.030	3.060	3.091	3.122	3.153	3.184	3.215	3.246	3.278	3.310	3.342
4	4.060	4.122	4.184	4.246	4.310	4.375	4.440	4.506	4.573	4.641	4.710
5	5.101	5.204	5.309	5.416	5.526	5.637	5.751	5.867	5.985	6.105	6.228
6	6.152	6.308	6.468	6.633	6.802	6.975	7.153	7.336	7.523	7.716	7.913
7	7.214	7.434	7.662	7.898	8.142	8.394	8.654	8.923	9.200	9.487	9.783
8	8.286	8.583	8.892	9.214	9.549	9.897	10.260	10.637	11.028	11.436	11.859
9	9.369	9.755	10.159	10.583	11.027	11.491	11.978	12.488	13.021	13.579	14.164
10	10.462	10.950	11.464	12.006	12.578	13.181	13.816	14.487	15.193	15.937	16.722
11	11.567	12.169	12.808	13.486	14.207	14.972	15.784	16.645	17.560	18.531	19.561
12	12.683	13.412	14.192	15.026	15.917	16.870	17.888	18.977	20.141	21.384	22.713
13	13.809	14.680	15.618	16.627	17.713	18.882	20.141	21.495	22.953	24.523	26.212
14	14.947	15.974	17.086	18.292	19.599	21.015	22.550	24.215	26.019	27.975	30.095
15	16.097	17.293	18.599	20.024	21.579	23.276	25.129	27.152	29.361	31.772	34.405
16	17.258	18.639	20.157	21.825	23.657	25.673	27.888	30.324	33.003	35.950	39.190
17	18.430	20.012	21.762	23.698	25.840	28.213	30.840	33.750	36.974	40.545	44.501
18	19.615	21.412	23.414	25.645	28.132	30.906	33.999	37.450	41.301	45.599	50.396
19	20.811	22.841	25.117	27.671	30.539	33.760	37.379	41.446	46.018	51.159	56.939
20	22.019	24.297	26.870	29.778	33.066	36.786	40.995	45.762	51.160	57.275	64.203
25	28.243	32.030	36.459	41.646	47.727	54.865	63.249	73.106	84.701	98.347	114.41
30	34.785	40.588	47.575	56.085	66.439	79.058	94.461	113.28	136.31	164.49	199.02
40	48.886	60.402	75.401	95.026	120.80	154.76	199.64	259.06	337.89	442.59	581.83
50	64.463	84.579	112.80	152.67	209.35	290.34	406.53	573.77	815.08	1,163.9	1,668.8

Period	12%	13%	14%	15%	16%	17%	18%	19%	20%	25%	30%
1	1.000	1.000	1.000	1.000	1.000	1.000	1.000	1.000	1.000	1.000	1.000
2	2.120	2.130	2.140	2.150	2.160	2.170	2.180	2.190	2.200	2.250	2.300
3	3.374	3.407	3.440	3.473	3.506	3.539	3.572	3.606	3.640	3.813	3.990
4	4.779	4.850	4.921	4.993	5.066	5.141	5.215	5.291	5.368	5.766	6.187
5	6.353	6.480	6.610	6.742	6.877	7.014	7.154	7.297	7.442	8.207	9.043
6	8.115	8.323	8.536	8.754	8.977	9.207	9.442	9.683	9.930	11.259	12.756
7	10.089	10.405	10.730	11.067	11.414	11.772	12.142	12.523	12.916	15.073	17.583
8	12.300	12.757	13.233	13.727	14.240	14.773	15.327	15.902	16.499	19.842	23.858
9	14.776	15.416	16.085	16.786	17.519	18.285	19.086	19.923	20.799	25.802	32.015
10	17.549	18.420	19.337	20.304	21.321	22.393	23.521	24.701	25.959	33.253	42.619
11	20.655	21.814	23.045	24.349	25.733	27.200	28.755	30.404	32.150	42.566	56.405
12	24.133	25.650	27.271	29.002	30.850	32.824	34.931	37.180	39.581	54.208	74.327
13	28.029	29.985	32.089	34.352	36.786	39.404	42.219	45.244	48.497	68.760	97.625
14	32.393	34.883	37.581	40.505	43.672	47.103	50.818	54.841	59.196	86.949	127.91
15	37.280	40.417	43.842	47.580	51.660	56.110	60.965	66.261	72.035	109.69	167.29
16	42.753	46.672	50.980	55.717	60.925	66.649	72.939	79.850	87.442	138.11	218.47
17	48.884	53.739	59.118	65.075	71.673	78.979	87.068	96.022	05.93	173.64	285.01
18	55.750	61.725	68.394	75.836	84.141	93.406	103.74	115.27	128.12	218.05	371.52
19	63.440	70.749	78.969	88.212	98.603	110.29	123.41	138.17	154.74	273.56	483.97
20	72.052	80.947	91.025	102.44	115.38	130.03	146.63	165.42	186.69	342.95	630.17
25	133.33	155.62	181.87	212.79	249.21	292.11	342.60	402.04	471.98	1,054.8	2,348.80
30	241.33	293.20	356.79	434.75	530.31	647.44	790.95	966.7	1,181.9	3,227.2	8,730.0
40	767.09	1,013.7	1,342.0	1,779.1	2,360.8	3,134.5	4,163.21	5,529.8	7,343.9	30,089.	120,393.
50	2,400.0	3,459.5	4,994.5	7,217.7	10,436.	15,090.	21,813.	31,515.	45,497.	280,256.	165,976.

Note: Factor calculation with calculator.

Set PMT = 1   Set PV = 0

Select N = number of required periods

Select I/Y = required interest rate

COMP FV = ?

If annuity in advance, calculate factor with BGN set on calculator.

Excel Spreadsheet

=FV (i, n, 1, PV, 0)

i = Decimal or %

1 in 3rd position for payment

PV as 0

1 = For beginning of period (5th position)

APPENDIX D

Present Value of an Annuity of $1, PV_{IFA} $PV_A = A \left[\dfrac{1 - \dfrac{1}{(1+i)^n}}{i} \right] = A \left[\dfrac{1 - (1+i)^{-n}}{i} \right]$

					Percent						
Period	1%	2%	3%	4%	5%	6%	7%	8%	9%	10%	11%
1	0.990	0.980	0.971	0.962	0.952	0.943	0.935	0.926	0.917	0.909	0.901
2	1.970	1.942	1.913	1.886	1.859	1.833	1.808	1.783	1.759	1.736	1.713
3	2.941	2.884	2.829	2.775	2.723	2.673	2.624	2.577	2.531	2.487	2.444
4	3.902	3.808	3.717	3.630	3.546	3.465	3.387	3.312	3.240	3.170	3.102
5	4.853	4.713	4.580	4.452	4.329	4.212	4.100	3.993	3.890	3.791	3.696
6	5.795	5.601	5.417	5.242	5.076	4.917	4.767	4.623	4.486	4.355	4.231
7	6.728	6.472	6.230	6.002	5.786	5.582	5.389	5.206	5.033	4.868	4.712
8	7.652	7.325	7.020	6.733	6.463	6.210	5.971	5.747	5.535	5.335	5.146
9	8.566	8.162	7.786	7.435	7.108	6.802	6.515	6.247	5.995	5.759	5.537
10	9.471	8.983	8.530	8.111	7.722	7.360	7.024	6.710	6.418	6.145	5.889
11	10.368	9.787	9.253	8.760	8.306	7.887	7.499	7.139	6.805	6.495	6.207
12	11.255	10.575	9.954	9.385	8.863	8.384	7.943	7.536	7.161	6.814	6.492
13	12.134	11.348	10.635	9.986	9.394	8.853	8.358	7.904	7.487	7.103	6.750
14	13.004	12.106	11.296	10.563	9.899	9.295	8.745	8.244	7.786	7.367	6.982
15	13.865	12.849	11.938	11.118	10.380	9.712	9.108	8.559	8.061	7.606	7.191
16	14.718	13.578	12.561	11.652	10.838	10.106	9.447	8.851	8.313	7.824	7.379
17	15.562	14.292	13.166	12.166	11.274	10.477	9.763	9.122	8.544	8.022	7.549
18	16.398	14.992	13.754	12.659	11.690	10.828	10.059	9.372	8.756	8.201	7.702
19	17.226	15.678	14.324	13.134	12.085	11.158	10.336	9.604	8.950	8.365	7.839
20	18.046	16.351	14.877	13.590	12.462	11.470	10.594	9.818	9.129	8.514	7.963
25	22.023	19.523	17.413	15.622	14.094	12.783	11.654	10.675	9.823	9.077	8.422
30	25.808	22.396	19.600	17.292	15.372	13.765	12.409	11.258	10.274	9.427	8.694
40	32.835	27.355	23.115	19.793	17.159	15.046	13.332	11.925	10.757	9.779	8.951
50	39.196	31.424	25.730	21.482	18.256	15.762	13.801	12.233	10.962	9.915	9.042

Percent

Period	12%	13%	14%	15%	16%	17%	18%	19%	20%	25%	30%	35%	40%	50%
1	0.893	0.885	0.877	0.870	0.862	0.855	0.847	0.840	0.833	0.800	0.769	0.741	0.714	0.667
2	1.690	1.668	1.647	1.626	1.605	1.585	1.566	1.547	1.528	1.440	1.361	1.289	1.224	1.111
3	2.402	2.361	2.322	2.283	2.246	2.210	2.174	2.140	2.106	1.952	1.816	1.696	1.589	1.407
4	3.037	2.974	2.914	2.855	2.798	2.743	2.690	2.639	2.589	2.362	2.166	1.997	1.849	1.605
5	3.605	3.517	3.433	3.352	3.274	3.199	3.127	3.058	2.991	2.689	2.436	2.220	2.035	1.737
6	4.111	3.998	3.889	3.784	3.685	3.589	3.498	3.410	3.326	2.951	2.643	2.385	2.168	1.824
7	4.564	4.423	4.288	4.160	4.039	3.922	3.812	3.706	3.605	3.161	2.802	2.508	2.263	1.883
8	4.968	4.799	4.639	4.487	4.344	4.207	4.078	3.954	3.837	3.329	2.925	2.598	2.331	1.922
9	5.328	5.132	4.946	4.772	4.607	4.451	4.303	4.163	4.031	3.463	3.019	2.665	2.379	1.948
10	5.650	5.426	5.216	5.019	4.833	4.659	4.494	4.339	4.192	3.571	3.092	2.715	2.414	1.965
11	5.938	5.687	5.453	5.234	5.029	4.836	4.656	4.486	4.327	3.656	3.147	2.752	2.438	1.977
12	6.194	5.918	5.660	5.421	5.197	4.988	4.793	4.611	4.439	3.725	3.190	2.779	2.456	1.985
13	6.424	6.122	5.842	5.583	5.342	5.118	4.910	4.715	4.533	3.780	3.223	2.799	2.469	1.990
14	6.628	6.302	6.002	5.724	5.468	5.229	5.008	4.802	4.611	3.824	3.249	2.814	2.478	1.993
15	6.811	6.462	6.142	5.847	5.575	5.324	5.092	4.876	4.675	3.859	3.268	2.825	2.484	1.995
16	6.974	6.604	6.265	5.954	5.668	5.405	5.162	4.938	4.730	3.887	3.283	2.834	2.489	1.997
17	7.120	6.729	6.373	6.047	5.749	5.475	5.222	4.988	4.775	3.910	3.295	2.840	2.492	1.998
18	7.250	6.840	6.467	6.128	5.818	5.534	5.273	5.033	4.812	3.928	3.304	2.844	2.494	1.999
19	7.366	6.938	6.550	6.198	5.877	5.584	5.316	5.070	4.843	3.942	3.311	2.848	2.496	1.999
20	7.469	7.025	6.623	6.259	5.929	5.628	5.353	5.101	4.870	3.954	3.316	2.850	2.497	1.999
25	7.843	7.330	6.873	6.464	6.097	5.766	5.467	5.195	4.948	3.985	3.329	2.856	2.499	2.000
30	8.055	7.496	7.003	6.566	6.177	5.829	5.517	5.235	4.979	3.995	3.332	2.857	2.500	2.000
40	8.244	7.634	7.105	6.642	6.233	5.871	5.548	5.258	4.997	3.999	3.333	2.857	2.500	2.000
50	8.304	7.675	7.133	6.661	6.246	5.880	5.554	5.262	4.999	4.000	3.333	2.857	2.500	2.000

Note: Factor calculation with calculator.

Set PMT = 1   Set FV = 0

Select N = number of required periods

Select I/Y = required interest rate

COMP PV = ?

If annuity in advance, calculate factor with BGN set on calculator.

Excel Spreadsheet

=PV (i, n, 1, FV, 0)

i = Decimal or %

1 in 3rd position for payment

FV as 0

1 = For beginning of period (5th position)

APPENDIX E: USING CALCULATORS FOR FINANCIAL ANALYSIS

This appendix is designed to help you use the following:

- Texas Instruments (BA II Plus)
- Hewlett-Packard (HP-10B II)
- Sharp (EL-738)

It provides only basic instructions for commonly used financial calculations. Familiarize yourself with the keyboard before you start.

Conventions for Key Sequences (Listed Vertically)

Numerical entries: 5.00

Primary keys: PMT

Secondary keys: {TAB}

- Designation is located above or below primary key
- Accessed by modifier key; e.g., 2nd ; purple or orange key for HP-10B II

Sign Changes

Many financial transactions entail an initial cash **outflow** (a payment) followed by subsequent cash **inflows** (receipts). Changes in cash flow patterns must be identified. For a negative cash flow (outflow) enter the appropriate number followed by the +/− key.

Annuities Due

The timing of cash flows is quite important in finance. A stream of payments is referred to as an annuity, with the usual assumption that the payments are at the end of each period; an **ordinary annuity.** When payments occur at the beginning of each period they are referred to as **annuities due.** This timing of cash flows must be identified in calculations.

BA II Plus	HP-10B II	EL-738
2nd		2ndF
{BGN}	{BEG/END}	{BGN/END}
2nd		
{SET}		
2nd		
{QUIT}		

Repeat to return to ordinary or END mode.

Before starting calculations it is important to.
- Clear the memory registers (otherwise errors usually result).
- Set the display format (number of decimals).
- Set the mode.
- Set the interest compounding frequency (best to set at once per period). Please reset the calculator defaults.

	BA II Plus	HP-10B II	EL-738
Clear calculator:			
Display	CE/C	C	ON/C
TVM Registers	2nd {CLR TVM}	{C ALL}	2ndF {CA}
Memory	2nd {MEM}	{C ALL}	2ndF {M-CLR}
	2nd {CLR Work}		0
Set decimal point:			
(4 is good for interest rates)	2nd {Format} 4 Enter	{DISP} 4	Setup 0 0 4
Floating decimal point:	2nd {Format} 9 Enter	{DISP} .	Setup 0 2
Set mode:	"ready to go"	"ready to go"	Mode 0
Set compounding frequency:	2nd {P/Y} 1 Enter ↓ 1 Enter 2nd {QUIT}	1 {P/YR}	"ready to go"
(Once per period)			

To get the interest factors for Appendixes A, B, C, and D. Tables are rounded.

	BA II Plus	HP-10B II	EL-738
Appendix A	1.000 PV	1.000 PV	1.000 PV
Future value of $1, FV_{IF}, compound value $i = 9\%$ or .09; $n = 5$	5.000 N	5.000 N	5.000 N
	9.000 I/Y	9.000 I/YR	9.000 I/Y
	CPT FV	FV	COMP FV
	Answer: −1.538624	Answer: −1.538624	Answer: −1.538624
Appendix B	1.000 FV	1.000 FV	1.000 FV
Present value of $1, PV_{IF}, discounted value $i = 9\%$ or .09; $n = 5$	5.000 N	5.000 N	5.000 N
	9.000 I/Y	9.000 I/YR	9.000 I/Y
	CPT PV	PV	COMP PV
	Answer: −0.6499314	Answer: −0.6499314	Answer: −0.6499314
Appendix C	1.000 PMT	1.000 PMT	1.000 PMT
Future value of an annuity of $1, FV_{IFA}, cumulative future value $i = 9\%$ or .09; $n = 5$	5.000 N	5.000 N	5.000 N
	9.000 I/Y	9.000 I/YR	9.000 I/Y
	CPT FV	FV	COMP FV
	Answer: −5.9847106	Answer: −5.9847106	Answer: −5.9847106
Appendix D	1.000 PMT	1.000 PMT	1.000 PMT
Present value of an annuity of $1, PV_{IFA}, cumulative present value $i = 9\%$ or .09; $n = 5$	5.000 N	5.000 N	5.000 N
	9.000 I/Y	9.000 I/YR	9.000 I/Y
	CPT PV	PV	COMP PV
	Answer: −3.8896513	Answer: −3.8896513	Answer: −3.8896513

Below, you can determine bond valuation, yield to maturity, net present value of an annuity, net present value of an uneven cash flow, internal rate of return for an annuity, and internal rate of return for an uneven cash flow.

Bond Valuation

Solve for P_b = Price of the bond

Given:

I = $80 annual coupon payments or 8% coupon ($40 semiannually)

P_n = $1,000 principal (par value)

N = 10 years to maturity (20 periods semiannually)

Y = 9.0% yield to maturity or required rate of return (4.5% semiannually)

You may choose to refer to Chapter 10 for a complete discussion of bond valuation.

Yield to Maturity

Solve for Y = Yield to maturity

Given:

P_b = 895.50 price of bond

I_t = $80 annual coupon payments or 8% coupon ($40 semiannually)

P_n = $1,000 principal (par value)

N = 10 years to maturity (20 periods semiannually)

You may choose to refer to Chapters 10 and 11 for a complete discussion of yield to maturity.

Net Present Value of an Annuity

Solve for PV = Present value of annuity

Given:

N = 10 years (number of years cash flow will continue)

PMT = \$5,000 per year (amount of the annuity)

r = I/Y (%) = 12% (cost of capital K_a)

Cost = \$20,000

You may choose to refer to Chapter 12 for a complete discussion of net present value.

	BA II Plus	HP-10B II	EL-738
Bond valuation:	40.00 PMT	40.00 PMT	40.00 PMT
	1,000.00 FV	1,000.00 FV	1,000.00 FV
	20.00 N	20.00 N	20.00 N
	4.50 I/Y	4.50 I/YR	4.50 I/Y
	CPT PV	PV	COMP PV
	Answer: −934.96	Answer: −934.96	Answer: −934.96
Yield to maturity: Price of bond (purchased) must be a negative cash flow.	895.50 +/− PV	895.50 +/− PV	895.50 +/− PV
	40.00 PMT	40.00 PMT	40.00 PMT
	1,000.00 FV	1,000.00 FV	1,000.00 FV
	20.00 N	20.00 N	20.00 N
	CPT I/Y	I/YR	COMP I/Y
	Answer: 4.83	Answer: 4.83	Answer: 4.83
	Multiply by 2 for annual rate = 9.65% (nominal).	Multiply by 2 for annual rate = 9.65% (nominal).	Multiply by 2 for annual rate = 9.65% (nominal).
	Setting {P/Y} to 2 achieves 9.65 directly.	Setting {P/Y} to 2 achieves 9.65 directly.	
	Advanced bond pricing functions are available for bonds purchased at times other than the coupon dates.		
NPV of an annuity:	5,000.00 PMT	5,000.00 PMT	5,000.00 PMT
	0.00 FV	0.00 FV	0.00 FV
	10.00 N	10.00 N	10.00 N
	12.00 I/Y	12.00 I/YR	12.00 I/Y
	CPT PV	PV	COMP PV
	Answer: −28,251.12	Answer: −28,251.12	Answer: −28,251.12
	+/−	+/−	+/−
	−	−	−
	20,000	20,000	20,000
	=	=	=
	Answer: \$8,251.12	Answer: \$8,251.12	Answer: \$8,251.12

Net Present Value of an Uneven Cash Flow

Solve for NPV = Net present value

Given:

N = 5 years (number of years cash flow will continue)

PMT = $5,000 (yr. 1); 6,000 (yr. 2); 7,000 (yr. 3); 8,000 (yr. 4); 9,000 (yr. 5)

$r = I/Y$ (%) = 12% (cost of capital K_a)

Cost = $25,000

You may choose to refer to Chapter 12 for a complete discussion of net present value concepts.

Internal Rate of Return for an Annuity

Solve for IRR = Internal rate of return

Given:

N = 10 years (number of years cash flow will continue)

PMT = $10,000 per year (amount of the annuity)

Cost = $50,000 (this is the present value of the annuity)

You may choose to refer to Chapter 12 for a complete discussion of internal rate of return.

Internal Rate of Return with an Uneven Cash Flow

Solve for IRR = Internal rate of return (return that causes present value of outflows to equal present value of the inflows)

Given:

N = 5 years (number of years cash flow will continue)

PMT = $5,000 (yr. 1); 6,000 (yr. 2); 7,000 (yr. 3); 8,000 (yr. 4); 9,000 (yr. 5)

Cost = $25,000

You may choose to refer to Chapter 12 for a complete discussion of internal rate of return.

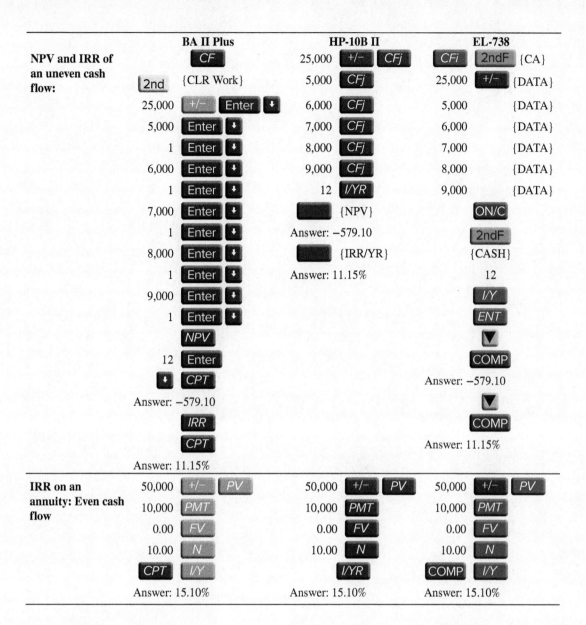

	BA II Plus	**HP-10B II**	**EL-738**
NPV and IRR of an uneven cash flow:	CF	25,000 +/− CFj	CFi 2ndF {CA}
	2nd {CLR Work}	5,000 CFj	25,000 +/− {DATA}
	25,000 +/− Enter ↓	6,000 CFj	5,000 {DATA}
	5,000 Enter ↓	7,000 CFj	6,000 {DATA}
	1 Enter ↓	8,000 CFj	7,000 {DATA}
	6,000 Enter ↓	9,000 CFj	8,000 {DATA}
	1 Enter ↓	12 I/YR	9,000 {DATA}
	7,000 Enter ↓	▭ {NPV}	ON/C
	1 Enter ↓	Answer: −579.10	2ndF
	8,000 Enter ↓	▭ {IRR/YR}	{CASH}
	1 Enter ↓	Answer: 11.15%	12
	9,000 Enter ↓		I/Y
	1 Enter ↓		ENT
	NPV		▼
	12 Enter		COMP
	↓ CPT		Answer: −579.10
	Answer: −579.10		▼
	IRR		COMP
	CPT		Answer: 11.15%
	Answer: 11.15%		
IRR on an annuity: Even cash flow	50,000 +/− PV	50,000 +/− PV	50,000 +/− PV
	10,000 PMT	10,000 PMT	10,000 PMT
	0.00 FV	0.00 FV	0.00 FV
	10.00 N	10.00 N	10.00 N
	CPT I/Y	I/YR	COMP I/Y
	Answer: 15.10%	Answer: 15.10%	Answer: 15.10%

Sources

Chapter 1

Finance in Action "The Foundations"
Source: Data from Bank of Canada, "Daily Noon Exchange Rates: 10 Year Look-up." bankofcanada.ca.

Table 1-1 Source: Adapted from "Report on Business," *The Globe and Mail,* May 2019.

Finance in Action "The Markets Reflect Value, Yields (Rates of Return), and Risk"
Source: Data from Bank of Canada, T-Bills, Series V39063; Commercial Paper, Series V39072. bankofcanada.ca.

Figure 1-2 Source: Data from Bank of Canada, Prime. www.bankofcanada.ca.

Chapter 2

Table 2-5 Source: Based on Company financial reports, TSX website, tsx.com.

Chapter 3

Table 3-3 Source: Adapted from Bank of Montreal annual reports, bmo.com; Royal Bank annual reports, rbc.com.

Chapter 5

Figure 5-5 Source: Statistics Canada, "Quarterly balance sheet and income statement, by industry,33-10-007-01, July, 2019. Reproduced and distributed on an "as if" basis with the permission of Statistics Canada.

Chapter 6

Figure 6-12 Source: Data from Bank of Canada, Prime. www.bankofcanada.ca.

Figure 6-13 Source: Data from Bank of Canada, Prime. www.bankofcanada.ca.

Figure 6-14 Statistics Canada, Quarterly balance sheet and income statement, by industry, 33-10-0007-01. Reproduced and distributed on an "as if" basis with the permission of Statistics Canada.

Chapter 8

Figure 8-1 Source: Statistics Canada, Quarterly balance sheet and income statement, by industry, Table: 33-10-0007-01, July 2019. Reproduced and distributed on an "as if" basis with the permission of Statistics Canada.

Figure 8-2 Source: Data from Bank of Canada, Canadian Prime, Series V80691311; U.S. Prime, Series V122148; bankofcanada.ca.

Figure 8-3 Source: Data from Bank of Canada Banking and Financial Statistics, 2019, www.bankofcanada.ca; V122246, V122241, V122254.

Figure 8-4 Source: Data from Bank of Canada, Prime V80691311, Paper V122491, bankofcanada.ca.

Chapter 11

Table 11-2 Sources: Perimeter Markets Inc., pfin.ca; DBRS, dbrs.com; Bloomberg. bloomberg.com; td.com/ca.

Chapter 13

Table 13-2 Sources: "Markets & Finance News," reuters.com/finance/markets; TMX Money, tmxmoney.com; Damodaran Online. "Data: Current," pages.stern.nyu.edu/~adamodar/New_Home_Page/datacurrent.html.

Finance in Action "Diversification: Go by Country or by Corporation" Source: William Goetzmann, Lingfeng Li, Geert Rouwenhorst (2008) *Long Term Global Market Correlations,* Yale ICF Working Paper No. 08-04. papers.ssrn.com/sol3/papers.cfm?abstract_id=288421.

Chapter 14

Figure 14-1 Source: Adapted in part from Statistics Canada, Tables: 36-10-0469-01, 36-10-0474-01 and 36-10-0475-01, and Bank of Canada Banking and Financial Statistics, November 2019. Reproduced and distributed on an "as is" basis with the permission of Statistics Canada.

Figure 14-2 Source: World Federation of Exchanges, 2018.

Figure 14-3 Source: Data from Bank of Canada Banking and Financial Statistics, January 2020.

Figure 14-4 Source: Data from Bank of Canada Banking and Financial Statistics, January 2020.

Figure 14-5 Source: Data from Bank of Canada Banking and Financial Statistics, January 2020.

Figure 14-6 Source: Data from Bank of Canada Banking and Financial Statistics, November 2019.

Figure 14-7 Source: Statistics Canada, Quarterly statement of changes in financial position and selected financial ratios, by industry, Table: 33-10-0008-01, 3rd quarter

2019. Reproduced and distributed on an "as is" basis with the permission of Statistics Canada.

Figure 14-8 Source: Statistics Canada, Table: 33-10-0008-01, 2019. Reproduced and distributed on an "as is" basis with the permission of Statistics Canada.

Figure 14-10 Source: Data from Bank of Canada Banking and Financial Statistics, November 2019; Statistics Canada, Table: 11-10-0076-01. Material used with the permission of the Bank of Canada. Reproduced and distributed on an "as is" basis with the permission of Statistics Canada.

Figure 14-11 Source:Investment Industry Regulatory Association of Canada, Statistics and Information, 2019, www.iiroc.ca.

Figure 14-12 Source: World Federation of Exchanges, 2019.

Figure 14-13 Source: Statistics Canada, International Investment Position, Table 36-10-0485-01, Third quarter 2019. Reproduced and distributed on an "as is" basis with the permission of Statistics Canada.

Finance in Action "Do Mutual Funds Achieve Superior Returns?" Source: Adapted from Burton G. Malkiel, "Returns from Investing in Equity Mutual Funds 1971 to 1991." From *The Journal of Finance,* vol. 50, issue 2, June 1995, 549–572. Copyright © 1995 the American Finance Association.

Chapter 15
Figure 15-3 Source: Investment Industry Association of Canada, Annual New Issues, 2018, www.iiac.ca.

Figure 15-4 Source: TMX MiG reports, 2019. www.tsx.com/listings/current-market-statistics/mig-archives.

Chapter 16
Figure 16-1 Source: Statistics Canada, Table: 33-10-007-01, Third quarter 2019. Reproduced and distributed on an "as is" basis with the permission of Statistics Canada.

Figure 16-3 Source: Data from Bank of Canada www.bankofcanada.ca, Series V122544, January 2020.

Chapter 18
Figure 18-2 Source: Statistics Canada, Table 33-10-0008-01, Third quarter 2019. Reproduced and distributed on an "as is" basis with the permission of Statistics Canada.

Chapter 19
Table 19-2 Source: Canadianwarrants.com.

Chapter 21
Figure 21-1 Source: Data from World Trade Statistical Review, 2019, Table A6, www.wto.org/statistics. Top 13 represent 58% of world total of $19.5 trillion.

Figure 21-2 Source: Data from World Trade Statistical Review, 2019, Table A6, www.wto.org. Top thirteen represent 60% of world total of $19.9 trillion. Commercial services add $5.5 trillion.

Figure 21-3 Source: Statistics Canada, CANSIM, Nov. 2019, Table 12-10-0011-01. Reproduced and distributed on an "as is" basis with the permission of Statistics Canada.

Figure 21-4 Source: Statistics Canada, Table 36-10-0014-01, 2018. Reproduced and distributed on an "as is" basis with the permission of Statistics Canada.

Figure 21-5 Source: Statistics Canada, Table 36-10-0485-01, third quarter 2019. Reproduced and distributed on an "as is" basis with the permission of Statistics Canada.

Figure 21-6 Source: Statistics Canada, Table 36-10-0008-01 & 36-10-0361-01, 2018. Reproduced and distributed on an "as is" basis with the permission of Statistics Canada.

Figure 21-7 Source: Statistics Canada, Table 36-10-0486-01, November 2019. Reproduced and distributed on an "as is" basis with the permission of Statistics Canada.

GLOSSARY

A

abnormal return A gain or loss above what should be expected, given the degree of risk inherent in an investment.

absolute priority rule Under the Bankruptcy Act, all senior claims on asset value must be settled in full before any value can be given to a junior claimant.

accounting The field of knowledge that provides a financial manager with much of the language of finance and with financial data.

accounts receivable Claims against customers for monies, goods, or services.

after-acquired property clause A clause whereby property purchased is placed under the original mortgage if purchased after the mortgage is executed.

aftermarket The market for a new security offering immediately after it is sold to the public.

aftertax cost of new debt A lower discount rate (than the cost of capital used in most capital budgeting decisions) representing greater certainty in the cash flow stream, because the costs associated with both leasing and borrowing are contractual and certain.

aftertax yield Determined for an investment by the formula: Investment yield (1 − tax rate).

agency theory Examines the relationship between the owners of the firm and their agents, the managers of the firm. Does management act in the best interests of shareholders?

agent One who sells, or "places," an asset for another party. An agent works on a commission or fee basis. Investment dealers sometimes act as agents for their clients.

aging of accounts receivables Analyzing accounts by the amount of time they have been on the books.

alternative trading systems (ATS) Exchanges that use the Internet to electronically match buy and sell orders automatically. These systems or networks have the sanction of securities commissions.

amalgamation A statutory combination of companies under one of the provincial or federal acts.

American Depository Receipts (ADRs) Receipts which represent the ownership interest in a foreign company's common shares that are held in trust in a New York bank. The depository receipts are in U.S. dollars while the shares are not. Many ADRs are listed on the NYSE and many more are traded in the over-the-counter market.

amortization Expensing of a cost (usually includes interest of a debt) over a number of periods. Generic term that includes depreciation and depletion.

annuity A series of consecutive payments or receipts of equal amount.

annuity in advance (or annuity due) A series of equal payments at the beginning of each period.

ARBS (arbitrageurs) Specialists in merger investments who attempt to capitalize on the difference between the value offered and the current market price of the acquisition candidate.

asset utilization ratios A group of ratios that measures the speed at which the firm is turning over or utilizing its assets. We measure inventory turnover, capital asset turnover, total asset turnover, and the average time it takes to collect accounts receivable.

asset-backed securities Current assets of a firm (receivables) are sold into a trust from which an investor receives the cash flow as the receivable payments are made. The firm gets immediate capital in exchange for its assets rolled into a trust, and frees up its capital tied up in these current assets.

assignment The liquidation of assets without going through formal court procedures. To effect an assignment, creditors must agree on liquidation values and the relative priority of claims.

asymmetric information An imbalance of pertinent information among investors and the management of firms can affect pricing in financial markets.

auction market A location where trading takes place in an open transparent manner, where all buyers and sellers have access to security prices.

average accounting return (AAR) This profitability measure is calculated as average earnings after tax divided by average book value.

average collection period The average amount of time accounts receivable have been on the books. It may be computed by dividing accounts receivable by average daily credit sales.

B

balance of payments The term refers to a system of government accounts that catalogues the flow of economic transactions between countries.

balance sheet A financial statement that indicates what assets the firm owns and how those assets are financed in the form of liabilities or ownership interest.

bank rate The rate of interest the Bank of Canada charges on loans to the chartered banks. It is a monetary tool used for management of the money supply.

bankers' acceptances Short-term securities that frequently arise from foreign trade. The acceptance is a draft drawn on a bank for approval for future payment and is subsequently presented to the payer.

bankruptcy The market value of a firm's assets is less than its liabilities, and the firm has a negative net worth. The term is also used to describe in-court procedures associated with the reorganization or liquidation of a firm.

basis point One basis point equals 1/100 of 1 percent.

bearer deposit notes Written promises to pay the individual in possession of the paper.

behavioural finance The study of psychological and sociological influences on financial decision making.

best efforts A distribution, also referred to as a marketed effort, in which the investment dealer agrees to work for a commission rather than actually underwriting (buying) the issue for resale. It is a procedure often used by smaller investment dealers with relatively unknown companies. The investment dealer is not directly taking the risk for distribution.

beta A measure of the volatility of returns on an individual stock relative to the market. Stocks with a beta of 1.0 are said to have risk equal to that of the market (equal volatility). Stocks with betas greater than 1.0 have more risk than the market, while those with betas of less than 1.0 have less risk than the market.

blanket inventory lien A secured borrowing arrangement in which the lender has a general claim against the inventory of the borrower.

bond indenture (See indenture.) A legal contract between the borrower and the lender that covers every detail regarding a bond issue.

bond rating Bonds are rated according to risk by Dominion Bond Rating Services and Standard and Poor's Rating Service. A bond that is rated AAA has the lowest risk, while a bond with a C rating has the highest risk. Coupon rates are greatly influenced by a corporation's bond rating.

bought deal An issue of securities that has been prepurchased by an investment dealer. The investment dealer has thus guaranteed proceeds to the issuing corporation, and the investment dealer bears the risk of holding or selling the security issue.

break-even analysis A numerical and graphical technique that is used to determine at what point the firm will break even (Revenue − Cost). To compute the break-even point, we divide fixed costs by price minus variable cost per unit.

brokers Members of organized stock exchanges who have the ability to buy and sell securities on the

floor of their respective exchanges. Brokers act as agents between buyers and sellers.

bull market A rising stock market. For our purposes, a bull market exists when stock prices are strong and rising, and investors are optimistic about future market performance.

business risk The risk related to the inability of the firm to hold its competitive position and maintain stability and growth in earnings. It is based on the nature of the firm's operations.

C

call feature Used for bonds and some preferred stock. A call or redemption feature, written into a bond indenture, allows the corporation to retire securities before maturity by forcing the bondholders to sell bonds back to it at a set price.

call option An option giving the holder the right to buy an underlying asset at a preset price.

Canadian Depository for Securities (CDS) An online, real-time national clearinghouse for money market, bond, and equity transactions. CDS is owned by the banks, investment dealers, and trust companies.

capital Sources of long-term financing that are available to the business firm.

capital (or finance) lease A long-term, noncancellable lease that has many of the characteristics of debt. Under CICA guidelines, the lease obligation must be shown directly on the balance sheet.

capital asset pricing model (CAPM) A model that relates the risk–return tradeoffs of individual assets to market returns. A security is presumed to receive a risk-free rate of return plus a premium for risk.

capital budgeting analysis The objective evaluation of long-term decisions to invest the firm's scarce resources.

capital budgeting decision One of three main decision areas of finance related to the acquisition of capital assets to create value for the firm.

capital cost allowance (CCA) Declining balance method of amortization allowed by the Income Tax Act as a tax-deductible expense.

capital markets Competitive markets for equity securities or debt securities with maturities of more than one year. The best examples of capital market securities are common stock, bonds, and preferred stock.

capital rationing Occurs when a corporation has more dollars of capital budgeting projects with positive net present values than it has money to invest in them. Therefore, some projects that should be accepted are excluded because financial capital is rationed.

capital structure The combination or weightings of the different liabilities and equities used to finance a corporation.

capital structure decision One of three main decision areas of finance related to the combination of debt and equity used by the firm.

capital structure theory The study of the relative importance of debt and equity in financing a firm. Early development of this theory was by Modigliani and Miller.

carrying costs The cost to hold an asset, usually inventory. For inventory, carrying costs include items such as interest, warehousing costs, insurance, and material-handling expenses.

cash budget A series of monthly or quarterly budgets that indicate cash receipts, cash payments, and the borrowing requirements for meeting financial requirements. It is constructed from the pro forma income statement and other supportive schedules.

cash conversion cycle The time between the initial outlay of funds for materials and the final collection of funds from clients.

cash discount A reduction in the invoice price if payment is made within a specified time period. An example would be 2/10, net 30.

cash flow A value equal to income after taxes plus noncash expenses. In capital budgeting decisions, the usual noncash expense is amortization.

cash flow cycle The pattern in which cash moves in and out of the firm. The primary consideration in managing the cash flow cycle is to ensure that inflows and outflows of cash are properly synchronized for transaction purposes.

CCA tax shield The reduction of taxes otherwise payable because the corporation can expense capital costs and therefore reduce taxable income.

certainty equivalent The adjustment of uncertain cash flows, as represented by a probability distribution, to a value that is considered equal and certain.

certificates of deposit (CD) Certificates offered by a bank, trust company, or other financial institution for the deposit of funds at a given interest rate over a specified time period.

clientele effect The effect of investor preferences for dividends or capital gains. Investors tend to purchase securities that meet their needs.

coefficient of correlation The degree of associated movement between two or more variables. Variables that move in the same direction are said to be positively correlated, while negatively correlated variables move in opposite directions.

combined leverage The total or combined impact of operating and financial leverage.

commercial paper An unsecured promissory note that large corporations issue to investors. The minimum amount is usually $25,000.

common equity The common stock or ownership capital of the firm. Common equity may be supplied through retained earnings or the sale of new common stock.

common shareholder Holders of common shares are the owners of the company. They have a residual claim to the earnings.

common stock Represents the ownership interest of the firm. Common shareholders have the ultimate right to control the business.

compensating balance A bank requirement that business customers maintain a minimum average balance. The required amount is usually computed as a percentage of customer loans outstanding or as a percentage of the future loans to which the bank has committed itself.

competition law A federal law that makes a merger or acquisition illegal if it "lessens competition substantially in a given market."

composition An out-of-court settlement in which creditors agree to accept a fractional settlement on their original claim.

compound value The future value of a single amount or an annuity when compounded at a given interest rate for a specified time period.

compounded semiannually A compounding period of every six months. For example, a five-year investment in which interest is compounded semiannually would indicate an *n* value equal to ten and an *i* value at one-half the annual rate.

consumer price index An economic indicator published monthly by Statistics Canada. It measures the rate of inflation for consumer goods.

contribution margin The contribution to fixed costs from each unit of sales. The margin may be computed as price minus variable cost per unit.

conversion The process of swapping one security for common shares in a corporation.

conversion feature A provision of a security that allows the swapping of that security for common shares under specified conditions.

conversion premium The market price of a convertible bond or preferred stock minus the security's conversion value.

conversion price The conversion ratio divided into the par value. This is the price of the common stock at which the security is convertible into shares. An investor would usually not convert the security into common stock unless the market price is greater than the conversion price.

conversion ratio The number of shares of common stock an investor receives if they exchange a convertible bond or convertible preferred stock for common stock.

conversion value The conversion ratio multiplied by the market price per share of common stock.

convertible exchangeable preferreds A form of preferred stock that allows the company to force conversion from convertible preferred stock into convertible debt. This can be used to allow the company to take advantage of falling interest rates or to allow the company to change aftertax preferred dividends into tax-deductible interest payments.

convertible security A security that may be traded into the company for a different form or type of security.

Convertible securities are usually bonds or preferred stock that may be exchanged for common stock.

corporate financial markets Markets in which corporations, in contrast to governmental units, raise funds.

corporate life cycle A curve illustrating the growth phases of a firm. The dividend policy most likely to be employed during each phase is often illustrated.

corporation A form of ownership in which a separate legal entity is created. A corporation may sue or be sued, engage in contracts, and acquire property. It has a continual life and is not dependent on any one shareholder for maintaining its legal existence. A corporation is owned by shareholders who enjoy the privilege of limited liability. There is, however, the potential for double taxation in the corporate form of organization, the first time at the corporate level in the form of profits, and again at the shareholder level in the form of dividends.

cost of capital The cost of alternative sources of financing to the firm. (See also weighted average cost of capital.)

cost-benefit analysis A study of the incremental costs and benefits that can be derived from a given course of action.

coupon rate The actual interest rate on the bond, usually payable in semiannual instalments. The coupon rate normally stays constant during the life of the bond and indicates what the bondholder's annual dollar income will be.

covariance A measure brought to a standardized scale known as the coefficient of correlation when divided by the standard deviations of two investments.

covenants Promises made by a firm to prevent weakening of the claims that debt holders have against the assets or cash flows of a borrowing firm.

credit terms The repayment provisions that are part of a credit arrangement. An example would be a 2/10, net 30 arrangement in which the customer may deduct 2 percent from the invoice price if payment occurs in the first 10 days. Otherwise, the full amount is due.

creditor committee A group of creditors established to run a business to avoid bankruptcy.

cross rates The relationship between two foreign currencies expressed in terms of a third currency (the dollar).

crown jewels A targeted company in a takeover may sell a prized division or asset (crown jewel), making the takeover less attractive to the buyer.

cum-rights The situation in which the purchase of a share of common stock includes a right attached to the stock. Also rights-on.

cumulative dividend (See cumulative preferred stock.)

cumulative voting Allows shareholders more than one vote per share. They are allowed to multiply their total shares by the number of directors being elected to determine their total number of votes. This system enables minority shareholders to elect directors even though they do not have 51 percent of the vote.

currency futures A futures contract that may be used for hedging or speculation in foreign exchange.

current cost (replacement cost) method A method of inflation-adjusted accounting. Financial statements are adjusted to reflect changing price levels using specific price indexes related to the specific types of goods being adjusted. This is shown as supplemental information in the firm's annual report.

current yield The yearly dollar interest payment divided by the current market price.

D

D & B A credit-rating agency that provides computer access to information contained in its database of more than 240 million businesses

Data Universal Number System (D-U-N-S) A unique, nine-digit code assigned by Dun & Bradstreet to each business in its information base.

dealer market A place where securities are sold out of the inventory of institutions by way of negotiation.

dealers Participants in the market who transact security trades over the counter from their own inventory of stocks and bonds. They are often referred to as market makers, since they stand ready to buy and sell their securities at quoted prices.

debenture A long-term unsecured corporate bond. Debentures are usually issued by large, prestigious firms having excellent credit ratings in the financial community.

debt utilization ratios A group of ratios that indicates to what extent debt is being used and the prudence with which it is being managed. Calculations include debt to total assets, times interest earned, and fixed-charge coverage.

debt/equity ratio A calculation of the capital structure of the firm; all liabilities to equity, debt obligations to equity, or long-term debt to equity.

decision tree A tabular or graphical analysis that lays out the sequence of decisions that are to be made and highlights the differences between choices. The presentation resembles branches on a tree.

decremental cash flows (outflow) The cash flows that are subtracted as a result of an investment decision.

deferred annuity An annuity that will not begin until sometime in the future.

degree of combined leverage (DCL) A measure of the total combined effect of operating and financial leverage on earnings per share. The percentage change in earnings per share is divided by the percentage change in sales at a given level of operation. Other algebraic statements are also used (see formula 5–10).

degree of financial leverage (DFL) A measure of the impact of debt on the earnings capability of the firm. The percentage change in earnings per share is divided by the percentage change in earnings before interest and taxes at a given level of operation. Other algebraic statements are also used, such as formula 5–5.

degree of operating leverage (DOL) A measure of the impact of fixed costs on the operating earnings of the firm. The percentage change in operating income is divided by the percentage change in volume at a given level of operation. Other algebraic statements are also used, such as formula 5–8.

demand loans Short-term, self-liquidating, variable rate loans generally repayable any time by the borrower or by "demand" from the financial institution.

derivatives Financial contracts that give the holder the right to buy or sell a particular commodity or asset at an established price at some time in the future.

diluted earnings per share EPS adjusted for all potential dilution from the issuance of any new shares of common stock arising from convertible bonds, convertible preferred stock, warrants, or any other options outstanding.

dilutive effect on shares The potential reduction in market share value as additional shares are issued.

discount rate The interest rate at which future sums or annuities are discounted back to the present.

discounted loan A loan in which the calculated interest payment is subtracted or discounted in advance. Because this lowers the amount of available funds, the effective interest rate is increased.

disinflation A levelling off or slowing down of price increases.

diversification Placing monies in a variety of investments that are somewhat unrelated (less than perfect positive correlation). Variability of returns, or risk, will be reduced.

divestiture The sale or spinoff of a subsidiary or a division of a company.

dividend capitalization model (See dividend valuation model.)

dividend declaration date The date on which a firm's board of directors announces the next dividend.

dividend payment date The day on which a shareholder of record will receive their dividend.

dividend record date Shareholders owning the stock on the holder-of-record date are entitled to receive a dividend. To be listed as an owner on the corporate books, the investor must have bought the stock before it went ex-dividend.

dividend reinvestment plans (DRIPs) Plans that provide the investor with an opportunity to buy additional shares of stock with the cash dividends paid by the company.

dividend tax credit Tax credit accorded to individuals receiving corporate dividends. Its purpose is to compensate for the fact that corporate earnings are taxed in the hands of the corporation and possibly again in the hands of the shareholder.

dividend valuation model A model for determining the value of a share of stock by taking the present value of an expected stream of future dividends.

dividend yield Dividends per share divided by market price per share. Dividend yield indicates the percentage return that a shareholder will receive on dividends alone.

DuPont system of financial analysis An analysis of profitability that breaks down return on assets between the profit margin and asset turnover. The second, or modified, version shows how return on assets is translated into return on equity through the amount of the firm's debt.

Dutch auction preferred stock A preferred stock security that matures every several weeks and is sold (reauctioned) at a subsequent bidding. The concept of Dutch auction means that the stock is issued to the bidder willing to accept the lowest yield, and then to the next lowest bidder, and so on until all of the preferred stock is sold.

E

earnings (net income or loss) The periodic value (not cash, necessarily) available to shareholders after expenses are subtracted from revenues.

earnings multipier Represents the relationship between earnings (usually current) and the market share price. Earnings times the multiplier gives the suggested market share price. Current market yields and future expected earnings influence the magnitude of the multiplier

earnings per share (EPS) The earnings available to common shareholders, divided by the number of common stock shares outstanding.

EBIT/EPS indifference point The amount of operating earnings required for one financing plan to equal an alternative financing plan with respect to the impact on earnings per share.

economic exposure This measure identifies the market value of assets and liabilities, denominated in a foreign currency, that is subject to possible change in market value because of fluctuations in exchange rates.

economic ordering quantity The most efficient ordering quantity for the firm. The EOQ allows the firm to minimize the total ordering and carrying costs associated with inventory.

economics The field of knowledge encompassing the workings of the economy, industries, and businesses and the models that try to explain how value is created, providing a structure for decision making.

effective rate of interest Yield that includes compounding effects over a given time period.

efficient frontier A line drawn through the optimum point selections in a risk–return tradeoff diagram. Each point represents the best possible tradeoff between risk and return (the highest return at a given risk level or the lowest risk at a given return level).

efficient markets Markets in which all available information is impounded into prices quickly and at minimal cost, expressed in degrees of efficiency based on whether information impounded is past, public, or private.

Electronic Communication Networks (ECNs) Exchanges that use the Internet to electronically match buy and sell orders automatically. These systems, or networks, have the sanction of securities commissions.

electronic funds transfer A system in which funds are moved between computer terminals without the use of written cheques.

euro The common currency shared by the 28 members of the European Monetary Union.

Eurobonds Bonds payable or denominated in the borrower's currency but sold outside the country of the borrower, usually by an international syndicate.

Eurocurrency Eurocurrency is a unit of currency held on deposit or traded outside the country issuing the currency.

Eurocurrency deposit An obligation from a financial institution to an individual, based on the holding of foreign currencies in a country other than the home country.

Eurodollar Dollars held on deposit by foreign banks and loaned out by those banks to anyone seeking dollars.

Eurodollar loans Loans from a foreign bank denominated in dollars.

European Economic and Monetary Union (EMU) A group of European countries that share a common currency (euro) and common interest rates. The common currency (euro) utilized by 19 countries is the third stage of economic and monetary union.

EVA Economic value added; a concept for financial decision making based on the formula EVA = Net operating profit after taxes (NOPAT) + [Capital × Cost of capital].

ex-dividend date Two business days before the holder-of-record date. On the ex-dividend date the purchase of the stock no longer carries with it the right to receive the dividend previously declared.

ex-rights date The date after which common shares no longer include rights. Trading of shares, ex-rights, occurs two business days before the actual ex-rights date.

exchange rate Foreign exchange rate. For example, the exchange rate between Canadian dollars and the euro is stated as dollars per euro or euros per dollar.

exercise price The price at which a warrant (or other, similar security) allows the investor to purchase common stock.

expectations hypothesis The hypothesis maintains that the yields on long-term securities are a function of short-term rates. The result of the hypothesis is that when long-term rates are much higher than short-term rates the market is saying it expects short-term rates to rise. Conversely, when long-term rates are lower than short-term rates the market is expecting short-term rates to fall.

expected value A representative value from a probability distribution arrived at by multiplying each outcome by the associated probability and summing up the values.

Export Development Corporation (EDC) Agency of the federal

government whose role is to facilitate the financing of Canadian exports through credit insurance, loan guarantees, special loans, and so forth.

expropriate The action of a country in taking away or modifying the property rights of a corporation or individual.

extension An out-of-court settlement in which creditors agree to allow the firm more time to meet its financial obligations, and a new repayment schedule is developed, subject to the acceptance of creditors.

external financing Corporate financing raised through sources outside the firm. Bonds, common stock, and preferred stock fall into this category.

external reorganization A reorganization under the formal bankruptcy laws in which a merger partner is found for the distressed firm. Ideally, the distressed firm should be merged with a strong firm in its own industry, although this is not always possible.

F

factoring receivables Selling accounts receivable to a finance company or a bank.

field warehousing An inventory financing arrangement in which collateralized inventory is stored on the premises of the borrower but is controlled by an independent warehousing company.

FIFO A system of writing off inventory into cost of goods sold in which the items purchased first are written off first. Referred to as first-in, first-out.

financial capital Financial claims on a firm or government, as opposed to real capital such as the plant and equipment.

financial futures market A market that allows for the trading of financial instruments related to a future time. A purchase or sale occurs in the present, with a reversal necessitated in the future to close out the position. If a purchase (sale) occurs initially, then a sale (purchase) will be necessary in the future.

financial intermediary A financial institution, such as a bank or a life

insurance company, that directs other people's money into investments such as government and corporate securities.

financial leverage A measure of the amount of debt used in the capital structure of the firm.

financial leverage Reflects the capital structure of the firm (mix of debt and equity [shares]).

financial markets The place of interaction for people, corporations, and institutions that either need money or have money to lend or invest.

financial risk The risk related to the inability of the firm to meet its debt obligations as they come due.

fiscal deficit Government expenditures are greater than government tax revenues, and the government must borrow to balance revenues and expenditures. These deficits act as an economic stimulus.

fixed costs Costs that remain relatively constant regardless of the volume of operations. Examples are rent, amortization, property taxes, and executive salaries.

float The difference between the corporation's recorded cash balance on its books and the amount credited to the corporation by the bank.

floating-rate bond A bond for which the interest payment rather than the price of the bond changes with market conditions.

floating-rate preferred stock The quarterly dividend on the preferred stock changes with market rates. The market price is considerably less volatile than it is with regular preferred stock.

floor value Usually equal to the pure bond value. A convertible bond will not sell at less than its pure bond value even when its conversion value is below the pure bond value.

flotation cost The distribution cost of selling securities to the public. The cost includes the underwriter's spread and any associated fees.

forced conversion Occurs when a company calls a convertible security that has a conversion value greater than the call price. Investors will take the higher of the two values and convert the security to common stock rather than take a lower cash call price.

foreign exchange rate The relationship between the values of two or more currencies. For example, the exchange rate between Canadian dollars and euros is stated as dollars per euro or euros per dollar.

foreign exchange risk A form of risk that results from a change in value of foreign exchange rates. This risk impacts on economic exposure.

Foreign Investment Review Agency A federal agency established in the early 1970s to review takeovers of large Canadian firms by foreigners. It was disbanded in 1985.

forward rate A rate that reflects the future value of a currency based on expectations. Forward rates may be greater than the current spot rate (premium) or less than the current spot rate (discount). One can contract at this rate.

forwards Customized contracts that fix the price of some commodity for delivery at a specified price, at a specified amount, and at a specified time in the future. Forwards generally cannot be resold.

four pillars of finance Traditional separation of financial institution roles in Canada among chartered banks, trusts, insurance companies, and securities dealers.

free cash flow Cash flow from operating activities, minus expenditures required to maintain the productive capacity of the firm, minus dividend payouts.

fronting loan A parent company's loan to a foreign subsidiary is channelled through a financial intermediary, usually a large international bank. The bank fronts for the parent in extending the loan to the foreign affiliate.

future value The value that a current amount grows to at a given interest rate over a given time period.

future value of an annuity The sum of the future value of a series of consecutive equal payments.

futures Standardized contracts that fix the price of some commodity for delivery at a specified place, at a specified price, and at a specified time in the future. Futures generally trade through a market and can be resold.

futures contract A contract to buy or sell a commodity at some specified price in the future.

G

general partnership A partnership in which all partners have unlimited liability for the debts of the firm.

going private The process by which all publicly owned shares of common stock are repurchased or retired, thereby eliminating listing fees, annual reports, and other expenses involved with publicly owned companies.

golden parachute Highly attractive termination payments made to current management in the event of a takeover of the company.

goodwill An intangible asset that reflects value above that generally recognized in the tangible assets of the firm. It arises when one firm acquires another for an amount greater than the acquired firm's book value.

gross profit Sales (revenues) less cost of goods sold (direct costs related to sales).

H

hedged A financial position structured with downside risk protection. .

hedging To engage in a transaction that partially or fully reduces a prior risk exposure by taking a position that is the opposite of your initial position. As an example, you buy some copper now but also engage in a contract to sell copper in the future at a set price.

historical book value per share The value of shareholders' equity based on past recording of equity investment and retained earnings.

historical or original-cost basis The traditional method of accounting, in which financial statements are developed based on original cost minus depreciation.

holding company A company that has voting control of one or more other companies. It often has less than a 50 percent interest in each of these other companies.

holding period or true yield to maturity (YTM) The rate of return, or yield, actually earned by an investor

for the period a financial security is owned (calculated after the fact).

homemade dividend Cash payment–like dividend determined by an investor by selling a portion of the investor's share holdings.

homemade leverage The use of leverage directly by investors in place of corporate leverage. It allows investors to bring into balance the value of unlevered and levered firms by providing the missing leverage themselves. Homemade leverage is part of the initial Modigliani and Miller approach.

hurdle rate The minimum acceptable rate of return in a capital budgeting decision.

I

IFRS (International Financial Reporting Standards) Rules established by members of the international accounting and auditing committees to standardize the preparation and reporting of financial statements. IFRS is mandatory for public companies but optional for private companies.

income trusts A trust controls "former" company assets that generate a stream of steady cash flows to the investor or unitholder. In exchange for the sale of these assets the firm receives a capital injection.

incremental cash flows (inflows) The identification of only those cash flows that are added as the result of an action or decision.

inflation The phenomenon of price increase with the passage of time.

inflation premium A premium to compensate the investor for the eroding effect of inflation on the value of the dollar. In the 1980s the inflation premium was 3 to 4 percent. In the late 1970s it was in excess of 10 percent.

information content (See dividend information content.)

initial public offering (IPO) The first time a corporation or government raises capital through the public markets.

insider trading Occurs when someone has information that is not available to the public and then uses this information to profit from trading in a company's common stock.

instalment loan A borrowing arrangement in which a series of equal payments are used to pay off the loan.

institutional investors Large investors such as pension funds and mutual funds.

interest factor The tabular value to insert into the various formulas. It is based on the number of periods (n) and the interest rate (i).

interest rate hedging Reduction of the risk of what interest rate one will pay (receive) at some time in the future. Financial futures can be employed.

interest rate parity theory A theory based on the interplay between interest rate differentials and exchange rates. If one country has a higher interest rate than another country after adjustments for inflation, interest rates and foreign exchange rates will adjust until the foreign exchange rates and money market rates reach equilibrium (are properly balanced between the two countries).

internal rate of return (IRR) A discounted cash flow method for evaluating capital budgeting projects. The IRR is a discount rate that makes the present value of the cash inflows equal to the present value of the cash outflows.

internal reorganization A reorganization under the formal bankruptcy laws. New management may be brought in and a redesign of the capital structure may be implemented.

internally generated funds Funds generated through the operations of the firm. The principal sources are retained earnings and cash flow added back from depreciation and other noncash deductions.

intrinsic value The true or inherent worth.

inventory profits Profits generated as a result of an inflationary economy, in which old inventory is sold at large profits because of increasing prices. This is particularly prevalent under FIFO accounting.

inverted yield curve A downward-sloping yield curve. Short-term rates are higher than long-term rates.

Investment Canada The replacement for the Foreign Investment Review Agency. It has a mandate to make Canada a more hospitable place for foreign investment.

investment dealer A financial organization that specializes in selling primary offerings of securities. Investment dealers can also perform other financial functions, such as advising clients, negotiating mergers and takeovers, and selling secondary offerings.

Investment Industry Regulatory Organization of Canada (IIROC) Professional association that advances the growth and development of the Canadian investment industry.

investment tax credit (ITC) For capital investments in certain industries or regions of the country, a specified percentage of the capital cost can be deducted from income taxes payable.

J

junk bond A bond that is not in default, but one that is of questionable quality and speculative in nature.

just-in-time inventory management (JIT) The production process credited to the Japanese whereby parts required on the assembly line arrive at the appropriate station at the exact moment they are required. This cuts down on inventories and requires high quality control.

L

letter of credit A credit letter, normally issued by the importer's bank, in which the bank promises to pay out the money for the merchandise when delivered.

level production Equal monthly production used to smooth out production schedules and employ labour and equipment more efficiently and at a lower cost.

leverage The use of fixed-charge items with the intent of magnifying the potential returns to the firm.

leveraged buyouts Existing management or an outsider makes an offer to "go private" by retiring all the shares of the company. The buying group borrows the necessary money, using the assets of the acquired firm as collateral. The buying group then repurchases all the shares and expects to retire the debt over time with the cash flow from operations or the sale of corporate assets.

leveraged leases The lessor for a large capital item may finance a portion with a loan from a financial institution.

LIBOR (London Interbank Offered Rate) An interbank rate applicable for large deposits in the London market. It is a benchmark rate, just like the prime interest rate in Canada. Interest rates on Eurodollar loans are determined by adding premiums to this basic rate. Most often, LIBOR is lower than the Canadian prime rate.

LIFO A system of writing off inventory into cost of goods sold in which the items purchased last are written off first. Referred to as last-in, first-out.

limited partnership A special form of partnership to limit liability for most of the partners. Under this arrangement, one or more partners are designated as general partners and have unlimited liability for the debts of the firm, while the other partners are designated as limited partners and are liable only for their initial contribution.

line of credit An established limit up to which a financial institution will lend funds if appropriate security is in place. Although generally available to the borrowing client at any time, the financial institution makes no formal guarantees.

liquidating dividend A final payment made to shareholders when a corporation is wound up or liquidated.

liquidation A procedure that may be carried out under the formal bankruptcy laws when an internal or external reorganization does not appear to be feasible and it appears that the assets are worth more in liquidation than through a reorganization. Priority of claims becomes extremely important in liquidation because it is unlikely that all parties will be fully satisfied in their demands.

liquidity The relative convertibility of short-term assets to cash. Thus, marketable securities are highly liquid assets, while inventory may not be.

liquidity premium theory This theory indicates that long-term rates should be higher than short-term rates. The premium of long-term rates over short-term rates exists because short-term securities have greater liquidity, and therefore higher rates have to be offered to potential long-term bond buyers to entice them to hold these less-liquid and more price-sensitive securities.

liquidity ratios A group of ratios that allows one to measure the firm's ability to pay off short-term obligations as they come due. Primary attention is directed to the current ratio and the quick ratio.

listing requirements Financial standards that corporations must meet before their common stock can be traded on a stock exchange. Listing requirements are not standard; instead, they are set by each exchange.

lockbox system A procedure used to expedite cash inflows to a business. Customers are requested to forward their cheques to a post office box in their geographic region, and a local bank picks up the cheques and processes them for rapid collection. Funds are then wired to the corporate home office for immediate use.

London Interbank Offered Rate (LIBOR) An interbank rate applicable for large deposits in the London market. It is a benchmark rate, just like the prime interest rate in Canada. Interest rates on Eurodollar loans are determined by adding premiums to this basic rate. Most often, LIBOR is lower than the Canadian prime rate.

M

majority voting All directors must be elected by a vote of more than 50 percent. Minority shareholders are unable to achieve any representation on the board of directors.

managing investment dealer An investment dealer who is responsible for the pricing, prospectus development, and legal work involved in the sale of a new issue of securities.

marginal cost of capital The cost of the last dollar of funds raised. It is assumed that each dollar is financed in proportion to the firm's optimum capital structure.

marginal principle of retained earnings The corporation must be able to earn a higher return on its retained earnings than a shareholder

would receive after paying taxes on the distributed dividends.

marginal tax rate The rate that applies to the last dollar of taxable income.

market efficiency Markets are considered to be efficient when (1) prices adjust rapidly to new information, (2) there is a continuous market in which each successive trade is made at a price close to the previous price (the faster the price responds to new information and the smaller the differences in price changes, the more efficient the market), and (3) the market can absorb large dollar amounts of securities without destabilizing the prices.

market for corporate control The possibility of leveraged buyouts, takeovers, and mergers is suggested as a control on management's tendencies to diverge from the goal of maximization of shareholder wealth.

market maker Participants in the market who transact security trades over the counter from their own inventory of stocks and bonds. They are often referred to as market makers, since they stand ready to buy and sell their securities at quoted prices.

market risk premium A premium over and above the risk-free rate. It is represented by the difference between the market return (Rm) and the risk-free rate (Rf), and it may be multiplied by the beta coefficient to determine the additional risk-adjusted return on a security.

market stabilization Intervention in the secondary markets by an investment dealer to stabilize the price of a new security offering during the offering period. The purpose of market stabilization is to provide an orderly market for the distribution of the new issue.

market value What someone is prepared to pay for a financial asset (or security).

market value maximization The concept of maximizing the wealth of shareholders. This calls for recognition not only of earnings per share but also of how they will be valued in the marketplace.

market value per share The price of a share traded on a public exchange by open auction.

market-determined share price The amount investors are willing to pay for their shares of a firm on the basis of trading in the capital market.

maturity date The date on which the bond is retired and the principal (par value) is repaid to the lender.

medium-term notes These debt instruments are like bonds but of a shorter time to maturity and are issued in a quicker manner through a POP prospectus.

merger The combination of two or more companies in which the resulting firms maintain the identity of the acquiring company.

merger premium The part of a buyout or exchange offer that represents a value over and above the market value of the acquired firm.

modified internal rate of return (MIRR) A discount methodology that determines the discount rate that will equate the future value of inflows, each growing at the cost of capital, with the initial investment.

money market Competitive market for securities with maturities of one year or less. The best examples of money market instruments are Treasury bills, commercial paper, and bankers' acceptances.

money market fund A fund in which investors may purchase units for as little as $500 or $1,000. The fund then reinvests the proceeds in high-yielding money market securities. Investors receive their pro rata portion of the interest proceeds daily as a credit to their units.

mortgage agreement A loan that requires real property (plant and equipment) as collateral.

multinational corporation (MNC) A firm doing business across its national borders. Some definitions require a minimum percentage (often 30 percent or more) of a firm's business activities to be carried on outside its national borders.

mutually exclusive The selection of one choice precludes the selection of any competitive choice. For example, several machines can do an identical job in capital budgeting. After one machine is selected, the other machines are not used.

N

net income (NI) approach Under the net income approach, it is assumed that the firm can raise all the funds it desires at a constant cost of debt and equity. Since debt tends to have a lower cost than equity, the more debt utilized, the lower the overall cost of capital and the higher the valuation of the firm.

net operating income (NOI) approach Under this approach, the cost of capital and valuation do not change with the increased utilization of debt. Under this proposition, the low cost of debt is assumed to remain constant with greater debt utilization, but the cost of equity increases to such an extent that the cost of capital remains unchanged.

net present value (NPV) The NPV equals the present value of the cash inflows minus the present value of the cash outflows, with the cost of capital used as a discount rate. This method is used to evaluate capital budgeting projects. If the NPV is positive, a project should be accepted.

net present value profile A graphic presentation of the potential net present values of a project at different discount rates. It is very helpful in comparing the characteristics of two or more investments.

net trade credit A measure of the relationship between the firm's accounts receivable and accounts payable. If accounts receivable exceed accounts payable, the firm is a net provider of trade credit; otherwise, it is a net user.

net worth or book value Shareholders' equity minus preferred share ownership. Basically, net worth is the common shareholders' interest as represented by common stock par value, contributed surplus, and retained earnings. If you take all of the assets of the firm and subtract its liabilities and preferred stock, you arrive at net worth.

nominal rate of interest Yield expressed without compounding effects over a given time period. Includes real return, inflation premium, and risk premium.

nonlinear break-even analysis Break-even analysis based on the assumption that cost and revenue relationships to quantity may vary at different levels of operation. Most of our analysis is based on linear break-even analysis.

nonvoting stock Stock that entitles the holder to an equal or greater dividend than voting stock but not to a vote on company business. Often issued to allow one party to maintain control of the company.

normal yield curve An upward-sloping yield curve. Long-term interest rates are higher than short-term rates.

O

Ontario Securities Commission (OSC) The regulatory body that oversees securities-related activities in Ontario. The OSC sets the standards for other provincial commissions because the majority of dollar volume of securities trading occurs in Toronto.

operating lease A short-term, nonbinding obligation that is easily cancellable.

operating leverage A reflection of the extent to which capital assets and fixed costs are utilized in the business firm.

operating leverage The degree to which capital assets and associated fixed costs are utilized by the firm

operating profit (earnings before interest and taxes) Revenues less variable and fixed costs.

optimum capital structure A capital structure that has the best possible mix of debt, preferred stock, and common equity. The optimum mix should provide the lowest possible cost of capital to the firm.

options Contracts that give the holder the right but not the obligation to buy or sell an underlying security at a set price for a given time period.

ordering costs Costs related to the processing of inventory into stock. Maintaining a relatively low average inventory in stock requires ordering many times, leading to high ordering costs.

over-the-counter (OTC) market Markets for securities (both bonds and stock) in which market makers, or dealers, transact purchases and sales of securities by trading from their own inventory of securities.

overnight, or call, money rate The interest rate at which financial institutions lend money to each other for a short period.

P

par value (face value) Sometimes referred to as the face value or the principal value of the bond. Most bond issues have a par value of $1,000 per bond. Older issues of common and preferred stock may also have an assigned par value.

parallel loan A Canadian firm that wishes to lend funds to a foreign affiliate (such as a Dutch affiliate) locates a foreign parent firm (such as a Dutch parent firm) that wishes to loan money to a Canadian affiliate. Avoiding the foreign exchange markets entirely, the Canadian parent lends dollars to the Dutch affiliate in Canada, while the Dutch parent lends euros to the Canadian affiliate in the Netherlands. At maturity, the two loans would each be repaid to the original lender. Notice that neither loan carries any foreign exchange risk in this arrangement.

participation provision A small number of preferred stock issues are participating with regard to corporate earnings. For such issues, once the common stock dividend equals the preferred stock dividend, the two classes of securities may share equally (or in some ratio) in additional dividend payments.

partnership A form of ownership in which two or more partners are involved. Like the sole proprietorship, a partnership arrangement carries unlimited liability for the owners. However, there is only single taxation for the partners, an advantage over the corporate form of ownership.

payback period (PP) A value that indicates the time period required to recoup an initial investment. The payback does not include the time-value-of-money concept.

payout ratio (See dividend payout.)

percent-of-sales method A method of determining future financial needs that is an alternative to the development of pro forma financial statements. We first determine the percentage relationship of various asset and liability accounts to sales, and then we show how that relationship changes as our volume of sales changes.

permanent current assets Current assets that will not be reduced or converted to cash within the normal operating cycle of the firm. Although from a strict accounting standpoint the assets should be removed from the current assets category, they generally are not.

perpetuity An investment without a maturity date.

pledging receivables Using accounts receivable as collateral for a loan. The firm usually may borrow 60 to 80 percent of the value of acceptable collateral.

point-of-sale terminals Computer terminals in retail stores that either allow digital input or use optical scanners. The terminals may be used for inventory control or other purposes.

poison pill A strategy that makes a firm unattractive as a potential takeover candidate. Poison pills may take many different forms.

portfolio effect The impact of a given investment on the overall risk-return composition of the firm. A firm must consider not only the individual investment characteristics of a project, but also how the project relates to the entire portfolio of undertakings.

pre-emptive right The right of current common shareholders to maintain their ownership percentage on new issues of common stock.

precautionary balances Cash balances held for emergency purposes. Precautionary cash balances are more likely to be important in seasonal or cyclical industries, where cash inflows are more uncertain.

preferred stock A hybrid security combining some of the characteristics of common stock and debt. The dividends paid are not tax-deductible expenses of the corporation, as is true of the interest paid on debt.

present value The current or discounted value of a future sum or annuity. The value is discounted back at a given interest rate for a specified time period.

present value model The determination of the value of assets based on their future "expected" cash flows.

present value of an annuity The sum of the present value of a series of consecutive equal payments.

price-earnings ratio (P/E) The multiplier applied to earnings per share to determine current value. The P/E ratio is influenced by the earnings and sales growth of the firm, the risk or volatility of its performance, the debt-equity structure, and other factors.

primary market Initial sale of corporate securities to investors when a corporation raises capital.

prime rate The rate a bank charges its most creditworthy customers.

private placement The sale of securities directly to a financial institution by a corporation. This eliminates the middleperson and reduces the cost of issue to the corporation.

privatization A process in which investment dealers take companies that were previously owned by the government to the public markets.

pro forma balance sheet A projection of future asset, liability, and shareholders' equity levels. Notes payable or cash is used as a plug, or balancing figure, for the statement.

pro forma income statement A projection of anticipated sales, expenses, and income.

profitability index This measure is the ratio of cash inflows to cash outflows in present value terms.

profitability ratios A group of ratios that indicates the return on sales, total assets, and invested capital. Specifically, users compute the profit margin (net income to sales), return on assets, and return on equity.

prospectus A document describing securities offered for sale to the public that includes the important information that has been filed with the appropriate provincial securities commission. It contains the list of officers and directors, financial reports, potential users of funds, and the like. It is for distribution to investors.

proxy Written authorization given by a shareholder to someone else to represent them and to vote their shares at a shareholders' meeting.

public financial markets Markets in which federal, provincial, and municipal governments raise money for public activities.

public placement The sale of securities to the public through the investment dealer–underwriter process. Public placements must be registered with the provincial securities commission.

public warehousing An inventory financing arrangement in which inventory, used as collateral, is stored with and controlled by an independent warehousing company.

purchase of assets A method of financial recording for mergers in which the difference between the purchase price and the adjusted book value is recognized as goodwill and is amortized over a maximum time period of 40 years.

purchasing power parity theory A theory based on the interplay between inflation and exchange rates. A parity between the purchasing powers of two countries establishes the rate of exchange between the two currencies. Currency exchange rates therefore tend to vary inversely with their respective purchasing powers to provide the same or similar purchasing power.

pure bond value The value of the convertible bond if its present value is computed at a discount rate equal to interest rates on straight bonds of equal risk, without conversion privileges.

put option Gives the holder the right to sell an underlying asset at a preset price.

R

ratio of bad debts to credit sales Bad debts as a percentage of credit sales. An indication of an aggressive or restrictive credit policy.

real capital Physical assets such as plant and equipment.

real rate of return The rate of return an investor demands for giving up the current use of their funds on a non-inflation-adjusted basis. It is payment for forgoing current consumption. Historically, the real rate of return demanded by investors has been of the magnitude of 2 to 3 percent. However, throughout the 1980s the real rate of return was higher at 5 to 7 percent.

real return bond A financial obligation that promises a coupon payment at a fixed yield above the inflation rate.

recapture The inclusion in income of the capital cost allowance (CCA) previously taken, when an asset pool closes and the last asset is sold for more than the undepreciated capital cost (UCC). Provided no capital gains occur, the difference between the sale price and the UCC is added to income.

refunding decision The process of retiring an old bond issue before maturity and replacing it with a new issue. Refunding occurs when interest rates have fallen and new bonds may be sold at lower interest rates.

reinvestment assumption An assumption must be made concerning the rate of return that can be earned on the cash flows generated by capital budgeting projects. The NPV method assumes the rate of reinvestment to be the cost of capital, while the IRR method assumes the rate to be the actual internal rate of return.

repatriation (of profits) Returning earnings to the multinational parent company in the form of dividends.

replacement cost The cost of replacing the existing asset base at current prices as opposed to original cost.

required rate of return That rate of return investors demand from an investment (securities) to compensate them for the amount of risk involved.

residual claim to income The basic claim that common shareholders have to income that is not paid out to creditors or preferred shareholders. This is true regardless of whether these residual funds are paid out in dividends or retained in the corporation.

residual theory of dividends This theory of dividend payout states a corporation will retain as much earnings as it may profitably invest. If any income is left after investments, the firm will pay dividends. This theory assumes that dividends are a passive decision variable.

resultant cash flows These are the cash flows that stem from a possible investment decision.

retractable feature A provision available with a security that entitles the holder to offer the security back to the issuer at a predetermined price at certain future dates.

revenue bond A bond based on an enterprise that generates a dependable stream of cash flow, and which acts, rather than the firm's assets, as the security for investors.

revolving credits Formal lines of credit.

rights offerings A sale of new common stock through a preemptive rights offering. Usually, one right will be issued for every share held. A certain number of rights may be used to buy shares of common stock from the company at a set price lower than the market price.

rights-on The situation in which the purchase of a share of common stock includes a right attached to the stock. Also cum rights.

risk A measure of uncertainty about the outcome from a given event. The greater the variability of possible outcomes, on both the high side and the low side, the greater the risk.

risk averse Having an aversion or dislike for risk. To induce most people to take larger risks, there must be increased potential for return.

risk premium A premium associated with the special risks of an investment. Of primary interest are two types of risk: business risk and financial risk. Business risk relates to the inability of the firm to maintain its competitive position and sustain stability and growth in earnings. Financial risk relates to the inability of the firm to meet its debt obligations as they come due. The risk premium also differs (is greater or less) for different types of investments (bonds, stocks).

risk-adjusted discount rate A discount rate used in the capital budgeting process that has been adjusted upward or downward from the basic cost of capital to reflect the risk dimension of a given project.

risk-free rate of interest A return on an investment that has no volatility and hence no risk. It is also the market price for the rent of money with no risk. Treasury bills are for practical purposes considered to be the risk-free rate of interest.

risk-free rate of return Rate of return on an asset that carries no risk. Treasury bills are often used to represent this measure, although longer-term government securities have also proved appropriate in some studies.

S

safety stock Inventory that is held in addition to regular needs to protect against being out of an item.

sale and leaseback An arrangement whereby a capital item is sold to a financial institution and then leased back from that financial institution. The arrangement may free monies and may allow for more effective use of the tax laws.

seasoned offering The sale of securities that add to the stock of similar securities already outstanding for a corporation or government.

secondary market The market for securities that have already been issued. It is a market in which investors trade back and forth with each other.

secondary offering The sale of a large block of stock in a publicly traded company, usually by estates, foundations, or large, individual shareholders.

secondary trading The buying and selling of publicly owned securities in secondary markets, such as the Toronto Stock Exchange and the over-the-counter markets.

secured claim A general category of debt, which indicates that the loan was obtained by pledging assets as collateral. Secured debt has many forms and usually offers some protective features to a given class of bondholders.

securities Evidence of financial obligation.

securitization of assets The issuance of a security that is specifically backed by the pledge of an asset.

security market line A line or formula that depicts the risk-related return of a security based on a risk-free rate plus a market premium related to the beta coefficient of the security.

segmentation theory A theory that government securities are divided into market segments by various financial institutions investing in the market. The changing needs, desires, and strategies of these investors tend to strongly influence the nature and relationship of short-term and long-term interest rates.

self-liquidating assets Assets that are converted to cash within the normal operating cycle of the firm. An example is the purchase and sale of seasonal inventory.

self-liquidating loan A loan expected to be repaid as assets are converted to cash within the normal operating cycle of the firm.

semistrong form Level of market efficiency that states that prices reflect all public information, such as announcements of company earnings forecasts.

semivariable costs Costs that are partially fixed but still change somewhat as volume changes. Examples are utilities and repairs and maintenance.

sensitivity analysis The altering of one variable at a time within an analysis to determine that variable's impact on the results of the analysis.

serial payments A bond may be paid off in instalments over the life of the issue.

shareholder wealth maximization Maximizing the wealth of the firm's shareholders through achieving the highest possible value for the firm in the marketplace. It is the overriding objective of the firm and should influence all decisions.

shareholders' equity The total ownership position of preferred and common shareholders.

shareholders' rights plan A protection plan against a creeping takeover whereby existing shareholders are allowed to buy newly issued shares at a substantial discount from market. This right is activated if a single investor acquires more than a stated percentage (often around 20 percent) of the company's outstanding shares without having reached any agreement with the company's board of directors.

simulation A method of dealing with uncertainty in which future outcomes are anticipated. The model may use random variables for inputs. By programming the computer to randomly select inputs from probability distributions, the outcomes generated by a simulation are distributed about a mean; instead of generating one return or net present value, a range of outcomes with standard deviations is provided.

sinking-fund provision A method for retiring bonds in an orderly process over the life of a bond. Each year or semiannually, a corporation sets aside a sum of money equal to a certain percentage of the total issue. These funds are then used by a trustee to purchase the bonds in the open market and retire them. This method prevents the corporation from being forced to raise a large amount of capital at maturity to retire the total bond issue.

sole proprietorship A form of organization that represents single-person ownership and offers the advantages of simplicity of decision making and low organizational and operating costs.

speculative premium The market price of the warrant (or option) minus the warrant's intrinsic value.

spontaneous source of funds Funds arising through the normal course of business, such as accounts payable generated from the purchase of goods for resale.

spot rate The rate at which the currency is traded for immediate delivery. It is the existing cash price.

statement of cash flows A required financial statement that outlines a company's cash flows over the course of a specified period.

statement of income or income statement A financial statement that measures the profitability of the firm over a time period. All expenses are subtracted from sales to arrive at net income.

step-up in the conversion price A feature that is sometimes written into the contract that allows the conversion ratio to decline in steps over time. This feature encourages early conversion when the conversion value is greater than the call price.

stock dividend A dividend paid in stock, rather than cash. A book transfer equal to the market value of the stock dividend is made from retained earnings to the capital stock. The stock dividend may be symbolic of corporate growth, but it does not increase the total value of the shareholders' wealth.

stock repurchase A corporate initiative to buy back its own shares. This decreases the number of shares outstanding.

stock split A division of shares by a ratio set by the board of directors. The par value is divided by the ratio set, and the new shares are issued to the current shareholders of record to increase their shares to the stated level. For example, a two-for-one split would increase your holdings from one share to two shares.

strip bond A bond in which the investor only receives the maturity or face value with all coupons removed.

strong form The level of market efficiency that states that all information, both private and public, is immediately reflected in stock prices.

subordinated debenture An unsecured bond in which payment to the holder occurs only after designated senior debenture holders are satisfied.

sunk costs Expenses already incurred that are not recoverable and are irrelevant in the capital budgeting decision process.

supernormal growth A rate of corporate growth that cannot be maintained indefinitely.

sustainable growth rate That level of growth in sales that can be maintained by a corporation without seeking additional debt or equity financing to support the increasing investment in assets.

swapped deposits Short-term securities offered by chartered banks that involve a foreign currency spot transaction, a foreign currency time deposit, and a forward contract. In effect, the purchaser lends money to the financial institution for investment in a foreign jurisdiction for a specified period. At maturity of the investment, the exchange rate is guaranteed.

sweetener (See financial sweetener.)

synergy The recognition that the whole may be equal to more than the sum of the parts; the "2 + 2 = 5" effect.

T

takeover tender offer An unfriendly acquisition that is not initially negotiated with the management of the target firm. A tender offer is usually made directly to the shareholders of the target firm.

targeted repurchase A targeted company in a takeover agrees to pay a premium to the acquiring company for the shares already purchased, to have them discontinue the acquisition. This is sometimes referred to as greenmail.

tax loss carry-forward A loss that can be carried forward for a number of years to offset future taxable income and perhaps be utilized by another firm in a merger or an acquisition.

tax savings or tax shield The reduction of taxes otherwise payable by the ability to lower taxable income. This takes the form of a deduction to which the taxpayer is entitled.

technical insolvency When a firm is unable to pay its bills as they come due.

temporary current assets Current assets that will be reduced or converted to cash within the normal operating cycle of the firm.

tender offer Rather than engage in a lengthy and expensive proxy fight, a potential buyer can elect to make a tender offer through a stock exchange directly to the target company's shareholders.

term deposit The lending of money to a financial institution for a specified time period and at a specified rate of interest.

term loan An intermediate-length loan in which credit is generally extended from one to seven years. The loan is usually repaid in monthly or quarterly instalments over its life, rather than with one single payment.

term structure of interest rates The term structure shows the relative level of short-term and long-term interest rates at a point in time for securities of equal risk.

terminal loss A deduction from income that is done when the last item in a CCA pool is sold and the sale price is less than the undepreciated capital cost (UCC). The difference is the amount of the deduction.

terms of exchange The buyout ratio or terms of trade in a merger or an acquisition.

three-sector economy Households, business, and government are the three sectors in the Canadian economy.

tight money A term to indicate time periods in which financing may be difficult to find and interest rates may be quite high by normal standards.

Toronto Stock Exchange (TSX) The largest organized security exchange in Canada.

trade credit Credit provided by sellers or suppliers in the normal course of business.

traditional approach to cost of capital Under the traditional approach, the cost of capital initially declines with the increased use of low-cost debt, but it eventually goes up due to the greater risk associated with increasing debt.

transaction exposure Foreign exchange gains and losses resulting from actual international transactions when the foreign funds are converted to Canadian dollars. These may be hedged through the foreign exchange market, the money market, or the currency futures market.

translation exposure The foreign-located assets and liabilities of a multinational corporation, which are denominated in foreign currency units and are exposed to losses and gains resulting from their treatment in the parent company's books, based on accounting rules and due to changing exchange rates. This is called accounting or translation exposure.

Treasury bills Short-term obligations of the federal government with maturities of up to one year.

trend analysis An analysis of performance that is made over a number of years to ascertain significant patterns.

trust receipt An instrument acknowledging that the borrower holds the inventory and proceeds for sale in trust for the lender.

U

undepreciated capital cost (UCC) The amount within a given CCA class (or pool) of assets available for tax-deductible amortization. The maximum amount of CCA that can be expensed in a given year in relation to a particular CCA class is the UCC multiplied by the applicable CCA rate. Special adjustments have to be made for in-year purchases and sales of assets in the class.

underpricing When new or additional shares of stock are to be sold, investment dealers will generally set the price at slightly below the current market value to ensure a receptive market for the securities.

underwriter The process of selling securities and, at the same time, assuring the seller a specified price. Underwriting is done by investment dealers and represents a form of risk taking. (See underwriting.)

underwriting spread The difference between the price that a selling corporation receives for an issue of securities and the price at which the issue is sold to the public. The spread is the fee that investment dealers and others receive for selling securities.

underwriting syndicate A group of investment dealers formed to share the risk of a security offering and also to facilitate the distribution of the securities.

unsecured debt A loan that requires no assets as collateral, but allows the bondholder a general claim against the corporation rather than a lien against specific assets.

V

variable costs Costs that move directly with a change in volume. Examples are raw materials, factory labour, and sales commissions.

W

warrant An option to buy securities at a set price for a given time period. Warrants commonly have a life of one to five years or longer, and a few are perpetual.

weak form The level of efficiency that states that prices reflect all of the information contained in the past price history.

weighted average cost of capital The computed cost of capital determined by multiplying the cost of each item in the optimal capital structure by its weighted representation in the overall capital structure and summing up the results.

white knight A firm that management calls on to help it avoid an unwanted takeover offer. It is an invited suitor.

working capital decision One of three main decision areas in finance, related to managing current assets and liabilities.

working capital management The financing and management of the current assets of the firm. The financial manager determines the mix between temporary and permanent current assets and the nature of the financing arrangement.

working capital position Current assets less current liabilities; reflected in the current ratio.

Y

yield The interest rate that equates a future value or an annuity to a given present value.

yield to maturity (y) The required rate of return on a bond issue. It is the discount rate used in present-valuing future interest payments and the principal payment at maturity. The term is used interchangeably with market rate of interest.

Z

zero sum game A financial position that nets out to zero from the gains and losses.

zero-coupon rate bond A bond that is sold at a deep discount from face value. The return to the investor is the difference between the investor's cost and the face value received at the end of the life of the bond.

INDEX